STUDY ANYWHERE
WITH YOUR TEXT AND FREE EBOOK

When you purchased a new copy of this text, you also received free access to an enhanced eBook. You now have the option of studying at home or on the go. The eBook is a portable version with everything that's in the book and more—including embedded study tools and questions, so you can make sure you are understanding the concepts presented in the book and not just passively reading about them. A sample:

- Tutorial-style interactive study exercises with answer-specific feedback
- Critical-thinking questions that ask you to apply your knowledge
- Labs that let you experience core concepts in social psychology
- "Behind the Citation" author videos that illuminate the importance of research
- Flashcards for in-the-moment practice of key terms
- Note-taking, highlighting, searching, and printing capabilities
- Demo at nortonebooks.com

To access the eBook, just follow the instructions on the card to the right. If you don't have a new copy of the book, you can purchase access to the eBook at nortonebooks.com.

Social Psychology

THIRD EDITION

Thomas Gilovich
Cornell University

Dacher Keltner
University of California, Berkeley

Serena Chen
University of California, Berkeley

Richard E. Nisbett
University of Michigan

W. W. NORTON & COMPANY • NEW YORK • LONDON

W. W. Norton & Company has been independent since its founding in 1923, when William Warder Norton and Mary D. Herter Norton first published lectures delivered at the People's Institute, the adult education division of New York City's Cooper Union. The firm soon expanded its program beyond the Institute, publishing books by celebrated academics from America and abroad. By midcentury, the two major pillars of Norton's publishing program—trade books and college texts—were firmly established. In the 1950s, the Norton family transferred control of the company to its employees, and today—with a staff of four hundred and a comparable number of trade, college, and professional titles published each year—W. W. Norton & Company stands as the largest and oldest publishing house owned wholly by its employees.

Editor: Sheri Snavely

Developmental Editor: Beth Ammerman

Project Editor: Carla L. Talmadge

Production Manager: Sean Mintus

Editorial Assistant: Catherine Rice

Managing Editor, College: Marian Johnson

Electronic Media Editor: Patrick Shriner

Electronic Media Assistant: Carson Russell

Marketing Manager, Psychology: Andrea Matter

Design Directors: Hope Miller Goodell, Chris Welch

Interior Designer: Lisa Buckley

Photo Editor: Michael Fodera

Photo Researcher: Jane Miller

Permissions Manager: Megan Jackson

Composition: Jouve North America

Manufacturing: Quad Graphics

Library of Congress Cataloging-in-Publication Data

Social psychology / Thomas Gilovich ... [et al.]. — 3rd ed.
    p. cm.
Rev. ed. of: Social psychology / Thomas Gilovich, Dacher Keltner, Richard E. Nisbett. 2nd ed. c2011.
Includes bibliographical references and index.
ISBN 978-0-393-91323-1 (hbk.)
1. Social psychology.   I. Gilovich, Thomas.   II. Gilovich, Thomas. Social psychology.
HM1033.G52 2013
302—dc23

2012024089

W. W. Norton & Company, Inc., 500 Fifth Avenue, New York, N.Y. 10110
www.wwnorton.com
W. W. Norton & Company Ltd., Castle House, 75/76 Wells Street, London W1T 3QT

3 4 5 6 7 8 9 0

About the Authors

THOMAS GILOVICH is Professor of Psychology and Co-Director of the Center for Behavioral Economics and Decision Research at Cornell University. He has taught social psychology for 30 years and is the recipient of the Russell Distinguished Teaching Award at Cornell. His research focuses on how people evaluate the evidence of their everyday experiences to make judgments, form beliefs, and decide on courses of action. He is a member of the American Academy of Arts and Sciences and a fellow of the American Psychological Society, the American Psychological Association, the Society for Personality and Social Psychology, the Society of Experimental Social Psychology, and the Committee for Skeptical Inquiry.

DACHER KELTNER is Professor of Psychology and the Director of the Greater Good Science Center at the University of California, Berkeley. He has taught social psychology for the past 18 years and is the recipient of the Distinguished Teaching Award for Letters and Sciences. His research focuses on the prosocial emotions (such as love, sympathy, and gratitude), morality, and power. Other awards include the Western Psychological Association's award for outstanding contribution to research, the Positive Psychology Prize for excellence in research, and the Distinguished Mentoring Award at UC Berkeley. He is a fellow of the American Psychological Association, the American Psychological Society, and the Society for Personality and Social Psychology. In 2008, the *Utne Reader* listed Dacher as one of the 50 visionaries changing the world.

SERENA CHEN is Professor of Psychology and the Marian E. and Daniel E. Koshland, Jr. Distinguished Chair for Innovative Teaching and Research at the University of California, Berkeley. She has taught social psychology for the past 15 years and is the recipient of the Distinguished Teaching Award from Berkeley's Social Science Division. Her research focuses on the impact of close relationships on the self and identity, and on the intrapersonal and interpersonal consequences of social power. She is a fellow of the Society of Personality and Social Psychology, and is the recipient of the Early Career Award from the International Society for Self and Identity. The American Psychological Society also identified her as a Rising Star.

RICHARD E. NISBETT is Theodore M. Newcomb Distinguished University Professor of Psychology at the University of Michigan and Research Professor at Michigan's Institute for Social Research. He has taught courses in social psychology, cultural psychology, cognitive psychology, and evolutionary psychology. His research focuses on how people from different cultures think, perceive, feel, and act in different ways. He is the recipient of the Distinguished Scientific Contribution Award of the American Psychological Association and the William James Fellow Award of the American Psychological Society and is a member of the National Academy of Sciences and the American Academy of Arts and Sciences.

Contents in Brief

Preface

A FRESH PERSPECTIVE IN SOCIAL PSYCHOLOGY

Social psychology illuminates and clarifies the nature of human beings and their social world. It is a science that offers novel insights into the foundations of moral sentiments, the origins of violence, and the reasons people fall in love. It offers basic tools for understanding how people persuade one another, why people trust each other and cooperate, and how people rationalize their undesirable actions. It offers science-based answers to questions human beings have been thinking about since we started to reflect on who we are: Are we rational creatures? How can we find happiness? What is the proper relationship of the individual to the larger society? How are we shaped by the culture in which we are raised?

After decades of collective experience teaching social psychology, we decided at the turn of the twenty-first century to put pen to paper (or rather fingers to keyboard) and write our own vision of this fascinating discipline. It was an ideal time to do so. Many new developments in the field were reshaping social psychology. Ten years of study had revealed how different kinds of culture—country of origin, regional culture, social class—shape human thought, feeling, and action. Evolutionary theory was helping to guide how social psychologists study things such as homicide, morality, and cooperation. Social psychologists were making inroads into the study of the brain. Specific areas of interest to us—judgment and decision making, emotion, altruism, and well-being—had emerged as well-defined areas deserving full treatment. The lure of writing a textbook, and the challenge in doing so, was to capture all of these new developments and integrate them with the timeless classics of social psychology that make it such a captivating discipline.

Our combined experience in teaching and conducting research in social psychology was substantially increased when Serena Chen signed on as coauthor. Serena brings to the project a decade and a half of experience in teaching social psychology. Her expertise in several core areas in the field—including the self, social cognition, attitudes and persuasion, and close relationships—gives our book an even more comprehensive and balanced view of the field. Writing this edition of our text, now as a gang of four, has been deeply rewarding. Our fascination with the field, and our pride in being a part of it, has been rekindled and magnified. It is gratifying to have this book reach the minds of the next generation of social psychology students.

THE STORY OF OUR SCIENCE

Whether students end up as teachers, salespeople, or talent agents, or as software designers, forest rangers, or book editors, other people are going to be the center of their lives. All of us grow up dependent on the members of our nuclear family (and in many cultural contexts, a larger extended family); we go through adolescence obsessed with our social standing and intensely focused on the prospects for romance and sexuality; and as adults we seek out others in the workplace, at clubs, in places of worship, and on holidays. Social psychologists spend their professional lives studying this intense sociality, examining how we act, think, and feel in all of these social encounters—and why we act, think, and feel that way. Above all else, we wanted our book to capture the fundamentally social nature of human life and to present the clever, informative, and sometimes inspiring methods that social psychologists have used to study and understand the social life around us.

In our teaching, we have found that many great studies in social psychology are simple narratives: the narrative of the person who felt compelled to harm another person in the name of science, the narrative of the clergyman who did not help someone in need because he was in a hurry, the narrative of the Southerner whose blood pressure rose when he was insulted in a hallway, the story of the young researcher who lived among hunter-gatherers in New Guinea to discover universal facial expressions. In our experience, teaching social psychology can bring so many "Aha!" moments—precisely because of these stories that are embedded within, and that inspire, our science.

To make sure students gain an understanding of the scientific process—and to ensure that they hone their critical thinking skills—we approach the subject of research methods in two ways. Chapter 2: The Methods of Social Psychology is an overview of the most important elements of conducting research in social psychology. It ties the methods of social psychology together by showing how many of them can be applied to a single problem—the nature of the "culture of honor." That chapter, and much of the rest of the book, is oriented toward providing the critical thinking skills that are the hallmark of social psychology. We show how the tools of social psychology can be used to critique research in the behavioral and medical sciences that the student reads about on the Web and in magazines and newspapers. More important, we show how the methods of social psychology can be used to understand everyday life and to figure out how to navigate new situations. We then embed the discussion of methodological issues throughout the book, in the context of various lines of research, melding the content of social psychology together with the means of uncovering that content and showing how the principles that underlie research can be used to understand ordinary events in people's lives.

Our coverage of research methods, and indeed our treatment of everything in the book, was designed to convey to the student that social psychology is a productive *scientific* enterprise. Much of the subject matter of social psychology—attraction, conformity, prejudice—readily engages the student's attention and imagination. The material sells itself. But in most textbook summaries of the field, the presentation comes across as a list of unconnected topics—as one intriguing fact after another. As a result, students often come away thinking of social psychology as all fun and games. That's fine up to a point. Social psychology *is* fun. But it is much more than that, and we have tried to show how the highlights of our field—the classic findings and the exciting new developments—are part of a scientific study of human nature that can sit with pride next to biology, chemistry, and physics and that is worthy of the most serious-minded student's attention.

The book's graphics are designed to complement and enhance the material covered in the text. We believe that students understand methodological issues best when they see them applied to questions that capture their interest, so our Scientific Method figures highlight the details of particularly informative experiments, bringing the parables of social psychology to life. You Be the Subject figures similarly help students get an insider's view of experimentation in social psychology and how it all works. Annotated figures help students read data graphics and understand the take-away points of the research. Throughout the text, Focus On boxes cover specific approaches to social psychology, including recent developments such as neuroscientific approaches to the social brain and the study of happiness, or positive psychology. These boxes allow the student to get a flavor of the trends in our field and can be elaborated as the instructor sees fit. We have tried to make sure that all of our field's varied methods—for example, archival analyses, semantic and affective priming, neuroimaging, and participant observation—are discussed in sufficient depth to give the reader an understanding of how they work and what their strengths and weaknesses are.

THE APPLICATION OF SOCIAL PSYCHOLOGY TO EVERYDAY LIFE

Possibly the easiest part of writing a social psychology textbook is pointing out to the student the enormous applied implications of what the field has to offer. We do a great deal of that pointing throughout the text. Each chapter begins with events in the real world that drive home the themes and wisdom of social psychology. For example, Chapter 3: The Social Self begins with the story of Eminem and his alter ego, Slim Shady. Chapter 12: Groups begins with a discussion of the protest movements that have come to be known as the Arab Spring—and how the uprisings were aided by the advent of social media. Chapter 14: Altruism begins with the story of Wesley Autrey, who jumped onto the tracks in front of an oncoming subway train to save the life of Cameron Hollopeter. What better way for the student to ponder the findings of social psychology than by relying on them to understand current events? Many of the Focus On boxes profile real-world applications of the wisdom of social psychology— for example, in understanding how black uniforms make professional athletes more aggressive or how meditation might shift a person's brain chemistry.

To bring into sharper focus the relevance of social psychology to daily living, we have four applied mini-chapters, or modules, at the end of the book. These modules bring science-based insight to bear on four areas of great importance to just about everyone: the latest findings on health and how science-based, practical techniques help us cope with stress during difficult times; the new science of behavioral economics and how it can help us lead more financially stable and rewarding lives; the latest discoveries in the study of human intelligence and education; and a new module on social psychological insights into how the legal system functions and how it can be improved. By some yardsticks, social psychology is only as good as the relevance of its findings to advancing human welfare. We believe that these four applied modules illustrate the great past successes and future promise of our field.

WHAT'S NEW IN THE THIRD EDITION

The cumulative nature of science requires revisions that do justice to the latest discoveries and evolving views of the field. Our Third Edition has much to offer in this regard. The student will learn about a great many new discoveries in social psychology. Here is a small sampling.

In Chapter 3: The Social Self, we include much additional theory and research developing the key notion that the self is fundamentally social and shifts as a function of the social context. We added sections describing research showing that both social comparison processes and self-control strategies can function automatically.

In Chapter 4: Social Cognition, we cover a topic that to this point has been (surprisingly) ignored in social psychology textbooks—construal level theory. Research in this area makes it clear that people sometimes construe events at a very low level, in terms of concrete details, and sometimes at a high level, in terms of more abstract features. How people construe an event, furthermore, influences such things as whether they tend to be happy or dissatisfied with an outcome, or whether they are optimistic or pessimistic about an upcoming event.

In Chapter 5: Social Perception, we present important work on how people can recall their past behavior or simulate their future actions by imagining themselves from the "outside," much as an observer would, or from the "inside," looking out at the environment. This simple difference in perspective has great influence on how people think, feel, and act.

In Chapter 6: Emotion, we present new findings documenting the social importance of touch (for example, in promoting cooperation in NBA teams), showing how mimicry is crucial to friendships, and showing how emotions like disgust are drivers of moral judgment.

Chapter 8: Persuasion covers the latest in social psychological approaches to political ideology, as well recent findings on barriers to persuasion.

Chapter 9: Social Influence has a new section on norms that integrates old ideas on the subject with newer research documenting how information about norms can be used to influence voting behavior, energy conservation, and binge drinking.

Chapter 12: Groups has a new section on power, which explores who tends to grab the reins of power and how having power influences what a person attends to and how a person tends to act toward others.

In Chapter 13: Aggression, we present remarkable new evidence linking inequality within a culture to levels of aggression, and we consider in more depth the topics of violence against women and of barriers to conflict resolution.

Chapter 14: Altruism presents new findings on how people from the upper classes are less altruistic in many respects than those from lower-class backgrounds, and on how altruism and cooperation are contagious, spreading from one person to another.

In making these changes, we have been careful to preserve the previous editions' insistence that each chapter stand alone, so that the chapters can be read in any order. We have done so stylistically by writing chapters that are complete narratives in their own right. Our chapters stand on their own theoretically as well, being organized around social psychology's emphasis on situationism, construal, and automaticity and highlighting important issues addressing what is universal about human behavior and what is variable across cultures. So although our table of contents suggests a particular order of covering the material, instructors will find it easy to present the topics in whatever order best suits their own preferences or needs.

ACKNOWLEDGMENTS

No book is written in a vacuum. Many people have helped us in the course of writing this text, starting with our families. Karen Dashiff Gilovich was her usual bundle of utterly lovable qualities that make the sharing of lives so enjoyable—and the difficulties of authorship so tolerable. Mollie McNeil was a steady source of kindness, enthusiasm, and critical eye and ear. Mark McDermott was an unequivocal source of support and stood ready as a sounding board. Sarah and Susan Nisbett were sounding boards and life-support systems. Mikki Hebl, Dennis Regan, and Tomi-Ann Roberts went well beyond the call of collegial duty by reading every chapter of early editions and providing us with useful commentary. In addition to giving us the considerable benefit of their good judgment and good taste, they also pointed out a few of our blind spots and saved us from an occasional embarrassing error.

We are also grateful to Jon Durbin, Vanessa Drake-Johnson, and Paul Rozin for bringing us together on this project and to Sheri Snavely for steering the book through its second and third editions. We have had a great deal of fun working together and have enjoyed the opportunity to think and write about the broad discipline that is social psychology. Thanks. We would also like to extend our deeply felt thanks to Beth Ammerman, whose talent (and endurance) as developmental editor is beyond impressive. We also owe a great deal to our tireless project editor Carla Talmadge, photo researcher Jane Miller, photo editor Michael Fodera, and production manager Sean Mintus. Our media editor, Patrick Shriner, has worked diligently to develop modern and high-quality media for our book, including the new interactive instructors' suite, student eBook, online tutorials, video, and online labs. We also are grateful for the marketing efforts of Andrea Matter and the Norton travelers who have worked to make this book a success.

Our thanks to the following people for their helpful suggestions and close reading of various chapters in the first, second, and third editions of the book.

Glenn Adams, *University of Toronto*

Craig Anderson, *Iowa State University*

Bob Arkin, *Ohio State University*

Clarissa Arms-Chavez, *Auburn University, Montgomery*

Joan Bailey, *New Jersey City University*

Miranda Barone, *University of Southern California*

Doris Bazzini, *Appalachian State*

Kristin Beals, *California State University, Fullerton*

Gordon Bear, *Ramapo College of New Jersey*

Elliott Beaton, *McMaster University*

Leonard Berkowitz, *University of Wisconsin–Madison*

Frank Bernieri, *Oregon State University*

Anila Bhagavatula, *California State University, Long Beach*

Susan Boon, *Calgary University*

Tim Brock, *Ohio State University*

Don Carlston, *Purdue University*

Sandra Carpenter, *University of Alabama*

Bettina Casad, *California Polytechnic State University, Pomona*

Nicholas Christenfeld, *University of California, San Diego*

Charlene Christie, *Oneonta College*

Eric Cooley, *Western Oregon University*

Alita Cousins, *Eastern Connecticut State University*

Karen Couture, *Keene State College*

Traci Craig, *University of Idaho*

Ken Cramer, *University of Windsor*

Chris Crandall, *University of Kansas*

Susan Cross, *Iowa State University*

George Cvetkovich, *Western Washington University*

Alex Czopp, *Western Washington University*

Deborah Davis, *University of Nevada, Reno*

Chris De La Ronde, *Austin Community College*

Ken DeMarree, *Texas Tech University*

Rachel Dinero, *Cazenovia College*

Pete Ditto, *University of California, Irvine*

Dan Dolderman, *University of Toronto*

John Dovidio, *Yale University*

David Duemler, *Lane Community College*

Richard P. Eibach, *Yale University*

Scott Eidelman, *University of Arkansas, Fayetteville*

Naomi Eisenberger, *University of California, Los Angeles*

Jack Feldman, *Georgia Institute of Technology*

Eli Finkel, *Northwestern University*

Marcia Finkelstein, *University of South Florida*

Madeleine Fugere, *Eastern Connecticut State University*

Azenett Garza-Caballero, *Weber State University*

Daniel Gilbert, *Harvard University*

Omri Gillath, *University of Kansas*

Tay Hack, *Angelo State University*

Jon Haidt, *University of Virginia*

Judith Harachiewicz, *University of Wisconsin, Madison*

Lisa Harrison, *California State University, Sacramento*

Todd Hartman, *Appalachian State University*

Lora Haynes, *University of Louisville*

Steve Heine, *University of British Columbia*

Edward Hirt, *Indiana University*

Zach Hohman, *California State University, Fullerton*

Gina Hoover, *Ohio State University*

Amy Houlihan, *Texas A&M, Corpus Christi*

Matthew I. Isaak, *University of Louisiana at Lafayette*

Kareem Johnson, *Temple University*

Kimberly Kahn, *Portland State University*

Andy Karpinski, *Temple University*

Iva Katzarska-Miller, *University of Kansas*

Sulki Kim, *California State University, Fullerton*

Leslie Kirby, *Vanderbilt University*

Marc Kiviniem, *University of Nebraska, Lincoln*

Stan B. Klein, *University of California, Santa Barbara*

Catalina E. Kopetz, *University of Maryland*

Ziva Kunda (deceased), *Waterloo University*

Marianne LaFrance, *Yale University*

Alan Lambert, *Washington University*

Jeff Larsen, *Texas Tech University*

Norman Li, *University of Texas, Austin*

Debra Lieberman, *University of Hawaii*

Anson (Annie) Long, *Indiana University of Pennsylvania*

Debbie S. Ma, *California State University, Northridge*

Doug McCann, *York University*

Connie Meinholdt, *Ferris State University*

Batja Mesquita, *University of Leuven*

Cynthia Mohr, *Portland State University*

Daniel Molden, *Northwestern University*

Mark Muravan, *University at Albany*

Mary Murphy, *University of California, Irvine*

Todd Nelson, *California State University, Stanislaus*

Angela J. Nierman, *University of Kansas*

Clark Ohnesorge, *St. Olaf College*

M. Minda Oriña, *St. Olaf College*

Bernadette Park, *University of Colorado*

Gerrod Parrott, *Georgetown University*

Ashby Plant, *Florida State University*

Jacqueline Pope-Tarrence, *Western Kentucky University*

Deborah Prentice, *Princeton University*

Mary Pritchard, *Boise State University*

Emily Pronin, *Princeton University*

Denise Reiling, *Eastern Michigan University*

Jane Richards, *University of Texas, Austin*

Jennifer Richeson, *Northwestern University*

Neal Roese, *University of Illinois at Urbana–Champaign*

Regina Roof-Ray, *Hartford Community College*

Alex Rothman, *University of Minnesota, Twin Cities Campus*

Darcy Santor, *Dalhousie University*

Constantine Sedikides, *University of Southampton*

Sohaila Shakib, *California State University, Dominguez Hills*

Gregory P. Shelley, *Kutztown University*

J. Nicole Shelton, *Princeton University*

Jeff Sherman, *Northwestern University*

Colleen Sinclair, *University of Missouri, Columbia*

Elizabeth R. Spievak, *Bridgewater State College*

Sue Sprecher, *Illinois State University*

Emily Stark, *Minnesota State University, Mankato*

Jeff Stone, *University of Arizona*

Justin Storbeck, *Queens College*

Michael Strube, *Washington University, St. Louis*

Kate Sweeny, *University of California, Riverside*

Lisa Szafran, *Syracuse University*

Lauren A. Taglialatela, *Kennesaw State University*

Chuck Tate, *San Francisco State University*

Warren Thorngate, *Carleton University*

Zakary Tormala, *Indiana University, Bloomington*

Jeanne Tsai, *Stanford University*

Jim Uleman, *New York University*

Naomi Wagner, *San Jose State University*

Nathan Westbrook, *California State University, Fullerton*

David Wilder, *Rutgers University*

Ben Wilkowski, *University of Wyoming*

Edward Witt, *Michigan State University*

Connie Wolfe, *Muhlenberg College*

Joseph Vandallo, *University of South Florida*

Leigh Ann Vaughn, *Ithaca College*

Marcellene Watson-Derbigny, *Sacramento State University*

Aaron Wichman, *Western Kentucky University*

Nancy Yanchus, *Georgia Southern University*

Jennifer Yanowitz, *University of Minnesota, Twin Cities Campus*

Janice Yoder, *University of Akron*

Jason Young, *Hunter College*

Randy Young, *Bridgewater State University*

Contents

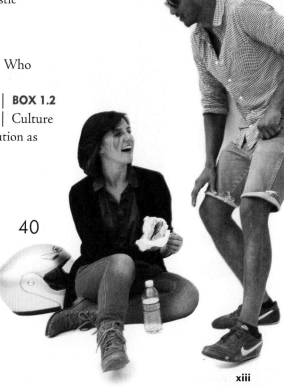

CHAPTER 5   Social Attribution: Explaining Behavior   152

CHAPTER 8   Persuasion   272

CHAPTER 9   Social Influence   308

Application Module 1 Social Psychology and Health 562

Application Module 2 Social Psychology and Personal Finance 574

Application Module 3 Social Psychology and Education 589

Social Psychology

THIRD EDITION

An Invitation to Social Psychology

WHEN ONE OF THE AUTHORS of this book was a teenager, the buses in the Southwestern city where he lived had signs over a row of seats reading "colored section." Around the same time, one of today's most distinguished social psychologists—the African-American Claude Steele—was prohibited from swimming in the public pools of Chicago (except on Wednesdays) because of his race. Meanwhile, black men with PhDs were stuck in low-status jobs—often as sleeping car porters or post office clerks.

Most white people at the time accepted such injustices and would not have thought of protesting these public policies, which strike the great majority of Americans today as appalling. And when black people in the South began to demand the right to vote without harassment as well as the right to use public accommodations such as restrooms and restaurants, many whites in both the South and the North initially regarded these demonstrations as disturbances of the peace. Were these people monsters? On the contrary, most of them were decent and kind, even in their interactions with individual black people.

But then newspapers and television began showing civil rights demonstrators being set upon by dogs and fire hoses. And when a black church in Birmingham was firebombed and four little girls were killed, public opinion in much of the country turned in favor of the demonstrators almost overnight. The same people who a few years before had merely accepted the status quo were now in favor of civil rights. In 1964, the Civil Rights Act was overwhelmingly passed by Congress and signed by Lyndon Johnson, a president from Texas.

Flash forward a few decades. Black people have now served as the CEOs of multibillion-dollar corporations and as presidents of major universities. Four of the ten most bankable movie actors of the last 20 years are black men. A black man, Colin Powell, has served as secretary of state and as chairman of the Joint

Chiefs of Staff, the highest military office in the United States. Another former secretary of state, Condoleezza Rice, is a black woman who grew up at the same time as the little girls who were killed in the church fire in Birmingham—and in a nearby neighborhood. Her successor was appointed by Barack Obama, the first U.S. president of African descent.

The history of race relations in the United States is full of both disturbing and uplifting episodes. But for social psychologists especially, it is also full of fascinating questions. How could one of the founders of the country, a beacon of eighteenth-century enlightenment, write that it is self-evident that all men are created equal—yet keep scores of slaves? Why were the Northern states not more magnanimous in their treatment of the defeated South after the end of the Civil War? Why did a dramatic social revolution in the South, overthrowing practices that were deeply engrained in the society, not produce a bloodbath? Why did the dismantling of many barriers to black success leave millions of blacks mired in abject poverty? How could countless white people move in a matter of a few years from acceptance of segregation to moral revulsion toward it?

In this book, you will read about theories and research findings that shed light on many of these questions. You will read about persuasion and attitude change, about people's capacity for self-deception, about the economic roots of social behavior, about the influence of culture, about the origins of and antidotes to racial prejudice, and about the sources of violence and the forces that can counter violence. You will also learn about the tools social psychologists use to address these questions—the scientific methods that allow them to supplement historical analysis, anthropological inquiry, and common sense. This chapter explains what social psychology is and what social psychologists study. It also presents some of the basic concepts of social psychology: the surprising degree to which social situations can influence behavior, the interpretive processes people use to understand situations, and the overlapping contributions of conscious and unconscious thinking to our understanding of the social world. Some recent developments in social psychology are also described here—namely, the application of evolutionary concepts to human behavior and the discovery of some significant differences in human cultures that frequently lead people in different societies to respond to the "same" situation in very different ways.

CHARACTERIZING SOCIAL PSYCHOLOGY

People have long sought explanations for human behavior. Stories, parables, and folk wisdom have been passed from generation to generation, attempting to explain why people do what they do and prescribing behaviors to avoid or follow. Social psychologists go beyond folk wisdom and try to establish a scientific basis for understanding human behavior. **Social psychology** can be defined as the scientific study of the feelings, thoughts, and behaviors of individuals in social situations.

social psychology The scientific study of the feelings, thoughts, and behaviors of individuals in social situations.

Why are people inclined to stereotype members of different groups? Why do people risk their lives to help others? Why do some marriages flourish and others fail? How do orderly crowds turn into violent mobs? These sorts of questions lie at the heart of social psychology, and careful research has provided at least partial answers to all of them. Some of the answers probably will not surprise you. For example, we tend to like people who like us, and the people we like generally have attitudes and interests that are similar to ours. When experimental findings reflect what our intuitions and folk wisdom say will happen, social psychologists elaborate that folk wisdom—they seek to discover when it applies and what lies behind the phenomenon in question. In contrast, other answers have been so counterintuitive that they surprised even the social psychologists who conducted the research. As you will see throughout this book, many of our most strongly held folk theories or intuitions fail to give complete answers to important questions. And others are just plain wrong. Social psychologists test these intuitions by devising studies and crafting experiments that successfully isolate the causes of behavior in social situations.

Explaining Behavior

In April 2004, more than a year after the start of the war in Iraq, CBS broadcast a story on *60 Minutes II* that exposed American atrocities against Iraqi prisoners in the Abu Ghraib prison near Baghdad. CBS showed photos of naked prisoners with plastic bags over their heads, stacked up in a pyramid and surrounded by laughing male and female American soldiers. Other photos showed hooded prisoners standing on narrow pedestals with their arms stretched out and electric wires attached to their bodies. CBS also reported that prisoners had been required to simulate sexual acts.

The reaction on the part of many Iraqis and others in the Arab world was to regard the acts as evidence that the United States had malevolent intentions toward Arabs (Hauser, 2004). Most Americans, too, were appalled at the abuse and ashamed of the behavior of the U.S. soldiers. Many of those who saw the photos on television or in the newspapers assumed that the soldiers who had perpetrated these acts were rotten apples—exceptions to a rule of common decency prevailing in the military and the general population.

But social psychologists were not so quick to make such an assumption. Indeed, thirty years before the atrocities at Abu Ghraib, Philip Zimbardo and his colleagues paid 24 Stanford University undergraduate men, chosen for their good character and mental health, to be participants in a study of a simulated prison

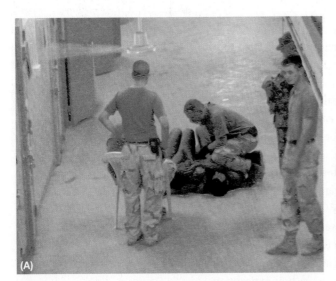 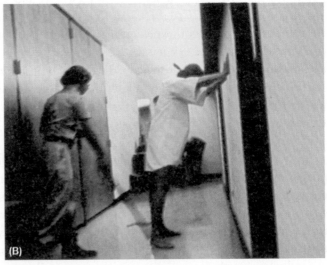

Prison Situations and Intimidation (A) Military guards at the Abu Ghraib prison in Iraq used torture, humiliation, and intimidation to try to obtain information from the prisoners. This included stripping them and making them lie naked in the prison corridors. (B) Such degradation echoes what happened in the Zimbardo prison study, as shown in this photo of a "guard" seeking to humiliate one of his prisoners at the simulated prison.

(Haney, Banks, & Zimbardo, 1973). The researchers flipped a coin to determine who would be a "guard" and who would be a "prisoner." The guards wore green fatigue uniforms and reflective sunglasses. The prisoners wore tunics with nylon stocking caps and had a chain locked around one ankle. The "prison" was set up in the basement of the psychology department, and the researchers anticipated the study would last for two weeks. But the guards quickly turned to verbal abuse and physical humiliation, requiring the prisoners to wear bags over their heads, stripping them naked, and requiring them to engage in simulated sex acts. The study had to be terminated after six days because the behavior of the guards produced extreme stress reactions in several of the prisoners.

Zimbardo today maintains that the balance of power in prisons is so unequal that they tend to be brutal places unless heavy constraints are applied to curb the guards' worst impulses. Thus, at both Abu Ghraib and Stanford, "It's not that we put bad apples in a good barrel. We put good apples in a bad barrel. The barrel corrupts anything that it touches" (quoted in Schwartz, 2004). Some might contend that the soldiers in Iraq were only following orders and that, left to their own devices, they would not have chosen to behave as they did. This may be the case, but it only pushes the question back one step: Why did they follow such orders?

Social psychologists seek to find answers to just such questions. They study situations in which people exert influence over one another, as well as the ways people respond to influence attempts of various kinds. Social psychologists are also interested in how people make sense of their world—how they decide what and whom to believe, how they make inferences about the motives, personalities, and abilities of other people, and how they reach conclusions about the causes of events.

Much of what social psychologists have learned about human behavior is invaluable. Social psychology now forms a significant part of the curriculum in many schools of business, public health, social work, education, law, and medicine. Social psychological research on such topics as judgment and decision making, social influence, and how people function in groups is relevant to all those fields. Social psychologists apply their knowledge to important questions concerning individuals and society at large, studying how to reduce stereotyping and prejudice in the classroom and workplace; how to make eyewitness testimony more reliable; how physicians can best use diverse sources of information to make a correct diagnosis; what goes wrong in airplane cockpits when there is an accident or near accident; and how businesses, governments, and individuals can make better decisions.

Research by social psychologists regularly influences government policy. For example, research on the effects of different kinds of welfare programs is used in shaping government assistance policies. Research also affects decisions by the courts. The landmark *Brown v. Board of Education* (1954) ruling that struck down school segregation in the United States drew heavily on social psychological research, which indicated that segregated schools were inherently unequal in their effects (and thus unconstitutional).

By the time you finish this book, you will have acquired a greater understanding of yourself and others. You will also have knowledge you can apply in your education, your career, and your interpersonal relationships.

Explaining Situations Social psychologists seek to understand how individuals act in relation to others in social situations and why. Is the father in this photo a particularly impatient person, or is his son being particularly obnoxious? If the son is being particularly obnoxious, how might the father best behave in order to encourage better behavior?

Comparing Social Psychology with Related Disciplines

Events like those at Abu Ghraib can be studied from many viewpoints, including those of anthropologists, criminologists, sociologists, and personality psychologists. Each type of professional takes a different approach to what happened and offers different kinds of explanations.

Personality psychology is a close cousin of social psychology, but it stresses individual differences in behavior rather than the social situation. Personality psychologists try to find a consistent pattern in the way an individual behaves across situations—to find an individual's position on a trait dimension. Thus social psychologists would examine the general situation at Abu Ghraib, in which orders were not clear but the guards were pressured to "soften up" the prisoners to get information about other insurgents and future attacks. Personality psychologists would instead look at whether certain traits and dispositions—for example, sadism or hostility—would predict cruel behavior across a range of situations.

Social psychology is also related to cognitive psychology, the study of how people perceive, think about, and remember aspects of the world. In fact, many psychologists call themselves cognitive social psychologists. Social psychologists differ from cognitive psychologists primarily in that the topics they study are usually social, for example, social behavior and perceptions of other people. Cognitive psychologists would be more likely to study categorization processes or memory for words or objects.

Sociology is the study of behavior of people in the aggregate. Sociologists study institutions, subgroups, bureaucracies, mass movements, and changes in the demographic characteristics of populations (for example, age, gender, socioeconomic status). Social psychologists sometimes do sociological work themselves, although they are likely to bring an interest in individual behavior to the study of aggregates. A sociologist might study how economic or government policy influences marriage and divorce rates in a population, whereas a social psychologist would be more likely to study why individuals fall in love, get married, and sometimes get divorced.

THE POWER OF THE SITUATION

Are we all capable of acts of brutality? In 1963 the philosopher Hannah Arendt suggested as much in her controversial book, *Eichmann in Jerusalem* (Arendt, 1963). Arendt described the trial of Adolf Eichmann, the notorious architect of Hitler's plan to exterminate the Jews in Nazi-occupied Europe. Advancing a very provocative thesis, Arendt described Eichmann as little more than a bureaucrat doing his job. While not condoning his actions (Arendt herself was Jewish), Arendt argued that Eichmann was not the demented, sadistic personality everyone expected (and that the prosecutor claimed he was), but instead a boring, unimaginative cog in a machine that he served with a resigned (if nevertheless perverse) sense of duty. Perhaps even more disturbing, the logical conclusion of Arendt's theory is that any one of us is capable of performing acts of brutality. Look at the person sitting closest to you right now. Do you think that he or she is capable of atrocities? Do you think that any situation could be so powerful that an ordinary person—even you—could act as Eichmann did in Nazi Germany or as the prison guards behaved at Abu Ghraib?

Arendt's book created a firestorm of indignant protests, and she was denounced for what many regarded as her attempt to exonerate a monster. But research has supported Arendt's unorthodox views about what she called "the banality of evil." This research raises a question that is central to the study of social psychology: How does the situation that people find themselves in affect their behavior?

Kurt Lewin, the founder of modern social psychology, was a Jewish Berliner who fled Nazi Germany in the 1930s and became a professor at the University of Iowa and then at MIT. Lewin was a physicist before becoming a psychologist, and he applied a powerful idea from physics to an understanding of psychological existence. He believed that the behavior of people, like the behavior of objects, is always a function of the field of forces in which they find themselves (Lewin, 1935). To understand how fast a solid object will travel through a medium, for example, we must know such things as the viscosity of the medium, the force of gravity, and any initial force applied to the object. In the case of people, the forces are psychological as well as physical. Of course the person's own attributes are also important determinants of behavior, but these attributes always interact with the situation to produce the resulting behavior.

The social equivalent of Lewin's concept of the field of forces is the role of the situation, especially the social situation, in guiding behavior. The main situational influences on our behavior, influences that we often misjudge or fail to see altogether, are the actions—and sometimes just the mere presence—of other people. Friends, romantic partners, even total strangers can cause us to be kinder or meaner, smarter or dumber, lazier or more hardworking, bolder or more cautious. They can produce drastic changes in our beliefs and behavior not only by what they tell us explicitly, but also by modeling through their actions what we should think and do, by subtly implying that our acceptability as a friend or group member depends on adopting their views or behaving as they do, or even by making us feel that our freedom is being encroached on by their influence attempts, thereby causing us to behave in ways that are the opposite of what we are being pressed upon to do. We rely on other people for clues about what emotions to feel in various situations and even to define who we are as individuals. All these effects have been shown in numerous studies demonstrating the power of the situation.

The Milgram Experiment

In the same year as the publication of Arendt's book, Stanley Milgram (1963, 1974) published the results of a now-classic experiment on social influence. Milgram advertised in the local newspaper for men to participate in a study on learning and memory at Yale University in exchange for a modest amount of money. (In subsequent experiments, women also participated; the results were similar.) When the volunteers—a mix of laborers, middle-class individuals, and professionals ranging in age from their 20s to their 50s—arrived at the laboratory, a man in a white lab coat told them they would be participating in a study of the

The Person or the Situation? Adolf Eichmann was apprehended in Argentina, where he had escaped after the end of World War II, and taken to Israel to stand trial for the murder of 6 million Jews. Here he stands with Israeli police in a bulletproof glass cage during his trial. Was Eichmann a brutal murderer or simply a bureaucrat following the orders of his superiors?

Kurt Lewin A pioneer of modern social psychology, Lewin stressed the importance of the field of forces, including the social situation, in affecting a person's behavior.

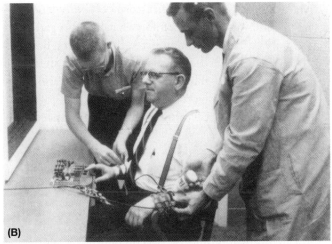

The Milgram Study To examine the role of social influence, Stanley Milgram set up a study in which participants believed they were testing a learner (actually a confederate) and punishing him with shocks when he gave the wrong answer. (A) Milgram's "shock machine." (B) The participant and experimenter attaching electrodes to the "learner" before testing begins.

effects of punishment on learning. There would be a "teacher" and a "learner," and the learner would try to memorize word pairs such as *wild/duck*. The volunteer and another man, a somewhat heavyset, pleasant-looking man in his late 40s, drew slips of paper to determine who would play which role. But things were not as they seemed: the pleasant-looking man was actually an accomplice of the experimenter, and the drawing was rigged so that he was always the learner.

The participant "teacher" was then instructed to administer shocks—from 15 to 450 volts—to the "learner" each time he made an error. Labels under the shock switches ranged from "slight shock" through "danger: severe shock" to "XXX." The experimenter explained that the teacher was to administer shocks in ascending 15-volt magnitudes: 15 volts the first time the learner made an error, 30 volts the next time, and so on. The teacher was given a 45-volt shock so that he would have an idea of how painful the shocks would be. What he didn't know was that the learner, who was in another room, was not actually being shocked.

Most participants became concerned as the shock levels increased and turned to the experimenter to ask what should be done. But the experimenter insisted they go on. The first time the teachers expressed reservations, they were told, "Please continue." If the teacher balked, the experimenter said, "The experiment requires that you continue." If the teacher continued to hesitate, the experimenter said, "It's absolutely essential that you continue." If necessary, the experimenter escalated to, "You have no other choice. You must go on." If the participant asked whether the learner could suffer permanent physical injury, the experimenter said, "Although the shocks may be painful, there is no permanent tissue damage, so please go on."

In the end, despite the learner's groans, pleas, screams, and eventual silence as the intensity of the shocks increased, 80 percent of the participants continued past the 150-volt level—at which point the learner mentioned that he had a heart condition and screamed, "Let me out of here!" Fully 62.5 percent of the participants went all the way to the 450-volt level, delivering everything the shock generator could produce. The *average* amount of shock given was 360 volts, *after* the learner let out an agonized scream and became hysterical.

Milgram and other experts did not expect so many participants to continue to administer shocks as long as they did. (A panel of 39 psychiatrists predicted that only 20 percent of the participants would continue past the 150-volt level and that only 1 percent would continue past the 330-volt level.) At first, some researchers even expressed suspicion as to whether Milgram's participants really believed that they were shocking the learner. To convince the scientific community that his participants took the situation seriously, Milgram invited social scientists to observe his experiments from behind a one-way mirror. The observers could scarcely believe what they were seeing. One of them reported:

> I observed a mature and initially poised businessman enter the laboratory smiling and confident. Within twenty minutes he was reduced to a twitching, stuttering wreck, who was rapidly approaching a point of nervous collapse. He constantly pulled on his earlobe and twisted his hands. At one point he pushed his fist into his forehead and muttered: "Oh God, let's stop it." And yet he continued to respond to every word of the experimenter and obeyed to the end. (Milgram, 1963, p. 377)

Milgram's study and its implications are described in more detail in Chapter 9. For now, the important question is, What made the participants in Milgram's study engage in behavior that they had every reason to suspect might seriously harm another person? Milgram's participants were not heartless fiends. Instead, the situation was extraordinarily effective in getting them to do something that would normally fill them with horror. For example, the experiment was presented as a scientific investigation—an unfamiliar situation for most participants. In all probability, the participants had never been in a psychology experiment before, and they had never been in a situation in which they were being asked to do something that could so severely harm another individual. The experimenter explicitly took responsibility for what happened (Adolf Hitler frequently made similar pledges during the years he marched his nation over a precipice). Moreover, participants could not have guessed at the outset what the experiment involved, so they were not prepared to resist anyone's demands. And as Milgram stressed, the step-by-step nature of the procedure was undoubtedly crucial. If the participant didn't quit at 225 volts, then why quit at 255? If not at 420, then why at 435?

"Evil is obvious only in retrospect."

—Gloria Steinem

Seminarians as Samaritans

A classic experiment by John Darley and Daniel Batson (1973) shows the importance of the situation even more simply. These investigators asked students at the Princeton Theological Seminary about the basis of their religious orientation to determine whether particular students were primarily concerned with religion as a means toward personal salvation or were more concerned with religion for its other moral and spiritual values. After determining the basis of their religious concerns, the psychologists asked each young seminarian to go to another building to deliver a short sermon. The seminarians were told what route to follow to get there most easily. Some were told that they had plenty of time to get to the building where they were to deliver the sermon, and some were told that they were already late and should hurry. On the way to deliver their sermon—on the topic of the Good Samaritan, by the way—each of the seminarians passed a man who was sitting in a doorway with his head down, coughing and groaning, and in

FIGURE 1.1 **Scientific Method: The Power of the Situation and Helping**

Hypothesis: The likelihood that an individual will help another person in need depends heavily on situational factors, such as being in a hurry.

Research Method:

1. Seminary student participants were primed to think about helping by being asked to deliver a talk on the Good Samaritan.

2. Some participants were told they had to rush, while others were told they had plenty of time to reach the location of the talk.

3. Participants then passed by a "victim" in obvious need of help.

Results:

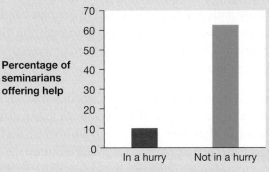

Percentage of seminarians offering help

Time pressure

CONCLUSION: The mundane fact of being in a hurry is such a powerful situational factor that it overrides people's helpful tendencies.

Source: Adapted from Darley & Batson (1973).

apparent need of help. It turned out that the nature of religious orientation was of no use in predicting whether the seminarians would offer assistance. But as you can see in **Figure 1.1**, whether seminarians were in a hurry or not was a very powerful predictor. The seminarians, it turned out, were pretty good Samaritans as a group—but only when they weren't in a rush.

The Fundamental Attribution Error

People are thus governed by situational factors—such as whether they are being pressured by someone or whether they are late—more than they tend to assume. At the same time, internal factors—the kind of person someone is—have much less influence than most people assume they do. You may be surprised by many of the findings reported in this book because most people underestimate the power of the external forces that operate on an individual and tend to assume, often mistakenly, that the causes of behavior can be found mostly within the person.

Psychologists call internal factors **dispositions**—that is, beliefs, values, personality traits, or abilities, whether real or imagined. People tend to think of dispositions as the underlying causes of behavior. Upon seeing a prison guard humiliating a prisoner, we may assume that the guard is a cruel person. Upon seeing a stranger in the street behaving angrily, we may assume that the person

dispositions Internal factors such as beliefs, values, personality traits, or abilities that guide a person's behavior.

is aggressive or ill tempered. Upon seeing an acquaintance being helpful, we may assume that the person is kinder than we had realized. Such judgments are valid far less often than we think. Seeing an acquaintance give a dollar to a beggar may prompt us to assume that the person is generous, but subsequent observations of the person in different situations might negate that assumption.

The failure to recognize the importance of situational influences on behavior, together with the tendency to overemphasize the importance of dispositions, or traits, was labeled the **fundamental attribution error** by Lee Ross (1977). Many findings in social psychology indicate that people should look for situational factors that might be affecting someone's behavior before assuming that the person has dispositions that match the behavior. As you read this book, you will become more attuned to situational factors and less inclined to assume that behavior can be fully explained by characteristics inherent in the individual. The ultimate lesson of social psychology is thus a compassionate one. Social psychology encourages us to look at another person's situation—to try to understand the complex field of forces acting on the individual—to fully understand the person's behavior.

fundamental attribution error The failure to recognize the importance of situational influences on behavior, and the corresponding tendency to overemphasize the importance of dispositions or traits on behavior.

"If you are like most people, then like most people, you don't know you're like most people."

—social psychologist Dan Gilbert

Channel Factors

Kurt Lewin (1952) introduced the concept of **channel factors** to help explain why certain circumstances that appear unimportant on the surface can have great consequences for behavior, either facilitating or blocking it. The term is also meant to reflect that such circumstances can sometimes guide behavior in a very particular direction by making it easier to follow one path rather than another. Consider a study by Howard Leventhal and others on how to motivate people to take advantage of health facilities' offerings of preventive care (Leventhal, Singer, & Jones, 1965). They attempted to persuade Yale students to get tetanus inoculations. To convince them that the inoculation was in their best interest, the researchers had them read scary materials about the number of ways a person could get tetanus (in addition to the proverbial rusty nail). To make sure they had the students' attention, the team showed them photos of people in the last stages of lockjaw. But not to worry—the students could avoid this fate simply by going to the student health center at any time and getting a free inoculation. Interviews showed that most participants formed the intention to get an inoculation. But only 3 percent did so. Other participants were given a map of the Yale campus with a circle around the health center and were asked to review their weekly schedule and decide on a convenient time to visit the center and the route they would take to get there. Bear in mind that these were seniors who knew perfectly well where the health center was, so such condescending treatment might produce little more than annoyance. In fact, it increased the percentage of students getting an inoculation ninefold, to 28 percent.

The channel factor in this case was the requirement to shape a vague intention into a concrete plan. A similar channel factor accounts for the use of public health services more generally. Attitudes about health; personality tests; demographic variables such as age, gender, and socioeconomic status; and other individual differences don't do a very good job of predicting who will use these services. The most powerful determinant of usage yet discovered is the distance to the closest facility (Van Dort & Moos, 1976).

channel factors Certain situational circumstances that appear unimportant on the surface but that can have great consequences for behavior, either facilitating or blocking it or guiding behavior in a particular direction.

Situations are often more powerful in their influence on behavior than we realize. Whether people are kind to others or not, whether they take action in their own best interest or not, can depend on subtle aspects of situations. We often overlook such situational factors when we try to understand our own behavior or that of others, and we often mistakenly attribute behavior to presumed traits, or dispositions (the fundamental attribution error).

THE ROLE OF CONSTRUAL

In his study of obedience, Milgram manipulated his participants' understanding of the situation they found themselves in by lulling them with soothing interpretations of events that were designed to throw them off the scent of anything that could be regarded as sinister. A "study participant" who had "chosen" to be in the "experiment" was "learning" a list of words with "feedback" that was given by the real participant in the form of electric shock.

A *participant* is someone who is acting freely; *learning* is a normal activity that often depends on *feedback*—a usually innocuous form of information. All this was taking place in an *experiment*—a benign activity carried out by trustworthy scientists. Our **construal** of situations and behavior refers to our interpretation of them and to the inferences, often unconscious, that we make about them. Whether we regard people as free agents or victims, as freedom fighters or terrorists, as migrant workers or illegal aliens, will affect our perceptions of their actions. And our perceptions drive our behavior toward them.

construal People's interpretation and inference about the stimuli or situations they confront.

Interpreting Reality

Look at **Figure 1.2**. Do you see a white triangle? Most people do. But in fact there is no white triangle. We construct a triangle in our mind out of the *gaps* in the picture. The gaps are located just where they would be if a triangle were laid over the outlined triangle and a portion of each of the three circles. That makes a good, clear image, but it's entirely a creation of our perceptual apparatus and our background assumptions about the visual world. These assumptions are automatic and unconscious, and they can be almost impossible to override. Now that you know the triangle is in your mind's eye and not on the page, do you still see it? Now look at **Figure 1.3**, a painting by surrealist artist Salvador Dali. Dali was a master at using the mind's tendency to construct meaningful figures from the gaps in an image. He created a number of well-known double images— paintings that could be perceived in two different ways, as in this painting.

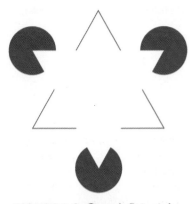

FIGURE 1.2 Gestalt Principles and Perception When viewing this figure, known as the Kanizsa triangle, people fill in the empty spaces in their mind and perceive a white triangle.

Our perceptions normally bear a resemblance to what the world is really like, but perception requires substantial interpretation on our part and is subject to significant error under certain conditions. What we see is not necessarily what is actually there but what is plausible—what makes a good, predictable "figure" in light of stored representations we have of the world and what makes sense in light of the context in which we encounter something. German psychologists in the early part of the twentieth century convincingly argued for this view in the case of visual perception. The theoretical orientation of those psychologists centered on the concept of *gestalt*, German for "form" or "figure." The basic idea of **Gestalt psychology** is that objects are perceived not by means of some passive and auto-

Gestalt psychology Based on the German word *gestalt*, meaning "form" or "figure," this approach stresses the fact that people perceive objects not by means of some automatic registering device but by active, usually unconscious interpretation of what the object represents as a whole.

FIGURE 1.3 Gestalt Principles in Art In his *Slave Market with Disappearing Bust of Voltaire*, Salvador Dali confronts the viewer with the bust of the French philosopher Voltaire (at center of painting). But on closer inspection, the bust is largely the product of the gap in the wall behind the two merchants. Their faces form Voltaire's eyes, and their collars form his nose and cheeks.

matic registering device, but by active, usually unconscious interpretation of what the object represents.

What's true for visual perception is even truer for judgments about the social world. Our judgments and beliefs are constructed from perceptions and thoughts, but they are not simple readouts of reality. A study conducted by Liberman, Samuels, and Ross (2002), using a game known as the **prisoner's dilemma** (discussed in greater detail in Chapter 14), showed in a concrete way how construal could operate to define a situation and dictate behavior. The game gets its name from the dilemma that would confront two criminals who had committed a crime together, were arrested, and were being questioned separately. Each prisoner could behave in one of two ways: confess the crime, hoping to get lenient treatment by the prosecutor; or deny the crime, hoping that the prosecutor would not bring charges or would fail to persuade a jury of his guilt. But of course the outcome that would result from the prisoner's choice would depend on the other prisoner's behavior. If both denied the crime—a "cooperative strategy"—both would stand a good chance of avoiding a harsh penalty. If one denied the crime and the other admitted it—a "defecting strategy"—the prisoner who admitted the crime would be treated leniently, but the denying prisoner would have the book thrown at him. If both admitted the crime, both would go to prison.

In psychology experiments, the game is usually played with monetary payoffs (rather than prison time!). The particular payoffs that Liberman and his colleagues used are shown in the matrix in **Figure 1.4.** If both participants cooperate (deny the crime) on a given trial, they both make some money; if both

prisoner's dilemma A situation involving payoffs to two people, who must decide whether to "cooperate" or "defect." In the end, trust and cooperation lead to higher joint payoffs than mistrust and defection.

Player 2's choice

	COOPERATE	DEFECT
COOPERATE	Player 1 gets 40¢ / Player 2 gets 40¢	Player 1 loses 20¢ / Player 2 gets 80¢
DEFECT	Player 1 gets 80¢ / Player 2 loses 20¢	Player 1 gets nothing / Player 2 gets nothing

Player 1's choice

FIGURE 1.4 Payoff Matrix for the Prisoner's Dilemma Payoffs differ based on whether both players cooperate, both players defect, or one cooperates and the other defects.

defect (admit the crime), neither gets anything. If one defects and the other doesn't, the defector wins big and the cooperator loses a small amount. As discussed in greater detail in Chapter 14, each player does better by defecting, no matter what the other player does (win 80 cents rather than 40 cents if the other player cooperates, get nothing rather than lose 20 cents if the other player defects). And yet if each player follows the logic of defecting and acts accordingly, both players are worse off (they each get nothing) than if they had both cooperated (they each would have gotten 40 cents).

Liberman, Samuels, and Ross (2002) asked Stanford University dormitory resident assistants to identify students in their dorms who they thought were particularly cooperative or competitive. Both types of students were then recruited to participate in a psychology experiment using the prisoner's dilemma game. Participants played the game in one of two experimental conditions: for half of them, the game was described as "the Wall Street game"; for the other half, it was described as "the community game." **Figure 1.5** shows how construal affected the results: the majority of students who were told they were playing the Wall Street game played it in a competitive fashion; the majority of students who were told they were playing the community game played it in a cooperative fashion. It seems reasonable to infer that the terminology that was used prompted different construals: the name *Wall Street* conjures up images of competitors struggling against one another for monetary advantage. The word *community* stirs up thoughts of sharing and cooperation. The situation exerted its influence through its effect on the way participants interpreted the meaning of the activity they were performing. Participants' presumed dispositions—whether they had been identified as highly competitive or highly cooperative—were of no use in predicting behavior.

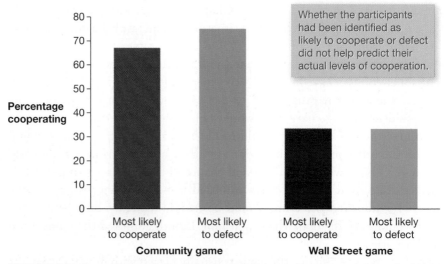

Whether the participants had been identified as likely to cooperate or defect did not help predict their actual levels of cooperation.

FIGURE 1.5 Construal and the Prisoner's Dilemma Percentage of Stanford University students who cooperated in the "the Wall Street game" versus "the community game." Resident advisers had previously identified them as being either likely to cooperate or likely to defect (compete). (Source: Adapted from Liberman, Samuels, & Ross, 2002.)

Schemas

How do we know how to behave in different kinds of situations? For example, if we are riding on an uncrowded train and someone asks us to give up our seat so he or she can sit, what prompts us to respond in a particular way? For that matter, how do we know how to behave in even the most ordinary situations, such as attending a college seminar? Although it usually seems as if we understand social situations immediately and directly, we actually depend on elaborate stores of systematized knowledge to understand even the simplest and most "obvious" situation. These knowledge stores are called **schemas**—generalized knowledge about the physical and social world, such as what kind of behavior to expect when dealing with a minister, a sales clerk, a professor, or a panhandler and how to behave in a seminar, at a funeral, at a McDonald's or a four-star restaurant, or when riding on a crowded or empty subway. There is even a schema—alleged to be universal—for falling in love.

schema A knowledge structure consisting of any organized body of stored information.

Schemas capture the regularities of life and lead us to have certain expectations we can rely on so that we don't have to invent the world anew all the time. We have a schema for "a party," for example. We expect people to act cheerful, excited, and maybe a little silly; and if it's a party attended by young people, there may be loud music, dancing, and a certain amount of rowdiness.

An early experiment by Solomon Asch (1940), another of the German founders of social psychology who immigrated to the United States in the 1930s, shows that schemas can sometimes operate very subtly to influence judgments. Asch asked two groups of undergraduates to rank various professions in terms of prestige. One of the professions was "politician." Before they gave their own ratings, the participants in one group were told that a sample of fellow students had previously ranked politicians near the top in prestige, whereas the participants in the

Schemas Our schemas—generalized knowledge about the physical and social world—help us know what is expected of us and how to behave in particular situations. (A) Our schema of a pizza shop leads us to order at a counter, wait for the pizza to be ready, and then either take it to an empty table or take it home to eat. (B) But our schema of a high-end restaurant leads us to be seated at a table with silverware, glasses, and a tablecloth; to choose what we want from a menu; to order at the table; and to be served food and wine by a waiter.

other group were told that their fellow students had ranked politicians near the bottom. This manipulation affected the participants' judgments substantially, but not because it changed their minds about politicians or because they were trying to conform. Asch was able to show that participants in the first group took the term *politician* to refer to statesmen of the caliber of Thomas Jefferson and Franklin D. Roosevelt. Participants in the second group were rating something closer to corrupt political hacks. It wasn't that the participants were blindly going along with the ratings of their peers. Rather, the different schemas activated by their peers' ratings served to define just what it was that participants were supposed to judge. Many of the persuasion attempts we are exposed to in the media have the goal not so much of changing the judgment of the object, but rather of changing the object of judgment. Advocates of legal abortion try to call up schemas related to *free choice*, while anti-abortion activists try to activate schemas related to *murder*. Affirmative action advocates encourage schemas related to *diversity*, and those opposed to affirmative action try to activate schemas related to *fairness*.

Stereotypes

Much work in social psychology has been dedicated to the study of stereotypes—schemas that we have for people of various kinds. Research on stereotyping examines the content of these person schemas and how they are applied and sometimes misapplied so as to facilitate, or derail, the course of interaction. We tend to judge individuals based on particular person schemas we have—stereotypes about a person's nationality, gender, religion, occupation, neighborhood, or sorority. Such summaries may be necessary to function efficiently and effectively. But they can be wrong, they can be applied in the wrong way and to the wrong people, and they can be given too much weight in relation to more specific information we have

Stereotypes and Construal Stereotypes are schemas about people of a certain kind. We construe people in light of the stereotypes they call up. Would you be surprised to know that the fellow in this picture is a wealthy lawyer who plays polo and frequents chic bars in Manhattan? None of these things is true, and you relied on your stereotypes to prevent you from entertaining those possibilities.

about a particular person (or would have if we didn't assume that the stereotype is all we need to know). The frequently pernicious role of stereotypes is the subject of an entire chapter of this book (Chapter 11).

 Although our understanding of situations often seems to be the result of a direct, unmediated registration of meaning, our comprehension of even the simplest physical stimulus is the result of construal processes that make use of well-developed knowledge structures. Such structures are called schemas when they summarize commonly encountered situations, and they are called stereotypes when they describe different types of people.

AUTOMATIC VERSUS CONTROLLED PROCESSING

How would you react if you saw a stranger at an airport carrying a backpack, looking agitated, and sweating profusely? In the post-9/11 world, you might fear that such a person might be carrying a bomb and that you could become a victim of a terrorist attack. The mind processes information in two ways when you encounter a social situation: one is automatic and unconscious, often based on emotional factors, and the other is conscious and systematic and more likely to be controlled by careful thought. Often, emotional reactions occur before conscious thought takes over. Thus your fearful reaction to the person with the backpack might automatically kick in without any special thought on your part. But when you start thinking systematically, you realize that he might have just come in from the summer heat, that he might be agitated because he is late for his plane, and that there is no reason to suspect that he might be carrying a bomb or threatening your safety in any other way.

Research by Patricia Devine and her colleagues has shown how automatic and controlled processing can result in incompatible attitudes in the same person toward members of outgroups (Devine, 1989a, 1989b; Devine, Monteith, Zuwerink, & Elliot, 1991; Devine, Plant, Amodio, Harmon-Jones, & Vance, 2002). People with low expressed prejudice toward an outgroup may nevertheless reveal feelings toward people in the outgroup that are almost as prejudiced as those of people who confess to explicit disliking of the group. For example, when white participants were asked to read words reminiscent of African-Americans and then rate a particular individual, race unspecified, about whom they read, they were more likely to report that the individual was hostile than if they had not read such words. And this was true whether or not they were willing to express anti-black attitudes in a questionnaire. The judgments of the "unprejudiced people" could thus be shown to be prejudiced when studied by a technique that examines unconscious processing of information. Furthermore, Anthony Greenwald and his colleagues showed that

Automatic Processing People often react quickly to frightening situations so that they can take immediate actions to save themselves from danger if necessary. The boy is handling the snake under the supervision of his teacher, but an automatic reaction is still visible. If the boy were to come across a snake in the grass, he would probably have a stronger automatic fear reaction.

the great majority of white people take longer to classify black faces with pleasant stimuli than to classify white faces with pleasant stimuli (Greenwald, McGhee, & Schwartz, 1998). This was true even for participants who showed no overt prejudice when asked about their attitudes. In general, automatic processes give rise to *implicit* attitudes and beliefs that cannot be readily controlled by the conscious mind; and controlled, conscious processing results in *explicit* attitudes and beliefs of which we are aware—though these may become implicit or unconscious over time. It's important to recognize that participants in these experiments were not necessarily dissembling. They likely were genuinely ignorant of the extent of the bias that was revealed by the implicit measures of attitude.

As another example of unconscious cognitive processes, consider the impact of social categories on judgments and behavior. Easily discriminable personal features, such as gender, race, and age, tend to trigger stereotypes that a person uses in forming judgments about other people, even when the person is unaware that these social categories have influenced the judgment in question (Blair, Judd, & Fallman, 2004; Brewer, 1988; Macrae, Stangor, & Milne, 1994). Even behavior can be unconsciously influenced by social categories. Bargh, Chen, and Burrows (1996) found that just mentioning words that call to mind the elderly (*cane, Florida*) causes college students to walk down a hall more slowly. And others have found that activating the concept of "professor" actually makes students do better on a trivia test (Dijksterhuis & van Knippenberg, 1998).

Types of Unconscious Processing

Two major types of unconscious processing have been identified, and both of them play an important role in producing beliefs and behaviors. Over 100 years ago, William James identified one type that is involved in what is now called "skill acquisition." If you have ever driven a car and realized that you haven't a clue as to what you have been doing—even what you have seen—for the last few minutes, you know about this type of automatic mental processing. As we learn and then overlearn certain skills, we can exercise them without being aware we are doing so. We also can carry them out without being distracted from other, conscious thoughts and processing.

The other type of automatic mental processing (associated with Sigmund Freud but with roots going well back into the nineteenth century) occurs when beliefs and behaviors are generated without our awareness of the cognitive processes behind them. In solving problems, sometimes we are well aware of the relevant factors we are dealing with and the procedures we are using to work with them. For example, when we solve mathematical problems ("Take half the base, multiply it by the height and . . ."), we usually know exactly what formula we are using. But these sorts of cognitive processes—where we are conscious of most of what is going on—are rarer than you might think. We often cannot correctly explain the reasons for our judgments about other people, our understanding of the causes of physical and social events, or what led us to choose one job applicant over another (or one romantic partner over another, for that matter).

In one experiment making this point about awareness, customers in a mall were asked to evaluate the quality of four nightgowns laid out in a row on a table (Nisbett & Wilson, 1977). No matter how the nightgowns were arranged, customers were by far most likely to give the highest rating to the last nightgown

William James One of the founders of psychology, James wrote about attention, memory, and consciousness, examining how overlearned behaviors can drop out of conscious awareness.

they examined. Yet when customers were asked whether the position of the night-gowns had influenced their judgments about quality, they responded with astonishment that the experimenter could think that they might have been influenced by such a trivial and irrelevant factor! Often we cannot even consciously identify some of the crucial factors that affect our beliefs and behavior. Experiments have shown that even when visual stimuli are presented so rapidly that people cannot report having seen them, the stimuli can still affect those people's beliefs and behavior (Zajonc, 2001).

Functions of Unconscious Processing

Why does so much mental processing take place outside of our awareness? Partly, it is a matter of efficiency. Conscious processes are generally slow and can run only serially—one step or one problem at a time. Automatic processes are typically much faster and can operate in parallel. When we recognize a face as belonging to a fourth-grade classmate, we have done so by processing numerous features (fore-head, eyes, chin, coloring, and so on) at the same time. Recognizing each feature one step at a time would leave us hopelessly mired in computation. And it's quite handy to be able to drive on autopilot while enjoying the scenery or carrying on a conversation. (Just make sure that the conversation is with someone physically in the car with you. Talking on a cell phone is a very different type of activity in many respects, and one that substantially increases your risk of having an accident.)

The efficiency of unconscious processes is not only convenient but also might have benefits for our survival. Consider the subtle influence of physiological factors, such as the body's position and movements. When a person encounters novel stimuli while the arm is flexed (bent back toward the shoulder), attitudes toward the stimuli tend to be favorable (Cacioppo, Priester, & Berntson, 1993). But when a person encounters novel stimuli while the arm is extended away from the body, the person tends to form more negative attitudes. Although people are completely unaware that they have incorporated this bodily information into their judgments, the muscular feedback from the arm positions gives "information" about whether the object is desirable or undesirable (based on a lifetime's experience embracing positive stimuli and pushing away negative stimuli). For our human ancestors, making instantaneous decisions about aversive stimuli, based on rapid, nonconscious integration of many sources of information, may often have been a matter of life or death.

In the study of social psychology, it is important to distinguish those social behaviors that appear to be the result of effortful, deliberate, and conscious processing from those that appear to be the result of effortless, automatic, and unconscious processing. Scientific research on human behavior is essential precisely because we can't simply ask people what caused them to behave as they did. Often they cannot really tell, and what they say may mislead rather than enlighten the researcher. Instead, social psychologists must craft experiments to isolate the true causes of people's behavior.

 Much of our behavior and many kinds of construal processes are carried out without our awareness, sometimes without awareness of even the stimuli to which we are responding. We tend to overestimate how accessible our mental processes are to our consciousness.

EVOLUTION AND HUMAN BEHAVIOR: HOW WE ARE THE SAME

Why do human beings generally live in family groups, assign roles to people on the basis of age, adorn their bodies, classify flora and fauna, and have rites of passage and myths? Evolution may explain such behaviors (Conway & Schaller, 2002).

Evolutionary theory has been around for about 150 years, ever since Charles Darwin's famous voyage to the Galápagos Islands and the discoveries he made about the modifications in animal and plant characteristics that had occurred over time. The theory has proved invaluable in understanding why organisms of all kinds have the properties they do, and how they come to have them. The key idea is that a process of **natural selection** operates on animals and plants so that traits that enhance the probability of survival and reproduction are passed on to subsequent generations. Organisms that die before they reproduce may just have bad luck, but they may possess characteristics that are less than optimal in the environments in which they find themselves. And these organisms that do not reproduce will not pass on these nonadaptive characteristics (through their genes) to a new generation. Those that do survive and reproduce give their genes a chance to live on in their offspring, along with the possibility that their characteristics will be represented in at least one more generation. Disadvantageous characteristics are selected against; characteristics better adapted to the environment are selected for.

Darwin himself assumed that natural selection is important for behavioral inclinations, just as it is for physical characteristics such as size, coloring, or susceptibility to parasites. And the number and importance of things that are universally true about humans is certainly consistent with the idea that much of what we share is at least partly the result of natural selection and is encoded in our genes. Recent developments in evolutionary theory and comparative biology, together with anthropological findings and studies by psychologists, have produced strong evidence that the theory of evolution can be quite helpful in explaining why people behave as they do.

natural selection An evolutionary process that molds animals and plants so that traits that enhance the probability of survival and reproduction are passed on to subsequent generations.

YOU ARE HERE

"There is grandeur in this view of life. . . . Whilst this planet has gone cycling on according to the fixed law of gravity, from so simple a beginning endless forms most beautiful and most wonderful have been, and are being, evolved."

—Charles Darwin

Human Universals

One theme that is consistent with evolutionary theory is that many human behaviors and institutions are universal, or very nearly so (Schaller, Simpson, & Kenrick, 2006). In the process of human evolution, we have acquired basic behavioral propensities—much as we have acquired physical features like bipedalism (having two legs)—that help us adapt to the physical and social environment. **Table 1.1** contains a list of reputed universals. Two things should be noted about the practices and institutions cited in Table 1.1, aside from their alleged universality. One is that humans share some of these characteristics with other animals, especially the higher primates. These include facial expressions (almost all of which we share with chimpanzees and some other animals), dominance and submission, food sharing, group living (true of all primates except orangutans), greater aggressiveness on the part of males (true of almost all mammals), preference for own kin (almost surely true of all animals), and wariness around snakes (true of all the large primates, including humans). The other, even more striking aspect of Table 1.1 is that the number of universals we share with other animals is (so far as we know) quite small. The bulk of Table 1.1 represents a large number of behaviors and institutions that appear to be effective adaptations for highly intelligent, group-living, upright-walking, language-using animals that are capable of living in almost any kind of ecology. These latter universals are compatible with an evolutionary interpretation (we are a particular kind of creature, qualitatively different from any other, with many adaptations so effective that they have become wired into our biology). But some theorists believe that the commonalities can be

TABLE 1.1 Universal Behaviors, Reactions, and Institutions

Some of the behaviors and characteristics that anthropologists believe hold for all human cultures, grouped into categories to show general areas of commonality.

Sex, Gender, and the Family

Copulation normally conducted privately	Sexual jealousy	Sexual regulation
Live in family (or household)	Marriage	Husband usually older than wife
Sexual modesty	Division of labor by gender	Males more physically aggressive
Females do more child care	Mother-son incest unthinkable	Incest prevention and avoidance
Preference for own kin	Sex differences in spatial cognition	

Social Differentiation

Age statuses	Classification of kin	Leaders
Ingroup distinguished from outgroup	Division of labor by age	

Social Customs

Baby talk	Pretend play	Group living
Dance	Rites of passage	Law (rights and obligations)
Dominance/submission	Taboo foods	Feasting
Practice to improve skills	Body adornment	Property
Hygienic care	Death rites	Rituals
Magic to sustain and improve life	Etiquette	Taboo utterances
Magic to win love	Gossip	Toys
Nonbody decorative art	Food sharing	

Emotion

Childhood fear of strangers	Wariness around snakes	Rhythm
Facial expressions of fear, anger, disgust, happiness, sadness, and surprise	Envy	Melody

Cognition

Aesthetics	Anthropomorphism of animals	Myths
Belief in supernatural, religion	Medicine	Taxonomy
Classification of flora and fauna	Language	Narrative

Source: Compiled by Donald Brown (1991), appearing in Pinker (2002).

Universal Facial Expressions Chimpanzees and humans express dominance and submission, anger and fear, through similar facial expressions. (A) The screaming chimp and (B) basketball coach Bobby Knight both have their mouths open and show their teeth in an aggressive display of dominance.

accounted for as simply the result of our species' superior intelligence. For example, every human group figures out for itself that incest is a bad idea and that classification of flora is useful.

Group Living, Language, and Theory of Mind

Group living contributed to survival in ages past, as groups provided protection from predators, greater success in finding foraging areas, access to mates, and other adaptive functions. The ability to produce and understand language has facilitated the ability to live in groups and to convey not only emotions and intentions to others but also beliefs, attitudes, and complex thoughts. There is strong evidence that infants are born prewired to acquire language, perhaps because of its importance to humans living together in groups (Pinker, 1994). All normal children learn language at developmental stages that are almost identical from one culture to another. At birth, all infants are able to produce the full range of possible sounds (phonemes) that exist in the totality of languages spoken anywhere on earth, and they babble all these sounds in the crib. Language acquisition consists of dropping all the "wrong" phonemes that are not used by the child's particular language. Thus children can learn to speak any language, depending on where they grow up; they can learn to speak their native language perfectly well even if they grow up with deaf parents who never speak at all; and twins can sometimes develop their own unique language in the crib, a language that follows rules of grammar in the same way as formally recognized languages do (Pinker, 1994, 2002). These findings indicate that there are general, inherited propensities to develop grammatical language.

Just as evolution has prepared humans to live together in groups and to communicate to promote survival and reproduction, it also may have provided humans with a **theory of mind**—the ability to recognize that other people have beliefs and desires. Children recognize before the age of 2 that the way to understand other people's behavior is to understand their beliefs and desires (Asch, 1952; Kuhlmeier, Wynn, & Bloom, 2003; Leslie, 2000; Malle, Moses, & Baldwin, 2001). By the age of 3 or 4, theory of mind is sophisticated enough that children can recognize when other people's beliefs are false (Wellman, 1990). Some of the most powerful evidence for a biologically based theory of mind comes from

theory of mind The understanding that other people have beliefs and desires.

Theory of Mind Temple Grandin is a high-functioning autistic woman who is a doctor of animal science and professor. As a child, she was mocked with the epithet "tape recorder" for her habit of constantly repeating things. She has described her understanding of the emotions and beliefs of other people as being so poor that she feels like "an anthropologist on Mars." She understands the pain and terror of animals sufficiently well, however, that she has been able to devise humane methods of slaughtering them.

the study of people who, through a genetic defect or physical or chemical trauma before or after birth, seem not to have one or to have only a weak version of one. Such a claim has been made about people with *autism*. Individuals with autism have deeply disordered abilities for interacting and communicating with others. They do not seem able to comprehend the beliefs or desires of others, including that the beliefs of others can be false (Perner, Frith, Leslie, & Leekam, 1989). Autistic children can have normal or even superior intellectual functioning but have less comprehension of people's beliefs and desires than children with Down syndrome, whose general intellectual functioning is far below normal. It seems plausible that evolution has provided us with information that is too universally essential to leave to chance or laborious trial-and-error learning. Given the importance of accurately understanding other people's beliefs and intentions, it would not be surprising that a theory of mind comes prewired.

Evolution and Gender Roles

Why is polygyny (one man, several wives) more common than polyandry (one woman, several husbands)? Why do women tend to care more than men about a potential partner's financial prospects? The evolutionary approach provides a possible answer to these questions in its theory of **parental investment**. In almost all mammalian species, the two sexes typically have different costs and benefits associated with the nurturing of offspring, largely because the number of offspring a female can have over the course of her lifetime is limited. The value of each child to her is therefore relatively high, and it is in the interest of her genes to see to it that each infant grows to maturity. For males, however, a nearly unlimited number of offspring is theoretically possible because so little energy is involved in creating them. A male can walk away from copulation and never see his mate or offspring again. Even if the male stays with the female and their offspring, however, his investment in the offspring is less than that of the female. As discussed in Chapter 10, many apparent differences between males and females are consistent with the implications that follow from this asymmetry. Evolution thus provides one way of looking at many seemingly universal tendencies related to sex, gender, and child rearing.

parental investment The evolutionary principle that costs and benefits are associated with reproduction and the nurturing of offspring. Because these costs and benefits are different for males and females, one sex will normally value and invest more in each child than will the other sex.

Avoiding the Naturalistic Fallacy

Evolutionary theory as applied to human behavior is controversial. The claim that there are biologically based differences between men and women in behaviors related to mate choice is particularly objectionable to some people. Such claims are controversial in part because they follow a long and embarrassing history of faulty assertions about biological differences that have been used to legitimize and perpetuate male privilege (Bem, 1993).

Even more objectionable, evolutionary theory has been invoked as justification for viewing the different human "races" almost as separate subspecies. Indeed, in the early twentieth century, Darwin's ideas were used to justify the struggle of some groups of people to achieve supremacy over others—the notion that might determines right. This so-called social Darwinist movement incorrectly interpreted "the survival of the fittest" to mean the survival of one human group in competition with another human group rather than one individual's struggle to survive and reproduce in its environment. Similarly distorted versions of Darwin's theory were also used to justify fascism and the ruthless domination of the weak by the strong.

Evolutionary claims about human behavior can also lead people to assume, mistakenly, that biology is destiny—that what we are biologically predisposed to do is what we inevitably will do and perhaps even should do. This claim—that the way things *are* is the way they *should be*—is known as the **naturalistic fallacy**, and it has no logical foundation. We are predisposed to do many things that we can overcome. Virtually all human societies are plagued by violence in everyday life, for example, but the incidence of it over the past few centuries has declined astronomically. The chances of being killed in various parts of England declined from the 13th century to the 20th by factors ranging from 10 to 100 (Pinker, 2011, p. 60). The most horrendous forms of torture, such as breaking all the bones in a person's body on the rack, are no longer practiced in Europe. Political leaders like Theodore Roosevelt and Winston Churchill did not hesitate to praise colonial wars and the damage done by them to subject peoples, but it would be unthinkable for their modern successors to express such sentiments. Civilization can be regarded as the never-ceasing attempt to modify much of what comes naturally, reducing the extent to which human life, as seventeenth-century philosopher Thomas Hobbes put it, is "poor, nasty, brutish, and short."

The fact that a theory can be misused is no reason to reject the theory itself in all its aspects. Indeed, the most important legacy of evolution for human beings is the great flexibility it allows for adaptation to distinctive circumstances. Caution about evolutionary claims is called for. What is not called for, however, is a rejection of evolutionary ideas out of hand.

Social Neuroscience

Evolutionary approaches to the study of social behavior alert us to the fact that everything that humans do or think takes place on a biological substrate. In recent years, social psychologists have begun to examine the biological grounding for all behavior: the brain. For example, intriguing conclusions have been reached about the areas of the brain that function most when we are feeling angry, fearful, or amorous (Heatherton, Macrae, & Kelley, 2004; Ochsner & Lieberman, 2001); when we're excited about the possibility of winning something valuable or worried about

naturalistic fallacy The claim that the way things *are* is the way they *should be*.

the prospect of losing it (Knutson et al., 2008; Tom, Fox, Trepel, & Poldrack, 2007); when we conclude that an action is morally reprehensible (Borg, Hyunes, Van Horn, Grafton & Sinnott-Armstrong, 2006; Borg, Lieberman, & Kiehl, 2008; Greene, Sommerville, Nystrom, Darley, & Cohen, 2001); and when we are solving various kinds of cognitive and social problems. While a person is experiencing different emotions or solving various problems, blood flows to the areas of the brain that are active. Using a technology known as functional magnetic resonance imaging (fMRI), scientists can take a picture of the brain that detects this blood flow and shows which brain regions mediate various feelings and behaviors.

In other lines of research, neuroscientists have provided a window into the development of social behavior by tracing the physical changes in the brain. For example, it turns out that a region of the brain that alerts people to danger is poorly developed until early adulthood (Decety & Michalska, 2010). This late development of an important brain region may help explain why adolescents take greater risks (in how they drive, for instance) than people in their mid-20s and beyond. Neuroscience has also revealed that later in life, the brain regions that mediate learning, notably the prefrontal cortex, decay particularly rapidly with increasing age. These findings help explain why the elderly find it more difficult to learn than do young people (Dempster, 1992; Raz et al., 1997); Shimamura, 1994).

Neuroscience not only tells us which areas of the brain function most when certain kinds of activities are taking place, but also informs us about how the brain, the mind, and behavior function as a unit and how social factors influence each of these components at the same time.

"Young man, go to your room and stay there until your cerebral cortex matures."

Evolutionary theory informs our understanding of human behavior just as it does our understanding of the physical characteristics of plants and animals. The many universals of human behavior suggest that some of these behaviors may be prewired—especially language and theory of mind. Differential parental investment of males and females may help us understand certain differences between men and women. Although misunderstandings and misapplications of evolutionary ideas sometimes make people suspicious of it, the theory has important implications for the field of social psychology.

CULTURE AND HUMAN BEHAVIOR: HOW WE ARE DIFFERENT

Despite the existence of universal human tendencies to have various emotions, customs, and forms of social organization, there is great flexibility among humans in the particular expression of these tendencies. The enormous behavioral flexibility of humans is tied to the fact that—together with rats—we are the most successful of all the mammals in our ability to live in virtually every type of ecosystem. Our adaptability and the range of environments we have evolved in have resulted in extraordinary differences between human cultures. Depending on the prevailing culture, humans may be more or less likely to cooperate with each other, to assign different roles to men and women, or to try to distinguish themselves as individuals.

FIGURE 1.6 **You Be the Subject: Self-Definition**

Write down ten things that describe who you are. You will have a chance to reflect on your answers later in this section.

1. I am _____
2. I am _____
3. I am _____
4. I am _____
5. I am _____
6. I am _____
7. I am _____
8. I am _____
9. I am _____
10. I am _____

Before you begin reading about the effects of culture on human behavior, complete the exercise in **Figure 1.6**. Really—do this. You will get much more out of the following discussion if you do.

Cultural Differences in Social Relations and Self-Understanding

Until fairly recently, psychologists regarded cultural differences as being limited primarily to differences in beliefs, preferences, and values. Some cultures regard the world as having been created by a supernatural force, some by impersonal natural forces, and some don't ponder the question much at all. The French like to eat fatty goose liver, the Chinese like to eat chicken feet, and the Americans like to eat cotton candy—and each group has trouble appreciating the tastes preferred by the other groups. These differences, while interesting, are not the sort of thing that would make anyone suspect that fundamentally different psychological theories are needed to account for the behavior of people in different societies.

But recent work shows that cultural differences go far deeper than beliefs and values. In fact, they extend all the way to the level of fundamental forms of self-conceptions and social existence and even to the perceptual and cognitive processes people use to develop new thoughts and beliefs (Henrich, Heine, & Norenzayan, 2010). Many of these differences are discussed throughout the book, but one set of interrelated dimensions is particularly central and needs to be introduced here.

To begin, read the following propositions. How plausible do you find each of them?

■ People have substantial control over their life outcomes, and they much prefer situations in which they have choice and control to those in which they do not.

- People want to achieve personal success. They find that relationships with other people can sometimes make it harder to attain their goals.
- People want to be unique, to be different from other people in significant respects.
- People want to feel good about themselves. Excelling in some ways and being assured of their good qualities by other people are important to personal well- being.
- People like their relations with others to be on a basis of mutuality and equality, but if some people have more power than others, most people prefer to be in the superior position.
- People believe that the same rules should apply to everyone—individuals should not be singled out for special treatment because of their personal attributes or connections to important people. Justice is, or should be, blind.

Hundreds of millions of people are reasonably well described by these propositions, but those people tend to be found in particular parts of the world—namely, Europe and many of the present and former nations of the British Commonwealth, including the United States, Canada, and Australia. These societies tend to be highly **independent** (or **individualistic**) **cultures** (Fiske, Kitayama, Markus, & Nisbett, 1998; Hofstede, 1980; Hsu, 1953; Markus & Kitayama, 1991; Triandis, 1995). Westerners think of themselves as distinct social entities, tied to each other by bonds of affection and organizational memberships to be sure, but essentially separate from other people and having attributes that exist in the absence of any connection to others. They tend to see their associations with other people, even their own family members, as voluntary and subject to termination once those associations become sufficiently troublesome or unproductive (**Table 1.2**).

independent (individualistic) cultures Cultures in which people tend to think of themselves as distinct social entities, tied to each other by voluntary bonds of affection and organizational memberships but essentially separate from other people and having attributes that exist in the absence of any connection to others.

TABLE 1.2 Independent versus Interdependent Societies

People in independent (individualistic) cultures have different characteristics than people in interdependent (collectivistic) cultures, as shown by the difference in emphasis on the individual and on the group.

Independent Societies	Interdependent Societies
Conception of the self as distinct from others, with attributes that are constant	Conception of the self as inextricably linked to others, with attributes depending on the situation
Insistence on ability to act on one's own	Preference for collective action
Need for individual distinctiveness	Desire for harmonious relations within group
Preference for egalitarianism and achieved status based on accomplishments	Acceptance of hierarchy and ascribed status based on age, group membership, and other attributes
Conviction that rules governing behavior should apply to everyone	Preference for rules that take context and particular relationships into account

But these characterizations describe other people less well. In fact, they provide a poor description of most of the world's people, particularly the citizens of East Asian countries such as China (Triandis, McCusker, & Hui, 1990), Japan (Bond & Cheung, 1983), and Korea (Rhee, Uleman, Lee, & Roman, 1995) as well as people from South Asian countries such as India (Dhawan, Roseman, Naidu, Thapa, & Rettek, 1995; Savani, Markus, & Conner, 2008) and Malaysia (Bochner, 1994), people from the Middle East (Greenberg, Eloul, Markus, & Tsai, 2012), and people from many Latin American countries. These societies represent more **interdependent** (or **collectivistic**) **cultures**. People in such cultures do not have as much freedom or personal control over their lives, and they do not necessarily want or need either (Sastry & Ross, 1998).

These differences in self-definition between people in independent and interdependent societies have important implications for the nature of their personal goals and strivings, values, and beliefs. Success is important to East Asians, but in good part because it brings credit to the family and other groups to which they belong rather than merely as a reflection of personal merit. Personal uniqueness is not very important to interdependent peoples and may in fact even be undesirable. In a clever experiment by Kim and Markus (1999), Korean and American participants were offered a pen as a gift for being in a study. Several of the pens were of one color and one pen was of another color. Americans tended to choose the unique color and Koreans the common color. Being unique and being better than others are not so important for interdependent people to feel good about themselves; moreover, feeling good about themselves is itself not as important a goal as it is for Westerners and other independent peoples (Heine, Lehman, Markus, & Kitayama, 1999). Interdependent people tend not to expect or even value mutuality and equality in relationships; on the contrary, they are likely to expect hierarchical relations to be the rule (Hsu, 1953; Triandis, 1987, 1995). They tend not to be universalists in their understanding of social norms; instead, they believe in different strokes for different folks. Justice should keep her eyes wide open, paying attention to the particular circumstances of each case that comes before her.

Who Are You?

Westerners' belief that they are self-contained is revealed by simply asking them to describe themselves (much as you were asked to do in Figure 1.6). Kuhn and McPartland (1954) invented a simple "Who Am I" test that asks people to list 20 statements that describe who they are. Americans' self-descriptions tend to be context-free answers referring to personality traits ("I'm friendly," "hardworking," "shy") and personal preferences ("I like camping"). When more interdependent participants respond to this test, however, their answers tend to refer to relationships with other people or groups ("I am Jan's friend") and are often qualified by context ("I am serious at work"; "I am fun-loving with my friends") (Cousins, 1989; Ip & Bond, 1995; Markus & Kitayama, 1991). Take a minute to look back at your own answers on the ten-question Who Am I test in Figure 1.6 and see what type of characterizations you emphasized.

Social psychologists Vaunne Ma and Thomas Schoeneman (1997) administered the Who Am I test to American university students and to four different groups living in Kenya—university students, workers in Nairobi (the capital city), and traditional Masai and Samburu herding peoples. Kenya was for decades

interdependent (collectivistic) cultures Cultures in which people tend to define themselves as part of a collective, inextricably tied to others in their group and placing less importance on individual freedom or personal control over their lives.

"Culture is an inherited habit."

—Francis Fukuyama

BOX 1.1 FOCUS ON CULTURE

Dick and Jane, Deng and Janxing

The first page of a reader for American children from the 1930s shows a little boy running with his dog. "See Dick run," the primer reads. "See Dick run and play." "See Spot run." The first page of a Chinese reader from the same era shows a little boy sitting on the shoulders of a bigger boy. "Big Brother loves Little Brother" reads the text. "Little Brother loves Big Brother." The difference between what the American child and the Chinese child of the 1930s were exposed to on the first day of class says much about the differences between their worlds. The American child is taught to orient toward action and to be prepared to live in a world where control and individual choice are possible. The Chinese child is more likely to be taught to be attuned to relationships. To the Westerner, it makes sense to speak of the existence of the person apart from any group. To East Asians (for example, Chinese, Japanese, and Koreans) and to many of the world's other peoples, the person exists only as a member of a larger collective—family, friends, village, corporation. People are related to one another like ropes in a net—completely interconnected and having no real existence without the connections (Munro, 1985).

Dick

See Dick.

See Dick run.

1

(A)

九　好朋友

小強是一個可愛的男孩子，

他是我的好朋友。

我們常常一同讀書，

一同玩耍，

大家很快樂。

(B)

Attention to Action versus Relationships (A) The Dick and Jane readers of the United States emphasize action and individualism, as shown on this page with the drawing of Dick running and the words, "See Dick. See Dick run." (B) East Asian readers are more likely to emphasize relationships, as seen in this Chinese reader in which two boys walk down the street with their arms around each other. The text says, "Xiao Zhiang is a very nice boy. He is my best friend. We always study together and play together. We have a lot of fun together."

a colony of Great Britain, and city dwellers, especially those who are educated, have had a great deal of exposure to Western culture. Kenyan students have been exposed still more to Western culture and are being educated in a Western tradition. In contrast, traditional African tribespeople are reputed to have little sense of themselves as individuals. Rather, their sense of self is defined by family, property, and position in the community. Tribespeople are constantly made aware of their roles and status in relation to family and other groups (Mwaniki, 1973).

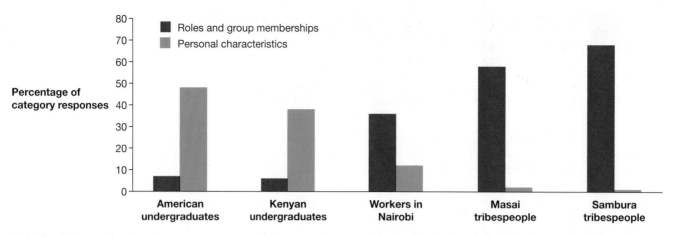

FIGURE 1.7 Self-Characterization The graph shows the percentage of "roles and group memberships" and "personal characteristics" responses on the "Who Am I" test by American undergraduates, Kenyan undergraduates, workers in Nairobi, Masai tribespeople, and Sambura tribespeople. (Source: Adapted from Ma & Schoeneman, 1997.)

Among traditional Kenyan tribespeople, the individualist is "looked upon with suspicion. . . . There is no really individual affair, for everything has a moral and social influence."

—Jomo Kenyatta (1938), first president of independent Kenya

Figure 1.7 shows how differently these four African groups view themselves. Traditional Masai and Samburu characterize themselves in terms of roles and group memberships, whereas Kenyan students are far more likely to mention personal characteristics. Kenyan students, in fact, differ only slightly from American students. Workers in Nairobi are in between the tribespeople and the students. This pattern of evidence, when considered in relation to the very large differences typically found between East Asian and Western students, suggests that modernization by itself does not produce substantial differences in self-conceptions. Rather, it is a Western orientation that seems essential to an independent conception of the self.

Individualism versus Collectivism in the Workplace

One of the first social scientists to measure the dimension of independence (or individualism) versus interdependence (or collectivism) was Geert Hofstede (1980), who surveyed the values of tens of thousands of IBM employees around the world. **Table 1.3** shows the sorts of values and beliefs that Hofstede examined and the differences he observed in individualistic versus collectivistic cultures. **Figure 1.8** displays these results geographically, showing the average degree of individualism expressed by the citizens of 67 countries. You can see that the countries of British heritage are the most individualistic, followed by the countries of continental Europe. East Asia, South Asia, Asia Minor, and Latin America are all relatively collectivistic.

Although Hofstede himself studied few East Asian societies, there is now a great deal of evidence about them. The research to date indicates that those cultures are very different from Western cultures. In a survey similar to Hofstede's, two professors in a business school in the Netherlands, Charles Hampden-Turner and Alfons Trompenaars, examined independence and interdependence among 15,000 middle managers from the United States, Canada, Great Britain, Australia, Sweden, the Netherlands, Belgium, Germany, France, Italy, Japan,

TABLE 1.3 Independent and Interdependent Cultures on the Job

People in independent and interdependent cultures tend to have different values and beliefs about job-related matters.

Independent Cultures	Interdependent Cultures
Want to get the recognition they deserve when they do a good job	Want the employer to have a major responsibility for their health and welfare
Want to have considerable freedom to adopt their own approach to the job	Want to work in a congenial and friendly atmosphere
Want to fully use their skills and abilities on the job	Want to be completely loyal to their company
Want to work in a department that is run efficiently	Believe that knowing influential people is more important than ability
Believe that decisions made by individuals are better than those made by groups	Believe that the better managers are those who have been with the company the longest time

Source: Adapted from Hofstede (1980).

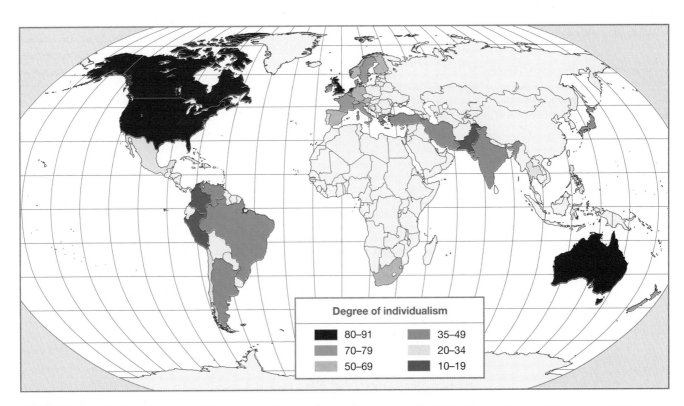

FIGURE 1.8 Individualism and Collectivism The map shows the degree of individualism and collectivism among IBM employees around the world, indicating greater individualism in Great Britain and in the United States, Canada, Australia, and New Zealand, all former British colonies. People in the countries represented in the very light blue were not surveyed by the researchers. (Source: Sabini, 1995, p. 261; based on data from Hofstede, 1980.)

BOX 1.2 **FOCUS ON CULTURE**

Individualism or Collectivism in Business Managers

Charles Hampden-Turner and Alfons Trompenaars (1993) studied individualism versus collectivism in thousands of business managers. To examine the value placed on individual distinctiveness and accomplishment versus harmonious relations within the group, they asked the business managers in their seminars whether business managers preferred

jobs in which personal initiatives are encouraged and individual initiatives are achieved

or

jobs in which no one is singled out for personal honor, but in which everyone works together.

To examine the acceptance of ascribed status (for example, age, family, religious background) as a basis for rewarding employees, Hampden-Turner and Trompenaars asked the business

managers whether they agreed with the following sentiment:

It is important for a manager to be older than his subordinates. Older people should be more respected than younger people.

To see whether their respondents felt there should be universal rules governing employer-employee relations or whether instead circumstances and specific situations should be taken into account, the investigators asked the business managers how they thought a manager should deal with an employee who had performed well for 15 years, but had recently become unproductive. If circumstances indicate it's unlikely that performance will improve, should the employee be dismissed on the grounds that

job performance should remain the grounds for dismissal, regardless of the age of the person and his previous record

or instead do you feel that

[it is] wrong to disregard the 15 years the employee has been working for the company. One has to take into account the company's responsibility for his life.

The cultures studied fell into three major clusters. East Asian managers were by far the most interdependent, or collectivistic, in their expressed values; managers from the British and former Commonwealth nations were the most independent, or individualistic (the United States and Canada were the most extremely independent); and managers from continental Europe were in between. What's more, the researchers found an interesting difference within Europe: people from the northwestern European nations of Sweden, the Netherlands, and Belgium were more individualistic than those from the more southern European nations of France, Italy, and Germany.

Singapore, and Korea (Hampden-Turner & Trompenaars, 1993). They presented these managers, who were attending seminars conducted by the investigators, with dilemmas in which individualistic values were pitted against collectivistic values. In line with Hofstede's results, they found that managers from East Asia, South Asia, and Latin America tended to hold collectivistic values; managers from British and former British colonies valued individualism; and managers from continental European nations valued a mix of individualism and collectivism. A sampling of the researchers' questions can be found in **Box 1.2**.

Culture and Gender Roles

Earlier, the discussion focused on some aspects of gender roles that are—or have been—universal. But gender roles vary greatly around the world and even within subcultures in the same country. Male dominance is one of the most variable aspects of gender roles. Some preliterate peoples, living lives much like those of people during the thousands of years of recent human evolution, are hunter-gatherers. The predominant male role is to hunt; the predominant female role is to gather plants. Despite the sharp demarcation of gender roles, such societies are relatively gender egalitarian. Indeed, the social structures are characterized by weak hierarchies in general, in which leaders have little power over others. Modern Western cultures are also relatively gender egalitarian, especially Scandinavian countries. Women constitute almost half the membership of the Parliament in Sweden. (Scandinavians, incidentally, have been relatively gender egalitarian for 1,000 years; the helmeted Viking woman of operas and cartoons was a reality.) Relative status of women in the rest of the world ranges from the Scandinavian extreme of equality to near-slavery conditions for women.

The kinds of sexual relations that are considered normal and appropriate also vary enormously. Overwhelmingly, polygyny, in which one man has several wives, and serial monogamy are the most common expectations among the world's subcultures—and that may have been the case for thousands of years. The traditional U.S. standard of lifetime monogamy is a rarity. The United States is considered decidedly prudish by many Western Europeans, for whom extramarital affairs are commonplace. The funeral of a recent president of France was attended by his wife and his mistress standing side by side. In some cultures women (and sometimes even men) who are suspected of having extramarital affairs are put to death. Indeed, in some of those cultures, a woman who is raped is expelled from the family circle or even killed. Homosexuals in some cultures may be sentenced to prison, a fate not uncommon in Europe until just a few generations ago.

It is a matter of some disagreement among social scientists whether the different sexual mores (norms) that characterize different cultures are merely arbitrary or whether most of them have economic or other practical roots. An example of an economic explanation concerns farmers in Nepal and Tibet who practice a form of polyandry—one wife with many husbands who are brothers. This system serves the economic goal of keeping scarce agricultural land in one family and produces just one set of related heirs per generation. A similar purpose was served by primogeniture, a common rule in Western Europe that only the firstborn male could inherit land. Otherwise, estates would be broken up into ever-smaller units and the original power of the landowning family would dwindle away to the status of ordinary peasants.

This book frequently returns to discussions of gender. Men and women differ in the way they understand themselves and in their emotions and motivations. But these differences are far from being constant across cultures—gender is constructed quite differently in different societies.

Some Qualifications

Societies differ in many ways, and it's not possible to put each society entirely in one box or another and say that some are independent in all respects and others are interdependent in all respects. Moreover, there are regional and subcultural differences within any large society. The U.S. South, for example, is more interdependent than much of the rest of the country in that family connections and community ties tend to be more important (Vandello & Cohen, 1999). However, the South has been described as more tolerant of character quirks and various kinds of social deviance than other regions of the country—clearly individualistic tendencies (Reed, 1990).

Moreover, the socialization within a given society of particular individuals or particular types of individuals may be oriented more toward independence or more toward interdependence. Gender socialization in our society is a good example (Kashima et al., 1995). While Dick is depicted in children's readers as running and playing (being independent), Jane is often shown caring for her dolls and cooking for others (being interdependent).

In many cultures, there are also social class differences in the independence versus interdependence dimension. Working-class people in modern societies are more interdependent than middle-class individuals. Working-class people have more interactions with their families than middle-class individuals do (Allan, 1979); their parenting styles emphasize conformity and obedience more than do those of middle-class individuals (Kohn, 1969); and they value personal uniqueness less than middle-class individuals do. A study by Stephens and her colleagues provides a striking example of the different values placed on uniqueness (Stephens, Markus, & Townsend, 2007). The researchers asked people how they would feel if a friend bought a car just like one they themselves had just bought. Middle-class people were likely to report that they would be disappointed because they like to be unique; working-class people were more likely to say they would be very happy to share that similarity with a buddy. Middle-class people also appear to care much more about exercising choice than do working-class people. Middle-class people were found to like an object that they had chosen better than one they were given; the reverse was true for working-class people (Stephens, Fryberg, & Markus, 2011). Class differences seem to be broad and deep enough that it is reasonable to regard them as genuine cultural differences.

As a final qualification to these broad generalizations, researchers have found that the same person can have a relatively independent orientation in some situations (for example, competing in a debate tournament) and a relatively interdependent orientation in others (for example, singing in a choir) (Gardner, Gabriel, & Lee, 1999; Kühnen & Oyserman, 2002; Trafimow, Triandis, & Goto, 1991).

Culture and Evolution as Tools for Understanding Situations

Both evolution and culture affect how people see the world and behave within it. The two together are complementary ways of understanding social relations. For the first several hundred thousand years of human existence, our ancestors were largely concerned with the necessities of surviving, reproducing, and nourishing their young in a fundamentally social environment. Such challenges may have resulted in the evolution of prewired inclinations toward certain behaviors and ways of thinking. But such inclinations are tools that can be applied flexibly or not at all. And many, if not most, of these tools are highly modifiable by culture (Sperber, 1996). Indeed, these tools *required* culture of some sort to develop naturally. Different ecologies and economies placed people in situations that differed markedly from one another and in turn produced different social systems and practices.

Evolution has given us all the capacity for an astonishingly wide range of behaviors. But whether a society develops a particular prewired option or not may depend on how adaptive the behavior is for the circumstances that confront the people in it (Sperber, 1996). Nature proposes, but culture disposes. Far from making us rigidly programmed automatons, evolution has equipped us with a large repertoire of tools for dealing with the enormous range of circumstances that humans confront. Cultural circumstances and our high intelligence determine which tools we develop and which tendencies we try to override.

 People in Western societies tend to be individualistic, or independent, whereas people in other societies are more likely to be collectivistic, or interdependent. Westerners tend to define themselves as having attributes that exist apart from their relations with other people. Non-Westerners tend to define themselves in terms of their relations with others. These differences have important implications for many of the most important phenomena of social psychology. Gender roles and sexual mores are examples of behaviors that differ widely from one culture to another. Evolution and culture each make important contributions to understanding human social behavior: evolution predisposes us to certain behaviors, but culture determines which behaviors are likely to be developed in particular situations.

Chapter Review

Summary

Characterizing Social Psychology

- *Social psychology* is the scientific study of the feelings, thoughts, and behaviors of individuals in social situations.

The Power of the Situation

- Social psychology emphasizes the influence of situations on behavior. People often find it difficult to see the role that powerful situations can play in producing their own and others' behavior, and so are inclined to overemphasize the importance of personal dispositions in producing behavior. The two tendencies together are called the *fundamental attribution error*.

The Role of Construal

- Social psychology also focuses on the role of *construal* in understanding situations. People often feel that their comprehension of situations is direct, without much mediating thought. In fact, even the perception of the simplest objects rests on substantial inference and the complex cognitive structures that exist for carrying it out.

- The primary tool people use for understanding social situations, and physical stimuli for that matter, is the *schema*. Schemas are stored representations of numerous repetitions of highly similar stimuli and situations. They tell us how to interpret situations and how to behave in them. *Stereotypes* are schemas of people of various kinds—police officers, Hispanics, yuppies. Stereotypes serve to guide interpretation and behavior, but they can often be mistaken or misapplied, and they can lead to damaging interactions and unjust behaviors.

Automatic versus Controlled Processing

- People's construals of situations are often largely automatic and unconscious. As a consequence, people are sometimes in the dark about how they reached a particular conclusion or why they behaved in a particular way.

Evolution and Human Behavior: How We Are the Same

- The evolutionary perspective focuses on practices and understandings that are universal and seem to be indispensable to social life, suggesting that humans are prewired to engage in those practices.

- Some evolutionary theorists have argued that differences between males and females may be explained by the differential *parental investment* required of the two sexes. They also talk about other universal characteristics that are more cognitive in nature, including *language*, which appears at the same stage of development in all cultures, as well as a *theory of mind*, which also develops early in normal people of all cultures.

Culture and Human Behavior: How We Are Different

- Behaviors and meanings can differ dramatically across cultures. Many of these differences involve the degree to which a society is *interdependent*, or *collectivistic*, in its social relations (having many relationships of a highly prescribed nature) versus *independent*, or *individualistic* (having fewer relationships of a looser sort). These differences influence conceptions of the self and the nature of human relationships and even basic cognitive and perceptual processes.

- Gender roles and sexual mores differ enormously across cultures. Even within the West, gender and sexual practices diverge significantly. Theorists differ in how strongly they believe this variability is arbitrary versus rooted in economic factors or some other aspect of the objective situation confronting the culture.

Key Terms

channel factors (p. 13)

construal (p. 14)

dispositions (p. 12)

fundamental attribution error (p. 13)

Gestalt psychology (p. 14)

independent (individualistic) cultures (p. 29)

interdependent (collectivistic) cultures (p. 30)

naturalistic fallacy (p. 26)

natural selection (p. 22)

parental investment (p. 25)

prisoner's dilemma (p. 15)

schema (p. 17)

social psychology (p. 5)

theory of mind (p. 24)

Further Reading

Darley, J. M., & Batson, C. D. (1973). From Jerusalem to Jericho: A study of situational and dispositional variables in helping behavior. *Journal of Personality and Social Psychology, 27*, 100–119. A classic experiment showing the power of "small" situational factors.

Doris, J. M. (2002). *Lack of character: Personality and moral behavior.* New York: Cambridge University Press. A philosopher shows the importance for the field of ethics of the fact that situational factors influence so powerfully behaviors that we consider moral or immoral.

Henrich, J., Heine, S. J., & Norenzayan, A. (2010). The weirdest people in the world? *Behavioral and Brain Sciences, 33*, 61–83. A documentation of the scores of important ways that people of European cultures differ from people of other cultures.

Ross, L., & Nisbett, R. E. (1991). *The person and the situation: Perspectives of social psychology.* New York: McGraw-Hill. A brief text reviewing some of the basic principles of social psychology.

The Methods of Social Psychology

RETAIL BUSINESS OWNERS ACROSS the Northern and Southern United States received the following letter from a job applicant who described himself as a hardworking 27-year-old man who was relocating to the letter-recipient's area from Michigan. Among a set of appropriate qualifications listed in the letter, the applicant described one rather striking blemish:

> There is one thing I must explain, because I feel I must be honest and want no misunderstandings. I have been convicted of a felony, namely manslaughter. You will probably want an explanation for this before you send me an application, so I will provide it. I got into a fight with someone who was having an affair with my fiancée. I lived in a small town, and one night this person confronted me in front of my friends at the bar. He told everyone that he and my fiancée were sleeping together. He laughed at me to my face and asked me to step outside if I was man enough. I was young and didn't want to back down from a challenge in front of everyone. As we went into the alley, he started to attack me. He knocked me down, and he picked up a bottle. I could have run away and the judge said I should have, but my pride wouldn't let me. Instead I picked up a pipe that was laying in the alley and hit him with it. I didn't mean to kill him, but he died a few hours later at the hospital.

Some of those contacted replied to the letter and complied with the applicant's requests, providing an application, the name of a contact person, or a phone number to call. Some even sent a note with their response.

In truth, however, the applicant was a fictional character created by two social psychologists in a carefully planned study (Cohen & Nisbett, 1997). The investigators measured how cooperative potential employers were with the applicant.

Defending One's Honor
Duels, like the one shown here between Aaron Burr and Alexander Hamilton, were practiced in the United States well into the nineteenth century.

If there was a note, they rated how sympathetic it seemed—how encouraging it was, how personal it was, and whether it mentioned an appreciation for the applicant's candor.

Cohen and Nisbett found some distinct patterns in the replies. Retailers from the South complied with the applicant's requests more than the retailers from the North did. And the notes from Southern businesses were much warmer and more sympathetic than those from the North. One Southern retailer wrote the following in her letter:

> As for your problem of the past, anyone could probably be in the situation you were in. It was just an unfortunate incident that shouldn't be held against you. Your honesty shows that you are sincere. . . .
>
> I wish you the best of luck for your future. You have a positive attitude and a willingness to work. Those are the qualities that businesses look for in an employee. Once you get settled, if you are near here, please stop in and see us.

No letter from a Northern employer was remotely as sympathetic toward the applicant.

Why were the Southerners seemingly so accepting of murder? You will find out in this chapter. More important, you will find out *how* the investigators found out. They employed most of the methods at the disposal of social psychologists—methods that deepen our understanding of human behavior and help us improve many types of social outcomes.

WHY DO SOCIAL PSYCHOLOGISTS DO RESEARCH (AND WHY SHOULD YOU WANT TO READ ABOUT IT)?

For the most part, people can get along perfectly well in everyday life without the benefit of findings from social psychology. The world is a reasonably predictable place: most of the situations we find ourselves in are similar to other familiar situations, and our observations about how people behave in those situations are accurate enough to allow us to navigate through the world with some confidence in the correctness of our predictions.

But many situations—interviews, initiations, dating—can contain surprises and pitfalls that social psychological research can help us anticipate and avoid. And even in familiar situations, our ideas about how people are likely to behave can be mistaken. Chapters 4, 5, and 12 describe some of these mistaken beliefs about social behavior and how those beliefs get formed.

Our opinions about *why* we behave as we do can also be mistaken (Nisbett & Wilson, 1977). As discussed in Chapter 1, many of the factors that influence our behavior are in fact hidden from us: they aren't represented in conscious, verbal forms but in nonconscious, nonverbal forms that aren't accessible to introspection. Fortunately, social psychology can tell us about the reasons not just for other people's behavior but for our own as well.

To see how social psychological research illuminates even ordinary aspects of human behavior and its causes, take a look at **Box 2.1**. Make your own guesses about the outcomes of the research described and then see how accurate those guesses are by looking at p. 46. When you have to predict the results of studies and *then* find out what they were, you avoid the **hindsight bias**, which refers to people's tendency after the fact to be overconfident that they could have predicted a given outcome (Bradfield & Wells, 2005; Fischhoff, Gonzalez, Lerner, & Small, 2005; Guilbault, Bryant, Brockway, & Posavac, 2004). Matching your predictions about Box 2.1 with the actual findings should serve as an antidote against thinking that social psychology findings are obvious. They are often obvious only in hindsight and not in foresight.

hindsight bias People's tendency to be overconfident about whether they could have predicted a given outcome.

 Social psychology shows us that some of our stereotypes about how people behave are mistaken; it also shows us how such beliefs are formed with sometimes faulty procedures. Our beliefs about the reasons for our own behavior can also be mistaken. Social psychological findings sometimes seem obvious, but often only after we know what they are. Hindsight bias mistakenly tells us that we knew about those findings all along.

HOW DO SOCIAL PSYCHOLOGISTS TEST IDEAS?

Social psychologists use a wide variety of methods to test hypotheses about human behavior. As you read about these methods in this chapter and see them applied elsewhere in the book, keep in mind that the logic underlying these methods is

"The scientific method itself would not have led anywhere, it would not even have been born without a passionate striving for clear understanding."

—Albert Einstein,
Out of My Later Years

BOX 2.1 FOCUS ON INTUITIVE SOCIAL PSYCHOLOGY

Predicting the Results of Social Psychology Studies

Predict how people would behave in each of these situations. (See p. 46 for answers.)

1. Does familiarity breed liking or contempt? Would you be likely to prefer a song you had heard many times on the radio or one you had heard less often?

2. Suppose some people were persuaded to lie about their beliefs about a certain matter. Would those people be more inclined to adjust their beliefs in the direction of the lie if paid a small amount of money, a large amount of money, or no money at all?

3. Suppose you knew that an acquaintance wanted a favor from you. Would you like the person better if (a) the person refrained from asking you the favor, (b) the person asked you to do the favor and you complied, or (c) the person asked you to do the favor and you turned the person down?

4. Suppose you got someone to think seriously for a few minutes about the inevitability of death. Would those thoughts be likely to make the person feel (a) more helpless, (b) less favorably inclined toward their fellow human beings, or (c) more patriotic?

5. Suppose a person endured a painful medical procedure. Would the person be less willing to undergo the procedure again if (a) the pain lasted for a long time, (b) the pain at its peak was particularly intense, (c) the first phase of the procedure was particularly painful, or (d) the final phase of the procedure was particularly painful?

6. Suppose male college students were asked to grade an essay written for an English class, and a picture of the female student who allegedly wrote the essay was attached to the essay. Would the grade be higher if (a) the student was very pretty, (b) the student was average looking, (c) the student was quite plain looking, or (d) the student grading the essay was about as good looking as the person who allegedly wrote the essay?

7. Suppose people were asked what a person should do if given the choice between an option with substantial potential gain but also substantial risk and another option that entails less potential gain but also less risk. Would people be more likely to recommend the risky choice if (a) they considered the choice by themselves or (b) they considered the choice in discussion with a small group—or (c) would it make no difference?

8. Suppose you asked one group of people to give their opinion about an issue after very brief consideration and asked another group to spend several minutes thinking about as many aspects of the issue as possible and then give their opinion. Which group do you think would have more extreme views on the topic: (a) the group asked immediately about their opinion or (b) the group asked to ponder a while before answering—or (c) would the amount of time thinking about the question make no difference?

9. Suppose you offered an award to some nursery school children if they would draw with magic markers, and all the children who were offered the award drew with them. Would these children be (a) more likely to play with the magic markers at a subsequent time than children never offered the award, (b) less likely, or (c) equally likely?

10. Suppose you asked a group of people to report 6 instances when they behaved in an assertive fashion, another group to report 12 instances when they behaved in an assertive fashion, and a third group to report 6 instances of some other behavior altogether, such as instances of introverted behavior. Which group would later report that they were most assertive: (a) the group asked for 6 instances of assertive behavior, (b) the group asked for 12 instances of assertive behavior, (c) the group asked about some other behavior—or (d) would it make little difference what the group was asked?

crucial for getting at the likely truth of propositions about social behavior. Even if you can't do a study to test a particular proposition, thinking through how you *would* test a given idea can lead you to new hypotheses that, on reflection, might seem preferable to your initial speculation.

Hypotheses are predictions about what will happen under particular circumstances. Hypotheses often test broader theories about behavior. A **theory** is a body of related propositions intended to describe some aspect of the world. In speaking casually, people may say that something is "just a theory," meaning it is a notion largely unsupported by facts. In science, including social science, theories generally have support in the form of empirical data, and they often have made predictions that are surprising except in light of the theory. In the history of science, many theories have led to a greater understanding of natural phenomena or to important real-life consequences. Evolutionary theory is supported by an enormous number of facts as well as nonintuitive predictions that have been confirmed by empirical observation. Bacterial adaptation to drugs, for example, is well understood in terms of evolutionary theory. Relativity theory in physics, which is also supported by a huge number of facts and accurate predictions, led to the development of the atomic bomb.

An example of a hypothesis born of a social psychological theory is the prediction that, if person A likes person B, who dislikes person C, person A will either come to dislike person C or begin to dislike person B. Such a hypothesis, which can be tested in a variety of ways, is an example of the sort of hypotheses that are generated by what is called balance theory, or the theory that people like to have consistent thoughts and behavior and will do substantial mental work to achieve such cognitive consistency. Hypotheses are tested by studies, which test predictions about what will happen in particular concrete contexts. Thus theories are more general than hypotheses, which are more general than findings from the studies that test them.

hypothesis A prediction about what will happen under particular circumstances.

theory A body of related propositions intended to describe some aspect of the world.

Observational Research

At the simplest level, research can be a matter of merely looking at a phenomenon in some reasonably systematic way with a view to understanding what is going on and coming up with hypotheses about why things are happening as they are. Charles Darwin was first and foremost a great observer of natural life, and his observations of finches in the Galápagos Islands led to his theory of evolution by natural selection.

Social psychologists themselves learn a great deal from observation. One such method of research, used by both psychologists and cultural anthropologists, is called *participant observation* and involves observing some phenomenon at close range. An anthropologist may live with a group of people for a long time, just noting what they do and coming up with guesses—sometimes inspired by conversations with the people being studied—about why those people do certain things or have certain beliefs. In the 1970s, for example, cultural anthropologist Shirley Brice Heath used participant observation to study preparation for schooling by middle-class and working-class families in a North Carolina town. She lived with the families—observing and taking part in their daily activities. She found remarkable differences between these two groups by living with them for lengthy periods. The middle-class families read to their children a great deal, included

Observational Methods The evolutionary psychologist and human behavioral ecologist Lawrence Sugiyama is shown here, with bow and arrow, involved in a particularly active form of participant observation.

How Accurate Were Your Predictions? (See Box 2.1 on p. 44)

1. Familiarity, in general, breeds liking. The more a person has been exposed to a stimulus, within broad limits, the more the person likes it. See Chapter 10.

2. People are more persuaded by the lies they tell if they are paid nothing or a small amount than if they are paid a lot. See Chapter 7.

3. We like people more if we do them a favor. See Chapters 7 and 9.

4. When people are reminded of their own mortality, they focus on the values they hold most dear, such as religion and love of country. See Chapter 7.

5. The duration of pain has little effect on people's willingness to experience a procedure again. See Chapter 6.

6. Males give higher grades to females who are good looking. See Chapter 10.

7. In general, group discussion shifts people toward more risky choices. See Chapter 12.

8. Thinking more about an issue makes people's opinions about the issue more extreme. See Chapter 9.

9. Rewarding children for doing something they would do anyway makes them less interested in doing it. Contracts turn play into work. See Chapter 7.

10. People report that they are more assertive if they are asked to think of a few instances of assertiveness rather than if they are asked to think of many. It's easier to come up with a few instances than many, and people use the effort they expend as an indicator of what they are really like. See Chapter 4.

them in dinner-table conversations, used the printed word to guide their behavior (recipes, game rules), and taught them how to categorize objects, how to answer "why" questions, and how to evaluate and make judgments about things. The working-class families didn't do those things as much, and although their children were reasonably well prepared for the early grades of school, their lack of preparation showed up in later grades, when they faced more complex tasks involving categorization and evaluation.

In the 1950s, the social psychologists Roger Barker and Herbert Wright studied how children in a Midwestern town interacted with their surroundings (Barker & Wright, 1954). They followed children around as they delivered the morning paper, went to school, played kick the can, did their homework, and went to church suppers. The study revealed a great deal about the way young people interact with their environments—the opportunities and constraints that came with their environments—and the factors that molded their characters.

Social psychologists often observe social situations in a semiformal way, taking notes and interviewing participants, but they typically design additional research to verify the impressions they get from participant observation. Observations are often misleading, so any tentative conclusions gleaned from observation should ideally be tested with other methods.

Archival Research

One type of research can be conducted without ever leaving the library (or the laptop). Using this method, researchers look at evidence found in archives of various kinds—record books, police reports, sports statistics, newspaper articles, and databases containing ethnographic (anthropological) descriptions of people in different cultures. For example, Nisbett (1993) and his colleagues studied FBI reports of homicides and found, as they had anticipated, that homicides were more common in the South than in the North. The FBI reports of homicide also included the circumstances of the homicide—murders committed in the context of another felony (for example, while robbing a convenience store) versus murders that are crimes of passion (for example, during a heated argument between neighbors or in the context of a lovers' triangle). Nisbett and colleague Dov Cohen analyzed the various types of murders and discovered that in the South, the most common kinds of homicide involved some type of insult—for example, barroom quarrels and cases of a man's girlfriend or wife leaving him for another man (Nisbett & Cohen, 1996). Other kinds of homicides are actually less common in the South than in the North. (One researcher was prompted to comment that as long as a Southerner stays out of the wrong bars and bedrooms, he's safer than a Northerner; Reed, 1981.) The observation that insult-related homicides are more common in the South led Cohen and Nisbett to begin a research program to study whether Southerners really do respond more aggressively to insults, or whether the higher rate of insult-related homicides was due to factors such as hot temperatures or lenient justice systems.

Surveys

One of the most common types of study in social psychology involves simply asking people questions. Surveys can be conducted using either interviews or written questionnaires. The participants can be a small collection of students or a large national survey. When the investigator is trying to discern the beliefs or attitudes of some group of people—freshmen at a particular university, Hispanics living in California, or the population of the United States as a whole—it is important that the sample of people in the survey be a *random sample* of the population as a whole. The only way to obtain a random sample is to give everyone in the population an equal chance of being chosen. If the university has a directory of students, a random sample can be obtained by finding out the total number of freshmen (say, 1,000) deciding how many to interview (say, 50) and then selecting every twentieth name from the directory and asking those people to participate in the survey (**Figure 2.1**).

A *convenience sample*—obtained, for example, by contacting people as they enter the library or e-mailing fraternity and sorority members—is not random and may be *biased* in some way. That is, it may include too many of some kinds of people and too few of others. Information based on biased samples is sometimes worse than no information at all. One notable example is a survey by the *Literary Digest*, based on more than a million respondents, that erroneously predicted that the Republican Alf Landon would defeat Franklin Delano Roosevelt in the 1936 presidential election. In fact, the election was one of the most dramatic landslides in history: Landon carried only two states. How could the survey have been so far off the mark? The sample was biased because it was drawn from telephone directories and automobile registrations. In 1936, wealthy people were more likely to own phones and cars than were poorer people as well as more likely to be Republicans.

You have probably seen the results of reader surveys in various magazines. Two-thirds *of Cosmopolitan* readers who went on a vegan diet say that they lost weight. Three-quarters of the readers of *Outside* magazine say that sex is more enjoyable outdoors. Sixty percent of respondents in a *Reader's Digest* poll claim they are happier after going to church than if they stay home and watch a football game on Sunday. Actually, all three results are fictional, and you should ignore each claim. But you should ignore claims like these even if they aren't made up. The people who take the time to respond to such polls are likely to be different from those who do not respond and therefore are unlikely to represent the population as a whole. *Cosmo* readers who lost weight may be more likely to respond to a survey about weight loss than those who did not lose weight. The criterion that everyone is equally likely to be in the sample is clearly not met, upping the odds that the survey results are misleading.

How many people would you need to sample in order to make inferences about a large population? In fact, the number of people needed to get a reasonably accurate count on some question—presidential preference, for example—is essentially independent of the size of the population in question. A sample of about 1,200 people from the entire adult population of the United States is sufficient to estimate the population value to a degree of accuracy of plus or minus 3 percent and to be 95 percent confident that the true value is within that range. The major

Population
Group you want to know about
(e.g., U.S. college students)

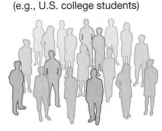

Random sample
Taken at random from the population (e.g., giving every student in the country an equal chance to be in the sample)

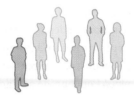

Convenience sample
Taken from some available subgroup in the population (e.g., students questioned as they come into the Student Union)

FIGURE 2.1 Sampling

national polls taken just before the presidential election generally come within 2 percent of the actual vote.

Cohen and Nisbett used surveys to pursue social psychological questions concerning attitudes toward violence (Nisbett & Cohen, 1996). One guess about why Southerners are more likely to commit homicide is that Southern attitudes might be more accepting of violence. But when Cohen and Nisbett looked at published national surveys of attitudes toward violence, they found few regional differences. For example, Southerners were no more likely than Northerners to agree with the sentiment that "an eye for an eye" is a justified retaliation, and Southerners were actually more likely to agree that "when a person harms you, you should turn the other cheek and forgive him." However, the researchers found that Southerners were more likely to favor violence in response to insults and to think that a man would be justified to fight an acquaintance who "looks over his girlfriend and talks to her in a suggestive way." Southerners were also more likely to approve of violence in response to threats to home and family, thinking, for example, that "a man has a right to kill a person to defend his house." The researchers also found that Southerners were more approving of violence in socializing children: they were more likely to say that spanking was a reasonable way to handle a child's misdeeds and more likely to say that they would encourage a child to beat up someone who was bullying him (see **Figure 2.2** for examples of the kinds of questions asked by Cohen and Nisbett).

In trying to explain this acceptance of violence in specific contexts, Cohen and Nisbett sought out anthropologists and historians. Several sources suggested that the South might be a "culture of honor." The U.S. North was settled by farmers from England, Holland, and Germany. The U.S. South was settled by herding peoples from the edges of Britain—Scottish, Irish, and Scotch-Irish from Ulster. Herding peoples throughout the world tend to be tough guys. They need to be because they can lose their livelihood—their herd—in an instant. They cultivate

---

FIGURE 2.2 You Be the Subject: Attitude toward Violence

Sometimes conflicts are resolved through fighting, and other times they are resolved nonviolently.

Imagine that a man named Fred finds himself in the following situations. In these situations, please indicate whether his starting a fight would be extremely justified, somewhat justified, or not at all justified.

1. Fred fights an acquaintance because that person looks over Fred's girlfriend and starts talking to her in a suggestive way.

2. Fred fights an acquaintance because that person insult's Fred's wife, implying that she has loose morals.

3. Fred fights an acquaintance because that person tells others behind Fred's back that Fred is a liar and a cheat.

On occasion, violent conflict involves shooting another person. Imagine that a man named Fred finds himself in the following situations. In these situations, indicate whether his shooting another person would be extremely justified, somewhat justified, or not at all justified.

4. Fred shoots another because that person steals Fred's wife.

5. Fred shoots another because that person sexually assaults Fred's 16-year-old daughter.

Results: Turn to p. 50 to see what your answers indicate.

a stance of being ready to commit violence at the merest hint that they might not be able to protect themselves, their homes, and their property. Insults must be prevented or retaliated against for a person to establish that he is not to be trifled with. Children are raised not to fear violence, to know how to protect themselves. This historical hypothesis guided the rest of Cohen and Nisbett's research.

Correlational Research

In understanding different types of research methods, one of the most important distinctions is that between correlational and experimental research. In **correlational research**, psychologists simply determine whether a relationship exists between two or more variables. **Experimental research** goes a step further, by enabling researchers to make strong inferences about how different situations or conditions affect people's behavior.

Correlation Is Not Causation Looking for correlations is an important way to begin a line of inquiry. However, once established, a correlation begs for further exploration. Does variable 1 causally influence variable 2, or is it the other way around—**reverse causation**, in other words? Or does some **third variable** influence both? In correlational research, we can never be sure about causality. For example, *TIME Magazine* (February 2004) published a cover story devoted to the proposition that love and sex are good for physical and mental health. The magazine quoted statistics showing that married people are happier than unmarried people. But the article left open a number of questions that should make a careful reader skeptical of the magazine's causal claims. Happier people may be more appealing to others and more likely to be married for that reason, so happiness may cause marriage rather than marriage causing happiness. This would be a case of reverse causality. Or perhaps good physical and mental health leads to greater likelihood of marriage as well as greater likelihood of being happy. In this case, the causal factor would be a third variable.

Correlational research cannot prove a causal relationship because of **self-selection**—that is, the investigator has no control over the level of a particular participant's score on a given variable. In effect, the participant has "chosen" the level of *all* variables—those that are measured and those that are not. For example, in the *TIME* study, the investigators did not choose whether a given person was married or not; participants in the study either were or were not married. And the investigators didn't know what other qualities each participant brought along with his or her marital status—a sunny or gloomy disposition, good or bad physical health. These various qualities are self-selected as opposed to investigator-selected.

In correlational research, investigators can look at only the degree of relationship between two or more variables. Strength of relationship can range from 0, meaning that the variables have no relationship at all, to 1, meaning that the covariation is perfect—the higher the level on one variable, the higher the level on the other—without exception. (In the latter case, the correlation is +1. If it were the case that being higher on one variable was perfectly associated with being lower on the other, the correlation would be −1.) By convention, a correlation of 0.2 indicates a slight relationship, a correlation of 0.4 a moderately strong relationship, and a correlation of 0.6 or higher a very strong relationship. **Figure 2.3** shows what are called scatterplots. Variable 1 is on the x-axis, and variable 2 is on

correlational research Research that does not involve random assignment to different situations, or conditions, and that psychologists conduct just to see whether there is a relationship between the variables.

experimental research In social psychology, research that randomly assigns people to different conditions, or situations, and that enables researchers to make strong inferences about how these different conditions affect people's behavior.

reverse causation When variable 1 is assumed to cause variable 2, yet the opposite direction of causation may be the case.

third variable When variable 1 does not cause variable 2 and variable 2 does not cause variable 1, but rather some other variable exerts a causal influence on both.

self-selection A problem that arises when the participant, rather than the investigator, selects his or her level on each variable, bringing with this value unknown other properties that make causal interpretation of a relationship difficult.

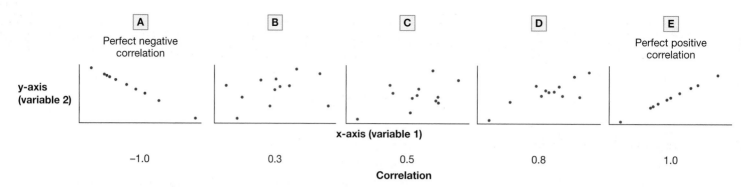

FIGURE 2.3 Scatterplots and Correlations

the y-axis. Each dot represents a case—for example, a study participant for whom you have a score on variable 1 and a score on variable 2. Panel A shows a perfect negative correlation, and panel E shows a perfect positive correlation.

Panel B in Figure 2.3 shows a correlation of 0.3, which corresponds, for example, to the correlation between the degree to which an individual is underweight, average, or overweight and the degree of incipient cardiovascular illness. Both the marked spread of the dots (their scatter) and the relatively shallow slope of the line that best fits the scatterplot show that the association is relatively weak. Consider the causal possibilities for the relationship in panel B. It is possible that something about being overweight causes cardiovascular illness. But it is also possible, for example, that people who are under stress tend to gain weight and also to develop cardiovascular symptoms. And it is possible that some underlying syndrome makes people prone both to be overweight and to develop cardiovascular illness. In either case, being overweight might play no causal role in cardiovascular illness (Jeffery, 1996).

Panel C in Figure 2.3 shows a correlation of 0.5, which is approximately the degree of association between height and weight. This correlation helps us understand the ambiguity of correlational findings. Height predicts weight, and weight predicts height, but you wouldn't say that one *causes* the other. Rather, a wide range of genetic and environmental factors causes both. Some of those factors undoubtedly make some people larger than others—influencing both height and weight. But some factors influence weight more than height, and vice versa. In any case, height does not cause weight, nor does weight cause height.

Panel D in Figure 2.3 shows a correlation of 0.8. This is about the degree of correlation that you would find between a person's score on the math portion of the Scholastic Aptitude Test on a first testing occasion and those obtained a year later. The association is quite strong, as indicated by the relatively slight scatter of the points around the line fitting the scatterplot and the relatively steep slope of that line. But it can't be said that the SAT score on the first occasion caused the score on the second occasion. Instead, it can be said that an underlying and undoubtedly highly complex set of factors involving genetics and social variables caused both scores to be similar for a given individual.

Try your hand at interpreting the correlational results in **Box 2.2**, which presents the results of numerous correlational studies for which scientists or the media have implied a clear causal connection. To be a good consumer of correlational research, you need to be able to evaluate such causal claims carefully. (Some possible responses to those causality claims are presented on p. 54.) For each

BOX 2.2   FOCUS ON SCIENTIFIC METHOD

Thinking about Correlations

Determine the nature of the correlation for each of these situations. (See p. 54 for answers.)

1. *TIME Magazine* (June 23, 2008, p. 102) reported that attempts by parents to control the portions their children eat will cause the children to become overweight. If the parents of overweight children stop controlling their portions, will the children get thinner?

2. Countries with higher average IQs have higher average wealth measured as average gross domestic product (GDP). Does being smarter make a country richer?

3. People who attend church have lower mortality rates than those who do not (Schnall et al., 2008). Does religion make people live longer?

4. People who have a dog are less likely to be depressed. If you give a dog to a depressed person, will the person get happier?

5. States with abstinence-only sex education have higher homicide rates. Does abstinence-only sex education cause aggression? If you give more informative sex education to students in those states, will the homicide rate go down?

6. Intelligent men have better sperm—more sperm and more mobile sperm (Arden, Gottfredson, Miller, & Pierce, 2008). Does this finding suggest that attending college, which improves intelligence, also improves sperm quality?

7. People who smoke marijuana are subsequently more likely to use cocaine than people who do not smoke marijuana. Does marijuana use cause cocaine use?

of the correlational findings listed, see if you can think of ways that the causal hypothesis could be tested in an experiment.

The Value of Correlational Findings   Correlational studies can be very helpful in alerting investigators to various possibilities for valid causal hypotheses about the nature of the world. Sometimes, too, these studies are a researcher's best option when an experimental study would be difficult or unethical. Researchers cannot randomly assign people to the levels of certain variables, such as gender, socioeconomic class, or intelligence. And they would not want to assign participants to a condition that held long-term risks. But correlational studies don't tell us about the direction of causality, and they don't tell us whether some third variable is driving the association between the two variables of interest.

Even if correlational studies cannot prove that a causal relationship exists, clever analysis of correlational data can be quite persuasive about the meaning of a relationship. Consider two examples.

1. *People who watch the local evening news—with its murders, fires, and other newsworthy mayhem—see more danger in the world than people who do not.* The most obvious explanation is that watching dangers on TV makes people feel more at risk. But could it be that people who are anxious watch local TV to justify their fearfulness? Or is there some third variable? For example, elderly people may have more anxiety about their lives and may have more time to watch TV. This study could be refined so that it potentially rules out the latter hypothesis. For example, the elderly may not be more likely to watch TV than younger people, and the elderly may be no more anxious about their lives than are younger people. These possibilities could be assessed by research. Ruling out one hypothesis does not prove

Longitudinal Studies Three participants in the "*Up* series" of documentary films by Michael Apted. The films are an ongoing longitudinal study that has traced the development of 14 British people from various socioeconomic backgrounds since 1964.

longitudinal study A study conducted over a long period of time with the same population, which is periodically assessed regarding a particular behavior.

independent variable In experimental research, the variable that is manipulated; it is hypothesized to be the cause of a particular outcome.

dependent variable In experimental research, the variable that is measured (as opposed to manipulated); it is hypothesized to be affected by manipulation of the independent variable.

random assignment Assigning participants in experimental research to different groups randomly, such that they are as likely to be assigned to one condition as to another.

control condition A condition comparable to the experimental condition in every way except that it lacks the one ingredient hypothesized to produce the expected effect on the dependent variable.

that the relationship is causal, but as other alternative explanations are tested and rejected, the nature of the relationship between the two variables may become clearer.

2. *People who watched a great deal of violent TV when they were 8 years old are more likely to be incarcerated for violence and other criminal behavior in adolescence and adulthood.* At first blush, it seems obvious that watching violent TV tends to make people more violent. On the other hand, it also seems obvious that people with more violent temperaments would be more likely to want to watch violent TV when younger and more likely to engage in criminal behavior when older. Note, however, that such a **longitudinal study** (one that studies people at two points in time) rules out the opposite direction of causality: nothing that happens when a person is 30 can affect anything the person did when younger. Again, clever analysis of data such as these, as discussed in Chapter 13, can make some interpretations much less plausible than others.

In this book, you will see many illustrations of the different types of inferences that can be drawn from correlational studies. You will also discover some of the clever ways that social psychologists have managed to circumvent the problems characteristic of correlational research.

Experimental Research

The best way to be sure about causality is to conduct an experiment. Experimental research requires an independent variable and a dependent variable. The **independent variable** is the one that is manipulated and is hypothesized to be the cause of a particular outcome. The **dependent variable** is measured (as opposed to manipulated) and is hypothesized to be the outcome of a particular causal process. In experiments, the researcher determines what the independent variable will be and what the levels for that variable will be. Dependent variables can be measured in many ways—by verbal reports (such as statements about degree of anger or anxiety), behavior (helping or not; getting an inoculation or not), physiological measures (heart rate or stress measures such as cortisol level), or neural measures (increased activity in the amygdala).

The great power of experiments comes from their ability to expose participants to different levels of the independent variable by **random assignment**. Random assignment ensures that participants are as likely to be assigned to one condition as to another and that, on average, except for the manipulation of the independent variable, there should be no differences across experimental groups. Random assignment also rules out the possibility of self-selection biases in samples. Also critical to experiments is a carefully crafted **control condition**, which is comparable to the experimental condition in every way except that it lacks the one ingredient hypothesized to produce the expected effect on the dependent measure.

As an example of a carefully designed experiment, let's go back to the findings that Southerners are more likely to commit homicide in situations where there has been an insult, and that Southerners are more likely to believe that violence is an appropriate response to an insult. Both of these findings are correlational: Southernness is associated with insult-related homicides, and Southernness is associated with the belief that violence is an appropriate response to an insult. To study further whether Southerners actually react more aggressively to an insult, Cohen and his colleagues performed a series of experiments (Cohen, Nisbett, Bowdle, & Schwarz, 1996; see **Figure 2.4**). The participants in their studies were all middle-class students at the University of Michigan; some students were Southerners, and some were Northerners. All of them believed they were participating in a study on the effects of time constraints on judgments of various kinds. After filling out a questionnaire, they were asked to take it down a long, narrow hallway lined with filing cabinets and leave it on a table at the end.

For some participants, a nasty surprise awaited near the end of the hallway. Another student stood in the hallway with a file drawer pulled out. For the participant to pass by, the student had to push the drawer in and move out of the way. Moments later, when the participant started back down the hall, the student had to get out of the participant's way again. This time the student slammed the drawer shut, pushed into the participant's shoulder, and said, "Asshole." (He then quickly exited behind a door labeled "Photo Lab" to avoid a physical confrontation. One participant actually ran after the student and rattled the door knob, trying to get at him. Would you care to guess the region of the country that participant was from?) Subjects in a control condition simply left the questionnaire on the

---

FIGURE 2.4 Scientific Method: Honor Experiments

Hypothesis: Members of a culture of honor, such as U.S. Southerners, will respond with more anger and aggression when insulted than will other people, such as U.S. Northerners.

Research Method:

1. Participants were asked to fill out a questionnaire, take it down a long, narrow hallway lined with filing cabinets, and leave it on a table at the end.

2. Some participants had to pass another student in the hall with a drawer pulled out. This student would have to close the drawer and move out of the way each time the participant passed. When the participant passed the student for the second time, the student slammed the file drawer shut, pushed into the participant's shoulder, and said, "Asshole."

Results: Southerners responded with more facial and bodily expressions of anger when insulted, and their testosterone level increased. Northerners did not show either of these responses.

CONCLUSION: Southerners do indeed experience more anger when insulted and are more biologically prepared for aggression.

1. It could be that parents try to control the portions that children eat if they are overweight. If so, the direction of causation is the reverse of that hypothesized by *TIME Magazine*. It could also be the case that less happy, more stressful families have more controlling parents and more overweight children, but there is no causal connection between the two. A third variable accounts for the correlation.

2. It could be that richer countries have better education systems and hence produce people who get higher IQ scores. In that case, wealth causes intelligence, rather than the other way around. It's also possible that some third factor, like physical health, influences both variables.

3. It could be that healthier people engage in more social activities of all kinds, including going to church. If so, the direction of causation runs opposite of the one implied. Or it could be that good social adjustment—a third variable—causes people both to engage in more social activities and to be healthier.

4. It could be that people who are depressed are less likely to do anything fun, like buying a pet. If so, the direction of causation is opposite to the one implied. (But in fact, giving a pet to a depressed person does improve the person's mood.)

5. It could be that states that are poorer are more likely to have higher homicide rates and states that are poorer are more likely to have abstinence-only sex education. Indeed, both are true. So there may be no causal connection at all between sex education and homicide. Rather, a third variable, such as poverty or something associated with it, may be causally linked to both and thus account for the correlation.

6. It could be that better physical health—a third variable—helps people to be smarter and helps sperm to be of better quality. Or some other factor could be associated with both intelligence and sperm quality, such as drug or alcohol use. So there might be no causal connection between intelligence and sperm quality.

table without incident. (The participants were, of course, randomly assigned to one or the other condition.) The study therefore had two independent variables: whether the participant was Northern or Southern, and whether the participant was insulted or not.

Several dependent variables were examined after the insult either did or did not take place. First, observers were positioned so that they could see the participant immediately after he was insulted. Insulted Southerners usually showed a flash of anger; insulted Northerners were more likely to shrug their shoulders or to appear amused. Second, participants were asked to read a story in which a man made a pass at another man's fiancée. Participants were asked to provide an ending for the story. Southerners who had been insulted were much more likely to provide a violent ending to the story than were Southerners who had not been insulted, whereas the endings provided by Northerners were unaffected by the insult. Third, the participants' level of testosterone, which mediates aggression in males, was tested both before and after the insult. The level of testosterone increased for Southerners who had been insulted, but it did not increase for Southerners who had not been insulted or for Northerners, whether insulted or not.

Fourth, as the participant walked back down the narrow hallway, another assistant to the experimenter walked toward him. This assistant was 6 feet 3 inches tall and weighed 250 pounds, and his instructions were to walk down the middle of the hall, forcing the participant to dodge out of his way. The dependent measure was how far away the participant was when he finally swerved out of the assistant's way. The investigators thought that the insulted Southerners would be put into such an aggressive mood that they would play "chicken" with the assistant, waiting until the last moment to swerve aside. And they did indeed. Northerners, whether insulted or not, swerved aside at a distance of about 5 feet from the assistant. Southerners, who have long been known for their politeness, stood aside at 9 feet if not insulted, but bulled ahead until 3 feet away if insulted.

The experiment by Cohen and colleagues is not an experiment in the full sense. Only one of the independent variables was created by random assignment, namely, whether the participant was insulted or not. The other independent variable was status as a Southerner or Northerner. Thus, technically, the Cohen study is correlational. The basic finding is that something about Southernness predisposes college men to respond aggressively to insults. The study can't tell us what the causally relevant aspect of Southernness is.

In many cases, however, experimental research can establish a causal relation between two variables. Recall from Chapter 1 the experiment in which John Darley and Daniel Batson (1973) found that seminary students in a hurry were less likely to offer aid to a victim. In that experiment, the main independent variable was whether or not the student was in a hurry. The dependent variable was whether or not the student stopped to help the victim. The seminary students were randomly assigned to be either in the "late" condition or the control ("not late") condition. Doing so ensured that participants in the two conditions were, on average, the same kind of people and thus showed that something related to being late is what caused such a large proportion of seminarians in the late condition to fail to help the apparent victim. Another example might be a study of the effects of violent media on children. A researcher could expose one group of young children to violent TV for a couple of hours while exposing a control group to innocuous programs that are emotionally vivid but not violent. The researcher could then see whether the "violent TV" group behaved in a more violent way afterward. If they did, these findings would support the hypothesis that violent TV leads to violence in later life (see Chapter 13).

Experimental research can sometimes answer the causality questions that are left unclear by purely correlational research, but not always. As mentioned earlier, in some cases an experiment might not be possible or ethical. We wouldn't want to assign 10-year-old children to watch lots of violent TV over a long period of time, for example. And we couldn't randomly assign some people to be married and others to remain single. However, investigators can take advantage of **natural experiments**, in which events occur that the investigator believes to have causal implications for some outcome. For example, we might measure people's happiness before and after they get married. And indeed, it turns out that people are happier after marriage than they were before (Argyle, 1999). These results are scarcely decisive, but they strongly suggest that married people are happier *because* they are married—not that they are married because they are cheerful. In another example, when television was first introduced in the United States, it was not broadcast to all communities across the country. Some communities had TV and others didn't. And whether or not a community received television was not determined by self-selection. This natural experiment therefore allowed investigators to draw relatively strong conclusions about the impact of television on people's habits and opinions.

7. It could be that people who take any kind of drug are more sensation seeking than other people and therefore engage in many kinds of stimulating behavior that are against the law. Smoking marijuana may not cause cocaine use, and cocaine use may not cause marijuana use. Rather, some third factor may influence both.

"Science walks forward on two feet, namely theory and experiment. Sometimes it is one foot which is put forward first, sometimes the other, but continuous progress is only made by the use of both."

—Robert Millikan, Nobel Prize in Physics, 1946

LOOKING BACK Social psychologists study phenomena by observational methods (though they usually do so to get an intuitive understanding with a view toward applying other methods), archival research involving records of various kinds, and surveys in which people are asked questions. The validity of surveys typically depends on using respondents who are randomly sampled from the population they represent. Correlational research, in which the investigator establishes whether there is a relationship between two variables, suffers from the problem of self-selection: the individuals being studied have "chosen" their level on each variable rather than being assigned a level by the investigator. Experimental research manipulates an independent variable and observes the effects of the manipulation on a dependent variable.

natural experiments Naturally occurring events or phenomena having somewhat different conditions that can be compared with almost as much rigor as in experiments where the investigator manipulates the conditions.

SOME OTHER USEFUL CONCEPTS FOR UNDERSTANDING RESEARCH

All research is not created equal. Just because someone has conducted a study does not mean you should accept the results as fact. What sets a well-designed study apart from a flawed one? In an experiment, random assignment and a control group can go a long way toward eliminating potential problems. But in designing any study, researchers also need to carefully consider certain types of validity and reliability, as well as the statistical significance of their findings.

External Validity in Experiments

The previous section points out the weaknesses of correlational studies, but experimental studies have weaknesses as well. Sometimes experiments can be so removed from everyday life that it can be hard to know how to interpret them

external validity An experimental
setup that closely resembles real-life
situations so that results can safely be
generalized to such situations.

(Aronson, Ellsworth, Carlsmith, & Gonzalez, 1990). When researchers don't know how to generalize the results obtained in an experiment to real-life situations, they say there is poor **external validity**. Experiments have poor external validity when the basic situation the participants are put into bears little resemblance to any real-life situation. When the purpose of the research is to generalize the results of an experiment directly to the outside world, external validity is critical. For example, if we wish to know whether TV violence makes children more aggressive, both the TV programs the children see and the types of behavior that could be called aggressive should resemble real TV shows, and the behavior examined should be behavior that children might actually engage in.

Poor external validity is not always fatal, however. Milgram's study of obedience discussed in Chapters 1 and 9 has poor external validity because most people in our society are almost never placed in a situation where an authority figure is commanding them to harm another person. Nevertheless, such things have happened in the world and will happen again. In other cases, investigators deliberately strip down a situation to its bare essentials to make a theoretical point that would be hard to make with real-world materials. For example, to find out how familiarity with a stimulus affects its attractiveness, Robert Zajonc (1968) and his colleagues presented Turkish words to Americans over a headset, presenting some of them many times and some of them only a few times. The experiment has poor external validity in that the situation is not like one ever encountered in real life. But the simplicity of the situation and the complete initial unfamiliarity of the Turkish words ensured that it was the sheer number of repetitions of the words that affected their attractiveness and not something else about the stimuli, such as how much they were liked beforehand. In research like Zajonc's, where the purpose is to clarify a general idea or theory, external validity is not essential.

One of the best ways to ensure the external validity of an experiment is to do a **field experiment**. Field experiments resemble laboratory experiments conceptually, but they take place in the real world, usually when the participants are not aware that they are participating in a study. An example would be an experiment in which researchers study the reactions of people who are asked to give up their seats on an uncrowded bus or train.

field experiment An experiment
set up in the real world, usually with
participants who are not aware that
they are in a study of any kind.

In one example of a field experiment, described at the beginning of this chapter, Cohen and Nisbett (1997) examined Southern and Northern merchants' reactions to a letter allegedly written by a job applicant who had been convicted of a felony. The felony in question was either a motor vehicle theft or, in the version you read, a homicide in the context of a love triangle. The dependent variable was the degree of responsiveness to the applicant's letter, ranging from no response at all to sending an encouraging letter and an application form. Southern businesses were much more encouraging of the man convicted of homicide than were Northern businesses. The experiment provides, in a field setting, evidence that Southern norms concerning violence in response to an insult are more accepting than Northern norms. Because there was no difference in the reactions of Southerners and Northerners to the letter that mentioned a theft, we know that Southerners are not just more forgiving of crimes generally. Thus the theft letter constitutes a control condition in this field experiment. And because the experiment's participants were potential employers who believed they were responding to a real applicant, its external validity is much higher than it would be if the participants had been asked to assess fictional job applicants in a laboratory setting.

Internal Validity in Experiments

Whatever the goal of an experiment, **internal validity** is essential. Internal validity is achieved when investigators know that only the manipulated variable—and no other external influence—could have produced the results. The experimental situation is held constant in all other respects, and participants in the various experimental conditions don't differ, on average, in any respect before they come to the laboratory. In Cohen and colleagues' insult experiment, if insulted Southerners had differed from noninsulted Southerners in some additional way, the investigators couldn't have concluded that the insult had caused the different behavior. It could have been something associated with the difference between the two groups before they ever arrived at the lab. Fortunately, there is an easy way to rule out such a possibility: random assignment of participants to experimental conditions. For example, the investigators can flip a coin to determine what condition the participant will be in or consult a random number table and assign the participant to the experimental condition if the next number is odd and to the control condition if the next number is even. With random assignment, researchers can be reasonably sure that the participants in one condition are not different, on average, from the participants in the other conditions. They will have the same average height, the same average degree of extraversion, the same attitudes (on average) toward capital punishment, and so on.

internal validity In experimental research, confidence that only the manipulated variable could have produced the results.

Internal validity also requires that the experimental setup seem realistic and plausible to participants. If it is implausible, if participants don't believe what the experimenter tells them, or if participants don't understand something crucial that is said to them, then internal validity is lacking and the experimenters can have no confidence in the results. In such cases, participants weren't responding to the independent variable as conceptualized by the experimenter but to something else entirely. Experimenters can help ensure that they meet the various criteria for internal validity by **debriefing** participants in pilot studies, that is, preliminary versions of the experiment. Debriefing may involve asking participants straightforwardly if they understood the instructions, found the setup to be reasonable, and so forth. Pilot study participants are generally told the purpose of the experiment and what the experimenters expected to find. Pilot participants can often provide useful information about how well the experiment is designed when they are brought in as consultants, so to speak, in the debriefing. Even after the experimental setup is finalized, debriefing is routine for the purpose of education—to let the participants know what questions are being studied, how the experiment addresses those questions, and why the results might have social value.

"Inquiry is fatal to certainty."

—Will Durant, philosopher

debriefing In preliminary versions of an experiment, asking participants straightforwardly if they understood the instructions, found the setup to be reasonable, and so forth. In later versions, debriefings are used to educate participants about the questions being studied.

Reliability and Validity of Tests and Measures

Reliability concerns the degree to which the particular way investigators measure a given variable—for example, intelligence or ratings of a person's charisma—is likely to yield consistent results. If you take an IQ test twice, do you get roughly the same score? Do two observers agree in their ratings of the charisma of world leaders or fellow fraternity members? Reliability is typically measured by correlations between 0 and 1. As a rule of thumb, ability tests are expected to have reliability correlations of about 0.8. Personality tests, such as measures of introversion, are expected to have that level of correlation or a little lower. People's

reliability The degree to which the particular way that researchers measure a given variable is likely to yield consistent results.

degree of agreement about the kindness or charisma of another person would be expected to show a correlation of at least 0.5.

measurement validity The correlation between some measure and some outcome that the measure is supposed to predict.

Measurement validity refers to the correlation between some measure and some outcome that the measure is supposed to predict. For example, IQ test validity is measured by correlating IQ scores with grades in school and with performance in jobs. If IQ scores predict behavior that requires intelligence, it can be inferred that the test is a valid measure of intelligence. Validity coefficients, as they are called, typically do not exceed 0.5. Personality tests rarely correlate with behavior in a given situation better than about 0.3. This result is surprising to most people, who expect that a measure of extraversion or aggression should predict quite well a person's behavior at a party or a hockey game.

Statistical Significance

statistical significance A measure of the probability that a given result could have occurred by chance.

When researchers obtain an empirical result—such as finding a correlation between two variables or observing that some independent variable affects a dependent variable in an experiment—they can test the **statistical significance** of the relationship. A finding has statistical significance if the probability of obtaining the finding by chance is less than some quantity. By convention, this quantity is usually set at 1 in 20, or 0.05, but probabilities can of course go much lower than that. Statistical significance is primarily due to (1) the size of the difference between groups in an experiment or the size of a relationship between variables in a correlational study and (2) the number of cases the finding is based on. The larger the difference or relationship and the larger the number of cases, the greater the statistical significance. All of the findings reported in this book are statistically significant (though not all are based on large effects).

 External validity refers to how closely an experimental setup resembles what people find in the real world. Internal validity refers to the extent to which investigators know that only the manipulated variable could have produced the results. Reliability of measures refers to the degree to which different instruments, or the same instrument at different times, produce the same values for a given variable. Measurement validity refers to the extent to which a measure predicts outcomes that it is supposed to measure. Statistical significance is a measure of the probability that a result could have occurred by chance.

BASIC AND APPLIED RESEARCH

basic science Science concerned with trying to understand some phenomenon in its own right, with a view toward using that understanding to build valid theories about the nature of some aspect of the world.

Science is of two broad types: basic science and applied science. **Basic science** isn't concerned with any particular real-world problem, but with trying to understand some phenomenon in its own right. Studies are conducted with a view toward using that understanding to build valid theories about the nature of some aspect of the world. Social psychologists who study the obedience of people to an authority figure in the laboratory are doing basic science—trying to understand the nature of obedience and the factors that influence it. They are not trying to find ways to make people less obedient to dubious authorities, though they may hope that their research is relevant to such real-world problems. Social psychologists who study the effect of being in a hurry on helping another person are interested in how situational factors affect people's behavior. They may also be interested in comparing the power of a particular situation with some other variable, such as a personality trait. They are not trying to find ways to make people more inclined to help people in need, though they may hope that their research would be relevant to such a goal.

Applied science is concerned with solving a real-world problem of importance. An example of applied research in social psychology might be a study of how to make preteens less susceptible to cigarette advertising. (One way is to make them aware of the motives of tobacco companies and of their cynical desire to make chumps of kids by getting them to do something that is not in their best interest.) Other social psychologists might try to convince people to use condoms to prevent the spread of sexually transmitted diseases (STDs). (One way is to have characters in soap operas talk about the use of condoms— a form of product placement, as it's known in the advertising industry; Bandura, 2004).

applied science Science concerned with solving some real-world problem of importance.

There is a two-way relationship between basic and applied research. Basic research can give rise to theories that can lead to **interventions**, or efforts to change people's behavior. For example, social psychologist Carol Dweck found that people who believe that intelligence is a matter of hard work study harder in school and get better grades than people who believe that intelligence is a matter of genes—that you either are intelligent or you are not, and you can't do much to change it (Dweck, Chiu, & Hong, 1995). Her basic research on the nature of beliefs about intelligence and their relationship to work in school prompted her to design an intervention with minority junior high students. She told some of them that their intelligence was under their control and gave them information about how working on school subjects actually changes the physical nature of the brain (Blackwell, Trzesniewski, & Dweck, 2007; Henderson & Dweck, 1990). Such students worked harder and got better grades than did students who were not given such information. Joshua Aronson and his colleagues have obtained similar results (Aronson, Fried, & Good, 2002; Good, Aronson, & Inzlicht, 2003).

intervention An effort to change people's behavior.

The direction of influence can also go the other way: applied research can produce results that feed back into basic science. For example, the applied research during World War II on how to produce effective propaganda led to an extensive program of basic research on attitude change. That program in turn gave rise to theories of attitude change and social influence that continue to inform basic science and to generate new techniques of changing attitudes in applied, real-world contexts.

Applied Research Tobacco companies spend a lot of money on advertising to encourage people to buy their cigarettes. Social psychologists can study how to counter that effect, as this public service advertisement by the California Department of Health Services is trying to do.

LOOKING BACK Basic science attempts to discover fundamental principles; applied science attempts to solve real-world problems. But there is an intimate relationship between the two: basic science can reveal ways to solve real-world problems, and science aimed at solving real-world problems can give rise to the search for basic principles that explain why the solutions work.

ETHICAL CONCERNS IN SOCIAL PSYCHOLOGY

Most people would want to conduct research geared to changing people's attitudes only if they believed the direction of change was for the better. We wouldn't support, or even want to allow, research that might have the effect of encouraging people to engage in dangerous behaviors. Similarly, most of us would not approve of a study in which participants were physically or psychologically harmed with little justification. For this reason, research conducted at universities has to go before an **institutional review board (IRB)** that examines research proposals and makes judgments about the ethical appropriateness of the research. Such boards must include at least one scientist, one nonscientist, and one person who is not affiliated with the institution. If some aspect of the study procedures is deemed overly harmful, that procedure must be changed before the research can be approved.

The key to the previous sentence is the word *overly*. Research may be allowed even if it does make people uncomfortable or embarrassed or cause physical pain, so long as the research is deemed sufficiently likely to yield scientific information of significant value and the discomfort or harm to the participants is not too great. For example, Milgram's research on obedience was conducted before IRBs came into existence; today it would be sure to get a thorough examination by an IRB, and it's not clear that it would be approved. On the one hand, there is no question that Milgram's research made some participants uncomfortable in the extreme; their psychological distress was manifest to observers. On the other hand, many (if not most) people would consider the knowledge gain to be enormous. It's not possible to think about Nazi Germany in the same way after knowing the results of the Milgram studies. Nor can we think the same way about the behavior of American soldiers involved in torturing Iraqi prisoners once we know about the studies. We can no longer blithely assume that ordinary, decent people would refuse to obey commands that are patently harmful. Different IRBs would undoubtedly reach different conclusions about the admissibility of the Milgram experiments today. What do you think? Would you permit research like Milgram's to be conducted?

In medical research, which is also governed by IRBs, a principle called **informed consent** governs the acceptability of research. Even if a given procedure is not known to be beneficial—indeed, even if there is a possibility that it will be less beneficial than other procedures or actually harmful in the short term—IRBs may allow the research to be conducted if the knowledge gain relative to the risk is deemed great enough. But participants must give their informed consent—their willingness to participate in light of their knowledge about all relevant aspects of the procedure.

Informed consent is also required for most psychological research. But for some research—namely, **deception research**—informed consent is not possible. John Darley and his colleagues could not have told their seminary participants the true nature of their study, or that the reason given for the hurry was bogus and the apparent victim was actually a stooge (or "confederate") who was merely pretending to be hurt as part of the experiment. Informed consent would have defeated the purpose of the experiment. If there is a good reason for deception, it is generally allowed by IRBs. An IRB, for example, gave permission for Cohen and his colleagues (1996) to deceive their Southern and Northern participants

institutional review board (IRB) A university committee that examines research proposals and makes judgments about the ethical appropriateness of the research.

informed consent Participants' willingness to participate in a procedure or research study after learning all relevant aspects about the procedure or study.

deception research Research in which the participants are misled about the purpose of the research or the meaning of something that is done to them.

and even to shove them and call them a dirty name. Participants themselves, when asked their opinion about what they were put through, generally understand the reasons for it and often say they learned more, and enjoyed the study more, than subjects who were not deceived or made uncomfortable (Smith & Richardson, 1983). For example, participants in the insult condition of Cohen and colleagues' study actually reported that they learned more and enjoyed themselves more than participants in the control condition did.

The debriefing procedure is particularly important when participants have been deceived or made uncomfortable. Experimenters owe participants a full accounting of what was done, what aspects of the procedure involved deception, why they were made uncomfortable, what the experiment was intended to examine, and what the potential is for valuable social contributions based on the research.

An understanding of the concepts discussed in this chapter is vital to appreciating the studies described in this book. When you read about an experiment, try to identify the independent and dependent variables and to think about whether the experiment has good external validity. Even more important, keep these methods in mind when you read about scientific findings in magazines and newspapers and on the Internet, since science reporting is often dubious on methodological grounds. In addition, familiarity with these methodological principles can help you in understanding other people's behavior and in guiding your own.

LOOKING BACK Ethical concerns about research are dealt with by institutional review boards. In research not involving deception, the procedures and purposes of experiments are explained to potential participants, and their informed consent is requested. Deception and even minor harm to participants are sometimes allowed when the potential gain to knowledge is considered to be great enough.

Chapter Review

Summary

Why Do Social Psychologists Do Research (and Why Should You Want to Read about It)?

- Social psychological research teaches people how to interpret and predict the outcomes of various social experiences and helps them understand their own behavior and that of others.

How Do Social Psychologists Test Ideas?

- Social psychologists often use *participant observation*, in which they place themselves in real situations to understand a social phenomenon better and to help them plan research that will test the hypotheses developed in observational settings.

- Social psychologists go to *archives* of various kinds to find information that helps them understand social phenomena. Such records include census reports, police reports, newspaper accounts, and historical and ethnographic records.

- *Surveys* ask people questions. *Random sampling* is essential for describing accurately the attitudes or behavior of people of a particular population: students at X university, the people of town Y, or the population of a country as a whole.

- *Correlational research* describes relationships between variables—for example, between age and support for welfare reform. Correlations can vary in strength from −1 to +1.

- *Self-selection* is a particular problem in correlational research, where the investigator is unable to choose the level of any variable for participants. Consequently, it's impossible to know if something associated with one of the measured variables is causing the correlation between two variables or if one of the variables is causing the other.

- In *experimental research*, the investigator manipulates different levels of the *independent variable* (the variable about which a prediction is made) and measures the effect of different levels on the *dependent variable*.

Some Other Useful Concepts for Understanding Research

- *External validity* refers to how closely the experimental setup resembles real-life situations. The greater the external validity, the more it is possible to generalize from the results obtained to real-life settings.

- *Field experiments* test hypotheses experimentally in real-life situations as opposed to the laboratory. Field experiments automatically have external validity.

- *Internal validity* refers to whether the experimenter can be confident that it is the manipulated variable only that accounts for the results, rather than some extraneous factor such as participants' failure to understand instructions.

- Participants in studies are normally *debriefed*; that is, investigators explain to them the purpose of the experiment and the likely knowledge gain.

- *Reliability* refers to the extent to which participants receive the same score when tested with a conceptually similar instrument or when tested at different times.

- *Measurement validity* refers to the degree to which some measure predicts what it is supposed to, such as the degree to which an IQ test predicts school grades.

Basic and Applied Research

- *Basic research* is intended to test theory. *Applied research* is intended to solve some real-world problem.

Ethical Concerns in Social Psychology

- *Institutional review boards* are committees set up to review research procedures to make sure that participants' privacy and safety are protected.

- *Informed consent* refers to the willingness of participants to take part in a study based on information presented to them before the study begins, informing them of the procedures they will undergo and any possible risks. Informed consent is not always possible, as when an experiment involves deception, where participants are misled about the purposes of a study.

Key Terms

applied science (p. 59)
basic science (p. 58)
control condition (p. 52)
correlational research
  (p. 49)
debriefing (p. 57)
deception research (p. 60)
dependent variable (p. 52)
experimental research (p. 49)
external validity (p. 56)

field experiment (p. 56)
hindsight bias (p. 43)
hypothesis (p. 45)
independent variable (p. 52)
informed consent (p. 60)
institutional review board
  (IRB) (p. 60)
internal validity (p. 57)
intervention (p. 59)
longitudinal study (p. 52)

measurement validity (p. 58)
natural experiments (p. 55)
random assignment (p. 52)
reliability (p. 57)
reverse causation (p. 49)
self-selection (p. 49)
statistical significance
  (p. 58)
theory (p. 45)
third variable (p. 49)

Further Reading

Aronson, E., Ellsworth, P. C., Carlsmith, J. M., & Gonzales, M. H. (1990). *Methods of research in social psychology* (2nd ed.). New York: McGraw-Hill. An excellent source of information about how to conduct research in social psychology.

Gilbert, D. T., Fiske, S. T., & Lindzey, G. (1998). *The handbook of social psychology* (4th ed., Vols. 1 and 2, part 2). New York: Oxford University Press. Advanced treatment of methods of research in social psychology.

IT'S YOUR TURN
TO BE APPRECIATED.
Donate to MARGS museum.

AMARGS

The Social Self

ON OCTOBER 17, 1972, Marshall Bruce Mathers III was born in Saint Joseph, a small town in Missouri. After being abandoned by his father, Marshall and his mother moved from city to city, often struggling to get by on welfare. Marshall was in his early teens when they finally settled in Detroit, Michigan. At around age 11, Marshall was introduced to hip hop music. By 14, he had dropped out of school and was performing amateur raps. In 1997, Marshall, increasingly known as Eminem, placed second in that year's Rap Olympics. A year later, he signed with the record label Aftermath Entertainment, headed by fellow rapper and record producer Dr. Dre. In 1999, Eminem introduced the world to his alter ego, Slim Shady, in his debut album, *The Slim Shady LP*. And, as the saying goes, the rest is (music) history. The album went triple platinum by the end of 1999 and catapulted Eminem to stardom.

Over the next decade, Eminem faced one controversy after another due to, among other things, lyrics laced with profanity and misogynist and homophobic sentiments, even as his record sales soared and he received multiple Grammy awards. During this same period, Eminem started an acting career, married and divorced the same woman twice, was arrested for assault and carrying a concealed weapon, nearly died from a drug overdose, and checked into and out of rehab.

Fans and critics alike eagerly awaited the 2008 release of Eminem's memoir, *The Way I Am*, chronicling the colorful life of the talented and controversial star. Unlike an autobiography, a memoir reflects a "looser" account of the writer's life. As the writer Gore Vidal put it: "A memoir is how one remembers one's own life, while an autobiography is history, requiring research, dates, facts double-checked." Vidal's view of memoirs describes Eminem's well. At the same time, it illustrates a central theme in social psychology: that reality is subjective,

Who Is Eminem? Like most people, Eminem—pictured here during a performance, arriving at the premiere of his movie *8 Mile*, and being arraigned on two felony weapons counts in 2000—has many different selves.

a product of our construals and interpretations of the social world. And that world includes ourselves. *The Way I Am* doesn't tell us who Eminem is in an objective sense; rather, it sheds light on who Eminem thinks he is. It tells us how Eminem makes sense of his own qualities and behaviors that, to the outside observer, can seem utterly incompatible. For example, the average person might find it puzzling that Eminem can spew forth profanity after profanity, knowing that his audience is filled with young, impressionable ears—and yet can be fiercely protective of his own children. But this seeming contradiction might make perfect sense to Eminem himself.

For each of us, as for Eminem, our self is in part a product of our construals, yet the self is fundamentally social in nature. We come to know ourselves through contributions from the immediate social environment, the surrounding culture, and our gender. Our self-esteem is often based on comparisons we make between ourselves and others. We regulate our behavior by initiating, altering, and controlling it in the pursuit of our goals, and we present ourselves to others in ways designed to get them to form particular impressions of us. Like Eminem's Slim Shady, most of us have alter egos—that is, second (and third, and fourth) selves—that characterize who we are in the presence of relevant audiences. This chapter explores these notions to draw a portrait of the self as it is constructed, maintained, and negotiated in the social environment.

NATURE OF THE SOCIAL SELF

The social psychological study of the self usually begins with William James. In his book *The Principles of Psychology* (1890), James introduced numerous self-related concepts and distinctions that continue to inspire research today. One of his most enduring contributions is reflected in the title of this chapter, "The *Social Self*." James coined the term the *social me* to refer to the parts of self-knowledge that are derived from social relationships. As you will see throughout this chapter, although the self can seem like the most individual, basic, and set-apart element of social life, it is a social entity through and through. Who a person is in one social context (with soccer buddies) is often not the same as who the person is in another social environment (with a romantic partner). As James articulated over a century ago, our sense of who we are is forged in our interactions with others, shaping, in turn, how we interact with others and how they see themselves.

Social psychologists today generally recognize three primary components of the self—the individual self, the relational self, and the collective self (Brewer & Gardner, 1996; Sedikides & Brewer, 2001). The **individual self** encompasses a person's beliefs about his or her unique personal traits, abilities, preferences, tastes, talents, and so forth. The focus of the individual self is on what sets the person apart from others. In contrast, relational and collective selves capture the social sides of the self, how the person is connected to others. The **relational self** refers to the sense of oneself in specific relationships—for example, as doting husband or black sheep of the family (Chen, Boucher, & Tapias, 2006). And the **collective self** refers to a person's identity as a member of the groups to which he or she belongs—for example, an Irish-Canadian, Episcopalian, gay urban male, Libertarian, weekend trainspotter, or member of Red Sox Nation (Deaux, Reid, Mizrahi, & Ethier, 1995; Hogg & Williams, 2000; Tajfel & Turner, 1986). In addition to beliefs about the traits that characterize who people are in their relationships and as group members, relational and collective selves include beliefs about the roles, duties, and obligations each of us assume in specific relationships and groups.

Recall from Chapter 1 that the prominence of different self-beliefs varies according to a person's culture of origin. In one study on culture and self-beliefs, American college students defined themselves primarily in terms of personal attributes (traits)—in other words, in terms of the individual self. In contrast, Japanese students were three times more likely than American students to define themselves in terms of their relationships and group memberships—in other words, relational and collective terms (Cousins, 1989). These cultural differences and their broader implications are discussed in more depth later in this chapter.

> "A man has as many social selves as there are individuals who recognize him. As many different social selves as there are distinct groups about whose opinions he cares."
>
> —William James

individual self Beliefs about our unique personal traits, abilities, preferences, tastes, talents, and so forth.

relational self Beliefs about our identities in specific relationships.

collective self Beliefs about our identities as members of social groups to which we belong.

LOOKING BACK The notion that the self is fundamentally social has long been recognized. As the social context shifts, so too does the nature of the self. The social self can be thought of as having three primary components: the individual self, the relational self, and the collective self, which may differ in prominence across individuals.

ORIGINS OF SELF-KNOWLEDGE

Across cultures, the search for the sense of self takes various forms. Socrates urged his fellow Athenians to examine the self, to find its essential and distinctive characteristics. Buddhist thought counsels people to transcend the material graspings of the self and its desires, illusions, and frustrations. Where does *your* sense of self come from? A social psychological answer to such a question points to numerous social origins of self-knowledge as well as to construal processes from which self-knowledge may be derived, nurtured, and maintained.

Family and Other Socialization Agents

Parents and other socialization agents (including grandparents, siblings, and teachers) teach children what they view as socially appropriate and valued attitudes and behaviors. This instruction happens directly, when parents insist that their children share, take turns, and say "thank you," as well as indirectly through modeling appropriate behavior. Socialization agents can also shape our sense of self. For example, by encouraging certain behaviors and providing opportunities for certain activities, socialization agents can influence the traits, abilities, and preferences that we come to associate with ourselves. Imagine a woman whose Jewish parents took her to synagogue every week as a child, who took Hebrew lessons, and who eventually had a Bat Mitzvah ceremony. Because her parents encouraged her to engage in such religious activities, it is not surprising that, as an adult, being Jewish is central to this woman's sense of self.

reflected self-appraisals Beliefs about what others think of our social selves.

Another way that family and other socialization agents shape the self is captured by the *symbolic interactionist* notion that we come to know ourselves through imagining what others think of us. The sociologist Charles H. Cooley (1902) coined the phrase "looking-glass self" to refer to the idea that other people's reactions to us serve as a mirror of sorts, reflecting our image so that we, too, can see it. In other words, self-knowledge is derived in part from **reflected self-appraisals**, our beliefs about others' appraisals of us. Throughout our lives, we experience direct or subtle reactions and appraisals from others. Parents praise our accomplishments. A romantic partner makes light of our fears. Teachers assign us a challenging task. Peers laugh heartily at our jokes. Reactions and appraisals like these convey to us that we are competent, are neurotic, have potential, or have a good sense of humor. In short, we see ourselves partly through the eyes of those around us.

Gaining self-knowledge through reflected self-appraisals might seem to suggest that we have little say in how we see ourselves. But the idea here is that we internalize how we *think* others appraise us, not necessarily how others *actually* see us. In fact, our reflected self-appraisals often do not correlate highly with the appraisals that others actually make of us (Felson, 1993; Kenny & DePaulo, 1993; Shrauger & Schoeneman, 1979; Tice & Wallace, 2005). Figuring out how and to what degree reflected self-appraisals influence people's sense of self can be tricky. For example, Amy's view of herself as a clumsy person could stem from her perception that her family and friends see her this way—but it's also possible that her view of herself as clumsy is actually what led her to perceive these reflected self-appraisals. Indeed, self-views often affect reflected self-appraisals rather than the other way around (Felson, 1993; Kenny & DePaulo, 1993). The upshot, then, is that although other people influence our sense of self through reflected self-appraisals, their impact may not be as simple and direct as the idea of the looking-glass self originally suggested.

Jennifer Pfeifer and her colleagues explored one way to examine whether reflected appraisals influence self-views, or vice versa—namely, by looking at the neural systems that are engaged when people think about and report on their self-views versus their reflected self-appraisals (Pfeifer, Masten, Borofsky, Dapretto, Fuligni, & Lieberman, 2009). Research suggests that activity in certain areas of the

BOX 3.1   FOCUS ON EVOLUTION

Siblings and the Social Self

What do most U.S. presidents, English and Canadian prime ministers, Oprah Winfrey, Bette Davis, and all of the actors who have portrayed James Bond (except Daniel Craig) have in common? What do Virginia Woolf, Ben Franklin, Charles Darwin, Mohandas Gandhi, Vincent Van Gogh, and Madonna have in common? The first group are firstborns. The second are later-borns. What does birth order have to do with our sense of self? According to Frank Sulloway (1996, 2001), a great deal. Sulloway has looked at sibling dynamics from an evolutionary perspective and arrived at a "born-to-rebel" hypothesis. Across species, Sulloway theorizes, sibling conflict—particularly when resources are scarce—is frequent, widespread, and on occasion deadly. Sand sharks devour one another before birth in the oviducts of the mother until one well-fed young shark emerges. Once a blue-footed booby drops below 80 percent of its body weight, its siblings exclude it from the nest, or worse, peck it to death. Infant hyenas are born with large canine teeth, which they often turn to deadly effect upon their newly born siblings. Even in humans, young siblings engage in frequent conflict, up to one squabble every 5 minutes (Dunn & Munn, 1985). You may remember long car trips in which the chief entertainment was sibling baiting.

Humans have evolved adaptations, or solutions, to threats to survival, and one such adaptation involves a means of resolving sibling conflict. According to the principle of diversification, siblings develop different traits, abilities, and preferences within the same family so that they can peacefully occupy different niches.

Throughout most of development, older siblings are larger and more powerful and often act as surrogate parents. They are invested in the status quo, which, not coincidentally, benefits them. ("Things were fine until you came along.") In contrast, younger siblings, with the "establishment" niche already occupied by their older sibling, develop in ways that make them inclined to challenge the family status quo. In a review of 196 studies of personality and birth order, Sulloway found that older siblings tend to be more assertive and dominant and more achievement-oriented and conscientious. These traits are consistent with older siblings' more assertive, powerful role in the family. In contrast, younger siblings tend to be more agreeable, and they are likely to be more open to novel ideas and experiences. This social self emerges as younger siblings learn to coexist with their more dominant older siblings (which accounts for their elevated agreeableness) and as

Sibling Conflict Firstborns like Prince William are often more responsible and more likely to support the status quo than younger siblings like Prince Harry, who often are more mischievous, more open to novel experiences, and more likely to rebel against authority.

they think of imaginative ways to carve out their own niche in the world (which accounts for their increased openness to experience). Charles Darwin is an excellent case study for Sulloway's hypothesis. The fifth of six children, Darwin developed perhaps the most revolutionary scientific theory in human history, one that challenged religious ideas about the creation of life on earth. To do so, he circumnavigated the globe on the ship HMS *Beagle*, often facing great dangers as he collected evidence that led to his original, paradigm-shifting theory of evolution.

brain, including the medial prefrontal cortex, is heightened during self-referential cognition, such as when people are asked to think about who they are (Lieberman, 2007). Reflected self-appraisal, however, also requires social perception—in particular, taking the perspective of others (what do others think about me?)—and thus brain regions that support perspective taking are also engaged (such as the temporal-parietal junction).

By subjecting participants to functional magnetic resonance imaging (fMRI) while they reported their self-views and reflected self-appraisals (their ratings of how they thought others viewed them), Pfeifer and colleagues were able to assess whether the neural systems involved in perspective taking were engaged even during the self-views task, suggesting that self-views are colored by reflected self-appraisals. In addition, the researchers included both early adolescent and adult participants, allowing them to see whether the influence of reflected self-appraisals on self-views is greater during adolescence, a developmental period during which the opinions and evaluations of others are of pronounced importance. Indeed, when asked to report their self-views, young adolescents exhibited greater activity relative to adults in neural systems relevant to *both* self-perception and perspective taking. In other words, adolescents but not adults spontaneously relied on reflected appraisals when reporting their self-views, suggesting that adolescents' sense of self is especially likely to be based on their beliefs about others' views of them.

Situationism and the Social Self

In the film *Zelig*, Woody Allen plays a character who automatically takes on the appearance of the people around him. Surrounded by a group of African-Americans, he begins to look black; in the presence of a group of elderly Greeks, he takes on their Mediterranean appearance. The humor of the film stems from how it makes light of a deeper truth: that our social self shifts dramatically from one situation to another. This notion that the social self changes across different contexts is consistent with the principle of situationism and is supported by abundant empirical evidence.

Aspects of the Self That Are Relevant in the Social Context What determines the nature of contextual shifts in the sense of self? Probably the greatest determinant is what is relevant, or appropriate, in the current situation. Students

Context and the Sense of Self In *Zelig*, Woody Allen takes on the appearance of those with whom he interacts, providing a dramatic illustration of how we often express different traits and characteristics when in different social contexts. (A) Zelig looks Chinese when he is next to a Chinese man. (B) Zelig takes on African-American features when he stands between two African-American men.

who are rebellious and free-spirited in the dorm will shift to a more sober and conventional demeanor around parents or professors. Someone who sees herself as relaxed and outspoken when with her close friends may be shy and inhibited when interacting with a group of new acquaintances. In situations where people experience a failure of some kind—for example, learning you have performed poorly on an exam—negative beliefs and feelings about the self come to the fore (Brown, 1998).

Markus and Wurf (1987) coined the term **working self-concept** to refer to the idea that only a subset of a person's vast pool of self-knowledge is brought to mind in any given context—the subset that is most relevant or appropriate in the current situation. The idea of a working self-concept is related to the earlier discussion of multiple levels for defining the self. Different situations are likely to bring to the fore different levels of self-definition. For example, Michael's working self-concept is likely to be infused with relational self-beliefs when he is spending time with his girlfriend, but with collective self-beliefs when he is hanging out with a bunch of fellow students watching his college football team play its longtime rival.

working self-concept Subset of self-knowledge that is brought to mind in a particular context.

Aspects of the Self That Are Distinctive in the Social Context William McGuire and Alice Padawer-Singer (1978) proposed another perspective on the effects of the current situation on our social self. According to their distinctiveness hypothesis, we highlight what makes us unique in a given social situation. To test this hypothesis, they asked sixth graders at different schools to spend 7 minutes describing themselves. On average, children wrote 11.8 statements, and these statements referred to their recreational activities, attitudes, friends, and school activities. (The children, incidentally, were more likely to refer to their dog when defining themselves than to all other family members combined!)

McGuire and Padawer-Singer examined these descriptions to see whether children defined themselves according to how they differed from their classmates. Indeed, they did (**Figure 3.1**). Thirty percent of children who were especially young or old compared with their classmates (that is, 6 months from the most common age of their classmates) mentioned their age in their self-definition, whereas only 19 percent of the other children did. Forty-four percent of children who were born outside of the United States mentioned this biographical

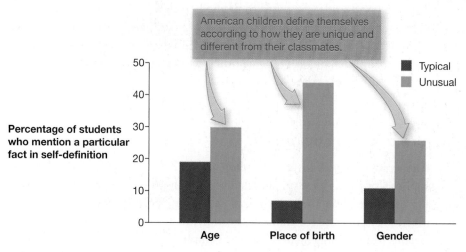

FIGURE 3.1 Distinctiveness and the Sense of Self (Source: Adapted from McGuire & Padawer-Singer, 1978.)

fact, whereas only 7 percent of those born in the United States mentioned that fact about themselves. Twenty-six percent of children of the minority gender in their class mentioned their gender as part of their self-definition compared with 11 percent of the majority gender (see also Cota & Dion, 1986). In the West at least, what's most central to your identity is what makes you distinct. Being white, for example, is likely to be often on Eminem's mind given that the world he occupies is filled with black artists.

Both Malleable and Stable? Most of us can easily distinguish among our individual, relational, and collective self-beliefs and would readily agree that our sense of self shifts depending on the context. Despite these shifts in our sense of self, however, most of us experience a sense of continuity in the self, the sense that we have a stable, core self. How can we reconcile what appear to be dueling notions of malleability and stability in the self?

There are several paths of reconciliation. First, although the content of the working self-concept varies across situations, core components of self-knowledge are likely to be on the top of the mind whenever a person thinks about the self (Markus, 1977). Thus, although Joo Young may see herself as painfully shy around members of the opposite sex but as outgoing with her girlfriends, she sees herself as a good listener no matter who she is around. Second, a person's overall pool of self-knowledge remains relatively stable over time, providing a sense of self-continuity, even as different pieces of self-knowledge come to the fore in different contexts (Linville & Carlston, 1994). Thus your belief that you are lazy may not characterize your working self-concept in a job interview, but it is nonetheless stored in memory (ready to be retrieved when you're lounging around watching television rather than doing the laundry) and therefore a stable part of how you see yourself.

Finally, although a person's sense of self may shift depending on the context, it's likely that these shifts conform to a predictable, stable pattern (English & Chen, 2007; Mischel & Shoda, 1995). Take a person who sees herself as confident around her friends, but as insecure around her overly critical mother. Although this person's sense of self clearly shifts according to the social context, it's not as if she is confident around her friends one day and insecure around them the next. In other words, the malleability in this individual's self is itself *stable*. Whenever she is around her friends, she tends to define herself as confident, whereas being around her mother reliably shifts her self-concept so that it includes being insecure. In short, the social self is defined by two truths: it is malleable, shifting from one context to another, but at the same time a person's social self has core components that persist across contexts.

Culture and the Social Self

The American Declaration of Independence and the *Analects* of the Chinese philosopher Confucius have shaped the lives of billions of people. Yet they reflect radically different ideas about the social self. The Declaration of Independence prioritized the rights and freedoms of the individual, and it protected those rights and liberties from infringement. Confucius emphasized the importance of knowing one's place in society, of honoring traditions, duties, and social roles, and of thinking of others before the self.

"We hold these truths to be self-evident, that all men are created equal, that they are endowed by their Creator with certain inalienable rights, that among these are Life, Liberty, and the pursuit of Happiness."

—Declaration of Independence

The differences reflected in these documents run deep in the cultures people inhabit. In Western societies, people are concerned about their individuality, about freedom, and about self-expression. Our adages reflect this: "The squeaky wheel gets the grease." "If you've got it, flaunt it." In Asian cultures, the homilies and folk wisdom encourage a different view of the self: "The empty wagon makes the most noise." "The nail that stands up is pounded down." Psychologists Hazel Markus, Shinobu Kitayama, and Harry Triandis have offered far-reaching theories about how cultures vary in the social selves they encourage and how these different conceptions of the self shape the emotions we feel, the motivations that drive us, and our ways of perceiving the social world (Markus & Kitayama, 1991; Triandis, 1989, 1994, 1995). These culture-based self-conceptions can influence numerous elements of the social self—including specific construal processes and self-esteem.

Cultures that promote an *independent self-construal* include much of the West, especially northwestern Europe and North America. In such cultures, the self is an autonomous entity that is distinct and separate from others (**Figure 3.2**, part A). The imperative is to assert uniqueness and independence. The focus is on internal causes of behavior. Together, these forces lead to a conception of the self in terms of traits that are stable across time and social context.

In contrast, in cultures that foster *interdependent self-construals*, the self is fundamentally connected to other people (Figure 3.2, part B). The imperative is for a person to find a place and fulfill appropriate roles within the community and other collectives—for example, within families and organizations. The focus is on

"A person of humanity wishing to establish his own character, also establishes the character of others."

—Confucius

BOX 3.2 FOCUS ON CULTURE AND NEUROSCIENCE

Culture and the Social Self in the Brain

When participants are asked to judge the self with respect to various trait dimensions, a certain region of the brain known as the medial prefrontal cortex is particularly active (Heatherton et al., 2006), suggesting that this part of the frontal lobe is involved in processes that represent self-knowledge. Ying Zhu and colleagues conducted a study using an interesting twist on this paradigm to ascertain whether many of the cultural differences in self-construal discussed in this chapter would be reflected in differences in neural activation (Zhu, Zhang, Fan, & Han, 2007). They had Chinese participants and Western Europeans rate the applicability of different traits to themselves, to their mothers, and to another person. For members of

both cultures, the assessments of self-trait similarity produced activation in the medial prefrontal cortex. But for Chinese participants, activation in this same region was also observed when participants were making the trait-mother comparisons. For the Westerners, in contrast, there was, if anything, a relative deactivation of the medial prefrontal cortex when they thought about their mothers. These findings seem to suggest that for people with interdependent self-construals, the same region of the brain represents the self and mother; they are merged within the brain. In contrast, for those with independent self-construals, the self and mother are quite distinct, all the way down to which neurons are activated in each person's brain.

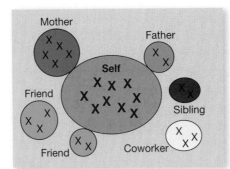

(A) Independent view of self

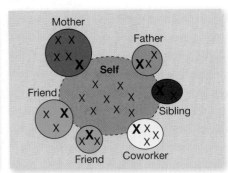

(B) Interdependent view of self

FIGURE 3.2 Views of the Self In the independent view of the self (A), the self is construed as a distinct, autonomous entity, separate from others and defined by distinct traits and preferences. In the interdependent view of the self (B), the self is construed as connected to others and defined by duties, roles, and shared preferences and traits.

Culture and Self-Concept In interdependent cultures, your social relationships are crucial in determining how you behave toward other people. These Japanese businessmen want to fit in with Western business associates. They attend a smile workshop to learn how to smile and behave as Western businessmen would expect so that their reactions won't be misunderstood by their Western associates.

the influence of the social context and the situation on current behavior. Together these forces lead to a self-conception in which the self is embedded within social relationships, roles, and duties. As emphasized in Chapter 1, this kind of self-construal is prevalent in many Asian cultures as well as in many Mediterranean, African, and South American cultures.

Some aspects of Eastern languages capture the interdependent self. For example, in Japanese, the word for *I*—meaning the person who is the same across situations and in relation to everyone—is almost never used. Instead, a Japanese man would use different words for *I* when talking with a colleague (*watashi*), his child (*tochan*), old college pals (*ore*), and close female friends (*boku*). Sometimes when referring to themselves, the Japanese use the word *jibun*, which originally meant "my portion"—reflecting the sense of self as a part of the whole—and which now would be translated "shared life space."

Gender and the Social Self

If different cultures promote different kinds of self-construals, what is the relationship between gender and the self-concept? In a review of the literature on the self-concept and gender, Susan Cross and Laura Madson (1997) marshaled evidence indicating that women in the United States tend to construe the self in more interdependent terms than men do—that is, in terms of connection to others. In contrast, men in the United States tend to prioritize difference and uniqueness, construing the self in more independent terms. The same gender differences are found among the Japanese (Kashima, Siegal, Tanaka, & Kashima, 1992).

The evidence for these basic differences in self-construal is manifold. When women describe themselves, they are more likely than men to refer to social characteristics and relationships (Maccoby & Jacklin, 1974). When asked to select photographs that are most revealing of who they are, women are more likely than men to select photos that include other people, such as friends and family members (Clancy & Dollinger, 1993). In social interactions, women tend to be more empathic and better judges of other people's personalities and emotions (Ambady, Hallahan, & Rosenthal, 1995; Bernieri, Zuckerman, Koestner, & Rosenthal, 1994; Davis & Franzoi, 1991; Eisenberg & Lennon, 1983; Hall, 1984). Men tend to be more attuned to their own internal responses, such as increased heart rate, whereas women are more attuned to situational cues, such as other people's reactions (Pennebaker & Roberts, 1992; Roberts & Pennebaker, 1995).

Where do these gender-related differences in self-construal come from? Socialization processes may be one influential source. Many agents of socialization guide women and men into differing self-construals. The media portray women and men differently, typically portraying men in positions of power and agency. Parents raise girls and boys differently. For example, parents tend to talk with girls more about emotions and being sensitive to others (Fivush, 1989, 1992). The friendships and groups that people form from the earliest ages also influence gender differences in self-construal. Starting at age 3 and continuing through the primary school years, girls and boys tend to play in gender-segregated groups that reinforce and amplify the differences in self-construal (Maccoby, 1990). Girls' groups tend to focus on cooperative games that are oriented toward interpersonal relationships (for example, mother and child). Boys' groups tend to emphasize competition, hierarchy, and distinctions among one another. As adults, gender-specific roles further amplify these differences. For example, even today, women take on most of the responsibilities for raising children, which calls on interdependent tendencies.

In addition, certain gender differences in the social self may have originated in human evolutionary history. Men were equipped physically and psychologically for hunting and aggressive encounters with other groups, whereas women were equipped physically and psychologically for nurturing the young. Thus an independent self-construal fits the roles largely fulfilled by males in our evolutionary history, and an interdependent self-construal is better tailored to the caregiving demands that fell disproportionately to females. Yet different cultures have very different ways of dealing with gender, and the past several generations have witnessed enormous changes in gender roles. Clearly, however much evolution may have contributed to gender differences in self-construal, these sorts of sex differences are not inevitable, and there are sharp limits to any evolutionary account of the role of gender in the nature of the self-concept.

Social Comparison

Sometimes people actively seek out information about themselves by making comparisons to other people. This is the central tenet of **social comparison theory**, an influential and enduring theory in social psychology put forward by Leon Festinger (Festinger, 1954; see also Suls & Wheeler, 2000; Wood, 1996). The essence of the theory is that when people have no objective standard they can use to evaluate their abilities or traits, they do so largely by comparing themselves with others. You can call yourself "honest" or "morally upright" if you don't lie to others or engage in ethically questionable behavior. But to be "rich," "smart," or a "top-notch tennis player" is to be wealthier, smarter, or a better tennis player than others.

Festinger noted, however, that there is no point in comparing yourself with Albert Einstein or Serena Williams, nor is it very helpful to compare yourself

social comparison theory The hypothesis that people compare themselves to other people in order to obtain an accurate assessment of their own opinions, abilities, and internal states.

with total novices. To get an accurate sense of how good you are at something, you must compare yourself with people who have approximately your level of skill. Numerous experiments have demonstrated that people are particularly drawn to comparisons with others roughly similar to themselves (Kruglanski & Mayseless, 1990; Suls, Martin, & Wheeler, 2002; Suls & Wheeler, 2000).

But we like to feel good about ourselves, so our search for similar targets of comparison tends to be biased toward people who are slightly inferior to or worse off than ourselves. All of this is a bit ironic because it leaves us in the position of saying, "Compared with people who are slightly worse at tennis than I am I'm pretty good!" or "Compared with people who are almost as conscientious as I am, I'm pretty darn conscientious!" These sorts of *downward* social comparisons help us define ourselves rather favorably, giving a boost to our self-esteem (Aspinwall & Taylor, 1993; Helgeson & Mickelson, 1995; Lockwood, 2002).

Do these sorts of biased social comparisons come at a cost? After all, we can learn a lot from people who are better than we are in various domains of life, and we sacrifice important opportunities for improvement if we engage only in downward social comparison. One influential study of breast cancer patients identified a strategy people use to get the emotional benefits of favorable comparisons without forfeiting the opportunity to learn from those who are better off (Taylor & Lobel, 1989). They do so by *comparing* themselves with those who are worse off ("I only had to have one set of lymph nodes removed") but initiating contact with those who are better off ("She seems to be in good spirits all the time, and I'd like to ask her over for lunch to find out how she does it").

Although downward social comparison may be more common, people sometimes engage in *upward* social comparison. We are particularly inclined to do so when we aspire to be substantially better at some skill or when we wish to improve a component of our personality (Blanton, Pelham, De Hart, & Kuyper, 1999). For example, in one study that examined the social comparisons made by a group of ninth graders, Blanton, Buunk, Gibbons, and Kuyper (1999) found that students most frequently chose to compare their grades with those of someone who had slightly better grades than they did, presumably with the hope that one day they might receive the higher grades of their better-performing classmates.

Given that different ability domains (say, intelligence versus athleticism) and different motives (feeling good about the self versus improving the self) call for different comparison targets, it might sound like a lot of work to choose a target that is suitable in a particular situation. As it turns out, people lessen this burden by relying on routinely used standards. For example, among college students, a best friend or a close sibling is a commonly used standard against which one compares the self. When people repeatedly compare themselves to a particular person, comparisons with this person become an automatic process—in other words, something that people don't consciously decide to do. In one study examining this notion of routine standards, some participants were asked to evaluate themselves on a series of personality attributes, and some participants were asked to evaluate a celebrity on the same attributes (Mussweiler & Rüter, 2003). Afterward, they engaged in a computer-based, lexical decision task in which they indicated whether each of a series of letter strings (such as CXRTON) was or was not a word as quickly as possible. Some of these letter strings spelled the name of the participant's best friend (each participant had identified this friend earlier). Participants who had been asked to evaluate themselves were faster than those who had evaluated a celebrity to respond to the name of their best friend in the subsequent lexical decision task, indicating that their best friends were on the top of their minds. In short, when people evaluate themselves, routinely used comparison targets—such as best friends—automatically spring to mind.

Narratives about the Social Self

Social comparisons represent one example of construal as a source of self-knowledge. Another comes from Dan McAdams's writings on the narrated self (McAdams, 2008). McAdams's central argument is that we are continually telling a particular story about our social self as we live our lives. Like a good novel, this narrated self has settings (where you grew up), characters (a generous mentor), plot twists and turns (your parents' divorce), dramatic themes (the quest for justice), and vivid images and scenes (when your girlfriend/boyfriend dumped you for your best friend). We tell these self-narratives, McAdams maintains, to important people in our lives—for example, a parent or a best friend. We tell them in part to integrate our many goals, to make sense of conflict, and to explain how we change over time. Eminem's memoir can be thought of as his narrated self, at least the version that existed when he wrote it. And your narrated self right now might focus on your process of choosing a particular life path—a career, a romantic partner, particular values. McAdams has found that self-narratives often involve powerful scenes of redemption and connecting to those who suffer. More vivid and engaging self-narratives, McAdams also finds, enable people to feel happy and fulfilled as they age.

"Very early, I knew that the only object in life was to grow."

—Margaret Fuller

Cross-cultural research finds that self-narratives vary across societies in intriguing ways. Dov Cohen and Alex Gunz (2002) asked Canadian and Asian students (a potpourri of students from Hong Kong, China, Taiwan, Korea, and various South and Southeast Asian countries) to tell stories about ten different situations in which they were the center of attention—for example, "being embarrassed." Canadians were more likely than Asians to reproduce the scene from their original point of view, looking outward from their own perspective. Asians were more likely to imagine the scene as an observer might, describing it from a third-person perspective. You might say that Westerners tend to experience and recall events from the inside out—with themselves at the center, looking out at the world. Easterners are more likely to experience and recall events from the outside in—starting from the social world, looking back at themselves as an object of attention (see also Chua, Leu, & Nisbett, 2005).

LOOKING BACK The social self originates from a variety of sources. Parents and other socialization agents—by virtue of what they teach us, what they encourage in us, how they react to us—help define who we are. The current situation matters as well: the social self shifts from one context to another. A person's culture of origin shapes the social self in profound ways: people from Western cultures—especially men in these cultures—define the self in independent terms, emphasizing uniqueness and autonomy; people from East Asian cultures, and women in many cultures, define the self in interdependent terms, emphasizing connection to others. Finally, the social self is shaped by comparing ourselves to others and constructing stories about our lives.

ORGANIZATION OF SELF-KNOWLEDGE

In his treatment of patients suffering from various neurological disorders, Oliver Sacks worked with a fascinating patient, William Thompson, who suffered from Korsakoff's syndrome (Sacks, 1985). Often the result of years of alcohol abuse, Korsakoff's syndrome destroys memory structures in the brain. Thompson was unable to remember things for more than a second or two. As a result, in each new situation, he would create false identities for the people he encountered, and his social self would move quickly from one identity to the next. Here is one exchange in which Thompson attributes a variety of identities to Oliver Sacks:

> "What'll it be today?" he says, rubbing his hands. "Half a pound of Virginia, a nice piece of Nova?"
>
> (Evidently he saw me as a customer—he often would pick up the phone on the ward, and say "Thompson's Delicatessen.")
>
> "Oh Mr. Thompson!" I exclaim. "And who do you think I am?"
>
> "Good heavens, the light's bad—I took you for a customer. As if it isn't my old friend Tom Pitkins. . . . Me and Tom" (he whispers in an aside to the nurse)
>
> "was always going to the races together."
>
> "Mr. Thompson, you are mistaken again."
>
> "So I am," he rejoins, not put out for a moment. "Why would you be wearing a white coat if you were Tom? You're Hymie, the kosher butcher next door. No bloodstains on your coat though. Business bad today? You'll look like a slaughterhouse by the end of the week!" (Sacks, 1985, p. 108)

As this exchange demonstrates, Thompson is utterly at sea in identifying the people who come into his world. He constructs identities for them that seem to have some plausibility at the moment but that are only loosely connected to any memories he might have about other people. Thompson's own social self also shifts with disorienting rapidity: one second he's in his role at Thompson's deli; seconds later, he's ready to go off gallivanting with his friend Tom.

This case study reveals that our social selves depend on our ability to remember, to know who we and other people are. Put another way, the knowledge that makes up our social self is stored in memory and capable of being retrieved and, in turn, it influences our thoughts, feelings, and behaviors. Given the enormous amount of self-knowledge each of us has, it would seem that this knowledge is stored in memory following some kind of organizational scheme or structure. Indeed, self-knowledge is thought to be organized around cognitive structures known as self-schemas.

self-schemas Cognitive structures, derived from past experience, that represent a person's beliefs and feelings about the self in particular domains.

Self-Schemas

The term **self-schema** refers to cognitive structures, derived from past experience, that represent a person's beliefs and feelings about the self in particular domains (Greenwald, 1980; Markus, 1977; Markus & Wurf, 1987). Take the domain of conscientiousness. Each of us has a self-schema representing our beliefs and feelings about how conscientious (or not) we are. These beliefs and feelings are based on our experiences in situations where conscientiousness was relevant (such as

"I don't know anybody here but the hostess—and, of course, in a deeper sense, myself."

studying for exams), experiences that are stored in memory as part of our conscientiousness self-schema. People vary in the precise content of this self-schema and in how elaborated it is. For instance, the self-schema of a person who views himself as very high (or low) in conscientiousness is likely to include more (or fewer) instances of past conscientious behavior, along with more elaborate beliefs about what it means to be high (or low) in conscientiousness, compared with the self-schema of a person for whom conscientiousness is not part of her self-conception at all.

Like the schemas we have about traits, other people, situations, and objects, the schemas we have about ourselves serve as more than simple storehouses of self-knowledge. They also serve an organizing function—they help us wade through and make sense of all the information that bombards us every day. This organizational function of self-knowledge is in keeping with a broad theme in this book: that our social knowledge—our attitudes, stereotypes, and expectations—organizes how we construe our social world. (Chapters 4 and 11 consider the impact of these various forms of social knowledge on how we process information and make judgments about the world.)

In one of the earliest papers exploring the idea of self-schemas, Hazel Markus (1977) hypothesized that if self-schemas exist, then a person who has a self-schema in a particular domain (a self-schema about extraversion or intellectual curiosity, perhaps) should process information in that domain more quickly, retrieve evidence consistent with the self-schema more rapidly, readily make predictions about his or her likelihood of engaging in schema-related behaviors, and interpret information that contradicts the self-schema in a biased, negative fashion. To test these hypotheses, Markus first identified participants who labeled themselves as either quite dependent or quite independent, and she called them "schematic" participants. She also identified "aschematic" participants: those who rated themselves moderately on the independent-dependent dimension and for whom neither dependence nor independence was important to their self-definition.

All participants returned to the laboratory three to four weeks later and rated how well they were described by a series of traits presented on a computer screen. The schematic participants judged schema-relevant traits as true or not true of themselves much more quickly than aschematic participants, suggesting that people are particularly attuned to information that maps onto a self-schema. The schematic participants also generated many more behaviors consistent with the schema-relevant traits, suggesting that past actions and experiences supporting the self-schema are abundant in memory and come readily to mind. Demonstrating that self-schemas allow people to make inferences about themselves, schematic participants were able to make more confident predictions about their future independence- or dependence-related behaviors. Finally, the schematic participants were more likely to refute feedback from a personality test that gave them information that contradicted their self-schemas—for example, challenging test feedback that told the independent participants that they were actually dependent—indicating that self-schemas influence our interpretation of incoming information.

Research has also shown that our rich network of self-schemas helps us remember information we encounter. More specifically, because information that is processed in reference to the self tends to be processed more deeply and integrated into our preexisting self-knowledge, we are better able to remember it. This is called the **self-reference effect** (Klein & Kihlstrom, 1986; Klein & Loftus, 1988),

self-reference effect The tendency for information that is related to the self to be more thoroughly processed and integrated with existing self-knowledge, thereby making it more memorable.

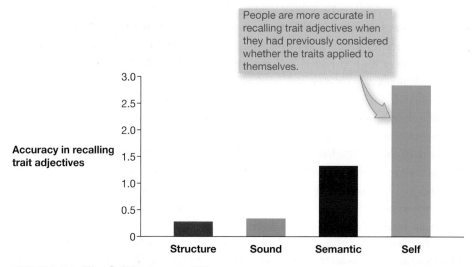

FIGURE 3.3 **The Self-Reference Effect** People are more accurate in recalling trait adjectives when they had previously considered whether the traits apply to themselves than when they had previously processed the adjectives according to their font style (structure), sound, or meaning. (Source: Adapted from Rogers, Kuiper, & Kirker, 1977.)

which is based on a fundamental principle of memory: information that is integrated into preexisting knowledge structures is more readily recalled.

In one of the first studies to document the self-reference effect, participants were presented with 40 trait adjectives (Rogers, Kuiper, & Kirker, 1977). For 10 of the adjectives, participants answered structural questions about the words—for example, whether the font was big or small. For another 10 adjectives, participants answered phonemic questions, addressing whether each adjective rhymed with another adjective. For an additional 10 adjectives, participants answered a semantic question, judging whether each adjective was a synonym or an antonym of another word. And finally, for still another 10 adjectives, participants indicated whether each word described themselves, thus processing each adjective in relation to the self. An hour later, after a few filler tasks, participants were asked to recall the original 40 traits.

Figure 3.3 presents the results. Information that was processed in reference to the self was better remembered. Research like this suggests that to the extent that you personalize how you perceive and understand events and objects in the environment—statements by political leaders, outcomes of athletic competitions, passing remarks made by some authority figure—you will be more likely to think about and remember that information.

Self-Complexity Theory

Most people possess numerous self-schemas corresponding to the most important components of themselves. Yet we have probably all encountered people who seem to define themselves in terms of just a few or even just a single dimension. This might be a classmate who is obsessed with getting into medical school and becoming a doctor, an aspiring Olympic athlete who practices 6 hours a day 7 days a week, or a friend who seems to live and breathe for her boyfriend. The self-definition of individuals like these seems to be dominated by a single self-schema. Does it matter how many self-schemas a person has?

According to Patricia Linville, both the number of self-defining domains a person has as well as the degree of overlap between different self-domains matter (Linville, 1985; 1987). **Self-complexity** is the term she uses to refer to how complex a person's self-knowledge is, as measured by the number of, and degree of overlap between, different self-schemas. People who are high in self-complexity tend to define themselves in terms of multiple domains (I'm a student, athlete, big sister, art aficionado, and Rihanna fan)—and these domains are relatively nonoverlapping (or distinct) in content. In contrast, people who are low in self-complexity possess fewer self-defining domains—and these domains are relatively overlapping in content. Take, for example, Nadia's self-schema for conscientiousness and her schema of herself as a student. Her belief that she tends to procrastinate is likely to be stored as part of both of these self-schemas, resulting in overlap between them.

Research suggests that a person's level of self-complexity can have important consequences, particularly when people are confronted with negative events or difficulties in a given life domain. Imagine learning that you did poorly on a midterm exam. If you're someone who is high in self-complexity—that is, you define yourself in terms of many nonoverlapping domains (for example, student, avid skier, devoted sorority sister, committed volunteer, enthusiastic fan of *Glee*)—the negativity that results from your poor exam grade is relatively contained, affecting only how you feel about yourself as a student. But if you're low in self-complexity—such that your identity as a student overlaps to a great extent with the few other identities you have—then the negativity associated with your poor exam grade is likely to lower your evaluations of yourself as a student as well as spill over and affect how you evaluate your other, overlapping identities. In short, putting all your "self eggs" in one basket can be risky in the face of threatening, self-relevant events.

LOOKING BACK Self-knowledge is stored in memory in an organized fashion. Self-schemas, the most basic organizational units, are cognitive structures that affect how we process and remember information, as well as how we make judgments about ourselves and the social world. Self-complexity is defined by the number and degree of overlap among a person's self-schemas. High self-complexity, which refers to having a relatively large number of nonoverlapping self-schemas, can serve a buffering function when people face a threat to one domain of the self.

SELF-ESTEEM

In 1987, California Governor George Deukmejian signed Assembly Bill 3659 into law. The bill allocated an annual budget of $245,000 for a self-esteem task force, charged with understanding the effects of self-esteem on drug use, teenage pregnancy, and high school dropout rates and with elevating schoolchildren's self-esteem. The initiative was based on the assumption that elevating self-esteem would help cure society's ills. Several findings support this assumption. People with low self-esteem are less satisfied with life, more hopeless, and more depressed (Crocker & Wolfe, 2001), and they are less able to cope with life's challenges, such as the social and academic demands of college (Cutrona, 1982). They tend to disengage from tasks following failure (Brockner, 1979), and they

self-complexity The tendency to define the self in terms of multiple domains that are relatively distinct from one another in content.

are more prone to antisocial behavior and delinquency (Donnellan, Trzesniewski, Robins, Moffitt, & Caspi, 2005). Raising self-esteem, the thinking was, just might produce healthier, more resilient children and a better society in the long run. By now, such a legislative act should strike you as something that could happen only in a Western culture (or perhaps California more specifically). Indeed, some rather pronounced cultural differences in self-esteem are examined later in this section. For the moment, however, let's examine the premise of the California task force—that elevating self-esteem is likely to yield many benefits to society. To do so, it's important to know what self-esteem is and where it comes from.

Trait and State Self-Esteem

self-esteem The positive or negative overall evaluation that each person has of himself or herself.

Self-esteem refers to the positive or negative overall evaluation people have of themselves. Researchers usually measure self-esteem with simple self-report measures like that in **Table 3.1**. As you can see from this scale, self-esteem represents how we feel about our attributes and qualities, our successes and failures, our self-worth. People with high self-esteem feel quite good about themselves. People with low self-esteem feel ambivalent about themselves; they tend to feel both good and bad about who they are. People who truly dislike themselves are rare and are typically found in specific clinical populations, such as severely depressed individuals.

Trait self-esteem is a person's enduring level of self-regard across time. Studies indicate that trait self-esteem is fairly stable: people who report high trait self-

---

TABLE 3.1 Self-Esteem Scale

Indicate your level of agreement with each of the following statements by using the scale below.

0 Strongly Disagree	1 Disagree	2 Agree	3 Strongly Agree

—— 1. At times I think I am no good at all.

—— 2. I take a positive view of myself.

—— 3. All in all, I am inclined to feel that I am a failure.

—— 4. I wish I could have more respect for myself.

—— 5. I certainly feel useless at times.

—— 6. I feel that I am a person of worth, at least on an equal plane with others.

—— 7. On the whole, I am satisfied with myself.

—— 8. I feel I do not have much to be proud of.

—— 9. I feel that I have a number of good qualities.

—— 10. I am able to do things as well as most other people.

To determine your score, first reverse the scoring for the five negatively worded items (1, 3, 4, 5, & 8) as follows: 0 = 3, 1 = 2, 2 = 1, 3 = 0. Then add up your scores across the 10 items. Your total score should fall between 0 and 30. Higher numbers indicate higher self-esteem.

Source: From Rosenberg (1965).

Elevated Self-Esteem People in the self-esteem movement feel that it is important for all children to have high self-esteem so that they will be happy and healthy. They have encouraged teachers to make every child a VIP for a day and coaches to give trophies to every child who plays on a team, whether the team wins or loses.

esteem at one point in time tend to report high trait self-esteem many years later; people who report low trait self-esteem at one point tend to report low trait self-esteem later (Block & Robins, 1993).

State self-esteem refers to the dynamic, changeable self-evaluations that are experienced as momentary feelings about the self (Heatherton & Polivy, 1991). Much as your working self-concept changes from one context to the next, so too does your state self-esteem, which rises and falls according to transient moods and specific construal processes that arise in different situations. For example, your current mood, either positive or negative, will shift your self-esteem up or down (Brown, 1998). When people experience a temporary setback, their self-esteem frequently takes a temporary dive—especially among those who have low self-esteem to begin with (Brown & Dutton, 1995). When college students watch their beloved college football team lose, their feelings of personal competence often drop (Hirt, Zillman, Erickson, & Kennedy, 1992). And children of average intelligence have lower self-esteem when they are in a classroom with academically talented children rather than with children who have lower academic abilities (Marsh & Parker, 1984). Comparing themselves with highly talented children makes them feel less able. Self-esteem also shifts during different stages of development. As males move from early adolescence (age 14) to early adulthood (age 23), self-esteem tends to rise. During the same period, females' self-esteem tends to fall (Block & Robins, 1993). Clearly, then, although one part of your self-esteem is quite stable, another part shifts in response to your current situation and broader life context.

Contingencies of Self-Worth

Let's think a bit more systematically about how your self-esteem is related to specific situations and to life domains that matter to you. Some of you may rest your feelings of self-worth and self-esteem on your academic achievements. For others,

contingencies of self-worth An account of self-esteem that maintains that self-esteem is contingent on successes and failures in domains on which a person has based his or her self-worth.

your self-esteem may be more closely tied to your physical fitness, being up on cultural trends, or your religious values.

To account for how self-esteem relates to different life domains, Jennifer Crocker and Connie Wolfe have proposed a **contingencies of self-worth** account of self-esteem (Crocker & Wolfe, 2001; see also Crocker & Park, 2003). Their model is based on the premise that self-esteem is contingent on—that is, rises and falls with—successes and failures in domains on which a person has based his or her self-worth. These investigators have focused on several domains that are important for self-esteem among college students in particular: family support, school competence, competition, virtue, social approval, physical appearance, and God's love, or what might be called religious identity (see also Crocker, Luhtanen, Cooper, & Bouvrette, 2003). A sample item measuring contingency in the domain of academic competence is "My self-esteem gets a boost when I get a good grade on an exam or paper." An item measuring contingency in the domain of others' approval is "I can't respect myself if others don't respect me." The domains that are most important to self-esteem vary from person to person. Similarly, cultures and subcultures also vary as to which domains are considered most important. For example, religious values are much more important to the self-esteem of African-Americans than to the self-esteem of European-Americans and Asian-Americans.

Our self-esteem depends heavily on our contingencies of self-worth. If things are going well in domains that are important to us, our self-esteem tends to rise; but if things are going badly in these domains, our self-esteem often plummets. To study the self-esteem of University of Michigan students who had applied to graduate school, Crocker and her colleagues (Crocker, Sommers, & Luhtanen, 2002) created a web page that contained an online questionnaire measuring self-esteem. They asked students to go to the website and fill out the questionnaire every day that they received a response from a graduate school—either an acceptance or a rejection. Needless to say, students in general had higher self-esteem on days when they received an acceptance and lower self-esteem on days when they received a rejection, but these effects were much larger for those students whose self-esteem was heavily contingent on academic competence.

At first glance, this work on contingencies of self-worth seems to offer some important lessons about cultivating higher self-esteem. First, it seems that to the extent that people can create environments that allow them to excel in domains related to their specific contingencies of self-worth, they will enjoy elevated self-esteem and its potential benefits. A second lesson might be that it is important for people to base their sense of self-worth on performance in many domains. This notion is reminiscent of self-complexity theory, which suggests that coping with failure may be easier among those who define the self in terms of multiple, non-overlapping domains. To Crocker and Park (2004), however, the most important lesson is that it is costly to pursue self-esteem in *any* domain. The costs of making self-esteem your primary goal include lowered feelings of autonomy (because you are controlled by self-esteem needs), less receptiveness to feedback that could be useful for learning and improvement (because such feedback threatens self-esteem), threatened relationships (because your self-esteem needs are prioritized over the needs of relationship partners), and heightened anxiety and stress (due to the fear of failure). Crocker and Park suggest that one way to avoid some of these costs is to replace self-esteem goals with alternative goals that include others or that involve contributing to something that is larger than the self.

Social Acceptance and Self-Esteem

In Crocker and colleagues' research on contingencies of self-worth, several of the domains that define people's self-worth—social approval, virtue, even competition—are social in nature. Mark Leary offers an especially social take on self-esteem, maintaining in his **sociometer hypothesis** that self-esteem is nothing but a readout of our likely standing with others. That is, self-esteem is an internal, subjective index of how well we are regarded by others and hence how likely we are to be included or excluded by them (Leary, Tambor, Terdal, & Downs, 1995). Leary notes that, as the most social of animals, we thrive when we are in healthy social relationships, and he reasons that we therefore need a way to quickly assess how we are doing socially. Our feelings of state self-esteem constitute just such an assessment. Leary notes that those things that make us feel good about ourselves—feeling attractive, competent, likable, and morally upright—are precisely those things that make others accept us (or reject us if we fall short). Elevated self-esteem indicates that we are thriving in our relationships; low self-esteem suggests that we are having interpersonal difficulties—or that we are in danger of having them. In this sense, low self-esteem is not something to be avoided at all costs; rather, it provides useful information about when we need to attend to our social relations or strengthen our social bonds.

"So, when he says, 'What a good boy am I,' Jack is really reinforcing his self-esteem."

sociometer hypothesis A hypothesis that maintains that self-esteem is an internal, subjective index or marker of the extent to which a person is included or looked on favorably by others.

In one test of the sociometer hypothesis, Leary and his colleagues led participants to believe that they were to perform a group task (Leary et al., 1995). Before the task, each participant was asked to write an essay about "what it means to be me" and "the kind of person I would most like to be." The experimenter then gave each person's essay to other participants (in another location), who were asked to indicate who they would like to work with in the group setting. The experimenter ignored the participants' actual preferences and randomly assigned some participants to a condition in which they had supposedly been passed over by the others and had to work alone, and other participants to a condition in which they were in high demand by others and worked with a group. Participants in the work-alone condition, who believed they had been excluded, reported lower levels of self-esteem than those included by the group. Our momentary feelings of self-worth strongly depend on the extent to which others approve of us and include us.

Culture and Self-Esteem

East Asian languages have no word that captures the idea of feeling good about oneself. The Japanese have a term now, but like the Japanese rendering for *baseball*—namely, *beisoboru*—the term for *self-esteem* is simply borrowed from English: *serufu esutiimu*. That it was Westerners who invented the term *self-esteem* reflects a long-standing concern in the West with the value of the individual. During the Enlightenment, in the eighteenth century, Western Europeans began to prioritize individuality, freedom, and rights, ideas that would weave their way into the Constitution of the United States (Baumeister, 1987; Seligman, 1988; Twenge, 2002). Nineteenth-century "transcendentalist" writers, including Ralph Waldo Emerson, Henry David Thoreau, and Margaret Fuller, continued this tradition and emphasized the dignity and power of the individual. Today, the emphasis on self-esteem in the West is higher than ever. Bookstores are filled with children's books about the importance of having a strong sense of self-worth. American parents today seek to raise independent and confident children—not the obedient children of 50 years ago (Remley, 1988). It comes as little surprise, then, that between 1968 and 1984, American college students reported greatly increased self-esteem (Twenge & Campbell, 2001).

Independent cultures foster higher levels of self-esteem than interdependent cultures. Compared with the world's more interdependent peoples—from Japan to Malaysia to India to Kenya—Westerners consistently report higher self-esteem and a more pronounced concern with evaluating the self (Dhawan, Roseman, Naidu, Thapa, & Rettek, 1995; Markus & Kitayama, 1991). It's not that Asians and other non-Westerners feel bad about themselves. Rather, they are more concerned with other ways of feeling good about themselves—for example, they are motivated toward self-improvement and commitment to collective goals (Crocker & Park, 2004; Heine, 2005; Norenzayan & Heine, 2004). Perhaps more dramatically, as people from interdependent cultures gain greater exposure to the West, this emphasis on self-worth rubs off on them and their self-esteem rises. As you can see in **Figure 3.4**, as Asian individuals become more immersed in Canadian life, they become more like Canadians in general with respect to self-esteem (Heine & Lehman, 2003).

So what is it about independent and interdependent cultures that creates these differences in self-esteem? A situationist hypothesis would be that people from Western cultures create social interactions that enhance self-esteem. Consistent with this notion, empirical studies find that situations described by Japanese as common in their everyday experience are regarded as less conducive of high self-esteem—by both Japanese and Americans—than situations common in the

"Who so would be a man must be a nonconformist. Hitch your wagon to a star. Insist on yourself; never imitate. The individual is the world."

—Ralph Waldo Emerson

"Independence is happiness."

—Susan B. Anthony

"Men resemble the times more than they resemble their fathers."

—Arab proverb

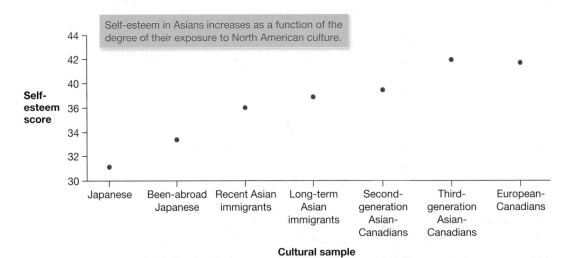

FIGURE 3.4 Cultural Change and Shifts in Self-Esteem The figure shows self-esteem for Japanese who live in Japan; for been-abroad Japanese (those who have spent time in a Western culture); for recent Asian immigrants (those who have moved to Canada within the last 7 years); for long-term Asian immigrants (those who have lived in Canada for more than 7 years); for second-generation Asian-Canadians (those who were born in Canada but whose parents were born in Asia); for third-generation Asian-Canadians (those who were born in Canada, whose parents were born in Canada, but whose grandparents were born in Asia); and for European-Canadians (Canadians whose ancestors were Europeans). (Source: Adapted from Heine & Lehman, 2003.)

United States (Kitayama, Markus, Matsumoto, and Norasakkunkit, 1997). For example, Japanese are much more often encouraged to engage in "assisted" self-criticism than are Americans. Japanese math teachers and sushi chefs, for example, critique themselves in sessions with their peers—not the sort of activities that tend to build self-esteem, however beneficial they might be to skill development. Situations reported by Americans as common in their country, by contrast, are regarded by both Americans and Japanese as more esteem-enhancing than situations common in Japan. For example, Americans are much more often praised for their achievements than are Japanese.

These cultural differences in the emphasis on promoting self-esteem versus working to improve the self have important consequences for how people respond to failures and setbacks (Heine et al., 2001). For example, Steven Heine and colleagues asked Canadian and Japanese students to take a so-called creativity test and then gave them false feedback about their performance. Some were told they had performed very well, and others were told they had performed very badly. The experimenter then gave the participants the opportunity to work on a similar task. The Canadians worked longer on the second task if they had succeeded at the first; the Japanese worked longer if they had failed. Canadians thus avoided being reminded of failure, and Japanese used the occasion to improve.

"America is a vast conspiracy to make you happy."

—John Updike

High Self-Esteem: Good or Bad?

Let's return to the California task force on self-esteem. Was it a good idea? Is having high self-esteem as beneficial as most Westerners think it is? Is low self-esteem uniformly bad, the source of negative outcomes in life? To be sure, there is considerable research suggesting that having high self-esteem is correlated with a variety of positive outcomes, as mentioned earlier. But the story is not as clear-cut as these correlations might suggest. For example, on the one hand, high-self-esteem individuals respond more adaptively to negative feedback, such as being less likely than their low-self-esteem counterparts to give up on a subsequent task (Sommer & Baumeister, 2002). On the other hand, negative feedback leads high-self-esteem people to define themselves in more independent ways, emphasizing their unique traits, goals, and accomplishments, which ends up having interpersonal costs. Namely, relative to low-self-esteem people, high-self-esteem people who received negative feedback (and subsequently defined themselves in independent ways) were liked less and rated more negatively on various trait dimensions (such as arrogance) by a new acquaintance with whom they had a brief interaction (Vohs & Heatherton, 2001).

Pointing to findings like these, Baumeister, Campbell, Krueger, and Vohs (2003) have questioned the importance of many of the findings that have fueled the self-esteem movement, such as those on academic performance. They have even raised questions about the direction of some of these effects; that is, self-esteem may be a consequence rather than a cause of such "outcomes." For example, accomplishments such as doing well in school may enhance people's self-esteem. Moreover, Baumeister and colleagues have suggested that high self-esteem may be linked to a variety of negative outcomes insofar as it may foster narcissism, a personality disorder defined by characteristics such as a grandiose self-concept, self-aggrandizing tendencies, and exploitativeness (Raskin & Terry, 1988). As you might expect, Baumeister's position on self-esteem is highly controversial, and other researchers have countered his position. For example, using a longitudinal

Dangers of High Self-Esteem
Narcissus was a mythological figure who was famously attractive and cruel to others. He fell in love with his own reflection so powerfully that he was unable to leave it, dying because he was unable to look away.

sample, Trzesniewski and colleagues found that high self-esteem as assessed in adolescence predicts positive outcomes 11 years later, including a greater likelihood of graduating from college and staying off unemployment, whereas low adolescent self-esteem is linked to negative outcomes in adulthood such as poorer mental and physical health, higher levels of criminal behavior, and worse economic prospects (Trzesniewski et al., 2006).

An important facet of this debate is that the literature has focused on comparisons between people with high versus low self-esteem. Yet it is increasingly clear that there are different types of high and low self-esteem. Indeed, narcissists have high self-esteem, but not all people with high self-esteem are narcissists, so there must be more than one kind of high self-esteem. For example, although securely held high self-esteem is linked to positive outcomes, high self-esteem that is essentially inflated egotism—that is, not warranted and hence rather tenuous and insecure—tends to have negative, potentially even dangerous consequences (Baumeister, Smart, & Boden, 1996). In particular, people with inflated, more egotistical high self-esteem react volatilely to threats to their self-esteem, using violent action to reassert their feelings of superiority and to dominate those who challenge them.

Further suggesting a link between certain forms of high self-esteem and violence, people who report elevated self-esteem and grandiosity also report greater aggressive tendencies (Wink, 1991). Hare (1993) has noted that psychopaths, who he estimates might be responsible for 50 percent of all serious crime, have grossly inflated views of their self-worth and at the same time are highly sensitive to insults and threats. Baumeister and colleagues further note that alcohol tends to elevate people's self-esteem and to increase the likelihood of aggression (Banaji & Steele, 1989) and that members of violent youth gangs tend to be assertive, defiant, and narcissistic, and they often resort to violence when they are disrespected or threatened. Baumeister and his colleagues even go so far as to suggest, drawing on historical scholarship, that slavery, terrorism, and genocide are products of the dangerous mixture of feelings of superiority and threats to the ego. Such provocative ideas serve as a caveat for the faith that Westerners place on raising people's self-esteem. In short, serious risks appear to be associated with promoting certain forms of high self-esteem.

LOOKING BACK Self-esteem represents people's overall evaluation of their traits, abilities, successes, and failures. Trait self-esteem is fairly stable, whereas state self-esteem fluctuates across different situations. People have different contingencies of self-worth: some people are more invested in intellectual ability, others in religious orientation, still others in sociability. According to sociometer theory, self-esteem is a gauge of a person's level of acceptance or rejection by others. People of non-Western cultures are less concerned with feeling positively about their attributes than are modern Westerners, and non-Westerners are more likely to seek out opportunities for self-improvement. Although high self-esteem may be largely beneficial, some types of elevated self-regard are associated with troublesome behavior tendencies.

MOTIVES DRIVING SELF-EVALUATION

Implicit in the preceding discussion of self-esteem is that people are motivated to view themselves positively. This motive, known as self-enhancement, influences numerous processes related to self-evaluation, including how people respond to negative feedback about the self and what evaluative information they seek out about themselves. Another key self-evaluative motive is self-verification.

Self-Enhancement

Whether you just found out your romantic interest in a coworker is not reciprocated, or you just received a less than stellar performance evaluation at work, it doesn't feel good to feel bad about yourself. It should come as no surprise, then, that self-enhancement, which refers to people's desire to maintain, increase, or protect their self-esteem or self-views (Leary, 2007; Sedikides & Gregg, 2008), is a powerful motive. To satisfy it, people use various strategies.

Self-Serving Construals As noted in the discussion of self-esteem, most people—at any rate, most Westerners—tend to have a positive view of themselves and, on average, their level of self-esteem is rather high. In fact, when asked to indicate how they compare with others in general on various traits and abilities, people consistently exhibit a pronounced **better-than-average effect**. That is, most people think they are above average in popularity, kindness, fairness, leadership, and the ability to get along with others, to name just a few characteristics (Alicke & Govorun, 2005). And it will surely be no surprise to you that most people think they are above-average drivers (Svenson, 1981). Indeed, a majority of drivers interviewed *while hospitalized for being in an automobile accident* rated their driving skill as closer to "expert" than "poor" (Preston & Harris, 1965; Svenson, 1981).

> **better-than-average effect** The finding that most people think they are above average on various trait and ability dimensions.

Why are people so upbeat about their talents and dispositions? Part of the answer has to do with how people interpret what it means to be kind, fair, athletic, or even a good driver. In short, self-serving construals are one means of pursuing self-enhancement. As Nobel Prize–winning economist Thomas Schelling once put it, "Everybody ranks himself high in qualities he values: careful drivers give weight to care, skillful drivers give weight to skill, and those who think that, whatever else they are not, at least they are polite, give weight to courtesy, and come out high on their own scale. This is the way that every child has the best dog on the block" (Schelling, 1978, p. 64). If people tend to construe particular trait or ability dimensions in terms of those things at which they excel, then most of them will end up convinced that they are above average. Indeed, construed in such self-serving ways, most people *are* above average.

David Dunning and his colleagues have shown that people engage in just this sort of self-serving construal of what it means to be, say, artistic, athletic, or agreeable and that such construals are an important part of the better-than-average effect. They have found, for example, that much stronger better-than-average effects are observed for ambiguous traits that are easy to construe in various ways (artistic, sympathetic, talented) than for unambiguous traits that are not (tall, punctual, muscular). Also, when people are given precise instructions about how they should interpret what it means to be, for example, artistic or athletic, the magnitude of the better-than-average effect diminishes dramatically (Dunning, Meyerowitz, & Holzberg, 1989).

People also take advantage of another sort of ambiguity that allows them to think highly of themselves, the ambiguity in which behaviors "count" in determining what someone is like. People tend to judge other people—how kind, outgoing, or athletic they are—by what they are like on average, but they tend to define themselves in terms of what they are like at their best. We tend to think of John's kindness as some middle ground between his warmest, most giving moments and the times when he has been rather cold; but what springs to mind when we think of our own kindness is the time when we *most* went out of our way to help someone else. If people (unknowingly) juggle the standards for what constitutes "talented," "considerate," or "agreeable," it should come as no surprise that they tend to think of themselves as above average (Williams & Gilovich, in press; Williams, Gilovich, & Dunning, in press).

Comparing or Reflecting? As discussed earlier, people sometimes make downward social comparisons—comparing themselves to inferior or worse-off others—to feel better about themselves. Doing so is a means of self-enhancement. But what happens when the only available comparison target we have is superior or better off than we are? Can self-enhancement motives still be served in such situations? Yes they can, as is captured in Abraham Tesser's (1988) **self-evaluation maintenance (SEM) model**. Tesser argues that people shift between two processes—reflection and comparison—in a way that allows them to maintain favorable views of themselves. In areas that are *not* especially relevant to our self-definition, we engage in *reflection*, whereby we flatter ourselves by association with others' accomplishments. For example, let's say you care very little about your athletic skills. When your friend scores the winning goal during a critical soccer match, you beam with pride, experience a boost to your self-esteem, and revel in her victory celebrations as if, in essence, it were your victory too. The closer you are to the triumphant person, the more likely you are to bask in reflected glory in this way (see Chapter 11).

However, when a domain *is* relevant to our self-definition, Tesser argues, we engage in *comparison*, assessing how our abilities or performance stack up to that of others. When we are superior to others, the comparison is downward, enabling us to maintain favorable self-views. But what if others outperform us? Comparing the self to outperforming others would have unflattering results. Such comparisons are particularly painful when the comparison target is a close associate. Is there anything we can do to protect our self-esteem in such challenging self-evaluative circumstances? There is indeed, but it takes some strategic maneuvering.

In one study that illustrates some of these strategies, Tesser and Smith (1980) had two pairs of friends, seated in four individual booths, play a word game with one another. Each participant had to guess four words based on clues provided by the three other participants. Each participant chose clues for the other participants from a list of ten clues clearly marked as to level of difficulty, and to keep participants from knowing the source of the clues, they were conveyed to the relevant participant by the experimenter. In the high-relevance condition, the task was described as a measure of verbal skills. In the low-relevance condition, the task was presented as a playful game. The researchers reasoned that the high-relevance condition should trigger comparison, leading participants to worry that others would succeed on the task and make their performance compare unfavorably. This concern should be higher for a friend than a stranger, since unflattering comparisons sting more with close than with distant others. Reflection should

self-evaluation maintenance (SEM) model A model that maintains that people are motivated to view themselves in a favorable light and that they do so through two processes: reflection and social comparison.

FIGURE 3.5 Scientific Method: Comparison and Self-Esteem

Hypothesis: Individuals will enable their friends' success in domains not relevant to them, but undermine their friends' performance in domains important to their self-esteem.

Research Method:

1. Two pairs of friends, seated in four individual booths, played a word game with one another in which each participant had to guess words based on clues provided by the three other participants.

2. Each participant chose clues from a list of ten clues clearly marked in terms of level of difficulty.

3. In the low-relevance condition, the task was presented as a playful game. In the high-relevance condition, the task was described as a measure of verbal skills.

Results: In the low-relevance condition, participants provided easier clues to a friend than to a stranger. In the high-relevance condition, participants provided clues to a friend that were every bit as hard as the clues they provided to a stranger.

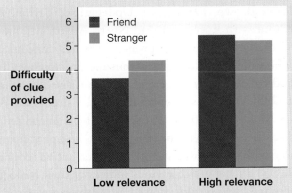

CONCLUSION: People bask in their friends' successes in domains not relevant to their self-esteem, but they seek to outperform their friends in domains important to their self-esteem.

Source: Adapted from Tesser & Smith (1980).

---

be triggered in the low-relevance condition such that participants could bask in the success of others, particularly if their friend succeeded. Given all of this, what kinds of clues do you think participants chose for their friends versus strangers— easy or difficult ones?

As you can see in **Figure 3.5**, when the word game was low in relevance (that is, when it was described as a playful game), participants provided easier clues to a friend than to a stranger, presumably to elevate their friend's performance and, through reflection, their own self-regard. Matters were quite different, however, when the word game was relevant to participants' self-concept. In this condition, participants provided clues to a friend that were every bit as hard as the clues they provided to a stranger. They did so, the theory goes, out of fear that a stellar performance by their friend, in particular, would make them look and feel bad in comparison. In short, one strategy for dealing with situations in which others may outperform you is to sabotage their performance. A nicer way to put this is that one way to ensure flattering comparisons is to close the gap between your performance and that of others. Hurting others' performance can help close this gap, but so could improving your own performance. The logic of Tesser's model

Anybody can sympathise with the sufferings of a friend, but it requires a very fine nature to sympathise with a friend's success.

—Oscar Wilde

suggests several other strategies as well: you could decrease your closeness to people who outperform you, thereby minimizing the sting of unflattering comparisons with them, or you could decrease the relevance of the domain in which they outperform you, thus increasing the appeal of reflection and dampening the sting of comparison (Erber & Tesser, 1994; Tesser, 1988).

Is Self-Enhancement Adaptive? All of this talk about the strategizing people do to ensure favorable self-views may make you wonder whether self-enhancement strivings are adaptive. Isn't having an honest and accurate understanding of oneself a hallmark of a person's mental health and happiness? Indeed, many important movements in psychology, such as the humanistic movement of Abraham Maslow and Carl Rogers, encourage us to accept our weaknesses, foibles, and flaws. In a controversial line of work, Shelley Taylor and Jonathon Brown have challenged this position. They argue that self-knowledge often includes positive illusions about the self—for example, that we are funnier, smarter, or warmer than we really are—and that such illusions, far from being detrimental, actually enhance well-being (Taylor & Brown, 1988, 1994; Updegraff & Taylor, 2000). Dozens of studies, carried out with Europeans and North Americans, have shown that people who are well adjusted are more prone to various illusions about the self relative to those who suffer from low self-esteem and unhappiness. In a laboratory context, Taylor and colleagues examined whether positive illusions have protective or detrimental biological consequences in stressful situations (Taylor, Lerner, Sherman, Sage, & McDowell, 2003). Participants high in the tendency to self-enhance (to hold positive illusions about themselves) and participants low in that tendency were faced with several stress-inducing tasks (such as counting backward by sevens from 9,095) during which various indices of their biological responses to stress were recorded. The results showed a healthier set of coping responses among high self-enhancers relative to low self-enhancers. For instance, high self-enhancers exhibited lower baseline levels of cortisol (a hormone associated with a stress response) and also showed less autonomic arousal during the stressful tasks.

Other researchers have questioned the notion that positive illusions promote adjustment and health, arguing instead that accurate rather than illusory self-beliefs foster well-being and other positive outcomes (Colvin & Block, 1994; Colvin & Griffo, 2008). They cite research showing that people who rate themselves more favorably than others do (that is, people who self-enhance) are seen by others as narcissistic (John & Robins, 1994). Other work shows that people who hold relatively accurate views of themselves—in that their ratings of themselves are similar to others' ratings of them—are judged by others more positively than are people who self-enhance (Colvin, Block, & Funder, 1995).

Perhaps the greatest challenge to Taylor and Brown's thesis about the benefits of positive illusions comes from cross-cultural research. This work demonstrates that East Asians are less likely to endorse positive illusions about the self than are Westerners (Heine, Lehman, Markus, & Kitayama, 1999; Kitayama, Markus, et al., 1997). For example, Japanese college students are less likely than American students to assume that they are better than average in important abilities, such as academic talent (Markus & Kitayama, 1991). Such cross-cultural evidence suggests that positive illusions do not automatically enhance well-being. They often do so for Westerners because a positive view of the self is a cherished cultural value. In contrast, personal well-being for East Asians appears to be more closely tied to interdependent values. For example, Mark Suh, Ed Diener, and

"Lord, I thank thee that I judge not—as others do."

—Puritan prayer

their colleagues have found that the well-being of East Asians is more dependent on fulfilling social roles and expectations and thus consistent with an interdependent self-construal (Suh, Diener, Oishi, & Triandis, 1998).

So are self-enhancing tendencies adaptive or not? At present, the answer to this question appears to be "it depends." For example, Robins and Beer (2001) showed that students who entered college with self-enhancing beliefs about their academic ability reported higher average levels of self-esteem and well-being over a four-year time period relative to their non-enhancing peers. However, self-enhancement tendencies were associated with a downward trajectory over the four-year period for both self-esteem and well-being. In essence, although self-enhancement was linked to greater self-esteem and well-being in the short term, the advantages associated with engaging in self-enhancement erode over time. The safest conclusion to draw at this point is that self-enhancement provides a number of benefits, but it can be taken too far and exact significant costs.

Self-Verification

Although a wealth of evidence indicates that self-enhancement is a powerful motive driving people's self-evaluative activities, it is not our only self-evaluative motive and we do not always seek to see ourselves through rose-colored glasses. The truth, at least our version of it, also matters. **Self-verification theory** holds that we strive for stable, subjectively accurate beliefs about ourselves because such beliefs give us a sense of coherence (Swann, 1990) and make us more predictable to ourselves and others, which helps interactions with others go more smoothly. More concretely, we strive to get others to confirm or verify our preexisting beliefs about ourselves. To illustrate, if you see yourself as extraverted, self-verification theory would predict that you will seek to get others to see you as extraverted as well. This holds true even for negative self-views. The idea is that if you truly believe you are, say, socially awkward, getting others to see this subjective truth bolsters your feelings of coherence and predictability.

self-verification theory A theory that holds that people strive for stable, subjectively accurate beliefs about the self because such beliefs give them a sense of coherence.

People engage in a number of self-verification strategies. We selectively attend to and recall information that is consistent with (and that therefore verifies) our self-views. People with negative self-views, for example, spend more time studying negative rather than positive feedback about themselves; they remember negative feedback better; and they prefer to interact with others who are likely to provide negative rather than positive feedback (Swann & Read, 1981; Swann, Wenzlaff, Krull, & Pelham, 1992).

Other self-verification strategies involve creating self-confirmatory social environments through our behavior. Our identity cues—such as our customary facial expressions, posture, gait, clothes, haircuts, and body decorations—signal to others important facets of our identity and increase the likelihood that others' impressions of the self will be verifying. Wearing a simple T-shirt conveys information about our political affiliations, our music preferences, the clubs we belong to, the holidays we take, our university, even our sexual attitudes. Samuel Gosling and his colleagues have found that even college students' dorm rooms—including the way clothes are folded (or not, as the case may be), the way books are arranged, and what is hanging on the walls—convey information about the self (Gosling, Ko, Mannarelli, & Morris, 2002) and thus may aid people in their self-verification efforts.

As many novels so vividly portray, people also choose to enter into relations that maintain consistent views of the self, even when those views are dark, ruinous,

Identity Cues and Self-Verification We create self-confirmatory social environments through the clothes we wear, hairstyles, jewelry, tattoos, and other identity cues. (A) A high school student wears his varsity jacket off the field, signaling his identity as an athlete. (B) Girls signal their youth and trendiness by donning Harajuku-inspired fashion while hanging out in the Harajuku district of Japan.

and tragic. These sorts of preferences guarantee that our personal lives will likely confirm our views of the self. In a study of intimate bonds, romantic partners who viewed each other in a congruent fashion—that is, whose perceptions of each other were in agreement—reported more commitment to the relationship, even when one partner viewed the other in a negative light (Swann, De La Ronde, & Hixon, 1994).

How might people integrate the self-enhancement and self-verification perspectives? One answer is that these two motives guide different processes related to self-evaluation. Self-enhancement seems to be most relevant to our emotional responses to feedback about the self, whereas self-verification determines our more cognitive assessment of the validity of the feedback (Swann, Griffin, Predmore, & Gaines, 1987). To test this hypothesis, Swann and colleagues gave participants with negative or positive self-beliefs negative or positive feedback. In terms of participants' evaluations of the accuracy and competence of the feedback—that is, the quality of the information—self-verification prevailed. Namely, participants with negative self-beliefs found the negative feedback most diagnostic and accurate, whereas participants with positive beliefs rated the positive feedback higher on these dimensions. All participants, however, felt good about the positive feedback and disliked the negative feedback. Our quest to verify our sense of ourselves, then, guides our assessment of the validity of self-relevant information, while our desire to think favorably about ourselves guides our emotional reactions to the same information.

 Self-evaluative activities such as seeking out evaluative feedback about the self can be driven by different motives, such as self-enhancement and self-verification. Self-enhancement strategies include self-serving construals and shifting back and forth between reflection and comparison processes depending on the self-relevance of the domain. When self-verification is our priority, we seek out appraisals and relationship partners that confirm our preexisting self-views, and we display cues that increase the likelihood that others will see us as we see themselves.

SELF-REGULATION: MOTIVATING AND CONTROLLING THE SELF

Self-regulation refers to the processes by which people initiate, alter, and control their behavior in the pursuit of their goals, whether the goal is doing well in school, being a good friend, improving your snowboarding skills, or getting in better shape (Carver & Scheier, 1982; Higgins, 1999; Muraven & Baumeister, 2000). Given that successful goal pursuit often requires resisting temptations, self-regulation also captures people's ability to delay gratification—that is, to prioritize their long-term goals (say, getting into graduate school) by forgoing short-term immediate rewards (say, a weeknight out on the town). Let's take a look at what the social psychological study of self-regulation has discovered about such efforts.

self-regulation Processes that people use to initiate, alter, and control their behavior in the pursuit of goals, including the ability to resist short-term awards that thwart the attainment of long-term goals.

Possible Selves

One perspective on self-regulation lies in the notion of **possible selves**, which refers to the kinds of people we hope to be in the future (Cross & Markus, 1991; Markus & Nurius, 1986). Possible selves, which are stored in memory like any other form of self-knowledge, have a self-regulatory function in that they serve as standards that can motivate goal-directed action. For example, you might imagine yourself ten years from now as an environmental scientist or as a lawyer seeking to redress injustice. This kind of self-knowledge can motivate present actions—learning organic chemistry or studying for the LSAT—that will help you get closer to your possible self. Research suggests that people who have rich ideas about possible selves are more optimistic and energetic and are less vulnerable to depression (Markus & Nurius, 1986).

possible selves Hypothetical selves that a person aspires to be in the future.

Although possible selves can incite action aimed at attaining them, it can take more than just imagining these selves for them to have such motivating effects. People have to feel that their possible selves are, in fact, attainable (Destin & Oyserman, 2009; Oyserman, Bybee, & Terry, 2006). To illustrate, if low-income students who aspire to become college-educated, high-achieving individuals perceive the path to attaining this self as filled with obstacles (insufficient financial resources) rather than supportive assets and opportunities (financial aid), then their hoped-for possible self is less likely to motivate action.

Self-Discrepancy Theory

A related perspective on how self-knowledge motivates and guides productive action is provided by Tory Higgins's **self-discrepancy theory** (Higgins, 1987). The theory posits that people hold not only beliefs about what they are actually like (**actual self**), but also beliefs about what they would ideally like to be (**ideal self**) and what they think they ought to be (**ought self**). Hence, ideal selves represent our hopes and wishes, whereas ought selves represent our duties and obligations. According to the theory, ideal and ought beliefs serve as self-guides, motivating people to close the gap between their actual self and these standards. When people feel they are failing to live up to these standards—in other words, when they perceive a discrepancy between their actual self and either their ideal

self-discrepancy theory A theory that behavior is motivated by standards reflecting ideal and ought selves. Falling short of these standards produces specific emotions—dejection-related emotions for actual-ideal discrepancies, and agitation-related emotions for actual-ought discrepancies.

actual self The self that people believe they are.

ideal self The self that embodies people's wishes and aspirations as held by themselves and by other people for them.

ought self The self that is concerned with the duties, obligations, and external demands people feel they are compelled to honor.

FIGURE 3.6 You Be the Subject: Ideal and Ought Selves

Write down some of your possible selves—that is, who you imagine being in the future.

_____

_____

_____

_____

_____

_____

Think about the extent to which the possible selves you describe are ideal selves you hope to achieve or ought selves you feel obligated to achieve.

Results: When people focus on how they fall short of their ideal selves, feelings of disappointment are triggered, whereas focusing on falling short of ought selves is likely to elicit anxiety.

or ought self—there are predictable emotional consequences. Specifically, discrepancies between the actual and the ideal self produce dejection-related affect, whereas discrepancies between the actual and the ought self give rise to agitation-related affect (**Figure 3.6**). To illustrate, when the judges disparage Samir's singing ability at an *American Idol* audition, the discrepancy between his actual self (a poor singer) and his ideal self (a rock star) arouses dejection-related emotions, such as disappointment and shame. When Mina loses patience with her ailing grandmother (actual self), she may feel agitation-related emotions such as guilt and anxiety if her ought self standards include being a patient and loving granddaughter.

Ideal and ought standards are associated with two fundamentally different approaches to goal pursuit. When people regulate their behavior with respect to ideal self standards, they tend to have a **promotion focus**, or a focus on attaining positive outcomes (Higgins, 1996). By contrast, when people regulate their behavior with respect to ought self standards, they tend to have a **prevention focus**, a focus on avoiding negative outcomes. When people are promotion-focused, they are particularly attuned to positive outcomes and are more inclined to engage in approach-related behaviors; when prevention-focused, people are especially sensitive to negative outcomes and exhibit avoidance-related tendencies.

Wide-ranging evidence supports Higgins's account of how ideal and ought selves can have different emotional and motivational consequences. When people are subtly induced to think about how they might approximate their ideal self—for example, by reading trait terms that capture their ideal self—they generally show elevated cheerful affect (Higgins, Shah, & Friedman, 1997; Shah & Higgins, 2001) and heightened sensitivity to positive outcomes (Brendl, Higgins, & Lemm, 1995). But if they think they will never become their ideal self, they tend to experience dejection-related emotions such as depression and shame and show reduced physiological arousal. In contrast, a prevention focus, triggered by associations to an ought self and any deviation from it, activates agitated affect (such as guilt or panic), elevated physiological arousal, avoidant behavior, and sensitivity to negative outcomes (Strauman & Higgins, 1987).

promotion focus Regulating behavior with respect to ideal self standards, entailing a focus on attaining positive outcomes and approach-related behaviors.

prevention focus Regulating behavior with respect to ought standards, entailing a focus on avoiding negative outcomes and avoidance-related behaviors.

Ego Depletion

Trying to live up to their ideal and ought self standards can be hard work for people. Often it requires controlling the impulse to engage in behavior that is detrimental to actualizing our ideal and ought selves. In fact, acts of self-control can be downright exhausting. Roy Baumeister, Kathleen Vohs, and their colleagues argue that when we attempt to control our behavior to live up to important standards, we often experience what they call **ego depletion** (Baumeister, Vohs, & Tice, 2007). Much as physical exercise can exhaust our muscles, self-control can exhaust us psychologically. This claim is based on the idea that self-control draws on a limited resource (Muraven & Baumeister, 2000). When we exercise self-control, we use up that precious resource so that less of it is available to sustain further acts of self-control.

In one study that illustrates the costs of self-control, participants were asked to rein in their emotions while watching an evocative film clip. Afterward, they were not able to squeeze a hand grip as long as control participants were. In another study, participants who exercised their will by eating healthy radishes instead of delicious-smelling cookies later gave up on an unsolvable puzzle faster than participants who did not exercise self-control and were allowed to indulge in the cookies (Baumeister, Bratslavsky, Muraven, & Tice, 1998). The notion that every time you engage in an act of self-control, your subsequent ability to regulate yourself suffers might make you want to throw in the towel. Not so fast. Researchers have discovered various factors that can counteract ego depletion effects. For example, cash incentives or other motives for good performance can counteract the negative effects of exerting self-control on a subsequent task (Muraven & Slessareva, 2003), as can being in a positive mood, presumably because of the empowering and energizing effects of positive emotions (Tice, Baumeister, Shmueli, & Muraven, 2007).

Research by Matthew Gailliot and his colleagues points to perhaps the most intriguing factor that may counteract ego depletion—namely, glucose (sugar). Shedding light on the biological underpinnings of ego depletion effects, these researchers hypothesized that self-regulation relies on circulating blood glucose levels. Thus, when people exert self-control, their blood glucose levels drop and they exhibit impaired self-control on subsequent tasks. And if blood glucose levels are somehow replenished after an initial self-control task, people no longer show ego depletion. Supporting these provocative ideas, Gailliot and his colleagues found that engaging in an initial self-control task—for example, suppressing one's emotions—does indeed appear to reduce circulating blood glucose levels, which in turn predict poorer performance on subsequent self-control tasks (Gailliot et al., 2007). To test whether a boost in blood glucose can counteract ego depletion effects, they had participants first engage in a self-control task and then drink Kool-Aid lemonade sweetened with either sugar (and hence glucose) or Splenda (which doesn't contain glucose). Participants who drank the Splenda-sweetened beverage showed the standard ego depletion effect on a later self-control task, whereas participants who drank the glucose-containing beverage did not. Overall, although the evidence indicates that exerting self-control is depleting, most situations do not completely wipe out our self-regulatory resources. With enough external or internal inducement (including glucose), we can override ego depletion.

ego depletion A state, produced by acts of self-control, in which people lack the energy or resources to engage in further acts of self-control.

Automatic Self-Control Strategies

Recent work by Ayelet Fishbach and her colleagues examines the self-control strategies people use to resist short-term temptations that can derail their long-term goals. One take-home point of this research is that although we certainly can and do implement self-control strategies deliberately, self-control strategies can also be deployed automatically, operating without our even realizing it. What are some examples of such automatic self-control strategies?

Imagine that you are trying to eat a healthier diet (long-term goal), but you are faced with a plate of warm and gooey chocolate chip cookies (temptation). Surely the alluring properties of the cookies and the immediate gratification they offer will put thoughts about eating healthy on the back burner, right? Across a series of studies, Fishbach, Friedman, and Kruglanski (2003) showed that, actually, quite the opposite can happen. That is, being faced with cookies may actually make you think more about your goal to eat healthily rather than less. The idea is that temptations (unhealthy foods) may become linked in memory to our goals (eating well) so that when the former is brought to mind, so too is the latter—and this can occur automatically. What's more, Fishbach and colleagues found that bringing goals to mind first has the effect of *diminishing* thoughts about temptations. Thus, being faced with temptations reminds us of our goals, while thinking about our goals puts temptations out of our minds. But before deciding you can abandon all deliberative efforts to resist temptations, note that the effects found in this research hold mainly when the goal in question is high in importance and among people who have had substantial past success in resisting goal-interfering temptations.

Automatic self-control strategies can influence behavior as well as thoughts, leading people to approach goals and to avoid temptations. In a clever set of studies demonstrating this effect, Fishbach and Shah (2006) measured how long it took participants to pull or push a lever in response to goal-related and temptation-related words (**Figure 3.7**). Pulling a lever toward the self is thought to represent approach tendencies, bringing an object closer to the self. In contrast, pushing a lever away from the self represents avoidance tendencies, moving an object further from the self. You see where this is going? Participants' pulling responses were quicker in response to goal-related words, but their pushing responses were

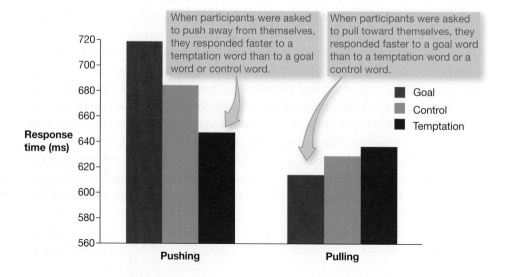

FIGURE 3.7 Automatic Self-Control Strategies Participants' response times for pushing a lever away from themselves versus pulling the lever toward themselves in response to self-generated goal, control, and temptation target words. (Source: From Fishbach & Shah, 2006.)

When participants were asked to push away from themselves, they responded faster to a temptation word than to a goal word or control word.

When participants were asked to pull toward themselves, they responded faster to a goal word than to a temptation word or a control word.

Response time (ms)

720
700
680
660
640
620
600
580
560

Goal
Control
Temptation

Pushing

Pulling

quicker in response to temptation-related words. And note, it's not as if participants were consciously deciding to pull and push more or less quickly. Instead, they showed automatic tendencies to approach goals and avoid temptations. Sound too good to be true? Well, there are some caveats. In particular, it's probably no surprise that these results held mainly for people who have been successful at regulating themselves in the past. But on a more encouraging note, these results mainly held true when temptations were very high in attractiveness—which of course is precisely when the automatic deployment of self-control strategies is most needed.

 Self-regulation refers to how people go about initiating, changing, and controlling their behavior in the pursuit of goals. Goal-directed actions can be motivated by standards in the form of possible selves, such as ideal and ought selves. Such actions can be either promotion- or prevention-focused. People tend to experience dejection-related emotions when they fall short of their ideal standards, and agitation-related feelings when they fail to meet their ought standards. Acts of self-regulation can be depleting, such that an initial act of self-control diminishes self-control ability on a subsequent task requiring self-control. Ego depletion effects can be counteracted by external and internal factors, including the ingestion of glucose. People may also have unintentional self-control strategies, such as automatic behavioral tendencies to approach goals and avoid temptations.

SELF-PRESENTATION

Alexi Santana entered Princeton University as a member of the class of 1993. He excelled in his classes, excelled in track, and was admitted to one of Princeton's most exclusive eating clubs. He dazzled his dormmates with his tales of being raised on a sheep farm in the wild canyons of southern Utah and his unusual habits—for example, he routinely arose at dawn and preferred to sleep on the floor.

The only trouble was that Alexi Santana was a fictitious identity. Santana was actually James Hogue, a 34-year-old drifter and former track star from Kansas City. Hogue had been convicted and served time for various crimes, including check forging and bicycle theft. He had gotten into Princeton thanks to a fraudulent application and had earned the admiration of his peers based on a completely fabricated identity. In a documentary called *Con Man*, Jessie Moss showed that Hogue had had a pattern of assuming false identities.

Hogue's story (or is it Santana's?) is an extreme version of a basic truth: our social self is often a dramatic performance in which we try to project a public self that is in keeping with our hopes and aspirations. This public self is one that we actively create in our social interactions and that is shaped by the perceptions of other people and the perceptions we want others to have of us (Baumeister, 1982; Mead, 1934; Schlenker, 1980; Shrauger & Schoeneman, 1979). The public self is concerned with **self-presentation**, that is, presenting who we would like others to believe we are—in Hogue's case, a brilliant track star. Another term for this concept is *impression management*, which refers to how we attempt to control the particular impressions other people form of us.

Sociologist Erving Goffman inspired the study of self-presentation with his keen observations about how we stake out our identity in the public realm,

self-presentation Presenting the person that we would like others to believe we are.

Self-Presentation James Hogue attended Princeton University on an academic scholarship under the assumed name of Alexi Santana. He constructed a false identity for himself at Princeton as a self-educated 18-year-old from Utah. Hogue is shown under arrest for forgery, wrongful impersonation, and falsifying records at Princeton.

face The public image of ourselves that we want others to believe.

something James Hogue had mastered (Goffman, 1959, 1967). Rather than doing controlled experiments, Goffman relied on naturalistic observations of how people behave in public settings. He spent time in mental institutions, noting how patients there seemed to ignore many rules of self-presentation—making unflattering comments about others and failing to observe the social niceties. Goffman wrote an entire chapter on what he called "response cries," like "Oops!" that we resort to when we have committed social gaffes and feel deeply embarrassed. These linguistic acts help reestablish social order when we have violated the rules of self-presentation and show how committed we are to the public self.

From these observations, Goffman arrived at what has been called a dramaturgic perspective on the social self: social interaction can be thought of as a drama of self-presentation, in which we attempt to create and maintain an impression of ourselves in the minds of others (Baumeister, 1982; Brown, 1998; Goffman, 1959; Leary & Kowalski, 1990; Schlenker & Leary, 1982). Critical to this drama, in Goffman's terms, is **face**, which refers to the public image of ourselves that we want others to believe. We may want others to think we are gifted but temperamental artists, that we have intellectual gifts that allow us to excel without studying, or that we are the object of many romantic interests. Social interactions are the stage on which we play out these kinds of claims, regardless of how true they are. Much like a play, the social drama of self-presentation is highly collaborative.

Public and Private Face
People may present themselves differently in public and private. (A) Kristen Stewart is not showing a carefully constructed public face when she is out running errands in Los Angeles, but (B) she does present a public face when she arrives at the premiere of one of her movies.

(A)

(B)

We depend on others to honor our desired social identities, and others likewise depend on us to honor their face claims.

Goffman's insights have shaped the study of the self in several lasting ways. For example, the concept of self-monitoring derives in part from Goffman's analysis of strategic self-presentation (Gangestad & Snyder, 2000; Snyder, 1974, 1979). **Self-monitoring** refers to people's tendency to monitor their behavior in such a way that it fits the demands of the current situation. High self-monitors carefully scrutinize situations, and they shift their self-presentation and behavior to fit the prevailing context. James Hogue was off the charts in terms of being a high self-monitor. Low self-monitors act in accordance with their internal inclinations, impulses, and dispositions, independent of the social context. High self-monitors are like actors, changing their behavior according to the people they are with. In contrast, low self-monitors are more likely to behave in accordance with their own traits and preferences, which suggests admirable candor and honesty. However, patients in a psychiatric hospital scored low on a self-monitoring scale, consistent with Goffman's early observations and his thesis that effective social functioning requires that we participate in some strategic self-presentation (Snyder, 1974).

self-monitoring The tendency for people to monitor their behavior in such a way that it fits situational demands (the current situation).

Protecting Your Own Face: Self-Handicapping

One of the complexities of strategic self-presentation is that people often don't live up to the public self they are trying to portray. For example, your claim about being the next great American writer will eventually be put to the test when you submit your prose for publication. Your claim about being the next great triathlete will eventually face the truth of the stopwatch and other competitors. The obvious risk of the public self is that we might not live up to it, and we risk embarrassing ourselves when that happens. To protect the self in these circumstances, we engage in various self-protective behaviors (**Box 3.3**).

One such behavior is **self-handicapping**, the self-defeating behaviors people engage in to protect their public selves and to prevent others from making unwanted inferences based on poor performance (Arkin & Baumgardner, 1985; Deppe & Harackiewicz, 1996; Hirt, McCrea, & Kimble, 2000; Jones & Berglas, 1978). Think of how often people engage in self-destructive behaviors when their

self-handicapping People's tendency to engage in self-defeating behavior in order to have a ready excuse should they perform poorly or fail.

BOX 3.3   FOCUS ON HEALTH

Dying to Present a Favorable Self

Thus far, you might think that self-presentation is a good thing. Erving Goffman himself wrote about how people's strategic self-presentation and how their honoring of other people's public claims are essential ingredients of harmonious communities. But our worries about our public image and the means by which we are guided by self-presentational concerns may be dangerous to our health (Leary, Tchividjian, & Kraxberger, 1994). Many practices that promote health are awkward or embarrassing and pose problems for our public identity. As a consequence, we avoid them. We sacrifice physical health to maintain a public identity defined by composure and aplomb. For example, between 30 and 65 percent of respondents reported embarrassment when buying condoms (Hanna, 1989). This embarrassment may deter sexually active teenagers from buying and using them,

thus increasing their risk of sexually transmitted diseases and unwanted pregnancies. Similarly, the fear of embarrassment at times prevents obese individuals from pursuing physical exercise programs or taking needed medications (Bain, Wilson, & Chaikind, 1989).

In other instances, we engage in risky behavior to enhance our public image and identity. Concerns about others' impressions and our own physical appearance are good predictors of excessive sunbathing, which increases the likelihood of skin cancer (Leary & Jones, 1993). Moreover, adolescents typically cite social approval as one of the most important reasons for starting to drink alcohol and smoke cigarettes (Farber, Khavari, & Douglass, 1980). And the same need for an enhanced public image motivates many cosmetic surgeries, which carry with them a variety of health risks.

---

public selves are on the line. Students will irrationally put too little effort into studying for an exam. Athletes party all night before the championship game. You may act too casually at a job interview or say shockingly inappropriate things on a first date. Why do we engage in such self-defeating behaviors? In Goffman's view, these actions provide an explanation for possible failure, thereby protecting the desired public self. If you don't perform as well as expected on an exam that you didn't prepare for, there is no threat to the claim you would like to make about your academic talents. Of course, people sometimes claim "self-handicaps" they have not experienced. Classrooms are filled with students who act as though they haven't studied terribly hard when in fact they did. The phenomenon is so common that students on at least one campus, Dartmouth College, have given the people who do it a name—"sneaky bookers."

In one of the first studies of self-handicapping, male participants were led to believe either that they were going to succeed or that they were going to have difficulty on a test they were scheduled to take (Berglas & Jones, 1978). Participants were then given the chance to ingest one of two drugs: the first would enhance their test performance; the second would impair it. Participants who felt they were likely to fail the test preferred the performance-inhibiting drug, even though it was likely to diminish their chances of success. Apparently, people would sometimes rather fail and have a ready excuse for it than go for success and have no excuse for their failure.

Protecting Others' Face: On-Record versus Off-Record Communications

Honesty is the best policy. Or is it? In Goffman's world of strategic self-presentation, honesty can be downright dangerous; it can threaten other people's attempts to present their desired public selves. Imagine that your best friend is in a band, and he thinks they are on the verge of making it big. When you first hear their music, it sounds clichéd and corny. Do you tell him so? Probably not directly, if you want to preserve your friendship. Instead, you might resort to polite "white lies" or some indirect and ambiguous language. Honest, direct statements, especially of a critical nature, threaten the public self that the individual (your friend) is trying to project, and it makes the honest speaker (you) come across as impolite and inconsiderate.

These ideas about protecting the public self have led to insightful analyses of language. Linguists Penelope Brown and Steven Levinson (1987) propose that there are two levels of communication. *On-record communication* includes the statements people make that they intend to be taken literally. Such statements tend to follow the rules of honest communication: they are direct, relevant, and delivered in a straightforward, sincere fashion (Clark, 1996; Grice, 1975). When a doctor delivers a dire prognosis or a financial advisor announces the loss of a family fortune, the doctor and financial advisor adhere to the rules of on-record communication.

When people need to deliver a message that threatens their public self or that of someone else (especially someone they like), they resort to *off-record communication*. Off-record communication is indirect and ambiguous; it allows us to hint at ideas and meanings that are not explicit in the words we utter. Off-record communication violates the rules of direct, honest communication with a variety of tactics, including rhetorical questions, exaggeration, understatement, or intentional vagueness, suggesting alternative interpretations of what is being said. Let's return to the hypothetical example of having to comment on your friend's music. Direct, on-record criticism threatens your friend's public self and your image as a kind friend. Instead of being direct ("Don't give up your day job"), self-presentation concerns are likely to lead you to off-record forms of communication. You might politely resort to obvious exaggeration ("OMG, you're the next Tupac"), vagueness ("Some of the rhythms are really interesting"), or jokey obliqueness ("You guys would be off the charts in Estonia"). In the drama of self-presentation, we break the rules of sincere communication to protect other people's public selves.

 Self-presentation involves people's efforts to get others to form particular desired impressions of them. Self-presentational efforts are more characteristic of high self-monitors, people who change their behavior based on the situation in which they find themselves. Low self-monitors attend more to their own preferences and dispositions, with little regard for the situation or what others think. People may self-handicap, or engage in self-defeating behaviors, to "save face"— in other words, to have excuses available should they fail. Finally, people may engage in off-record communication, merely hinting at disagreement or disapproval, to save other people's face.

Chapter Review

Summary

Nature of the Social Self

- The social self can be thought of as having three primary components: the *individual self*, the *relational self*, and the *collective self*, which may differ in prominence across individuals.

Origins of Self-Knowledge

- The social self has several foundations, including socialization by family members and other important people. *Reflected self-appraisals*, our beliefs about what others think of us, help us gain self-knowledge. The social self is shaped by construal processes.

- The social self is shaped by the current situation in many ways. For example, people in Western cultures tend to define themselves according to what distinguishes them from others in the social context.

- The self is profoundly shaped by whether people live in independent or interdependent cultures.

- Women generally emphasize their relationships and define themselves in an interdependent way, and men generally emphasize their uniqueness and construe themselves in an independent way.

- People rely on *social comparison* to learn about their own abilities, attitudes, and personal traits.

- The social self can also be thought of as a narrative, or story, that we tell to make sense of our goals, conflicts, and changing identities.

Organization of Self-Knowledge

- *Self-schemas*, the most basic organizational units of self-knowledge, help guide construal of and memory for social information.

- People differ in their levels of *self-complexity*. More complex self-representations enable us to be more resilient in response to negative, self-relevant events.

Self-Esteem

- *Trait self-esteem* tends to be a stable part of identity, and *state self-esteem* changes according to different contextual factors, such as personal failure or the poor performance of a beloved sports team.

- Our self-esteem is defined by particular domains of importance, or *contingencies of self-worth*, and by our being accepted by others.

- Self-esteem is more important and elevated in Western than in East Asian cultures.

- Studies have linked various forms of antisocial behavior with narcissistic forms of self-esteem.

Motives Driving Self-Evaluation

- The motives for self-evaluation include the desire for self-enhancement and for self-verification.

- The motivation to have elevated self-esteem guides the maintenance of relationships that allow us to engage in favorable social comparisons and provide esteem-enhancing pride taken in relationship partners' successes.

- Having a stable set of self-beliefs gives people a sense of coherence and predictability.

Self-Regulation: Motivating and Controlling the Self

- *Possible selves*, which represent who people aspire to be, can motivate action aimed at attaining them.

- *Self-discrepancy theory* investigates how people compare their *actual self* to both their *ideal* and *ought selves* and the emotional consequences of such comparisons.

- When people regulate their behavior with respect to ideal self standards, they have a *promotion focus* for attaining positive outcomes. When people regulate their behavior with respect to ought self standards, they have a *prevention focus* for avoiding negative outcomes.

- Self-control can produce a state of *ego depletion*, which makes it harder to exert further self-control.

- Self-control strategies can be implemented automatically, such as when long-term goals automatically spring to mind when people are faced with temptations that can thwart these goals.

Self-Presentation

- *Self-presentation* theory considers the self to be a dramatic performer in the public realm. People typically seek to create and maintain a favorable public impression of themselves. *Face* refers to the public image people want others to believe about them. People engage in *self-monitoring* to ensure that their behavior fits the demands of the social context.

- People protect their public self through *self-handicapping behaviors*, which can explain away possible failure.

- Face concerns and self-presentation shape social communication. *On-record communication* is direct; *off-record communication* is indirect and subtle.

Key Terms

actual self (p. 95)
better-than-average effect (p. 89)
collective self (p. 67)
contingencies of self-worth (p. 84)
ego depletion (p. 97)
face (p. 100)
ideal self (p. 95)
individual self (p. 67)
ought self (p. 95)
possible selves (p. 95)

prevention focus (p. 96)
promotion focus (p. 96)
reflected self-appraisals (p. 68)
relational self (p. 67)
self-complexity (p. 81)
self-discrepancy theory (p. 95)
self-esteem (p. 82)
self-evaluation maintenance (SEM) model (p. 90)
self-handicapping (p. 101)

self-monitoring (p. 101)
self-presentation (p. 99)
self-reference effect (p. 79)
self-regulation (p. 95)
self-schemas (p. 78)
self-verification theory (p. 93)
social comparison theory (p. 75)
sociometer hypothesis (p. 85)
working self-concept (p. 71)

Further Reading and Films

Allen, W. (Director). (1983). *Zelig* [Motion picture]. United States: Orion Pictures Corporation. "Human chameleon" Leonard Zelig (Woody Allen) soars to celebrity in the 1920s and 1930s with his unexplained ability to transform himself into anyone he meets.

Dennis, N. F. (1955/2002). *Cards of identity*. Normal, IL: Dalkey Archive Press. A novel about a group of people who change others' identities by surrounding them with evidence supporting the new identity.

Higgins, E. T. (2011). *Beyond pleasure and pain: How motivation works*. New York: Oxford. A far-reaching account of how motivation works, including the role of "ideal" and "ought" selves in motivating behavior.

Taylor, S. E. (1989). *Positive illusions: Creative self-deception and the healthy mind*. New York: Basic Books. A recounting of the various illusions psychologically healthy people hold about themselves and the world.

CHAPTER 4

Social Cognition: Thinking about People and Situations

EARLY IN THE MORNING ON June 28, 1993, New York State troopers on Long Island's Southern State Parkway noticed a Mazda pickup truck with no license plates. When they motioned for the driver to pull over, he sped off, leading them on a 25-minute chase that ended when the Mazda slammed into a utility pole. After arresting the driver, the officers noticed a foul odor emanating from under a tarp in the back of the truck. When the tarp was removed, the officers discovered the badly decomposed body of a 22-year-old woman. Subsequent investigation implicated the driver, Joel Rifkin, in the murders of 16 other women, making him the most prolific serial killer in New York State history.

Those who knew Rifkin expressed shock at the news. One neighbor told reporters, "When I would come home at 1 or 2 in the morning, if I saw the garage light on, I'd feel safe because I knew Joel was around." A second neighbor said he was "simply a gentle young man." Classmates asserted he was "not the kind of guy who would do something like this."

As this story makes clear, social judgments can have serious consequences. Mistaking a serial killer as someone who's "gentle" and "safe" to be around can be a lethal mistake. More generally, effective action requires sound judgment about the world around us. "How will my professor react if I ask for more time?" "Are they developing nuclear weapons?" "Will my boyfriend be faithful?" "Is it worth it?"

This chapter's discussion of social cognition—and sources of error in judgment about the social world—proceeds in five parts. Each focuses on a critical aspect of social judgment: (1) Our judgments are only as effective as the quality of the information on which they are based, yet the information available to

Errors in Social Judgment
Although Joel Rifkin was the most prolific serial killer in New York's history, his neighbors insisted that he was "a gentle young man" who was "not the kind of guy who would do something like this."

us in everyday life is not always accurate or complete. (2) The way information is presented, including the order in which it is presented and how it is framed, can affect the judgments we make. (3) We don't just passively take in information. We often actively seek it out, and a pervasive bias in our information-seeking strategies often distorts the conclusions we reach. (4) Our preexisting knowledge, expectations, and mental habits can influence the construal of new information and thus substantially influence judgment. (5) Two mental systems—intuition and reason—underlie social cognition, and their complex interplay determines the judgments we make.

WHY STUDY SOCIAL COGNITION?

The field of social cognition is the study of how people think about the social world and arrive at judgments that help them interpret the past, understand the present, and predict the future. Social psychologists have long been interested in cognition. Indeed, one of the earliest and most fundamental principles of social psychology is the construal principle introduced in Chapter 1: If we want to know how a person will react in a given situation, we must understand how the person experiences that situation. Social stimuli rarely influence people's behavior directly; they do so indirectly through the way they are interpreted and construed.

The example that began this chapter does more than testify to the importance of social judgments in everyday life. It also highlights the fact that our judgments are not always flawless. We trust some people we shouldn't. We make some investments that turn out to be unwise. Some of our mistakes are harmless and others have dire consequences, but all of them can help us figure out how to do better next time. They are informative to psychologists as well because they provide particularly helpful clues about how people think about other individuals and make inferences about them. They give psychologists hints about the strategies, or rules, people follow to make judgments—both those that turn out to be successful and those that lead to disaster. The strategy of scrutinizing mistakes has a long tradition in psychology. Perceptual psychologists study illusions to illuminate general principles of perception, and psycholinguists study speech errors to learn about speech production. Whether rare or common, mistakes often reveal a great deal about how a system works by showing its limitations. Thus researchers interested in social cognition have often explored the limitations of everyday judgment.

"Many complain about their memory; few about their judgment."

—La Rochefoucauld

THE INFORMATION AVAILABLE FOR SOCIAL COGNITION

Social cognition depends first of all on information. Understanding other people depends on accurate information; but sometimes people have little or no information on which to base their assessments, sometimes the available information is misleading, and sometimes the way that they acquire information affects their thinking unduly. Each of these circumstances presents special challenges to achieving an accurate understanding of others.

Minimal Information: Inferring Personality from Physical Appearance

Sometimes people have very little information on which to base a judgment, but that rarely stops them from making inferences about a person or situation. Consider the impressions we form of complete strangers based on the briefest glances. One of the most interesting things about such impressions is how quickly we make them. The term *snap judgment* exists for a reason. In a telling empirical demonstration of this fact, Janine Willis and Alex Todorov (2006) showed participants a large number of faces and had them rate how attractive, aggressive, likable, trustworthy, and competent each person seemed. Some participants were given as much time as they wanted to make each rating, and their estimates were used as the standard of comparison—as the most confident impressions an individual could form based solely on photographs. Other participants were asked to make the same ratings, but after seeing each face for only a second, half a second, or a tenth of a second. How well did these hurried judgments correspond with the more reflective assessments? As you can see in **Table 4.1**, remarkably well. A great deal of what we conclude about people based on their faces is determined almost instantaneously.

Perceiving Trust and Dominance What is it that people so quickly think they see in another's face? To find out, Todorov and his colleagues (Todorov, Said, Engell, & Oosterhof, 2008) had participants rate a large number of photographs of different

---

TABLE 4.1 Correlations between Time-Constrained Trait Judgments Based on Facial Appearance and Judgments Made without Time Constraints

Trait Judgment	EXPOSURE TIME		
	100 ms	500 ms	1,000 ms
Trustworthiness	0.73	0.66	0.74
Competence	0.52	0.67	0.59
Likability	0.59	0.57	0.63
Aggressiveness	0.52	0.56	0.59
Attractiveness	0.69	0.57	0.66

Note: All correlations were significant, $p < 0.001$.

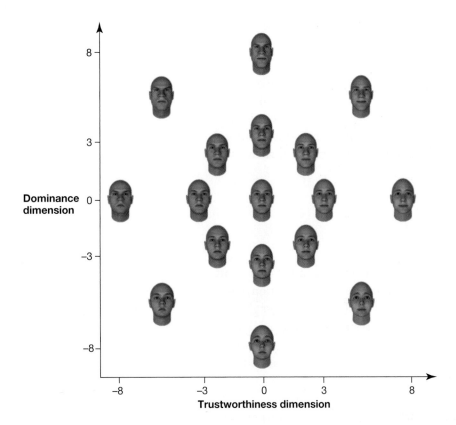

FIGURE 4.1 Judging Faces
Computer-generated faces showing variation on the two independent dimensions of trustworthiness (x-axis) and dominance (y-axis).

faces, all with neutral expressions, on the personality dimensions people most often spontaneously mention when describing faces. When they looked at how all these judgments correlated with one another, they found that two dimensions tend to stand out. One is a positive-negative dimension, involving such assessments as whether someone is seen as trustworthy or untrustworthy, aggressive or not aggressive. The other dimension centers around power, involving such assessments as whether someone seems confident or bashful, dominant or submissive. It appears, then, that people are set to make highly functional judgments about others—whether they should be approached or avoided (dimension 1) and where they are likely to stand in a status or power hierarchy (dimension 2). Todorov has used computer models to generate faces that represent various combinations of these two dimensions, including faces that are more extreme on each trait dimension than would ever be encountered in real life (**Figure 4.1**). In these faces, we can see the hypermasculine features, such as a very pronounced jaw, that make someone look dominant and the features, such as the shape of the eyebrows and eye socket, that make someone look trustworthy.

If you look at the faces that are seen as trustworthy and not dominant, you'll notice that the trustworthy, nondominant faces tend to look like baby faces. Indeed, extensive research by Leslie Zebrowitz and her colleagues has shown that adults with such baby-faced features as large round eyes, a large forehead, high eyebrows, and a rounded, relatively small chin are assumed to possess many of the characteristics associated with the very young (Berry & Zebrowitz-McArthur, 1986; Zebrowitz & Montepare, 2005). They are judged to be relatively weak, naive, and submissive, whereas those with small eyes, a small forehead, and an angular, prominent chin tend to be judged as strong, competent, and dominant (**Figure 4.2**).

Theoretically, it makes sense that people would consider adults with baby faces to be relatively harmless and helpless. The renowned ethologist Konrad Lorenz (1950) speculated that the cuteness of the young in many mammalian species triggers a hardwired, automatic reaction that helps ensure that the young and helpless receive adequate care. The automatic nature of our response to infantile features makes it more likely that we would overgeneralize and come to see even adults with such features as trustworthy and friendly. These assessments have dramatic implications: baby-faced individuals receive more favorable treatment as defendants in court (Zebrowitz & McDonald, 1991) but have a harder time being seen as appropriate for "adult" jobs such as banking (Zebrowitz, Tenenbaum, & Goldstein, 1991).

FIGURE 4.2 You Be the Subject: Personality Ratings Based on Appearance

Review these photos and circle where you think each person would fall on the personality scales below.

Personality Rankings

Weak	1	2	3	4	5	6	7	8	9	10	**Strong**
Naive	1	2	3	4	5	6	7	8	9	10	**Competent**
Submissive	1	2	3	4	5	6	7	8	9	10	**Dominant**

Weak	1	2	3	4	5	6	7	8	9	10	**Strong**
Naive	1	2	3	4	5	6	7	8	9	10	**Competent**
Submissive	1	2	3	4	5	6	7	8	9	10	**Dominant**

Results: If you are like most people, you judged the person in the top photo (which is more "babyish" according to the criteria used by Zebrowitz et al.) to be lower on these personality dimensions than the person in the bottom photo.

The Accuracy of Snap Judgments How accurate are the snap judgments we make of people based on their appearance or upon witnessing very brief samples of their behavior? Are people with baby faces, for example, really more likely to be weak or submissive? It's easy to imagine how being treated by others as weak and submissive might encourage something of a dependent disposition. It's also easy to imagine how a strong jaw might elicit deference from others, thereby encouraging a forceful, dominant stance toward the world. But are the facial features people associate with different personality traits valid cues to those traits?

That question awaits a fully satisfactory answer. The current evidence is mixed. Some investigators report moderately high correlations between the judgments made about people based on their facial appearance and those individuals' own reports of how approachable, extraverted, and powerful they are (Berry, 1991; Berry & Brownlow, 1989; Penton-Voak, Pound, Little, & Perrett, 2006). But similar studies have found no connection between judgments based on facial appearance and self-reports of agreeableness and conscientiousness (Pound, Penton-Voak, & Brown, 2007). And when behavioral observations rather than self-ratings are used as the criterion of accuracy, evidence that people can accurately assess other people's personalities based on facial appearance alone is even harder to find (Zebrowitz, Andreoletti, Collins, Lee, & Blumenthal, 1998; Zebrowitz, Voinescu, & Collins, 1996). Perhaps the fairest summary of current research in this area is that people's snap judgments about facial appearance may hold a kernel of truth, but it is a very small kernel.

Sometimes, however, it is more important to predict not what a person's true personality is, but rather what other people in general think. In these cases, the pertinent question boils down to how well snap judgments predict more considered consensus opinion. And the evidence indicates that they predict rather well. For example, in one study, participants were shown, for 1 second, pictures of the Republican and Democratic candidates in U.S. congressional elections and asked to indicate which candidates looked more competent. Those judged to be more competent by most of the participants won 69 percent of the races (Todorov, Mandisodza, Goren, & Hall, 2005). The person judged to be more competent might not actually be more competent; what matters in predicting the outcome of elections is not what is really true, but what the electorate believes to be true.

In another line of research, participants were shown "thin slices" of professors' performance in the classroom (that is, three 10-second silent video clips) and asked to rate the professors on a variety of dimensions, such as how anxious, competent, active, professional, and warm they seemed. A composite of these relatively quick assessments correlated significantly with students' evaluations of their professors at the end of the semester (Ambady & Rosenthal, 1993). Whether individual professors who are evaluated by their students as warm and competent actually are warm and competent can't be known, but judgments based on very brief exposure to the professors' behavior in the classroom predicted students' end-of-semester evaluations rather well.

Misleading Firsthand Information: Pluralistic Ignorance

Some of the information we have about the world, including our immediate impressions of others, comes to us through direct experience. The rest comes to us secondhand, through gossip, news accounts, biographies, textbooks, and so on. In many cases, the information collected firsthand is more accurate because it has the advantage of not having been filtered by someone else, who might slant things in a particular direction. But firsthand experiences can also be deceptive, as when we are inattentive to information about events that occur before our eyes or when we misconstrue such events. Our own experience can also be unrepresentative, as when we judge what the students are like at a given university from the one student we encounter during a tour of the campus or we conclude what "the people" are like in a foreign country from the few we encounter at hotels, restaurants, or museums.

Finally, some of the firsthand information we acquire is information we extract from other people's behavior. But people's behavior sometimes springs from a desire to create an impression that is not a true reflection of their beliefs or traits, and such discrepancies can lead to predictable errors in judgment. Consider the following familiar scenario (Miller & McFarland, 1991): A professor finishes a discussion of a difficult topic by asking, "Are there any questions?" Many students are completely mystified, but no hands are raised. The befuddled students conclude that everyone else understands the material and that they alone are confused.

This is just one example of a phenomenon known as **pluralistic ignorance**. The phenomenon arises whenever people act in ways that conflict with their private beliefs because of a concern for the social consequences. It is embarrassing to admit that you did not understand a lecture when you suspect that everyone

pluralistic ignorance Misperception of a group norm that results from observing people who are acting at variance with their private beliefs out of a concern for the social consequences—actions that reinforce the erroneous group norm.

else did. However, when everyone follows that logic, an illusion is created and everyone misperceives the group norm. People conclude from the illusory group consensus that they are deviant, and this misperception reinforces the difficulty of acting in accordance with what they really believe.

Pluralistic ignorance is particularly common in situations where "toughness" is valued, leading people to be afraid to show their kinder, gentler impulses. Gang members, for example, have been known privately to confess their objections to brutal initiation procedures and the lack of concern for human life, but they are afraid to say so because of the fear of being ridiculed by their peers. The result is that few of them realize how many of their fellow gang members share their private reservations (Matza, 1964).

Nicole Shelton and Jennifer Richeson (2005) examined another form of pluralistic ignorance, one with profound implications for interactions between members of different ethnic groups. The researchers predicted that individuals might worry that someone from another ethnic group would not be interested in talking to them. Initiating conversation would therefore seem risky, something they might want to avoid due to fear of being rejected. As a result, no opening gesture is made and no contact is established. But how do people interpret the missed opportunity? When Shelton and Richeson asked students a series of focused questions to probe this issue, they found that although the students tended to attribute their own failure to initiate contact to their fear of rejection, they assumed that the other person didn't initiate contact because of a lack of interest in establishing friendships across ethnic lines. And when both people assume the other is not interested, neither one makes the effort to become friends.

Misleading Secondhand Information

Do you believe that global warming is caused by humans? That Walt Disney was anti-Semitic? That your roommate's father is a good parent? Different people will have different answers to such questions, of course. But their different responses are alike in one important respect: all are based to a large extent on secondhand information. Few of us have any firsthand knowledge of the links between industrialization and climatological data. None of us knows firsthand what Walt Disney thought about Jews. Similarly, for most people, knowledge of their roommate's father is restricted to whatever stories the roommate has told about him.

Because so many of our judgments are based on secondhand information, a comprehensive understanding of social cognition requires an analysis of how accurate this information is likely to be. What are some of the variables that influence the accuracy of secondhand information? What factors reduce the reliability of secondhand information, and when are these factors likely to come into play?

Ideological Distortions Transmitters of information often have an ideological agenda—a desire to foster certain beliefs or behaviors in others—that leads them to accentuate some elements of a story and suppress others. Sometimes such motivated distortion is relatively "innocent": the person relaying the message fervently believes in it but chooses to omit certain inconvenient details that might detract from its impact. For example, when prepping Harry Truman for his 1947 speech on the containment of the Soviet Union, Undersecretary of State Dean Acheson remarked that it was necessary to be "clearer than the truth."

"Here it is—the plain, unvarnished truth. Varnish it."

Of course, not all distortions are so innocent. People often knowingly provide distorted accounts for the express purpose of misleading. Republicans trumpet all manner of misleading statistics to make the Democrats look bad, and the Democrats do likewise to the Republicans. In areas of intense ethnic strife, such as Kashmir, Congo, Gaza, and Rwanda, all sides wildly exaggerate their own righteousness and inflate tales of atrocities committed against them (even though the reality is bad enough).

Distortions in the Service of Entertainment: Overemphasis on Bad News One of the most pervasive reasons for distortion in secondhand accounts is the desire to entertain. On a small scale, this happens in the stories people tell one another, sometimes exaggerating to make them more interesting. Being trapped in an elevator with 20 people for an hour is more interesting than being trapped with 6 people for 15 minutes. So we round up, generously.

On a larger scale, the desire to entertain distorts the messages people receive through the mass media. One way that print and broadcast media can attract an audience is to report— indeed, overreport—negative, violent, and sensational events. Bad news tends to be more newsworthy than good news—or, as the news world puts it, "If it bleeds, it leads."

To be sure, the media provide a distorted view of reality. In the world as seen through the media, 80 percent of all crime is violent; in the real world, only 20 percent is violent (Center for Media and Public Affairs, 2000; Marsh, 1991; Sheley & Askins, 1981). In addition, news coverage of crime does not correlate with the rise and fall of the crime rate. There is just as much coverage during the best of times as there is during the worst of times (Garofalo, 1981; Windhauser, Seiter, & Winfree, 1991). The world as presented in motion pictures and television dramas is even more violent (Gerbner, Gross, Morgan, & Signorielli, 1980).

Positive and Negative Information in the Media
The media are more likely to report negative than positive information because the public seems more interested in the negative. The media thoroughly covered the devastation left by the 2011 earthquake in Japan. But people learned much less about relief efforts to help the victims and the way the Japanese helped one another, as shown in this photo where ordinary citizens carry elderly people to a shelter.

Effects of the Bad-News Bias The most frequently voiced concern about the bad-news bias is that exposure to such a distorted view of reality can lead people to believe they are more at risk of victimization than they really are. To find out whether this concern is valid, investigators have conducted surveys that ask people how much television they watch and then ask them questions about the prevalence of crime (for example, "How likely do you think it is that you or one of your close friends will have their house broken into during the next year?" or "If a child were to play alone in a park each day for a month, what do you think that child's chances are of being the victim of a violent crime?").

Such studies have consistently found a positive correlation between the amount of time spent watching television and the fear of victimization. As with all correlational studies, however, this finding by itself is difficult to interpret. Perhaps there is something about the kind of people who watch a lot of television—besides their television habits—that makes them feel so vulnerable. To address this problem, researchers have collected a variety of other measures (income, gender, race, residential location) and examined whether the findings hold up when these other variables are statistically controlled. When this is done, an interesting pattern emerges. The correlation between television-viewing habits and perceived vulnerability is substantially reduced among people living in low-crime neighborhoods, but it remains strong among those living in high-crime areas (Doob & MacDonald, 1979; Gerbner et al., 1980). People who live in dangerous areas and do not watch much television feel safer than their neighbors who watch a lot. Thus the violence depicted on television can make the world appear to be a dangerous place, especially when the televised images are similar to certain aspects of a person's environment.

TV Violence and Belief in Victimization Viewing crime shows such as *Dexter* makes people feel unsafe. People who don't watch much TV feel safer than those living in the same neighborhood who do watch TV frequently.

Differential Attention to Positive and Negative Information The tendency of the news media to hype bad news raises a more fundamental psychological question: Why is it in the media's interest to do so? Are audiences simply more interested in, titillated by, or receptive to negative information? The answer seems to be yes: even if positive and negative information are presented in equal measure, they do not have symmetrical effects (see Chapter 7).

Consider the following situation: You have just delivered a speech in a class on rhetoric. Seven of your classmates compliment you on your presentation; one comments that your introduction lacked punch. If you are like most people, you will find yourself obsessed with the one negative comment, even though it was outnumbered by the complimentary remarks.

This all-too-common reaction reflects a pervasive human tendency that has implications for our very survival. That is, we may be more attentive to negative information than to positive information because the former has more implications for our well-being. Some negative events constitute threats to survival and therefore need to be attended to quickly and thoroughly. Organisms that fail to do so put themselves at risk. To be sure, many positive events, such as eating, also have survival implications, but they are usually not as urgent. A morsel of food not eaten now can be eaten later; a predator that is not avoided now never will be. The result is that people may be more vigilant for potential threats than for potential benefits (Dijksterhuis & Aarts, 2003; Hansen & Hansen, 1988; Pratto & John, 1991; see also Baumeister, Bratslavsky, Finkenauer, & Vohs, 2001; Forgas, 1992; Rozin & Royzman, 2001).

 The quality of people's judgments derives in part from the quality of the information on which their judgments are based. Sometimes we have very little information at our disposal, as when we must make snap judgments about other people based only on their physical appearance and the tiniest samples of their behavior. Research indicates that the snap judgments people make show remarkable agreement with one another. The information available to us for closer examination may contain a number of potential biases. Even firsthand information can be biased, as when people behave in ways that do not reflect their true attitudes. Information received secondhand can also lead to errors, as when communicators distort information in the interest of profit or ideology. We are inclined to attend more to threatening stimuli than to unthreatening stimuli, and this bias may account for the media's overreporting of negative, violent, and sensational stories.

HOW INFORMATION IS PRESENTED

To understand the powerful impact of how information is presented, we only need to consider the marketing and advertising of products. In an economy of abundance, companies can easily produce enough to satisfy the needs of society, but they find it useful to stimulate sufficient "need" so that there will be a larger demand for their products. By manipulating the messages people receive about various products through marketing, producers hope to influence consumers' buying impulses. The key to successful marketing, in turn, is not simply the selection of *what* information to present, but *how* to present it. It is an article of faith among advertisers that the way information is presented has a powerful influence on what people think and do.

Social psychologists have confirmed the validity of this conviction, finding time and time again that slight variations in the presentation of information—*how* it is presented and even *when* it is presented—can have profound effects on people's judgments.

Order Effects

How happy are you with your life in general? How many dates have you been on in the past month?

If you are like most people, there may have been some connection, but not a strong one, between your responses to the two questions. After all, there is much more to life than dating. Indeed, when survey respondents were asked these two questions in this order, the correlation between their responses was only 0.32.

But when another group of respondents was asked the two questions in the opposite order, the correlation between their responses was more than twice as strong—0.67. Asking about their recent dating history in the first question made them very aware of how that part of their life was going, which then had a notable effect on how they answered the second question (Strack, Martin, & Schwarz, 1988; see also Haberstroh, Oyserman, Schwarz, Kiihnen, & Ji, 2002; Schwarz, Strack, & Mai 1991; Tourangeau, Rasinski, & Bradburn, 1991).

Results such as these provide striking confirmation of something many people grasp intuitively—namely, that the order in which items are presented can have a powerful influence on judgment. That is why we all worry so much about whether we should go on first or last in any kind of performance. Sometimes the information presented first exerts the most influence, a phenomenon known as a **primacy effect**. On other occasions, the information presented last has the most impact, a phenomenon known as a **recency effect**.

Order effects are not limited to public performances and opinion polls, of course, but are pervasive in everyday social life. In one study, Solomon Asch (1946) asked people to evaluate a hypothetical individual described in the following terms: intelligent, industrious, impulsive, critical, stubborn, and envious. The individual was rated favorably, no doubt because of the influence of the two very positive terms that began the list—*intelligent* and *industrious*. A second group read the same trait adjectives in the opposite order and formed a much less favorable impression. Thus there was a substantial primacy effect. Traits presented at the beginning of the list had more impact than those presented later on. Etiquette books (and your parents) are right: first impressions are crucial.

Order effects arise for a number of reasons. Some arise because of information-processing limitations. Primacy effects, for example, often result from a tendency to pay great attention to stimuli presented early on, but then to lose focus during the presentation of later items. In Asch's experiment, for example, it is impossible to miss that the person described in the first list is intelligent and industrious; but once an initial positive impression is formed, it is easy to gloss over the person's stubbornness and envy. Recency effects, in contrast, typically result when the last items are easiest to recall. Information remembered obviously receives greater weight than information forgotten, so later items sometimes exert more influence on judgment than information presented earlier.

Order effects also arise because the initial information affects how later information is construed. All of the traits in Asch's experiment have different shades of meaning, and how each is construed depends on the information already encountered. Take the word *stubborn*. When it follows positive traits, such as *intelligent* and *industrious*, people interpret it charitably, as steadfast or determined. In contrast, when it follows *envious*, it is seen more negatively, as closed-minded or rigid (Asch & Zukier, 1984; Biernat, Manis, & Kobrynowicz, 1997; Hamilton & Zanna, 1974; Higgins & Rholes, 1976).

Framing Effects

Order effects like those just discussed are a type of **framing effect**. That is, the way information is presented, including the order of presentation, can "frame" the way it is processed and understood. Asking survey respondents first about how many dates they have had recently invites them to consider this information when evaluating how happy they are with their lives in general.

Order effects are a type of "pure" framing effect. The frame of reference is changed even though the content of the information is exactly the same in the two versions; only the order is different. Consider the (probably apocryphal)

"It's not just compared to the table, damn it. This is a small portion."

story of the monk whose request to smoke while he prayed was met with a disapproving stare by his superior. When he mentioned this to a friend, he was told: "Ask a different question. Ask if you can pray while you smoke." The request is the same in both versions. But there is a subtle difference in the frame of reference. The latter presupposes smoking; the former does not.

Spin Framing Framing effects are not limited to the order in which information is presented. Advertisers, for example, try to induce consumers to frame a buying decision in terms favorable to the product being advertised. They do so by using what might be called spin framing, a less pure form of framing that varies the content, not just the order, of what is presented. A company with a competitive edge in quality will introduce information that frames the issue as one of quality. Another company with an edge in price will feature information that frames the issue as one of savings.

Participants in political debates likewise try to frame the discussion by spinning, or highlighting some aspects of the relevant information and not others. Thus we hear advocates of different positions talk of "pro-choice" versus "the right to life," "terrorists" versus "freedom fighters," "illegal aliens" versus "undocumented workers," even "torture" versus "enhanced interrogation." The power of such terms to frame the relevant issues led the United States in 1947 to change the name of the *War* Department to the more benign-sounding *Defense* Department.

Politicians (and some polling organizations with a political mission) also engage in spin framing when they conduct opinion polls to gather support for their positions. People are more likely to say they are in favor of repealing a "death" tax than an "inheritance" tax. And asking people whether they are in favor of "tax relief" is almost guaranteed to elicit strong support because the very word *relief* implies that taxes are a burden that one needs relief from (Lakoff, 2004). Shading survey questions in a particular way has been shown to influence public

Spin Framing Is this U.S. soldier in Afghanistan a "liberator" or a member of an "occupying army"? The words used to describe him highlight different information, which affects how people react to him.

opinion dramatically on a host of policy issues. Because it is so easy to slant public opinion questions in a particular direction, it is important to know who sponsored a particular poll, as well as the exact wording of the questions. As former Israeli Prime Minister Shimon Peres noted, opinion polls are "like perfume—nice to smell, dangerous to swallow."

Positive and Negative Framing Nearly everything in life is a mixture of good and bad. Ice cream tastes great, but it is full of saturated fat. Loyalty is a virtue, but it can make a person blind to another's faults. The mixed nature of most things means that they can be described, or framed, in ways that emphasize the good or the bad, with predictable effects on people's judgments. A piece of meat described as 75 percent lean is considered more appealing than one described as 25 percent fat (Levin & Gaeth, 1988), and students feel much safer using a condom described as having a 90 percent success rate than one described as having a 10 percent failure rate (Linville, Fischer, & Fischhoff, 1993). Note that exactly the same information is provided in each frame (pure framing); only the focus is different. Note also that there is no "correct" frame. It is every bit as valid to state that a piece of meat is 75 percent lean as it is to state that it is 25 percent fat. Similarly, consider **Figure 4.3**: if you are like most people, you would probably be willing to pay much more to restore the forest than you would to grow more trees.

These sorts of framing effects influence judgments and decisions of the greatest consequence, even among individuals with considerable expertise on the topic in question. In one study, for example, over 400 physicians were asked whether they would recommend surgery or radiation for patients diagnosed with a certain type of cancer. Some were told that of 100 previous patients who had the surgery, 90 lived through the postoperative period, 68 were still alive after a year, and 34 were still alive after five years. Eighty-two percent of these physicians recommended surgery. Others were given exactly the same information, but it was framed in different language: that 10 died during surgery or the postoperative period, 32 had died by the end of the first year, and 66 had died by the end of five years. Only 56 percent of the physicians given the information in this form recommended surgery (McNeil, Pauker, Sox, & Tversky, 1982).

Because negative information tends to attract more attention and have greater psychological impact than positive information (Baumeister et al., 2001; Rozin & Royzman, 2001), information framed in negative terms tends to elicit a stronger response. To some extent, the results just described reflect that tendency. Ten people dying sounds more threatening than 90 out of 100 surviving. More direct

(A) Positive framing: How much would you pay to grow more trees?

(B) Negative framing: How much would you pay to restore what has been lost?

FIGURE 4.3 Positive and Negative Framing How information is framed has a powerful influence on the responses it elicits. Because negative information typically has greater impact, people tend to be more inclined to pay more to restore what was lost (B) than to bring about the same benefit anew (A).

support for this idea comes from studies that have examined people's reactions to losses versus unrealized gains (Tversky & Kahneman, 1981). People hate losing things much more than failing to have them in the first place.

Temporal Framing

Imagine that one of your friends e-mails you today and asks if you can come over next Saturday at 9:00 a.m. to help him move. You're free that day and he's a good friend, so of course you say you'll help him out. Now imagine that on a Saturday morning at 8:30 a.m., your friend e-mails to ask if you can come over in half an hour and help him move. It's cold out and you still feel sleepy, so you write back saying you're not feeling well—or maybe you don't write back at all, pretending that you never saw the e-mail. Why were you so eager to help when asked a week in advance, but so reluctant when asked on the moving day?

You probably have experienced similar feelings of being at odds with a decision made by an earlier version of yourself. Your earlier self might have thought it was a good idea to take an extra-heavy course load this semester, but now your present self is frazzled, sleep deprived, and overworked. How could you have thought this would be a good idea? Or an earlier self might have thought that an Outward Bound experience would be the perfect way to spend a chunk of your precious summer vacation, but once you are up in the mountains, the bad food and the onslaught of mosquitoes makes you wonder what you were thinking earlier.

Why do things often seem like brilliant ideas at one time and terrible ideas at another? The key to understanding these sorts of disagreements within ourselves is to recognize that actions and events come framed within a particular time perspective. They belong to the distant past, the present moment, the immediate future, and so on. And according to **construal level theory**, the temporal perspective from which people view events has important and predictable implications for how they construe them (Fiedler, 2007; Liberman, Sagristano, & Trope, 2002; Trope & Liberman, 2003, 2010). Any action or event can be thought of at a low level of abstraction, rich in concrete detail—for example, chewing your food, carrying a friend's chair up the stairs, or giving a panhandler a dollar. But it can also be thought of at a higher level of abstraction, rich in meaning but stripped of detail—dining out, helping a friend move, or being generous. It turns out that we tend to think of distant events, those from long ago or far off in the future, in abstract terms and of events close at hand in concrete terms. Next week you'll be dining out, or helping a friend move; but right now you're chewing your food, or later this afternoon you'll be carrying your friend's chair up the stairs.

This difference in construal has important implications for what people think and how they act in their everyday lives, and it explains inconsistent preferences. Things that sound great in the abstract are sometimes less thrilling when fleshed out in all their concrete detail, so we regret making some commitments. We think of a heavy course load a year from now as "furthering my education" or "expanding my horizons." That sounds great, so we accept the challenge. But we experience the heavy course load during the semester itself as "studying" or "spending time in the library," which is less inspiring, so we question the earlier decision to take on this burden. But sometimes the abstract level can be less desirable than the concrete, producing the opposite sort of inconsistency. You might swear that you'll stick to your diet no matter what (because you don't want to "pig out"), yet when

construal level theory A theory that outlines the relationship between psychological distance and the concreteness versus abstraction of thought. Psychologically distant actions and events are thought about in abstract terms; actions and events that are close at hand are thought about in concrete terms.

you're standing in front of the buffet, you find it so easy to indulge (because you're only "sampling the various options").

This influence of near and far events applies to dimensions other than time (Trope & Liberman, 2010). Things can be close or far in space (at your college campus versus in Barbados) and close or far socially (something that will happen to you versus something that will happen to a distant acquaintance). Far or near on these other dimensions has the same effect on construal as far or near in time. For example, NYU students tended to think of "climbing a tree" as "holding onto branches" when the climbing was to take place 3 miles from campus, but as "getting a good view" when it was to take place 3,000 miles away on the West Coast. Similarly, "going to the dentist" was seen as "getting a cavity filled" nearby but as "protecting one's teeth" in far-off Los Angeles (Fujita, Henderson, Eng, Trope, & Liberman, 2006).

 The way information is presented, including the order in which it is presented, can affect judgment. Primacy effects occur when information presented first has more impact than information presented later, often because the initial information influences the way later information is construed. Recency effects occur when information presented later has more impact, especially when later information is easier to remember than earlier information. People are susceptible to many framing effects in information presentation. Sometimes communicators deliberately spin information so as to influence our judgment by changing the frame of reference. The temporal framing of an event—whether it will occur soon or far in the future—also influences how we think of it; far-off events are construed in more abstract terms, and imminent events are construed more concretely.

HOW WE SEEK INFORMATION

Suppose a friend gives you a bunch of potted plants for your dorm room or apartment, saying, "I'm not sure, but they might need frequent watering. You should check that out." How would you do that? If you are like most people, you would water them often and see how they do. What you would *not* do is give a lot of water to some, very little to the others, and compare the results.

Confirmation Bias

When evaluating a proposition (a plant needs frequent watering; a generous allowance spoils a child; Hispanics place a high value on family life), people more readily, reliably, and vigorously seek out evidence that would support the proposition rather than information that would contradict the proposition. This is known as the **confirmation bias** (Klayman & Ha, 1987; Skov & Sherman, 1986). In one study that examined this tendency, one group of participants was asked to determine whether working out the day before an important tennis match makes a player more likely to win. Another group was asked to determine whether working out the day before a match makes a player more likely to lose. Both groups could examine any of four types of information before coming to a conclusion— the number of players in a sample who worked out the day before and won their

confirmation bias The tendency to test a proposition by searching for evidence that would support it.

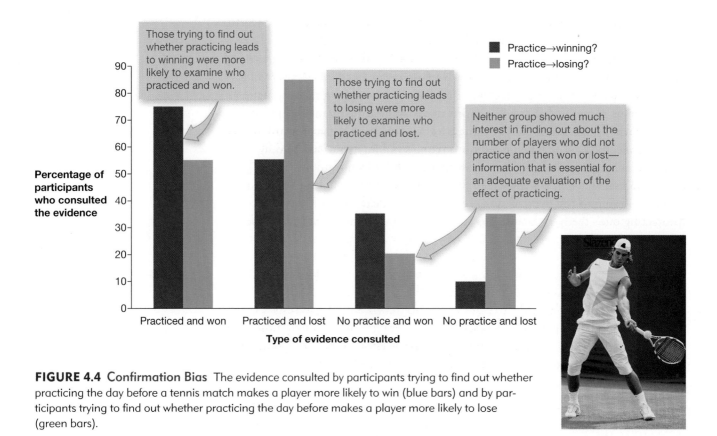

FIGURE 4.4 Confirmation Bias The evidence consulted by participants trying to find out whether practicing the day before a tennis match makes a player more likely to win (blue bars) and by participants trying to find out whether practicing the day before makes a player more likely to lose (green bars).

match, the number of players who worked out and lost, the number of players who did not work out the day before and won, and the number of players who did not work out and lost. In fact, all four types of information are needed to make a valid determination. You have to calculate and compare the success rate among those who did work out the day before the match with the success rate among those who did not. If the first ratio is higher than the second, then working out the day before increases the chances of winning.

But participants tended not to seek out all of the necessary information. Instead, as **Figure 4.4** makes clear, participants were especially interested in examining information that could potentially confirm the proposition they were investigating. Those trying to find out whether practicing leads to winning were more interested in the number of players who practiced and won than were those trying to find out whether practicing leads to losing—and vice versa (Crocker, 1982).

This tendency to seek out confirming information can lead to all sorts of false beliefs because a person can find supportive evidence for almost anything (Gilovich, 1991; Shermer, 1997). Are people more likely to come to harm when there is a full moon? There will certainly be many months in which hospital ERs are unusually busy during the full moon. Do optimistic people live longer? You can probably think of some very elderly people who are unusually upbeat. But evidence consistent with a proposition is not enough to draw a firm conclusion because there might be even more evidence against it—more days with empty ERs during the full moon, more pessimists living long lives ("grumpy old men"). The danger of the confirmation bias, then, is that if we look mainly for one type of evidence, we are likely to find it. To truly test a proposition, we must seek out the evidence against it as well as the evidence for it.

In the social realm, the confirmation bias often leads people unwittingly to ask questions that shape the answers they get, thereby providing illusory support for what they're trying to find out. In a particularly telling study, one group of participants was asked to interview someone and determine whether the target was an extravert; another group was asked to determine whether the target was an introvert (Snyder & Swann, 1978). Participants selected their interview questions from a list provided. Those charged with determining whether the target was an extravert tended to ask questions that focused on sociability ("In what situations are you most talkative?"), whereas those charged with determining whether the target was an introvert tended to ask questions that focused on social withdrawal ("In what situations do you wish you could be more outgoing?"). Of course, if you ask people about times when they are most sociable, they are likely to answer in ways that will make them seem relatively outgoing, even if they are not. And if you ask about their social reticence, they will almost certainly answer in ways that make them seem relatively introverted—again, even if they are not. In a powerful demonstration of this tendency, the investigators tape-recorded the interview sessions, edited out the questions, and then played the responses to another, uninformed set of participants. These latter participants rated those who had been interviewed by someone testing for extraversion as more outgoing than those who had been interviewed by someone testing for introversion.

Motivated Confirmation Bias

In the preceding examples—and fairly often in daily life—the individuals who fall prey to the confirmation bias feel no particular motivation to confirm a particular outcome. As far as they are concerned, they are simply testing a proposition. Even so, they end up engaging in a biased, and potentially misleading, search for evidence.

But sometimes, of course, people deliberately search for evidence that confirms their preferences or expectations. Someone who wants a given proposition to be true may energetically sift through the pertinent evidence in an effort to uncover information that confirms its validity. In such cases, information that supports what a person wants to be true is readily accepted, whereas information that contradicts what the person would like to believe is subjected to critical scrutiny and often discounted (Dawson, Gilovich, & Regan, 2002; Ditto & Lopez, 1992; Gilovich, 1983, 1991; Kruglanski & Webster, 1996; Kunda, 1990; Pyszczynski & Greenberg, 1987).

In one notable examination of this tendency, proponents and opponents of capital punishment read about studies of the death penalty's effectiveness as a deterrent to crime. Some read state-by-state comparisons purportedly showing that crime rates are not any lower in states with the death penalty than in states without the death penalty, but they also read about how crime rates within a few states went down as soon as the death penalty was put in place. Other participants read about studies showing the exact opposite: state-by-state comparisons that made the death penalty look effective and before-and-after comparisons that made it look ineffective. Those who favored the death penalty interpreted the evidence, whichever set they were exposed to, as strongly supporting their position. Those opposed to the death penalty saw just the opposite. Both sides jumped on the problems associated with the studies that contradicted their positions, but they readily embraced the studies that supported them. Their preferences tainted how they viewed the pertinent evidence (Lord, Ross, & Lepper, 1979).

 People's efforts to acquire needed information are often tainted by two pronounced types of confirmation bias. One type occurs when we look for evidence consistent with propositions or hypotheses we wish to evaluate. To evaluate propositions satisfactorily, however, it is necessary to examine evidence both for it and against it. The other type of confirmation bias occurs when we want a given proposition to be true, so we seek out evidence that confirms our beliefs or preferences and explain away evidence that contradicts them.

TOP-DOWN PROCESSING: USING SCHEMAS TO UNDERSTAND NEW INFORMATION

What is being described in the following paragraph?

> The procedure is quite simple. First you arrange things into different groups. Of course, one pile may be sufficient, depending on how much there is to do. If you have to go somewhere else due to lack of facilities, that is the next step; otherwise you are pretty well set. (Bransford & Johnson, 1973, p. 400)

Not so easy to figure out, is it? *What* is arranged into different groups? *What* facilities might be lacking? Most people find it difficult to understand what the paragraph is about. But suppose it had the title "Washing Clothes." Now read the paragraph again. Suddenly it is no longer so mystifying. Each sentence makes perfect sense when construed from the perspective of doing the laundry.

Understanding the paragraph involves using what we already know to make sense of new information. What we know about doing laundry helps us comprehend what it means to "arrange things into different groups" and to "go somewhere else due to lack of facilities." Similarly, what we know about human nature and about different contexts allows us to determine whether another person's tears are the product of joy or sadness. What we know about norms and customs enables us to decide whether a gesture is hostile or friendly.

Perceiving and understanding the world involves the simultaneous operation of **bottom-up** and **top-down processes**. Bottom-up processes consist of taking in relevant stimuli from the outside world—text on a page, gestures in an interaction, sound patterns at a cocktail party, and so on. At the same time, top-down processes filter and interpret bottom-up stimuli in light of preexisting knowledge and expectations. The meaning of stimuli is not passively recorded; it is actively *construed*.

Preexisting knowledge is necessary for understanding, and it is surely required for inferences and judgments. Indeed, as the laundry example makes clear, understanding and judgment are inextricably linked. They both involve going beyond currently available information and extrapolating from it. Psychologists who study inferences and judgments, then, have been interested in how people use their stored knowledge.

One principle psychologists have discovered is that stored information is not filed away bit by bit. Instead, information is stored in coherent configurations,

bottom-up processes "Data-driven" mental processing, in which an individual forms conclusions based on the stimuli encountered through experience.

top-down processes "Theory-driven" mental processing, in which an individual filters and interprets new information in light of preexisting knowledge and expectations.

or schemas, in which related information is stored together. Information about Hillary Rodham Clinton, secretary of state, is tightly connected to information about Hillary Rodham Clinton, Wellesley grad; Hillary Rodham Clinton, former First Lady; Hillary Rodham Clinton, presidential candidate; and Hillary Rodham Clinton, best-selling author (Bartlett, 1932; Markus, 1977; Nisbett & Ross, 1980; Schank & Abelson, 1977; Smith & Zarate, 1990). You no doubt have schemas for all sorts of things, such as a fast-food restaurant (chain, so-so food, bright primary colors for decor, limited choices, cheap), a party animal (boisterous, drinks to excess, exuberant but none-too-graceful dancer), and an action film (good guy establishes good guy credentials, bad guy gains the upper hand, good guy triumphs and bad guy perishes in eye-popping pyrotechnical finale).

The Influence of Schemas

The various schemas we all possess affect our judgments in many ways: by directing our attention, structuring our memories, and influencing our construals (Brewer & Nakamura, 1984; Hastie, 1981; Taylor & Crocker, 1981). Without schemas, our lives would be a buzzing confusion; but schemas can sometimes lead us to mischaracterize the world.

Attention Attention is selective. We cannot focus on everything, and the knowledge we bring to a given situation allows us to direct our attention to the most important elements and to ignore the rest. The extent to which our schemas and expectations guide our attention was powerfully demonstrated by an experiment in which participants watched a videotape of two "teams" of three people, each passing a basketball back and forth. The members of one team wore white shirts, and the members of the other team wore black shirts. Each participant was asked to count the number of passes made by the members of one of the teams. Forty-five seconds into the action, a person wearing a gorilla costume strolled into the middle of the action (**Figure 4.5**). Although a large black gorilla might seem hard to miss, only half the participants noticed it! The participants' schemas about what is likely to happen in a game of catch directed their attention so intently to some parts of the videotape that they failed to see a rather dramatic stimulus that they did not expect to see (Simons & Chabris, 1999).

Memory Because schemas influence attention, they also influence memory. We are most likely to remember those stimuli that have most captured our attention. Indeed, former *New York Times* science writer Daniel Goleman has referred to memory as "attention in the past tense" (Goleman, 1985). The influence of schemas on memory is also important for judgment—and hence subsequent action. After all, many judgments are not made immediately; rather, they are made later and based on information retrieved from memory.

Researchers have documented the impact of schemas on memory in many experiments (Fiske & Taylor, 1991; Hastie, 1981; Stangor & McMillan, 1992). In one study, students watched a videotape of a husband and wife having dinner together (Cohen, 1981). Half the students were told that the woman in the tape was a librarian, the other half that she was a waitress. The students later took a quiz that assessed their memory of various features of what they had witnessed. The central question was whether the students' memories were influenced by their stereotypes (schemas about particular groups in society) of librarians and

FIGURE 4.5 Scientific Method: Selective Attention

Hypothesis: Our expectations guide our attention, making it hard to see what we don't expect.

Research Method:

1. Participants watched a video of two teams passing a basketball back and forth.

2. The viewers were asked to count the number of times the basketball was passed by members of one of the teams.

3. Forty-five seconds into the action, a person wearing a gorilla costume strolled into the middle of the action.

© 2005, Daniel J. Simons

Results: Half of the participants did not notice the person in the gorilla costume.

CONCLUSION: We cannot focus on everything, so we direct our attention to what we believe is most important and ignore the rest.

waitresses. They were asked, for example, whether the woman was drinking wine (librarian stereotype) or beer (waitress stereotype) and whether she had received a history book (librarian) or romance novel (waitress) as a gift. The tape had been constructed to contain an equal number of items consistent and inconsistent with each stereotype.

Did students' preexisting knowledge affect what they recalled? It did indeed. Students who thought the woman was a librarian recalled librarian-consistent information more accurately than librarian-inconsistent information; those who thought she was a waitress recalled waitress-consistent information more accurately than waitress-inconsistent information. Information that fits a preexisting schema often enjoys an advantage in recall (Carli, 1999; Zadny & Gerard, 1974).

This study shows that schemas might influence memory by affecting the **encoding** of information—how information is filed away in memory—because schemas might affect what information people attend to and how they initially interpret and store that information. But schemas might also influence the **retrieval** of information, or how information is extracted from a storehouse of knowledge.

Social psychologists have good reason to believe that schemas influence encoding because we know that they direct attention. One way to find out whether schemas influence retrieval as well would be to provide people with a schema *after* they have been exposed to the relevant information, when it obviously cannot influence encoding. Many experiments have used this tactic. The typical result is that providing a schema after the relevant information has been encountered does not affect memory as much as providing it beforehand (Bransford & Johnson, 1973; Howard & Rothbart, 1980; Rothbart, Evans, & Fulero, 1979; Wyer, Srull, Gordon, & Hartwick, 1982; Zadny & Gerard, 1974). Nonetheless, occasionally schemas provided after information has been encountered do have a substantial

encoding Filing information away in memory based on what information is attended to and the initial interpretation of the information.

retrieval The extraction of information from memory.

effect (Anderson & Pichert, 1978; Carli, 1999; Cohen, 1981; Hirt, 1990). Thus the appropriate conclusion seems to be that schemas influence memory through their effect on both encoding and retrieval, but the effect on encoding is typically much stronger.

Construal Schemas affect not only what information we attend to and remember but also the way we interpret, or construe, that information. To understand how this works, meet Donald, who may seem to you like a contestant in an "Extreme" sports competition. Actually, Donald is a fictitious person who has been used as a stimulus in numerous experiments on the effect of prior knowledge on social judgment:

> Donald spent a great amount of his time in search of what he liked to call excitement. He had already climbed Mt. McKinley, shot the Colorado rapids in a kayak, driven in a demolition derby, and piloted a jet-powered boat—without knowing very much about boats. He had risked injury, and even death, a number of times. Now he was in search of new excitement. He was thinking, perhaps, he would do some skydiving or maybe cross the Atlantic in a sailboat. By the way he acted one could readily guess that Donald was well aware of his ability to do many things well. Other than business engagements, Donald's contacts with people were rather limited. He felt he didn't really need to rely on anyone. Once Donald made up his mind to do something it was as good as done no matter how long it might take or how difficult the going might be. Only rarely did he change his mind even when it might well have been better if he had. (Higgins, Rholes, & Jones, 1977, p. 145)

In one early study featuring Donald as the stimulus, students participated in what they thought were two unrelated experiments (Higgins et al., 1977). In the first, they were shown a number of trait words projected on a screen as part of a perception experiment. Half of the participants were shown the words *adventurous*, *self-confident*, *independent*, and *persistent* embedded in a set of ten traits. The other half were shown the words *reckless*, *conceited*, *aloof*, and *stubborn*. After completing the "perception" experiment, the participants moved on to the second study on "reading comprehension," in which they read the short paragraph about Donald and rated him on a number of trait scales. (The paragraph is intentionally ambiguous about whether Donald is an adventurous, appealing sort or a reckless, unappealing person.) The investigators were interested in whether the words that participants encountered in the first experiment would lead them to apply different schemas and thus affect their evaluations of Donald.

As the investigators expected, participants who had previously been exposed to the words *adventurous*, *self-confident*, *independent*, and *persistent* formed more favorable impressions of Donald than did those who had been exposed to the less flattering words. Thus participants' schemas about traits like adventurousness and recklessness influenced the kind of inferences they made about Donald.

The broader point is that information stored in the brain can influence how people construe new information. This is most likely to occur when the stimulus, like many of Donald's actions, is ambiguous (Trope, 1986). In such cases, we must rely more heavily on top-down processes to compensate for the inadequacies of the information obtained from the bottom up.

Behavior So far you've seen how schemas can influence people's attention, memory, and interpretations of information. Can they also influence behavior? The answer is a resounding yes. Many studies have shown that certain types of behavior are elicited automatically when people are exposed to stimuli in the environment that bring to mind a particular schema. In one especially notable experiment, described as an investigation of "language proficiency," participants were asked to perform a sentence completion task. They were given 30 sets of 5 words each and asked to form a grammatical English sentence using 4 of the 5 words. For half the participants, embedded within these 150 words were many that are stereotypically associated with the elderly—*gray, wrinkle, Florida, bingo,* and so on. These words were chosen to bring to mind the schema of the elderly among these participants. The remaining participants were exposed to neutral words that are not associated with the elderly, so their schema of the elderly was not primed. The experimenter then thanked the participants for their efforts, and the study, the participants believed, was over.

But it had just begun. A second experimenter covertly timed how long it took each participant to walk from the threshold of the laboratory to the elevator down the hall. The investigators had predicted that merely activating the concept of the elderly for some of the participants would make them walk more slowly down the hallway because "slow" is a trait associated with the elderly. Amazingly, it did. Participants who had performed the sentence completion task using numerous words associated with the elderly took 13 percent longer to walk to the elevator (Bargh et al., 1996; see also Cesario et al., 2006).

Further studies of this sort have found that similarly activating the trait of rudeness makes people behave more assertively (Bargh et al., 1996), and activating the goal of achievement leads people to persevere longer at difficult tasks (Bargh, Gollwitzer, Lee-Chai, Barndollar, & Trotschel, 2001). Playing German music in a liquor store appears to boost sales of German wine at the expense of French wine, whereas playing French music appears to boost sales of French wine—even if customers do not realize what type of music is being played (North, Hargreaves, & McKendrick, 1999).

In another set of demonstrations, Dutch social psychologists Ap Dijksterhuis and Ad van Knippenberg exposed students to stimuli meant to bring to mind the schema for a social group associated with intellectual accomplishment (professors) or the schema for a social group not noted for refined habits of mind (soccer hooligans). Those exposed to the professor cues subsequently performed better on a test of general knowledge than those shown cues associated with soccer hooligans (Dijksterhuis & van Knippenberg, 1998).

More remarkable still, Dijksterhuis, van Knippenberg, and their colleagues demonstrated that activating the stereotype of professor or supermodel led participants to perform in a manner *consistent* with the stereotype, but activating a

Priming Activating stereotypes like professor or supermodel may lead people to construe themselves along the lines of the stereotyped group and to act the way they think someone in the group would act. Activating a specific instance of the group, however, such as (A) Albert Einstein or (B) Claudia Schiffer, tends to have the opposite effect since people compare themselves to these specific people and feel that they aren't much like them at all.

specific (extreme) example of the stereotyped group (for example, Albert Einstein or Claudia Schiffer) led participants to perform in a manner *inconsistent* with the stereotype. That is, they performed worse on the general-knowledge test when Einstein was brought to mind and better when Claudia Schiffer was (Dijksterhuis & van Knippenberg, 1998). These results fit the general tendency for the activation of schemas to produce behavior in line with the schema in question because the activation affects construal. People think of themselves as more intelligent (and act that way) when viewing themselves—however implicitly—through the "lens" of a professor than they do when viewing themselves through the lens of a fashion model. The activation of *specific members* of a stereotyped group, in contrast, tends to yield behavior that contrasts with the stereotype in question (Herr, 1986; Schwarz & Bless, 1992). Individual examples tend to serve as standards of judgment—in this case, Einstein serves as a very high standard (making people feel unintelligent), and Claudia Schiffer serves as a relatively low standard (making people feel smart).

Which Schemas Are Activated and Applied?

In the librarian/waitress experiment described earlier, there is little doubt about which schema participants will apply to the information they encounter in the videotape. The experimenter informs them that the woman is a librarian (or waitress), and they know nothing else about her. It stands to reason, then, that they would view the videotape through the "lens" of their librarian (or waitress) schema. In real life, however, the situation is often more complicated. For instance, one might know that besides being a librarian, the woman is a triathlete, a Republican, and a gourmet cook. Which schema (or combination of schemas) is likely to be thought of, or "activated"?

Recent Activation Schemas can be brought to mind, or activated, in various ways. Recent activation is one of the most common and important ways of doing so. If a schema has been brought to mind recently, it tends to be more accessible and hence ready for use (Ford & Kruglanski, 1995; Herr, 1986; Sherman, Mackie, & Driscoll, 1990; Srull & Wyer, 1979, 1980; Todorov & Bargh, 2002). **Priming** is the term researchers typically use to refer to procedures that momentarily activate a particular schema.

Recall the "Donald" study conducted by Tory Higgins and his colleagues (Higgins et al., 1977). Participants who had previously been exposed to trait adjectives such as *adventurous* formed more favorable impressions of the fictional Donald than did those who had been exposed to adjectives such as *reckless*. By exposing participants to words implying adventurousness or recklessness, the researchers were trying to prime participants' schemas for the traits *adventurous* and *reckless*. Of course, schemas can be activated by stimuli other than words. People's judgments and behavior have been shown to be influenced by schemas primed by features of the surrounding environment (Aarts & Dijksterhuis, 2003; Gosling, Ko, Mannarelli, & Morris, 2002; Kay, Wheeler, Bargh, & Ross, 2004), cultural symbols, such as a country's flag (Carter, Ferguson, & Hassin, 2011; Ferguson & Hassin, 2007; Hassin, Ferguson, Shidlovsky, & Gross, 2007), the pursuit of a goal (Aarts, Gollwitzer, & Hassin, 2004), a significant other (Shah, 2003), feedback from one's own body (Jostmann, Lakens, & Schubert,

prime To momentarily activate a concept and hence make it accessible. (Also used as a noun—a stimulus presented to activate a concept.)

BOX 4.1 FOCUS ON EVOLUTION

Knowledge, Learned and Innate

Are schemas always attained by learning, or are at least some of them innate—prewired because they are so useful to all humans in all circumstances? This is one of the most enduring controversies in philosophy and psychology. Socrates believed that much knowledge is a priori, that is, prior to experience. His most famous attempt to show this principle was his quizzing of a stable boy whose answers, Socrates maintained, showed an innate understanding of the Pythagorean theorem. His demonstration has never convinced many people. The most famous philosopher of relatively modern times who endorsed the concept of a priori knowledge is Immanuel Kant, who maintained that concepts such as causality had to exist prior to experiential knowledge. In contrast, most philosophers over the last hundred years or so have presumed that all knowledge is derived from experience. A clear exception is Charles Sanders Peirce, who maintained that learning itself would be impossible without innate knowledge structures guiding us toward hypotheses that can be tested by experience.

Twentieth-century psychology was, in general, heavily opposed to the concept of a priori knowledge. A chief tenet of learning theory was that any stimulus could be connected to any other stimulus and result in learning. This is the psychological position the psychologist Steven Pinker has derided as the "blank slate" view of human nature. This view holds that all knowledge and belief are derived from experience. There exists at least one unquestioned exception to such a rule. John Garcia showed that all animals, including humans, who eat a food with a distinctive taste not previously experienced and who become ill as much as 24 hours later, will have a revulsion to that food in the future. Apparently there exists a knowledge structure, not dependent on experience, to the effect that "unusual foods followed by gastrointestinal upset are noxious and to be avoided." Others have maintained that there are many such knowledge structures. Some stimulus connections are readily learned because the organism is "prepared" to learn them (Seligman, 1970). Other connections cannot be learned, because the

organism is "counterprepared" to learn them. For example, pigeons will starve to death before they can learn that not pecking at a light will result in a food reward.

One exception to the blank-slate psychology of the twentieth century was Carl Jung, who held that certain "archetypes" such as the concept of initiation are universal and exist prior to experience. Another exception was the developmental psychologist Jean Piaget, who maintained that developmental stages of thought were universal, resulting in so-called formal operations including the rules of logic. Piaget believed that humans are prepared genetically to learn such rules of inference.

The topic remains a lively one for debate. Proponents of innate schemas insist that unguided learning is normally difficult or impossible, and opponents maintain that it is all too easy to wave one's hands and say that a given belief would have required genetically prepared knowledge structures.

2009; Lee & Schwarz, 2011), and even a passing smell (Holland, Hendricks, & Aarts, 2005).

Frequent Activation and Chronic Accessibility You may have noticed that people differ in the schemas they tend to use when evaluating others. College professors are often concerned with whether someone is smart, sales managers with whether someone is persuasive, and those involved in the entertainment business with whether someone has charisma. As these examples illustrate, the role of the evaluator or the context in which a target person is encountered often influences which traits or schemas are used. But sometimes the schema is simply determined by habit: if a person uses a particular schema frequently, it may become chronically accessible and therefore likely to be used still more frequently in the future. A frequently activated schema functions much like a recently activated one: its heightened accessibility increases the likelihood that it will be applied to understanding a new stimulus.

In one study that examined the impact of chronic accessibility on information processing, participants were recruited for two supposedly unrelated experiments (Higgins, King, & Mavin, 1982). In the first, they were simply asked to list the traits of five people—two male friends, two female friends, and themselves. This part of the experiment was designed to identify what schemas were most accessible for each participant. Any trait schema that was listed in three or more of a given participant's descriptions was considered a highly accessible, or chronically accessible, schema.

About two weeks later, the participants returned for the second, supposedly unrelated experiment and were greeted by a different experimenter. They were asked to read a brief hypothetical description of another person, but they did not know the description had been individually crafted for each participant to include certain behaviors reflecting some traits that were highly accessible for them and other behaviors reflecting less accessible traits. After reading the description, the participants were asked to write their own description of the type of person they thought the target person was. These descriptions were then scored for whether they included behaviors that exemplified the chronically accessible and relatively inaccessible traits for each participant. Consistent with the idea that people's chronically accessible schemas strongly influence their evaluations of others, participants' descriptions of the target person contained more behaviors reflecting their chronically accessible traits (55 percent) than behaviors exemplifying their less accessible traits (31 percent). The chronically accessible schemas each of us brings to a social encounter thus have a significant impact on how we perceive the encounter.

Consciousness of Activation: Necessary or Not? Carefully conducted interviews with participants at the end of many priming experiments have found that very few (and, in many cases, none) of them suspected that there was any connection between the two parts of the study—the initial priming phase and the subsequent judgment phase. This finding raises the question of how conscious a person must be of a stimulus for it to effectively prime a given schema. Research suggests a clear-cut answer: not at all. A great many studies have shown that stimuli presented outside of conscious awareness can prime a schema sufficiently to influence subsequent information processing (Bargh, 1996; Debner & Jacoby, 1994; Devine, 1989b; Draine & Greenwald, 1998; Ferguson, 2008; Ferguson, Bargh, & Nayak, 2005; Greenwald, Klinger, & Liu, 1989; Klinger, Burton, & Pitts, 2000; Lepore & Brown, 1997; Neuberg, 1988; Shah, 2003).

In one study, researchers showed a set of words to participants on a computer screen so quickly that it was impossible to discern what the words were (Bargh & Pietromonaco, 1982). (When participants in a control condition were asked simply to guess what each word was, they were unable to do so, guessing fewer than 1 percent of the words correctly.) Participants were shown either mainly hostile words (for example, *hate, whip, stab, hostile*) or mainly nonhostile words (for example, *water, long, together, every*). Immediately afterward, the researchers asked participants to read a short paragraph about an individual who had committed a number of moderately hostile acts and then to rate that person on a number of trait dimensions. The participants who had previously been exposed to predominantly hostile words rated the target person more negatively than did those exposed to predominantly nonhostile words. They did so, mind you, even though they were not consciously aware of the words to which they

subliminal Below the threshold of conscious awareness.

had been exposed. Thus schemas can be primed even when the presentation of the activating stimuli is **subliminal**—that is, below the threshold of conscious awareness.

Similarity, or Feature Matching

An activated schema cannot guide the interpretation of new information unless an association is made between the schema and the incoming information. But what determines whether an activated schema is applied and used to make sense of new information?

The most common determinant of whether a particular schema is applied and used in interpreting new information is the degree of similarity, or "fit," between critical features of the schema and the incoming stimulus (Andersen, Glassman, Chen, & Cole, 1995; Higgins & Brendl, 1995). Suppose you are taking a drive through the countryside and you see a rather large, formally dressed group of people assembled on a hill. Whether you apply a wedding or a funeral schema to help you interpret the scene will surely depend on whether they are wearing black or more festive attire, whether a supply of champagne is packed in ice, and so on. The features of the situation tell you what kind of situation it is, and then you apply the relevant schema to assist with further interpretation of what you encounter (Holyoak & Thagard, 1995; Read, 1984, 1987; Spellman & Holyoak, 1992).

One study illustrating this feature-matching process is similar to the "Donald" study described earlier, but with a twist (Banaji, Hardin, & Rothman, 1993). As in the earlier study, participants in this experiment were first exposed to written stimuli meant to activate a trait schema—in this case, participants' schema for dependence. Control participants were exposed to neutral stimuli. Afterward, participants were asked to form an impression of a target person as part of a supposedly unrelated reading comprehension task. The target was described as behaving in ways that were weakly associated with dependence. Participants rated the target on various dimensions, including dependence-related ones (for example, passive, cooperative). The additional twist in this study, though, was that the target was male for half the participants (Donald) but female for the other half (Donna). Previous priming studies would lead one to expect that participants

"But, seriously . . . "

The Availability Heuristic People often judge the likelihood of an event by how readily pertinent examples come to mind. (A) While tornadoes are equally common in Kansas and Nebraska, people tend to think that they are more common in Kansas because tornadoes in Kansas come more readily to mind thanks to our familiarity with (B) *The Wizard of Oz*, in which a tornado in Kansas whisks Dorothy and Toto to the land of Oz.

most people, thinking about a tornado in Kansas immediately brings to mind the one that whisked away Dorothy and her little dog Toto in *The Wizard of Oz*.

We can't prevent ourselves from assessing the ease with which examples from Nebraska and Kansas come to mind, and once we've made such assessments, they seem to give us our answer. It is easier to think of a tornado in Kansas (never mind that it was fictional) than one in Nebraska, so we conclude that Kansas probably has more tornadoes. The implicit logic seems compelling: if examples can be quickly brought to mind, there must be many of them. Usually that's true. It's easier to think of male presidents of Fortune 500 companies than female presidents, easier to think of successful Russian novelists than successful Norwegian novelists, and easier to think of instances of German military aggression than Swiss military aggression precisely because there are more male presidents, more successful Russian novelists, and more instances of German military aggression. The availability heuristic, therefore, normally serves us well. The ease with which relevant examples can be brought to mind (that is, how "available" they are) is indeed a reasonably accurate guide to overall frequency or probability.

But the availability heuristic is not an infallible guide. Certain events may simply be more memorable or retrievable than others, making availability a poor guide to true number or probability. Nebraska has as many tornadoes as Kansas, but none of them are as memorable as the one in *The Wizard of Oz*. In an early demonstration of the availability heuristic, Kahneman and Tversky (1973a) asked people whether there are more words that begin with the letter *r* or more words that have *r* in the third position. A large majority thought that more words begin with *r*, but in fact more words have *r* in the third position. Because words are stored in memory in roughly alphabetical fashion, words that begin with *r* (*rain, rowdy, redemption*) are easier to recall than those with *r* as the third letter (*nerd, harpoon, barrister*). The latter words, although more plentiful, are harder to access.

Disentangling Ease of Retrieval from the Amount of Information Retrieved As noted earlier, the availability heuristic involves judging the frequency of an event, the size of a category, or the probability of an outcome by how *easily* relevant instances can be brought to mind (Schwarz & Vaughn, 2002). Note that it is not simply an assessment of the *number* of instances that are retrieved. But how do we know that? After all, not only do people have an easier time thinking of words that begin with *r*, but they also can think of many more of them. How do we know that people arrive at their answers by consulting their experience of how easy it is to think of examples rather than by simply comparing the number of examples they are able to generate? It is difficult to distinguish between these two explanations because they are so tightly intertwined. If it is easier to think of examples of one category, we will probably also think of more of them.

An ingenious experiment by Norbert Schwarz and his colleagues managed to untangle the two interpretations (Schwarz et al., 1991). In the guise of gathering material for a relaxation-training program, students were asked to review their lives for experiences relevant to assertiveness. The experiment involved four conditions. One group was asked to list 6 occasions when they had acted assertively, and another group was asked to list 12 such examples. A third group was asked to list 6 occasions when they had acted unassertively, and the final group was asked to list 12 such examples. The requirement to generate 6 or 12 examples of either behavior was carefully chosen: thinking of 6 examples would be easy for nearly everyone, but thinking of 12 would be extremely difficult.

Notice how this experimental setup disentangles the *ease* of generating examples and the *number* of examples generated. Those who have to think of 12 examples of either assertiveness or unassertiveness will think of more examples, but they will find it hard to do so. What, then, has a greater effect on judgment? To find out, the investigators then asked the participants to rate their own assertiveness. As Kahneman and Tversky would have predicted, the results indicated that it is the ease of generating examples that seems to guide people's judgments (**Table 4.2**). Those who provided 6 examples of their assertiveness subsequently rated themselves as more assertive than those who provided 12 examples, even though the latter thought of more examples. Similarly, those who provided 6 examples of their failure to be assertive subsequently rated themselves as less assertive than those who provided 12 examples. Indeed, the effect of ease of generation was so strong that those who thought of 12 examples of unassertiveness rated themselves as more assertive than those who thought of 12 examples of assertiveness! Apparently, the difficulty of coming up with 12 occasions when they acted unassertively convinced participants in the former group that they must be pretty assertive after all.

TABLE 4.2 The Availability Heuristic

This table shows average ratings of participants' own assertiveness after they were asked to think of 6 or 12 examples of their assertiveness or unassertiveness.

Number of Examples	TYPE OF BEHAVIOR	
	Assertive	Unassertive
6	6.3	5.2
12	5.2	6.2

Source: Adapted from Schwarz et al. (1991).

Biased Assessments of Risk One area where the availability heuristic rears its head in everyday life harks back to the earlier discussion of negative information being overreported in the news, which has the unfortunate effect of making many people more fearful than might be appropriate. But not all hazards are equally overreported; some receive more news coverage than others. As a result, if people assess risk by how easily they can bring examples of various hazards to mind, their assessments should be predictable from how much press attention different hazards receive (Slovic, Fischoff, & Lichtenstein, 1982).

For example, do more people die each year by homicide or suicide? As you have surely noticed, homicides receive much more press coverage, so most people think they are more common. In reality, however, suicides outnumber homicides in the United States by a margin of 3 to 2. Are people more likely to die by accident or disease? Statistics indicate that disease claims more than 16 times as many lives as accidents, but because accidents (being more dramatic) receive disproportionate press coverage, most people erroneously consider them to be as lethal as disease. Finally, do more people die each year in fires or drownings? Again, fires receive disproportionate media attention, so most people think that fires claim more lives than drownings. In reality, there are more drownings each year than deaths by fire.

People typically overestimate the frequency of dramatic events that claim the lives of many people at once. Deaths due to plane crashes, earthquakes, and tornadoes are good examples. In contrast, people underestimate the commonness of "silent" deaths that quietly claim individual lives, such as deaths resulting from emphysema and strokes. People also underestimate the lethality of maladies they frequently encounter in nonfatal form—deaths from vaccinations, diabetes, and asthma. Because everyone knows healthy asthmatics and healthy diabetics, it is easy to lose sight of the number of lives that have been lost to these afflictions. Lists of the most overestimated and underestimated hazards are provided in **Table 4.3**, which shows that death from accidents tends to be overestimated and death from disease underestimated.

Biased Estimates of Contributions to Joint Projects Another example of how the availability heuristic can distort everyday judgment involves the dynamics of joint projects. People sometimes work together on a project and then afterward

---

TABLE 4.3 Biased Assessments

This table shows the most notable biases in the perceived commonness of causes of death.

Most Overestimated	Most Underestimated
All accidents	Smallpox vaccination
Motor vehicle accidents	Diabetes
Tornadoes	Lightning
Flood	Stroke
All cancers	Asthma
Fire	Emphysema
Homicide	Tuberculosis

Source: Adapted from Slovic, Fischoff, & Lichtenstein (1982).

decide who gets the bulk of the credit. You work with someone on a class project and turn in a single paper. Whose name is listed first? You and an acquaintance are hired to write a computer program for a lump-sum payment. How do you split the money?

With the availability heuristic in mind, social psychologist Michael Ross predicted that people would tend to overestimate their own contributions to such projects. After all, because we devote so much energy and attention to our own contributions, they should be more available than the contributions of everyone else. He and Fiore Sicoly conducted several studies that verified this prediction (Ross & Sicoly, 1979). In one study, married couples were asked to apportion responsibility for various tasks or outcomes in their everyday life—how much each contributed to keeping the house clean, maintaining the social calendar, starting arguments, and so on. The respondents tended to give themselves more credit than their partners did. In most cases, when the estimates made by the two participants were summed, they exceeded the logically allowable maximum of 100 percent. (In our favorite example, a couple was asked to estimate their relative contributions to making breakfast. The wife stated that her share was 100 percent on the reasonable grounds that she bought the food, prepared it, set the table, cleared the table, and washed the dishes. The husband estimated his contribution to be 25 percent—because he fed the cat!)

But how do we know that it is the availability heuristic rather than some sort of motivational bias that gives rise to this phenomenon? In other words, maybe people overestimate their contributions simply because they want to see themselves, and have others see them, in the most favorable light. This would certainly be the logical conclusion if the effect held true only for positive items. But Ross and Sicoly found that the overestimation of a person's own contributions held for negative outcomes (such as starting arguments) as well as positive outcomes (such as taking care of the house), making it clear that availability played a large role in this effect.

Availability's Close Cousin: Fluency Just as examples of some categories are easier to think of than others, some individual stimuli are easier to process than others. Psychologists have a term for this—**fluency**, which refers to the ease or difficulty associated with information processing. A clear image is easy to process, or fluent. An irregular word (for example, *imbroglio*) is hard to process, or disfluent. The subjective experience of fluency, much like the subjective sense of availability, influences all sorts of judgments people are called on to make (Jacoby & Dallas, 1981; Oppenheimer, 2008). For example, we judge fluent names to be more famous, fluent objects to be more prototypical members of their categories, and common adages that rhyme to be more valid and truthful than those that don't (Jacoby, Woloshyn, & Kelley, 1989; McGlone & Tofighbakhsh, 2000; Whittlesea & Leboe, 2000). Fluency also influences the perceived difficulty of a task that is being described. When the font (typeface) of a recipe is hard to read, people estimate that the dish would be harder to cook (Song & Schwarz, 2008).

In addition to such direct effects on judgment, fluency appears to influence *how* people process relevant information. In many respects, the feeling of fluency (or disfluency) has the same effect as being in a good (or bad) mood (see Chapter 7). A feeling of disfluency while processing information leads people to take something of a "slow down, be careful" approach to making judgments and decisions. In one study that examined this tendency, participants were given the Cognitive

fluency The feeling of ease associated with processing information.

FIGURE 4.7 You Be The Subject: Cognitive Reflection Test

Some participants were asked to answer the following questions from the Cognitive Reflection Task (Frederick, 2005) presented in a font that was easy to read. Try it. What are the answers to these two questions?

1. In a lake, there is a patch of lily pads. Every day, the patch doubles in size. If it takes 48 days for the patch to cover the entire lake, how long would it take for the patch to cover half the lake?_____ days

2. If it takes 5 machines 5 minutes to make 5 widgets, how long would it take 100 machines to make 100 widgets?_____ minutes

Other participants were presented with the questions in a font that was difficult to read. Try them again.

1. IN A LAKE, THERE IS A PATCH OF LILY PADS. EVERY DAY, THE PATCH DOUBLES IN SIZE. IF IT TAKES 48 DAYS FOR THE PATCH TO COVER THE ENTIRE LAKE, HOW LONG WOULD IT TAKE FOR THE PATCH TO COVER HALF THE LAKE? _____ DAYS

2. IF IT TAKES 5 MACHINES 5 MINUTES TO MAKE 5 WIDGETS, HOW LONG WOULD IT TAKE 100 MACHINES TO MAKE 100 WIDGETS? _____ MINUTES

CONCLUSION: The effort participants put into reading the disfluent font carried over to their approach to solving the problems, putting them into a more deliberative mind-set. They were therefore more likely to see that it would take 47 days for the lily pads to cover half of the lake and that it would take 5 minutes for the 100 machines to make 100 widgets.

Source: Adapted from Alter et al. (2007).

Reflection Task (Frederick, 2005) printed in either a normal, easy-to-process font or a degraded font (**Figure 4.7**). Performing well on the Cognitive Reflection Task requires stifling an immediate gut feeling to get the correct answer to each question. For example: "A bat and ball cost $1.10 in total. The bat costs $1 more than the ball. How much does the ball cost?" You need to think beyond the immediate response of 10 cents to arrive at the correct response of 5 cents ($0.05 + $1.05 = $1.10). The participants in the study answered more questions correctly when the questions were presented in a degraded, and hence disfluent, font (Alter, Oppenheimer, Epley, & Eyre, 2007). The difficulty of merely reading the question caused these participants to slow down, giving their slower, more analytical processes a chance to catch up with their immediate intuitive response.

The Representativeness Heuristic

We all sometimes find ourselves wondering whether someone is a member of a particular category. Is he gay? Is she a Republican? In making such assessments, we automatically assess the extent to which the person in question *seems* gay or Republican. In so doing, we rely on what Kahneman and Tversky (1972) have dubbed the representativeness heuristic. Instead of focusing on the true question of interest—"Is it likely that this person is a Republican?"—we ask, "Does this person seem Republican?" or "Is this person similar to my prototype of a Republican?" The use of the representativeness heuristic thus reflects an implicit assumption that *like goes with like*. A member of a given category ought to resemble the category prototype; an effect ought to resemble its cause.

The representativeness heuristic is generally useful in making accurate judgments about people and events. Members of certain groups often resemble the

The Representativeness Heuristic Both (A) Ted Bundy, who was convicted of committing multiple murders of young women, and (B) Scott Peterson, who was convicted of killing his pregnant wife, were clean-cut, educated professionals, characteristics that are not part of our prototype of a murderer. Because of the representativeness heuristic, people were surprised to learn that these men were, in fact, the perpetrators.

base-rate information Information about the relative frequency of events or of members of different categories in the population.

group prototype (the prototype must come from somewhere), and effects often resemble their causes. The degree of resemblance between person and group, or between cause and effect, is thus often a helpful guide to group membership and causal status. The strategy is effective to the extent that the prototype has some validity and the members of the category cluster around the prototype.

But even when the prototype is valid, the representativeness heuristic can create difficulties if people rely on it exclusively. The problem with the representativeness heuristic is that a strong sense of resemblance can blind us to other potentially useful sources of information. One source of useful information, known as **base-rate information**, concerns knowledge about relative frequency. How many members of the category in question are there relative to the members of all other categories? The individual in question is more likely to be a Republican if the local population includes a lot of Republicans. But a strong sense of representativeness sometimes leads people to ignore base-rate likelihood, which could (and should) be put to good use.

The Resemblance between Members and Categories: Base-Rate Neglect Many studies have documented this tendency for people to ignore or underutilize base-rate information when assessing whether someone belongs to a particular category (Ajzen, 1977; Bar-Hillel, 1980; Ginosar & Trope, 1980; Tversky & Kahneman, 1982). In one of the earliest studies, Kahneman and Tversky (1973b) asked participants to consider the following description of Tom W. that was supposedly written during Tom's senior year in high school by a psychologist who based his assessment on Tom's responses on personality tests. The participants were also told that Tom is now in graduate school.

> Tom W. is of high intelligence, although lacking in true creativity. He has a need for order and clarity and for neat and tidy systems in which every detail finds its appropriate place. His writing is rather dull and mechanical, occasionally enlivened by somewhat corny puns and by flashes of imagination of the sci-fi type. He has a strong drive for competence. He seems to have little feel and little sympathy for other people and does not enjoy interacting with others. Self-centered, he nonetheless has a deep moral sense. (Kahneman & Tversky, 1973b, p. 238)

One group of participants was asked to rank nine academic disciplines (for example, law, computer science, social work) in terms of how likely it was that Tom chose them as his field of specialization. A second group was asked to rank the nine disciplines in terms of how similar they thought Tom was to the typical student in each discipline. A final group was never shown the description of Tom; these participants merely estimated the percentage of all graduate students in the United States who were enrolled in each of the nine disciplines.

How should the participants assess the likelihood that Tom would choose each discipline for graduate study? They should certainly assess how similar Tom is to the type of person who pursues each field of study—that is, they should consider how representative Tom is of the people in each discipline. But representativeness is not a perfect guide. Some of the least lawyerly people study law, and some of the least people-oriented individuals pursue social work. Because representativeness is not a perfect guide in this context, any additional useful information should also be considered, such as what proportion of all graduate students choose each field—that is, base-rate information. Clearly, Tom W. is more likely to have pursued a discipline that has a thousand students on campus than one that has ten. A savvy judgment, then, would somehow combine representativeness with an assessment of the popularity of each field.

Table 4.4 provides the rankings of the nine disciplines by each of the three groups of participants—those asked to assess likelihood, similarity, and base rate. Note that the rankings of the *likelihood* that Tom chose to study each of the disciplines are virtually identical to the rankings of how *similar* Tom is to the students in each discipline. In other words, the participants' responses were based entirely on how much the description of Tom resembled the "typical" student in each field. By basing their responses exclusively on representativeness, the participants failed to consider the other source of useful information—base-rate frequency. As you can also see from Table 4.4, the likelihood rankings did not correspond at all to what the participants knew about the overall popularity of each of the fields. Useful information was ignored.

It should be pointed out, however, that although base-rate neglect is often observed, it is not inevitable or universal (Bar-Hillel & Fischhoff, 1981). Certain circumstances encourage the use of base-rate frequency. Two circumstances stand out as having the greatest impact. The first is whether the base-rate information has some causal significance to the task at hand (Ajzen, 1977; Tversky & Kahneman, 1982). For example, if you were given a description of an individual's academic strengths and weaknesses and asked to predict whether the person passed an exam, you would not be indifferent to the fact that 70 percent of the students who took the exam failed (that is, that the base rate of failure was 70 percent). Note that the base rate has causal significance in this case: the fact that 70 percent

---

TABLE 4.4 The Representativeness Heuristic

Participants ranked nine academic disciplines in terms of the likelihood that Tom W. chose that graduate field, the perceived similarity between the description of Tom W. and the typical student in that field, or the number of graduate students enrolled in each field.

Discipline	Likelihood	Similarity	Base Rate
Business administration	3	3	3
Computer science	1	1	8
Engineering	2	2	5
Humanities and education	8	8	1
Law	6	6	6
Library science	5	4	9
Medicine	7	7	7
Physical and life sciences	4	5	4
Social science and social work	9	9	2

Source: Adapted from Kahneman & Tversky (1973b).

of the students failed means the exam was difficult, and the difficulty of the exam is part of what *causes* a person to fail. People use the base rate in such contexts because its relevance is obvious. When the base rate is not causally relevant, as in the Tom W. experiment, its relevance is less obvious. If twice as many people major in business as in the physical sciences, it would be *more likely* that Tom W. is a business major, but it would not *cause* him to be a business major. The relevance of the base rate is thus less apparent.

Another way to improve people's use of base-rate information is to change their fundamental approach to the problem. People typically try to assess whether someone belongs to a particular category by taking an "inside" view of the task and focusing on details of the particular case at hand. Who is this person, and what "type" does he or she resemble? But it is possible to take an "outside" view of the problem. Suppose, for example, that you are asked to predict the undergraduate majors of a large number of students, not just Tom W. The details about each individual might now seem less important, and the significance of other, purely "statistical" considerations, such as base-rate frequency, might become more apparent. In the extreme case, if everyone in a sample of 20 resembled a pre-law student, most people would nevertheless hesitate to guess that all were pre-law students. Indeed, circumstances that encourage an outside perspective have been shown to reduce base-rate neglect and other biases of human judgment (Gigerenzer, 1991; Griffin & Tversky, 1992; Kahneman & Lovallo, 1993; Kahneman & Tversky, 1982b, 1995).

The Planning Fallacy A common pitfall that results from adopting an inside view is the tendency to be unrealistic about how long it takes to complete a project. This tendency, known as the **planning fallacy**, is something of a paradox because people's overly optimistic assessments about their ability to finish a current project exist side by side with their knowledge that the amount of time needed in the past has typically exceeded their original estimates. Students, for example, often confidently assert that they will have all assignments done well in advance of an exam so that they can calmly and thoroughly review the material beforehand. However, it is distressingly common for this anticipated calm review to give way to feverish cramming. Students aren't the only victims of the planning fallacy. Even your textbook authors, who know about the planning fallacy, have fallen prey to it when estimating how long it would take to write an article. And don't even ask how long they thought it would take to finish this textbook.

The error is illustrated more dramatically by setbacks in large-scale building projects. When the people of Sydney, Australia, decided in 1957 to build their iconic opera house, the original estimates were that it would be completed by 1963 and cost $7 million. It opened in 1973 at a cost of $102 million. Similarly, when Montreal was named host of the 1976 summer Olympics, the mayor announced that the entire Olympiad would cost $120 million and that many events would take place in a stadium with a first-of-its-kind retractable roof. The Olympics, of course, went on as planned in 1976, but the stadium did not get its roof until 1989. Moreover, the final cost of the stadium was $120 million, the amount budgeted for the entire Olympics!

To shed light on the planning fallacy, psychologists Roger Buehler, Dale Griffin, and Michael Ross (1994) conducted a number of studies of people's estimates of completion times. In one study, students in an honors program were asked to predict as accurately as possible when they would turn in their theses. They were

planning fallacy The tendency for people to be unrealistically optimistic about how quickly they can complete a project.

The Planning Fallacy People typically estimate that projects will be completed sooner than they actually are—even when they are aware of past efforts that took much longer than originally estimated to complete. (A) It took ten years longer than estimated to complete construction of the Sydney Opera House. (B) The Central Artery/Tunnel Project (the "Big Dig") in Boston was plagued by unforeseen problems that dramatically delayed completion of the project.

also asked to estimate what the completion date would be "if everything went as poorly as it possibly could." Fewer than a third of the students finished by the time they had estimated. More remarkably, fewer than half finished by the time they had estimated for the worst-case scenario.

Follow-up experiments laid the blame for people's optimistic forecasts on the tendency to approach the task from an exclusively inside perspective. In one study, participants were asked to verbalize their thoughts as they were trying to estimate how long a task would take. Nearly all of their thoughts were about various plans and scenarios whereby the project would be finished. Only a precious few dealt with the participants' track record on previous tasks. Thus the inside perspective (What steps are required to complete *this* project?) crowds out the potentially informative outside perspective (How often do I get such things done on time?). People have personal histories that would be helpful in accurately estimating completion times. They just don't use them. When Buehler and his colleagues asked people how often they completed tasks by the time they initially expected, the average response was only a third of the time.

The Resemblance between Cause and Effect The representativeness heuristic also affects people's assessments of cause and effect (Downing, Sternberg, & Ross, 1985; Gilovich & Savitsky, 2002). In particular, people are predisposed to look for and accept causal relationships in which like goes with like. Big effects are thought to have big causes, small effects to have small causes, complicated effects to have complicated causes, and so on. This assumption is often validated by everyday experience. Being hit with a small mallet typically produces a smaller bruise than being hit with a large mallet. Resolving the complicated mess in the Middle East will probably require complex, sustained negotiation, not some simple suggestion that has yet to be made. But sometimes small causes create big effects, and vice versa: tiny viruses give rise to devastating diseases like malaria or AIDS; splitting the nucleus of the atom releases an awesome amount of energy.

BOX 4.3   FOCUS ON CULTURE

Predictions East and West

The philosopher Ludwig Wittgenstein had this to say about the direction of the future: "When we think about the future of the world, we always have in mind its being where it would be if it continued to move as we see it moving now. We do not realize that it moves not in a straight line ... and that its direction changes constantly."

As it turns out, Wittgenstein was a little too ready to say "we." Whereas Westerners, or at any rate Americans, are indeed inclined to predict that the world will move in whatever direction it now moves, East Asians are likely to expect the world to reverse direction. Ji, Nisbett, and Su (2001) point to a tradition in the East, dating back thousands of years, that emphasizes change. The *Tao* (the Way) envisions the world as existing in one of two states at any given time—*yin* and *yang* (light and dark, male and female, and so on)—that alternate with one another. The fact that the world is in one state is a strong indication that it is about to be in the other state. The black dot inside the white swirl and the white dot inside the black swirl of the Tao sym-

bol remind us that the seed of the future is to be found in the present.

Ji and her colleagues reasoned that the tradition of the *Tao* would cause East Asians to judge events as being likely to reverse course rather than to continue moving in their current direction. They tested this hypothesis in several ways. In one study, they asked participants to read brief stories and predict how they would turn out. For example, participants read about a poor young man and were asked how likely it was that he would become rich. The Americans thought it was not so likely; the Chinese thought it was more likely. In another study, Ji and her colleagues showed various time trends to participants. The graphs were alleged to be recent movements in a variety of indicators that participants would be likely to know nothing about—for example, world economic growth rate and world cancer death rate. Trends were shown as either decidedly increasing or decidedly decreasing. American respondents were overwhelmingly likely to predict that the trends would continue in the same direction they were going. Chinese

The Tao Symbol

respondents were much more likely than Americans to predict that the trends would reverse course—to move down if they had been going up and to move up if they had been going down. And who do you think bets the stock market will go up when it's in a bull mood and down when it's in a bear mood? You guessed it: the Americans bet the current direction; the Chinese bet the opposite (Ji, Zhang, & Guo, 2008).

Health and medicine are areas in which the impact of representativeness on causal judgments is particularly striking. Many people think that you should avoid milk if you have a cold and potato chips if you suffer from acne. Why? Because milk seems so representative of phlegm, and the greasiness of potato chips seems so representative of the oily skin that often accompanies acne. To be sure, people are affected by what they eat—people gain weight by eating lots of fat and can develop an orange tint to the skin by consuming too much carotene. But sometimes we take this belief that "you are what you eat" to almost magical extremes. In one experiment, college students were asked to make inferences about the attributes of members of (hypothetical) tribes (Nemeroff & Rozin, 1989). One group was told about a tribe that ate wild boar and hunted sea turtles for their shells; a second group was told about a tribe that ate sea turtles and hunted wild boar for their tusks. The students' responses indicated that they assumed that the characteristics of the food would "rub off" on the tribe members. Members of the turtle-

TABLE 4.5 Representativeness and Astrological Signs

This table shows the personality traits that are supposedly characteristic of people born under 9 of the 12 astrological signs.

Astrological Sign	Personality Characteristics
Aries (the Ram)	Quick-tempered; headstrong
Taurus (the Bull)	Plodding; prone to rage
Gemini (the Twins)	Vacillating; split personality
Cancer (the Crab)	Attached to their homes
Leo (the Lion)	Proud; leader
Virgo (the Virgin)	Modest; retiring
Libra (the Scales)	Well balanced; fair
Scorpio (the Scorpion)	Sharp; secretive
Capricorn (the Goat)	Hardworking; down to earth

Source: Adapted from Huntley (1990); Read et al. (1978).

eating tribe were considered better swimmers and more generous; those who ate boar were thought to be more aggressive and more likely to have beards.

Another area in which representativeness affects causal judgments is in the realm of pseudoscientific belief systems. Consider, for example, the case of astrological signs and representative personality traits. A central tenet of astrology is that an individual's personality is influenced by the astrological sign under which the person was born. The personalities associated with specific astrological signs are listed in **Table 4.5**. Notice the resemblance between the features we associate with each sign's namesake and those that supposedly characterize individuals born under that sign. Were you born under the sign of the lion (Leo)? Then you are likely to be a proud, forceful leader. Born under the sign of the ram (Aries)? Then you tend to be headstrong and quick-tempered. Born under the sign of the virgin (Virgo)? Then you are inclined to be modest and retiring.

The personality profiles that supposedly accompany various astrological signs have been shown time and again to have absolutely no validity (Abell, 1981; Schick & Vaughn, 1995; Zusne & Jones, 1982). Why, then, is astrology so popular? Part of the reason is that astrology takes advantage of people's use of the representativeness heuristic. Each of the personality profiles has some superficial appeal because each draws on the intuition that like goes with like. Who is more inclined to be vacillating than a Gemini (a twin)? Who is more likely to be fair and well balanced than a Libra (the scales)?

The Joint Operation of Availability and Representativeness

The availability and representativeness heuristics sometimes operate in tandem. For example, a judgment that two things belong together—that one is representative of the other—can make an instance in which they do occur together particularly available. The joint effect of these two heuristics can thus create an **illusory correlation** between two variables, or the belief that they are correlated when in

illusory correlation The belief that two variables are correlated when in fact they are not.

fact they are not. A judgment of representativeness leads us to expect an association between the two entities, and this expectation in turn makes instances in which they are paired unusually memorable.

A classic set of experiments by Loren and Jean Chapman illustrates this point nicely (Chapman & Chapman, 1967). The Chapmans were struck by a paradox observed in the practice of clinical psychology. Clinicians often claim that they find various projective personality tests helpful in making clinical diagnoses, but systematic research on these tests has shown many of them to be completely lacking in validity. (Projective tests require people to respond to very unstructured and ambiguous stimuli, such as the famous Rorschach inkblots, and thus "project" their personalities onto what they see.) Why would intelligent, conscientious, and well-trained clinicians believe that such tests can diagnose psychopathologies when they cannot? Why, in other words, do some clinicians perceive an illusory correlation between their clients' pathologies and their responses on such tests?

To find out, the Chapmans first asked numerous clinicians about which specific test responses by their clients tended to indicate which specific pathological conditions. Much of their work focused on the Draw-a-Person Test, in which the client simply draws a picture of a person, and the therapist interprets the picture for signs of various psychopathologies. The clinicians reported that they observed many connections between particular drawings and specific pathological conditions—drawings and pathologies that seem, intuitively, to belong together. People suffering from paranoia, for example, were thought to be inclined to draw unusually large or small eyes. People insecure about their intelligence were thought to be inclined to draw a large (or small) head.

To investigate these illusory correlations further, the Chapmans gathered a sample of 45 Draw-a-Person pictures—35 drawn by psychotic patients in a nearby hospital and 10 drawn by graduate students in clinical psychology. They then attached a phony statement to each picture that supposedly described the pathological condition of the person who drew it. Some came with the description "is suspicious of other people," others with the description "has had problems of sexual impotence," and so on. The Chapmans were careful to avoid any correlation between the nature of a drawing and the pathological condition attached to each. For example, "is suspicious of other people" appeared just as often on pictures with unremarkable eyes as on pictures with large or small eyes.

These pictures (with accompanying pathological conditions) were then shown to college students who had never heard of the Draw-a-Person Test. Although the study was carefully designed so that there was no connection between the pictures and pathological conditions, the students nonetheless "saw" the same relationships reported earlier by the clinical psychologists. To the students, too, it seemed that prominent eyes were likely to have been drawn by individuals who were suspicious of others. This finding suggests, of course, that the clinical psychologists were not detecting any real correlations between pathological conditions and responses on the Draw-a-Person Test. Instead, they were "detecting" the same illusory correlations that the undergraduate students were detecting—illusory correlations produced by the joint operation of availability and representativeness. Certain pictures are representative of specific pathologies (for example, prominent eyes and paranoia),

"For what it's worth, next week all your stars and planets will be in good aspect for you to launch an invasion of England."

and therefore instances in which the two are observed together (for example, a paranoid individual drawing a person with large eyes) will be particularly noteworthy and memorable.

In a final study, the Chapmans simply asked another group of students to indicate the extent to which various conditions (suspiciousness, impotence, dependence) "called to mind" different parts of the body (eyes, sexual organs, mouth). Tellingly, their responses matched the correlations reported by the earlier groups of clinicians and students.

The Chapman and Chapman studies and a great many other investigations of intuitive judgment make it clear that the intuitive system produces many errors—some of them far from trivial in their consequences. Is it possible to increase the sway of the rational system at the expense of the intuitive system? The answer is yes, and you are doing it now in your studies at your university. Many of the errors discussed in this chapter can be reduced by training in statistics and research methods (Nisbett, Fong, Lehman, & Cheng, 1987). Moreover, some of the framing effects discussed earlier can be reduced by training in economics (Larrick, Morgan, & Nisbett, 1990). Such training increases the scope and sophistication of our rational faculties and the likelihood that they will intervene to override or offset a mistake spawned by the intuitive system. So although our errors may be disconcerting, they can be reduced markedly by training.

 Two mental systems guide our judgments and decisions: one akin to intuition and the other akin to reason. The intuitive system operates quickly and automatically, while the rational system tends to be more deliberate and controlled. These systems can lead to the same judgments, they can lead to opposite judgments, or the intuitive system may produce a satisfying judgment so quickly that the rational system is never engaged. The intuitive system uses heuristics to make its quick assessments, which can sometimes bias judgment. The availability heuristic may lead to biased assessments of risk and biased estimates of people's contributions to joint projects. The representativeness heuristic may result in base-rate neglect and mistaken assessments of cause and effect. When these two heuristics operate together, they can lead to an illusory correlation between two variables.

Chapter Review

Summary

Why Study Social Cognition?

- By studying errors of judgment we can understand how we make judgments and learn to avoid mistakes.

The Information Available for Social Cognition

- Sometimes we have very little information but make judgments anyway—as when people make personality judgments based on physical appearance

- Mistaken inferences can arise from *pluralistic ignorance*, which tends to occur when people are reluctant to express their misgivings about a perceived group norm; their reluctance in turn reinforces the false norm.

- Information received secondhand often does not provide a full account of what happened or may stress certain elements at the expense of others.

- Positive information is more likely to be reported and tends to receive much more weight in people's judgments than negative information.

How Information Is Presented

- How information is presented can affect judgment. The *order* in which information is presented can be important. When the information presented first is more influential, there is a *primacy effect*, which often results because the initial information affects the way subsequent information is interpreted. When information presented last is more influential, there is a *recency effect*, which usually results from such information being more available in memory.

- Order effects are a type of *framing effect*. Others include the "spinning" of information by varying the language or structure of the information that is presented.

- The temporal framing of an event also influences how we think of it. Far-off events are construed in more abstract terms, and imminent events are construed more concretely.

How We Seek Information

- People tend to examine whether certain propositions are true by searching for information consistent with the proposition in question. This *confirmation bias* can lead people to believe things that aren't true because evidence can generally be found to support even the most questionable propositions.

- People are sometimes *motivated* to find evidence supporting a preexisting conclusion.

Top-Down Processing: Using Schemas to Understand New Information

- *Schemas* influence our interpretation of information. They are important *top-down* tools we use to understand the world, as opposed to the *bottom-up* tools of perception and facts retrieved from memory.

- Schemas guide attention, memory, the construal of information, and can directly prompt behavior.

- The likelihood that a given schema will be applied depends on how well the incoming information matches the critical features of the schema. Sometimes irrelevant similarities between the available information and a schema lead us to apply the schema inappropriately.

- In general, the more recently and the more frequently a schema has been "activated," the more likely it is to be applied to new information. We need not be consciously aware of a schema to be influenced by it.

Reason, Intuition, and Heuristics

- People have two systems for processing information: an *intuitive* system and a *rational* system. Intuitive responses are based on rapid, associative processes, whereas rational responses are based on slower, rule-based reasoning.

- Intuitive *heuristics*, or mental shortcuts, provide us with sound judgments most of the time, but they sometimes lead us into errors of judgment.

- We use the *availability heuristic* when we judge the frequency or probability of some event by how readily relevant instances come to mind. It can encourage us to overestimate how much we have contributed to group projects, and it can lead us to overestimate the risks posed by memorable hazards.

- The *fluency* we experience when processing information can influence the judgments we make about it. Disfluent stimuli lead to more reflective judgment.

- We use the *representativeness heuristic* when we try to categorize something by judging how similar it is to our conception of the typical member of the category or when we try to make causal attributions by assessing how similar an effect is to a possible cause. Sometimes we overlook highly relevant considerations such as *base-rate information*—how many members of the category there are in a population.

- The "inside" perspective on judgment leads to errors such as the *planning fallacy*, which we could avoid by taking an "outside" perspective and attending to our history of finishing similar tasks in a given time.

- Operating together, availability and representativeness can produce potent *illusory correlations*, which result when we think that two variables are correlated, both because they resemble each other and because the co-occurrence of two similar events is more memorable than the co-occurrence of two dissimilar events.

Key Terms

availability heuristic (p. 136)
base-rate information (p. 142)
bottom-up processes (p. 124)
confirmation bias (p. 121)
construal level theory (p. 120)
encoding (p. 126)
fluency (p. 140)

framing effect (p. 117)
heuristics (p. 136)
illusory correlation (p. 147)
planning fallacy (p. 144)
pluralistic ignorance (p. 112)
primacy effect (p. 117)
prime (p. 129)

recency effect (p. 117)
representativeness heuristic (p. 136)
retrieval (p. 126)
self-fulfilling prophecy (p. 134)
subliminal (p. 132)
top-down processes (p. 124)

Further Reading

Gilbert, D. (2006). *Stumbling on happiness*. New York: Knopf. This book focuses on happiness but also offers a penetrating and engaging review of how the mind works.

Gilovich, T. (1991). *How we know what isn't so: The fallibility of human judgment in everyday life*. New York: Free Press. A study of how the general principles of human judgment can lead people to hold all sorts of questionable and erroneous beliefs.

Hastie, R., & Dawes, R. (2001). *Rational choice in an uncertain world: The psychology of judgment and decision making*. Thousand Oaks, CA: Sage. An informative overview of scholarship on judgment and decision making.

Kahneman, D. (2011). *Thinking, fast and slow*. New York: Farrar, Straus and Giroux. An engaging overview of intuitive and rational thought by one of the foremost contributors to the field of judgment and decision making.

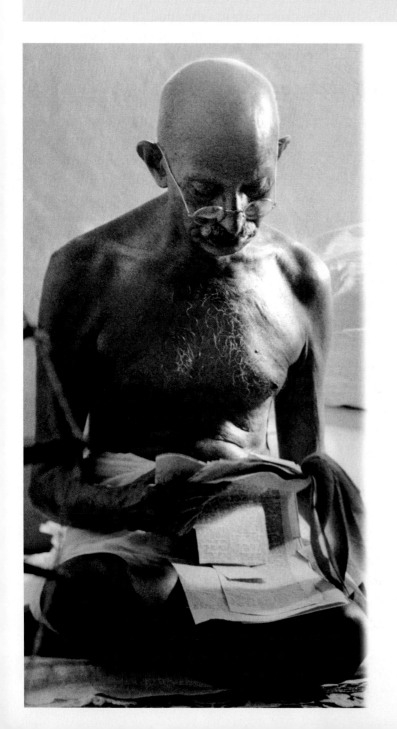

What made Gandhi Gandhi.

Social Attribution: Explaining Behavior

FROM 1995 TO 2009, BILL GATES was the richest person in the world. (He is now second to Mexican telecom mogul Carlos Slim.) Gates dropped out of Harvard at the ripe old age of 19 to start a company called Microsoft, which he soon built into the most profitable corporation in the world. Why do you think he was able to invent tremendously creative and powerful software at such a young age and build such a hugely successful company? Most people would say he must be one of the smartest people who ever lived. But Bill Gates is not one of the people who would say that.

Instead, as science writer Malcolm Gladwell informs us in his book *Outliers*, Gates would tell you that in 1968, when he was in eighth grade, he was bored with his Seattle public school. His parents happened to be well-off enough to put him into a private school called Lakeside, which just happened to have a time-sharing computer terminal that linked the school's computer club (at a time when few colleges, let alone high schools, had computer clubs) to a mainframe computer in downtown Seattle. Back then, most computers still required a clumsy punch-card system for data entry; but Lakeview's terminal, like most computers today, used a more efficient keyboard system. Gates became one of a tiny handful of teenagers in the world who were able to do real-time programming in 1968.

Gates's luck kept on running for the next six years. Lakeside was rich but soon ran out of money to pay for expensive mainframe time. By coincidence, Monique Rona, one of the founders of a company called Computer Center Corporation (CCC), had a son at Lakeside. Her company offered to let the Lakeside Computer Club have free programming time in exchange for testing the company's software. CCC went bankrupt shortly thereafter, but by then Gates and his friends managed to persuade a local firm called ISI (Information

Bill Gates (A) Bill Gates as a fledgling entrepreneur. (B) Bill Gates after he became primarily a philanthropist.

Sciences, Inc.) to let them have free computer time as payment for helping the firm develop a payroll program. Gates by this time was spending 20 to 30 hours a week programming.

Gates also established a connection to the University of Washington, which happened to have one computer that was free for the little-used period from 3 a.m. to 6 a.m. Gates lived close enough to the university that he could sneak out of bed at night and walk to the computer center. (Years later, Gates explained to his mother why she had found it so difficult to wake him up in the mornings.)

The next fortuitous event was that one day ISI needed programmers who were familiar with a particular type of software that would be needed to handle a new job setting up a computer system for a power station in Bonneville, Washington. Gates and his pals happened to be familiar with the software, so they went to work at Bonneville under the supervision of a brilliant master of programming. (Gates's high school was indulgent enough to let him skip the spring term of his senior year to do the work.) By the time Gates got to Harvard, he had spent many thousands of hours programming, almost certainly more than any freshman there and probably more than any freshman anywhere. Gates was a brilliant guy, but he could not have started Microsoft at 19 if he had not had such unusually fortunate experience with programming beginning when he was 13.

This kind of difference between the causal attributions of the observer (that's you) and the actor (Bill Gates) is commonplace. The observer is inclined to attribute actions, especially highly distinctive ones, to properties of the actor, such as personality traits and abilities. The actor is more inclined to attribute the same action to situational factors. In this chapter, you will read about the process of causal attribution—the ways that people try to understand why others, as well as they themselves, do the things they do.

People engage in causal attribution because they need to draw inferences about others and themselves based on their behavior, but the true meaning of an action may not be clear. Was Robert kind to his new employer because he's a genial person or because he was just currying favor? Did the congresswoman visit the new senior citizens' center because she has a real interest in the elderly, or was she just trying to win votes?

This chapter examines how people explain the behavior they witness (or hear about) in others and what effect their explanations have on the judgments they make about others. The chapter also examines how people understand the causes of their own behavior and how this understanding influences both their immediate emotional experience and their subsequent behavior. These are the concerns of **attribution theory**, or the study of how people understand the causes of events.

attribution theory An umbrella term used to describe the set of theoretical accounts of how people assign causes to the events around them and the effects that people's causal assessments have.

FROM ACTS TO DISPOSITIONS: INFERRING THE CAUSES OF BEHAVIOR

In class one day, you listen as a student gives a long-winded answer to a question posed by your professor. When the student is finally finished, your professor says, "Good point," and then proceeds to expand on the topic. You can't help wondering, "Did she really think it was a good point, or was she just trying to encourage student participation? Or was she trying to boost her standing on ratemyprofessors. com?" The way you answer these questions explains this particular action by your professor. It also helps make sense of many of her other actions in the course—such as whether she calls on this student often, or whether she seems consistently solicitous of students' opinions in general.

Causal attribution is the process people use to explain both their own and others' behavior. Understanding causal attributions is crucial to understanding

causal attribution Linking an event to a cause, such as inferring that a personality trait was responsible for a behavior.

Causal Attribution Causal attribution is central to much of social life, ranging from casual speculation to formal decision-making situations such as a trial.

everyday social behavior because we all make causal attributions many times a day, and the attributions we make can greatly affect our thoughts, feelings, and future behavior.

The Pervasiveness and Importance of Causal Attribution

When you ask someone out for a date but are rebuffed ("No thanks, I have a cold"), you do not simply take the response at face value. You wonder whether the person really has a cold or is just giving you the brush-off. Similarly, when you get back an exam, you are not simply happy or sad about the grade you received. You make an attribution. You might decide that you are smart and hardworking, or you might decide that you're not so good at this subject or that the test was unfair. Attributions are a constant part of mental life. You may ask yourself such questions as: "Why was my interview so short? Did the interviewers conclude that I obviously have what it takes, or were they just not interested?" "Why does everything work out so well for my roommate, while I have to struggle to get by?"

Concluding that someone won't go out with you because she's sick leads to an entirely different set of emotional reactions than concluding that she finds you unappealing. And attributing a bad grade on an exam to a lack of ability leads to unhappiness and withdrawal, whereas attributing failure to a lack of effort often leads to more vigorous attempts to study harder and more effectively in the future. Indeed, systematic research on causal attribution has shown that people's explanations have tremendous consequences in a number of areas, including health and education.

Explanatory Style and Attribution

A group of investigators led by Chris Peterson and Martin Seligman has examined the impact of attributions on academic success by relating a person's explanatory style to long-term academic performance. **Explanatory style** refers to a person's habitual way of explaining events, and it is assessed along three dimensions: internal/external, stable/unstable, and global/specific. To assess explanatory style, researchers ask respondents to imagine six different good events that might happen to them ("You do a project that is highly praised") and six bad events ("You meet a friend who acts hostilely toward you") and to provide a likely cause for each. Respondents are then asked if each cause (1) is due to something about them or something about other people or circumstances (internal/external), (2) will be present again in the future or not (stable/unstable), and (3) is something that influences other areas of their lives or just this one (global/specific). An explanation that mentions an *internal* cause implicates the self ("There I go again"), but an *external* cause does not ("That was the pickiest set of questions I've ever seen"). A *stable* cause implies that things will never change ("I'm just not good at this"), whereas an *unstable* cause implies that things may improve ("The cold medicine I was taking made me groggy"). Finally, a *global* cause is something that affects many areas of life ("I'm stupid"), whereas a *specific* cause applies to only a few ("I'm not good with names").

In the research by Seligman, Peterson, and their colleagues, the three dimensions of internal/external, stable/unstable, and global/specific are combined to

explanatory style A person's habitual way of explaining events, typically assessed along three dimensions: internal/external, stable/unstable, and global/specific.

form an overall explanatory style index, which is then correlated with an outcome variable of interest, such as students' GPAs. A tendency to explain negative events in terms of internal, stable, and global causes is considered a pessimistic explanatory style, and it is related to a variety of undesirable life outcomes. For example, students with a pessimistic explanatory style tend to get lower grades than those with a more optimistic style (Peterson & Barrett, 1987).

Peterson and Seligman have also studied the relation between different explanatory styles and health. In one study, they examined whether a person's explanatory style as a young adult could predict physical health later in life (Peterson, Seligman, & Vaillant, 1988; see also Peterson, 2000). The study took advantage of the fact that members of Harvard's graduating classes from 1942 to 1944 took part in a longitudinal study that required them to complete a questionnaire every year and submit medical records of periodic physical examinations. Using the medical records, judges scored each person's physical health on a 5-point scale, where "1" means the person was in good health and "5" means the person was deceased. This was done for all participants when they reached the ages of 25, 30, 35, and so on.

The physical health of the men at each of these ages was then correlated with their explanatory style as young men, which was assessed by having judges score their descriptions of their most difficult experiences during World War II. (These descriptions were the men's responses to a question they had been asked in 1946, when they were all recent college graduates.) The correlations, after statistically controlling for the respondents' initial physical condition at age 25, are reported in **Table 5.1**. As a quick glance at the table indicates, explanatory style during young adulthood is a significant predictor of physical health in later life. (Explanatory style does not correlate with health at ages 30 to 40, most likely because nearly all of the respondents were in generally good health at those ages, so there was nothing to predict. Thus, regarding one of the most important outcomes there can be—whether we are vigorous or frail, alive or dead—our causal attributions seem to matter. The tendency to make external, unstable, and specific attributions for

"A pessimist sees the difficulty in every opportunity; an optimist sees the opportunity in every difficulty."

—Sir Winston Churchill

TABLE 5.1 Does Explanatory Style Early in Life Predict Later Physical Health?

The correlation between explanatory style at age 25 and physical health at seven points in life; earlier physical health is controlled statistically.

Age	Correlation
30	0.04
35	0.03
40	0.13
45	0.37*
50	0.18
55	0.22*
60	0.25*

Source: Peterson, Seligman, & Vaillant (1988).
*Denotes statistically significant correlation.

FDR, Elected U.S. President for Four Terms FDR's optimistic attributional style undoubtedly contributed to his being the only major political figure in U.S. history to be successful in politics after incurring a severe physical handicap.

failure presumably makes us less prone to despair and encourages more of a can-do outlook that promotes such behaviors as flossing our teeth, exercising, and visiting the doctor—behaviors that can lead to a longer, healthier life.

Attributions about Controllability A second group of researchers, led by Bernard Weiner and Craig Anderson, has conducted research that reinforces the idea that people's attributional tendencies have a powerful effect on their long-term outcomes. But these investigators emphasize whether an attribution implies that an outcome is controllable, not whether its consequences are global or specific. On the one hand, attributions for failure that imply controllability—for example, a lack of effort or a poor strategy—make perseverance easier because we can always try harder or try a new strategy (Anderson, 1991; Anderson & Deuser, 1993; Anderson, Krull, & Weiner, 1996). If we view outcomes as beyond our control, on the other hand, it's tempting to simply give up—indeed, it's often rational to do so.

Research inspired by these findings has shown that people can be trained to adopt more productive attributional tendencies for academic outcomes—in particular, an inclination to attribute failure to a lack of effort—and that doing so has beneficial effects on subsequent academic performance (Dweck, 1975; Forsterling, 1985). The effects are both substantial and touching. Blackwell, Dweck, and Trzesniewski (2004) report tough junior high school boys crying when made to realize that their grades were due to a lack of effort rather than a lack of brains. Making people believe they can exert control over events that they formerly believed to be outside their control restores hope and unleashes the kind of productive energy that makes future success more likely (Crandall, Katkovsky, & Crandall, 1965; Dweck & Reppucci, 1973; Peterson, Maier, & Seligman, 1993; Seligman, Maier, & Geer, 1968).

Gender and Attribution Style This type of training might be put to good use to undo some inadvertent attributional training that takes place in elementary school classrooms across the United States and that appears to give rise to a troubling gender difference in attributional style. That is, boys are more likely than girls to attribute their failures to lack of effort, and girls are more likely than boys to attribute their failures to lack of ability (Dweck, 1986; Dweck, Davidson, Nelson, & Enna, 1978; Lewis & Sullivan, 2005; Ryckman & Peckham, 1987). Carol Dweck and her colleagues have found that this difference results in part from boys and girls being subtly taught different ways to interpret both their successes and their failures (Dweck et al., 1978). They observed teachers' feedback patterns in fourth- and fifth-grade classrooms and found that although girls, on average, outperform boys in school, negative evaluations of girls' performance were almost exclusively restricted to intellectual inadequacies ("This is not right, Lisa"). In contrast, 45 percent of the criticism of boys' work referred to nonintellectual factors ("This is messy, Bill"). Positive evaluation of girls' performance was related to the intellectual quality of their performance less than 80 percent of the time; for boys, it was 94 percent of the time. Dweck and her colleagues argue from these data that girls learn that criticism means they may lack intellectual ability, whereas boys learn that criticism means they haven't worked hard enough or paid enough attention to detail. Similarly, girls are likely to suspect that praise may be unrelated to the intellectual quality of their performance, whereas boys learn that praise means their intellectual performance was excellent.

Dweck and her colleagues performed an experiment in which they gave students feedback of the kind girls typically receive in the class or the kind boys typically receive. They found that both boys and girls receiving the kind of comments typically given to girls were more likely than those receiving feedback typically given to boys to view subsequent failure feedback as reflecting their ability. So, whatever other reasons there may be for boys crowing about their successes and dismissing their failures, they are aided in this pattern by the treatment they receive in the classroom. And whatever motivational factors operate for girls, their more modest attributions are likewise shaped by the feedback they receive in school.

 People differ in their individual explanatory styles. That is, people differ in whether they tend to make attributions that are external or internal, stable or unstable, global or specific. Attributional style predicts academic success as well as health and longevity. Belief in the controllability of outcomes is important, and beliefs about the controllability of academic outcomes can be altered by training. Boys and girls learn to draw different conclusions about academic outcomes: boys receive feedback indicating that success is due to ability and failure is due to insufficient effort or to incidental factors, whereas girls receive feedback indicating the reverse.

THE PROCESSES OF CAUSAL ATTRIBUTION

Does she really like me, or is she just pretending she does because I'm rich and famous? Does that candidate really believe what she is saying, or is she just saying that to win votes? Is he really a jerk, or is he just under a lot of pressure? These types of questions run through people's heads every day. How we answer these questions—how we assess the causes of observed or reported behavior—is not capricious; rather, such assessments follow rules that make them predictable. These rules have evolved to serve many functions—namely, to help us understand the past, illuminate the present, and predict the future. Only by knowing the cause of a given event can we grasp the true meaning of what has happened and anticipate what is likely to happen next.

For example, our perception of how much control another person has over his or her actions is one important factor in how we judge that person. When a person offers an excuse for problematic behavior, it typically yields more pity and forgiveness if it involves something beyond the person's control ("I had a flat tire") than if it involves something controllable ("I needed to take a break") (Weiner, 1986). And people who are opposed to a gay lifestyle express more favorable attitudes toward gays if they consider homosexuality an inescapable result of a person's biology rather than a lifestyle choice (Whitely, 1990).

Another particularly important focus of attributional analysis is determining whether an outcome is the product of something within the person (that is, an internal, or "dispositional," cause) or a reflection of something about the context or circumstances (that is, an external, or "situational," cause). Ever since Kurt Lewin (see Chapter 1) pointed out that behavior is a function of both the person

"If we're being honest, it was your decision to follow my recommendation that cost you money."

and the situation, all theories of attribution have been concerned with people's assessments of the relative contributions of these two types of causes (Heider, 1958; Hilton & Slugoski, 1986; Hilton, Smith, & Kim, 1995; Jones & Davis, 1965; Kelley, 1967; Medcoff, 1990). How do we figure out whether someone acted a certain way? Was it primarily because that's who he is, or largely because of the situation he faced?

Frequently, the distinction between internal and external is straightforward. You might win the pot in your weekly poker game because you're a better player than everyone else (internal cause), or maybe you simply were lucky and got the best cards (external cause). Knowledge and skill clearly reside within a person, and luck is something completely beyond a person's influence. In the case of poker, the internal/external dichotomy is easy to grasp.

In other contexts, however, the distinction isn't so clear. We might say that someone became a rock-and-roll guitarist because of a deep love of the instrument (internal cause) or because of the desire for fame and fortune (external cause). But aren't love and desire both inner states? And if so, why is the love of playing the guitar considered an internal cause, whereas the desire for fame and fortune considered an external cause? The answer is that loving to play the guitar is not something shared by everyone, or even most people, so it tells us something characteristic and informative about the person. It thus makes sense to refer to the cause as something personal or internal. Most people, however, seem to find the prospect of fame attractive (why else would there be so many reality TV shows?), and even more find the prospect of wealth attractive. Doing something to achieve fame and fortune, then, tells us little about the person in hot pursuit of either. So in this case, it makes sense to refer to the cause as something impersonal or external. Determining whether certain actions are the product of internal versus external causes thus requires assessments of what most people are like and what most people are likely to do.

Attribution and Covariation

> "The logic of science is also that of business and life."
>
> —John Stuart Mill

When scientists attempt to nail down the cause of some phenomenon, they try to isolate the one cause that seems to make a difference in producing the effect. That is, they try to identify the cause that seems always to be present when the effect or phenomenon occurs and always seems to be absent when the phenomenon does not occur. For example, to determine whether ulcers are caused by a bacterium, a medical researcher might determine whether individuals who are given the bacterium develop ulcers and whether individuals who have ulcers improve after taking a suitable antibiotic.

> "The whole of science is nothing more than refinement of everyday thinking."
>
> —Albert Einstein

To a considerable degree, this is how people assess causality in their everyday lives (Cheng & Novick, 1990; Fiedler, Walther, & Nickel, 1999; Forsterling, 1989; Hewstone & Jaspers, 1987; Kelley, 1973; Nisbett & Ross, 1980; White, 2002). When your friend states that she likes her statistics class, you automatically try to figure out why: "Is she a math fan?" "Is it taught by a gifted teacher?" What does your friend say about other math classes or about her classes in general? What do other students in her statistics class say about it?

covariation principle The idea that behavior should be attributed to potential causes that co-occur with the behavior.

In considering these questions, people use what attribution theorists have dubbed the **covariation principle** (Kelley, 1973). That is, we try to determine what causes—internal or external, symptomatic of the person in question or applicable to nearly everyone—"covary" with the observation or effect we are trying to explain. Psychologists believe that three types of covariation information are particularly significant: consensus, distinctiveness, and consistency.

Consensus refers to what most people would do in a given situation—that is, does everyone behave the same way in that situation, or do few other people behave that way? Is your friend one of a precious few who likes her statistics class, or do most students like the class? All else being equal, the more an individual's reaction is shared by others (when consensus is high), the less it says about that individual and the more it says about the situation. **Distinctiveness** refers to what an individual does in different situations—that is, whether a behavior is unique to a particular situation or occurs in many situations. Does your friend seem to like all math classes, or even all classes in general, or does she just like her statistics class? The more someone's reaction is confined to a particular situation (when distinctiveness is high), the less it says about that individual and the more it says about the specific situation. **Consistency** refers to what an individual does in a given situation on different occasions—that is, whether the behavior is the same now as in the past or whether it varies. Does your friend have favorable things to say about today's statistics class only, or has she raved about the course all semester? The more an individual's reaction is specific to a given occasion (when consistency is low), the harder it is to make a definite attribution either to the person or to the situation. The effect is likely due to some less predictable combination of circumstances.

Putting the three sources of information together, a situational attribution is called for when consensus, distinctiveness, and consistency are all high (see **Table 5.2**). When everyone likes your friend's statistics class, when she claims to like no other math class, and when she has raved about the class all semester, there must be something special about that class. In contrast, a dispositional attribution

consensus What most people would do in a given situation—that is, whether most people would behave the same way or few or no other people would behave that way.

distinctiveness What an individual does in different situations—that is, whether the behavior is unique to a particular situation or occurs in all situations.

consistency What an individual does in a given situation on different occasions—that is, whether next time under the same circumstances, the person would behave the same or differently.

TABLE 5.2 Covariation Information

Putting covariation information to work by using consensus, distinctiveness, and consistency information. How do you explain a friend's enthusiastic comments about her statistics class? Does she have idiosyncratic tastes (internal attribution), or is the class a gem (external attribution)?

Attribution	Consensus	Distinctiveness	Consistency
An **external attribution** is likely if the behavior is:	High in **consensus**: Everyone raves about the class.	High in **distinctiveness**: Your friend does not rave about many other classes.	High in **consistency**: Your friend frequently raves about the class.
An **internal attribution** is likely if the behavior is:	Low in **consensus**: Hardly anyone raves about the class.	Low in **distinctiveness**: Your friend raves about all classes.	High in **consistency**: Your friend has raved about the class on many occasions.

Covariation and Attribution A person in the audience watching Chris Rock perform a comedy routine, as here, may be laughing because of his own disposition or the situation. If you can observe the person on a number of occasions at comedy clubs and find that he always laughs at Chris Rock routines (high consistency), that he rarely laughs at other comedians' jokes (high distinctiveness), and that most people laugh when Chris Rock performs (high consensus), covariation principles will lead you to attribute the person's laughter to the situation rather than to his disposition.

is called for when consensus and distinctiveness are low but consistency is high. When few other students like her class, when she claims to like all math classes, and when she has raved about the course all semester, her fondness for the course must reflect something about her.

To verify that people do indeed use covariation information in these ways, attribution researchers have presented participants with statements such as "John laughed at the comedian. Almost everyone who hears the comedian laughs at him [indicating consensus]. John does not laugh at many other comedians [indicating distinctiveness]. In the past, John has almost always laughed at the same comedian [indicating consistency]." The participants are then asked to indicate whether they think the event (John's laughing) was due to the person (John), the situation (the comedian), the circumstances (the details surrounding the performance that particular day), or some combination of these factors.

These studies have revealed that people do in fact apply the logic of covariation (Forsterling, 1989; Hewstone & Jaspers, 1983; Hilton et al., 1995; McArthur, 1972; White, 2002). Participants tend to make situational attributions when consensus, distinctiveness, and consistency are high and to make dispositional attributions when consensus and distinctiveness are low but consistency is high. The only surprising finding in these studies is that participants are sometimes only modestly influenced by consensus information. They respond to whether or not everyone laughed at the comedian, but rather mildly. This finding reflects a common tendency to focus more on information about the person (here, distinctiveness and consistency) at the expense of information that speaks to the influence of the surrounding context (here, consensus).

Attribution and Imagining Alternative Actors and Outcomes

The judgments people make are not always based on what has actually happened; sometimes we also base them on what we *imagine* would happen under different situations or if a different individual were involved. For example, in considering the high rates of obedience in Stanley Milgram's experiments (see Chapters 1 and 9), you might try to imagine what you would do if you were a participant. You might have difficulty imagining that you would administer so much electric shock to the victim. In other words, you would believe that a change in the participant—in particular, if *you* were the participant—would lead to a change in the outcome. Hence, you would conclude that it must have been the person, not the situation, that was responsible for the behavior.

The Discounting and Augmentation Principles Sometimes the information available to us suggests that either of two (or more) causes might be responsible for a given behavior. Someone interviews for a job and seems quite personable. Is that the way she really is, or is she just putting on a good face for the interview? We are not well equipped to make an attribution when we have not had the opportunity to see how this person behaves in other situations or to witness how other people behave in exactly the same situation.

In these situations, people typically use their general knowledge about the world to infer how most people would behave in the situation in question, and they combine that knowledge with a bit of logic to arrive at an attribution. The logic is known as the **discounting principle**, according to which our confidence that a particular cause is responsible for a given outcome must be reduced (discounted) if there are other plausible causes that might have produced it (Kelley, 1973). Either a sunny disposition or the desire to land a job is sufficient to make someone act personably in an interview. By pure logic, then, a confident attribution cannot be made. But we supplement the pure logic with our knowledge of people. That knowledge tells us that nearly everyone would act in a personable manner to get the job offer, so we can't be confident that the applicant's disposition is all that sunny. We thus discount the possibility that what we've seen (a personable demeanor) tells us something about the person involved (she's personable) because we imagine that nearly everyone would act similarly in that context.

discounting principle The idea that people should assign reduced weight to a particular cause of behavior if other plausible causes might have produced it.

Extending the logic just a bit leads to a complementary **augmentation principle**, by which we can have greater (augmented) confidence that a particular cause is responsible for a given outcome if other causes are present that we imagine would produce the *opposite* outcome. Typically, we can be more certain that a person's actions reflect what that person is really like if the circumstances would seem to discourage such actions. If someone advocates a position despite being threatened with torture for doing so, we can safely conclude that the person truly believes in that position.

augmentation principle The idea that people should assign greater weight to a particular cause of behavior if other causes are present that normally would produce the opposite outcome.

One important implication of the discounting and augmentation principles is that it can be difficult to know what to conclude about someone who behaves "in role," but easy to figure out what to think about someone who acts "out of role." In one of the earliest attribution studies (Jones, Davis, & Gergen, 1961), participants witnessed another person acting in either an extraverted or introverted manner during an interview. Half of the participants were led to believe the person was interviewing for a job as a submariner, a position that required close contact with many people over a long period of time and thus favored extraverted personalities. The other participants thought he was interviewing for a job as an astronaut, which involved long periods of solitude and thus favored an introverted personality. (Note that this study was published in 1961, when space flight involved a single astronaut in a tiny capsule.)

In short, half the participants witnessed behavior that conformed to the dictates of the situation—someone who exhibited the appropriate trait for the job. Because the behavior fit the situation in these instances, it should be difficult to judge whether the behavior truly reflected the person being interviewed. In contrast, the other participants witnessed behavior that defied the dictates of the situation—someone who exhibited the inappropriate trait for the job. Because the behavior varied from what the situation called for, it should be seen as a clear reflection of the interviewee's true self.

When the participants subsequently rated the interviewee on a host of trait dimensions related to introversion/extraversion, their judgments closely followed the logic of the discounting and augmentation principles. As shown in **Figure 5.1**, participants responded as if they had learned nothing about the person's degree of extraversion if he behaved in a fashion that would be considered "in role" (see the middle two bars). Out-of-role behavior prompted more extreme judgments (see the two outer bars). Someone who acts outgoing when he should be subdued is assumed to be a true extravert; someone who acts withdrawn when he should be outgoing is assumed to be a true introvert.

FIGURE 5.1 Discounting and Augmentation Out-of-role behavior is seen as more informative of a person's true self than in-role behavior. The figure shows the perceived extraversion of a person who acted in an introverted or extraverted manner while interviewing for a position that favored introversion (astronaut) or extraversion (submariner). (Source: Adapted from Jones, Davis, & Gergen, 1961.)

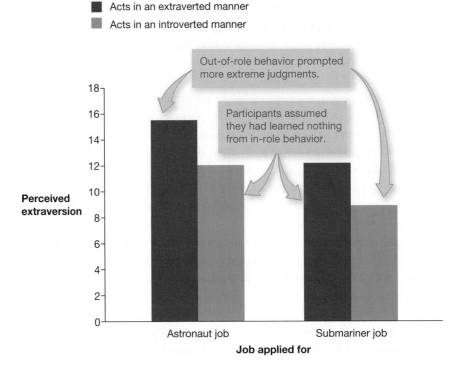

counterfactual thoughts Thoughts of what might have, could have, or should have happened "if only" something had been done differently.

The Influence of What Almost Happened In making causal assessments, people sometimes consider whether a given outcome is likely to have happened if the circumstances were slightly different. Our attributions are thus influenced by our knowledge of what has actually happened in the past as well as by our **counterfactual thoughts** (thoughts *counter* to the facts) of what might have, could have, or should have happened "if only" a few minor things were done differently (Johnson, 1986; Kahneman & Tversky, 1982a; Roese, 1997; Roese & Olson, 1995; Sanna, 2000). "If only I had studied harder" implies that a lack of effort was the cause of a poor test result. "If only the Republicans had nominated a different candidate" implies that the candidate, not the party's principles, was responsible for defeat.

Consider, for example, an experiment in which participants read about a woman who went to lunch with her boss to celebrate her promotion (Wells & Gavanski, 1989). The woman's boss ordered for her; but not knowing she suffered from a rare allergy to wine, he ordered a dish made with a wine sauce. The woman fell ill shortly after the meal, went into convulsions, and died en route to the hospital. Some participants read a version of this story in which the boss had considered ordering a different dish that did not contain wine. The others read a version in which the alternative dish her boss had considered also contained wine. The participants were then asked several questions about the cause of the woman's death.

The investigators predicted that the participants' attributions would be influenced not only by what happened in the scenario, but by what *almost* happened. Those who read that the woman's boss almost ordered a dish without wine would readily imagine a chain of events in which she was just fine, and thus they would come to view the boss's choice of meals as causally significant. In contrast, if the dish the boss almost ordered also contained wine, the participants would not readily imagine a different outcome, so they would be likely to see the boss's choice of meals as less causally significant. As **Figure 5.2** indicates, that is exactly what happened.

Emotional Effects of Counterfactual Thinking Our attributions influence our emotional reactions to events, and it therefore stands to reason that our counterfactual thoughts do as well. Our emotional reaction to an event tends to be more intense if it almost did not happen—a phenomenon known as **emotional amplification**. Would you feel worse, for example, if someone you loved died in a plane crash after switching her assigned flight at the last minute or after sticking with her assigned flight? Most people say that a last-minute switch would make the loss harder to bear because of the thought that it "almost" did not happen. In general, the pain or joy we derive from any event tends to be proportional to how easy it is to imagine the event not happening.

Given that our thoughts about "what might have been" exert such a powerful influence on our reactions and attributions, a key question becomes what determines whether a counterfactual event seems like it "almost" happened. Some of the most common determinants are time and distance. Suppose, for example, that someone survives a plane crash in a remote area and then tries to hike to safety. Suppose he hikes to within 75 miles of safety before dying of exposure. How much should the airline pay his relatives in compensation? Would your estimate of the proper compensation change if the individual made it to within one-fourth of a mile of safety? It would for most people. Those led to believe he died a quarter mile from safety recommended an average of $162,000 more in compensation than those who thought he died 75 miles away (Miller & McFarland, 1986). Because he almost made it (within a quarter mile), his death seems more tragic and thus more worthy of compensation.

This psychology of coming close leads to something of a paradox in Olympic athletes' emotional reactions to winning a silver or bronze medal. An analysis of the smiles and grimaces that athletes exhibited on the medal stand at the 1992 summer Olympics in Barcelona, Spain, revealed that silver medalists, who finished second, seemed to be less happy than the bronze medalists, or third-place finishers, they had outperformed (Medvec, Madey, & Gilovich, 1995; see **Figure 5.3**). This finding was replicated at the 2004 Olympic Games in Athens, Greece (Matsumoto & Willingham, 2006). This effect appears to result from silver medalists being consumed by what they did not receive (the coveted gold medal), whereas bronze medalists focus on what they did receive (any medal). (Those who finish fourth in Olympic competition receive no medal at all.) Indeed, analyses of the athletes' comments during postevent interviews confirmed the suspected difference in their counterfactual thoughts. Silver medalists were more focused on how they could have done better "if only" a few things had gone differently, whereas bronze medalists were more inclined to state that "at least" they received a medal. Second place can thus be a mixed blessing. The triumph over many can get lost in the defeat by only one.

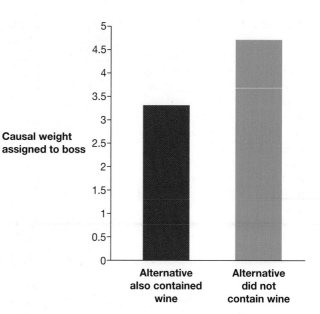

Causal weight assigned to boss

Alternative also contained wine

Alternative did not contain wine

FIGURE 5.2 **The Role of Imagined Outcomes in Causal Attribution** The causal significance of the boss's choice of meals as seen by participants who read that the boss almost ordered a different dish that did or did not also contain wine. (Source: Adapted from Wells & Gavanski, 1989.)

emotional amplification A ratcheting up of an emotional reaction to an event that is proportional to how easy it is to imagine the event not happening.

Hypothesis: People's emotional responses to events are influenced by their thoughts about "what might have been."

Research Method:

1. Researchers videotaped all televised coverage of the 1992 summer Olympic games in Barcelona, Spain.

2. College students who didn't know anything about the games examined the athlete's smiles and grimaces and rated how happy each athlete appeared.

3. The students rated the athletes shown immediately after finishing their events and when shown on the podium.

Results: Silver medalists, who finished second, seemed less happy than the third-place bronze medalists.

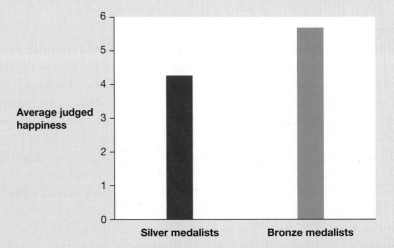

CONCLUSION: People react to events based not only on what they are, but also on what they are not. Silver medals are often experienced as *not* a gold medal, and so may be enjoyed less than bronze medals, which are often experienced as *not* an also-ran.

The Influence of Exceptions versus Routines Another determinant of how easy it is to imagine an event not happening is whether it resulted from a routine action or a departure from the norm. In one study that examined this idea, participants read about a man who was severely injured when a store he happened to be in was robbed. In one version of the story, the robbery took place in the store where the man most often shopped. In another version, the robbery took place in a store he decided to visit for "a change of pace." When participants were asked how much the victim should be compensated for his injuries, those who thought the injuries were sustained in an unusual setting recommended over $100,000 more in compensation than did those who thought they were sustained in the victim's usual store (Miller & McFarland, 1986). The injuries were presumably more tragic because it was so easy to see how they could have been avoided.

The Anguish of What Might Have Been It is especially upsetting when someone dies who was not supposed to be in a particular situation. (A) The bullfighter José Cubero, known as Yiyo, died in the bullring after substituting at the last minute for another bullfighter. (B) In the Israeli army, soldiers are forbidden to trade missions, no matter how compelling the circumstances. The reasoning is that if a soldier dies on a mission that he was not supposed to go on, the family will feel even greater anguish at his "needless death," and the soldier who should have gone will feel enormous guilt at still being alive.

This kind of reasoning helps explain why those who put themselves in considerable danger, such as bullfighters and fighter pilots, often have informal rules against changing places with someone else. Changing places is thought to be asking for trouble. The death some years ago of the Spanish matador Yiyo seemed particularly tragic, in part because he violated the unwritten code of his profession and served as a last-minute replacement for another matador (Miller & Taylor, 1995). The extra anguish that accompanies such tragedies may make them particularly memorable and therefore reinforce the superstition that switching spots somehow increases the chances of disaster by "tempting fate" (Risen & Gilovich, 2007, 2008). In less ominous circumstances, the same processes are at work in the belief that you should never change lines at the grocery store or depart from your initial hunch on a multiple-choice test. Because we "kick ourselves" when our new line slows to a crawl or when our initial hunch was right, such occasions may be particularly memorable, and we may overestimate how often a change of heart leads to a bad outcome (Kruger, Wirtz, & Miller, 2005; Miller & Taylor, 1995).

 A primary aspect of causal attribution involves assessing how much the person or the situation is responsible for a given event. People make such assessments by employing the logic of covariation. We consider the distinctiveness and consistency of a person's behavior, as well as whether other people would have behaved similarly. When the person's behavior is not unique to a particular situation, when the person behaves consistently in those circumstances, and when not everyone behaves in that way, we feel confident that it is something about the person that caused the behavior. When behavior is distinctive and consistent and most people behave in the same way as the person, we tend to attribute the behavior to the situation. We also rely on our psychological insight to make attributions. When someone stands to gain from a particular behavior, we attribute the behavior to what the person stands to gain and not to the person's underlying disposition. But when someone behaves in a way that conflicts with self-interest, we are inclined to attribute the behavior to the person's dispositions. Moreover, counterfactual thoughts about events that "almost" occurred influence our causal attributions and emotional reactions to events that did occur.

ERRORS AND BIASES IN ATTRIBUTION

The attributions people make are sometimes less than fully rational. Our hopes and fears sometimes color our judgment, we sometimes reason from faulty premises, and we are occasionally misled by information of questionable value and validity. In other words, our causal attributions are occasionally subject to predictable errors and biases. Indeed, since the initial development of attribution theory in the late 1960s and early 1970s, social psychologists have made considerable progress in illuminating some of the pitfalls of everyday causal analysis.

The Self-Serving Attributional Bias

self-serving attributional bias The tendency to attribute failure and other bad events to external circumstances, but to attribute success and other good events to oneself.

"Success has a thousand fathers; failure is an orphan."

—Old saying

One of the most consistent biases in causal assessments is one you have no doubt noticed time and time again: people are inclined to attribute their own failure and other bad events to external circumstances, but to attribute their successes and other good events to themselves—that is, they are subject to a **self-serving attributional bias** (Carver, DeGregorio, & Gillis, 1980; Greenberg, Pyszczynski, & Solomon, 1982; Mullen & Riordan, 1988). Think for a moment about two of your classes, the one in which you've received your highest grade and the one in which you've received your lowest. In which class would you say the exams were the most "fair" and constituted the most accurate assessment of your knowledge? If you're like most people, you'll find yourself thinking that the exam on which you performed well was the better test of your knowledge (Arkin & Maruyama, 1979; Davis & Stephan, 1980; Gilmour & Reid, 1979). Students tend to make external attributions for their failures ("The professor is a sadist," "The questions were ambiguous") and internal attributions for success ("Man, did I study hard"; "I'm smart"). Research has shown that professors do the same thing when their manuscripts are evaluated for possible publication (Wiley, Crittenden, & Birg, 1979). (However, papers by the authors of this textbook are rejected only because of theoretical bias, unfair evaluation procedures, or the simple narrow-mindedness of reviewers.)

Consider your favorite athletes and their coaches. How do they explain their wins and losses, their triumphs and setbacks? Richard Lau and Dan Russell (1980) examined newspaper accounts of the postgame attributions of professional athletes and coaches and found that attributions to one's own team were much more common for victories than for defeats. In contrast, attributions to external elements (bad calls, bad luck, and so on)

"There might have been some carelessness on my part, but it was mostly just good police work."

were much more common for defeats than for victories. Overall, 80 percent of all attributions for victories were to aspects of one's own team, but only 53 percent of all attributions for defeats were to one's own team. Only 20 percent of attributions for victories were to external elements, whereas 47 percent of attributions for defeats were to external elements (see also Roesch & Amirkhan, 1997).

You no doubt have observed this tendency to attribute success internally and failure externally (**Box 5.1**), and you no doubt can readily explain it: people exhibit a self-serving bias in their attributions because doing so makes them feel good about themselves (or at least prevents them from feeling bad about themselves). The self-serving attributional bias, then, is a motivational bias—motivated by the desire to maintain self-esteem (see Chapter 3). What could be simpler?

Actually, things are not so simple. Even a completely rational person, unaffected by motivations to feel good, might make the same pattern of attributions and be justified in doing so (Wetzel, 1982). After all, when we try to succeed at something, any success is at least partly due to our efforts and thus warrants our taking some of the credit. Failure, on the other hand, usually occurs *despite* our efforts and therefore requires looking elsewhere, perhaps externally, for its cause. A fully rational individual, then, might exhibit a self-serving pattern of attribution because success is generally so much more tightly connected than failure to our intentions and effort.

To see this pattern more clearly, consider an experimental paradigm that reliably elicits the self-serving attributional bias (Beckman, 1970). Participants in these studies are required to tutor a student who is having difficulty mastering some material. (In some of these studies, the participants are real teachers, and in others they are college students.) After an initial round of tutoring, the student is assessed and found to have done poorly. A second round of tutoring follows,

"First, I'd like to blame the Lord for causing us to lose today."

Self-Serving Bias Athletes often attribute victory to their own skills and defeat to external factors. (A) When the Boston Red Sox were defeated by the New York Yankees, they may have attributed their defeat to external factors, such as bad calls or even the "Curse of the Bambino" (Babe Ruth's revenge after the Red Sox sold his contract to the Yankees). (B) When the Red Sox defeated the Yankees in game 7 of the American League Championship series in 2004 and went on to win the World Series that year, they most likely attributed their victories to their personal qualities and skills.

BOX 5.1 FOCUS ON DAILY LIFE

Self-Serving Attributions

The magnitude of the self-serving attributional bias can be seen in various public documents. When corporations send end-of-year letters to their shareholders, how do you think they account for their corporation's triumphs and tribulations? One study found that CEOs claimed credit for 83 percent of all positive events and accepted blame for only 19 percent of all negative events (Salancik & Meindl, 1984). Or consider the accident reports motorists file with their insurance companies after being involved in an auto accident. The externalizing here can be downright comic. "The telephone pole was approaching; I was attempting to swerve out of its way when it struck my car," was how one motorist explained his mishap. "A pedestrian hit me and went under my car," stated another (MacCoun, 1993).

These data, of course, require a disclaimer. Unlike the more controlled laboratory studies of the self-serving attributional bias, the corporate reports and insurance forms are for public consumption. Perhaps the authors of these reports don't really believe what they are saying; they're just hoping others will swallow it. These examples should thus be taken as illustrations of the self-serving attributional bias, not as solid evidence for it. The real evidence comes from the more carefully controlled studies described in the text.

and then an additional assessment is made. For half the participants, the student's performance on the second assessment remains poor; for the other half, the student shows marked improvement. Such studies typically reveal that the teachers tend to take credit if the student improves from session to session, but they tend to blame the student if the student continues to perform poorly. In other words, people make an internal attribution for success (improvement) but an external attribution for failure (continued poor performance).

It may seem as if the teachers are trying to feel good about themselves and are making less than rational attributions to do so. But that is not necessarily the case. Suppose researchers programmed a computer, devoid of any feelings and hence having no need to feel good about itself, with software that allowed it to employ the covariation principle. What kind of attributions would it make? It would receive these inputs: (1) the student did poorly initially, (2) the teacher redoubled his or her efforts or changed teaching strategy (as most people do after an initial failure), and (3) the student did well or poorly in the second session. The computer would then look for a pattern of covariation between the outcome and the potential causes that would tell it what sort of attribution to make. When the student failed both times, there would be no correlation between the teacher's efforts and the student's performance (some effort at time 1 and poor performance by the student; increased effort at time 2 and continued poor performance). Because an attribution to the teacher could not be justified, the attribution would be made to the student. When the student succeeded the second time, however, there would be an association between the teacher's efforts and the student's performance (some effort at time 1 and poor performance; increased effort at time 2 and improved performance). An attribution to the teacher would therefore be fully justified.

"We permit all things to ourselves, and that which we call sin in others, is experience for us."

—Ralph Waldo Emerson, *Experience*

As this example indicates, we shouldn't be too quick to accuse others of making self-serving attributions just to make themselves feel good. It can be difficult to tell from the pattern of attributions alone whether someone has made an attribution to protect self-esteem; such a pattern could be the result of a purely rational analysis.

The Fundamental Attribution Error

Try to recall your initial thoughts about the individuals who delivered the maximum level of shock in Milgram's studies of obedience (see Chapters 1 and 9). The participants were asked to deliver more than 400 volts of electricity to another person, over the victim's protests, as part of a learning experiment. Nearly two-thirds of all participants did so. Note that a straightforward application of the covariation principle would lead to a situational attribution in this case and not an inference about the participants' character or personalities. Because virtually all of these participants gave high levels of shock in the face of protests by the "learner," and nearly two-thirds were willing to deliver everything the machine could produce (that is, consensus was high), their behavior doesn't say much about the individual people involved, but rather speaks to something about the situation that made their behavior (surprisingly) common.

If you are like most people, however, you formed a rather harsh opinion of the participants, thinking of them as unusually cruel and callous, perhaps, or as unusually weak. If so, your judgments reflected a second way that everyday causal attributions often depart from the general principles of attributional analysis. There seems to be a pervasive tendency to see people's behavior as a reflection of the kind of people they are, rather than as a result of the situation they find themselves in.

The tendency to attribute people's behavior to elements of their character or personality, even when powerful situational forces are acting to produce the behavior, is known as the fundamental attribution error (Ross, 1977). It is called "fundamental" both because the problem people are trying to solve (figuring out what someone is like from a sample of behavior) is so basic and essential and because the tendency to think dispositionally (to attribute behavior to the person while ignoring important situational factors) is so common and pervasive.

Experimental Demonstrations of the Fundamental Attribution Error Social psychologists have devised a number of experimental paradigms to examine the fundamental attribution error (Gawronski, 2003; Gilbert & Malone, 1995; Lord, Scott, Pugh, & Desforges, 1997; Miller, Ashton, & Mishal, 1990; Miller, Jones, & Hinkle, 1981; Vonk, 1999). In one of the earliest studies, students at Duke University were asked to read an essay about Fidel Castro's Communist regime in Cuba (Jones & Harris, 1967). Half of the participants read a pro-Castro essay, and half read an anti-Castro essay, supposedly written in response to a directive to "write a short, cogent essay either defending or criticizing Castro's Cuba as if you were giving the opening statement in a debate." Afterward, the participants were asked to rate the essayist's general attitude toward Castro's Cuba. Because the essayist was thought to have been free to write an essay that was either supportive or critical of Castro's Cuba, it is not surprising that those who read a pro-Castro essay rated the writer's attitude as being much more favorable toward Cuba than those who read an anti-Castro essay (**Figure 5.4**).

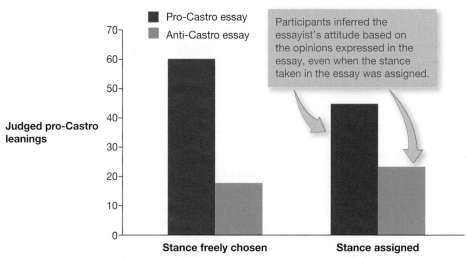

FIGURE 5.4 **The Fundamental Attribution Error** Participants' ratings of the essayists' true attitude toward Castro's Cuba; higher numbers indicate more of an assumed pro-Castro attitude. (Source: Adapted from Jones & Harris, 1967.)

However, the results from other participants in this experiment *are* surprising. These other participants read the same essays, but they were told that the stance taken (pro- or anti-Castro) had been assigned, not freely chosen. These participants' ratings of the essayist's true attitude were less extreme. Nevertheless, they still drew inferences about the essayist's attitude: those who read a pro-Castro essay thought the author was relatively pro-Castro, and those who read an anti-Castro essay thought the author was relatively anti-Castro (see the right-hand portion of Figure 5.4). From a purely logical perspective, these inferences are unwarranted. If individuals are assigned to write on a given topic, what they write cannot be taken as an indication of what they really believe. In thinking that the essays reflected the authors' true beliefs, participants showed that they were making the fundamental attribution error.

You might object to this conclusion and question how much support such studies provide for the fundamental attribution error. After all, when people are compelled to say something that is inconsistent with their beliefs, they normally distance themselves from their statements by subtly indicating that they do not truly believe what they are saying (Fleming & Darley, 1989). But the essays contained no distancing cues, so participants legitimately may have inferred that the essays reflected something of the essayists' true attitudes.

Other demonstrations of the fundamental attribution error get around these problems by allowing plenty of room for such distancing behaviors. In those studies, participants are randomly assigned to one of two roles: questioner or responder (Gilbert & Jones, 1986; Van Boven, Kamada, & Gilovich, 1999). The questioner's job is to read a series of questions over an intercom to the responder, who then answers with one of two entirely scripted responses. Thus the responders' answers are not their own and should not be considered informative about their true personalities. The added twist in this study is that after reading each question, the questioners themselves—with instructions from the experimenter—indicate to the responder which of the two responses he or she is to make. Thus the questioners are affecting the responders' behavior. For example, in response to the question, "Do you consider yourself to be sensitive to other

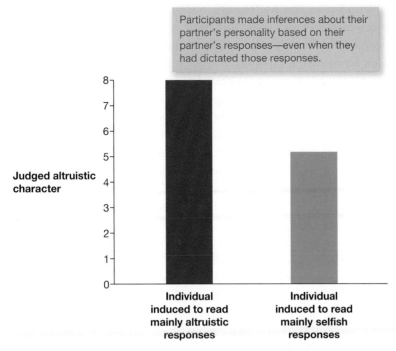

Participants made inferences about their partner's personality based on their partner's responses—even when they had dictated those responses.

Judged altruistic character

Individual induced to read mainly altruistic responses

Individual induced to read mainly selfish responses

FIGURE 5.5 **The Perceiver-Induced Constraint Paradigm** *Participants' average trait ratings of individuals that they themselves had directed to respond in an altruistic or selfish manner. Higher numbers indicate greater assumed altruism. (Source: Adapted from Van Boven, Kamada, & Gilovich, 1999.)*

people's feelings?" the questioner signals to the responder which of these two answers to give: "I try to be sensitive to others' feelings all the time. I know it is important to have people one can turn to for sympathy and understanding. I try to be that person whenever possible" (altruistic response) or "I think there are too many sensitive, 'touchy-feely' people in the world already. I see no point in trying to be understanding of another if there is nothing in it for me" (selfish response).

After reading a list of these questions to the responder and eliciting a particular response, the questioners in one such study were asked to rate the responder on a set of personality traits (trustworthiness, greediness, kindheartedness). The investigators found that the questioners drew inferences about the responders—even though they had directed the responders to answer as they did! Responders led to recite mainly altruistic responses were rated more favorably than those led to recite mainly selfish responses (**Figure 5.5**). Note also that this occurred even though the responders could have (and may have) tried through tone of voice to distance themselves from the responses they were asked to give (Van Boven et al., 1999).

The Fundamental Attribution Error and Perceptions of the Advantaged and Disadvantaged An inferential problem we all face in our daily lives is deciding how much credit to give to those who are succeeding in life and how much blame to direct at those who are not. How much praise and respect should we give to successful entrepreneurs, film stars, and artists? And to what degree should we hold the impoverished among us accountable for their condition? The discussion thus far about the fundamental attribution error suggests that people tend to assign too much responsibility to the individual for great accomplishments and terrible mistakes and not enough responsibility to the particular situation, broader societal forces, or pure dumb luck.

An ingenious laboratory experiment showed that people are indeed quick to commit the fundamental attribution error in such situations (Ross, Amabile, & Steinmetz, 1977). From a broader perspective, it also suggested that we often fail to see the advantages that some people enjoy in life and the disadvantages that others must overcome. In the study, participants took part in a quiz-game competition much like the television show *Jeopardy*. Half the participants were assigned the role of questioner and the other half the role of contestant. The questioner's job was to think of challenging but not impossible general-knowledge questions ("Who were the two coinventors of calculus?" "Who played the role of Victor Laszlo in the film *Casablanca?*"), and the contestant was to answer the questions (see answers on the next page).

From a self-presentation standpoint, the questioners had a tremendous advantage. It was relatively easy for the questioners to come off well because they could focus on whatever personal knowledge they happened to have and could ignore their various pockets of ignorance. Everybody has *some* expertise, and the questioners could focus on theirs. The contestants, however, suffered from the disadvantage of having to field questions about the questioners' store of knowledge, which typically did not match their own.

Thinking logically, people should correct appropriately for the relative advantages and disadvantages enjoyed by the questioners and contestants, respectively. Thus, if asked to rate the questioners' and contestants' general knowledge and overall intelligence, anyone watching the quiz show should be reluctant to make any distinction between the participants in these two roles: any difference in their *apparent* knowledge and intelligence could so easily be explained by their roles. But that was not what happened. Predictably, the unfortunate contestants did not answer many of the questions correctly. The contestants came away quite impressed by the questioners' abilities, rating them more highly than their own. And when the quiz game was later reenacted for a group of observers, they, too, rated the questioners' general knowledge more highly than that of the contestants (**Figure 5.6**). Notice that the only people not fooled by the questioners' performance were the questioners themselves, who rated their own general knowledge and intelligence as roughly equal to the average of the student body. This aspect of the results almost certainly occurred because the questioners knew they had skipped over yawning gaps in their knowledge base in order to come up with whatever challenging questions they could offer.

This experiment serves as a caution about the inferences we all draw in our everyday lives. On average, the very successful among us have worked harder and exercised more talent and skill than the unsuccessful. The successful thus deserve our admiration—on average. But this experiment teaches us not to lose sight of the invisible advantages that many people enjoy and the equally invisible disadvantages that others must struggle to overcome. By dint of birth and connections, for example, some people start out in life with considerable financial resources. Making even more money is not terribly difficult for them because they already have a sizable stake. Conversely, few things are as challenging as making money when you must start from scratch. Thus our attributions for success and failure in life, and the traits we infer as a result, should reflect the relative advantages and disadvantages that different individuals have experienced (see, for example, **Box 5.2**). The case of Bill Gates, which opened this chapter, makes this point quite clear.

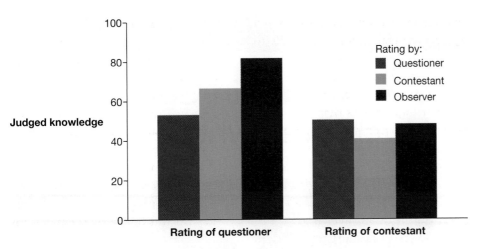

Answers to Quiz-Show Game
Questions on the Previous Page
Isaac Newton and Gottfried von
Leibnitz; Paul Henreid.

FIGURE 5.6 Role-Conferred Advantage and Disadvantage The bars show ratings of the general knowledge of the questioner and contestant in the quiz-show experiment. Participants thought the questioners were more knowledgeable than the contestants even though they knew they had been randomly assigned to their roles and that the questioners had a much easier task. (Source: Adapted from Ross, Amabile, & Steinmetz, 1977.)

Causes of the Fundamental Attribution Error

Why are people so quick to see someone's actions as reflecting the person's inner traits and enduring character? A tendency so strong and so pervasive probably is not due to a single cause but is more likely the result of several causes acting jointly. Indeed, social psychologists have identified several psychological processes that appear to be responsible for the fundamental attribution error.

Motivational Influence and the Belief in a Just World One reason we are likely to attribute behavior to people's traits and dispositions is that dispositional inferences can be comforting. The twists and turns of life can be unsettling. A superbly qualified job candidate may be passed over in favor of a mediocre applicant with the right connections. A selfless Good Samaritan may be stricken with cancer and experience a gruesome death. These events produce anxiety that tempts us to think such things couldn't happen to us. But we can minimize the perceived threat to ourselves in several ways, and one of them is to attribute people's outcomes to something about them rather than to fate or chance (Burger, 1981; Walster, 1966). More broadly, by thinking that people "get what they deserve," that "what goes around comes around," or that "good things happen to good people and bad things happen to bad people," we can reassure ourselves that nothing bad will happen to us if we are the right kind of person living the right kind of life. Thus people tend to attribute behavior and outcomes to dispositions in part because they are *motivated* to do so.

Social psychologists have studied this impulse as part of their examination of the **just world hypothesis**—the belief that people get what they deserve in life and deserve what they get (Lambert, Burroughs, & Nguyen, 1999; Lerner, 1980; Lipkus, Dalbert, & Siegler, 1996). Victims of rape, for example, are often viewed as responsible for their fate (Abrams, Viki, Masser, & Bohner, 2003; Bell, Kuriloff, & Lottes, 1994), as are victims of domestic abuse (Summers & Feldman,

just world hypothesis The belief that people get what they deserve in life and deserve what they get.

BOX 5.2 FOCUS ON SPORTS AND ACADEMICS

How to Succeed at Hockey in Canada and at Math Pretty Much Everywhere

A disproportionate number of Canadian hockey stars—the very best of the very best—were born in January, February, or March. Could being born in a cold month somehow be an advantage for playing a winter sport like hockey? If so, what mechanism could account for that connection? Could it be a player's astrological sign? Might it be that Capricorn, Aquarius, and Pisces people are particularly speedy or insensitive to being roughed up? In England, in the premier soccer league, about twice as many players were born between September and November as were born between June and August. Could it be that Virgos, Libras, and Scorpios have more endurance or ability to aim their heads at a projectile than Geminis, Cancers, and Leos?

The correct explanation is both more prosaic and more thought provoking. January 1 is the cutoff date for being able to play hockey at a given age level. A child born January 5 is almost a year older than a child born December 27. And that age difference means a huge difference in strength and agility. The child with an early birth date is going to play better from the word go, get more attention from coaches, and be more likely to move up to a higher league. And that latter difference is decisive: although the older child's initial edge in size, agility, and coordination will eventually disappear, it puts him on a different "track" that makes it likely that he will continue to reap the benefits, all through childhood and adolescence, of playing against better players and receiving better coaching. The cutoff for age-level play for soccer in England is September 1, so it's the fall-born child who is going to have the advantage over other children. Brilliant Bill and his brother Plodding Pete differ in their skills for a completely arbitrary rea-

Wayne Gretzky The great Canadian hockey player Wayne Gretsky. You will not be surprised by his birthday: January 26.

son. The accident of birth, not innate ability, is what lies behind the skill difference.

What's true for sports is also true for academics. The Trends in International Mathematics and Science Study is a test given to fourth-graders around the world. Children born at opposite ends of the cutoff date differ by as much as 12 percentile points (Bedard & Dhuey, 2006). So a given fourth-grader who could score at the 90th percentile if born soon after the cutoff date might score at only the 78th percentile if born later. That could be the difference between being admitted to an advanced math curriculum or not, which in turn could mean the difference between going to an elite college or a less prestigious one, which in turn . . .

In *Outliers*, Malcolm Gladwell presents case after case of highly successful

people who had unseen advantages. We attribute their accomplishments to their native talent or to an unusual capacity for hard work. Undoubtedly, more successful people are, on average, more talented and hardworking; but often they have had advantages that, if we knew about them, would cause us to be less likely to make wholly dispositional attributions for their success.

And to what does Gladwell attribute his astonishing success as a science writer—one who often has more than one book at a time on the *New York Times* bestseller list? Among other things, he chalks it up to reading work by social psychologists on the fundamental attribution error, particularly Ross and Nisbett's (1991/2011) *The Person and the Situation* (Gladwell, 2011).

1984). This insidious tendency reaches its zenith in the claim that if no defect in a victim's manifest character or past actions can be found, the tragic affliction must be due to some flaw or transgression in a "past life." Thus, for example, it has been argued that children who have been sexually abused are likely to have been sex offenders themselves in a past life (Woolger, 1988). Such beliefs show how far people will go to maintain their belief in a just world. Research in this area has also shown that people tend to "derogate the victim"—that is, they rate unfavorably the character of those who suffer unfortunate outcomes that are completely beyond their personal control (Jones & Aronson, 1973; Lerner & Simmons, 1966; Lerner & Miller, 1978). "Since I'm a good person, I don't have to worry that I will have the terrible fate of that bad person."

"The employees have to assume a share of the blame for allowing the pension fund to become so big and tempting."

People Are Often More Salient than Situations What influences whether a potential cause springs to mind or how readily it springs to mind? One important determinant is how much the cause stands out perceptually, or how *salient* it is (Lassiter, Geers, Munhall, Ploutz-Snyder, & Breitenbecher, 2002; Robinson & McArthur, 1982; Smith & Miller, 1979). Elements of the environment that more readily capture our attention are more likely to be seen as potential causes of an observed effect. And because people are so noticeable and interesting, they tend to capture our attention much more readily than other aspects of the environment. Situations, if attended to at all, may be seen as mere background to the person and his or her actions. This is particularly true of various social determinants of a person's behavior (customs, social norms) that are largely invisible. Attributions to the person, then, have an edge over situational attributions in everyday causal analysis.

The importance of perceptual salience in our attributions has been demonstrated in many ways. In one study, participants watched a videotape of a conversation between two people. Some participants saw a version of the tape that allowed them a view of only one of the individuals; others saw a tape that allowed them to see both individuals equally well. When asked to assign responsibility for setting the tone of the conversation, those who could see only one individual assigned more responsibility to that individual than did those who could see both equally well (Taylor & Fiske, 1975). In another set of studies, one person in a videotaped conversation was made highly salient by being brightly lit on camera or by wearing a dramatically striped shirt. Those who witnessed the videotaped conversation made more dispositional attributions for the behavior of the salient individual than they did for the behavior of the nonsalient individual (McArthur & Post, 1977).

Attribution and Cognition Perceptual salience explains some instances of the fundamental attribution error better than others. It explains the results of the quiz-show study, for example, because the decisive situational influence—that the questioner could avoid areas of ignorance but the contestant could not—was invisible and therefore had little impact on people's judgments. But what about the attitude attribution studies in which participants knew that a writer had been assigned to argue for the particular position advocated in an essay? Here, the situational constraints were far from invisible. Why didn't the participants discount appropriately and decide that the target person's

Perceptual Salience and Attribution The fundamental attribution error is made in part because people are more salient than situations. If the people in this photo were to engage in a particular behavior—say, break out in song, tell embarrassing anecdotes, or complain about the weather—observers would be likely to assume that the behavior in question reflects the disposition of the woman in the center more than it reflects the others' dispositions because her red clothing and her uncovered face make her stand out.

behavior was perfectly well accounted for by the situational constraints and thus refrain from making any inference about the person at all? The answer is that the cognitive machinery people draw on when using the discounting principle doesn't work that way.

Let's review the logic of the discounting principle, depicted in **Figure 5.7A**. By that logic, we simultaneously weigh what we've seen (or heard or read) about the person's behavior and the context of that behavior to figure out what kind of person we're dealing with—that is, to draw a dispositional inference. What is puzzling about the fundamental attribution error, then, is why we don't give enough weight to the situational information when we know (as did the participants in the earlier example of attitude attribution) that it is sufficient to produce the observed behavior.

That would indeed be a puzzle if, in fact, people reasoned along the lines depicted in Figure 5.7A. But research by Dan Gilbert makes it clear that we don't reason that way at all. Instead, we reason in the manner depicted in Figure 5.7B, which suggests that our failure to discount sufficiently for situational influences is not so puzzling after all (Gilbert, 2002). Gilbert has shown that we do not weigh behavioral and situational information simultaneously; instead, we observe the behavior in question and initially identify what that behavior is and what it means. For example, we see a certain pattern of gaze, a certain constriction of the muscles around the eyes, and a certain upturn of the corners of the mouth, and we must identify whether we're seeing nervousness or bemusement (Trope, 1986). We see one person in the arms of another, and we must decide whether the latter is carrying, helping, or kidnapping the other (Vallacher & Wegner, 1985).

Once we've identified what we've seen, we immediately—and automatically—characterize the person based on the behavior observed (Carlston & Skowronski, 1994; Moskowitz, 1994; Newman, 1993; Todorov & Uleman, 2003; Uleman, 1987; Winter & Uleman, 1984). Initially, someone who acts in a hostile manner is seen as hostile regardless of what prompted the hostility; someone who acts in a compassionate manner is seen as compassionate, again, regardless of what may have prompted the compassion. Then, but only upon reflection, we consciously and deliberately take in what we know about the prevailing situational constraints and adjust our initial dispositional inference if warranted. Thus the situational information is taken into account sequentially, after an initial dispositional inference has been made (see Figure 5.7B).

The primacy of the initial characterization of the person gives it one of its advantages. The situational information is not taken into account on its own terms, but is used to adjust the initial dispositional inference. Such adjustments, unfortunately, tend to be insufficient, so the initial characterization of the person is weighted too heavily. Moreover, because the initial characterization of the person happens automatically, it does not require much energy to perform and cannot easily be altered. The adjustment requires deliberate effort, attention, and energy to perform and so it can easily be short-circuited. When people are tired, unmotivated, or distracted, they should thus be more likely to commit the fundamental attribution error (or make a larger error) because the adjustment stage is shortened or skipped altogether.

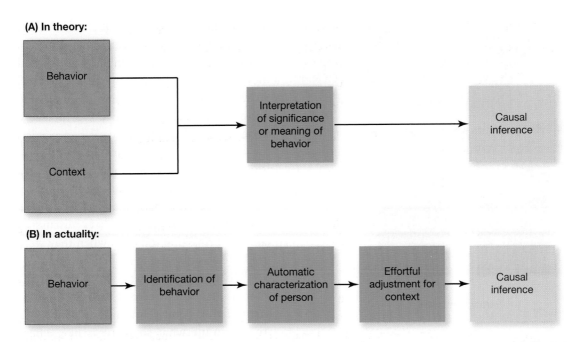

(A) In theory:

Behavior

Context

Interpretation of significance or meaning of behavior

Causal inference

(B) In actuality:

Behavior → Identification of behavior → Automatic characterization of person → Effortful adjustment for context → Causal inference

FIGURE 5.7 Inferring Dispositions According to the discounting principle, a potential cause is discounted as a possible cause of a particular outcome if other causes might have produced the outcome. (A) In theory, people should simultaneously weigh both the other person's behavior and the surrounding context to arrive at an explanation of such behavior. (B) In actuality, people tend to spontaneously make a dispositional inference and adjust for the context only with effort. The resulting inference is likely to be biased toward dispositional causes.

Gilbert has conducted a number of experiments that demonstrate the automatic nature of dispositional inference and the deliberate nature of people's efforts to take situational information into account. In one study, participants were shown a videotape, without the sound, of a young woman engaged in a conversation with another person. The woman appeared anxious throughout: "She bit her nails, twirled her hair, tapped her fingers, and shifted in her chair from cheek to cheek" (Gilbert, 1989, p. 194). Half the participants were told that the woman was responding to a number of anxiety-inducing questions (about her sexual fantasies or personal failings, for example). The other participants were told that she was responding to questions about innocuous topics (world travel or great books, for example). Gilbert predicted that all participants, regardless of what they were told about the content of the discussion, would witness the woman's anxious demeanor and immediately and automatically assume that she was an anxious person. Those told that she was discussing anxiety-producing topics, however, would then deliberatively adjust their initial characterization and conclude that maybe she was not such an anxious person after all. Those told that she was discussing a series of bland topics would not make such an adjustment and would conclude that she was an anxious person.

So far, this is just a standard attribution experiment. But Gilbert added a wrinkle. He gave another two groups of participants the same information he gave the first two, but he had these groups memorize a list of words while watching the videotape. Gilbert reasoned that this extra demand on their attention would make them less able to carry out the deliberative stage of the attribution process, in which they would adjust their initial characterization of the person to account

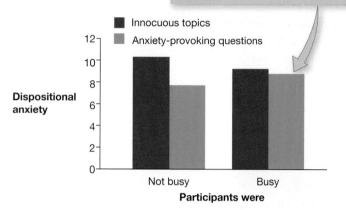

Observers who were kept busy by having to memorize a list of words did not correct their initial, automatic impression that the person was anxious and did not take into account the nature of the material being discussed.

■ Innocuous topics
■ Anxiety-provoking questions

FIGURE 5.8 Adjusting Automatic Characterizations Observers had to judge how generally anxious a person was who appeared anxious while discussing either innocuous or anxiety-provoking topics. (Source: Adapted from Gilbert, 1989.)

for situational constraints. If so, then those who thought that the young woman was discussing anxiety-provoking topics should nevertheless rate her as being just as anxious as those who were told she was discussing innocuous topics. As **Figure 5.8** indicates, that is just what happened. When participants were busy memorizing a list of words, they did not have the cognitive resources needed to adjust their initial impression, so they rated the woman as just as anxious when they were told she was discussing anxiety-provoking topics as when they were told she was discussing innocuous topics.

Gilbert's work shows us that the fundamental attribution error is a basic component of the cognitive machinery people use to determine what someone is like. There are two reasons we have a strong tendency to make overly dispositional attributions. First, we use information about situational influence to adjust an immediate dispositional characterization; and such adjustments, like adjustments of all sorts, tend to be insufficient. Second, the adjustment phase requires energy and attention, so it can be disrupted by anything that tires or distracts. Because our lives are so busy and complicated and we are so often preoccupied with planning our own actions and self-presentations, we frequently lack the resources to do justice to the correction phase of attributional analysis (Geeraert, Yzerbyt, Corneille, & Wigboldus, 2004).

Salient Situations It stands to reason that we would focus initially on the person and only later adjust to account for the situation because people are compelling stimuli of considerable importance to us. But what about those occasions when it is the situation that has the most importance? What happens, for example, when we see someone react to a new ride at an amusement park and we want to know whether the ride is scary or not? Do we immediately and automatically characterize the situation (the ride is terrifying) based on the behavior we've seen (these people are terrified), and only later correct this initial situational inference in light of what we know about the individuals involved (they're rookies who've never been to a first-rate amusement park)? Research suggests that we do indeed. When people are primarily interested in finding out about the situation in which they observe someone behave (and are less interested in the person engaged in the behavior), the attributional sequence that Gilbert so carefully revealed is reversed. In such cases, people will automatically and effortlessly draw strong inferences about the situation (Krull, 1993; Krull & Dill, 1996; Krull & Erickson, 1995).

The Consequences of the Fundamental Attribution Error Does it matter that we are susceptible to the fundamental attribution error? Indeed it does. We make the error many times a day, and the results can be unfortunate. Here's just one example: People—including employers and college admissions officers—often assume that they can learn a lot about a person's traits and abilities from a 30-minute unstructured interview. But interviews tell us only about the person's *apparent* traits and abilities in a *single situation*. And in fact, the validity of the unstructured interview is virtually nil: the correlation between judgments based on interviews and the subsequent judgments based on job or school performance is only 0.10 (Hunter & Hunter, 1984).

A more accurate prediction of future performance would require information based on a wide array of situations: letters summarizing experience about the candidate in a range of situations, reports of previous job performance, high school GPA (which in turn is based on performance in everything from labs to ability to concentrate on homework to mastery of material as revealed by exams). Such information is not infallible, but it often predicts future behavior with reasonable accuracy. Correlations between these types of "input" information and later outcomes are typically much higher, on the order of 0.3 to 0.5. When we rely on one or two interviews, we set ourselves up for disappointment: we hire and admit people who aren't as terrific as we thought and pass up people who would have been much more satisfactory.

If the fundamental attribution error is so pervasive and consequential, why are we so susceptible to it and so unaware of it? For one thing, we are not very good at assessing the validity of our own judgments. We can explain after the fact almost any failure of prediction—and we do so in a way that prevents us from seeing our errors. Jane didn't work out very well; but she had some personal problems that came up shortly after she was hired, and her boss was difficult to get along with. And our decision to choose Jane prevented us from seeing that other people would have been more satisfactory.

A second reason is that situations and persons are often confounded. Sometimes people behave as we expect not because they have the broad traits or abilities we mistakenly identify, but because we see them only in situations that prompt the behavior we wrongly use as evidence about general dispositions. We see Rachel only at parties, when she seems nice and fun to be around, but we don't know about the trials she inflicts on her roommates. We see Professor Jones only in his statistics classroom, where he seems stiff and boring and none too pleasant, but we don't see him being fun, kind, and helpful with his student advisees. Such errors usually cause no harm, so they don't prompt us to look for how we went wrong.

The Actor-Observer Difference in Causal Attributions

It may have occurred to you that exactly how oriented we are toward either the person or the situation depends on whether we're engaged in the action ourselves or observing someone else engaged in the action. In the role of "actor," we're often more interested in determining what kind of situation we are dealing with. In the role of "observer," in contrast, we're often interested in determining what kind of person we are dealing with. By this logic, actors should be more likely than observers to make situational attributions for a particular behavior. Indeed, there is considerable evidence for just such a difference (Jones & Nisbett, 1972; Pronin, Lin, & Ross, 2002; Saulnier & Perlman, 1981; Schoeneman & Rubanowitz, 1985; Watson, 1982).

In one of the most straightforward demonstrations of this **actor-observer difference** in attribution, participants were asked to explain why they chose the college major that they did or why their best friends chose the major that they did. When the investigators scored the participants' explanations, they found that participants more often referred to characteristics of the person when explaining someone else's choice than when explaining their own choice, and they referred more often to

actor-observer difference A difference in attribution based on who is making the causal assessment: the actor (who is relatively disposed to make situational attributions) or the observer (who is relatively disposed to make dispositional attributions).

the specifics of the major when explaining their own choice than when explaining someone else's choice. You might attribute your own decision to major in psychology, for instance, to the facts that the material is fascinating, the textbooks beautifully written, and the professors dynamic and accessible. In contrast, you might attribute your friend's decision to major in psychology to "issues" he needs to work out (Nisbett, Caputo, Legant, & Maracek, 1973; see also **Box 5.3**).

This phenomenon has significant implications for human conflict, both between individuals and between nations. Married couples, for example, often squabble over attributional differences. A husband may mention a late meeting or unusually heavy traffic to explain why an errand did not get done, whereas his wife may be more inclined to argue that he is lazy, inattentive, or "just doesn't care" (see Chapter 10). Similarly, at the national level, the United States is likely to explain the stationing of its troops in so many locations across the globe as a necessary defense against immediate and future threats. Other countries may be more inclined to see it as a manifestation of U.S. "imperialism."

BOX 5.3   FOCUS ON MEMORY

The Mind's Eye

As far back as the late nineteenth century, psychologists have noted that when people remember past experiences, they tend to do so from one of two perspectives. Sometimes we remember events from a first-person perspective in which we "see" in our mind's eye what we saw when we actually experienced the event in question. We see our teacher praising us in front of the class, the look on our father's face when he uttered the words "getting divorced", the football as it sails toward us in the end zone. But sometimes we remember events from a third-person perspective in which we see *ourselves* in the mental image, much like an observer would. We see ourselves beaming that day in the classroom, the tears on our cheeks when our parents split up, or our exultant touchdown celebration.

Do these different perspectives influence people's judgments in the same way that having an actor's or observer's perspective influences people's causal attributions? They do. People make more dispositional attributions for their own behavior when they recall the episode from a third-person perspective rather than a first-person perspective (Frank &

Gilovich, 1989). First-person memories also tend to be more detail focused, so they encourage a bottom-up, low-level construal of the event in question, whereas third-person memories encourage a top-down, high-level construal (Libby & Eibach, 2011). If you remember going over Chapter 1 of this book from a first-person perspective, you're likely to think that you were "reading"; if you remember it from a third-person perspective, you're likely to think that you were "studying." This can have all sorts of influences on people's attributions. For example, people who suffer from low self-esteem are more likely to make "I'm no good" overgeneralizations when recalling a failure experience from a third-person instead of a first-person perspective (Libby, Valenti, Pfent, & Eibach, 2011).

People adopt these same two perspectives when anticipating or imagining future events, and the consequences are similar. Students who imagine completing an academic assignment from a third-person perspective tend to think of it more as "pursuing my education" than "doing my homework," so they end

up being more motivated to do the work (Vasquez & Buehler, 2007).

In the most remarkable demonstration of the influence of visual perspective on people's thoughts and behavior, Lisa Libby, Richard Eibach, and their colleagues asked voters in Ohio to picture themselves voting in the 2004 presidential election from either a first- or a third-person perspective. Those who did so from a third-person perspective reported feeling more enthusiastic about the prospect of voting and saw themselves as more committed to this key element of participatory democracy (high-level construal). When Libby, Eibach, and colleagues followed up after the election to see who actually voted, those who had earlier thought of voting from a third-person perspective were 25 percent more likely to do so than those who had thought of it from a first-person perspective (Libby, Shaeffer, Eibach, & Slemmer, 2007). Just as actors and observers can view the same behavior very differently, actors can view their own behavior very differently as well, depending on whether they think of it from the inside out (first-person perspective) or the outside in (third-person perspective).

Like the fundamental attribution error, the actor-observer difference has no single cause. Several processes give rise to it. First, assumptions about what needs explaining can vary for actors and observers. When asked, "Why did you choose the particular college major that you did?" a person might reasonably interpret the question to mean "Given that you are who you are, why did you choose the particular college major that you did?" The person is taken as a given and therefore need not be included as part of the explanation. This is much like Willie Sutton's explanation of why he robbed banks: "Because that's where the money is." He takes it as given that he's a crook and thus interprets the question as one about why he robs *banks* rather than filling stations. Notice, in contrast, that when asked about another person ("Why did your roommate choose his or her particular college major?"), the nature of the person cannot be taken as given and is thus "fair game" in offering an explanation (Kahneman & Miller, 1986; McGill, 1989).

Second, the perceptual salience of the actor and the surrounding situation is different for the actor and the observer (Storms, 1973). The actor is typically oriented outward, toward situational opportunities and constraints. Observers, in contrast, are typically focused on the actor and the actor's behavior. Because people tend to make attributions to potential causes that are perceptually salient, it stands to reason that actors will tend to attribute their behavior to the situation, and observers will tend to attribute that same behavior to the actor.

Third, note that actors and observers differ in the amount and kind of information they have about the actor and the actor's behavior (Andersen & Ross, 1984; Jones & Nisbett, 1972; Prentice, 1990; Pronin, Gilovich, & Ross, 2004). Actors know what intentions influenced them to behave in a certain way; observers can only guess at those intentions. Actors are also much more likely to know whether a particular action is typical of them or not. An observer may see someone slam a door and conclude that he's an angry person. The actor, in contrast, may know that this is an unprecedented outburst and hence does not warrant such a sweeping conclusion. (In the attribution language used earlier, the actor is in a much better position to know if the behavior is *distinctive* and thus merits a situational rather than a dispositional attribution.)

The Actor-Observer Difference People often explain their own actions in terms of the situation, and the actions of others in terms of the person. This demonstrator hurls a Molotov cocktail after riot police fired tear gas. He would probably see his actions as a response to an untenable situation, while others might see him as an aggressive and criminal hooligan.

Our attributions are subject to predictable errors and biases. We often exhibit a self-serving attributional bias, attributing success to the self and failure to the situation. We exhibit the fundamental attribution error when we attribute behavior to a person's dispositions rather than to the situation, even when there are powerful situational factors that we ought to consider. Actors are more likely than observers to attribute behavior to the situation, whereas observers are more likely than actors to attribute behavior to the actor's disposition.

CULTURE AND CAUSAL ATTRIBUTION

Much of what psychologists know about how people understand the behavior of others is undoubtedly universal. People everywhere are likely to imagine outcomes that could have occurred in understanding what happened and why. People everywhere probably prefer to maintain the view that they live in a just world. All people undoubtedly perceive the causes of their own behavior somewhat differently

FIGURE 5.9 Attention to the Social Situation How much do the expressions of the background individuals influence people's impressions of the focal individual? Masuda and his colleagues found that Japanese participants are more influenced by the surrounding faces than are American participants.

than they perceive the causes of other people's behavior. But there are some basic differences in how people from different cultures understand the causes of behavior. Some of these differences could be anticipated on the basis of what has been discussed already about cultural differences in perception and in characteristic social relations.

Cultural Differences in Attending to Context

Most of the world's people tend to pay more attention to social situations and the people who are involved in them than do Westerners. The kinds of social factors that are merely background for North Americans appear to be more salient to people from other cultures (Hedden et al., 2000; Ji, Schwarz, & Nisbett, 2000). In a particularly telling experiment, Takahiko Masuda and his colleagues showed Japanese and American participants cartoon figures having various expressions on their faces (Masuda, Ellsworth, Mesquita, Leu, & van de Veerdonk, 2004; see **Figure 5.9**). The central, target face was always surrounded by smaller, less salient faces with expressions that were unlike those of the target. For example, the target might appear to be happy, whereas most of the surrounding faces might appear to be sad. The Japanese participants' judgments about the facial expression of the target were more influenced by the surrounding faces than were the judgments of the Americans. A happy face surrounded by sad faces was judged less happy by Japanese participants than by American participants, and a sad face surrounded by happy faces was judged less sad.

Asians and Westerners also differ in how much attention they give to context, even when perceiving inanimate objects. Kitayama, Duffy, Kawamura, and Larsen (2002) asked Japanese and American participants to examine a square with a line drawn at the bottom (**Figure 5.10**). They then led their participants to another part of the room, showed them a square of a different size, and asked them either to draw a line of the same length as the original or to draw a line having the same length *in relation to* the original square. Americans were better at the absolute

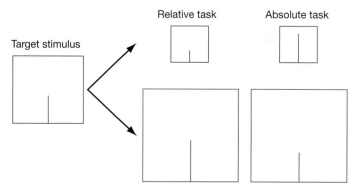

FIGURE 5.10 Sensitivity to Context and the Framed Line Task Participants are shown the target stimulus and then, after a brief interval, are asked to draw a vertical line at the bottom of an empty box. In the relative task, the line must be drawn in the same *proportion* to the box as it was originally. In the absolute task, the new line must be exactly the same length as the original line. Japanese participants are better at the relative task, and American participants are better at the absolute task. (Source: Adapted from Kitayama, Duffy, Kawamura, & Larsen 2002.)

judgment, which required ignoring the context, whereas Japanese were better at the relative judgment, which required paying attention to the context.

Hedden and his colleagues (Hedden, Ketay, Aron, Markus, & Gabrieli, 2008) used functional magnetic resonance imaging (fMRI) to examine activation of fronto-parietal activity in the brain, which is associated with difficult perceptual judgments. There was more activity in that region for East Asians when they made judgments about absolute line length and thus had to ignore the context, and more activity in that region for Westerners when they made proportional judgments and thus had to pay attention to the context.

Causal Attribution for Independent and Interdependent Peoples

Given the pronounced difference between Asians' and Westerners' attention to context, it should come as no surprise to learn that Asians are more inclined than Westerners to attribute behavior to the situation.

For example, attributions for the outcomes of sports events are not the same in independent cultures as they are in interdependent cultures. As discussed earlier in the chapter, coaches and players on sports teams in the United States tend to see positive outcomes as the result of the abilities of individual players and the actions of coaches ("We've got a very good keeper in Bo Oshoniyi, who was defensive MVP of the finals last year") (Lau & Russell, 1980). In contrast, the attributions of Hong Kong coaches and players are more likely to refer to the other team and the context ("I guess South China was a bit tired after having played in a quadrangular tournament") (Lee, Hallahan, & Herzog, 1996).

Other work shows that Westerners see dispositions and internal causes where Asians see situations and contexts. Morris and Peng (1994) showed participants animated cartoons of an individual fish swimming in front of a group of fish. In some scenes, the individual fish scooted off from the approaching group; in other scenes, the fish was joined by the group and they swam off together; in still other scenes, the individual fish joined the group. Participants were asked why these events occurred. Americans tended to see the behavior of the individual fish as internally caused, and Chinese were more likely to see the behavior of the individual fish as externally caused (see also Kashima, Siegal, Tanaka, & Kashima, 1992; Rhee, Uleman, Lee, & Roman, 1995; Shweder & Bourne, 1984).

These differences in causal perception are probably due to differences in cultural outlook that in turn result in differences in what is attended to. As Markus and Kitayama (1991) put it, "If [like Asians] one perceives oneself as embedded within a larger context of which one is an interdependent part, it is likely that other objects or events will be perceived in a similar way." Westerners, in contrast, are more likely to see themselves as independent agents; consequently, they are more inclined to see people, animals, and even objects as behaving in ways that have relatively little to do with situational context.

Culture and the Fundamental Attribution Error

Is it reasonable to assume that the fundamental attribution error occurs in all cultures? After all, nearly everyone wishes to live in a just world; other people and their dispositions are everywhere more salient and capture attention more readily than the situation; and all people have the same basic cognitive machinery. The error does indeed seem widespread. For example, Jones and Harris's (1967) finding that people assume that a speech or essay by another person represents that person's own opinion on the topic, despite the presence of obvious situational demands, has been demonstrated in many societies, including China (Krull et al., 1996), Korea (Choi & Nisbett, 1998), and Japan (Kitayama & Masuda, 1997).

But in fact there is evidence that the fundamental attribution error is more widespread and pronounced for Westerners than for Easterners. Westerners pay little attention to situational factors in circumstances in which Asians pay considerable attention to them and grant their influence. For example, in a variant of the Jones and Harris setup, participants are first asked to write an essay favoring a particular position before seeing someone else write a similar essay. With this direct experience of being required to advocate a particular position, Koreans recognize how powerful the situation is and as a result make no assumption about the attitudes of a target individual whom they subsequently observe (Choi & Nisbett, 1998). American participants, in contrast, learn nothing from the experience of being pressured to support a particular view. They are just as likely as control participants to assume that the coerced target believes what he or she said.

Koreans are also more likely to recognize the implications of consensus information: if many people behave in a particular way in a given situation, they recognize that the situation is probably the main determinant of behavior (Cha & Nam, 1985). Americans' attributions tend to be less influenced by consensus information. Finally, there is evidence that Asians are less likely to make an initial dispositional inference in circumstances where such inferences are made by the great majority of Westerners (Na & Kitayama, in press). In this study, participants were presented with information about someone that might lead them to make an inference about the person's personality (such as "She checked twice to see if the gas was on in the stove before she left," which might lead a participant to infer that she was *careful*). When participants were later shown a picture of the person along with the word *reckless*, the American participants exhibited a pattern of brain activity associated with surprise, but the Korean participants did not. Thus Asians are not just more likely to notice situational cues that might correct a dispositional inference, they might also be less likely to make a dispositional inference in the first place. Gilbert's (1989, 2002) claim that dispositional inferences are normally automatic and inevitable may not apply as consistently to people from interdependent cultures.

In a similar study, Al-Zahrani and Kaplowitz (1993) found that Saudi Arabian students were more collectivistic in orientation than Americans. Saudi Arabian students should therefore be less likely to show the fundamental attribution error in their causal explanations. The researchers gave brief readings describing morally positive and negative behaviors to Saudi Arabian students and American students and asked them to indicate the degree to which they thought the behaviors were caused by something internal to the person versus something external. The responses showed that the American attributions were more internal than the Saudi attributions.

There are also differences in attributional tendencies among American subcultures. Researchers have determined how often people mention traits in their descriptions of themselves and other people. (Using traits to describe a person is similar to making an internal attribution, since both traits and internal attributions imply something about the person being considered.) Puerto Rican children use fewer traits when describing themselves than do Anglo-American children (Hart, Lucca-Irizarry, & Damon, 1986) and are less likely to use traits to describe other people's behavior (Newman, 1991). Zarate, Uleman, and Voils (2001) found that Mexican-Americans and Mexicans were also less likely to make trait inferences than were Anglo-Americans.

Priming Culture

In today's world of highly mobile populations, many people have spent significant parts of their lives in both independent and interdependent societies. These individuals offer psychologists an opportunity to better understand cultural influences on attribution. For example, Hong Kong has been the location for several fruitful cultural studies because the British governed Hong Kong for 100 years. The culture there is substantially Westernized, and children learn English when they are quite young.

People in Hong Kong, it turns out, can be encouraged to think in either an interdependent way or an independent way when presented with images that suggest one culture or the other. Hong, Chiu, and Kung (1997) showed some participants the U.S. Capitol building, a cowboy on horseback, and Mickey Mouse. They showed other participants a Chinese dragon, a temple, and men writing Chinese characters using a brush. They also showed a control group of participants neutral pictures of landscapes. Next the investigators showed all participants the animated cartoons of an individual fish swimming in front of a group of other fish (devised by Morris and Peng, 1994) and asked them why they thought this was happening. Participants who were shown the American pictures gave more reasons having to do with motivations of the individual fish and fewer explanations having to do with the other fish or the context than did participants who saw the Chinese pictures. Participants who saw the neutral pictures first gave explanations that were in between those of the other two groups.

Other natural experiments are made possible by the fact that many people living in North America are of Asian descent and think of themselves as partly Asian and partly Western. In one study, researchers asked Asian-American participants either to recall an experience that made their identity as an American apparent to

Priming Culture To prime Western associations and individualistic attributions, investigators might show participants a photo of (A) the U.S. Capitol building or (B) an American cowboy roping a steer. To prime Asian associations and collectivist attributions, the investigators might show participants a photo of (C) a Chinese temple or (D) a Laotian dragon.

them or to recall an experience that made their Asian identity salient. They then showed the students a group of highly abstract cartoon vignettes suggesting physical movements, such as an object falling to the bottom of a container of liquid, and asked them to rate how much they thought the object's movement was due to dispositional factors (for example, shape, weight) versus contextual factors (for example, gravity, friction). Participants who had their American identity primed rated causes internal to the objects as more important than did participants who had their Asian identity primed (Peng & Knowles, 2003; see also Benet-Martinez, Leu, Lee, & Morris, 2002).

Social Class and Attribution

social class The amount of wealth, education, and occupational prestige a person and his or her family enjoy.

So far this section has looked at how people from different countries and ethnic backgrounds vary in their tendencies to attribute events to situational versus dispositional causes. Recent studies find that another form of culture—social class—influences attribution in important ways. **Social class** refers to the amount of wealth, education, and occupational prestige a person and his or her family enjoy. Families with higher socioeconomic status enjoy greater wealth, education, and occupational prestige than those from less privileged backgrounds. And it turns out that within a particular culture or ethnicity, people from different ends of the socioeconomic spectrum arrive at very different causal explanations for events.

In a series of studies, Michael Kraus and his colleagues have found that lower-class or working-class individuals resemble individuals from interdependent cultures in their attributional tendencies. In other words, they are more likely than those higher up the socioeconomic ladder to attribute events to situational factors and less likely to offer dispositional explanations (Kraus, Piff, & Keltner, 2009). In one study, people from different class backgrounds were presented with a graph portraying an important political event—the recent rise in economic inequality in the United States. Lower-class individuals attributed this economic event to contextual factors (such as the absence of educational opportunity), whereas upper-class and upper-middle-class individuals were more likely to favor dispositional causes (such as a lack of effort or talent on the part of those whose incomes are falling) in explaining economic changes in the United States.

The study also found that when asked to make attributions for positive life outcomes (getting into a desired graduate program) and negative life outcomes (suffering a health problem), lower- and working-class individuals were more likely to invoke situational causes, and those higher up the socioeconomic ladder were more likely to invoke dispositional causes. And when presented with the facial expression example described earlier, where a target individual expresses emotion that differs from the emotions expressed by surrounding individuals, those lower on the socioeconomic spectrum were more likely to be swayed by the emotions of the individuals in the surrounding context when explaining a focal individual's emotions. Investigators believe that these class differences are found because lower-social class individuals, like Asians, live in worlds where attention to other people is more necessary for effective functioning than it is for higher-social class individuals.

Dispositions: Fixed or Flexible?

So do Asians think like "social psychologists," putting great emphasis on situational determinants of behavior, whereas Westerners think like "personality psychologists," putting more emphasis on dispositional determinants? Not quite. It may be more accurate to say that Asians think in both of these ways. Asians and Westerners both use the same dimensions of judgment—essentially the "Big Five" personality dimensions of extraversion, neuroticism, agreeableness, conscientiousness, and openness to experience—to understand other people. And the evidence shows that these dimensions play almost as much of a role in judging people's personalities, including one's own, for Asians as they do for Westerners (Cheung et al., 2001; McCrae, Costa, & Yik, 1996; Piedmont & Chase, 1997; Yang & Bond, 1990). Norenzayan, Choi, and Nisbett (1999) asked Korean and American college students a number of questions intended to tap their theories about the causes of behavior and found that although Koreans and Americans rated the importance of personality the same, the Koreans reported situations to be more important than did the Americans.

Ara Norenzayan and his colleagues also asked their participants several questions about their beliefs regarding how fixed or flexible personality is—whether it is something about them that can't be altered much or whether it can be changed. The Koreans considered personalities to be more malleable than the Americans did. The belief that personality is malleable, of course, is consistent with the view that behavior is substantially influenced by external factors.

The view that personality is changeable is also consistent with the view—much more characteristic of interdependent peoples than of independent peoples—that abilities can be changed by environmental factors and through effort (Dweck, 1999; Dweck, Chiu, & Hong, 1995; Dweck, Hong, & Chiu, 1993). Americans report valuing education more than Asians do—but American students spend much less time studying than do Asian students (Stevenson & Stigler, 1992). The belief in the value of effort to overcome inadequacy is deeply rooted in the cultures of China, Korea, and Japan.

Thus the processes of making attributions and forming impressions are in many ways the same and in many ways quite different across cultures. Asians and other interdependent peoples live in more interconnected social worlds than do Westerners. And probably as a consequence, they are attuned to more of their environment. Embedded in a social web themselves, interdependent peoples are inclined to see the contexts in which other people, and even other animals and objects, exist (**Box 5.4**). Asians, like Westerners, do tend to make the fundamental attribution error. But they err to a lesser degree, presumably because they are more attuned to situational contexts and are more likely to correct their judgments when the context is highlighted in some way (Choi & Nisbett, 1998).

People in interdependent cultures pay more attention to social situations and the people within these situations than do Westerners. Asians as well as Westerners are susceptible to the fundamental attribution error, but Westerners are more susceptible to it. For individuals reared in both interdependent and independent cultures, it is possible to prime the different ways of perceiving and attributing behavior. Social class also influences attributional tendencies: lower- and working-class individuals are more likely to attend to the surrounding circumstances, whereas upper-middle- and upper-class individuals are more likely to make dispositional attributions.

BOX 5.4 FOCUS ON INTERNATIONAL RELATIONS

One Cause or Many?

An international conflict occurred between China and the United States when a Chinese fighter plane collided with a U.S. surveillance plane in 2001 and the surveillance plane was forced to land on a Chinese island without receiving permission from the ground. Demanding an apology for the incident from the United States, the Chinese held captive the crew of the surveillance plane. The Americans refused, asserting that the accident was caused by the recklessness of the Chinese fighter pilot.

Political scientist Peter Hays Gries and social psychologist Kaiping Peng argued that the conflict was intensified by the two adversaries' very different conceptions of causality (Gries & Peng, 2002). They noted that to the Chinese, the insistence that there was such a thing as *the* cause of the accident was hopelessly limited in its per-

spective. Relevant to the accident were a host of considerations, including the fact that the United States was, after all, spying on China and there was a history of interaction between the particular surveillance plane and the particular fighter pilot. Given the complexity and ambiguity of causality, the Chinese believed that the very least the United States could do would be to express its regrets that the incident had occurred. The presumed ambiguity of causality may lie behind Eastern insistence on apology for any action that results in harm to someone else, no matter how unintentionally and indirectly. Ultimately, the "regret" formula was the one that the two countries hit upon to resolve the impasse, but likely few people on either side understood the role played in the conflict by the differing conceptions of causality identified by Gries and Peng.

BEYOND THE INTERNAL/EXTERNAL DIMENSION

Everyday causal analysis often requires people to determine whether a given action is mainly due to something about the person involved or to the surrounding situational context. But this person/situation question is not the only one we ask, and it is not the whole story of everyday causal analysis. We often ask ourselves additional questions about people's behavior to arrive at a more nuanced understanding of its meaning and to enable us to make more refined predictions about future behavior. In particular, we're often interested in understanding a person's intentions (Heider, 1958; Jones & Davis, 1965; Malle, 1999).

Think of it this way: People engage in causal analysis to make the world more predictable—to find the "glue" that holds all sorts of varying instances of behavior together. Sometimes that glue is a trait in the person—for example, her kindness explains her long hours at the soup kitchen, her unfailing politeness to everyone in the residence hall, and her willingness to share her notes with others in her class. At other times the glue is provided by knowing someone's intentions—for example, the long hours in the library, the ingratiating behavior toward the professor, and the theft of another student's notes all come together and make sense if we know that the individual has a particularly strong desire to get a good grade (Malle, Moses, & Baldwin, 2001; Searle, 1983).

Empirical studies of everyday explanations of behavior attest to the significance people attach to understanding the reasons for a given behavior. Roughly

80 percent of the time, for example, people explain intentional actions by referring to the actor's reasons (Malle, 2001). Reasons for action, of course, are many and varied, but the overwhelming majority of the reasons offered to explain behavior fall into two classes: desires and beliefs. Why did the senator endorse an amendment banning the burning of the American flag? Because she *wants* to be reelected, and she *believes* she needs to appease her constituents. Why does the neighbor put up with his wife's abusive insults? Because he doesn't *want* to be alone, and he *believes* no one else would be interested in him.

Beliefs and wants give rise to intentional action, so it stands to reason that to understand the behavior of others, we have to understand what they're seeking and what they believe will allow them (or not allow them) to get it. Understanding others' beliefs and desires is central to the *theory of mind* that is so obviously necessary to a full understanding of other people and is developed at such an early age that many people believe it is "hardwired" in the human brain (see Chapter 1).

 When we want to understand a person's intentions, the attributional question we are most inclined to ask concerns the *reason* for the person's behavior. Understanding a person's reasons for a particular action, in turn, often requires understanding the person's beliefs and desires.

Chapter Review

Summary

From Acts to Dispositions: Inferring the Causes of Behavior

- People constantly search for the causes of events, and their attributions affect their behavior. We all have different *explanatory styles*, which tend to be stable over time. Some people have a pessimistic style, attributing good outcomes to external, unstable, and local causes and bad outcomes to internal, stable, and global causes. This style is associated with poor health, poor performance, and depression.

The Processes of Causal Attribution

- We all use the *covariation principle* to make attributions. When we know that a person engages in a given behavior across many situations and that other people tend not to engage in the behavior, we are likely to attribute the behavior to the person. When we know that the person engages in the behavior only in a particular situation and that most people in that situation also engage in the behavior, we tend to attribute the behavior to the situation.

- *Counterfactual thoughts* can powerfully affect attribution. People often perform mental simulations, adding or subtracting elements about the person or the situation and using these simulations to guide their attributions. Joy or pain in response to an event is *amplified* when it is easy to see how things might have turned out differently.

- Our ability to imagine what others would likely do in a given situation allows people to make use of the *discounting* and *augmentation principles*. If situational constraints could plausibly have caused an observed behavior, we discount the role of the person's dispositions. If strong forces were present that would typically inhibit the behavior, we assume that the actor's dispositions were particularly powerful.

Errors and Biases in Attribution

- People's attributions are not always fully rational. We sometimes attribute events to causes that flatter us beyond what the evidence calls for—exhibiting the *self-serving attributional bias*.

- *The fundamental attribution error* is the tendency to attribute behavior to real or imagined dispositions of the person and to neglect influential aspects of the situation confronting the person. Even when it ought to be obvious that the situation is a powerful influence on behavior, we often attribute behavior to presumed traits, abilities, and motivations.

- One of the reasons we make such erroneous attributions is due to the *just world hypothesis*. We like to think that people get what they deserve and that bad outcomes are brought about by bad or incompetent people.

- Another reason for the fundamental attribution error is that people and their behavior tend to be more salient than situations.

- A final reason for the fundamental attribution error is that attribution appears to be a two-step process. We typically characterize people immediately and automatically in terms consistent with their behavior, and only later do we adjust this initial characterization to take account of the impact of prevailing situational forces.

- There are *actor-observer differences* in attributions. In general, actors tend to attribute their behavior much more to situations than do observers, partly because actors can usually see the situations they confront better than observers can.

Culture and Causal Attribution

- There are marked cultural differences in susceptibility to the fundamental attribution error. Interdependent peoples are less likely to make the error than independent peoples, in part because their tendency to pay attention to context encourages them to look to the situation confronting the actor.

- When bicultural people are primed to think about one culture or the other, they make causal attributions consistent with the culture that is primed.

- Lower-class individuals, like people from interdependent cultures, tend to make more situational attributions compared with middle-class and upper-class individuals.

Beyond the Internal/External Dimension

- Much of the time, people are concerned with more than whether to attribute behavior to the situation versus the person. We are interested in discerning the intentions and reasons that underlie a person's behavior.

Key Terms

actor-observer difference (p. 181)
attribution theory (p. 155)
augmentation principle (p. 163)
causal attribution (p. 155)
consensus (p. 161)
consistency (p. 161)

counterfactual thoughts (p. 164)
covariation principle (p. 160)
discounting principle (p. 163)
distinctiveness (p. 161)
emotional amplification (p. 165)
explanatory style (p. 156)

just world hypothesis (p. 175)
self-serving attributional
   bias (p. 168)
social class (p. 188)

Further Reading

Gilbert, D. T. (1995). Attribution and interpersonal perception. In A. Tesser (Ed.), *Advanced social psychology* (pp. 99–147). New York: McGraw-Hill. An insightful and enjoyable analysis of how people make attributions for one another's behavior.

Roese, N. J., & Olson, J. M. (1995). *What might have been: The social psychology of counterfactual thinking*. Mahwah,

NJ: Erlbaum. A compendium of some of the most important work on counterfactual thinking.

Ross, L., & Nisbett, R. E. (1991/2011). *The person and the situation: Perspectives of social psychology*. London: Pinter & Martin.

Conditions apply. See in store for details

Emotion

ONE DAY IN A NAZI CONCENTRATION CAMP, the attending staff was clearing a gas chamber of corpses. As they disposed of the stiffening bodies, they discovered a 16-year-old girl at the bottom of the pile, breathing and very much alive. The medical doctor on hand, Miklos Nyiszli, and his staff were overwhelmed by feelings of sympathy. Instinctively, they offered the young girl a coat to keep her warm. They fed her warm broth and tea. They put their heads together to think of ways to save the young girl, to help her escape her inevitable death in the Nazi master plan. They settled upon the idea of hiding the young girl amid the German women working in the camp. Were this to happen, the girl might somehow eventually find her freedom. Nyiszli pitched this idea to the commandant at the concentration camp, but the officer was unmoved. He quickly disposed of the young girl using his method of choice—she was shot in the back of the neck.

The writer George Orwell, author of the novels *1984* and *Animal Farm*, also experienced such a "sympathy breakthrough" during his experiences in combat. Orwell fought against fascists in the Spanish Civil War in the 1930s. One day in Spain, Orwell had a fascist in his sight. With gun loaded and aimed, he was poised to shoot his adversary. As the soldier raced by, panting, half dressed, clutching his pants with his hand and stumbling, Orwell simply could not pull the trigger. Later Orwell reflected, "I did not shoot partly because of the detail of the trousers. I had come to shoot 'fascists'; but a man who is holding up his trousers isn't a 'Fascist', he is visibly a fellow creature, similar to yourself, and you don't feel like shooting him."

Sympathy breakthroughs like those experienced by Nyiszli and Orwell are surprisingly common during combat. Often in face-to-face encounters with adversaries, soldiers who have been trained to kill will abandon the mind-set

George Orwell The writer George Orwell fought fascists in the Spanish Civil War in the 1930s.

"We all know that emotions are useless and bad for our peace of mind and our blood pressure."

—B. F. Skinner

and rules of war. They ignore the orders of superiors. They refuse to kill. They often collapse in sorrow at the harm they have caused.

Many lessons can be derived from such sympathy breakthroughs. One lesson is that sympathy is a powerful trigger of altruistic behavior—a theme explored in more detail in Chapter 14. A more general lesson is that emotions are important guides of thought and action. Once set in motion, emotions wield powerful influences on what people perceive, how they reason, what they deem right and wrong, and what matters to them. During sympathy breakthroughs, for example, soldiers shift radically in how they construe combat; they no longer view their adversaries as enemies, but instead as fellow human beings. Once set in motion, emotions trigger action: they impel people to respond to specific goals, threats, and opportunities in the environment. Sympathy breakthroughs have led soldiers to shift out of a fight-or-flight pattern of action to one of altruism and concern.

The philosopher Jean Paul Sartre called these effects of emotions "magical transformations." Any situation can be construed in multiple ways and can call forth a variety of actions. Emotions are magical transformations in that they powerfully and immediately shift the individual to specific ways of thinking and acting. When you feel sad, the emotions you feel shape every facet of your mind and action, from how you look at your surroundings to the tone of your voice to the way you act in the world. The same is true of other emotions, like pride or enthusiasm, anger or compassion.

For over 2,000 years, many writers in the traditions of Western thought have been wary of the power of emotions, of the magical transformations in thought and action they can bring about (Oatley, 2004). The emotions have long been viewed as disruptive of harmonious social bonds, and as enemies of reason and sound moral judgment. Social psychology has arrived at a different conclusion, revealing that although emotions can indeed disrupt sound reasoning and make people behave irrationally, they can also aid reason and are vital to healthy relationships, sound functioning, and effective pursuit of the good life.

This chapter is structured around four enduring questions about emotions: To what extent are emotions universal, and to what extent do they vary across cultures? What is the role of emotions in social relationships? How do emotions influence our reasoning? And finally, what is happiness? Before tackling these questions, let's first define *emotion*, which is no simple task.

CHARACTERIZING EMOTION

Light is something everyone knows when they see it, but it is exceptionally hard to define. The same is true of the emotions. When you experience cold feet before making a speech or going on a first date, what is that experience like? What happens when a stranger's anonymous kindness moves you to tears? What are emotions, and how do they differ from more general feelings of, say, well-being or despair? What differentiates one type of emotion from another?

Emotions can be defined as brief, specific, socially oriented states. They are *brief* in that they last for seconds or minutes, not hours or days. Facial expressions of emotion typically last between 1 and 5 seconds (Ekman, 1992). Many of the physiological responses that accompany emotion—sweaty palms, the blush, and goose bumps, for example—last dozens of seconds or minutes. In contrast, the moods that we experience—for example, when we feel irritable or blue—last for hours and even days. Emotional disorders, such as depression, last for weeks or months.

Emotions are also *specific*: we feel emotions about specific people and events—the politician whose rhetoric angers you, the kind friend whose act of generosity fills you with gratitude, the ill relative whose demise makes you sad. Philosophers call the focus of an emotional experience its "intentional object." When you're angry, for example, you usually have a very clear sense of what you're angry about (for example, the embarrassing story your dad has told about your first date).

Finally, emotions typically help individuals achieve their *social goals*. Emotions motivate us to act in specific ways that affect important relationships and help us navigate our social environment (DeSteno & Salovey, 1996; Frijda & Mesquita, 1994; Keltner & Haidt, 1999; McCullough, Kilpatrick, Emmons, & Larson, 2001; Oatley & Jenkins, 1992; Parrott, 2001; Salovey & Rodin, 1989; Salovey & Rothman, 1991; Tiedens & Leach, 2004). Gratitude motivates us to reward others for their cooperative actions. Guilt motivates us to make amends when we have harmed other people. Anger impels us to right social wrongs and restore justice. Of course, not every episode of emotion is beneficial. Some outbursts of anger, for example, produce undesirable outcomes. (If, in anger, you make sarcastic comments to a traffic cop, you might find yourself much worse off than when you started.) But in general, emotions motivate appropriate goal-directed behavior that makes for stronger social relationships.

The Components of Emotion

In a well-known parable from India, six blind men are asked to determine what an elephant looks like by touching different parts of its body. They come to different conclusions depending on the part of the body they touch. The blind man who touches the leg observes that the elephant must look like a pillar, a blind man who touches the tail suggests the elephant looks like a rope, and the blind man who touches the tusk suggests the elephant looks like a solid pipe. What we make of objects depends on our vantage point and the information we take in.

In many ways, emotion researchers are like these blind men in the parable. Emotions involve many components, and the claims that scientists have made about emotions depend on what component of emotion is in focus. For example, William James, one of the founding figures in the field of psychology, argued that the essence of an emotion, what determines its experience and differentiates it from other emotions, is its bodily response (James, 1884). In other words, for James, emotions are defined by shifts in our heart rate, in our sweaty palms or blush, and in our muscle tension and movements of the viscera. According to Charles Darwin, emotions are defined by their accompanying expressive behaviors, their gestures, facial muscle movements, vocalizations, and postural movements. These behaviors and movements signal to others the nature of the individual's internal

emotions Brief, specific psychological and physiological responses that help humans meet goals, many of which are social.

state, thereby helping to coordinate smooth or effective interaction (or at least heading off potentially catastrophic misunderstanding).

Although emotions certainly involve these physiological components, there is now consensus that emotions arise as a result of **appraisal processes**, through which we evaluate events and objects in our environment according to their relation to our current goals (Lazarus, 1991; Smith & Ellsworth, 1985). The appraisals that trigger different emotions, known as **core-relational themes**, are fairly similar across cultures (Lazarus, 1991; Mauro, Sato, & Tucker, 1992; Mesquita, 2003; Mesquita & Ellsworth, 2001; Mesquita & Frijda, 1992; Scherer, 1997). For example, appraisals of loss trigger sadness in most parts of the world, violations of rights trigger anger, expressions of affection trigger love, and witnessing undeserved suffering triggers compassion (Boucher & Brandt, 1981; Rozin, Lowery, Imada, & Haidt, 1999).

In the **primary appraisal stage**, unconscious, fast, and automatic appraisals of whether the event is consistent or inconsistent with the person's goals give rise to general pleasant or unpleasant feelings (LeDoux, 1993; Mischel & Shoda, 1995; Zajonc, 1980). These more automatic appraisals are triggered by stimuli of significance to our survival—smiling and angry faces, snakes, pleasant and unpleasant sounds, bad odors, loud sounds (Dimberg & Öhman, 1996; Murphy & Zajonc, 1993).

In the **secondary appraisal stage**, more specific and deliberative appraisals transform initial pleasant or unpleasant feelings into more specific emotions, such as fear, anger, pride, gratitude, or sympathy (Barrett, 2006; Lazarus, 1991; Roseman, 1991; Russell, 2003; Smith & Ellsworth, 1985). The individual takes stock of the situation and figures out who is responsible for the event, whether it is consistent with social norms, how fair it is, and the extent to which effective action can be taken to deal with the event. Such appraisals will determine, for example, whether the individual feels anger, sadness, or guilt in the face of a negative turn of events (Smith & Ellsworth, 1985), or a sense of fear or challenge when faced with uncertainty and obstacles.

Appraisal processes get emotions going. Once under way, emotions involve several response systems. Specific emotions are associated with patterns of activation in regions of the brain and the release of neurotransmitters like dopamine and oxytocin (Davidson, Pizzagalli, Nitzschke, & Kalin, 2003). Emotions engage responses in your body—patterns of respiration, cardiovascular response, muscle movement, even activation in the immune system (Levenson, 2003). We express our emotions with facial expressions, voice (Scherer, Johnstone, & Klasmeyer, 2003), posture, and physical touch (Hertenstein, 2002), as well as in language, art, poetry, and music, which give shape to our conscious experience of emotion (Barrett, Mesquita, Ochsner, & Gross, 2007; Oatley, 2003; Wilson & Gilbert, 2008). When feeling different emotions, we see our lives and the world through an emotion-tinted lens, selectively perceiving emotion-congruent events in our current environment and recalling emotion-related episodes from the past (Niedenthal, 2008).

To illustrate the many components of emotion, consider what has been learned in the study of sympathy, what Miklos Nyiszli and George Orwell probably felt during their sympathy breakthroughs in the midst of war (Goetz, Keltner, & Simon-Thomas, 2010). Social psychologists now know that specific regions of the brain—a part of the frontal lobes known as the orbitofrontal cortex and an old part of the middle of the brain known as the periaqueductal grey—are

appraisal processes The ways people evaluate events and objects in their environment based on their relation to current goals.

core-relational themes Distinct themes, such as danger or offense or fairness, that define the core of each emotion.

primary appraisal stage An initial, automatic positive or negative evaluation of ongoing events based on whether they are congruent or incongruent with an individual's goals.

secondary appraisal stage A subsequent evaluation in which people determine why they feel the way they do about an event, consider possible ways of responding to the event, and weigh future consequences of different courses of action.

activated during feelings of sympathy. People feeling sympathy show a slowing of their heart rate, which is thought to allow the individual to attend to the needs of others and enable more altruistic behavior (see Chapter 14). Sympathy is signaled in vocalizations and patterns of touch. Momentary feelings of sympathy break down "us" versus "them" distinctions and lead people to believe in their shared humanity with others (Oveis, Horberg, & Keltner, 2010). Though the scientific study of emotion is a relatively new branch of social psychology, it has focused on many different kinds of responses, revealing answers to age-old questions about human nature.

"Nothing's either good or bad but thinking makes it so."

—William Shakespeare, *Hamlet*

 Emotions are brief, specific experiences that help people meet social goals. Emotions involve many components. They arise out of primary appraisal processes—quick, automatic evaluations of whether a stimulus is good or bad—and more complex secondary appraisal processes—for example, determining who is responsible or whether the event is fair. Emotions are reflected in different kinds of expressive behavior, in our language, in physiological responses in the brain and body, and in how we think.

UNIVERSALITY AND CULTURAL SPECIFICITY OF EMOTION

As Charles Darwin circumnavigated the globe on the *Beagle*, he encountered the Fuegians of Tierra del Fuego, Chile, a people living in hunter-gatherer conditions. The Fuegians greeted Darwin and his colleagues naked and with arms flailing wildly. This emotional expression dumbfounded the crew members of the *Beagle*—except for Darwin. Darwin took it to be a greeting display, one of affection, and was the first to make friends with the Fuegians by reciprocating their friendly chest slaps. Darwin's experience of this first encounter illustrates the central question in this section: To what extent are expressions of emotion universal, and how do they vary across cultures? The Fuegians developed a specific way of expressing affection to strangers—flailing their arms. Underlying this idiosyncratic expression, though, are important elements that appear to be universal (open-handed gestures that convey warmth and kindness).

Evolutionary and cultural approaches arrive at different answers to the question of the universality and cultural variability of emotional expression. An evolutionary approach assumes that the many components of emotion—facial expression, vocalization, physiological response—enable adaptive responses to the threats to survival and opportunities faced by all humans (Ekman, 1992; Nesse, 1990; Öhman, 1986; Tooby & Cosmides, 1992). The reasoning is that emotions such as fear enable adaptive responses to threats to survival, whereas emotions such as love, compassion, and jealousy help people form and maintain reproductive relationships just as critical to gene replication (Keltner, 2009). By implication, the components of emotion, including facial expression, should be universal.

In contrast, the cultural approach assumes that emotions are strongly influenced by values, roles, institutions, and socialization practices and that these vary across different cultures (Ellsworth, 1994; Markus & Kitayama, 1991; Mesquita, 2003; Oatley, 1993). As a result, people in different cultures should express their emotions in very different ways. As the next section demonstrates, scientific

BOX 6.1 **FOCUS ON NEUROSCIENCE**

Felt and False Smiles

Are smiles emotional or not? This seemingly modest question has been the subject of intense debate among emotion researchers. How can the smile be the primary signal of positive emotion, as Ekman (1993) asserts, and at the same time occur during anger, disgust, or grief? Answers to these kinds of questions can be found in *The Mechanism of Human Facial Expression*, published in 1862 by a French physician named Duchenne de Boulogne. In this book, Duchenne detailed the results of his research on stimulating the facial muscles with electrical currents. He identified the actions of two muscles: (1) the *zygomatic major* muscle, which pulls the lip corners upward, and (2) the *orbicularis oculi*, which surrounds the eye and in contracting causes crow's-feet to form, the upper cheek to raise, and a pouch to form under the lower eyelid.

Based on this anatomical distinction, Ekman has coined the term the *Duchenne smile*, which is the smile that involves the action of the *orbicularis oculi* and tends to be associated with the experience of positive emotion. Research has shown that the Duchenne smile differs in many ways from smiles that do not involve this muscle action. Duchenne

Different Kinds of Smiles (A) A polite, non-Duchenne smile; and (B) a Duchenne, or enjoyment, smile, as demonstrated by Paul Ekman.

smiles tend to last between 1 and 5 seconds, and the lip corners tend to be raised to equal degrees on both sides (Frank, Ekman, & Friesen, 1993). Duchenne smiles tend to be associated with activity in the left anterior portion of the brain, whereas non-Duchenne smiles are associated with activity in the right anterior portion of the brain (Ekman & Davidson, 1993; Ekman, Davidson, & Friesen, 1990). This is consistent with a rich literature showing that positive emotions are more strongly associated with activation in the left side of the brain (Davidson et al., 2003). Duchenne smiles are associated with pleasure, whereas in some studies, non-Duchenne smiles have been shown to be associated with negative emotion (Hess, Banse, & Kappas, 1995; Keltner & Bonanno, 1997; Ruch, 1995).

studies of emotional expression reveal support for both perspectives—that how humans express emotion is at once universal, and subject to striking cultural variations.

Darwin and Emotional Expression

In 1872, Charles Darwin published *The Expression of Emotions in Man and Animals*, a book that he wrote feverishly in four months. In it, Darwin proposed that human emotional expression is similar to that of other mammals—a thesis in keeping with his theory of evolution, which held that humans share an evolutionary history with other mammals. In making his case, Darwin proposed his **principle of serviceable habits**, which maintains that expressions of human emotion that we observe today derive from habitual patterns of behavior that proved useful in the evolution of our primate and mammalian predecessors. For

principle of serviceable habits
Charles Darwin's thesis that emotional expressions are remnants of full-blown behaviors that helped our primate and mammalian predecessors meet important goals in the past.

example, the observable signs of anger—the furrowed brow and display of teeth, the tightened posture and clenched fists, the fierce growl—are vestiges of threat displays and attack behavior observed in our mammalian relatives that were useful in conflicts and aggressive encounters.

Darwin's analysis generated three hypotheses about emotional expression. First, it posits universality. Darwin reasoned that because all humans have the same 30 to 40 facial muscles and have used these muscles to communicate similar emotions in our evolutionary past, people in all cultures should communicate and perceive emotion in a similar fashion. A second prediction concerns the similarity between our emotional expression and that of our primate and mammalian ancestors. Darwin reasoned that because humans share an evolutionary history with other primates and mammals, our emotional expressions should resemble the emotional expressions of other species. In support of this thesis, Darwin drew fascinating parallels between human emotion and the expressions of animals in the London Zoo as well as those of his favorite dogs at home. Finally, Darwin argued that blind individuals, lacking the rich visual input a culture provides in how to display emotion, will still show similar expressions as sighted individuals because the tendency to express emotions in particular ways is encoded in the human nervous system.

Signaling Intentions Darwin believed that animals signal their intentions through displays such as (A) this dog signaling his hostile intentions toward another dog and (B) this dog signaling submission to another dog.

The Universality of Facial Expression

Interested in gathering data about the universality of emotional expression, Darwin queried English missionaries living in other cultures about whether they had observed expressions not seen in Victorian England. The result? They had not. Of course, his question was rather biased and may have encouraged the answer he sought. Nevertheless, approximately 100 years later, his work served as inspiration for an important series of studies carried out by Sylvan Tomkins, Paul Ekman, Wallace Friesen, and Carroll Izard (Ekman, Sorenson, & Friesen, 1969; Izard, 1971; Tomkins, 1962, 1963).

Cross-Cultural Research on Emotional Expression The most notable research in this area is the work by Paul Ekman and Wallace Friesen. To test Darwin's universality hypothesis, Ekman and Friesen initially took more than 3,000 photos of people well trained in expression, such as actors, as they portrayed anger, disgust, fear, happiness, sadness, and surprise according to Darwin's descriptions of the expressions. In a first set of studies, the researchers presented photos of these six emotions to people in Japan, Brazil, Argentina, Chile, and the United States. The participant's task was to select from six emotion terms the one that best matched the feeling the person was showing in each photo. The results? A home run for Darwin. Across these five cultures, accuracy rates were typically between 80 and 90 percent for the six emotions; the rate of chance guessing (randomly selecting one term out of six) was 16.7 percent (Ekman et al., 1969). The critics, however, were unconvinced. They noted a fundamental flaw in this study: participants in these cultures had all seen Western media, and they may have learned how to identify the expressions through their exposure to U.S. actors portraying those emotions. The universality in judging emotion that Ekman and Friesen documented may have been merely the result of participants from these countries sharing in the same media culture.

Charles Darwin In addition to developing the theory of evolution, Charles Darwin studied emotional expressions in nonhuman species and humans. He sought to document that human emotional expressions have their parallels in other species and are universal to people of all cultures.

Ekman and Friesen thus faced a stiff challenge: to find a culture that had little or no exposure to Westerners or to Western media. In accomplishing this goal, Ekman went to Papua New Guinea to study the Fore (pronounced *FOR-ay*), a hill tribe living in Stone Age conditions. Ekman lived with the tribe for six months. The Fore who participated in Ekman's study had seen no movies or magazines, did not speak English or Pidgin (a combination of English and a native language), had never lived in Western settlements, and had never worked for Westerners. After gaining approval for his study from the local witch doctor, Ekman devised an emotion-appropriate story for each of the six emotions. For example, the sadness story was: "The person's child had died, and he felt sad." He then presented photos of three different expressions along with a story that matched one of the expressions and asked participants, both adults and children, to match the story to an expression (Ekman & Friesen, 1971). Here chance guessing would have yielded an accuracy rate of 33 percent. The Fore participants, however, achieved accuracy rates between 80 and 90 percent in judging the six emotions. In another task, Ekman videotaped the posed expressions of Fore participants as they imagined being the individual in the six emotion-specific stories and then presented these clips to Western college students, who selected from six emotion terms the one that best matched the Fore's pose. U.S. college students correctly interpreted the posed expressions of the Fore, with the exception of fear (**Figure 6.1**). Subsequent studies in dozens of cultures have consistently found that people from cultures that differ in religion, political structure, development, and self-construals nevertheless agree in how they label the photos depicting anger, disgust, fear, happiness, sadness, and surprise (Ekman, 1984, 1993; Elfenbein & Ambady, 2002, 2003; Izard, 1971, 1994).

Ekman's study was a catalyst for a tremendous upsurge in the scientific study of emotion, but it was not without its limitations. For example, the study (as well as almost all judgment studies) is vulnerable to the free-response critique: the

Facial Expressions
Groundbreaking studies by Ekman, Friesen, and Izard identified these six facial expressions as universal.

FIGURE 6.1 Scientific Method: Universality of Facial Expressions

Hypothesis: Facial expressions of emotion have been shaped by evolution and are universal.

Research Method:

1. American actors were photographed showing expressions that conveyed emotions such as happiness, sadness, disgust, anger, and fear.
2. These photographs were then shown to members of the isolated and preliterate Fore tribe in New Guinea.
3. All participants who saw the photos were asked to pick the emotion story that matched each photograph.
4. Then the procedure was reversed. New Guinea tribesmen were photographed portraying various facial expressions, and American college students were asked to pick the emotion label that matched each photograph.

Happiness   Disgust

Results: Fore and American participants reliably judged the emotion expressed in the photos at much higher levels of accuracy than expected by chance.

CONCLUSION: Facial expressions of emotion are universal.

Source: Adapted from Ekman, Sorenson, & Friesen (1969).

---

researchers provided the terms with which participants labeled the facial expressions. If given the chance to label the faces in their own words (with free responses), perhaps people from different cultures would choose different terms that reflect culture-specific concepts. For example, people from interdependent cultures are more likely to think of positive emotions by using socially engaging terms (for example, "harmony") rather than disengaging terms (for example, "pride") (Kitayama, Karasawa, & Mesquita, 2004). If the Fore had been allowed to label the photos with their own words, they might have labeled a smile as "gratitude" rather than "happiness" or labeled it with some concept that does not map onto Western conceptions of emotion. But in fact, when participants in different cultures are allowed to use their own words to label facial expressions, they show high degrees of similarity (Haidt & Keltner, 1999; Izard, 1971).

Emotional Expression in Other Animals What about Darwin's second claim, that human emotional expressions resemble those of our mammalian relatives, given our shared evolutionary history? This idea has a firm anatomical foundation: our closest primate relatives, chimpanzees, have facial musculatures very similar to our own (Matsumoto, Keltner, Shiota, O'Sullivan, & Frank, 2008). This second idea of Darwin's has proved remarkably fruitful in helping researchers understand the origins of different emotional expressions. For example, chimps show threat displays and whimpers that are surprisingly similar to our own displays of anger and sadness. When affiliating in friendly fashion, nonhuman primates show a teeth-revealing display known as the "silent bared teeth display" that resembles our smile, but when playing and wrestling, they show the "open mouth pant hoot," the predecessor to the human laugh (Preuschoft, 1992).

Research on the parallels between human and nonhuman displays helped reveal the deeper functions of a seemingly most human emotion—embarrassment. Initial studies of people in embarrassing situations (making funny faces, sucking on pacifiers in front of friends) have identified the distinct nonverbal display of embarrassment. When people feel embarrassed, they shift their gaze down; they smile in a compressed, self-conscious way; they often touch their faces; and they move their heads down and typically to the left, exposing their necks (Harris, 2001; Keltner, 1995). What is the meaning of these behaviors? Careful cross-species comparisons revealed that human displays of embarrassment resemble appeasement displays in other mammals (Keltner & Buswell, 1997). Embarrassment signals remorse for social transgressions, prompting forgiveness and reconciliation when people violate social norms (Miller, 1992, 1996; Miller & Leary, 1992; Miller & Tangney, 1994; Parrott & Smith, 1991). In one study, participants observed an individual knocking over a supermarket display (Semin & Manstead, 1982). In one condition, he seemed visibly embarrassed; in the other condition, he was unperturbed. Participants more favorably evaluated the person who showed embarrassment.

In more recent studies, individuals who display greater embarrassment or blushing in social interactions, as opposed to other emotions, are more likely to be trusted, cooperated with, and given resources by a stranger (Feinberg, Willer, & Keltner, 2012; van Dijk, de Jong, & Peters, 2009). These social benefits of embarrassment cast a new light on many everyday social phenomena. When people are just getting to know one another, they often embarrass themselves with self-deprecating stories. Perhaps they are embarrassing themselves as a way of demonstrating commitment to the social contract, and to elicit trust in new friends and potential romantic partners. When defendants first appear in a courtroom, there is often considerable concern about the degree to which they show remorse, a self-conscious emotion related to embarrassment. (Some defendants are better at

Embarrassment and Appeasement and the Maintenance of Social Bonds To maintain harmonious social relations, humans may exhibit displays that are reminiscent of appeasement displays in nonhuman species. (A) This woman shows the typical elements of an embarrassment display—downward gaze, a compressed smile, and face touching—that trigger others to forgive. (B) This prairie dog lies on its back and extends its arms and legs toward the other animal, a sign of appeasement.

it than others. The talented actor Mark Wahlberg was a self-admitted delinquent who reports that the best acting he ever did was in juvenile court.)

Emotional Expression among the Blind A final line of research by Jessica Tracy and her colleagues on the expression of pride brings together Darwin's ideas about universality, cross-species similarities, and the expressions made by those without eyesight. Pride is the feeling associated with achievement—with gaining in status through socially valued actions. The emotion is reliably signaled with some of the dominance-related behaviors seen in other mammals: expansive posture, head movements up and back, arm thrusts upward (Tracy & Robins, 2004). When Jessica Tracy and Rick Robins traveled to Burkina Faso, in Africa, they found that a remote tribe readily identified displays of pride as being of that emotion (Tracy & Robins, 2007). In another recent study, Jessica Tracy and David Matsumoto carefully analyzed the emotional expressions of sighted and blind Olympic athletes just after they had either won or lost a judo competition (Tracy & Matsumoto, 2008). Sure enough, after victory, sighted and blind athletes alike threw their arms in the air with chest out as an expression of pride. After losing, both groups of athletes dropped their heads and slumped their shoulders in a display of shame and dejection. The athletes hailed from more than 20 countries, suggesting that these shame and pride displays are universal.

Cultural Specificity of Emotion

All of the findings just discussed—from cross-cultural research, research in animals other than humans, and research in blind individuals—are consistent with Darwin's thesis that human emotion evolved out of the patterns of expressive behavior in our mammalian relatives (Ekman, Friesen, & Ellsworth, 1982a, 1982b; Elfenbein & Ambady, 2002, 2003; Matsumoto et al., 2008; Mesquita & Frijda, 1992). However, when anthropologists began studying different cultures, it wasn't hard to find examples of cultural variation in emotional expression. For example, the Inuit of Alaska (colloquially referred to as Eskimos) were never observed to express anger (Briggs, 1960), and seventeenth-century Japanese wives of Samurai soldiers would smile upon receiving the news that their husbands had died nobly in battle.

One way to think about how cultures vary in their emotional expression is that cultures develop **emotion accents**—that is, highly stylized, culturally specific ways of expressing particular emotions (Elfenbein & Ambady, 2002). In a study conducted in India and the United States, for example, participants were asked to judge two expressions of embarrassment, shown in **Figure 6.2** along with the rates at which members of the two cultures identified the two expressions as embarrassment (Haidt & Keltner, 1999). As you can see, members of both cultures were likely to interpret the expression on the left as embarrassment. But Indian participants also readily perceived the tongue bite—an emotion accent in India—as embarrassment, while U.S. college students were bewildered by this display and saw little embarrassment in it.

This kind of research indicates that there is clearly a great deal of variability in how members of different cultures express their emotions. The deeper challenge is to show exactly how these expressions differ. Empirical studies have risen to this challenge, documenting several ways that members of different cultures vary in their emotional expression.

emotion accents Culturally specific ways that individuals from different cultures express particular emotions, such as the tongue bite as an expression of embarrassment in India.

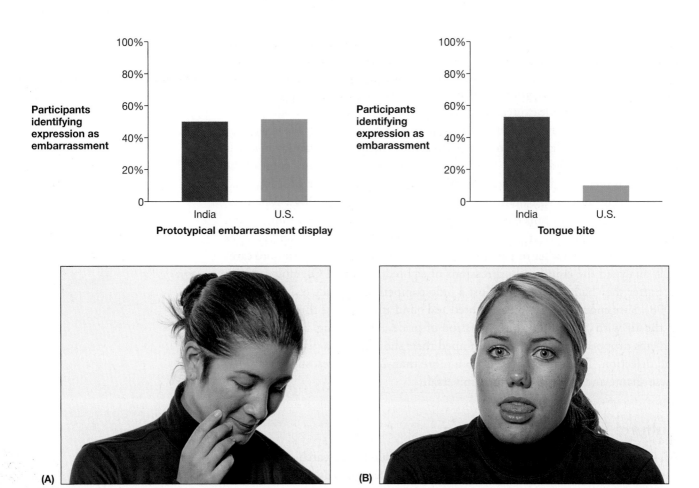

FIGURE 6.2 Universality and Cultural Variation in Emotional Expression People in the United States and India agree in their judgments of a prototypical embarrassment display (A), but only people in India recognize the ritualized tongue bite as a display of embarrassment (B). (Source: Adapted from Haidt & Keltner, 1999.)

Culture and Focal Emotions If you have traveled to another country, you may have come to the conclusion that cultures seem to be defined by particular emotions: Mexico is a proud culture, Tibet a kind one, Japan a modest one. This intuition was shared by early anthropologists, who often described cultures as angry cultures, shame- or guilt-prone cultures, or gentle cultures. Batja Mesquita has taken this idea further, making the important point that cultures vary in which emotions are focal. **Focal emotions** are the more common emotions in the everyday lives of the members of a culture, presumably experienced and expressed with greater frequency and intensity (Mesquita, 2003). For example, for individuals from cultures that value honor, sexual and family insults are highly charged events and trigger higher levels of anger than in members of cultures that do not prioritize honor (Rodriguez Mosquera, Fischer, & Manstead, 2000, 2004). Anger appears to be a more focal emotion in honor-based cultures.

Or consider the expression of self-conscious emotions like embarrassment and shame. Self-conscious emotions express modesty, an appreciation of others' opinions, and a sense of how the self is located within a social collective. These qualities of the self-conscious emotions are consistent with the core concerns in interdependent cultures—to maintain harmony and be mindful of others. Therefore it might be expected that shame and embarrassment would be more focal

focal emotions Emotions that are especially common within a particular culture.

emotions in more interdependent cultures, and recent studies have confirmed these expectations. For example, cultures vary in the extent to which they **hypercognize** emotions—that is, in the number of words they use to represent different emotions (Russell, 1991). In Tahiti, for example, there are 46 separate terms that refer to anger. In China, a highly interdependent culture, there are at least 113 words that describe shame and embarrassment, suggesting that the hypercognized self-conscious emotions are highly focal in the daily conversations of the Chinese (Li, Wang, & Fischer, 2004).

Members of interdependent cultures might also be expected to express shame and embarrassment in more intense, nonverbal behavior displays. Indeed, in the study of sighted and blind Olympic judo competitors described earlier, Jessica Tracy and David Matsumoto revealed cultural differences in the expression of these emotions. Athletes from more interdependent cultures, such as China and Japan, showed more intense head droops and shoulder shrugs of shame in response to losing than did individuals from independent cultures, such as the United States (Tracy & Matsumoto, 2008). When an emotion fits the self-construal or value of a particular culture, people develop a richer language to communicate the emotion and express it in more intense nonverbal displays.

Culture and Ideal Emotions Recently, Jeanne Tsai and her colleagues have offered another way of thinking about how emotions vary systematically across different cultures (Tsai, 2007; Tsai, Knutson, & Fung, 2006). In her affect valuation theory, Tsai reasons that cultures vary in the emotions they value or idealize. Emotions that promote specific cultural values and ideals are cherished more; as a result, those emotions play a more prominent role in the social lives of individuals.

For example, Tsai and colleagues reason that in the United States, excitement is greatly valued. Excitement enables individuals to pursue a cultural ideal of self-expression and achievement. In contrast, many East Asian cultures attach greater value to feelings of calmness and contentedness because these positive emotions more readily enable the individual to fold into harmonious relationships and groups (Kitayama, Karasawa, & Mesquita, 2004; Kitayama, Markus, & Kurokawa, 2000; Kitayama, Mesquita, & Karasawa, 2005; see also Mesquita, 2001; Mesquita & Karasawa, 2002). The different emotions that are valued readily translate into striking cultural differences in emotional behavior. Americans, for example, compared with East Asians, are more likely to participate in risky recreational practices (for example, mountain biking); to advertise consumer products with intense smiles of excitement; to get addicted to excitement-enhancing drugs (cocaine); and to express preferences for upbeat, exciting music rather than soothing, slower songs and for children's books that feature highly excited protagonists (Tsai, 2007). All of these differences in social practice, Tsai reasons, flow out of the value placed on excitement in America.

One clear prediction about emotional expression is that in Western European cultures, joy and excitement should be more frequently expressed, whereas in East Asian cultures, greater restraint will be placed on the expression of these positive emotions. Paul Ekman proposed that cultures vary in their **display rules**, culturally specific rules that govern how, when, and to whom we express emotion (Ekman & Friesen, 1969). People can *de-intensify* their emotional expression—for example, suppressing the urge to laugh at a friend's fumbling on a romantic quest. People can *intensify* their expression—for example, smiling widely upon receiving yet another unfashionable sweater from Grandma. They can *mask* their

hypercognize To represent a particular emotion with numerous words and concepts.

display rules Culturally specific rules that govern how and when and to whom people express emotion.

Neutralizing Expressions
According to the display rules of poker, this woman masks any feelings about her cards with a neutral poker face.

negative emotion with a polite smile. And they can *neutralize* their expression with a poker face.

Consistent with Tsai's thinking about the different value placed on excitement in the East versus the West, several studies reveal that people from more interdependent cultures de-intensify their outward expression of excitement. For example, anthropologist Catherine Lutz observed that in the interdependent Ifaluk people, who live on a small island in Micronesia, children were actively discouraged from expressing their excitement (Lutz, 1988). In many Asian cultures, it is inappropriate to speak of personal enthusiasms; and in these cultures, people may also de-intensify their expressions of pleasure at personal success. Across dozens of cultures, people from more interdependent cultures report being more likely to suppress positive emotional expression than individuals from independent cultures (Matsumoto et al., 2008; Mesquita & Leu, 2007). People from interdependent cultures are more likely to temper their experience of positive emotion with negative emotions (Schimmack, Oishi, & Diener, 2002). And Tsai herself has found that in responding to emotional stimuli of various kinds, people from independent cultures are more likely to show intense smiles of excitement (Tsai & Levenson, 1997). Intending no real offense, people from India have been known to refer to Americans as dogs. It's just that Americans are always saying, "Wow, wow!"

 Charles Darwin inspired dozens of studies finding that human emotional expression is universal, is seen in other species, and is evident in the blind. At the same time, it is clear that emotional expression varies across cultures. Cultures have specific emotion accents, such as the tongue bite in India for embarrassment. Cultures vary in the emotions that are focal, and they express focal emotions more intensely. Cultures vary in the emotions that they value, and they regulate emotions that are less valued with specific display rules—that is, the rules governing how and when to express emotions.

EMOTIONS AND SOCIAL RELATIONSHIPS

Iraneus Eibl-Eibesfeldt was a German ethologist—a scientist who studies social behavior in naturalistic contexts—who devoted his career to the careful observation of hunter-gatherer peoples in New Guinea, Africa, and other locations. He did so in the spirit of Charles Darwin, seeking to discover universal patterns of social relationship. In summing up his thousands of hours of observations, Eibl-Eibesfeldt concluded that emotions are the grammar of social relationships (1989). That is, emotions are the basic elements of warm attachments between parents and children, sibling play and conflict, flirtations between young women and men, and encounters of dominance and submissiveness between rivals.

This claim is in keeping with a central thesis of this chapter—that emotions are profoundly social (Tiedens & Leach, 2004). The expression of emotion helps coordinate social interactions. Emotions, as you shall see, help guide judgments and decisions that are made in the service of important social goals, such as to maintain fair relationships. Emotions are indeed a kind of a social language, one that helps form and maintain important relationships. Let's now look more specifically at how emotions fulfill these roles in romantic relationships, in friendships, and within and between groups.

Emotions in Friendship and Intimate Relationships

Kirsten Lindsmith and Jack Robinson are like many couples in their 20s, trying to navigate the complexities of a romantic relationship (Harmon, 2011). They haggle over the housework, struggle to communicate with each other, and fumble for words to describe what their future together might be. What adds to the challenges of romantic life for Kirsten and Jack is that they both have been diagnosed with Asperger's syndrome. People with Asperger's, or Aspies, can reason like well-adjusted adults, and their language is untouched by their condition. What they struggle with is emotion, the grammar of social life. People with Asperger's don't communicate emotion as readily in the face and voice, and they prove to be less effective in reading the emotions of others. As a result, Aspies like Kirsten and Jack often struggle in close relationships. This section follows the story of Kirsten and Jack and related scientific studies that reveal how emotions are important to romantic relationships and friendships.

Emotions in Personal Relationships Emotions often determine the quality and stability of romantic relationships. If this couple keeps up the humor and mirth and other positive emotions throughout their marriage, they will be less likely to divorce.

Touch and Closeness For Kirsten and Jack, touch is something they largely avoid. Jack is overwhelmed by the sweaty feeling of holding Kirsten's hand and prefers to avoid such contact. Nor does he like to kiss—it feels like he's "mashing his face" against hers. Touch is often absent in their relationship, thereby depriving them of one of the languages of social connection.

Recent studies have documented that people can readily communicate many emotions through tactile contact, much as they can through facial expression (Hertenstein, Keltner, App, Bulleit, & Jaskolka, 2006). In this research, a toucher and a touchee sat at a table separated by a black curtain, which prevented all communication between the two participants other than touch. The toucher attempted to convey different emotions by making contact with the touchee for 1 second on the forearm. Upon being touched, the touchee, as in the Ekman studies, selected which emotion had been communicated from a list of emotion terms. As you can see in **Figure 6.3**, people in the United States and Spain could reliably communicate prosocial emotions such as love, compassion, and gratitude with brief tactile contact. Moreover, Spaniards, a high-touch culture, proved to be better at communicating emotion through touch. This finding fits with studies suggesting that individuals from interdependent cultures are better able to communicate emotion through touch. For example, in one study of friends talking in a café, British friends were not observed to touch at all, Americans touched each other twice, and Puerto Ricans touched each other 180 times (Jourard, 1966).

People rely on this rich language of touch (the right kind) to promote closeness in friendships and intimate relationships in three different ways. First, touch provides rewards to others; it is as pleasurable as a bright smile or a taste of chocolate. The right kind of touch stimulates specific cells under your skin—the largest organ in your body—that trigger activation in the orbitofrontal cortex, a brain region involved in the representation of rewards (Rolls, 2000).

A second way that touching builds closeness is that it soothes in times of stress. Touch reduces levels of the stress hormone cortisol (Francis & Meaney,

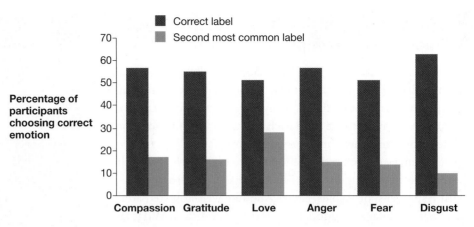

FIGURE 6.3 **Communicating Emotion through Touch** With a brief touch to the forearm, participants could reliably communicate different emotions to a stranger. (Source: Adapted from Hertenstein et al., 2006.)

1999). In one study, married women anticipating an electric shock showed decreased threat-related activity in stress-related regions of the brain (for example, the right anterior insula, superior frontal gyrus, and hypothalamus) when holding the hand of a spouse, but not that of a stranger (Coan, Schaefer, & Davidson, 2006).

A third way that touch promotes closeness is that it encourages reciprocity, a foundation of friendships and intimate bonds. Nonhuman primates spend up to 20 percent of their day grooming, and they systematically share food with other non-kin who have groomed them earlier in the day. In humans, friendly patterns of touch have been found to increase compliance with requests (Willis & Hamm, 1980) and cooperation toward strangers in economic games (Kurzban, 2001). In a recent study of touch among professional basketball players in the National Basketball Association, Michael Kraus and his colleagues coded all of the touches—high fives, fist bumps, head slaps, and bear hugs—that teammates engaged in during one game at the beginning of the 2008 season (Kraus, Huang, & Keltner, 2010). Even though each player on average touched his teammates for about 2 seconds during the game, that touch proved critical to the cohesiveness of the team. The more players touched each other, the more the teams were cooperative on the court (for example, helping out in defending the other team, making good passes to one another), and the better the team played at the end of the season.

Touch and Cooperation on the Basketball Court Basketball teams in which teammates touch each other more play better. Here the USA basketball team celebrates a gold medal with many kinds of touch.

Emotional Mimicry When Kirsten has strong emotional responses, Jack is often unresponsive and unmoved. This behavior diverges from the tendency for people to imitate and mimic the emotions of others and to synchronize their actions with the actions of others (Hatfield, Cacioppo, & Rapson, 1994). People tend to touch their own faces more when they see others touch theirs (Chartrand & Bargh, 1999), and they also tend to (unknowingly) mimic subliminally presented smiles in photos (Dimberg &

BOX 6.2   FOCUS ON CULTURE

Flirtation and the Five Kinds of Nonverbal Display

Flirting is the pattern of behavior, both verbal and nonverbal, conscious and at times out of awareness, that communicates our attraction to a potential romantic partner.

Givens (1983) and Perper (1985) spent hundreds of hours in singles bars, charting the flirtatious behaviors that predict romantic encounters. They found that in the initial attention-getting phase, men roll their shoulders and engage in exaggerated motions to show off their resource potential, raising their arms to let others admire their well-developed pecs and washboard abs, or ordering a drink in a way that lets others see their flashy Rolex watch. Women smile coyly, preen, flick their hair, and walk with arched back and swaying hips. In the recognition phase, the potential romantic partners lock their gaze on each other, expressing interest by raised eyebrows, singsong voices, and laughter. In the touching phase, the potential romantic

partners move close, and they create opportunities to touch with provocative brushes of the arm, pats on the shoulder, or not-so-accidental bumps against one another. Finally, in the keeping-time phase, the potential partners express and assess each other's interest by lining up their actions. When they are mutually interested, their glances, gestures, and laughter mirror each other's, and their shoulders and faces are aligned.

What is the nonverbal language of flirtation, or of other interactions for that matter? Paul Ekman and Wallace Friesen (1969) have organized the rich language of nonverbal behavior, so evident in flirtation, into five categories. The first is *affective displays*, or emotional expressions, which we have seen are universal. The other four categories of nonverbal behavior are more likely to vary across cultures. There are *emblems*, which are nonverbal gestures that directly translate to a word. Well-known emblems in English include the peace sign, the thumbs-up sign, the rubbing of one forefinger with the other to say "shame on you," and, in the late 1960s, the raised, clenched fist for Black Power. Researchers have analyzed over 800 emblems throughout the world, and surely there are many more. Emblems often do not have the same meaning in different cultures. For example, the gesture in which you form a circle with your thumb and forefinger means "OK" in the United States, "money" in Japan, "zero" in France, and "let's have sex" in parts of Mediterranean Europe. When accepting an invitation to dinner in Greece, be careful not to make this gesture.

Illustrators are nonverbal behaviors that we use to make our speech vivid, engaging, and easy to visualize. We rotate our hands in the air and use dramatic fist shakes to indicate the power of our convic-

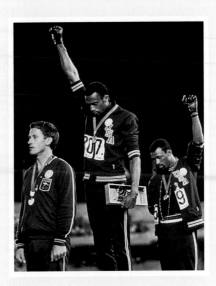

Black Power American athletes at the 1968 Olympics in Mexico City raise their fists and display the emblem for Black Power.

tions. We raise our eyebrows when uttering important phrases, we nod our head, and we move our torso to show empathy.

Regulators are nonverbal expressions we use to coordinate conversation. We look and point at people to whom we want to speak. We look away and turn our bodies away from those we wish would stop speaking.

Finally, there are *self-adaptors*, which are the nervous, seemingly random behaviors people engage in when tense, as if to release nervous energy. People touch their noses, twirl their hair, jiggle their legs, and rub their chins. The author Joseph Conrad suggested that people always touch their faces when entering public places. Try the experiment yourself. See how frequently people touch their faces when entering a restaurant or bar. Be sure to include an appropriate baseline of comparison.

Flirting Can you tell from the woman's nonverbal language what she is trying to convey?

Öhman, 1996), the postures of high-power individuals, and even the postures of sculptures in a museum (Oatley, Keltner, & Jenkins, 2006). We are especially likely to imitate the emotions of others. Simply hearing another person laugh can trigger laughter (Provine, 1992). We blush when we see a friend blushing (Shearn, Bergman, Hill, Abel, & Hinds, 1992). Our tendency to mimic the emotions of others is one way we come to understand what other people feel (Niedenthal, Mermillod, Maringer, & Hess, 2010).

Consider the case of laughter, one of the most common emotional behaviors in friendships and romantic relationships. Jo-Anne Bachorowski has devoted years to unlocking the mysteries of laughter, spending hundreds of hours analyzing the acoustic profiles—the rhythm, pitch, and variability—of different laughs (Bachorowski & Owren, 2001). She has catalogued different kinds of laughs. You may be embarrassed to learn (or feel validated, as the case may be) that men are much more likely than women to produce "grunt" laughs that sound like the noises that emanate from the gorilla compound at the local zoo. And within milliseconds of participating in amusing tasks, the laughs of friends but not strangers begin to mimic each other (Smoski & Bachorowski, 2003).

Emotional mimicry produces closeness. In a yearlong study of roommates in college by Cameron Anderson and his colleagues, new roommates came to the laboratory at the fall and spring of the academic year and at each visit reported their emotional reactions to different evocative stimuli, such as humorous or disturbing film clips (Anderson, Keltner, & John, 2003). The roommates' emotions became increasingly similar (compared with those of two randomly selected individuals) over the course of the year. This emotional mimicry, furthermore, predicted increased closeness in friendships. Presumably, mimicry establishes similarity between individuals, which, as described in Chapter 10, increases closeness and liking.

Piercarlollo Valdesolo and David DeSteno have produced experimental evidence showing that nonverbal mimicry increases liking between strangers. In their study, participants completed an exercise with a confederate that created an opportunity to mimic one another in a synchronized fashion (Valdesolo & DeSteno, 2011). The participant and the confederate sat across from one another with earphones on and listened to rhythmic patterns of tones. They were asked to tap their fingers to the tones. In one condition, the participant and confederate listened to the same patterns of tones and therefore mimicked each other's tapping at the same moments in time; in the other condition, they listened to different patterns of tones and tapped their fingers in different rhythms. At the end of the experiment, participants whose tapping mimicked the confederate's tapping reported feeling more similar to the confederate, expressed higher levels of compassion for the confederate, and were more likely to help the confederate complete a dull task later in the study. Basic physical mimicry seems to promote increased closeness among non-kin.

Some cultures depend on mimicry more than others to establish rapport. Sanchez-Burks, Bartel, and Blount (2009) had employees of a large Southwestern firm undergo mock interviews in which they were instructed to do their best to impress the interviewer favorably. Interviewees were either Anglo-Americans or Hispanics. In one condition, the interviewer mimicked the behavior of the interviewee: if the interviewee crossed his leg, the interviewer crossed his leg. In another condition, the interviewer never mimicked the interviewee. A group of observers then rated the interviewees' performance. The no-mimicking condition made no difference to raters' judgments about how impressive the interviewee was. But Hispanics were rated much higher than Anglo-Americans in the condition where the interviewer had established rapport by mimicking the interviewee's behavior.

Oxytocin and Trust Distraught over his emotional struggles with Kirsten, Jack, an avid consumer of knowledge related to chemistry, schemed about inventing a drug to help them with their difficulties. He focused on a pharmacological use of oxytocin, a neuropeptide composed of nine amino acids that is produced in the hypothalamus and released into the brain and bloodstream. Receptors for oxytocin are found in the olfactory system, limbic-hypothalamic system, brain stem, and regions of the spinal cord that regulate the cardiovascular system. Oxytocin is involved in uterine contractions, lactation, maternal bonding, and sexual interaction (Carter, 1998). And still other studies suggest that Jack was on the right track in his thinking: oxytocin is a trigger of closeness.

In nonhuman species, oxytocin increases pair-bonding and caregiving behavior. Comparisons between prairie voles, which display pair bonding, and closely related montane voles, which do not, reveal differences in the location of oxytocin receptors in the brain of each species (Carter, 1998; Insel, Young, & Zuoxin, 1997). Injection of oxytocin into the montane vole promotes preferences for single partners in this otherwise promiscuous rodent (Williams, Insel, Harbaugh, & Carter, 1994).

In humans, new studies are revealing oxytocin to be a source of closeness and trust. One of the most dramatic studies involved the trust game (Kosfeld, Heinrichs, Zak, Fishbacher, & Fehr, 2005). In the trust game, participants are given a certain amount of money—say, $10—and must give some portion of that money to a stranger. The experimenter then triples the value of that gift, and the stranger gives some portion of this new sum back to the original participant. Like so many endeavors in life, participants in the game have to trust the other person with initial acts of generosity in the hopes of stimulating more mutually beneficial relationships. In one condition, participants inhaled oxytocin before playing. In the other condition, they inhaled a saline solution. As you can see in **Figure 6.4**, participants given a nasal blast of oxytocin were more than twice as likely to give away the maximal amount of money.

Other emotions, including love, also seem to be related to oxytocin (Gonzaga, Turner, Keltner, Campos, & Altemus, 2006; Taylor, 2002). To explore this possibility, Gian Gonzaga and his colleagues first explored the nonverbal signals of romantic love and sexual desire in young romantic partners, guided by the ideas of Darwin described earlier. From videotaped conversations between romantic partners, these researchers found that when feeling love, romantic partners displayed brief, coordinated patterns of smiling, mutual gaze, affiliative, open hand gestures, and open posture. When feeling desire, in contrast, they showed a variety of lip-related actions, including puckers, lip licks, wipes, and tongue protrusions (Gonzaga, Keltner,

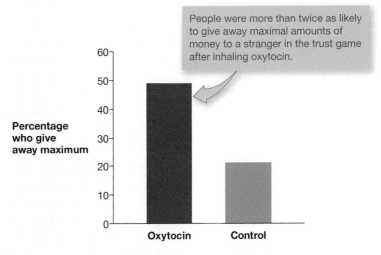

People were more than twice as likely to give away maximal amounts of money to a stranger in the trust game after inhaling oxytocin.

FIGURE 6.4 Effect of Oxytocin on Trust and Generosity (Source: Adapted from Kosfeld et al., 2005.)

Londahl, & Smith 2001; Gonzaga et al., 2006). And in a second study of women recalling an experience of warmth toward another person, intense displays of love but not desire were associated with greater release of oxytocin into the bloodstream (Gonzaga et al., 2006).

Emotional Intelligence Kirsten and Jack struggle with many different components of emotion, from touch to emotional mimicry. Even the simplest of tasks—putting emotions into words—proves challenging. When Kirsten struggles to find words to express her emotions to Jack, she describes the experience as the "blue screen of death"—the screen one sees when a computer crashes in Windows. She simply cannot find words to articulate her emotional life. When Jack offers a comment on Kirsten's cooking, it's often too blunt, making her cry. He in turn is mystified by her emotional reactions.

In summing up the emotional difficulties of Kirsten and Jack, Peter Salovey and John Mayer would suggest that they need to cultivate emotional intelligence (Salovey & Mayer, 1990). Emotional intelligence captures how well people use their emotions in their daily lives. Think of it as the extent to which people have mastered the grammar of social life—emotion. In more specific terms, emotional intelligence is defined by four skills: (1) an ability to accurately perceive others' emotions, (2) an ability to understand one's own emotions, (3) an ability to use current feelings in making decisions, and (4) the ability to manage one's emotions in ways that are fitting to the current situation. As Kirsten and Jack recognize, they struggle with these skills and their relationship suffers as a result.

People with high levels of emotional intelligence, by contrast, are able to put their emotions to good use, and they enjoy strong relationships (for a review, see Mayer, Barsade, & Roberts, 2008). For example, children who are high in emotional intelligence at age 5 prove to be better adjusted socially, as rated by their teachers, three years later. Adolescents who score higher on emotional intelligence report having more friends. Young adults who score higher on measures of emotional intelligence have more constructive and cooperative interactions with their romantic partners. Late in life, adults who score higher on measures of emotional intelligence enjoy greater respect and status at work and are perceived to be better workplace citizens. Individuals experience healthier social relationships, then, when they are able to perceive their own and others' emotions and to put them to good use in social interactions.

Emotions within and between Groups

The story of Jack and Kirsten highlights how central emotions are to the face-to-face dynamics of friendship and romantic relationships. It is hard to imagine a friendship getting off the ground without feelings of liking and gratitude, or a romantic relationship taking flight without feelings of love, desire, and compassion (Ellis, 1992; Trivers, 1971).

Group life is also highly emotional. Just think of the collective delight and euphoria of fans at a football game that's going their way, or activists at a political rally, or members of a congregation at church. Think of the social anxieties of the young teen, self-consciously trying to fit into a clique of friends. Think, in contrast, of the rage between groups on the battlefield. Emotions are an important part of group dynamics.

Emotions and Role Negotiation within Groups One of the central dimensions of an individual's role within a group is that person's status, as discussed in Chapter 12. The benefits of having high status are many, and the costs of negotiating status can be high. Conflicts over who is higher in a group's hierarchy are often violent and even deadly in humans and nonhumans alike. As a result, many nonhuman species rely on nonverbal displays to establish hierarchy. Apes pound their chests, frogs croak, stags roar endlessly for hours, chimps flash their fangs, and deer lock their horns. These kinds of ritualized displays enable group members to establish who has power and who doesn't in less costly fashion than direct aggressive encounter. Do you think we humans are beyond such chest pounding and roaring? Perhaps, but humans do negotiate their places within group hierarchies through emotional displays.

For example, anger is clearly a high-power emotion, conveying force and strength. And several studies support the notion that expressions of anger lead to gains in power within groups. People attribute elevated status and power to individuals displaying anger (Knutson, 1996). In turn, people assume that high-power people respond to difficulties with anger (Tiedens, 2001). High-power negotiators who display anger are more likely to get their way and prompt more subordinate behaviors in their counterparts (Sinaceur & Tiedens, 2006; Van Kleef, De Dreu, Pietroni, & Manstead, 2006). One experiment even found that people attributed greater power to leaders, such as Bill Clinton, who displayed anger as opposed to other emotions (Tiedens, 2001). An old adage of trial lawyers states that when you have the law on your side, you should argue the law; when you have the facts on your side, you should argue the facts; and when you have neither on your side, you should pound the table!

Is there a low-power emotional counterpart to anger? One possibility is embarrassment. Among the Awlad'Ali, a nomadic tribe living in Egypt, being in the presence of someone more powerful is a source of embarrassment and shame, or *hasham*. In this culture, the experience of *hasham*, as well as its display in the kind of embarrassment-related gaze and modest smiles described earlier, signals to group members the individual's subordinate status and dependence on others (Abu-Lughod, 1986). The display *of hasham* is a way in which people act out lower-status positions. In experimental research, people who display embarrassment are judged to be of lower status and physically smaller (Ketelaar, 2005). Much as anger signals power within groups, embarrassment signals submissiveness.

Emotion and Group Boundaries When African-American children first attended white schools in the South following *Brown v. Board of Education of Topeka* (1954), the Supreme Court decision that made segregation illegal, they were greeted with violent protests from white crowds. Most astonishing in the films of these historic moments is the emotion—facial expressions of anger, fists thrust into the air, and shrieks of rage. As readily as emotions unite people, they also can divide groups.

Diane Mackie and Eliot Smith argue in their intergroup emotion theory that group members experience emotions toward other groups according to their identification with their own group and their feeling of strength or weakness relative to the outgroup (Mackie, Silver, & Smith, 2004). They have found that anger and contempt are felt toward outgroups when group members feel that their group is stronger than the outgroup and when the members are passionately identified with their own group. For example, U.S. citizens were particularly enraged following the 9/11 terrorist attacks when they identified as Americans and felt that America was much stronger than the terrorists. By contrast, group members are more likely to feel fear when they feel weak in relation to the outgroup.

Emotions divide groups through a second process known as infrahumanization (Cortes, Demoulin, Rodriguez, Rodriguez, & Leyens, 2005). **Infrahumanization** is the tendency for ingroup members to deny outgroup members full human standing. Emotions play a critical role in infrahumanization. Group members may attribute similar levels of more basic emotions, such as anger or disgust, to their own group and to outgroups; but they assume that their own group members are more likely than outgroup members to experience more complex, sophisticated emotions such as pride or sympathy (Cortes et al., 2005). These more complex emotions involve more uniquely human cognitive capacities—a sense of self, taking others' perspectives—and are especially important in how group members define their own group's identity. Outgroup members who exhibit secondary emotions may even be punished, because in doing so they threaten other people's ethnocentric views (Vaes, Paladino, Castelli, Leyens, & Giovanazzi, 2003). As you might imagine, infrahumanization can readily feed into violence toward outgroup members.

 Emotions are vital to social relationships. In the development of friendships and romantic partnerships, touch offers a rich language of emotional connection, through its capacity to reward, to soothe, to encourage reciprocity, and to communicate emotions such as compassion and gratitude. Emotional mimicry promotes closeness. The neurochemical oxytocin increases trust, generosity, and commitment. Emotional intelligence, the ability to use emotions effectively, is beneficial to relationships. Emotions are powerful forces in group dynamics. Emotions such as anger and embarrassment signal different levels of power and help group members find their place within social hierarchies. People's universal tendency to fail to attribute the more human emotions (pride, compassion, and regret, for example) to outgroups can readily give rise to aggression and violence.

EMOTIONS AND SOCIAL COGNITION

Many of your most important decisions—what job to take, whom to marry, which neighborhood to live in—are based on gut feelings, emotions that are engaged during decision making. For most Western philosophers, this is not a desirable state of affairs. For the past 2,500 years, philosophers have argued that our emotions are less sophisticated ways of perceiving the world than our logic and higher reasoning (Haidt, 2001; Oatley, 2004). Our metaphors of emotion reveal this bias: we speak of emotions as forms of insanity ("I'm mad with love") and disease ("I'm sick with envy") rather than forms of clarity, reason, and health. According to this line of thought, the individual functions better when reason is the master of the passions.

That view is changing. Twenty-five years of research suggest that emotions generally have principled, systematic effects on cognitive processes and contribute to reasonable judgments of the world (Clore, Gasper, & Garvin, 2001; Clore & Parrott, 1991; Forgas, 1995, 2003; Isen, 1987; Lerner & Keltner, 2001; Loewenstein & Lerner, 2003; Rozin, 1996). Not only do experiments lead to

infrahumanization The tendency to be reluctant to attribute more complex emotions, such as pride or compassion, to outgroup members.

this conclusion, so too do studies of individuals who have suffered injuries to emotion-processing areas of the brain. Damage to the frontal lobes, which are connected to the amygdala and other brain regions involved in emotion, often results in the inability to rely on current emotions to make sound decisions. A person with frontal lobe damage, for example, will fail to consult feelings of fear and anxiety when facing decisions and as a result may take inappropriate risks (Damasio, 1994). Individuals with frontal lobe damage will often be unable to access feelings of sympathy when seeing another person suffer, and they may exhibit alarmingly cool behavior toward others in need (Blair, Jones, Clark, & Smith, 1997).

"Reason is and ought to be the slave of passion."

—David Hume

Emotions Provide Information for Judgments

Most serious judgments in life are complex. For instance, a thorough answer to a question about how satisfied you are with your life might lead you to think about whether you're meeting your goals of getting prepared for a career, whether your health is good, whether your finances will ever be in order, how serious the risks of global warming are, and so on. Given this complexity, Norbert Schwarz and Jerry Clore have argued that we often rely on a simpler assessment that is based on our current feelings, asking ourselves, "How do I currently feel about it?" This account of how emotions influence judgment is called the **feelings-as-information perspective** (Clore, 1992; Clore & Parrott, 1991; Schwarz, 1990; Schwarz & Clore, 1983). Its basic assumption is that emotions provide us with rapid, reliable information about events and conditions within our current environment—gut feelings, so to speak—that shape our most important judgments.

In a first test of this feelings-as-information perspective, Schwarz and Clore (1983) studied the potent effects that bright, sunny days and gloomy, overcast days have on the emotional lives of people in the Midwest. They telephoned people in Illinois on either a cloudy day or a sunny day. They asked participants, "All things considered, how satisfied or dissatisfied are you with your life as a whole these days?" Participants had to indicate their satisfaction on a 10-point scale, where 10 was "completely satisfied with life." In one condition, researchers simply asked participants about their mood and life satisfaction on that day. The researchers predicted that participants who were called on a sunny day would be happier and would report greater life satisfaction than participants who were called on a gloomy day. In a second condition, before being asked about mood and life satisfaction, other participants were asked, "How's the weather down there?" Schwarz and Clore reasoned that this question would lead those participants to attribute their current mood and life satisfaction to the weather and not to use their feelings in evaluating their life satisfaction (**Table 6.1**). Finally, at the end of this brief survey, participants indicated how happy they felt at that moment.

When asked only about their mood and life satisfaction, the participants' responses confirmed Schwarz and Clore's feelings-as-information hypothesis: people were happier when called on sunny days than when called on overcast, gray days, and they also indicated greater life satisfaction. In contrast, when participants were initially asked about the weather, they tended to discount the

feelings-as-information perspective A theory that since many judgments are too complex for people to thoroughly review all the relevant evidence, they rely on their emotions to provide them with rapid, reliable information about events and conditions within their social environment.

TABLE 6.1 Feelings as Information

People often use their current feelings to make complex social judgments. In a study of the feelings-as-information hypothesis, Schwarz and Clore asked people to indicate how happy they were with life on an overcast day or a sunny day.

	Not Attributing Feelings to the Weather	Attributing Feelings to the Weather
Happiness		
Sunny	7.43	7.29
Overcast	5.00	7.00
Life Satisfaction		
Sunny	6.57	6.79
Overcast	4.58	6.71

Source: Adapted from Schwarz & Clore (1983).

relevance of their feelings related to the weather and thus reported equivalent levels of life satisfaction whether the day was sunny or gloomy.

This study set the stage for subsequent experiments that have revealed how people rely on different emotions to make important judgments and decisions. In keeping with the feelings-as-information perspective, people in a bad mood are more likely to arrive at negative judgments about consumer products, political figures, and economic policies (Forgas & Moylan, 1987). Several studies, for example, have focused on anger and lend credence to the old notion that when people are angry about something—say, a bad day at work—that emotion is likely to influence all sorts of judgments. Simply recalling an angry event in the past can cause people to rely on that emotion to blame others for current problems and to assume that unfair things will happen to them in the future (DeSteno, Petty, Wegener, & Rucker, 2000; Feigenson, Park, & Salovey, 2001; Keltner, Ellsworth, & Edwards, 1993; Lerner, Goldberg, & Tetlock, 1998; Quigley & Tedeschi, 1996).

Still other emotions feed into judgments. People in a state of fear perceive greater risk in their environment, pay more attention to those threats, and offer pessimistic estimates about the bad things that are likely to happen to them in the future (Lerner & Keltner, 2001; Mineka, Rafaeli, & Yovel, 2003). In a national field experiment conducted right after the 9/11 terrorist attacks, people who were induced to feel fear (as opposed to anger) about the attacks perceived greater risks in their environment, related not just to terrorism but to other matters as well, such as the possibility of a flu epidemic (Lerner & Gonzalez, 2005; Lerner, Gonzalez, Small, & Fischhoff, 2003).

Do emotions always guide people's judgments? Not according to Joseph Forgas, who has found that we are most likely to rely on our emotions when we make more complex judgments ("How will global warming influence the American economy 20 years from now?") as opposed to simple judgments ("Is my car's tire flat?") and when we do not have preexisting schemas to guide our judgment (Forgas, 1995, 2000). People are most likely to be guided by their emotions in judgments of complex matters where they do not have previous norms or ideas to guide them.

Emotions and Moral Judgment

When asking jurors to render legal judgments, judges in the United States encourage them to put aside their emotions in judging the guilt or innocence of the defendant and in making decisions about sentence length and punitive damages. This view of emotion is rooted in Western suspicions about the influence of emotions, but according to Jonathan Haidt, it is naive. Haidt claims that emotions are essential guides to our moral decisions (Haidt, 2001). As an example, read the following scenario, and decide whether you think the action described is right or wrong:

> Mark and Julie are brother and sister. They are traveling together in France on a summer vacation from college. One night they are staying alone in a cabin near the beach. They decide that it would be interesting and fun if they tried making love. At the very least it would be a new experience for each of them. Julie was already taking birth control pills, but Mark uses a condom, too, just to be safe. They both enjoy making love, but they decide not to do it again. They keep that night as a special secret, which makes them feel even closer to each other.

When asked whether such actions are wrong, nearly all college students immediately say yes, typically with pronounced disgust (Haidt, 2001). They're in good company. All cultures around the world view incest as immoral (Brown, 1991). When pressed to explain why Julie and Mark's encounter is wrong, people may reason that it is dangerous to inbreed, only to remember that Julie and Mark are using birth control. They may contend that each would be hurt emotionally, but recall that it was clearly specified that Julie and Mark were not harmed in any way by the event. Eventually, when all of their possible reasons have been refuted, people may simply say, "I can't explain why, I just know this is wrong" (**Figure 6.5**).

Haidt argues that people's responses to the Julie and Mark scenario reveal the two systems that are engaged when people make moral judgments about right or wrong, of virtue and character. First, people experience gut feelings that orient them to the nature of the moral wrongdoing (Batson, Engel, & Fridell, 1999; Greene & Haidt, 2002; Haidt, 2003). People then rely on more deliberative processes—assessments of costs and benefits, causal attributions, considerations of prevailing social norms—to arrive at a final moral judgment of right or wrong. But emotions are primary drivers of moral judgment (**Box 6.3**).

FIGURE 6.5 You Be the Subject: Emotions and Moral Judgment

Try Jonathan Haidt's demonstration of the role of emotion in moral judgment on a friend.

1. Read the "Mark and Julie" scenario to one or more friends, and pay close attention to their facial expressions and voices as they listen.

2. Then ask your friends to explain why it is wrong.

3. Refute each argument (as in the text).

Results: Such responses demonstrate that a person's emotional reactions often determine their judgment of morality. People do not reason their way to moral judgment; they feel their way.

BOX 6.3   FOCUS ON NEUROSCIENCE

The Moral Brain

One of the most compelling demonstrations of Haidt's two-system theory of moral judgment is that offered by neuroscientist and philosopher Joshua Greene and his colleagues (Greene, Sommerville, Nystrom, Darley, & Cohen, 2001). They used a methodology now known as "trolleyology," which presents participants with morally compelling scenarios and asks for quick decisions. In this instance, Greene's participants worked through a variety of moral scenarios while images of their brains were gathered with fMRI technologies. Participants judged different moral and nonmoral dilemmas in terms of whether they considered the action to be appropriate or not. Some of the moral dilemmas were likely to engage mainly impersonal, rational calculation, whereas others had more personal, emotional implications. An example of the more impersonal type is the well-known "trolley dilemma," in which the participant imagines a runaway trolley headed for five people who will be killed if it proceeds on its present course. The only way to save them is to hit a switch that will turn the trolley onto another set of tracks, where it will kill one person instead of five. The participant is asked whether it is appropriate to hit the switch and save five lives. Most participants answer yes with only a little hesitation.

In the more emotionally evocative "footbridge dilemma," five people's lives are again threatened by a trolley, but in this case the participant is asked to imagine standing next to a very heavy stranger on a footbridge over the trolley tracks. The participant is told that pushing the stranger off the bridge and onto the tracks would kill the stranger, but his dead body would cause the train to veer off its course and thus would save the lives of the five other individuals. (The participant's own weight, it is explained, is insufficient to send the trolley off the track.) Is it appropriate to push the stranger off the footbridge? The same two options are presented in the trolley dilemma and the footbridge dilemma—one death or five deaths—but in the footbridge dilemma the action is highly personal. The participant must imagine using his or her own hands to push the stranger to his gruesome death.

As participants responded to several different dilemmas of this sort in Greene and colleagues' study, fMRI techniques ascertained which parts of each participant's brain were active. Consistent with Haidt's two-system theory, the personal moral dilemmas activated regions of the brain that previous research had found to be involved in emotion. The impersonal moral dilemmas and the nonmoral dilemmas activated brain regions associated with working memory, regions centrally involved in deliberative reasoning.

Haidt proposes that several emotions guide moral judgment. *Self-critical* emotions, such as shame, embarrassment, and guilt, arise when we have violated social norms and moral codes or ideas about virtue and character (Baumeister, Stillwell, & Heatherton, 1994; Higgins, 1987; Keltner & Anderson, 2000; Keltner & Buswell, 1997; Tangney, Miller, Flicker, & Barlow, 1996). Emotions like embarrassment and guilt motivate us to make amends for our inappropriate actions. People who are "shameless," who are less likely to experience emotions like embarrassment and guilt, are more likely to engage in violence and criminal behavior (Beer, Heerey, Keltner, Scabini, & Knight, 2003; Blair et al., 1997; Keltner, Moffitt, & Stouthamer-Loeber, 1995). *Other-praising* emotions, most notably gratitude and "elevation," or awe, signal our approval of others' moral virtues (Haidt, 2003; Keltner & Haidt, 2003; McCullough et al., 2001).

More empirical attention has been given to *harm-related* emotions like sympathy, concern, and compassion. These emotions motivate prosocial behavior toward people who suffer or are vulnerable, as discussed in Chapter 14 (Batson & Shaw, 1991; Eisenberg et al., 1989). Recent studies find that momentary feelings of compassion lead individuals to see the common humanity they share with others, which encourages more prosocial behavior (Oveis et al., 2010). Sympathy also sways moral judgments in the realm of punishment (Rudolph, Roesch, Greitemeyer, & Weiner, 2004; Weiner, Graham, & Reyna, 1997). People who attribute a criminal defendant's immoral action to contextual causes (for example, an impoverished environment or abusive family background) are more likely to feel sympathy and to recommend less severe forms of punishment that focus on reforming the character of the defendant, whereas people who blame the defendant and feel anger are more likely to recommend harsher forms of punishment (Lerner et al., 1998; Quigley & Tedeschi, 1996). Compassion makes people less punitive in nonlegal settings as well (Condon & DeSteno, 2011).

The best studied of the moral emotions are *other-condemning* emotions, such as anger and disgust. We feel these emotions in response to others' immoral acts. But empirical studies find that anger and disgust tend to be involved in different moral domains. Unfair violations of rights and freedoms, such as when people are not allowed to speak their mind or are not given fair access to an opportunity, are more likely to trigger anger than disgust (Rozin et al., 1999; Vasquez, Keltner, Ebenbach, & Banaszynski, 2001). By contrast, disgust tends to arise when people condemn others for being impure in body, mind, or character (Haidt, Koller, & Dias, 1993; Wheatley & Haidt, 2005).

Several studies find that feelings of disgust amplify, or intensify, judgments that impure actions are morally wrong (and not just a matter of personal choice). For example, people who morally condemn cigarette smoking and meat consumption are particularly likely to find these acts disgusting (Rozin & Singh, 1999). People led to feel disgust by viewing images of gore are more likely to morally condemn impure acts (for example, leaving sweat on an exercise machine) and praise pure acts such as meditating (Horberg, Oveis, Keltner, & Cohen, 2009). Feelings of disgust tend to heighten prejudice toward groups that might be construed as impure—namely, homosexual men—but not other outgroups (Dasgupta, DeSteno, Williams, & Hunsinger, 2009; Inbar, Pizarro, & Bloom, in press). This effect is so strong that people standing near a trash can sprayed with a putrid-smelling scent expressed more negative attitudes toward gay men (Inbar, Pizarro, & Bloom, 2012).

Emotions Influence Reasoning

Emotions thus feed into people's judgments by acting as guides to how good or bad something is, about how fair things are, and about whether there is risk to worry about. Our immediate emotional responses also serve as intuitive guides to our moral judgment. How we feel about something often determines what we think about it.

Emotions also influence the very processes we use in reasoning, as indicated by research on the **processing style perspective.** Consider how emotions might influence the use of stereotypes, which are automatic, effort-saving tools for judging others. Galen Bodenhausen has found that people induced to experience sadness

processing style perspective
A theory that different emotions lead people to reason in different ways—for example, that anger facilitates reliance on preexisting heuristics and stereotypes, whereas sadness facilitates more careful attention to situational details.

are less likely to stereotype others than are people feeling anger (Bodenhausen, Sheppard, & Kramer, 1994). Sadness appears to make people more astute, careful judges of others, and anger less so.

How, then, do positive emotions influence the creativity and complexity of our reasoning? People tend to assume that positive emotions are sources of simplistic or lazy thinking. Think of a creative genius—a van Gogh, Woolf, Beethoven, or Darwin—and odds are that you imagine their creative acts as having been produced during moments of struggle, tension, somberness, and even despair.

Alice Isen (1987, 1993) suggests that this view of creativity is wrong, contending that happiness prompts people to think in ways that are flexible and creative. In her studies, Isen induces positive emotion with trivial events. She gives participants little bags of candy. Participants find a dime. They are asked to give associations for positive words. They watch an amusing film clip. These subtle ways of making participants feel good produce striking changes in their reasoning. When given one word (for example, *carpet*) and asked to generate a related word, people feeling positive emotions generate more novel associations (for example, *fresh* or *texture*) than people in a neutral state, who tend to produce more common responses (for example, *rug*). People feeling positive moods categorize objects in more inclusive ways, rating fringe members of categories (for example, *cane* or *purse* as an example of clothing) as better members of that category than do people in a neutral state, whose categories tend to be more narrowly defined. These effects of positive emotion have important social consequences. Negotiators in a positive mood are more likely to reach an optimal agreement that incorporates the interests of both sides, because positive moods allow opponents to think flexibly about the positions and interests of the other side (Carnevale & Isen, 1986; Forgas, 1998b).

Extending Isen's findings, Barbara Fredrickson has advanced her **broaden-and-build hypothesis** regarding positive emotions (Fredrickson, 1998, 2001). Fredrickson proposes that positive emotions broaden our thoughts and actions to help us build emotional and intellectual resources such as empathy or the acquisition of knowledge. These increases in intellectual resources, in turn, build our social resources, such as friendships and social networks. Fredrickson and her colleagues have found that when people are led to experience positive emotions (by watching an amusing film clip, for example), they broaden and build in several ways (Fredrickson, 2001; Waugh & Fredrickson, 2006). People feeling positive emotion, for example, rate themselves as more similar to outgroup members, suggesting that they broaden their way of looking at themselves in relation to people from different groups. Within developing relationships, people feeling positive emotion see greater overlap between their self-concepts and the self-concepts of their friend or romantic partner.

broaden-and-build hypothesis
The hypothesis that positive emotions broaden thought and action repertoires, helping people build social resources.

 Emotions influence social cognition in powerful ways. People consult their emotions as information in making judgments about life satisfaction, how fair things are, and how much risk is in the environment. Emotions are also powerful intuitions that feed into our moral judgments, shaping our judgments of punishment and wrongdoing. Emotions shape how we reason, a process perhaps most evident in the broaden-and-build hypothesis, which shows that positive emotions lead to broadened, more creative thought patterns that in turn help build intellectual and social resources.

HAPPINESS

It is only fitting to conclude this chapter by asking a question that has long preoccupied philosophers and laypeople alike: What is happiness? The Declaration of Independence refers to inalienable rights, among them "life, liberty, and the pursuit of happiness." Various philosophers have considered happiness to be one of the highest aims of living and a critical metric for assessing the moral quality of human action and the fairness of economic and political systems.

Over time, the meaning of happiness has changed (McMahin, 2006). In early Greek life, happiness was believed to be achieved through ethical behavior, in being temperate, fair, and dutiful. In the Middle Ages, as plagues and wars darkened the times, happiness was thought to be found in the afterlife, in communion with God when the soul was liberated from the passions of earthly life. In the eighteenth-century Enlightenment, people sought out happiness in hedonistic experiences or in actions that advanced the happiness of as many people as possible (the idea of the greater good). And recent studies reveal great cultural variation in the meaning of happiness. Americans are likely to associate happiness with personal achievement (Yuchida & Kitayama, 2009). As you might anticipate, people in East Asian cultures more often think of happiness as an experience to be found in harmonious interactions with others and in fulfilling duties (Kitayama, Karasawa, & Mesquita, 2004).

What, then, is happiness? What determines if we will experience pleasure? Can we predict what will make us happy? What actually brings us lasting happiness?

The Determinants of Pleasure

Pleasure is a core element of many experiences of happiness. But what makes for a pleasurable experience? Barbara Fredrickson (1998) and Daniel Kahneman (1999) have found some surprising answers to this question. In their research, they have people experience pleasure in different ways. For example, in one study, participants watched pleasurable films, such as a comedy routine or a puppy playing with a flower (Fredrickson & Kahneman, 1993). While watching these clips, the participants used a dial to rate their second-by-second pleasure. The researchers then correlated these second-by-second ratings with the participants' ratings of their overall pleasure at the end of the clip. The question of interest was: How do participants' immediate reports of pleasure predict their overall recollections of pleasure?

This study and others like it have documented three determinants of people's overall assessments of pleasure. First, the *peak moment* of pleasure associated with an event—for example, that burst of joy as you eat an ice-cream sundae—strongly predicts how much pleasure you will associate with the event. Second, how you feel at the *end* of the event also strongly predicts your overall reports of pleasure. If you are planning a backpacking trip through Europe or a first date, make sure that last day (or last 5 minutes) is extremely pleasurable. Finally, and somewhat surprisingly, the length of the pleasurable experience is unrelated to overall reports of pleasure, a bias called **duration neglect**. Whether a neck massage lasts 20 minutes or 60 minutes, whether a first date lasts 1 hour or 10, seems to have little sway over our experience of pleasure. What matters is whether the peak moment and ending are good. The same principle holds for negative experiences. Remembered pain is predicted by peak and end discomfort, not by its duration (Kahneman, 1999).

duration neglect The relative unimportance of the length of an emotional experience, be it pleasurable or unpleasant, in judgments of the overall experience.

Knowing What Makes Us Happy

Can people reliably predict what will make them happy and what will bring them despair? These kinds of predictions are profoundly important. We burn the midnight oil at work on the assumption that career success will bring lasting joy. We choose graduate schools, careers, vacations, and marriage partners based on the sense that one option will bring more happiness than others. In deciding what career or romantic partner to choose, we may begin with practical questions, but we are very likely to come back to the basic question: What will make us happy? Regrettably, the answer to this question is usually not as simple as we would like it to be.

In research on **affective forecasting**, Daniel Gilbert and Timothy Wilson have documented a variety of biases that undermine our attempts to predict what will make us happy (Gilbert, Brown, Pinel, & Wilson, 2000). Take one study that examined the expected and actual impact of breaking up with a romantic partner (Gilbert, Pinel, Wilson, Blumberg, & Wheatley, 1998). People who had not experienced a romantic breakup, called "luckies," reported on their own overall happiness and then predicted how unhappy they would be two months after a romantic breakup. This estimate was compared with the happiness of people who had recently broken up, labeled "leftovers." As seen in **Figure 6.6**, leftovers were just as happy as luckies, but luckies predicted that they would be much less happy two months after a breakup than leftovers actually were. People overestimated how much a romantic breakup would diminish their life satisfaction.

A related study looked at the predicted and actual effects of getting tenure (Gilbert et al., 1998). As you may know, professors are evaluated around six years into their job and either given tenure (which means they have a permanent position at the university) or sent packing. The tenure process is fraught with anxiety, but many of these tenure-related anxieties may be misguided. Five years after the tenure decision, professors who did not get tenure were not significantly less

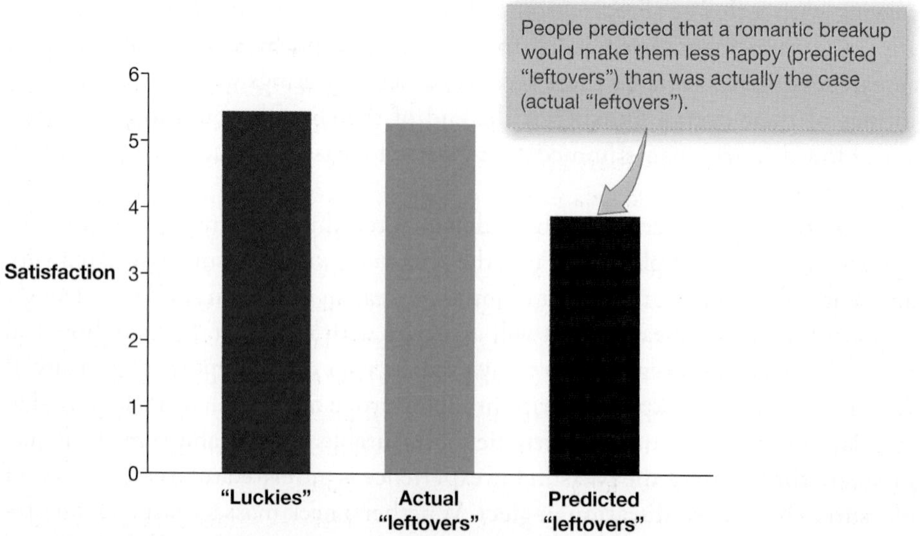

affective forecasting Predicting future emotions—for example, whether an event will result in happiness or anger or sadness, and for how long.

People predicted that a romantic breakup would make them less happy (predicted "leftovers") than was actually the case (actual "leftovers").

FIGURE 6.6 Do We Know What Makes Us Happy? Daniel Gilbert and his colleagues asked whether people are accurate in their judgments of how happy they will be following a romantic breakup. The results were consistent with their claims about biased affective forecasting. (Source: Adapted from Gilbert et al., 1998.)

happy than those who did. Once again, predictions differed from reality. Young assistant professors predicted a level of happiness five years after getting tenure that was far above what was actually observed in professors who did get tenure. And assistant professors expected a level of happiness five years after a denial of tenure that was far below what was actually observed in professors who had been recently denied tenure.

A variety of biases interfere with people's attempts to predict the level of their future happiness. One is **immune neglect** (Gilbert et al., 1998). We are often remarkably resilient in responding to painful setbacks, largely because of what Gilbert and Wilson call the "psychological immune system," which allows us to rise above the effects of negative experience and trauma. We find the silver lining, the humor, the potential for growth, insight, and positive change in the face of painful setbacks and traumatic experiences, and these "immune-related" processes allow us to return to satisfying lives in the face of negative experiences. However, when estimating the effects of traumatic events like breakups or failures at work, we fail to consider these processes, how effectively they will take hold, or how quickly they will exert their effects. Instead, we assume that we will be devastated by traumatic negative events. As a consequence, we inaccurately predict our future happiness.

Another bias is **focalism**: we focus too much on the main elements of significant events, such as the initial despair after learning that we have been denied tenure, and we neglect to consider how other aspects of our lives also shape our satisfaction (Wilson, Wheatley, Meyers, Gilbert, & Axson, 2000). We tend to assume that once a particular event happens—for example, once we ace our GREs, get married, or have children—we will be truly happy. What we forget to consider is that after those exam scores arrive, after our wedding, or after the arrival of our children, many other events—such as problems on our job, conflicts with our spouse, or difficulties with our children—will also influence our happiness.

immune neglect The tendency for people to underestimate their capacity to be resilient in responding to difficult life events, which leads them to overestimate the extent to which life's difficulties will reduce their personal well-being.

focalism A tendency to focus too much on a central aspect of an event while neglecting to consider the impact of ancillary aspects of the event or the impact of other events.

"Nothing in life is as important as you think it is at the moment you are thinking of it."

—Psychologist and Nobel laureate Daniel Kahneman

The Happy Life

The final question about happiness may be the most important of all: What brings people happiness in their lives? Finding sound answers to this question not only helps you fare better in your personal relationships and career but also helps you live longer. Sonja Lyubomirsky, Laura King, and Ed Diener reviewed several hundred studies of the correlates and consequences of happiness (Lyubomirsky, King, & Diener, 2005). Their conclusion is that happiness is good for marriage. Marriage expert John Gottman has observed that for marriages to fare well, partners need to experience and express five positive emotions for every negative one (Gottman, 1993). Marriages with higher ratios of laughter, gratitude, appreciation, love, and kindness to anger, contempt, and fear are more likely to last. Happiness also makes for more creative and better-performing workers, which makes sense in light of the influences of positive emotion on creative thought. Happiness also helps people live longer. One well-known study found that nuns who at age 20 reported greater happiness in personal narratives as they entered the convent were more likely to live into their 80s and 90s than nuns who reported being less happy in their narratives (Danner, Snowdon, & Friesen, 2001).

What, then, are the sources of happiness? One way to answer the question is to look at the broad demographic and cultural factors that make for happier individuals. Do you have any intuitions about who is happier: women or men? It turns out that gender matters little in the realm of happiness: women are about as happy as men. The same is true for age: although people become a bit happier as they age, in general age has a weak effect on happiness. So much for midlife crises.

What about money? Here the story is more complicated and not what you might expect. In wealthier countries, money is related to life satisfaction, but not powerfully so. College undergraduates now state that earning a lot of money is the primary reason for going to college. (A whopping 74 percent reported this reason in one recent survey, up from 24 percent 20 years ago. It remains to be seen whether the recent collapse of the financial industry causes students to rethink their career plans.) But for people who have attended college, more money buys them only a bit more satisfaction with their lives (Myers, 2000b). And some recent research suggests that the pursuit of material gain as a central purpose in life actually makes people less happy (Lyubomirsky, 2007). And studies indicate that money does shape life satisfaction for people who have little. People from poorer nations are less happy than those in rich nations. This may be because people in disadvantaged countries often suffer from a lack of jobs, poor nutrition, diseases, and civil strife that are correlated with extreme poverty.

Broader ideological factors matter as well. In surveys of individuals from various countries, people are happier in independent cultures, in cultures where individuals have rights (such as the right to vote), and in countries where there is more rather than less economic equality (Diener, 2000). These survey studies point to broad forces that enable people to be happy: some degree of economic well-being, equality, freedom, and individual rights.

And finally, as you might have guessed, scientists who study happiness all agree that the most powerful source of happiness is relationships (Lyubomirsky, 2007). All kinds of relationships—romantic relationships, friendships, family connections, neighborhood ties—lift people's spirits. In the 1970s and 1980s in the United States, married people were twice as likely to say that they were "very happy" (48 percent) than were unmarried people (24 percent). Moreover, contact with friends consistently correlates strongly with levels of life satisfaction (Myers, 1999). We are social beings, and having strong social bonds brings great satisfaction.

Cultivating Happiness

People devote a great deal of energy to being happier and to trying to make their children, friends, coworkers, and romantic partners happier—and for good reason. The literature suggests that cultivating happiness makes for healthier families, workplaces, communities, and cultures. Can we choose to live in ways that make us happier? In a recent theoretical paper, Sonja Lyubomirsky, Ken Sheldon, and David Schkade (2005) say yes. In their survey of the literature on the genetic and environmental determinants of happiness, they suggest that about half of the variation among individuals in happiness is due to genetic factors. Studies of identical and fraternal twins, for example, find that identical twins, genetically the same, are about twice as similar in their levels of happiness as fraternal twins. Another 10 percent of the variation in happiness is due to the quality of the current environment—the neighborhood you grow up in; whether your country is at war; the rights, freedoms, and opportunities you enjoy. The remaining 40 percent of variation in happiness is shaped by the activities people choose, the patterns of thought that they develop, the ways that they handle stress, and the relationship style they cultivate with others.

So what does social psychology have to say about the freely chosen paths to happiness? One clear piece of wisdom concerns how people handle stressful times. Deeply stressful times—difficulties at work, trying times in a marriage, the loss of a loved one, turbulent times with parents and children—are part of living. And if these kinds of stresses are chronic, they can make you less happy, wear down your immune system, and lead to poor health.

One strategy for cultivating happiness is to create a narrative of your life, during good times and bad. Write about the emotions of life's trials and tribulations. James Pennebaker and his colleagues have conducted dozens of studies in which they have had participants write about the emotions associated with traumas they

---

BOX 6.4   FOCUS ON POSITIVE PSYCHOLOGY

Nirvana in Your Brain

Ever since the Buddha found enlightenment when meditating under a bo tree 2,500 years ago, billions of people have turned to meditation to find peace and happiness. There are many kinds of meditation practices, but they share certain principles. They encourage you to mindfully slow down your breathing to a healthy, steady rhythm with deep exhalations, which reduces stress-related cardiovascular arousal. Many meditation practices encourage a mindful attention to different sensations in your body. They likewise encourage nonjudgmental awareness of the stream of thoughts flowing through your mind. And many meditation practices—for example, those popularized by the Dalai Lama—encourage training the mind in loving kindness or compassion. Here the meditator extends feelings of compassion to family members, friends, loved ones, strangers, the self, and ultimately adversaries, to encourage a more compassionate stance toward fellow human beings.

Does meditation work? Neuroscientist Richard Davidson has been seeking a rigorous answer to that question. In one line of work, he has studied Tibetan monks, who spend as much as 4 or 5 hours a day quietly and devotedly meditating. Upon scanning the brain of a Tibetan monk, he found that this individual's resting brain showed levels of activation in the left frontal lobes—regions of the brain involved in positive emotion—to be literally off the charts. In another observation, Davidson blasted the monk with a loud burst of white noise to assess the startle response of the monk. For most people, this kind of stimulus activates an ancient and powerful startle response, the strength of which is a good indicator of how stressed out the individual is. The monk didn't even blink.

These benefits are not enjoyed only by monks who have devoted their lives to meditation. When Davidson, Jon Kabat Zinn, and colleagues had software engineers train in the techniques of mindfulness meditation—an accepting awareness of the mind, loving kindness toward others—six weeks later these individuals showed increased activation in the left frontal lobes. They also showed enhanced immune function as evident in the magnitude of the immune response in the skin to a flu shot (Davidson et al., 2003). In similarly motivated work, Barbara Fredrickson and her colleagues have found that practicing mindfulness meditation, with a focus on being mindful of breathing and extending loving kindness to others, boosts happiness several weeks later (Fredrickson, Cohn, Coffey, Pek, & Finkel, 2008).

have experienced (Pennebaker, 1989, 1993; Pennebaker, Hughes, & O'Heeron, 1987; Smyth, 1998). Researchers have used this procedure with people who are bereaved or divorced, who have experienced devastating earthquakes, who are Holocaust survivors, and, more recently, who were directly affected by the 9/11 terrorist attacks. People who write about the most difficult emotions associated with the trauma, compared with people who write in more factual fashion about the same trauma, benefit in many ways. They are less likely to visit the doctor, they experience elevated life satisfaction, they show enhanced immune function, they report fewer absentee days at work or school, and they do better in school (Pennebaker, 1993).

Putting your emotions into words helps for several reasons. First, people who give narrative structure to their emotions gain insight into their interior life, which points to effective ways to deal with their troubles and difficulties (Pennebaker, Mayne, & Francis, 1997). Pennebaker and his colleagues laboriously coded participants' written narratives, and they found that the increased use of insight words, such as "I now see" or "perspective," correlate with increased benefits. Second, putting emotions into words reduces the distress associated with not expressing your emotions. Inhibiting the expression of emotion has been shown to increase heart rate and blood pressure (Gross, 1998), and chronically elevated blood pressure can lead to health problems (Sapolsky, 1994). Expressing emotions should help bring your blood pressure back to normal. Finally, labeling emotions also helps us identify the causes of those emotions, thus reducing the extent to which they color our judgments of irrelevant domains (Keltner, Locke, & Audrain, 1993; Wilson & Brekke, 1994; Wilson, Centerbar, & Brekke, 2002). If you know that your frustration is due to a prima donna at work, that feeling is less likely to influence your view of other facets of your life. It also appears that writing about more positive life themes, such as your most important goals, has similar benefits (Emmons, McCullough, & Tsang, 2003; King & Miner, 2000). For example, Laura King and her colleagues had undergraduates write about their future best possible selves and then weeks later measured their well-being and health. This act of envisioning a hopeful future centering on a better self increased students' reports of well-being and reduced their reports of problematic health symptoms. And writing about goals and values has been found to improve the academic functioning of minority junior high students (Cohen, Garcia, Apfel, & Master, 2006; Oyserman, Bybee, & Terry, 2006).

A second piece of wisdom is to cultivate the many positive emotions that are so vital to personal well-being and relationships. A life that is rich with positive emotions—amusement, gratitude, love, and contentment—is one of the clearest paths to life satisfaction. You might start your pursuit of happiness with gratitude. For many social theorists, including Adam Smith and Charles Darwin, gratitude is the glue of cooperative communities. The expression of gratitude rewards others for their generous acts, and feeling gratitude promotes happiness. Sonja Lyubomirsky (2007) had people count five blessings once a week and found that these grateful individuals, compared with appropriate control individuals, reported higher levels of happiness and health several weeks later. Simply reflecting on the meaningful things that life offers—the pleasures of friendship, an unusually beautiful day, a terrific meal—increased well-being. Reflecting on reasons for being grateful leads to increased happiness and fewer problematic health symptoms measured several weeks later (Emmons et al., 2003).

The same is true of other positive emotions. Forgiving someone increases well-being and reduces stress-related physiology (Lawler et al., 2003). Increasing laughter and play in your relationships makes for more satisfying bonds. Cultivating feelings of contentment and interest make for long-term gains in overall well-being (Fredrickson, 2001). The path to a happy life is through the emotions.

 Our retrospective experiences of pleasure are based on peak and end pleasures, but not on the duration of the pleasurable experience. People can have difficulty predicting whether they will be happy in the future: they are often more resilient than they think, and they also tend to focus on certain aspects of future events while neglecting other aspects that will also be important in the future. Being happy is good for your relationships, your work life, and your health. Some broad demographic factors (gender, age, income) matter little in shaping our happiness; others (equality, rights, a minimum level of economic well-being) matter a lot. Finally, happiness can be cultivated through writing narratives of tough times and cultivating positive emotions such as gratitude, laughter, and forgiveness.

Chapter Review

Summary

Characterizing Emotion

- The experience of emotion is generally brief, lasting only seconds or minutes; moods often last for hours or days.

- Emotions are usually specific to people and events, and motivate individuals to achieve specific goals.

- *Appraisal processes* are the construal processes that trigger emotions. In the *primary appraisal stage*, we evaluate whether ongoing events are congruent with our goals. In the *secondary appraisal stage*, we determine why we feel as we do and what to do about it, considering different ways of responding and possible consequences.

- Emotions involve expressive processes, enabling us to communicate our feelings and reactions through facial expression, touch, the voice, and art.

- Language enables us to label our emotions, and emotion shapes our attention, memories, and judgments.

Universality and Cultural Specificity of Emotion

- There are universal aspects to emotion based on evolutionary factors; emotions enable us to respond quickly and effectively to threats and opportunities related to survival.

- Paul Ekman's studies revealed that people in dramatically different cultures judge expressions of anger, disgust, fear, happiness, sadness, and surprise in a highly similar fashion.

- There are cultural differences in when and which emotions are expressed. Some cultures develop specific ways of expressing a particular emotion, known as an *emotion accent*. Cultures vary in which emotions are *focal*, or common in everyday experience. Cultures vary in how many words they have in their language to describe emotion. And cultures vary in which emotions are highly valued, or idealized.

Emotions and Social Relationships

- With brief touches we can communicate emotions like love, compassion, and gratitude, which are vital to intimate relationships.

- We often mimic the expressive behaviors and emotions of others, and this process brings us closer to others.

- A chemical known as oxytocin, which circulates through the brain and bloodstream, promotes trust and devotion.

- Emotional intelligence, which captures four ways in which people use emotions wisely, predicts healthier social relationships of every kind.

- The expression of some emotions, like anger, gives people high status within groups, whereas emotions such as embarrassment confer lower status.

- Emotions establish group boundaries. People have been shown to *infrahumanize* outgroup members: they attribute basic emotions like anger and disgust to outgroups, but assume that outgroups do not so readily experience the more complex emotions, like embarrassment.

Emotions and Social Cognition

- The *feelings-as-information perspective* says that emotions provide rapid and reliable information for judgments when we don't have time to evaluate complex information. Studies have found that momentary emotions influence judgments of life satisfaction and risk.

- Emotions influence moral judgments in powerful ways. Feelings of disgust make us judge impure behaviors (for example, cigarette smoking) as wrong.

- The *processing style perspective* says that emotions lead us to process information in different ways. Positive emotions lead to the use of heuristics and stereotypes; negative emotions lead to more systematic and detailed assessments. The *broaden-and-build hypothesis* holds that positive emotions broaden our thought, prompting us to see greater similarities with individuals from other groups, and build stronger relationships.

Happiness

- Our overall assessments of pleasure seem closely tied to the peak and end of a pleasurable stimulus and, surprisingly, have little to do with its duration. Our ability to predict the sources of happiness turns out to be suspect, in part because of two biases: *immune neglect* and *focalism*.

- Many objective factors, such as gender, age, and money, have small effects on our happiness. Sociocultural factors, such as relationships and social equality, have substantial effects on our happiness.

- A new science of happiness says that happiness promotes healthy marriages and helps people live longer.

- About 40 percent of a person's happiness is due to the habits and practices that the individual chooses to cultivate. Writing about times of difficulty and stress makes for healthier adjustment, as does cultivating positive emotions such as gratitude.

Key Terms

affective forecasting (p. 224)
appraisal processes (p. 198)
broaden-and-build hypothesis (p. 222)
core-relational themes (p. 198)
display rules (p. 207)
duration neglect (p. 223)

emotion accents (p. 205)
emotions (p. 197)
feelings-as-information perspective (p. 217)
focal emotions (p. 206)
focalism (p. 225)
hypercognize (p. 207)

immune neglect (p. 225)
infrahumanization (p. 216)
primary appraisal stage (p. 198)
principle of serviceable habits (p. 200)
processing style perspective (p. 221)
secondary appraisal stage (p. 198)

Further Reading

Damasio, A. R. (1994). *Descartes' error: Emotion, reason, and the human brain*. New York: Free Press. An early neuroscientific approach to how emotions influence our most important decisions.

Darwin, C. (1872/1998). *The expression of emotions in man and animals* (3rd ed.). New York: Oxford University Press. Darwin's classic on the evolution of the expressions of different emotions.

Keltner, D. (2009). *Born to be good: The science of a meaningful life*. New York: W. W. Norton & Company. A recent statement about the evolution of positive emotions like love, awe, compassion, and mirth.

Oatley, K. (2004). *Emotions: A brief history*. Malden, MA: Blackwell. A review of how we have thought about emotions over 2,000 years of Western civilization.

CHAPTER 7

Attitudes, Behavior, and Rationalization

THROUGHOUT THE UNITED STATES' long and painful military involvement in Vietnam—a conflict that split the nation into "hawks" and "doves," consumed the energies of three administrations, and ultimately cost the lives of 58,000 U.S. soldiers—the government put a positive spin on the enterprise. It maintained that there was "light at the end of the tunnel," that Communist North Vietnam would soon be vanquished, that a satisfactory peace agreement would soon be struck, and that the South Vietnamese regime that the United States was supporting would soon be able to defend itself. But despite repeated positive pronouncements of this sort, many government officials had doubts about the U.S. effort in Vietnam and the prospects for success. Their doubts often surfaced as key decisions needed to be made, such as whether to increase the number of U.S. soldiers stationed in South Vietnam or whether to initiate a bombing campaign against North Vietnam.

Lyndon Johnson, the U.S. president responsible for the largest buildup of American troops in Vietnam, employed an interesting tactic to deal with those in his administration who had begun privately to express such doubts and to waver from the administration's policy on the war (Halberstam, 1969). Johnson would send the doubters on a "fact-finding" mission to Vietnam, nearly always with a group of reporters in tow. This might seem like a risky move on Johnson's part, because if any of these less-than-staunch supporters expressed their doubts to the press, the administration's policies would be undermined. But Johnson knew they would not express their doubts publicly and instead would prefer to try to influence administration policy from the inside. Unwilling to express their doubts to the public and confronted by criticism of the war effort by reporters, the doubters would be thrust into the position of publicly *defending* administration policy. This public advocacy, Johnson reasoned, would serve to lessen their doubts and help turn the skeptics in his administration into advocates. Known

Public Advocacy and Private Acceptance Despite the continuing problems in fighting the Vietnam War, U.S. president Lyndon Johnson publicly declared that the war was going well and insisted that his advisers and cabinet members also publicly express their support and confidence. (A) Defense Secretary Robert McNamara had reservations about the war that may have been alleviated by the constant necessity of defending it. Here he is shown briefing the press on U.S. air attacks. (B) To bolster morale, Johnson himself spoke to U.S. troops in South Vietnam, while U.S. general William Westmoreland, South Vietnamese general Nguyen Van Thieu, South Vietnamese premier Nguyen Coo Ky, and U.S. secretary of state Dean Rusk looked on.

as an unusually savvy politician, Johnson was using some very clever psychology—psychology that is explored in this chapter—to win support for his policy.

Johnson's strategy highlights some important questions about the consistency between attitudes and behavior, especially whether the consistency between the two is the result of attitudes influencing behavior or behavior influencing attitudes. Both types of influence exist. Those with strong pro-environment attitudes are more likely to vote Green or Democratic than Republican. Thus attitudes influence behavior. But everyone knows that people rationalize, so behavior influences attitudes as well. Environmentally minded individuals who drive gas-guzzling cars tend to convince themselves that automobile exhaust contributes very little to air pollution or global warming—or that they don't drive that much anyway.

The relative strength of these two effects is worth pondering. Which is stronger: the effect of

Behavior Can Influence Attitudes Many people who consider themselves environmentalists nonetheless drive gas-guzzling SUVs. Driving a vehicle that is not fuel efficient can lead those who are concerned about the environment to convince themselves that there is not much connection between fuel efficiency and air pollution or climate change.

attitudes on behavior or the effect of behavior on attitudes? It's a difficult question to answer, but decades of research on the topic have shown that the influence of attitudes on behavior is a bit weaker than most people suspect, and the influence of behavior on attitudes is much stronger than most suspect. So Johnson was right: get budding skeptics to publicly endorse the policy, and they will be skeptics no longer. More generally, give people a slight nudge to behave in a particular way, and their attitudes typically follow.

This chapter examines what social psychologists have learned about the consistency between attitudes and behavior. Research shows that attitudes are often surprisingly poor predictors of behavior, but it also specifies the circumstances in which they predict behavior rather well. The chapter also examines several "consistency theories" that explain why people tend to maintain consistency among their attitudes and between their attitudes and behavior. But let's start with the basics: what are attitudes, and how are they measured?

THE THREE COMPONENTS OF ATTITUDES

In the most general sense, an **attitude** is an evaluation of an object along a positive-negative dimension. At the core, then, attitudes involve *affect*—that is, how much people like or dislike an object, be it a politician, a landscape, an athletic shoe, an entrée, or themselves. Nearly all objects trigger some degree of positive or negative emotion, which constitutes the affective component of attitudes (Bargh, Chaiken, Raymond, & Hymes, 1996; Breckler, 1984; Cacioppo & Berntson, 1994; Fazio, Jackson, Dunton, & Williams, 1995; Fazio, Sanbonmatsu, Powell, & Kardes, 1986; Zanna & Rempel, 1988).

Most attitude theorists maintain that attitudes involve more than affect (Breckler, 1984; Eagly & Chaiken, 1998; Zimbardo & Leippe, 1991). Attitudes also involve *cognitions*, thoughts that typically reinforce a person's feelings. These include knowledge and beliefs about the object, as well as associated memories and images. Your attitude about a favorite city, for example, includes knowledge about its history and its most appealing neighborhoods and landmarks, as well as special times you've spent there.

Finally, attitudes are associated with specific *behaviors* (Fishbein & Ajzen, 1975). Most generally, the affective evaluation of good versus bad is connected to a behavioral tendency to approach versus avoid. When specific attitudes are primed—brought to mind, even unconsciously—people are more likely to act in ways consistent with the attitude (Chen & Bargh, 1999). Neuroscientific studies indicate that our attitudes activate particular regions in the brain—areas of the motor cortex—that support specific actions (Preston & de Waal, 2002). When you see a young child crying or a delicious-looking hot fudge sundae, your mind prepares your body for the actions of caretaking or consumption. Thus attitudes are associated with specific intentions and actions.

MEASURING ATTITUDES

It won't surprise you to learn that attitudes are most commonly measured through simple survey questions. Indeed, attitude questionnaires may be the most widely used methodology in social psychology. When researchers want to know how participants feel about members of other groups, their romantic partners, themselves, the president, and so on, they usually just ask them. More specifically, researchers typically ask their participants to rate an attitude object on a **Likert scale**, named after Rensis Likert, its inventor. The Likert scale lists a set

attitude An evaluation of an object in a positive or negative fashion that includes the three elements of affect, cognition, and behavior.

Likert scale A numerical scale used to assess people's attitudes; it includes a set of possible answers with labeled anchors on each extreme.

of possible answers with anchors on each extreme—for example, 1 = never, 7 = always. To determine attitudes toward the use of cell phones while driving, for example, participants might be asked to respond on a scale of 1 to 7, where 1 is the least favorable answer ("It's never acceptable") and 7 is the most favorable ("It's always acceptable"). You've probably responded to many of these kinds of queries yourself. Yet when it comes to many complex attitudes—for example, your attitude toward gay marriage, the Tea Party, or hedge fund managers—responses to these sorts of simple scales are likely to miss some important elements.

To understand why, consider the following questions: How much do you value freedom? How strongly do you feel about the need to reduce discrimination? How important is a less polluted environment? If an investigator asked these questions of a random selection of individuals, odds are that most responses would be very positive. But surely people differ in the strength and depth of their attitudes toward these issues. How, then, can social psychologists better capture the richness of people's attitudes if traditional Likert scales sometimes fail to differentiate people with stronger and weaker attitudes?

One approach, developed by Russell Fazio, is to measure the *accessibility* of the attitude—that is, how readily the attitude can be activated in the individual's mind, thereby guiding thought and behavior (Fazio, 1995; Fazio & Williams, 1986). Fazio and his colleagues measure the accessibility of attitudes by assessing the time it takes the individual to respond to the attitude question; this measure is known as the **response latency**. A person who takes 750 milliseconds to respond affirmatively to a question such as "Do you approve how the president is handling the economy?" is likely to have a stronger attitude on this topic than an individual who takes several seconds. In a study conducted five months before Ronald Reagan and Walter Mondale squared off in the 1984 presidential election, for example, Fazio and Williams (1986) measured how long it took participants to answer how good a president each of the opposing candidates would make. The time it took participants to respond to this question was a strong predictor of who they believed won the first debate between the two candidates and, more important, which candidate they voted for six months later.

A second way to assess the strength and importance of a person's attitude is to determine the *centrality* of the attitude to the individual's belief system (Krosnick & Petty, 1995). To assess attitude centrality, researchers measure a variety of attitudes within a domain and calculate how strongly each attitude is linked to the others. For example, in a study of social and political attitudes, a researcher might ask you your attitudes toward abortion, stem cell research, offshore drilling, gay marriage, sex education in high school, a clean environment, drug legalization, taxation, and subsidizing the automobile industry. If an attitude is very important to you, it should be highly correlated with your attitudes toward certain other issues. For example, if abortion is a defining social issue for you, as it is for many, then your attitude toward abortion is likely to be strongly correlated with your attitudes toward stem cell research and sex education, and perhaps even with your attitudes toward gay marriage and taxation.

Other ways of measuring attitudes do not rely on explicit self-reports. Investigators often use **implicit attitude measures** when there is reason to believe that people may be unwilling or unable to report their true attitudes. Chapter 11, on stereotypes and prejudice, discusses in some detail two widely used implicit measures—affective priming and the implicit association test, or IAT. Implicit measures like these also allow researchers to tap *automatic attitudes*—that is,

response latency The time it takes an individual to respond to a stimulus, such as an attitude question.

implicit attitude measures Indirect measures of attitudes that do not involve self-report.

BOX 7.1 **FOCUS ON NEUROSCIENCE**

Is the Bad Stronger than the Good?

At the core of our attitudes is a positive or negative response to an attitude object, whether it's an old friend's voice, a roommate's messy pile of dishes, or the smell of freshly cut grass. Pioneering research by neuroscientist Joseph LeDoux has found that one part of the brain—the amygdala—is central to this initial, core component of our attitudes (LeDoux, 1989, 1993, 1996). This almond-shaped region of the brain receives sensory information about a stimulus from the thalamus and then provides information about the positive or negative valence, or value, of the object. This evaluation occurs, remarkably, before the mind has categorized the object in question. Thus, even before we know what an object is, we have a gut feeling about it. When the amygdala is damaged, animals no longer have appropriate evaluations of objects: they eat feces, attempt to copulate with members of other species, and show no fear of threatening stimuli such as snakes or dominant animals.

LeDoux's research raises another interesting question: Are our quick positive and negative evaluations of stimuli comparable with respect to their strength? Reviews by Shelley Taylor (1991), Paul Rozin and Edward Royzman (2001), Roy Baumeister and his colleagues (Baumeister, Bratslavsky, Finkenauer, & Vohs, 2001), and John Cacioppo and Wendy Gardner (1999) have all yielded the same answer: negative evaluations are stronger than positive evaluations. It would certainly make evolutionary sense for an organism to be more vigilant about avoiding harm than seeking pleasure, to be more watchful for danger signs than for cues to opportunity. Food or mating opportunities not realized today might be realized tomorrow; if a predator is not avoided today, there is no tomorrow. A pronounced negativity bias might therefore increase the chances of survival.

Consider a few generalizations supporting the conclusion that the bad is stronger than the good. Negative stimuli, such as frightening sounds or noxious smells, elicit more rapid and stronger physiological responses than positive stimuli, such as delicious tastes. Losing $20 is more painful than winning $20 is pleasurable. Negative trauma, such as the death of a loved one or sexual abuse, can change the individual for a lifetime; positive events don't appear to have equivalent effects. Or consider Paul Rozin's observation about contamination: The briefest contact with a cockroach will spoil a delicious meal, but the inverse—making a pile of cockroaches delicious by spicing it up with your favorite foods—is unimaginable (Rozin & Royzman, 2001).

Contamination A cockroach on food spoils a delicious meal. (Note that the meal does not make the cockroaches suddenly seem appetizing.)

In related work, Tiffany Ito, John Cacioppo, and their colleagues presented participants with positively valenced pictures—for example, photographs of pizza or of a bowl of chocolate ice cream—and negatively valenced slides—for example, photographs of a mutilated face or a dead cat (Ito, Larsen, Smith, & Cacioppo, 1998). As they did so, they recorded participants' electrocortical activity on the scalp and studied brain regions known to be involved in evaluative responses to stimuli. They discovered a clear negativity bias in evaluation: the negative stimuli generated greater brain activity than the positive or neutral stimuli. It seems that the bad is indeed stronger than the good.

people's immediate evaluative reactions that they may not be conscious of, or that may conflict with their consciously endorsed attitudes. Researchers also sometimes use nonverbal measures of attitudes, such as people's smiling behavior or degree of physical closeness, as indices of positive attitudes toward others. Researchers can also measure physiological indicators, such as the increased heart rate and sweaty palms associated with fear, to capture people's attitudes. **Box 7.1**, for example, describes how patterns of brain activity recorded from the surface of the scalp reveal the strength of people's positive and negative attitudes.

Attitudes have three elements—affect, cognition, and behavior. Researchers have developed many ways to measure attitudes, from explicit self-reports to physiological measures.

PREDICTING BEHAVIOR FROM ATTITUDES

Most academic discussions of how well attitudes predict behavior begin with a remarkable study conducted by Richard LaPiere in the early 1930s (LaPiere, 1934). LaPiere spent two years touring the United States with a young Chinese couple, visiting numerous hotels, auto camps, restaurants, and cafés. Although prejudice and discrimination against Chinese individuals were common at the time, it is reassuring to learn that LaPiere and his traveling companions were denied service by only one of the 250 establishments they visited. Maybe anti-Chinese prejudice wasn't so strong after all.

To find out, LaPiere wrote to all of the establishments they had visited and asked whether their policy was to serve "Orientals." Approximately 90 percent of those who responded said they would not, a response rate that is stunningly inconsistent with what LaPiere actually observed during his earlier tour of the country. This result was unfortunate in human terms because it indicated that anti-Chinese prejudice was indeed rather robust. And it was unfortunate from the perspective of psychological science because it suggested that attitudes do not predict behavior very well. To a scientific discipline that had treated attitudes as powerful determinants of people's behavior, this news was truly surprising—and rather unsettling.

Attitudes Do Not Always Predict Behavior This store in Elk City, Idaho, displays a sign declaring "No Earth Firster or Sympathizer Allowed." The store owners may indeed intend to bar environmentalists from the store, but if someone walked into the store wearing a "Save the Whales" T-shirt, would they really deny that person service?

Note that this inconsistency was not some fluke associated with the particulars of LaPiere's study. Many experiments conducted over the next several decades yielded similar results. Indeed, a much-cited review in the 1960s of the existing literature on attitudes and behavior concluded, "The present review provides little evidence to support the postulated existence of stable, underlying attitudes within the individual which influence both his verbal expressions and his actions" (Wicker, 1969, p. 75).

Most people find this result surprising. Why? Why do we think that people's attitudes are strong predictors of their behavior when careful empirical studies reveal that they are not? Part of the reason is that we see plenty of evidence every day that attitudes and behavior go together. People who picket abortion clinics have attitudes opposed to abortion. People who show up at the local bowling alley have positive attitudes toward the sport. Families with a large litter of kids (usually) have positive attitudes about children. Evidence of a tight connection between attitudes and behavior is all around us. But this evidence only tells us that if people behave in a certain way, they are likely to have a positive attitude toward that behavior. This does not mean, however, that people with a positive attitude toward a given behavior are likely to behave in a manner consistent with their attitude. What is not so obvious in everyday life are the many instances of people with positive attitudes toward bowling who do not bowl or people with positive attitudes toward kids who do not have children.

After all, people might have many reasons for failing to act on their attitudes. And once you are aware of all of these reasons, the finding that attitudes so often fail to predict behavior may no longer seem so surprising. Even more important is to gain an understanding of *when* attitudes are likely to be highly predictive of behavior and when they are not (Glasman & Albarracín, 2006).

Attitudes Sometimes Conflict with Other Powerful Determinants of Behavior

Suppose you were asked to predict the strength of the relationship between people's attitudes toward dieting and their success in dieting. Would you expect a strong relationship? Probably not. Eating less is determined by too many things other than a person's attitude about dieting, including eating habits, individual physiology, and whether a roommate is pigging out—as well as the person's attitudes toward other things, such as Ben & Jerry's ice cream, Krispy Kreme donuts, and french fries.

What is true about attitudes toward dieting is also true about attitudes in general. They all compete with other determinants of behavior. The situationist message of social psychology (and of this book) suggests that attitudes do not always win out over these other determinants, and hence attitudes are not always so tightly connected to behavior.

One particularly potent determinant of a person's actions that can weaken the relationship between attitudes and behavior is an individual's understanding of the prevailing norms of appropriate behavior. You might relish the idea of talking excitedly with the person next to you in the movie theater or lecture hall, but let's hope you refrain from doing so out of the recognition that it just isn't done. Others would disapprove. Similarly, the hotel and restaurant owners in LaPiere's study may have wanted to turn away the Chinese couple but refrained from doing so out of concern about how it would look and the scene it might cause.

Attitudes Are Sometimes Inconsistent

Many people report having a hard time pinning down their attitude toward the actor Russell Crowe. They acknowledge great admiration for his skill as an actor, but they just don't like him. This highlights two important facts about attitudes. First, attitudes may conflict with one another. We might like great acting but dislike arrogance. Second, the different components of an attitude may not always align. In particular, there can be a rift between the affective component (what we feel about Russell Crowe) and the cognitive component (what we think about him). When the affective and cognitive components of an attitude are inconsistent, it's hardly surprising that the attitude may not predict behavior very well. The cognitive component might determine the attitude we express, but the affective component might determine our behavior (or vice versa). The restaurant and hotel owners from LaPiere's study, for example, might have thought it was bad for their business to serve Chinese individuals; but the feelings aroused by a living, breathing Chinese couple may have made it hard to deny them service.

"I do not like thee, Dr. Fell.
The reason why I cannot tell.
But this I know and know full well.
I do not like thee, Dr. Fell"

—Nursery rhyme written in 1680 by satiric poet Tom Brown after being threatened with dismissal by the dean of his college, one Dr. Fell of Christ-church, Oxford University

Inconsistent Attitudes Attitudes may not be good predictors of behavior, because people often have different attitudes that conflict with one another. Elliot Spitzer, disgraced former governor of New York, had campaigned on the importance of high ethical standards among public officials and vowed to "change the ethics of Albany." He resigned after it was revealed that he was a frequent customer in a high-priced prostitution operation. Did he think his involvement with prostitutes was wrong but did it anyway, or did he view participation in the sex trade as ethically acceptable?

Introspecting about the Reasons for Our Attitudes

Consider your attitude toward someone you're attracted to. Why are you attracted to that person? If you put this question to yourself, a number of factors are likely to spring to mind: "He's cute." "She's ambitious." "She's easy to be with."

But sometimes it's not so easy to know exactly why we like someone. It may not be because of specific, readily identifiable attributes; we may simply share some indescribable chemistry. When we introspect about the reasons, however, we may focus on what is easy to identify, easy to justify, and easy to capture in words—and thus miss the real reasons for our attraction. Timothy Wilson and his colleagues have empirically tested this idea by asking students about the person they were dating. Participants in one group were simply asked for an overall evaluation of their relationship. Those in another group were first asked to list why they felt the way they did and then to give an overall evaluation of their relationship. The researchers then contacted the participants again nearly nine months later and asked about the status of their relationship. The attitudes of participants in the first group, who evaluated the relationship without considering the reasons, were much more accurate predictors of the current status of the relationship than were those of participants who had introspected about their reasons for liking their partners (Wilson, Dunn, Bybee, Hyman, & Rotondo, 1984). Thinking about why we like someone can sometimes lead to confusion about what our true feelings really are.

Wilson has shown that this effect applies far beyond our attitudes toward romantic partners and that introspecting about the reasons for our attitudes about all sorts of things can undermine how well those attitudes guide our behavior. The cause in all cases is the same: introspection may lead us to focus on the easiest-to-identify reasons for liking or disliking something at the expense of the *real* reasons for our likes and dislikes. When people are induced to think carefully about the reasons they prefer one product over another (as opposed to simply stating a preference), they are more likely to regret their choice later (Wilson et al., 1993), and their choices are less likely to correspond to the "true" value of the product as determined by experts (Wilson & Schooler, 1991).

Does this mean that introspection is always (or even typically) harmful and that we should forgo careful analysis and always go with our gut? Not at all. In deciding whether to launch a military campaign, for example, it is imperative for analysts to leave no stone unturned and to exhaustively consider the reasons for and against the idea from all angles. In addition, in many cases the real reasons for our attitude are perfectly easy to identify and articulate, and in those cases introspection produces no rift between the variables we think are guiding our attitude and those that actually are. The contaminating effect of introspection is limited to those times when the true source of our attitude is hard to pin down—as when the basis of our attitude is largely affective. In such cases, a cognitive analysis is likely to seize on seemingly plausible but misleading cognitive reasons.

When the basis of our attitude is largely cognitive, however, the search for reasons is more likely to yield the real reasons, and introspection is unlikely to diminish the relationship between attitude and behavior (Millar & Tesser, 1986; Wilson & Dunn, 1986). Thus, introspecting about your reasons for liking a certain artist may create a rift between your expressed attitude and your subsequent behavior, but introspecting about why you would prefer one digital camera over another is unlikely to create such a rift.

Attitudes Are Sometimes Based on Secondhand Information

What is your attitude toward Bali? Secretary of State Hillary Clinton? The British royal family? Chances are you have attitudes about all three, perhaps even very strong ones. Yet, you've probably never been to Bali, have never met Secretary Clinton, and have never been in the presence of British royalty. This creates the possibility that your attitude may be a bit off the mark and may not match how you would behave if you actually went to Bali, met Secretary Clinton, or were confronted by Queen Elizabeth II. Similarly, the hotel and restaurant managers in LaPiere's study may have had little or no previous exposure to Chinese individuals, and what they imagined so-called Orientals were like may not have matched the actual Chinese couple they encountered. Thus their abstract attitude toward Orientals did not predict the behavioral response elicited by this particular Chinese couple.

Numerous experiments have shown that attitudes based on direct (firsthand) experience predict subsequent behavior much better than those derived indirectly (secondhand). In one of the earliest studies, Dennis Regan and Russ Fazio (1977) measured Cornell University students' attitudes about a housing shortage that caused some freshman students to spend the first month or two of the year sleeping on cots in a dormitory lounge. Some of the students had firsthand experience with the housing crisis because they were the ones forced to sleep on the cots; others had merely heard or read about the crisis. The students were then given an opportunity to act on their attitudes by signing a petition, writing a letter, or joining a committee.

Clearly, the students who were directly affected by the crisis were more likely to take action, but that was not the focus of the study. Instead, Regan and Fazio were interested in whether the *correlation* between the students' attitudes and their overt behavior was higher among the directly affected students than among the others. It was. Among the directly affected students, those with strong attitudes about the crisis were much more likely to take relevant action than those with less strong opinions. Among students who were not directly affected, this relationship was much weaker.

Additional studies have shown this effect to be very reliable. Attitudes about participating in psychological research predict actual participation much more strongly among those who have previously taken part in research than among those who have not (Fazio & Zanna, 1978). Attitudes about solving intellectual puzzles predict who will attempt to solve them more strongly among those who have previously tried such puzzles (Regan & Fazio, 1977). And attitudes about flu shots predict who will get inoculated more strongly among those who have received flu shots in the past (Davidson, Yantis, Norwood, & Montano, 1985).

When the attitude we have about some object or event is based on firsthand experience, our attitude may turn out to be a rather telling guide to our subsequent actions after all.

The Mismatch between General Attitudes and Specific Targets

Typically, the attitudes people express are about general classes of things—the environment, pushy people, French cooking, or global trade. But the attitude-relevant behavior that is typically assessed deals with a particular instance of that class—donating to Greenpeace, reacting to a specific pushy individual, ordering foie gras, or picketing a meeting of the World Trade Organization. Because of such a great mismatch between general attitudes and specific instances of real behavior, it is no wonder that attitudes do not always predict behavior particularly well.

Several studies have shown that consistency between attitudes and behavior is higher when the attitude and behavior are at the same level of specificity. Highly specific attitudes typically do a better job of predicting specific behaviors, and general attitudes typically do a better job of predicting how a person behaves "in general" across a number of different instances of, say, environmentalism, political activism, or xenophobia (Ajzen, 1987). In LaPiere's study, for example, the attitudes expressed by the various merchants were rather general—whether they would serve Orientals. But the behavior, of course, involved one specific Chinese couple with a specific demeanor dressed in a specific fashion. Perhaps the results would have been different if LaPiere had asked the merchants whether they would serve a well-dressed Chinese couple who seemed pleasant and agreeable. If you want to predict a specific type of behavior accurately, you have to measure people's attitudes toward that specific type of behavior.

The broader point here is that what most people usually think of as attitudes toward different classes of people, places, things, and events are often expressions of attitudes toward a prototype of a given category. Therefore, if we encounter a specific situation or person who doesn't fit the prototype, our behavior is not likely to reflect our stated attitude. Our general attitude doesn't apply to *that* sort of person. Consider a study in which male college students were asked about their attitudes toward gay men (Lord, Lepper, & Mackie, 1984). The researchers also elicited from each student his stereotype of the "typical" gay man. Two months later, a different experimenter approached the students and asked if they would be willing to show some visiting students around campus. One of the visitors, "John B.," was described in such a way that the participants would think he was gay. For half the participants, the rest of the description of John B. was crafted to fit their own individualized stereotype of a male homosexual; for the other half, it was not. What the investigators found was that the students' willingness to show John B. around campus was strongly predicted by their attitudes toward gay men (those with positive attitudes said they were willing; those with negative attitudes said they were not), but only if John B. matched their prototype of a gay individual. If John B. did not fit their image of a gay

General Attitudes and Specific Targets A person with a general attitude about income inequality may not participate in the Occupy Wall Street movement. But someone with more specific attitudes about the causes of the 2008 recession or the *Citizens United* Supreme Court decision is more likely to join in protest, like this person protesting in New York City.

person, their attitudes toward gays did not predict whether they were willing to show him around campus (see also Lord, Desforges, Ramsey, Trezza, & Lepper, 1991).

"Automatic" Behavior That Bypasses Conscious Attitudes

The influence of an attitude on behavior is sometimes conscious and deliberate: we reflect on our attitudes and then decide how to behave. But often our behavior is more reflexive than reflective, and the surrounding context elicits the behavior automatically.

To be sure, sometimes our automatic behavior is consistent with—indeed, caused by—our attitudes. In fact, one of the purposes of attitudes is to allow us to respond quickly, without having to do much weighing of pros and cons. We go with our gut feeling. But some types of automatic behavior bypass our attitudes altogether, as when we jump away from something that looks like a snake in the grass. When such actions are elicited directly and mindlessly from the surrounding context, the connection between our conscious attitudes and our behavior is necessarily weak. As noted in Chapter 4, one of the strongest and most influential research trends in social psychology over the past two decades has been uncovering more and more instances in which our behavior is automatically elicited by stimuli present in the environment. Recall, for example, the experiment that found that people primed with the concept of the elderly walked more slowly down a hallway without being aware they were doing so. Such findings highlight another limitation to how well attitudes predict behavior: automatic behavior that bypasses our conscious attitudes can conflict with those attitudes without our knowing it.

 Attitudes can be surprisingly weak predictors of behavior. The inconsistency between attitude and behavior may occur because attitudes sometimes conflict with social norms about appropriate behavior, because different attitudes can conflict with one another or the affective and cognitive components of an attitude may conflict, because introspecting about the reasons behind our attitudes can cause confusion about our true feelings, because our attitudes are not always based on firsthand experience, because general attitudes sometimes do not correspond to the specific action that is required in a given situation, and because some behavior is automatic and bypasses conscious thought altogether.

PREDICTING ATTITUDES FROM BEHAVIOR

Many young people resent being sent to church, temple, or mosque, often with the complaint, "Why do I have to go? I don't believe any of this stuff." And many of them have been told, "It doesn't matter if you believe it. What's important is that you continue with your studies and your prayers." Some resist to the very end and abandon all religious rituals and practices the minute their parents give them permission to opt out. But a remarkable number stick with it and eventually find themselves genuinely holding some of the very religious convictions and sentiments they originally resisted. Over time, mere outward behavior can give way to genuine inner conviction.

The previous section presented the first part of the story about the connection between attitudes and behavior: attitudes can predict behavior, but not as strongly as most people would suspect. The second part of the story, as illustrated by the religion example just described, is that behavior can powerfully influence attitudes. Social psychological research over the past half century has documented time and time again the surprising extent to which people tend to bring their attitudes in line with their actions. This urge reflects the powerful tendency to justify, or rationalize, our behavior and to minimize any inconsistencies between our attitudes and actions.

Why does our behavior so powerfully influence our attitudes? A number of influential theories have been put forward to explain this relationship. As a group, they are referred to as cognitive consistency theories, and they attempt to account for some of the most common sources of rationalization people use to bring their attitudes in line with their actions.

Balance Theory

balance theory A theory holding that people try to maintain balance among their beliefs, cognitions, and sentiments.

The earliest consistency theory was Fritz Heider's **balance theory**. Heider (1946) claimed that people try to maintain balance among their beliefs, cognitions, and sentiments. If your two friends like each other, everything is fine and balanced. But if your two friends detest each other, you've got a problem: you have an imbalanced set of relationships on your hands. According to Heider, you will exert psychological energy to achieve or restore balance in this set of relationships. You may, for example, decide you like one friend less or conclude that their dislike of each other is a misunderstanding based on a relatively trivial issue.

In a threesome (or triad), things are balanced if the product of the three sentiments (+ for liking, − for disliking) is positive. If my enemy (−) is disliked by a particular person (−), balance is achieved by my liking that person (+): $(-) \times (-) \times (+) = +$. You'll recognize that advertisers take advantage of this desire for balance. They may have a beloved celebrity (+) say positive things (+) about a burger establishment or brand of basketball shoe, which puts psychological pressure on you to like that type of burger or shoe: $(+) \times (+) \times (+) = +$.

Support for Heider's balance theory comes from two types of studies: studies that establish two relationships in a triad and then elicit people's inferences about the third, and studies that present various balanced and imbalanced relationships and then examine how well people remember them or how comfortable they are with them. People remember balanced relationships better and rate them more favorably, and they "fill in" unspecified relations by assuming balance (Gawronski, Walther, & Blank, 2005; Hummert, Crockett, & Kemper, 1990; Insko, 1984). It would be easier to

Balance Theory To maintain balance, a fan of Beyonce's may like—and even buy—products she endorses.

remember that Piers and Sharon from *America's Got Talent* get along with each other but both have a hard time with Howie than to recall that Sharon likes Howie but Piers doesn't. And if someone you know loves basketball, then you're likely to assume her best friend does too.

Cognitive Dissonance Theory

By far the most influential consistency theory—and one of the most influential theories in the history of social psychology—is Leon Festinger's theory of **cognitive dissonance** (Festinger, 1957). Like Heider, Festinger argued that people are troubled by inconsistency among their thoughts, sentiments, and actions and that they will expend psychological energy to restore consistency. More specifically, Festinger thought that an aversive emotional state—dissonance—is aroused whenever people experience inconsistency between two cognitions. And when the cognitions are about a person's own behavior (for example, "I just failed to live up to my vow"), the person is troubled by the inconsistency between their cognitions and their behavior as well. This unpleasant emotional state motivates efforts to restore consistency. According to Festinger, people try to do so by changing the cognition to make it more consistent with the behavior.

cognitive dissonance theory A theory that maintains that inconsistencies among a person's thoughts, sentiments, and actions create an aversive emotional state (dissonance) that leads to efforts to restore consistency.

But what counts as cognitive inconsistency, and in what circumstances does it arise? And how exactly do people try to get rid of the inconsistency when it does arise? The tremendous amount of research that Festinger's theory inspired has attempted to answer these questions, leading to a greater understanding of psychological conflict and rationalization. To develop a sense of the kinds of inconsistency that people find troubling, and to get a flavor for the diverse phenomena that can be explained by the theory of cognitive dissonance, let's look at some of the classic experiments on the subject—experiments that have inspired generations of social psychologists.

Decisions and Dissonance Even a moment's reflection tells us that all hard decisions arouse some dissonance. Because the decision is hard, the rejected alternative must have some desirable features, the chosen alternative must have some undesirable features, or both. These elements are inconsistent with the choice that is made and hence produce dissonance (Brehm, 1956). If you move to Los Angeles from a small town in the Midwest in pursuit of good weather, you'll enjoy the sun, but the dirty air and hours spent in traffic will likely arouse dissonance. According to Festinger, once you've made an irrevocable decision to move to L.A., you'll exert mental effort to reduce this dissonance. You'll rationalize. You'll maintain that the lack of visibility is mainly due to haze, not pollution, and you'll tell your friends how much you've learned from the audiobooks you play on your car stereo during your long commute.

Numerous experiments have documented this tendency for people to rationalize their decisions. In one study, the investigators interviewed bettors at a racetrack, some just before and some just after placing their bets (Knox & Inkster,

Rationalizing Decisions, Reducing Dissonance After placing a bet at the track, as here at the Kentucky Derby, people are likely to concentrate on the positive features of the horse they bet on and to downplay any negative features. This rationalization process gives them greater confidence in the choice they made.

1968). The investigators reasoned that the act of placing a bet and making an irrevocable choice of a particular horse would cause the bettors to reduce the dissonance associated with all the negative features of the chosen horse (doesn't do well on a wet track) and all the positive features of the competing horses (the perfect distance for one horse, the best jockey on another). Dissonance reduction should be reflected in greater confidence on the part of those interviewed right *after* placing their bets. Consistent with these predictions, bettors who were interviewed as they waited in line to place their bets gave their horses, on average, a "fair" chance of winning the race; those who were interviewed after they had placed their bets and were leaving the ticket window gave their horses, on average, a "good" chance to win. One participant provided some extra commentary that serves as something of a window on the process of dissonance reduction. This participant had been interviewed while waiting in line (before placing his bet), but then, emerging from the ticket window, he approached another member of the research team and said, "Are you working with that other fellow there? Well, I just told him that my horse had a fair chance of winning. Will you have him change that to a good chance? No, by God, make that an excellent chance." Making hard decisions triggers dissonance, which in turn triggers processes of rationalization that make us more comfortable with our choices. Similar findings have been observed in elections: voters express greater confidence in their candidates when interviewed after they have voted than when interviewed right beforehand (Frenkel & Doob, 1976; Regan & Kilduff, 1988).

Festinger argued that dissonance reduction takes place only after an irrevocable decision has been made. He maintained, for example, that "there is a clear and undeniable difference between the cognitive processes that occur during the period of making a decision and those that occur after the decision has been made. Reevaluation of alternatives in the direction of favoring the chosen or disfavoring the rejected alternative . . . is a post-decision phenomenon" (Festinger, 1964, p. 30).

The evidence from the betting and election studies seems to support Festinger's contention. But his claim is at odds with other things we know about people. One of humankind's distinguishing characteristics is the ability to anticipate the future. If, in the process of making a decision, we see blemishes associated with what is emerging as our favorite option, why not start the process of rationalization beforehand so that dissonance is minimized or eliminated altogether (Wilson, Wheatley, Kurtz, Dunn, & Gilbert, 2004)?

Indeed, more recent research has established that the same sorts of rationalization and distortion that occur after people make a decision also subconsciously take place *before* they make the decision. This research has shown that whether choosing restaurants, vacation spots, consumer goods, or political candidates, once people develop a slight preference for one option over the others, they distort subsequent information to support their initial preference (Brownstein, 2003; Brownstein, Read, & Simon, 2004; Russo, Medvec, & Meloy, 1996; Russo, Meloy, & Medvec, 1998; Simon, Krawczyk, & Holyoak, 2004; Simon, Pham, Le, & Holyoak,

Leon Festinger In studying how people bring their attitudes in line with their behavior, Leon Festinger developed cognitive dissonance theory.

2001). Thus the small size of a particular Italian restaurant tends to be rated as a plus by those leaning toward Italian food ("nice and intimate"), but as a minus by those leaning toward a big burger joint ("we won't be able to talk without everyone overhearing us"). Festinger appears to have been right that decisions evoke dissonance and dissonance reduction, but these processes occur more often and more broadly than he anticipated—they occur both before and after decisions are made.

Effort Justification The element of dissonance theory that rings most true to many people is the idea that if you pay a high price for something—in dollars, time, or effort—and it turns out to be disappointing, you're likely to experience dissonance. As a result, you're likely to devote mental energy to justifying what you've done. The most familiar

Fraternity Hazing and Commitment Fraternities try to increase their members' commitment to the group by having them undergo difficult and embarrassing initiation rituals like the one shown here.

effort justification People's tendency to reduce dissonance by justifying the time, effort, or money they have devoted to something that has turned out to be unpleasant or disappointing.

example of **effort justification** on campus, perhaps, is fraternity hazing. Someone who undergoes a painful or humiliating initiation ritual will have a need to believe it was all worthwhile, and one way to do so is to extol the virtues of being in that particular fraternity. The Greek system, in other words, capitalizes on cognitive dissonance.

This sort of *sweet lemons rationalization* ("it's really not so bad") can be seen in many other contexts, of course. Religious groups require their members to contribute a great deal of time and money to their organizations. Certain high-end restaurants may secure their reputations as the very best places to dine by charging their customers exorbitant prices. Those who don't have pets often suspect that pet lovers exaggerate the pleasure they get from their animals to offset all the early morning walking, poop scooping, and furniture wrecking. And those who choose not to have children suspect that homebound, sleep deprived, overtaxed parents are fooling themselves when they say that nothing in life brings greater pleasure (Eibach & Mock, 2011).

The role of dissonance reduction in such situations was explored in an early study in which female undergraduate students signed up for an experiment thinking it involved joining an ongoing discussion group about sex (Aronson & Mills, 1959). When they arrived, however, the students were told that not everyone can speak freely and comfortably about such a topic, so potential participants needed to pass a screening test to join the group. Those assigned to a control condition simply read aloud a list of innocuous words to the male experimenter. Those assigned to a "mild" initiation condition read aloud a list of mildly embarrassing words—for example, *prostitute, petting, virgin*. Finally, those assigned to the "severe" initiation group had to read aloud a list of quite obscene words and a passage from a novel describing sexual intercourse.

All participants were then told they had passed their screening test and could join the discussion group. The group was meeting that very day, but because everyone else had been given a reading assignment beforehand, the participants were told that it was best if they just listened in on this session. Then, over headphones in a nearby cubicle, the participants heard a stupefyingly boring discussion of the sex life of invertebrates. Not only was the topic not what the participants

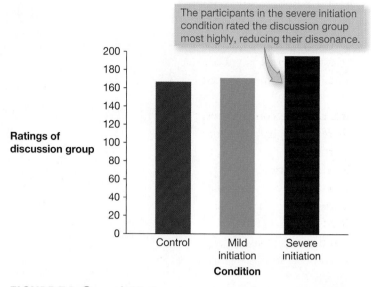

The participants in the severe initiation condition rated the discussion group most highly, reducing their dissonance.

FIGURE 7.1 Group Initiation and Liking for the Group
Ratings of a discussion group by participants who experienced no initiation, a mild initiation, or a severe initiation to join the group. (Source: Adapted from Aronson & Mills, 1959.)

induced (forced) compliance
Subtly compelling individuals to behave in a manner that is inconsistent with their beliefs, attitudes, or values, in order to elicit dissonance—and therefore a change in their original attitudes or values.

had in mind when they signed up for a discussion group about sex, but the members of the discussion group "contradicted themselves and one another, mumbled several non sequiturs, started sentences that they never finished, hemmed, hawed, and in general conducted one of the most worthless and uninteresting discussions imaginable" (Aronson & Mills, 1959, p. 179).

The investigators predicted that the discussion would be boring and disappointing to all the participants but that it would produce dissonance only for those who had undergone a severe initiation to join the group. The cognition "I suffered to get into this group" is inconsistent with the realization that "this group is worthless and boring." One way for the participants in the severe initiation condition to reduce dissonance would be to convince themselves that the group and the discussion were not so boring after all. And that's just what they did. When the experimenters asked participants at the end of the study to rate the quality of the discussion on a number of scales, those in the severe initiation condition rated it more favorably than those in the other two conditions (**Figure 7.1**).

Induced Compliance and Attitude Change Dissonance theory can also explain what often happens as a result of **induced (forced) compliance**—that is, when people are induced to behave in a manner that is inconsistent with their beliefs, attitudes, or values. Most people will feel some discomfort with the mismatch between their behavior and their attitudes. One way to deal with the inconsistency—the easiest and most likely way, given that the behavior cannot be taken back—is for people to change their original attitudes or values. This was the core idea behind Lyndon Johnson's stratagem, described in the opening to this chapter: when doubters in his administration gave press conferences in which they publicly defended the administration's position, the inconsistency between their private doubts and their public comments led them to dispel their doubts.

Numerous experiments have demonstrated the power of induced compliance to shift a person's original attitudes. In the very first experiment that demonstrated such an effect, Leon Festinger and Merrill Carlsmith (1959) had participants engage in what can only be described as experimental drudgery for an hour (loading spools on a tray over and over, turning pegs on a pegboard one-quarter turn at a time). Participants in the control condition were sent immediately afterward to see someone from the psychology department who interviewed them about their experience as research volunteers. When asked how much they enjoyed the experiment, they gave quite low ratings. No surprise there.

Participants in two other conditions were told that the experiment was about how people's performance on a task is influenced by their expectations about it beforehand. These participants were led to believe that they were in a control, "no expectation" condition, but that other subjects were told beforehand that the study was either very interesting or boring. Looking rather sheepish, the experimenter explained that the next participant was about to show up and needed to be told that the study was interesting. This was usually done, the experimenter explained, by a confederate posing as a participant. But the confederate was absent, putting the experimenter in a bit of a jam. Would you, the experimenter asked the participant, play the role usually played by the confederate and tell the next participant that the experiment is interesting? The experimenter offered the participant either $1 or $20 for doing so.

In this "play within a play," the true participants think they are confederates. What is most important to the experiment, and what is readily apparent to the participants, is that they have just lied (nearly every participant agreed to the request) and said that a mind-numbingly boring study is interesting. Festinger and Carlsmith argued that this act would produce dissonance for those participants who were given only $1 for the assignment. Their words were inconsistent with their beliefs, and $1 was not enough to justify the lie. Those given $20 could at least tell themselves that they were justified in lying (and that just about anyone else would have lied too) because the pay was good and the lie was of little consequence (**Figure 7.2**).

FIGURE 7.2 Scientific Method: Induced Compliance and Attitude Change

Hypothesis: Participants induced to say something they don't believe with little incentive to do so will come to believe what they say.

Research Method:

1. Participants worked on a series of boring tasks.

2. Participants were then asked to tell another person that the tasks were interesting and enjoyable. Some participants were paid $1 to do so; others were paid $20. Control participants were not asked to tell the other person that the tasks were interesting.

3. Later, participants reported to someone seemingly unconnected to the experiment how much they enjoyed the task they had worked on.

Results: Participants in the $1 condition rated the tasks as more enjoyable than those in the control or $20 conditions, who did not differ significantly from one another:

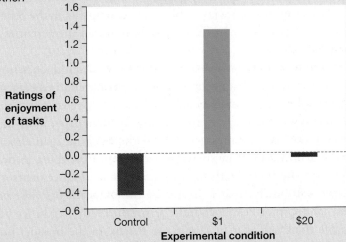

CONCLUSION: Saying something that we don't believe, and doing so with little justification ($1 instead of $20), produces dissonance. Dissonance is an unpleasant internal state that leads people to change their original attitudes or beliefs.

Source: Adapted from Festinger & Carlsmith (1959).

BOX 7.2 **FOCUS ON INTELLECTUAL HISTORY**

Blaise Pascal, Cost-Benefit Analysis, and Cognitive Consistency Theory

In a single stroke Pascal, the seventeenth-century French mathematician and Catholic philosopher, gave rise to both modern cost-benefit analysis (comparing the total expected costs and benefits of different options and choosing accordingly) and to cognitive consistency theory. Why should people believe in God? Benefit: if God exists and we believe in God, then we are likely to behave in such a way as to have eternal life. Cost: not much. In fact, behaving in a godly way is likely to have earthly benefits. Why should people *not* believe in God? Benefit: not much, indeed probably loss stemming from failing to behave in a godly way. Cost: eternal damnation. Now, anyone who accepts the logic of this argument would agree that it would be foolhardy not to wager that God exists and choose to believe in God. The benefits clearly outweigh the costs.

The problem is, logically concluding that it pays to believe in God may not be enough to make a person truly believe. Pascal recognized that some people will say, "Try as I might, I simply cannot believe. What can I do?" As a solution, Pascal essentially invented cognitive consistency theory, advising nonbelievers to behave as believers do: pray, light candles, attend church. If they behaved in such a way, Pascal reasoned, then their beliefs would change to be consistent with the behavior. Problem solved. (But note that although Pascal was on to something very important about people's need for cognitive consistency, scholars such as Voltaire and Diderot had no difficulty spotting and articulating the logical flaws in Pascal's argument for believing in God.)

Festinger and Carlsmith predicted that participants in the $1 condition would rationalize their behavior—that is, they would reduce their dissonance—by changing their attitude about the task they had performed. If they convinced themselves that the task was not uninteresting after all, their lie would not really be a lie. Consistent with these predictions, when participants in the $1 condition were later asked by the person from the psychology department to evaluate their experience, they rated the task more favorably than participants in the other conditions did. Only the participants in the $1 condition rated the activities above the neutral point.

There is a very important lesson here about the best way to influence someone else's attitudes, a lesson that has important implications for child rearing, among other things. If you want to persuade people to do something (take school seriously, protect the environment, refrain from using foul language) and you want them to internalize the broader message behind the behavior, you should use the smallest amount of incentive or coercion necessary to get them to do it. In other words, don't go overboard with the incentives. If the inducements are too substantial, people will justify their behavior by the inducements (like participants in the $20 condition of Festinger and Carlsmith's study), and they will not need to rationalize their behavior by coming to believe in the broader purpose or philosophy behind it. But if the inducements are just barely sufficient (as in the $1 condition), people's need to rationalize will tend to produce a deep-seated attitude change in line with their behavior. So if you're going to pay your children for doing their homework, be sure you pay them the least amount necessary to get them to do it.

Induced Compliance and Extinguishing Undesired Behavior The flip side of this idea involves the use of mild versus severe punishments and is illustrated by experiments using what is known as the "forbidden toy" paradigm (Aronson & Carlsmith, 1963; Freedman, 1965; Lepper, 1973). In one experiment of this type, an experimenter showed children at a nursery school a set of five toys and asked the children to tell him how much they liked each one. The experimenter then explained that he would have to leave the room for a while, but he would be back soon. In the meantime, the child was free to play with any of the toys except for the child's second favorite. Half the children were told not to play with the forbidden toy and that the experimenter would "be annoyed" if they did. This was the *mild threat* condition. In the *severe threat* condition, the children were told that if they played with the forbidden toy, the experimenter "would be very angry" and "would have to take all of my toys and go home and never come back again."

While the experimenter was gone, each child was covertly observed, and none played with the forbidden toy. Aronson and Carlsmith predicted that not playing with the forbidden toy would produce dissonance, but only for the children in the mild threat condition. For them, not playing with the toy would be inconsistent with the fact that it was highly desirable, an inconsistency that Aronson and Carlsmith predicted the children would resolve by derogating the toy—by convincing themselves that it wasn't so great after all. Those who received the severe threat should experience no such dissonance, because not playing with it was justified by the threat they received. Thus there was nothing to cause them to derogate the toy. To find out if their predictions were correct, Aronson and Carlsmith had the children reevaluate all five toys when the experimenter returned. As expected, the children in the severe threat condition either did not change their opinion of the forbidden toy or liked it even more than before (**Figure 7.3**). In contrast, many of those in the mild threat condition viewed the toy less favorably. Thus the threat of severe punishment will keep children from doing something you don't want them to do; but they will still, later on, want to do it. The threat of

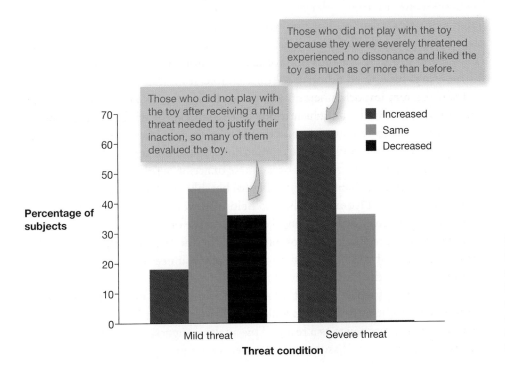

FIGURE 7.3 Derogation of the Forbidden Toy The percentage of children in the mild and severe threat conditions whose opinion of the forbidden toy increased, stayed the same, or decreased. (Source: Adapted from Aronson & Carlsmith, 1963.)

mild punishment—if it's just enough of a threat to keep them from doing it—can bring about psychological change, such that they will no longer be tempted to do what you don't want them to do.

When Does Inconsistency Produce Dissonance?

Festinger's original statement describing when people will experience dissonance has some problems. Festinger thought that people would experience dissonance whenever they held two inconsistent cognitions. But what constitutes inconsistency? Is it really inconsistent to refrain from playing with an attractive toy if an authority figure asks you not to? Apparently it is, given the results obtained by Aronson and Carlsmith (and later investigators). But what's so jarringly unpleasant about such inconsistency? We often refrain from doing things that we know we would find enjoyable, even when we have no compelling reason (like a severe threat) to refrain from doing them. Which of these situations are likely to induce dissonance and which are not?

One of the earliest and most significant contributors to the understanding of cognitive dissonance, Eliot Aronson, offered a solution to this question. A particular inconsistency will arouse dissonance, Aronson argued, if it implicates our core sense of self (Aronson, 1969; Sherman & Gorkin, 1980). People like to think of themselves as rational, morally upright, worthy individuals, and anything that challenges such assessments is likely to arouse dissonance. Expending great effort to join a boring group calls into question our wisdom and rationality; telling another student that a boring task is interesting challenges our integrity.

To understand the sorts of cognitions likely to challenge our sense of judgment and personal character, it is useful to think about when *someone else's* actions make us question *that person's* character—or better still, to think of the justifications someone else could offer that would *prevent* us from questioning his or her judgment or moral fiber. Imagine that you ask a tech-savvy friend to help you with a computer problem, but he says no. How harshly would you judge him? The answer probably depends on several factors. First, you wouldn't blame him if he could not have acted otherwise—for example, if he was at work and his boss wouldn't let him leave. He had no choice. Second, you probably wouldn't blame him much if he could justify his actions (see Chapter 5); perhaps he had to console a distraught roommate or spend the evening studying for an important exam. He *could* have helped out—he had some choice in the matter—but it's clear that doing so would not have been the best course of action, and you react accordingly. Third, you would probably judge him more harshly in rough proportion to how much harm resulted from his failure to help. You would (understandably) think worse of him if you ended up failing a course because of it than if you were simply prevented from checking Facebook or surfing the Internet. Finally, you wouldn't blame him much if you never told him how badly you needed his help, so he had no way to foresee the harm he might cause.

This analysis of when we hold other people responsible for their actions provides some insight into when we will hold *ourselves* responsible for our actions and experience dissonance as a result. This analysis suggests, in other words, that we ought to experience dissonance whenever we act in ways that are inconsistent

with our core values and beliefs and (1) the behavior was freely chosen, (2) the behavior was not sufficiently justified, (3) the behavior had negative consequences, and (4) the negative consequences were foreseeable.

Free Choice The critical role of freedom of choice has been apparent since the very earliest dissonance experiments and has been demonstrated most often and most clearly in the induced-compliance paradigm. In the first demonstration of this kind, students at Duke University were offered either $0.50 or $2.50 to write an essay in favor of a state law banning Communists from speaking on college campuses. (This experiment was done in the mid-1960s, and both payments may now seem low; for comparable amounts today, it would be reasonable to multiply these amounts by a factor of 8: $4 and $20, respectively.) Because the law was at variance with the U.S. Constitution's guarantee of freedom of speech, nearly all students were opposed to it, and their essays thus conflicted with their true beliefs. For half the participants, their freedom to agree (or decline) to write such an essay was emphasized. For the other half, it was not. There was no dissonance effect among these latter participants. Indeed, those paid $2.50 later expressed attitudes more in favor of the ban than did those paid $0.50 (presumably because writing the essay was associated with the good feelings that accompany the larger reward). In the free-choice group, however, the standard dissonance effect was obtained: those paid $0.50 changed their attitude more than those paid $2.50 (Linder, Cooper, & Jones, 1967).

Insufficient Justification This last experiment, like all of the induced-compliance studies, also demonstrates the importance of insufficient justification in producing dissonance. If a person's behavior is justified by the existing incentives, even behavior that is dramatically in conflict with the person's beliefs and values will not produce dissonance—or the rationalizations that arise to combat it. Those paid $2.50 (about $20 today) for writing an essay that was inconsistent with their true beliefs felt no pressure to change their attitudes because their behavior was psychologically justified by the large cash payment. Those paid only $0.50 (about $4 today) had no such justification and thus felt the full weight of their inconsistency. Thus it appears that most of us are willing to sell our souls for money; and if the money is good enough, we don't even need to justify the sale.

Negative Consequences If nothing of consequence results from actions that are at variance with our attitudes and values, it is easy to dismiss them as trivial. Indeed, a number of experiments have demonstrated that people experience dissonance only when their behavior results in harm of some sort. One such study used Festinger and Carlsmith's paradigm (described earlier) in which participants were induced to tell someone that a boring experiment was very interesting. The participants received either a small or a large incentive for doing so. Half the time, the confederate seemed convinced that the boring task really was going to be interesting, and half the time the confederate clearly remained unconvinced ("Well, you're entitled to your own opinion, but I don't think that I have ever enjoyed an experiment, and I don't think that I will find this one much fun."). Note that there were no negative consequences when the person appeared unconvinced: no one was deceived. Thus, if negative consequences are necessary for the arousal of cognitive dissonance, the standard dissonance effect should occur only when the person is convinced. That was exactly what the researchers found: the boring task was rated more favorably only by participants who were offered little incentive to lie to another person who appeared to believe the lie (Cooper & Worchel, 1970; Nel, Helmreich, & Aronson, 1969).

Foreseeability We typically do not hold people responsible for harm they have done if the harm was not foreseeable. If a dinner guest who is allergic to peanuts becomes ill after eating an entrée with a peanut sauce, we do not hold the host responsible if the guest never informed the host of the allergy. As this example suggests, it may be the *foreseeable* negative consequences of our actions that generate cognitive dissonance. Negative consequences that are not foreseeable do not threaten a person's self-image as a moral and decent person, so they may not arouse dissonance.

This hypothesis has been verified in experiments that induced participants to write an essay in favor of a position they disagreed with (for example, that the size of the freshman class at their university should be doubled). If any negative consequences of such an action (for example, the essays are to be shown to a university committee charged with deciding whether to implement the policy) are made known to the participants after the fact, there is no dissonance and hence no attitude change in the direction of the essay they wrote. But if the negative consequences were either foreseen (participants knew beforehand that their letters would be shown to the committee) or foreseeable (participants knew beforehand that their letters *might* be shown to such a committee), the standard dissonance effect was obtained (Cooper, 1971; Goethals, Cooper, & Naficy, 1979).

Self-Affirmation and Dissonance

If dissonance results from challenges or threats to people's sense of themselves as rational, competent, and moral, then it follows that they can ward off dissonance not only by dealing directly with the specific threat itself but also indirectly by taking stock of their other qualities and core values. Claude Steele and his colleagues have argued that this sort of **self-affirmation** is a common way that people cope with threats to their self-esteem (Cohen, Aronson, & Steele, 2000; Correll, Spencer, & Zanna, 2004; McQueen & Klein, 2006; Schmeichel & Martens, 2005; Sherman & Cohen, 2002, 2006; Steele, 1988; Steele, Spencer, & Lynch, 1993): "Sure, I might have violated a friend's confidence, but I am very

self-affirmation Bolstering our identity and self-esteem by taking note of important elements of our identity, such as our important values.

empathetic when other people are having difficulties." "I know I drive an SUV, but no one attends church services more regularly than I do." By bolstering themselves in one area, people can tolerate a bigger hit in another.

In one of the cleverest demonstrations of the effects of self-affirmation, Steele (1988) asked science majors and business majors at the University of Washington to participate in an experiment using the post-decision dissonance paradigm (see pp. 245–247), in which participants have to choose between two objects of similar value. In a control condition, both groups showed the usual dissonance effect: finding hidden attractions in the chosen alternative and hidden flaws in the unchosen alternative. But in another condition, the experimenters had the business and science majors put on white lab coats before rendering their final evaluations. Steele predicted that wearing a lab coat would affirm an important identity for the science majors, but not for the business majors. The results supported his predictions. The business majors reduced dissonance just as much as participants in the control condition; the science majors did not. If you feel good about yourself, you don't sweat the small stuff like minor decisions.

Is Dissonance Universal?

This section has discussed cognitive dissonance as if it were a cross-culturally universal phenomenon. Is it? There is substantial evidence on the question, yielding some interesting answers. Heine and Lehman (1997) used the free-choice, self-affirmation paradigm in which they asked all participants to choose between two objects (CDs, in this case), but first gave some of the participants self-affirmation in the form of positive feedback on a personality test. Heine and Lehman's participants were Japanese and Canadian, and the researchers wanted to see if the dissonance effect was the same in people from these two different cultures. The results for the Canadians were similar to those in earlier studies: participants exhibited a substantial dissonance effect in the control condition, finding previously unnoticed attractions in the chosen CD and previously unnoticed flaws in the unchosen one, but they showed no dissonance effect if they were given positive feedback about their personalities. The Japanese participants, in contrast, were unaffected by the self-affirmation manipulation. More striking still, they showed no dissonance effect in *either* condition, which led Heine and Lehman to conclude that cognitive dissonance might be a phenomenon unique to Westerners. But Sakai (1981), using an induced-compliance paradigm in which participants were persuaded to do something they didn't want to do, found dissonance effects for Japanese participants—if they were led to think that other students were observing their behavior.

Do these findings imply that East Asians may experience dissonance in the induced-compliance paradigm but not in the free-choice paradigm? That would be messy. Fortunately, there's another way to reconcile the two sets of results. As this book emphasizes throughout, East Asians, along with many other people in the world, are more attuned to other people and their reactions than are Westerners. If East Asians exhibit dissonance effects in the induced-compliance paradigm because they question their actions when others are observing them, then they should also exhibit dissonance effects in the free-choice paradigm if they are led to think about other people's possible reaction to their choice.

Following this logic, Kitayama, Snibbe, Markus, and Suzuki (2004) asked Japanese and Canadian participants to choose between two CDs. In one condition (the standard condition investigators have used for nearly 60 years), participants were asked, after ranking a large number of CDs, to choose between two of the middle-ranked CDs. In the other condition, participants were also asked to rank the presumed preferences of the "average college student." In this way, the researchers "primed," or made salient, a "meaningful social other." This manipulation made no difference for the Canadians, but it made a great deal of difference for the Japanese. The Japanese showed almost no dissonance effect in the standard condition, but they showed an even larger dissonance effect than the Canadians in the socially primed condition.

The different triggers of dissonance reduction in the East versus the West was illustrated even more dramatically in yet another study in which the investigators asked participants to choose between two CDs (Kitayama, Snibbe, Markus, & Suzuki, 2004). For some participants, hanging right in front of them at eye level was the poster shown in **Figure 7.4**. The poster was allegedly a figure from another, unrelated experiment, and the investigators' intention was to see whether the schematic faces in it might prime the concept of other people and hence prompt the Japanese participants to show a strong dissonance effect. The poster had the expected effect: in the standard free-choice condition, the Japanese showed no evidence of dissonance reduction, but in the poster condition they did. American participants actually showed slightly less dissonance reduction in the poster condition than in the standard condition.

Hoshino-Browne, Zanna, Spencer, and Zanna (2004) observed a similar effect of social priming when they asked participants to choose a CD either for themselves or for a friend. Euro-Canadians, as well as Asian-Canadians who only weakly identified themselves as Asians, showed much larger dissonance effects when choosing for themselves than when choosing for a friend; but Asian-Canadians who strongly identified themselves as Asians showed much larger dissonance effects when choosing for a friend than when choosing for themselves.

It appears that post-decision dissonance may indeed be universal, but the conditions that prompt it may be very different for different peoples. For independent Westerners, it may be prompted by a concern about one's ability to make an adequate choice that reflects well on one's decision-making ability; for Easterners and perhaps other interdependent peoples, it may be prompted by a concern about one's own ability to make choices that would be approved by others.

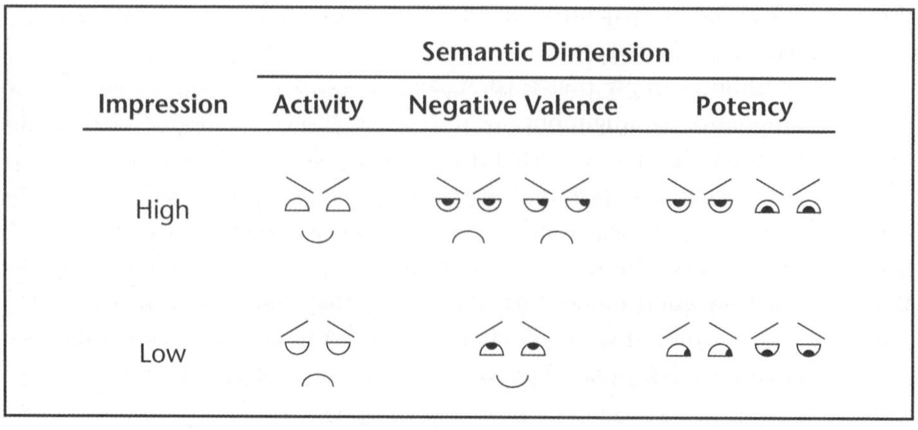

FIGURE 7.4 Culture and Priming The poster used by Kitayama and colleagues (2004) to prime the idea of "social others." The labels were included simply to make the poster look like part of another, unrelated experiment.

Impression	Semantic Dimension		
	Activity	Negative Valence	Potency
High			
Low			

Behavior can have a powerful impact on our attitudes, largely because people like their attitudes to be consistent with one another and with their behavior. When there is inconsistency among cognitions, values, or actions, dissonance is likely to be aroused. We can reduce dissonance by changing our attitudes to be in line with our behavior. Dissonance is more pronounced when the inconsistency implies that the self is deficient in some way. Therefore, when we can affirm the self somehow, we are less susceptible to dissonance. Different circumstances arouse dissonance in people of different cultures.

SELF-PERCEPTION THEORY

Like all prominent theories that have been around for a long time, dissonance theory has faced many theoretical challenges and has had to withstand numerous critiques. One critique, however, stands out above all others in its impact: Daryl Bem's self-perception theory (Bem, 1967, 1972). The theory began as an alternative account of all of the dissonance findings, but it has important implications for self-understanding more generally, and it offers novel explanations for many real-life choices and behaviors.

Inferring Our Own Attitudes

According to Bem's **self-perception theory**, people do not always come to know their own attitudes by "looking inward" and discerning what they think or how they feel about something. Rather, they often look outward, at their behavior and the context in which it occurred, and *infer* what their attitudes must be. Self-perception works just like social perception. People come to understand themselves and their attitudes in the same way that they come to understand others and their attitudes.

At first glance, this idea seems bizarre—as implausible as the old joke about two behaviorists who've just finished having sex: One turns to the other and says, "That was great for you, how was it for me?" The theory feels wrong on a gut level because we're convinced that sometimes we "just know" how we feel about something, and we don't need to engage in any process of inference to find out. On closer inspection, however, self-perception theory makes more sense, in part because Bem concedes that sometimes we can just introspect and figure out our attitudes. It is only when our prior attitudes are "weak, ambiguous, and uninterpretable," he argues, that "the individual is functionally in the same position as an outside observer" (Bem, 1972, p. 2). The caveat is helpful. Most of us can remember times when we figured out how we felt about something by examining our behavior. "I guess I was hungrier than I thought," you might say, after downing a second Double Whopper with cheese. The key question, then, is whether the inference process that constitutes the core of self-perception theory applies only to such trivial matters as these or whether such processes are engaged when we grapple with attitudes of substance—for example, about volunteering to fight in Afghanistan or to work in a political campaign or to help underprivileged children.

Bem's account of the dissonance effects observed in previous studies is quite simple. He argues that people in these studies are not troubled by any unpleasant state of arousal like dissonance; they merely engage in a rational inference process.

self-perception theory A theory that people come to know their own attitudes by looking at their behavior and the context in which it occurred and *inferring* what their attitudes must be.

"How do I know what I think until I hear what I say?"

—Anonymous

They do not *change* their attitudes in these studies; rather, they infer what their attitudes must be. People value what they have chosen more after having chosen it because they infer that "if I chose this, I must like it." People form tight bonds to groups that have unpleasant initiation rituals because they reason that "if I suffered to get this, I must have felt it was worth it." And people who are offered little incentive to tell someone that a task was interesting come to view the task more favorably because they conclude that "there's no other reason I would say this is interesting if it wasn't, so it really must be." In support of this explanation, Bem showed that when *observer-subjects* read descriptions of dissonance experiments and are asked what attitude a participant would have had, the observer-subjects replicate the attitudes of the actual participants. They assume, for example, that a person who was paid only $1 to say that working on a boring task was interesting would have more favorable attitudes toward the task than a person paid $20. Bem reasoned that if the observers come up with the same inferences about attitudes as the attitudes reported by the actual participants, there is no reason to assume that the participants themselves arrived at their beliefs because they were motivated to reduce dissonance.

Testing for Arousal

Dissonance theory posits that the inconsistency between behavior and prior attitudes (or values) produces an unpleasant physiological state that motivates people to reduce the inconsistency. If there is no arousal, there is no attitude change. Self-perception theory, in contrast, contends that no arousal is involved: people coolly and rationally infer what their attitudes must be in light of their behavior and the context in which it occurred. Therefore, any decisive test to determine which of the two theories is more accurate should focus on whether people experience arousal in the standard dissonance paradigms (for example, the induced-compliance paradigm) and in similar everyday situations.

Considerable evidence indicates that, as dissonance theory predicts, acting at variance with our true beliefs does indeed generate arousal (Elliot & Devine, 1994; Galinsky, Stone, & Cooper, 2000; Harmon-Jones, 2000; Norton, Monin, Cooper, & Hogg, 2003; Waterman, 1969). If arousal is generated in dissonance experiments, it should be possible to influence the impact of that arousal—that is, whether it will lead to attitude change or not by altering how it is interpreted (Cooper, Zanna, & Taves, 1978; Losch & Cacioppo, 1990). Researchers have done so in experiments using "misattribution" manipulations (see Chapter 6). In one study, participants were given a drug (in reality, a placebo) and told that it would have no effect, that it would make them feel tense, or that it would make them feel relaxed (Zanna & Cooper, 1974). The participants then wrote, under free-choice or no-choice conditions, an essay arguing that inflammatory speakers should be barred from college campuses, a position with which they strongly disagreed. Among participants who were told that the drug would have no effect, the investigators expected to see the standard dissonance result—greater attitude change in favor of banning inflammatory speakers on the part of those who freely chose to write the essay as opposed to those in the no-choice condition. As the middle bars in **Figure 7.5** show, the results confirmed the researchers' expectations.

But the results from the other conditions are more telling. The investigators predicted that the standard dissonance effect would disappear when participants

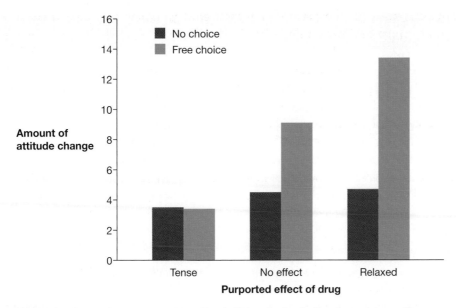

FIGURE 7.5 Does Arguing against One's Prior Attitude Produce Arousal? The amount of attitude change in the direction of a previously objectionable proposition on the part of participants who wrote essays—under free-choice and no-choice conditions—in support of the proposition. Before writing these essays, participants were given a pill and told that it would make them tense, that it would have no effect, or that it would make them relaxed. (Source: Adapted from Zanna & Cooper, 1974.)

were told (incorrectly) that the drug would make them tense. Those who freely chose to write the essay would experience the arousal state of dissonance, but they would attribute it to the drug and thus feel no compulsion to change their attitude to get rid of their unpleasant physiological state. It would go away, they were led to believe, as soon as the drug wore off. As the leftmost bars in Figure 7.5 show, that prediction, too, was confirmed. And what about the participants who were told that the drug would relax them? Those who freely chose to write the essay would experience arousal, an internal state inconsistent with the experimenter's earlier statement that the drug would make them feel relaxed. The researchers predicted that this would make them think, however implicitly, "I must *really* have done something wrong if I am this upset"—thoughts that should set in motion particularly powerful efforts at dissonance reduction. This prediction was also confirmed. As the rightmost bars in Figure 7.5 reveal, the greatest difference between participants in the free-choice and no-choice conditions—that is, the largest dissonance effect—was observed among participants who had been told that the drug would make them feel relaxed.

Reconciling the Dissonance and Self-Perception Accounts

The experiment just described speaks volumes about the relative merits of dissonance theory and self-perception theory. It is clear that behavior that is inconsistent with prior attitudes does indeed generate arousal (Croyle & Cooper, 1983; Elkin & Leippe, 1986) and that the effort to dispel that arousal motivates the types of attitude change found in dissonance experiments (Harmon-Jones, Brehm, Greenberg, Simon, & Nelson, 1996). In that sense, Festinger was right.

BOX 7.3 FOCUS ON EDUCATION

The Overjustification Effect and Superfluous Rewards

If you dropped in on a family dinner in a foreign land and heard a parent tell a child that he had to eat his *pfunst* before he could eat his *pfeffatorst*, you would immediately conclude that the child did not like the *pfunst* but loved *pfeffatorst*. Things that people do only to get something else are typically things they do not particularly like. But what happens when the child actually likes *pfunst*? Because the parents are making the child eat *pfunst* in order to have the privilege of eating *pfeffatorst*, the child may conclude that maybe *pfunst* isn't so great after all.

Self-perception theory makes just such a prediction, and this tendency to devalue those activities that we perform in order to get something else is known as the *overjustification* effect (Lepper, Greene, & Nisbett, 1973). The justification for performing the activity is overly sufficient: we would do it because it's inherently rewarding (or, more generally, for "intrinsic" reasons) but also because there is an external payoff for doing it ("extrinsic" reasons). Because the extrinsic reasons would be sufficient to produce the behavior, we might discount the intrinsic reasons for performing it and conclude that we don't much like the activity for its own sake.

Particularly intriguing evidence for the overjustification effect comes from a study of children's choice of activities in school. Elementary schoolchildren were shown two attractive drawing activities. In one condition, the children were told they could first do one drawing activity and then the other. In a second condition, they were told they *must* first do one activity *in order to* do the other (in both conditions, the experimenters counterbalanced which activity came first). For several days after this initial drawing session, the experimenters put out both drawing activities during the school's free-play period and covertly observed how long the children played with each activity. Children who earlier had simply drawn first with one and then the other played with both activities equally often. But those who earlier had used one *in order to* use to the other tended to avoid the former (Lepper, Sagotsky, Dafoe, & Greene, 1982). Their intrinsic interest in the first drawing activity had been undermined.

The overjustification effect has important implications for how rewards should be used in education and child rearing. It is common practice, for example, to reward children for reading books, getting good grades, or practicing the piano. That's fine if the child wouldn't otherwise read, study, or practice. But if the child has some interest in these activities to begin with, the rewards might put that interest in jeopardy. In one powerful demonstration of this danger, researchers introduced a set of novel math games into the free-play portion of an elementary school curriculum. As **Figure 7.6** indicates, the children initially found them interesting, as indicated by the amount of time the children chose to play with them at the outset of the experiment (baseline phase). Then, for several days afterward, the investigators instituted a "token economy" program whereby the children could earn points redeemable for prizes by playing with the math games. The more they played with the math games, the more points they earned. The token-economy program was effective in increasing how much the children played the games (see the bar in the treatment phase). But what happened when the token-economy program was terminated

Dissonance theory is the proper account of the phenomena observed in these experiments (and their real-world counterparts), not self-perception theory.

But note the irony here: the experiment that most powerfully supports the cognitive dissonance interpretation depends on the very processes of inference that lie at the core of self-perception theory. When participants in that experiment implicitly reasoned, "I'm aroused, but the experimenter told me the drug would make me anxious, so therefore . . . ," they were—just as self-perception theory predicts—making inferences about what was going on inside of them. Self-perception theory may not provide an accurate account of what happens when people behave in a way that challenges their sense of self as a moral and rational person, but it does capture some very important aspects of how the mind works.

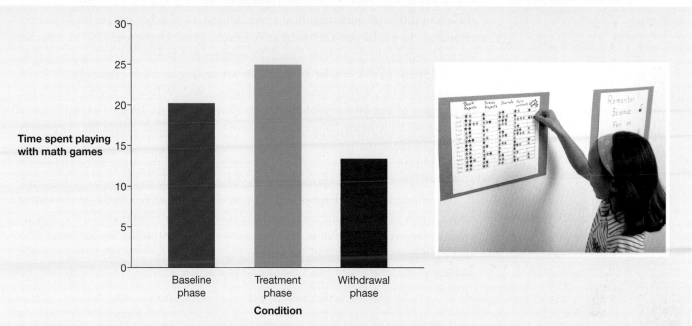

FIGURE 7.6 **The Effects of Superfluous Rewards** The amount of time elementary schoolchildren spent playing math games originally (baseline phase), when they received rewards for playing them (treatment phase), and afterward (withdrawal phase). (Source: Adapted from Greene, Sternberg, & Lepper, 1976.)

and the children no longer earned points for playing the games? Would they still play with them? As the bar on the right in the figure indicates, they did not. Having once received rewards for these activities, the children came to see them as something done only to get a reward, and their original interest was diminished (Greene, Sternberg, & Lepper, 1976).

Such findings don't imply that giving out rewards is always a bad thing. People aren't always intrinsically motivated, and when they aren't, rewards are often the best way to get them to do something they would not otherwise do. Rewards can also be administered in ways that minimize their negative impact. For instance, rewards can be performance

contingent—that is, based on how well someone performs. These have been shown to be less likely to decrease interest in an activity than task-contingent rewards, which are simply based on doing a task or not (Deci & Ryan, 1985; Harackiewicz, Manderlink, & Sansone, 1984; Sansone & Harackiewicz, 2000).

A consensus has thus emerged among social psychologists that both dissonance reduction processes and self-perception processes occur and influence people's attitudes and broader views of themselves. Dissonance reduction processes are activated when people's behavior is inconsistent with preexisting attitudes that are clear-cut and of some importance. Self-perception processes, in contrast, are invoked when behavior "clashes" with attitudes that are relatively vague or of little import (Chaiken & Baldwin, 1981; Fazio, Zanna, & Cooper, 1977).

This consensus view might make it seem as if self-perception processes are relegated to the trivial fringe of social life. They are not. Self-perception processes may be engaged primarily when our prior attitudes are weak or unclear, but a considerable body of research has made it abundantly clear that a surprising proportion of our attitudes *are* rather weak and ambiguous. Although self-perception processes typically influence unimportant attitudes more than important ones, at times they do influence important attitudes—and important subsequent behavior. Self-perception manipulations, for example, have been shown to influence such significant phenomena as whether we are likely to contribute to the public good (Freedman & Fraser, 1966; Uranowitz, 1975), whether we are likely to cheat to reach a goal (Dienstbier & Munter, 1971; Lepper, 1973), our judgment of the precise emotion we are feeling and how strongly we feel it (Dutton & Aron, 1974; Schachter & Singer, 1962; White & Kight, 1984), our assessment of our own personality traits (Schwarz et al., 1991; Tice, 1993), and whether we truly enjoy an activity we have engaged in our entire life (Lepper & Greene, 1978).

In addition, the core principle of self-perception theory—that we use whatever cues we have available to us to figure out what we think and how we feel, including knowledge of the surrounding context and how we've acted—is consistent with a tremendous amount of recent evidence that our thoughts and feelings are affected by, even grounded in, our physical states and bodily movements. This area of inquiry, on "embodied" cognition and emotion, is currently being pursued actively in many areas of psychology and is worth examining in some detail.

The Embodied Nature of Cognition and Emotion

A variety of physical actions are associated with various psychological states. When people are happy, they tend to smile; if they don't like something, they're inclined to push it away; and if they agree with something, they are likely to nod their heads up and down. This is the behavioral component of attitudes discussed earlier: these motor actions of smiling, pushing, and nodding *are important parts of* our attitudes. As a result, if people are induced to make the bodily movements associated with certain attitudes, beliefs, or emotions, they might come to have, or find it easier to have, those very attitudes, beliefs, or emotions. That is, in figuring out what we think, feel, or believe, we draw on whatever cues are available to us—including what our bodies are doing—without being consciously aware that we are doing so.

In one early demonstration of this effect, Gary Wells and Richard Petty (1980) had students ostensibly test a set of headphones by moving their heads up and down or side to side while listening to music and radio editorials. When later asked about the viewpoints advocated in the editorials, the students indicated that they agreed with them more if they had listened to them while nodding their heads up and down than if they had listened to them while shaking their heads from side to side. We nod our heads at things we approve of, and this lifelong association leads us to view more favorably those things we encounter while nodding (Epley & Gilovich, 2001; Forster & Strack, 1996).

In a similar vein, Fritz Strack and his colleagues had some students hold a marker with their teeth, which creates a smiling expression (see **Figure 7.7** and try it). Others were asked to hold the marker between their top lip and nose, creating an expression akin to a frown. While holding the marker in one of these ways, the participants were asked to rate how amused they were by a number of cartoons. As you can probably anticipate, students who held the marker in their teeth (the smilers) thought the cartoons were more amusing than did students in the control

FIGURE 7.7 You Be the Subject: Self-Perception Affected by Movement

Try positioning a pen or pencil in the two ways shown below.

Watch a funny TV show while in the first position; after the first commercial break, switch to the second position. Was the TV show more or less amusing before or after the commercial break?

Results: Research evidence suggests that the physical movements we engage in while evaluating stimuli can affect how those stimuli are evaluated (see **Box 7.4** for further discussion).

condition, and those who held the marker atop their upper tip (the frowners) thought the cartoons were less amusing (Strack, Martin, & Stepper, 1988).

Other researchers have explored the implications of our tendency to push away things we find aversive and pull toward us things we find appealing (see Chapter 1). Because extending the arm is closely associated with negative stimuli, and flexing the arm is associated with positive stimuli, being induced to make these bodily movements can have predictable effects on attitudes. In one study, John Cacioppo, Joseph Priester, and Gary Berntson (1993) showed Ohio State University students a series of 24 Chinese ideographs while they were either pressing down on a table (arm extension) or lifting up on a table from underneath (arm flexion). The students evaluated the ideographs presented while they flexed their arms more favorably than those presented while they extended their arms (see also Chen & Bargh, 1999). Other studies using this procedure have shown that flexing the arm fosters creative insight on various problem-solving tasks (Friedman & Forster, 2000) and makes people more inclined to accept their initial attempt at estimating unknown values (Epley & Gilovich, 2004).

All of these effects challenge the idea (as self-perception theory does) that our attitudes, knowledge, and beliefs are stored as abstract propositions or representations in the brain. They support an alternative view that our attitudes and beliefs, and even the most abstract concepts, are partly "embodied" in the physical movements associated with those attitudes, beliefs, or concepts (Barsalou, 2008; Niedenthal, Barsalou, Winkielman, Krauth-Gruber, & Ric, 2005). Part of the attitude of disapproval or the belief that we don't like something is represented in the physical act of pushing away. Even our understanding of sentences like "He raced down the corridor" is grounded in the physical act of running. When people

BOX 7.4 FOCUS ON COGNITIVE SCIENCE

Embodied Metaphors

Abstract concepts are often grounded in concrete ideas, typically in simple, physical metaphors (Lakoff & Johnson, 1980). We say that we "see" what you mean when we understand what you mean, that things are "looking up" when we're optimistic, that she has a "warm" personality when she is kind and outgoing, and so on. Given the embodied nature of cognition, these metaphorical relationships suggest the possibility that simply feeling certain physical sensations might activate the more complex ideas to which they are linked, with predictable effects on people's thoughts, feelings, and actions. In support of this idea, Zhong & Leonardelli (2008) had participants recall either a time they had been socially excluded or a time they were welcomed by others and then asked them to estimate the temperature of the room. Supporting the idea of being "cold and lonely," those who had just thought of a time they had been rejected estimated that the room was significantly cooler. In another study, participants were asked to fill out a survey attached to a lightweight or heavy clipboard, a survey that involved estimating the value of various monetary currencies (the Japanese yen, the Swiss franc, and so on). Those who reported their estimates on a heavy clipboard thought the currencies were more valuable, reinforcing the idea of weight as a metaphor for importance (Jostmann, Lakens, & Schubert, 2009). Investigators have also shown that we feel closer to others when holding a warm cup of coffee than when holding a cup of iced coffee (Ijerman & Semin, 2009).

Other studies have shown that people feeling morally "impure" as a result of

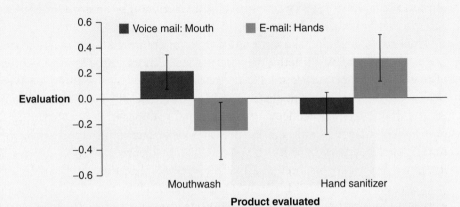

FIGURE 7.8 Is Moral Purification Tied to the Manner of the Misdeed? The amount participants who lied over voice mail or e-mail were willing to pay (in standardized units, or number of standard deviations above or below average) for cleaning products geared to the mouth or the hand. (Source: From Lee & Schwarz, 2010.)

recalling a past misdeed apparently also feel physically dirty because they are more likely to select an antiseptic hand wipe instead of a pencil as a token gift for having participated in the experiment (Zhong & Liljenquist, 2006). The precise nature of these influences was demonstrated in a remarkable study that examined how they might play out differently when different parts of the body are involved in a misdeed (Lee & Schwarz, 2010). All participants were asked to imagine that they were competing with a colleague for promotion at a law firm and that they had found a document that the colleague had lost. Returning the document to the colleague would help the colleague's career but hurt the participant's. Participants were instructed to leave a voice mail message or type an e-mail message stating that they could

not find the document (in other words, to lie). Afterward, as part of an allegedly unrelated study, the participants indicated how much would pay for a variety of household products, including mouthwash and hand sanitizer. Remarkably, those who *spoke* the lie over the phone apparently felt their mouths were unclean because, as shown in **Figure 7.8**, they put a high value on the mouthwash. Those who *typed* their lie, in contrast, apparently felt their hands were unclean because they placed a high value on the hand sanitizer. As the authors noted, their findings "indicate that the embodiment of moral purity is specific to the motor modality involved in a moral transgression, making purification of the 'dirty' body part more desirable than purification of other body parts" (Lee & Schwarz, p. 1424).

read such a sentence, motor regions associated with running become ever so slightly activated, and when they read "Raymond picked up the Easter egg," brain areas involved in grasping become activated (Speer et al., 2009). This explains why people who have had botox injections (which smooth out wrinkles in the face by immobilizing facial muscles) have a hard time processing sentences containing emotion. Without being able themselves to mimic the emotional expressions as they are reading, the very concepts of sad, angry, and so on are a bit harder to access and comprehend (Havas et al., 2010).

Thus the seemingly abstract, cognitive act of comprehension is not abstract at all. To understand something—whether an abstract proposition, a sentence of text, or a possible future state of the world (like the Cubs winning the World Series)—people must mentally "try it on" or simulate it. And what our bodies are doing or how they are feeling can facilitate or impede the act of simulation, influencing what we think and feel. Consider the remarkable (and distressing) finding that people believe more in the reality of global warming and consider it a more serious environmental threat on hot days than they do on cooler days (Li, Johnson, & Zaval, 2011; Risen & Critcher, 2011). In one study, participants were inside a laboratory where the thermostat was set to either 81 or 73 degrees. Respondents in the warmer room expressed greater belief in the reality of global warming. The effect was quite strong—strong enough that conservatives in a warm room expressed the same concern about the problem as liberals in a cold room. In other words, the effect of the temperature of the room was comparable in magnitude to the effect of political attitudes. It thus seems that to get a handle on the idea of global warming, we must mentally simulate it, and we do so much more easily when we feel warm (Risen & Critcher, 2011).

 Self-perception theory maintains that people infer their attitudes from their behavior, thus providing an alternative explanation of why people often change their attitudes when the attitudes conflict with their actions. Experimental evidence, however, has shown that arousal is indeed generated when behavior is inconsistent with attitudes and that this arousal does indeed often motivate attitude change. Nevertheless, researchers have reconciled dissonance theory and self-perception theory, showing that dissonance theory best explains attitude change for preexisting clear-cut attitudes, whereas self-perception theory best explains attitude change for less clear-cut attitudes. Recent research on embodied cognition indicates that people draw on all sources of information—not just the actions they have performed but also the precise movements of the body—as part of the very act of comprehending ideas and determining their attitudes and opinions.

BEYOND COGNITIVE CONSISTENCY TO BROADER RATIONALIZATION

The core of dissonance theory is the idea that people find psychological inconsistency uncomfortable and therefore engage in psychological work to lessen the discomfort. Other tensions, of course, can produce similar types of psychological discomfort and elicit similar efforts at rationalization and justification. Two relatively recent theories have been offered to explain how we respond to two such sources of discomfort. One deals with the discomfort that comes from thinking about the problems associated with the broader social and political system to which we are committed. The other deals with the extreme discomfort—indeed, the terror—that comes with thinking about the inevitability of death.

System Justification Theory

Chapter 3 discusses people's need to think well of themselves, or what some have called ego justification motives (Jost, Banaji, & Nosek, 2004). Chapter 11 discusses people's need to think well of the groups to which they belong, or group justification motives. But beyond the desire to think highly of our own talents, virtues, and habits or to take pride in being, say, a Canadian, a Californian, a Christian, or a Cowboys fan, we want to think highly of the broader political and social systems we are part of—we want to see them as fair, just, and desirable (Jost & Banaji, 1994; Jost et al., 2004).

Those who have studied these tendencies have noted that social and political systems do not serve everyone's needs equally. Those who benefit the most from a given system, such as those who are wealthier and occupy more powerful positions in society, have both a psychological and an economic incentive to defend the system. Those who don't benefit from the system (or are even disadvantaged by it) obviously do not have an economic incentive to defend the system, but they do have a psychological incentive to do so. According to **system justification theory**, believing that the world is or should be fair, combined with abundant evidence of inequality, can generate a fair amount of ideological dissonance. Extolling the virtues of the prevailing system is typically an easier way of reducing that dissonance than bringing about effective change. Protest is hard; justification is easy.

system justification theory The theory that people are motivated to see the existing political and social status quo as desirable, fair, and legitimate.

Common observations that seem to support system justification theory are the fact that women often feel that they deserve lower pay than men doing the same work (Jost, 1997; Major, 1994) and the fact that low-income groups in the United States do not necessarily support more egalitarian economic policies over the status quo (Fong, 2001; Jost, Pelham, Sheldon, & Sullivan, 2003). Some of the most interesting support for the system justification perspective comes from studies that look at compensatory stereotypes, or beliefs that those who occupy less privileged roles in a society nonetheless derive a number of compensatory benefits: "Low-income people may be poor, but they're happier than the wealthy." "Women may not have much power, but they're nicer, warmer, and more socially connected than men." Exposure to such stereotypes is thought to give ideological support to the status quo, making people more accepting of current gender roles and more accepting of the broader sociocultural status quo (Jost & Kay, 2005; Kay & Jost, 2003).

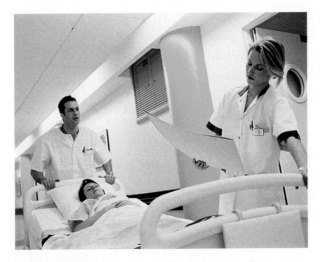

System Justification To defend the broader social and political systems to which they belong, economically disadvantaged people often defend their own disadvantage. Female nurses like the one depicted here sometimes admit to feeling that they deserve to make less money than their male counterparts doing the same work.

Terror Management Theory

Humans may be the only organisms that know with certainty that they will die. That's not such a blessing. Indeed, many people find that thinking about the inevitability of their own death—really thinking about it and letting it sink in—brings on a level of anxiety that verges on debilitating. People need to deal with that potentially crippling anxiety in order to get on with life. **Terror management theory (TMT)** specifies the processes people use to do so. The most common way that people deal with the problem is simply to deny it—to maintain that it is only their bodies and this particular earthly existence that will come to an end. Most people the world over believe they will go on living in some form after their lives on earth have ended. But beyond this common form of what has been called "the denial of death" (Becker, 1973), people can derive some solace from believing that although they personally will cease to exist, many of the things they value will live on. For many people, this sort of indirect immortality is achieved by thinking about their role as parent. They won't live on, but their children and grandchildren will. This is probably why men who are reminded of the inevitability of their own death express an interest in having more children (Wisman & Goldenberg, 2005).

TMT further emphasizes that people try to achieve symbolic immortality by thinking of themselves as connected to a broader culture, worldview, and set of values. You will certainly die at some point, but many of the things you value most—America; freedom and democracy; Christianity, Buddhism, or Islam; or even your alma mater or favorite sports team—will live on long after. To the extent that people are closely connected to such institutions, they symbolically live on along with them. Therefore, people will most vigorously embrace their broader worldview and cultural institutions when they are reminded of their own inevitable death. Of course, to live on, even symbolically, with a broader cultural institution, we must maintain solid and meaningful connections to that institution. Terror management theory therefore further maintains that, to do so, we strive to achieve and maintain high self-esteem by meeting or exceeding the standards specified by the values, norms, and roles of a given cultural worldview. By meeting those standards, we satisfy the criteria of being meaningfully connected to that worldview, allowing us to feel symbolically immortal.

Terror management theorists have tested their ideas by subjecting participants to manipulations that make their own mortality more salient. The most common manipulation is to have participants write out responses to two directives: (1) "Briefly describe the emotions that the thought of your own death arouses in you," and (2) "Jot down, as specifically as you can, what you think will happen to *you* as you physically die." In other studies, the same objective has been accomplished by having participants fill out surveys either in front of a funeral home or at a control location not associated with death or by showing participants pictures of fatal car accidents or control photographs not connected to death.

Consistent with the tenets of TMT, mortality salience manipulations have been shown to make people more hostile to people who criticize their country (Greenberg et al., 1990), more committed to their ingroups and more hostile to outgroups (Dechesne, Greenberg, Arndt, & Schimel, 2000; Greenberg et al., 1990), more eager to punish those who challenge prevailing laws and established procedures (Rosenblatt, Greenberg, Solomon, Pyszczynski, & Lyon, 1989), and more reluctant to use cultural artifacts such as a crucifix or the U.S. flag for a mundane, utilitarian purpose (Greenberg, Simon, Porteus, Pyszczynski, & Solomon, 1995). Making death salient, in other

terror management theory (TMT) The theory that people deal with the potentially paralyzing anxiety that comes with the knowledge of the inevitability of death by striving for symbolic immortality through the preservation of a valued worldview and the conviction that they have lived up to its values and prescriptions.

"I don't want to live on in my work; I want to live on in my apartment."

—Woody Allen

"The future's uncertain and the end is always near."

—The Doors, *Roadhouse Blues*

Mortality Salience and Nationalism The outpouring of nationalist sentiment observed right after the 9/11 attacks on the World Trade Center and the Pentagon, like this display of flags at Pepperdine University, may have been partly fueled by the very salient reminder of our own mortality that the attacks provided.

words, makes people want to uphold the values of the institutions they identify with and that will live on after them.

It isn't difficult to think of potential political implications of terror management concerns. For example, in the run-up to the 2004 U.S. presidential election, survey respondents were asked their opinions about either the Democratic challenger, John Kerry, or the incumbent Republican president, George W. Bush. Some did so after the usual mortality salience manipulation, others after writing about their experience with dental pain. Because Bush, as the incumbent president, was the head of the country and was seen by many as the leader of the fight against al-Qaeda and other terrorist organizations, the investigators predicted that survey respondents would be more favorable to Bush and less favorable to Kerry after a mortality salience manipulation. As **Figure 7.9** indicates, this prediction was confirmed (Landau, Solomon, Greenberg, Cohen, & Pyszczynski, 2004). Further support for this idea comes from an analysis of public opinion polls during that election that showed that support for Bush tended to go up whenever the terrorist threat level announced by the Department of Homeland Security went up. Presumably, heightened threat warnings made the public's mortality very salient (Wilier, 2004).

Terror management concerns are certainly not unique to Americans. Iranian respondents read statements allegedly issued by either a radical ("The U.S. represents the world power that Allah wants us to destroy") or a peaceful Islamist ("One should treat other humans with respect and care, no matter what racial, ethnic, or religious background"). Some did so after a mortality salience manipulation, others after a control procedure. Participants in the mortality salience condition expressed more support of the radical Islamist statements than did participants in the control condition (Pyszczynski et al., 2006).

Considerable evidence also supports TMT's contention that awareness of the inevitability of death increases striving for self-esteem (Arndt, Schimel, & Goldenberg, 2003; Kasser & Sheldon, 2000; Taubman-Ben-Ari, Florian, & Mikulincer, 1999). In a particularly telling study, participants in one condition read an essay stating that the consensus scientific opinion regarding reports of near-death experiences—the feeling of leaving and looking down at one's body, of moving down a long, brightly lit tunnel, and so on—is that these experiences are exactly what we would expect, given the makeup of the brain, and that they do not suggest in any way that there might be life after death. Participants in another condition read that the consensus scientific opinion was just the opposite: that reports like these point to the plausibility of some sort of life after death. All participants then received favorable feedback about themselves from very dubious sources, such as horoscopes and questionable personality tests, and then rated the validity of the feedback they received. Those who read the essay that cast doubt on life after death rated the feedback as more valid than those who read the essay that encouraged belief in an afterlife. In other words, if we can believe that there is life after death, we needn't be so concerned with living on symbolically, so the need for self-esteem is reduced (Dechesne et al., 2003).

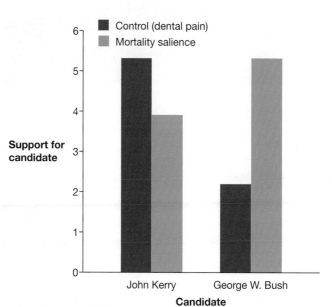

FIGURE 7.9 Mortality Salience and Support for Candidates in the 2004 U.S. Presidential Election Survey respondents reported their attitudes toward presidential candidates John Kerry and George W. Bush either under normal survey conditions or after a mortality salience manipulation.

 People's tendencies to rationalize go beyond their attempts to resolve personal cognitive inconsistencies. People are motivated to see the broader social and political systems in which they live as fair and just and good. They are also motivated to deal with the anxiety that comes from the knowledge of human mortality, and they often do so by adhering more closely to their worldviews.

Chapter Review

Summary

The Three Components of Attitudes

- *Attitudes* are primarily evaluations of attitude objects along a negative or positive dimension, and they include three elements: *affect* (emotion), *cognition* (thoughts and knowledge), and *action tendencies* (behavior).

Measuring Attitudes

- Attitudes can be measured with self-report *Likert scales*, and their strength or importance assessed with response latencies that capture *attitude accessibility* (how readily the attitude can become active in an individual's mind). Attitude linkage measures gauge *attitude centrality* (how closely an attitude is correlated to attitudes about other issues), and *implicit measures* tap into attitudes that people are unaware they have or may be unwilling to report.

Predicting Behavior from Attitudes

- It can be surprisingly difficult at times to predict behavior from attitudes, because attitudes are sometimes *ambiguous* or *inconsistent*; attitudes sometimes *conflict* with other powerful determinants of behavior; attitudes are sometimes based on *secondhand information* about the object; attitudes and the attitude targets we actually confront may be at different *levels of generality*; and some of our behavior is *automatic*.

Predicting Attitudes from Behavior

- Behavior can have substantial effects on attitudes. Most of the research showing such effects grew out of *cognitive consistency theories*, which stress how much people value consistency among their various attitudes and between their attitudes and behavior.
- *Balance theory* specifies that people desire balance among their beliefs and sentiments and thus prefer to hold attitudes that make sense with their other attitudes and to behave in ways that align with their attitudes.
- *Cognitive dissonance theory* is based on the idea that people experience *dissonance*, or discomfort, when attitudes and behavior are inconsistent. People often try to reduce the dissonance they are feeling by bringing their attitudes in line with their behavior.
- After making a choice between two objects or courses of action, people engage in dissonance reduction by finding new attractions in the chosen alternative and previously undetected flaws in the unchosen alternative.
- People engage in *effort justification* when they exert effort toward some goal and the goal turns out to be disappointing. They justify their expenditure of energy by deciding that the goal is truly worthwhile.
- People attempt to reduce dissonance in *induced-compliance* situations. For example, when induced by another person to argue for a position at variance with their true attitudes, people who are poorly compensated for doing so feel that they must justify their behavior and typically do so by changing their attitudes to align better with their behavior.
- Inconsistency between attitudes and behavior should produce dissonance only when there *is free choice* (or the illusion of it) to engage in the behavior, there is *insufficient justification* for the behavior, the behavior has *negative consequences*, and the consequences were *foreseeable*.
- We can offset or reduce the negative effects of psychological inconsistency, and of threats to self-identity and self-esteem more generally, by engaging in *self-affirmation*—that is, by affirming other important elements of our identity, such as our important values.
- Dissonance is apparently universal, but there are cultural differences in the conditions that prompt people to experience it. For example, the Japanese tend to experience post-decision dissonance only when asked to think about what another person would choose.

Self-Perception Theory

- *Self-perception theory* is based on the premise that people change their attitudes to align with their behavior because they observe their behavior and the circumstances in which it occurs, and then they infer, just as an observer might, what their attitudes must be.

■ Whereas self-perception may play a role in generating the effects in some dissonance experiments, evidence indicates that there is often a motivational component as well. Self-perception appears to account for attitude change when attitudes are weak or unclear to begin with, and more motivated dissonance reduction is invoked when attitudes are more strongly held.

■ Bodily sensations are often incorporated into our judgments about an object or our appraisal of a situation. For example, we believe communications more when we read them while pulling on something than while pushing on something.

Beyond Cognitive Consistency to Broader Rationalization

■ According to *system justification theory*, people are motivated to justify the broader political and social systems of which they are a part. One way they do so is through stereotypes that play up the advantages of belonging to relatively disadvantaged groups, such as the belief that the poor are happier than the rich.

■ The knowledge that we are all destined to die can elicit paralyzing anxiety. *Terror management theory* maintains that people often cope with this anxiety by striving for symbolic immortality through their offspring and through their identification with institutions and cultural worldviews that live on after their own death.

Key Terms

attitude (p. 235)
balance theory (p. 244)
cognitive dissonance theory (p. 245)
effort justification (p. 247)
implicit attitude measures (p. 236)

induced (forced) compliance (p. 248)
Likert scale (p. 235)
response latency (p. 236)
self-affirmation (p. 254)
self-perception theory (p. 257)

system justification theory (p. 266)
terror management theory (TMT) (p. 267)

Further Reading

Eagleman, D. (2011). *Incognito: The secret lives of the brain.* New York: Random House. An accessible and entertaining examination of how much of everything we do is done without conscious intervention.

Festinger, L. (1957). *A theory of cognitive dissonance.* Stanford, CA: Stanford University Press. The original statement of one of the most influential theories in the history of social psychology.

Pyszczynski, T. A., Solomon, S., & Greenberg, J. (2003). *In the wake of 9/11: The psychology of terror.* Washington, DC: American Psychological Association. An application of terror management theory to the events that followed the terrorist attacks on the World Trade Center and the Pentagon.

Wilson, T. D. (2002). *Strangers to ourselves: Discovering the adaptive unconscious.* Cambridge, MA: Harvard University Press. An insightful review of current thinking about the impact of nonconscious processes on human behavior.

Persuasion

IN 1964, THE SURGEON GENERAL RELEASED his advisory committee's Report on Smoking and Health. This report detailed a scientifically established relationship between smoking tobacco and lung cancer. Since then, this country has witnessed one of the great persuasion battles of our time. The U.S. government has spent billions of dollars on public service announcements in print, on television and radio, and on the Internet portraying the perils of smoking. And the tobacco industry has countered, spending billions of dollars extolling the pleasures of smoking. The battle over smoking has been expensive and passionate and continues to this day. Meanwhile, millions of lives are being lost, and millions of people are beginning or continuing to smoke.

Public service ads aimed at persuading people to stop smoking are graphic, powerful, and backed by highly credible, prestigious, and expert sources from the medical profession and the government. These ads have made people aware of the high risks of smoking, including the facts that one out of every three cancer-related deaths is related to smoking, that smoking causes between 400,000 and 500,000 premature deaths each year in the United States, that smoking increases the chances of early impotence in men, and that women who smoke are four times as likely to have serious side effects from birth control pills and to suffer from fertility problems. And these public service ads have had an impact: in the 1950s, about 50 percent of all Americans smoked. Today, just over 20 percent of Americans smoke (Centers for Disease Control and Prevention, 2010).

But why do those 20 percent continue to smoke, despite being fully aware of the significant health risks of smoking? The $13 billion that the tobacco industry spends each year on advertising is no doubt partially responsible for the large number of people who still smoke. One especially effective campaign promoting smoking was the "Joe Camel" campaign in which Joe Camel, a cartoon mascot of Camel cigarettes, appeared on billboards, in magazines, and on promotional

Advertising and Smoking (A) In 1985, the R. J. Reynolds Company introduced an advertising campaign for Camel cigarettes that featured the "cool" cartoon character Joe Camel. The ads appealed to children and led to a huge increase in the sales of cigarettes to children and teenagers. The Federal Trade Commission successfully sued R. J. Reynolds for targeting children and forced the company to end the Joe Camel campaign. (B) Public service ads were created to persuade people to stop smoking. This Cancer Country ad parodies the Marlboro cigarette ads in which cowboys are smoking cigarettes and looking rugged and manly and instead stresses the connection between smoking and cancer.

"The object of oratory alone is not truth, but persuasion."

—Thomas Babington Macaulay

"The receptive ability of the masses is very limited, their understanding small; on the other hand, they have a great power of forgetting. This being so, all effective propaganda must be confined to a very few points which must be brought out in the form of slogans until the very last man is enabled to comprehend what is meant by any slogan. If this principle is sacrificed by the desire to be many sided, it will dissipate the effectual working of the propaganda, for the people will be unable to digest or retain the material that is offered them."

—Adolf Hitler

items such as T-shirts. Soon after the start of the campaign, Camel's market share among underage smokers rose from 0.5 to 32.8 percent. Another successful campaign increased sales of Virginia Slims cigarettes. The product slogan, "You've come a long way, baby," targeted women and linked smoking Virginia Slims cigarettes to women's quest for success, independence, and thinness. After the introduction of the Virginia Slims campaign, smoking by 12-year-old girls more than doubled.

This story about the battle over smoking, about the millions of people who have kicked the habit as well as the large numbers of people who continue to smoke, reveals the two overarching themes of this chapter: our susceptibility to persuasion and our resistance to it. People can be remarkably susceptible to persuasion. Charismatic leaders like Nelson Mandela, Martin Luther King Jr., or Mohandas (Mahatma) Gandhi can stir the masses to bring about radical social change in the absence of significant institutional power or money. Political protests such as those in Tunisia, Egypt, and Libya during the recent "Arab Spring" speak to how quickly groups of people can change the attitudes of many in ways that lead to profound societal changes.

At the same time, people can also be remarkably resistant to persuasion. It is estimated that only 1 percent of prisoners of war in the Korean War altered their political beliefs, even though they were tortured and indoctrinated in the most extreme ways (Zimbardo & Leippe, 1991). And many well-financed and skillfully designed campaigns to encourage people to practice safe sex often fail, as do anti-drug programs (Aronson, Fried, & Stone, 1991). People can be stubbornly resistant to changing their minds, even when their health or economic well-being is affected.

This chapter is organized around a central question: Why, in response to attempts at persuasion ranging from political indoctrination to door-to-door religious proselytizing, do people sometimes change their minds, whereas at other times they do not? What are the mechanics of attitude change? How do persuasive messages change people's attitudes, often in lasting and significant ways? And how do people resist attitude change? Before considering why attitudes change and why they do not, this chapter considers why people have them in the first place.

FUNCTIONS OF ATTITUDES

What purposes do attitudes serve? One answer is that they guide behavior—a valid assumption, although attitudes guide behavior less powerfully than most people suspect (see Chapter 7). Researchers have, however, highlighted four other functions of attitudes (Eagly & Chaiken, 1998; Pratkanis, Breckler, & Greenwald, 1989) and have illustrated the importance of attitudes in areas as wide-ranging as food preferences and the fear of death.

The Utilitarian Function of Attitudes

Attitudes serve what has been called a **utilitarian function**—that is, they alert us to rewarding objects we should approach and to costly or punishing objects we should avoid (Ferguson & Zayas, 2009). When you become aware of an attitude you hold—say, toward the smell of dinner, the sight of the library, a highly critical peer, or a person you feel fondly toward—you are by definition aware of positive and negative information about the attitude object. These attitudes are often activated by our current goals—for example, to get good grades or to find a romantic partner—and trigger actions that help us pursue our goals (Ferguson, 2008). Imagine that the goal to get a good grade on your psychology exam is on your mind. Because of that goal, your attitudes toward objects relevant to achieving this goal (the library, books) should become more positive. And it turns out this change can occur automatically, even if you do not consciously decide to evaluate the library positively (Ferguson & Bargh, 2008). Not surprisingly, when your attitudes toward goal-relevant objects are positive, you are more likely to engage in goal-relevant behavior (for example, going to the library). In short, attitudes make us evaluatively ready to achieve the goals that matter to us.

Our food preferences also illustrate the utilitarian function of attitudes. Here our dietary likes and dislikes help us eat foods that are beneficial to survival and avoid foods that are potentially dangerous. The preference for sweet foods—no doubt one of our strongest positive attitudes—helps us identify foods of nutritional value, such as foods that provide vitamin C, which humans, unlike many mammals, do not synthesize in their body. Our strong distaste for bitter foods helps us avoid the toxins that tend in nature to taste bitter (Profet, 1992; Rozin & Kalat, 1971). Interestingly, women are particularly sensitive to bitter tastes and pungent smells during the first trimester of pregnancy. Their experience of "morning sickness" prevents them from eating these foods and thus protects the fetus from being exposed to dangerous toxins at a particularly vulnerable stage of development (Profet, 1992).

utilitarian function An attitudinal function that serves to alert people to rewarding objects and situations they should approach and costly or punishing objects or situations they should avoid.

Attitudes and Associations
Our attitudes alert us to rewarding objects—or threatening or neutral ones. A positive attitude toward a beautiful woman may help sell a car if an association is created between the woman and the car. Here an attractive model poses next to a sports car, thereby pairing the emotionally arousing stimulus of the beautiful woman with the car.

The idea that attitudes serve utilitarian functions has helped shed light on why humans prefer certain natural settings in different parts of the world (Orians & Heerwagen, 1992). Evolutionary psychologists have reasoned that people prefer landscapes that have water, lush trees and bushes, semi-open space, ground cover, and distant views to the horizon. These kinds of environments offered our ancestors reliable sources of water, opportunities for hunting animals and gathering food, shelter, and the means to detect and hide from predators. We have positive attitudes toward these kinds of environments today, the argument goes, because of the evolutionary advantages these attitudes conferred on those who possessed and acted on them.

In modern life, advertisers have put the utilitarian function of attitudes to good use. Researchers have shown that attitudes toward fairly neutral objects can be modified by pairing that object with a stimulus that generates a strong positive or negative reaction (Petty & Wegener, 1998). People's attitudes toward political slogans, consumer products, persuasive messages, and other people can be changed when paired with emotionally arousing stimuli such as pleasing odors, electric shock, harsh sounds, or pleasant pictures (Gresham & Shimp, 1985; Janis, Kaye, & Kirschner, 1965; Razran, 1940; Staats & Staats, 1958; Zanna, Kiesler, & Pilkonis, 1970). Ads that use animals, babies, or sexually alluring young women and men are more likely to sell products than those that use less intrinsically rewarding objects, such as cartoons or historical figures (Pratkanis & Aronson, 2000).

The Ego-Defensive Function of Attitudes

ego-defensive function An attitudinal function that enables people to maintain cherished beliefs about themselves and their world by protecting them from contradictory information.

Aside from signaling rewards and threats, attitudes also serve an **ego-defensive function**, protecting us from unpleasant facts or emotions. We develop certain attitudes, this reasoning holds, to maintain cherished beliefs about ourselves or our world. One way that we protect our valued beliefs is addressed in terror management theory (see Chapter 7). This account holds that our fear of dying leads us to adopt or cling to attitudes that reflect cultural worldviews out of a belief that if we do so, part of us will survive death. For example, research has shown that when their mortality is somehow made salient, people tend to exhibit more positive evaluations of their own group versus other groups, greater patriotism, increased religious conviction, greater conformity to cultural standards, and a greater inclination to punish moral transgressors. Whereas a strong desire to live is instinctive in humans, death is one of life's few certainties and thus is a source of many of our strongest attitudes and deepest values.

Guided by a similar logic, John Jost and his colleagues have argued that political conservatism is a form of motivated or ego-defensive cognition that helps people ward off certain anxieties (Jost, Glaser, Kruglanski, & Sulloway, 2003). Summarizing dozens of studies spanning several decades and different cultures, these researchers identify two core values to

"It's broccoli, dear."
"I say it's spinach, and I say the hell with it."

political conservatism. The first is resistance to change. Conservatives express greater qualms about change of any kind, whether it takes the form of political revolution, changes in social conventions or sexual identities, or even artistic change or scientific advance. A second core dimension of conservatism is the endorsement of inequality. Societies bring about inequalities in resources and opportunities (although they vary in the degree of inequality). Conservatives are more willing to accept these inequalities.

So where do these two core values of conservatism come from? According to Jost and colleagues, these core values are attempts to manage fear and uncertainty. Conservatives consistently show higher levels of fear than people who hold other political beliefs: they judge the world to be a more dangerous place, react more quickly to danger-related words, and even are more prone to nightmares. Conservatives also show less interest in new technological innovations, unfamiliar music, changes in job requirements—all things that require some tolerance of uncertainty. To ward off fear and uncertainty, conservatives gravitate to attitudes and beliefs that envision a structured and orderly world, and this behavior gives rise to their core values—resistance to change and tolerance of inequality.

Survival and Preferred Landscapes Some evolutionary psychologists claim that people have evolved a preference for landscapes that have water, semi-open space, ground cover, and distant views to the horizon because these environments provided survival advantages to our ancestors. This view of the Husch Vineyards in California shows such preferred characteristics.

The Value-Expressive Function of Attitudes

A third idea about why we have attitudes, the **value-expressive function**, captures a more social dimension of attitudes: that attitudes help us express our most cherished values, usually in groups where these values can be supported and reinforced. If you were to predict which first-year students at your college would join various groups on your campus—the Korean Christian group, the Tea Party, the Students for Diversity, Take Back the Night, and so on—surely those students' social attitudes would be a big help in making predictions. The same is true of which Facebook sites you visit and which "tweets" you receive. We all join groups, in part, to express our attitudes. These groups are known as our **reference groups**—that is, groups whose opinions matter to us and that affect our opinions and beliefs.

The value-expressive function of attitudes accounts for a variety of phenomena. For example, children in the United States express an early allegiance to the Democratic or Republican Party, in part to express the values of a very important group, the family (Niemi & Jennings, 1991). People who are committed to having low prejudice are more likely to associate with groups that promote those attitudes, and they feel guilt and shame when their actions contradict their attitudes toward minority groups (Devine, Monteith, Zuwerink, & Elliot, 1991; Devine, Plant, Amodio, Harmon-Jones, & Vance, 2002; Plant & Devine, 1998). Our commitment to the idea that people in the groups we join share our attitudes can even lead to certain forms of bias: within political groups, people tend to overestimate the similarity between their own attitudes and the attitudes of their leaders (Judd, Kenny, & Krosnick, 1983).

value-expressive function An attitudinal function whereby attitudes help people express their most cherished values—usually in groups in which these values can be supported and reinforced.

reference groups Groups whose opinions matter to a person and that affect the person's opinions and beliefs.

Value Expression and Reference Groups Our membership in reference groups allows us to freely express our attitudes with like-minded others. (A) At a gay wedding in Tel Aviv, Israel, individuals express their support of gay marriage. (B) Here the Shades of Praise gospel choir performs in New Orleans, relying on one of the oldest ways to express convictions collectively—singing.

Theodore Newcomb's study of student attitudes at Bennington College richly illustrates the value-expressive function of attitudes (Newcomb, 1958). Newcomb studied all 600 students who attended Bennington, an isolated, experimental liberal arts college in pastoral Vermont—brand new at the time of Newcomb's study in the mid-1930s. The school was left-leaning in its politics, and it was run by charismatic, liberal professors. The students, on the other hand, were largely from upper-class, Protestant, Republican families. The question was: Would the students' conservative background or the liberal context in which they were immersed for several years prevail in shaping their political attitudes?

As it turns out, the experience at Bennington College shaped the students' political attitudes profoundly and in a lasting fashion (which may, in part, account for your parents' ambivalence about your departure to college). In a four-year period, most students' political conservatism changed dramatically. This attitude change played out in their voting preferences, as you can see in **Figure 8.1**. First-year students were much more likely to prefer the Republican candidate; fourth-year students, the Democratic or radical left-wing candidate. And in a follow-up

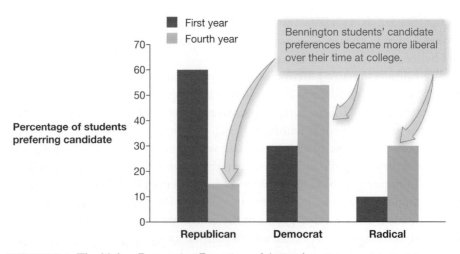

FIGURE 8.1 The Value-Expressive Function of Attitudes (Source: Adapted from Newcomb, 1958.)

study of 129 students about 25 years later, 60 percent of these former students voted for the more liberal presidential candidate, John F. Kennedy, in his election against Richard Nixon. This finding suggests that the changes these women underwent during college stayed with them throughout their lives.

Other findings attest to the value-expressive function of holding liberal attitudes at Bennington College. Most notably, liberal students tended to garner greater respect from their Bennington peers and to be better integrated into college groups than the conservative students. The conservative students, in contrast, were less likely to be leaders in the eyes of their peers, and they felt more alienated at the college and were likely to spend more time at home. Whether students became liberals or remained conservatives, their attitudes reflected a deep value-expressive function.

The Knowledge Function of Attitudes

A fourth function of attitudes is the **knowledge function**, by which attitudes help organize our understanding of the world. Our attitudes guide what we attend to and remember. They make us more efficient, and sometimes more biased, perceivers of the complex social situations we experience. Most typically, we pay attention to and recall information that is consistent with our preexisting attitudes (Eagly & Chaiken, 1998).

For example, in one study by Lepper, Ross, Vallone, and Keavney (unpublished data), supporters of Jimmy Carter and Ronald Reagan, as well as undecided voters, watched a videotape of a debate between the two candidates during the 1980 presidential campaign. Members of these three groups answered a simple question: Who won the debate? As you can see in **Figure 8.2**, students' preexisting attitudes led partisans to very different conclusions about who emerged victorious. Carter supporters thought Carter had won. Reagan supporters were more strongly convinced that Reagan had won. And the undecided voters were split, although more of them concluded that Reagan had prevailed.

knowledge function An attitudinal function whereby attitudes help organize people's understanding of the world, guiding how they attend to, store, and retrieve information.

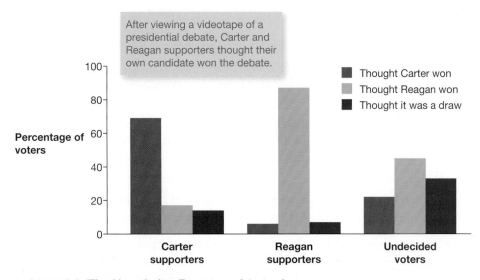

FIGURE 8.2 The Knowledge Function of Attitudes Partisans believe their own candidates prevail in debates, even when viewing the same video. (Source: Adapted from Lepper, Ross, Vallone & Keavney, unpublished data.)

This theme, that our attitudes lead us to seek out and selectively attend to information that bolsters our preexisting attitudes, comes up again and again in social psychology. Our preexisting beliefs and attitudes about a person or group of individuals lead us to selectively recall information that is consistent with those beliefs and attitudes (Fiske & Taylor, 1981; Stangor & McMillan, 1992; see Chapter 4). We like physically attractive individuals, and we interpret their actions more favorably (Dion, Berscheid, & Walster, 1972; see Chapter 10). In contrast, prejudicial attitudes toward different outgroups lead us to interpret the actions of members of those groups negatively, in ways that are consistent with our prejudices (Hamilton & Trolier, 1986; see Chapter 11).

Clearly, a bit of irony is at work here. Our attitudes are built on our experiences and our acquisition of knowledge. Yet eventually our attitudes become entrenched, and they bias us toward being more attentive to new information that supports our attitudes. In the service of efficiency, our attitudes sometimes cause us to sacrifice objectivity.

 Our attitudes serve four functions that are vital to our daily living. They help us identify rewards and threats, they help us avoid unpleasant realities about life and who we are, they are part of why we belong to different groups, and they are powerful guides to our construal of the social world.

PERSUASION AND ATTITUDE CHANGE

The scientific community overwhelmingly agrees that humans are causing the surface of the earth to warm and that this global warming probably will yield catastrophic events—frequent hurricanes that dwarf Katrina (the scourge of New Orleans), rising sea levels (which could put vast parts of coastal states like Florida under water and eliminate many tropical islands), melting polar ice caps, rampant wildfires, and the disappearance of thousands of species. It is also quite clear that all of us can do many things to cut our carbon emissions, a primary source of global warming. Here are just a few:

- We can drive our cars less and rely more on bikes or public transportation.
- We can fly less on vacations.
- We can cut red meat from our diet (you'd be surprised how much that can help).
- We can use energy-efficient light bulbs, toilets, heating systems, and solar panels, all things that right now cost more than the conventional options but that yield many benefits in the long run.
- We can turn off computers and lights when not in use.
- We can buy local produce or grow our own food (this can help reduce carbon emissions because trucking isn't required to deliver the food).

Now imagine that you were charged with the task of producing a public service campaign to persuade people to adopt these habits. This challenge would not be as difficult as changing people's sexual practices to curb AIDS, as has been attempted in African countries. Still, there are plenty of barriers to changing attitudes and behaviors related to cutting carbon emissions. People would have to change old habits (like driving their cars), give up strong preferences (those mouth-watering double cheeseburgers), and adjust their daily routine, taking extra time out of their day to use public transportation or shop at the farmer's market. So what kind of green campaign would you design? The literature on persuasion suggests that there is no simple, one-solution-fits-all means of persuasion. In fact, there are multiple routes to persuasion, and the message that you would craft should depend on whom you are trying to persuade.

A Two-Process Approach to Persuasion

Two important theoretical models were developed in the 1980s to explain how people change their attitudes in response to persuasive messages. The two models, Shelly Chaiken's **heuristic-systematic model** of persuasion (Chaiken, 1980; Chaiken, Liberman, & Eagly, 1989) and Richard Petty and John Cacioppo's **elaboration likelihood model** (**ELM**) of persuasion (Petty & Cacioppo, 1979, 1984, 1986), were developed independently and employ different vocabularies. But essentially they are quite similar (**Figure 8.3**). For the sake of convenience, the following discussion is organized around the elaboration likelihood model.

The ELM starts from the assumption that there are two routes to persuasion. Through the **central route** (known as the **systematic route** in Chaiken's model), people think carefully and deliberately about the content of the message. They attend to the logic and cogency (how convincing the argument is) of the arguments contained in the message as well as to the evidence and principles that are cited, and they retrieve relevant experiences, memories, and images. All of this elaborate thinking can lead the individual to change an attitude or not, based on a careful sifting of the arguments and other evidence presented in the message.

heuristic-systematic model A model of persuasion that maintains that there are two different routes of persuasion: the systematic route and the heuristic route.

elaboration likelihood model (ELM) A model of persuasion that maintains that there are two different routes of persuasion: the central route and the peripheral route.

central (systematic) route A persuasive route wherein people think carefully and deliberately about the content of a message, attending to its logic, cogency, and arguments as well as to related evidence and principles.

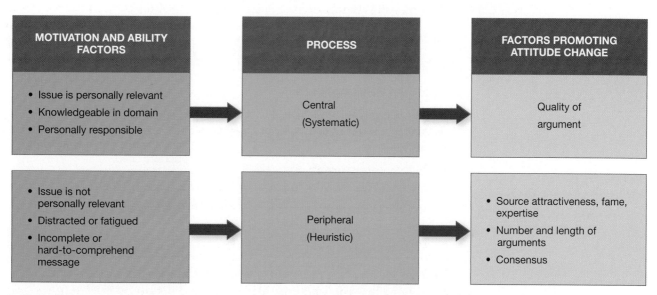

FIGURE 8.3 A Two-Process Approach to Persuasion According to Petty and Cacioppo's elaboration likelihood model, there are two routes to persuasion: a central route and a peripheral route. The routes are engaged by different levels of motivation and ability to attend to the message, and they promote attitude change by different factors. Chaiken's model refers to these two processes as the systematic and heuristic routes, respectively. Note, too, that any persuasion variable—such as communicator expertise—can bring about attitude change through both central and peripheral routes to persuasion.

peripheral (heuristic) route A persuasive route wherein people attend to relatively simple, superficial cues related to the message, such as the length of the message or the expertise or attractiveness of the communicator.

Through the **peripheral route** (known as the **heuristic route** in Chaiken's model), people primarily attend to superficial aspects of the message that are tangential to its substance. Cues tangential to the content of the message—for example, the communicator's expertise or apparent credibility—can be considered as forms of evidence when processed in a deliberate, thoughtful fashion. But when persuasion occurs through the peripheral route, the individual is swayed by these cues without giving much thought to the message itself. Here the individual might consider how long the message is or how expert the communicator seems. Using the peripheral route, the individual relies on relatively simple communication heuristics, or rules of thumb, to justify attitude change. Thus the person might change his or her attitude toward red meat because "a lot of people seem to be saying you shouldn't eat it" or "because there are a lot of arguments against it." Or peripheral cues might change the individual's basic emotional reaction to the attitude object that is the focus of the persuasive message (**Figure 8.4**). An attractive or credible communicator, for example, might make the receiver feel more positively toward the attitude object—such as public transportation—simply by eliciting general feelings of liking or attraction.

What determines whether we will go through the central or peripheral route in responding to a persuasive message? One factor is our *motivation* to devote time and energy to a message. When the message has personal consequences for us, for example, we are more likely to go through the central route and carefully work through the arguments and any other evidence in the message. A second factor is our *ability* to process the message in depth. When the message is clear and we have sufficient time, we are able to process it deeply. When we have little motivation and little ability to process the message, we instead attend to the easy-to-process peripheral cues associated with the message—for example, the appearance and credentials of the communicator.

FIGURE 8.4 You Be the Subject: Central and Peripheral Persuasion Tactics

Go to www.thegreenguide.com

List the central persuasion tactics: the strength, cogency, and clarity of the evidence.

____
____
____
____
____
____

List the peripheral persuasion tactics: the attractiveness and credibility of the source, and the number of arguments and supporters cited.

____
____
____
____
____
____

Results: You may have gravitated to areas of the website that are important or relevant to you in some way (perhaps a section on travel). In these areas, you probably were more attuned to and more influenced by arguments and evidence—central persuasion tactics. In areas less relevant to you (perhaps the section on gardening), you may have been more influenced by peripheral tactics, such as the beauty of the imagery.

Let's look at some specific examples. Three factors make the central route to persuasion more likely: (1) the *personal relevance* of the message—that is, whether it bears on our goals, concerns, and well-being; (2) our *knowledge* about the issue—the more we know, the more likely we are to scrutinize the message with care and thoughtfulness; and (3) whether the message makes us feel *responsible* for some action or outcome—for example, when we have to explain the message to others. In contrast, peripheral processing is triggered by factors that (1) reduce our motivation or (2) interfere with our ability to attend to the message carefully (Eagly & Chaiken, 1993; Petty & Cacioppo, 1986; Petty & Wegener, 1998). Thus, when people are distracted—for example, if they are carrying out some other task—they are more likely to attend primarily to the peripheral cues of the message. People who are tired, who are in an uncomfortable posture, or who are given messages that are incomplete or hard to comprehend are also more likely to focus on the peripheral cues of a message (Kiesler & Mathog, 1968; Petty & Wegener, 1998).

To test the ELM approach to persuasion, researchers typically first generate strong and weak arguments related to an issue. They then present these strong and weak arguments as part of a message. They also vary the potency of various peripheral cues associated with the message, such as the number of arguments offered or the communicator's fame. Finally, they typically vary a factor, such as the personal relevance of the issue, to manipulate the likelihood that the individual will process the message centrally or peripherally. If participants process the message via the central route to persuasion, they should be influenced mainly by the strong and not the weak arguments. The strength of the arguments should be less important for individuals who are attending only to the peripheral cues of the message, however, since these participants should be more affected by such things as the number of arguments and the fame of the communicator.

Consider one study that varied the strength of the arguments, the relevance of the issue, and a peripheral cue, the expertise of the source of the persuasive message. In this study, participants read either eight weak arguments or eight strong arguments in support of a comprehensive exam to be implemented at their school (Petty, Cacioppo, & Goldman, 1981). Personal relevance was manipulated by notifying the participants that this exam would be initiated either the following year, which would mean the participants would have to take the exam, or in ten years (presumably) after the students' graduation. Finally, source expertise was varied: half of the participants were told the arguments were generated by a local high school class, and half were told that the arguments were generated by the "Carnegie Commission on Higher Education" chaired by a Princeton University professor.

Take a close look at **Figure 8.5**. You can see that when the message was not relevant to the students—that is, when the exam was to be implemented ten years later—the expertise of the source mattered, but the strength of the argument did not matter as much. The participants with scant motivation to attend to the message gave little thought to the quality of the arguments, but they were moved by whether the arguments were produced by a high school class or a professorial committee. The results differed for participants who would have to take the exam; for them, the message was clearly relevant. They were more persuaded by strong than by weak arguments, but they were less influenced by whether the communicator was an expert.

In this comprehensive exam study, high personal relevance was linked to being persuaded by the strength of the arguments, whereas low personal relevance led

"Of the modes of persuasion furnished by the spoken word there are three kinds. The first kind depends on the personal character of the speaker; the second on putting the audience into a certain frame of mind; the third on the proof, provided by the words of the speech itself."

—Aristotle

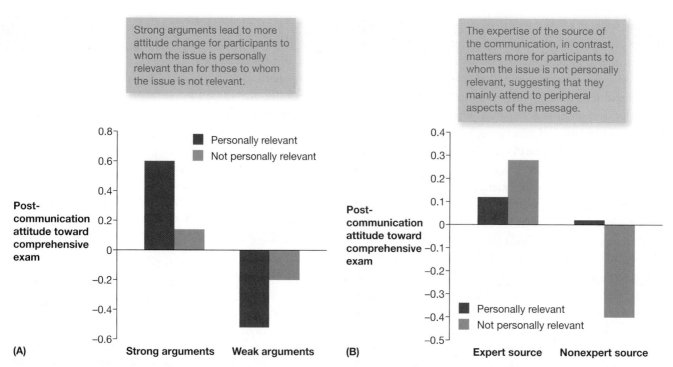

FIGURE 8.5 Central or Peripheral Route to Persuasion Attitude change can be brought about by strong arguments when people are motivated and by the expertise of the communicator when people aren't motivated. (Source: Adapted from Petty & Cacioppo, 1986, p. 154.)

participants to be persuaded by source expertise. Note, though, that both the ELM and HSM argue that persuasion variables such as argument strength and source expertise are not tied to a single route of persuasion. Instead, persuasion variables can serve multiple roles, affecting persuasion through either the central (systematic) or peripheral (heuristic) route depending on the circumstances (Chen & Chaiken, 1999; Petty, 1997; Petty & Brinol, 2008). To illustrate, it is certainly the case that the expertise of the source of a persuasive message often changes people's attitudes through the peripheral route, given how little effort it takes to notice that someone is an expert. But if people are highly motivated and have the ability to think carefully, source expertise could function as an argument whose strength is evaluated: if its strength is judged to be high, persuasion is enhanced, but if strength is perceived to be low, then persuasion is hindered. Source expertise could also affect persuasion through the central route by biasing (for example, making more favorable) the thoughts people generate about an attitude object or issue (Chaiken & Maheshwaren, 1994; Tormala, Brinol, & Petty, 2007).

Overall, the routes to persuasion are twofold. Some circumstances or messages prompt thoughtful integration of new arguments and evidence into people's belief systems, thus promoting attitude change. At other times we engage in less effortful thinking and are more persuaded by superficial cues—the beauty or charm of the communicator, for example—or even by subliminal cues (**Box 8.1**). If you're interested in more enduring attitude change, however, your best bet is to convince people through the central route. Using the central route, people attend to the message more carefully, and its effects are more pronounced. The central, compared to the peripheral, route of persuasion is thought to bring about

BOX 8.1   FOCUS ON MODERN LIFE

A Subliminal Route to Persuasion?

In 1990, the rock band Judas Priest was tried for contributing to the suicide deaths of Ray Belknap and James Vance. Prosecutors alleged that the men had been led down the path to suicide by the subliminal message "Do it" that the band had embedded into one of its songs. Can subliminal messages have such powerful effects? Might subliminal messages be a third, implicit or unconscious, route to persuasion?

Subliminally presented stimuli can activate certain concepts and even shape people's everyday thoughts, feelings, and actions (Dijksterhuis, Aarts, & Smith, 2005). Consider a pair of laboratory experiments suggesting that subliminal persuasion attempts may be effective. In one, pictures of a target person were shown to participants immediately after a subliminal presentation of either a pleasant image (for example, a child playing with a doll) or an unpleasant one (for example, a bloody shark). When later asked to evaluate the target person, those for whom the target was paired with positive subliminal images provided more favorable evaluations than those exposed to negative images (Krosnick, Betz, Jussim, & Lynn, 1992). In a study that directly examined the impact of subliminal messages on behavior, participants were told not to drink anything for 3 hours before arriving at the experiment (Strahan, Spencer, & Zanna, 2002). Upon arrival, half the participants were allowed to quench their thirst and half were kept thirsty. Participants were then subliminally primed, some with words related to thirst (*thirst, dry*) and some with neutral words (*pirate, won*). They were then allowed to drink as much as they wanted of each of two beverages. Thirsty participants who were primed with thirst-related words drank significantly more than thirsty participants primed with neutral words. A follow-up study using the same procedure found that subliminal messages can even influence a person's *choice* of beverage. Specifically, the two beverages that participants were offered were described as sports drinks—one labeled Super-Quencher and the other Power-Pro. When asked at the end of the experiment how many discount coupons for the two drinks they would like, thirsty participants who were exposed to thirst-related subliminal messages requested 24 percent more of the Super-Quencher coupons than thirsty participants exposed to neutral subliminal messages.

Should we be alarmed that advertisers, political campaign managers, or rock bands might try to alter our behavior by bombarding us with messages we can't see? Maybe not. The outside world and the laboratory environment differ in a number of important ways that make these effects less likely to be so strong in daily life. The focus of the persuasion attempt in these studies is typically something that people have no firm opinion about, such as a new sports drink. It's one thing to shift people's attitudes and behavior with respect to neutral stimuli; it's another thing entirely to shift people's attitudes and behavior with respect to more familiar, psychologically significant stimuli—for example, to get Republicans to vote for a Democratic candidate or to induce Coke drinkers to switch to Pepsi. In addition, the subliminal message in the laboratory is presented right before the target attitude or behavior is assessed, and the individual encounters no competing messages in the interim. That's almost never the case in the real world. A subliminal command to "Drink Coke" could conceivably motivate people to leave their seats to get a drink; but once in the lobby, with advertisements for all sorts of merchandise screaming at them, they might be as likely to drink Pepsi as Coke or even to order a candy bar instead of a beverage.

In fact, no studies have ever demonstrated that subliminal stimuli induce people to do something they are opposed to doing. There is no reason to believe that being subliminally primed with the words "Do it" would lead anyone not already comfortable with the idea of suicide to kill himself. Nor is there any reason to believe that Democrats can be subliminally induced to vote Republican, Apple enthusiasts to buy a Dell, or clean-cut adolescents to join a cult.

Subliminal Advertising In a television ad run by the Republicans during the 2000 presidential election, the word *RATS* was quickly flashed on the screen in a subliminal attack on Al Gore, the Democratic candidate, and his Medicare plan.

attitude change that is more enduring, more resistant to persuasion, and more predictive of behavior (Eagly & Chaiken, 1993; Mackie, 1987; Petty, Haugtvedt, & Smith, 1995).

Now that you have a better sense of how persuasive messages work, let's look at some more specific investigations of how—and how well—persuasion works. Many of these studies were inspired by an influential approach to attitude change developed by Carl Hovland and his colleagues at Yale University starting in the 1940s and 1950s (Hovland, Janis, & Kelley, 1953). Their Yale School approach, which was stimulated by their work on mass communication for the army during World War II, broke down the persuasive message into three components: (1) the who, or source of the message; (2) the what, or content of the message; and (3) the whom, or target of the message.

Source Characteristics

Perhaps more than ever, the rich, the famous, and the good-looking are spokespeople for social causes. For example, actor Matt Damon is cofounder and a highly visible spokesperson for water.org, an organization devoted to getting clean water to impoverished countries. What are the effects of having such striking spokespeople for different causes? These kinds of questions, concerning *who* delivers the message, are called source characteristics. **Source characteristics** are independent of the actual content of the message and, within the framework of the ELM, can be powerful means for changing people's attitudes.

Persuasion and Celebrity Endorsements Advertisers often use celebrities to endorse and advertise their products, public service announcements, and social campaigns, believing that the person who delivers the message is an important factor in convincing people to buy their products or join the cause. A recent example is Lady Gaga's highly publicized anti-bullying campaign.

Attractiveness One important source characteristic is the *attractiveness* of the communicator. The lead singer of U2, Bono, has emerged as the best-known spokesperson for the plight of African nations, just edging out Angelina Jolie. Glamorous movie stars regularly appear in public service announcements—for example, urging teens to read, stay in school, or avoid bullying or taking drugs. From one perspective, these campaigns make no sense, for beauty (or celebrity) has no logical connection to the trustworthiness of an opinion about a consumer product or risky behavior. But here the ELM helps: attractive communicators can promote attitude change through the peripheral route of persuasion. For example, we like and trust physically attractive people (see Chapter 10) and, for good or ill, this simple fact can make us more likely to endorse the attitudes they communicate.

Social psychological research shows that attractive communicators are more persuasive than less attractive communicators (Petty & Cacioppo, 1986). Attractive communicators could lead to persuasion through the central route—for example, by increasing the favorability of people's effortful thinking about the position they are endorsing. However, most research on source attractiveness has shown that attractive communicators are particularly persuasive to people for whom the message is not important and who have little knowledge in the domain, circumstances that make people more likely to attend to peripheral cues like a source's attractiveness (Chaiken, 1980; Petty, Cacioppo, & Schumann, 1983; Wood & Kallgren, 1988).

Credibility A second influential source characteristic is the *credibility* of the communicator. Credibility refers to the combination of expertise and trustworthiness of the communicator. Advertisers try to use credibility to their advantage. Ads for toothpaste and aspirin cite the testimonials from medical professionals who endorse the product. Actors who play doctors on television and who have no obvious knowledge about medicine have even been brought in to endorse health-related products. ("I'm not a real doctor, but I play one on TV.") Is this an effective tactic? What would the ELM predict? As you may have anticipated, such communicators produce more attitude change in circumstances that promote the peripheral route to persuasion. Thus communicators perceived to be high in credibility produce more persuasion when the topic is of little personal relevance to the target or when the target is distracted, since such a target would not be paying much attention to the message itself (Kiesler & Mathog, 1968; Petty, Cacioppo, & Goldman, 1981; Rhine & Severance, 1970). A target who happens to be highly motivated and able to think carefully may still be susceptible to source credibility. The target may, for example, interpret the high credibility of the source as a strong argument in favor of changing his or her attitude toward the position the credible source is endorsing.

The Sleeper Effect What about all the noncredible communicators who crowd the airwaves these days—the crackpots maintaining that the Holocaust never happened, that AIDS is not caused by sexual contact, or that global warming is a hoax? Do these messages fall on deaf ears? An early study by Hovland and Weiss (1951) suggests otherwise. In this study, participants first rated the likelihood that a nuclear submarine would be built in the near future (at the time, they did not exist). Five days later, participants read an essay about the imminence of nuclear submarines and were told the essay was written either by the highly credible physicist Robert Oppenheimer, the "father of the atomic bomb," or by a noncredible journalist who worked for *Pravda*, the propaganda newspaper of the former Soviet Union. As you might expect, the Oppenheimer essay led to greater attitude change than the essay by the less credible *Pravda* writer, even though the content of the essay was exactly the same.

Much more surprising, however, was that four weeks later, the participants who had read the essay by the *Pravda* writer, although unmoved initially, actually shifted their attitudes toward the position he advocated. This latter effect came to be known as the **sleeper effect**—that is, messages from unreliable sources exert little influence initially but over time have the potential to shift people's attitudes. Careful research by Anthony Pratkanis, Tony Greenwald, and their colleagues has identified how the sleeper effect works. It seems that over time, people dissociate the source of the message from the message itself. You hear some loose

Credibility and Persuasion If people believe that a communicator is sincere, knowledgeable, and trustworthy, they are more likely to believe the message. Martin Luther King Jr. is pictured here at the Lincoln Memorial during the March on Washington in August 1963 as he is about to give his "I Have a Dream" speech. His actions in the months leading up to the rally, as well as his strong and poetic words and dramatic presentation, contributed to his credibility and ability to persuade.

"Every time a message seems to grab us, and we think, 'I just might try it,' we are at the nexus of choice and persuasion that is advertising."

—Andrew Hacker

sleeper effect An effect that occurs when messages from unreliable sources initially exert little influence but later cause individuals' attitudes to shift.

cannon on talk radio arguing forcibly against the evidence for global warming. Initially, you discount his message because of his lack of credibility. But over time, the message has the chance to influence your views because you dissociate the source of the message from its content. More important, when cues that challenge the noncredible source *precede* the message—for example, when the trustworthiness of the communicator is called into question at the get-go—the sleeper effect does not occur (Pratkanis, Greenwald, Leippe, & Baumgardner, 1988). In this case, people develop a negative reaction to the ensuing message and counterargue against it, thus reducing its impact.

Message Characteristics

message characteristics Aspects of the message itself, including the quality of the evidence and the explicitness of its conclusions.

Ever since Aristotle, philosophers have sought to elucidate the principles of persuasive messages, taught today in courses on rhetoric and marketing. What are the **message characteristics** that make a communication persuasive? By now you should anticipate what the ELM might say: that it depends on the audience's motivation and ability to process the message.

Arguing against Self-Interest
Patrick Reynolds, the grandson and heir of the late R. J. Reynolds (founder of the R. J. Reynolds Tobacco Company, the second-largest tobacco company in the United States and manufacturer of such brands as Camel, Kool, Winston, and Salem cigarettes), is shown speaking to students about the dangers of smoking. He watched his father and older brother both die of emphysema and lung cancer brought on by cigarette smoking and decided to devote his life to antismoking advocacy. His antismoking speeches and support for a smoke-free society have high credibility given his family history and the fact that his arguments, if effective, would ultimately reduce his inheritance.

Message Quality As you saw in Figure 8.3, *high-quality messages* are more persuasive in general and are especially so for people who find the message relevant, who have knowledge in the domain, and who feel responsible for the issue. What, then, makes for high-quality messages? In general, higher-quality messages convey the desirable yet novel consequences of taking action in response to the message (Burnstein & Vinokur, 1973); they often appeal to core values of the audience (Cacioppo, Petty, & Sidera, 1982); and they are straightforward, clear, and logical (Chaiken & Eagly, 1976; Leippe & Elkin, 1987).

In general, you will produce more attitude change if you make your conclusions explicit (Hovland, Lumsdaine, & Sheffield, 1949) and if you explicitly refute the opposition, thereby giving the receiver of the message material to use in counterarguing against subsequent opposing messages (Hass & Linder, 1972; Petty & Wegener, 1998). And you will be more persuasive if you argue against your own self-interest. For example, Walster, Aronson, and Abrahams (1966) found that a message delivered by a prison inmate advocating longer prison sentences was more persuasive than a message in which the same prisoner argued for shorter sentences. When someone argues in a direction contrary to obvious self-interest, the source of the message is perceived to be more sincere.

Vividness What about the truth of persuasive messages (**Box 8.2**)? Do facts stand a chance when pitted against vivid but improbable statements? Research by Hamill, Wilson, and Nisbett (1980) suggests that *vivid information* embedded in a personal narrative with emotional appeal can be more persuasive than statistical facts that are objectively more informative. In their study, the researchers first assessed participants' attitudes toward welfare. In one condition, participants read a vivid, gripping story about a woman who was a lifetime welfare recipient. This story was based on one Ronald Reagan told to great effect about a "welfare queen," a lifetime recipient of welfare who exploited the system to enjoy a life of

Lie to Me

The popular television show *Lie to Me* is based on the research of social psychologist Paul Ekman, who did the early studies of the universality of facial expression. Lying, of course, is one of the most challenging acts of persuasion: to get someone to believe the opposite of what you actually believe. Ekman, Bella DePaulo, and others have discovered certain clues to discern whether someone is lying or telling the truth. When people lie, they are more likely to show speech hesitations, face touches, micro-expressions of negative emotion, leg jiggles, speech dysfluencies (when two words get mixed up and form new words), sudden rises in the pitch of the voice, and increased eye contact (DePaulo, Lanier, & Davis, 1983; Ekman, O'Sullivan, Friesen, & Scherer, 1991; Mehrabian & Williams, 1969; Riggio & Friedman, 1983).

How good are we at catching liars? It turns out that we are surprisingly inept at this important task. Ekman and his colleagues have presented videotapes of people lying and telling the truth to thousands of people (Ekman & O'Sullivan, 1991). Participants simply had to indicate whether each person was lying or telling the truth. Whereas chance guessing would yield accuracy rates of 50 percent, people were correct, on average, only 57 percent of the time. This same research yielded interesting answers about who's particularly good at catching liars. What's your guess? Contrary to what you might expect, those sages of the human character—judges, clinicians, and psychological scientists—proved no better than the average person. The one group that shone in their ability to catch liars was secret service agents, because they get a sound training in the social psychology of lying just reviewed.

comfort and leisure. In another condition, participants were given facts about welfare: that the average stay was two years and that only 10 percent of welfare recipients received welfare for four years or more. In a third condition, participants were given both the vivid narrative and the facts. In this condition, it should have been clear that the case they read about was quite atypical of welfare recipients in general. Which message do you think would lead to more attitude change: the vivid but unrepresentative story or the plain facts? You no doubt are anticipating the punch line: students were much more likely to change their attitudes after hearing the vivid story—even when they also had the cold statistics. The facts did little to alter their attitudes.

Vivid images abound in the media, and apparently to great effect. Messages warning of global warming depict baby polar bears floating perilously on melting blocks of ice in the sea. The nightly news highlights the single murder, kidnapping, or fire in its local coverage. ("If it bleeds, it leads"; see Chapter 4.) More generally, the power of vivid images is evident in the **identifiable victim effect**. Vivid, flesh-and-blood victims are often more powerful sources of persuasion than abstract statistics (Collins, Taylor, Wood, & Thompson, 1988; Shedler & Manis, 1986; Taylor & Thompson, 1982). For example, Ryan White contracted HIV at age 13 and struggled nobly with the disease until succumbing some six years later. Following his death, the U.S. Congress passed the Ryan White Care Act, which funds the largest set of services for people living with

"The death of a single Russian soldier is a tragedy. The death of a million soldiers is a statistic."

—Joseph Stalin

identifiable victim effect The tendency to be more moved by the plight of a single, vivid individual than by a more abstract number of individuals.

The Identifiable Victim Effect
People are often more persuaded to act on behalf of a cause by portrayals of clearly identifiable victims, such as the children in this compelling ad for UNICEF.

AIDS in the country. It is clear that Ryan's moving, noble six-year struggle with AIDS did more to shift people's attitudes about the disease than any amount of statistics or medical argument.

Fear What does fear do for persuasive communications? Let's return to our hypothetical question about running a carbon emissions reduction campaign. Should you scare the daylights out of people with images of refugees, food shortages, wildfires, and flooded coastal areas? The ELM offers somewhat competing notions regarding fear and persuasion. On the one hand, intense fear could disrupt the careful, thoughtful processing of the message, thus reducing the chances of persuasion. On the other hand, the right kind of fear might heighten the participant's motivation to attend to the message, thus increasing the likelihood of attitude change.

What does the evidence say? In general, it is advisable to make ad campaigns frightening and also to provide information about how to act on that fear (Boster & Mongeau, 1984). In a study that first lent support to this recommendation, Howard Leventhal and his colleagues tried to change the smoking habits of participants in one of three ways. Some participants were shown a graphic film of the effects of lung cancer, which included footage of a lung operation in which the blackened lung of a smoker was removed. Other participants were given a pamphlet with suggestions about how to quit smoking. A third group was shown the film and given the pamphlet (Leventhal, Watts, & Pagano, 1967). Participants who saw the scary film reduced their smoking more than did those who just read the pamphlet (and thus did not have their motivation to quit increased by a fear induction). Fear by itself can be persuasive. But participants who both saw the film and read the pamphlet decreased their smoking the most, as you can see in **Figure 8.6**, which presents participants' self-reports of their

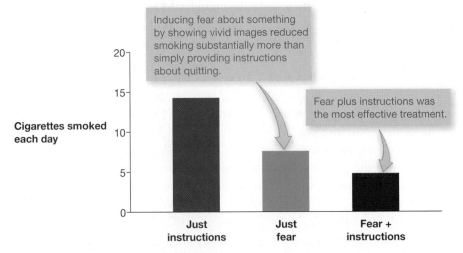

Inducing fear about something by showing vivid images reduced smoking substantially more than simply providing instructions about quitting.

Fear plus instructions was the most effective treatment.

FIGURE 8.6 Fear and Persuasive Messages Moderate levels of fear lead to attitude change. (Source: Adapted from Leventhal, Watts, & Pagano, 1967.)

daily smoking behavior one month after the intervention. In general, persuasive messages that provide information that can be acted on can be highly effective (Leventhal, 1970; Leventhal et al., 1967; Robberson & Rogers, 1988). However, it is possible to frighten people so much that they will choose to deny the danger rather than act to combat it, especially if there is no clear recommendation about how to deal with the threat (Becker & Josephs, 1988; Job, 1988; Rogers & Mewborn, 1976).

Culture Vividness and fear aren't the only factors that make a message persuasive. How a message is targeted to a particular cultural group also matters. Thus the sort of message content we find in the media of independent and interdependent societies differs substantially. Marketing experts Sang-pil Han and Sharon Shavitt analyzed the advertisements in American and Korean news magazines and women's magazines (Han & Shavitt, 1994). They found that the American ads emphasized benefits to the individual ("Make your way through the crowd" or "Alive with pleasure"), whereas Korean ads focused on benefits to collectives ("We have a way of bringing people closer together" or "Ringing out the news of business friendships that really work"). Han and Shavitt also conducted experiments in which they manipulated the content of advertisements and measured their effectiveness. They found that the individual-oriented ads were more effective with American participants and that the collective-oriented ads were more effective with Korean participants.

(A)

(B)

Message Characteristics and Targeting Messages may differ based on the times and culture. Messages are often targeted to collective concerns in interdependent societies and to individual concerns in independent societies. Similarly, messages may vary at different times in the same society. (A) During World War II, U.S. army posters stressed collective concerns. (B) In recent times, army recruitment posters highlight individual characteristics cultivated by military service, such as individual strength.

Receiver Characteristics

Communication by its very nature always involves both a communicator and someone who receives the message. Consistent with the ELM, receivers who are more personally involved, knowledgeable, and responsible respond to messages quite differently from those who are less motivated. More generally, certain people are more vulnerable, or amenable, to persuasion. **Receiver characteristics** such as personality, mood, and age can matter, often in surprising and significant ways.

Need for Cognition One facet of personality that influences the likelihood of attitude change is called the *need for cognition* (Cacioppo, Petty, Feinstein, & Jarvis, 1996), which refers to the degree to which people like to think deeply about things. People high in the need for cognition like to think, puzzle, ponder, and consider multiple perspectives on issues. This is the kind of person who passes his or her time on the subway reading *Scientific American* or completing complex puzzles. People low in the need for cognition don't find thought and contemplation to be that much fun. As you might imagine, people with a high need for cognition are more persuaded by high-quality arguments and are relatively unmoved by peripheral cues of persuasion (Cacioppo, Petty, & Morris, 1983; Haugtvedt & Petty, 1992).

Persuasion and Mood The mood of an audience can affect whether a message will lead to attitude change. In Germany in the 1930s, Adolf Hitler staged rallies like this Hitler Youth rally to create a mood of strength and unity that would encourage people to support his ideas.

Mood A second important audience characteristic is *mood*. People who are good at communication go to great lengths to create a particular mood in their audience. Hitler staged enormous rallies for his most important speeches, surrounded by bold Nazi banners, awesome displays of military strength, and thousands of supporters signaling in unison. His intent was to stir the emotions of his audience to make them more receptive to his ideas. Persuasive communicators create other kinds of audience moods than the somber atmosphere of Nazi rallies. Ronald Reagan, known as "the great communicator," was famous for his disarming, infectious humor during his speeches and press conferences. (During one visit to a university, students were giving him the silent treatment because he cut state funding for colleges. After walking past ranks of these silent protesters, Reagan turned, put a finger to his mouth, and said, "Shhh.")

Studies have found that people who were exposed to persuasive messages while eating or listening to beautiful music were more likely to change their attitudes, presumably through the peripheral route of persuasion (McGuire, 1985). Mood can affect persuasion through the central route as well. For instance, work by Duane Wegener and Richard Petty strongly suggests that persuasive efforts through the central route are more likely to be successful when the mood of the message matches the mood of the receiver. Specifically, more pessimistic, counterattitudinal messages tend to prompt greater message processing in sad or depressed people, whereas uplifting, optimistic, pro-attitudinal messages prompt greater message processing in happy people (Bless et al., 1996; Mackie & Worth, 1989; Wegener & Petty, 1994; Wegener, Petty, & Smith, 1995).

Age Finally, what about the *age* of the audience? As you might have guessed, younger people are more susceptible to persuasive messages than are adults or the elderly (Sears, 1986). This finding has great real-world significance. For example, one of the main sources of Ronald Reagan's political success was the overwhelming support he received from the 18 to 25 age group, the same demographic group that would back Barack Obama in overwhelming numbers 28 years later. This young age group is quite malleable in its political allegiances.

Another real-world application of the age effect in persuasion has to do with relying on children as witnesses in legal cases. How seriously should courts take the testimony of young children—for example, in child abuse cases—if their attitudes can be so readily altered by motivated attorneys and misleading questions (Loftus, 1993, 2003)? A final problem concerns the extent of advertising directed at young children. Given that advertising, and the media more generally, can shape people's attitudes and does so more for the young than for the old, perhaps we should worry about the immense amount of advertising that is directed at children aged 16 and younger.

David Sears has drawn on this link between age and susceptibility to persuasion as part of a broader commentary on the persuasion literature (Sears, 1986). Most studies of attitude change involve participants who are students in their first couple of years in college. These individuals are at a developmental stage that is very dynamic, as illustrated by the Bennington College study, and they are particularly prone to attitude change. And as people age, their attitudes become less malleable. Sears poses a thorny question: Does the literature on attitude change generalize to other age groups? It is likely, he concludes, that the persuasion literature overestimates the extent to which our attitudes can be changed by would-be persuaders. The final section of this chapter elaborates on this theme and discusses instances in which people resist attitude change.

Let's now return to your campaign to change people's everyday habits to reduce carbon emissions. How might the literature on persuasion help you? Perhaps the most important lesson is to tailor your message according to the individual receiving the message. Certain people—including those for whom global warming is personally relevant, who know quite a bit about the crisis, who feel a sense of personal responsibility about it, and who have a high need for cognition—are likely to go through the central route, responding to the deeper substance of the message. For people like this, there is no substitute for high-quality messages, ones that are logical and clear, that make subtle rather than heavy-handed recommendations, and that appeal to clear consequences and values.

For many other people, and in many contexts, the peripheral route to persuasion is likely to be a better bet. For example, the peripheral route is likely to be more effective for younger audiences, for those who know less about global warming, and for people who don't think that global warming is relevant to their lives. Here you might resort to attractive environmentalists (Matt Damon), highly credible ones (Nobel Prize–winning scientists), and messages that have the weight of various communication heuristics working in your favor.

The elaboration likelihood and heuristic-systematic models spell out two ways of processing persuasive messages. When motivation and ability are high, persuasion is likely to occur through the central (systematic) route, whereby people are persuaded on the basis of a careful, systematic analysis of a message, such as the strength of its arguments. When motivation and ability are low, attitude change tends to occur through the peripheral (heuristic) route, whereby people are persuaded by easy-to-process cues such as the sheer number of arguments and communicator attractiveness. Messages tend to be more effective if they are clearly laid out, if they refute opposing messages, if they match recipients' cultural values, and if they are vivid. Recipients of a message who have a high need for cognition are more likely to process messages through the central route. Moreover, recipients who are in a good mood are more persuadable than those who are not, and younger people are more persuadable than older people.

THE MEDIA AND PERSUASION

We all live in a media-saturated world. A recent compilation of studies found that the average American adult watches 4.34 hours of TV and video a day, surfs the Internet on average for 2.47 hours, listens to an average of 1.34 hours of radio, and reads newspapers or magazines for an average of 0.44 hours (eMarketer, 2011). All told, over half of Americans' waking hours are spent in contact with the media, which significantly exceeds the time they spend in face-to-face social interaction with friends and family.

Given our media-saturated lives, it's easy to imagine that almost all of our attitudes are shaped by mass communication. Decisions to buy a Dell or an Apple laptop or Levi's or Gap jeans could be guided by commercials recently seen on TV or heard on the radio. Which candidate we choose in the voting booth could be guided by recent political ads. Indeed, many conspiracy theories are based on the notion that our daily life is controlled by all-pervasive media organizations, owned and operated by a hidden and nefarious elite. Are we really so susceptible to media influence?

third-person effect The assumption by most people that "other people" are more prone to being influenced by persuasive messages (such as those in media campaigns) than they themselves are.

In what is known as the **third-person effect**, most people assume that "other people" are more prone to being influenced by persuasive campaigns than they themselves are—that others do not share their powers of rational analysis and restraint (Duck & Mullin, 1995; Hoorens & Ruiter, 1996; Perloff, 1993; Vallone, Ross & Lepper, 1985). In one study of the third-person effect, participants judged the likely impact of three media presentations on themselves and on other respondents (Innes & Zeitz, 1988). For all three presentations—a political ad campaign, a story about levels of violence portrayed in the media, and a campaign designed to deter people from associating with individuals who drink and drive—participants rated others as more likely to be influenced than themselves.

So how powerful are the media in actually shaping our attitudes? Documenting the effects of the media on people's attitudes is no simple task. Researchers have done some experiments, but more typically they have relied on survey methodologies whereby people report which programs and ads they have seen. Retrospective self-reports, however, are notoriously fallible. If participants say they have seen some ad, or say they have not, how can researchers be sure? How can they be certain that viewers saw the ad under the same conditions? And once again, what about self-selection effects? For example, highly motivated citizens are more likely to tune in to political ads than are less motivated citizens (Iyengar, 2004). Any effect of the ad campaign is confounded by these differences in political motivation.

Notwithstanding these difficulties, many studies attest to the power of the media. For example, research has shown that violence in the media and video games does indeed make people more aggressive (see Chapter 13). But the effects of the media are not always as robust as you might imagine. Let's study a few examples of how the media sometimes produce surprisingly little attitude change. This review serves as a platform for considering how people resist persuasive attempts.

The Surprisingly Weak Effects of the Media

William McGuire reviewed the evidence regarding the effects of intensive media campaigns on fairly specific behaviors and found remarkably small, sometimes nonexistent, effects (McGuire, 1985, 1986). His conclusions have generally stood the test of time. People are often quite independent-minded in the face of the media glut. Let's look at three specific cases in which the media have had surprisingly weak or nonexistent effects.

Consumer Advertising   Advertising in the United States is a multibillion-dollar industry. Do the captivating Nike or Abercrombie & Fitch commercials make you go out and buy their products? McGuire claims they don't. When researchers have looked carefully at the correlation between the ad budget of a product and its market share—that is, the proportion of consumers who buy a product—they have found a very weak or nonsignificant correlation. Even when such effects do occur, they are usually short-lived and typically last less than one year (Bird, 2002; Landes & Rosenfield, 1994). How much a company spends on a product may have little direct effect on whether people buy it. Ads do have other effects, however, that may indirectly influence purchasing behavior. Ads have been shown to increase product loyalty, product awareness, and warm or excited feelings about the product, all of which may in turn influence purchasing behavior (McGuire, 1986).

Political Advertising   What about political ads? As elections draw near, our TVs become filled with dramatic and, at times, controversial political ads. Here numerous studies by political scientists have challenged conventional wisdom: most studies document no significant correlation between the amount a candidate spends on an election and success in the election (Jacobson, 1978; Levitt, 1994). A study of the 1976 Democratic presidential primaries did find a correlation between a candidate's expenditures and the number of votes obtained, but only during the early stages of the campaign. Other variables, such as the candidate's previous success, were more important in predicting the candidate's ultimate success (Grush, 1980). Relevant studies indicate that political ads have very small effects on voting behavior (Kaid, 1981). They mainly influence late-deciding voters, and they are as likely to influence voters against as for the advertised candidate. Work by Ansolabehere and Iyengar (1995) suggests that certain kinds of ads, most notably negative ads that aggressively critique the opponent, may turn potential voters off from voting. As support for this claim, these authors note the

Political Advertising In presidential elections, billions of dollars are spent in creating positive ads that play up the strengths and likability of the candidate.

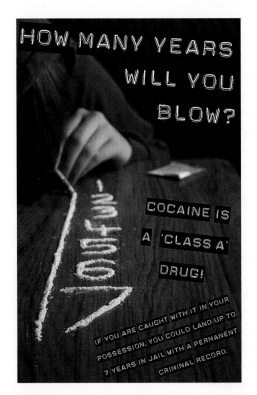

Public Service Ads Public service ads try to persuade people to avoid drugs or alcohol or cigarettes or unsafe sex and instead to engage in healthy and productive behaviors. This antidrug ad was part of a campaign to encourage kids to choose not to take drugs.

historical rise in negative ads and the drop in voter turnout in presidential elections. In 1960, voter turnout for the presidential election was 62 percent; by 1988, it had slipped to 50 percent (although it did rise to 57 percent in the 2008 election). In a careful study of the 1992 Senate campaigns, Ansolabehere and Iyengar divided campaigns into negative ones (defined by attack advertisements) and positive ones (defined by ads offering reasons to vote for a given candidate). The positive Senate campaigns averaged a higher voter turnout (57 percent) than the negative campaigns (49.7 percent).

Public Service Announcements Public service announcements (PSAs) are inserted into television breaks and urge the public to follow beneficial health or social practices. They present compelling arguments against taking drugs or smoking cigarettes or engaging in unsafe sex. Other PSAs encourage parents to read to their children, to play with them, and to praise them. Do these have much effect on later behavior? Again, the answer appears to be no (Tyler, 1984). Careful studies have found that well-designed, heavily exposed campaigns against drug abuse, for example, have had little impact on children's knowledge about the dangers of drugs or, more important, their drug-taking behavior (Schanie & Sundel, 1978). This includes the D.A.R.E. campaign, an extremely expensive and widely used program to discourage drug use. A recent longitudinal study found that children who participated in the D.A.R.E. program in sixth grade did not differ in how much they smoked cigarettes, drank alcohol, or used illegal drugs when they were 20 years old compared with appropriately matched comparison children who did not participate in D.A.R.E. (Lynam et al., 1999).

Though standard mass communication efforts often have little impact, some novel methods of persuasion have proved effective. For example, when adolescents are taught by the use of scenarios how to turn away requests for unprotected sex, reports of unprotected sex and rates of sexually transmitted diseases (STDs) go down (Jemmott, Jemmott, & Fong, 1998; Jemmott, Jemmott, Braverman, & Fong, 2005).

The Media and Conceptions of Social Reality

Studies have largely supported McGuire's provocative claim that the media's persuasive efforts often have little impact on people's attitudes and behaviors, in particular when the ads in question target specific behaviors. Our behaviors, after all—whether we buy the BlackBerry or iPhone, whether we engage in safe sex or not—are determined by a complex combination of forces. It seems unlikely that out of the white noise of the competing messages from the media that bombard us each day, one message in particular would prompt us to take specific action.

Others have argued, however, that the media have an even more unsettling influence: they shape our very conception of social reality (Eibach, Libby, & Gilovich, 2003). Specific advertisements may not lead us to buy specific products, but they might lead us to a conviction that personal happiness is to be found in materialistic pursuits. Political ads may not lead us to vote for a particular candidate, but they may lead us to conclude that the country is going downhill.

Political scientist Shanto Iyengar refers to this effect of the media as **agenda control**: the media shape what you think is important and true. For example, the prominence of issues in the news media—fear of crime or concern about traffic congestion or worry about the economy—is correlated with the public's perception that those issues are important (Dearing & Rogers, 1996; Iyengar & Kinder, 1987). In one experiment, viewers saw a series of newscasts. In one condition, they saw three stories dealing with U.S. dependence on foreign energy sources; in another, six such stories; and in a final condition, no stories like this. When exposed to no news about dependence on foreign energy, 24 percent of the viewers cited energy as one of the three most important problems facing the country. This percentage rose to 50 percent for the participants who saw three stories on the subject and to 65 percent for the participants who saw six stories (Iyengar & Kinder, 1987). So a politician in office should hope that news reports focus on things that are going well at the time, and a politician who wishes to defeat the incumbent should hope that the media focus on things that are not going well (**Box 8.3**).

George Gerbner and his colleagues have explored the agenda control thesis by coding the content of television programs and looking at the attitudes of heavy television viewers (Gerbner, Gross, Morgan, & Signorielli, 1986). It should come as no surprise that the world depicted on TV scarcely resembles social reality. On prime-time programs, for example, males outnumber females by a factor of 3 to 1. Ethnic minorities, young children, and the elderly are underrepresented. Crime is wildly more prevalent per unit of time on prime-time television than in the average U.S. citizen's real life. And heavy television viewers—namely, those who watch 5 hours or more per day—construe social reality much like the reality they view on television. Heavy television viewers tend to endorse more racially prejudiced attitudes. They assume that women have more limited abilities than men. They overestimate the prevalence of violent crime and assume that the world is quite dangerous and sinister. And they overestimate the number of physicians

agenda control Efforts of the media to select certain events and topics to emphasize, thereby shaping which issues and events people think are important.

BOX 8.3   FOCUS ON THE MEDIA

The Hostile Media Phenomenon

On July 23, 2008, with the presidential race heating up and the gap between John McCain and Barack Obama narrowing, John McCain sat down to talk with Sean Hannity of Fox News. Along with a discussion of the war in Iraq, the central topic they covered was media bias. McCain and Hannity claimed that the media were treating Barack Obama uncritically, in biased fashion, reacting to him as if he were a rock star rather than looking critically at his political agenda. This allegation of media bias was in part political ploy, but also a tendency long observed in politicians and citizens alike. President George W. Bush liked to refer to the media as "the filter," expressing the conviction that the mainstream media reported on his presidency through a biased political lens that reflected badly on his views and agenda. Richard Nixon felt that the media were run by an elite Jewish clique. The thesis that the media are ideologically biased regularly produces best sellers that appeal to liberals and conservatives alike. An entire organization, Fairness and Accuracy in Reporting (FAIR; www.fair.org), is devoted to documenting bias in the media (for example, showing that conservatives are more likely to appear as experts on news shows like *Nightline*).

Research by Robert Vallone, Lee Ross, and Mark Lepper (1985) suggests that we all tend to believe that the media are biased against our preferred causes. According to these researchers, most people believe that they see the world in a reasonable, objective fashion. By implication, if a media outlet attempts to present both sides of an issue, it must be biased. This basic tendency to perceive the media as hostile is a regularity in the political theater of presidential politics and a common feature of our perception of the media. For example, in one telephone survey conducted three days before the 1980 presidential election, among Jimmy Carter supporters who felt that the media had favored one candidate in its coverage, 83 percent thought that it favored Reagan. In contrast, for Reagan supporters who felt the media had been biased, 96 percent felt that the media had favored Carter.

and lawyers in the population. Of course, these findings could be the result of self-selection effects. Perhaps more prejudiced, cynical, and ignorant people watch more television in the first place, and these individual differences are producing such results.

Guided by the agenda control thesis, Shelly Grabe, L. Monique Ward, and Janet Shibley Hyde have asked whether exposure to media makes women more vulnerable to body image problems, a central threat to the health and well-being of young women (Grabe, Ward, & Hyde, 2008). Females in today's magazines, television shows, and movies are thinner than females in the real-life population; many meet the body weight criteria for anorexia. Experimental studies have looked at the short-term effects of being exposed to images of thin females in the media, and correlational studies have looked at whether girls and women who consume high levels of media have body image problems. Regrettably, both kinds of evidence find that women who are exposed to images of thin females in the media are more likely to accept this thin ideal as normal, to feel dissatisfied about their own bodies, and to engage in problematic eating behaviors.

 Media persuasion effects—at any rate, advertising effects—are weaker than people might assume, even though most of us believe that the media are quite effective, at least for other people. The greatest effects of the media seem to involve influencing our conceptions of reality and exerting agenda control—that is, making us feel that some issues are particularly important.

RESISTANCE TO PERSUASION

The media seem to have their greatest effects indirectly in shaping our most basic assumptions about social reality. But why don't they have more powerful effects on what we purchase, who we vote for, or whether we follow the wisdom of campaigns seeking that we live in healthier ways? Why are the effects of the media generally small and sometimes even nonexistent? Part of the answer lies in the fact that many of the important principles of social psychology—the power of our perceptual biases, of preexisting commitments, and of prior knowledge—serve as sources of independent thought and significant forces of resistance in the face of persuasive attempts.

Attentional Biases and Resistance

When the Office of the Surgeon General issued its 1964 report linking smoking to lung cancer, it would seem to have provided incontrovertible evidence about the health risks of smoking, requiring smokers and nonsmokers alike to shift their attitudes toward smoking. And yet, after the release of the report, 40 percent of smokers found the report flawed compared with 10 percent of nonsmokers. We all would like to think that we can absorb data and information in relatively unbiased fashion (Pronin, Gilovich, & Ross, 2004) and that if we learned that a habit was dangerous to our health, we would alter our attitudes toward that habit accordingly. But our minds sometimes respond selectively to information in a way that maintains our original attitudes.

Let's break this assertion down a bit. First, several studies indicate that people are inclined to *attend selectively* to information that confirms their original attitudes (Eagly & Chaiken, 1998; Sweeney & Gruber, 1984). That is, we tune in to information that reinforces our attitudes, and we tune out information that contradicts them. In one illustrative study, students who either supported or opposed the legalization of marijuana listened to a message that advocated legalization (Kleinhesselink & Edwards, 1975). The message contained 14 arguments: 7 were strong and difficult to refute (and clearly appealing to the pro-marijuana students), and 7 were silly and easy to refute (and very attractive to the anti-legalization students). The students heard the message over earphones accompanied by a continual static buzz. To combat this problem, students were allowed to press a button to eliminate the buzz for 5 seconds, thus revealing the information they preferred to attend to—arguments that were consistent with their attitudes or that opposed their position.

As you might have anticipated, the pro-legalization students pushed the button more often when the speaker was delivering the strong arguments in favor of legalization—wanting to hear the information that would reinforce their preexisting attitudes. The anti-legalization students, in contrast, were more likely to push the button while the speaker offered up the easy-to-refute arguments in favor of legalization, the very information that would reinforce their position. In a similar study, students who were asked to write essays about federal funding for abortion or the use

of nuclear energy tended to select as reference material for their essays magazine articles that supported their opinion (McPherson, 1983). During presidential elections, many people are more inclined to read newspapers, blogs, and websites that support their preferred candidate and to avoid those that support the opposition.

Not only do we selectively attend to and seek out information that supports our attitudes, we also *selectively evaluate* the information we take in. Specifically, we are prone to look favorably on information that supports our attitudes and critically on information that contradicts our attitudes. For example, in one study, Ziva Kunda (1990) had female and male students read a story presented as a *New York Times* article that detailed how caffeine consumption in females is associated with an increased risk of fibrocystic disease. Half of the participants were high-caffeine users—fans of lattes, cappuccinos, and on hot days Diet Coke or Mountain Dew. The other participants were low-caffeine users. The female high-caffeine users, of course, should have considered the article most threatening and thus should have greeted it with the greatest skepticism. As you can see in **Figure 8.7**, this expectation was confirmed. Independent of caffeine use, the male participants found the article fairly convincing, as did the females who used little caffeine. Only the high-caffeine-using females were less convinced by and more critical of the article.

In related research, Peter Ditto and colleagues have shown that people are more critical of evidence that violates cherished beliefs about their personal health (Ditto & Lopez, 1992). Patients who receive diagnoses indicating that they are unhealthy are more likely to downplay the seriousness of the diagnosis and the validity of the test that produced the diagnosis (Ditto, Jemmott, & Darley, 1988). In a clever extension of this work, Ditto and Lopez (1992) gave undergraduates a test of a fictitious medical condition called "TAA deficiency" that was supposedly associated with pancreatic disorders later in life. The test was simple: to put saliva on a piece of yellow paper and observe whether it would change color in

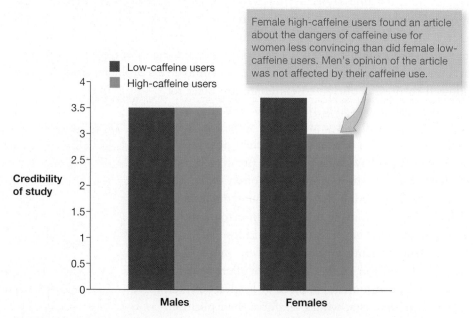

FIGURE 8.7 Selective Evaluation People who are personally motivated will derogate information that challenges cherished beliefs. (Source: Adapted from Kunda, 1990.)

the next 20 seconds. In the deficiency condition, participants were told that if the paper remained the same color (yellow), they had the medical condition; in the no-deficiency condition, participants were told that if the paper changed to a dark green, they had the medical condition. The paper remained yellow throughout the study. Clearly, participants in the deficiency condition would be motivated to see the paper change color, and they should be disturbed by the evidence they were confronted by—that the paper remained yellow. And indeed, these participants took almost 30 seconds longer than participants who received more favorable evidence to decide that their test was finished. Given our tendency to selectively attend to and evaluate incoming messages in ways that confirm our preexisting attitudes, it is no wonder the media has such difficulty in producing attitude change. Most messages, it would seem, are preaching to the choir.

Previous Commitments and Resistance

Many persuasive messages fail because they cannot overcome the target's previous commitments. For example, recent empirical research reveals that our political allegiances are often passed from parent to child and seem to be part of our DNA (**Box 8.4**). Political ads that try to convince potential voters to shift their political allegiances must, in effect, convince voters to abandon these deep commitments—not a likely outcome. Similarly, antidrug campaigns are designed to reduce the drug-taking behavior of individuals who may be engaging in a habitual act that is embedded in a way of life and a community of friends.

There is also evidence that public commitments make people resistant to attitude change (they also make people resistant to conformity; see Asch's line judgment studies in Chapter 9). In some studies, participants are asked to make public statements regarding their attitudes (Kiesler, 1971; Pallak, Mueller,

---

BOX 8.4 FOCUS ON BIOLOGY

The Genetic Basis of Attitudes

One of the deepest sources of our commitment to important attitudes and our resistance to persuasive messages is our genes. Work by Abraham Tesser (1993), of the University of Georgia, suggests that our attitudes are in part inherited. To support this claim, Tesser examined the attitudes of monozygotic (identical) twins, who share 100 percent of their genes, and the attitudes of dizygotic (fraternal) twins, who share 50 percent of their genes. For most attitudes surveyed, the identical twins' attitudes were more similar than those of fraternal twins. This was true, for example, for attitudes about the death penalty, jazz, censorship, divorce, and socialism. Moreover, researchers found that the more heritable attitudes were also more accessible, less susceptible to persuasion, and more predictive of feelings of attraction to a stranger who shared those attitudes. Of course, there is no gene for attitudes toward censorship or socialism; the hereditary transmission must occur through some other element of temperament, such as a fear of novelty (which might make you dislike jazz but be more tolerant of censorship), impulsivity, or a preference for risk taking.

More recent research by James Fowler and his collaborators has found that genes account not only for politically relevant attitudes, as Tesser documented, but for political participation (Fowler, Baker, & Dawes, 2008). More specifically, they found that identical twins were more likely to resemble each other than were fraternal twins in sharing party affiliations and in their likelihood of voting in an election in Los Angeles. No wonder it's often hard to shift people's political attitudes and voting preferences; doing so would require changing a basic part of who they are.

Dollar, & Pallak, 1972). When participants make public commitments to their attitudes—as people do every day when they discuss politics and social issues with their friends—they are more resistant to subsequent counterattitudinal messages than are control participants.

Why might public commitments increase people's resistance to persuasive communications? The most obvious reason is that it is hard to back down from a public commitment, even when evidence is presented against the position we took. Another reason is not so obvious: public commitments engage us in more extended thought about a particular issue, which tends to produce more extreme, entrenched attitudes. Abraham Tesser's **thought polarization hypothesis** supports this reasoning. To test his hypothesis, Tesser measured participants' attitudes toward social issues, such as legalizing prostitution (Tesser & Conlee, 1975). He then had the participants think for a few moments about the issue. When they stated their attitudes toward the same issue a second time, they routinely gave stronger ratings: both opponents and proponents became polarized. The repeated expression of attitudes has led to more extreme attitudes in a variety of domains, including attitudes toward people, artwork, fashions, and football strategies (Downing, Judd, & Brauer, 1992; Judd, Drake, Downing, & Krosnick, 1991; Tesser, Martin, & Mendolia, 1995). A caveat is in order here, however. Increased thought about an attitude object can lead to more moderate attitudes for people who have previously had little motivation to think about the issue or little preexisting knowledge about the issue (Judd & Lusk, 1984).

Knowledge and Resistance

According to the ELM approach to attitude change, prior knowledge makes people scrutinize messages much more carefully. People with a great deal of knowledge are more resistant to persuasion. Such people have more beliefs, emotions, and habits tied up with their attitudes, which should make their attitudes more resistant to change. This intuition has been borne out in the experimental literature (Haugtvedt & Petty, 1992; Krosnick, 1988; Lydon, Zanna, & Ross, 1988; Zuwerink & Devine, 1996). For example, in a study of attitudes toward environmental preservation, Wendy Wood (1982) divided students into two groups: those who were pro-preservation and knew a lot about the issue and those who were pro-preservation but less knowledgeable about the subject. In a second session, she exposed these two groups of students to a message opposed to environmental preservation. The students with a great deal of knowledge about the environment moved only a little in their attitudes, and they counterargued a great deal in response to the message, relying on what they already knew and strongly believed about the issue. The less knowledgeable students, however, shifted their attitudes in the direction of the anti-preservation message, for they had less knowledge to rely on to counterargue against the message.

Attitude Inoculation

Thus far, this section has examined how people's belief systems—their biases, commitments, and preexisting knowledge—make them resistant to attitude change. This resistance is due to the more general tendency to selectively attend to, and favorably evaluate, evidence that supports preexisting attitudes. Certain

thought polarization hypothesis
The hypothesis that more extended thought about a particular issue tends to produce more extreme, entrenched attitudes.

techniques can be used to further these tendencies to resist persuasion—or to instill them in people with less commitment, knowledge, and confidence in their opinions.

William McGuire has developed such a technique, which finds inspiration in a rather unusual source: the inoculations we receive against viruses. When we receive an inoculation, we are exposed to a weak dose of the virus. Exposure to this small dose of the virus stimulates our immune system, which then is prepared to defend against exposure to larger doses of the virus. McGuire believed that resistance to persuasion could be encouraged in a similar fashion, by **attitude inoculation**—small attacks on our beliefs that would engage our attitudes, prior commitments, and knowledge structures and thereby counteract the larger attack (McGuire & Papageorgis, 1961).

attitude inoculation Small attacks on people's beliefs that engage their attitudes, prior commitments, and knowledge structures, enabling them to counteract a subsequent larger attack and be resistant to persuasion.

In studies attesting to the efficacy of attitude inoculation, McGuire first assessed participants' endorsements of different cultural truisms, such as "It's a good idea to brush your teeth after every meal if at all possible" or "The effects of penicillin have been, almost without exception, of great benefit to mankind" (McGuire & Papageorgis, 1961). More than 75 percent of the participants checked 15 on a 15-point scale to indicate their agreement with truisms like these.

Then came the intervention. McGuire and Papageorgis exposed participants to a small attack on their belief in the truism. For example, in the toothbrushing case, the participants might read, "Too frequent brushing tends to damage the gums and expose the vulnerable parts of the teeth to decay." In some conditions, the researchers asked the participants to refute that attack by offering arguments against it; this was the attitude inoculation. In other conditions, the researchers asked the participants to consider arguments in support of the truism. Then, some time between 1 hour and 7 days later, the researchers asked the participants to read a three-paragraph, full-scale attack on the truism.

Figure 8.8 presents data that attest to the immunizing effectiveness of attitude inoculation. As you can see in the first column, before the attack, participants strongly endorsed the truism. The subsequent, forceful attack did indeed reduce the belief in the truism for those people who faced no initial attack (the second column). But having earlier refuted a mild attack against the truism led people to substantially resist the subsequent stronger attack (the third column). Furthermore, counterarguing against the initial attack was clearly more effective than generating arguments that supported the truism (the fourth column).

Think how useful attitude inoculation might be. For example, in smoking prevention programs, adolescents might be presented with pro-smoking arguments likely to be advanced by peers and advertisements (for example, "Smoking is about freedom and maturity") and then encouraged to counterargue against these pressures—a clear example of attitude inoculation.

Changes in Attitude Certainty

In the preceding discussion of resistance to persuasion, the implication has been that if people resist a persuasive appeal, their attitude toward the target object has not changed. But in most research in this area, "no attitude change" means that no change has occurred in the direction or extremity of the target attitude. But is it possible that other facets of the attitude are changed, even though the attitude remains, say, moderately negative? A growing body of research by Tormala,

FIGURE 8.8 Scientific Method: Attitude Inoculation

Hypothesis: Defending small attacks on core attitudes makes people resistant to persuasion.

Research Method:

1. Researchers assessed participants' endorsements of a cultural truism.

2. Participants then experienced a small attack on their belief in the truism.

3. In the attitude inoculation condition, the researchers asked participants to offer arguments against the attack. In other conditions, the researchers asked the participants to consider arguments in support of the truism.

4. Between one hour and seven days later, the researchers asked the participants to read a full-scale attack on the truism.

Results: Before the attacks, participants strongly endorsed the truism. The full-scale attack reduced the belief in the truism for participants who faced no initial attack (second bar). But participants in the attitude inoculation condition substantially resisted the subsequent stronger attack (third bar). Attitude inoculation was more effective than generating arguments in support of the truism (fourth bar).

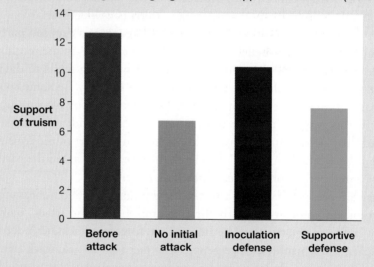

CONCLUSION: Attitude inoculation, in which people use preexisting attitudes, commitments, and knowledge to come up with counterarguments, makes people more resistant to attitude change.

Source: Adapted from McGuire & Papageorgis (1961).

Petty, and their colleagues (Tormala & Petty, 2002; Tormala, Clarkson, & Petty, 2006) suggests that the conviction or certainty with which an attitude is held may change even if the direction and extremity of an attitude do not. Understanding factors that influence attitude certainty is important because attitudes higher in certainty predict behavior better (Fazio & Zanna, 1978), stand up to persuasive appeals better (Wu & Shaffer, 1987), and persist longer over time (Bassilli, 1996). When and how exactly might resistance to persuasion influence attitude certainty?

In a typical experiment investigating this question, participants are exposed to a counterattitudinal persuasive message (a message arguing in favor of an issue that participants are known or safely assumed to be against) and are asked to argue against the message. Both before and after this exercise, researchers assess the certainty with which participants hold their attitude on the relevant issue. Studies like this have shown that when people resist persuasion (that is, the direction and extremity of their attitude do not change), the process of resisting it can increase *or* decrease attitude certainty. Resistance enhances attitude certainty when people perceive that they have resisted persuasion, that the message they resisted was strong, and that the source of the message was credible (Tormala & Petty, 2002; Tormala & Petty, 2004a, 2004b). If people do not perceive themselves as having resisted persuasion (even if their attitudes indicate that they did), or if they see the resisted message as weak and its source noncredible, attitude certainty does not increase.

On the flip side, resistance to persuasion can decrease attitude certainty if people feel like they did a bad job of resisting a persuasive message, coming up with weak arguments against the message (Tormala, Clarkson, & Petty, 2006). They may feel this way even when the direction and extremity of their attitude did not change in response to the message. Furthermore, when people perceive that they did a poor job resisting persuasion, the relevant attitude is less likely to predict behavior and leaves them more vulnerable to future counterattitudinal persuasive messages. The irony, then, is that initial resistance to persuasion can at times lead the relevant attitude to be more susceptible to subsequent persuasive attempts. Overall, this research represents an important direction for the literature on resistance to persuasion; resisting persuasion involves more than whether the direction and extremity of attitudes are changed.

 Media efforts and attempts by others to change people's attitudes are not as effective as most of us believe. People often selectively attend to and evaluate information that confirms their original attitudes and beliefs, and they ignore or criticize information that disconfirms them. Preexisting commitments to political ideologies or values increase resistance to counterattitudinal messages and persuasion. Attitude inoculation, or small attacks on our beliefs, can make us resistant to attitude change since the small attacks give us the chance to muster arguments we can use when faced with stronger attacks on our beliefs and attitudes. Finally, resistance to persuasion may involve changes in the conviction with which an attitude is held, even as the direction and extremity of the attitude remain intact.

Chapter Review

Summary

Functions of Attitudes

- Attitudes serve several functions. They serve a *utilitarian function*, signaling rewards and punishments. They serve an *ego-defensive function*, protecting people from undesirable beliefs and emotions. They serve a *value-expressive function*, reflecting values that people want others, especially their *reference groups*, to acknowledge. And attitudes serve a *knowledge function*, organizing how people construe the social world and guiding how people attend to, store, and retrieve information.

Persuasion and Attitude Change

- Both the *heuristic-systematic model* of persuasion and the *elaboration likelihood model* of persuasion hypothesize that there are two routes to persuasion. Factors determining which route is used include motivation, or how important the message is to the person, and ability to process the message.

- When using the *central (systematic) route* to persuasion, people attend carefully to the message, and they consider relevant evidence and underlying logic in detail. People are especially likely to go through this route when the message is relevant to them, when they have knowledge in the domain, and when the message evokes a sense of personal responsibility. When going through the central route, people are more persuaded by high-quality messages.

- In the *peripheral (heuristic) route to persuasion*, people attend to superficial aspects of the message. They use this route when they have little motivation or time or ability to attend to its deeper meaning. In this route, people are persuaded by source characteristics, such as attractiveness and credibility of the communicator, and message characteristics, such as how many arguments there are and whether the conclusions are explicit.

- The elements of the persuasive process can be broken into three components: the *source* of the message, the *content* of the message, and the *target* of the message.

- A noncredible source is unlikely to induce immediate attitude change, but with time, a *sleeper effect* may occur, in which attitude change occurs after time has passed and the message has become dissociated from its source.

- Vivid communications, including images of *identifiable victims*, are usually more effective than matter-of-fact ones, and fear-evoking communications that provide fear-reducing courses of action produce more attitude change than either non-fear-evoking communications or fear-evoking communications that do not provide fear-reducing courses of action.

- Message content often varies in independent and interdependent societies. Ads in independent cultures emphasize the individual, and ads in interdependent societies emphasize the collective.

- The target, or audience, of a message also affects whether a particular message is effective and whether attitude change occurs. Audience, or *receiver*, characteristics include the need for cognition (that is, how deeply people like to think about issues), mood, and age.

The Media and Persuasion

- According to the *third-person effect*, most people believe that other people are more likely to be influenced by the media than they are. But in fact, the media have surprisingly weak effects on most people. This is true in the case of consumer advertising (which rarely leads to long-lived effects), political advertising (which has small effects on most voters and mainly affects late-deciding voters), and public service announcements (which are unlikely to have a lasting impact on behavior unless they are also accompanied by specific suggestions and practice in avoiding negative behaviors).

- The media are most effective in *agenda control*—that is, in shaping what people think about. They do so through the number of stories and discussions they present on various issues—such as terrorism, moral values, war, the environment, or the economy—that therefore are likely to be present in people's minds.

Resistance to Persuasion

- People can be resistant to persuasion because of preexisting biases, commitments, and knowledge. People selectively attend to and evaluate information in accordance with their original attitudes, tuning in information that supports their preexisting attitudes and beliefs and tuning out information that contradicts them.

- Public commitment to a position helps people resist persuasion. Just thinking about an attitude object can produce *thought polarization*, or movement toward extreme views that can be hard for a communicator to alter.

- People with more knowledge are more resistant to persuasion because they are able to counterargue against messages that take an opposite position to what they know and believe.

- Resistance to persuasion can be encouraged through *attitude inoculation*, exposing a person to weak arguments against his or her position and allowing the person to generate arguments against it.

- Even if the direction and extremity of a person's attitude remain intact, resistance to persuasion may change the certainty with which the person holds the attitude.

Key Terms

agenda control (p. 297)

attitude inoculation (p. 303)

central (systematic) route (p. 281)

ego-defensive function (p. 276)

elaboration likelihood model (ELM) (p. 281)

heuristic-systematic model (p. 281)

identifiable victim effect (p. 289)

knowledge function (p. 279)

message characteristics (p. 288)

peripheral (heuristic) route (p. 282)

receiver characteristics (p. 292)

reference groups (p. 277)

sleeper effect (p. 287)

source characteristics (p. 286)

third-person effect (p. 294)

thought polarization hypothesis (p. 302)

utilitarian function (p. 275)

value-expressive function (p. 277)

Further Reading and Films

Eagly, A. H., & Chaiken, S. (1993). *The psychology of attitudes*. Fort Worth, TX: Harcourt Brace & Company. An excellent overview of the literature on attitudes.

Orwell, G. (1990). *1984*. New York: Signet (originally published in 1945). A superb consideration of propaganda by a great novelist and essayist.

Pratkanis, A. R., & Aronson, E. (2000). *Age of propaganda*. New York: Freeman. An overview of the empirical science of the media and propaganda.

Riefenstahl, L. (Director). (1934). *Triumph of the will* [Motion picture]. Germany: Leni Riefenstahl-Produktion. An unnerving documentary of the Nazi Party rally at Nuremberg in 1934, showing Adolf Hitler's persuasive power as an orator as he whips a large number of people into an emotional state.

Zimbardo, P. G., & Leippe, M. R. (1991). *The psychology of attitude change and social influence*. New York: McGraw-Hill. An excellent and engaging treatment of attitudes and persuasion.

CHAPTER 9

Social Influence

A YOUNG WOMAN IN 1980 would be more likely to be seen smoking a cigar than wearing a tattoo. Before the late 1980s, tattoos were rarely seen on anyone besides sailors and prison inmates. Now they can be found on architects, homemakers, even doctors, professors, and judges. A study published in 2007 by the Pew Research Center found that approximately 40 percent of those under 40 have at least one tattoo, and 10 percent of Americans over 40 years of age have one. These figures were probably too low by the time they were published (and they are almost certainly too low now), but they do reflect the surge in the popularity of tattoos over the past few decades.

The sudden rise in the popularity of tattoos is a compelling demonstration of the power of social influence. After all, the millions of people who went to their local tattoo parlor and paid for a permanent image somewhere on their body did not all suddenly sense the virtues of body art on their own. Instead, they influenced one another. To be sure, the influence sometimes was implicit ("Look at that cool butterfly Jill has on her ankle") and other times explicit ("Check out our sorority letters on my ankle; you should get them too").

Social influence, whether explicit or implicit, is likely to account for prison guards abusing inmates (see Chapter 1), schoolchildren failing to stop a bully, or soldiers suppressing their fear and charging into battle. Sometimes people consciously decide to copy others or go along with their demands or requests; other times they just go along without awareness that their behavior is modeled on that of others. This chapter explores the different types of social influence—implicit and explicit—operating in everyday social life.

The topic of social influence highlights, as much as any other in social psychology, an important theme first raised in Chapter 1 of this book: that many seemingly minor and subtle details of a given situation can profoundly affect

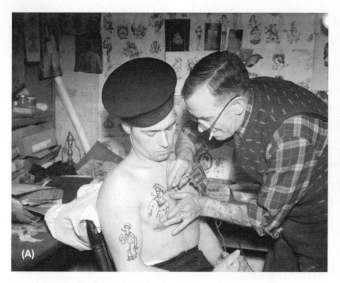

Social Influence and Fashion Social influence affects what we do and say and how we present ourselves to others. (A) In the 1940s, tattoos were rarely seen on anyone other than sailors and soldiers. (B) Today, tattoos are rather common, on both men and women.

people's behavior. As a result, the study of social psychology changes forever the way we view human behavior—whether it be the behavior of bona fide heroes like the firefighters who charged into the World Trade Center to rescue those trapped inside or, at the other end of the spectrum, those who become suicide bombers or participate in acts of genocide, such as the Holocaust in Europe or, more recently, the massacres in the Darfur region of Sudan.

In examining social influence, then, this chapter discusses a number of "situationist classics" in social psychology—experiments that have become well known, both in the field of psychology and in the broader culture, for revealing how seemingly inconsequential elements of a social situation can have surprisingly powerful effects on people's behavior. The results of these experiments have surprised and intrigued generations of students, forcing them to rethink some of their basic assumptions about human nature.

WHAT IS SOCIAL INFLUENCE?

social influence The many ways that people affect one another, including changes in attitudes, beliefs, feelings, and behavior that result from the comments, actions, or even the mere presence of others.

Social influence, broadly speaking, refers to the many ways that people affect one another. It involves changes in attitudes and behavior that result from the comments, actions, or even the mere presence of others. Social influence is a subject to which everyone can relate. Other people routinely try to influence us—whether it be a friend's pressure to go out drinking; Madison Avenue's efforts to get us to adopt the latest fashion; a charity's plea for our time or money; or a parent's, politician's, or priest's attempts to shape our moral, political, or religious values. We are also often the agents of social influence, as when we unconsciously smile at someone for actions we like and frown at someone for actions we dislike, or when we deliberately try to coax a friend into doing us a favor. Effective dealings with others require knowing when to yield to their attempts to influence us and when—and how—to resist. Being effective also demands that we exercise some skill in our attempts to influence others.

Social psychologists distinguish among several types of social influence. The one most familiar to the average person is **conformity**, which social psychologists define as changing one's behavior or beliefs in response to some real (or imagined) pressure from others. As noted earlier, the pressure to conform can be implicit, as when you decide to toss out your loose-fitting jeans in favor of those with a tighter cut (or vice versa) simply because other people are doing so. But conformity pressure can also be explicit, as when members of a peer group pointedly encourage one another to smoke cigarettes, try new drugs, or push the envelope on some new extreme sport.

conformity Changing one's behavior or beliefs in response to explicit or implicit pressure (whether real or imagined) from others.

When conformity pressure is explicit, it shades into another type of social influence called **compliance**, which social psychologists define as responding favorably to an explicit request by another person. Compliance attempts can come from people with some power over you, as when your boss or professor asks you to run an errand, or from peers, as when a classmate asks to borrow your notes. Compliance attempts from powerful people often are not as nuanced and sophisticated as those from peers, because they don't have to be. (Think how much easier it would be for your professor to persuade you to loan her $20 than it would be for a stranger sitting next to you in the classroom.)

compliance Responding favorably to an explicit request by another person.

Finally, another type of social influence, which social psychologists refer to as **obedience**, occurs when the power relationship is unequal and the more powerful person issues a command rather than a request, to which the less powerful person submits.

obedience In an unequal power relationship, submitting to the demands of the more powerful person.

CONFORMITY

If you went back in time to the 1930s and visited any commuter train station, you would notice a number of similarities to and differences from today's commuting scene. One important similarity is that most people (alas, not everyone) would keep to the right, so that collisions and inconvenience are kept to a minimum. But at least two important differences would stand out: nearly all the commuters in the 1930s were men, and nearly all of them wore hats. The transition from a predominantly male workforce in the 1930s to today's more egalitarian workplace was the product of all sorts of forces, large and small, many of them brought to fruition very deliberately and at great cost to the individuals involved. But what about the hats? Was their disappearance over the years deliberate? If so, who did the deliberating? It's hard to resist the conclusion that this trend was much more mindless—that most people simply copied the clothing choices of everyone else.

Is a tendency to go along with others a good thing or a bad thing? In today's Western society, which prizes autonomy and uniqueness, the term *conformity* connotes something bad to most people. If someone called you a conformist, for instance, you probably wouldn't like it. And some types of social influence *are* bad. Going along with a crowd to pull a hurtful prank, try a dangerous new drug, or drive a vehicle while intoxicated are good examples. Other types of conformity are neither good nor bad, as when we conform to the norm to wear athletic shorts very short (as in the 1970s) or very long (as in the 1990s). Still other types of

Conformity Pressures in Daily Life Conformity to what others are doing can be seen in these images of commuters from the 1930s and today. Nearly all of the commuters from the '30s wore hats on their way to work, but very few do today.

conformity are clearly beneficial, both to ourselves (because we don't have to consider every possible action) and to others (because conforming eliminates potential conflict and makes human interaction so much smoother). Conformity plays a big part, for example, in getting people to suppress anger; to pay taxes; to form lines at the theater, museum, and grocery store; and to stay to the right side of the sidewalk or roadway. Would any of us really want to do away with those conformist tendencies? Indeed, evolutionary psychologists and anthropologists have argued that a tendency to conform is generally beneficial. We may be well served by doing what others are doing in the same situation, unless we have a good reason not to (Boyd & Richerson, 1985; Henrich & Boyd, 1998).

Automatic Mimicry

As the cartoon on this page illustrates, sometimes we mindlessly imitate other people's behavior. It is often said that yawning and laughter are contagious, but a great deal of other behavior is as well. Like it or not, we are often subconscious copycats.

The tendency to reflexively mimic the posture, mannerisms, facial expressions, and other actions of those around us has been examined experimentally. In one study, undergraduates at New York University took part in two 10-minute sessions in which each of them, along with another participant, was asked to describe various photographs from popular magazines such as *Newsweek* and *Time*. The other participant was, in reality, a confederate of the experimenter, and there was a different confederate in each of the two sessions. The confederate in one session frequently rubbed his or her face, whereas the confederate in the other session continuously shook his or her foot. As the participant and confederate went about their business of describing the various photographs, the participant was surreptitiously videotaped. Doing so allowed the investigators to

"I don't know why. I just suddenly felt like calling."

determine whether participants tended to rub their faces in the presence of the face-rubbing confederate and shake their feet in the presence of the foot-shaking confederate. The videotapes were taken of the participants only—the confederates were not visible on the tape—so the judges timing how long participants rubbed their faces or shook their feet were unaffected by knowledge of what the confederates were doing.

As predicted, the participants tended to mimic (conform to) the behavior exhibited by the confederate. They shook their feet more often when in the presence of a foot-shaking confederate and rubbed their faces more often when in the presence of a face-rubbing confederate (**Figure 9.1**). Follow-up studies have shown that this tendency to mimic others is particularly strong among people who have an empathic orientation toward others or who have a need to affiliate with others, and when the others in question are well liked (Chartrand & Bargh, 1999; Lakin & Chartrand, 2003; Leighton, Bird, Orsini, & Heyes, 2010; Stel et al., 2010).

Why Do We Mimic? But why do people mindlessly copy others' behavior? There appear to be two reasons. William James (1890) provided the first explanation by proposing his principle of **ideomotor action**, whereby merely thinking about a behavior makes its actual performance more likely. Merely thinking about eating a bowl of gourmet ice cream, for example, makes us more likely to actually open the freezer, take out the ice cream, and indulge. And merely thinking that we might type the wrong letter on the computer keyboard makes us more likely to type that very letter (Wegner, 1994; Wegner, Ansfield, & Pilloff, 1998). The principle of ideomotor action is based on the fact that the brain regions responsible for perception overlap with those responsible for action. When this principle is applied to mimicry, it means that when we see others behave in a particular way, the idea of that behavior is brought to mind (consciously or otherwise) and makes us more likely to behave that way ourselves.

The second reason we reflexively mimic others is to prepare for interaction with them, interaction that is likely to go more smoothly if we establish some

ideomotor action The phenomenon whereby merely thinking about a behavior makes its actual performance more likely.

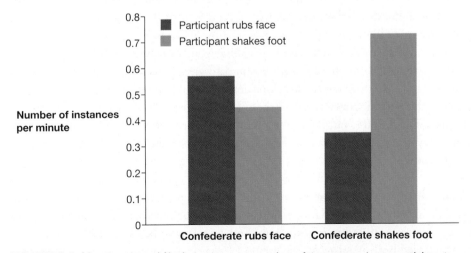

FIGURE 9.1 Unconscious Mimicry Average number of times per minute participants performed an action (face rubbing, foot shaking) while in the presence of someone performing that action or not. (Source: Adapted from Chartrand & Bargh, 1999.)

Ideomotor Action and Conformity When we see others behave in a particular way, we may unconsciously mimic their postures, facial expressions, and behavior. Before the signing of the 1995 Mideast Peace Accord, Bill Clinton, Israeli Prime Minister Yitzhak Rabin, Egyptian President Hosni Mubarak, and King Hussein of Jordan all adjusted their ties, as Yasser Arafat, who was not wearing a tie, looked on.

rapport. Chapter 4 discusses a study in which participants who were led to think about old people acted more like old people themselves, taking longer to walk out of the laboratory to the elevator. It's as if the very idea of old people made them mindlessly prepare for being around the elderly by slowing down their own movements. This idea receives support from follow-up studies showing that the tendency to automatically adopt the behavior of members of different social categories holds true only for those with a positive attitude toward the group in question—that is, those who might be expected to want to interact with members of the category and have the interaction go well. Individuals with positive attitudes toward the elderly tended to walk more slowly when the category "elderly" was primed, but those with negative attitudes toward the elderly tended to walk faster (Cesario, Plaks, & Higgins, 2006).

It appears, then, that we tend to mimic others as a way of laying the groundwork for smooth, gratifying interaction. And it works! Studies have found that people tend to like those who mimic them more than those who do not, even when they are not aware of being mimicked (Chartrand & Bargh, 1999). What's more, individuals who have been mimicked tend to engage in more prosocial behavior immediately afterward—such as donating money to a good cause or leaving larger tips to the person who mimicked them (van Baaren, Holland, Kawakami, & van Knippenberg, 2004; van Baaren, Holland, Steenaert, & van Knippenberg, 2003). Mimicry seems to be a helpful first step on the road to harmonious interaction and goodwill.

Cultural Differences in Mimicry Cultures differ in how much they expect mimicry in social interactions and in how much they are thrown off when the people they interact with fail to mimic them. Sanchez-Burks, Bartel, and Blount (2009) interviewed both Anglo-American and Hispanic-American middle managers in a large corporation. The interview resembled a job interview, and participants had a chance to win a large amount of money if they performed particularly well.

In some of the sessions, the interviewer deliberately mirrored the interviewee's behavior: he crossed his legs when the interviewee crossed his or hers, rested his chin on his hand when the interviewee did that, and so on. In other interviews, the interviewer was careful to avoid mirroring the interviewee. Being attuned to the emotions and behavior of others is more characteristic of Hispanic cultures than of Anglo-American cultures, and Sanchez-Burks and his colleagues believed that such attunement includes sympathetically mirroring the behavior of others. The researchers therefore anticipated that the Hispanic interviewees would do better in the interview when the interviewer mirrored their behavior than when he or she did not. Their findings confirmed this expectation. When the interviewer mirrored a Hispanic interviewee, the interviewee reported less anxiety and was rated more highly by observers than when the interviewer did not do any mirroring. For Anglo-American interviewees, it made no difference whether the interviewer mirrored their behavior or not.

Informational Social Influence and Sherif's Conformity Experiment

An early conformity experiment by Muzafer Sherif (1936) dealt with a type of conformity that is somewhat less automatic and reflexive. Sherif was interested in how groups influence the behavior of individuals by shaping how reality is perceived. He noted that even our most basic perceptions are influenced by frames of reference. (In the well-known Müller-Lyer illusion reproduced in **Figure 9.2**, for example, one vertical line appears longer than the other because of how the lines are "framed" by the two sets of arrows.) Sherif designed his experiment to examine the circumstances in which other people serve as a *social* frame of reference.

Sherif's experiment was built around the autokinetic illusion, the illusion that a stationary point of light in a completely darkened environment is moving. Ancient astronomers noted this phenomenon, which occurs because in complete darkness there are no other stimuli to help the viewer sense where the light is located. Perhaps, Sherif thought, other people would fill the void and serve as a frame of reference against which the viewer could assess his or her perceptions of the light's movement. To begin, Sherif put individual participants in a darkened room, presented them with a stationary point of light on trial after trial, and had them estimate how far it "moved" each time. What he found was that some people thought, on average, that the light moved very little on each trial (say, 2 inches), and others thought it moved a good deal more (say, 8 inches).

Sherif's next step was to bring several participants into the room together and have them call out their estimates. He found that people's estimates tended to converge over time. Those who individually had thought the light had moved a fair amount soon lowered their estimates; those who individually had thought it had moved very little soon raised theirs (**Figure 9.3**). Sherif argued that everyone's individual judgments quickly fused into a group norm, and the norm influenced how far the light was seen to move. A follow-up experiment reinforced his interpretation, finding that when participants were brought back for individual testing up to one year later, their judgments still showed the influence of their group's earlier responses (Rohrer, Baron, Hoffman, & Swander, 1954).

Social psychologists typically interpret the behavior of Sherif's participants as the result of **informational social influence**, or the use of other people—their

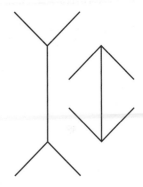

FIGURE 9.2 The Müller-Lyer Illusion In the Müller-Lyer illusion, the framing of the vertical lines by the arrows affects how people perceive their lengths. Even though the two vertical lines are exactly the same length, the vertical line on the left appears longer than the vertical line on the right because of its outward-pointing "fins" at the top and bottom, as opposed to the inward-pointing fins at the top and bottom of the line on the right.

informational social influence The influence of other people that results from taking their comments or actions as a source of information about what is correct, proper, or effective.

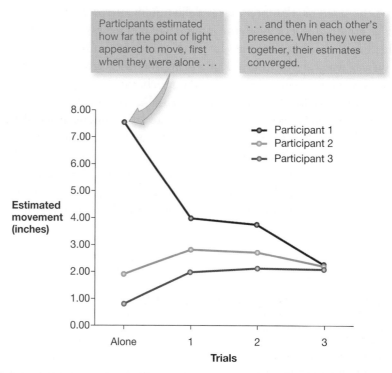

Participants estimated how far the point of light appeared to move, first when they were alone . . .

. . . and then in each other's presence. When they were together, their estimates converged.

FIGURE 9.3 Informational Social Influence Sherif's conformity experiment used the autokinetic effect to assess group influence. Participants' estimates tended to become more similar over time. (Source: Adapted from Sherif, 1936.)

comments and actions—as a source of information about what's likely to be right, proper, or effective (Deutsch & Gerard, 1955). We want to be right, and the opinions of other people are a useful source of information we can draw on to "get it right." The tendency to use others as a source of information is most pronounced when we are uncertain of how to behave or what is factually correct. We are more likely to conform in a foreign country than our own, and we are more likely to conform to others' views on subjects we have vague ideas about, such as macroeconomic policy, than on subjects we have clear opinions about, such as the relative quality of Buffalo's climate versus Honolulu's. Note that the task Sherif asked his participants to perform was about as ambiguous as it gets, so informational social influence was at its peak. The light, in fact, did not move at all; it just appeared to move. And that appearance, being so uncertain and ambiguous, was readily influenced by the expressed judgments of others (see also Baron, Vandello, & Brunsman, 1996; Levine, Higgins, & Choi, 2000; Tesser, Campbell, & Mickler, 1983).

Normative Social Influence and Asch's Conformity Experiment

You may be thinking to yourself, "What's the big deal here? Why *wouldn't* participants conform to one another's judgments? After all, the task was impossible, and no one could have felt confident in his or her own estimates. Why *not* rely on others?" If you had such thoughts, you were pursuing a line of reasoning advanced by another pioneer of conformity research, Solomon Asch. Asch thought that Sherif's experiment, although informative about a certain type of conformity, did not speak to those situations in which there is a clear conflict between an individual's own

Solomon Asch A pioneer of conformity research, Asch studied the effect of normative social influence.

judgment and that of the group. It does not apply, for example, to the experience of knowing that you have consumed too much alcohol to drive safely while your peers are urging you to get behind the wheel ("Come on. Don't be a wimp, you'll be fine"). Asch predicted that when there is a clear conflict between a person's own judgment and the judgments advanced by the group, there will be far less conformity than that observed by Sherif. Asch was right. But the reduced rate of conformity was not what made his experiment one of the most famous in the history of psychology. What made his study so well known was how often participants *did* conform, even when they thought the group was out of its collective mind.

You may already be familiar with Asch's experiment (Asch, 1956). Eight individuals were gathered together to perform a simple perceptual task—to determine which of three lines was the same length as a target line (**Figure 9.4**).

FIGURE 9.4 **Scientific Method: Normative Social Influence**

Hypothesis: Participants conform to the opinions expressed by the majority even when they know the majority is incorrect.

Research Method:

1. One true participant (the man in the middle) and seven confederates were asked to say which of the three test lines was the same length as the target line.

2. On some trials, the confederates unanimously responded incorrectly, making the true participant doubt his own judgment (he is seen leaning forward to take another look at the lines).

A B C

Test lines   Target line

Results: The true participant conformed to the erroneous majority on a third of the trials.

CONCLUSION: To avoid the disapproval of the group, many participants conformed to the judgments of the majority rather than express their own judgment.

Source: Adapted from Asch (1956).

Each person called out his judgment publicly, one at a time. The task was easy enough that the experience was uneventful—at first.

On the third trial, however, one individual found that his private judgment was at odds with the expressed opinions of everyone else in the group. That one individual was the only true participant in the experiment; the seven others were confederates instructed by Asch to respond incorrectly. The confederates responded incorrectly on 11 more occasions before the experiment was over; and the question was, how often would the participant forsake what he knew to be the correct answer and conform to the incorrect judgment rendered by everyone else? Here there was no ambiguity, as there was in Sherif's experiment; the right answer was clear to participants (when individuals in a control group made these judgments by themselves, with no social pressure, they almost never made a mistake).

As Asch predicted, there was less conformity in his study than in Sherif's, but the rate of giving in to the will of the group was still surprisingly high. Three-quarters of the participants conformed to the erroneous majority at least once. Overall, participants conformed on a third of the critical trials. The reason that Asch's experiment has had such impact is not simply that the results are surprising: they are disturbing to many people as well. We like to think of people, ourselves especially (Pronin, Berger, & Molouki, 2007), as sticking to what we think is right rather than following the herd, and we worry about people abandoning the dictates of their own conscience to follow others into wrongheaded or potentially destructive behavior.

As this discussion implies, informational social influence does not seem to be the main source of conformity pressure in Asch's experiment. There is undoubtedly some informational social influence at work here; the erroneous judgments called out by the majority were for lines that were between one-half and three-fourths inch off the correct answer. Thus some participants may have questioned their own judgment and regarded the confederates' responses as informative. But again, in the absence of social pressure, control participants got the answer right nearly 100 percent of the time; so the primary reason people conformed was to avoid standing out, negatively, in the eyes of the group (**Box 9.1**). Social psychologists refer to this as **normative social influence**, or the desire to avoid the disapproval, criticism, or ostracism that other people might deliver (Deutsch & Gerard, 1955). People are often reluctant to depart from the norms of society, or at least the norms of those subgroups they care most about, because they fear the social consequences (Cialdini, Kallgren, & Reno, 1991). The normative social pressures in Asch's experiment are sufficiently intense that the participants found themselves in a wrenching dilemma: "Should I say what I truly think it is? But what would everyone else think? They all agree, and they all seem so confident. Will they think I'm nuts? Will they interpret my disagreement as a slap in the face? But what kind of person am I if I go along with them? What the #@!$% should I do?"

To get an idea of the intensity of the participants' dilemma, imagine the following scenario. As part of a discussion of Asch's experiment, your social psychology professor shows an overhead of the target line and the three test lines and reports that although the right answer is line B, the confederates all say it's C. As your professor begins to move on from the basics of Asch's experiment, one student raises his hand and announces with conviction, "But the right answer *is* C!"

What would happen? Doubtless everyone would chuckle, making the charitable assumption that the student was trying to be funny. But if the student insisted

normative social influence The influence of other people that comes from the individual's desire to avoid their disapproval, harsh judgments, and other social sanctions (for example, barbs, ostracism).

BOX 9.1 FOCUS ON HEALTH

Bulimia and Social Influence

Why do young women engage in binge eating and then purging by vomiting or using laxatives? The phenomenon is relatively new. Such behavior, known as bulimia, was virtually unheard of until about 45 years ago. Does it exist because the fashion industry and media have persuaded women to want to be thinner than it is natural for them to be (see Chapter 10)? Is it because depression and anxiety have increased in recent decades? Is it because body image and self-esteem have worsened?

All of these factors may play a role in the current epidemic of bulimia, but another factor is social influence. Christian Crandall (1988) studied sorority women at a large Midwestern university and found that the more bulimic a woman's friends were, the more bulimic she was likely to be. As Crandall learned, this relationship was not because bulimic women discovered each other and became friends while nonbulimic women sought out peers who preferred to keep their food down. Early in the school year, when women had known one another for only a short time, there was no association between the level of a woman's engagement in bulimic activity and the level of her friends' engagement in such activity. But over the course of the year, women in now-established friendship groups (not *new* groups of friends) came to have similar levels of bulimia.

Crandall studied two sororities and found two slightly different patterns of influence. In one sorority, women who differed in their level of bulimic activity from the average level in the sorority were less likely to be popular. Crandall inferred from this that there was an "appropriate" or normative level of bulimia in that sorority, and deviations from it *in either direction* were punished by rejection. In the other sorority, more binge eating (up to quite a large amount) was associated with more popularity. In that sorority, Crandall concluded, there was pressure toward considerable binge eating, and those most inclined to binge were rewarded with acceptance and popularity.

Thinness and Social Influence When some members of a sorority engage in binge eating and purging to stay thin, pressures on other members of the sorority to do likewise can be intense.

that the confederates' answer was correct, the chuckles would turn to awkward, nervous laughter, and everyone would turn toward the professor in an implicit plea to "make this awkward situation go away." In subsequent lectures, most people would avoid sitting by the individual in question, and a buffer of empty seats would surround him. (And, of course, lunch invitations, dating opportunities, and offers to join a fraternity or other social clubs would diminish as well.) *That* is the fate that Asch's participants felt they risked if they departed from the majority's response. Perhaps, then, it's no great surprise that participants so often chose not to take the risk and conformed to the majority response (Janes & Olson, 2000; Kruglanski & Webster, 1991; Levine, 1989; Schachter, 1951). Let's now consider when and why these conformity pressures are likely to be especially potent.

Factors Affecting Conformity Pressure

Several generations of researchers have examined the characteristics of the group and the characteristics of the task that influence the tendency to conform. This research has provided a clearer understanding of when the tendency to conform will be particularly strong and when it will not. Both informational and normative social influence have proved to be powerful forces: as either source of influence intensifies, so does the rate of conformity.

Group Size It's surely no surprise that conformity increases as the size of the group increases. Larger groups exert both more normative influence and more informational social influence than smaller groups. What *is* surprising, perhaps, is that the effect of group size levels off pretty quickly (**Figure 9.5**). Research using Asch's paradigm, for example, has shown an increase in conformity as the size of the group increases, but only to a group size of three or four; after that, the amount of conformity levels off (Campbell & Fairey, 1989; Gerard, Wilhelmy, & Conolley, 1968; Insko, Smith, Alicke, Wade, & Taylor, 1985; Rosenberg, 1961).

"'The way to get along,' I was told when I entered Congress, 'is to go along.'"

—John F. Kennedy

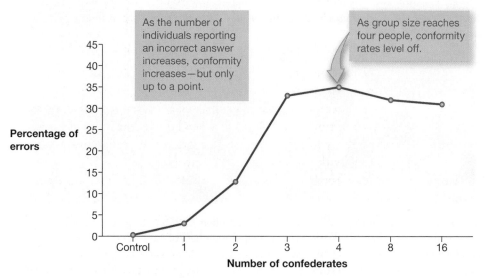

FIGURE 9.5 The Effect of Group Size on Conformity (Source: Adapted from Asch, 1951.)

The effect of group size makes sense, of course, from the standpoint of both informational and normative social influence. The larger the number of people who venture a particular opinion, the more likely it has merit. But only to a certain point. The validity of information increases only if the opinions are independent of one another. If not, the opinions of additional people do not offer any real information, and the more people there are, the less likely it is that their views are independent. Also, the larger the group, the more people one stands to displease. But here, too, the impact of group size goes up only to a certain point. A person can feel only so much embarrassment, and the difference between being viewed as odd, foolish, or difficult by 2 versus 4 people is psychologically much more powerful than the difference between being viewed that way by 6 versus 8 or by 12 versus 14.

Group Unanimity A striking effect was observed in Asch's original studies when the unanimity of the group was broken. Recall that in the basic paradigm, the participant went along and reported the wrong answer a third of the time. That figure dropped to 5 percent when the true participant had an ally—that is, when just one other member of the group deviated from the majority. This effect occurs because the presence of an ally weakens both informational social influence ("Maybe I'm not crazy after all") and normative social influence ("At least I've got someone to commiserate with"). This effect also suggests a powerful tool for protecting independence of thought and action. If you expect to be pressured to conform and want to remain true to your own beliefs, bring an ally along.

Note that the other individual who breaks the group's unanimity doesn't need to offer the correct answer—just one that departs from the group's answer. Suppose the right answer is the shortest of the three lines, and the majority claims it's the longest. If the fellow dissenter states that it's the middle line, it reduces the rate of conformity, even though the participant's own view hasn't been reinforced. What matters is the break in unanimity. This fact has important implications for free speech. It suggests that we might want to tolerate loathsome and obviously false statements ("The Holocaust never happened"; "The president is a child molester"; "The World Trade Center attacks were a government hoax") not because what is said has any value, but because it liberates *other people* to say things of value. The presence of voices, even bizarre voices, that depart from conventional opinion frees the body politic to speak out and thus can foster productive political discourse.

Expertise and Status Imagine that you were a participant in Asch's experiment and that the other participants who were inexplicably stating what you thought was the wrong answer were all former major-league batting champions. If you proceeded on the assumption that a player can't lead the league in hitting without exceptional eyesight, you most likely would grant the group considerable authority and go along with their opinion. In contrast, if the rest of the group were all wearing Coke-bottle eyeglasses, you would be unlikely to take their opinions seriously.

As this thought experiment illustrates, the expertise and status of the group members powerfully influence the rate of conformity. Expertise and status often go together, of course, because people grant greater status to those with special expertise, and we often assume (not always correctly) that those with high status have considerable expertise (Koslowsky & Schwarzwald, 2001). To the extent

"It takes a great deal of bravery to stand up to our enemies, but just as much to stand up to our friends."

—Albus Dumbledore, in *Harry Potter and the Sorcerer's Stone*

"If there is any principle of the Constitution that more imperatively calls for attachment than any other it is the principle of free thought—not free thought for those who agree with us but freedom for the thought that we hate."

—Oliver Wendell Holmes

Expertise, Status, and Social Influence When the United States was preparing to invade Iraq to unseat Saddam Hussein and secure his putative weapons of mass destruction in March 2003, the U.S. administration sent Secretary of State Colin Powell to speak to the delegates of the United Nations because he had great credibility. Powell presented what he believed were the facts about Iraq's weapons of mass destruction and hoped to convince the delegates of the need to invade Iraq.

that these characteristics can be separated, however, expertise primarily affects informational social influence. Experts are more likely to be right, so we take their opinions more seriously. Status, in contrast, mainly affects normative social influence. The disapproval of high-status individuals can hurt more than the disapproval of people we care less about.

Many researchers have examined the effect of expertise and status on conformity (Cialdini & Trost, 1998; Crano, 1970; Ettinger, Marino, Endler, Geller, & Natziuk, 1971). One of the earliest and most intriguing studies used a paradigm quite different from Asch's. Torrance (1955) gave the members of navy bombing crews—pilot, navigator, and gunner—a number of reasoning problems, such as this horse-trading problem:

A man bought a horse for $60 and then sold it for $70. He later repurchased the horse for $80 and then, changing his mind yet again, sold it for $90. How much money did he make on his series of transactions? (Answer on p. 323.)

The crews then had to report one answer for the whole group. Torrance monitored the group's deliberations and found that if the pilot (who generally held the highest status) originally came up with the correct solution, the group eventually reported it as their answer 91 percent of the time. If the navigator offered the correct answer, the group reported it 80 percent of the time. But if the lowly gunner offered the correct answer, the group offered it up only 63 percent of the time. The opinions of higher-status individuals thus appear to carry more weight with the group as a whole (Foushee, 1984).

Culture As this book emphasizes throughout, people from interdependent cultures are much more concerned about their relations with others and about fitting into the broader social context than are people from independent cultures. People reared in interdependent cultures are therefore likely to be more susceptible to both informational social influence (they consider the actions and opinions of others more telling) and normative social influence (they consider the high regard of others more important). Thus people from interdependent cultures might be expected to conform more than those from independent cultures.

Evidence supports this contention. In one early test of cross-cultural differences in conformity, Stanley Milgram (1961) conducted experiments using Asch's paradigm in Norway and France. Milgram maintained that Norwegians emphasize group cohesiveness and politeness, whereas the French enjoy conversational combat and don't shrink from disagreements. Just as he expected, Milgram found that the Norwegian participants conformed more than the French participants.

But why study Norway and France (other than that both are delightful places to visit and conduct research)? In the examination of independent versus interdependent cultures throughout this book, France and Norway have not loomed large in the discussion. What about the greater independent/interdependent divide that exists between a broader sample of the world's regions? A more systematic analysis of the results of experiments using the Asch paradigm in 133 different studies in 17 countries found that conformity does indeed tend to be greater in interdependent countries than in independent countries (Bond & Smith, 1996). The individualism that is highly valued in American and Western European societies has given individuals in those societies a greater willingness to stand apart from the majority. And the willingness to resist the influence of the majority may be increasing. More recent conformity experiments in the United States and Great Britain using Asch's procedure have tended to find lower rates of conformity (Bond & Smith, 1996; Perrin & Spencer, 1981).

Answer to Horse Problem on p. 322
$20.
Amount paid = $140 ($60 + $80).
Amount received = $160 ($70 + $90).

Tight versus Loose Cultures Michele Gelfand and her colleagues (2011) have pursued a distinction between cultures that overlaps somewhat with the independence/interdependence dimension but differs enough that it deserves a name of its own: tightness versus looseness. Conformity to social norms lies at the heart of this construct. Some cultures, which Gelfand calls "tight," have very strong norms regarding how people should behave and do not tolerate departure from those norms. Other cultures are "loose": their norms are not so strong, and their members tolerate more deviance.

In a highly ambitious study, Gelfand and her colleagues studied a number of variables in 33 nations. They found that, compared with loose nations, tight nations are more likely to have governments that are autocratic or dictatorial, to punish dissent, to have sharp controls on what can be said in the media, to have more laws and higher monitoring to ensure that the laws are obeyed, and to inflict more punishment for disobedience of laws. If a nation was tight on one of these dimensions, it tended to be tight on all; if it was loose on one of the dimensions, it tended to be loose on all. Tight countries include India, Germany, People's Republic of China, South Korea, Japan, Austria, Portugal, Britain, Turkey, and Italy. Loose countries include Greece, Hungary, Israel, the Netherlands, Ukraine, New Zealand, and Brazil.

Gelfand and colleagues surveyed people in each of the 33 countries, asking them about the appropriateness of arguing, crying, laughing, singing, flirting, reading a newspaper, and several other behaviors in each of 15 different situations or places, including a bank, doctor's office, restaurant, funeral, library, elevator,

Tight versus Loose Cultures (A) As this picture of French boys lined up for school illustrates, some cultures are relatively "tight": they have strong norms about how people should behave and tolerate very little leeway in deviating from those norms. (B) Other cultures are relatively "loose": their norms are not as stringent, as this more chaotic line indicates.

and movie theater. The tighter the nation's laws and norms, the fewer behaviors were allowed in these various situations. The researchers also asked people if their country had many social norms, whether others would strongly disapprove if someone acted inappropriately, and so forth. Again, the tighter the nation, the more its citizens pointed to tight constraints.

Why are some nations tight and some loose? Gelfand and colleagues found that tighter nations tend to have higher population densities, fewer natural resources, less-certain food supplies, less access to safe water, more risk of natural disasters, more territorial threats from neighbors, and higher prevalence of pathogens. It appears, then, that behavioral constraints are associated with, and perhaps partly caused by, ecological constraints.

Gender To grow up as a boy or girl in a given society is to grow up in a slightly different culture. Societies differ tremendously in how they socialize boys and girls, but all societies sex-type to some degree. If there are cultural differences in conformity, should we expect gender differences as well? Perhaps. Women are raised to value interdependence and to nurture important social relationships more than men are, whereas men are raised to value and strive for autonomy and independence more than women are. So we might expect women to be more subject to social influence and thus to conform more than men do.

However, people are more likely to conform when they're confused by the events unfolding around them. And if women are taught to attend to relationships, and hence are more likely to be the "experts" on human relationships, their greater sophistication about relationships may give them the confidence necessary to resist the influence of the majority.

The research findings are what you might expect given these two opposing considerations. Reviews of the literature on gender differences in conformity have shown that women tend to conform more than men—but only a bit (Bond & Smith, 1996; Eagly, 1987; Eagly & Carli, 1981; Eagly & Chrvala, 2006). The difference tends to be greatest when the situation involves face-to-face contact, like that in Asch's original study. But the difference also seems to be strongly influenced by the specific content of the issue at hand. For instance, would you be more likely to conform to other people when they assert that the atomic number of beryllium is 62 or when they assert that the most important ingredient in a good sandwich is horseradish? If you're like most people, you know more about sandwiches than about the periodic table, so you would be more likely to stand your ground when discussing lunchtime meals. Analyses of the specific contexts in which men and women differ in the tendency to conform reveal just this effect (Sistrunk & McDavid, 1971). Thus women tend to conform more in stereotypically male domains (for example, on questions about geography or deer hunting), whereas men tend to conform more in stereotypically female domains (for example, on questions about cosmetics or child rearing). So it should be no surprise that, overall, men and women tend to differ in conformity, but only slightly.

Difficulty (or Ambiguity) of the Task A comparison of Asch's and Sherif's experiments highlights the difficulty of the task and hence how challenging it is to arrive at a confident answer. When the judgment at hand is unambiguous and easy to make, informational social influence is virtually eliminated. Only normative social influence is at work, and resistance to the group is stronger (Allen, 1965;

Baron et al., 1996). As noted earlier, for example, you're less likely to act decisively and assertively when you are visiting a foreign country and are uncertain about what is called for in a given situation. When the "right" thing to do is unclear, people are particularly inclined to rely on others for guidance.

Anonymity While an easy task eliminates informational social influence, the ability to respond anonymously eliminates normative social influence. For example, when the true participant in Asch's paradigm is allowed to write his judgments on a piece of paper instead of saying them aloud for the group to hear, conformity drops dramatically. When nobody else is aware of his judgment, he has no need to fear the group's disapproval. This highlights an important distinction between the impact of informational and normative social influence. Informational social influence, by influencing how people come to see the issues or stimuli before them, tends to influence **internalization**, or our private acceptance of the position advanced by the majority (Kelman, 1958). We don't just mimic a particular response; we adopt the group's perspective. Normative social influence, in contrast, often has a greater impact on public compliance than on private acceptance. To avoid disapproval, we sometimes do or say one thing but continue to believe another.

internalization Private acceptance of a proposition, orientation, or ideology.

The Interpretive Context of Disagreement The most surprising aspect of Asch's experiment is that the participants conformed to the erroneous judgments of a group of strangers. Why would the participants care so much about what these other people think of them? They've never seen these people before and likely will never see them again. If people conform this much to the questionable judgment of strangers, surely they would conform even more to the judgments of those they know well, care about, and must deal with in the future (Lott & Lott, 1961; Wolf, 1985).

What can explain this curious feature of Asch's experiment? The key is to notice that participants in Asch's experiment faced a double whammy. First, they had to confront the fact that everyone else saw things differently than they did. Second, they had no basis for understanding *why* everyone else saw things differently. ("Could I be mistaken? No, it's as plain as day. Could they be mistaken? I don't see how, because they're not any farther away than I am and it's so clear. Are they unusual? No, they don't look much different from me or anyone else.")

Knowing why our opinions are different ("They don't see the lines the way I do because they're wearing distorting glasses") lessens both informational and normative social influence. Informational social influence is lessened because the explanation can diminish the group's impact as a source of information ("They're biased"). Normative social influence is lessened because we can assume that those in the majority are aware of why we differ from them. For instance, if we have different views on some burning political issue of the day, those we disagree with might think we're biased, selfish, or have different values, but at least they won't think we're crazy. In Asch's situation, in contrast, the participants faced the reasonable fear that if they departed from everyone else's judgment, their behavior would look truly bizarre and everyone would think they were nuts.

The important point here is that it is difficult to act independently when we don't know what to make of things. It's easier to stand our ground when we have a clear understanding of what might be causing others to make different judgments from our own (Ross, Bierbrauer, & Hoffman, 1976).

The Influence of Minority Opinion on the Majority

There was a time in the United States when people owned slaves, when women were not allowed to vote, and when children worked long hours for scandalously low pay in unhealthy conditions. But small groups of abolitionists, suffragettes, and child welfare advocates saw things differently than their peers and worked tirelessly to change public opinion about each of these issues. And they succeeded. In each case the broader public changed its views, and important legislation was passed. Minority opinion became the majority opinion.

Examples like these remind us that although conformity pressures can be powerful, majority opinion does not always prevail. Conformity pressure can be resisted, and minority voices can be heard clearly enough to change the prevailing majority opinion. How do minority opinions come to influence the majority? Are the sources of influence the same as those that majorities bring to bear on minorities?

In the first experimental examination of these questions, Serge Moscovici and his colleagues had participants in a group setting call out whether a color was green or blue (Moscovici, Lage, & Naffrechoux, 1969). The border between blue and green, of course, is not always clear, but the critical stimuli shown to the participants were ones that the participants, when tested alone, nearly always thought were blue. The experimenter showed participants these stimuli in the presence of a minority of respondents (confederates of the experimenter) who responded "green"; the experimenter then recorded how the true participants responded.

"Give me a firm place to stand and I will move the world."

—Archimedes of Syracuse

Minority Influence on the Majority Minority opinions can influence the majority through consistent and clear messages that persuade the majority to systematically examine and reevaluate its opinions. (A) British suffragette Emmeline Pankhurst presented her views in favor of women's right to vote to an American crowd in 1918. (B) Rosa Parks refused to give up her seat at the front of a bus in Montgomery, Alabama, in December 1955. Her actions resulted in a citywide bus boycott that eventually led the U.S. Supreme Court to declare that segregation was illegal on the city bus system.

When the minority varied their responses randomly between "green" and "blue," the participants said "green" after the others did so only 1 percent of the time, about the same as when they responded alone. But when the minority responded with "green" consistently, the true participants responded likewise 8 percent of the time. But that was not the only effect the minority had. When the participants thought the experiment was over, the experimenter introduced them to a second experimenter who, they were told, was also interested in color vision. This second experimenter showed participants a series of blue-green colors and recorded where each participant, individually, thought blue left off and green began. What Moscovici and his colleagues found was that participants who had earlier been exposed to a consistent minority now identified more of these stimuli as green—their sense of the border between blue and green had shifted. Thus, when the minority opinion was consistent, it had both a direct effect on participants' responses in the public setting and a latent effect on their subsequent, private judgments.

Further investigation of minority influence in paradigms like Moscovici's has shown that minorities have their effect primarily through informational social influence (Moscovici, 1985; Nemeth, 1986; Wood, Lundgren, Ouellette, Busceme, & Blackstone, 1994). People in the majority are typically not terribly concerned about the social costs of stating their opinion out loud—they have the majority on their side, and normative social influence is minimized. But they might wonder why the minority keeps stating its divergent opinion. This can lead the majority to consider the stimulus more carefully, leading to a level of scrutiny and systematic thought that can produce genuine change in attitudes and beliefs. Thus majorities typically elicit more conformity, but it is often of the public compliance sort. In contrast, minorities typically influence fewer people, but the nature of the influence is often deeper and results in true private acceptance (Maass & Clark, 1983).

 Conformity can occur in response to implicit or explicit social pressures and can be the result of automatic mimicry, informational social influence, or normative social influence. Group size influences conformity, but it appears to reach maximum effect at around four people. Unanimity also is crucial in conformity, and a single ally can help an individual hold out against the group. People from more interdependent cultures conform more than people from more independent cultures, and women conform slightly more than men. More difficult tasks lead to more conformity, and plausible explanations for why others might hold views different from our own tend to reduce conformity. Conformity pressures notwithstanding, minorities often do have an influence, primarily through informational social influence.

OBEDIENCE TO AUTHORITY

The study of when and why people obey the commands of someone in authority has been dominated by the most famous set of social psychological experiments ever conducted—those of Stanley Milgram. Milgram's experiments are so well known, in fact, that "they have become part of our society's shared intellectual legacy—that small body of historical incidents, biblical parables, and classic literature that serious thinkers feel free to draw on when they debate about human nature or contemplate human history" (Ross, 1988).

The Setup of the Milgram Experiments

Milgram's research on obedience began as an investigation of conformity. He was intrigued by Asch's findings but wondered about their limitations in much the same way that Asch had wondered about the limitations of Sherif's findings. Recall that Asch thought it only natural that people would readily conform to others' responses when they didn't have a firm opinion themselves. But what would happen, he wondered, if there was a clear conflict between the individual's personal convictions and the group's response? Asch found considerable conformity even then, which surprised him. Milgram's findings surprised Milgram even more.

Milgram was interested in whether the kind of pressures observed in Asch's paradigm were powerful enough to lead people to do something far more significant than report an incorrect line length. He wondered what would happen if he asked participants to deliver electric shocks whenever a subject performing a task (in reality the experimenter's confederate) responded incorrectly. Would participants conform here, when doing so involved hurting another human being?

This is an interesting question, but Milgram never pursued it. The reason is that he first needed to obtain data from a control group to see how willing participants would be to deliver electric shock when there was no pressure to conform (Evans, 1980). And that's where he got his surprising result, one that entirely changed his research agenda. A surprisingly large percentage of his participants were willing to do something they thought was hurting another human being, even when there was no group of other participants leading the way.

Recall from Chapter 1 the basic procedure of Milgram's experiments. After responding to an ad in a New Haven newspaper, participants in Milgram's study reported for an experiment on learning. A "random" draw was rigged so that the participants always became the "teacher" and the confederate always became the "learner." The teacher's job was to administer an electric shock every time the learner—a genial, middle-aged man who was strapped into a chair with his arm on a shock delivery apparatus—made a mistake and reported the wrong word from a list of word pairs presented at the beginning of the study (for example, glove/book, grill/detergent, anvil/pope). Teachers were briefly strapped to the chair themselves and given a 45-volt shock so they would know that the shocks were painful. The teacher started off by delivering 15 volts after the learner's first mistake and then increasing the shock in 15-volt increments after each subsequent mistake. As the mistakes accumulated, participants found themselves required to deliver 255, 300, and 330 volts of electricity—all the way up to 450 volts. (In reality, no electric shock was delivered to the learner.) If a participant expressed reservations or tried to terminate the experiment, the experimenter would respond with a carefully scripted set of responses—"Please continue," "The experiment requires that you continue," "It is absolutely essential that you continue," "You have no other choice; you must go on."

Stanley Milgram Using a "shock generator" that looked real but was actually just a prop, Milgram studied whether participants would continue to obey instructions and shock a learner even after believing that the learner was in grave distress as a result of the shocks.

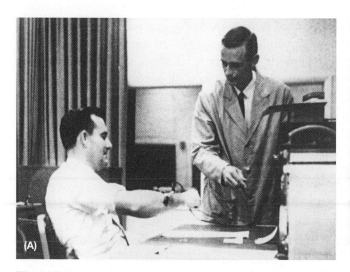 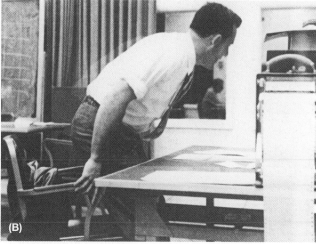

The Milgram Experiment Participants were led to believe that the shock generator had 30 levels of shock, ranging from "slight shock" to "danger: severe shock" to "XXX." (A) A participant being given a sample shock of 45 volts (this was the only real shock in the experiment). (B) A participant standing up to ask the experimenter if he could stop the experiment.

The great surprise in these studies was that people continued to obey the experimenter's orders and to shock the confederate. In the remote-feedback version of the experiment, in which the learner was in an adjoining room and could not be heard except when he vigorously pounded on the wall after a shock of 300 volts, 66 percent of the participants continued the learning experiment and delivered the maximum shock of 450 volts. In the voice-feedback version, the participants could hear a series of increasingly desperate pleas by the learner—including screaming that he had a heart condition—until finally, ominously, he became silent. Despite these cues that the learner was suffering, 62.5 percent of the participants delivered the maximum shock (Milgram, 1965, 1974).

Opposing Forces

Milgram's participants found themselves in an agonizing conflict, caught between two opposing sets of forces. On the one hand were the forces compelling them to complete the experiment and to continue delivering shock (Reeder, Monroe, & Pryor, 2008). Among these forces was a sense of fair play—they had agreed to serve as participants, they had already received payment for doing so, and they felt that they now had to fulfill their part of the bargain. Some participants may also have been motivated by the reason they had agreed to be participants in the first place—to advance science and the understanding of human behavior. Another important motivating factor was normative social influence—in this case, the desire to avoid the disapproval of the experimenter or of anyone else associated with the experiment whom they imagined they might encounter on their way out. Closely related to this concern was the very human desire to avoid "making a scene" and upsetting others (Goffman, 1966; Miller, 1996).

On the other hand, several powerful forces compelled the participants to want to terminate the experiment. Foremost among these was the moral imperative to stop the suffering of the learner (Burger, Girgis, & Manning, 2011). Participants may have felt a specific desire not to hurt the genial man they had met earlier, as well as a more abstract reluctance to hurt others. Some participants were also probably concerned about what would happen if something went wrong. "What if he dies or is permanently injured?" "Will there be a lawsuit?" Still others may have wondered about the prospect of having to walk out with the learner after everything was over and the embarrassment (even retaliation) it might bring. And how could the participants be sure that the roles wouldn't be reversed? At the moment, they occupied the teacher role; but what if there was a new round that called for *them* to be strapped into the shock machine?

Specifying these opposing forces acting on participants contributes to an understanding of why they responded the way they did and why the whole experience was so stressful. How might the rate of obedience change if the strength of these opposing forces were modified (Blass, 2000, 2004; Miller, 1986)? This is exactly the question Milgram tried to answer through a comprehensive series of studies in which he conducted important variations on the original.

Tuning In the Learner Milgram directed his initial efforts at increasing the forces that compelled people to terminate the experiment. These forces were all triggered by an awareness of the learner's suffering, so Milgram tried to increase them by making the learner more prominent—or, in his words, by "tuning in the learner." (Participants spontaneously tried to do the opposite—that is, to deal with their own discomfort by tuning *out* the learner, sometimes literally turning away from him in their chair.) In the *remote-feedback* version of the experiment, the teacher could neither see nor hear the learner (except for one episode of vigorous pounding). In the *voice-feedback* version, the learner was still not in view; but he and his vigorous protests were clearly audible, so that the teacher was constantly aware of him. In a *proximity* version, the learner received his shock in the same room where the participant delivered it, from only 1.5 feet away. Finally, in the *touch-proximity* version, the participant was required to force the learner's hand onto the shock plate (a sheet of insulation kept the participant from being shocked, too). **Figure 9.6** shows the effect of these manipulations. As the learner became more and more present and "real," the teachers found it increasingly difficult to deliver the shocks, and obedience rates diminished.

One lesson to be drawn from this experiment is chilling: the more removed we are from others, the easier it is to hurt them. Consider, for example, the military technologies that allow individuals to inflict harm on others from a great distance. Combat is often no longer hand to hand. A mere push of a button can guide a predator drone to a target or fire a missile from an underground silo a continent away. The remoteness of the victims in such cases makes the harm done to them abstract, so the emotional brakes on aggression are weakened dramatically.

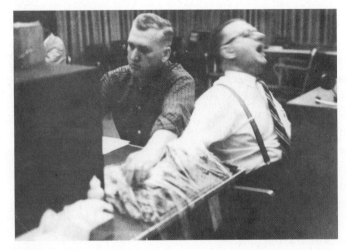

Tuning In the Learner In a "touch-proximity" condition, participants were required to force the learner's hand onto the shock plate, which reduced the participants' obedience rates.

Tuning Out the Experimenter Another way to influence obedience in Milgram's paradigm is to strengthen or weaken the "signal" coming from the experimenter and thus strengthen or weaken the forces acting on participants to complete the experiment. Milgram conducted several variations on this theme as well. In the standard version of the study, the experimenter was present in the same room, right next to the partici-

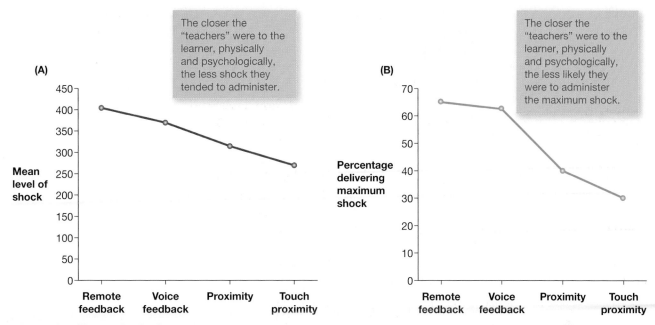

(A)

The closer the "teachers" were to the learner, physically and psychologically, the less shock they tended to administer.

Mean level of shock
[y-axis: 0, 50, 100, 150, 200, 250, 300, 350, 400, 450]
[x-axis: Remote feedback, Voice feedback, Proximity, Touch proximity]

(B)

The closer the "teachers" were to the learner, physically and psychologically, the less likely they were to administer the maximum shock.

Percentage delivering maximum shock
[y-axis: 0, 10, 20, 30, 40, 50, 60, 70]
[x-axis: Remote feedback, Voice feedback, Proximity, Touch proximity]

FIGURE 9.6 Tuning In the Learner The effect of experimental manipulations that make the learner more and more salient on (A) the mean level of shock participants delivered and (B) the percentage of participants who delivered the maximum amount of shock. (Source: Adapted from Milgram, 1965.)

pant. In an *experimenter-absent* version, the experimenter gave the initial instructions alongside the participant but then left the room and issued his orders over the telephone. By physically removing himself from the scene, the experimenter lost much of his influence.

Another way to diminish the experimenter's power is to alter his authority. In one version, for example, an "ordinary person" (seemingly another participant, but in reality a confederate) was the one who delivered the orders to increase the shock level each time the learner made a mistake. In still another version, two experimenters initially instructed the participant to shock the victim. At one point, however, one of the two experimenters announced that he found the proceedings objectionable and argued with the other experimenter, who continued to urge the participant to complete the experiment.

Figure 9.7 shows the results of these manipulations. As the experimenter became less salient and less of an authority in the participant's mind, it became easier for the participant to defy him, so the rate of obedience declined. Notice that this series of experimental variations had a more pronounced effect than the "tuning in the learner" series (compare Figures 9.6 and 9.7). Making it *easier* for participants to disobey thus seems to be more effective than increasing their *desire* to disobey. This distinction provides an important clue to understanding the surprising levels of obedience observed in Milgram's experiments.

Tuning Out the Victim
Missiles can be fired from pilotless ("drone") aircraft by a person located thousands of miles away. This distance can make the harm more abstract and orders to fire less likely to be questioned.

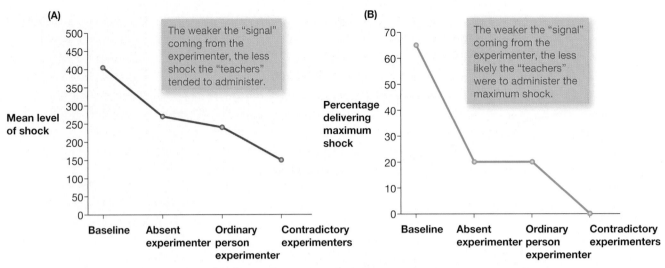

FIGURE 9.7 Tuning Out the Experimenter The effect of experimental manipulations that make the experimenter less and less salient on (A) mean level of shock participants delivered and (B) the percentage of participants who delivered the maximum amount of shock. (Source: Adapted from Milgram, 1965.)

Would You Have Obeyed?

As mentioned in Chapter 1, no one anticipated the widespread obedience that Milgram found. A group of psychiatrists predicted that fewer than 1 percent of all participants—a pathological fringe—would continue until they delivered the maximum amount of shock. This failure of prediction is matched by an equally noteworthy failure of after-the-fact insight: almost no one believes, even after hearing the basic results and all the experimental variations, that he or she would deliver very high levels of shock. Thus, although Milgram's experimental variations give us some understanding of when and why people engage in such surprising behavior, they do not give us a fully satisfying explanation. As one social psychologist put it, the experiments do not pass a critical "empathy test" (Ross, 1988). They do not lead us to empathize fully with the obedient participants and take seriously the possibility that *we* would also obey to the end—as most participants did. A truly satisfying explanation might not convince us that we would *surely* do so, but it should at least convince us that we *might* act that way.

Milgram's work is often mentioned in discussions of how people sometimes obey the directives of malevolent government officials and engage in sadistic, demeaning torture, such as that observed at Abu Ghraib, or commit hideous crimes against humanity, such as those witnessed during the Holocaust in Nazi Germany, in the "ethnic cleansing" in Bosnia, or in the massacres in Rwanda or Darfur. Explanations of such incomprehensible cruelties vary along an "exceptionalist-normalist" continuum. The exceptionalist thesis is that such crimes are perpetrated only by "exceptional" people—that is, exceptionally sadistic, desperate, or ethnocentric people. Many Germans were virulent anti-Semites. The Serbs harbored long-standing hatred and resentment against the Bosnians. The Rwandan Hutus had a score to settle with the Tutsis. The normalist thesis, in contrast, is that everyone is capable of such destructive obedience and that given the right circumstances, almost anyone would commit such acts (**Box 9.2**).

Milgram's research, of course, is typically taken to support the normalist position. Milgram himself certainly took this position. When asked by Morley Safer on the CBS show *60 Minutes* whether he thought something like the Holocaust could happen in the United States, Milgram offered this opinion:

> I would say, on the basis of having observed a thousand people in the experiment and having my own intuition shaped and informed by these experiments, that if a system of death camps were set up in the United States of the sort we had seen in Nazi Germany, one would be able to find sufficient personnel for those camps in any medium-sized American town. (quoted in Blass, 1999, p. 955)

Let's take a closer look.

They Tried but Failed One of the reasons people think they would never behave the way the average participant in Milgram's experiments behaved is that they misunderstand exactly how the average participant acted (Ross, 1988). People conjure up images of participants blithely going along with the experimenter's commands, increasing the shock level from trial to trial, being relatively inattentive to the learner's situation. Indeed, Milgram's experiments have often been described as demonstrations of "blind" obedience.

But that's not what happened. Participants did not mindlessly obey. Nearly all tried to disobey in one form or another. Nearly everyone called the experimenter's attention to the learner's suffering in an implicit plea to stop the proceedings. Many stated explicitly that they refused to continue (but nonetheless went on with the experiment). Some got out of their chair in defiance, only to sit back down moments later. The participants tried to disobey, but they just weren't particularly good at it. As Lee Ross (1988) put it, "the Milgram experiments have less to say about 'destructive obedience' than about ineffective and indecisive *disobedience*."

This distinction is critical. Most of us have had the experience of having good intentions but being unable to translate those intentions into effective action. We have *wanted* to speak up more forcefully and effectively against racist or sexist remarks, but we were too slow to respond or the words didn't come out right. Or we have *wanted* to reach out to those who are ignored at social gatherings but were distracted by all that was going on and our own social needs. Most of us can relate to being good-hearted but ineffective, but not to being uncaring.

A chilling parallel to the behavior of Milgram's participants can be found in the behavior of some (and only some) of the German soldiers called on to execute Polish Jews during World War II (Browning, 1992). Members of German Reserve Police Battalion 101, for example, were mostly individuals who hoped to avoid the inevitable violence of the war by volunteering for police duty in the German city of Hamburg. After the invasion of Poland, however, they were removed from Hamburg and made to serve as military police in occupied Poland. Most of what they were called on to do was harmless, routine police work. But on July 13, 1942, the men were roused from their barracks before dawn and taken to the outskirts of the village of Józéfow, where they were given their gruesome orders—to round up all the Jewish men, women, and children from the village, send all able-bodied young men to a work camp, and shoot the rest.

Most were shocked and repelled by their orders. Many resisted. But their resistance, like that of Milgram's participants, was feeble. Some occupied themselves with petty errands or moved to the back of the battalion, hoping to avoid being called on

BOX 9.2 FOCUS ON TODAY

Would Milgram Get the Same Results Now?

If you conducted Milgram's experiments today, would you get the same results? Some argue that today's more intense media coverage of such events as the abuses at Abu Ghraib prison or the dubiously accurate intelligence reports about weapons of mass destruction before the 2003 invasion of Iraq have made people less trusting of authority and thus less likely to obey instructions to harm another individual. Perhaps, but it is a difficult idea to test because ethical concerns make it impossible to replicate Milgram's experiments today. All psychological research must now be approved by an institutional review board (see Chapter 2), whose job it is to make sure that any proposed research will not cause undue stress to the participants or harm them in any way. Few, if any, review boards would approve a replication of Milgram's experiments.

Jerry Burger of Santa Clara University did the next best thing, however, by con-ducting a near replication of Milgram's basic experiment to investigate whether the tendency to obey authority has changed since Milgram's time (Burger, 2009; Burger, Girgis, & Manning, 2011). Burger identified a critical moment in the proceedings when disobedience was most likely—just after the participant had (supposedly) delivered 150 volts of electricity and the learner protested and demanded to be released. It was some-thing of a now-or-never moment: four of five participants who did not stop at this point never stopped at all.

Burger saw an opportunity. It would be ethically dubious to put people through the stress of deciding between disobey-ing the experimenter or administering 300 or 400 volts of electricity. But the procedure is not so stressful—and hence is ethically more acceptable—up to the 150-volt level. After all, until that point the learner hasn't protested, and the pain caused by the shocks, the participants are likely to presume, can't be that bad. Burger therefore sought and received permission from Santa Clara's review board to replicate Milgram's basic experi-ment up to that point only.

Burger also took several steps to safe-guard the welfare of his participants. First, individuals who were interested in participating were asked over the phone if they had ever been diagnosed with a psychiatric disorder, were currently in psychotherapy or taking medication for anxiety or depression, or had ever expe-rienced any serious trauma. Anyone who answered yes to any of these questions was not allowed to participate. Second, those who passed this initial screening were told they would receive $50 for two 45-minute sessions. In the first ses-sion, participants filled out a number of psychological scales, such as the Beck Depression Inventory, and then were interviewed by a licensed clinical psychol-ogist. If the psychologist detected any

to take part. Others took part in the roundup but then refrained from shooting if no one was watching. Still others fired but missed intentionally. What they *didn't* do was state assertively that they wouldn't participate, that what they were being asked to do was wrong. They tried to find an easy way to disobey, but there was no easy way.

In the case of Milgram's experiments, participants experienced difficulty in try-ing to halt the proceedings partly because the experimenter was not playing by the normal rules of social life. The participants offered *reasons* for stopping the experiments, but the experimenter largely ignored those reasons, making mini-mally responsive statements such as "The experiment requires that you continue." Participants were understandably confused and uncertain about how to act. And as noted in the discussion of conformity, people are unlikely to act decisively when they lack a solid grasp of the events happening around them. What are we to do when charged with administering electric shock to "teach" someone who is no longer trying to learn anything, at the insistence of an authority figure who seems unconcerned about the learner's predicament? How are we to respond when events have stopped making sense?

These questions have important implications for those real-world instances of destructive obedience with which we should be most concerned. Many of the most

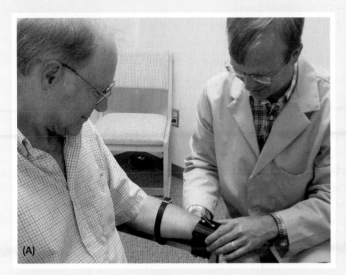

Revisiting Milgram In Jerry Burger's partial replication of the Milgram experiments, participants faced the same conflict over whether to administer increasing levels of shock (up to 165 volts) to the "learner" or to call a halt to his suffering by refusing to continue.

sign in the participants' questionnaire responses or in their face-to-face interviews that they might not be up to the challenge of being in the study, they were paid their $50 right then and excluded from the second session.

Those who made it past both screenings were run through a replication of the voice-feedback version of Milgram's experiment. The results were essentially the same as those obtained by Milgram himself. In Burger's study, 70 percent of the participants were willing to administer the next level of shock (165 volts) after hearing the learner's protest. This compares with 82 percent of Milgram's participants—not a statistically significant difference. Men and women were equally likely to continue past the critical 150-volt level, and whether participants obeyed the experimenter was unrelated to how they scored on personality scales measuring empathy or their desire to control events in their lives. Today, people seem to react to pressure to obey the same way they did almost 50 years ago.

hideous episodes of genocide, for example, have occurred right after large-scale social upheaval. Without reliable norms of appropriate behavior, people are less able to muster the confidence required for decisive action to stop such atrocities.

Release from Responsibility Participants' ineffectiveness in stopping the experiment meant that they were trapped in a situation of terrible conflict and stress. They knew that what was happening should not continue, yet they couldn't bring it to an end. They were therefore desperate for anything that would reduce their stress. Fortunately for the participants (but unfortunately for the learner, if he really had been receiving electric shock), the experimenter provided something to reduce their stress by taking responsibility for what was happening. When participants asked, as many did, "Who is responsible for what happens here?" the experimenter responded, "I am responsible." Participants seized on this as a justification for their actions, and the stress they were experiencing was significantly reduced.

We have all been in similarly stressful, confusing situations in which we wanted the stress and confusion to end. "My friends are making me uncomfortable by savagely teasing that guy in our English class, but they'll think I'm a jerk if I speak out." "Everyone's popping those pills as if they weren't harmful, and they'll think

I'm a wimp if I don't too." It is always tempting in such situations to grab at anything that would make the dilemma "go away." "Maybe the guy in our class really does deserve it, and I'm being too sensitive." "Maybe the pills really are harmless, and I'm blowing things out of proportion."

Of course, the cover, or "out," that the experimenter provided in Milgram's experiments worked only because participants viewed the person taking responsibility as a legitimate authority. People wouldn't allow just anyone to take responsibility and then assume that everything was okay. If you were approached by a strange character on campus who said, "Quick, help me set fire to the psychology building. I'll take full responsibility," you almost certainly would refuse to pitch in. In Milgram's experiments, however, participants believed they could legitimately transfer responsibility to the experimenter. He was a representative of science; and in nearly all variations of Milgram's paradigm, he was affiliated with Yale University, a respected institution (although obedience was still high when the experimenter operated out of a storefront in downtown Bridgeport). These aspects of the situation made it easier for participants to reduce their own stress over what was happening by assuming that the experimenter knew better and was ultimately responsible for what happened.

The cover provided by authorities has implications for some of the worst acts of destructive obedience in history. In Nazi Germany, in Rwanda, and at Abu Ghraib, the demands to obey were issued by authority figures who either explicitly took responsibility or whose position supported an assumption of responsibility. And such claims of responsibility have nearly always been legitimized by some overarching ideology. Whether it is based on nationalism, religious ideology, or ethnic identity, every example of such organized aggression has been draped in a legitimizing ideology that seeks to present otherwise hideous actions in a way that makes them seem like morally appropriate behavior (Staub, 1989; Zajonc, 2002).

Step-by-Step Involvement Keep in mind as well that the participants in these experiments did not deliver 450 volts of electricity right away. Instead, each participant first administered only 15 volts to the learner. Who wouldn't do that? That's feedback, not punishment. Then 30 volts. No problem there either. Then

Legitimacy of Experiment To see how participants would react if the experiment were not conducted at Yale and the authority seemed less legitimate, Milgram had the participants report to "Research Associates of Bridgeport," located above a storefront in downtown Bridgeport and inside a seedy office. Obedience rates declined somewhat but remained high even under these conditions.

45, 60, 75—each step is a small one. Once participants started down this path, though, it was hard to stop, and they administered more and more shock. Indeed, the increments were so small that if a certain level of shock seemed like too much, why wouldn't the previous level also have been too much (Gilbert, 1981)?

It is important to recognize the powerful influence of the step-by-step nature of participants' obedience in the experiments. Most of us have had the experience of gradually getting in over our heads in this way. We may tell a "little white lie"—one that sets in motion a cascade of events that requires more and more deception. (Many a sitcom plot rests on this very sequence.) Or we may dig in our heels over a small matter in a dispute—and later find it hard to back down because of our initial stubbornness. Our behavior often creates its own momentum, and it's hard to know in advance where it will lead. Milgram's participants can certainly be forgiven for not foreseeing how everything would unfold. Would any of us have seen it any more clearly?

The parallels between this element of Milgram's procedure and what happened in Nazi Germany are striking (**Box 9.3**). German citizens were not asked, out of the blue, to assist with or condone the deportation of Jews, Gypsies, homo-

---

BOX 9.3   FOCUS ON HISTORY

Step-by-Step to Genocide

Anti-Jewish laws and policies of the German government before and during World War II. Note the gradual nature of anti-Jewish statutes and policies.

1. April 1, 1933
Boycott of Jewish businesses is declared.

2. April 7, 1933
Law for the Restoration of the Professional Civil Service authorizes the dismissal of most non-Aryan civil servants (especially those with Jewish parents or grandparents).

3. September 22, 1933
Reestablishment of Reich Chamber of Culture leads to the removal of non-Aryans from organizations and enterprises related to literature, the press, broadcasting, music, and art.

4. September 15, 1935
Reich Citizenship Law defines citizens of the Reich as only those who are of German or kindred blood.

5. September 16, 1935
Law for the Protection of German Blood and German Honor forbids marriage between Jews and nationals of German or kindred blood and declares marriages conducted in defiance of this law void, forbids relations outside of marriage between Jews and nationals of German or kindred blood, and forbids Jews from employing in their household female nationals of German or kindred blood who are under age 45.

6. November 16, 1936
Jews are prohibited from obtaining passports or traveling abroad, except in special cases.

7. April 1938
Jews are forced to register with the government all property valued at 5,000 marks or more.

8. July 25, 1938
Fourth Decree of the Reich Citizenship Law terminates the licenses of Jewish physicians as of September 30, 1938.

9. September 27, 1938
Fifth Decree of the Reich Citizenship Law allows Jewish legal advisers to attend professionally only to the legal affairs of Jews.

10. October 5, 1938
Jewish passports and ration cards are marked with a J.

11. January 1, 1939
All Jews are required to carry a special ID card.

12. July 1940
Purchases by Jews are restricted to certain hours and stores; telephones are taken away from Jews.

13. September 19, 1941
Jews are forced to display the Jewish badge prominently on their clothing and with few exceptions are not allowed to use public transportation.

14. October 14, 1941
Massive deportation of German Jews to concentration camps begins.

15. October 23, 1941
Jewish emigration is prohibited.

16. January 20, 1942 (the Wansee Conference)
Nazi leaders decide that 11 million Jews (every Jew in Europe) are to be killed.

sexuals, and communists to the death camps. Instead, the rights of these groups were gradually stripped away. First, certain business practices were restricted, then travel constraints were imposed, and then citizenship was narrowed; only later were people loaded into boxcars and sent to the death camps. The Nazis would doubtless have had a much harder time if they had started with the last step. Their own citizens would probably have been less cooperative; more of their victims would probably have resisted more actively. It is telling in this regard that the most vigorous defiance of the Nazis' genocide plans tended to take place not in Germany, but in the countries Germany overran. Among the many reasons for this difference may well have been that Germany carried out the "final solution" much faster in the conquered countries than in Germany itself.

 Many factors contribute to people's willingness to obey leaders who demand immoral behavior. Several elements of the situation may make obedience easier to understand: a person's attempts to disobey are often blocked; the person in authority often takes responsibility for what happens; and once the obedience begins, there is typically no obvious stopping point. But when the circumstances lead the individual to be "tuned in" to the victim, obedience decreases substantially. When the circumstances lead the individual to "tune out" the person in authority, obedience is also greatly reduced.

COMPLIANCE

Milgram's research demonstrates how common it is for people to obey the insistent commands of someone in a position of authority—and why they so often do so. But attempts to influence behavior often come from people with no special authority or status. Charities urge us to give money. Con men try to get us to go along with their schemes. Salespeople want us to buy their products. Friends ask us for favors. If you want someone to do something, and you have no power over the person and only your wits to help you, what approach should you take? Or, if you're worried about being taken advantage of by those who have their own (and not your) best interests at heart, what techniques should you watch out for? Social psychologists have studied different strategies for eliciting compliance, and their research gives us some clues about how (and how effectively) these strategies work.

Compliance attempts come in roughly three types: those directed at the mind, those directed at the heart, and those based on the power of norms (which, given the impact of informational and normative influence, appeal to both the mind and the heart). People can be led to do things because they come to see good reasons for doing so, because their feelings guide them to do so, or because everyone else is doing so. Of course, these types of influence are not so neatly separable, and many compliance attempts are a blend of the three approaches.

Reason-Based Approaches

When someone does something for us, we usually feel compelled to do something for that person in return. Indeed, all societies that have ever been studied possess a powerful **norm of reciprocity**, according to which people should benefit those

norm of reciprocity A norm dictating that people should provide benefits to those who benefit them.

who benefit them (Fiske, 1991; Gouldner, 1960). This norm also exists in many bird and mammal species. For example, when one monkey removes parasites from another's back, the latter typically returns the favor, thus helping to cement the social bond between them.

When someone does us a favor, it creates an obligation to agree to any reasonable request that person might make in turn. To fail to respond is to violate a powerful social norm and run the risk of social sanction (Cotterell, Eisenberger, & Speicher, 1992). Indeed, the English vocabulary is rich in derogatory terms for those who do not uphold their end of the norm of reciprocity: *sponge, moocher, deadbeat, ingrate, parasite, bloodsucker, leech.* If you do a favor for someone, that person is likely to agree to a reasonable request you subsequently make because of the fear of being seen as a sponge, moocher, and so on. This may be why restaurant customers often leave larger tips when the server gives them a piece of candy (Strohmetz, Rind, Fisher, & Lynn, 2002).

The influence of the norm of reciprocity in eliciting compliance was demonstrated with particular clarity in a simple experiment in which two individuals were asked to rate a number of paintings, supposedly as part of an experiment on aesthetics (Regan, 1971; see also Whatley, Webster, Smith, & Rhodes, 1999). One of the individuals was a real participant; the other was a confederate of the experimenter. In one condition, the confederate returned from a break in the procedure with two sodas and offered one to the participant. "I asked (the experimenter) if I could get myself a Coke, and he said it was OK, so I bought one for you, too." In another condition, the confederate returned empty-handed. Afterward, during another pause in the experiment, the confederate asked the participant for a favor. He explained that he was selling raffle tickets for which the prize was a new car and that he stood to win $50 if he sold the most raffle tickets. He then proceeded to ask if the participant was willing to buy any raffle tickets, which cost 25 cents apiece: "Any would help, the more the better." (To make sure all participants had the means to purchase some tickets, they had already been paid—in quarters!—for participating in the study.)

In a testament to the power of the norm of reciprocity, participants who were earlier given a Coke by the confederate bought twice as many raffle tickets as those who were not given a Coke (or were given a Coke by the experimenter, to control for the possibility that simply receiving a Coke may have put participants in a good mood and it was that, and not the compulsion to reciprocate, that had increased compliance). Thus doing a favor for someone creates an uninvited debt that the recipient is obligated to repay. Businesses and other organizations often try to take advantage of this pressure by preceding their request with a small gift. Insurance agents give out calendars or return-address labels. Pollsters who want you to complete a survey send it along with a dollar. Cult members offer a flower before giving their pitch. Our hearts sink when we see these gifts coming, and we often go to great lengths to avoid them—and the obligations they bring.

"All contacts among men rest on the schema of giving and returning the equivalent."

—G. Simmel

"There is no duty more indispensable than that of returning a kindness."

—Cicero

Reciprocity and Grooming among Mammals Reciprocity helps promote group living and reduce aggression, as evidenced by grooming in macaques.

The Reciprocal Concessions, or the Door-in-the-Face, Technique Robert Cialdini, social psychology's most innovative contributor to the literature on compliance, has explored a novel application of the norm of reciprocity. The inspiration for his decision to conduct research on the technique is best introduced in his own words:

> I was walking down the street when I was approached by an eleven- or twelve-year-old boy. He introduced himself and said that he was selling tickets to the annual Boy Scouts circus to be held on the upcoming Saturday night. He asked if I wished to buy any at five dollars apiece. Since one of the last places I wanted to spend Saturday evening was with the Boy Scouts, I declined. "Well," he said, "if you don't want to buy any tickets, how about buying some of our big chocolate bars? They're only a dollar each." I bought a couple and, right away, realized that something noteworthy had happened. I knew that to be the case because: (a) I do not like chocolate bars; (b) I do like dollars; (c) I was standing there with two of his chocolate bars; and (d) he was walking away with two of my dollars. (Cialdini, 1984, p. 47)

Cialdini's experience with the Boy Scout led him to articulate a general compliance technique whereby people feel compelled to respond to a concession with one of their own (Cialdini et al., 1975; O'Keefe & Hale, 1998, 2001; Reeves, Baker, Boyd, & Cialdini, 1991). First, you ask someone for a very large favor that he or she will certainly refuse, and then you follow that request with one for a more modest favor that you are really interested in receiving. The idea is that the drop in the size of the request will be seen as a concession, a concession that the target of the request must match to honor the norm of reciprocity. The most available concession is to comply with the second request. Another way of looking at this reciprocal concessions technique is that the first favor is so large and unreasonable that the person asked inevitably refuses, slamming the door in the face of that request but then keeping it open just a crack for the subsequent, smaller request. The combination of making a large request followed immediately by a smaller request is hence also known as the **door-in-the-face technique** (or **reciprocal concessions technique**).

Cialdini demonstrated the power of this technique in a field study on the Arizona State University campus. Members of Cialdini's research team, posing as representatives of the "County Youth Counseling Program," approached students and asked if they would be willing to chaperone a group of juvenile delinquents on a day trip to the zoo. Not surprisingly, the overwhelming majority, 83 percent, refused. But the experience—and the response rate—was much different for another group of students who had first encountered a much larger request. They were first asked whether they would be willing to counsel juvenile delinquents for 2 hours a week for the next two years. All of them refused, at which point they were asked about chaperoning the trip to the zoo. Now, 50 percent of the students agreed to chaperone—triple the rate of the other group (Cialdini et al., 1975). A series of carefully crafted follow-up studies revealed that the pressure to respond to what was perceived as a concession was responsible for the dramatic increase in compliance. For example, this technique does not work when the two requests are made by different individuals. In that case, the second, smaller request is not seen as a concession, so it does not create the same obligation.

door-in-the-face technique (reciprocal concessions technique) Asking someone for a very large favor that he or she will certainly refuse and then following that request with one for a smaller favor (which tends to be seen as a concession that the target will feel compelled to honor).

Want to use this technique in your own life? Then consider an experiment in which professors were asked if they would be willing to meet for "15 to 20 minutes" to discuss a topic of interest to a student. When faced with this request by itself, 57 percent agreed. But 78 percent agreed to the request when it was preceded by another request—to spend "2 hours a week for the rest of the semester" with the student (Harari, Mohr, & Hosey, 1980).

The That's-Not-All Technique Another technique that uses the norm of reciprocity in a similar way, the **that's-not-all technique**, may be more familiar to you. Suppose you're at an electronics store and have asked about a plasma TV you've been wanting. You're told it costs $1,299 and comes with a three-year warranty. After a moment in which you say nothing, the salesperson says, "And that's not all; it also comes with a free DVD player!" An add-on like this may strike you as a gift from the store or the salesperson and therefore create some pressure to reciprocate. This sort of pressure can result in increased sales.

Jerry Burger has demonstrated the effectiveness of this technique. At an arts fair on the Santa Clara University campus, half of the individuals who approached the booth of the Psychology Club bake sale were told that one cupcake and two medium-sized cookies cost a total of 75 cents. The other half of the participants were initially told that each cupcake cost 75 cents, and then, before they responded whether they wanted one or not, they were told that the price included two medium-sized cookies. Seventy-three percent of the participants in the latter, "that's-not-all" condition purchased the snacks, compared with only 40 percent in the control "all-at-once" condition (Burger, 1986; Burger, Reed, DeCesare, Rauner, & Rozolis, 1999; Pollock, Smith, Knowles, & Bruce, 1998).

The Foot-in-the-Door Technique All of us perform certain actions because they are consistent with our self-image. Environmentalists take the time to recycle (even when sorely tempted to toss a bottle or can into the trash) because that's part of what it means to be an environmentalist. Skiers rise early to tackle fresh snow (even when they really want to sleep in) because that's what real skiing enthusiasts do. This suggests that if requests can be crafted to appeal to a person's self-image, the likelihood of compliance can be increased.

One way to pull this off is to employ what's known as the **foot-in-the-door technique**. In a sense, it is the opposite of the door-in-the-face technique because it starts with a small request to which everyone complies (which allows the person making the request to get a foot in the door) and then follows up with a larger request involving the real behavior of interest. The idea is that the initial agreement to the small request will lead to a change in the individual's self-image as someone who does this sort of thing or who contributes to such causes. The person then has a reason for agreeing to the subsequent, larger request: "It's just who I am."

In the first systematic examination of the foot-in-the-door technique, the investigators knocked on doors in a California neighborhood and asked homeowners

Foot-in-the-Door Technique After getting the customer to agree to a test drive, it may be easier for the salesperson to "close the deal" and get the customer to buy the car.

whether they would be willing to have a large billboard sign bearing the slogan "Drive Carefully" installed on their lawn for one week (Freedman & Fraser, 1966). One group of residents was shown a picture of the sign and how large and unattractive it was, so not surprisingly only 17 percent agreed to the request. Another group of residents was approached with a much smaller request—to display in a window of their home a 3-inch-square sign bearing the words "Be a safe driver." Virtually all of them agreed to do so. Two weeks later, when this group was asked to display the billboard on their lawn, a staggering 76 percent of them agreed to do so.

To examine the breadth of this effect, the investigators included another condition in which the first request (signing a petition) was unlike the second and involved a different issue (keeping California beautiful). Even with these differences in the two requests, agreeing to the first request led nearly half the respondents to agree to the second, larger request. Perhaps we should be even more careful than we already are about agreeing to the requests that others make of us. Agreeing to do the most trivial favors can set us up to give in to much larger requests (Burger, 1999; Burger & Guadagno, 2003; Schwartzwald, Bizman, & Raz, 1983).

Notice the similarity between the foot-in-the-door technique and the step-by-step nature of the requests made by Milgram in his study of obedience. In both studies, getting participants to comply with a small and unobjectionable action (signing a petition, administering 30 volts of electricity) paves the way to much more serious behavior. The similarity between the two experiments also shows that taking away a reason for *not* doing something can be as powerful as providing a reason for doing it. Having administered, say, 160 volts of electricity takes away a reason for refusing to administer 175 volts. After all, what's so different about the two levels of shock? And consenting to an earlier request to display a small sign takes away a reason for refusing to put up a much larger sign ("No thanks, I don't do that sort of thing.").

Another technique that works in precisely this way involves legitimizing the tiniest imaginable contribution. Charities might solicit money, for example, by ending their request with the words "even a penny would help." Such a request invalidates the thought that "I can't really afford to give." What's more, most people would be reluctant to make a very small donation once they have decided to give. Indeed, research on the effectiveness of this technique shows that such "even a penny" appeals substantially increase the percentage of individuals who donate but do not lower the amount that is typically given (Brockner, Guzzi, Kane, Levine, & Shaplen, 1984; Cialdini & Schroeder, 1976; Reeves, Macolini, & Martin, 1987; Weyant, 1984). The net result is that such appeals increase overall charitable giving.

Emotion-Based Approaches

Cognitive, or reason-based, appeals can be effective in obtaining compliance, but so can affective, or emotion-based, approaches.

Positive Mood Suppose you want to ask your dad for a new computer, a new amplifier for your guitar, or simply to borrow the family car for a road trip. When would you ask? When he's just come home from work in a foul mood, cursing his boss and his suffocating job? Or after he's just landed a promotion and a big raise? It doesn't take an advanced degree in psychology to know that it's better to ask when he's in a good mood. When people are in a good mood, they feel expansive, charitable, and affirmative, so they're more likely to agree to such requests. Even little children know to ask someone for a favor when that person is in a good mood.

The wisdom of this approach has been verified in countless experiments. In one study, participants received a telephone call from someone who claimed to have spent her last dime on this very ("misdialed") call and who asked if the participant would dial the intended number and relay a message (Isen, Clark, & Schwartz, 1976). In one condition, no more than 20 minutes before receiving the call, participants were given a free sample of stationery to put them in a positive mood. In another condition, participants did not receive a free sample before receiving the call. When the request was made of individuals who were not given the free sample, only 10 percent complied. But the compliance rate shot up dramatically among participants who received the request a few minutes after receiving the gift (**Figure 9.8**), and then it declined gradually as the delay between the gift and the request increased.

Feeling good clearly makes people more likely to agree to requests and, more generally, to help others. This effect has been shown in experiments that have lifted participants' moods by telling them they did well on a test, having them think happy thoughts, giving them cookies, or playing cheerful music. Participants are then confronted with requests to make change, donate to charity, help with experiments, give blood, and tutor students (Carlson, Charlin, & Miller, 1988; Isen, 1999).

Positive moods tend to increase compliance for two main reasons. First, our mood colors how we interpret events. We are more likely to view requests for favors as less intrusive and less threatening when we're in a good mood. We give others the benefit of the doubt, possibly looking on someone who asks to borrow our notes not as an irresponsible or lazy individual who doesn't deserve to be bailed out, but as a victim of circumstance who could get back on track with a little assistance (Carlson et al., 1988; Forgas, 1998a, 1998b; Forgas & Bower, 1987).

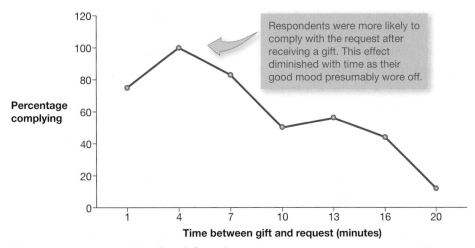

FIGURE 9.8 Positive Mood and Compliance Percentage of respondents who agreed to help a stranger by making a telephone call and relaying a message 1 to 20 minutes after receiving a small gift. (Source: Adapted from Isen, Clark, & Schwartz, 1976.)

Positive Mood and Requests When people are in a good mood, they are more likely to agree to requests. Those attending this benefit for UNICEF are therefore more likely to donate money to the organization.

Another reason a good mood increases compliance involves what's known as mood maintenance. Pardon the tautology, but it feels good to feel good, and we typically want the feeling to last as long as possible (Clark & Isen, 1982; Wegener & Petty, 1994). And one way to sustain a good mood is to do something for another person (Dunn, Aknin, & Norton, 2008). Or, stated differently, one way to wreck a good mood is to turn down a request and invite all sorts of self-recrimination ("What kind of heartless person am I?") that pollutes and erodes a positive mental state. Several studies point to mood maintenance as an important component of the impact of a positive mood on compliance. In one study, participants were first either given cookies (which put them in a good mood) or not given cookies. They were then asked (by someone other than the person who provided the cookies) if they would be willing to assist with an experiment by serving as a confederate. Half the participants were told the job of confederate would involve *helping* the "true" participant in the experiment; the other half were told it would involve *hindering* the participant. Having received a cookie (and being in a good mood) increased the compliance rate when the task involved helping the participant, but not when it involved hindering the participant (Isen & Levin, 1972). Helping another person promotes feeling good; hurting someone does not.

Negative Mood If a good mood increases compliance, does a bad mood decrease it? It surely can, but even the slightest introspection reveals that certain types of bad moods are likely to *increase* compliance, not decrease it. And people know this and use it to their advantage. Suppose, for example, that your boyfriend or girlfriend was flirting too much with someone (alas, not you, or it wouldn't be too much), and you point out the offense. Would that be a good time to ask your partner for something? You bet it would! When people feel guilty, they're often motivated to do whatever they can to get rid of that awful feeling. So at least one type of bad mood, centered around feelings of guilt, should increase compliance.

Social psychologists have demonstrated a strong, positive association between guilt and compliance in many experiments in which participants have been led to feel guilty by being induced to lie, break a camera, knock over stacks of carefully arranged index cards, or injure an adorable laboratory rat (Carlsmith & Gross, 1969; Darlington & Macker, 1966; O'Keefe & Figgé, 1997; J. Regan, 1971; D. T. Regan, Williams, & Sparling, 1972). In a particularly clever test of the effect of guilt on compliance, researchers asked Catholics to donate to the March of Dimes when they were either on their way into church for confession or on their way out. The presumption was that those on their way in were rehearsing their sins and thus feeling guilty; those on their way out had done penance for their sins and so were no longer plagued by guilt. As the investigators predicted, those solicited on the way in gave more money than those solicited on the way out (Harris, Benson, & Hall, 1975).

Another study of guilt and compliance made it clear that other, related emotions can lead to increased compliance as well. In this experiment, participants were recruited to assist in a supposed study of growth and development (J. Regan, 1971). The study was described as already having run for six weeks, and the participant's task was to monitor a voltage meter (located to the participant's left) to make sure the stimulation delivered to a 2-month-old albino rat (located to the participant's right) "stayed at the pre-determined mild level." Meanwhile, the experimenter was stationed in an adjoining room, where he was supposed to be measuring the rat's pulse but actually was secretly monitoring the participant's every move. As the experiment got under way, all participants performed the assigned task—for a while. But because the voltage meter registered the same 109 to 110 volts moment after monotonous moment, pretty soon all participants turned their attention to the rat itself. When they did, the experimenter delivered an intense shock through the floor of the rat's cage, causing the rat to jump and squeal in pain and the voltage meter to shoot up from 110 to 140 volts. The experimenter then called out from the adjoining room, "Something's wrong . . . his pulse is wild . . . [with a tone of frustration] Six weeks!" The experimenter then proceeded to terminate the experiment and sent the participant to the department secretary to receive the promised payment. While at the secretary's office, the participant received an appeal to donate to a charitable cause.

The unsettling experience with the rat, of course, was designed to make participants feel guilty (because their inattentiveness apparently caused the rat to receive too much shock and thus jeopardized the experiment). It also allowed researchers to find out whether the participants' guilt would increase the amount they gave to the charitable cause. It did. Participants who thought their actions had led to the fiasco donated nearly three times as much money as the participants who went through the procedure uneventfully because nothing bad happened to the rat. Once again, guilt increased compliance.

But another condition of the experiment yielded a telling result. Participants in this condition also witnessed the rat jump and squeal; but it happened at a random moment, not right after they had turned their attention away from their assigned task. And they heard the experimenter yell from the adjoining room, "There has been a short circuit in here . . . This isn't your fault at all." These participants, then, had no reason to feel guilty over what had happened, yet they ended up donating just as much as the guilty participants. Apparently, *witnessing* harm is enough to enhance the impulse to "do good"; one need not be the cause of the harm. Thus simply feeling upset, or even sad, can lead to an increase in people's willingness to comply with requests.

These results suggest that bad moods tend to increase compliance in part because we don't want to feel bad, so we jump at the opportunity to do something to brighten our mood. According to the **negative state relief hypothesis**, doing something for someone else, especially when we do it for a good cause, is one way to make ourselves feel better (Cialdini, Darby, & Vincent, 1973; Cialdini & Fultz, 1990; Cialdini et al., 1987). We often help others, in other words, to help ourselves.

Negative State Relief Oskar Schindler saved the lives of 1,200 Polish Jews during the Holocaust. Initially driven by the desire for easy profits, he took over a Jewish factory and ran it with cheap Jewish labor. Perhaps in a desire for negative state relief or from sheer humanitarianism, he used the millions he made from the cheap labor to bribe officials to save those who were slated for death. He is pictured here in Tel Aviv with some of those he saved and their descendants.

negative state relief hypothesis The idea that people engage in certain actions, such as agreeing to a request, to relieve their negative feelings and feel better about themselves.

Do not take the research on negative state relief to mean that it is the sole reason for the link between bad moods and increased compliance. Although people's desire to improve their mood may be the most consistent and powerful motive at play, there are other considerations as well. Even if we desire relief from guilt, sadness, and embarrassment equally, the behaviors we are willing to engage in to achieve that relief may be different for some of these emotions. Guilt and sadness can both lead to withdrawal—which can interfere with compliance—but the circumstances that elicit withdrawal are likely to be very different for the two states. When sad, you might be reluctant to be around those who are happy; when feeling guilty, you might want to avoid anyone or anything that reminds you of your transgression.

Another type of bad mood, that produced by anger, is likely to be another story entirely. People sometimes revel in their anger and hence, at least for a time, may be less interested in seeking relief from it. So although all sorts of bad moods increase compliance because doing someone a favor promises relief from a negative state, the precise profile of the relationship between mood and compliance is likely to be different for different types of bad moods. Historically, social psychologists who have studied compliance have focused on the effects of the rather pronounced difference between being in a good mood and being in a bad mood. But research that distinguishes among the different varieties of good and bad moods is proving to be informative in related areas of social psychology, and the field of compliance awaits the results of similar, more fine-grained investigations (Lerner, Gonzalez, Small, & Fischhoff, 2003; Lerner, Small, & Loewenstein, 2004; Tiedens & Linton, 2001).

Norm-Based Approaches

As studies of conformity have shown, people copy one another. People with overweight friends tend to have trouble keeping their weight down as well (Hill, Rand, Nowak, & Christakis, 2010); teenage girls exposed to pregnant teenagers are more likely to become pregnant themselves (Akerlof, Yellen, & Katz, 1996); how well older people plan for retirement is greatly influenced by their coworkers' plans (Duflo & Saez, 2003); and student drinking is connected to student perceptions of how much other students drink (Lewis & Neighbors, 2004). Clearly, people conform to the behavior of those around them, a tendency that can be harnessed to get them to comply with explicit requests or implicit suggestions. That's why advertisers assert that "More and more people are switching to . . ." or "Nine out of ten people use. . . ."

Effective Norm-Based Appeals Letting people know what others are doing can also be used to advance the public good. Consider a norm-based approach to energy use that was studied in California (Schultz, Nolan, Cialdini, Goldstein, & Griskevicius, 2007). Homeowners received messages indicating how much energy they had used (in kilowatt-hours per day) in previous weeks, as well as what the average energy use was in the neighborhood. The effect of this simple intervention was clear-cut and immediate: those who consumed more energy than average significantly reduced their use of energy.

But what about the households that used *less* energy than average? Did telling them that their neighbors tended to be less conscientious make them more wasteful? Yes, it did, but the investigators had a simple remedy at hand that preserved

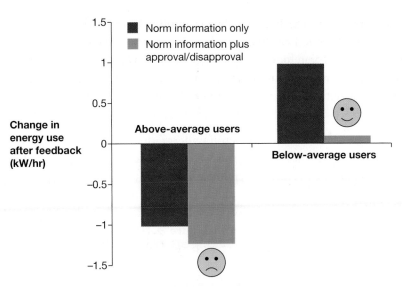

FIGURE 9.9 Using Norms to Conserve Energy Telling above-average energy consumers how much energy they use and how much the average household uses significantly reduced energy consumption (bars on the left). Providing this information to below-average energy consumers led to significantly greater energy consumption, unless it was accompanied by a simple symbol of approval (bars on the right). (Source: Adapted from Schultz et al., 2007.)

the gains among above-average energy users while undoing the damage caused to the habits of below-average users. The usage information given to half of the households was accompanied by a small sign of approval or disapproval (a happy or sad face), depending on whether the residents' energy use was better or worse than average. The signal of approval was enough to maintain the superior conservation efforts of those who might otherwise have slacked off (**Figure 9.9**).

Another ecologically minded norm-based approach was directed at persuading hotel guests to reuse their towels and thus conserve water and energy. The investigators found that when the small card (one you've doubtless seen many times yourself) urging guests to reuse their towels contained a statement that a majority of past guests had chosen to reuse their towels, a significantly higher percentage complied. Interestingly, the rate of compliance increased even further when the card stated that a majority of guests who "stayed in this room" reused their towels (Goldstein, Cialdini, & Griskevicius, 2008).

Telling people about social norms is likely to be most effective when the norm is misunderstood—when people overestimate the popularity of destructive behavior or underestimate the popularity of constructive behavior. Student drinking is a case in point, an example of the phenomenon of pluralistic ignorance described in Chapter 4. On campuses across the United States, students think that binge drinking is much more common than it actually is and that "teetotaling" or moderate drinking is much less common than it is (Perkins, Haines, & Rice, 2005). In one study, Deborah Prentice and Dale Miller (1993) examined the discrepancy between private attitudes and public norms about alcohol at Princeton University. They thought there might be a discrepancy between the two for the following reasons:

> The alcohol situation at Princeton is exacerbated by the central role of alcohol in many of the university's institutions and traditions. For example, at the

eating clubs, the center of social life on campus, alcohol is on tap 24 hours a day, 7 days a week. Princeton reunions boast the second highest level of alcohol consumption for any event in the country after the Indianapolis 500. The social norms for drinking at the university are clear: Students must be comfortable with alcohol use to partake of Princeton social life. (Prentice & Miller, 1993, p. 244)

Prentice and Miller asked Princeton undergraduates how comfortable they felt about drinking habits at Princeton, as well as how comfortable they thought both their *friends* and the *average undergraduate* felt about campus drinking habits. If the students were suffering from pluralistic ignorance on this issue, they would indicate that they were less comfortable with drinking than they supposed most students were. The results, shown in **Figure 9.10**, indicate that this is exactly what happened. Hidden discomfort with alcohol existed side by side with perceived popular support.

Efforts to stem excessive alcohol consumption by providing students with accurate information about their peers' drinking have proved to be quite effective (Neighbors, Larimer, & Lewis, 2004; Perkins & Craig, 2006; Schroeder and Prentice, 1998). In one study, students attending regularly scheduled club or organizational meetings typed into wireless keypads information about their own drinking behavior and their beliefs about the drinking habits of their peers. Their aggregate responses were immediately projected for all to see, giving everyone telling information about actual drinking behavior on campus—and correcting widespread misunderstandings of how much and how often other students drink. Follow-up online surveys conducted one and two months later revealed that students who received this information reported drinking significantly less

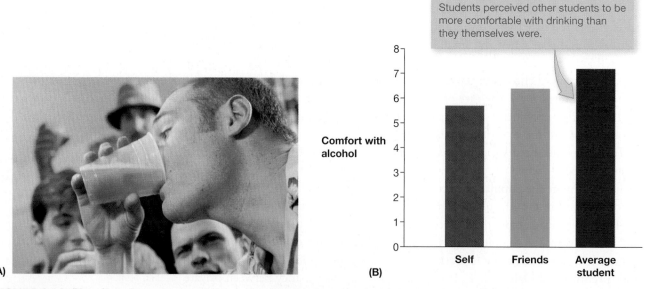

(A)

(B)

FIGURE 9.10 Pluralistic Ignorance (A) University students believe that drinking alcohol is more popular among their peers than it really is. Because of this belief, they censor their own reservations about drinking, thus furthering the illusion that alcohol is so popular. (B) Princeton University students' ratings of their own and other students' comfort with campus drinking habits at Princeton. (Source: Adapted from Prentice & Miller, 1993.)

than they had previously, and less than students in a control group (LaBrie, Hummer, Neighbors, & Pedersen, 2008).

Descriptive and Prescriptive Norms In constructing norm-based compliance appeals, it is important to be aware that there are two kinds of norms. **Descriptive norms** are simply that—descriptions of what is typically done. **Prescriptive norms**, often called **injunctive norms**, are what one is supposed to do. Descriptive norms correspond to what *is*; prescriptive norms correspond to what *ought to be*. University administrators often say that students should get eight or nine hours of sleep (prescriptive norm), but most students sleep much less (descriptive norm).

It is also important in constructing an effective appeal to be sure that the two norms are not placed in conflict with each other. A common mistake is to try to strengthen the pull of the prescriptive norm by stating how infrequently it is followed. "Isn't it a shame that so few people . . ." vote in elections, eat a healthy diet, get screened for cancer, you name it. Making such an appeal is understandable, but note that it inadvertently pits a descriptive norm against the prescriptive norm it is trying to highlight (Sieverding, Decker, & Zimmerman, 2010). By telling people what a shame it is that so few people vote, you are telling them that few people vote. Given the power of descriptive norms, such information is likely to make people *less* likely to vote, not more likely. Indeed, those involved in get-out-the-vote campaigns now know that it is more effective to emphasize how many people vote, not how few (Gerber & Rogers, 2009).

A particularly ingenious investigation of the importance of aligning prescriptive and descriptive norms was conducted in Petrified Forest National Park in Arizona, where visitors sometimes take samples of petrified wood home with them as souvenirs. If everyone took samples, of course, there would soon be no Petrified Forest to visit. To examine the most effective ways to deal with the problem, the investigators rotated different warning signs at various locations in the park. One sign had the usual emphasis on the severity of the problem, stating, "Many past visitors have removed petrified wood from the park, changing the state of the Petrified Forest," and accompanied by pictures of visitors taking wood. An alternative, positively framed sign stated, "The vast majority of past visitors have left the petrified wood in the park, preserving the natural state of the Petrified Forest," and was accompanied by pictures of visitors admiring and photographing a piece of petrified wood. The investigators placed specially marked pieces of wood along trails near these signs and monitored how many of them were stolen over the course of the experiment. In a remarkable demonstration of the importance of aligning prescriptive and descriptive norms, the theft rate was over four times lower when the signs emphasized how few people take petrified wood from the park (Cialdini, Demaine, Sagarin, Barrett, Rhoads, & Winters, 2006).

Descriptive and Prescriptive Norms in Conflict By telling people they shouldn't remove petrified wood from the Petrified National Forest (prescriptive norm), park officials are communicating that stealing petrified wood is something that people do (descriptive norm).

BOX 9.4 FOCUS ON POSITIVE PSYCHOLOGY

Resisting Social Influence

"I'd rather be a free man in my grave /
Than living as a puppet or a slave."
—Reggae legend Jimmy Cliff

People don't always conform, comply, and obey. They sometimes engage in heartening, even heroic, acts of independence—refusing to go along with misguided peers, defying the demands of a corrupt boss, or blowing the whistle on unethical business practices. What enables people to hold their ground, obey their conscience, and resist being influenced by others?

The pressure to give in to others can be offset by the tendency for people to resist attempts to restrict their freedom to act or think as they wish. According to **reactance theory**, people experience an unpleasant state of arousal when they believe their freedoms are threatened, and they often act to reduce this unpleasant arousal by reasserting their prerogatives (Brehm, 1956). If your parents tell you that you cannot dye your hair, does your desire to have it dyed diminish or increase? Reactance theory predicts that the moment you feel your freedom is being taken away, it becomes more precious and your desire to maintain it increases.

But once motivated to resist, what factors might increase your ability to stand firm? Recall some of the lessons of Asch's and Milgram's experiments. For example, one important variable is practice. In Milgram's experiments, many participants wanted to disobey and even tried to do so, but they weren't very good at it. Maybe if they had been trained to disobey when

the situation called for it, they would have done a better job. There is evidence that the Christians who tried to save Jews during the Holocaust tended to be people who had a history of helping others, either as part of their job or as volunteers. Those who did the most to help often did not have any higher regard for their Jewish neighbors than did those who did little: they were simply more practiced in reaching out and providing aid.

Another way to increase the ability to resist social influence is to have an ally. In Asch's experiments, having just one additional person who departed from the majority was enough to drastically reduce conformity. Indeed, the most important lesson of Asch's research is just how difficult it can be to be the *lone* holdout. People also need to be wary of potentially slippery slopes. The stepwise procedure in Milgram's experiments may have played an important role in the surprising levels of obedience observed in those studies. It's often easiest to resist influence from the start, rather than giving in and hoping to put a stop to things later on. As the Catholic Church teaches, "Avoid the near occasion of sin."

Keep in mind, too, that many influence attempts are based on appeals to emotion. A particularly effective strategy for dealing with these types of appeals is simply to put off a response. If there is a "first law" of emotional experience, it is that emotions fade. Therefore, the compulsion to give in because you are caught up in a particular emotion can be diminished simply by waiting to respond. After the initial emotions dissipate, you can then

decide whether to comply with a request on the merits of the idea, not on the basis of an intense emotional state.

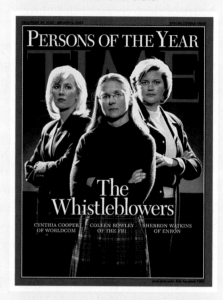

Resisting Social Influence The women pictured on this cover of *Time* magazine all refused to go along with those who were knowingly covering up wrongdoing. Cynthia Cooper (left) was a vice president of the internal audit department of WorldCom who discovered an accounting fraud and confronted the company's controller with her findings. Coleen Rowley (center) was an FBI agent who told her superiors before 9/11 that the flight training of known suspects may have constituted a terrorist threat. Sherron Watkins (right) was a vice president of corporate development at Enron who identified fraud at the company and wrote a letter to her boss detailing her suspicions rather than pretending that nothing was wrong.

reactance theory The idea that people reassert their prerogatives in response to the unpleasant state of arousal they experience when they believe their freedoms are threatened.

LOOKING BACK

Reason-based approaches induce compliance by providing good reasons for people to comply with a request. One of these reasons is the norm of reciprocity, by which people feel compelled to benefit those who have benefited them. In the door-in-the-face (or reciprocal concessions) technique, people who have refused a large request are then induced to agree to a smaller request. In the that's-not-all technique, people are induced to buy an expensive product because a gift has been added to the deal. In the foot-in-the-door technique, people comply with a small request and then are induced to grant a larger request. Emotion-based approaches also can lead to compliance. People who are in a positive mood are more likely to comply with a request in order to maintain their good mood. In contrast, according to the negative state relief hypothesis, people who feel guilty or sad are also likely to comply with a request in order to feel better. Norm-based approaches capitalize on people's tendencies to look to others for guidance. People are responsive to both descriptive and prescriptive norms, but it is important that norm-based appeals do not pit the two against each other.

Chapter Review

Summary

What Is Social Influence?

- There are three types of social influence. *Conformity* involves a change in a person's attitudes or behavior in response to (often implicit) pressure from others. *Obedience* involves giving in to the commands of an authority. *Compliance* involves going along with explicit requests made by others.

Conformity

- There are three sources of conformity. Sometimes conformity is mindless and automatic, elicited by mere perception of someone else's behavior. Other times, people conform because of *informational social influence*—that is, they view the actions of others as informative about what is best to do. Still other times, people conform because of *normative social influence*—that is, out of concern for the social consequences of their actions.

- Several characteristics of a group affect conformity pressure. The larger the *group size*, the greater its influence—but only up to about four people. *Unanimous groups* exert far more social influence than those with even a single dissenter. Moreover, the greater the *expertise* and *status* of group members, the greater their influence.

- Culture and gender affect conformity. People from more interdependent cultures are more likely to conform than people from independent cultures are. Women are somewhat more likely to conform than men, but both men and women conform more in domains in which they have less knowledge.

- Several task factors affect conformity pressure. The more *difficult* and *ambiguous* the task, as in the autokinetic experiment, the greater the conformity. When people's responses are *anonymous*, they are less affected by others' responses. Finally, when people have *satisfying explanations* of others' judgments, they are less affected by others' responses.

- The direction of influence is not always from the majority to the minority. Sometimes *minority influence* can be substantial, especially when the minority expresses consistent views.

Obedience to Authority

- The study of obedience has been dominated by the experiments of Stanley Milgram, who documented the surprising willingness of most people to go along with seemingly harmful commands of an authority.

- Participants in obedience experiments are caught in a conflict between two opposing forces: *normative social influence* and *moral imperatives*. The balance between these forces shifts toward the former when participants tune out the learner and tune in the experimenter.

- Although Milgram's results strike nearly everyone as wildly counterintuitive, they can be rendered less surprising by considering the *stepwise nature* of his commands, the (mostly ineffective) *attempts to terminate* the experiment made by most participants, and the ability of participants to place the burden of *responsibility* on the experimenter, not themselves.

Compliance

- Compliance with the requests of others may be elicited through *reason-based*, *emotion-based*, and *norm-based techniques*.

- Powerful reason-based approaches include invoking the *norm of reciprocity* by, for example, doing a favor for someone or making a concession (the *door-in-the-face technique*) or using the *foot-in-the-door technique* by first getting someone to agree to a small request before making the more substantial request that is really wanted.

- Powerful emotion-based approaches include getting the targeted person in a good mood, which is likely to increase compliance because of *mood maintenance* and because of the influence of the good mood on how the request is interpreted.

- Compliance may also result from a desire for *negative state relief* because an act of compliance may reduce guilt or sadness.

- Norm-based appeals take advantage of people's inclinations to look to others for guidance about how to act.

Usually, people are reluctant to stray too far from the mainstream, so information about what others are doing can have considerable impact. Most people are also motivated to "do the right thing," so information about prescriptive norms can also have great impact. Information about descriptive and prescriptive norms should not be presented as conflicting.

Key Terms

compliance (p. 311)
conformity (p. 311)
descriptive norms (p. 349)
door-in-the-face technique (reciprocal concessions technique) (p. 340)
foot-in-the-door technique (p. 341)
ideomotor action (p. 313)

informational social influence (p. 315)
internalization (p. 325)
negative state relief hypothesis (p. 345)
normative social influence (p. 318)
norm of reciprocity (p. 338)

obedience (p. 311)
prescriptive (injunctive) norms (p. 349)
reactance theory (p. 350)
social influence (p. 310)
that's-not-all technique (p. 341)

Further Reading

Blass, T. (2004). *The man who shocked the world: The life and legacy of Stanley Milgram.* New York: Basic Books. A comprehensive and informative summary of the most famous experiments in the history of psychology.

Cialdini, R. B. (2000). *Influence: Science and practice* (4th ed.). Boston: Allyn & Bacon. A very engagingly written treatment of many of the most common and effective compliance techniques and an analysis of how and why they work.

Gladwell, M. (2000). *The tipping point: How little things can make a big difference.* Boston: Little, Brown. Best-selling treatment of how social trends develop and change.

Thaler, R. H., & Sunstein, C. R. (2008). *Nudge: Improving decisions about health, wealth, and happiness.* New Haven: Yale University Press. An analysis of how psychological knowledge of compliance and decision making can be used to craft more effective social policies.

CHAPTER 10

Relationships and Attraction

IN THE PILOT EPISODE OF ABC'S HIT SERIES *MODERN FAMILY*, viewers are introduced to Claire and Phil, parents in a household that, although modern in terms of clothing, language, and technology, is not so different from the conventional families we saw on television in the '50s and '60s—those depicted in *Leave It to Beaver*, *Father Knows Best*, or *I Love Lucy*. Claire and Phil are both white, have been married for 16 years, and have their three biological children in tow. Phil is the sole breadwinner (although in keeping with the detachment from reality characteristic of so many TV shows, he hardly ever does any actual work). Chaos ensues as the oldest daughter, Hayley, brings home her first boyfriend.

We then meet Jay, a gruff 50-something-year-old with a well-concealed heart of gold; his beautiful young Colombian wife of six months, Gloria; and her son from a previous marriage, Manny. More chaos ensues as people keep assuming Jay is Gloria's father and Manny declares his love for a girl out of his league.

We are then introduced to Cam and Mitchell, a gay couple, as they return to Los Angeles with their newly adopted Vietnamese infant daughter, Lily. Still more chaos, this time centered on which of the two men is best suited for the more feminine sides of raising a child and how they should break the news of the adoption to Mitchell's apparently not-so-accepting family.

When Cam and Mitchell arrive at a family gathering, we discover that Mitchell's family consists of all the other characters we met earlier. Jay is his dad—and Claire's. This makes Claire's three kids and Lily cousins; Manny, Claire's stepbrother; and Gloria, although younger, Claire's stepmother. Modern indeed.

The series captures the complications that can arise in the superextended families we so often see in today's world. And despite the chaos—in this show at least, and so often in real life—it all works. The show was a hit from the first

Modern Family As seen in this recent hit series, families can be quite diverse, and people form all sorts of romantic bonds.

episode because viewers, whatever their own family circumstances, found it so easy to imagine being a part of this particular extended family—and liking what they imagined.

What can *Modern Family* tell us about the topic of this chapter, relationships and attraction? For one thing, it shows us that human beings can find themselves romantically attracted to all sorts of people: people of the same or different sex, people from different cultures, and people spanning a considerable age range. It also shows us that all sorts of relationships, even all sorts of family relationships, "work." They work in the sense of helping to meet the needs of the individuals involved.

This chapter examines a broad range of enduring relationships—with parents, friends, and romantic partners, and with members of the same and opposite sex. Much of the chapter focuses on interpersonal relationships, attachments in which bonds of family or friendship or love or respect or hierarchy tie together two or more individuals over an extended period of time. In such relationships, the individuals generally engage in activities together and have joint memories of shared experiences. Research has shown that these relationships are central to everyday human functioning.

CHARACTERIZING RELATIONSHIPS

In studying relationships, researchers face certain challenges that are not as common in other areas of social psychology (Bradbury & Karney, 1993; Finkel & Eastwick, 2008; Gonzalez & Griffin, 1997; Karney & Bradbury, 1995). For example, many studies of relationships are not true experiments with random assignment of participants to different conditions. Instead, they use longitudinal methods to examine the dynamics that unfold over time in preexisting relationships. Investigators attempt to understand, for example, what factors early in a relationship make for happier or more problematic bonds. This kind of research faces the challenging methodological problem of *self-selection*, which occurs whenever investigators cannot assign participants to the conditions that are to be compared. When participants "select" their own condition, we can never know whether an observed difference between two conditions is a reflection of the different experiences of the people in those conditions or is simply a result of different types of people tending to gravitate to each of the two conditions. For example, couples who make special efforts to celebrate their anniversaries may be less likely to get divorced than couples who don't. But is the failure to celebrate anniversaries a cause of discord, or is it that people who are not getting along don't celebrate their anniversaries?

The Importance of Relationships

Many people from Western cultures define themselves in independent (individualistic) terms, focusing on how they are different and separate from others. Nevertheless, human nature is profoundly social, and a person's identity and sense of self are shaped by social relationships (see also Chapter 3). Indeed, human beings (and other animals) have what appears to be a biological need to belong in relationships.

It is self-evident that humans have biologically based needs for food, oxygen, warmth, and safety. Without nutritional intake, air, or water, we die. Roy Baumeister and Mark Leary claim that the same is true of relationships: we have a need to be embedded in healthy relationships (Baumeister & Leary, 1995). They offer a number of arguments to support their claim that we all have a need (not a desire, but a need) to belong.

Arguments for the Need to Belong Baumeister and Leary point out the likely evolutionary basis of our tendency to seek out social relationships. There is a great deal of consensus that relationships help individuals and offspring survive, thus contributing to the increased likelihood of the replication of the individual's genes. Long-term romantic bonds evolved, to a large extent, to facilitate reproduction and to raise human offspring, who are especially vulnerable and dependent for many years (Diamond, 2003; Ellis, 1992). Parent-offspring attachments help ensure that infants and children are protected and will survive until they can function independently (Bowlby, 1982). Friendship evolved as a means for non-kin to cooperate and to avoid the costs and perils of competition and aggression (Trivers, 1971).

If relationships have an evolutionary basis, then they can be expected to have many universal features. Similar kinds of dynamics should exist between romantic partners, between parents and children, between siblings, and between friends in different cultures around the world. Pioneers in the field of human ethology, who studied hunter-gatherer groups in their natural environments, documented patterns of social behavior that appear to be universal—caregiving between mother and child, wrestling between siblings, flirtation by young people who are

"We are all in this together, by ourselves."

—Lily Tomlin

"No more fiendish punishment could be devised, were such a thing physically possible, than that one should be turned loose in society and remain absolutely unnoticed by all the members thereof."

—William James

courting, affection between romantic partners, dominance displays between adolescent males (Eibl-Eibesfeldt, 1989). This chapter considers in detail both the universality and cultural variation in human relationships.

Baumeister and Leary also note that if the need to belong is truly a need, it should be satiable. That is, when people are thirsty or hungry, they drink and eat—but only to a point. And the same appears to be true of our social lives. Consider one kind of relationship that is important to us all—friendship. In Western European cultures, college students tend to restrict their meaningful interactions to, on average, about six friends (Wheeler & Nezlek, 1977). It seems that we satisfy our need for friendship with a limited number of close friends, and once that need is satisfied, we no longer seek it in others. But if the need to belong is not satisfied in existing relationships, people will seek to satisfy it in other relationships. Observational studies in prisons, for example, find that prisoners suffer great anguish at the loss of contact with their family. As a result, they often form substitute families based on kinship-like ties with other prisoners (Burkhart, 1973).

Evidence for the Need to Belong Perhaps the strongest support for the need to belong comes from evidence showing how vital relationships are to our physical and mental well-being. That is, when the need to belong is not met over a long period of time, people tend to suffer profoundly negative consequences. For example, in a classic series of experiments, Harry Harlow (1959) raised baby rhesus monkeys without contact with other rhesus monkeys but with access to two "mother surrogates"—props vaguely resembling monkeys (**Figure 10.1**). The monkeys raised in isolation were in no way normal when they reached adolescence. As adolescents, they were highly fearful, could not interact with their peers, and engaged in inappropriate sexual behaviors—for example, attacking potential mates or failing to display typical sexual positions during copulation.

A natural experiment with elephants makes a similar point. A natural experiment involves an accidentally produced set of conditions (rather than conditions created by an experimenter) that largely avoids self-selection problems. Elephants in some areas of Africa have been slaughtered for the ivory in their tusks, leaving young elephants to grow up on their own. These adolescent elephants prove to

Universality of Relationships (A, B) Siblings in different cultures all play, support, and fight with each other, although the specific kinds of play, support, and conflict may vary according to the culture. (C) Parents in different cultures show similar kinds of attachment behaviors, including patterns of touch and eye contact.

FIGURE 10.1 Scientific Method: Harlow's Monkeys and Their "Mothers"

Hypothesis: Infant monkeys will form an attachment to a surrogate mother that provides warmth and comfort rather than one that provides nutrients.

Research Method: Infant rhesus monkeys were put in a cage with two different "mothers":

1. One was made of cloth and looked like a monkey, but could not give milk.

2. The other was made of wire, but could give milk.

 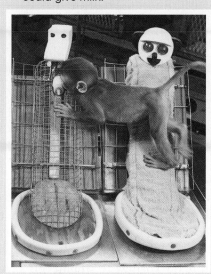

Results: The monkeys clung to the cloth mother and went to it for comfort in times of threat. The monkeys approached the wire mother only when hungry.

CONCLUSION: Infant monkeys will prefer and form an attachment to a surrogate mother that provides warmth and comfort over a wire surrogate mother that provides nutrients.

be quite antisocial and aggressive toward members of their own species as well as others; they kill rhinoceroses for sport, for example. African gamekeepers have solved the problem of the wild elephants by importing adult elephants to show the adolescents how to be elephants.

In humans, mortality rates are higher for divorced, unmarried, and widowed individuals (Lynch, 1979). Admissions to hospitals for psychological problems are 3 to 23 times higher for divorced than for married individuals, depending on the study and nature of the psychological problems in question (Bloom, White, & Asher, 1979; Hughes & Waite, 2009). Suicide rates are higher for single and divorced individuals (Rothberg & Jones, 1987), as are crime rates (Baumeister & Leary, 1995). Having support from others also strengthens our cardiovascular, immune, and endocrine systems (Oxman & Hull, 1997; Uchino, Cacioppo, & Kiecolt-Glaser, 1996; see also Application Module 1).

Relationships and the Sense of Self

Beyond being crucial to our physical and emotional well-being, our social relationships shape our very sense of who we are. Susan Andersen, Serena Chen, and their colleagues have explored one important way that relationships are central

The Need to Belong There is an evolutionary basis for the need to belong. Not only do elephant parents feed and protect young elephants, but they teach them appropriate social behavior that enables them to live in groups. If the young elephants grow up without adults, they are likely to become antisocial and aggressive and have difficulty living in groups.

to our identities by examining what they call our relational selves—that is, the beliefs, feelings, and expectations about ourselves that derive from our relationships with significant others in our lives (Andersen & Chen, 2002). When we encounter someone who reminds us of a significant other, the specific "self" we tend to be when we're around this significant other is activated, including associated beliefs, feelings, and expectations that then shape our interactions with the new individual, often outside of our awareness. For example, your mother may have often criticized your efforts and accomplishments. Around her, your relational self would be defined by a sense of inadequacy and feelings of shame. When you encounter someone who reminds you of your mother—say, a supervisor at work or a traffic court judge—you're likely to transfer these beliefs, feelings, and interaction patterns to that person, and they will shape the content of the new relationship.

To document how past relationships shape current interactions, Hinkley and Andersen had participants write down 14 descriptive sentences about a positive significant other and a negative significant other. Participants then wrote 20 sentences that described what they were like with that person (Hinkley & Andersen, 1996). Two weeks later, participants were given a description of another person who either resembled the participant's own positive or negative significant other or, in a control condition, the positive or negative significant other of another participant. They then wrote 14 statements describing themselves at that moment.

Participants exposed to a new person similar to their significant other were more likely to describe themselves in terms that resembled what they are like with that significant other than were participants in the control condition. For example, if a participant listed traits like "silly" and "irreverent" when describing what she was like with her father, these traits were more likely to appear in her self-description two weeks later after simply encountering someone who reminded her of her father. Thus, encountering people who remind us of significant others changes how we think about ourselves in the current situation, often at an automatic level, and shapes the more immediate, accessible thoughts we have about ourselves.

Besides activating specific self-beliefs and feelings, the relational self also shapes our current interactions. In one illustrative study, participants interacted with a target person who resembled a positive or negative significant other of the participant (Berk & Andersen, 2000). Participants liked the target who resembled a positive significant other more than the target who resembled a negative significant other, and the well-liked target was more likely to show positive emotion toward the participant. The process seems to be that (1) the target reminds me of good old X, (2) I therefore like the target, (3) so I express positive affect toward the target, and (4) as a consequence, the target expresses positive affect toward me.

Different Ways of Relating to Others

Although many types of relationships contribute to our well-being and shape our sense of ourselves and the way we relate to others, different kinds of relationships have different kinds of effects on these outcomes. We obviously behave in very different ways with a new romantic partner, with friends from our ultimate Frisbee team, with a minister or rabbi, or with our supervisors at work (Fiske, 1992; Moskowitz, 1994). Although this chapter focuses on interpersonal relationships such as those among friends or romantic partners, it is necessary to understand some important distinctions among different types of relationships.

Communal and Exchange Relationships   The incredible economic growth that China and India have witnessed in the past decade has brought about significant cultural changes. Millions of young people have left their villages and moved to the large cities that have mushroomed in these new economic superpowers. A quiet village life of friends and family has been replaced by one of interacting mostly with strangers and bosses with whom they have no personal connection. How best to think about these changes in psychological terms?

Margaret Clark and Judson Mills argue that two fundamentally different types of relationships—communal relationships and exchange relationships—arise in different contexts and are governed by different norms (Clark, 1992; Clark & Mills, 1979, 1993). **Communal relationships** are those in which the individuals feel a special responsibility for one another and often expect that their relationship will be long term. Communal relationships are based on a sense of "oneness" and family-like sharing of common identity (Fiske, 1992). People in communal relationships, such as close friends, come to resemble one another in the timing of their laughter and their specific emotional experiences. In communal relationships, individuals give and receive according to the principle of need—that is, according to who has the most pressing need at any given time. Prototypical examples of communal relationships are relations between family members and between close friends—the kinds of relationships that are the social fabric of communal life in small villages.

Exchange relationships, in contrast, are trade-based relationships, often short term, in which individuals feel no special responsibility toward one another. In exchange relationships, giving and receiving are governed by concerns about equity (you get what you put into the relationship) and reciprocity (what you give is returned in kind). Examples of exchange relationships include interactions with salespeople and bureaucrats, or with workers and supervisors in a business organization.

The distinction between communal and exchange relationships highlights notable cultural differences in patterns of relationships. First, societies differ

"Sticks in a bundle are unbreakable."

—Kenyan proverb

communal relationships Relationships in which the individuals feel a special responsibility for one another and give and receive according to the principle of need; such relationships are often long term.

exchange relationships Relationships in which individuals feel little responsibility toward one another; giving and receiving are governed by concerns about equity and reciprocity.

"O.K., who else has experienced the best-friend relationship as inadequate?"

widely in which approach they generally prefer. People in East Asian and Latin American societies are inclined to take a communal approach to many situations in which people in European and Commonwealth countries would be inclined to take an exchange approach. Consider the question, raised in Chapter 1, of how businesspeople would treat an employee who had put in 15 good years of service but over the past year had fallen down on the job and showed little chance of getting back on track. East Asians tended to feel that the company had an obligation to treat the employee as family and keep him on the payroll. Western businesspeople were more likely to feel that the relationship was purely contractual, or exchange based, and that the employee should be let go. There are differences among Western nations, however: people from Catholic countries are more likely to take a communal stance than people from Protestant countries. Indeed, even within the United States, Catholics are more likely than Protestants to take a communal stance in relationship matters (Sanchez-Burks, 2002, 2004; Sanchez-Burks, Nisbett, & Ybarra, 2000).

Reward and Social Exchange Theories of Interpersonal Relationships The important distinction between communal and exchange relationships notwithstanding, many social psychologists believe that even the most intimate relationships are based to some extent on exchange. Indeed, one of the most widely accepted theories of interpersonal relationships has the virtue of simplicity: people tend to like and gravitate toward those who provide them with rewards (positive exchange). The rewards don't have to be tangible or immediate, and they don't have to come from direct interaction. But according to this reward framework, we tend to like those who make us feel good (Clore & Byrne, 1974; Lott & Lott, 1974).

You might test the reward theory yourself: Think of all your friends, and ask yourself whether reward theory helps explain your liking of them. Some of the rewards are easy to identify. Your friendship with one person, for example, may make you part of a clique to which you would otherwise not belong. You may like another person because she is hilarious and you have fun when you're around her. For many of your friends, however, the rewards may be more indirect and less obvious. Indeed, the very best friends are those whose rewards may be the most indirect of all: they are the ones who make you feel good about yourself when you are around them.

Note that the reward framework helps answer one of the most basic and practical of questions: What can you do to get others to like you? According to the exchange perspective, the answer is clear: reward them. Make other people feel good when they are around you. This approach is similar to the advice given by Dale Carnegie in his book *How to Win Friends and Influence People* (which has sold 15 million copies since its first printing in 1937): to win friends, "Dole out praise lavishly."

It might seem that such a strategy would backfire. People surely see through most efforts to gain favor and resent the attempt to influence them. Wealthy individuals, for example, are surely alert to the existence of "gold diggers" who fake affection in an effort to part them from their money. But the term *gold digger* probably wouldn't even exist if a great many of them were not successful in

"Love is often nothing but a favorable exchange between two people who get the most of what they can expect, considering their value on the . . . market."

—Erich Fromm

"A proposal of marriage in our society tends to be a way in which a man sums up his social attributes and suggests to a woman that hers are not so much better as to preclude a merger or a partnership in these matters."

—Erving Goffman

"We always do believe in praise of ourselves. Even when we know it is not disinterested, we think it is deserved."

—David Lodge, *Thinks*

their quest. Their success suggests that ingratiation may be more effective than it "should" be. Flattery may get you pretty far after all (Jones, 1964; Vonk, 2002).

The reward framework is a variant of a broader theory that views much of human interaction as social exchange (Kelley & Thibaut, 1978; Rusbult, 1983). **Social exchange theory** starts with the assumption that people are motivated to maximize their own feelings of satisfaction. People seek out rewards in their interactions with others, and they are willing to pay certain costs to obtain them. Typically, people desire interactions or relationships in which the rewards exceed the costs. Such interactions yield a net gain. If rewarding interactions are not available, however, an individual is likely to seek out those interactions in which the costs exceed the rewards by the smallest amount. More generally, social exchange theory maintains that people tend to pursue those interactions that yield the most favorable difference between rewards and costs. Central to the theory is the notion of "shopping around": social exchange theorists see people as shopping around for the interactions that offer the most favorable trade-offs of costs and benefits. Note, however, that the combination of too many rewards and too few costs is not necessarily attractive, either. Indeed, **equity theory** maintains that people are also motivated to pursue fairness, or equity, in which individuals have an equal share of rewards and costs.

social exchange theory A theory based on the idea that all relationships have costs and rewards, and that how people feel about a relationship depends on their assessments of its costs and rewards and the costs and rewards available to them in other relationships.

equity theory A theory that maintains that people are motivated to pursue fairness, or equity, in their relationships; rewards and costs are shared roughly equally among individuals.

Attachment Styles

Attachment theory was first advanced by John Bowlby, an early advocate of an evolutionary approach to human behavior (Bowlby, 1982; Hazan & Shaver, 1994; Mikulincer & Shaver, 2003; Simpson & Rholes, 1998). The central thesis of Bowlby's theory is that our early attachments with our parents and other caregivers shape our relationships for the rest of our lives.

attachment theory A theory about how our early attachments with our parents shape our relationships for the rest of our lives.

Bowlby noted that unlike many mammals, human infants are born with few survival skills. In fact, they are the most vulnerable offspring on earth, requiring several years to reach even a limited amount of independence. They survive, Bowlby noted, by forming intensely close attachments to parents or parental figures. Evolution has given infants a variety of traits that promote parent-offspring attachments, including the heartwarming smiles, laughs and coos, and facial features that evoke love and devotion (Berry & McArthur, 1986; McArthur & Baron, 1983). Likewise, evolution has led to a variety of parental traits that promote attachment—most notably, strong feelings of parental love and protective instincts toward their infants (Fehr, 1994; Fehr & Russell, 1991; Hazan & Shaver, 1987, 1994; Hrdy, 1999).

Early in development, children rely on their parents for a sense of security, which allows them to explore the environment and to learn. A child's confidence in the secure base that the parents provide stems in part from the parents' availability and responsiveness to the child's ever-shifting emotions. Over time, children develop internal "working models" of themselves and of how relationships function based on their parents' availability and responsiveness (Baldwin, Keelan, Fehr, Enns, & Koh-Rangarajoo, 1996; Collins & Read, 1994; Pietromonaco & Feldman-Barrett, 2000). Internal working models of the self include individuals' beliefs about their lovability and competence, while internal working models of how relationships work reflect individuals' beliefs about other people's availability, warmth, and ability to provide security. These working models, Bowlby claimed,

"Ezra, I'm not inviting you to my birthday party, because our relationship is no longer satisfying to my needs."

originate early in life and shape our relationships from cradle to grave, giving rise to distinct styles of attachment.

Inspired by Bowlby's ideas, Mary Ainsworth classified the attachment patterns of infants according to how the children responded to separations and reunions with their caregivers, both in the laboratory and in the home (Ainsworth, 1993; Ainsworth, Blehar, Waters, & Wall, 1978). Using an experimental procedure that came to be known as the strange situation, Ainsworth had infants and their caregivers enter an unfamiliar room containing many interesting toys. As the infant explored the room and began to play with some of the toys, a stranger walked in. The stranger remained in the room, and the caregiver quietly left. Returning after 3 minutes, the caregiver greeted and comforted the infant if he or she was upset. The separation typically caused infants to be distressed. Infants whose caregivers responded quickly and reliably to their distress cries, as assessed by outside observers, were typically securely attached. Such infants were comfortable in moving away from their caregivers to explore a novel environment—with the occasional glance back at the caregiver to make sure things were okay. These children felt safe even though they weren't in contact with their caregiver. Caregivers who were not so reliable in their responses to their infants—sometimes intruding on the child's activities and sometimes rejecting the child—tended to have infants who showed anxious attachment; these infants were likely to cry or show anger when placed in novel environments and were less comforted by contact with their caregiver when it occurred. Caregivers who rejected their infants frequently tended to produce children with an avoidant attachment style. In a strange situation, the avoidant child might not seek out the caregiver and might even reject attention when it was offered.

The Strange Situation Mary Ainsworth set up an experimental situation in which she was able to measure infants' attachment to their caregivers. (A) A mother and child enter an unfamiliar room with many interesting toys. The infant explores the room and plays with the toys. In the meantime, a stranger enters the room and then the mother leaves. (B) When the mother returns to the room, she picks up the infant and comforts him if he is upset that she has left the room. (C) The mother then puts the infant down, and the infant is free to return to playing with the toys—or he might react by crying and protesting the separation.

Classifying Attachment Styles Researchers have since developed self-report measures to classify adults' attachment styles (for example, Bartholomew & Horowitz, 1991; Brennan, Clark, & Shaver, 1998; Hazan & Shaver, 1987). Analyses of people's responses to these measures reveal two dimensions that capture most of the variation in adult attachment—anxiety and avoidance (**Figure 10.2**). As the names suggest, the first dimension refers to the amount of anxiety and fear a person feels about rejection and abandonment within close relationships. The second dimension, avoidance, refers to whether a person is comfortable with or avoids intimacy in primary adult relationships. Where a person falls on these two dimensions yields four specific attachment styles. Individuals who score low on both anxiety and avoidance have a **secure attachment style**: they are confident about their relationship, are comfortable with intimacy, and want to be close to others during times of threat and uncertainty.

All other combinations yield attachment patterns with some degree of insecurity. Those who are anxious but not avoidant are said to have **anxious-preoccupied** attachments. They are comfortable with and seek out intimacy but do so mainly out of a fear of rejection and abandonment. This attachment style can lead to a type of "clinginess" that is not associated with a great deal of satisfaction for either member of the relationship. Those who are avoidant but not anxious are said to have **dismissive-avoidant** attachments. They exhibit compulsive self-reliance, prefer distance from others, and react to rejection by being quick to distance themselves even further from the source of the rejection. Finally, individuals who score high on both anxiety and avoidance are said to have a **fearful-avoidant** attachment style. These individuals tend to have mixed feelings about close relationships, wanting very badly to have close connections with others, but feeling uncertain and unworthy of others' affection and therefore uncomfortable with intimacy.

secure attachment style An attachment style characterized by feelings of security in relationships. Individuals with this style are comfortable with intimacy and want to be close to others during times of threat and uncertainty.

anxious-preoccupied style An attachment style characterized by dependency or "clinginess." People with an anxious-preoccupied style tend not to have a positive view of themselves, but they value and seek out intimacy.

dismissive-avoidant style An attachment style characterized by independence and self-reliance. People with a dismissive-avoidant style seek less intimacy with others and deny the importance of close relationships.

fearful-avoidant style An attachment style characterized by ambivalence and discomfort toward close relationships. People with a fearful-avoidant style desire closeness with others but feel unworthy of others' affection and so do not seek out intimacy.

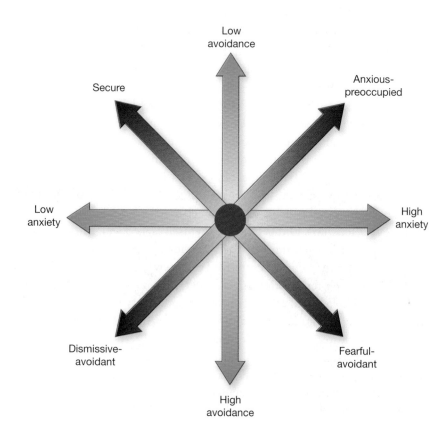

FIGURE 10.2 Attachment Styles The attachment styles that characterize different people tend to fall along the two dimensions of anxiety and avoidance.

Stability of Attachment Styles A central principle of attachment theory is that these attachment styles are established early and are stable throughout a person's life; that is, the attachments you form as a child shape the way you relate as an adult to your romantic partners, your children, and your friends. Evidence supports this provocative thesis: important early life events are associated with later attachment styles. Brennan and Shaver (1993) found that anxious individuals were more likely to have experienced the death of a parent, abuse during childhood, or the divorce of their parents. In a 40-year longitudinal study of women who graduated in 1960 from Mills College in Oakland, California, Klohnen and Bera (1998) found that women who classified themselves as avoidant at age 52 had also reported greater conflict in the home 30 years earlier at age 21.

What's more, individuals classified as secure, avoidant, or anxious at age 1 tend to be similarly classified in early adulthood (Fraley & Spieker, 2003). A four-year longitudinal study found that 70 percent of adults reported the same attachment style across all four years of the study (Kirkpatrick & Hazan, 1994). Secure individuals were particularly likely to remain secure (83.3 percent remained secure across the four years).

You might expect that a secure attachment style would predict more positive life outcomes. You would be right (Cooper, Shaver, & Collins, 1998). Securely attached individuals report the greatest relationship satisfaction (Shaver & Brennan, 1992). In a four-year longitudinal study, secure individuals were less likely to have experienced a romantic breakup (25.6 percent) over the period under study than avoidant individuals (52.2 percent) or anxious individuals (43.6 percent). In the Mills College study, secure individuals were more likely to be married at age 52 than were avoidant individuals (82 percent versus 50 percent) and to report fewer marital problems. Moreover, several studies have documented especially high rates of depression, eating disorders, maladaptive drinking, and substance abuse in those with an anxious attachment style (Mikulincer & Shaver, 2003).

If you have become concerned while reading this that your future relationships are doomed because you've had some negative relationship experiences that have left you feeling insecurely attached, don't despair. Although attachment theorists assume that people's early experiences shape their relationships throughout life, and there is evidence pointing to some degree of stability in attachment styles, the amount and nature of the stability to be expected is rather complex. First, there is the question of whether people tend to have the same attachment style across all of their relationships—with parents, friends, siblings, and romantic partners. Mark Baldwin and his colleagues (Baldwin et al., 1996) asked undergraduates to list ten important relationships in their lives and then had them indicate the attachment style (secure, anxious-ambivalent, or avoidant) that best characterized them in each of these relationships. Did people see themselves as having the same attachment style across all or even most of their relationships? On the contrary, more than 50 percent of participants characterized themselves as having all three attachment styles across their ten relationships. Moreover, consistent with the idea that people have multiple kinds of attachment working models stored in their memories, Baldwin and colleagues found that different attachment styles can be momentarily primed or activated—in effect, leading a person to respond in, say, a securely attached manner even if she is typically avoidant in most of her relationships.

A second question is whether a person's attachment style within a given relationship is stable across time. The evidence described earlier points to some degree of stability, but it is a moderate degree of stability at most. Overall, given

BOX 10.1   FOCUS ON CULTURE

Building an Independent Baby in the Bedroom

If you are a white, middle-class North American, odds are you slept by yourself in your own bedroom from infancy on. And that probably seems perfectly normal to you. Normal, maybe; common, definitely not. There are few cultures in the world where such a sleeping arrangement is customary. In an article titled "Who Sleeps with Whom Revisited," Shweder, Jensen, and Goldstein (1995) describe the sleeping arrangements of people in many of the world's cultures. The sleeping arrangements predict fairly well how independent and individualistic a given culture is. In Japan, most children sleep with their parents until they are adolescents. In the non-Western, nonindustrial world, it is virtually unheard of for a very young child not to sleep with his or her parents, and such a practice would be regarded as a form of child abuse. Even in the United States, 55 percent of African-American children less than 1 year of age sleep with a parent every night, and 25 percent of African-American children 1 to 5 years old sleep with a parent. In a white, predominantly blue-collar community in Appalachian Kentucky, 71 percent of children between the ages of 2 months and 2 years were found to sleep with their parents, as well as 47 percent of children between 2 and 4 years of age.

This study reveals the extent to which interdependent and independent self-construals permeate social behavior. In more interdependent cultures, young children are much more likely to sleep side by side with their parents than in independent cultures. While psychologists can only speculate about the effects these patterns of sleep have on attachment patterns, we might expect secure attachments in the independent cultures to be defined by greater independence and autonomy than secure patterns in interdependent cultures.

that most people appear to have different attachment styles with different relationship partners, and given that the stability of attachment style within any particular relationship is a matter of degree, it would be safe to conclude that there is room for change in a person's attachment style even within a specific relationship.

The findings described here about attachment apply most readily to modern Western cultures (Morelli & Rothbaum, 2007). In cultures that place less value on autonomy, infants who are left in a room without their mothers may be more fearful about exploring the environment, and the reunion with their mother may be much more turbulent. This observation does not imply that such children are insecurely attached. Instead, it means they are being socialized to be interdependent with others, especially with family members.

Relationships are essential to our social adjustment. Our need to belong in relationships is an evolved, universal motive that shapes our thoughts and actions. If not satisfied, that need can have highly negative consequences for our well-being. Our sense of self, or our relational self, shifts according to whether the people around us remind us of a significant other. In communal relationships, generally of long duration, people are concerned with each other's needs; in contrast, exchange relationships are governed by concerns over equity and are often of short duration. The reward theory of interpersonal relationships maintains that people tend to like those who provide them with rewards. Social exchange theory maintains that people generally desire interactions in which rewards exceed costs, whereas equity theory maintains that people seek equity, or equally shared rewards and costs. Our way of relating to our intimate others has origins in our early bonds with our parents. This attachment can exert considerable influence on our current relationships, on how we act toward others and appraise events within our relationships, and on our personal well-being.

ATTRACTION

Forming relationships thus seems to be instinctive and necessary to the well-being of humans and other animals. But why are we drawn to some people and not to others? It is sometimes hard to figure out why two people are attracted to each other and get along so well. And although we typically know whether we like someone, we are often at a loss to explain why. To be sure, we know that we like people who are nice to us, make us laugh, share our values, and so on. But these obvious influences notwithstanding, sometimes we are drawn to some people and repulsed by others for reasons we can't explain.

What are the most powerful determinants of whether you will like someone? What is the underlying basis of good or bad "chemistry"? And, in particular, what leads two people to be romantically attracted to each other? Some of the answers may surprise you. Many of the variables that you might expect to influence attraction do indeed have an effect—but sometimes a much more powerful effect than you would have guessed.

Proximity

propinquity Physical proximity.

Who are your best friends on campus? Are they the people who were on your hall freshman year? Are they the ones you encountered most often in class? Are they your peers on the track team, drama club, or debate society? Something that *has* to influence whether people become friends or lovers is simple physical proximity, also called **propinquity**. And, in fact, the most enduring friendships are forged between people whose paths cross frequently.

"Despite the fact that a person can pick and choose from a vast number of people to make friends with, such things as the placement of a stoop or the direction of a street often have more to do with determining who is friends with whom."

—William Whyte, *The Organization Man*

Studies of Proximity and Attraction A number of studies have demonstrated the effects of proximity on who become friends and romantic partners. Remember that these studies are important not so much because they demonstrate that a relationship between proximity and attraction exists (most people would guess that anyway), but because they demonstrate how *strong* the relationship is. As one person put it, "Cherished notions about romantic love notwithstanding, the chances are about 50–50 that the 'one and only' lives within walking distance" (Eckland, 1968).

One study of propinquity was conducted at MIT in the 1940s, in a married student housing project known as Westgate West (Festinger, Schachter, & Back, 1950). The project was built to house returning American servicemen and their families after World War II. The housing project consisted of 17 ten-unit apartment buildings that were isolated from other residential areas of the city. The incoming students were randomly assigned to their residences, and few of them knew one another beforehand. **Figure 10.3** shows the layout of the Westgate West apartment houses.

The investigators conducted a sociometric survey, asking each resident to name the three people they saw socially most often in the entire housing project. The effect of proximity was striking: two-thirds of those listed as friends lived

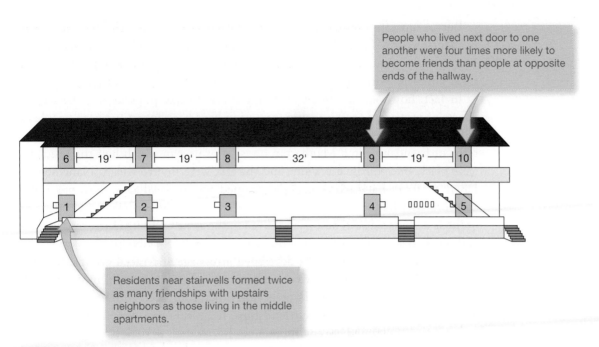

People who lived next door to one another were four times more likely to become friends than people at opposite ends of the hallway.

Residents near stairwells formed twice as many friendships with upstairs neighbors as those living in the middle apartments.

FIGURE 10.3 Proximity and Friendship Diagram of an MIT apartment complex. (Source: Adapted from Festinger, Schachter, & Back, 1950.)

in the same building as the respondent, even though those in the same building represented only 5 percent of the residents of Westgate West. More striking still was the pattern of friendships *within* each building. Note that the physical distance between apartments was quite small—19 feet between the doorways of adjacent apartments and 89 feet between those at the ends of each hallway. Nevertheless, even within such a confined space, greater proximity led to more friendships. Forty-one percent of those living in adjacent apartments listed one another as friends, compared with only 10 percent of those living at opposite ends of the hallway.

Proximity presumably leads to friendship because it facilitates chance encounters. If so, then pure physical distance should matter less than what might be called **functional distance**, the tendency of an architectural layout to encourage contact between certain people and discourage it between others. The MIT study shows just how important functional distance is. As Figure 10.3 indicates, the stairs are positioned such that upstairs residents will encounter the occupants of apartments 1 and 5 much more often than the occupants of the middle apartments. And in fact, the residents of apartments 1 and 5 formed twice as many friendships with their upstairs neighbors as did those living in the middle apartments. Notice also that the residents of apartments 1 and 6 and apartments 2 and 7 are equally distant from one another physically. They reside directly above one another. But the stairs that pass the door of apartment 1 make it and apartment 6 vastly closer from a functional perspective. Are the residents of apartments 1 and 6 more likely to become friends than the residents of apartments 2 and 7? Absolutely. The residents of apartments 1 and 6 were 2.5 times more likely to become friends than were the residents of apartments 2 and 7. Thus it is functional distance more than physical distance that is decisive. Proximity promotes friendship because it (literally) brings people together.

functional distance The tendency of an architectural layout to encourage or inhibit certain activities, including contact between people.

But are any cautions in order? You may be wondering about the diversity of the residents in the MIT study. Perhaps proximity has a powerful effect on friendship formation in homogeneous groups, but not in heterogeneous groups in which it must "compete" with factors such as similarity of age, race, ethnicity, or religion.

In fact, however, in studies involving more diverse populations, the largest effects of proximity on friendship formation have been found between people of *different* races, ages, or social classes. One study, for example, examined the patterns of friendships in a Manhattan housing project in which half the residents were black, one-third were white, and the rest were Puerto Rican (Nahemow & Lawton, 1975). Each ethnic group contained people of all ages. Both proximity and similarity had strong effects on who befriended whom. Eighty-eight percent of those designated as a "best friend" lived in the same building as the respondent, and nearly half lived on the same floor. Yet the effect of proximity was especially pronounced in friendships that developed *across* age and racial groups. Seventy percent of the friendships between people of different ages and races involved people who lived on the same floor as each other, compared with only 40 percent of the same-age and same-race friendships. It appears that people are willing to look beyond the immediate environment to find friends of their own age and race; their friendships with people of a different age or race, on the other hand, tended to be those that fell in their laps.

Proximity, Availability, and Anticipating Interaction Why is the effect of proximity on friendship so great? The first reason, just discussed, is that proximity makes contact more likely.

Another reason, one that follows directly from the first, is that people tend to give those they expect to interact with the benefit of the doubt. Simply knowing that we will interact with someone makes us like that person more. In one demonstration of this effect, women at the University of Minnesota were given information about the personalities of two other students—one who would later join them in a discussion of student dating habits and another with whom they would have no contact (Darley & Berscheid, 1967). The two personality profiles were made equivalent through counterbalancing: half the participants were told they would meet one student, and the other half were told they would meet the other student, so that the nature of the description could not be the cause of any result obtained. Even so, participants liked the person they expected to meet significantly more.

This initial positive stance toward others is likely to create a cycle in which the favorable expectations of each partner are reinforced by the positive behavior of the other. The powerful effects of proximity on friendship are one result. Because we know we must occasionally interact with those next door or down the hall, we make an effort to have our initial encounters go well. As a result, most initial interactions are rewarding and help advance friendships.

The Mere Exposure Effect Robert Zajonc has offered what is arguably the simplest, most basic explanation of why proximity, and the frequent contact that comes with proximity, leads to liking: the **mere exposure effect** (Zajonc, 1968). Zajonc contends that the more you are exposed to something, the more you tend to like it. This may strike you as implausible. After all, what about all those pop tunes on the radio that seem to become more irritating each time you hear them? And why are there sayings like "Familiarity breeds contempt"? Upon reflection,

mere exposure effect The finding that repeated exposure to a stimulus (for example, an object or person) leads to greater liking of the stimulus.

The Influence of Mere Exposure on Liking It may seem hard to believe, but many now-revered landmarks elicited anything but reverence initially. (A) When the Eiffel Tower was completed in Paris, France, in 1889, to commemorate the French Revolution's centennial, a group of artists and intellectuals, including Alexandre Dumas, Guy de Maupassant, and Emile Zola, signed a petition calling it "useless and monstrous" and "a disgraceful column of bolts." (B) San Francisco's TransAmerica building likewise elicited negative reactions initially; renowned *San Francisco Chronicle* columnist Herb Caen angrily suggested knitting a giant tea cozy to cover the spire.

however, Zajonc's claim makes more sense. You probably recall hating a song that played all the time on the radio when you were younger, only to discover some nostalgic virtue in it when you hear it now.

Researchers have generated a massive amount of empirical support for the claim that mere repeated exposure facilitates liking (Bornstein, 1989; Moreland & Beach, 1992; Zajonc, 1968). Some of the most striking (though less convincing) evidence is correlational. There is a remarkable correlation between how frequently people are exposed to various items (words, fruits, cities, chemical elements) and how much they like those items. For example, there is a strong correlation between people's preference for various letters in the English alphabet and how often they appear in the language (Alluisi & Adams, 1962). It is hard to imagine that the English language contains so many *e*'s or *r*'s just because people like those letters. It's more plausible that people like them because they are exposed to them so often.

To test the mere exposure effect in an experimental setting, Zajonc (1968) created a stimulus set of Turkish words that were utterly unfamiliar to his participants—for example, *kadirga*, *afworbu*, and *lokanta*. Different words within this set were then shown to his participants 0, 1, 2, 5, 10, or 25 times. Afterward, the participants were asked to indicate the extent to which they thought each word referred to something good or bad. The more times participants saw a given word, the more they assumed it referred to something good. Zajonc replicated this experiment with Chinese pictographs (symbols used in Chinese writing) and college yearbook photos as stimuli (in the latter case, subjects judged how much they thought they would like the person). The mere exposure effect was supported each time.

Further evidence for the mere exposure effect is based on the observation that the image each of us has of our own face is not the same as the image our friends have of us. Because we typically see ourselves in the mirror, the image we have of ourselves is a mirror image, whereas our friends typically see our "true" image. Thus, if simple exposure induces liking, we should prefer our mirror image, and our friends should prefer our true image. And when an experiment showing participants' mirror-image and true-image photographs was conducted, that's exactly what happened (Mita, Dermer, & Knight, 1977) (**Figure 10.4**).

Perhaps the most intriguing test of the mere exposure effect was done with albino rats (Cross, Halcomb, & Matter, 1967). One group of rats was raised in an environment where selections of Mozart's music were played for 12 hours each day. A second group was exposed to an analogous schedule of music by Schoenberg. The rats were then placed individually in a test cage that was rigged so that the rat's presence on one side of the cage would trip a switch that caused previously unheard selections of Mozart to be played, whereas the rat's presence on the other side would generate new selections of Schoenberg. The rats were thus able to "vote with their feet" and express a preference for the quintessentially classical music of Mozart or the modern, atonal compositions of Schoenberg. The results support the mere exposure effect: rats raised on a musical diet of Mozart moved significantly more often to the side of the cage that caused Mozart to be played, whereas those raised on a diet of Schoenberg moved to the side that caused Schoenberg's music to be played (**Figure 10.5**). (Rats in a control condition with no initial exposure to music later exhibited a preference for . . . you guessed it, Mozart.)

But *why* does mere repeated exposure lead to liking? It seems there are two explanations. First, people find it easier to perceive and cognitively process

---

FIGURE 10.4 You Be the Subject: The Mere Exposure Effect

Which image do you prefer, the one on the left or the one on the right?

Results: People prefer true photos of others, but mirror-image photos of themselves. (The one on the right is the true image.)

Explanation: People see themselves when they look in the mirror, which means that they are familiar with a reverse image of themselves—and this is the image they generally prefer. They see others, however, as they truly are and usually prefer this true image to a mirror image.

FIGURE 10.5 Scientific Method: Mere Exposure and Musical Preferences

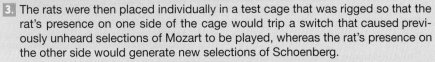

Hypothesis: Exposure leads to liking.

Research Method:

1. One group of rats was raised for the first 52 days of life in an environment in which Mozart was played for 12 hours each day (specifically, *The Magic Flute*, Symphonies 40 and 41, and the Violin Concerto No. 5).

2. A second group of rats was exposed to an analogous schedule of atonal music by Schoenberg (specifically, *Pierrot Lunaire*, *A Survivor from Warsaw*, *Verklärte Nacht*, *Kol Nidre*, and Chamber Symphonies 1 and 2).

3. The rats were then placed individually in a test cage that was rigged so that the rat's presence on one side of the cage would trip a switch that caused previously unheard selections of Mozart to be played, whereas the rat's presence on the other side would generate new selections of Schoenberg.

Results: Rats raised on a musical diet of Mozart moved significantly more often to the side of the cage that led to Mozart being played, whereas those raised on a diet of Schoenberg moved more often to the side that led to Schoenberg's music being played.

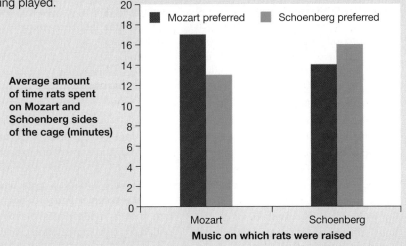

Average amount of time rats spent on Mozart and Schoenberg sides of the cage (minutes)

Music on which rats were raised

The height of the bars represents the average number of minutes the rats who had earlier been exposed to either Mozart or Schoenberg chose to inhabit a side of their cage that led to Mozart or Schoenberg being played.

CONCLUSION: Exposure leads to liking. Being exposed to Mozart led to a preference for Mozart's music. Being exposed to Schoenberg led to a preference for Schoenberg's music.

Source: Adapted from Cross, Halcomb, & Matter (1967).

familiar stimuli—the processing of familiar stimuli is more "fluent." And because people find the experience of fluency inherently pleasurable, those positive feelings make the stimuli more appealing (Reber, Schwarz, & Winkielman, 2004; Winkielman & Cacioppo, 2001; see also Chapter 4).

Robert Zajonc offered a second interpretation that draws on some of the most fundamental psychological processes, those involved in classical conditioning. Upon repeated exposure to a thing or a person with no negative consequences, we learn to associate the stimulus with the absence of anything negative and form

BOX 10.2 FOCUS ON POSITIVE PSYCHOLOGY

The Basis of Beauty

What makes the Golden Gate Bridge so aesthetically pleasing? Why do mathematicians describe certain proofs as "beautiful"? And why are pandas and harp seals considered more adorable than mollusks and vultures? Thinkers throughout the ages have pondered and argued about the nature of aesthetic beauty. Those who have taken the *objectivist* view, the ancient Greeks especially, argue that beauty is inherent in the properties of objects that produce pleasant sensations in the perceiver. Their goal has been to identify the stimulus features that have such effects—balance, proportion, symmetry, contrast. All of these and others have been put forward as important elements of beauty. Other scholars, those who subscribe to the *subjectivist* view, argue that "beauty is in the eye of the beholder," and therefore the search for general laws of beauty is futile.

Psychologists have recently offered a different view, one that attributes aesthetic pleasure to perceptual and cognitive fluency (Reber, Schwarz, & Winkielman, 2004), or how easily information can be processed. Some objects are more easily identified than others (perceptual fluency), and some are more easily interpreted, defined, and integrated into existing semantic knowledge (cognitive fluency). The core idea is that the more fluently an object is processed, the more positive the aesthetic experience. An important part of this argument is that people experience pleasure when processing fluent stimuli. Electromyography (EMG) recordings of people's faces reveal more activation of the zygomaticus major (the "smiling muscle") when

they are exposed to fluent stimuli rather than disfluent stimuli (Winkielman & Cacioppo, 2001). Another critical part of the argument is that all of the features that objectivists regard as inherently pleasing—symmetry, contrast, and so on—tend to increase perceptual fluency.

Symmetrical patterns are processed efficiently and, as noted on p. 385, symmetrical faces are considered particularly good looking—as are symmetrical structures like the Eiffel Tower, the Chrysler Building, and the Golden Gate Bridge. Objects characterized by high contrast can be recognized especially quickly, and laboratory studies have found that such stimuli are judged especially attractive—as are flowers, goldfinches, and the photographs of Ansel Adams (Reber, Winkielman, & Schwarz, 1998). Aside from the impact of these classic aesthetic features, this perspective maintains that anything that increases the fluent processing of an object ought to increase its aesthetic appeal. Previous exposure to a stimulus makes it easier to process, and mere repeated exposure leads to greater liking. Prototypical members of a category are processed fluently, and people find "average" faces attractive—as well as average automobiles, birds, and fish (Halberstadt & Rhodes, 2000, 2003).

But how does this explain people's aesthetic appreciation of complicated stimuli, such as Beethoven's Symphony No. 9, the Bilbao Museum, or the ceiling of the Sistine Chapel? Simple stimuli are surely processed more fluently than complex stimuli, but the simplest things are not always the most pleasing. True enough. What seems to be particularly appealing

Positive Psychology Symmetrical stimuli are easy to process (that is, they're fluent) and, like fluent stimuli in general, tend to be experienced as aesthetically pleasing. The symmetry of the Golden Gate Bridge may be one reason it is regarded as one of the most beautiful bridges in the world.

is "simplicity in complexity." People seem to like those things that are processed more easily than one might expect given their overall complexity. Processing a simple image fluently is often unsatisfying, but a complex image or sound pattern that is made accessible by some underlying structure often yields the greatest sensation of aesthetic pleasure.

The fluency perspective on aesthetic beauty thus occupies a middle ground between the objectivist and subjectivist views. Beauty is indeed in the eye of the beholder, but not in the sense that it is completely arbitrary and variable from person to person. Rather, beauty lies in the processing experience of the beholder, an experience that is strongly determined by how objective stimulus properties influence perceptual and cognitive fluency.

a comfortable, pleasant attachment to the stimulus. Mere repeated exposure thus leads to attraction because it is reinforcing. This conditioning process helps organisms distinguish stimuli that are "safe" from those that are not (Zajonc, 2001). Thus, the more often people are exposed to something, the more they tend to like it.

Similarity

Another important determinant of attraction is similarity: people tend to like other people who are similar to themselves (Berscheid & Reis, 1998; Byrne, 1961; Byrne, Clore, & Smeaton, 1986; Caspi & Herbener, 1990; Locke & Horowitz, 1990; Ptacek & Dodge, 1995; Rosenblatt & Greenberg, 1988). After all, "Birds of a feather flock together." Not that friends agree about everything, of course. Agreement on core political values is likely to have more of an impact on whether you like someone than whether you root for the same baseball team or agree on the best musical groups of the 1990s.

Studies of Similarity and Attraction The impact of similarity on attraction has been demonstrated in many ways. Couples who intend to marry are quite similar to each other on an extremely wide range of characteristics. In one study, the members of 1,000 engaged couples—850 of whom eventually married—were asked to provide information about themselves on 88 characteristics (Burgess & Wallin, 1953). The investigators then compared the average similarity of the couples with the similarity of random "couples" created by pairing individual members of one couple with individual members of another couple. This analysis revealed that members of engaged couples were significantly more similar to one another than members of random couples on 66 of the 88 characteristics. Furthermore, for none of the characteristics were the members of engaged couples more *dissimilar* than the randomly created "couples." The similarity of engaged couples was strongest for demographic characteristics (such as social class and religion) and physical characteristics (such as health and physical attractiveness; see **Box 10.3**) and was less strong—but still present—for personality characteristics (such as leadership and sensitivity). Subsequent research that has focused on personality per se has also shown that married couples exhibit considerable similarity in the behaviors indicative of such core personality characteristics as extraversion and genuineness (Buss, 1984). Moreover, interracial and interethnic couples tend to be more similar to each other in terms of their personality traits than are couples of the same race and ethnicity. People may compensate for dissimilarity on one dimension by seeking out greater similarity on others (Rushton & Bons, 2005).

A second type of evidence that supports the link between similarity and attraction comes from studies in which individuals are thrown together for an extended period of time. In one study, Theodore Newcomb recruited male University of Michigan transfer students to live for a year, rent free, in a large house in exchange for filling out questionnaires a few hours each week (Newcomb, 1956, 1961). Newcomb made sure that none of the students knew one another beforehand. Among the questionnaires they filled out were several that asked them to indicate how much they liked each of their housemates. To an increasing degree over the course of the 15-week study, as students got to know one another better and better, the students' liking of one another was predictable from how similar they were (see also Griffitt & Veitch, 1974).

Another type of evidence supporting the proposition that people are attracted to those who are similar to themselves comes from the "bogus stranger" paradigm (Byrne, 1961; Byrne et al., 1986; Byrne, Griffitt, & Stefaniak, 1967; Byrne & Nelson, 1965; Griffitt & Veitch, 1971; Tan & Singh, 1995). In these experiments, participants are given the responses to attitude or personality questionnaires supposedly filled out by someone else (but really created by the experimenter to

BOX 10.3   FOCUS ON DAILY LIFE

Do Couples Look More Alike over Time?

Many people claim that not only do the two people in a couple tend to look like each other, but they look more alike the longer they have been together. There are many reasons why this might be so. People who live together may adopt similar styles of dress and grooming. They doubtless have similar diets, which may make them look more alike over time. They obviously live in the same region of the country, and because of climatic factors, they may acquire the same suntan and the same number of wrinkles.

Perhaps most interesting from a psychological perspective, couples also experience many of the same emotions. The death of a child devastates both parents; winning the lottery brings elation to both. More generally, a downbeat household is typically one in which both members are unhappy; an upbeat household is one in which both are happy. Eventually, a lifetime of experiencing the same emotions may have similar effects on the face and physical bearing of each member of the couple. As someone once said, "After age 40, we all have the faces we deserve." A happy lifetime tends to produce "crow's feet" around the eyes; an unhappy one tends to leave creases

around the outside of the mouth. Thus people who live together and experience the same emotions may converge in facial appearance.

Is there truth to this idea? Robert Zajonc and his colleagues have collected evidence indicating that there is indeed (Zajonc, Adelmann, Murphy, & Niedenthal, 1987). They enlisted the help of 12 married couples to see whether they came to look more alike over time. The members of each couple were 50 to 60 years old, and they provided both current photos of themselves and photos taken during their first year of marriage, approximately 25 years earlier. The photos were cropped and reproduced so that extraneous identifying information, such as style of dress and type of film, was eliminated. Judges who were unaware of who was married to whom were then asked to assess how much each of the men resembled each of the women (for both the current and older photos).

To check for the possibility that older people as a whole are simply more alike, Zajonc and his colleagues established a set of control couples by pairing members of different couples with one another and then assessing the similarity

Physical Similarity Over time, the members of a couple tend to look like each other, perhaps because of initial physical similarities, but also because of shared diet, living conditions, and emotional experiences.

of these "random" couples. Contrary to the notion that older people are generally more homogeneous in appearance, there was no tendency for these random couples to converge in appearance over time. This set them apart from the actual couples, who looked significantly more alike roughly 25 years into their marriages than they did as newlyweds. Thus, not only do we seek mates who are similar to ourselves, we become even more similar in appearance over time.

show a given level of similarity to the participants' own responses). After reading the responses of the bogus stranger, the participants rate him or her on several dimensions, including their liking of the person in question. In study after study of this type, the more similar the stranger is to the participant, the more the participant likes him or her.

But Don't Opposites Attract?   Although most people accept the idea that similarity fosters attraction, they also endorse the opposite theory of **complementarity**— that opposites attract. The idea is that individuals with different characteristics should complement each other and thus get along well. It does seem that a dependent person might profit from being with someone who is nurturing or that a

complementarity The tendency for people to seek out others with characteristics that are different from and that complement their own.

person who is quiet might get along with someone who likes to talk. The yin and yang of two divergent personalities *ought* to create a successful unity.

But notice that the effect of complementarity on attraction, if it exists, is surely more limited in scope than that of similarity. Unlike similarity, for example, there is no reason to expect that complementarity of attitudes, beliefs, or physical characteristics will lead to attraction. The complementarity hypothesis really makes sense only for those traits for which one person's needs can be met by the other (Levinger, 1964). Someone who is dependent can have his or her needs taken care of by a partner who is nurturing. But someone who is a hard worker probably won't want to be with someone who is lazy, and someone who values honesty is not likely to associate with a habitual liar. Thus we might reasonably expect to find complementarity in such traits as dependence-nurturance or introversion-extraversion, but not in such traits as honesty, optimism, or conscientiousness.

What does the evidence tell us? Although a few studies have been offered in support of the complementarity hypothesis (Wagner, 1975; Winch, 1955; Winch, Ktanes, & Ktanes, 1954, 1955), many of them have been criticized for their methodological problems (Katz, Glucksberg, & Krauss, 1960), and many more studies have failed to provide evidence for the hypothesis (Antill, 1983; Boyden, Carroll, & Maier, 1984; Levinger, Senn, & Jorgensen, 1970; Meyer & Pepper, 1977; Neimeyer & Mitchell, 1988).

Thus similarity appears to be the rule and complementarity the exception. Even when two people seem to represent a perfect example of complementarity, they are likely to complement each other on only one or two features of their personalities. Their other characteristics are likely to be similar or unrelated.

Why Does Similarity Promote Attraction? Interactions with people who share our beliefs, values, and personal characteristics tend to be rewarding and thus tend to increase our attraction toward them. For one thing, interactions with similar others are often rewarding simply because they tend to go smoothly. Two people who share a religious faith, for example, often find common ground when they watch a movie, listen to the news, or take a vacation together. Two atheists tend to do likewise. But if the believer and the atheist are paired, their views will often clash, putting their enjoyment of the movie, news, or vacation at risk.

In addition, people who share our beliefs and values validate those beliefs and values. We often enjoy interacting with similar others because they reinforce our beliefs, outlooks, ideologies, and goals—they don't make us question these important parts of ourselves. This effect is perhaps easiest to appreciate by considering our interactions with people who do *not* share our beliefs and attitudes. If you've ever had a contentious political discussion, you know that interacting with someone who challenges our beliefs and assumptions can be unsettling, and this often makes us dislike the person associated with such unsettling feelings. An experiment that used a polygraph to monitor people's physiological reactions makes this point nicely (Clore & Gormly, 1974). The participants were confronted by a confederate who either agreed or disagreed with their attitudes. Not surprisingly, the participants tended to like the confederate who agreed with their views more than the confederate who disagreed with them. More important, the amount of arousal the participants experienced while listening to the confederate predicted the strength of their affective reactions. The more aroused they were while hearing the confederate agree with them, the more they liked the confederate; the more aroused they were while hearing the confederate disagree with them, the more they disliked the confederate.

"Jack Sprat could eat no fat. His wife could eat no lean. And so between them both you see, they licked the platter clean."

—Mother Goose nursery rhyme

"We are so in sync. I was just about to ask you for a divorce."

B. Smaller

Finally, people tend to think that most of their beliefs, values, tastes, and habits are the "right" ones to have. The logical result is that we tend to think that people who are similar to us have the right qualities, just like we do. In contrast, someone who disagrees with us will strike us as "unreasonable" (Pronin, Gilovich, & Ross, 2004). And who wants to be around someone who's unreasonable?

Physical Attractiveness

Not surprisingly, one of the most powerful determinants of interpersonal attraction is physical attractiveness. After all, who receives the most attention at parties, at the health club, or at the checkout line in the grocery store? Attractive people have an advantage in winning other people's attention and affection. Because a person's physical appearance is so visible—and visible so *immediately*—it affects our instantaneous, gut reaction to someone we meet for the first time. A person's keen intelligence and strong moral fiber can be demonstrated, but it usually takes time. Beauty is obvious right away. Partly for this reason, empirical research indicates that a person's looks play an even more important role in interpersonal attraction than intuition might suggest.

Before considering the relevant research findings, it is worthwhile (and bracing for those of us who aren't so attractive) to keep in mind some important caveats. First, although certain features are deemed attractive by most people, there is considerable variability in what individual people find attractive. Second, although people are predisposed to like those who are physically attractive, the reverse is also true. People tend to find those they like more attractive than those they don't like (Kniffin & Wilson, 2004). Further, happy couples tend to perceive each other as physically attractive even if other people don't see them that way (Murray & Holmes, 1997; Murray, Holmes, & Griffin, 1996). Finally, although some people are considered good looking throughout their lives, physical attractiveness is less stable than most of us think (Zebrowitz, 1997; Zebrowitz, Olson, & Hoffman, 1993). People who are unattractive in their teens sometimes bloom in young adulthood, while the looks of the kings and queens of the high school prom often fade.

Impact of Physical Attractiveness The most frequently documented finding about the impact of physical attractiveness in everyday life—and the least surprising—is that attractive individuals are much more popular with members of the opposite sex than are their less attractive counterparts. This effect has been shown in studies that correlate various indices of popularity, such as dating frequency and friendship ratings, with physical attractiveness (Berscheid, Dion, Walster, & Walster, 1971; Curran & Lippold, 1975; Feingold, 1984; Reis, Nezlek, & Wheeler, 1980); in investigations in which blind dates are later asked how attracted they are to their partners (Brislin & Lewis, 1968; Curran & Lippold, 1975; Walster, Aronson, Abrahams, & Rottman, 1966); and in studies of online and speed dating in which participants indicate how attracted they are to individuals they can see in photographs or face to face (Alterovitz & Mendelsohn, 2009; Asendorpf, Penke, & Back, 2011; Eastwick & Finkel, 2008; Luo & Zhang, 2009; Riggio & Woll, 1984; Woll, 1986).

But attractive individuals benefit in other areas as well. An essay supposedly written by an attractive author is typically evaluated more favorably than one attributed to an unattractive author (Anderson & Nida, 1978; Cash & Trimer, 1984; Landy & Sigall, 1974; Maruyama & Miller, 1980). Other studies have shown that each 1-point increase (on a 5-point scale) in physical attractiveness is worth approximately $2,000 in additional annual salary (closer to $3,500 in inflation-adjusted dollars; Frieze, Olson, & Russell, 1991; Hamermesh & Biddle, 1994; Roszell, Kennedy, & Grabb, 1989; see also Cash & Kilcullen, 1985). Men are more likely to come to the aid of an injured female if she is good looking (West & Brown, 1975). And jurors often give attractive defendants a break (Efran, 1974); even when convicted, attractive criminals receive lighter sentences from judges (Gunnell & Ceci, 2010; Sigall & Ostrove, 1975; Stewart, 1980). In one study, for example, participants recommended prison sentences that were 86 percent longer for unattractive defendants than for attractive defendants (Sigall & Ostrove, 1975). Crime may not pay, but the wages are clearly better for those who are good looking.

"Beauty is life's E-Z Pass."

The Halo Effect Attractive individuals also benefit from a **halo effect**, the common belief—accurate or not—that attractive individuals possess a host of positive qualities beyond their physical appearance. Thus people may endeavor to date, mate, and affiliate with the physically attractive not only because of their looks but also because of many other attributes attractive people are thought to have. In experiments that require people to make inferences about individuals depicted in photographs, good-looking men and women were judged to be happier, more intelligent, and more popular and to have more desirable personalities, higher incomes, and more professional success (Bar-Tal & Saxe, 1976; Dion, Berscheid, & Walster, 1972; Eagly, Ashmore, Makhijani, & Longo, 1991; Feingold, 1992b; Jackson, Hunter, & Hodge, 1995; Moore, Graziano, & Millar, 1987). The only consistently negative inferences about physically attractive individuals are that they are immodest and less likely to be good parents (Bar-Tal & Saxe, 1976; Dion et al., 1972; Wheeler & Kim, 1997). Attractive women are sometimes also seen as vain and materialistic (Cash & Duncan, 1984; Dermer & Theil, 1975; Podratz, Halverson, & Dipboye, 2004).

This halo effect appears to vary in predictable ways across different cultures. In independent cultures such as the United States, physically attractive individuals are assumed to be more dominant and assertive than their less attractive counterparts. In interdependent cultures such as Korea, attractive individuals are thought to be more generous, sensitive, and empathic than unattractive individuals (Wheeler & Kim, 1997).

Is there any validity to these beliefs? Given the preferential treatment that physically attractive people often receive, it would be surprising if there were not some impact on their development. Indeed, there is evidence that physically attractive individuals enjoy advantages on certain personality dimensions one might expect. Physically attractive people seem to be somewhat happier, less stressed, and more satisfied with their lives, and they perceive themselves as having greater control over what happens to them (Diener, Wolsic, & Fujita, 1995; Umberson & Hughes, 1987).

Some of the personality correlates of physical attractiveness were revealed in an experiment in which participants had 5-minute telephone conversations

halo effect The common belief—accurate or not—that attractive individuals possess a host of positive qualities beyond their physical appearance.

"Not to worry—I'm going to put our best-looking people on the job."

with members of the opposite sex. The experimenters rated all participants for physical attractiveness. Because the conversations took place over the phone, however, the participants themselves did not know what the person they were talking to looked like. Still, when the participants rated their partners afterward on a number of personality dimensions, those who had been deemed attractive by the experimenters were rated as more likable and socially skilled than their less attractive counterparts (Goldman & Lewis, 1977). A lifetime of easier, rewarding social encounters appears to instill in attractive individuals the confidence and social skills that bring about more rewarding interactions in the future (Langlois et al., 2000; Reis et al., 1982).

But what happens when the attractiveness of the conversation partner is known? Because much of the population is so taken with physical beauty and because those who are physically attractive are thought to possess a host of other desirable characteristics, people may make a greater effort when dealing with someone who is good looking. They may listen better and be more responsive, more energetic, and more willing to express agreement with an attractive person. The net result is that attractive people may be given an advantage that makes it easier for them to come across as socially skilled—even when they are not. In other words, the physical attractiveness stereotype may give rise to a self-fulfilling prophecy—a tendency for people to act in ways that bring about the very thing they expect to happen (see Chapters 4 and 11). This phenomenon was demonstrated in an experiment in which men were asked to have a get-acquainted conversation with a woman over the phone. Each male participant was given a photograph supposedly taken of his conversation partner. In reality, the photos were chosen to be quite attractive for half the participants and unattractive for the others. The conversations were tape-recorded, and when just the woman's comments—and *only* the women's comments—were played to other participants who were not shown the woman's photo and thus had no preconceptions about her appearance, a rather stunning result emerged. They rated the woman who had talked to someone who thought she was attractive as being warmer and more socially poised than the woman who had talked to someone who thought she was unattractive (Snyder, Tanke, & Berscheid, 1977). Once again, the deck is stacked in favor of the physically attractive: people talk to them in ways that bring out their warmth and confidence, thereby confirming the stereotype that they are socially skilled.

Gender and the Impact of Physical Attractiveness Physical attractiveness affects men and women differently. One glance at the newsstand, even by a visitor from Mars, would reveal that attractive women's faces and bodies predominate in the visual media. In short, the world tends to focus on and evaluate women's attractiveness more than men's.

It should be no surprise, then, that attractiveness is more important in determining women's life outcomes than men's. Obesity, for example, negatively affects women's social mobility, but not men's. Overweight girls are less likely to be accepted to college than their average or thin peers (Wooley & Wooley, 1980). Women deemed unattractive at work experience more negative outcomes than similarly unattractive men (Bar-Tal & Saxe, 1976). And physical attractiveness matters more for women than it does for men when it comes to popularity, dating prospects, and even marriage opportunities (Margolin & White, 1987). Simply growing up in an area that has fluoridated water, which improves the look and quality of one's teeth, is associated with a 4 percent average increase in a woman's annual earnings in adulthood but has no effect on a man's earnings (Glied & Neidell, 2008).

So beauty can translate into power for women. It functions as a kind of currency that women can use in obtaining financial and social resources. Barbara Fredrickson and Tomi-Ann Roberts (1997) have argued that these kinds of external rewards encourage women's preoccupation with their own attractiveness, even coaxing them to adopt a kind of outsider's perspective on their physical selves. What Freud called women's vanity may be more appropriately viewed as a survival tactic in a world that so heavily emphasizes women's physical attractiveness.

The Universality of Physical Attractiveness Okay, so physical attractiveness is important; but what is it that people find attractive? What do people who are considered attractive look like? What features set them apart from everyone else?

This question might seem impossible to answer. After all, doesn't it depend on who is doing the judging—on an individual's unique preferences as well as the more general tastes of the prevailing culture or historical era? In short, doesn't the assessment of what is attractive vary enormously from person to person, culture to culture, and era to era?

To be sure, there is considerable variation from person to person as to specific preferences (Beck, Ward-Hull, & McLear, 1976; Wiggins, Wiggins, & Conger, 1968) as well as substantial variation in preferences between cultures and subcultures and across historical periods (Darwin, 1871; Fallon, 1990; Ford & Beach, 1951; Hebl & Heatherton, 1997; see **Box 10.4**). But such variation does not mean that all determinants of physical attractiveness are arbitrary or subject to the whims of fashion. People in Western cultures widely agree on who is attractive and who is not (Cross & Cross, 1971; Iliffe, 1960; Langlois et al., 2000), but they aren't alone; people from different cultures and subcultures tend to share their assessments as well (Cunningham, Roberts, Barbee, Druen, & Wu, 1995; Langlois et al., 2000; Rhodes et al., 2001). Asians, blacks, and whites, for example, share roughly the same opinions of which Asian, black, and white faces they find attractive (Bernstein, Lin, & McClellan, 1982; Maret, 1983; Maret & Harling, 1985; Perrett, May, & Yoshikawa, 1994; Thakerar & Iwawaki, 1979).

Moreover, infants prefer to look at faces that adults consider attractive more than at faces that adults consider unattractive. In experiments, infants as young as 3 months were shown slides of two human faces side by side. Adults had previously judged one of the faces as attractive and the other as unattractive. The slides were typically shown to the infant for 10 seconds, and the amount of time the infant spent looking at each one was recorded by someone who was unaware of which face, the one on the left or right, was the attractive one. Looking time was interpreted as an index of the infant's preference. In several studies, infants showed a clear preference for attractive over unattractive faces (Langlois et al., 1987; Langlois, Ritter, Roggman, & Vaughn, 1991; Samuels & Ewy, 1985; Slater et al., 1998). By the end of the first year, when infants' behavioral repertoires are more advanced, they are more inclined to play contentedly with an adult stranger who is attractive than with an adult who is unattractive.

BOX 10.4 FOCUS ON HEALTH

The Flight to Thinness

Anyone who has seen the paintings of Renoir or Rubens is aware of how times have changed when it comes to the ideal weight for women. This shift has received a great deal of media attention in recent years because much of the world, the United States in particular, is obsessed with thinness. And it's an unhealthy obsession at that, having been blamed for the alarming increase in such eating disorders as bulimia and anorexia nervosa in young women (Brumberg,

1997). Society's current preference for thin women is something of an anomaly, given the historical preference for heavier physiques. To be sure, heaviness was not always viewed as negatively as it is now. Just consider this claim by the eighteenth-century French gourmand Brillat-Savarin: "To acquire a perfect degree of plumpness . . . is the life study of every woman in the world" (Shapin, 2006).

The modern trend toward thinness has been documented in a number of ways.

Researchers examined photographs of women appearing in *Vogue* and *Ladies' Home Journal* over the course of the twentieth century, computing the relative size of the women's busts and waists. The bust-to-waist ratio declined markedly across this time span, indicating a turning away from a more voluptuous standard of female beauty (Silverstein, Perdue, Peterson, & Kelly, 1986). Analyses of *Playboy* centerfolds and Miss America contestants over the latter half

Preferred Body Types In the United States today, most women wish to be thin. But people for centuries preferred women with a heavier body type and more curves, as shown in the paintings of Peter Paul Rubens in the early seventeenth century and Auguste Renoir in the early twentieth century. (A) Rubens's *Venus before a Mirror* (1614–1615). (B) Renoir's *Blond Bather* (1919). The trend toward ever-thinner figures continues in recent times and can be seen in these images of a sex symbol from the 1950s and '60s: (C) Marilyn Monroe; and today, (D) Keira Knightley.

reproductive fitness The capacity to get one's genes passed on to subsequent generations.

Biology and Attraction What then are the features that adults and children, across cultures, find physically attractive? Most attempts to address this question have been guided by biological, or evolutionary, theorizing and have focused on romantic or sexual attraction. The central idea is that we have evolved to have a preference, or "taste," for people whose physical features signify health or, more generally, **reproductive fitness**—the capacity to pass one's genes to subsequent generations. By mating with reproductively fit individuals, people maximize the chances of their own genes being passed on.

of the twentieth century have revealed a similar trend toward slenderness (Garner, Garfinkel, Schwartz, & Thompson, 1980; Wiseman, Gray, Mosimann, & Ahrens, 1992). This trend is captured more vividly, perhaps, by the reaction of model Elizabeth Hurley at an exhibition of the clothes worn by a sex symbol of another era: "I've always thought Marilyn Monroe looked fabulous, but I'd kill myself if I was that fat" (*Allure* magazine, January 2000).

To try to make sense both of the historical norm and the contemporary deviation, Judith Anderson examined the preferred female body type in 54 cultures (Anderson, Crawford, Nadeau, & Lindberg, 1992). She and her colleagues found a relationship between body-weight preferences and the reliability of the food supply across cultures: in cultures with a relatively uncertain food supply, moderate to heavyset women were considered more desirable. But in cultures with very reliable supplies of food, a relatively thin body type was generally preferred. And it is hard to imagine a culture with a more stable food supply and a more pronounced infatuation with slender bodies than that of the contemporary United States.

And get this! What Anderson found cross-culturally over long time periods has also been found among individuals over much shorter time periods. Leif Nelson and Evan Morrison asked male students who were entering a cafeteria (and were presumably hungry) to indicate what body weight they "personally consider ideal in a member of the opposite sex." The hungry participants entering the cafeteria expressed a preference for a significantly heavier female body type than did the sated participants leaving the cafeteria (Nelson & Morrison, 2005).

The current obsession with thinness also appears to be characterized by some unfortunate misperceptions. In one telling study, male and female undergraduates were shown a series of nine drawings of body types ranging from very thin to very heavy (Fallon & Rozin, 1985). The participants were asked to identify the body types along a continuum that represented (1) their own current body type, (2) the body type they would most want to have, (3) the body type they thought would be most attractive to the opposite sex, and (4) the body type of the opposite sex that they personally found most attractive (this time, of course, on a set of line drawings of the opposite sex). The male students, on average, thought that their current body type was precisely as heavy as the ideal body type. Moreover, they also believed that their body type was most attractive to female University of Pennsylvania students (although the women actually preferred a more slender male physique than the men anticipated). The results were quite different for the female students. The women judged themselves to be considerably heavier than their own ideal and considerably heavier than what they thought would be most attractive to men. Perhaps the most disturbing finding is that the women in this study thought that what was most attractive to men was a body type considerably more slender than what the men actually preferred. An unfortunate pair of "thought bubbles" spring immediately to mind: a women standing next to a man worrying that "I'd feel more comfortable around him if only I lost a few pounds," while the man is simultaneously thinking, "She looks great, but she would look even better if she'd gain a few pounds."

But why would women think that men are more attracted to slender physiques than they actually are? Most explanations center on the mass media, which inundate women with images of rail-thin supermodels, actresses, and newscasters. There may be considerable truth to this claim, but it begs an additional question: Why would the media perpetuate an image of an ideal body type that neither men nor women truly think is ideal? One explanation places the blame on the fashion industry. Designers want their clothes to take center stage, not the models wearing them, and a curvaceous figure more often than not "spoils the line." Stated differently, many clothes look better (or at least top fashion designers believe they look better) on lanky women. The net result, according to this interpretation, is a society that is quite literally making itself sick (through excessive dieting, anorexia, or bulimia) in the service of the narrow interests of the fashion industry.

Following the evolutionary thesis, we should be attracted to people whose features signify reproductive fitness and not to people whose features might indicate disease or reproductive problems. Thus we might expect people to steer clear of facial features that are too unusual—for example, eyes placed so close together that the person looks like a Cyclops, or so far apart that the person looks like an extraterrestrial. At the extremes, such features could reflect genetic problems or indicate that something has gone wrong during early development—both of which could make the person's offspring poor evolutionary prospects.

Preferred Facial Features

(A) Queen Nefertiti, of prebiblical times, was considered physically attractive in her time—and in ours. Her clear skin, widely spaced and large eyes, small nose and chin, full lips, and high eyebrows are features deemed attractive in all eras. (B) These same features can be found in many people considered very attractive today, such as Angelina Jolie.

There is evidence that people do indeed find unusual facial features unattractive and that they are drawn to "average" faces (**Figure 10.6**). Either photographic or computer technology can be used to create a composite (or average) face out of any number of individual faces (Galton, 1878; Langlois & Roggman, 1990; Said & Todorov, 2011). People typically consider such composite faces of both men and women as more attractive than the average individual face in the set of faces from which they were constructed, and this effect is stronger the more individual faces are put into the composite. To a significant extent, then, the more average, or typical, a face is, the more attractive it is. (Perhaps, then, we should not be envious of those who are physically attractive because, after all, they are "just average.")

This does not mean that averageness is all there is to attractiveness, however (Rhodes, 2006; Said & Todorov, 2011). Many people are attractive precisely because of something extreme about them. The "bee stung" lips of supermodels depart from the norm, and people with strikingly colored eyes are thought to be especially attrac-

---

FIGURE 10.6 Scientific Method: Attraction to Average Faces

Hypothesis: People are attracted to average faces.

Research Method:

1. Researchers created an average face by dividing each individual face into small squares (at right, four of the many tiny squares are shown).

2. Each square was assigned a number based on a shade of gray.

3. Researchers then averaged the shades of gray across the two photos to create an averaged configuration of the two individual photos and continued averaging even more individual faces with the newly created face.

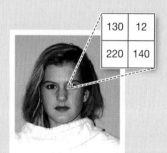

 + 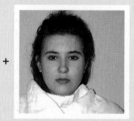 /2 =

Results: Participants found the average faces to be more attractive than the individual faces from which they had been constructed.

CONCLUSION: Faces that are close to the average of all faces are judged more attractive.

FIGURE 10.7 Attraction to Exaggerated Features To further explore attraction to average faces, Perrett, May, and Yoshikawa (1994) made three different kinds of composite faces: (A) a face created by averaging 60 faces, (B) a face created by averaging only the 15 most attractive of these faces, and (C) a face created by calculating the differences between the first two composites and then exaggerating these differences by 50 percent. Participants found the exaggerated face to be the most attractive.

tive by most people. To explore this question, one study used three types of composite faces: (1) an *average* composite that was constructed by averaging all the faces from a pool of 60 photographs, (2) an *attractive* composite formed by averaging only the photographs of the 15 faces previously judged to be most attractive, and (3) an *attractive + 50 percent* composite that was created by calculating the point-by-point differences between the average and attractive composites and then exaggerating these differences by 50 percent (Perrett et al., 1994; see also **Figure 10.7**).

If averageness were all there was to attractiveness, then the average composite should be the most attractive because it was created by averaging a greater number of faces. In addition, any composite that is exaggerated away from the average should be perceived as less attractive than an average face. Yet neither of these results was obtained. Instead, participants judged the attractive composite to be significantly more attractive than the average composite, and the attractive + 50 percent composite was judged to be even more attractive than either of the simple composites.

Another feature that plays an important role in judgments of physical attractiveness is bilateral symmetry. Bilaterally symmetrical individuals in a variety of animal species have been shown to have an advantage in sexual competition (Manning & Hartley, 1991; Markow & Ricker, 1992; Moller, 1992a). In humans, facial attractiveness is correlated with the degree of bilateral symmetry (Scheib, Gangestad, & Thornhill, 1999; Thornhill & Gangestad, 1993).

Biologists believe that departures from symmetry typically result from injuries to an organism in utero (before birth), particularly injuries caused by exposure to parasites (Hubschman & Stack, 1992; Moller, 1992b; Polak, 1993) and by infectious diseases experienced by the mother during pregnancy (Livshits & Kobyliansky, 1991). In addition, bilaterally symmetrical adults tend to have fewer respiratory and intestinal infections than do their less symmetrical peers (Thornhill & Gangestad, 2005). Bilateral symmetry thus seems to serve as a signal of an organism's ability to resist disease. Therefore, according to evolutionary theory, bilaterally symmetrical individuals should be sought out by potential mates.

Thus, two features that signal health and reproductive fitness—averageness and bilateral symmetry—are important determinants of perceived attractiveness. Each of these effects, by the way, exists independently of the other: averageness affects attractiveness ratings when symmetry is statistically controlled, and vice versa. This is important to establish because a face that is "average" in configuration will also be highly symmetrical. These findings attest to the value of a biological approach to attraction, one that examines the reproductive significance of features that contribute to attractiveness.

Sex Differences in Mate Preferences

Any discussion of the biology of attraction leads inevitably to the question of whether there are sex differences in the basis of what is considered attractive. Do men and women look for different things in a mate? Evidence indicates that they do. But do these differences arise because of biology and evolution, or are they the result of social and cultural influences? The core ideas laid out by evolutionary psychologists and some of the evidence they offer to advance their claims are presented here, along with a critique of the evolutionary approach from an alternative, sociocultural perspective.

Investment in Offspring Evolutionary psychologists claim that evolution favors fundamentally different preferences in women and men because of the different investments each sex typically makes in offspring. Women tend to invest much more, even before the child's conception. Men contribute infinitesimally small sperm, which contain little more than genetic material for the potential zygote; women provide a much larger ovum, which contains both genetic material and nutrients the zygote needs in the initial stages of life. Because of this difference, ova are much more "expensive" to produce, and the average woman produces only 200 to 250 mature ova in her lifetime, compared with the millions of sperm the average man produces each *day*. After conception, of course, in utero development takes place entirely within the woman, taxing her physiologically and preventing her from conceiving another child for at least nine months (during which time her male partner is able—biologically—to conceive a large army). After the child is born, an extended period of nursing further taxes the woman and drastically reduces her fertility, thus increasing the time until she is likely to produce additional offspring.

Biologists have observed throughout the animal kingdom that the sex that invests the most in the offspring is almost always more "selective" in choosing a mate than the sex that invests less. Males typically must compete more vigorously among themselves (**intrasex competition**) for females' attention and affection (**intersex attraction**). Because of their direct competition with one another, evolution has favored males with greater size. Due to the pressures of intersex attraction, the male is typically the louder, gaudier member of the species. (Of course, humans are something of an exception in this regard: more effort goes into managing and accentuating women's appearance, although in some societies men have been the more extensively adorned sex.)

Consider, too, those species—such as the Panamanian poison-arrow frog—in which the *male* invests more in the offspring. Is the typical pattern of behavioral sex differences found so widely in the animal kingdom reversed in such species?

intrasex competition Direct competition between two or more males or two or more females for access to members of the opposite sex.

intersex attraction The interest in and attraction toward a member of the opposite sex.

Absolutely. The females in these species are typically larger than their male counterparts, and they compete with one another more fiercely for the favors of the relatively choosy males (Trivers, 1985).

Thus one of the most straightforward predictions from evolutionary psychology is that women ought to be more selective in their choice of mates; or, stated the other way, men should be more indiscriminate than women. This hypothesis conforms to both the historical record and to everyday observation: in virtually all societies in which this issue has been systematically studied, the average man appears ready to jump into bed much more quickly and with a much wider range of potential partners than the average female. (Note that in the world's oldest profession, prostitution, it is nearly always a man making the payment.) A number of studies make this point empirically, the most ambitious being a cross-cultural study with over 16,000 participants from societies all over the globe. Men and women in this study were asked, "Ideally, how many different sexual partners would you like to have?" over various time intervals, ranging from one month to the rest of their lives. Across every time interval and in all regions of the world, men expressed a desire for a greater number of sexual partners (Schmitt, 2003).

What Do Men Want? What Do Women Want? In humans, what do men find attractive in a mate? And if women are indeed more discriminating than men, what do women find attractive in a potential mate? From an evolutionary perspective, if men are to reproduce successfully, they need to find mates who are fertile. But how does one spot a fertile woman? There are no direct cues, but because women experience a relatively narrow window of lifetime fertility (the much-discussed "biological clock"), there is at least one reasonably good indirect cue—youth. Men should thus be drawn to youth and the cues associated with youth—smooth skin, lustrous hair, full lips, and a figure in which the waist is much narrower than the hips (Singh, 1993).

The key reproductive facts confronting women are much different. Although the quality of a man's sperm tends to decline a bit in older age, men typically continue to be fertile throughout life, so there is less evolutionary pressure for women to be attracted to youthful men. Instead, given the demands of nine months of gestation and years of breast-feeding, a critical task confronting women in our ancestral past was to acquire a mate who had resources and who could be counted on to invest them in their children. According to evolutionary psychologists, then, women should be attracted to men who either possess material resources or the characteristics associated with acquiring them—physical strength, industriousness, and social status.

This proposed asymmetry in mate selection has been examined systematically in studies of personal ads and online dating sites in the United States, Canada,

"It is a truth universally acknowledged, that a single man in possession of a good fortune, must be in want of a wife."

—Jane Austen, *Pride and Prejudice*

"Will he ever be able to produce revenue again?"

> "I love a cute guy walking down the street checking me out. . . . I have blonde shoulder-length hair, a nice toushie [sic], and brown bedroom eyes."

> "I am looking for someone to spoil. To be blunt I work for an investment firm and I make quite a bit of money. I am looking for a sweet, cute girl/woman to take care of financially."

> —Personal ads from *Craig's List*

and India (Alterovitz & Mendelsohn, 2009; Gustavsson, Johnsson, & Uller, 2008; Harrison & Saeed, 1977; Kenrick & Keefe, 1992; Rajecki, Bledsoe, & Rasmussen, 1991). These studies reveal an overwhelming tendency for men to seek youth and beauty and to offer material resources, but for women to seek resources and accomplishment and to offer youth and beauty. (For more extensive evidence, see Feingold, 1990, 1992a.)

This trend also emerged in a survey of over 10,000 participants from 37 different cultures (Buss, 1989, 1994), including respondents from the West (Germany, the Netherlands, Israel, and Brazil), from industrialized regions in non-Western countries (Shanghai, China, and Tehran, Iran), and from more rural societies (the Gujarati Indians and South African Zulus). Notably, when asked what they desire in a mate, both men and women in *all* cultures rated kindness and intelligence more highly than either physical attractiveness or earning potential. Nevertheless, just as evolutionary psychologists would predict, men in nearly every culture rated physical attractiveness as more desirable in a mate than women did (**Figure 10.8A**). And in *every* culture, men preferred marriage partners who were younger than they were (Figure 10.8B). Women consistently preferred partners who were older than they were and consistently assigned greater importance than men did to various indices of a potential mate's ability to provide material resources, such as having "good financial prospects," "social status," and "ambition-industriousness" (Figure 10.8C).

Critique of Evolutionary Theorizing on Sex Differences in Attraction The empirical evidence on sex differences in attraction probably is not much of a surprise. Are these findings, then, a triumph of evolutionary theorizing? Should the theory be judged based on how well it fits with data such as these?

This is not an easy question. Consistency with the available data is certainly one criterion by which theories are judged. Yet nearly all of these results can be explained without reference to reproductive fitness or any inherited male/female differences. For example, the tendency for women in all known cultures to be attracted to men bearing status and material resources might very well be the result of a flexible, nonbiological adaptation to an environment in which women in all cultures find themselves. Because men everywhere have, on average, greater physical size and strength and do not experience the restrictions of pregnancy and nursing, men may have disproportionate control over material resources in virtually all cultures. Being economically vulnerable, women might quite rationally be more concerned with material needs than men are (Eagly & Wood, 1999; Wood & Eagly, 2002).

> "The mind is not sex-typed."

> —Margaret Mead

One implication of this difference in material resources is that in societies where the two sexes have relatively equal power, the greater female emphasis on finding a mate with status and economic resources should be lessened. In a reanalysis of the cross-cultural data collected by evolutionary psychologists, Wood and Eagly (2002) found just this pattern. The greater the gender equality in a society (as indicated by United Nations data on income differential, the proportion of women in the national legislature, and so on), the less importance women placed on earning capacity in a potential mate. Gender equality did not affect how much importance men placed on women's attractiveness, however.

Biology? Or Culture? If the most frequently cited evidence in support of the evolutionary approach to sex differences in attraction can be so easily questioned,

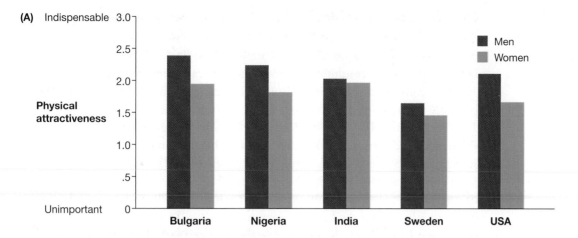

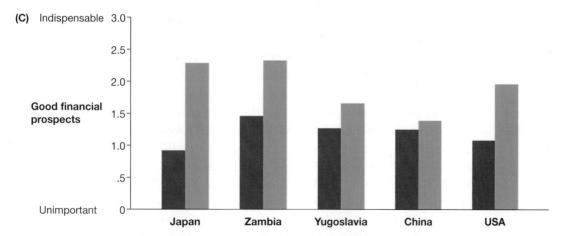

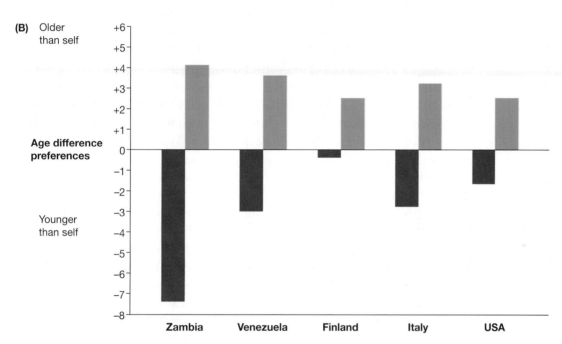

FIGURE 10.8 Differences in Male and Female Mating Preferences The bars show representative findings from a cross-cultural survey of mating preferences. (The importance of physical attractiveness and good financial prospects was rated on a 4-point scale ranging from "indispensable" to "unimportant." Age difference preferences are simply the respondents' average preferred age difference between self and spouse.) (Source: Adapted from Buss, 1989.)

why buy into the approach at all? Evolutionary psychologists would respond that the best way to deal with this problem is the way it is always handled in science—by examining what happens across a range of conditions in an effort to obtain a nuanced pattern of results that no other theory can accommodate.

To examine what happens across a broad range of conditions was, of course, precisely the point of the ambitious cross-cultural studies described earlier (Buss, 1989; Schmitt, 2003). The guiding logic has surface appeal: if the predicted sex differences show up in culture after culture, they are unlikely to be the result of socialization practices (which, for many practices and institutions, vary widely from culture to culture). But as just discussed, the strength of this argument can be questioned. The uniformity across cultures may be the indirect result of relatively simple differences between men and women in size and strength, and in gestation and lactation, that ultimately result in certain behavioral patterns—not the direct result of genetically inherited behavioral tendencies. In the end, cross-cultural studies like those described here cannot overcome the problems they were designed to address. Ultimately, these studies never overcome the problem of resting on a sample size of one—the human species.

Meanwhile, bear in mind that the broader theory of evolution is unsurpassed in its ability to explain many of the complicated behavioral patterns observed throughout the animal kingdom. Biological accounts of human behavior will always spark controversy, and we should remain skeptical of glib, overreaching accounts (Bem, 1993). Still, it would be hard to maintain that evolution has shaped the behavioral tendencies of every plant and animal on earth—but not those of humans.

What, then, would count as truly unambiguous support for the evolutionary framework? The answer is simple: any empirical result that would not be discovered without the guidance of evolutionary theory and that all other accounts would have difficulty explaining. As it turns out, there are some findings that fit the bill. Recall the earlier discussion of bilateral symmetry and its relationship to physical attractiveness. People seek out symmetrical individuals, the argument goes, because symmetry is a sign of "good genes," and combining a sexual partner's good genes with our own increases the chances that our own genes will survive and be passed on in future generations. This logic has led investigators to propose that symmetry ought to be especially preferred in potential mates when the probability of conception is relatively high (the only time, after all, when issues of genetic transmission are relevant). Thus, in one study, women who were at various phases of their menstrual cycles were asked (we're not kidding) to sniff a number of T-shirts that had earlier been worn by a group of men who varied in their degree of bilateral symmetry. As the investigators anticipated, the T-shirts of the symmetrical men were judged to have a better aroma than those of less symmetrical men—but only by those women who were close to the ovulation phase of their menstrual cycle (Gangestad & Thornhill, 1998; Thornhill & Gangestad, 1999; Thornhill et al., 2003). It is unlikely that anyone, without the help of evolutionary theory, would ever have predicted or sought to test such a relationship.

Evidence also shows that women's preferences may change in other ways at different points in their menstrual cycles. For example, it has been argued that the "strong jaw" of particularly masculine-looking male faces is also a sign of good genes. But women generally rate slightly *feminized* male faces as most attractive (Perrett et al., 1998)—*except* when they are ovulating and the chances of conception are highest. Near ovulation, their preferences tend to shift toward more masculinized faces (Penton-Voak et al., 1999; see **Figure 10.9**). Additional studies along these lines have shown that women during the ovulatory phase of their menstrual cycle (1) can more quickly recognize male faces as male (but not female faces as female) than during other times of the month; (2) would prefer (again, during ovulation) to have a "fling" with a man with a lower, more masculine voice (Puts, 2005); and (3) prefer men who pursue more confident, assertive, and competitive tactics of self-presentation (Gangestad, Simpson, Cousins, Garver-Apgar, & Christensen, 2004; Macrae, Alnwick, Milne, & Schloerscheidt, 2002).

Where a woman is in her menstrual cycle also appears to influence the behavior of the men around her. In one study, men were asked to smell the T-shirts worn by women at different points in their cycles. Those exposed to the scent of a woman near ovulation had higher levels of testosterone than those exposed to a woman at other points of her menstrual cycle (Miller & Maner, 2010). In another study, men who interacted with a female confederate who was near the ovulatory phase of her cycle were both more likely to mimic her nonverbal behavior and more likely to take risks in a decision-making task in her presence, presumably in an effort to make a favorable impression (Miller & Maner, 2011).

Studies like these, that assess changes in judgments of attractiveness across biologically meaningful conditions, provide the strongest evidence to date for the evolutionary approach to human attraction. They take us far beyond simple empirical demonstrations of male and female differences that most people have already observed in their daily lives.

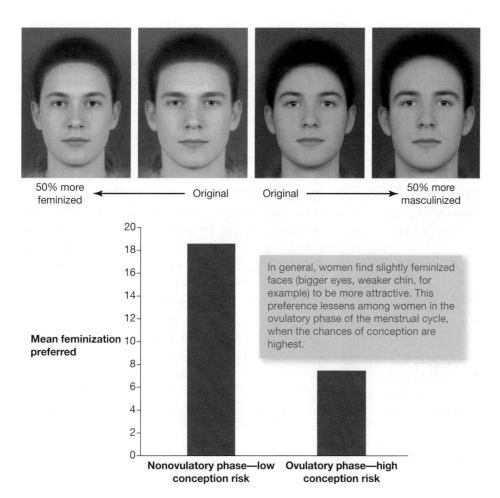

50% more feminized ← Original   Original → 50% more masculinized

In general, women find slightly feminized faces (bigger eyes, weaker chin, for example) to be more attractive. This preference lessens among women in the ovulatory phase of the menstrual cycle, when the chances of conception are highest.

Mean feminization preferred

Nonovulatory phase—low conception risk   Ovulatory phase—high conception risk

FIGURE 10.9 Women's Judgments of Male Attractiveness across the Menstrual Cycle
The photos depict faces that have been altered to be 50 percent more feminized (left) from the original photo and 50 percent more masculinized (right). Women were asked to select the one face they thought was most attractive from a set of five such faces that varied from 50 percent masculinized to 50 percent feminized. The graph shows that the women tended to select somewhat feminized faces overall, but the mean degree of feminization of the selected face was less for women who were at a stage in their cycle when pregnancy was especially likely.

LOOKING BACK Proximity to others means that we tend to encounter them more; and the more we encounter people, the more we tend, through mere exposure, to like them. Also, when people know they will interact frequently with one another, they typically assume the best of one another and do their best to make sure their interactions go smoothly. People are also more inclined to like those who are similar to themselves than people who are dissimilar to themselves. Similar others validate our beliefs and values; they have qualities we like, and our interactions with them tend to be less marred by conflict. Physically attractive individuals are more popular with the opposite sex than are less attractive people, are evaluated more positively, and tend to have better social skills. The effects of physical attractiveness appear to be based in part on biological predispositions: certain elements of physical attractiveness may indicate reproductive fitness.

ROMANTIC RELATIONSHIPS

Throughout history and across different cultures, the reasons for marrying have varied dramatically (Coontz, 2005). In hunter-gatherer cultures, parents "married off" their children to members of other nearby tribes. This practice had the effect, whether intended or not, of ensuring more cooperative trading relationships between groups and also reducing the likelihood of genetic problems that can stem from "inbreeding." For much of Western European history as well, marriages were arranged, again by parents, to consolidate ties with other families and ensure that property and wealth stayed within families. And in some cultures, arranged marriages are still common.

But for most of the roughly 2.3 million couples who get married each year in the contemporary United States (and the vast majority of all North Americans marry), marriage is about romance—about love. So what is this thing we call love? What do people look for in a romantic partner, and what makes them fall in love? How does love change over the course of a long-term relationship? And

Marriage across Cultures Wedding ceremonies vary in the specifics but are practiced throughout different cultures. Here we see ceremonies in (A) Lapland, Scandinavia; (B) Gondar, Ethiopia; and (C) Shanghai, China.

what determines which way a relationship will go—toward contentedness and happiness or toward dissatisfaction and breakup?

What Is Love?

According to one prominent analysis of love, Robert Sternberg's **triangular theory**, the nature of love results from the interplay of three elements: passion, intimacy, and commitment (Sternberg, 1986).

triangular theory of love A theory that states that love has three major components—passion, intimacy, and commitment—which can be combined in different ways.

Early in the relationship, romantic partners experience intense, at times all-consuming feelings of passion, or sexual arousal, for each other. The intensity of romantic passion is expressed in a host of metaphors that capture its single-mindedness and loss of control: lovers feel "knocked off their feet," "hungry" for each other, and "mad" or "crazy" with desire (Lakoff & Johnson, 1980). These feelings of passion are registered in specific patterns of touch, cuddling, and sexual behavior and fluctuate for women with rising levels of certain sex hormones—estrogen in particular (Konner, 2003).

Importantly, people feel this early passion uniquely for a preferred romantic partner. Eli Finkel and colleagues have pioneered the speed-dating approach to the study of early desire (Finkel & Eastwick, 2008). In this research, a dozen or so young women and a dozen or so young men arrive at the lab and engage in a series of rapid-fire, 2-minute get-acquainted conversations with all of the members of the opposite sex. After each of these supercharged interactions, the participants rate their sexual desire and felt chemistry for one another. Finkel and colleagues have found that when one individual feels unique desire and chemistry for another, those feelings are reciprocated (Eastwick, Finkel, Mochon, & Ariely, 2007). Speed daters who felt chemistry for many other people actually generated little desire or chemistry in others. Apparently, people can detect whether interest is targeted or promiscuous.

Surveys indicate that with increasing time together, early passion ebbs and a second element of the romantic relationship becomes more prominent—a deep sense of intimacy (Acevedo & Aron, 2009; Sprecher & Regan, 1998). Couples feel increased comfort and security from the sense of being close and knowing each other better and better. With increasing intimacy, romantic partners include their partner's perspectives, experiences, and characteristics more and more into their own self-concept (Aron & Aron, 1997; Aron, Aron, & Allen, 1989; Aron & Fraley, 1999). In one study of this "second phase," married couples first rated 90 trait adjectives for how accurately they described themselves and their spouse (Aron, Aron, Tudor, & Nelson, 1991). After a brief distracter task, participants viewed each trait on a computer screen and were asked to indicate as quickly as possible whether the trait was "like me" or "not like me." As you can see in **Figure 10.10**, participants were faster to identify traits on which they were similar to their spouse and slower to ascribe traits to themselves that their partner did not also possess. With increasing intimacy, it is as if the two partners become one.

The third element of love in Sternberg's theory is commitment (Frank, 1988; Gonzaga, Keltner, Londahl, & Smith, 2001). A long-term commitment entails many sacrifices—forgoing other flirtations, relationships, and reproductive opportunities; commitment of resources to one another; and pragmatic demands of coordinating two sets of interests, values, friends, and career aspirations.

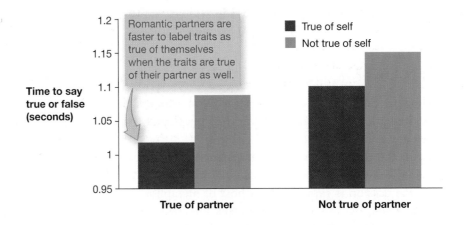

FIGURE 10.10 Construing Close Others as We Construe Ourselves When we fall in love, do our identities merge with our romantic partners? As one way to answer this question, the Arons and their colleagues had romantic partners label traits as true or not true of the self. Some traits were also true of their partner; others were not. (Source: Adapted from Aron, Aron, Tudor, & Nelson, 1991.)

The different types of love that arise from the various combinations of these three components can be conceptualized as a triangle like the one depicted in **Figure 10.11**. The points of the triangle correspond to the types of love that arise from a single component alone. For example, passion without intimacy or commitment is pure infatuation; intimacy without passion or decision/commitment is simple liking; and decision/commitment without passion or intimacy is what Sternberg calls "empty" love. The sides of the triangle, then, correspond to the types of love that arise from the combination of two components. For example, intimacy and commitment without passion is the essence of companionate love. Finally, inside the triangle lies consummate love, or the love that is experienced if two people feel passionate, intimate, and committed to each other. Consummate love is the ideal type of love that most people say they strive to experience at some point in their lives.

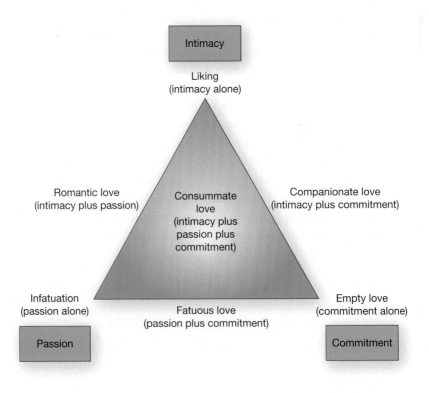

FIGURE 10.11 Triangular Theory of Love Sternberg's triangular theory of love, with different types of love conceptualized as different combinations of the three basic components of passion, intimacy, and commitment. (Source: Adapted from Sternberg, 1988.)

An Investment Model of Romantic Satisfaction

Just about everyone would like to know what factors determine whether a relationship, once begun, will last. One attempt to capture why some long-term romantic relationships survive and others don't is provided by Caryl Rusbult's **investment model of interpersonal relationships** (Rusbult, 1980, 1983). A flowchart of the investment model is presented in **Figure 10.12**. Once partners are in a long-term romantic bond, three ingredients make them more committed to each other: rewards, the relative absence of alternative partners, and investments in the relationship.

The first and most obvious determinant of enduring commitment is *rewards*, a variable discussed earlier in this chapter. When romantic partners are asked to rate the rewards they receive from their relationship as well as what they provide to the other, one of the strongest determinants of romantic satisfaction in long-term relationships is how much they get out of the relationship (Cate, Lloyd, Henton, & Larson, 1982). In fact, John Gottman, a leading marriage researcher, maintains that for long-term romantic relationships in the United States to steer clear of divorce, rewarding experiences must outweigh negative experiences by a factor of 5 to 1 (Gottman, 1993).

Simple rewards, however, are not enough. Whether or not *alternative partners* are available is another strong contributor to the enduring commitment a partner feels. The fewer alternatives a romantic partner has, the more committed he or she tends to feel, and the more likely the partner is to remain in the relationship. For example, in questionnaire studies, romantic partners who report few potential alternative partners are less likely to break up later on (White & Booth, 1991). A person may stick with a relationship that is not terribly satisfying if it is the only game in town. In contrast, people sometimes leave gratifying relationships in pursuit of others who appear to be even more promising. (Think of the multiple marriages of the gorgeous movie star or the wealthy entrepreneur.)

The third determinant of commitment is the *investments* that the couple has put into the relationship. A person is more likely to remain in a relationship if he or she has invested heavily in it. Investments can be direct, such as the time,

investment model of interpersonal relationships A model of interpersonal relationships that maintains that three things make partners more committed to each other: rewards, few alternative partners, and investments in the relationship.

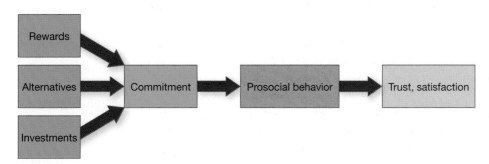

FIGURE 10.12 Rusbult's Investment Model of Romantic Commitment According to Rusbult's model, three factors determine how committed romantic partners are: how many rewards they derive from the relationship, the available romantic alternatives, and how much they have invested in the relationship. More committed partners, in turn, are more likely to engage in prosocial behavior, like forgiveness, and are more likely to feel trust and satisfaction in the bond.

TABLE 10.1 Measuring the Elements of the Commitment Model of Romantic Relationships

To assess how strong the bonds between romantic partners are, researchers ask the partners to respond to statements that reveal possible alternative romantic partners, investment in the relationship, commitment to the relationship, and satisfaction with the relationship.

Element of Model	Sample Item
Alternatives	"All things considered, how attractive are the people other than your partner with whom you could become involved?"
Rewards	"Are there special activities associated with your relationship that you would in some sense lose or that would be more difficult to obtain if the relationship were to end (for example, shared friends, child rearing, recreational activities, job)?"
Investments	"Have you devoted your time and effort and money to buying and improving the home you share, cultivating friendships, rearing children, or building a business together, which would be lost or damaged if the relationship were to end?"
Commitment	"For how much longer do you want your relationship to last?"
Satisfaction	"All things considered, to what degree do you feel satisfied with your relationship?"

effort, caring, and love given to the relationship. Or they can be indirect, such as the shared memories, mutual friends, and shared possessions that are part of having a life together.

In empirical tests of Rusbult's investment model, romantic partners have typically been asked to report on the three determinants of their commitment (rewards, alternative partners, and investments), their level of commitment, and how satisfied they are in their relationship (**Table 10.1**) every six months or so for a couple of years (Berg & McQuinn, 1986; Rusbult, 1983; Simpson, 1987). In these longitudinal studies, each of the three determinants of commitment predicts a couple's decision to stay or leave. Other studies find that more committed partners enjoy more satisfying and stable bonds. When asked to describe their relationship, the more committed partners are more likely to use plural pronouns, such as *we* (Agnew, Van Lange, Rusbult, & Langston, 1998). Highly committed partners were also found to be more likely to engage in prosocial behaviors like self-sacrifice and accommodation, rather than retaliation, in the face of demands from their partner (Wieselquist, Rusbult, Agnew, & Foster, 1999).

Marital Dissatisfaction

It is widely known that roughly one-half of first marriages in the United States now end in separation or divorce (Martin & Bumpass, 1989; Myers, 2000a). Less widely known is the finding that marriages are less satisfying today than they were 30 years ago (Glenn, 1991; Myers, 2000a). Marital conflict stimulates adrenal and pituitary stress responses, which are known to cause cardiac problems and inhibit immune responses (Kiecolt-Glaser, Malarkey, Cacioppo, & Glaser, 1994). And unhappy marriages leave a disturbing legacy: children of divorced parents are more likely to experience greater personal and academic difficulties, both during childhood and later in adulthood (Amato & Keith, 1991; Wallerstein, Lewis, & Blakeslee, 2000). Given that romantic dissatisfaction is so widespread and has such far-reaching effects, learning what predicts romantic dissatisfaction and divorce is an important enterprise.

Predictors of Dissatisfaction and Divorce One way to understand unhappy romantic relationships is to ask whether certain kinds of people or certain circumstances make marital dissatisfaction or divorce more likely. Does the kind of person you marry matter? What about a couple's social class or age?

To answer these questions, researchers relate measures of marital satisfaction to measures of personality and background. They have learned, first, that personality matters. Neurotic people, who tend to be anxious, tense, emotionally volatile, and plaintive, have less happy romantic relationships and are more likely to divorce (Karney & Bradbury, 1997; Karney, Bradbury, Fincham, & Sullivan, 1994; Kurdek, 1993). For similar reasons, people who are highly sensitive to rejection have greater difficulties in intimate relationships (Downey & Feldman, 1996; Downey, Freitas, Michaelis, & Khouri, 1998; see also Murray, Holmes, MacDonald, & Ellsworth, 1998). Moreover, romantic partners and friends who are sensitive to rejection respond with greater hostility when feeling rejected by intimate others (Ayduk, Downey, Testa, Yen, & Shoda, 1999; Downey, Feldman, & Ayduk, 2000; Downey et al., 1998).

Certain demographic factors also predict problems in romantic relationships. Most notably, individuals from lower socioeconomic backgrounds are more likely to divorce (Williams & Collins, 1995). Socioeconomic status (SES) refers to the combination of educational background, wealth, and occupational prestige of a person and his or her family (see Chapter 5). Being from a lower socioeconomic background is more likely to introduce into the relationship financial difficulties and the burdens of finding gratifying and stable work, some of the primary reasons that marriages break up (Berscheid & Reis, 1998).

Finally, people who marry at a younger age are more likely to divorce. There are several possible explanations for this finding. For example, younger people may not be as effective at being partners in long-term romantic relations. Or people who marry young may not be as effective at choosing the right romantic partners.

The Four Horsemen of the Apocalypse As romantic partnerships mature, they revolve more and more around conversations and emotional exchanges about parenting, children, finances, and intimacy. Are there telltale signs in couples' patterns of communication that indicate that a relationship is in trouble? To answer this question, John Gottman and Robert Levenson have pioneered the interaction dynamics approach to studying gay, lesbian, and heterosexual relationships. This approach identifies the specific emotions

"I hope when I grow up I'll have an amicable divorce."

and patterns of communication that predict dissatisfaction and, ultimately, dissolution (Gottman & Levenson, 1992; Levenson & Gottman, 1983).

Gottman and Levenson videotaped married partners engaged in intense conversations in the laboratory and then studied the videos carefully for clues to romantic dissatisfaction. In a conflict discussion task, partners talked for 15 minutes about an issue they both recognized as a source of intense conflict in their relationship, and they tried their best to resolve it. Gottman and Levenson then coded the interactions for anger, criticism, defensiveness, stonewalling, contempt, sadness, and fear, as well as several positive behaviors, including affection, enthusiasm, interest, and humor.

In one long-term study, Gottman and Levenson followed the marriages of 79 couples from Bloomington, Indiana, over many years. Based on their observations, they identified "the Four Horsemen of the Apocalypse"—that is, the four negative behaviors that are most harmful to relationships: criticism, defensiveness, stonewalling, and contempt.

Gottman and Levenson find, just as you would expect, that married individuals who continually carp and find fault with their partners have less satisfying marriages. The same is true of people who are prone to defensiveness and stonewalling (resisting dealing with problems). When romantic partners are unable to talk openly and freely about their difficulties without being defensive—refusing to consider the possibility that something they are doing might contribute to the conflict—they are in trouble. This is especially true of men. To the extent that the male partner stonewalls, withdraws, and denies the issues his partner brings up, there is often great dissatisfaction in the relationship. In contrast, the more partners disclose to each other, the more they tend to like each other (Collins & Miller, 1994).

Contempt, the emotion felt when one person looks down on another, is particularly toxic to romantic bonds. **Figure 10.13** shows how frequently couples who did or did not eventually divorce were observed to express contempt (Gottman & Levenson, 1999). The couples who eventually divorced expressed more than twice as much contempt as the couples who stayed together. A wife's expression of contempt is especially predictive of dissatisfaction and divorce.

Gottman and Levenson's studies are susceptible to the problem of self-selection mentioned at the beginning of this chapter: do married couples get divorced because they express contempt and other negative emotions, or do they express these emotions because their relationship is on rocky ground? Additional findings by Gottman and Levenson indicate that negative communication patterns may in fact contribute directly to divorce. In the study of 79 couples from Indiana, Gottman and Levenson used measures of the four toxic behaviors (criticism, defensiveness, stonewalling, and contempt) early in the relationship to predict who would stay together and who would be divorced 14 years later. Remarkably, based on these four measures gathered from a 15-minute conversation, they could predict with 93 percent accuracy who would get divorced (Gottman & Levenson, 2000).

Dangerous Attributions Certain construal tendencies are also related to the maintenance of romantic bonds. One construal tendency associated with dissatisfaction is *blame*. In a review of 23 studies, Bradbury and Fincham (1990) looked at the relationship between romantic partners' causal attributions and

FIGURE 10.13 Scientific Method: Contempt and Marital Dissatisfaction

Hypothesis: Contempt and feelings of superiority harm intimate relationships.

Research Method:

1. Researchers coded facial expressions of contempt from a 15-minute conversation between married partners.

2. They then related the number of contempt expressions to the likelihood that the couple would eventually divorce or stay together.

Results: Married partners who expressed more contempt were more likely to be divorced 14 years later than married partners who expressed less contempt.

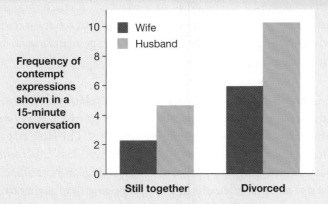

CONCLUSION: Contempt and derisive feelings toward your romantic partner are toxic for the relationship.

Source: Adapted from Gottman & Levenson (1999).

their relationship satisfaction. They found that dissatisfied, distressed couples make attributions that cast their partner and their relationship in a negative light (Karney & Bradbury, 2000; McNulty & Karney, 2001). Distressed couples attribute rewarding, positive events in their relationships to unstable causes that are specific, unintended, and selfish. For example, a distressed partner might interpret a partner's unexpected gift of flowers as the result of a whim, particular to that day, and anticipate the gift to be followed by some selfish request. Happier couples tend to attribute the same positive events to stable causes that are general, intended, and selfless. A satisfied romantic partner thus might attribute a gift of flowers to his or her partner's enduring kindness. Similarly, happier partners attribute negative events—the forgotten anniversary or sarcastic comment—to specific and unintended causes, whereas distressed partners attribute the same kinds of negative events to stable and global causes and see their partners as blameworthy and selfish.

Creating Stronger Romantic Bonds

Now that some of the most common trouble spots in relationships have been identified, let's turn to the kinds of things you can do to build healthier romantic bonds. You already have some clues. You might be wise to marry when a bit older; to avoid highly anxious, rejection-sensitive, neurotic individuals when choosing a partner; to minimize criticism, defensiveness, stonewalling, and contempt in your interactions; and to try to interpret your partner's actions in a praiseworthy fashion.

Capitalize on the Good Are there healthy patterns of conversation that foster more satisfying bonds? Shelly Gable and her colleagues argue that it is particularly important to capitalize on the good—to share what is good in your life with your partner (and vice versa) (Gable, Gonzaga, & Strachman, 2006; Gable, Reis, Impett, & Asher, 2004). In their research, Gable and colleagues found that individuals who received active, constructive "capitalization" from their significant others reported greater relationship satisfaction (Gable et al., 2004). Such responses are evident when one partner responds to the other's good news with engaged enthusiasm. For example, at the news of a partner's forthcoming art show, the actively constructive partner might ask questions about what pieces to show and whom to invite—questions that reveal an active engagement in such an important development in the partner's life.

Be Playful Courtship and the early phases of a relationship involve unusual levels of fun: late-night dancing, candlelit exchanges of poetry, weekend getaways, summer trips, and other exhilarating activities. The later stages, especially when children are involved, become oriented around less inherently enjoyable activities—diaper changing, house cleaning, bill paying, and chauffeuring children to soccer practice and piano lessons. It's not surprising that having children, while bringing many joys, typically leads to a drop in romantic satisfaction (Myers, 2000a). In fact, married partners typically do not return to their previous level of satisfaction until the children leave home. (A point nicely made in an exchange between a priest, a rabbi, and a minister on when life begins: the priest says at conception, the rabbi says at birth, and the minister says when the dog dies and the last child goes away to college.)

Correlational studies show that behaviors as simple as using nicknames (Baxter, 1984) or teasing while negotiating a conflict (Keltner et al., 1998) can keep play alive and make couples happier. Humor and laughter—the right kind—can de-escalate intense conflicts to more peaceful exchanges (Gottman, 1993). Experimental work by Art Aron and his colleagues attests to the benefits of a bit of exhilarating silliness in a marriage (Aron, Norman, Aron, McKenna, & Heyman, 2000). In their study, spouses who had been married for several years engaged in one of two tasks. In a playfully arousing condition, partners were tied together at the knees and wrists with Velcro straps, and they were required to move a soft ball positioned between their heads across a long mat. In the other condition, each partner had to push a ball on his or her own to the middle of the mat with a stick. Spouses reported significantly higher marital satisfaction after engaging in the novel, amusing joint task, both compared with participants in the other condition and compared with a baseline assessed earlier. Unusual, playful activities are arousing—and spouses often misattribute their arousal to their feelings about their partner, thereby enhancing both partners' satisfaction with the relationship.

Keys to Good Relationships (A) Shared laughter and play are vital to healthy relationships. (B) Open communication and disclosure during conflicts are more helpful than stonewalling.

Illusions and Idealization in Romantic Relationships Sandra Murray and her colleagues have collected evidence that a tendency to idealize one's romantic partner is another important ingredient in a satisfying intimate bond (Murray & Holmes, 1993, 1997; Murray, Holmes, Dolderman, & Griffin, 2000; Neff & Karney, 2002). In one study, married couples and dating partners rated themselves and their partners on 21 traits related to virtues (for example, understanding, patient), desirable attributes within romantic relationships (for example, easygoing, witty), and faults (for example, complaining, distant) (Murray et al., 1996). Murray and her colleagues then compared the participants' ratings of their partners' virtues and faults to their ratings of their satisfaction in the relationship. Individuals who idealized their romantic partners—that is, rated the partner higher on these traits than the partner did him or herself—were more satisfied with their relationships. Individuals also reported greater relationship satisfaction when their partners idealized them.

In other studies, Murray and John Holmes (1999) have examined how people idealize their romantic partners. In one study, people were asked to write about their partners' greatest fault. Satisfied partners engaged in two forms of idealization. First, they saw virtue in their partner's faults. For example, an individual might write that his or her partner was melancholy, but that melancholy quality gave the partner a depth of character that was incomparably rewarding. Second, satisfied partners were more likely to offer "yes, but" refutations of the fault. For example, a satisfied partner might write that her husband did not like to hold down a steady job, but at least that gave him more time to help out at home (see a possible neuroscientific explanation in **Box 10.5**).

> "Love to faults is always blind, Always is to joy inclined, Lawless, winged, and unconfined, And breaks all chains from every mind."
>
> —William Blake

Love and Marriage in Other Cultures (Most of Them, in Fact)

To a degree that is hard for modern Westerners to comprehend, some of our generalizations about love and marriage do not apply to most of the world's cultures, nor even to most Western cultures until relatively modern times. Although

BOX 10.5 FOCUS ON NEUROSCIENCE

This Is Your Brain in Love

As the work of Murray and colleagues suggests, the mind does amazing things when in love, turning faults into charming idiosyncrasies (Murray & Holmes, 1999). What does your brain do during love? Recently, neuroscientists and relationship researchers have joined forces to answer this question, and their answers are both intuitive and surprising. In these studies, fMRI images of the brain's pattern of activation are gathered while a person looks at a picture of a romantic partner or is in the throes of feeling intense love (Fisher, Aron, & Brown, 2006). Not surprisingly, these neuroimaging methods reveal that romantic love is associated with activation in reward regions of the brain (the ventral striatum)—regions rich with receptors for oxytocin (which promotes trust and love; see Chapter 6) and dopamine (which promotes approach-related behavior).

What may surprise you, though, is that romantic love also deactivates our friend the amygdala, a region of the brain associated with the perception of threat (again, see Chapter 6). It appears that in the throes of love, the brain disables your ability to see what is threatening or dangerous about the new love. This finding may help your parents understand why you might fall in love with someone who does not quite live up to their standards. Your brain simply isn't reacting to potential signs of risk in your new love—the fondness for motorcycles, the odd tattoos, the disregard for conventional society. These neuroscience findings also help shed light on what the brain might be doing as you turn your partner's faults and flaws (which in others might activate the amygdala) into pleasing virtues, as Murray and colleagues found.

romantic love seems to be experienced in almost every culture, it has generally not been regarded as a prerequisite to marriage (Dion & Dion, 1993). The more typical pattern is a marriage arranged by parents. A young man's parents and a young woman's parents come to an agreement about the suitability of the pair for each other, and they announce the marriage transaction to their children. We mean *transaction* in a very economic sense: often the prospective bride's parents provide a dowry or, somewhat less often, the groom's parents pay a "bride price." This custom is still observed today in much of South, East, and Southeast Asia and in much of Africa.

Love, even if not in the romantic sense, frequently follows marriage; and many cultures have an expression for this development, such as "Loves comes in the pillow." In other words, the postromantic feelings of companionability, affection, and commitment are expected to follow rather than precede marriage. You might be surprised to learn that some historians believe that the idea that romantic love should precede marriage is relatively recent, emerging only in the past 500 years or so. Before that, and for a long time after that in some countries, arranged marriage was the tradition.

Arranged marriages avoid some of the pitfalls of marrying for romantic love, including mismatches between the couple's socioeconomic status and religion—two factors associated with relatively high rates of divorce. They also make it more likely that in-laws will regard one another with respect—a stance perhaps less likely when the in-laws are dragged together for reasons having nothing to do with mutual regard. The lack of expectation that there should be romantic love also makes it less likely that the common, gradual transformation from romantic to companionate love will be a source of disappointment and discontent. Finally, most cultures with arranged marriages provide social supports that extend far beyond the immediate family. And the relationships are likely to be deeper than the replaceable kind that are common in the highly mobile modern Western world.

 Romantic relationships are a human universal, essential to our well-being, but in today's world they can be a difficult enterprise. Personality and demographic factors predict unhappiness in marriage, as do toxic behaviors like criticism, defensiveness, stonewalling, contempt, and blame. The science of relationships is also yielding important insights into successful and rewarding relationships: partnerships make it when the individuals capitalize on the good, choose to be playful, and see their partner in a flattering light.

Chapter Review

Summary

Characterizing Relationships

- Relationships come into being when individuals depend on one another for help in meeting life's demands.

- There is a biologically based *need to belong*, evident in the evolutionary benefits and universality of different relationships and in the negative consequences that accompany the absence of relationships.

- Relationships shape the sense of self and how social events are remembered and explained. People have certain *relational selves*, or beliefs, feelings, and expectations that derive from their relationships with particular other people. When one of these is activated by a particular person, that person is seen in light of the relevant relational self.

- Clark and Mills have contrasted *communal relationships* that are often long term with *exchange relationships* that are often of short duration and are governed by concerns of equity.

- We tend to like those who provide us with the greatest rewards. *Social exchange theory* holds that people pursue those interactions that provide the most favorable difference between rewards and costs.

- John Bowlby's *attachment theory* holds that early in development, children rely on their parents for a sense of security. Attachment styles vary along the two dimensions of anxiety (fear of rejection) and avoidance (discomfort with intimacy). For example, people with a *secure attachment style* are neither anxious nor avoidant; they are comfortable with intimacy and, when stressed, wish to be close to other people. Attachment styles are somewhat stable over the life span and can have wide-ranging effects on an individual's well-being.

Attraction

- *Proximity*, or sheer closeness of contact, leads to attraction. Three reasons for the power of proximity are sheer *availability, anticipation of interaction*, and the *mere exposure effect*.

- *Similarity* also leads to attraction. Studies invariably find that people like individuals who resemble them more than individuals who do not. There is scant evidence that "opposites attract."

- *Physically attractive* people are much more popular with the opposite sex, earn more money, and receive lighter sentences for crimes. Because of the *halo effect*, they are believed to have many positive qualities that go beyond their physical appearance.

- Physical appearance affects the lives of women more than men. At work, for example, women deemed unattractive fare much worse than men considered unattractive.

- Evolutionary psychologists argue that we are attracted to features that signify *reproductive fitness*—the capacity to reproduce our genes in future generations if we were to mate and have children with a person who possesses those features. These include physical characteristics that signal vitality, fertility, and likely reproductive success.

- In species in which parental investment is greater for the female, the males must compete vigorously among themselves (*intrasex competition*) for access to choosy females. The males also must compete for the females' attention (*intersex attraction*) and so are typically the louder and gaudier of the species.

- Evolutionary psychologists believe that differential parental investment by men and women leads men to prefer women whose physical appearance gives the impression that they will be fertile. Women are attracted to men who can be expected to provide for them and their children—men who are strong, industrious, and have social status.

- Though much evidence supports the hypotheses of evolutionary psychologists, most of the human findings can be explained without resorting to an evolutionary explanation. The strongest support for the evolutionary approach to attractiveness in humans comes from studies showing that women increase their preference for attractive (or at least symmetrical) and masculine men during the ovulatory phase of their menstrual cycles, when they have a higher probability of conceiving.

Romantic Relationships

- Romantic relationships are an important part of social life, and they are important to our satisfaction with our lives and even our physical health. According to the triangular theory of love, romantic love is founded on passion, intimacy, and commitment.

- According to the investment model of relationships, happy romantic relations are affected by *commitment*, which is a function of *rewards* in the relationship, *alternatives* to the relationship, and *investments* in the relationship.

- Longitudinal research has identified several factors that predict romantic problems. Divorce and marital dissatisfaction are often caused by *marrying young, criticism, defensiveness, stonewalling, contempt*, and *blame*.

- Research has also uncovered some important elements of satisfied romantic relationships. Happy couples *capitalize* on the good events in their lives, they *have fun*, and they have more *positive illusions* about their partners.

- In many cultures, marriages are arranged by a couple's parents. Love—not necessarily the romantic kind—is expected to follow marriage.

Key Terms

anxious-preoccupied style (p. 365)
attachment theory (p. 363)
communal relationships (p. 361)
complementarity (p. 376)
dismissive-avoidant style (p. 365)
equity theory (p. 363)
exchange relationships (p. 361)

fearful-avoidant style (p. 365)
functional distance (p. 369)
halo effect (p. 379)
intersex attraction (p. 386)
intrasex competition (p. 386)
investment model of interpersonal
    relationships (p. 395)

mere exposure effect (p. 370)
propinquity (p. 368)
reproductive fitness (p. 382)
secure attachment style (p. 365)
social exchange theory (p. 363)
triangular theory of love (p. 393)

Further Reading

Bowlby, J. (1969/1982). *Attachment and loss*. Vol. 1. *Attachment* (2nd ed.). New York: Basic Books. A seminal theoretical statement about the evolution of different attachment processes.

Etcoff, N. L. (1999). *Survival of the prettiest: The science of beauty*. New York: Doubleday. An application of evolutionary theory to understanding what people consider beautiful and why.

Fredrickson, B. L., & Roberts, T. (1997). Objectification theory: Toward understanding women's lived experiences and mental health risks. *Psychology of Women Quarterly, 21,* 173–206. An analysis of the broad-based effects on women of the great emphasis placed on their physical attractiveness.

Gottman, J. (1993). *Why marriages succeed or fail*. New York: Simon & Schuster. Includes great tips for happy marriages.

I AM GAY

AND THIS IS WHERE I PLAY

We have always been a part of this community.

Gay and straight, we play ball together, and see each other at the barbershop and church. It's time to treat us with the love we deserve.

CHAPTER 11

Stereotyping, Prejudice, and Discrimination

CRISTÓBAL COLÓN, KNOWN TO MOST of us as Christopher Columbus, was no doubt in an exceptionally good mood on the morning of October 12, 1492, when he went ashore in the Bahamas on Guanahani Island, which he promptly renamed San Salvador. It had been 11 weeks since he set sail from Spain in his effort to find a western route to Japan, China, and the East Indies. Now he had spotted land, and the glory he sought was ensured, as was his appointment as viceroy and governor-general of all territories he might discover.

It is understandable, then, that Colón was rather expansive in his journal that day. His good mood was reflected in his description of the inhabitants of San Salvador (Columbus, 1492/1990):

They swam out to the ships' boats where we were and brought parrots and balls of cotton thread and spears and many other things, and they bartered with us for other things which we gave them, like glass beads and hawks' bells. In fact they took and gave everything they had with good will. . . . They were well built, with handsome bodies and fine features. Their hair is thick, almost like a horse's tail. . . . They do not carry arms and do not know of them because I showed them some swords and they grasped them by the blade and cut themselves. . . . They are all fairly tall, good looking and well proportioned.

They ought to make good slaves.

Colón's journal entry on that day touches on the main ideas in this chapter—stereotyping, prejudice, and discrimination. He was well on his way toward developing a (rather favorable) stereotype of those he encountered, characterizing the islanders as a whole on the basis of those individuals he happened to meet that day. Nevertheless, he was immediately prejudiced against the islanders, whose appearance and customs differed from those of his own people.

407

Stereotyping Outgroups
Upon landing on an island in the Bahamas, Christopher Columbus was greeted by the natives and offered gifts of welcome, as shown in this German engraving. Yet Columbus was prejudiced against the indigenous people because they differed from Europeans; he stereotyped them as a group that would make good slaves, and he treated them as such.

And he felt no need to treat them as he would treat his crew or other Europeans, as his chilling statement "They ought to make good slaves" makes clear.

We may be tempted to dismiss Colón's reactions as outdated and to believe that surely people are more enlightened today. In some ways, they are (Devine, Plant, & Blair, 2001; Pinker, 2011; Swim & Campbell, 2001). Slavery still exists but no longer as a sanctioned, state-sponsored enterprise. Moreover, the world is now more truly multicultural than it has ever been. Members of different races, ethnicities, and religions live and work alongside one another more peacefully and productively than ever before. And of course, in 2008 the United States elected its first African-American president, a triumph that nearly all pioneers of the civil rights movement said they never thought would happen in their lifetime.

Despite such progress, however, it is abundantly clear that the human tendencies to stereotype, harbor prejudice, and engage in discrimination are still with us. The awful events in Darfur, Rwanda, Bosnia, and Somalia and the long-standing conflicts in the Middle East or Kashmir clearly show that intergroup enmity and conflict continue to be distressingly common elements of the human condition. Nor are such problems confined to other, more troubled parts of the world. Stereotyping, prejudice, and discrimination prevail in the United States, too, as evidenced by videotapes of police officers brutalizing members of minority groups, as well as the countless instances of minorities being pulled over by the police for no cause or being passed over by cab drivers and potential employers.

The continued existence of ethnic, religious, and racial animosity challenges us all to understand the underlying causes of intergroup tension. Where do stereotypes, prejudice, and discrimination come from? Why do they persist? What can be done to eliminate or reduce their impact?

Any serious attempt to address these questions must begin with the recognition that most likely there will never be a single, comprehensive theory of stereotyping, prejudice, or discrimination. The causes of each of these phenomena are many and varied, and any satisfactory account of them must incorporate numerous elements. This chapter therefore focuses on three general perspectives that shed light on these issues. The *economic perspective* identifies the roots of much intergroup hostility in the competing interests that set many groups apart from one another. The *motivational perspective* emphasizes the psychological needs and wishes that lead to intergroup conflict. The *cognitive perspective* traces the origin of stereotyping to the same cognitive processes that allow people to categorize, say, items of furniture into distinct classes of chairs, couches, and tables. This perspective takes into account the frequent conflict between people's consciously held beliefs and values and their quick, reflexive reactions to members of specific racial, ethnic, occupational, or other demographic groups.

Note that these three perspectives are exactly that—perspectives, not sharply defined categories. In addition, they should be seen not as competing accounts but as complementary elements of a more complete analysis. Sometimes the same phenomenon or the same empirical finding can be considered an example of both an economic influence and a motivational influence. Nevertheless, despite the sometimes fuzzy boundaries between them, the distinctions are useful for the purpose of organizing and thinking clearly about the various causes of stereotyping, prejudice, and discrimination—as well as some ways that intergroup conflict may be lessened.

CHARACTERIZING INTERGROUP BIAS

Do you believe that Asians are industrious, that Italians are temperamental, that Muslims are fanatical, or that Californians are "laid back"? Such beliefs are **stereotypes**—beliefs that certain attributes are characteristic of members of particular groups. They can be positive or negative, true or false. And whether valid or not, they are a way of categorizing people (Lee, Jussim, & McCauley, 1995). Stereotyping involves thinking about a person not as an individual, but as a member of a group, and projecting what (you think) you know about the group onto your expectations about the individual.

Some stereotypes have some truth to them and others don't. Consider the old joke that heaven is a place where you have an American house, a German car, French food, British police, an Italian lover, and everything is run by the Swiss. Hell, on the other hand, is a place where you have a Japanese house, a French car, British food, German police, a Swiss lover, and everything is run by the Italians. The Swiss bureaucracy is indeed more widely praised than the Italian, and automobile magazines rave more about what's rolling off the assembly lines at BMW and Audi than at Peugeot and Renault. Some stereotypes are accurate. On the other hand, is there any reason to be especially wary of German police? There certainly was during the 1930s and 1940s, but has German law enforcement been particularly likely to encroach on civil liberties since then? Maybe, maybe not. Are Italian lovers to be preferred to Swiss? You make the call.

But stereotypes about Swiss administrators, German police, or Italian lovers (again, whether valid or not) are not what concern social psychologists (Judd & Park, 1993). Most of the concern with stereotyping has focused on the kinds of stereotypes considered the most questionable and those most likely to give rise to the most pernicious forms of prejudice and discrimination.

Prejudice refers to an attitudinal and affective response toward a certain group and its individual members. Negative attitudes have received the most attention, but it's also possible to be positively prejudiced toward a particular group. Prejudice involves *prejudging* others because they belong to a specific category.

stereotypes Beliefs that certain attributes are characteristic of members of particular groups.

"I speak French to my ambassadors, English to my accountant, Italian to my mistress, Latin to my God and German to my horse."

—Frederick
the Great of Prussia

prejudice A negative attitude or affective response toward a certain group and its individual members.

discrimination Unfair treatment of members of a particular group based on their membership in that group.

Discrimination refers to negative or harmful behavior directed toward members of particular groups. It involves unfair treatment of others—treatment based not on their character or abilities but on their membership in a group.

Roughly speaking, stereotyping, prejudice, and discrimination refer to the belief, attitudinal, and behavioral components, respectively, of negative intergroup relations. Stereotyping, prejudice, and discrimination often go together. People are more inclined to injure those they hold in low regard. But the components of intergroup bias need not all occur together. A person can discriminate without prejudice, for example. Jewish parents sometimes say they don't want their children to marry outside the faith, not because they have a low opinion of other groups, but because they are concerned about assimilation and its implications for the future of Judaism. Members of nearly all ethnic groups have harbored similar sentiments out of the same concern about preserving a cultural identity or way of life. Thus ingroup favoritism can arise in the absence of outgroup enmity. Sometimes, of course, statements that "I have nothing against them, but . . ." are merely cover-ups of underlying bigotry. At other times, they are doubtless sincere (Lowery, Unzueta, Knowles, & Goff, 2006).

It is also possible to be prejudiced and yet not discriminate, particularly when a culture frowns on discrimination. Civil rights laws in the United States are specifically designed to uncouple prejudiced attitudes and discriminatory actions. The threat of punishment is intended to keep people's discriminatory impulses in check.

Modern Racism

Throughout much of the world, the norms about how different groups of people are to be viewed and treated have changed. In Western countries in particular, it is not legally acceptable to engage in many forms of discrimination that were common half a century ago, nor is it socially acceptable to express the sorts of prejudices and stereotypes that were common until relatively recently. This change has created conflict in many people between what they really think and feel and what they think they *should* think and feel (or

Stereotyping, Prejudice, and Discrimination Stereotyping, prejudice, and discrimination often go together. (A) Stereotypes of African-Americans as more likely to break the law can be combined with anti-black sentiment to lead to discrimination, such as a tendency for police officers to be more likely to pull over African-American drivers. (B) Stereotypes linking Islam with extremism can lead to negative reactions toward Muslims and Islamic institutions.

what they believe is prudent to say or do publicly). For many, it has also created a conflict between competing beliefs and values (for example, a belief in equal treatment versus a desire to make up for past injustice through affirmative action) or between competing abstract beliefs and gut-level reactions (for example, a belief that we ought to feel the same toward members of all groups versus some hard-to-shake resistance to that belief). In addition, as recent research has shown, some of our reactions to other groups are unconscious and automatic, and these responses may differ from our more thoughtful beliefs and attitudes. These sorts of conflicts have inspired social psychologists to develop new theoretical accounts to explain this modern, more constrained, more conflicted sort of prejudice.

This theoretical shift is particularly noteworthy with respect to accounts of race relations in the United States. Some have argued that old-fashioned racism has largely disappeared in the United States but has been supplanted by a subtler, more modern counterpart (Kinder & Sears, 1981; McConahay, 1986; Sears, 1988; Sears & Henry, 2005; Sears & Kinder, 1985; see Haddock, Zanna, & Esses, 1993, and Swim, Aiken, Hall, & Hunter, 1995, for similar accounts of homophobia and sexism, respectively). In one example of this theoretical shift, **modern racism** is defined as a rejection of explicitly racist beliefs (for example, that there are genetic differences between racial groups in intelligence) while maintaining an enduring suspicion of, discomfort with, or animosity toward African-Americans.

modern racism Prejudice directed at other racial groups that exists alongside rejection of explicitly racist beliefs.

Gaertner and Dovidio (1986; Dovidio & Gaertner, 2004) have explored the conflicts and inconsistencies that often accompany modern racism. They note that many people hold strong egalitarian values that lead them to reject prejudice and discrimination, and yet they also harbor unacknowledged negative feelings and attitudes toward minority groups that stem from ingroup favoritism and a desire to defend the status quo (Sidanius & Pratto, 1999). Whether these individuals will act in a prejudiced or discriminatory manner depends on the details of the situation. If the situation offers no justification or "disguise" for discriminatory action, their responses will conform to their egalitarian values. But if a suitable rationalization is readily available, the modern racist's prejudices will emerge.

In an early experimental test of this idea, participants were in a position to aid a white or black individual in need of medical assistance (Gaertner & Dovidio, 1977; see also Dovidio, Smith, Donella, & Gaertner, 1997; Saucier, Miller, & Doucet, 2005). If the participants thought they were the only one who could help, they came to the aid of the black victim somewhat more often (94 percent of the time) than they did for the white victim (81 percent). But when they thought that other people were present and their inaction could be justified on nonracial grounds ("I thought somebody else with more expertise would intervene"), they helped the black victim much less often than the white victim (38 percent versus 75 percent). In situations such as this, the prejudice or discrimination is "masked," and the individual remains comfortably unaware of being racist. Thus modern racism shows itself in subtle ways. The modern racist would never join the Ku Klux Klan but might consistently give black passersby a wider berth. Such a person might never utter a racist word but might never support any social policy designed to aid black Americans, either.

In another telling study, white participants evaluated black and white applicants to college (Hodson, Dovidio, & Gaertner, 2002). Participants whose scores on the Attitudes toward Blacks Scale indicated that they were high or low in explicit prejudice toward blacks rated white and black applicants the same when the applicants excelled on all pertinent dimensions or were below par on all dimensions. But when the applicants excelled on certain dimensions and were below average on others, the ratings of prejudiced and unprejudiced participants diverged: the prejudiced participants rated the black applicants less favorably than did the unprejudiced participants. In these latter cases, prejudiced participants' discriminatory responses could be defended as nondiscriminatory—that is, they could be hidden—by claiming that the dimensions on which the black applicants fell short were more important than those on which they excelled.

However, when the desire to appear unprejudiced is sufficiently strong—when, say, the audience might be particularly disapproving—the *opposite* result is sometimes observed: bias directed at the ingroup. In one study, white participants first read that "some admissions procedures are alleged to be biased, and activist groups are pressuring colleges all over the country to review and reevaluate their admissions criteria." When they then read the application folders of black applicants who were strong on some dimensions and weak on others, they rated them *more* favorably than they rated comparable white applicants, and they did so by judiciously choosing which dimensions of accomplishment should receive more weight (Norton, Vandello, & Darley, 2004; see also Harber, 1998; Norton, Sommers, Apfelbaum, Pura, & Ariely, 2006).

Benevolent Racism and Sexism

Statements like "Some of my best friends are _____" (fill in the blank) or "I'm not sexist; I love women!" illustrate a common conviction that stereotypes must be negative to be harmful. In fact, however, many of our "isms" (racism, sexism, ageism) are ambivalent, containing both negative and positive features (Czopp & Monteith, 2006; Devine & Elliot, 1995; Ho & Jackson, 2001). Someone might believe, for example, that Asians are colder and more rigid than whites—and at the same time believe they are more intellectually gifted. Similarly, someone might believe that women are less competent and intelligent than men—and at the same time believe women are warmer and have better social skills.

In their work on ambivalent sexism, Peter Glick and Susan Fiske (2001a, 2001b) have interviewed 15,000 men and women in 19 nations and found that benevolent sexism (a chivalrous ideology that offers protection and affection to women who embrace conventional roles) often coexists with hostile sexism (dislike of women who are viewed as usurping men's power). Glick and Fiske argue that even these partly positive stereotypes aren't necessarily benign. Ambivalent sexist or racist attitudes may be particularly resistant to change. The favorable features of such belief structures enable the stereotype holder to deny any prejudice. (Think of the trucker who romanticizes women so much he decorates his mud flaps with their likeness.) By rewarding women and minorities for conforming to the status quo, benevolent sexism and racism inhibit progress toward equality. In other words, those who hold ambivalent attitudes tend to act positively toward members of outgroups only if they fulfill their idealized image of what such people should be like—say, the happy housewife or the *Playboy* centerfold. Those who deviate tend to be treated with hostility (Lau, Kay, & Spencer, 2008).

Measuring Attitudes about Groups

The most straightforward way to assess how people feel about various groups is, of course, to ask them. And indeed, in the United States and elsewhere, public opinion polls have frequently asked respondents about their attitudes toward members of other groups. A number of systematic attitude scales also have been developed for this purpose, such as the Attitudes toward Blacks Scale (Brigham, 1993), the Modern Racism Scale (McConahay, Hardee, & Batts, 1981), the Internal Motivation to Respond Without Prejudice Scale (Plant & Devine, 1998), and many more. However, because people may be unwilling or unable to express their convictions accurately, social psychologists have developed new methods of assessing people's stereotypes and prejudices (Wittenbrink & Schwarz, 2007). Surveys of people's attitudes toward certain groups cannot always be trusted, because respondents may not think it's acceptable to express what they really feel or because what people report verbally is only a part of their stance toward members of other groups. Given that so many forms of prejudice are ambivalent, uncertain, or hidden—even from the self—they are not likely to be revealed through self-report (Crandall & Eshleman, 2003). Social psychologists have therefore employed a number of physiological measures of prejudice and stereotyping (Amodio, 2008; Amodio et al., 2004; Amodio & Lieberman, 2009) and have developed some widely used indirect measures, two of which are discussed here. (For overviews of a wider set of implicit measurement procedures, see Gawronski & Payne, 2010; Wittenbrink & Schwarz, 2007.)

The Implicit Association Test (IAT) Anthony Greenwald and Mazarin Banaji (1995) have pioneered a technique called the **Implicit Association Test (IAT)** for revealing subtle, nonconscious prejudices, even among those who advocate universal equality and high regard for all groups. The technique works like this: a series of words and/or pictures are presented on a computer screen, and the respondent is told to press a key with the left hand if the picture or word conforms to one rule and to press another key with the right hand if it conforms to another rule. You can try a noncomputerized version in **Figure 11.1**. Or you can see whether you hold any implicit stereotypes or prejudice toward a variety

Implicit Association Test (IAT)
A technique for revealing nonconscious prejudices toward particular groups.

FIGURE 11.1 You Be the Subject: The Implicit Association Test (IAT)

First, as you read each word in the column below, tap your left index finger if it is either a female name or a "weak" word, and tap your right index finger if it is either a male name or a "strong" word.

Martha
Vigorous
Jason
Small
David
Powerful
Karen
Delicate
Gloria
Feather
Tony
Mighty
Matthew
Wispy
Rachel
Robust
Amy
Fine
George
Flower
Betsy
Stout
Charlene
Iron

Then repeat the procedure, but now as you read each word, tap your left index finger if it is either a female name or a "strong" word, and tap your right index finger if it is either a male name or a "weak" word.

Did you find yourself tapping faster as you read the words the first time or the second?

of groups by taking some of the IATs online at https://implicit.harvard.edu/implicit/research/.

Greenwald and Banaji argued that respondents would be faster to press one key for members of a particular group and words stereotypically associated with that group than to press the same key for members of that group and words that contradict the stereotype associated with that group. It's easy to respond quickly when the category members and the attributes associated with the group are signaled with the same hand, rather than signaled with different hands.

The same general procedure is used to assess implicit prejudice, but in this case participants are first asked to press one key for both positive words and either photos or the names of people in one group, and another key for both negative words and people in another group. People prejudiced against old people, for example, should be faster to press the appropriate key when the same key is used for old faces and negative words (because old people are viewed negatively) and slower when the same key is used for old faces and positive words. Participants then repeat the procedure with the pairings of the two groups and positive/negative words switched. A nonconscious prejudice toward old people would be captured by the difference between the average time it takes to respond to old faces/positive words and the average time it takes to respond to old faces/negative words.

Millions of people have taken the IAT on the web. Among other results, researchers have found that both young and older individuals show a pronounced prejudice in favor of the young over the old, and about two-thirds of white respondents show a strong or moderate prejudice for white over black (Nosek, Banaji, & Greenwald, 2002). In addition, about half of all black respondents also show some prejudice in favor of white faces.

An important question, however, is whether a person's responses on the IAT are predictive of behavior that is more significant than pressing computer keys (Amodio & Devine, 2006; Brendl, Markman, & Messner, 2001; Karpinski & Hilton, 2001). Although the test has its critics (Blanton & Jaccard, 2008; Blanton et al., 2009), there is evidence that IAT responses do correlate with other measures of prejudice (Lane, Banaji, Nosek, & Greenwald, 2007; Rudman & Ashmore, 2007). In one study, participants in a brain-imaging machine were shown pictures of black and white faces. The participants' earlier IAT responses were significantly correlated with heightened neural activity in the amygdala (a brain center associated with emotional learning and evaluation) in response to the black faces. Their scores on a more traditional, conscious measure of prejudice, the Modern Racism Scale, were not correlated with this difference in neural activity, suggesting that the IAT assessed an important component of attitudes that participants were unable or unwilling to articulate (Phelps et al., 2000). In another study, participants interacted with a white experimenter, took the IAT, and then interacted with a black experimenter. The participants' IAT scores, it turns out, predicted the discrepancy between how much they spoke to the white versus the black experimenter, how often they smiled at the white versus the black experimenter, and the number of speech errors and hesitations they exhibited when interacting with the white versus the black experimenter (McConnell & Leibold, 2001).

Priming and Implicit Prejudice Social psychologists have also measured prejudices that individuals might not know they have, or that they may wish to deny, by using a number of **priming** (mental activation) procedures. The logic of these procedures is simple: If I show you the word *butter* and then ask you to tell me, as quickly as you can, whether a subsequent string of letters is a word, you'll recognize that *bread* is a word more quickly than you'll recognize that *car* is a word because of your preexisting association between bread and butter. Similarly, if you associate nuns with virtue and charity, you are likely to respond quickly to positive terms (*good, benevolent, trustworthy*) after seeing a picture of a nun. But if you have negative associations to nuns as, say, strict, rigid, or cold, you are likely to respond more quickly to negative terms (*mean, unhappy, unbending*) after seeing a picture of a nun. An implicit measure of prejudice can thus be derived by comparing a person's average reaction time to positive and negative words preceded by faces of members of the target category (compared with "control" trials in which positive and negative words are preceded by faces of noncategory members). As discussed later in this chapter, numerous studies using these priming methods have shown that people often have subtle prejudices against various target groups that they would steadfastly deny having (Banaji, Hardin, & Rothman, 1993; Bessenoff & Sherman, 2000; Dijksterhuis, Aarts, Bargh, & van Knippenberg, 2000; Dovidio, Kawakami, & Gaertner, 2002; Fazio & Hilden, 2001; Friese, Hofmann, & Schmitt, 2008; Gawronski, Cunningham, LeBel, & Deutsch, 2010). And there is no reason to assume that people are lying when they deny such prejudices: they simply may not have conscious access to many of their attitudes and beliefs.

priming A procedure used to increase the accessibility of a concept or schema (for example, a stereotype).

In much of today's Western world, prejudice and discrimination are frowned upon. This trend has led to an explicit rejection of prejudiced attitudes that nonetheless is sometimes accompanied by subtle and often nonconscious discriminatory behavior. The schism between what people consciously maintain and how they sometimes feel or act has led to the development of various indirect measures of attitudes toward different groups. These include the Implicit Association Test and priming procedures, which measure the degree to which different groups trigger positive or negative associations.

THE ECONOMIC PERSPECTIVE

Not surprisingly, some of the most intense intergroup tensions arise between groups that vie for the same limited resource. Israelis and Palestinians claim ownership of much of the same small strip of land and, to put it mildly, they have some difficulty getting along. Immigrants from Mexico and Central America face some of the harshest discrimination from those U.S. citizens who see them as threats to their own jobs. Philippine, Sri Lankan, and African workers in rich Gulf countries like Qatar and the United Arab Emirates have been known to draw sharp lines between their own groups and all others.

These observations highlight the core tenets of the economic view of prejudice and discrimination. According to the economic view, groups develop prejudices about one another and discriminate against one another when they compete for material resources. Religious groups, racial groups, and cultural groups all stand ready to protect and promote their own interests by lashing out at those they perceive to be threatening them.

Realistic Group Conflict Theory

realistic group conflict theory
A theory that group conflict, prejudice, and discrimination are likely to arise over competition between groups for limited resources.

One version of the economic perspective has been dubbed **realistic group conflict theory** because it acknowledges that groups sometimes confront real conflict over what are essentially economic issues (LeVine & Campbell, 1972). According to this theory, prejudice and discrimination often arise from competition over limited resources. The theory predicts, correctly, that prejudice and discrimination should increase under conditions of economic difficulty (King, Knight, & Hebl, 2010). When there is less to go around or when people are afraid of losing what they have, competition intensifies. The theory also predicts that prejudice and discrimination should be strongest among groups that stand to lose the most from another group's economic advance. For example, people in the working class in the United States exhibited the most anti-black prejudice in the wake of the civil rights movement (Simpson & Yinger, 1985; Vanneman & Pettigrew, 1972). Working-class jobs were most at risk once millions of black Americans were allowed to compete more freely for entry-level manufacturing jobs in companies from which they had previously been excluded.

Realistic group conflict theory also specifies some of the ways that conflict between groups is likely to play out. First of all, a pronounced **ethnocentrism** develops—that is, the other group is vilified and one's own group is glorified. Anyone who has ever played pickup basketball knows this phenomenon well. An opponent whose antics seem intolerable instantly seems more likable once that person becomes a teammate. More generally, people in the outgroup are often thought of in stereotyped ways and are treated in a manner normally forbidden by one's moral code. At the same time, loyalty to the ingroup intensifies, and a "circle the wagons" mentality develops. For example, in the wake of the 9/11 attacks on the World Trade Center, many people reported that different racial groups in the United States seemed to pull together more than they had beforehand. In an experimental investigation of this tendency, telling white students that the attacks were directed at all Americans, regardless of race and class, served to reduce prejudice toward African-Americans (Dovidio et al., 2004).

ethnocentrism Glorifying one's own group while vilifying other groups.

The Robbers Cave Experiment

Many of these elements of ethnocentrism that are brought about by intergroup competition were examined in one of social psychology's classic studies. In 1954, Muzafer Sherif and his colleagues carried out an ambitious experiment far from the confines of the psychology laboratory (Sherif, Harvey, White, Hood, & Sherif, 1961). Twenty-two fifth-grade boys were taken to Robbers Cave State Park in southeastern Oklahoma (so named because the outlaws Belle Starr and Jesse James were thought to have hidden there). The boys had signed up for a two-and-a-half-week summer camp experience that, unbeknownst to them, was also a study of intergroup relations. The research team spent over 300 hours screening boys from the Oklahoma City area to find 22 who were "average" in nearly every respect: none had problems in school, all were from intact, middle-class families, and there were no notable ethnic group differences among them. The boys, none of whom knew each other beforehand, were divided into two groups of 11 and taken to separate areas of the park. Neither group even knew of the other's existence—initially.

"Without knowledge of the roots of hostility we cannot hope to employ our intelligence effectively in controlling its destructiveness."

—Gordon Allport

Competition and Intergroup Conflict In the first phase of the experiment, the two groups independently engaged in activities designed to foster group unity (for example, pitching tents, preparing meals) and took part in common camp activities such as playing baseball, swimming, and putting on skits. Considerable cohesion developed within each group, and each chose to give itself a name—the Eagles and the Rattlers. A consistent hierarchical structure also emerged within each group, such that "effective initiators"—the boys who made suggestions that the others accepted—were rated most popular.

In the second phase, the Eagles and Rattlers were brought together for a tournament. The boys were told that each member of the winning team would receive a medal and a highly coveted pocket knife (a type of reward that researchers would be unlikely to hand out to young boys today!). Members of the losing team would get nothing. The tournament lasted five days and consisted of such activities as baseball, touch football, tug-of-war, cabin inspections, and a treasure hunt. The competitive nature of the tournament was designed to encourage each group to see the other as an impediment to the fulfillment of its own goals and hence as a foe. And that is exactly what happened.

From the very first competitive encounter, and with steadily increasing frequency throughout the tournament, the two groups hurled insults at each other, calling those in the other group "bums," "cowards," "stinkers," and so on. Although such terms may be tame by today's trash-talking standards, they are clearly not terms of endearment, and they differ markedly from the self-glorifying and congratulatory comments the boys made about members of their own group. The expression of intergroup hostility, moreover, was not limited to words. The Eagles captured and burned the Rattlers' flag, which of course brought about a retaliatory theft of the Eagles' flag. Food fights broke out in the dining area, raids were conducted on each other's cabins, and numerous challenges to engage in physical fights were issued.

It is particularly interesting to note how the internal dynamics of the two groups changed as they became locked into this competitive struggle. Boys who were either athletically gifted or who advocated a more aggressive stance toward the other group tended to gain in popularity. The initial leader of the Eagles, for example, had neither of these characteristics, and he was essentially deposed by someone who was more athletic and more of a firebrand.

In addition to diligently recording episodes of hostility, the investigators conducted a number of more tightly controlled assessments of how favorably the

The Robbers Cave Experiment Muzafer Sherif divided 10-year-old boys into two groups to observe how the groups would relate to each other. (A) During an early phase of the study when the two groups competed for prizes, they reacted hostilely toward each other. (B) In a later phase, the groups had to work together to accomplish goals that neither could accomplish alone, such as pulling a truck to get it started. (C) Working on these superordinate goals led the boys to set aside their differences and become friends.

boys tended to look on members of their own group while derogating members of the other group. In one assessment, the investigators scattered a large quantity of beans around a field and asked the two groups to pick up as many as they could in a 1-minute period. The group collecting the most would receive $5. When the contest was over, but before the winner was announced, an image of each boy's collection of beans was briefly projected on a wall, and everyone was asked to estimate the number of beans that the boy had collected. In reality, the same quantity of beans (35) was always shown, but this was impossible to discern because of the brief duration of the projection and the large quantity of beans shown. The boys' estimates revealed clear ingroup favoritism: each group estimated that boys in *their* group had collected more beans than boys in the other group.

Reducing Intergroup Conflict through Superordinate Goals   The third and final part of the experiment is in many respects the most important. It was devoted to assessing ways to reduce the conflict between the two groups. First, on seven occasions over the next two days, the two groups were simply brought together in various noncompetitive settings to see whether their hostility would dissipate. It did not. Simple contact between the two groups just led to more name calling, jeering, food fights, and insults.

Given that simple noncompetitive contact did not reduce intergroup friction, the investigators contrived to confront the boys with a number of crises that could be resolved only through the cooperative efforts of both groups. For example, the water supply to the camp was disrupted, and the entire length of pipe from the reservoir to the campgrounds had to be inspected to find the source of the problem—a task made much more manageable if all the boys in both groups were assigned to inspect a given segment of the line. Also, a truck carrying supplies for a campout at a distant area of the park mysteriously "broke down." How to get it running again? The investigators had left a large section of rope near the truck in the hope that the boys might try to pull the truck to get it started. One of the boys said, "Let's get our tug-of-war rope and have a tug-of-war against the truck." In doing so, members of both groups intermingled throughout the length of rope and pulled it together.

Relations between the two groups quickly showed the effects of these **superordinate goals**—that is, goals that could not be achieved by either group alone but could be accomplished by both working together. Name calling abruptly dropped off and friendships between members of the two groups developed. When the study was completed, the boys insisted that everyone return to Oklahoma City on the same bus rather than on the separate buses by which they had arrived. And when the bus pulled over at a roadside diner, the group that had won $5 in the bean collection contest—the Rattlers—decided to spend their money on malted milks for everyone, Eagles included. The hostility produced by five days of competition was erased by the joint pursuit of common goals, resulting in a happy ending.

The Robbers Cave experiment offers several important lessons. One is that neither differences in background nor differences in appearance nor prior histories of conflict are necessary for intergroup hostility to develop. All that is required is that two groups enter into competition for goals that only one can achieve. Another lesson is that competition against "outsiders" often increases group cohesion. Note that this tendency is often exploited by political demagogues who invoke the specter of outside enemies to try to stamp out dissension or to deflect

superordinate goals Goals that transcend the interests of any one group and that can be achieved more readily by two or more groups working together.

attention from problems or conflict within the group itself. The final lesson points to how intergroup conflict can be diminished. To reduce the hostility that exists between certain groups, policy makers should think of ways to get them to work together to fulfill common goals. Simply putting adversaries together "to get to know one another better" is usually not enough (Bettencourt, Brewer, Croak, & Miller, 1992; Brewer & Miller, 1988; Stephan & Stephan, 1996; Wilder, 1986). It is the pursuit of superordinate goals that keeps everyone's eyes on the prize and away from meddlesome subgroup distinctions.

Evaluating the Economic Perspective

The economic perspective "works" in the sense that it fits nicely with what we see around us as the successes and failures of intergroup relations. Consider race and ethnic relations in the United States and the effort to build harmonious relations between groups with long histories of conflict and suspicion. Where have efforts toward integration been most successful? Many analysts cite the integration of blacks, Hispanics, Native Americans, and whites in the military (as well as many white subgroups that have not always looked on one another favorably, such as Irish, Italians, Slavs, Jews, and Catholics). The success of integration in the military makes perfect sense in light of the lessons learned from the Robbers Cave experiment. Different ethnic and religious groups in the military are in the equivalent of phase 3 of the Robbers Cave experiment. Their whole purpose is to be ready to defend the United States against a common outside enemy. They must therefore engage in cooperative, interdependent action to accomplish shared goals—precisely the set of circumstances that brought about healthy intergroup functioning in the Robbers Cave experiment. In such circumstances, the group or category to which a person belongs recedes in importance, and what he or she can contribute to the joint effort becomes more prominent (Gaertner, Mann, Dovidio, Murrell, & Pomare, 1990; Gaertner, Murrell, & Dovidio, 1989; Miller & Brewer, 1986).

Integration of the Military
Integration of different racial and ethnic groups has been remarkably successful in the U.S. military, where soldiers cooperate to accomplish the shared goal of defending the nation.

What implications do Sherif's findings have for race and ethnic relations on college campuses? For many students, minorities and majority alike, the college years are the first time they have had close and sustained contact with members of other ethnic groups. How well does it work? The first thing to note is that the conditions of intergroup contact are not as favorable in the classroom as they are on the battlefield. Although students will assist their close friends to help them achieve higher grades, rarely do students feel a strong cooperative bond with their classmates in general. Few students ask themselves, "Is there anything I can do to increase the mean grade of everyone else in the class?" Rather, the common reliance on curved grading can encourage a competitive struggle of all against all in which another student's triumph is seen as a threat to one's own grade.

Because of these conditions, the integration effort on college campuses may be less successful than it has been in the military. Indeed, students, faculty, and administrators on countless college campuses are discussing what, if anything,

BOX 11.1 FOCUS ON EDUCATION

The "Jigsaw" Classroom

If the competitive atmosphere of most classrooms exacerbates racial and ethnic tensions in integrated schools, what would happen if the classroom were made less competitive? Might a more cooperative learning environment improve academic performance and intergroup relations in integrated settings?

Social psychologist Elliot Aronson developed a cooperative learning procedure to find out. When the public school system in Austin, Texas, was integrated in 1971, the transition was not smooth. A disturbing number of physical confrontations took place between black, Hispanic, and white children, and the atmosphere in the classrooms was not what proponents of integration had hoped it would be. The superintendent of schools invited Aronson to do something to improve matters. Mindful of the lessons of the Robbers Cave experiment, Aronson wanted to institute procedures that would unite students in the common goal of mastering a body of material, rather than competing for the highest grades and the teacher's attention. He and his colleagues came up with something called the "jigsaw" classroom (Aronson, Stephan, Sikes, Blaney, &

Snapp, 1978; Aronson & Thibodeau, 1992).

In the jigsaw classroom, students are divided into small groups of roughly six students each. Every effort is made to balance the groups in terms of ethnicity, gender, ability level, leadership, and so on. The material on a given topic is then divided into six parts, and each student is required to master one part (and only one part) and teach it to the others. For a lesson on Barack Obama, for example, one student might be responsible for Obama's early years in Hawaii and Indonesia, another for his time as a law professor at the University of Chicago, a third for his accomplishments in the Illinois state legislature, a fourth for his historic presidential election campaign, and a fifth for his White House years. By dividing the material in this way, Aronson ensured that no student could learn the entire lesson without help from peers. Each student's material must, like the pieces of a jigsaw puzzle, fit together with all the others for everyone in the group to learn the whole lesson.

Each student's dependence on the others in the group dampens the usual competitive atmosphere and encourages the students to work cooperatively

toward a common goal. To the extent that the groups are ethnically heterogeneous, members of different ethnic groups gain the experience of working with one another as individuals rather than as representatives of particular ethnic groups.

The effectiveness of the jigsaw classroom has been assessed in field experiments that compare students in classrooms that use the jigsaw procedure with those in classrooms that teach the same material in the usual fashion. These studies have typically found that students in the jigsaw classrooms like school more and develop more positive attitudes toward different ethnic groups than do students in traditional classrooms (Slavin, 1995).

Thus, the lessons learned from the Robbers Cave experiment, that intergroup hostility can be diminished by cooperative activity directed at a superordinate goal, have profound practical significance. A simple classroom procedure derived from these lessons—one that can be used in conjunction with traditional, more individualistic classroom exercises—can both boost academic performance and facilitate positive ethnic relations.

---

ought to be done about the tendency for students of different races or ethnic origins to inhabit rather different niches in the university. Many students segregate themselves almost exclusively with other members of their own race or ethnic group in their choice of residence, dining hall, and even fields of study. To be sure, many students—perhaps most—of different ethnic groups do mix on college campuses, and the effort to integrate college campuses on the whole has been a great success. However, the integration effort at the university may have lagged behind that in the military—a result that a close look at the Robbers Cave experiment would lead us to expect (**Box 11.1**).

Prejudice can arise from realistic conflict between groups over scarce resources. The Robbers Cave experiment serves as an instructive model of this sort of conflict, showing how otherwise friendly boys could turn into enemies when placed in groups competing for limited resources. The enmity between the groups evaporated when they had to cooperate to achieve superordinate goals of value to both groups. This result has considerable implications for managing potentially troublesome intergroup relations around the globe.

THE MOTIVATIONAL PERSPECTIVE

Intergroup hostility, it turns out, can develop even in the absence of competition. In the Robbers Cave experiment, there were signs of increased ingroup solidarity when the two groups first learned of each others' existence—*before* they were engaged in, or even knew about, the organized competition. Midway through phase 1 of the experiment, when the two groups were still being kept apart, they were allowed to get within earshot of one another. The mere fact that another group existed made each set of boys take their group membership much more seriously. Both groups quickly became territorial, referring to the baseball field as "*our* diamond" rather than "the diamond" and a favorite swimming spot as "*our* swimming hole." The Eagles, who beforehand had not found it necessary to have a group name, quickly settled on the name *Eagles* once they learned that there was another group of boys in the park. Furthermore, when the two groups learned about each other's existence, both wanted to "run them off" and "challenge them."

That these developments took place before any competition had been arranged indicates that intergroup hostility can develop merely because another group exists. The existence of group boundaries among any collection of individuals, then, can be sufficient to initiate group discrimination.

The Minimal Group Paradigm

People's readiness to adopt an "us/them" mentality has been extensively documented in experiments employing the **minimal group paradigm** pioneered by Henri Tajfel (Tajfel & Billig, 1974; Tajfel, Billig, Bundy, & Flament, 1971; see also Ashburn-Nardo, Voils, & Monteith, 2001; Brewer, 1979; Yamagishi, Mifune, Liu, & Pauling, 2008). It is an experimental setup in which researchers create groups based on arbitrary and seemingly meaningless criteria and then examine how the members of these "minimal groups" are inclined to behave toward one another. The participants first perform a rather trivial task and are then divided into two groups, ostensibly on the basis of their responses. In one type of task, for example, participants estimate the number of dots projected briefly on a screen. Some participants are told they belong to a group of "overestimators," and others are told they belong to a group of "underestimators." In reality, the participants are randomly assigned to the groups, and they learn only that they are assigned to a particular group—they never learn who else is in their group or who is in the other group. Thus, what it means to be part of a "group" is boiled down to the bare minimum.

In the second part of the experiment, the participants are taken individually to cubicles and are asked to assign points, redeemable for money, to successive pairs of their fellow participants. They do not know the identity of those to whom they are awarding points; they know only a participant's "code number" and group membership. Participants are asked to assign points to, say, "Number 4 of the overestimator group" and "Number 2 of the underestimator group." Some

minimal group paradigm An experimental paradigm in which researchers create groups based on arbitrary and seemingly meaningless criteria and then examine how the members of these "minimal groups" are inclined to behave toward one another.

of the options participants can choose provide relatively equal outcomes for members of both groups but with slightly more for the member of the outgroup; some choices offer to maximize what the ingroup member can receive but still result in more points for the members of the outgroup; and some maximize the relative ingroup advantage over the outgroup but don't provide much in the way of absolute reward for members of the ingroup.

Numerous experiments have shown that a majority of participants are interested more in maximizing the *relative* gain for members of their ingroup than in maximizing the absolute gain for their ingroup. A moment's reflection reveals just how extraordinary this choice is. The participants do not know who the ingroup and outgroup members are; the choices are never for themselves; and, of course, the basis for establishing the two groups is utterly trivial. Yet they still exhibit a tendency to favor their minimal ingroup. Moreover, they are willing to do so at a cost to the ingroup, which earns fewer points than it would if the focus were on absolute gain rather than "beating" the other group. That ingroup favoritism emerges in this context is testimony to how easily we slip into thinking in terms of *us* versus *them* (Brewer & Brown, 1998). And if history has taught us anything, it is that the us/them distinction, once formed, can have enormous—and enormously unfortunate—implications.

Social Identity Theory

Studies using the minimal group paradigm have shown the pervasiveness and tenacity of ingroup favoritism, but what does it have to do with the *motivational* perspective on prejudice? Might it not reflect a purely cognitive tendency to divide the world into categories of *us* and *them*? Just as all children quickly learn to distinguish the self from all others, might we not all learn to distinguish "my side" from the "other side"?

Much of the psychology behind ingroup favoritism might very well reflect cognitive influences. The us/them distinction may be one of the basic cuts people make in dividing up and organizing the world. Still, the ingroup favoritism observed in the minimal group situation cannot be the product of cognition alone. For that we need a motivational theory—a theory to explain why, once the us/them distinction is made, *we* are treated better than *they*. Some divisions into *we* and *they* have the sorts of material or economic implications discussed earlier, and those implications often provide motivation enough for people to treat ingroup members better than outgroup members. But not all motivations are economic, and certainly no meaningful economic implications are riding on the ingroup/outgroup partition in the minimal group paradigm. To explain that sort of ingroup favoritism, a much broader motivational theory is needed.

The most widely recognized theory that attempts to explain the ubiquity of ingroup favoritism, even when the ingroups and outgroups do not differ in any significant way, is Henri Tajfel and John Turner's **social identity theory** (Tajfel & Turner, 1979; see also Spears, 2011; Stroebe, Spears, & Lodewijkx, 2007). The theory rests on the undeniable fact that people's self-esteem derives not only from their personal identity and accomplishments, but also from the status and accomplishments of the various groups to which they belong. Being "an American" is an element of the self-concept of most Americans, and with it comes the pride associated with, say, the Bill of Rights, U.S. economic and military clout, and the

"Cruelty and intolerance to those who do not belong to it are natural to every religion."

—Sigmund Freud

social identity theory A theory that a person's self-concept and self-esteem derive not only from personal identity and accomplishments but also from the status and accomplishments of the various groups to which the person belongs.

Social Identity Theory People derive their sense of identity not only from their individual accomplishments but also from those of the groups to which they belong. (A) These delegates at the Republican National Convention identify with the Republican Party. (B) These individuals derive part of their identity from belonging to the community of surfers.

accomplishments of American scientists, industrialists, athletes, and entertainers. With it, too, comes the shame associated with American slavery and the treatment of Native Americans. Similarly, being a gang member, a professor, a film buff, or a surfer means that our identity and esteem are intimately tied up with the triumphs and shortcomings of our fellow gang members, academics, film buffs, and surfers.

Boosting the Status of the Ingroup Because our self-esteem is based in part on the status of the various groups to which we belong, we might be tempted to do what we can to boost the status and fortunes of these groups and their members. Therein lies a powerful cause of ingroup favoritism: feeling better about the group leads us to feel better about ourselves. Evidence in support of this thesis comes from studies that have assessed participants' self-esteem after they have had an opportunity to exhibit ingroup favoritism in the minimal group situation. As expected, those who had been allowed to engage in intergroup discrimination had higher self-esteem than those who had not been given the opportunity to discriminate (Lemyre & Smith, 1985; Oakes & Turner, 1980). Other research has shown that people who take particularly strong pride in their group affiliations are more prone to ingroup favoritism when placed in a minimal group situation (Crocker & Luhtanen, 1990). And people who are highly identified with a particular group react to criticism of the group as if it were criticism of the self (McCoy & Major, 2003).

Basking in Reflected Glory Social identity theory also receives support from the everyday observation that people go to great lengths to announce their affiliation with a certain group when that group is doing well. Sports fans, for example, often chant, "We're number 1!" after a team victory. But what does *"We're* number 1*"* mean? It is a rare fan indeed who does anything other than cheer or heckle referees and opposing players. Yet countless fans want to be connected to the effort when the outcome is a victory. Not so after a loss.

Robert Cialdini refers to this tendency to identify with a winning team as **basking in reflected glory**. He investigated the tendency by recording how often

basking in reflected glory The tendency for people to take pride in the accomplishments of those with whom they are in some way associated, as when fans identify with a winning team.

Basking in Reflected Glory
Sports fans, like these University of Colorado students, passionately identify with their team and feel joyous when the team wins and dejected when it loses. To connect themselves to the team, fans often wear team jerseys to the game—and to class or work the next day if the team wins.

students wore their school sweatshirts and T-shirts to class after their football team had just won or lost a game. As expected, students wore the school colors significantly more often following victory than after defeat. Cialdini and his colleagues also tabulated students' use of first-person ("We won") and third-person ("They lost") pronouns following victory and defeat. The inclusive *we* was used significantly more often after a win, and the more restrictive *they* was used more often after a loss (Cialdini et al., 1976). As social identity theory predicts, the triumphs and failings of the groups with which we affiliate affect our self-esteem—even when the group is simply a favorite sports team (Hirt, Zillman, Erikson, & Kennedy, 1992). We therefore have an incentive to identify with such groups when they do well but to distance ourselves from them when they lose.

Derogating Outgroups to Bolster Self-Esteem To bask in reflected glory is to use ingroup identity to bolster self-esteem. But does derogating outgroups boost self-esteem? Does tearing down another group make people feel better about their own group—and hence themselves? Several studies have shown how stereotyping and prejudice can boost or maintain self-esteem in this way. In one study, half of the participants had their self-esteem threatened by being told they had just performed poorly on an intelligence test; the other half were told they had done well (Fein & Spencer, 1997). The participants then watched a videotaped interview of a job applicant. The content of the videotape made it clear to half of the participants (none of whom was Jewish) that the applicant was Jewish, but not to the other half. Participants were later asked to rate the job applicant. Among participants whose self-esteem had been threatened, those who thought she was Jewish rated her more negatively than did those who were not told she was Jewish; no such difference was found among those whose self-esteem had not been threatened (**Figure 11.2A**). In addition, the participants who had their self-esteem threatened and had "taken it out" on the Jewish applicant experienced an increase in their self-esteem from the time they received feedback on the intelligence test to the end of the experiment (Figure 11.2B). Stereotyping and derogating members of outgroups appear to bolster self-esteem.

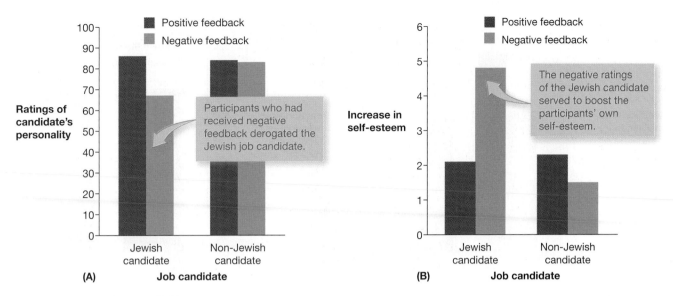

FIGURE 11.2 Bolstering Self-Esteem Average ratings of a job candidate's personality and the increase in raters' self-esteem, depending on whether or not the candidate was identified as Jewish and whether the rater had earlier received positive or negative feedback. (Source: Adapted from Fein & Spencer, 1997.)

A rather stunning demonstration of this tendency was reported by Lisa Sinclair and Ziva Kunda (1999). In their study, (non-black) participants were either praised or criticized by a white or black doctor. Sinclair and Kunda predicted that the participants would be motivated to cling to the praise they received but to challenge the criticism—and that they would use the race of their evaluator to help them do so. In particular, they thought that individuals who received praise from a black doctor would tend to think of him more as a doctor (a prestigious occupation) than as a black man, whereas those who were criticized by a black doctor would tend to think of him more as a black man than as a doctor.

To test their predictions, Sinclair and Kunda had their participants perform a lexical decision task right after receiving their feedback from the doctor. That is, the researchers flashed a series of words and nonwords on a computer screen and asked the participants to indicate, as fast as they could, whether each string of letters was a word. Some of the words were associated with the medical profession (for example, *hospital, prescription*) and some were associated with common stereotypes of blacks (for example, *rap, jazz*). Sinclair and Kunda reasoned that if the participants were thinking of their evaluator primarily as a doctor, they would recognize the medical words faster; if they were thinking of their evaluator primarily as a black man, they would recognize the words associated with the black stereotype faster.

As **Figure 11.3** shows, that is exactly what happened. Participants were particularly fast at recognizing words associated with the black stereotype when they had been criticized by the black doctor, and they were particularly slow to recognize those words when praised by the black doctor (Figure 11.3A). When he criticized them, in other words, participants saw him as a black man—something they did not do so readily when he praised them. The reverse was true for the medical words (Figure 11.3B). Participants were particularly fast at recognizing medical words when they had been praised by the black doctor, and they were particularly slow to do so when criticized by the black doctor.

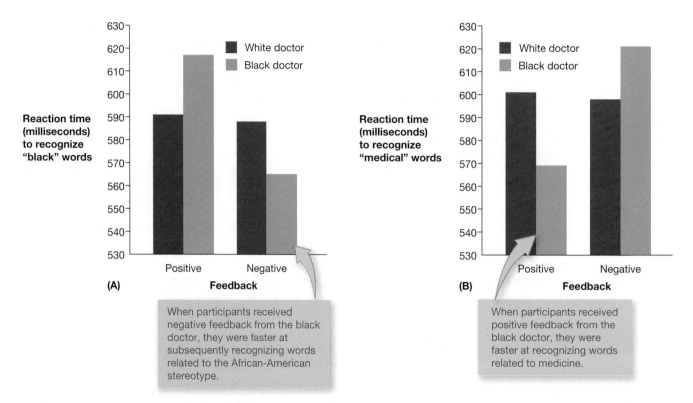

FIGURE 11.3 Self-Esteem and Racial Prejudice Participants were either praised or criticized by a white or black doctor. Reaction times to "black" words and "medical" words after criticism or praise by white doctors were virtually the same. But this was not true for reaction times after criticism or praise by black doctors. (Source: Adapted from Sinclair & Kunda, 1999.)

Frustration-Aggression Theory

frustration-aggression theory

A theory that elaborates the idea that frustration leads to aggression.

Anyone who has ever been stuck in traffic on the way to an important meeting is familiar with one of the most consistent and powerful laws of psychology, a law captured in **frustration-aggression theory**. Simply put, frustration leads to aggression. The probability of blaring the horn or swearing at a nearby motorist is much higher when the smooth transit to one's destination is blocked. Extending this idea to the study of prejudice and discrimination leads to another motivational account of prejudice and discrimination: people are particularly likely to vilify outgroups under conditions that foster frustration and anger. Note that the theory is a good illustration of the sometimes blurry line between economic and motivational accounts of stereotyping and prejudice. If the source of frustration is the very group to which prejudice and discrimination are directed—that is, if outgroup members are perceived as getting in the way of the individual's goals—frustration-aggression theory is both an economic and a motivational account. But sometimes the source of frustration is not the targeted group—it can be an overheated room (Miller & Bugelski, 1948) or recalling an earlier experience that elicited anger (DeSteno, Dasgupta, Bartlett, & Cajdric, 2004). In these cases, the motivation is not economic competition, and the two accounts diverge.

From Generalized to Targeted Aggression By itself, the link between frustration and aggression cannot explain the origins of prejudice and discrimination because frustration leads to *generalized* aggression. The link between frustration and aggression doesn't explain why hard times should lead to aggression targeted at specific groups.

Another fact from everyday experience provides the rest of the explanation. Often we cannot lash out at the true source of our frustration without getting into further difficulty, so we *displace* our aggression onto a safer target. The person who is denied a raise at work takes it out on the kids at home. Thus frustration-aggression theory predicts that hardship will generate malevolence directed at minority groups that, by virtue of being outnumbered and in a weaker position, constitute particularly safe and vulnerable targets. The classic example is anti-Semitism. Throughout history, Jews have been welcomed and accepted into numerous societies that, when times got tough, suddenly targeted Jews as scapegoats and directed their anger at the Jewish community.

In one of the most frequently cited studies of frustration and displaced aggression, Carl Hovland and Robert Sears (1940) examined the relationship between the price of cotton and the number of lynchings of blacks in the South between 1882 and 1930. Cotton was enormously important to the Southern economy during this period, so Hovland and Sears assumed that times were good and frustrations low when the price was high, and that times were tough and frustrations high when the price was low. Sure enough, they observed a strong negative correlation between the price of cotton in a given year and the number of lynchings that took place that year. Lean times saw numerous lynchings; good times, relatively few.

A reanalysis of Hovland and Sears's data that used more modern statistical techniques in some ways provides even stronger support for the frustration-aggression account (Hepworth & West, 1988). The investigators found the same negative correlation reported previously, but unlike Hovland and Sears, they also found a similar—though weaker—negative correlation between economic conditions in the South and the number of lynchings *of whites*. This result fits the frustration-aggression account because frustration increases generalized aggression. But the fact that the relationship is stronger for blacks than for whites is also consistent with the idea that frustration leads to aggression that tends to be displaced toward relatively powerless groups.

Displaced Aggression Four white police officers were charged with using excessive force in the racially motivated beating of Rodney King, a black man, after they stopped him for a traffic violation. After the officers were acquitted in April 1992 by an all-white jury, the black community erupted in violence. Unable to lash out at the police or the jury, they took out their anger and frustration by rioting and looting stores in predominantly black neighborhoods.

Evaluating the Motivational Perspective

The strength of the motivational perspective is that it builds on two undeniably important elements of the human condition. First, people readily draw the us/them distinction, and the various groups to which an individual belongs are intimately connected to the motive to enhance self-esteem. Second, people tend to react to frustration with aggression and often direct their aggression at the "safest" and least powerful targets in a given society. Social psychologist Roger Brown once likened conflict between groups to "a sturdy three-legged stool" because it rests on the pervasive and enduring human tendencies to glorify the ingroup, to form societies in which there are unequal distributions of resources, and to stereotype members of different groups (Brown, 1986, p. 533). Both the motivational and economic perspectives have shown how readily people will reward their own and penalize outsiders—leg number 1.

Both perspectives also speak to how an unequal distribution of resources can sow the seeds of intergroup hostility—leg number 2. To examine leg number 3 of Brown's stool—stereotyping—the next section considers the cognitive perspective.

 People are inclined to favor ingroups over outgroups—even when the basis of group membership is trivial—in part because people identify with their groups and feel good about themselves when they feel good about their groups. Threats to self-esteem also result in the denigration of outgroup members. A variant of frustration-aggression theory maintains that frustration is more likely to result in aggression toward the relatively powerless.

THE COGNITIVE PERSPECTIVE

From the cognitive perspective, stereotyping is inevitable. It stems from the ubiquity and necessity of categorization. People categorize nearly everything, both natural (bodies of water—creek, stream, river) and artificial (cars—sports car, sedan, SUV). Even color, which arises from continuous variation in electromagnetic wavelength, is perceived as distinct categories.

All of this categorizing has a purpose: it simplifies the task of taking in and processing the incredible volume of stimuli that confronts us. The American journalist Walter Lippmann, who is thought to have given us the term *stereotype*, stated:

> The real environment is altogether too big, too complex, and too fleeting, for direct acquaintance. We are not equipped to deal with so much subtlety, so much variety, so many permutations and combinations. . . . We have to reconstruct it on a simpler model before we can manage with it. (Lippmann, 1922, p. 16)

Stereotypes provide us with those simpler models that allow us to deal with the "great blooming, buzzing confusion of reality" (Lippmann, 1922, p. 96). More generally, according to the cognitive perspective, stereotypes are a natural result of the way our brains are wired to store and process information.

Stereotypes and the Conservation of Mental Reserves

According to the cognitive perspective, stereotypes are useful cognitive categories that allow people to process information efficiently (Macrae & Bodenhausen, 2000). If so, we should be particularly inclined to use them when we are overloaded, tired, or mentally taxed in some way—that is, when we are in need of a shortcut. Several experiments have demonstrated exactly that (Kim & Baron, 1988; Macrae, Hewstone, & Griffiths, 1993; Pratto & Bargh, 1991; Stangor & Duan, 1991; Wigboldus, Sherman, Franzese, & van Knippenberg, 2004). In one intriguing demonstration, students were shown to be more likely to invoke stereotypes when tested at the low point of their circadian rhythm. "Morning people," when tested at night, were more likely to invoke a common stereotype and conclude, for example, that a person charged with cheating on an exam was guilty if he was an athlete. "Night people," when tested in the morning, were more

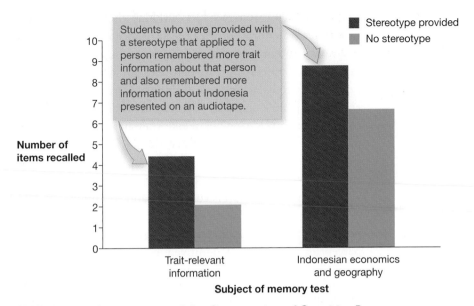

Students who were provided with a stereotype that applied to a person remembered more trait information about that person and also remembered more information about Indonesia presented on an audiotape.

- ■ Stereotype provided
- ■ No stereotype

Number of items recalled

Subject of memory test

Trait-relevant information

Indonesian economics and geography

FIGURE 11.4 Stereotypes and the Conservation of Cognitive Resources
Stereotypes facilitate recall of stereotype-consistent information and conserve cognitive resources that can be used to aid performance on other tasks. (Source: Adapted from Macrae, Milne, & Bodenhausen, 1994.)

likely to conclude that a person charged with dealing drugs was guilty if he was black (Bodenhausen, 1990). Thus people are most likely to fall back on mindless stereotypes when they lack mental energy.

If the use of stereotypes conserves intellectual energy, then encoding information in terms of relevant stereotypes should furnish extra cognitive resources that can be applied to other tasks. In one test of this idea, students were asked to perform two tasks simultaneously. One required them to form an impression of a (hypothetical) person described by a number of trait terms presented on a computer screen (for example, *rebellious, dangerous, aggressive*). The other task involved monitoring a tape-recorded lecture on the economy and geography of Indonesia. For half of the students, the presentation of the trait terms was accompanied by an applicable stereotype (for example, *skinhead*); for the remaining students, the trait terms were presented alone. The key questions were whether the applicable stereotype would facilitate the students' later recall of the trait terms they had seen and, more important, whether it would also release extra cognitive resources that could be devoted to the lecture on Indonesia. To find out, the students were given a brief quiz on the contents of the lecture ("What is Indonesia's official religion?" "Jakarta is found on which coast of Java?").

As the experimenters anticipated, the use of stereotypes eased the students' burden in the first task and thereby facilitated their performance on the second (**Figure 11.4**). Students who were provided with a stereotype not only remembered the relevant trait information better but also performed better on the surprise multiple-choice test on Indonesia (Macrae, Milne, & Bodenhausen, 1994).

Construal Processes and Biased Assessments

The upside of stereotypes is that they conserve cognitive resources. But as is often the case, the benefit comes at a cost. What is gained in efficiency is paid for by occasional inaccuracy and error. In particular, not all category members are

"Why it is we never focus on the things that unite us, like falafel?"

well captured by a stereotype. Invoking the stereotype may save time and effort, but it can lead to mistaken impressions and unfair judgments about individuals. In addition, biased information processing can help explain why even stereotypes completely lacking in validity nevertheless develop and endure. If people suspect—because of what they have been told, or the implications of a joke they heard, or a hard-to-interpret performance difference—that a particular group of people might differ from other groups in some way, it is shockingly easy to construe pertinent information in such a way that their suspicion is confirmed and solidified.

The cognitive perspective on stereotyping does more than point out the obvious fact that stereotypes can distort our perceptions of others. Cognitively oriented social psychologists also seek to identify the precise construal processes that give rise to such distortions. What kind of faulty reasoning processes give rise to inaccurate stereotypes? How, in other words, might a well-meaning person, lacking any malice, nonetheless come to hold the kind of troublesome and inaccurate convictions that are at the heart of the most worrisome stereotypes? How might such beliefs arise from cognitive processing alone? To answer these questions, we must consider the kinds of construal processes that are invoked once individuals are perceived as belonging to different groups.

Accentuation of Ingroup Similarity and Outgroup Difference There is an apocryphal story about a man who owned a farm near the Russian–Polish border. European history being what it is, the farm had gone back and forth under the rule of each country many times. Indeed, after the most recent boundary was drawn, the farmer was uncertain whether he lived in Poland or Russia. To settle the issue, the farmer saved up to have a proper survey conducted and his national identity established. The surveyor worked long and hard, making the most careful measurements. When the survey was finished, the farmer, scarcely able to contain his anticipation, asked, "Well, do I live in Russia or Poland?" The surveyor replied that although remarkably near the border, the entire farm was located in Poland. "Good," the farmer stated, "I don't think I could take those harsh Russian winters."

The point of the story, of course, is that although an arbitrary national border cannot affect the weather at a fixed location, arbitrary categorical boundaries can have significant effects on the human mind. Although few people would make an error like the one in this story, research has shown that merely dividing a continuous distribution into two groups leads people to see less variability within each group and more variability between the two. In one early experiment, participants were shown a series of lines in which the adjacent lines varied from one another in length by a constant amount (Tajfel & Wilkes, 1963). When the series was split in half to create two groups, the participants tended to underestimate the differences between adjacent lines within each group and to overestimate the difference between the adjacent lines that formed the border between the groups. In more social tests of this idea, participants are divided into two "minimal" groups. They then fill out an attitude questionnaire twice—once to record their own attitudes and once to record how they think another ingroup or outgroup member might respond. Participants consistently assume that their beliefs are more similar to those of another ingroup member than to those of an outgroup member—even when group membership is arbitrary (Allen & Wilder, 1979; Wilder, 1984).

The remarkable thing about this result is *not* that people assume more similarity between members within a group than across groups. That only makes sense. After all, why categorize members into groups in the first place if the members of each group are not, on average, more similar to one another than they are to the members of the other group? What *is* remarkable, and potentially troubling, is that people make such assumptions even when the groups are formed arbitrarily or when they are formed on the basis of a dimension (for example, skin color) that may have no bearing on the particular attitude or behavior under consideration. In these circumstances, the pure act of categorization distorts our judgment.

The Outgroup Homogeneity Effect Think of a group to which you do not belong: Islamic fundamentalists, stamp collectors, heroin addicts, Winnebago owners. It is tempting to think of such groups as a unitary *they*. We tend to call to mind an image of such groups in which all members think alike, act alike, even look alike. We also tend to assume that an outgroup's within-group similarity is much stronger than our own ingroup's. *They* all think, act, and look alike. *We* don't. This tendency is called the **outgroup homogeneity effect**.

One study examined the outgroup homogeneity effect by showing Princeton and Rutgers students a series of videos of other students making decisions, such as whether to listen to rock or classical music or whether to wait alone or with other participants during a break in an experiment. Half of the Princeton and Rutgers students were told that the students shown on the tape were from Princeton; half were told they were from Rutgers. After watching the tape, the participants estimated the percentage of students at the same university who would make the same choices as those they had seen on the tape. The results indicated that the participants assumed more similarity among outgroup members than among ingroup members. Princeton students who thought they had witnessed the behavior of a Rutgers student were willing to generalize that behavior to other Rutgers students. In contrast, Princeton students who thought they had witnessed the behavior of a Princeton student were less willing to generalize. The opposite was true for Rutgers students. People see more variability of habit and opinion among members of the ingroup than they do among members of the outgroup (Quattrone & Jones, 1980; see also Bartsch, Judd, Louw, Park, & Ryan, 1997; Linville, 1982; Linville, Fischer, & Salovey, 1989; Ostrom & Sedikides, 1992; Park & Judd, 1990; Park & Rothbart, 1982; Read & Urada, 2003; Simon et al., 1990).

It is easy to understand why the outgroup homogeneity effect occurs. For one thing, we typically have much more contact with fellow members of an ingroup than with members of an outgroup, so we have greater opportunity to encounter evidence of divergent opinions and habits among ingroup members. Indeed, sometimes *all* we know about outgroup members is what their stereotypical characteristics are reputed to be. But differences in the number of interactions make up only half the story. The nature of the interactions we have with ingroup and outgroup members is likely to be different as well. Because we share the same

outgroup homogeneity effect
The tendency for people to assume that within-group similarity is much stronger for outgroups than for ingroups.

Overcoming the Outgroup Homogeneity Effect We often think of outgroups as having members who all think, dress, and act alike. We might expect that all Hasidic bands would be alike, but we would soon realize that this Hasidic reggae band differs from other Hasidic bands, as well as from mainstream bands, and that individual differences also exist within the band. We see lead singer Matisyahu dressed in traditional Hasidic garb while the other members of his band are not.

group membership, we do not treat an ingroup member as a representative of a group. It is the person's idiosyncratic likes, dislikes, talents, and shortcomings that are front and center in the interaction. Not so with outgroup members. We often treat an outgroup member as a representative of a group, so the person's unique characteristics recede to the background.

Distinctiveness and Illusory Correlations Although the cognitive perspective emphasizes the role of pure cognition in the formation and maintenance of stereotypes, it is not always clear where impartial information processing leaves off and passions, motives, and self-interest begin. The tendency to see outgroups as more homogeneous than ingroups, for example, may be largely due to the cognitive processes just described, but the effect is sometimes accentuated by the wish to think of an ingroup as more diverse, multifaceted, and nonconformist than other groups.

But at least one type of stereotyping bias does arise from cognitive processes alone. People sometimes "see" correlations (relationships) between events, characteristics, or categories that are not actually related—a phenomenon referred to as illusory correlation (Fiedler, 2000; Fiedler & Freytag 2004; Garcia-Marques & Hamilton, 1996; Hamilton & Sherman, 1989; Hamilton, Stroessner, & Mackie, 1993; Klauer & Meiser, 2000; Shavitt, Sanbonmatsu, Smittipatana, & Posavac, 1999; Stangor & Lange, 1994; see also Chapter 4). Some illusory correlations result simply from the way we process unusual events.

Distinctive events capture attention. We would notice if a student were to attend a lecture wearing a clown outfit—or nothing at all. Because we attend more closely to distinctive events, we are also likely to remember them better, and as a result they may become overrepresented in our memory. These processes have important implications for the kinds of stereotypes that are commonly associated with minority groups. By definition, minority groups are distinctive to most members of the majority, so minority group members stand out. Note also that negative behaviors, such as robbing, assaulting, and murdering, are (fortunately) much less common than positive behaviors, such as lawn mowing, saying thank you, and obeying traffic signs, so negative behaviors are distinctive as well. Negative behavior on the part of members of minority groups is therefore doubly distinctive and doubly memorable. And because negative behavior by the majority or positive behavior by the minority is not as memorable, negative actions by the minority are likely to seem more common than they really are. Minority groups are therefore often thought to be responsible for more problematic behavior than they actually engage in.

An experiment by David Hamilton and Robert Gifford (1976) demonstrates the impact of **paired distinctiveness**—the pairing of two distinctive events that stand out even more because they co-occur. Participants were shown a series of 39 slides, each one describing a positive or negative action initiated by a member of "group A" or "group B." ("John, a member of group A, visited a sick friend in the hospital." "Bill, a member of group B, always talks about himself and his problems.") The groups were completely fictional, so any judgments made about them could not be the result of any preexisting knowledge or experience on the part of the participants. Two-thirds of the actions were attributed to group A, thus making A the majority group. Most of the actions attributed to each group were positive, and they were distributed equally: 9 of 13, or 69 percent, of the actions attributed to group B were positive, as were 18 of 26, or 69 percent, of the actions attributed to group A. There was thus no correlation between group membership and the likelihood of positive or negative behavior.

paired distinctiveness The pairing of two distinctive events that stand out even more because they co-occur.

FIGURE 11.5 Scientific Method: Distinctiveness and Illusory Correlation

Hypothesis: Two distinctive events stand out, are better remembered, and leave even more of an impression because they co-occur.

Research Method:

1. Participants were shown a series of slides, each of which described a positive or negative action initiated by a member of group A or group B.

2. Two-thirds of the actions were attributed to group A, making A the majority group. Most of the actions attributed to each group were positive (equally true of both groups).

Results: Members of the minority group were thought to be disproportionately responsible for the negative behaviors.

Members of the minority group were rated more highly on negative traits and less highly on positive traits than members of the majority group.

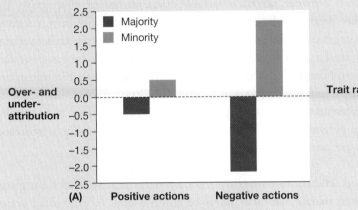

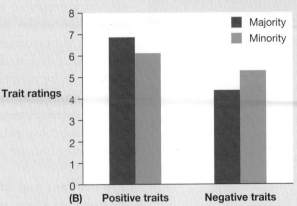

CONCLUSION: Jointly distinctive events (minority status and rare behavior) stand out and form the basis of illusory correlations.

Source: Adapted from Hamilton & Gifford (1976).

After viewing the entire series of slides, participants were shown just the behaviors they had seen earlier—that is, with no names or groups attached—and were asked to indicate the group membership of the person who had performed each one. They were also asked to rate the members of the two groups on a variety of trait scales. Both measures indicated that the participants had formed a distinctiveness-based illusory correlation. They overestimated how often a negative behavior was performed by a member of group B (the smaller group), and they underestimated how often such a behavior was performed by a member of group A (the larger group; see **Figure 11.5A**). As a result, they also rated members of the larger group more favorably (Figure 11.5B).

To show that paired distinctiveness, rather than something about negative behavior, had produced their results, Hamilton and Gifford showed that an illusory correlation was also obtained when positive behaviors were less common. Under these circumstances, participants overestimated how often a *positive* behavior was associated with the smaller group.

In generalizing Hamilton and Gifford's results to the types of rich, consequential, and firmly held stereotypes seen in the everyday world, keep two important points in mind. The first is that their results are particularly impressive because they were obtained in a laboratory context that excluded elements that might encourage illusory correlations in everyday life. In particular, when members of

Paired Distinctiveness Because eating a tremendous number of hot dogs is unusual, a non-Japanese observer who witnessed Takeru Kobayashi's triumph in an annual hot dog eating contest might wonder whether the Japanese are particularly fond of hot dogs.

"Stereotypic beliefs about women's roles, for example, may enable one to see correctly that a woman in a dark room is threading a needle rather than tying a fishing lure, but they may also cause one to mistakenly assume that her goal is embroidery rather than cardiac surgery."

—Dan Gilbert

different ethnic groups come together, they are often acutely aware of one another's ethnicity. And when you are especially aware of a person's ethnicity and that person proceeds to do something unusual, ethnicity is often the first thing that comes to mind to account for the action. If you have seen few Polynesians in your life, for instance, but you see a Polynesian curse at the bank teller who is serving your line, you will be tempted to conclude that something about being Polynesian was at least partly responsible for the incident. ("I guess that's just the way they are.") Of course, if a member of your own ethnic group were to display the same behavior, you would be unlikely to consider the person's ethnicity as a possible explanation (Risen, Gilovich, & Dunning, 2007).

But one feature of Hamilton and Gifford's work does not fit real-world stereotyping so well. Their analysis predicts that people should be prone to develop illusory correlations between any two variables that are jointly distinctive. But people don't do so. Being left-handed and being a vegetarian are both relatively rare, but our culture has no stereotype of southpaws being particularly averse to eating meat. Nor are Latinos thought to be particularly likely to be gay, or Asians thought to be particularly likely to snowboard. Thus, although Hamilton and Gifford's provocative analysis captures something real and important about some illusory correlations, it overpredicts. More work needs to be done to specify *which* jointly distinctive pairings are likely to form the core of commonly held stereotypes, and which are not.

Expectations and Biased Information Processing Because of the outgroup homogeneity effect, people are more likely to assume that an individual action is typical of a group if the group is not their own. But regardless of whether it's an ingroup or outgroup under consideration, people do not generalize equally from everything they see. Some acts (an epileptic seizure, for example) discourage generalization from the individual to the group no matter who the actor is; other acts (rudeness, for example) invite it. In general, people are more likely to generalize behaviors and traits that they already suspect may be typical of the group's members. Stereotypes can therefore be self-reinforcing. Actions that are consistent with an existing stereotype are noticed, deemed significant, and remembered, whereas those at variance with the stereotype may be ignored, dismissed, or quickly forgotten (Bodenhausen, 1988; Kunda & Thagard, 1996; von Hippel, Sekaquaptewa, & Vargas, 1995).

Stereotypes also influence how the details of events are interpreted. In one striking demonstration of this effect (Duncan, 1976; see also Dunning & Sherman, 1997; Kunda & Sherman-Williams, 1993; Plant, Kling, & Smith, 2004; Sagar & Schofield, 1980), white participants watched a videotape of a heated discussion between two men and were asked, periodically, to code the behavior they were watching into one of several categories (for example, "gives information," "playing around," "aggressive behavior"). At one point in the video, one of the individuals shoved the other. For half the participants, a black man shoved another man; for the other half, a white man did the shoving. The race of the person made a difference in how the action was interpreted. When perpetrated by a white man, the incident tended to be coded as more benign (as "playing around," for example). When perpetrated by a black man, it was coded as a more serious action (as "aggressive behavior," for example).

The results of this study are remarkable because the participants saw the shove with their own eyes. The influence of stereotypes is likely to be even greater when the episode is presented to people secondhand and is therefore more open to differential construal. In one study, for example, participants listened to a play-by-play account of a college basketball game and were told to focus on the exploits of one player in particular, Mark Flick. Half the participants saw a photo of Mark that made it clear he was African-American, and half saw a photo that made it clear he was white. When participants rated Mark's performance, their assessments reflected commonly held stereotypes about black and white basketball players. Those who thought Mark was African-American rated him as more athletic and as having played better; those who thought he was white rated him as having exhibited greater hustle and as having played a more savvy game (Stone, Perry, & Darley, 1997).

Studies such as these make it clear that people do not evaluate information even-handedly. Instead, information that is consistent with a group stereotype typically has more impact than information that is inconsistent with it.

Explaining Away Exceptions

If every rule has an exception, the same is true for stereotypes. Groups known for their intellectual talents nonetheless include a few dolts. Groups renowned for their athletic abilities are sure to include a klutz or two. Evidence contradicting a stereotype is almost certain to be encountered, even if the stereotype is largely accurate. Of course, if the stereotype is invalid, evidence of disconfirmation is encountered that much more often. What happens when people encounter such contradictory evidence? Do they abandon their stereotypes or hold them less confidently?

How people respond to stereotype disconfirmation varies with factors such as how emotionally involved they are in the stereotype, whether they hold the stereotype in isolation or belong to a group that preaches it, and so on. One thing is clear, however: people do not give up their stereotypes easily. As numerous studies have demonstrated, people evaluate disconfirming evidence in a variety of ways that have the effect of dampening its impact. An understanding of these processes provides some insight into one of the most vexing questions about stereotypes—namely, why they so often persist in the face of evidence that would seem to contradict them.

Subtyping The first thing to note is that no stereotype contains an expectation of perfectly consistent behavior. Groups thought to be dishonest, lazy, or carefree are thought to be dishonest, lazy, or carefree *on average*, or more dishonest, lazy, or carefree than other groups. It is not expected that all of their members behave in those ways all the time. This loophole allows people to remain unmoved by apparent disconfirmations of their stereotypes because anyone who acts at variance with the stereotype is simply walled off into a category of "exceptions." Psychologists refer to this tendency as **subtyping** (Queller & Smith, 2002; Richards & Hewstone, 2001; Weber & Crocker, 1983). Sexists who believe that women are passive and dependent and should stay home to raise children are likely to subcategorize assertive, independent women who choose not to have children as "militant" or "strident" feminists, thereby leaving their stereotype of women largely intact. Similarly, racists who maintain that African-Americans can't excel outside of sports and entertainment are unlikely to be much troubled by the likes of, say, Barack Obama ("He's half white") or Attorney General Eric Holder ("His parents were immigrants from Barbados"). To the racist mind,

subtyping Explaining away exceptions to a given stereotype by creating a subcategory of the stereotyped group that can be expected to differ from the group as a whole.

Explaining Away Exceptions
People who hold negative stereotypes of ethnic groups sometimes dismiss examples of individuals who don't conform to the stereotype as exceptions or members of relatively rare subtypes.

they are merely the "exceptions that prove the rule." (Incidentally, if you've ever wondered how an exception can prove a rule—it can't. The expression uses the word *prove* in its less common sense: "to test.")

The tendency to subtype reflects a more general truth: evidence that supports a stereotype is treated differently from evidence that refutes it. Supportive evidence tends to be accepted at face value, whereas contradictory evidence is often critically analyzed and discounted. One way we do so is by attributing behavior consistent with a stereotype to the dispositions of the people involved and attributing inconsistent behavior to external causes (Crocker, Hannah, & Weber, 1983; Deaux & Emswiller, 1974; Kulik, 1983; Swim & Sanna, 1996; Taylor & Jaggi, 1974). An anti-Semite who believes that Jews are "cheap" is likely to dismiss a Jew's acts of philanthropy as due to a desire for social acceptance, but to attribute any pursuit of self-interest as a reflection of some "true" Jewish character. Thus, episodes consistent with a stereotype reinforce its perceived validity; those that are inconsistent with it are deemed insignificant (Pettigrew, 1979).

Concrete versus Abstract Construal Another way we differentially process supportive and contradictory information is by varying how concretely or abstractly we encode the actions of people from different groups. Almost any action can be construed at different levels of abstraction (Vallacher & Wegner, 1987). If you see someone lifting an individual who has fallen, you could describe the action less abstractly as exactly that—an act of lifting. Alternatively, you could say, more abstractly, that the person was "helping" the fallen individual. More broadly still, you might see the person as "helpful" or "altruistic." These different levels of abstraction carry different connotations. The more concrete the description, the less it says about the individual involved. Nearly anyone can lift, but not everyone is altruistic. Thus, if people's evaluations are guided by their preexisting stereotypes, we might expect them to describe actions that are consistent with a stereotype in abstract terms (thus reinforcing the stereotype), but to describe actions that are inconsistent with it in concrete terms (thus avoiding a potential challenge to the stereotype). Stereotypes may insulate themselves from disconfirmation, in other words, by influencing the level at which relevant actions are encoded (von Hippel et al., 1995).

This prediction was tested in a study that took place during the annual *palio* competition in Ferrara, Italy (Maass, Salvi, Arcuri, & Semin, 1989). The *palio* are horse-racing competitions that have taken place in various Italian towns since the thirteenth century (with a brief interruption during the time of the Black Plague). The races pit different teams, or *contrade*, against one another and take place in the context of an elaborate festival in which supporters of each *contrada* root for their team. In the weeks leading up to the *palio*, feelings of intergroup competition run high.

Before one such *palio* competition, the supporters of two *contrade*, San Giorgio and San Giacomo, were shown a number of sketches depicting a member of their own *contrada* or of the rival *contrada* engaged in an action. The *contrada* membership of the person depicted was established simply by having the color of the

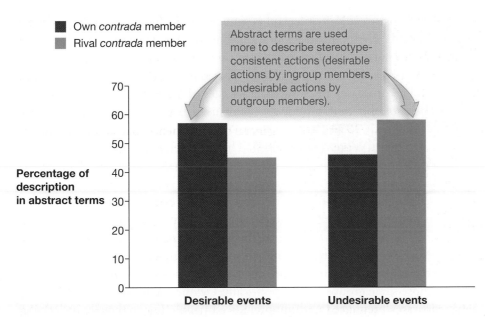

Legend:
- ■ Own *contrada* member
- ▮ Rival *contrada* member

Abstract terms are used more to describe stereotype-consistent actions (desirable actions by ingroup members, undesirable actions by outgroup members).

Percentage of description in abstract terms (y-axis: 0, 10, 20, 30, 40, 50, 60, 70)

x-axis: Desirable events, Undesirable events

FIGURE 11.6 Stereotypes and the Encoding of Behavior Events that are consistent with preexisting stereotypes are encoded at a more abstract, and therefore more meaningful, level than events that are inconsistent with preexisting stereotypes. The figure depicts the percentage of abstract versus concrete terms used to describe desirable and undesirable actions by members of the ingroup and outgroup. Abstract terms consist of state verbs or trait terms (for example, *hates, hateful*), and concrete terms consist of descriptive and interpretive action verbs (for example, *hits, hurts*). (Source: Adapted from Maass, Salvi, Arcuri, & Semin, 1989.)

protagonist's shirt match that of one *contrada* or another. Some of the sketches portrayed desirable actions (for example, helping someone), and some portrayed undesirable actions (for example, littering). After inspecting each sketch, the participants were asked to describe what it depicted, and their responses were scored for level of abstraction.

The results revealed a clear bias (**Figure 11.6**). Actions consistent with a participant's preexisting orientation (that is, positive actions by a member of one's own *contrada* or negative actions by a member of the rival *contrada*) were described at a more abstract level than actions inconsistent with the participant's preexisting orientation (that is, negative actions by a member of one's own *contrada* or positive actions by a member of the rival *contrada*). This asymmetry feeds the tendency to perceive the ingroup in a favorable light. Abstractly encoding events that fit one's stereotypes lends them greater import; concretely encoding events that violate one's preferences or expectations renders them less consequential. Thus, "cheating" someone is more significant than "taking" something from someone, "helping" someone is more significant than "lifting" someone, and "showing concern" about someone is more significant than "visiting" someone.

Automatic and Controlled Processing

As mentioned earlier in this chapter, some of the cognitive processes that give rise to stereotyping and prejudice are deliberate, elaborate, and mindful—that is to say, conscious. Subtyping, for example, is often a conscious process (Devine & Baker, 1991; Kunda & Oleson, 1995; Weber & Crocker, 1983). Other cognitive processes, in contrast, give rise to stereotyping and prejudice rapidly and automatically, without much conscious attention and elaboration. This is likely to be the case for distinctiveness-based illusory correlations and the outgroup homogeneity effect.

In the past 25 years, researchers have explored the interplay between automatic and controlled processes and how together they give rise to the way people react to members of different groups (Bodenhausen, Macrae, & Sherman, 1999; Devine & Monteith, 1999; Fazio & Olson, 2003; Sherman et al., 2008; Sritharan & Gawronski, 2010; Wittenbrink, 2004). This research has shown that our reactions to different groups of people are to a surprising degree guided by quick and automatic mental processes that we can override but not eliminate. This research has also highlighted the common rift that exists between our immediate, reflexive reactions to outgroup members and our more reflective responses.

Patricia Devine (1989b) examined the joint operation of automatic and controlled processes by investigating the schism that exists for many people between their knowledge of racial stereotypes and their own personal beliefs and attitudes toward those same groups. More specifically, Devine sought to demonstrate that what separates prejudiced and nonprejudiced people is not their knowledge of derogatory stereotypes, but whether they resist the stereotypes. To do so, she relied on the distinction between automatic processes, which we do not consciously control (such as the use of binocular disparity to judge distance), and controlled processes, which, as the name suggests, we direct more consciously. The activation of stereotypes is typically an automatic process; thus, stereotypes can be triggered even if we don't want them to be. Even a nonprejudiced person will, under the right circumstances, access an association between Muslims and fanaticism, blacks and criminality, and WASPs and emotional repression, because those associations are present in our culture. Whereas a bigot will endorse or employ such stereotypes, a nonprejudiced person will employ more controlled cognitive processes to suppress them—or at least try to.

To test these ideas, Devine selected groups of high- and low-prejudiced participants on the basis of their scores on the Modern Racism Scale. To show that these two groups do not differ in their automatic processing of stereotypical information, she presented to each participant a set of words, one at a time, so briefly that they could not be consciously identified. She showed some of the participants neutral words (*number, plant, remember*) and other participants words stereotypically associated with blacks (*welfare, jazz, busing*). Devine hypothesized that although the stereotypical words were presented too briefly to be consciously recognized, they would nonetheless prime the participants' stereotypes of blacks. To test this hypothesis, she next presented the participants with a written description of an individual who acted in an ambiguously hostile manner (to highlight hostility, a feature of the African-American stereotype). In one incident, for example, the target individual refused to pay his rent until his apartment was repaired. Was he being needlessly belligerent or appropriately assertive? The results indicated that he was seen as more hostile—and more negative overall—by participants who had earlier been primed by words designed to activate stereotypes of blacks (words, it is important to note, that were not otherwise connected to the concept of hostility). Most important, this result was found equally for prejudiced and nonprejudiced participants. Because the stimulus words unconsciously activated their stereotypes, the nonprejudiced participants were caught off guard and were unable to suppress the automatic processing of stereotypical information.

To demonstrate that prejudiced and nonprejudiced individuals differ primarily in their *controlled* cognitive processes, Devine next asked her participants to list characteristics of black Americans. As predicted, the two groups differed substantially in the output of this consciously controlled procedure: prejudiced participants listed many more negative characteristics stereotypically associated with blacks than did nonprejudiced participants. Thus, even though both prejudiced and nonprejudiced individuals have stored in their minds the same negative stereotypes of black Americans (as shown in the first part of Devine's study), prejudiced individuals believe them and are willing to voice those beliefs, whereas nonprejudiced individuals reject them.

Subsequent investigations have qualified one element of Devine's research: automatic negative stereotypes associated with members of various stigmatized groups appear to be more easily activated among prejudiced individuals than among nonprejudiced individuals (Fazio, Jackson, Dunton, & Williams, 1995; Lepore & Brown, 1997; Wittenbrink, Judd, & Park, 1997). Nevertheless, even among nonprejudiced individuals, there is often a rift between the beliefs and sentiments elicited by automatic processes and those elicited by more controlled processes. One study examined the areas of the brain that were activated when white participants were shown pictures of black faces and white faces (Cunningham et al., 2004; see also Lieberman, Hariri, Jarcho, Eisenberger, & Bookheimer, 2005). The key manipulation in this study was the amount of time participants were exposed to the black and white faces. When shown the faces for only 30 milliseconds, the participants exhibited greater activation in the amygdala (which registers emotional response) after exposure to black faces than after exposure to white faces. Furthermore, the amount of amygdala activation was related to participants' implicit prejudice as measured by the IAT. But when the faces were shown for 525 milliseconds, participants showed no difference in amygdala activation when exposed to black versus white faces. This result suggests that these participants—all of whom had expressed a strong desire to avoid prejudice—initially had an automatic response to black versus white faces that they then tried to control. Indeed, at 525 milliseconds, black faces caused more activity in the prefrontal cortex—an area of the brain associated with cognitive and behavioral regulation—than did white faces.

The implications of the rift between people's automatic and controlled reactions to members of a different racial group were further investigated by Dovidio, Kawakami, and Gaertner (2002). These researchers first used a priming procedure like that described on p. 415 under "Priming and Implicit Prejudice" to assess white participants' implicit prejudice toward blacks and also measured their explicit attitudes with the Attitudes toward Blacks Scale (Brigham, 1993). They then had the participants engage in two 3-minute conversations, one with a white student and one with a black student. They videotaped and later scored these conversations, once with the sound removed and once with all channels included, for the amount of friendliness exhibited by the participant.

Dovidio and colleagues predicted that the explicit measure of prejudice would predict ratings of the participants' friendliness made from the full videotape because those ratings would be primarily determined by what participants said, and people can readily control what they say. But they expected that the implicit measure of prejudice would predict participants' nonverbal friendliness—that is, the ratings of participants' friendliness made from the video channel only—because nonverbal behavior is harder to control. And that's precisely what happened. Participants' scores on the Attitudes toward Blacks Scale predicted how differentially friendly they were to the white and black students as assessed from the full videotape. These scores were also related to how differentially friendly the participants themselves thought they were. But their scores on the implicit measure of prejudice (their reaction times) predicted how differentially friendly they were to the white and black students as assessed from the video-only ratings. These scores were related to how friendly *their conversation partners* thought they had been. Explicit measures of prejudice, it seems, can predict controlled behavior, but implicit measures may do a better job of predicting automatic behavior (see also Fazio et al., 1995).

The results of another study of people's automatic reactions to members of stigmatized groups are rather disturbing. Payne (2001) had participants decide as quickly as possible whether an object depicted in a photo was a handgun or a hand tool (for example, pliers). Each photograph was immediately preceded by a picture of either an African-American or a white face. Payne found that the participants (all of whom were white) were faster to identify a weapon as a weapon when it was preceded by an African-American face and faster to identify a hand tool as a hand tool when it was preceded by a white face (see also Payne, Lambert, & Jacoby, 2002; see **Figure 11.7**).

Is this pattern the result of automatic prejudice toward African-Americans on the part of white participants? That is, is the recognition of handguns facilitated by African-American faces because both handguns and African-Americans are

---

FIGURE 11.7 Scientific Method: Stereotypes and Categorization

Hypothesis: Social attitudes can influence basic categorization processes.

Research Method:

1. White participants were shown a white or black face.

2. Immediately after viewing a face, participants were shown an object and asked to identify it as a gun or a tool as quickly as possible.

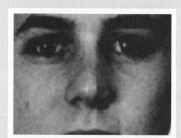

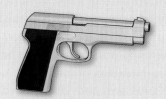

Results: Participants identified guns more quickly and mistook tools for guns more often after being primed with black faces.

CONCLUSION: Implicit stereotypes influence identification and categorization.

Source: Adapted from Payne, Lambert, & Jacoby (2002).

evaluated negatively by white participants? Or is this effect due to automatic stereotyping? That is, is the facilitation caused by a stereotypical association between handguns and African-Americans that exerts its effect even among nonprejudiced individuals?

The good news (limited good news, perhaps, but good news nonetheless) is that it appears to be the latter. Charles Judd, Irene Blair, and Kristine Chapleau (2004) replicated Payne's experiment with four types of target stimuli that varied in whether they were viewed positively or negatively and whether they were stereotypically associated with African-Americans. Specifically, the stimuli associated with African-Americans consisted of pictures of handguns (negative) and sports equipment (positive), and the stimuli not associated with African-Americans consisted of pictures of insects (negative) and fruit (positive). Judd and his colleagues found that African-American faces facilitated the recognition of both positive and negative stereotypical items (handguns and sports equipment), but not the non-stereotypical items (insects and fruits), regardless of whether they were positive or negative.

A similar conclusion emerges from studies with even more chilling implications for the everyday lives of African-Americans (**Box 11.2**). This research was inspired by the tragic death of Amadou Diallo, a black African immigrant who

BOX 11.2   FOCUS ON THE LAW

Stereotypical Facial Features and the Death Penalty

The election of Barack Obama as the 44th president of the United States highlights the often ambiguous nature of race. Although the child of a white mother and black father, Obama is almost always referred to as the first African-American president, not the first biracial president. This is no doubt a legacy of the "one-drop rule": historically, individuals were considered black if they had any trace of black ancestry at all. Various Southern states used this standard to back the notorious Jim Crow laws that enforced racial segregation and restricted the rights of blacks. But now that society has moved beyond the one-drop rule, we are left with the difficult issue of "who counts" as black, white, Asian, Hispanic, and so on. Indeed, many biologists question whether racial categories make any sense at all—that is, whether race really exists (Bamshad & Olson, 2003).

The psychology behind the one-drop rule notwithstanding, race-based judgments about others often differ in intensity depend-ing on how much an individual's physical features conform to a stereotype. African-American faces with more stereotypically African features (darker skin, fuller lips, more flared nostrils) elicit prejudiced reactions more readily than faces with less stereotypical features (Livingston & Brewer, 2002; Ma & Correll, 2011). Furthermore, both black and white individuals with more stereotypically African features are assumed to have traits associated with common stereotypes of African-Americans (Blair, Judd, Sadler, & Jenkins, 2002). In the most consequential manifestation of this tendency, individuals with stereotypically African features tend to receive harsher sentences than those with less stereotypically African features (Blair, Judd, & Chapleau, 2004), and blacks accused of capital crimes are more likely to end up on death row if they have stereotypically African features (Eberhardt, Davies, Purdie-Vaughns, & Johnson, 2006).

Automatic Reactions and Stereotyping White police officers in New York City attempted to question Amadou Diallo, a black West African immigrant who had gone outside his apartment building to get some air and who seemed to fit the description of the serial rapist they were looking for. Diallo ran up the steps of his building and then reached inside his jacket for what police believed was a gun but was actually his wallet. Reacting out of fear that Diallo was about to start firing a weapon, the four police officers fired 41 shots, striking the innocent Diallo 19 times and killing him.

in 1999 was riddled with 19 bullets by police officers who said afterward that they thought, incorrectly, that he was reaching for a gun. In these studies, participants watched a video game in which, at unpredictable moments, a target individual—sometimes white, sometimes African-American—popped up out of nowhere holding either a gun or some other object (Correll, Park, Judd, & Wittenbrink, 2002; Correll, Urland, & Ito, 2006; Ma & Correll, 2011; Payne, 2006). Participants were instructed to "shoot" if the target individual was holding a gun and to press a different response key if he was not. Because participants were instructed to respond as quickly as possible, they were bound to make occasional mistakes. The pattern of mistakes is shown in **Figure 11.8**, and it is clear that participants treated African-American and white targets differently. They made both types of mistakes—shooting an unarmed target and not shooting an armed target—equally often when the target individual was white. But for African-American targets, participants were much more likely to make the mistake of shooting if the target was unarmed than failing to shoot if the target was armed. Notably, the same effect was obtained in a follow-up experiment with African-American participants. Prolonged experience with these sorts of shoot/don't shoot decisions, either through laboratory exposure or real-world police work, seems to diminish the tendency to shoot unarmed blacks more than unarmed whites, but the reaction time differences (faster to decide to shoot an armed black and not to shoot an unarmed white) tend to persist (Correll, Park, Judd, Wittenbrink, Sadler, & Keesee, 2007; Payne, 2006; Plant & Peruche, 2005; Plant, Peruche, & Butz, 2005).

Evaluating the Cognitive Perspective

Critics of the cognitive perspective have said that although the approach has made strides in advancing psychologists' understanding of intergroup conflict, the recent emphasis on reaction-time methods and brief, reflexive phenomena may lead us to lose sight of the causes of the truly disturbing manifestations of

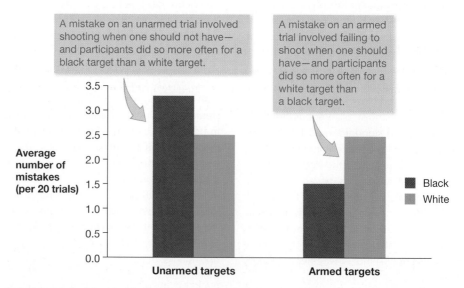

FIGURE 11.8 Automatic Stereotyping and Prejudice Participants were shown images of an armed or unarmed individual who appeared suddenly on a computer screen. They were told to respond as quickly as possible by pressing one button to "shoot" an armed individual and another button if the individual was unarmed. (Source: Adapted from Correll, Park, Judd, & Wittenbrink, 2002.)

prejudice and discrimination that are all-too-common elements of real-world experience. Indeed, when ethnic groups in Africa, the Middle East, Indonesia, and elsewhere are bent on subjugating or exterminating one another, and when police officers in countries the world over brutalize minorities with alarming frequency, reaction-time assessments of subtle prejudices can seem rather removed from the heart of the matter. Critics have also noted that many of the effects documented in this literature are very short-lived. Seeing someone who belongs to a particular ethnic group may automatically activate our stereotypical associations to that group, but the activation is typically brief. One team of investigators reported that they could find no trace of stereotype activation after a mere 10 minutes of interaction with a member of a minority group (Kunda, Davies, Adams, & Spencer, 2002).

As important as it is to keep these concerns in mind, it's also important to note that a great deal of damage can be done on the basis of people's initial, quick responses, as the shooting studies just reviewed make abundantly clear. It is surely no consolation to Amadou Diallo's family to know that the cognitive operations that made the police officers think Diallo was reaching for a gun rather than a wallet would have soon been overridden by more level-headed processes. And however brief these initial, automatic processes might be, they can get the ball rolling in an unfortunate direction. They can be the seeds from which deeper sorts of prejudice and discrimination are sown.

Furthermore, social psychologists working from the cognitive perspective have done the most to make it clear that we all tend to stereotype and that we all have the capacity to harbor troubling prejudices—prejudices we are often unaware we have. Subjecting yourself to implicit measures of prejudice like the IAT (see Figure 11.1) can yield undeniable evidence that you have certain negative associations to particular groups that you would rather not have. That knowledge can be the first step toward overcoming prejudice.

Stereotypes help people make sense of the world and process information efficiently, freeing us to use cognitive resources for other work. But they can also cause us to make many errors, such as seeing outgroup members as more homogeneous than they actually are. Our expectations of what a group of people is like can lead us to process information in ways that make stereotypes resistant to disconfirmation, as we explain away information that violates a stereotype and subcategorize those who don't fit the stereotype. Stereotypes can result from both automatic and controlled processing. Even people who do not express prejudicial views may reflexively respond to individuals on the basis of their unconscious stereotypes and prejudices.

BEING A MEMBER OF A STIGMATIZED GROUP

So far, this chapter has been concerned with the perpetrators of prejudice (who, it should be clear by now, can include all of us). But what about the victims of prejudice? They, of course, pay an unfair price in terms of numerous indicators of material and psychological well-being—health, wealth, employment prospects, and longevity among them. What's more, members of stereotyped or stigmatized groups are typically aware of the stereotypes that others hold about them, and this awareness also can have negative effects on them (Crocker, Major, &

Steele, 1998; Herek, 1998; Jones et al., 1984; Pinel, 1999; Shelton, Richeson, & Salvatore, 2005). Social psychologists have focused on two burdens that come with knowing that others may be prejudiced against one's group—attributional ambiguity and stereotype threat. Members of stereotyped groups can also have a very difficult time dispelling common stereotypes about them because those who hold the stereotypes act in ways that tend to elicit the very behavior that lies at the heart of the stereotype.

Attributional Ambiguity

As discussed in Chapter 5, people want to know the causes of events around them in order to achieve a sense that they live in an ordered, predictable world. But this sense is threatened for members of stigmatized groups because they cannot tell whether many of their experiences have the same causes as those of everyone else or whether they are the result of prejudice. "Did my officemate get the promotion instead of me because I'm so overweight?" "Would the state trooper have pulled me over if I were white?" "Did I get that fellowship because I'm Latino?" These sorts of questions may be particularly vexing with respect to negative outcomes, but they are also disconcerting in the context of positive outcomes. When someone has to wonder whether an accomplishment is the product of an affirmative action policy, it can be difficult to completely "own" it and reap the full measure of pride it would ordinarily afford.

In one study that examined this sort of attributional predicament, African-American and white students received flattering or unflattering feedback from a white student in an adjacent room (Crocker, Voelkl, Testa, & Major, 1991). Half the participants were led to believe that this other student could see them through a one-way mirror, and half were led to believe they could not be seen (because a blind covered the mirror). Whether or not they could be seen had no effect on how white students reacted to the feedback. But it did affect how black students reacted. When black students thought the other person could not see them—and therefore didn't know their race—their self-esteem went down from the unflattering feedback and was boosted by the positive feedback. When they thought the other person could see them, in contrast, their self-esteem was not injured by the bad news, nor was it enhanced by the good news. Thus, this study indicates that members of stigmatized groups live in a less certain world, not knowing whether to attribute positive feedback to their own skill or to others' condescension and not knowing whether to attribute negative feedback to their own error or to others' prejudice.

Stereotype Threat

An extensive program of research initiated by Claude Steele and his colleagues speaks dramatically to a second difficulty confronting members of stigmatized groups (Steele, 1997; Steele, Spencer, & Aronson, 2002). In particular, this research has shown that the performance of members of stigmatized groups can be impaired by **stereotype threat**—the fear that they will confirm the stereotypes that others have regarding a group of which they are a member. In one study, Steven Spencer, Claude Steele, and Diane Quinn (1999) looked at the effect on women's math test scores of making salient the stereotype that women do not

stereotype threat People's fear of confirming the stereotypes that others have regarding a group of which they are a member.

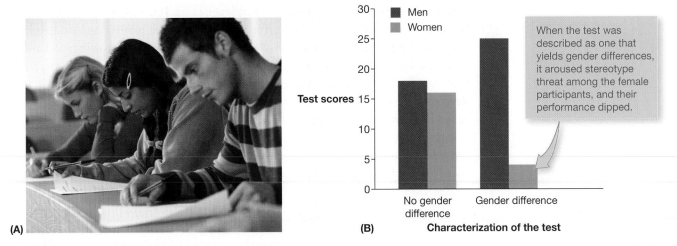

Test scores

Men
Women

When the test was described as one that yields gender differences, it aroused stereotype threat among the female participants, and their performance dipped.

(A)

(B) **Characterization of the test**

No gender difference

Gender difference

FIGURE 11.9 Stereotype Threat and Performance Math test performance by men and women when the test was described as one that yields gender differences (and hence aroused stereotype threat among women) or was described as one that does not yield gender differences. (Source: Adapted from Spencer, Steele, & Quinn, 1999.)

perform well in mathematics. In one condition, participants were told there was no gender difference on a particular test they were about to take. Other participants were told that there was a gender difference in favor of men. As can be seen in **Figure 11.9**, men and women performed equivalently when told there was no gender difference on the test, but women performed worse than men when they were told that there was a gender difference.

It's not necessary to be so blatant in the manipulation of stereotype threat for it to have an effect. Michael Inzlicht and Talia Ben-Zeev (2000) had university women take a math test either in the company of two other women or in the company of two men. Those who took the test with other women got 70 percent of the problems right on average. Those who took the test with men got 55 percent right on average.

Claude Steele and Joshua Aronson (1995) examined the sensitivity to stereotype threat on the part of African-American students. Playing on a stereotype that questions blacks' intellectual ability, they gave black and white Stanford University students a difficult verbal test taken from the Graduate Record Exam. Half of the students were led to believe that the test was capable of measuring their intellectual ability, and half were told that the investigators were in the early stages of trying to develop the test and that nothing could be learned about intellectual ability from their scores. This manipulation had no effect on the performance of white students. In contrast, African-American students did as well as white students when they thought it was the test that was being tested, but they performed much worse than white students when they thought their intellectual ability was being tested. Here too, a blatant manipulation was not required to produce a significant effect on the performance of African-Americans. In a follow-up study, it was enough simply to have participants indicate their race at the top of the page to cause African-American students' performance to be worse than in a control condition in which they did not indicate their race (Steele & Aronson, 1995).

It seems that no one is safe from stereotype threat. Joshua Aronson and his colleagues (1999) showed that the math performance of white males deteriorated when they were reminded of Asian proficiency in math. And in a particularly clever experiment, Jeff Stone and his colleagues had college students perform a laboratory golf task that was described as a measure of "natural athletic ability," "sports intelligence," or "sports psychology" (Stone, Lynch, Sjomeling, & Darley, 1999). White and black students performed equally well in the "sports psychology" condition. But black students performed significantly worse when it was described as a test of "sports intelligence," and white students performed worse when it was described as a test of "natural athletic ability."

Stereotype threat appears to undermine performance in a number of ways. Stereotype threat leads to increased arousal, which can directly interfere with performance on complex tasks (Ben-Zeev, Fein, & Inzlicht, 2005) and serve as a source of distraction that interferes with concentration on the task at hand (Cheryan & Bodenhausen, 2000). Furthermore, knowing that one's group is "suspect" in the eyes of others tends to elicit negative thinking (Cadinu, Maass, Rosabianca, & Kiesner, 2005), which can both directly undermine performance and lead individuals to "play it safe" by being more obsessed with avoiding failure than reaching for success (Seibt & Forster, 2004).

Although everyone is vulnerable to some type of stereotype threat based on their group memberships, Steele (1997) maintains that the vulnerability of African-Americans has particular potential for damage. Stereotype threat can result in poorer overall academic performance, which undermines confidence, rendering the individual still more susceptible to stereotype threat. This vicious cycle can result in "disidentification" from academic pursuits, as students who feel the threat most acutely opt out of academics altogether and identify other areas in which to invest their talent and energy and from which to derive their self-esteem.

Self-Fulfilling Prophecies

Members of a stigmatized group often feel trapped in invalid and unfair stereotypes because the majority's stereotypical beliefs can create a self-fulfilling prophecy—that is, people act toward members of certain groups in ways that encourage the very behavior they expect. Thinking that members of a particular group are hostile, an individual may act toward them in a guarded manner, thereby eliciting a coldness that the individual sees as proof of their hostility (Shelton & Richeson, 2005). A teacher who thinks that members of a particular group lack intellectual ability may fail to offer them adequate instruction, thereby increasing the chances that they will indeed fall behind their classmates. As Robert Merton, who coined the term *self-fulfilling prophecy*, once said, "The specious validity of the self-fulfilling prophecy perpetuates a reign of error. For the prophet will cite the actual course of events as proof that he was right from the very beginning" (Merton, 1957, p. 423).

The trap that's sprung by certain types of self-fulfilling prophecies was powerfully illustrated in an experiment in which white Princeton students interviewed both black and white men pretending to be job applicants (Word, Zanna, & Cooper, 1974). The interviews were monitored, and it was discovered that the students (the white interviewers) unwittingly treated black and white applicants differently. When the applicant was black, the interviewer tended to sit farther away, to hem and haw throughout the session, and to terminate the proceedings

"Oppression has no logic—just a self-fulfilling prophecy, justified by a self-perpetuating system."

—Gloria Steinem

earlier than when the applicant was white. This is not the type of environment that inspires self-possession and smooth interview performance.

Sure enough, the second phase of the experiment showed just how difficult it had been for the black applicants. Interviewers were trained to treat *new* applicants, all of whom were white, the way that either the white or the black applicants had been treated earlier. These interviews were tape-recorded and later rated by independent judges. Those applicants who had been interviewed in the way the black applicants had been interviewed earlier were evaluated more negatively than those who had been interviewed the way the white applicants had been interviewed. In other words, by placing black applicants at a disadvantage, the white interviewers confirmed their negative stereotypes of blacks. Similar results have been obtained in interview studies of homosexual job applicants (Hebl, Foster, Mannix, & Dovidio, 2002).

 Victims of stereotyping can suffer attributional ambiguity, not knowing whether performance feedback is genuine or based on their group membership. They can suffer from stereotype threat, performing worse because they are afraid of affirming a stereotype that exists about their group. They can also find it difficult to overcome a commonly held stereotype because others act toward them in a way that elicits behavior consistent with the stereotype and suppresses behavior inconsistent with the stereotype, making the stereotype self-fulfilling.

REDUCING STEREOTYPES, PREJUDICE, AND DISCRIMINATION

This chapter began with a discussion of the progress that has been made in intergroup relations in the United States and across much of the globe—and how much further we must go to achieve true equality of opportunity for all citizens of the world. What has contributed to the improved relations we have witnessed thus far, and what principles can we draw on to advance further?

Many factors—including specific legal interventions, broad economic developments, and seemingly incidental sociological trends—have brought about improved relations between gays and straights, blacks and whites, Latinos and Anglos, and numerous other groups. One factor that is both cause and consequence of these developments is the increased day-to-day interaction between members of different groups. When people interact frequently, it becomes easier to see one another more as individuals and less as representatives of particular groups. As Barack Obama put it in his 2008 inaugural address, "As the world grows smaller, our common humanity shall reveal itself."

But simple contact between broad cross sections of different groups is not the be-all and end-all of harmonious relations, and some types of contact are more helpful than others. Numerous studies were conducted to assess the effect of the Supreme Court's desegregation decision in *Brown v. the Board of Education of Topeka* (1954) on race relations in U.S. schools. The initial studies did not provide strong support for what came to be known as the "contact hypothesis"—the straightforward idea that bringing together students of different races and ethnicities would reduce prejudice and discrimination. One review of the

Reducing Prejudice Advocates of the "contact hypothesis" maintain that greater familiarity with members of stigmatized groups can reduce prejudice directed toward those groups, particularly when the increased contact takes place under certain favorable conditions.

relevant literature found that in a majority of the studies that looked at the effect of integration on interracial attitudes, an *increase* in prejudice was observed (Stephan, 1986).

This was not an encouraging finding, to be sure, but in many ways, it is not surprising either. After all, simply bringing the Rattlers and Eagles together did not reduce the animosity between the two groups at Robbers Cave. Contact between different groups is likely to be more positive and more productive if certain conditions are met. First, the different groups need to have equal status. If one group feels superior and the other resentful, then harmonious, productive interactions are unlikely to be the norm. Second, as in the Robbers Cave study, productive intergroup interactions are facilitated if the different groups have a shared goal that requires their cooperative interaction—and thus promotes a common ingroup identity (Gaertner & Dovidio, 2000, 2009; Nier, Gaertner, Dovidio, Banker, & Ward, 2001; West, Pearson, Dovidio, Shelton, & Trail, 2009). Third, a community's broader social norms need to support intergroup contact. If children of different races, religions, and ethnicities go to school with one another but their parents send them begrudgingly and rarely miss an opportunity to speak ill of the "other" children, the students themselves are unlikely to reach out across group boundaries. On the other hand, merely knowing that someone in one's group is friends with a member of an outgroup—and what that implies about perceived social support for contact with the outgroup—is sufficient to reduce stereotyping and outgroup derogation (Wright, Aron, McLaughlin-Volpe, & Ropp, 1997). Finally, the contact should encourage one-on-one interactions between members of the different groups. Doing so puts each person's identity as an individual in the foreground and downplays a person's group membership. An analysis of numerous studies on the effect of desegregation, involving tens of thousands of students in over 25 different nations, found that when most of these conditions are met, contact between members of different groups does indeed tend to be effective in reducing prejudice (Pettigrew & Tropp, 2000, 2006, 2008). And university students who are assigned roommates of a different race report reduced anxiety about cross-race interactions and register a significant improvement on implicit measures of attitudes toward the other group (Shook & Fazio, 2008).

Note, though, that even if increased intergroup contact were entirely effective in eliminating prejudice, the ideas discussed in this chapter make it clear that other prejudices and animosities are at risk of arising anew. Powerful elements of human nature encourage stereotyping, prejudice, and discrimination—forces that require constant attention if relations between different groups are to remain harmonious. Resources are finite, and realistic conflict over who should get them guarantees that there will always be conflict between groups (the economic perspective). Also, people need to feel valued and have a sense of self-worth, a sense that stems in part from the groups to which they belong. Thus, even when conflict over scarce resources is diminished, these motivational concerns can sour intergroup relations (the motivational perspective). And what psychologists have learned about how the mind works makes it clear that people categorize and make inferences in a way that sharpens distinctions between groups and can serve to exacerbate intergroup conflict (the cognitive perspective).

Thus the capacity to stereotype, harbor prejudice, and act in a discriminatory fashion is present in all of us, and the responsibility for reducing intergroup hostility and conflict lies with each of us as well. Intergroup harmony requires constant attention. We must all do our part as citizens to make sure, at a societal level, that civil rights laws are honored and enforced, that media depictions of different groups are not biased, and that different groups are given more opportunities to work together to achieve common goals rather than compete against one another for scarce resources. Moreover, on an individual level, we must all do our part to overcome our fear that members of other groups don't really want to interact with us (Shelton & Richeson, 2005); only when we reach out and interact with members of other groups as individuals will group boundaries begin to lose their significance. Such positive interactions can replace the troublesome associations we inherit from slanted media depictions or bigoted acquaintances with the more positive associations that come from person-to-person, equal-status contact.

 Contact between members of different groups can go a long way toward reducing group stereotypes and intergroup hostility. Intergroup contact is particularly likely to be beneficial when members of different groups interact as equals, work together to try to accomplish common goals, and come together on a one-on-one basis—and when these interactions are supported by broader societal norms.

Chapter Review

Summary

Characterizing Intergroup Bias

- *Stereotypes* are generalizations about groups that are often applied to individual group members. *Prejudice* involves a negative attitude and emotional response to members of a group. *Discrimination* involves negative behavior toward an individual because of the person's membership in a group.

- Blatant, explicit racism in much of the world is now relatively rare. But *modern racism*, whereby people hold overtly egalitarian attitudes while unconsciously holding negative attitudes and exhibiting more subtle forms of prejudice, still exists.

- *Benevolent racism and sexism* consist of attitudes the individual thinks of as favorable toward a group but that have the effect of supporting traditional, subservient roles for members of disadvantaged groups.

- In recent years, there have been successful efforts to measure people's nonconscious attitudes with "implicit" measures. The *Implicit Association Test* compares reaction times when outgroup pictures (or words) and positive items are in the same response category versus when outgroup pictures (or words) and negative items are in the same category. Another implicit measure involves *priming* with a picture of a member of some group. If the prime increases the time it takes to recognize subsequently presented positive words and decreases the time it takes to recognize subsequently presented negative words, prejudice toward the group is revealed.

- Three approaches to studying prejudice and discrimination are the economic perspective, the motivational perspective, and the cognitive perspective.

The Economic Perspective

- One version of the *economic perspective* is *realistic group conflict theory*, which reflects the fact that groups are sometimes in competition for scarce resources and that this conflict can lead to prejudice and discrimination. The classic Robbers Cave experiment put two groups of boys in competition at a camp. Soon the groups were expressing open hostility toward each other. When the groups were brought together in noncompetitive situations where they

had to cooperate to achieve *superordinate goals*—goals that could be achieved only when the two groups worked together—the hostility dissipated.

The Motivational Perspective

- According to the *motivational perspective*, sometimes poor relations between groups occur simply because there *are* two groups, and an us/them opposition results. This phenomenon occurs even in the *minimal group paradigm*, where people find out they are members of one of two groups that have been defined in a trivial and arbitrary way. People favor members of their own group over members of the other group, even when it actually costs their group something to "beat" the opposition.

- *Social identity theory* attempts to explain ingroup favoritism, maintaining that self-esteem is derived in part from group membership and group success.

- *Frustration-aggression theory* maintains that when people are frustrated in their attempt to reach a goal, they often lash out at less powerful individuals or groups. Challenges to a person's self-esteem can have similar effects, and experiments have shown that people express more antagonism toward outgroup members when they have suffered a blow to their self-esteem.

The Cognitive Perspective

- The *cognitive perspective* focuses on stereotypes, which are a form of categorization. People rely on them all the time, but especially when they are tired or overtaxed.

- Several construal processes lead to inaccurate stereotypes. We tend to assume that outgroups are more *homogeneous* than our ingroups are, leading to the *outgroup homogeneity effect*. We also often engage in *biased information processing*, seeing aspects of other groups that confirm our stereotypes and failing to see facts that are inconsistent with them.

- Distinctive groups (because they are in the minority) are often associated with distinctive (rare) behaviors. This *paired distinctiveness* results in our attributing illusory properties to such groups, creating illusory correlations.

- Encountering contradictory evidence about group members may not change our ideas about the group, because we treat the evidence as an exception that proves the rule. Behavior consistent with a stereotype is often attributed to the dispositions of the group members, whereas behavior that is inconsistent with a stereotype is often attributed to the situation. We tend to code favorable evidence about ingroup members more abstractly and the same sort of evidence about outgroup members less abstractly. The converse is true for unfavorable evidence.

- We sometimes respond to outgroup members reflexively, relying on *automatic processes* whereby prejudice is unleashed outside of our awareness. Often these automatic reactions can be corrected by conscious, *controlled processes*.

Being a Member of a Stigmatized Group

- Members of stigmatized groups suffer from *attributional ambiguity*. They have to ask whether others' negative or positive behavior toward them is due to prejudice or to some factor unrelated to their group membership.

- The performance of members of stigmatized groups can be impaired by *stereotype threat*—the fear that they will confirm others' stereotypes.

- We often unknowingly create *self-fulfilling prophecies*—acting toward people in such a way as to bring about the very behavior we expect of them.

Reducing Stereotypes, Prejudice, and Discrimination

- Contact between members of different groups can lessen intergroup animosity, especially if the contact involves one-on-one interactions between individuals of equal status, if it encourages the cooperative pursuit of superordinate goals, and if it is supported by the prevailing norms in each group.

Key Terms

basking in reflected glory (p. 423)
discrimination (p. 410)
ethnocentrism (p. 416)
frustration-aggression theory (p. 426)
Implicit Association Test (IAT) (p. 413)
minimal group paradigm (p. 421)

modern racism (p. 411)
outgroup homogeneity effect (p. 431)
paired distinctiveness (p. 432)
prejudice (p. 409)
priming (p. 415)
realistic group conflict theory (p. 416)

social identity theory (p. 422)
stereotypes (p. 409)
stereotype threat (p. 444)
subtyping (p. 435)
superordinate goals (p. 418)

Further Reading

Allport, G. (1954). *The nature of prejudice*. Reading, MA: Addison-Wesley. A classic treatment of prejudice, with emphasis on racial prejudice in the United States.

Herek, G. M. (1998). *Stigma and sexual orientation: Understanding prejudice against lesbians, gay men, and bisexuals*. Thousand Oaks, CA: Sage Publications. A social psychological look at prejudice and discrimination directed at sexual minorities.

Obama, B. (1995). *Dreams from my father: A story of race and inheritance*. New York: Random House. Best-selling memoir of America's first African-American president.

Steele, C. S. (2010). *Whistling Vivaldi: How stereotypes affect us and what we can do*. New York: W. W. Norton. Insightful account of stereotype threat and its influence in a great many areas of contemporary life.

CHAPTER 12

Groups

ON DECEMBER 17, 2010, Mohamed Bouazizi, a Tunisian street vendor, set himself on fire to protest the harassment and humiliation he was subjected to by government officials. Images of his self-immolation were captured by passersby and posted on YouTube, tapping into the anger of countless Tunisians over human rights abuses and setting off protests throughout the country. Aided by announcements spread through social media, the protests gained in intensity, eventually forcing President Ben Ali to flee the country on January 14. The phenomenon that came to be known as the Arab Spring had begun.

Two weeks later in Egypt, protesters inspired by what had happened in Tunisia gathered in Cairo and many other cities across the country to demand the ouster of Egyptian President Hosni Mubarak. As bloggers spread information about torture by members of the Egyptian army and police, messages posted on Facebook, Twitter, and a host of other short messaging services alerted the population to the time and place of street protests and provided tactical advice about how protesters should conduct themselves. The government attempted to shut down Internet service throughout the country to stem the protests, but its efforts to do so were ineffective. On February 11, President Mubarak resigned, ending his 30-year grip on power.

The events in Tunisia and Egypt in turn led to antigovernment protests in Libya aimed at ending the autocratic rule of Muammar Gaddafi. The opposition grew into an armed insurrection that, with aerial support provided by NATO countries, defeated Gaddafi's forces and drove him from power. After being on the run for nearly two months, Gaddafi was killed by rebel forces while trying to flee his hometown of Sirte.

Uncertain as of this writing is the fate of protests and rebellions in other Arab countries, including Syria and Yemen, where the protests and government

Group Uprisings (A) The "Arab Spring" of 2011 saw popular uprisings in many Arab countries, including this protest in Tahrir Square, Cairo. (B) The protests were aided by many new forms of social media, and they raise all sorts of questions about what exactly constitutes a "group."

crackdown have been especially intense. Another question involves the ultimate success of the Arab Spring. Thus far, this remarkable string of uprisings has brought forth heartwarming stories of people risking their lives to make their democratic dreams a reality. It has also produced heartbreaking images of brutal repression of those dreams in countries—including Bahrain, Yemen, and Syria—where the rulers have held tight to their grip on power. It has also produced worrisome images from the newly freed countries of different groups turning on one another, such as fundamentalist Muslims attacking Coptic Christians in Cairo. Will we all look back on the Arab Spring as a historic awakening of democratic yearnings in that part of the world and as the beginning of the end of a host of despotic regimes? Will the leaders of the provisional governments in the countries that have successfully rebelled have the wisdom to make the right decisions necessary to build and sustain true democracies?

Regardless of how these uncertainties are resolved, the events of the Arab Spring highlight several issues of significance to this chapter. One is the centrality and importance of groups in human events. No single person can overthrow a government and install another; collective action is required. This chapter therefore explores how groups function, how they make decisions, and how the processes of group decision making can sometimes impede the effort to find the best course of action. It also examines how people achieve positions of leadership within a group, as well as the effects of power on people with authority. Finally, the chapter explores how orderly groups can devolve into unruly mobs when individual identity is diminished and the typical constraints on people's behavior are lessened.

Perhaps the first issue to tackle is the very definition of a group. Who were these masses of protestors who took to the streets in Tunisia, occupied Tahrir Square in Cairo, and risked their lives in clashes with soldiers in so many countries across the Arab world? Do those who occupy a square for one night constitute a group?

What about if they march together from the square? Does that make them more of a group? And what about people whose only connection is through Facebook or Twitter? Can they be said to constitute a group?

THE NATURE AND PURPOSE OF GROUP LIVING

Humans and all large primates (except the orangutan) live in groups, so group life must offer us some advantages in the struggle for survival. These advantages, however, are not well understood, because different mammalian species have successfully pursued both solitary and group lifestyles. Wolves live in groups but bears do not, and neither of these species appears any worse off for the particular lifestyle it has pursued.

Still, it is generally maintained that life with others offered our human ancestors protection from predators, efficiency in acquiring food, assistance with rearing children, and defense against human aggressors—benefits that humans are less equipped to do without than are, say, bears or orangutans. It is also generally maintained that these benefits are so crucial to survival that we have a psychological need to be with others and belong to groups (Baumeister & Leary, 1995; Correll & Park, 2005).

So what, exactly, is a group? This is not an easy question, since there are so many different types of groups, and the different types don't always share many features. The members of a baseball team are clearly a group, but most people do not consider the members of a large lecture course to be a group. Similarly, most people would say that the individuals riding together in an elevator are not a group. But suppose the elevator breaks down, and those inside must figure out how to escape or summon help. Most would say that the individuals in the elevator now seem more like a real group. But why?

A group has been described as "a collection of individuals who have relations to one another that make them interdependent to some significant degree" (Cartwright & Zander, 1968, p. 46). Thus the people in the functioning elevator do not make up a group because they are not very interdependent. But once the elevator breaks down and they must decide on joint action (or whether to take joint action), they become interdependent and hence more of a group. Note that interdependence varies along a continuum; therefore, so should whether or not a collection of people constitutes a group (McGrath, 1984). And to most people, this idea seems right. The members of a family are more of a "real" group than are participants in a seminar, and they in turn are more of a group than are students in a large lecture course. By this reasoning, a nation's citizens make up something of a group, but they are less of a group than are the members of a tribe or band, who interact with one another more frequently and are more directly dependent on one another.

SOCIAL FACILITATION

Let's begin the examination of groups by considering one of the simplest, most basic questions about social life: What effect does the presence of other people have on human performance? That is, does the presence of others typically help

> "No man is an island, entire of itself; every man is a piece of the continent, a part of the main."
>
> —John Donne

or hinder performance, or does it exert no effect at all? To address this question, let's consider it in more personal and vivid terms. Suppose you are by yourself trying to perfect a skill—practicing the piano, developing a topspin lob for your tennis game, or working through the intricacies of conjugating Latin verbs. You feel you are making progress when someone else takes a seat nearby and proceeds to observe—a perfect stranger, your mother, or even, say, Oprah Winfrey or George Clooney. What does this other person's presence do to your performance? Does it give you the energy and focus necessary to bring your performance to new heights? Or do you become so nervous and distracted that your performance suffers?

Social Facilitation and Competition Performance is typically enhanced in the presence of others when the activity is well learned. Here Lance Armstrong is energized by the presence and cheering of the spectators as he competes in the 2004 Tour de France.

social facilitation Initially a term for enhanced performance in the presence of others; now a broader term for the effect—positive or negative—of the presence of others on performance.

Initial Research

Norman Triplett (1898) is often credited with being the first person to experimentally examine the effect of other people's presence on human performance. Triplett was something of a bicycling enthusiast (or "wheelman," as they were known at the time). After reviewing speed records put out by the Racing Board of the League of American Wheelmen, Triplett noticed that the fastest times were recorded when cyclists competed directly against one another on the same track at the same time. Much slower speed records were obtained when cyclists raced alone against the clock. Thus Triplett believed that the presence of others tended to facilitate human performance.

Triplett realized, however, that the cycling records were not the best test of his hypothesis, so he conducted what is widely referred to as social psychology's first experiment. He invited a group of 40 children to his laboratory and had them turn a fishing reel as fast as they could. Each child did so on six trials with rest periods in between. On three of the trials the child was alone, and on three trials another child was alongside doing the same thing. Under these more controlled conditions, Triplett found that the children tended to turn the reel faster when in the presence of another child engaged in the same activity. The presence of others appeared to facilitate human performance. Research on this subject thus came to be known as **social facilitation** research.

A number of subsequent experiments reinforced Triplett's findings and extended them in two important ways. First, the same effects were obtained when the others present were not doing the same thing (that is, not "coacting"), but were merely present as an audience of passive observers (Gates, 1924; Travis, 1925). Second, the same effect was also observed in a vast number of animal species, indicating that the phenomenon is quite general and fundamental. For example, animals as diverse as dogs, fish, armadillos, opossums, and frogs have been shown to eat more when in the presence of other members of the same species than when alone (Boice, Quanty, & Williams, 1974; Platt & James, 1966; Platt, Yaksh, & Darby, 1967; Ross & Ross, 1949; Uematsu, 1970). Other studies have shown that ants dig more earth (Chen, 1937), fruit flies do more preening (Connolly, 1968), and centipedes run faster through mazes (Hosey, Wood, Thompson, & Druck, 1985) when together than when alone. For both humans and other animals, then, much of the research on this topic indicates that the presence of others facilitates performance.

Unfortunately, however, numerous exceptions emerged soon after Triplett's original findings. Floyd Allport (1920), for example, asked students at Harvard and Radcliffe to refute philosophical arguments as best they could in a 5-minute period. The students provided higher-quality refutations when working alone than when working in the presence of another student. The presence of others has also been shown to inhibit performance on arithmetic problems, memory tasks, and maze learning (Dashiell, 1930; Pessin, 1933; Pessin & Husband, 1933). And the presence of other members of the same species has sometimes been found to inhibit the performance of animals (Allee & Masure, 1936; Shelley, 1965; Strobel, 1972).

Resolving the Contradictions

Putting all of these findings together, it seemed for a time that the best answer to the question "What is the effect of the presence of others on performance?" was that it sometimes helps and sometimes hurts. That is not a terribly satisfying answer. It's about as helpful as a political pundit saying that the Republicans will regain the presidency in the next election . . . but then again they might not. That might be all you expect from a political forecaster, but you probably want more from research psychologists who study the effects of the presence of others on performance.

Zajonc's Theory Fortunately, a more satisfying understanding was eventually obtained when social psychologist Robert Zajonc proposed an unusually elegant theory to account for all of the divergent findings on this topic. Zajonc (1965) argued that the presence of others, indeed the *mere* presence of others, tends to facilitate performance on simple or well-learned tasks, but it hinders performance on difficult or novel tasks. Even more important, Zajonc's theory explained *why* the presence of others has these effects.

Robert B. Zajonc

Zajonc's theory has three components (**Figure 12.1**). First, the mere presence of others makes a person more aroused. (More generally, the mere presence of another member of the same species tends to arouse any organism.) Other people are dynamic and unpredictable stimuli, capable of doing almost anything at any time. We therefore need to be alert, or aroused, in their presence so we can react to what they might do.

Second, arousal tends to make a person more "rigid," in the sense that the person becomes even more inclined to do what he or she is already inclined to do. In the language Zajonc used, arousal makes a person more likely to make a **dominant response**. Think of it this way: In any situation, you can respond in a variety of ways, and the possible responses can be arranged in a hierarchy according to their likelihood of occurrence. Whatever you are most inclined to do in that situation is at the top of the hierarchy and is thus the "dominant response." When aroused, Zajonc argued, people are even more inclined to make that dominant response.

The third component of Zajonc's theory links the increase in dominant response tendencies to the facilitation of simple tasks and the inhibition of complex tasks. For easy or well-learned tasks, the dominant response—your reflexive response—is likely to be the correct response. Indeed, that is tantamount to what it means for a task to be easy or well learned. Thus the presence of other people, by facilitating your dominant response, facilitates the correct response and

dominant response In an individual's hierarchy of responses, the response he or she is most likely to make.

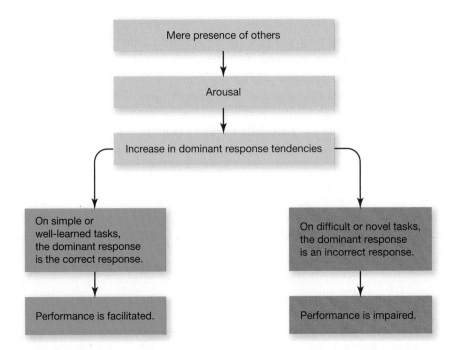

FIGURE 12.1 Zajonc's Model of Social Facilitation The presence of others (indeed, their *mere* presence) increases arousal and facilitates dominant response tendencies. This improves performance on easy or well-learned tasks but hinders performance on difficult or novel tasks.

improves performance (**Box 12.1**). In contrast, for difficult or novel tasks, the dominant response is unlikely to be the correct response. Again, that is what it means for a task to be difficult or novel. Thus the presence of others facilitates an *incorrect* response and hinders performance.

Testing the Theory Zajonc's theory provided a remarkably accurate summary of the diverse findings that existed at the time. Like any theory, however, Zajonc's needed to be subjected to more stringent tests. The existing findings did not offer a sufficiently rigorous test; after all, the theory was based on the existing findings and therefore *had* to be consistent with them. Thus, since its publication, Zajonc's theory has been tested in a variety of ways on numerous occasions, and it has held up extremely well.

In one of these tests, Zajonc and his colleagues placed cockroaches in the start box of one of two mazes and then shone a light at the start box (Zajonc, Heingartner, & Herman, 1969). Cockroaches instinctively flee from light and head toward a dark area; in this case, the cockroaches would try to reach the dark goal box. In the simple maze (a "runway"), getting to the darkened chamber was easy. The cockroach needed only to do what it does instinctively: run directly away from the light (its dominant response). In contrast, getting to the darkened chamber in the complex maze was more of a challenge: the cockroach had to do more than follow its instincts and flee from the light; it had to execute a turn. Two features of this setup were especially important. First, because cockroaches invariably run from light, doing so is clearly their dominant response. Second, Zajonc created two different conditions: in one, the dominant response led to the goal (the simple maze); in the other, it did not (the complex maze).

Zajonc had his cockroaches run one of these two mazes either alone or with another cockroach. He predicted that cockroaches running the simple maze

BOX 12.1   FOCUS ON DAILY LIFE

Social Facilitation of Prejudice

It is generally believed that prejudiced individuals are less likely to show their prejudice in most public settings. To do so, the logic goes, is to risk others' disapproval. But if some forms of prejudice represent dominant response tendencies, they might sometimes be facilitated in the presence of others—even when those others disapprove of prejudice.

In one study that examined this idea, students were seated in front of a computer and shown, very briefly, pairs of images—a black or white face followed by a picture of a gun or a hand tool. The students were asked to indicate as quickly as possible whether the second image was a gun or a tool (see Chapter 11). If they didn't respond within a

half second, they were informed that they did not respond quickly enough. This procedure was repeated over and over, and the experimenters recorded, as a measure of prejudice, the number of mistakes participants made. In particular, they were interested in how often a hand tool was mistakenly identified as a gun when it was preceded by a black face compared to when it was preceded by a white face. Some participants performed this task alone, not expecting to interact with anyone in the experiment. Others performed the task expecting to share their responses with others after they were finished.

The investigators found that participants made 13 percent more ste-

reotypic errors (calling a tool a gun if it was preceded by a black face), but not significantly more non-stereotypic errors (calling a tool a gun if it was preceded by a white face), when they expected to interact with others than when they did not (Lambert et al., 2003). To be sure, this result can be explained without reference to social facilitation (perhaps expecting to compare their results with others later on simply distracted participants and therefore made it harder for them to control their prejudices). But it is consistent with the social facilitation account, and the investigators were inspired to conduct the research by previous work on social facilitation.

---

would get to the goal box more quickly when together than when alone, but that those running the complex maze together would take longer to reach the chamber. Indeed, that is exactly what happened: the presence of another cockroach facilitated performance on the simple maze but hindered performance on the complex maze (**Figure 12.2**).

Coacting versus Mere Presence Finally, to show that the *mere* presence of another cockroach has these effects—as opposed to competition or some other, more complex factor than the presence of others of the same species—Zajonc added a condition in which the cockroach ran the maze not with another cockroach running alongside, but with other cockroaches merely present as a passive "audience." To create this condition, Zajonc built a set of Plexiglas boxes, or "grandstands," that flanked the two mazes and then filled them with observer cockroaches. Again, as Figure 12.2 indicates, the results were exactly as predicted: the presence of the observing cockroaches facilitated performance on the simple maze but inhibited performance on the complex maze.

Now, having validated Zajonc's theory in experiments such as this, psychologists can apply it to the real world by making more precise predictions than beforehand about what ought to happen in everyday life (Ben-Zeev, Fein, & Inzlicht, 2005; Thomas, Skitka, Christen, & Jurgena, 2002). An experiment

Why cockroaches give lousy surprise parties.

Hypothesis: The presence of other members of the same species will improve performance on an easy task and hinder performance on a difficult task.

Research Method:

1. Researchers placed cockroaches in the start box of two mazes and shone a light that caused the cockroaches to head toward a dark area (the goal box).

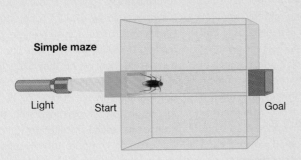

Simple maze

Light   Start   Goal

Complex maze

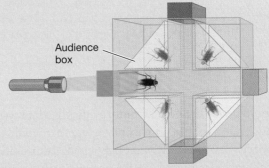

In the **simple maze**, the cockroach need only follow its dominant response and run directly away from the light to get to the goal.

In the **complex maze**, the cockroach's dominant response does not easily lead it to the goal. The cockroach must execute a turn.

2. The cockroaches ran one of these two mazes alone, with another cockroach, or with an audience of cockroaches behind a transparent wall.

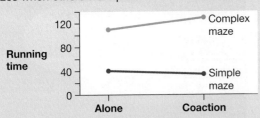

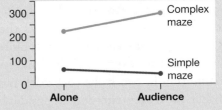

Audience box

Results: The cockroaches took less time to run simple mazes when others were present, but more time to run complex mazes when others were present.

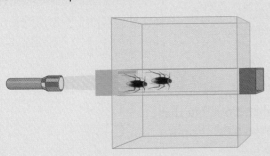

Average time (in seconds) taken by cockroaches to negotiate simple or complex mazes when alone or alongside another cockroach.

Average time to negotiate simple or complex mazes when alone or in the presence of an audience.

CONCLUSION: Social facilitation effects can be observed widely in the animal kingdom. For cockroaches, as for humans, the presence of others increases dominant response tendencies, leading to better performance on easy tasks and worse performance on difficult tasks.

Source: Adapted from Zajonc, Heingartner, & Herman (1969).

conducted in a university pool hall is a particularly informative example of such a real-world extension (Michaels, Blommel, Brocato, Linkous, & Rowe, 1982). Students playing recreational pool were unobtrusively observed and deemed skilled or unskilled based on their performance. Zajonc's theory, again, predicted that the presence of an audience would make the skilled players perform better (for them, the task is easy) but make the unskilled players perform worse (for them, the task is difficult). To test this prediction, the experimenters walked up to the pool tables and watched. As expected, the good players did even better than before, and the poor players did even worse.

Mere Presence or Evaluation Apprehension?

Zajonc's theory remains to this day the most compelling and widely accepted account of social facilitation. Few theorists question Zajonc's contention that the presence of others increases arousal, and virtually no one disputes the claim that the presence of others tends to facilitate performance on easy tasks and to hinder performance on difficult tasks (Geen, 1989; Guerin, 1993; Sanna, 1992; Thomas et al., 2002). One element of Zajonc's theory, however, is disputed—whether it is the *mere* presence of other people that increases arousal. When most people reflect on why they would be aroused in the presence of others, it is not just the presence of others that seems decisive. Instead, **evaluation apprehension**—a concern about looking bad in the eyes of others, about being evaluated—seems to be important (Blascovich, Mendes, Hunter, & Salomon, 1999; Cottrell, Wack, Sekerak, & Rittle, 1968; Seta & Seta, 1992).

evaluation apprehension People's concern about how they might appear in the eyes of others—that is, about being evaluated.

Testing for Evaluation Apprehension A number of social psychologists have argued that evaluation apprehension is the critical element underlying social facilitation. To evaluate this contention experimentally, there must be three conditions: one with the subject performing alone, one with the subject performing in front of an evaluative audience, and one with the subject performing in front of an audience that cannot evaluate the subject's performance. In one such experiment, the investigators cleverly built "from scratch" a response hierarchy in their participants so that they would know exactly what the dominant and subordinate responses were (Cottrell et al., 1968). The participants were given a list of ten nonsense words, such as *nansoma*, *paritaf*, or *zabulon*. The participants were asked to pronounce two of the ten words once, two words twice, two words 5 times, two words 10 times, and two words 25 times. They were thus much more familiar with some of the words than with others. After this initial training phase of the experiment, the test phase began. Now the participants were told that these same words would be flashed on a screen very briefly (some so briefly they might not be visible), and their task would be to identify each word as it was shown. If they could not identify a word, they should guess. Unbeknownst to the participants, none of the target words was actually shown, and they were reduced to guessing on every trial (this task is thus known as a *pseudo-recognition* test).

The participants performed this task either (1) alone, (2) in the presence of two fellow students who watched the proceedings attentively, or (3) in the presence of blindfolded "observers." The blindfolds in the latter, mere presence condition were supposedly to prepare the blindfolded individuals for an experiment in perception, but in reality they were to make it clear to the participants that these individuals could not evaluate them. The researchers were interested in

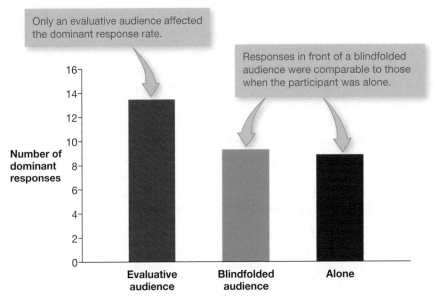

Only an evaluative audience affected the dominant response rate.

Responses in front of a blindfolded audience were comparable to those when the participant was alone.

FIGURE 12.3 Evaluation Apprehension and Social Facilitation Average number of dominant responses made by participants who were responding alone, next to a blindfolded audience (who therefore couldn't monitor or evaluate their performance), or next to an attentive audience (who could evaluate their performance). (Source: Adapted from Cottrell, Wack, Sekerak, & Rittle, 1968.)

how often the participants guessed a dominant word (those they had pronounced 25 times) and how this rate varied across the three conditions. The results, shown in **Figure 12.3**, highlight the importance of evaluation apprehension. Individuals performing in front of an evaluative audience made more dominant responses than those performing alone; those performing in front of a blindfolded audience did not. Thus the audience that could not evaluate what was going on had no effect on performance. This experiment seems to demonstrate conclusively that it is the concern about others as a source of evaluation, not their mere presence, that is responsible for social facilitation. But maybe there is less to this demonstration than meets the eye.

Testing for Mere Presence The experiment just described appears to have included the three conditions necessary to distinguish between the mere presence and evaluation apprehension accounts of social facilitation: an alone condition, a condition with another person merely present, and a condition with a potentially evaluative person present. But appearances can be deceiving. Although participants in the alone condition were alone in an objective sense (no one else was physically present), they may not have been psychologically alone. After all, they were in an experiment, one in which they were asked to perform a strange task. It seems likely that they would feel apprehensive about the prospect of their performance being surreptitiously recorded (which it was!). Thus the alone condition used in this study may not have been a "true" alone condition. To adequately test Zajonc's theory, then, it is essential to create a condition in which participants feel truly alone.

In an ingenious experiment, Hazel Markus (1978) managed to create a true alone condition. When participants arrived individually for the experiment, they were told to go into an adjoining room to wait for the other participants to arrive. While there, they were to put on the necessary attire for the experiment. In particular, they were asked to (1) take off their own shoes, (2) put on a pair of lab socks over their own socks, (3) put on a pair of oversized lab shoes, and (4) put on a similarly oversized lab coat. The participants did all this and waited, in vain, for the "other participants" to arrive. In reality, there were no other participants. After 10 minutes, the experimenter reappeared and stated that the other participants were apparently not coming, and the experiment would have to be scratched. The participants were then instructed to change back into their own clothes.

Unbeknownst to the participants, all of this changing of clothes was surreptitiously observed and timed through a one-way mirror. Markus was interested in how quickly participants could perform the novel tasks of putting on and taking off the unfamiliar lab coat, socks, and shoes, as well as how quickly they could perform the well-learned tasks of taking off and putting on their own, very familiar, shoes. Participants did this in one of three conditions: alone, with another person watching attentively, or in the mere presence of a repairman working on a piece of apparatus with his back to the participant.

Notice how the alone condition in this experiment improves on those used in previous studies. Not only is the subject physically alone, but there is no reason to worry about being observed or evaluated. From the participant's perspective, the experiment has yet to begin, and therefore there is no cause for evaluation apprehension. The subject believes that he or she is both physically and psychologically alone.

Even though the participants did not think they were "performing," Zajonc's theory predicts that they should change their own clothes faster and the novel clothes more slowly when in the mere presence of another person. As shown in **Table 12.1**, that is exactly what happened. Participants took off and put on their own shoes more quickly, and the experimenter's shoes, socks, and coat more slowly, when in the presence of another person—even when the other person had his back turned and was unable to observe. Thus, when a true alone condition is included, an effect of the mere presence of another person can be observed. Note again that the effects were stronger for an attentive audience than for a merely present audience, but that is not a problem for the theory. It just means that evaluation apprehension can add to a person's arousal and thus compound the effect of mere presence. Overall, these results and those of similar investigations (Cottrell et al., 1968; Platania & Moran, 2001; Rajecki, Ickes, Corcoran, & Lenerz, 1977; Schmitt, Gilovich, Goore, & Joseph, 1986) strongly support Zajonc's theory.

TABLE 12.1 Social Facilitation and the Effect of an Audience

The amount of time, in seconds, participants took to change each item of clothing varied based on whether they were changing their own clothing or novel lab clothing and whether they were alone or in the presence of another person who was ignoring them (merely present) or evaluating them (attentive audience).

	Alone	Merely Present Audience	Attentive Audience
Well-Learned Tasks (Own Shoes)	16.5	13.5	11.7
Novel Tasks (Lab Shoes, Socks, and Coat)	28.8	32.7	33.9

Source: Adapted from Markus (1978).

Further Perspectives on Social Facilitation

In light of the research by Zajonc and Markus, it seems safe to say that the mere presence of others is sufficient to increase arousal and thus facilitate performance on well-learned tasks and inhibit performance on novel tasks. At the same time, an interesting and healthy debate continues about *why* the mere presence of others has such effects. Some social psychologists have argued, in fact, that it is not the mere presence of another person that has these effects, but something that always accompanies the awareness of the mere presence of another. They have put forward a **distraction-conflict theory** of social facilitation based on the idea that being aware of another person's presence creates a conflict between attending to that person and attending to the task at hand. They believe that this attentional conflict is arousing, and that *this* arousal underlies the standard social facilitation effects (Baron, 1986; Baron, Moore, & Sanders, 1978; Groff, Baron, & Moore, 1983; Huguet, Galvaing, Monteil, & Dumas, 1999; Sanders, 1981). Thus far, not enough supportive data have been collected to settle the issue (Guerin, 1993). But intriguingly, researchers have shown that nonsocial distractions (for example, being required to perform two tasks simultaneously) can generate effects just like the standard social facilitation effects (Sanders & Baron, 1975).

One hundred years of research on social facilitation has also made it clear that people are complex stimuli and that their presence can have a variety of effects that often overlay the more basic mere presence effects focused on here. People are often very concerned about making a good impression, and this evaluation apprehension can intensify arousal and lead to more pronounced social facilitation effects. At times, however, the presence of others can mask the typical social facilitation effects. If those who are present belittle effort and devalue accomplishment, then performance will be inhibited even on simple tasks. In many work settings, for example, employees have powerful norms against working too hard, and "rate busters" are made to feel the wrath of the group, so that output suffers on even the simplest tasks (Homans, 1965). Similarly, African-American students sometimes put out less effort—and hence don't perform as well—in the presence of other African-Americans in order to avoid "acting white" (Ogbu, 1991; Ogbu & Davis, 2003). And consider Erving Goffman's rather charming example of adolescent boys riding a carousel. When others are present, the boys engage in a variety of behaviors designed to convey "role distance," or lack of interest in the carousel (Goffman, 1961). If such a desire to maintain role distance were to emerge in a performance setting, it would surely impede output, regardless of how energizing the presence of others might be.

Perhaps the most common pattern of responses that runs counter to the social facilitation effects discussed in this section is what social psychologists call **social loafing**, or the tendency to exert less effort when working on a group task in which individual contributions cannot be monitored (Hoeksema-van Orden, Gaillard, & Buunk, 1998; Karau & Williams, 1995; Latané, Williams, & Harkins, 1979; Plaks & Higgins, 2000; Price, Harrison, & Gavin, 2006; Sanna, 1992; Shepperd, 1995; Shepperd & Taylor, 1999; Williams, Harkins, & Latané, 1981). If you and your friends have to move a couch up a flight of stairs, for example, you might be tempted to coast a bit and hope that your friends' more vigorous efforts will get the job done. In these situations, people often loaf because their contributions are not seen as crucial to the success of the effort and because their individual contributions—and hence they themselves—cannot be assessed.

distraction-conflict theory A theory based on the idea that being aware of another person's presence creates a conflict between attending to that person and attending to the task at hand, and that this attentional conflict is arousing and produces social facilitation effects.

social loafing The tendency to exert less effort when working on a group task in which individual contributions cannot be monitored.

Practical Applications

The basic pattern of facilitation of simple tasks and inhibition of complex tasks is reliable enough to warrant some practical advice. Of greatest relevance to student life, perhaps, is the obvious recommendation for how to study. Study alone. When the material is unfamiliar and must be committed to memory, it is best to do so without the arousal and distraction brought on by the presence of others. Study groups may be helpful for reviewing or for dividing up and summarizing vast amounts of material, and groups can be invaluable when some members have information or approaches that the others do not, but the hard work of absorbing and integrating new ideas should be done alone. Then, once the material is assimilated, sitting cheek by jowl with the other students in the examination room should aid performance.

Another potentially important practical application involves the way workspaces might be designed. If the tasks to be accomplished are simple or repetitive (and the workforce is highly motivated), then the setting should be designed so that people are in contact with one another. Such a design reaps the benefits of social facilitation of simple tasks. If the tasks to be performed are challenging and ever-changing, however, it may be wise to give everyone the luxury of privacy. Such a design avoids the costs of social inhibition of performance on complex tasks.

Dominant Responses and Social Facilitation People tend to do better on well-learned tasks but worse on difficult or poorly mastered tasks in the presence of others. Presumably, the children who know the material well will do better on these standardized tests in the presence of other test takers because their dominant responses will be the correct responses. But children who don't know the material well will be more likely to give incorrect answers in the presence of others.

 LOOKING BACK Even the most minimal group situation—the mere presence of a single other person—can influence performance. The presence of others is arousing, and arousal accentuates a person's existing performance tendencies. Easy tasks are made easier, and difficult tasks are made more difficult.

GROUP DECISION MAKING

When people come together in groups, one of the most important things they do is make decisions. Groups that cannot decide what to do or how to act do not function well. They wallow, bicker, and often split apart. It should come as no surprise, then, that social psychologists have spent considerable energy studying how—and how well—groups make decisions (Hinsz, Tindale, & Vollrath, 1997; Kerr, MacCoun, & Kramer, 1996; Laughlin, Hatch, Silver, & Boh, 2006; Levine & Moreland, 1990, 1998; Sommers, 2006).

Much of this research on group decision making has been guided by the assumption that decisions made by groups are typically better than those made by individuals. Many heads are better than one. And indeed, when groups and individuals are presented with problems for which there are precise, factual answers (such as the horse-trading problem discussed in Chapter 8), groups are more likely than the average individual to arrive at the solution (Laughlin, 1988; Laughlin & Ellis, 1986).

When people "come together . . . they may surpass, collectively and as a body, the quality of the few best. . . . When there are many who contribute to the process of deliberation, each can bring his share of goodness and moral prudence."

—Aristotle

Yet in many contexts, group decisions are no better than those rendered by individuals. The key to understanding such contexts is to recognize that although arriving at a best possible solution to a problem may be the *group's* most important goal, it may not be the most important goal for any of the individual group members. Individuals may be more concerned with how they will be judged by everyone else, how they can avoid hurting someone's feelings, how they can dodge responsibility if things go wrong, and so on. When people get together to make group decisions, some predictable social psychological processes unfold that can subvert the stated goal of arriving at the best possible choice.

Groupthink

In informal settings where social harmony is all-important and the costs of making an incorrect decision are not so great, it is hardly surprising that defective decision making sometimes results from group pressures to reach a unanimous decision. But what happens when life and death are literally at stake, and the incentives to "get it right" are high? In those contexts, surely people wouldn't go along with faulty reasoning merely to preserve group harmony or to avoid embarrassment, would they? Yes, they would—and they do.

Irving Janis carefully analyzed a number of decisions made at the very highest levels of government and found evidence of just this sort of calamitous group decision making (Janis, 1972, 1982; see also Esser, 1998). Here are a few of the fiascos Janis looked at:

- The Kennedy administration's attempt to foster the overthrow of Fidel Castro's regime by depositing a group of CIA-trained Cuban refugees on the beaches of Cuba's Bay of Pigs but failing to provide air cover. (The refugees were captured in short order, thus humiliating the United States internationally, both for its role in trying to undermine a sovereign nation and for initially denying its involvement in the affair.)
- The Johnson administration's decision to increase the number of U.S. soldiers fighting in Vietnam. (This policy failed to advance U.S. objectives in the region and substantially increased the number of lives lost.)
- The conclusion by the U.S. naval high command that extra precautions were not needed at Pearl Harbor despite warnings of an imminent attack by the Japanese. (This had severe repercussions on December 7, 1941, the "day of infamy," when the Japanese destroyed U.S. ships at the Pearl Harbor naval base in a surprise attack.)

groupthink A kind of faulty thinking by highly cohesive groups in which the critical scrutiny that should be devoted to the issues at hand is subverted by social pressures to reach consensus.

Janis maintained that these calamitous decisions were made because of **groupthink**, a kind of faulty thinking by highly cohesive groups in which the critical scrutiny that should be devoted to the issues at hand is subverted by social pressures to reach consensus. Other investigators have made the same claim about other disasters, such as the ill-fated launches of the space shuttles *Challenger* and *Columbia* (Esser & Lindoerfer, 1989; Glanz & Schwartz, 2003; see **Box 12.2**).

Symptoms and Sources of Groupthink According to Janis, groupthink is a sort of psychological diminishment characterized by a shallow examination of infor-

BOX 12.2 **FOCUS ON GOVERNMENT**

Groupthink in the Bush Administration

Groupthink seems to have played a role in the miscalculations that plagued the Bush administration's decision to invade Iraq in 2003. A report by the U.S. Senate Intelligence Committee identified groupthink as one factor that led the Bush administration to err so badly in its claim that Iraq possessed weapons of mass destruction (WMD). Specifically, the report concluded that many of the groups involved in assessing the threat posed by Iraq "demonstrated several aspects of groupthink: examining few alternatives, selective gathering of information, pressure to conform within the group or withhold criticism, and collective rationalization" (Select Committee on Intelligence, 2004). The committee also found fault with administration analysts for failing to put in place common safeguards against groupthink, "such as . . . 'devil's advocacy,' and other types of alternative or competitive analysis."

Unfortunately, this tendency by policy-making groups to seek support for existing views rather than subject them to critical scrutiny is sufficiently common that the U.S. military has its own name for the phenomenon—*incestuous amplification*, which *Jane's Defense Weekly* defines as "a condition in warfare where one only listens to those who are already in lock-step agreement, reinforcing set beliefs and creating a situation ripe for miscalculation."

mation, a narrow consideration of alternatives, and a sense of invulnerability and moral superiority (Janis, 1972). Especially under the direction of a strong leader, groups may ignore or reject alternative viewpoints, discourage others from coming forward with other ideas and assessments, and end up believing in the wisdom and moral correctness of their proposed solutions. Thus the very source of a group's potentially superior decision making—the airing of differing opinions and the presentation of varied facts and perspectives—never comes into play (**Figure 12.4**).

The historical record shows that social psychological forces have had a hand in numerous instances of faulty decision making, sometimes with disastrous consequences. Less clear, however, is whether these psychological processes cluster together to produce a recognizable condition of groupthink (Choi & Kim, 1999; Henningsen, Henningsen, Eden, & Cruz, 2006; Turner & Pratkanis, 1998). Do such conditions as cohesiveness, insularity, and high stress tend to occur together, or are they separate variables that tend to inhibit effective decision making? And are the various sources and symptoms of groupthink *essential* ingredients of this sort of faulty decision making? Questions like these have not been adequately resolved, and the evidence gathered to test Janis's thesis has been mixed at best (Aldag & Fuller, 1993; Longley & Pruitt, 1980; McCauley, 1989; Tetlock, Peterson, McGuire, Chang, & Feld, 1992). Nonetheless, his observations have been useful in identifying social factors that can lead to calamitous decisions as well as factors that can improve group decision making.

For example, strong, directive leaders who make their preferences known sometimes intimidate even the most accomplished group members and stifle vigorous discussion (McCauley, 1998). Also, just as Janis contends, at times the issue that must be decided is so stressful that groups seek the reassurance and comfort of premature or illusory consensus. And both strong leaders and the drive to find consensus breed **self-censorship**, or the decision to withhold information or opinions. Janis reports that Arthur Schlesinger, a member of President

self-censorship The tendency to withhold information or opinions in group discussions.

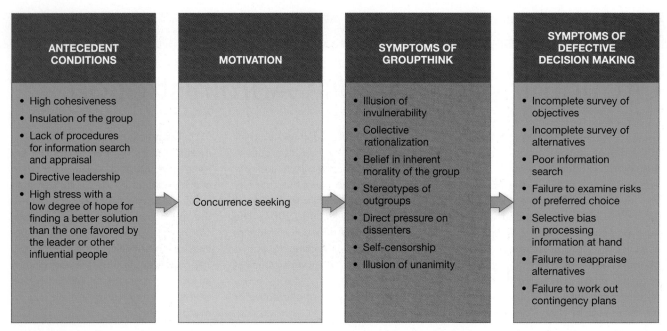

FIGURE 12.4 Elements of Janis's Groupthink Hypothesis Certain conditions lead decision-making groups to be excessively concerned with seeking consensus, which detracts from a full, rational analysis of the existing problem. (Source: Adapted from Janis & Mann, 1977, p. 132.)

Kennedy's inner circle during the Bay of Pigs deliberations, was ever afterward haunted "for having kept so silent during those crucial discussions in the Cabinet Room. . . . I can only explain my failure to do more than raise a few timid questions by reporting that one's impulse to blow the whistle on this nonsense was simply undone by the circumstances of the discussion" (Janis, 1982, p. 39). Some of the participants in that fiasco have written that the pressures to agree with the unsound plan were so great because the group was a newly created one, and the participants were reluctant to step on one another's toes. In contrast, by the time they came together to deliberate over subsequent crises, they had been around the block with one another and were more willing to offer and accept criticism without worrying so much about threatening their relationship with the group.

Preventing Groupthink Even though the theory may be less than precise, Janis's suggestions for how to improve group deliberations have been shown to have merit. Freer, more vigorous discussion is likely to take place, for example, if the leader refrains from making his or her opinions or preferences known at the beginning. Groups can also avoid the tunnel vision and illusion of consensus that Janis describes by making sure the group is not cut off from outside input. Individuals who have not been privy to the early stages of a discussion can provide a fresh perspective as well as put the brakes on any rash actions that might otherwise develop. Finally, a similar safeguard against rash action and unsound argumentation is to designate one person in the group to play devil's advocate—to be given every incentive to name any and all weaknesses in the group's proposed plan of action.

In addition to his analysis of foreign policy fiascos, Janis examined a number of highly successful decisions, including the Kennedy administration's handling of the Cuban missile crisis, and claimed that the deliberations leading to these decisions were not marked by symptoms of groupthink. In the case of the Cuban missile crisis, Janis discovered how John Kennedy and his advisers sought to avoid another fiasco after the Bay of Pigs incident early in his administration. Severely embarrassed by that event, Kennedy took steps to ensure that all policies would be evaluated more thoroughly from then on. He frequently excused himself from the group so as not to constrain the discussion. He brought in outside experts to critique his advisers' analysis and tentative plans, and he appointed specific individuals (his brother, Robert Kennedy, and Theodore Sorensen) to act as devil's advocates. These safeguards seem to have paid off because the negotiations that kept Soviet missiles out of Cuba were one of the enduring highlights of the tragically short Kennedy administration.

Preventing Groupthink John F. Kennedy's cabinet met during the Cuban missile crisis to try to resolve the impasse with the Soviets over Soviet missiles in Cuba. They took steps to avoid groupthink by encouraging vigorous debate and making recommendations based on unbiased analysis.

Groupthink in Other Cultures Groupthink can take different forms in non-Western cultures. The drive toward harmony is greater, for example, in East Asian cultures such as Japan than in Western cultures such as the United States (Nisbett, 2003). Groupthink in places like Japan can be so great, in fact, that even at scientific meetings there is rarely true debate or any other exchange that might appear confrontational or cause anyone to lose face. Japanese scientists who are familiar with Western norms of scientific discourse believe that their own science suffers from not giving ideas a public airing. In fact, Japanese science seems to be underperforming, given the amount of money spent on scientific research in that country (French, 2001). Still, Japanese corporations are in general highly effective, and in some industries they are the most competitive in the world. How is this possible if open and free debate does not take place? Japanese managers have meetings where they discuss policy issues, but these discussions may only appear to be like Western meetings. Nothing is really debated; instead, participants simply nod their approval of the proposal that is brought to them. This behavior sounds like a recipe for disaster, but it turns out that managers typically discuss matters with everyone individually before the meeting to find out their views. The frank exchange goes on before the meeting, consensus is achieved as a result of these individual encounters, and the larger meeting is then little more than a rubber stamp. Although this procedure of one-on-one discussion and consensus finding may be different from procedures to improve group decision making in Western organizations, it appears to be helpful in preventing groupthink.

Group Decisions: Risky or Conservative?

Implicit in all the concern over avoiding groupthink is the suspicion that groups are often too rash—that decisions made by groups are often riskier and less thoroughly thought out than those made by individuals. But popular culture tends to hold precisely the opposite belief—namely, that groups abhor risk and tend to adopt middle-of-the-road solutions. Thus, in the United States at least, we tend to celebrate the swashbuckling CEO or politician who breaks free of institutional inertia and "takes chances" and "gets things done." So which is it?

Do groups tend to make riskier or more risk-averse decisions than individuals? What type of error do we invite—risky or conservative—when we turn over a difficult decision to a group?

An MIT graduate student, James Stoner, put this very question to the test in 1961 by having participants make decisions about various choice dilemmas. That is, they had to render advice to a set of hypothetical individuals considering various risky courses of action. In one scenario, for example, an engineer had to decide whether to stay in his current job, which paid a moderate salary, or take a position with a new firm in which, if successful, he could earn a great deal more money. Should he stick with the security of his current firm or take a gamble on the new job? Here is the dilemma in full (adapted from Stoner, 1961):

> Mr. A., an electrical engineer who is married and has one child, has been working for a large electronics corporation since graduating from college five years ago. He is assured of a lifetime job with a modest, though adequate, salary, and liberal pension benefits upon retirement. On the other hand, it is very unlikely that his salary will increase much before he retires. While attending a convention, Mr. A. is offered a job with a small, newly founded company that has a highly uncertain future. The new job would pay more to start and would offer the possibility of a share in the ownership if the company survived the competition of the larger firms.
>
> Imagine that you are advising Mr. A. Listed below are several probabilities or odds of the new company's proving financially sound.
>
> Please check the lowest probability that you would consider acceptable to make it worthwhile for Mr. A to take the new job.
> ___ The chances are 1 in 10 that the company will prove financially sound.
> ___ The chances are 3 in 10 that the company will prove financially sound.
> ___ The chances are 5 in 10 that the company will prove financially sound.
> ___ The chances are 7 in 10 that the company will prove financially sound.
> ___ The chances are 9 in 10 that the company will prove financially sound.
> ___ Place a check here if you think Mr. A should not take the new job no matter what the probability.

As you can see, participants were asked to give their advice by specifying the likelihood of success that would be necessary for the engineer to decide to take the job with the new company. If the new company was sure to succeed, clearly the engineer should take it because it would pay more money; if it was sure to fail, the engineer should stay put. Participants had to decide what the new firm's chances had to be to make the switch worthwhile.

Stoner's participants rendered such decisions for 12 different choice dilemmas. First they did so individually, and then they met with other participants to discuss each dilemma and arrive at a consensus answer. Stoner then compared the group odds with the average odds specified by each individual. He expected the group to insist on higher odds of success (that is, to make a more conservative recommendation) than the average odds specified individually by each group member. He found just the opposite. The groups tended to recommend riskier courses of action than did the individual group members. Stoner, and many after him, concluded that groups tend to make riskier decisions than individuals, a pattern that came to be known as the **risky shift** (Stoner, 1961; Wallach, Kogan, & Bem, 1962). And the group members weren't just feigning boldness to appear courageous to everyone else. When participants were subsequently asked to render new *individual*

risky shift The tendency for groups to make riskier decisions than individuals would.

decisions, the group discussion had left its mark. These later individual recommendations tended to be riskier than what these same individuals had recommended originally.

But as with the findings on social facilitation, the initial, clear picture of whether groups make riskier decisions than individuals soon became murky. Several follow-ups to Stoner's work found decisions made by groups that were more cautious or "risk averse" than those made by individuals. Groups sometimes insist on greater odds of success, in other words, before they are willing to recommend a risky course of action. Indeed, such a result was even found on two of Stoner's 12 original choice dilemmas. But the notion that groups sometimes make riskier decisions than individuals and sometimes make less risky decisions is hardly satisfying. Can't social psychologists tell us when groups tend to be risky and when they tend to be more cautious?

"It's agreed, then, that we move forward on the philodendron."

The key to discovering whether there is any higher-order clarity is to examine, in detail, the kind of issues that tend to elicit conservative group decisions and the kind that tend to induce risky decisions. You've already seen an example of an issue for which group discussion tends to make everyone riskier. Now consider a choice dilemma for which group discussion tends to make everyone more cautious (adapted from Stoner, 1961):

> Mr. C., a married man with a 7-year-old son, can provide his family with all the necessities of life, but few of the luxuries. Mr. C.'s mother recently died, leaving his son (that is, her grandson) a small inheritance she had accumulated by scrimping and saving, making regular donations to a savings account at her local bank. Mr. C. would like to invest his son's inheritance in the stock market. He is thinking about investing in a group of "blue-chip" stocks and bonds that should earn a 6 percent return on investment with reasonable certainty. However, he recently received a reliable tip about a new biotech company that has excited all the venture capitalists. If things go as well as predicted, he could more than quadruple his son's investment in the company within the first year; if things do not go well, however, he could lose the money and join the long list of those who have been burned by investing in high-tech start-ups.

How does this example differ from the earlier one? Many people report that their first reaction to the two scenarios is very different. In the first, stay-or-switch-jobs dilemma, they find themselves thinking, "Go for it. Don't be stuck in a dead-end job all your life; you'll regret it later." In contrast, when reading the second scenario, they find themselves thinking, "Not so fast! You shouldn't put your son's (and his grandmother's) legacy at risk."

Group Polarization

Researchers hypothesized that group discussion has the effect of making people more inclined to go in the direction they are already predisposed to go. If the issue is one that prompts most people to be inclined toward risk, talking it over with other members of a group may make everyone even more risk seeking. If the issue is one that prompts most people to be reluctant to take a chance, talking it over group polarization The tendency for group decisions to be more extreme than those made by individuals. Whatever way the individuals are leaning, group discussion tends to make them lean further in that direction.

may make everyone even more conservative. Rather than an overall risky shift, in other words, there is a **group polarization** effect. That is, group decisions tend to be more *extreme* than those made by individuals. Whatever way the majority of the individuals are leaning, group discussion tends to make them lean further in that direction (Moscovici & Zavalloni, 1969; Myers & Bishop, 1971; Zuber, Crott, & Werner, 1992).

The same result holds true even when groups discuss issues that have nothing to do with risk. In one study, for example, French students expressed their opinions about General Charles de Gaulle and about Americans, first individually and then again after having discussed them in groups. The results? Their initially positive sentiments toward de Gaulle became even more positive, and their initially negative sentiments toward Americans became even more negative (Moscovici & Zavalloni, 1969). It appears that we are more likely to hear the term *ugly American* from a group of foreigners than from a collection of individual foreigners.

But why does group discussion lead to more extreme inclinations by group members? Why don't the individuals in the group simply conform to the group average, with the result that group discussion does not tend to move the group in one direction or the other? Subsequent research indicates that two causes work in concert to produce group polarization. One involves the persuasiveness of the information brought up during group discussion; the other involves people's tendency to try to claim the "right" position in the distribution of opinions within the group. Let's consider each explanation in turn.

The "Persuasive Arguments" Account When trying to decide whether to pursue a risky or conservative course of action, people consider the different arguments in favor of each course. It stands to reason that when people are predisposed to take chances in a given situation, they can think of more and better arguments in favor of risk. When people are predisposed to play it safe, in contrast, they can think of more and better arguments that favor caution. But any one person is unlikely to think of *all* the arguments in favor of one alternative or the other. Thus, when the issue is discussed by the group, each person is likely to be exposed to new arguments. This expanded pool of arguments, in turn, is likely to be skewed in favor of risk when the people are already predisposed toward risk on the issue in question but skewed in favor of caution when people are already predisposed to play it safe.

The net result, then, is that group discussion tends to expose the average person to even more arguments in favor of the position that the average person was already inclined to take. This exposure only serves to strengthen those initial inclinations, and group polarization is the inevitable result. This explanation suggests that personal, face-to-face discussion is not necessary to produce group polarization. All that should be required is exposure to the pool of arguments that true group discussion tends to elicit. Several studies have tested this idea by having participants read the arguments of other group members in private so that they are exposed to the arguments without knowing who in the group might have advanced them. In support of the persuasive arguments interpretation, these studies have tended to show that reading others' arguments is sufficient to produce group polarization (Burnstein & Vinokur, 1973; Burnstein, Vinokur, & Trope, 1973; Clark, Crockett, & Archer, 1971).

The "Social Comparison" Interpretation Although exposure to the full pool of arguments is sufficient to induce group polarization, other social psychological processes also give rise to the same outcome. Foremost among them is the very human tendency to compare ourselves with everyone else. "Am I as smart as most people here?" "Do my neighbors all drive better cars than I do?" "Am I getting as much out of life as everyone else?" Recall from Chapter 3 Leon Festinger's (1954) social comparison theory, which argues that when objective standards for self-evaluation are not available, people judge themselves in relation to others. An extensive body of research inspired by Festinger's theory has shown that such comparisons are extremely common, are often automatic (Mussweiler, 2003), and have important consequences (Suls & Wheeler, 2000; Wood, 1989).

Consider how these comparisons might lead to group polarization. When evaluating an issue for which people are inclined to take risks (a career choice early in life), people are likely to think they are more tolerant of risk than the average person. In this case, riskiness is valued, and people like to think of themselves as having more than an average amount of a valued trait. When considering an issue for which people are inclined to be cautious (investing money that belongs to a beloved relative), however, most people are likely to think they are more risk averse than the average person. People tend to think, in other words, that they are farther out on the correct side of the opinion distribution on most issues.

But what happens when all of the individuals in a group are inclined to make the same choice—say, a risky choice—and are also inclined to think of themselves as more likely than average to take risks? Many of them will find, inevitably, that their tolerance of risk is closer to average than they thought—perhaps even below average. This realization leads some individuals to attempt to show that they are in fact more risk tolerant than average. The group as a whole, then, becomes a bit riskier on those issues for which a somewhat risky approach initially seemed warranted. Similarly, the group would become a bit more conservative on those issues for which a somewhat cautious approach seemed warranted. In other words, the desire to distinguish oneself from others by expressing a more extreme opinion in the "right" direction leads predictably to the group polarization effect. As one journalist put it, "People are always trying to outdo one another; if everyone in a group agrees that men are jerks, then someone in the group is bound to argue that they're assholes" (Kolbert, 2009).

This interpretation can be tested by doing just the opposite of what was done to test the persuasive arguments account: expose people to everyone else's positions without conveying the content of any of the arguments for or against one position or another. As predicted, when people are told only about others' positions and not the basis of those positions, the group polarization effect is observed (Teger & Pruitt, 1967). Notably, the group polarization effect in this experiment was weaker than usual, as would be expected if both persuasive arguments and social comparison contribute to the effect.

Valuing Risk One more piece of the puzzle needs to be explained. Social psychologists have provided perfectly satisfactory accounts of why group discussion tends to intensify group members' initial leanings. But why do group members tend to lean so often in the risky direction? Recall that in Stoner's original investigation, a shift toward greater risk was observed on 10 of the 12 scenarios, a predisposition toward risk that has been replicated in countless subsequent studies.

The logic of both the persuasive arguments and social comparison interpretations leads to the inescapable inference that people—or, at least, the American college students who have made up the bulk of the participants in these studies—must typically value risk taking over caution. It is not hard to show that this is the case. When American participants read descriptions of people, some described as risk takers and others not, they assume that the risk takers possess a variety of favorable traits such as intelligence, confidence, and creativity as well (Jellison & Riskind, 1970). Also, when participants are asked to specify the level of risk they are comfortable with in a given situation, the level of risk the average person is comfortable with, and the level of risk the person they *most admire* is comfortable with, the latter is assumed to be comfortable with the greatest risk (Levinger & Schneider, 1969).

The high value Americans place on risk is typically attributed to the broader culture of the country. The hard-edged capitalism that is such an integral feature of U.S. life requires an active encouragement of risk and a willingness to take on the possibility of failure. (Note that two-thirds of all new businesses in the United States go under within a year.) Thus Americans celebrate the stories of people like J. C. Penney, who went bankrupt twice before making his fortune, or Ted Turner, who bet the ranch on his vision of a global, 24-hour television news service (CNN). Some have even argued (in what may be a shaky contention) that the American love affair with risk is part of our biological makeup. Because America is a nation of immigrants, the argument goes, we inherited the genes of those who took a chance on life in the New World—a gamble not taken by those who had a cautious outlook (Farley, 1986).

By this logic, a risky shift after group discussion should occur more often among U.S. participants than among participants in other cultures that do not value risk as highly. And that is indeed the case. In studies conducted in Uganda and Liberia, the recommendations made by participants in response to the choice dilemma scenarios tended to be more cautious than those made by U.S. participants, and the recommendations did not become riskier after group discussion (Carlson & Davis, 1971; Gologor, 1977).

Polarization in Modern Life

How do the phenomena just discussed affect group decision making on controversial issues in modern life? What would a group of university administrators concerned about declining support for affirmative action think about affirmative action policies after a group discussion? How would a group of people who are alarmed about the rise of radical Islam feel about the proper policies to combat Islamic terrorism after talking things over together?

Note that these issues are unlike those typically studied in the research literature on group polarization. They are not the sort for which people generally lean in the same direction. They are, after all, contentious public policy questions, so there are strong advocates for all sides on each issue. The movement toward the extremes found in the group polarization literature depends on most people leaning in a general direction—toward riskiness on one issue, caution on another. It might seem, then, that there is no basis for predicting what effect discussion might have on the group members' attitudes about public policy disputes.

But here appearances are deceiving. Although the issues under discussion are indeed subject to contentious debate, the people most likely to meet in a group to discuss them are those who share the same general perspective, concerns, and preferences. They would therefore tend to lean in the same direction on the issues. Thus the lessons of group polarization would indeed apply. When homogeneous groups come together, their discussions are likely to lead to even stronger attitudes than the ones the group members came in with (Schulz-Hardt, Frey, Luthgens, & Moscovici, 2000).

Is this a problem? At the very least, group homogeneity robs the group of one of its greatest potential strengths—the give and take of *different* perspectives and sources of information that allow the best course of action to be discerned (Surowieki, 2004). Heterogeneous groups tend to outperform homogeneous groups when it comes to making the most effective decisions. (Note, however, that this effect is not as strong as might be supposed, in part because of a tendency for group members to talk about information they *share*—information that is often easier to talk about and that leads to more congenial discussion—rather than information unique to one person or another; Kelly & Karau, 1999; Postmes, Spears, & Cihangir, 2001; Stasser, 1999; Stasser & Titus, 1985). This effect was anticipated by the founding fathers of the United States, who spoke passionately about the evils of opinion homogeneity and took steps (the much-praised checks and balances) to guard against the tyranny of the majority. Their view, strongly validated by subsequent social psychological research, was that deliberative bodies function best when they provide for the airing of competing views.

To the modern mind, group polarization may be particularly troubling because of the possibility that contemporary life may encourage dialogue primarily among like-minded individuals. At one level, much of the world is more heterogeneous and multicultural than it has ever been, and more varied voices are heard in public debate. But at the same time, it has become easier and easier to screen our inputs to hear only those voices we want to hear. For our nightly news, we can choose from the cacophony of niche programming (geared toward those with conservative views or liberal views) and select those programs offering the opinions we already hold. Rather than reading a metropolitan newspaper serving the diverse interests of a broad community, we can carefully tailor the information and opinions we receive from the Internet to fit our preexisting preferences. And rather than coming together to discuss the issues of the day with a broad spectrum of the general public, we can sit at home and discuss them with a set of like-minded individuals who contribute to the same blog or are all signed up to the same Internet chat group (McKenna & Bargh, 1998). Research has shown, for example, that more than 80 percent of the links on the most popular political websites and blogs are to other, like-minded sites—conservative blog to conservative blog, liberal website to liberal website (Sunstein, 2007).

Such a restricted range of inputs would be problem enough even if it only reinforced our preexisting beliefs. But the literature on group polarization makes it clear that group discussion among like-minded individuals doesn't just reinforce existing opinion; it makes it more extreme. Thus modern communication technologies such as the Internet may incubate extremism. The various hate groups that make extensive use of Internet communication were certainly not created by the Internet. Nevertheless, this mode of communication, and the group polarization it fosters, might well feed such extremist views.

"The differences of opinion, and the jarrings of parties . . . promote deliberation and circumspection; and serve to check the excesses of the majority."

—Alexander Hamilton, *The Federalist*

LOOKING BACK Groupthink can lead to defective decision making since people in highly cohesive groups may censor their reservations, ignore or reject alternative viewpoints, and succumb to ingroup pressures. To avoid this problem, the group should encourage the airing of all viewpoints, leaders should refrain from stating their opinions at the outset, and someone should be designated to play devil's advocate. Group decision making can also lead to group polarization, in which group decisions tend to be more extreme than those made by individuals due to the force of persuasive arguments and social comparison. To avoid the growing polarization in the modern world and to promote well-reasoned decisions, it is important to have a dialogue among diverse groups of people and to air a full range of opinions.

LEADERSHIP AND POWER

People in cultures that value egalitarianism, such as the United States and Canada, often like to think that much of their group life is nonhierarchical and has no real leaders or positions of rank. Sure, there are presidents of sororities and student bodies, captains of fire departments and football teams, and CEOs of charitable foundations and Fortune 500 companies. But to many people it seems that often in group life there are no leaders; each individual is granted the same status and enjoys equal voice and power.

Nothing could be further from the truth. Social hierarchies are a natural part of group life, as are leaders and people who are led. When children as young as age 2 join their first groups—their packs of friends in preschool—some quickly rise to the top rungs of status, while others do not. When middle-school children form groups of friends at summer camp, they quickly identify the leaders and those who are more likely to follow (Savin-Williams, 1977). Even in one of the most egalitarian groups in society, the college dorm, within the first week of living together hallmates quickly agree on who are the leaders on their floor—and who are not (Anderson, John, Keltner, & Kring, 2001).

Groups readily evolve into hierarchies because having leaders helps solve some of the difficulties inherent in group living (Anderson & Brown, 2010). The allocation of resources can give rise to intense conflict between group members—and a social hierarchy offers rules for dividing up resources that, although often unfair (those on top get more), are one means of avoiding or at least decreasing that strife. Group decision making can sometimes be unmanageably complex—and hierarchies provide a shared notion of who guides group discussion and how decisions are made. The collective actions in which groups engage demand that individual behaviors be coordinated—and having leaders helps enable more effective collective action. Finally, group life often requires that individuals sacrifice their own interests to benefit the group—and leaders (charismatic leaders in particular) can help motivate selfless action.

Given that leaders and hierarchies are an inevitable part of group life, at least two important questions arise: Who rises to positions of leadership? And what happens to leaders once in positions of power? Let's consider what the research literature has to say about each.

Who Becomes a Leader?

How do people rise to positions of leadership within social hierarchies? This question may be of more than passing interest to you, particularly in light of the many advantages that people in the upper echelons enjoy. For example, as people rise in socioeconomic status (SES)—that is, their level of education and wealth and occupational prestige—they are less likely to suffer from depression and anxiety and are more likely to enjoy improved health and a greater life expectancy (Adler et al., 1994; Williams & Collins, 1995).

So who tends to rise to the top in groups? Is it survival of the fittest? The strongest? The most cunning? The influential Italian philosopher Niccolò Machiavelli offered his own hypotheses in his book, *The Prince*, the most influential book ever written on the nature of leadership. His thesis was that people rise to positions of leadership by being deceptive, by ruthlessly pitting competitors against one another, and by coercion, fear, and manipulation rather than affection and honesty (Machiavelli, 1532/2003).

Fortunately, social psychological studies of how people rise through the ranks have proved Machiavelli wrong. One important determinant of leadership is expertise and skill relevant to the goals of the group; there is no substitute for having specific talents that enable groups to achieve their specific goals (Anderson & Brown, 2010; French & Raven, 1959). The scientist with new insights into sequencing DNA is likely to rise in a biotech firm; the basketball player who has mastered all the subtle skills that make teams better—the timely pass, the well-positioned screen, defensive help, or clutch shot—is more likely to become captain. Cameron Anderson and Gavin Kilduff have found that groups tend to quickly choose as leaders those individuals who demonstrate knowledge and skill in tasks central to the group's identity (Anderson & Kilduff, 2009). When our leaders have the knowledge and skill that enable better group performance, we benefit as individuals.

Of course, leadership is not based on expertise, knowledge, and technical skill alone. Successful groups are cohesive; they function smoothly together, and the whole is greater than the sum of the parts. Thus individuals who have the social skills to build strong, cooperative relations among group members also increase their chances of rising to positions of leadership. In summer camps, the more socially dynamic, outgoing children tend to become leaders (Savin-Williams, 1977). In fraternities, the more humorous, playful members who are adept at telling stories assume positions of leadership (Keltner, Young, Heerey, Oemig, &

Power and Intimidation High-power individuals often feel less constrained by social rules about appropriate behavior than do low-power individuals. Lyndon Johnson approaches Senator Theodore Green more closely than is socially acceptable, touches his arm, and leans in close to his face as he seeks to intimidate him into voting the way Johnson wants him to.

Monarch, 1998). In college dorms and in social groups on college campuses, the highly extraverted individuals, who are socially engaged and adept at building and maintaining relationships, quickly gain respect and status from their peers (Anderson et al., 2001). In the workplace, highly extraverted individuals tend to acquire positions of leadership (Judge, Bono, Hies, & Gerhardt, 2002), and emotionally intelligent individuals—those who can read the moods and needs of others—make more effective managers (Côté & Miners, 2006). Even in our close primate relatives, the socially skilled chimpanzees and bonobos who build strong alliances, negotiate conflicts between subordinates, and ensure just allocations of resources are the ones who acquire and maintain elevated positions of rank in their primate hierarchies (de Waal, 1986).

Finally, alongside expertise and social skills, an individual who can provide rewards to the group is more likely to rise to positions of leadership. Empirical studies find that individuals who selflessly share resources with others are actually more likely to rank highly in social hierarchies (for example, Anderson & Brown, 2010; Willer, 2009). This tendency to grant authority to the more generous group members works to the benefit of the group as a whole.

What Is Power?

As people assume leadership positions, they experience many things: increased wealth and prestige, the respect of colleagues, more responsibilities at work, the challenges of managing individuals in groups, and that great intangible that so many in history have lusted after—power. And with power, a person's behavior is likely to change in many ways, some of them not at all obvious.

To understand the influence of power on social behavior, it is important to define power more carefully. **Power** is typically defined as the ability to control one's own outcomes and those of others and the freedom to act (Fiske, 1993; Kelley & Thibaut, 1978). Power is related to three other kinds of social rank— status, authority, and dominance—but it is not synonymous with them. **Status** is the outcome of an evaluation of attributes that produces differences in respect and prominence, which in part determines an individual's leadership position and power within a group (French & Raven, 1959; Kemper, 1991). But it is possible to have power without status (for example, the corrupt politician) and status without relative power (for example, a religious leader in a slow-moving line at the Department of Motor Vehicles). **Authority** is power that derives from institutionalized roles or arrangements or formalized positions within a hierarchy (Weber, 1947). But power, of course, can exist in the absence of formal roles (for example, within informal social groups). **Dominance** is behavior enacted with the goal of acquiring or demonstrating power. Yet power can be attained without any attempt to establish dominance (as with leaders who attain their positions through their efforts to instill goodwill in the group and benefit the group).

How Does Power Influence Behavior?

Much of human history, it seems, has been characterized by astonishing abuses of power. Consider the horrifying genocides perpetrated by despotic leaders—the likes of Hitler, Stalin, Mao Zedong, Pol-Pot, Idi Amin, and Saddam Hussein. Consider also the much less horrifying but still troublesome impulsive actions

power The ability to control our own outcomes and those of others; the freedom to act.

status The outcome of an evaluation of attributes that produces differences in respect and prominence, which in part determines an individual's power within a group.

authority Power that derives from institutionalized roles or arrangements.

dominance Behavior enacted with the goal of acquiring or demonstrating power.

of so many leaders—Bill Clinton's reputation-ruining affair with intern Monica Lewinsky, Dominique Strauss-Kahn's boorish behavior toward so many women, famed basketball coach Bobby Knight's tendency to abuse his players (and members of the press). And then there are the outrageous excesses of Hollywood celebrities and record-industry stars covered so assiduously by the tabloid press. This impulsive, often immoral side to power is reflected in time-honored sayings: "Power corrupts." "Money [a source of power] is the root of all evil." And it begs for a social psychological explanation.

The **approach/inhibition theory** of power offers one account of how power can lead to this sort of behavior (Keltner, Gruenfeld, & Anderson, 2003; Keltner, Van Kleef, Chen, & Kraus, 2008). If, as noted earlier, power involves a lack of constraint and the freedom to act as one wishes, when you experience elevated power you should be less concerned about the evaluations of others and more inclined to engage in approach-related behavior to satisfy your goals and desires (Guinote, 2007). In contrast, reduced power is associated with increased constraint and a vulnerability to the actions of others. As a result, the experience of reduced power should make a person more vigilant and careful in making judgments and decisions and more inhibited in social behavior. Experiences of elevated power, in effect, give the green light to the pursuit of an individual's goals and desires. Reduced power is more like a yellow light: caution is in order.

The approach/inhibition theory of power yields two central hypotheses. The first concerns the influence of power on how people perceive others. High-power individuals, inclined to go after their own goals, are predicted to be a little less systematic and careful in how they judge other people (Brauer, Chambres, Niedenthal, & Chatard-Pannetier, 2004; Vescio, Snyder, & Butz, 2003). In keeping with this hypothesis, high-power individuals are more likely to thoughtlessly stereotype others, rather than carefully attending to individuating information (Fiske, 1993; Goodwin, Gubin, Fiske, & Yzerbyt, 2000; Neuberg & Fiske, 1987; see also Vescio, Snyder, & Butz, 2003). They are less accurate judges of others' emotions (Gonzaga, Keltner, & Ward, 2008). This may be one reason that males, who on average have disproportionate power in the world, tend to be a bit less accurate than females in judging expressive behavior (Henley & LaFrance, 1984; LaFrance, Henley, Hall, & Halberstadt, 1997; but see also Hall, 1984).

Perhaps the most dramatic demonstration of the empathy failures associated with elevated power was provided by Joseph Magee and his colleagues (Magee, Galinsky, Inesi, & Gruenfeld, 2006). These investigators first induced people to feel relatively powerful or powerless by having them recall a time when they exerted control over another person or when they were controlled by someone else. Participants then performed a simple perspective-taking task: they were asked to draw the letter *E* on their forehead so that someone across from them could read it. This task requires the participant to take the other person's perspective and draw the *E* in reverse. As you can see in **Figure 12.5**, participants feeling a surge of power were much less likely to spontaneously draw the *E* in a way that took the other person's perspective. Power reduces the ability to empathize.

The influence of power on social perception can have unfortunate consequences. Theresa Vescio and her colleagues, for example, have found that powerful men who stereotype female employees by focusing exclusively on their weaknesses tend to devote fewer resources to those employees (Vescio, Gervais, Snyder, & Hoover, 2005), evaluate female employees more negatively in masculine contexts, and anticipate less success by female employees than by male employees (Vescio,

approach/inhibition theory A theory that maintains that high-power individuals are inclined to go after their goals and make quick judgments, whereas low-power individuals are more likely to constrain their behavior and attend to others carefully.

"Power is the ultimate aphrodisiac."

—Henry Kissinger

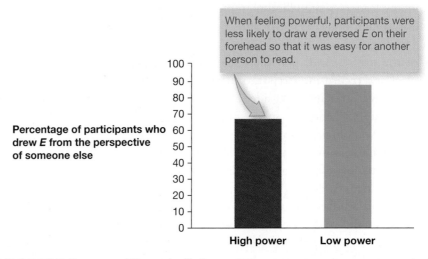

FIGURE 12.5 Power and Empathy Failures Power diminishes our capacity to take the perspective of others. (Source: Magee, Galinsky, Inesi, & Gruenfeld, 2006.)

Snyder, & Butz, 2003). In a similar vein, the experience of power leads high-prejudice whites to focus to a greater extent on the weaknesses of black employees relative to other employees (Vescio, Gervais, Heidenreich, & Snyder, 2006).

Are there costs to the heightened vigilance that low-power individuals maintain as they carefully attend to others? Indeed there are. The experience of reduced power makes people less flexible in their thought and less able to shift their attention to meet different demands of the task at hand (Smith & Trope, 2006). For example, in a series of studies, Pamela Smith and her colleagues induced people to feel elevated power or diminished power by priming them with low- or high-power words (*obey*, *dominate*) or having them recall an experience of low or high power (Smith, Jostmann, Galinsky, & van Dijk, 2008). Participants then worked on a variety of cognitive tasks. In one task, participants saw different words flashed in a sequence and were asked to determine whether a current word on the screen matched the word presented two trials earlier. In another, the Stroop task, participants had to name the color of the ink in which a word was written ("sedan")—a task made more difficult on trials in which the word itself referred to a different color ("blue"). Performance on these tasks requires considerable cognitive flexibility and control. In the Stroop task, for example, the participant must ignore the meaning of the word when naming the color of the ink in which it is written. As predicted, the individuals randomly assigned to feel relatively powerless proved less effective in performing these cognitive tasks. The vigilant and narrowed focus that comes with a sense of reduced power diminishes an individual's ability to think flexibly and creatively (**Figure 12.6**).

A second core hypothesis of approach/inhibition theory is that power should make people behave in disinhibited (less constrained) and at times more inappropriate ways. That is, do you think that only CEOs, politicians, and rock stars exhibit sexually inappropriate behavior? Think again. Social psychologists have found that just giving people the faintest sniff of power—for example, by having them recall an experience when they had power or having them read power-related words (that is, priming people with ideas of power)—leads them to act in sexually assertive and potentially problematic ways. Dispositionally high-power individuals or individuals who are primed with feelings of power are more likely

FIGURE 12.6 You Be the Subject: Strike the Pose of Power

Alpha female and male primates at your local zoo are well known for their power displays—chest pounding and physical expansion to show greater power; cowering and postural contraction to show submissiveness. Using the body to signal leadership and rank within social hierarchies is not restricted to our primate relatives; it's seen regularly in human life, too. We express leadership and power through displays of increased physical size, including expanding the chest and shoulders and raising the arms over the head. And we express weakness and low rank by shrinking—caving in our chests and constricting our shoulders to make our bodies small.

Can you become more powerful by striking a pose? Dana Carney and her colleagues think so (Carney, Cuddy, & Yap, 2010). Carney and her colleagues asked whether participants who assumed high- or low-power poses would experience some of the qualities of power discussed so far. In one study, participants were hooked up to physiological recording devices on their arm and leg and were directed to assume either two high-power postures or two low-power postures for 1 minute each. (They were told to hold these postures to eliminate error in the physiological measurements.) Holding the body in the high-power postures led to increases in testosterone levels, a hormone known to increase dominant behaviors and aggression. Holding the body in the low-power postures, in contrast, increased levels of cortisol in participants, a stress hormone that increases vigilant and inhibited behavior and is known to be activated in submissive individuals. It also changed their approach to risk: participants who held their bodies in a high-power posture were much more likely to take a chance on gambling away money.

Try adopting one of the power displays depicted in these photos. After holding the posture on the left for a while, do you feel slightly more powerful and authoritative?

to touch others and approach them closely, to have sexual ideas running through their minds, to feel attraction for a stranger, to overestimate other people's sexual interest in them, and to flirt in an overly forward fashion (Bargh, Raymond, Pryor, & Strack, 1995; Kuntsman & Maner, 2011; Rudman & Borgida, 1995). In one survey of 1,261 employees, the higher an individual's rank in the organization, the more likely he or she was to report having had sexual affairs when married (Lammers, Stapel, & Galinsky, 2011). Power is indeed the ultimate aphrodisiac (**Box 12.3**).

In contrast, low-power individuals tend to inhibit themselves in a variety of ways (for example, Guinote, Judd, & Brauer, 2002). Individuals with little power often constrict their posture and dampen their expressive behavior

BOX 12.3 FOCUS ON BUSINESS

Power, Profligacy, and Accountability

In 2001 and 2002, Enron, an energy-trading company based in Houston, Texas, collapsed in spectacular fashion. Once one of the most lauded companies in the world, it proceeded to lose billions of dollars in stockholders' assets and had to lay off thousands of workers, largely due to fraudulent accounting practices. Most emblematic of the Enron managers who exhibited corruption, greed, and immorality was Jeffrey Skilling.

Fresh from earning an MBA from Harvard University, Skilling was hired at Enron and saw himself as the company visionary, specializing in creating new energy markets. He was aggressive, brash, and out of control. He shouted profanities at financial analysts who questioned his proposals. He took his favorite employees on outrageous vacations—in one, he and his friends trashed expensive SUVs in the Australian outback. He frequented Enron parties with strippers and eventually divorced his wife to marry his secretary, whom he quickly promoted to a new job with an annual salary of $600,000. He had difficulties

with alcohol. Eventually, his reckless, deceptive business practices took their toll and helped fuel the Enron demise.

One way to understand the Enron collapse is to consider the context and culture of the firm and how it encouraged the brash, reckless, and illegal practices that led to the company's downfall. A similar culture was said to exist in many of the multinational banks and Wall Street investment firms whose actions led to the severe recession of 2008. It is a culture that feeds the sense of power and the feeling of being a "master of the universe" (Wolfe, 1987). Institutions that encourage such feelings offer a valuable lesson about the perils of unchecked power and its disinhibiting effects.

A different approach to trying to understand the actions of Skilling, his colleagues at Enron, and some of their peers in the banking industry is to think about the kinds of people who actively pursue positions of power and how their drive for power might make them more likely to act so greedy or reckless. David Winter and his colleagues took this approach.

They used college students' interpretations of the ambiguous social situations portrayed in Thematic Apperception Test scenes to measure the students' need for power (Winter, 1973, 1988; Winter & Barenbaum, 1985). They found that the students with a high need for power were more likely to become officers of their dorms, fraternities, and university organizations, and they were more likely to seek high-power careers—for example, in the law. These students are also more likely to engage in profligate, disinhibited behaviors reminiscent of Jeffrey Skilling's reckless actions: they are more likely to gamble, drink, and seek one-night stands.

Winter and his colleagues also documented an important factor that constrains the disinhibiting effects of power: accountability. Accountability refers to the condition in which one individual feels responsible to others. When individuals with a high need for power experience life events that enhance accountability—for example, having children—they are less likely to engage in profligate behaviors like gambling or drinking.

(Ellyson & Dovidio, 1985). Low-power individuals tend to refrain from speaking up: they inhibit their speech and clam up and withdraw during group interactions, thus depriving the group of important information and alternative perspectives (Holtgraves & Lasky, 1999; Hosman, 1989; Moreland & Levine, 1989).

Perhaps most unsettling are studies showing that elevated power is associated with increased antisocial behavior. For example, high-power individuals are more likely to violate politeness-related communication norms: they are more likely to interrupt, speak out of turn, and act rudely at work (DePaulo & Friedman, 1998; Pearson & Porath, 1999). And consider a study in which two low-power fraternity members and two high-power members were brought to the laboratory and asked to tease each other by making up nicknames and telling amusing stories about one another (**Figure 12.7**). Although teasing can be a harmless way for friends to pass the time, in this study high-power fraternity members teased low-power targets in more aggressive and humiliating ways, whereas low-power fraternity members were quite restrained in how they

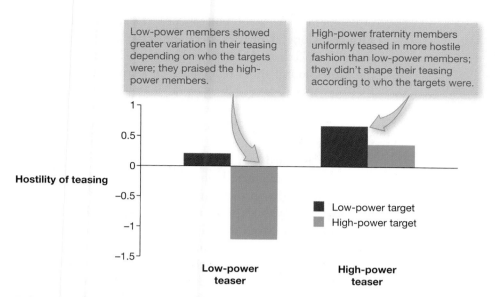

Low-power members showed greater variation in their teasing depending on who the targets were; they praised the high-power members.

High-power fraternity members uniformly teased in more hostile fashion than low-power members; they didn't shape their teasing according to who the targets were.

FIGURE 12.7 An Approach/Inhibition Theory of Power and the Dynamics of Teasing The approach/inhibition theory of power holds that high-power individuals are more impulsive in their behavior, whereas low-power individuals are more likely to inhibit their behavior and shift it according to social context. In this study, high- and low-power fraternity members teased each other in groups of four by making up nicknames about each other. (Source: Adapted from Keltner, Young, Heerey, Oemig, & Monarch, 1998.)

teased their high-power brothers (Keltner et al., 1998). Across a wide variety of contexts—school playgrounds, hospital settings, the workplace—high-power individuals are more likely to tease in hostile fashion (Keltner, Capps, Kring, Young, & Heerey, 2001).

Power disinhibits more harmful forms of aggression as well, leading to violent behavior against the relatively powerless. For example, power asymmetries between coworkers increase the likelihood of sexual harassment (Studd, 1996). The prevalence of rape rises with a culture's acceptance of male dominance and the subordination of females (Reeves-Sanday, 1997). The incidence of hate crimes against minority groups rises in direct proportion to the numerical advantage the majority enjoys in the local environment over the minority (Green, Wong, & Strolovitch, 1996).

The research does not portray power in a flattering light. High-power individuals tend to act in an overly direct, impulsive, and even aggressive fashion. High-power individuals are more likely to engage in unethical behavior and to be more critical of others than they are of themselves for committing such acts, thus revealing blindness to their own moral failings (Lammers et al., 2011). The research on power provides insight into a number of disturbing trends in society—the child abuse perpetrated by some Catholic priests, the excessive bonuses that CEOs permit themselves to take while their companies are going down the tubes, or the senator who uses public funds to finance his out-of-town trysts. These tendencies are all the more alarming when we consider the influence that powerful people have over our lives.

What are we to do? Research suggests that we should be careful about who gains power because power seems to encourage individuals to express their underlying inclinations, both good and bad. If the person is inclined toward malevolent

"The fundamental concept in social science is Power, in the same sense that Energy is the fundamental concept in physics. . . . The laws of social dynamics are laws which can only be stated in terms of power."

—Bertrand Russell

"You see what power is— holding someone else's fear in your hand and showing it to them!"

—Amy Tan

"I'm not a machine, Deborah.
I can't just turn my greed on and off."

or competitive behavior, power will increase the likelihood of such behavior. But, on the other hand, if the person is more ethical and concerned about the public good, power will amplify the expression of those tendencies. In a study that illustrates this tendency, Serena Chen and her colleagues preselected participants who were either self-interested and exchange-oriented or more compassionate and communally oriented (Chen, Lee-Chai, & Bargh, 2001). Each participant was then randomly assigned to a high-power or low-power position in a clever, subtle manner: high-power individuals were seated in a snazzy leather professorial chair during the experiment; low-power individuals were seated in a plain chair. Participants were then asked to complete a long questionnaire with the help of another participant, who was late. Consistent with the idea that power amplifies the expression of preexisting tendencies, the communal-oriented participants with high power took on the lion's share of completing the task. In contrast, the exchange-oriented participants with high power acted in more self-serving fashion, leaving more of the task for the other participant. The effects of power, then, depend on who holds it. Power corrupts the corruptible.

 Power is the freedom to act and the ability to control one's own outcomes and those of others. Knowledgeable, outgoing, and socially adept people tend to assume positions of leadership within a group. Power tends to make individuals less careful in their thoughts about others and more impulsive in their behavior.

DEINDIVIDUATION AND THE PSYCHOLOGY OF MOBS

Consider the following quite similar reactions to two very different events in San Francisco. The first involved the tragic circumstances surrounding the murders of Mayor George Moscone and Supervisor Harvey Milk in 1978. On November 27 of that year, Milk's political rival Dan White shot and killed both Moscone and Milk, San Francisco's first openly gay supervisor, in City Hall. In a rather swift trial, White's lawyers argued that he was minimally responsible for his deeds because of severe depression. His lawyers claimed that his depression led him to subsist on a junk-food diet, which further "diminished his capacity" to distinguish right from wrong. These tactics, ridiculed in the press as the now-infamous "Twinkie defense," were nonetheless effective. Instead of a first-degree murder conviction, White was found guilty of the lesser charge of voluntary manslaughter and faced a maximum sentence of eight years in prison. With good behavior, he would be eligible for parole in less than five years. (White ended up serving a little over five years, but 22 months after his release from prison, he committed suicide.)

The verdict infuriated members of San Francisco's gay community. Many thought the verdict would have been more severe if a supervisor other than Harvey Milk had been slain. The evening of the verdict, gay activists organized a peaceful protest march, but events quickly got out of hand. It began with several

The Psychology of Mobs (A) Upon learning of the killing of Harvey Milk and George Moscone by Dan White, a mob of demonstrators gathered to mourn their passing. (B) When Dan White was given a light sentence in his trial for the murder, demonstrators again took to the streets, rioting and setting cars on fire in protest of what they saw as a travesty of justice.

demonstrators smashing the glass windows and doors of city hall. Over the pleas of rally organizers urging calm, the crowd began to chant, "Kill Dan White! Get Dan White!" Vandalism and violence soon intensified. When police moved in to quell the disturbance, a battle ensued. The demonstrators threw rocks and bottles at police, set fire to numerous police cars, and looted nearby stores. In the end, 12 police cars were gutted by fire, 20 police officers were injured, and 70 demonstrators needed medical attention. Eight people were arrested. As unfortunate and destructive as the rioting was, it nevertheless strikes most people as understandable. However much they might disapprove, most observers would not think of the rioters' actions as insane: they were lashing out against a justice system they thought had failed.

Now consider the striking similarity to events that erupted in the same city three years later in response to a much less understandable cause: the San Francisco 49ers' *victory* over the Cincinnati Bengals in Super Bowl XVI, a victory that earned the city its first professional championship in any sport. Within minutes of the game's conclusion, giddy fans poured out of homes and bars and into the streets to celebrate. At first it was all harmless, celebratory stuff—horns blared, beer was chugged, champagne was sprayed. As the evening wore on, however, events took a more sinister turn, eventually echoing what had transpired in the aftermath of the Dan White verdict. Bonfires were started in an intersection and atop a car. When police tried to restore order, they were met with a barrage of stones, bricks, and bottles. Before the streets were cleared, 8 police officers and 100 others were treated for injuries, and 70 arrests were made.

Deindividuation and the Group Mind

These two events in San Francisco's history, as well as a great many similar events around the world, challenge us to understand how large groups of people are sometimes transformed into unruly mobs. How can peaceful gatherings spin out of control and become violent? Why do law-abiding citizens, when immersed in

Emergent Properties of Groups Some behaviors surface only when people are part of a group and submerge their individual identities into the group. The people in this flash mob converged at this store after receiving e-mails telling them when and where to gather. Their screams and raised arms reflect the fact that they are in a group—behavior that would be highly unlikely if each of them were there alone.

"Whoever be the individuals that compose it, however like or unlike be their mode of life, . . . their character, or their intelligence, the fact that they have been transformed into a crowd puts them in possession of a sort of collective mind."

—Gustav LeBon

deindividuation The reduced sense of individual identity accompanied by diminished self-regulation that comes over people when they are in a large group.

a crowd, engage in acts of destruction they would never commit alone? How can we understand the psychology of "the mob"?

Social psychologists have addressed these questions in the context of examining the *emergent properties of groups*—behaviors that emerge only when people are in groups. People do things in groups that they would never do alone. Indeed, we often hear people say that a group has "a mind of its own." As a result, the behavior of large groups of people is more than the sum of the behavioral tendencies of its individual members. You might dance, sing, and play air guitar at rock concert with all your friends, but you'd be much less likely to do so if the band were playing a private concert just for you. We do things in groups that we'd never do alone.

One of the first people to offer an extensive analysis of the psychology of the mob was a French sociologist, Gustav LeBon (1895). LeBon thought that people tended to lose their higher mental faculties of reason and deliberation when they were in large groups: "By the mere fact that he forms part of an organised crowd, a man descends several rungs in the ladder of civilization" (p. 52). For LeBon, this descent stems from the collection of individual, rational minds giving way to a less reflective "group mind."

Social psychologists have expanded on LeBon's ideas by examining how the thought patterns of individuals change when they come together in large groups and how these changes make them more susceptible to group influence. Most of the time, we feel individuated—that is, we feel individually identifiable by others, we consider ourselves individually responsible for our actions, and we are concerned with the propriety and future consequences of our behavior. But as a number of social psychologists have noted, we often experience a loss of individual identity—a sense of **deindividuation**—when we're in a large group (Diener, 1980; Festinger, Pepitone, & Newcomb, 1952; Prentice-Dunn & Rogers, 1989; Singer, Brush, & Lublin, 1965; Zimbardo, 1970). When in large crowds, we sometimes feel "lost in the crowd," caught up in what is happening in the moment, and have a diminished sense of responsibility for our actions.

A Model of Deindividuation

Philip Zimbardo (1970) proposed a theoretical model of deindividuation that specifies how certain conditions create the kind of psychological state that promotes the impulsive and often destructive behaviors observed in mobs (**Figure 12.8**). Perhaps the most important of these conditions are the anonymity that individuals enjoy by blending in with a large group and the diffusion of responsibility that occurs when there are many people to share the blame. These conditions, along with the arousal, heightened activity, and sensory overload that often accompany immersion in a large group, lead to the internal state of deindividuation. The deindividuated state is characterized by diminished self-observation and self-evaluation and a lessened concern with how others evaluate us.

Thus a deindividuated person is less aware of the self, more focused on others and the immediate environment, and hence more responsive to behavioral

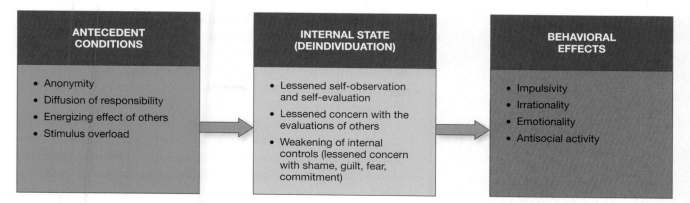

ANTECEDENT CONDITIONS	INTERNAL STATE (DEINDIVIDUATION)	BEHAVIORAL EFFECTS
• Anonymity • Diffusion of responsibility • Energizing effect of others • Stimulus overload	• Lessened self-observation and self-evaluation • Lessened concern with the evaluations of others • Weakening of internal controls (lessened concern with shame, guilt, fear, commitment)	• Impulsivity • Irrationality • Emotionality • Antisocial activity

FIGURE 12.8 **A Theoretical Model of Deindividuation** Certain antecedent conditions lead to an internal state of deindividuation, which in turn leads to behavioral effects that in other situations would be kept under control. (Source: Adapted from Zimbardo, 1970.)

cues—for good or for bad. Being in a deindividuated state lowers the threshold for exhibiting actions that are typically inhibited. People are more likely to engage in a host of impulsive behaviors, both because there is more of a "push" to do so (because of increased arousal and many impulsive others to imitate) and because the constraints that usually "pull" them back from such actions are weakened (because of a lessened sense of evaluation and responsibility).

What emerges is the kind of impulsive, irrational, emotional, and occasionally destructive behavior that people think of as characteristic of mobs. This kind of behavior often creates its own momentum and is less responsive to stimuli that might, if a person were alone, bring it under control, thereby leading to behavior that is difficult to stop. Thus Zimbardo's model of deindividuation is not an account of mob violence per se. Instead, it is a theoretical analysis of crowd-induced *impulsive* behavior—behavior that because of its very impulsivity often turns violent (Spivey & Prentice-Dunn, 1990).

One implicit element in the model is that people often find the impulsivity that accompanies deindividuation to be liberating. Zimbardo argues that people go through much of their lives in a straitjacket of cognitive control. Living under such constraints can be tiresome and stifling, so people sometimes yearn to break free and act more spontaneously and impulsively. In support of this idea, Zimbardo notes that virtually all societies try to safely channel the expression of this need by scheduling occasions when people are encouraged to "let loose." We see this in harvest rites in agrarian cultures, carnivals in religious societies, galas and festivals throughout history, and, perhaps, in the mosh pits and use of intoxicants at modern rock concerts.

Deindividuation and Rioting
When people are in a group and angry, they may let go of self-control and give in to impulses to wreak havoc. Normally law-abiding citizens merge into this crowd and break windows and smash cars with little thought to personal responsibility or the law.

Testing the Model

It should be noted at the outset that the psychology of the mob and other emergent properties are extremely difficult to study. People are on their best behavior when they enter a scientific laboratory, so it's difficult to create a laboratory

Deindividuation and Impulsive Behavior During carnivals and festivals, people tend to "let loose" and relax their usual control over their behavior. A woman lets go of her inhibitions during a Mardi Gras parade in New Orleans.

situation where they will act impulsively and destructively. Also, there are ethical constraints against putting people in situations where aggressiveness and acts of destruction are likely. Therefore, some of the most informative research on the subject takes place out in the world and not in the laboratory (for exceptions, see Lea, Spears, & de Groot, 2001; Postmes & Spears, 1998).

This research, whether in the real world or in a laboratory setting, also involves very few controlled experiments. Instead, it often involves the examination of archives—data originally gathered with no thought to its relevance to deindividuation. Investigators use these records to search for predicted correlations between the various antecedent conditions and resultant behaviors.

Because these empirical tests are not controlled experiments, they do not control for, or rule out, various alternative interpretations of the results. Indeed, you might think of other explanations having nothing to do with deindividuation for some of the empirical results reported here. Even so, it is important to ask whether any one alternative interpretation can account for *all* of the relevant findings. If each finding requires a *different* alternative explanation, but all fit the model of deindividuation, the deindividuation account is the most likely and most parsimonious interpretation.

Suicide Baiting Imagine that you are on your way to class when you notice a disturbance up ahead. When you get closer, you find that everyone is looking up at one of the top floors of a high-rise dormitory. It appears that a student is halfway out an open window and threatening to jump. What do you do? Try to stop the poor soul from jumping? Call for help?

Hard as it may be to believe, people occasionally do just the opposite—they engage in suicide baiting, urging the individual to jump. Is suicide baiting more likely when many individuals are gathered below? In other words, are people more likely to engage in suicide baiting when they feel deindividuated?

To answer these questions, researchers examined 15 years of newspaper accounts of suicidal jumps and averted jumps (Mann, 1981). They found 21 instances of attempted suicide, and suicide baiting occurred in 10 of them. They then analyzed the data to determine whether two variables associated with deindividuation—the cover of darkness and the presence of a large group of onlookers—are related to whether suicide baiting occurred. As shown in **Figure 12.9**, suicide baiting was more than twice as likely when the crowd size exceeded 300. Also, suicide baiting was more than four times as likely if the episode took place after 6 p.m. As people feel more anonymous, either by being lost in a large crowd or under the cloak of darkness, they are more inclined to taunt and egg on a potential suicide.

Although it is possible to question some of the details of these analyses (for example, why were the cutoffs set at 300 people and 6 p.m.?) and to suggest alternative interpretations (the larger the group, the more likely it is to contain a psychopath who starts the taunting), the data are nevertheless consistent with the idea that variables that lead to deindividuation also lead to antisocial behavior.

The Conduct of War Wars have always been a part of what English novelist and scientist C. P. Snow calls the "long and gloomy history of man." The conduct of warfare, however, has varied enormously from culture to culture and

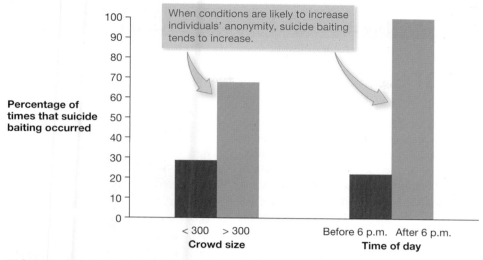

When conditions are likely to increase individuals' anonymity, suicide baiting tends to increase.

Percentage of times that suicide baiting occurred

100
90
80
70
60
50
40
30
20
10
0

< 300   > 300
Crowd size

Before 6 p.m.   After 6 p.m.
Time of day

FIGURE 12.9 Deindividuation and Suicide Baiting (Source: Adapted from Mann, 1981.)

epoch to epoch. Warfare practices vary in their ferocity, for example. At the high end of the ferocity scale, we find head-hunting, ritualistic torture, and the systematic slaughter of civilian noncombatants. At the very low end would be what Tom Wolfe (1979) has described as single-combat warfare: the David and Goliath battles in which the warring parties select a single warrior to do battle with each other. The losing side pays a price in territory or some other form of wealth, but less damage is done to both groups.

Is the brutality of warfare related to deindividuation? The theory predicts that it should be. It should be easier for people to let go of the usual prohibitions against barbarity when they feel anonymous and unaccountable for their actions. To determine whether such a relationship exists, the warfare practices of 23 non-Western cultures were investigated (Watson, 1973). Each culture was examined for whether its warriors were deindividuated before battle (that is, whether they wore masks or war paint) and for how aggressively they waged war (that is, did they torture the enemy; did they fight to the death in all battles?). As predicted, there was a strong correlation between deindividuation and aggressiveness in warfare. Among those cultures whose warriors changed their appearance before battle, 80 percent were deemed particularly aggressive; among those cultures whose warriors did not change their appearance, only 13 percent were deemed especially aggressive. When warriors are disguised in battle, they fight more ferociously (**Box 12.4**).

Warfare and Deindividuation
Warriors in tribes that deindividuate themselves before battle by wearing war paint and war masks tend to engage in more brutal warfare practices.

Halloween Mayhem To American readers, one of the most familiar occasions for uninhibited and impulsive behavior is Halloween night. The destructive acts that occur on that holiday range from mild episodes of egg throwing to much more serious hooliganism. One group of social psychologists decided to take advantage of the Halloween atmosphere to conduct an ambitious test of the

BOX 12.4 **FOCUS ON HISTORY**

Celts and Warfare

The ancient Romans were terrified of the Gauls, who fought savagely and with little thought to self-preservation. Depending on your point of view, Gallic fighters were either extremely individuated or extremely deindividuated: they fought naked! The Romans eventually succeeded in pushing them to the far corners of the empire, where they became Bretons, Welsh, Irish, and Scots and in modern times have been known as Celts. For many centuries the Scots painted their faces blue in battle (as you may have seen in the film *Braveheart*), and they were regarded as ferocious fighters. Their descendants, the so-called Scotch Irish (some Scottish, some Irish, and some Scots who had settled in Northern Ireland), were the main settlers of Appalachia and the U.S. South. Body paint was no longer required for them to maintain their reputations as fearsome fighters, first against the Native Americans and then in the Civil War, when they out-generaled and out-soldiered the North. The tradition has continued into the twenty-first century. Southerners are heavily overrepresented in the U.S. military.

Fierce Scotsman A statue of Scottish leader William Wallace, whose life is depicted in the film *Braveheart*.

role of deindividuation in antisocial behavior (Diener, Fraser, Beaman, & Kelem, 1976). They set up research stations in 27 homes throughout the city of Seattle and monitored the behavior of over 1,000 trick-or-treaters. At each participating house, the children were told they could take one piece of candy from a large bowl sitting on a table in the entrance to the house. Next to the bowl of candy was a bowl filled with coins. The experimenter then excused herself from the scene and covertly monitored the children's actions from afar. Would the children take just their allotted single piece of candy, or would they take more—perhaps even some coins?

The investigators examined the influence of two variables connected to deindividuation. First, the children arrived either individually or in groups, and the investigators expected that those in groups would feel more anonymous and therefore would be more likely to transgress. Second, the experimenter purposely "individuated" a random sample of children arriving both alone and in groups. In particular, the experimenter, before departing, asked each child his or her name and address and then repeated this information aloud for emphasis. Individuating the children—that is, identifying them by name so they would no longer feel anonymous—was predicted to inhibit any temptation to transgress.

As **Figure 12.10** shows, both variables had the anticipated effect. The children who arrived in groups were much more likely to transgress than those who were alone, regardless of whether they were anonymous or not. Children who were anonymous were much more likely to transgress than those who were individuated, regardless of whether they were alone or in groups. Putting these two findings together, the children in anonymous groups were the most likely to transgress.

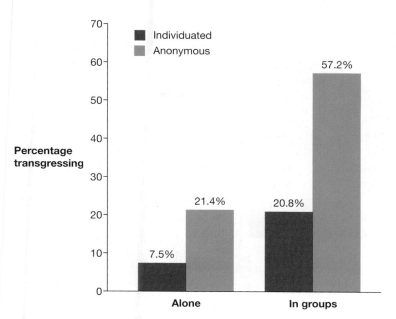

FIGURE 12.10 Deindividuation and Transgression The percentage of trick-or-treaters who transgressed was affected by whether they had been asked to give their name (individuated condition) or not (anonymous condition) and whether they were alone or in a group.

Summary of the Evidence The strength of each of the studies mentioned thus far lies in the "realness" and significance of the dependent variables—suicide baiting, warfare practices, and stealing. Unfortunately, with but one exception, all of the results are correlational findings, so the researchers cannot be sure of what is responsible for the relationship. The one exception is the Halloween study. Part of the study was correlational: some participants showed up alone, and others arrived in groups. Perhaps being in a group does indeed cause a person to feel deindividuated and therefore to be more likely to act out, but perhaps rowdier people simply prefer to trick-or-treat with others. The other half of the study, however, is a true experiment and does not suffer from this self-selection problem. Children were randomly assigned to the anonymous and individuated conditions, so the researchers can be sure that *on average* the two groups consisted of the same type of children. The tendency of anonymous children to act out can therefore confidently be attributed to anonymity per se and not to the kind of children who seek out anonymity.

Self-Awareness and Individuation

If "losing ourselves" in a crowd and becoming deindividuated makes us more likely to behave impulsively, it stands to reason that being especially self-conscious would have the opposite effect. Anything that focuses attention on the self, such as being in front of a camera, seeing ourselves in a mirror, or wearing a name tag, may lead to **individuation** and make us particularly inclined to act carefully and in accordance with our sense of propriety. This is just what **self-awareness theory** predicts. When people focus their attention inward on themselves, they become concerned with self-evaluation and how their current behavior conforms to their internal standards and values (Duval & Wicklund, 1972).

individuation An enhanced sense of individual identity produced by focusing attention on the self, which generally leads people to act carefully and deliberately and in accordance with their sense of propriety and values.

self-awareness theory A theory that maintains that when people focus their attention inward on themselves, they become concerned with self-evaluation and how their current behavior conforms to their internal standards and values.

Individuation and Self-Awareness Anything that focuses attention on the self and individual identity is likely to lead to heightened concern with self-control and propriety. Name tags on these people at a business conference lead to individuation and, most likely, restrained behavior.

spotlight effect People's conviction that other people are attending to them—to their appearance and behavior—more than they actually are.

Studies of Self-Awareness Many experiments have shown that people do indeed act in ways that are more consistent with their enduring attitudes and values when they have been made self-conscious by being placed in front of a mirror or an attentive audience (Beaman, Klentz, Diener, & Svanum, 1979; Carver, 1974; Carver & Scheier, 1981; Duval & Lalwani, 1999; Froming, Walker, & Lopyan, 1982; Gibbons, 1978; Scheier, Fenigstein, & Buss, 1974). In one study, college students were asked to solve a series of anagrams and told to stop when a bell sounded. In a control condition, nearly three-quarters of them fudged a bit by continuing to work beyond the bell. But in a condition that caused participants to be made self-aware by working in front of a mirror, fewer than 10 percent cheated (Diener & Wallbom, 1976). Although most students *say* that cheating is a bad thing, it appears to take some self-awareness to get them to act on that belief. Note that because being in a state of self-awareness is the flip side of feeling deindividuated, all of these experiments that support self-awareness theory also provide indirect support for the model of deindividuation.

Self-Consciousness and the Spotlight Effect The negative relationship between self-consciousness and deindividuation raises the question of how self-conscious people typically are in the normal course of events. There are pronounced individual differences, of course, in how focused people are on themselves and in how much they believe others are focused on them as well (Fenigstein, Scheier, & Buss, 1975). But there is also reason to believe that the typical level of self-consciousness is fairly high, particularly when others are around. People begin to feel deindividuated only in the presence of a large crowd. This is why, as noted earlier, it has been assumed that people enjoy feeling deindividuated—it is a welcome break from the usual self-conscious state.

Evidence that people are indeed prone to a high level of self-consciousness comes from research on the **spotlight effect**—that is, people's conviction that other people are attending to their appearance and behavior more than is actually the case (**Figure 12.11**). People who make an insightful comment in a group discussion, for example, believe that others will notice their comment and remember it better than others actually do. People who suffer an embarrassing mishap, such as triggering an alarm in a public building or falling down while entering a lecture hall, think others are judging them more harshly than they actually are (Epley, Savitsky, & Gilovich, 2002; Fortune & Newby-Clark, 2008; Gilovich, Kruger, & Medvec, 2002; Gilovich, Medvec, & Savitsky, 2000; Savitsky, Epley, & Gilovich, 2001).

In one of the clearest demonstrations of the spotlight effect, participants who arrived individually for an experiment were asked to put on a T-shirt sporting a picture of the pop singer Barry Manilow. Despite obvious signs of displeasure, everyone did so. They then reported to another room down the hall where, upon entering, they found a group of fellow students filling out questionnaires. After leaving the room moments later, the participants were asked to estimate the percentage of those other students who would be able to recall the person pictured

FIGURE 12.11 **You Be the Subject: Spotlight Effect**

Imagine that you go to a dinner party and discover that everyone except you brought a gift for the host.

1. Rate how harshly you would be judged by the host for this omission:

Totally fine 0 1 2 3 4 5 6 7 8 9 10 **Unforgivable**

2. Rate how harshly you would judge a guest who failed to bring a gift:

Totally fine 0 1 2 3 4 5 6 7 8 9 10 **Unforgivable**

Which ratings are lower?

Result: Did you assign a higher number for rating 1 than rating 2? In part because of the spotlight effect, most people think that their own actions (the social blunder, in this case) stand out more than they acually do.

on the T-shirt. As predicted, the participants overestimated how much they had stood out in their new shirt. They estimated that roughly half of the other students would be able to identify that it was Barry Manilow pictured on their shirt, when in fact only about a quarter were able to do so (Gilovich et al., 2000).

LOOKING BACK Social psychologists have examined the relationship between self-consciousness and behavior from two directions. Research on deindividuation has shown that the diminished sense of self-awareness that sometimes occurs when we are immersed in large groups makes us get caught up in ongoing events and encourages impulsive—and sometimes destructive—actions. Research on self-awareness and the spotlight effect has shown how carefully we typically monitor our own behavior with an eye toward what others might think and how our awareness of self encourages us to act with a greater sense of propriety.

Chapter Review

Summary

The Nature and Purpose of Group Living

- Human beings, like all large primates except the orangutan, are group-living animals who influence and must get along with others.

Social Facilitation

- The presence of other people sometimes improves human performance and sometimes hinders it, but in predictable ways. Research on *social facilitation* has shown that the presence of others is arousing, and that arousal increases people's tendencies to do what they are already predisposed to do. On easy tasks, people are predisposed to respond correctly, so increasing this tendency facilitates performance. On novel or difficult tasks, people are not predisposed to respond correctly, so arousal hinders performance by making them more likely to respond incorrectly.

- A number of clever experiments have indicated that the *mere presence* of others leads to social facilitation effects, although other factors, including *evaluation apprehension*, can intensify them. Moreover, *distraction-conflict theory* explains social facilitation by noting that awareness of another person can distract an individual and create a conflict between attending to the other person and to the task at hand, a conflict that is itself arousing.

- *Social loafing* is the tendency to exert less effort on a group task when individual contributions cannot be monitored.

Group Decision Making

- *Groupthink* is the tendency for members of cohesive groups to deal with the stress of making highly consequential decisions by pursuing consensus more vigorously than a critical analysis of all available information. Groupthink has been implicated in the faulty decision making that has led to various policy fiascos.

- Group decision making is affected by how cohesive a group is, how directive its leader is, and ingroup pressures that can lead to the rejection of alternative viewpoints and *self-censorship*, the tendency for people to refrain from expressing their true feelings or reservations in the face of apparent group consensus.

- Exchanging views with fellow group members can lead to more extreme decisions and make people more extreme in their attitudes. The *risky shift* refers to those cases in which groups make riskier decisions than individuals.

- Group discussion tends to create *group polarization*: initial leanings in a risky direction tend to be made riskier by group discussion, and initial leanings in a conservative direction tend to be made more conservative.

- Group polarization is created in part because group discussion exposes members to a greater number *of persuasive arguments* in favor of the consensus opinion than they would have thought of themselves. It is also produced through *social comparison*, whereby people compare their opinions and arguments with those of others when there are no objective standards of evaluation.

- People from cultures that place a high value on risk are more likely to make risky decisions after group discussion than people from cultures that do not value risk as highly.

- Polarization is a particularly common outcome in homogeneous groups, and it may be a particular problem in the modern world because people are likely to read newspapers and watch news programs that fit their preexisting views. This polarization may be further reinforced through communication on the Internet, which makes it increasingly easy for people to find like-minded others and to exchange information solely with those who share their opinions.

Leadership and Power

- Power involves a sense of control and the freedom to act. It derives from interpersonal sources, such as a person's position of authority or expertise, as well as individual factors—in particular, the ability to engage with others socially and build strong alliances.

- As an account of how power can lead to excesses and abuses, the *approach/inhibition theory* of power holds that elevated power makes people look at things more simplistically and act in more disinhibited ways.

Deindividuation and the Psychology of Mobs

- Large groups of people sometimes transform into unruly mobs. This may happen because the anonymity and diffusion of responsibility that people often feel in large groups can lead to a mental state of *deindividuation* in which they are less concerned with the future, with

normal societal constraints on behavior, and with the consequences of their actions.

- The deindividuated state of getting lost in the crowd stands in marked contrast to how people normally feel, which is quite individually identifiable. *Self-awareness theory* maintains that focusing attention on the self leads people to a state of *individuation*, marked by careful deliberation and concern with how well their actions conform to their internal moral standards.

- Most people overestimate how much they personally stand out and are identifiable to others. This phenomenon is known as the *spotlight effect*.

Key Terms

approach/inhibition theory (p. 479)
authority (p. 478)
deindividuation (p. 486)
distraction-conflict theory (p. 464)
dominance (p. 478)
dominant response (p. 457)

evaluation apprehension (p. 461)
group polarization (p. 472)
groupthink (p. 466)
individuation (p. 491)
power (p. 478)
risky shift (p. 470)

self-awareness theory (p. 491)
self-censorship (p. 467)
social facilitation (p. 456)
social loafing (p. 464)
spotlight effect (p. 492)
status (p. 478)

Further Reading

Janis, I. L. (1983). *Groupthink: Psychological studies of policy decisions and fiascoes*. Boston: Houghton-Mifflin. The classic formulation of the theory of groupthink, with supportive evidence.

Hackman, R. (2010). Group performance. In S. T. Fiske & D. T. Gilbert (Eds.), *The Handbook of social psychology* (5th ed.). Hoboken, NJ: Wiley. A state-of-the-art, comprehensive review of social psychological influences on performance in groups.

Sunstein, C. R. (2003). *Why societies need dissent*. Cambridge, MA: Harvard University Press. An important application of social psychological research on group polarization to the free exchange of ideas and opinion formation in the modern world.

Surowieki, J. (2005). *The wisdom of crowds*. New York: Random House. Best-selling account of how and why the aggregate of many independent opinions can be tremendously accurate.

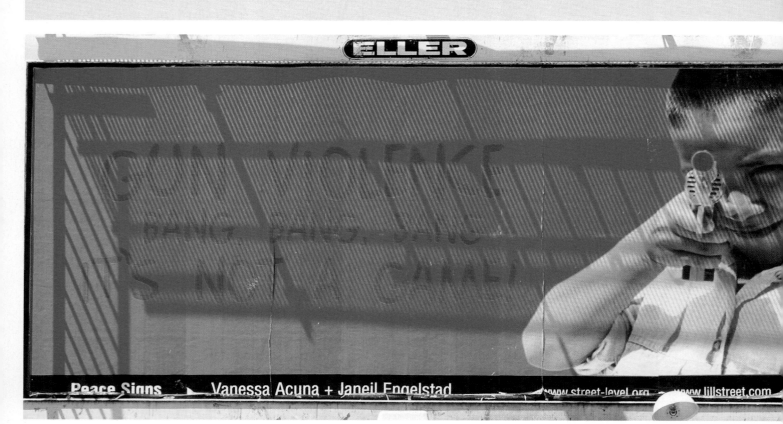

CHAPTER 13

Aggression

ON THE EVENING OF APRIL 6, 1994, Odette and Jean-Baptiste, a Rwandan husband-and-wife pair of physicians, were enjoying a drink with a friend while listening to the radio. Just after eight o'clock, they heard that the plane carrying President Juvenal Habyarimana of Rwanda, a Hutu, had been shot down near Kigali, Rwanda's capital. Odette knew there was going to be trouble. Unlike the Hutu president or her husband, Odette was a Tutsi, and she had witnessed several massacres of her people at the hands of the Hutus, a people with whom they shared a language, religion, and history of living together. She was worried that the incident would fuel anti-Tutsi sentiment among the majority Hutus.

Tragically, she proved to be right. In the 100 days that followed, Hutus would massacre approximately 800,000 Tutsis and moderate Hutus (Gourevitch, 1998). Many of the massacres were carried out by militiamen known as the *interahamwe*. They set up roadblocks throughout Rwanda, pulled Tutsis from their cars, and killed them. In small Rwandan towns, Hutus turned on their Tutsi neighbors, brutally killing them with machetes. Hutu schoolteachers massacred their Tutsi students. Even Tutsis taking sanctuary in churches were massacred. Throughout the rolling hills of Rwanda, flocks of crows and buzzards signaled where massacres had taken place.

Regrettably, massacres like the Rwanda genocides are a recurring part of history. In 2003 in Darfur, Sudan, several groups, desperate because of drought and starvation, attacked the Sudanese government. The government's response resembled the Rwandan genocide. Government-sponsored armed militias pursued a scorched-earth strategy in dealing with the rebels: they burned villages, raped women, and slaughtered tens if not hundreds of thousands of people.

Based on the sheer number of people killed by their fellow human beings, the twentieth century was the most violent in history. Rwanda and Darfur were

Mass Murder Genocide did not end with the Nazi murder of millions. It has also occurred in the former Yugoslavia, in Cambodia, in Rwanda, and in Sudan, among other places. (A) An open grave of 10,000 naked bodies was found at the Bergen-Belsen concentration camp when the British liberated the camp in April 1945. (B) A church in Nitarama, Rwanda, holding the remains of 400 Tutsis killed by the Hutu *interahamwe* was discovered by a United Nations team in September 1994.

just two of several large-scale genocides. How do social psychologists make sense of this type of violence, and other forms of violence considered in this chapter—school shootings, homicide, rape, and the violence in families? How do different situational factors produce aggression, and how does people's construal of complex situations give rise to violence? What factors promote group conflict—and, more important, what factors can pave the way for greater peace?

Explanations for why aggression occurs vary according to whether it is hostile or instrumental aggression. **Hostile aggression** refers to behavior motivated by feelings of anger and hostility and whose primary aim is to harm another, either physically or psychologically. Clearly, the genocide in Rwanda emerged in part for purely hostile reasons: Hutus seeking revenge on Tutsis out of anger about past hostilities. **Instrumental aggression**, in contrast, refers to behavior that is intended to harm another in the service of motives other than pure hostility. People harm others, for example, to gain status, to attract attention, to acquire wealth, and to advance political and ideological causes. Some of the genocide in Rwanda was committed in the pursuit of political purposes: the Hutus were seeking to displace the more powerful Tutsis. Many acts of aggression involve a mix of hostile and instrumental motives. A football player who intentionally harms another might do so out of aggressive emotion (hostile aggression) or for a variety of instrumental reasons—for example, to foster a reputation for fearlessness, to help his team win, or to make the kind of plays that secure a place on the team or that earn a lucrative contract.

hostile aggression Behavior intended to harm another, either physically or psychologically, and motivated by feelings of anger and hostility.

instrumental aggression Behavior intended to harm another in the service of motives other than pure hostility (for example, to attract attention, to acquire wealth, or to advance political and ideological causes).

SITUATIONAL DETERMINANTS OF AGGRESSION

In considering the massacres of Rwanda and Darfur, it is striking how quickly peaceful, stable relations between groups can turn to aggression. Just as the right atmospheric and ecological conditions can instantly transform a healthy forest into a roaring inferno, the right mix of situational factors can give rise to violence, whether it takes place between different ethnic or religious groups, groups of adolescent boys encountering each other on a Friday night, athletic teams on the field, or children on grade-school playgrounds.

The idea that situational factors produce aggressive behavior might seem counterintuitive. It is quite easy to believe that aggression arises because of aggressive people—the bullies, sociopaths, and criminal personalities among us. Without doubt, there is a grain of truth to this belief; but social psychology suggests that it is also wise to consider situational factors to understand why aggression happens. For example, scientists have discovered that certain genes may predispose people to aggression, but these genes lead to aggressive behavior only when certain circumstances occur in the individual's life (**Box 13.1**). The important point is that certain circumstances and situations release people's aggressive tendencies. So let's take on social psychology's challenge and think about situational factors that give rise to violence. One such factor—heat—has been a particular focus of research.

BOX 13.1   **FOCUS ON GENES AND ENVIRONMENT**

Nature or Nurture? It's Both

Many biological factors predispose certain individuals to act aggressively (White, 1997; Yudko, Blanchard, Henne, & Blanchard, 1997). For example, testosterone, a male sex hormone, tends to be associated with higher levels of aggression: delinquents have higher levels of testosterone than college students (Banks & Dabbs, 1996), and members of rowdier fraternities have higher levels than members of more responsible fraternities (Dabbs, 2000).

Research by Avshalom Caspi, Terrie Moffitt, and their colleagues indicates that aggression might best be thought of as the interaction between situational factors and genetically based individual differences (Caspi et al., 2002). Caspi, Moffitt, and colleagues tested for the two forms of the monoamine oxidase A (MAOA) gene. Monoamine oxidase is an enzyme that metabolizes certain neurotransmitters in the synapses between neurons in the brain, allowing for smooth communication between neurons. In nonhuman species, individuals with a defective, short form of the MAOA gene have been shown to be more aggressive, suggesting that this gene may predict aggressive behavior in humans. Caspi and colleagues identified men with this defective short form of the gene, which was 37 percent of their sample, and those with the long form of the gene. To capture situational factors, they also identified men who had or had not been mistreated by their parents as children— one of the most potent circumstances that gives rise to violence in adulthood.

Overall, the defective MAOA gene alone did not affect whether the boys committed violent crimes (rape, assault, robbery) by age 26. This finding suggests that genetic predispositions of the individual alone do not determine whether the individual engages in aggression. The catalyst of aggressive behavior proved to be the combination of the short form of the MAOA gene and a family environment of physical abuse. Boys who had the defective gene *and* were mistreated as children were three times as likely to have been convicted of a violent crime by age 26 as the boys who had the defective gene but had not been mistreated. Although those with the gene for low MAOA activity who had also suffered mistreatment were only 12 percent of the population of boys in the study, they were responsible for 44 percent of the group's convictions for violent crime. Some 85 percent of the boys with the short form of the MAOA gene who were severely mistreated developed some form of antisocial behavior. The important lesson of this telling study is that nature requires nurture to shape behavior.

Heat and Aggression In Spike Lee's movie *Do the Right Thing*, on a very hot day a confrontation between whites and blacks begins in this restaurant and escalates into a race riot.

"I pray thee good Mercutio,
let's retire;
The day is hot, the Capulets
abroad.
And, if we meet, we shall not
'scape a brawl,
For now, these hot days, is the
mad blood stirring."

—Shakespeare, *Romeo and Juliet*

Heat

The first line of Spike Lee's movie *Do the Right Thing* comes from a radio newscaster who says, "It's hot out there, folks." It's early in the morning, and the main characters, clad in T-shirts and shorts, are already uncomfortable and sweating profusely. By the end of the day, tensions between African-Americans and Italian-Americans escalate, and a race riot ensues.

People have long believed that moods and actions are closely tied to the weather. Perhaps the most widely assumed connection is between heat and aggression. We think of angry people as "boiling over," "steamed," and "hot under the collar." And indeed, anger literally raises the temperature of the body because of increases in blood pressure and the distribution of blood to certain parts of the body, such as the hands. But the connection between anger and heat may also have to do with what the ambient temperature does to people's emotions and actions.

Are people more aggressive when it's hot? As early as the nineteenth century, social theorists observed that violent crime rates were higher in southern France and southern Italy, where the temperatures are hotter, than in northern France and northern Italy. Of course, other factors—such as levels of unemployment, per capita income, ethnic composition, or average age—might also have produced these regional differences in aggression.

Craig Anderson has provided evidence that higher-than-normal temperatures are associated with increased aggression (Anderson, 1987, 1989). First, there are higher rates of violent crimes in hotter regions. Anderson examined the crime rates of 260 cities throughout the United States. For each city, he identified the number of days in which the temperature exceeded 90 degrees Fahrenheit. The number of hot days (above 90 degrees) was a strong predictor of elevated violent crime rates but not nonviolent crime rates. This was true even when Anderson controlled for the city's level of unemployment, per capita income, and average age of its citizens (Anderson, 1987).

People are also more violent during hot months, such as July and August, than during cooler months, such as January and February (the one exception is December, when violent crime rates also rise—so much for holiday cheer). In **Figure 13.1**, for example, you can see that murder and rape increase during the summer months. Moreover, one of the cleverest studies of heat and aggression found that major league baseball pitchers are more likely to hit batters as the weather gets hotter and hotter (Reifman, Larrick, & Fein, 1991). This is especially true when the pitcher's teammates have been hit by the opposing pitcher earlier in the game (Larrick, Timmerman, Carton, & Abrevaya, 2011). This effect cannot be attributed to reduced competence; neither wild pitches nor walks go up with the temperature (see also Kenrick & MacFarlane, 1984).

These findings point to a potentially unsettling consequence of climate change: that as the temperature of the earth rises, people might expect to see increases in violence throughout the world. Recently, climate scientists have addressed this possibility, and the results are one more reason to be concerned about climate change. Solomon Hsiang and his colleagues looked at data for the past 50 years and found that during what are known as El Niño years in tropical countries—when the weather is especially hot and dry—the likelihood of civil conflict rises dramatically (Hsiang, Meng, & Cane, 2011).

What is it about high temperatures that makes people more aggressive? One explanation assigns a prominent role to attributional processes (see Chapter 5). According to the misattribution perspective, people are aroused by the heat, but they are largely unaware that it is the source of their arousal. When they encounter circumstances that prompt anger—say, a frustrating driver or an irritating romantic partner—they attribute their arousal to that person, and this misattributed arousal gives rise to amplified feelings of anger and aggression. Another possibility is that heat triggers not just undifferentiated arousal, but specific feelings of anger in particular—angry feelings that increase the likelihood of all kinds of aggressive behavior. This explanation is considered in greater detail later in this chapter.

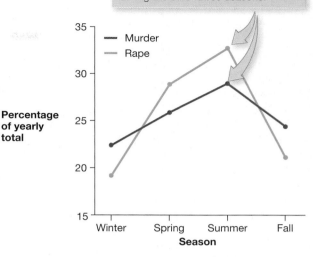

FIGURE 13.1 Effects of Season on Violent Behavior Do the hot months of summer make people more aggressive? Various studies of aggressive behaviors throughout different months of the year indicate that they do. (Source: Adapted from Anderson, 1989, p. 82.)

Media Violence

The Western media are saturated with images of aggression. The average American child watches 3 to 4 hours of television a day, and many of the programs children watch are violent. Prime-time television programs have, on average, about five to six violent acts per hour, and about 90 percent of the programs that children watch portray at least some violence (Gerbner, Gross, Morgan, & Signorielli, 1986). By age 12, the average viewer of American television has seen about 100,000 acts of violence, from car crashes on reality police shows to murders and beatings on weekly crime or courtroom dramas to dead bodies on the nightly news. Some estimates are that the average high school graduate in America has seen 13,000 killings on TV, not to mention those they see in movies, in video games, and on websites.

Does the violence portrayed in the media make people more aggressive? Every year, concerned citizens urge the entertainment industry to stop depicting so much violence. Journalists routinely decry the violence on television and in the movies. Do these movements receive support from scientific evidence linking violent media to aggressive behavior?

Several strands of evidence indicate that people who campaign against media violence are correct in their basic assumption—that exposure to media violence increases aggressive behavior. Let's start with copycat violence—that is, the imitation of specific violent acts depicted in the media (**Box 13.2**). In March 1981, John Hinckley Jr. attempted to assassinate President Ronald Reagan, shooting him in the chest and, by many accounts, impairing Reagan's ability to lead the country in the months afterward. What investigators soon discovered was unnerving evidence about the nature of copycat violence. Hinckley had seen Martin Scorsese's movie *Taxi Driver*, which starred Robert De Niro as a violent sociopath who attempts to kill a politician to win the love of a young prostitute

BOX 13.2   FOCUS ON THE MEDIA

Copycat Violence

David Phillips (1986) has gathered evidence indicating that one type of copycat violence, suicide—the ultimate form of violence against the self—is a very real phenomenon. In a first study, Phillips identified 35 suicides reported in the U.S. media from 1947 to 1968 and examined the suicide rates in the following months. He compared the suicide rates of those months with the rates observed during the same months in the years before and after each suicide. This comparison allowed him to control for the effects of weather and season on aggressive behavior.

In 26 of the 35 widely reported suicides, the suicide rate rose substantially more in the month following the suicide than in the two comparison months. For example, Marilyn Monroe's widely publicized overdose in August 1962 was followed by a 12 percent increase in suicides in the United States and a 10 percent increase in Great Britain. Phillips also observed a strong positive correlation between the amount of media coverage the suicide received and the increase in the suicide rate. That is, the more newspaper space was devoted to a suicide, the greater the increase in copycat suicides. And more detailed analyses suggested that people were not killing themselves out of grief over the death of beloved celebrities; people even imitated the suicides of despised individuals, such as a leader of the Ku Klux Klan.

Of course, Phillips could not measure a number of variables that might have affected suicide rates. For example, were particularly depressive or aggressive people—that is, those more inclined initially to harm themselves or others—most likely to imitate the publicized acts of violence and commit suicide? Phillips's data do not tell us. But even if depressed or aggressive people are more likely to commit copycat suicide, Phillips's claim about imitative suicide still holds. It may simply be that the effect is particularly pronounced among certain segments of the population.

played by Jodie Foster. In Hinckley's hotel room was a letter addressed to Jodie Foster; in it, Hinckley declared that he was going to kill President Reagan for her.

How prevalent is copycat violence? Social psychology offers one answer to this question, not only for the short term, but over much of the life span as well. Laboratory studies have examined the effects of exposure to media violence on aggression immediately afterward (Anderson et al., 2003; Geen, 1998). In these studies, participants typically view aggressive films and then are given an opportunity to act in an aggressive fashion—for example, by shocking a confrontational confederate (for a review, see Berkowitz, 1993). The results of these studies indicate that watching aggressive films does indeed make people more aggressive. For example, one study showed that watching aggressive films compared with control films made juvenile delinquents staying at a minimum-security penal institution more aggressive (Leyens, Camino, Parke, & Berkowitz, 1975). In another study, male college students behaved more aggressively toward a female when they were angered and exposed to violent media imagery (Donnerstein, 1980; Donnerstein & Berkowitz, 1981). Exposure to violent pornography in particular increases the endorsement of aggression against women (Allen, Emmers-Sommer, Gebhardt, & Giery, 1995).

By controlling the specific kinds of violent media participants view, these experimental studies have uncovered the sorts of media violence that are most likely to lead to aggression. People tend to be more aggressive, for example, after seeing films in which they identify with the perpetrator of the violent act (Leyens & Picus, 1973). People are also more likely to be aggressive after watching violent films that portray justified violence—that is, violence perpetrated against "bad people" (Berkowitz, 1965). However, when participants are led to direct their

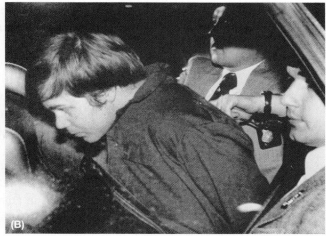

Copycat Violence Violence in the media sometimes is imitated in real life. (A) In the film *Taxi Driver*, Robert De Niro's character tries to assassinate a politician. (B) John Hinckley Jr. attempted to assassinate President Ronald Reagan after seeing the film.

attention away from the aggressive content of the violent film—for example, by focusing on the aesthetic features of the film—they are less likely to be aggressive (Leyens, Cisneros, & Hossay, 1976).

Building on these studies of the short-term effects of media violence, further research has focused on its long-term effects. The work of psychologists such as Rowell Huesmann and Leonard Eron and their colleagues in many different countries makes a strong case that early exposure to media violence leads to aggressive behavior later in life. Consider one study in which Eron and Huesmann assessed the television viewing habits of 211 boys in Columbia County, in upstate New York, from childhood to adulthood (Huesmann, Moise-Titus, Podolski, & Eron, 2003). They wanted to know whether each boy's preference for watching violent TV at age 8 as reported by his mother would predict how much criminal activity he would engage in by age 30. One potential problem with this study is that perhaps aggressive boys at age 8 like to watch violent TV. If so, any relationship between violent TV watched at age 8 and subsequent aggression could be attributed to the aggressiveness of the boy and not to watching violent TV. Huesmann and Eron therefore controlled for how aggressive the child was at age 8 to look at the "pure" relations between violent TV watched at age 8 and subsequent aggressive behavior. As **Figure 13.2** shows, children who preferred to watch violent TV at age 8 were more likely to engage in serious criminal activity by age 30. This is solid, though not conclusive, evidence that it was the violent TV, rather than the participants' initial aggressiveness, that resulted in their greater criminal activity.

Violent Video Games

New technologies—websites, YouTube, and video games—have introduced new opportunities for people to be exposed to aggressive imagery. For example, about 85 percent of American teens play video games regularly (Anderson & Bushman,

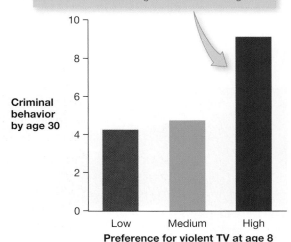

Men who liked to watch violent TV at age 8, holding constant how aggressive they were at that age, were more likely to commit serious criminal acts at age 30 than were men who had little or moderate liking for violent TV at age 8.

FIGURE 13.2 Preference for Media Violence and Aggressiveness The y-axis scale for criminal behavior reflects two measures: number of criminal convictions and seriousness of each crime. (Source: Adapted from Huesmann, 1986.)

2001). A recent nationally representative sample (Gentile, 2009) found that the average American between the ages of 8 and 18 spends about 13 hours a week playing video games. Boys, as you might expect, play more on average (just over 16 hours) than girls (about 9 hours). This same survey found that about 8 percent of American children are obsessive in their playing of video games, playing an average of 24 hours a week and showing many symptoms of addiction. For example, playing games gives them a high, they feel withdrawal symptoms when they don't play, and playing games creates conflicts within the family and in their personal lives.

Two such aficionados of video games were Eric Harris and Dylan Klebold. They played violent video games habitually, and their favorite was the game *Doom*. Harris, in fact, created a custom version of *Doom* in which two shooters, armed with extra weapons and unlimited ammunition, would gun down an array of helpless victims who could not fight back. A short time later, on April 20, 1999, Harris and Klebold's actions mirrored their video game world. Harris and Klebold planted bombs and took several guns and massive amounts of ammunition to their school, Columbine High School, in Littleton, Colorado. There they killed 12 of their classmates and 1 teacher, as well as injuring another 23 students, before killing themselves.

Are video games the cause of this kind of violence? Certainly not the only cause, and many in the video game industry vehemently argue that there is *no* relationship between playing video games and violence. In a May 12, 2000, interview on CNN, Doug Lowenstein, then president of the Interactive Digital Software Association, stated, "There is absolutely no evidence, none, that playing a violent video game leads to aggressive behavior." Yet research by Craig Anderson and Brad Bushman and their colleagues indicates otherwise and suggests that we have reason to worry about the prevalence of video games in youth culture today (Anderson & Bushman, 2001; Anderson & Dill, 2000).

In one study, 43 undergraduate women and men with an average amount of experience playing video games were randomly assigned to play one of two games (Bartholow & Anderson, 2002). Some played *Mortal Kombat*, a video game in

Video Games and the Columbine Massacre (A) An image from a violent video game. The correlation between playing violent video games and aggressive thoughts and behavior documented in the laboratory may play out in real life. (B) Eric Harris and Dylan Klebold spent hours playing the violent video game *Doom*. Some observers have speculated that spending so much time playing the game may have contributed to the boys' decision to plant bombs and shoot their classmates at Columbine High School in Littleton, Colorado. Here, cameras in the school cafeteria on April 20, 1999, showed Harris and Klebold armed with guns and getting ready to shoot their fellow students, who were huddled beneath the tables. They killed 12 students and 1 teacher before killing themselves.

which the player chooses to be one character and attempts to kill six other characters. The more killings and the more violent the deaths, the more points the participant wins. Others played *PGA Tournament Golf*, a video game in which players complete 18 holes of simulated golf, choosing appropriate clubs and shots best suited to the simulated wind conditions, sand traps, and trees. All participants played several rounds of one of these games against a confederate. When participants lost, they were punished by the confederate with a burst of white noise. When participants won, they punished the confederate with a burst of white noise. The study found that participants who had played *Mortal Kombat* gave longer and more intense bursts of white noise to their competitor than those who had played the golf game.

In a review of 35 studies like the one just described, Anderson and Bushman documented five disturbing effects of playing violent video games (Anderson & Bushman, 2001). Playing violent video games (1) increases aggressive behavior; (2) reduces prosocial behavior, such as helping or altruism; (3) increases aggressive thoughts; (4) increases aggressive emotions; and (5) increases blood pressure and heart rate, physiological responses associated with fighting and fleeing. These effects were observed in children and adult women as well as in men.

Social Rejection and Aggression

The Columbine massacre prompted intense reflection in the United States, and many hypotheses about the origins of the shooting spree, including the one just considered—that violent video games increase aggressive behavior. Another hypothesis that emerged after the massacre was social rejection—Harris and Klebold felt socially rejected by the more popular students at school, and their shooting rampage was a reaction to their feelings of ostracism. Following the massacre, the Department of Education sponsored a research-based report that agreed with this hypothesis, concluding that school shooters like Harris and Klebold tend to feel rejected by their peers. (For an alternative account that attributes the Columbine massacre to Klebold and Harris's pathological tendencies, see Cullen, 2009.)

How might social rejection trigger aggression, even on the scale of the Columbine massacre? Geoff MacDonald and Mark Leary have proposed an answer (MacDonald & Leary, 2005). Throughout the long course of human evolution, MacDonald and Leary reason, being socially rejected from the group was akin to a death warrant, given our profound dependence on others for food, shelter, defense, and affection. Given the many evolutionary advantages to being integrated into groups, social rejection came to activate a threat defense system, which involves stress-related cardiovascular arousal; the release of the stress hormone cortisol; feelings of distress and pain; and, most relevant to the current discussion, defensive aggressive tendencies. Early in primate evolution, this threat defense system was attuned to cues of physical aggression, such as a predator's attack, and it enabled our predecessors to fare well in aggressive encounters. As humans evolved into the most social of primates, social cues—hearing someone gossip about us, seeing an acquaintance's sneer or contemptuous eye roll, hearing a superior's critical tone of voice—acquired the power to trigger this threat defense system and its associated feelings and tendencies, including the tendency to act aggressively.

Dozens of studies reveal how chronic social rejection, such as that experienced by Harris and Klebold, sets in motion a set of feelings that can lead to extreme aggression. For example, social rejection stimulates feelings of pain: people who feel rejected report higher levels of chronic physical pain, physical ailments, and even greater pain during childbirth (MacDonald & Leary, 2005). To study experimentally the painful consequences of rejection, Kip Williams has developed the ball-tossing paradigm, which may remind you of the politics of playing four square on your grade-school playground many years ago. In this paradigm, one participant plays a ball-tossing game with two confederates. At a predetermined time in the experiment, the two confederates stop throwing the ball to the participant and throw the ball only to each other for 5 painful minutes. Sure enough, being rejected in this game triggers feelings of distress, shame, self-doubt, and a submissive, slouched posture (Williams, 2007).

In a neuroimaging study conducted by Kip Williams, Naomi Eisenberger, and Matthew Lieberman (Eisenberger, Lieberman, & Williams, 2003), participants believed that they were playing the ball-tossing game with two other people. (In actuality, they were playing against a computer that had been programmed by the experimenter.) When the participant experienced the virtual form of rejection, fMRI images revealed that a region of the brain known as the anterior cingulate, which processes physically painful stimuli, lit up. In other words, social rejection activates the same regions of the brain involved in processing physical pain. Supporting the idea that social pain is similar in nature to physical pain, Nathan de Wall and his colleagues have found that acetaminophen, the active ingredient in Tylenol, diminishes social pain just as it does physical pain (de Wall et al., 2010).

Alongside feelings of pain, social rejection also increases the likelihood of aggression. People who report a chronic sense of rejection are more likely to act aggressively in their romantic relationships, even resorting to physical abuse (Dutton, 2002). In important experimental work, Jean Twenge and her colleagues have found that individuals who were led to imagine a lonely, socially rejected future, compared with appropriate control individuals, were more likely to administer unpleasant noise blasts to strangers who had nothing to do with the participant's sense of social rejection (Twenge, Baumeister, Tice, & Stucke, 2001). Putting these findings together, MacDonald and Leary have argued that social rejection is a root cause of school shootings, like that at Columbine, that are tragically all too common these days in the United States and other countries, such as Scotland and Germany (Leary, Kowalski, Smith, & Phillips, 2003).

Income Inequality

Short-term factors such as heat and exposure to violent media have thus been shown to result in higher levels of aggression, as have important social conditions of the individual's life such as his or her experience of social rejection. Social psychologists are also interested in whether more enduring conditions in the individual's life influence levels of aggression, such as the presence of green spaces in the individual's neighborhood (**Box 13.3**) and prevailing economic conditions. Consider one such economic factor—levels of income inequality, or the degree to which the wealthy differ from the poor in their yearly income and net wealth. Some countries are characterized by high economic inequality: the highest-paid professionals—executives, lawyers, and financial managers—have yearly incomes in the millions and make vastly more than the average worker. The United States is characterized by fairly extreme inequality: almost 100 countries out of 136

BOX 13.3   FOCUS ON THE ENVIRONMENT

Green Neighborhoods Make for More Peaceful Citizens

The current environmentalist movement was inspired by philosophers such as Henry David Thoreau and Ralph Waldo Emerson, who were known as the transcendentalists. These writers found great calm and peace in being out in the woods. Their writings inspired a young naturalist, John Muir, whose experiences as a young man in the Sierra Nevada mountains led him to found the Sierra Club and argue on behalf of state and national parks, which he helped create.

Social psychologists have recently begun to examine how the availability of nature and green spaces influences our psychological functioning. Recent experiments have found, for example, that a walk in the woods (as opposed to a walk through a town) enables adults to perform better on a measure of concentrated attention (Berman, Jonides, & Kaplan, 2008) and that reports of experiences in nature are the best predictor, compared with other recreational activities, of calming down from the stress of work (Korpela & Kinnunen, 2009).

These findings raise a question: might green spaces make for less violent neighborhoods? Social psychologist Frances Kuo thinks so. In one line of research, Kuo has studied police reports of violence occurring near 98 low-rise buildings that are part of the Ida Wells housing project in Chicago (Kuo & Sullivan, 2001). Some of the buildings were surrounded by trees and lawns, others by asphalt and a lack of greenery. The residents in these 98 buildings came from similar backgrounds, were enduring similar levels of unemployment and economic hardship, and were randomly assigned to the buildings they lived in. Kuo discovered that the likelihood of violent crime was lower near apartments surrounded by green spaces. In experimental research, Kuo has allowed children with attention deficit disorder, who are more prone to aggressive acts, to go for a walk of comparable length and physical exertion in one of three places: in a green park, in a quiet neighborhood, or in noisy downtown Chicago (Taylor & Kuo, 2009). She found that children scored better on a measure of concentration only after the walk in the park. Green spaces seem to calm people's minds, enabling them to handle the frustrations of daily living better.

reported on by the Central Intelligence Agency have less of a gap between the rich and the poor (Central Intelligence Agency, 2011).

Does economic inequality increase violence? Researchers Wilkinson and Pickett think so (Wilkinson & Pickett, 2009). In their research, they measure the degree of inequality in terms of the difference in percentage of wealth owned by the richest in a society (usually the top 20 percent) compared with that owned by the poorest in the society (usually the bottom 20 percent). They then look at whether regional inequality—in a country, state, or county—correlates with the prevalence of different kinds of violence. Indeed it does. In countries characterized by high economic inequality, such as Bolivia, Iran, Kenya, and the United States, the average citizen is much more likely to be murdered, assaulted, or raped than in countries with less economic inequality, such as Germany, Taiwan, Ireland, and Norway. In addition, children in countries with greater income inequality are more likely to experience conflict with their peers and to report being victims of bullying (**Figure 13.3**). If states within the United States are classified according to their levels of economic inequality, the pattern repeats itself at the state level. Rates of homicide, for example, are higher in U.S. states with high levels of economic inequality (such as Louisiana and California) than in those with low levels of economic inequality (such as Utah and Wisconsin).

Social psychologists have offered several explanations for the connection between income inequality and violence. Wilkinson and Pickett note that the

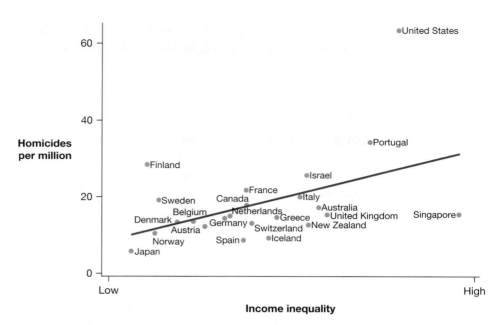

FIGURE 13.3 Income Inequality and Homicide Rates in Several Industrialized Countries Homicides are more likely in countries where there is greater income inequality between the rich and the poor. (Source: From Wilkinson & Pickett, 2009.)

powerful feelings of social rejection felt by individuals at the bottom in unequal societies might trigger violence, and this explanation has been bolstered by recent empirical findings. Another possibility is that inequality undermines the cohesiveness of a neighborhood, state, or country—that is, the feeling of trust and goodwill individuals have toward one another. Robert Sampson and his colleagues (Sampson, Raudenbush, & Earls, 1997) have found that more violent crime occurs in less cohesive neighborhoods. Evolutionary psychologists Martin Daly, Margot Wilson, and Shawn Vasdev (2001) contend that inequality throws males into competition for economic resources and access to females—two sources of conflict that often lie behind murder and other crimes.

 Many situational factors increase the likelihood of violence. These include high temperature, media and video game violence, social rejection, and economic inequality.

CONSTRUAL PROCESSES AND AGGRESSION

Thus far, this chapter has shown that several situational factors make people more aggressive. Of course, as this book emphasizes throughout, situations do nothing by themselves. Rather, their influence is channeled through construal processes. Many people live in extreme heat, see violent images in movies or on video games, and encounter horrific social rejection and income inequality without acting aggressively. This raises the intriguing question explored in this section: what particular construals of stimuli such as heat or social rejection give rise to aggressive behavior? The answer to this question goes back to some of the earliest studies of aggression, and it leads to a social psychologist's discovery that one construal process in particular—seeing the world through the lens of anger—is a powerful cause of aggressive behavior.

The Frustration-Aggression Hypothesis

In the late 1930s and 1940s, Neal Miller and John Dollard offered a simple account of aggression that was based largely on laboratory studies of rats (Dollard, Doob, Miller, Mowrer, & Sears, 1939; Miller, 1941). Miller and Dollard argued that *the* determinant of aggression is **frustration**, the thwarting of an individual's attempts to achieve some goal. Individuals act aggressively (or at least have the desire to act aggressively), Miller and Dollard maintained, when they feel thwarted in their attempt to reach that goal.

frustration The internal state that accompanies the thwarting of an attempt to achieve some goal.

Miller and Dollard proposed that aggression increases in direct proportion to (1) the amount of satisfaction the person anticipates receiving from meeting the goal (before it is blocked), (2) how completely the person is prevented from achieving the goal, (3) how frequently the person is blocked from achieving the goal, and (4) how close the individual believes he or she is to achieving the goal (Miller, 1941). In a study that illustrates some of these principles (and may remind you of your own experience with aggression), a confederate cut in front of individuals waiting patiently in line to see a movie. In one condition, the target was twelfth in line; in another condition, the target was second in line, about to purchase a ticket and therefore closer to 2 hours of anticipated pleasure. As predicted by the frustration-aggression hypothesis, the target who was second in line was much more aggressive in response to the confederate who cut in line than the person who was twelfth in line (Harris, 1974).

Critiques of the Frustration-Aggression Hypothesis

The frustration-aggression hypothesis is an important first step toward understanding the causes of aggression. When an individual feels blocked in the pursuit of a goal, aggression is more likely. As compelling as this account may be, closer examination reveals several problems with it (Berkowitz, 1993).

A first criticism has called into question the hypothesis that all aggressive behaviors follow from frustration, or the perceived thwarting of goal-directed activity. Consider again the relationship between heat and aggression. How does heat block an individual's goals? Research findings suggest that aggression can also follow stimuli that do not directly block goal-directed behavior. When animals are shocked, for example, they often aggress against others in their vicinity (Berkowitz, 1993). When people are exposed to extreme levels of pollution, they are also more likely to act aggressively (Rotton & Frey, 1985). And some forms of instrumental aggression, such as bullying, are not the direct product of the blocking of goals (Olweus, 1979, 1980). For example, bullies often act aggressively against weaker peers out of a desire to get attention, raise their status, or show off. In each of these cases, the stimulus that produces aggression has nothing to do with blocking an individual's goals. Some kind of construal other than the perceived thwarting of goals must account for how these stimuli give rise to aggression.

learned helplessness Passive and depressed responses that individuals show when their goals are blocked and they feel that they have no control over their outcomes.

A second problem with the frustration-aggression hypothesis is that frustration does not necessarily lead to aggression. Frustration can lead to other responses, again depending on how the individual construes the source of frustration. The best example here comes from the literature on **learned helplessness**, the passive and depressive responses some people show when their goals are blocked and they believe that they have no control over their outcomes (Seligman, 1975). In a series of frequently cited studies, dogs were shocked and prevented from escaping the pain. After repeated exposure to this uncontrollable, negative stimulus, the dogs did not react with aggression; instead, they collapsed into a pitiable state of helplessness and resignation.

A Neo-Associationistic Account of Aggression

The two critiques of the frustration-aggression hypothesis highlight how important construal processes are to the initiation of aggressive behavior. It is not just having our goals blocked that leads to aggression; it is how we interpret the events that seem to have prevented us from reaching those goals. To take one example, acts that we construe as having been intentionally harmful are more likely to make us aggressive than equally harmful acts that we construe as accidental (Worchel, 1974). Observations such as these set the stage for Leonard Berkowitz's neo-associationistic account of aggression, which maintains that anger-related construals are the key process that makes people respond aggressively to aversive stimuli.

Berkowitz (1989) has argued that any aversive event can elicit an aggressive response: pain, hunger, fatigue, humiliation, rejection, anxiety, insults—you name it. For example, in one of his studies, participants who held their arms horizontally for several painful minutes offered harsher, more hostile assessments of their mothers and romantic partners than did control subjects (Berkowitz & Troccoli, 1990). The critical determinant is whether the event produces unpleasant feelings of anger. Anger is associated with thoughts of assigning blame, fight-or-flight physiology, and feelings of injustice and revenge. Once activated, these thoughts, feelings, and physiological reactions make intentional harm against another—aggression—more likely (**Figure 13.4**). This line of thinking helps illuminate when different features of the situation lead to violence and when they do not. To return to the heat example, sometimes extreme heat does not trigger anger (for example, it might prompt relaxation), and in these instances, it will not lead to aggressive behavior. Other times, however, extreme heat does trigger feelings of anger, and at such times it does make people act aggressively.

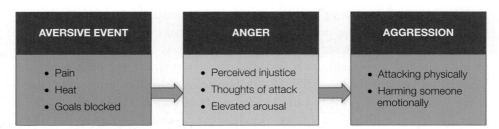

FIGURE 13.4 The Neo-Associationistic Account of Aggression This theory holds that aggression occurs following aversive events that make people angry. (Source: Adapted from Berkowitz, 1989.)

BOX 13.4 **FOCUS ON SPORTS**

The Effect of Uniform Color on Aggression

The tendency to act more aggressively when a weapon is nearby reinforces a core lesson of social psychology—the situationist message that seemingly small changes in the environment can have a substantial impact on behavior. This tendency also raises the question whether other environmental cues might foster or inhibit aggression. For example, might the clothes people wear influence how they behave, including whether they behave aggressively? Might the menacing black shirts worn by Hitler's S.S. (*Schutzstaffel*) have made it easier for them to brutalize the populace of conquered lands?

Support for such a possibility comes from research on the effect of uniform color on aggressiveness in professional sports (Frank & Gilovich, 1988). The investigators began by examining the penalty records of all teams in professional football (the NFL) and ice hockey (the NHL) from 1970 to 1985. As shown in the accompanying figure, the black-uniformed teams consistently ranked near the top in penalties every year.

As pronounced as this tendency might be, however, it cannot tell us whether wearing black actually causes players to be more aggressive. There are two other possibilities. First, because of some negative stereotypes involving the color black (for example, cinematic villains typically dress in black), players in black uniforms may look more intimidating even if they play no differently than players on other teams. Thus players in black uniforms may be more likely than others to be penalized for marginal infractions. Second, the finding may simply be a selection effect; that is, the managers of certain teams, believing that aggressiveness pays off in victories, may both recruit particularly aggressive players and, incidentally, give them black uniforms to foster an aggressive image.

The latter interpretation can be ruled out. By a convenient twist of fate, several teams switched uniforms from non-black to black during the period under investigation, and all experienced a corresponding increase in penalties. One team, the NHL's Pittsburgh Penguins, changed uniform colors in the middle of a season, so the switch was not accompanied by any changes in players, coaches, or front-office personnel. Nevertheless, the Penguins averaged 8 penalty minutes in the blue uniforms they wore before the switch and 12 penalty minutes in the black uniforms they wore after—a 50 percent increase.

Follow-up laboratory experiments have provided support both for perceptions of aggressiveness and actual aggressiveness of players in black (**Figure 13.5**). Thus the tendency for black-uniformed teams to draw so many penalties appears to be the joint effect of a bias on the part of referees and a tendency for players wearing black to act more aggressively (Frank & Gilovich, 1988).

But does wearing black always make people more aggressive? Probably not. The effect seems to be limited to contexts that are already associated with confrontation and aggression. Thus the black clothing worn by Catholic clerics and Hasidic Jews may not make them any more aggressive, but the black shirts worn by Hitler's S.S. might very well have contributed to their brutality.

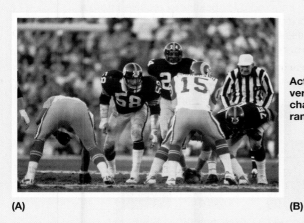

(A)

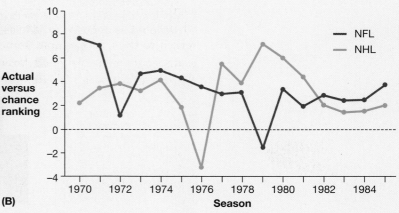

(B)

FIGURE 13.5 Uniform Color and Aggression (A) The Pittsburgh Steelers, wearing black uniforms, were known for their aggressive play. (B) Penalty records of black-uniformed teams in the NFL and NHL from 1970 to 1985. (Note that the hockey season always stretches across two calendar years; thus, "1985" corresponds to the 1985–1986 season.) Points on the graph represent the difference between the average ranking of the black-uniformed teams and the average to be expected based on chance alone (represented by the dotted horizontal line at 0). (Source: Adapted from Frank & Gilovich, 1988.)

Weapons and Violence

People today live in an era in which weapons are everywhere. Worldwide, roughly 650 million guns are in the hands of nonmilitary citizens (Small Arms Survey, 2011). This same survey found that in the United States, there were nearly 89 guns for every 100 citizens in 2007. Gun control is one of the most divisive political issues in the United States today. Opponents of gun control see the possession of firearms as a constitutionally guaranteed right to bear arms. Advocates of gun control believe that restricting the purchase and use of guns would reduce the incidence of lethal aggression.

Berkowitz has gathered data that might be used by advocates of gun control (**Figure 13.6**). According to Berkowitz, guns serve as powerful cues that prime anger-related construals, making aggression more likely. To test his hypothesis,

---

FIGURE 13.6 Scientific Method: Priming of Anger-Related Aggression

Hypothesis: Aggression is more likely when anger is experienced in situations that include images or objects that prime violent thoughts.

Research Method:

1. A male participant and a confederate worked on a series of problems and took turns evaluating each other's performance by delivering between one and ten shocks. The participant believed that more shocks were delivered for performances that most needed improvement.

2. Participants unwittingly assigned to the "neutral" condition were shocked by the confederate once, whereas participants assigned to the "anger" condition were shocked several times.

3. The participant then watched the confederate work on the problems and gave his evaluation of the confederate's performance in the form of shocks. In a "no object" condition, no objects were near the shock machine. In a "neutral object" condition, badminton rackets and shuttlecocks were near the shock machine. In a "gun" condition, a revolver and a shotgun were sitting near the shock machine.

Results: Participants who were angered by shocks they received from a confederate were more likely to retaliate with shocks when there were violent weapons as opposed to harmless objects near the shock machine.

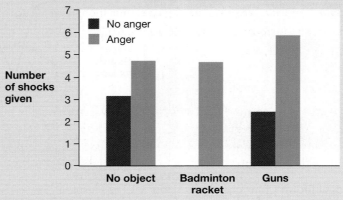

CONCLUSION: Weapons primed more aggressive behavior when combined with preexisting anger.

Source: Adapted from Berkowitz & LePage (1967).

Berkowitz had male participants engage in an experiment with a male confederate on "the effects of physiological stress upon work" (Berkowitz & LePage, 1967). The participant and confederate worked on a series of problems and took turns "evaluating each other's performance." They did so by delivering between one and ten shocks, having been instructed to deliver more shocks for performances that most needed improvement.

The researchers had the participants work on the problems first. Unknown to the participants, the confederate delivered shocks based on whether the participants had been assigned to a neutral or anger condition (not based on their actual performance). The confederate shocked those assigned to the neutral condition one time and those assigned to the anger condition seven times. The participant then watched the confederate work on the problems and gave his evaluation of the confederate's performance in the form of shocks under one of three conditions. In a "no object" condition, no objects were near the shock machine. In a "neutral object" condition, badminton rackets and shuttlecocks were near the shock machine. In a "gun" condition, a revolver and a shotgun lay near the shock machine—rather unusual experimental props, to say the least. According to the neo-associationistic account of aggression, participants who were angry and primed to think aggressive thoughts by the presence of the guns should be particularly aggressive toward the confederate. These participants administered more shocks than those in the other experimental conditions.

It's critical to note that the aggression-priming effect of the guns was observed only in the condition in which subjects were made angry; the guns had no effect if participants were not angry (see also Frodi, 1975; Turner & Leyens, 1992). That is, guns make people aggressive when they are combined with or elicit anger-related construals, as Berkowitz maintained. In further support of this point, a recent study found that hunters do not become more aggressive when presented with images of guns, because they construe guns as objects for recreation rather than for violence (Bartholow, Anderson, Carnagey, & Benjamin, 2005).

 LOOKING BACK People's construals of situations can be crucial in determining whether they act aggressively. We do not become aggressive every time one of our goals is blocked; instead, experiences that prompt us to feel anger lead to aggressive behavior. When we feel angry, stimuli that prime thoughts of aggression, such as weapons, increase our aggressive tendencies.

CULTURE AND AGGRESSION

Anthropologists have long noted dramatic cultural variation in levels of aggression. People in certain cultures have been observed to be kind, peaceful, and cooperative. Alaskan Inuits, for example, have been described as rarely expressing anger or aggression and as remarkably kind in their actions with others. People in other cultures have been portrayed as violent, belligerent, and aggressive. Among the Yanomami, who live in the Amazon, aggression is encouraged in children, intra-tribal fighting with spears and knives is a weekly source of injury and death, and rape and war are considered an intrinsic part of human nature (Chagnon, 1997).

The challenge for social psychologists, of course, is to bring cultural differences in aggression into the laboratory and find explanations for them. The cultural

Culture and Aggression There are cultural as well as individual differences in the expression of aggression. (A) The Alaskan Inuits rarely express anger or aggression. (B) The Yanomami encourage aggression in their children and are known for their violent raids against their enemies.

perspective on aggression holds that certain values, as well as habitual ways of construing the self and others, make members of one culture more aggressive and violent than others, or more prone to specific kinds of aggression. Let's look at two distinct lines of research that illustrate the cultural approach to aggression.

The Culture of Honor

Richard Nisbett and Dov Cohen have explored regional differences in violence in the United States (Cohen & Nisbett, 1997; Cohen, Nisbett, Bowdle, & Schwarz, 1996; Nisbett, 1993; Nisbett & Cohen, 1996). Nisbett and Cohen argue that a **culture of honor** is prevalent in the U.S. South; men in such cultures tend to be concerned about their reputation for toughness, machismo, and the willingness and ability to avenge a wrong or insult. These concerns give rise to firm rules of politeness and other means by which people recognize the honor of others, thus lending stability to social relations and reducing the risk of violence. The downside of the concern with honor is that it makes people particularly sensitive to slights and insults and makes them feel obligated to respond with violence to protect or reestablish their honor.

Chapter 2 presents several lines of evidence using a variety of methods that indicate that when their honor is slighted, Southerners are more likely than Northerners to respond with aggression (Nisbett & Cohen, 1996). In archival research, Nisbett and his colleagues found that murders in the context of a felony were about equally common in the North, South, and Southwest; but honor-related homicides, those that occurred as a result of an argument or perceived insult, were far more common in the South and Southwest than in the North (**Figure 13.7**). To examine participants' sensitivity to slights and insults, Cohen and his colleagues exposed Southerners and Northerners to an insult in the context of a laboratory study. Insulted students from Southern states showed more anger in their facial expressions than did students from the North (Cohen et al., 1996), showed higher levels of testosterone and cortisol, shook another person's hand more firmly, and refused to move out of the way of an imposing confeder-

culture of honor A culture that is defined by its members' strong concerns about their own and others' reputations, leading to sensitivity to slights and insults and a willingness to use violence to avenge any perceived wrong or insult.

The rates of felony-related murders are similar in different regions of the United States . . .

. . . but argument-related murders are much more common in the U.S. South and Southwest than in other regions of the United States.

White male homicide offender rates (per 100,000)

Non-South South and Southwest

Felony-related murders

Non-South South and Southwest

Argument-related murders

FIGURE 13.7 The Culture of Honor and Homicide Homicide rates point to a sensitivity to slights and insults that characterizes a culture of honor in the South and Southwest. (Source: Adapted from Nisbett & Cohen, 1996, p. 21; based on data from Fox & Pierce, 1987.)

ate walking toward them in a narrow hallway. In a field experiment, Cohen and Nisbett (1997) found that some Southern employers actually expressed a good deal of warmth toward a potential job applicant who confessed to having been convicted of manslaughter after defending his honor.

What are the deeper origins of this culture-related variation in aggression? Why is honor-related homicide more common in the South? Could it just be the higher temperatures there? It's not likely, because honor-related homicides are more common in the relatively cool mountain regions of the South than in the relatively hot lowlands. Could it be the brutal history of slavery? Again, it's not likely, and for the same geographical reason. Homicide is more common in the highlands, where slavery was relatively uncommon, than in the lowlands, where slavery was ubiquitous.

Instead, Nisbett and Cohen (1996) argue that the culture of honor in the South is a variant of a culture found worldwide among people who earn their living by herding animals. Herders are susceptible to losing their entire wealth in an instant if someone steals their cows, pigs, or sheep. Farmers, in contrast, are susceptible to no such rapid and catastrophic loss—at least not at the hands of another person. The vulnerability of the herder means that he has to develop a tough exterior and make it clear that he is willing to take a stand against the slightest threat, even an insult or a joke at his expense. This difference fits the pattern of violence in the United States because the North was founded primarily by farmers from England, Germany, and the Netherlands, whereas the South was founded primarily by Scottish and Irish settlers (and especially the Scotch-Irish of Northern Ireland—Celtic peoples who had herded, rather than farmed, since prehistoric times). Thus the people in the Southern highlands, where the herding culture continued to be a major economic activity until quite recently, were more likely to be violent than those in the lowlands, where settlers had taken advantage of the rich soil to become farmers.

Rape-Prone Cultures

Rape of the Sabine Women
Rape is a disturbingly common form of violence, in particular during times of violence and in contexts where women occupy positions of low power. Such was the case in the legend of the rape of Sabine women who were forced to marry the Romans who conquered their town and raped them.

rape-prone cultures Cultures in which rape tends to be used as an act of war against enemy women, as a ritual act, and as a threat against women so that they will remain subservient to men.

In 1990, Nobel Prize–winning economist Amartya Sen estimated that there were 100 million missing women in the world (Sen, 1990). Women, holding constant their country of origin and class background, are more likely to enjoy longer life expectancies than men, so a given population should include more women than men. But in some countries, particularly those where women experience an unequal status in relation to men, women are more vulnerable to patterns of negligence and violence and are underrepresented in the population—hence the estimate of "missing" women (Kristof & WuDunn, 2009). For example, in some countries parents are less likely to immunize their daughters than their sons, or to take daughters to the hospital, and as a result girls are more likely to die early deaths due to curable sicknesses. In Pakistan, young girls may be killed by local villagers for acts of disobedience. Bride burning—the practice of punishing a young woman for offering too small a dowry to the groom's family in marriage—claims the lives of thousands of young women in India every year. And the sexual trafficking of young girls into prostitution—widespread throughout the world—claims the lives of thousands of girls as young as age 8 or 9 each year.

One of the most disturbing and common acts of violence against women is rape, the coercive forcing of sex by one person (overwhelmingly male) upon another (typically female). Rape is often used as an instrument of terror during war, as it was in the genocides in Bosnia, Rwanda, and Darfur. But acts of rape are not limited to the madness of war. The latest estimates from the organization UN Women (2011) are that sexual violence and rape are disturbingly common in marriages around the world. A survey of 86 countries found that on average about 20 percent of women experience sexual violence or rape in a romantic relationship at some time in their lives. In some countries, this rarely happens: for example, only 2.7 percent of women in Cambodia reported such an experience. In other countries, the statistics are staggering: in Ethiopia, 58.6 percent of women reported experiencing at least one episode of sexual violence in an intimate relationship.

What makes rape more prevalent in one culture than another? And how can such a question be tackled empirically? Peggy Reeves Sanday (1981, 1997) relied on archival records to study the cultural determinants of rape. She read descriptions provided by historians and anthropologists of 156 cultures dating back to 1750 BCE and continuing to the 1960s. She looked carefully for references to rape in these accounts and identified what she called **rape-prone cultures**. She defined such cultures according to whether they used rape as (1) an act of war against enemy women; (2) a ritual act—for example, as part of a wedding ceremony or of an adolescent male's rite of passage to adulthood; and (3) a threat against women so that they will remain subservient to men.

Of the 156 cultures Sanday studied, 47 percent were classified as rape free, in that there were no reports of rape in the accounts of the culture; 18 percent as rape prone; and 35 percent as rape present, where rape occurs but not as a ritual, threat, or act of war. It would be no surprise, however, if these figures underestimated the prevalence of rape proneness across cultures. They are based largely on anthropologists' observations, and rape is one of the most difficult acts to observe as well as a taboo subject in many cultures.

Putting these concerns aside, let's look at some of Sanday's specific findings. One question she addressed was what sexual attitudes predicted the prevalence of rape across the 156 cultures. For example, is there more rape in more sexually repressed cultures, because individuals resort to rape to gratify their sexual desire? Sanday did not find a higher incidence of rape in these cultures. She assessed the extent of each culture's sexual repressiveness according to the prevalence of post-partum (the period shortly after the birth of a child) taboos and premarital sex taboos. The prevalence of rape in each culture was unrelated to these sexually restrictive beliefs or practices.

What about the general level of violence in the culture? If rape at its core is an act of violence, then it should be more prevalent in more aggressive, violent cultures. This prediction would fit with Berkowitz's account of aggression; that is, members of highly aggressive, hostile cultures, where anger-related ideas are in the air, so to speak, should be more prone to commit aggressive acts, including rape. This indeed proved to be the case. Rape-prone cultures were more likely to have high levels of violence, a history of frequent warfare, and an emphasis on machismo and male toughness.

Finally, many scholars have treated rape as an act of dominance, a means of subordinating women, relegating them to lower-status positions. This approach suggests that rape may be more prevalent in cultures whose women have lower status. This prediction, too, proved to be true. Women in rape-prone cultures were less likely to participate in education and political decision making than were women in rape-free cultures. Women in rape-free cultures were more empowered and more likely to be granted equal status with men. Consider the Mbuti Pygmies as an illustration of these findings (Turnbull, 1965). In this (reportedly) nearly rape-free society, there is minimal interpersonal violence and fighting. Great prestige is attached to the raising of children, and women's contribution to society is valued. Women and men assume different duties, but they have equal standing. And women and men participate equally in political decision making.

 Cultures differ greatly in their propensity toward aggression of various kinds. Members of cultures of honor, which frequently were herding cultures in the past, are more inclined to commit violence when insulted. Cultures that are prone to rape are characteristically those that devalue women and have extreme gender inequality.

EVOLUTION AND AGGRESSION

For many people, the term *evolution* brings to mind a violent struggle for survival and the opportunity to reproduce. And indeed, evolutionary theorists have used various approaches to offer new insights into the origins of aggression.

Violence in Stepfamilies

Throughout the world, literature is full of tales of wicked stepparents who abuse their children. In the animal kingdom, "step-relations" seem similarly prone to violence. To take one example, when male lions acquire a new mate, they routinely kill all of the female's cubs from prior relations. Evolutionary psychologists Margo Wilson and Martin Daly suggest that these tendencies in our mammalian forebears have left their trace in human nature as well (Daly & Wilson, 1996; Wilson, Daly, & Weghorst, 1980).

Natural selection, Daly and Wilson reason, rewards those parents who devote resources to their own offspring. All the behaviors related to parental care—from filial love to breast-feeding—assist the survival of our own offspring, thereby increasing our **inclusive fitness**—that is, our own survival plus that of individuals carrying our genes. But parental care is costly, as any parent of a newborn will tell you; it requires time, effort, and material resources. In evolutionary terms, these expenditures are offset by the gains of having offspring—namely, the survival of our genes. Stepparents, in contrast, incur the same costs with no enhancement of their inclusive fitness, since they do not share genes with their stepchildren.

Survey research consistently finds that relations between stepparents and stepchildren tend to be more distant and conflict laden, and less committed and satisfying, than relations between parents and their genetic offspring (Hobart, 1991). The archival evidence is even more sobering. Daly and Wilson (1996) found that in the United States, children who are younger than 2 years of age are 100 times more likely to suffer lethal abuse at the hands of stepparents than at the hands of genetic parents, and in Canada, they are 70 times more likely to suffer lethal abuse from stepparents than from genetic parents. These findings hold, it is important to note, even when researchers control for a variety of likely contributing causes, such as poverty, youth of the mother, length of time the couple has lived together, number of children in the home, or reporting biases. In a study of a South American foraging people, 43 percent of children raised by a mother and stepfather died before their fifteenth birthday; that is more than twice the rate of death (19 percent) of children raised by two genetic parents. (This statistic does not imply that the stepchildren were killed; but at the very least, they were more likely to have been denied resources—for example, food and physical care—that were made available to genetic offspring.)

inclusive fitness The evolutionary tendency to look out for ourselves, our offspring, and our close relatives together with their offspring, so that our genes will survive and be passed on in future generations.

Violence against Stepchildren Literature and fairy tales in particular abound with tales of stepchildren treated badly by their stepmothers, as illustrated in (A) Cinderella, who becomes the scullery maid for her stepmother and stepsisters; and (B) Hansel and Gretel, who are sent out to die in the forest at the urging of their stepmother.

Gender and Aggression

When we hear about school shootings or think about teen violence, or when we read about the genocides and rapes in Rwanda and Darfur, these acts of aggression are almost always committed by young men. Physical aggression is, in fact, from early childhood to old age, the most marked and stubborn gender difference in behavior. In the United States, 99 percent of all people arrested for rape, 88 percent of all those arrested for murder, 92 percent arrested for robbery, and 87 percent arrested for aggravated assault are men (Kimmel, 2004). Men are also overwhelmingly the victims of violence.

Women, of course, are also aggressive, but in different ways. Women seem to exceed men in "relational aggression"—they gossip, form alliances, and exclude others (Coie et al., 1999; Dodge & Schwartz, 1997; McFayden-Ketchum, Bates, Dodge, & Pettit, 1996). Many female readers will remember with a wince the vicious ways girls can behave toward one another in middle school: speaking behind people's backs, tarnishing reputations, and the like. Obviously, this kind of aggression can be extremely hurtful emotionally. It does appear that while young men are more prone to acts of physical aggression—many of them profiled in this chapter—young women are more prone to acts of emotional aggression.

Scene from the Movie *Mean Girls* Although men commit most of the acts of physical aggression, women are more likely to engage in what is known as relational or emotional aggression.

Both evolutionary and cultural theorists have considered men's greater levels of physical aggression. Let's first look at an evolutionary approach to the tendency for men to engage in more physical violence. Evolutionists reason that during the period of evolutionary adaptation in early human history, men were hunters and protectors and almost exclusively the ones to engage in violent, intertribal warfare. Women, by contrast, were much more likely to be caretakers of infants and children. This basic division of labor in our evolutionary past helps illuminate why males are so much more aggressive today. They were the ones who developed greater upper body strength, greater muscle mass, and a greater tendency toward aggressive behavior, because certain demands of survival—finding sources of meat, defending against attacks—required these features. Women, as caretakers, developed greater abilities to empathize and care—forces that inhibit aggressive behavior and produce greater altruistic behavior (see Chapter 14).

Evolutionists also reason that the men's ability to mate generally depended on their status within the social hierarchy (Daly & Wilson, 1988). High-status men were much more successful than low-status men in terms of their reproductive success, or number of offspring. Thus, some men had offspring with many women, whereas other men's chances for reproduction were much more uncertain. By contrast, reproductively healthy women who wanted to pass on their genes were, almost without exception, able to do so. This basic difference in reproductive patterns required men to evolve strategies—including violence—for outcompeting other males to gain access to mates. This competition may account in part for much of the violence seen around the world: men are 20 times as likely to kill other men as women are to kill other women (Daly & Wilson, 1988).

The Psychopath in Film
In *Silence of the Lambs*, actor Anthony Hopkins portrayed murderer Hannibal Lecter in a way that is in keeping with findings showing that psychopaths lack empathy for others' suffering.

Cultural theorists counter by arguing that men are socialized into different roles that differentially prioritize physical aggression. Parents, teachers, media sources, and social institutions systematically, and often unwittingly, cultivate more aggressive tendencies in men. Consider, for example, how young boys are treated from the first moments of life. In short, they are expected to be more aggressive. When parents are presented with a video of an infant looking startled, if the infant is described as a boy, the parents say the infant is angry. If the same infant is described as a girl, the parents say the infant is fearful (Condry & Condry, 1976). Mothers talk more about emotions with their daughters than with their sons, and such conversations may cultivate greater empathy in women (Fivush, 1991). Empathy proves to be a critical source of prosocial behavior (see Chapter 14) and is profoundly lacking in the most violent of human beings (**Box 13.5**). The one exception to this parenting trend is anger, which mothers are more likely to mention in labeling the emotions of their sons. In effect, from very early in life, anger and aggressive reactions are made more salient to young boys than to young girls. Given that anger is a primary determinant of aggression, this socialization process might account for at least some of the gender differences in aggression considered in this chapter.

 Evolutionary theory leads social psychologists to expect that stepparents are more likely than genetic parents to aggress against children. It also leads to the expectation that males will be more aggressive than females—in part because aggression can be helpful in attaining status and access to females. Males are in general more physically aggressive than females, and females are in general more relationally or emotionally aggressive. Some cultural theorists argue that evolutionary arguments are unnecessary to explain these differences and that socialization practices are explanation enough.

BOX 13.5 **FOCUS ON MENTAL HEALTH**

The Cold-Hearted Psychopath

What would many Hollywood thrillers be like without the cold-hearted killer, such as Dr. Hannibal Lecter in *Silence of the Lambs*? The inspiration for these characters is a clinical category known as psychopaths—people, usually male, who are prone to extreme patterns of violence and who make up the majority of individuals in prisons who have been convicted of violent crime (Hare, 1991). A long-standing assumption is that psychopaths have profound empathy deficits, lacking any feeling for those they harm.

Recent scientific study reveals a more nuanced picture, suggesting that while psychopaths are as adept as the average person in understanding the emotions of others, they have deficits in responding emotionally to the suffering of others. The key scientist studying psychopaths is James Blair (Blair, Mitchell, & Blair, 2005), who finds that psychopaths cognitively understand the emotions of others quite well. For example, when shown photos of facial expressions of emotion, psychopaths do as well as appropriate comparison individuals in identifying emotions from the face. They also prove to be quite adept at assessing the mental states of other people; they can reliably infer what other people are thinking. They do show empathic deficits in their responses to others' sadness, however. Show a photo of a sad face to the average adult, and that person will respond with a galvanic skin response, a measure of the sweat response in the palms that indicates a physiological reaction to the other person's suffering. By contrast, psychopaths show no such physiological response to the sadness of others, but they do show such galvanic skin response to other emotionally evocative images, such as images of guns. From Blair's research, we can conclude that psychopaths understand quite well the emotions and mental states of others, but they lack feeling for the suffering of others.

CONFLICT AND PEACEMAKING

This chapter begins with an account of the Rwandan genocide, a story that seems to repeat itself with discouraging regularity in human history. In the aftermath of that genocide, Rwandans went through a process of reconciliation, following principles similar to those used in post-apartheid South Africa to help blacks and whites move beyond a history of violence to a more peaceful society. In Rwanda, formal court proceedings convicted several leaders of the genocide. In informal "truth and reconciliation" gatherings in Rwandan villages, Hutu perpetrators apologized to relatives of their victims, who were given a public arena to air their rage. Today, by most accounts, Rwanda is a stable and peaceful society. Although tensions and bitterness persist, levels of aggression and conflict between the Hutus and Tutsis are low.

One lesson from Rwanda is that groups can so quickly fall into conflict, a state in which their goals are incompatible with one another. And just as quickly, the same groups can shift to more peaceful relations defined by minimal violence and a sense of shared purpose. This lesson repeats itself in the conflicts of human history. In World War II, the Japanese and Germans were mortal enemies of the United States. Today, they are two of the United States' strongest allies.

What does social psychology have to say about these transitions between conflict and peacemaking? Some empirically tested insights speak to the power of construal as a source of conflict and peacemaking.

Misperception

The frenzy toward genocide in Rwanda was stirred by a manifesto known as the Hutu Ten Commandments, which was published in a widely read newspaper, the *Kangura*, and spread like wildfire by local radio stations. The Hutu Ten Commandments warned of the dangers of the Tutsis, insisting that Tutsi women were secret agents bent on Hutu demise, that Hutu men who married or employed Tutsi women were traitors, and that Hutus who did business with a Tutsi were enemies of the Hutu people. These and other rumors and fears led Hutus to form deadly misperceptions of the Tutsi people that helped fuel the genocide. This sort of misperception is not unique to Rwanda; it is common in wartime propaganda and the rhetoric that accompanies international crises. As conflicts escalate between groups, adversaries misperceive one another in several ways, forming what have been called "mirror images" of one another (Bar-Tal, 1990). It is common for both sides in escalating conflicts to attribute belligerence, imperialism, and inhuman qualities to another. These images of the enemy serve as ready justification for aggression.

Intergroup conflict and the misinformation campaigns that often foster it can lead to **dehumanization**, the tendency to think of opponents in nonhuman terms. Group members come to assume that individuals from other groups are less capable of experiencing emotions like compassion or embarrassment that enable cooperative relations; they assume that their group alone is capable of feeling such humanizing and moral sentiments (Leyens et al., 2001). As the conflict escalates, group members dehumanize their opponents by likening them to nonhuman species, in particular those that are filthy or disgusting (pigs, rats, insects).

Alongside this tendency to dehumanize, the parties in conflict often consider their strife as a fight between good and evil (Bar-Tal, 1990). Group members

dehumanization The tendency to attribute nonhuman characteristics to groups other than one's own—for example, by referring to them as rats, dogs, pigs, or vermin.

have a powerful tendency to think of their own group as moral and good, and the other side as immoral and evil (Brewer & Kramer, 1985). Conflicts between groups over concrete matters—trade routes, levels of compensation, territory, peace treaties—are quickly seen in moral terms.

Besides justifying aggression, these kinds of construals can have several regrettable consequences that amplify social conflict and make peacemaking more difficult. First, they can lead opponents to overlook areas of agreement with each other (Ross & Ward, 1995). For example, in survey studies, Lee Ross and his colleagues recruited opponents in ideological conflicts over such issues as abortion or the death penalty, as well as in geopolitical conflicts like those in Northern Ireland and the Middle East. Ross and colleagues asked members of both sides to provide their own attitudes and to estimate the attitudes of their opponents (Robinson, Keltner, Ward, & Ross, 1995). These data revealed that group members systematically overestimate the extremity of their opponents' attitudes; that is, they assume the other side is made up of fanatical extremists, when in fact many people on the other side are more moderate in their convictions. In doing so, group members tend to overestimate the differences between the two groups. Whereas the attitudes of opponents in social conflicts typically inhabit a fair amount of common ground, group members assume there is little or none. Studies of negotiations reveal a similar tendency: negotiators typically underestimate the amount of common ground in their attitudes and preferences and tend to settle for less desirable outcomes than might actually be available (Thompson & Hrebec, 1996).

A closely related tendency, and another barrier to more peaceful relations, arises when group members assume that their opponents' interests are the exact opposite of their own; any gain for one side means a loss to the other (Plous, 1985). In the context of negotiation, this situation leads to a tendency known as **reactive devaluation**: the mere fact that the other side has offered a concession is enough to reduce its attractiveness (Ross & Stillinger, 1991). To study this phenomenon, Ross and colleagues examined ongoing tensions between university students and administrators regarding their university's investments in South African–based companies in the 1980s. At the time, an apartheid system legally segregated whites and blacks in South Africa. Whites, although in the numerical minority, held positions of power and lived comfortable lives. Most blacks lived in impoverished townships and had little political power. Many U.S. college students demanded that their universities sell their investments in South African–based companies.

In response to this kind of protest, administrators at Stanford University were considering, and in fact were about to adopt, a plan wherein Stanford would divest its funds from companies that did not meet certain standards regarding opportunities for blacks in South Africa. Ross and Stillinger measured students' evaluations of this partial divestment plan, both before and after the university administration had put forward the plan. **Figure 13.8** shows strong evidence of reactive devaluation. Before the university adopted the partial divestment plan, when students were considering its merits in the abstract, they felt it was a significant and positive move, particularly compared with an

reactive devaluation The tendency to attach less value to an offer in a negotiation once the opposing group makes it.

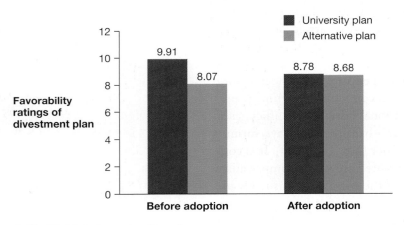

FIGURE 13.8 Reactive Devaluation in a Social Conflict Students rated two plans for divesting university funds from South African companies. Before the university administrators ultimately proposed one plan, the students saw great value in it; after the administrators proposed the plan, the students saw less value in it.

alternative plan that involved initiating an investment in companies that had left South Africa. But after Stanford had adopted the partial divestment plan and it was no longer an abstract proposal, students evaluated it much less favorably. The mere fact that "the other side" was known to have adopted the plan was enough to make students regard it as less acceptable. When parties to a conflict react in this way, it can be difficult indeed to reach a satisfactory resolution.

Simplistic Reasoning and Rhetoric

In the heat of conflict, group members are prone to misperceive their opponents and distrust their actions and proposed resolutions. Psychologist Phil Tetlock has found that this kind of simplistic reasoning can lead to simplistic rhetoric as well, which can also contribute to escalating conflicts on the international stage.

Tetlock proposes that adversaries in conflicts can reason and speak to one another in relatively complex or simple fashion. The complexity (or simplicity) of a position in a conflict is defined by two qualities: (1) the level of differentiation, or number of principles and arguments in the position; and (2) the level of integration, or connections drawn between the different principles and arguments. Those taking complex positions in conflicts consider many arguments and principles, even opposing ones, and draw many connections between them. Simpler positions involve fewer arguments—in particular, very few from the other side—and few connections between pieces of information. For example, a complex position on gay marriage would involve many principles (ideas about individual rights, views of marriage, legal precedent) and factual arguments (economic consequences of legalizing gay marriage, data related to family outcomes in gay and straight families, policy implications of legalizing gay marriage) as well as various connections between them (how legal precedent might influence tax-related benefits for gay citizens if they were allowed to marry). A simple position on gay marriage might be that it should be allowed in order to honor the principle of equality, or that it is unacceptable because marriages involve only relations between a man and woman.

How does the complexity or simplicity of reasoning influence group conflict? To answer this question, Tetlock and colleagues have coded the complexity of politicians' reasoning from their speeches and interviews. Who do you think engages in more complex rhetoric, incumbents seeking reelection or challengers? In an analysis of selected papers and speeches of ten presidents, from McKinley to Carter, only one of the ten candidates was more complex while on the campaign trail than while speaking as an elected president: Herbert Hoover (Tetlock, 1981). Politicians are more simplistic and extremist while wooing potential voters on the campaign trail and more complex as elected officials, when dealing with the give-and-take of policy making.

Who do you think is more complex, liberals or conservatives? (Your answer, of course, probably depends on your own political affiliation.) It turns out that extremists on both sides are less complex in their public rhetoric than moderate liberals and moderate conservatives. In one study, Tetlock coded the interviews of 89 members of the British House of Commons and found that extreme socialists and extreme conservatives were less complex than moderate socialists or moderate conservatives (Tetlock, 1984).

Most relevant to the subject of conflict resolution, Tetlock and colleagues have found that the complexity of reasoning and rhetoric may actually pave the way for more effective peacemaking. In the study of British politicians, more complex politicians on both the right and the left deemphasized differences between the

"You campaign in poetry and you govern in prose."

—former New York Governor Mario Cuomo

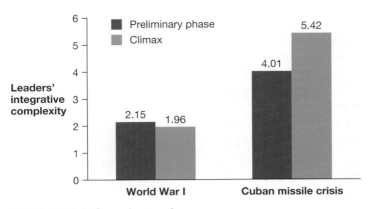

FIGURE 13.9 Complexity of Rhetoric In international crises, leaders who speak in ways that are more complex, taking into consideration the other side's views, are more likely to avoid escalating conflicts.

two parties, expressed tolerance of their opponents' views, and resisted blaming their opponents for England's woes at that time. That is, they avoided the misperceptions and polarization discussed in this section. In other research, Suedfeld and Tetlock examined the complexity of political leaders' rhetoric during two crises: the buildup to World War I in 1914 and the 1962 Cuban missile crisis, in which U.S. President John F. Kennedy and Soviet Premier Nikita Khrushchev averted a nuclear encounter (Suedfeld & Tetlock, 1977). **Figure 13.9** shows that between the preliminary phase of the conflict and the climax that led to war, the complexity of the political leaders' rhetoric decreased. In the crisis that was successfully resolved, the complexity of the leaders' rhetoric increased between the preliminary phase of the conflict and the climax.

Communication and Reconciliation

Often in the heat of conflict, or in the aftermath of aggression, the adversaries tend to stop communicating, to separate themselves from one another. Politicians fighting over a budget deal hunker down with their own party, formulating strategy. Warring nations expel diplomats and end formal communication. In divorce proceedings, the husband and wife are told not to communicate with each other, no matter what the intention.

This tendency to avoid our adversaries flies in the face of one of the most potent tools for reducing conflict: face-to-face communication (Frank, 1988). Numerous empirical studies find that simply allowing adversaries to communicate reduces levels of competition and aggression and increases the chances of finding satisfying resolutions to many kinds of conflict (Thompson, 2005). Communication no doubt reduces the misperceptions of opponents, to which disputants are prone, and paves the way for peacemaking and cooperation.

As adversaries communicate, they often show a powerful tendency to reconcile, to make amends for their differences and acts of harm, and to return to more peaceful relations. Our primate relatives exhibit instinctual tendencies toward reconciliation (de Waal, 1996). For example, in the heat of conflict, chimpanzees display submissive posture and vocalizations to one another, actions that trigger conciliation behaviors such as grooming, open-handed gestures, and even embraces. Humans resort to more complex reconciliation behaviors—confessions, apologies, signs of remorse—that trigger a sense of forgiveness, leading to reduced feelings of revenge and increased acceptance of the other person (McCullough, 2008).

This process of reconciliation is a powerful tool for reducing conflict and aggression. In Rwanda, face-to-face reconciliation—as in South Africa at the end of apartheid—was probably critical to the peacemaking after the genocide. Families fare better over time if the parents actively pursue strategies that encourage forgiveness during family conflicts (McCullough, Fincham, & Tsang, 2003). Even just imagining the act of forgiving a perpetrator of harm can reduce the fight-or-flight physiology of anger, which is a trigger of aggression (Lawler et al., 2003).

Social psychological studies of reconciliation have led to an innovative approach adopted by the criminal justice system (McCullough, 2008). In many jurisdictions, the perpetrator and victim of violent crimes are usually separated (often for very good reason) and therefore do not have an opportunity to communicate and reconcile. As an alternative to this approach, in programs focused on restorative justice, professionals who are highly trained in counseling and the law mediate conversations between perpetrators and victims. These conversations are based on several principles. The offender takes responsibility for the crime (in the court of law, offenders often resist making such confessions). The offender tries to "undo" the crime through apology or acts of reparation. And the offender and victim are encouraged to engage in a respectful dialogue with one another. As difficult as these conversations sound, they are often highly effective. Victims of crime who participate in restorative justice programs report many fewer thoughts of revenge than do appropriate comparison individuals and are more than twice as likely to forgive the offender and to report that the criminal justice system is fair (Sherman & Strang, 2007).

Moving toward a Less Violent World?

People the world over have witnessed massive amounts of violence in the past 100 years, in the form of wars and genocides. But despite the dispiriting news we hear daily, psychologist Steven Pinker has offered a different perspective on our current times (Pinker, 2007). Pinker argues that we are enjoying one of the least aggressive, most cooperative periods in human history. The data he draws on to make this claim are broad in scope. For example, people are dramatically less likely to die in today's wars as opposed to those in the past. Murder rates have also fallen precipitously in every European culture that has been analyzed, and recently in the United States as well. In fifteenth-century England, for example, the annual murder rate was 24 per 100,000 people; in 1960 England, it was 0.6 per 100,000. The "enhanced interrogation" techniques used by the United States at various times since the World Trade Center attacks in 2001 have drawn criticism from many parts of the world; but several hundred years ago, much more brutal torture was the norm, and it was often a form of public entertainment.

How do we explain such broad cultural shifts in violence and the more humane treatment of our foes? One explanation is that the world has become substantially more interconnected: our interests are more intertwined with those of people from other communities, states, and nations. Globalization has made businesses multinational. Solutions to global warming and many other environmental problems will require treaties that involve many countries. Many college campuses in the United States and Canada draw students from all over the world. People communicate with others in distant lands over the Internet, on Facebook, on Twitter, and through Skype. People are much more likely to marry and form friendships with people from different backgrounds. This expanding interdependence has given rise to greater cooperation among nations, states, and communities (Wright, 2000). Cooperation, Pinker argues, has short-circuited more aggressive tendencies and given rise to greater prosocial behavior.

 Several construal biases—dehumanization, misperceiving common ground, simplistic reasoning and rhetoric—can escalate group conflict. Reconciliation processes can be a powerful tool for increasing peacemaking tendencies during conflict.

Chapter Review

Summary

Situational Determinants of Aggression

- *Hostile aggression* is motivated by anger and hostility, having the primary aim of harming others, either physically or psychologically. *Instrumental aggression* is behavior intended to achieve some goal.

- *Heat* affects levels of violence. Hotter cities have higher rates of violent crime, and more violence occurs during hot months than during cool months.

- *Media violence* has been shown to cause violence and aggression in real life. When a highly publicized suicide occurs, copycat suicides follow. Longitudinal studies show that children who watch more violence on TV commit more serious crimes as adults than do children who watch less violence. Watching violence on TV also causes more violent behavior in the short run. Violent video games also increase the likelihood of violence.

- *Social rejection* is a powerful elicitor of aggressive tendencies.

Construal Processes and Aggression

- According to the *frustration-aggression hypothesis*, when attempts at achieving goals are blocked, aggression ensues.

- An alternative hypothesis is the *neo-associationistic model*, which states that people respond aggressively to an aversive stimulus only when they make anger-related construals about that stimulus.

- Construal processes affect both anger and aggression. Acts that seem intentional are more likely to cause aggression than identical acts that do not seem intentional.

Culture and Aggression

- People in many parts of the world, including many people in the U.S. South, adhere to a *culture of honor*, meaning that they are inclined to respond to insults and actions that convey malicious intentions with violence or threats of violence. Such cultures are especially likely wherever there is a history of herding, with its greater attendant risks of losing all wealth.

- In *rape-prone cultures*, levels of violence tend to be high in general, and rape is used as a weapon in battle. In such cultures, rape is used as a ritual act and as a threat to keep women subservient to men. Relatively rape-free cultures tend to grant women equal status.

Evolution and Aggression

- Evolutionary theory provides a useful perspective on *family violence*. Stepchildren are more subject to abuse than genetic offspring, who can carry on the genetic line.

- Violent and aggressive acts are more likely to be committed by men than by women. Women are likely to be aggressive in different ways than men, using *relational aggression* such as gossip and ostracism to hurt others emotionally rather than violence.

Conflict and Peacemaking

- Groups in conflict tend to *misperceive* the other side as extremist and overestimate their differences, *dehumanize* the opponent, assume the other side's actions are motivated by hostility, and *reactively devalue* any offers or concessions.

- More complex reasoning involving more evidence and integration of ideas promotes peacemaking in international conflicts.

- Communication is a powerful way to reduce conflict.

Key Terms

culture of honor (p. 514)

dehumanization (p. 521)

frustration (p. 509)

hostile aggression (p. 498)

inclusive fitness (p. 518)

instrumental aggression (p. 498)

learned helplessness (p. 510)

rape-prone cultures (p. 516)

reactive devaluation (p. 522)

Further Reading

Berkowitz, L. (1993). *Aggression*. New York: McGraw-Hill. A comprehensive overview of the social psychological study of aggression.

Nisbett, R. E., & Cohen, D. (1996). *Culture of honor: The psychology of violence in the South*. Boulder, CO: Westview Press. This book summarizes years of work on the culture of honor.

CHAPTER 14

Altruism and Cooperation

IN A FEW SECONDS ON JANUARY 2ND, 2007, WESLEY AUTREY became a national hero. The 50-year-old construction worker was waiting with his two young daughters to catch a subway train at the 137th and Broadway station in New York City. As they waited, a young film student, Cameron Hollopeter, collapsed to the ground, suffering from what appeared to be a seizure. Autrey and two women rushed to help the young student, who was twisting and convulsing on the ground. With a borrowed pen, Autrey managed to pry Hollopeter's mouth open and clear his respiratory passages so that he could recover his breath and strength.

Autrey's heroics were just beginning. Hollopeter stood up, staggered to the platform's edge, and then fell onto the tracks, landing face down between two rails. The lights of an oncoming train appeared. Autrey had to make a split-second decision: jump onto the tracks with his daughters waiting nearby, or let the train run over Hollopeter? Autrey chose to jump. He landed on the tracks and lay on top of Hollopeter. The train's brakes screeched, but it could not stop in time: five cars of the train rolled over Autrey and Hollopeter. As the crowd screamed and cried, Autrey called out, asking those nearby to tell his two young daughters that their father was okay. The train had missed Autrey by one inch, leaving grease smears on his blue cap.

In the aftermath of the event, Autrey was celebrated as a hero. He appeared on the daily television shows, was named one of *TIME Magazine*'s 100 most influential people, received a standing ovation at President George W. Bush's State of the Union address, and was awarded the Bronze Medallion, New York City's highest award for excellence in citizenship. Of it all, Autrey said, "I don't feel like I did something spectacular; I just saw someone who needed help. I did what I felt was right."

Extraordinary Altruism Wesley Autrey jumped on the New York subway tracks to save a fallen man in the face of an oncoming train. He is pictured here (A) with his children and (B) at the State of the Union address.

Altruism in Rwanda Paul Rusesabagina, acting manager of the Mille Collines Hotel in Kigali, Rwanda, saved over a thousand people from massacre by sheltering them at the hotel, bribing the *interahamwe*, and appealing to influential contacts.

ALTRUISM

Reports of people risking their lives for strangers in need, as Autrey did, are not rare. Even during the unspeakable violence of the Rwandan genocide, discussed in Chapter 13, individuals engaged in inspiring acts of concern for others. Paul Rusesabagina, a Hutu, was the acting manager of the Mille Collines, the most prestigious hotel in the capital city of Kigali. As the massacres unfolded, he hid over a thousand people (both Tutsis and moderate Hutus) at the hotel. Each day, the Hutu *interahamwe* would arrive and demand to take some of the Tutsis away. And each day Rusesabagina would plead and ply them with beer and money to prevent further massacres. Around the clock he frantically called and faxed influential contacts, appealing for their help. Often risking his own life and those of his children and wife, he pleaded and schemed time and time again for the survival of his guests.

Autrey's and Rusesabagina's actions are clear examples of **altruism**—unselfish behavior that benefits others without regard to consequences for the self. Humans are prone to feelings of compassion that lead us to behave in ways that benefit others who are suffering, often at a cost to ourselves. At the same time, we don't always act on such prosocial feelings. Many forces can inhibit altruistic action, including basic tendencies toward self-preservation and fear of embarrassment (say, by misinterpreting a mundane situation as an emergency). When do we act altruistically, and when don't we?

Empathic Concern: A Case of Pure Altruism?

During the Los Angeles riots of 1992, Reginald Denny, a white truck driver, was being beaten severely by four black youths. Several black residents who lived near the area saw the beating live on television and rushed to the scene to save Denny's life, risking their own lives in the process. What motivates this kind of action?

altruism Unselfish behavior that benefits others without regard to consequences for the self.

Compassion by Strangers Often even strangers will respond to an individual's distress and offer aid without thought of rewards or danger. (A) During the riots in Los Angeles in 1992, Reginald Denny was pulled from his truck and severely beaten. (B) Upon seeing the incident on television, Bobby Green (pictured here) and several other local residents rushed to the scene to rescue him.

In an important line of research, Daniel Batson has made a persuasive case for a selfless, other-oriented state that motivates altruistic behavior like that displayed by Wesley Autrey, Paul Rusesabagina, and Reginald Denny's saviors (Batson & Shaw, 1991). Batson begins by proposing that in any altruistic action, several motives are likely to be in play. Two of these motives are essentially selfish (egoistic); a third is more purely oriented toward unselfishly benefiting another person.

The first selfish motive is the **social rewards** motive. Those motivated by social rewards act altruistically with an eye toward how it will look to others (Campbell, 1975; Nowak & Sigmund, 1998; Nowak, Page, & Sigmund, 2000). Altruistic action earns people the esteem and respect of others, two very desirable social rewards. Mark van Vugt and his colleagues have found, for example, that group members will give greater social status and power to other group members who act altruistically (Hardy & van Vugt, 2006). We reward people's altruistic actions in many other ways—praise, awards, and even mentions in the media—perhaps to increase the cohesiveness and goodwill in our groups.

A second selfish motive for helping is the **personal distress** motive. People are motivated to help others in need in order to reduce their *own* distress (Cialdini & Fultz, 1990; Cialdini & Kenrick, 1976). From the first moments of life, in fact, we respond to others' distress with our own distress. For example, in one study, 1-day-old infants heard a tape recording of their own crying, the crying of another 1-day-old, or the crying of an 11-month-old (Martin & Clark, 1982). One-day-olds cried the most in response to the cries of another 1-day-old. Later in life, too, when we see someone crying, experiencing physical pain, or stuck in an embarrassing situation, we usually experience our own feelings of personal distress. Neuroscientific studies find that when we watch someone else experience pain, the pain regions of the brain are activated (Singer et al., 2004). The resulting feelings lead us to act in ways that return us to a more peaceful state. The most direct way to alleviate our own personal distress is to reduce the distress of the other person, and helping behavior is one way to accomplish that aim.

social rewards Benefits like praise, positive attention, tangible rewards, honors, and gratitude that may be gained from helping others.

personal distress A motive for helping those in distress that may arise from a need to reduce our *own* distress.

empathic concern Identifying
with another person—feeling and
understanding what that person is
experiencing—accompanied by the
intention to help the person in need.

Finally, there is **empathic concern**, the feeling people experience when identifying with the person in need, accompanied by the intention to enhance the other person's welfare. When we encounter another person in need or in pain, we not only experience our own feelings of distress but also imagine what that person must be experiencing. As we grow older, taking the other's perspective in this way results in an empathic state of concern, which motivates us to help that person address the needs and thus enhance his or her welfare, even at our own expense. This experience of empathic concern, Batson's reasoning goes, produces a selfless or other-oriented altruism. It is the split-second feeling that led Wesley Autrey to help the young student on the subway tracks and led Paul Rusesabagina to risk his life and the lives of his family to help the Tutsis.

Empathy versus Personal Distress Now comes the tricky part. How can researchers demonstrate that behavior can be motivated by empathic concern? Batson and his colleagues have taken an imaginative approach to this question in experiments that expose participants to another person in distress. The experiments are set up so that egoistic motives—to reduce personal distress or gain social rewards—would lead to little helping behavior. At the same time, the participant is led to empathize with the person in need. If an empathic concern produces helping, even in the face of egoistic opportunities to avoid it, we can confidently infer that there is an empathy-based form of helping that is not selfishly motivated. Let's see how this empirical strategy has played out in three studies.

The first study pitted the selfish motive of reducing personal distress against the motive of empathic concern by allowing participants to escape their aversive arousal by simply leaving the experiment. The researchers anticipated that if participants still helped, they must have been motivated by empathic concern (Batson, O'Quin, Fultz, Vanderplas, & Isen, 1983). Participants were told that they would interact with another participant of the same sex. The other participant was to complete several trials of a digit-recall task and to receive a shock after each mistake. In the easy-escape condition, the participant was required to watch the confederate receive only two of the ten shocks, and the participant was then free to leave the experiment while the confederate finished the study. In this condition, if participants were guided primarily by the egoistic motive to reduce personal distress, there should be relatively little helping behavior—the participant could simply leave. In the difficult-to-escape condition, the participant was told it would be necessary to watch the other person take all ten shocks.

After the first two trials, the confederate, made up to look a little pale, asked for a glass of water, mentioned feelings of discomfort, and recounted a traumatic shock experience from childhood. At this time, the participant provided self-reports of distress-related emotions (feeling upset, worried, perturbed) and empathic concern (feeling sympathetic, compassionate, tender). Batson and his colleagues used these self-reports to divide participants into those who were feeling egoistic distress and those who were feeling empathic concern. At this point in the experiment, the experimenter turned to the participant to ask whether he or she would be willing to sit in for the confederate, taking some of this person's shocks. If there is such a thing as altruism based on empathic concern, Batson and colleagues reasoned, then they should see substantial levels of altruism (agreeing to sit in for the confederate) on the part of participants who felt empathic concern for the confederate, even when they could simply leave the experiment and escape their empathic distress. The investigators' observations were consistent with this reasoning. Those participants who mostly felt distress and could escape the situation took few shocks on behalf of the confederate. Those participants who felt empathic concern, however, volunteered to take more shocks, even when they could simply leave the study.

Those still skeptical about the idea of pure altruism based on empathic concern might have a few reservations about Batson's study. First of all, empathic concern was not manipulated; instead, Batson and his colleagues identified empathic participants according to their self-reports. Perhaps there was a selection bias in this study—that is, the high-empathy participants might just be more helpful in general for reasons other than a selfless response to the confederate in need. Second, the experimenter knew how the participant acted, so a social rewards account of this study cannot be ruled out. Perhaps participants who took more shocks on behalf of the confederate hoped to impress the experimenter or wanted to avoid embarrassing themselves by leaving a person in obvious need. It would be much more telling to show that there are substantial rates of helping when doing so is completely anonymous. That notion motivated Batson's next study.

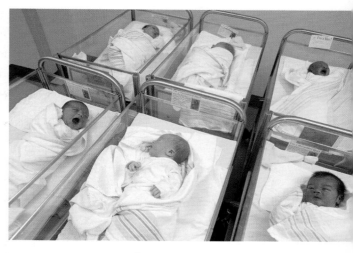

Empathy among Newborns
When newborns hear another newborn cry, they feel the distress of the other baby and will also begin to cry, as seen in this photo of newborns in a hospital nursery.

Anonymous Altruism In this study, Batson and colleagues asked female participants to form an impression of another person based on some information that person wrote while seated in another cubicle (Fultz, Batson, Fortenbach, McCarthy, & Varney, 1986). The communicator, a student confederate who called herself Janet Arnold, wrote two notes to the participant, expressing supposedly honest information about herself. The task of the listener (the actual participant) was to form as accurate an impression of Janet as possible. This time, empathic concern was manipulated. In the low-empathy condition, the participant was told to be as objective as possible when reading the notes, to concentrate on the facts at hand. In the high-empathy condition, the participant was told to imagine as vividly as possible how the communicator—the other person—felt. In the first note to the participant, Janet confessed to feeling out of place at her new home at the university. In the second note, Janet expressed a strong need for a friend, and she rather forthrightly asked the participant if she'd like to hang out a bit.

After receiving the second note, the participant was told that Janet had finished and left the study. At this point, the experimenter gave the participant a form that described another "long-term relationship study" and asked whether the participant would like to spend time at some later date in the future with Janet Arnold. In the low-social-evaluation condition, Janet's notes were delivered in sealed envelopes, and the experimenter did not read them. Similarly, the participant indicated how much time she would spend with Janet on a form that she enclosed in a sealed envelope to be sent to the professor conducting the study (who was never to meet the participant). Neither the experimenter nor Janet would know of the participant's response. In contrast, in the high-social-evaluation condition, both the experimenter and the participant read Janet's notes, and Janet and the experimenter would know how much time the participant said she would be willing to spend with Janet. The critical dependent measure was the number of hours the participant volunteered to spend with Janet. As you can see in **Figure 14.1**,

FIGURE 14.1 Scientific Method: Empathy and Altruism

Hypothesis: Empathy promotes altruistic behavior.

Research Method:

1. Female participants were seated at separate cubicles and asked to engage in an impression formation task. The communicator (a confederate), supposedly a student named Janet Arnold, wrote two notes to the participant, expressing supposedly honest information about herself. The task of the listener (the actual participant) was to form as accurate an impression of the communicator as possible.

2. In the low-empathy condition, the participant was told to be as objective as possible when reading the notes, to concentrate on the facts at hand.

3. In the high-empathy condition, the participant was told to imagine as vividly as possible how the communicator—the other person—felt.

4. Then the experimenter gave the participant a form that described another long-term relationship study and asked whether the participant would like to spend time with the other communicator, our lonely Janet Arnold.

5. In the low-social-evaluation condition, Janet's notes were delivered in sealed envelopes and not read or known by the experimenter. Similarily, the participant indicated how much time she would spend with Janet on a form that she enclosed in a sealed envelope.

6. In the high-social-evaluation condition, the experimenter and the participant read Janet's notes, and Janet and the experimenter were privy to the participant's indication of how much time she would spend with Janet.

Results: Participants who were encouraged to feel empathy for another student, Janet, who reported feeling lonely, volunteered to spend more time with her, even in the low-social-evaluation condition, where their volunteering was anonymous.

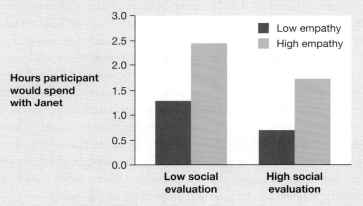

CONCLUSION: Even in anonymous conditions where no social reward can be gained, empathy promotes altruistic behavior.

Source: Adapted from Fultz, Batson, Fortenbach, McCarthy, & Varney (1986).

participants in the high-empathy condition volunteered to spend more time with her, even when no one would know of their action.

Physiological Indicators of Empathy One final study is especially helpful in assessing whether, as Batson supposes, some kind of selfless state motivates altruistic behavior. Particularly strong evidence for such a motive would be to show that empathic concern has a distinct physiological signature that predicts whether a person will act altruistically. To study this question, Nancy Eisenberg

BOX 14.1 FOCUS ON SOCIAL TRENDS

Are Young Adults Today Less Empathetic than Those a Generation Ago?

Since the time of the pharaohs, people have complained that civilization is in decline and that the younger generation is not living up to the admirable standards set by the generations before them. This lament rarely has any basis in fact, for most of us would agree that people today are at least as compassionate, productive, and virtuous as they were in generations past—when people watched gladiatorial battles to the death, enjoyed public hangings, and owned slaves. Stephen Pinker (Pinker, 2011) has shown that over the eons, violence has been steadily decreasing while sympathy with our fel-low human beings is increasing. But evidence suggests that quite recently, levels of empathic concern may have declined. Sara Konrath and colleagues compiled the results from 72 studies involving 13,737 college students in the United States who had filled out a self-report scale that measures empathic concern (Konrath, O'Brien, & Hsing, 2011). This seven-item scale includes statements such as "I often have tender, concerned feelings for people less fortunate than me." People who often feel high levels of empathic concern tend to be interested in other people; they have more positive attitudes toward other species; and time and time again, as Dan Batson would predict, they act in more prosocial ways. For example, they are more likely to give money to homeless people, carry someone's belongings, volunteer for charity, and return incorrect change. Konrath synthesized studies spanning 30 years, from 1979 to 2009, to compare how empathetic college students are today with how empathetic college students were 30 years ago. Her result: college students' reports of how much empathy they feel for other people have dropped significantly over the last 30 years.

and her colleagues showed a videotape of a woman and her children who had recently been in an accident to second graders, fifth graders, or college students (Eisenberg et al., 1989). The children in the film missed school while they recovered from their injuries in the hospital. As the participants watched this moving film clip, their facial expressions were recorded on videotape and continuous measures of heart rate were taken. After watching the videotape, the participants were given the opportunity to help by taking homework to the recovering children during their recess (and thus sacrificing their playtime, which was highly valued by the younger participants). Eisenberg and her colleagues found that both children and college students who felt sympathy and concern in response to the accident victims (or empathic concern, in Batson's terms) showed eyebrows that were pulled in and upward, a concerned gaze, and heart rate deceleration—a physiological response that is the opposite of the heart rate acceleration associated with a fight-or-flight response. These participants were also more likely to help. In contrast, participants who reported distress while watching the videotape showed a pained wince in the face and heart rate acceleration, and they were less likely to help. Thus, empathic concern produces more helping behavior than distress; it also appears to do so in part through a different physiological response.

"Our earth is degenerate in these latter days; bribery and corruption are common; children no longer obey their parents; and the end of the world is evidently approaching."

—From an Assyrian clay tablet engraved 4,800 years ago

Empathic Concern and Volunteerism Dan Batson's research shows that feelings of empathic concern and sympathy increase the likelihood that people will act altruistically, helping those who suffer. These feelings also appear to be a primary determinant of other prosocial behaviors. For example, Allen Omoto and Mark Snyder have studied **volunteerism**, which they define as nonmonetary

volunteerism Nonmonetary assistance an individual regularly provides to another person or group with no expectation of compensation.

assistance that people provide with no expectation of receiving any compensation (Omoto & Snyder, 1995; Penner, Dovidio, Piliavin, & Schroeder, 2005). In the United States, estimates indicate that over 61 million people—close to 30 percent of the population—volunteer, providing companionship to the elderly, mentoring troubled children, or assisting the sick and dying (Omoto, Malsch, & Barraza, 2009). As with altruism, volunteerism has many motives, including a desire for social rewards and a desire to reduce personal distress. But Omoto and colleagues have found that self-reports of feelings of empathic concern also predict the likelihood that an individual will engage in volunteerism (Omoto et al., 2009).

Recent evidence suggests that volunteerism is good for your health. Stephanie Brown and her colleagues studied a sample of 423 elderly married couples over the course of five years and found that volunteerism increases longevity (Brown, Nesse, Vinokur, & Smith, 2003). At the beginning of the study, the researchers assessed the degree to which each partner offered help to other people—for example, by doing errands, shopping, or providing childcare for neighbors. The participants also indicated how often they received this kind of help from people other than their spouses, to capture how much they were the beneficiaries of volunteerism. Brown and colleagues then followed these participants for five years and kept track of who died (as 145 of them did during the study). Remarkably, people who gave more to other individuals were less likely to die during the five years of the study, when controlling for the participant's initial health, gender, and social contacts. And how about the recipients of help? They were no less likely to die than people who did not receive help. It may indeed be better to give than to receive.

What cultivates empathic concern in people? What produces the Wesley Autreys and Paul Rusesabaginas of the world, or the good-hearted citizens who make sacrifices and volunteer for others? One answer comes from the remarkable work of the Oliners (Oliner & Oliner, 1988), who interviewed over 100 rescuers from World War II, individuals who risked their lives to save Jews during the Nazi Holocaust. (Sam Oliner himself was saved by such a person in Poland as a young boy.) In the course of these interviews, rescuers reported that altruism and compassion were highly valued in their homes. Rescuers reported that their parents and grandparents frequently told stories from their own lives and from their culture in which altruism was a theme. Altruism was a central theme in the books the family read and the teachings they discussed. In their dinner-time conversations about the events of the day, they discussed things through the lens of altruism and concern for other people. Altruism was explicitly invoked as an important ethical principle. Empathic concern apparently is a powerful force for good in human societies and can be passed from parents to children.

Situational Determinants of Altruism

Thus far, social psychology has documented a state—empathic concern—that motivates altruistic action and volunteerism. But people don't always act on their empathic concern. Consider the horrifying tragedy that befell Kitty Genovese. In the early morning hours of March 13, 1964, Winston Moseley stalked Kitty Genovese as she walked home in Queens, New York. He tackled her in front of a bookstore near her apartment and stabbed her in the chest. As she screamed for help, lights went on and several windows opened in the surrounding apartments. From his seventh-floor window, one neighbor yelled, "Let that girl alone!"

Moseley left the woman, only to return a short while later. He stalked his screaming victim to a stairwell in her apartment house, stabbed her eight more times, and sexually assaulted her. New York police received their first call about the incident at 3:50 a.m., 30 minutes after the cries of distress first awakened neighbors. By the time they arrived, Kitty Genovese was beyond help.

Thirty-eight of the neighbors admitted to having heard her screams. Many of them must have felt the pangs of empathic concern. But no one intervened aside from the neighbor who yelled from afar. Not a single person called the police. Instead, investigators heard explanations such as "I was tired"; "We thought it was a lover's quarrel"; "We were afraid." One couple simply watched the assault from behind curtains in their dimly lit apartment.

The Kitty Genovese incident shocked the American public. Like Stanley Milgram's studies of obedience to authority (see Chapters 1 and 8), the incident also raises fundamental questions about human nature. Are we really that callous to the suffering of others? The findings that we have reviewed on empathic concern, altruism, and volunteerism suggest not. Kitty Genovese's murder moved several social psychologists to attempt to understand the processes that dampen our empathic concern, inhibit altruistic action, and make people reluctant to intervene during emergencies.

Failure to Intervene in an Emergency Kitty Genovese was a young woman who was stalked and killed in Queens in front of her apartment as her neighbors watched from their windows and failed to intervene.

Darley and Batson's Good Samaritan Study No research better reveals the powerful situational determinants of altruism than a classic study by John Darley and Daniel Batson from 1973 (discussed briefly in Chapter 1). Their study was modeled on the timeless tale of the Good Samaritan, which concerns different reactions to a man who has been robbed, stripped, and left in a ditch. In the Bible story, a busy priest first walks by. Despite being a religious leader and supposedly concerned with those in need, he fails to stop and help the man. Next a Levite, another religious functionary, arrives and also avoids the man. Finally, a resident of Samaria, a member of a group that followed different religious customs and was despised by mainstream society, sees the half-dead man. The Samaritan stops, helps the man, takes him to an inn, and provides money for clothes and food to restore the victim's strength.

Darley and Batson's study, inspired by the Good Samaritan parable, makes for an even better story than the classic tale itself. The lesson is that subtle situational factors, such as whether you are on time or late, powerfully determine whether you will help someone in need.

Darley and Batson (1973) asked students attending Princeton Theological Seminary to give a talk to undergraduate students at another location on the Princeton campus. In one condition, the seminary students were told that the topic of the talk would be the jobs that seminary students typically find upon graduating. In a second condition, they were to give a talk on the tale of the Good Samaritan. The experimenter then gave them a map of the Princeton campus and showed them the building where they were to give their talk. In one condition, the no-hurry condition, participants were told they had plenty of time to get to the designated room. In a moderate-hurry condition, it was clear that the seminary students would have to hustle a bit to be on time. In the high-hurry condition, the seminarians were told they were already a bit late for the students waiting to hear their words of wisdom.

As the seminarians crossed the Princeton campus, their path led them past a man (actually a confederate) who was slumped over and groaning in a passageway. When the seminary students got within earshot, the man complained that he was having trouble breathing. The man was visibly and audibly in distress. The question was: What proportion of seminary students in the various conditions would stop to help the man?

The topic of the talk had no statistically significant effect on the seminary students' likelihood of helping the man in distress. The largest effect was produced by the most subtle of variables: whether or not the students were late. Seminary students who were not in a hurry were more than six times as likely to stop and attend to the suffering man as those who were in a hurry to give a talk. Only 10 percent of the students in the high-hurry condition stopped to help (see Figure 1.1 in Chapter 1).

Like so many of the classic studies in social psychology, this one offers lasting lessons about how powerful situations can be. Being late made it unlikely that the very people we would expect to exhibit altruism—students studying to be spiritual leaders—would do so. The study itself has many compelling features: the use of seminary students as participants, the naturalistic setting, the assessment of real behavior as the dependent measure. Let's now look at other kinds of situational factors that affect the likelihood of altruistic behavior.

Audience Effects One important determinant of whether people will stop to offer help to others in need is the presence of other people. Researchers who have studied **bystander intervention**—that is, how likely it is for people to intervene in an emergency—have found that people are less likely to help when other people are around (Latané & Nida, 1981). In part, the presence of other bystanders at emergencies reduces the likelihood of helping because of a **diffusion of responsibility**. Knowing that others have seen the emergency, each bystander is likely to assume that others will intervene, indeed may be better positioned to intervene, and thus each person feels less responsibility for helping the victim. The witnesses of the Kitty Genovese murder may have seen other apartment dwellers' lights go on, or they may have seen others in the windows, and they may have assumed that someone else would help. The end result is a disturbing lack of action.

Consider one of the best known of the studies of audience constraints on helping, a study by John Darley and Bibb Latané inspired by the Kitty Genovese tragedy (Darley & Latané, 1968). College students sat in separate cubicles discussing the problems associated with living in an urban environment. They engaged in this conversation over an intercom system, which allowed only one participant to talk at a time. One of the discussants, a confederate (one of the authors of this book, as it happens), early on described his difficulties in adjusting to urban life and mentioned that he had problems with seizures from time to time, especially when under stress. Then, after everyone else had spoken, the confederate took his second turn. As he did so, he became increasingly loud and incoherent; he choked and gasped. Before falling silent, he uttered the following words:

> If someone could help me out it would it would er er s-s-sure be sure be
> good . . . because er there er er a cause I er I uh I've got a a one of the
> er sei-er-er things coming on and and and I could really er use some help
> so if somebody would er give me a little h-help uh er-er-er-er-er c-could
> somebody er er help er uh uh uh (choking sounds) . . . I'm gonna die er er
> I'm gonna die er help er er seizure er (chokes, then quiet). (Darley & Latané,
> 1968, p. 379)

bystander intervention Giving assistance to someone in need on the part of those who have witnessed an emergency. Bystander intervention is generally reduced as the number of observers increases, because each person feels that someone else will probably help.

diffusion of responsibility A reduction of the sense of urgency to help someone involved in an emergency or dangerous situation under the assumption that others who are also observing the situation will help.

In one condition, participants were led to believe that their discussion group consisted of only two people (the participant and the victim). In another condition, the conversation was among three people (the participant, the future victim, and another person). And in a final condition, the audience was the largest: the conversation apparently involved six people (the participant, the victim, and four other people).

The question, of course, was whether the other students would leave their cubicles to help the victim, who was presumably suffering from a potentially lethal epileptic seizure. The presence of others had a strong effect on helping rates. Eighty-five percent of the participants who were in the two-person condition, and hence the only witness of the victim's seizure, left their cubicles to help. In contrast, 62 percent of the participants who were in the three-person condition and 31 percent of those in the six-person condition attempted to help the victim (**Box 14.2**). The presence of other people, at least of strangers, strongly inhibits helping behavior (Latané & Nida, 1981).

Several types of studies have pursued this question: whether people are less likely to help when other people are around or when they are alone (for a review, see Latané & Nida, 1981). In some studies, people witnessed a victim who was in danger or in pain. For example, participants might witness a person who had passed out in a subway. In other studies, participants witnessed a staged theft in a liquor store or on the beach. Across these kinds of studies, 75 percent of people helped when they were alone compared with 53 percent who helped when they were in the presence of others.

These studies of audience effects have typically examined whether the presence of strangers reduces helping behavior. But what about the presence of friends? Many real-world observations would suggest that the presence of friends might boost levels of altruism. For example, soldiers readily risk their lives to save their combat buddies. Good friends in grade school often stand up to bullies on the playground when their friends are nearby.

BOX 14.2   FOCUS ON DAILY LIFE

Likelihood of Being Helped

A given bystander is less likely to help in an emergency situation if other bystanders are around. But what are the chances of your receiving help from *any* of the bystanders? When there are more bystanders, there are more people who might help. Consider the "seizure" study described in this chapter. When participants thought they were alone, they helped 85 percent of the time. When they thought there was one other person who might help, they intervened 62 percent of the time. If there really had been two bystanders, each of them with a 62 percent chance of intervening, the victim would have received help 86 percent of the time—virtually identical to the rate of receiving help with one bystander (probability of receiving help = $1 - .38^2 = .86$). When participants thought there were four other people who might render assistance, they intervened 31 percent of the time. Again, had there really been five bystanders, each of them with a 31 percent chance of intervening, the victim would have received help 85 percent of the time (probability of receiving help = $1 - .69^5 = .85$). Does this mean that it doesn't matter whether there are many or few people around? Not so fast. These studies have also measured how quickly people come to the aid of someone in distress, and they have consistently found that single bystanders act more quickly than the *quickest* person to react in a group of bystanders. And when you're in an emergency situation, a lack of speed can kill.

Mario Mikulincer and Phil Shaver have collected evidence suggesting that the presence of friends may indeed increase altruistic action (Mikulincer, Shaver, Gillath, & Nitzberg, 2005). In their study, participants first completed a task in which they judged whether ten strings of letters made up actual words. In the midst of this task, they were presented with the name of an acquaintance, of a friend they did not feel a close attachment to, or of a person (usually a friend) to whom they felt strongly attached. In the third condition, the investigators reasoned, the prosocial tendencies associated with a sense of a secure attachment should be activated (see Chapter 10). Participants then moved on to "another study" in which they were given the task of evaluating another participant, actually a confederate, who had to complete a sequence of upsetting tasks. They watched the poor confederate look over gory photos, hold a rat, hold her arm in near-freezing water, and finally handle a large, hairy tarantula. In the middle of this last task, the confederate gave up and asked whether the actual participant might be able to take over. Those participants who had been exposed to their close friend's name felt more empathic concern for the confederate than participants who were exposed to the other names. They were also more likely to volunteer to hold the spider. Whereas groups of strangers appear to inhibit altruistic responses to emergencies, friends can evoke our nobler tendencies.

Victim Characteristics Needless to say, altruism is not blind nor indiscriminate. People are most likely to help when the harm to the victim is clear and the need is unambiguous (Clark & Word, 1972; Gaertner & Dovidio, 1977). Researchers have studied altruistic intervention when a person in need either screams or remains silent. Bystanders help victims who scream and make their needs known between 75 and 100 percent of the time, but they help silent victims only between 25 and 40 percent of the time.

That said, one powerful determinant of helping is whether anything about the victim suggests that it might be costly to render assistance. The greater the costs associated with helping, studies reveal, the less likely people are to act altruistically. In one study on this theme, carried out on a subway train in Philadelphia, a "victim" (actually a confederate) staggered across the car, collapsed to the floor, and then stared up at the ceiling (Piliavin & Piliavin, 1972). In one condition, a trickle of blood was seen to flow from the victim's chin. In the other condition, there was no blood on the victim. The researchers believed that bystanders would find it more costly to help the bleeding victim, who would likely expose the helper to greater trauma and might require greater medical care. The influence of such anticipated costs was reflected in the results of this study. When the victim was bleeding, he received help 65 percent of the time; when he was not bleeding, he received help 95 percent of the time. Even though the bleeding victim's need was more apparent, the likely costs of helping inhibited altruistic intervention.

More enduring characteristics of the victim also powerfully influence rates of helping. For one thing, the gender of the victim matters. In general, women tend to receive more help than men (Latané & Nida, 1981). But this behavior varies according to the victim's appearance. More attractive women and women dressed in conventionally feminine attire tend to receive more help from passersby (Piliavin & Unger, 1985). There are at least two explanations of this result. Women dressed in feminine attire fit the gender stereotype of being more dependent and helpless—and thus in greater need of help. In addition, male passersby may view their intervention as a foot in the door for a possible romantic involvement with an attractive woman in need.

People are also more likely to help similar others (Dovidio, 1984; Dovidio & Gaertner, 1981), including those from their own racial or ethnic group (Latané & Nida, 1981). For example, in recent work by Joan Chiao and her colleagues, African-Americans responded with greater empathy and more altruistic inclinations when viewing the suffering of African-Americans as opposed to European-Americans. Only the suffering of participants' own group members activated a region of the frontal lobes known as the medial prefrontal cortex, which is involved in empathic response (Mathur, Harada, Lipke, & Chiao, 2011). Other species appear to respond altruistically only to their own group. Several nonhuman primates will give up the opportunity to eat and partially starve themselves if their action will terminate a shock that is being administered to a member of their own species—something they will not do for members of other species (Preston & de Waal, 2002).

Construal Processes and Altruism

What would go through your mind if you encountered a person slumped over in a hallway while on your way to a talk, or if you witnessed someone passing out on the subway? What is it about being late, or hearing unambiguous cries of distress, or being in the presence of others that influences our inclination to help? In other words, what are the construal processes that influence whether we help or not?

In everyday life, many instances of distress are surprisingly ambiguous. A loud apparent dispute between a man and a woman overheard on the street might be careening toward violence and require intervention. But perhaps it's a non-threatening lovers' spat, or just two thespians acting out a dramatic scene from a play. A group of adolescent boys may be pummeling a smaller boy—or perhaps they're just playfully wrestling.

Pluralistic Ignorance Bystanders may do nothing if they are not sure what is happening and don't see anyone else responding. Here, this crowd of children may collectively arrive at the conclusion that the boys are just playing when bullying may be taking place given the ambiguous responses of other kids.

Helping in Ambiguous Situations Given the ambiguity of many emergencies, helping requires the potential helper to perceive first that a person is suffering and that intervention is needed. The victim's behavior provides clues about whether help is needed. When a victim's distress is not salient, the victim is less likely to receive help. As discussed earlier, when people in need vocalize their distress with loud cries, they are much more likely to be helped (Clark & Word, 1972; Schroeder, Penner, Dovidio, & Piliavin, 1995). Similarly, another study found that people are more likely to help when they are aware of the events leading up to the victim's distress (Piliavin, Piliavin, & Broll, 1976). When the situation is vivid and dramatic, the bystander is more likely to notice what is happening and to understand what is going on. In the more vivid condition, participants saw another person, a confederate, faint and slowly regain consciousness. In the less vivid condition, the participant saw only the aftermath of the incident—a confederate just regaining consciousness. Participants were much more likely to

"I said, 'I'm not on duty! I just came back to get my flip-flops.'"

come to the individual's aid (89 percent versus 13 percent) when they saw the entire drama unfold, so that they could understand the full nature of the problem.

The surrounding social context also plays an important role in determining whether bystanders conclude that assistance is called for. A form of pluralistic ignorance (see Chapter 5) occurs when people are uncertain about what is happening and assume that nothing is wrong because no one else is responding or appears concerned. There are strong norms to maintain a calm and collected demeanor in public, especially during emergencies. It is embarrassing, after all, to be the one who loses composure when there is no actual danger. When everyone in a potentially dangerous situation behaves as if nothing is amiss, each person will tend to mistake the others' calm demeanor as a sign that no emergency is taking place (Latané & Darley, 1968).

In one study that examined the role of pluralistic ignorance in bystander intervention, researchers asked participants to fill out a stack of questionnaires in a laboratory room (Latané & Darley, 1968). The participants did so in one of three conditions: alone, in a room with two passive confederates exhibiting the calm demeanor that was intended to produce pluralistic ignorance, or with two other genuine participants. As participants in these three conditions filled out their questionnaires, a rather strange and unnerving thing happened that presumably should serve as a clear signal of likely danger: smoke started to filter into the room from beneath a door, filling the laboratory room.

When participants were alone and had no input from other participants as to what was happening, 75 percent of them left the room and reported the smoke to the experimenter. (What could the other 25 percent of the participants have been thinking?) In the two other conditions, pluralistic ignorance took hold, and participants were less likely to assume that something was amiss. With three real participants, only 38 percent of the participants left to report the smoke. And remarkably, with two passive confederates showing no signs of concern, only 10 percent reported the smoke to the experimenter.

Anecdotal evidence from this study suggests that participants construed the smoke differently in the three conditions. Participants who did not report the smoke to the experimenter consistently told the experimenter that they did not believe it was dangerous. One participant ventured the hypothesis that it was truth gas! The students who did report the smoke construed it as a sign of imminent danger.

Combating Pluralistic Ignorance Bystanders are less likely to fall prey to pluralistic ignorance when they can clearly see one another's initial expressions of concern (and before their initial expressions are covered up out of the desire to seem less alarmed). This hypothesis was tested in a study in which participants were led through a construction-filled hallway to a lab (Darley, Teger, & Lewis, 1973). As they walked to the lab, they passed several stacks of wooden frames used in construction and a workman who seemed to be doing repairs. Once in the lab room, the participants began the ostensible task of the experiment—they were to do their best drawing of a model horse. Darley and his colleagues varied the degree to which participants would be able to see others' nonverbal expressions, those reliable signals of concern about a possible emergency. In the control condition, the participant was alone. In another condition, two participants were seated facing each other as they drew the model horse. With this alignment, they would see each other's immediate, spontaneous expressions of emotion when the emergency occurred. In a final condition, participants were seated back-to-back. Here they had no visual access to each other's immediate reactions.

As the participants labored over their drawings, they suddenly heard a loud crash and the workman crying out in obvious pain, "Oh, my leg!" The results of this study make it clear that seeing others' spontaneous emotional expressions reduces the effects of pluralistic ignorance. Ninety percent of the participants who were alone left the room to help the workman. Eighty percent of the participants who were seated face-to-face did so. But only 20 percent of the participants who were seated back-to-back left to help. Not having others' initial, unguarded reactions to help interpret the incident as a true emergency, these participants collectively assumed that nothing was wrong.

So how do you improve the chances of getting help when you need it? According to John Darley, who studied the factors affecting bystander intervention for more than a decade, two things are likely to be effective: (1) make your need clear—"I've twisted my ankle and I can't walk; I need help"; and (2) select a specific person—"You there, can you help me?" By doing so, you overcome the two greatest obstacles to intervention: you prevent people from concluding there is no real emergency (thereby eliminating the effect of pluralistic ignorance), and you prevent them from thinking that someone else will help (thereby overcoming diffusion of responsibility).

Culture and Altruism

Imagine that it's late at night, and you need assistance. Where do you think you would be more likely to receive help: in a large metropolis or in a small rural town? In a poor or a rich neighborhood? Near a church, or far away from a place of worship? Each of these questions involves the influence of different kinds of culture—geographical region, social class, and religiousness—on altruism. The prevalence of altruistic behavior varies in dramatic and sometimes surprising ways with these types of cultural influences.

Altruism in Urban and Rural Settings All across the world, people are moving out of small villages in the country to large cities. And recent studies suggest that the communities they are leaving behind might be kinder and more altruistic. Survey research indicates that people in rural areas report higher levels of empathic concern (Smith, 2009). Does that translate to different levels of altruistic behavior? To investigate this question, researchers have systematically examined helping rates in rural and urban environments. Nancy Steblay (1987) reviewed 35 studies that permitted comparisons of helping rates in rural and urban environments. She looked at the helping rates in communities of different sizes, ranging from fewer than 1,000 to more than 1 million. In all, 17 opportunities to offer assistance were created experimentally, typically in naturalistic settings. Researchers examined whether people would grant simple requests (for example, give the time of day), whether they would intervene to stop a crime, and whether they would help people in need (such as an injured pedestrian).

Steblay's analysis showed that strangers are significantly more likely to be helped in rural communities than in urban areas. The effect of population size was particularly pronounced in towns with populations between 1,000 and 50,000.

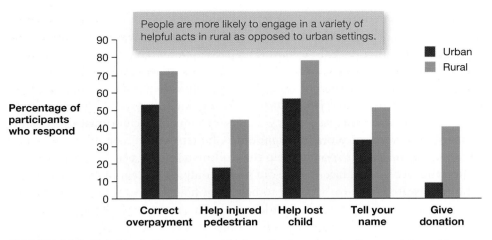

FIGURE 14.2 Helping in Rural versus Urban Environments (Source: Adapted from Steblay, 1987.)

Thus, you're much more likely to be helped in a town of 1,000 than of 5,000; in a town of 5,000 than of 10,000; and so on. Once the population rises above 50,000, however, there is little effect of increasing population. For a better picture of these results, consider the specific findings presented in **Figure 14.2**. As the figure shows, people are more likely to engage in a variety of helping behaviors in rural environments.

Let's dissect this finding a bit. You might ask which matters most: a person's current context or the context in which the person was brought up. For example, if you were brought up in a small rural town but currently live in a big city, which setting is more likely to influence whether you will help someone in need? The current situation wins hands down. In analyzing these 35 studies, Steblay found that the participant's current context, rural or urban, was a much stronger predictor of helping behavior than the person's rural or urban background. This finding is another nod to the power of the current situation.

What accounts for this rural-urban difference in helping rates? Researchers have offered three explanations. Stanley Milgram (1970) attributed it to stimulus

Helping in the Country People living in rural settings (A) are more likely to help others than people in the city (B), as shown here in the different responses to people in need.

overload. The amount of stimulation in modern urban environments is so great that no one can attend to all of it. As you walk down a city street, for example, the traffic, the construction, the swarms of people are, in combination, too much to take in fully. You narrow your focus, both in terms of attention and in terms of what circumstances you recognize as having a claim on your thoughts, feelings, and actions. There are simply too many inputs, so you shut down a bit and are less likely to attend to the needs of others and less likely to act altruistically.

A second explanation might be labeled the diversity hypothesis. Earlier we noted that people are more likely to help others who are similar to themselves. Urban areas, of course, are made up of more diverse populations. Thus, on average, you're more likely to encounter someone similar to yourself in a rural environment than in an urban environment. This may contribute to the observed urban-rural difference in helping rates. The third explanation is that more people are likely to be around to help in urban areas than in more rural environments, so a diffusion of responsibility may discourage people from helping in urban areas.

Social Class and Altruism In June of 2010, Bill Gates and investment guru Warren Buffet launched "the giving pledge" with great fanfare and media buzz. They asked that the wealthiest individuals in the United States give at least half of their wealth to charity. Warren Buffet pledged to give away 99 percent of his wealth by the end of his life. More than 40 of America's richest individuals soon followed suit, including Larry Ellison of Oracle and Mark Zuckerburg of Facebook. By some estimates, if the wealthiest Americans honored the giving pledge, charities would receive some $600 billion.

The giving pledge raises an intriguing question about altruism: Who gives more, the rich or the poor? Social scientists talk about the rich and the poor in terms of social class, an important cultural identity. Social class shapes the neighborhood you grow up in, the kind of schools you attend, the clubs your parents belong to, the food you eat, the clothes you wear, and even the music you prefer. Working-class individuals prefer music—country-western for example—that emphasizes struggle and overcoming obstacles; upper-class individuals prefer music—alternative rock, for example—that highlights individuality and freedom of expression (Snibbe & Markus, 2005).

Social psychologists measure social class as the combination of three factors: your family wealth, the educational level that you and your parents attain, and the prestige of your work and that of your parents (e.g., Kraus, Piff, & Keltner, 2011). These three elements of social class are correlated (yes, most of you will earn more by working hard and achieving a college degree). Together they give an individual a sense of his or her position in the class hierarchy as someone from an upper-class, middle-class, or lower-class background.

So how does social class influence levels of altruism? Are the Gates and Buffets of the world the rule, or the exception to the rule? When it comes to altruism, it turns out that individuals who have less give more, at least in terms of the proportion of their income that they give away to charity. Nationwide surveys of charitable giving in America find that wealthy individuals give away smaller proportions of their income to charity than do the poor (Greve, 2009). For example, a study by an organization called Independent Sector (2002) found that individuals making less than $25,000 per year gave away an average of 4.2 percent of their income, whereas those making over $100,000 per year gave away only 2.7 percent. It would seem that the Gates and Buffets are exceptions.

What investigators have learned about empathic concern and altruism sheds light on why the poor may give more than the rich. Specifically, Michael Kraus, Paul Piff, and their colleagues reason that a relative scarcity of resources leads lower-class individuals to be empathically attuned to others and to seek to build strong relationships that help them adapt to their more unpredictable, taxing, and at times threatening environments (Kraus et al., 2011). Upper-class individuals, by contrast, enjoy more abundant resources and opportunities that enable them to be more independent of others. In keeping with this theorizing, lower-class individuals prove to be more empathetic than upper-class individuals in a variety of ways that assess empathy: they are better judges of the emotions of a stranger with whom they have just interacted, they are better judges of a friend's emotions, and they are more accurate in their inferences about what emotions are expressed in photographs (Kraus, Côté, & Keltner, 2010).

Given these class-related differences in empathy, are lower-class people more likely to act in a prosocial fashion? Indeed, Piff and colleagues have found that they are (Piff, Kraus, Côté, Cheng, & Keltner, 2010). In one study, for example, people from different class backgrounds played the dictator game, an economic game in which they received 10 points and were asked to give some portion of those points to a stranger. The points that participants had at the end of the experiment determined their chances to win a lottery to be conducted at a later time, when all participants had completed the study. On average, participants gave away 41 percent of their points, and lower-class individuals gave away more of their points to a stranger than did members of the upper class.

A second study tied the tendency for lower-class individuals to act in more prosocial fashion to their tendency to feel more empathic concern for strangers in need. In this study, participants were given the chance to help an obviously distressed confederate who had arrived late for the experiment and therefore needed the participant's assistance to complete required tasks. Before this opportunity to provide help, participants watched either a neutral film clip (a relatively uninteresting scene from the movie *All the President's Men*) or a moving portrayal of the suffering of children living in poverty. Showing the film about poor children was intended to induce upper-class participants to feel the same level of empathic concern typical of lower-class individuals, which the investigators predicted would lead them to help more. The findings supported these predictions. **Figure 14.3** shows the class difference in prosocial behavior discussed earlier: after watching a neutral film clip, lower-class individuals offered to do more of the other participant's tasks than upper-class participants did. When upper-class individuals are

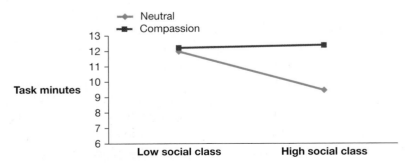

FIGURE 14.3 Social Class and Altruism Lower-class people help more than upper-class people, except when both groups are made to feel compassion. (Source: From Piff, Kraus, Côté, Cheng, & Keltner, 2010.)

made to feel compassion, however, they respond in the same prosocial fashion as their lower-class counterparts.

Religion, Ethics, and Altruism People the world over define themselves in terms of religion—as Muslims, Protestants, Methodists, Unitarians, Jews, Catholics, Mormons, Buddhists, Hindus, or Sikhs. Many others who avoid formal religion still define themselves as spiritual people who believe in forces that transcend the physical laws of nature. Like social class, religion can shape almost every facet of social life, ranging from whom you marry to your moral beliefs.

The world's major religions emphasize compassion, altruism, and treating others, even strangers and adversaries, with kindness (**Table 14.1**). This conduct is seen in such religious practices as tithing and tending to those who suffer. It is seen in moral codes such as the golden rule—that we treat others as we would like to be treated. It is seen in the texts of the major religions, which encourage a prosocial stance toward others through fables and time-honored passages. Admittedly, many of the world's religions include stories of taking revenge, putting people to death for seemingly trivial offenses, and treating nonbelievers in cruel ways. Still, these troublesome elements aside, all religions stress compassion and the need to treat others—at least some others—well.

Does exposure to religious concepts make people more prosocial? Recent research by Ara Norenzayan and Azim Shariff addresses this question (Norenzayan & Shariff, 2008; Shariff & Norenzayan, 2007). In a first study, participants were presented with sequences of five words, randomly arranged, and asked to generate sentences using four of those words. In a religion prime condition, the five words always included at least one word with religious meaning, such as *Spirit, divine, God, sacred,* and *prophet*. For example, in this condition participants would read "Felt she eradicate the spirit" and create the sentence "She felt the spirit." In a neutral prime condition, participants did the same task of unscrambling sentences, but none of the words had religious meaning. Participants then received ten Canadian dollars and were asked to give some amount away to a stranger. **Figure 14.4** shows the powerful effect of being primed by religious

TABLE 14.1 The Golden Rule across Cultures and Religions

Matthew 7:12	"In everything, therefore, treat people the same way you want them to treat you, for this is the Law and the Prophets." (*New American Standard Bible*, 1995)
Sextus the Pythagorean	"What you wish your neighbors to be to you, you will also be to them."
Buddhism	"Putting oneself in the place of another, one should not kill nor cause another to kill."
Tibetan Buddhism	"If you want others to be happy, practice compassion. If you want to be happy, practice compassion." (Dalai Lama)
Hinduism	"One should never do that to another which one regards as injurious to one's own self." (*Mahabharata*)
Muhammad	"Hurt no one so that no one may hurt you."
Taoism	"He is kind to the kind; he is also kind to the unkind."

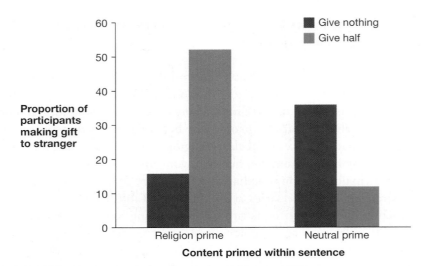

FIGURE 14.4 Religion and Altruism Being primed with religious concepts leads to greater generosity. (Source: Adapted from Norenzayan & Shariff, 2008.)

concepts like "divine" or "sacred." Participants in the neutral prime condition were more than twice as likely to give nothing to a stranger as compared to those in the religion prime condition (36 percent versus 16 percent). By contrast, people who were primed with religious concepts were more than four times as likely to treat a stranger as an equal by giving half of the money to the stranger (52 percent versus 12 percent).

Shariff and Norenzayan also examined whether secular, nonreligious concepts related to kindness and ethical behavior generate similar levels of generosity. In what they called a "civic" condition, participants unscrambled sentences that included words related to the secular institutions and ideas that build more cooperative societies, words like *civic*, *jury*, *court*, *police*, and *contract*. These words also generated high levels of generosity in the economic game—as much generosity, in fact, as the religious words prompted. It seems that the emphasis on fairness and cooperation and equality, seen in both religious traditions and secular treatments of ethics, can do a great deal to elicit prosocial behavior.

Evolution and Altruism

Few behaviors are more problematic to explain from an evolutionary perspective than altruism. Natural selection favors behaviors that increase the likelihood of survival and reproduction. Altruistic behavior, by its very nature, is costly; it devotes precious resources to others that could be used for ourselves or our genetic relatives. The costs of altruism can include the ultimate sacrifice. Consider the fates of four college-aged friends who took a day off from their jobs at a summer camp in upstate New York to relax at a swimming hole near some scenic waterfalls. While walking down a steep path to get there, one of them slipped and fell into a whirlpool. When he was sucked down under the raging, foamy water, each of his three friends was moved by altruistic concerns and, in succession, jumped into the river to save the others. They all died. Individuals guided by unbounded altruism would not have fared well in evolutionary history.

BOX 14.3   FOCUS ON POSITIVE PSYCHOLOGY

Spending Money on Others Brings Greater Happiness than Spending on the Self

People work hard to earn money to gratify their desires. Right? When Elizabeth Dunn and her colleagues surveyed several hundred college students, they found that to be the pervasive belief (Dunn, Aknin, & Norton, 2008). When they conducted a nationally representative survey of 632 Americans, they found that spending on personal matters (bills, gifts for the self) outpaced more prosocial forms of spending (gifts to others and charity) by a factor of 10 ($1,713.91 annually versus $145.96 annually). But these researchers also documented that more prosocial forms of spending bring greater boosts of happiness than self-focused spending. In one survey, they found that personal spending did not correlate with happiness, whereas prosocial spending did, independent of income. In a second study, six weeks after receiving a bonus, prosocial spending, again in the form of gifts to others and to charity, predicted increases in happiness, whereas personal spending did not.

Finally, Dunn and colleagues conducted a telling experiment. Forty-six participants first rated their overall happiness in the morning. They then received an envelope with a sum of money in it and were instructed to spend it. In the personal spending condition, participants were asked to use the money to pay a bill or buy themselves a gift by 5 p.m. of that day. In the prosocial spending condition, participants were asked to make a charitable donation, or buy a gift for someone else by 5 p.m. Participants were contacted after 5 p.m. and asked to report on their happiness. The participants in the prosocial spending condition reported being happier than they had been in the morning, whereas those people in the personal spending condition did not. It pays to be generous.

How, then, have evolutionary theorists accounted for altruistic behavior, which surely exists? Two evolutionary explanations have been offered: kin selection and reciprocity.

Kin Selection   One evolutionary explanation for altruism is based on the concept of **kin selection**, which refers to the tendency for natural selection to favor behaviors that increase the chances of survival of genetic relatives (Hamilton, 1964). Recall from Chapter 13 that inclusive fitness is the evolutionary tendency for people to look out for themselves, their offspring, and their close relatives as well as *their* relatives' offspring, ensuring that their genes survive. Thus, from the perspective of kin selection, people should be more likely to help those who share more of their genes, helping siblings more than first cousins, first cousins more than second cousins, and so on. By helping relatives survive, people help their own genes pass to future generations.

The kin selection thesis is that we should have a highly developed capacity to recognize kin. This ability would help us determine whom to help and whom to ignore. Indeed, there is evidence that at least some nonhuman animals reared apart can recognize their kin through specific visual cues and smells (Rushton, Russell, & Wells, 1984). Human mothers can recognize their new babies from photographs, even when they have had very little contact with the baby (Porter, Cernoch, & Balogh, 1984), and from smells left by the baby on T-shirts (Porter, Cernoch, & McLaughlin, 1983). (To our knowledge, there is no evidence that fathers are equally capable of identifying their own offspring.)

The more obvious prediction from kin selection theory is that we should direct more of our helping behavior toward kin than toward non-kin. There is support

kin selection The tendency for natural selection to favor behaviors that increase the chances of survival of genetic relatives.

for this hypothesis as well. Take two cases in the animal world. Mockingbirds have been observed to be more likely to feed hungry nestlings that are not their own but that are more closely related than other hungry nestlings (Curry, 1988). Ground squirrels, when sensing that a predatory coyote or weasel is in the vicinity, are more likely to emit an alarm call—thus putting themselves in danger by calling the predator's attention to their own location—in order to warn a genetic relative or a squirrel they have lived with than they are to warn unrelated squirrels or squirrels from other areas (Sherman, 1985).

In humans, genetic relatedness seems to influence helping as well. Across many cultures, people report receiving more help from close kin than from more distant relatives or nonrelatives (Essock-Vitale & McGuire, 1985). When hypothetical situations are described to them, people report being more willing to help closely related individuals (especially those young enough to have children) than more distantly related individuals or strangers (Burnstein, Crandall, & Kitayama, 1994). In a study of kidney donations, donors were about three times as likely to engage in this altruistic act for a relative (73 percent) than for nonrelatives (27 percent) (Borgida, Conner, & Manteufel, 1992). In a puzzle task that required cooperation, identical twins, who share all their genes, were found to cooperate about twice as often (94 percent) as fraternal twins (46 percent), who share only half of their genes (Segal, 1984; see also Burnstein, 2005). A recent neuroimaging study found that young mothers responded with activation in the orbitofrontal cortex—a region of the brain involved in prosocial emotion and approach behavior—to pictures of their own young babies but not to pictures of other equally cute babies (Nitschke et al., 2004).

Reciprocity Genetic relatedness, then, is a powerful determinant of people's helping behavior. But what about helping those who are not our kin? We often go to great lengths to help our friends. We give them money, let them sleep at our apartments and eat out of our refrigerators, help them move, and so on. And sometimes we put our lives on the line to help them, as did the young people who died trying to save their friend from drowning. Even more compelling, perhaps, is how often we help total strangers. People will dive into icy waters to save people they've never met, give money anonymously to charities, and engage in all sorts of more ordinary, less costly behaviors such as giving up a seat on a bus or taking the time to help someone cross a street. Such actions can be accounted for in part by reciprocity and cooperation, which form the basis of the second major evolutionary explanation for altruism.

In traditional, preliterate societies, individuals living in groups were best able to survive when they cooperated with one another. To explain how cooperation evolved, evolutionary theorists most commonly use the concept of **reciprocal altruism**, or the tendency to help other individuals with the expectation that they will be likely to help in return at some other time (Trivers, 1971). Cooperation among non-kin provides many benefits that increase the chances of survival and reproduction for both parties. Reciprocal altruism reduces the likelihood of dangerous conflict, helps overcome problems arising from scarce resources, and offers a basis for individuals to form alliances and constrain more dominant individuals (Preston & de Waal, 2002).

There is some evidence for the mutual helping that is the essence of reciprocal altruism. Vampire bats need blood meals to survive and may starve to death if they do not have a blood meal after 60 hours. Researchers have found that satiated bats

reciprocal altruism The tendency to help others with the expectation that they are likely to help us in return at some future time.

will regurgitate blood to feed bats that have given to them in the past but will not make a donation to a bat that has not been a donor itself (Wilkinson, 1990). In his observations of chimpanzees and bonobos, Frans de Waal (1996) has found that primates are disposed to share food with other primates who share with them, to look after each other's offspring, and to systematically groom other primates who have groomed them earlier. Reciprocity is a rule of primate social behavior.

In humans, the impulse to reciprocate is a powerful motive, and the tendency to return favors appears to be a human universal (Gouldner, 1960). Consider the following experiment. Researchers mailed Christmas cards to numerous complete strangers. About 20 percent reciprocated by sending their own Christmas cards back to the senders, whom they had never met (Kunz & Woolcott, 1976). Either the participants had too few friends to accommodate the stacks of Christmas cards they bought, or they felt compelled by the norm of reciprocity to respond with a Christmas card to the sender. Thus altruistic behavior directed toward non-kin appears to follow rules related to reciprocity and is an important part of the social contract.

Reciprocal Altruism Vampire bats will regurgitate blood to feed starving bats that have given blood to them in the past, but they will not give blood to bats that have not helped them in the past.

People's altruistic tendencies are the unselfish behaviors that benefit others. People may act altruistically for selfish motives, such as reducing distress or gaining social rewards, but some acts of altruism are based on a more selfless state of empathic concern. Researchers have examined a number of subtle but powerful situational determinants of whether or not people help others. The presence of other bystanders may lead to a diffusion of responsibility in which everyone assumes someone else will help. Characteristics of the victim also affect whether people will help, and people are more likely to help women and similar others. Moreover, construal processes influence helping; in particular, pluralistic ignorance can lead people to be less likely to help. People in rural settings and those from lower-class backgrounds are more likely to help than people in urban settings or from upper-class backgrounds. Two evolutionary concepts that can account for the existence of altruism are kin selection and reciprocity.

COOPERATION

The tendency for humans to cooperate is part of our evolutionary heritage. From archaeological studies of the bones of animals our hominid predecessors killed for food, we know that those early humans hunted in cooperative groups (Mithen, 1996). The profound vulnerability of our offspring—born prematurely to accommodate their enormous brains—required cooperative child care; both parents shared the burdens of raising such dependent offspring (Konner, 2003). The inclination to cooperate for common goals is almost a defining attribute of humans.

One of the most striking aspects of human relations is how quickly competitive relationships can become cooperative (and vice versa). In World War II, the mortal enemies of the United States were the Germans and Japanese. Shortly after the end of the war, they became strong allies. During the Rwandan genocide, Hutus sought to annihilate Tutsis; since then, the two groups have become more collaborative. It is an important lesson of history, how readily people shift from competition and aggression to cooperation.

Cooperation During World War I, instances of cooperation took place between enemy soldiers, as during this informal Christmas truce in 1914. Soldiers from both sides emerged from their trenches and fraternized in no-man's-land, as shown in this lithograph published in 1915.

The Prisoner's Dilemma Game

Core principles that account for how and why humans cooperate have been examined through the use of an experimental paradigm known as the prisoner's dilemma game (also see Chapter 1). Imagine being in an experiment in which you are ushered into a small cubicle by the experimenter, who informs you that there is another participant (whom you will never meet) in a cubicle nearby. Both you and the other participant are required to make a simple decision: independently, you must choose to "cooperate" with each other (do what will benefit both of you) or "defect" (do what will disproportionately benefit yourself). You will be paid for your participation, and your compensation will depend on the choices you make. If both of you cooperate, you will each receive $5. If both of you defect, you will each get $2. If one cooperates and the other defects, the defector will receive $8, and the cooperator will not receive anything. The experimenter says that you will be paid as soon as each of you makes your choice, and reiterates that you and the other subject will never meet. What do you do?

From the perspective of maximizing your own self-interest, the best, or "rational," choice is to defect. Whatever your partner does, you make more money by defecting than by cooperating. To see this, consult the summary of payoffs presented in **Figure 14.5**. If your partner cooperates, you receive $8 by defecting but only $5 by cooperating. If your partner defects, you receive $2 by defecting and nothing by cooperating. Defection thus "dominates" cooperation. So why not defect?

Here's the catch: the payoffs are the same for both players, so if both reason this way and choose to defect, they receive

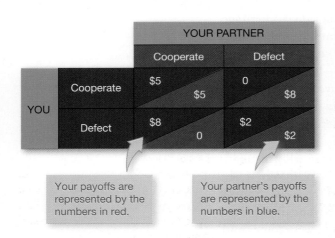

FIGURE 14.5 Payoff Matrix for Prisoner's Dilemma Game

only $2 rather than the $5 that would be theirs through mutual cooperation. The "best" choice for each individual player (defection) is a terrible choice from the standpoint of the two players in combination.

Countless individuals have participated in over 2,000 experiments of just this type, involving what is known as the prisoner's dilemma game. On the surface, the prisoner's dilemma game seems to hold little promise for teaching us anything significant about real human interaction. Unlike many real-world situations, the game offers no range of cooperative to competitive behaviors to choose from; instead, there are only two behaviors—cooperate or defect. In addition, participants are not allowed to discuss the choices beforehand, and they are never permitted to explain or justify them afterward. Overall the game seems too limited, too artificial, to tell us anything significant about real-world cooperation and competition.

Looks may be deceiving, however. As simple as the prisoner's dilemma seems, it nevertheless captures the essential features of many significant real-world situations (Dawes, 1980; Schelling, 1978). Consider a real-world analogue: India and Pakistan have been engaged in an arms race for decades. Like nearly all such struggles, the contest is ultimately futile because its structure is that of the prisoner's dilemma. Each country must decide whether to spend more on armaments or to stop spending money on more arms and enjoy a significant economic "peace dividend," as the United States did following the breakup of the Soviet Union. However, regardless of what the other does, it is "better" to acquire more arms. (If India freezes its acquisition of weapons, Pakistan can achieve an edge by spending more. If India builds up its arsenal, Pakistan has to spend more to avoid vulnerability.) Nonetheless, because the new weapons systems developed by one side are quickly matched by the other, the net effect is waste. The two countries pay dearly for a military balance that was attainable for less expense.

Developing Cooperative Relationships Here a Tutsi woman in Rwanda coexists peacefully with a Hutu man who had killed people close to her.

BOX 14.4 FOCUS ON NEUROSCIENCE

The Cooperative Brain

Cooperation is vital to human survival, but it is an inherently fragile arrangement. When we cooperate, we risk being exploited by others. Often, the rewards of cooperation are to be enjoyed much later—for example, when we cooperate with colleagues on a long-term project. James Rilling and his colleagues have found that the brain may be wired to enable cooperation in the face of these kinds of uncertainties (Rilling et al., 2002). They have shown that during acts of cooperation, our brains fire as if we are receiving rewards. In their study, 36 women played the prisoner's dilemma game over the Internet with another player. The researchers used fMRI technology to scan the brains of these women when they cooperated with the stranger—which was their most common choice. They found that reward-related regions of the brain (the nucleus accumbens, ventral caudate, and ventromedial/orbitofrontal cortex) lit up when the women cooperated. These regions of the brain are rich in dopamine receptors and are activated by all sorts of rewards, such as sweet tastes, pleasant smells, pictures of tropical vacations, and pleasing touches. Cooperation, it seems, is inherently rewarding.

Thus, although the prisoner's dilemma game may seem sterile and artificial on the surface, it captures a great many difficult real-world choices between cooperation and competition. Thousands of studies using the prisoner's dilemma game provide some telling insights into how people make these difficult choices, illuminating why people or groups or countries would be likely to defect or cooperate and suggesting what might be done to foster cooperative relations.

Situational Determinants of Cooperation

Do you choose to work with people who tend to be intensely competitive or with more cooperative types? Do you play basketball with highly competitive players or with cooperative individuals who are more interested in a good game than in coming out on top? Are you in a romantic relationship with someone who is interested in winning arguments—who views love as war, as the old saying goes—or someone who sees relationships as a matter of mutual benefit and collaboration? An important study by Kelley and Stahelski (1970) suggests that the cooperative or competitive outcomes in your relationships may, without your knowledge, depend as much or more on your behavior as on the behavior of the people you deal with. This study found that competitive people create more competitive interactions and thus come to construe their counterparts as also being competitive—which in turn justifies their own competitive behavior.

Upon arriving at the laboratory, participants were shown the prisoner's dilemma game and the payoff matrix in Figure 14.5. Was the goal to beat the other person or to maximize mutual gain? Some participants made it clear that they thought competition was the goal; others indicated that they thought cooperation was the goal. The experimenters paired off cooperators with cooperators, cooperators with competitors, and competitors with competitors and had the participants play several rounds of the game. After a certain number of trials, the players had to judge whether their partners were competitors or cooperators, as assessed earlier.

What happened in these various combinations? A revealing tale emerged about how contagious competition is. First, the competitors made everyone, including the cooperators, more competitive. Wouldn't you be competitive if your partner consistently defected on you, enjoying high rewards at your expense? Second, whereas cooperators were fairly accurate in their judgments whether they were interacting with a cooperator or a competitor, competitors were not. Competitive participants, who made others more competitive, mistakenly assumed that everyone was competitive.

Kelley and Stahelski's findings reveal that highly competitive individuals create competitive interactions with those individuals around them, and they even make more cooperative people more adversarial. Yet in real life, of course, we often know a lot about the people we choose to enter into relationships with, whether it is a romantic partnership, a business deal, or a political negotiation. Word spreads about a person's **reputation**, which social psychologists define as the beliefs, evaluations, and impressions about an individual's character that develop within a group or social network (Emler, 1994). In the daily banter, joking, and gossip that is so important to group life, we often spread information about whether another group member is cooperative or competitive, a central component of an individual's reputation (Frank, 1988; Keltner, Van Kleef, Chen, & Kraus, 2008).

reputation The beliefs, evaluations, and impressions people hold about an individual within a social network.

In many studies using the prisoner's dilemma game, participants play with a stranger whom they know nothing about. But what happens if they are given information about the other player's cooperative or competitive nature? Is their behavior influenced by this knowledge? To examine the effects of reputation, some studies have added certain twists to the game so that participants do know something about the other player. As you would expect, when people know a player's history of cooperation, they play games like the prisoners' dilemma game very differently depending on what that history tells them. Participants will readily cooperate and give resources to an interaction partner whom they know to have a history of cooperation, but they will compete and choose not to give resources to interaction partners known to be greedy or competitive (Wedekind & Milinski, (2000).

Construal Processes and Cooperation

Construal factors matter a great deal in shaping interactions toward more cooperative or competitive outcomes. In a compelling demonstration of the power of construal in shaping levels of cooperation, Steve Neuberg (1988) had male undergraduates participate in a standard prisoner's dilemma experiment. Before doing

---

BOX 14.5   FOCUS ON POSITIVE PSYCHOLOGY

Is Cooperation Contagious?

Popular movies and inspiring ads have centered on the "pay it forward" concept—that is, when we cooperate, we inspire others to be more cooperative in subsequent situations. Is cooperation contagious? For years, James Fowler and Nicholas Christakis have been gathering evidence on the contagious nature of human behavior and have discovered that behaviors like smoking, anxiety, happiness, and obesity spread through communities from one person to another (Christakis & Fowler, 2009). We are a mimetic species prone to imitating the behaviors of others around us (see Chapter 8). Using an economic game, Fowler and Christakis have found that cooperative acts inspire others to be more cooperative in ensuing situations (Fowler & Christakis, 2010).

In the study, participants played several rounds of an economic game in groups of four, in each round playing

with an entirely new set of participants. In each round of the game, the participant was given 20 money units (MUs) and allowed to give some amount, between 0 and 20, to the group. Each MU the participant gave to the group was translated to an increase of 0.4 MU for each of the four group members. This means that each gift of 1 MU would cost the giver 0.6 MU personally but benefit each other group member. If participants kept all their MUs, they would end the game with 20 MUs. If they each gave all their MUs to the group, each member would end the game with 32 MUs. This method created the usual dilemma—that behaviors costly to the self are beneficial for the group—and allowed Fowler and Christakis to examine how cooperative gifts to other players by a player in one round might influence those other players' levels of generosity in subsequent rounds. They found that for every MU

Pay It Forward The movie *Pay It Forward* centers on the theme of how one individual's generosity leads to other acts of generosity.

---

a player gave, his or her partners would give 0.19 MUs more on average to a *new* set of players in the next round, and 0.07 MUs on average to still other players in the round after that, two times removed from the original round.

so, however, the participants were subliminally "primed" with one of two different sets of stimulus words, ostensibly as part of another experiment. For one group, Neuberg flashed 22 hostile words (for example, *competitive*, *hostile*, *unfriendly*) for 60 milliseconds—too fast for anyone to "see" them and consciously register what they were, but long enough, research has shown, for them to leave a subconscious impression. He showed another group a list of neutral words (for example, *house*, *looked*, *always*) for an equally brief period. The question was whether exposure to the hostile words would lead participants to look out for their own interests, on the assumption that "it's a dog-eat-dog world out there."

Exposure to the hostile words affected the participants' actions. Eighty-four percent of the participants exposed to the hostile words defected on a majority of the trials in the subsequent prisoner's dilemma game; only 55 percent of the participants exposed to the neutral words did so. This study gives reason for concern about the kinds of stimuli to which people are commonly exposed. The ideas in the air—the competitive and aggressive images we see in the media, in video games, in films—may foster a more competitive society.

Based on the results of Neuberg's study, it might seem that the way we explicitly label situations might influence levels of competition and cooperation. If we think of international crises as buildups to war, diplomatic solutions may become less likely. When lawyers treat divorce settlements as adversarial and as opportunities to get their client the best outcome at the expense of the estranged spouse, entrenched bitterness seems inevitable.

In a striking demonstration of the power of labels, Liberman, Samuels, and Ross (2002) conducted a study, discussed in Chapter 1, in which they labeled the prisoner's dilemma game in one of two ways. Half of the participants were told they were going to play the "Wall Street" game, and the other half were told it was the "community" game. Everything else about the experiment was the same for the two groups. What might seem to be a trivial change of labels had a dramatic effect on the participants' behavior. Those playing the community game cooperated on the opening round twice as often as those playing the Wall Street game. Moreover, these initial differences were maintained throughout the subsequent rounds of the experiment. The Wall Street label doubtless made the participants adopt a perspective that made maximizing their own profits paramount. In contrast, the community label no doubt conjured up a different set of images and motives that increased the appeal of maximizing the participants' joint outcomes.

Culture and Cooperation

Given how labels and hence construals shape levels of cooperation, you might expect cultural factors to have a similar influence on the tendency to cooperate or compete. Consider the influence of a relatively specific subculture on cooperation—the discipline you choose to study in college and eventually apply in your own career. One of the most popular majors on campus is economics. Economic theory assumes that people are rational actors who always act in self-interested ways, attempting to maximize their own gains. Many people think this is a cynical view of the human condition; but in keeping with the ideas of eighteenth-century philosopher Adam Smith, economists have assumed that people and society are best served if individuals are allowed to selfishly pursue their own ends. The storekeeper and restaurateur will succeed to the extent that they serve their patrons well, simultaneously improving their customers' lives and doing well themselves by charging as much as a competitive market will allow.

Does training in the discipline of economics encourage people to act more competitively? The results of several studies indicate that it does (Carter & Irons, 1991; Frank, Gilovich, & Regan, 1993; Marwell & Ames, 1981). In one study, Cornell undergraduates who were majoring in economics and in a variety of other disciplines participated in a single-trial prisoner's dilemma game in which researchers took great pains to ensure that each person's response remained anonymous (Frank, Gilovich, & Regan, 1993). Seventy-two percent of the economics majors defected on their partners, whereas only 47 percent of those majoring in other disciplines defected. In a random sample of over 1,000 professors in 23 disciplines, participants were asked how much money they gave annually to public television, the United Way, and other charitable causes (Frank, Gilovich, & Regan, 1993). The economists were twice as likely as the members of all the other academic disciplines to free ride on the contributions of their fellow citizens—that is, to give nothing at all to charity while presumably enjoying services such as public television to the same extent as everyone else. The subculture that people are immersed in appears to powerfully influence their inclination to cooperate with others or look after themselves.

To take a broader look at the prevalence of cooperation in different cultures around the world, Joseph Henrich and his colleagues recruited individuals from 15 different small societies to play the ultimatum game, a close relative of the prisoner's dilemma game (Henrich et al., 2001). In the original version of the ultimatum game, an *allocator* is given a certain amount of money (say, $10) and told to keep a certain amount and allocate the rest to a second participant, a *responder*. The responder can then choose to either accept or reject the allocator's offer. If the responder accepts, he or she receives what was offered and the allocator keeps the balance. If the responder rejects the offer, neither player receives anything.

In Henrich and colleagues' version of the study, the participants were foragers, slash-and-burn farmers, nomadic herding groups, and individuals in settled, agriculturalist societies in Africa, South America, and Indonesia. What they were allowed to offer an anonymous stranger differed—in some cultures it was money, in others a cherished good such as tobacco. In all cases, the researchers attempted to make rewards equal to approximately the same fraction of a daily wage in each culture.

"Every individual, therefore, endeavors as much as he can . . . to employ his capital in the support of domestic industry, and so to direct that industry that its produce may be of greatest value; every individual necessarily labours to render the annual revenue of the society as great as he can. He . . . neither intends to promote the public interest, nor knows how much he is promoting it. By . . . directing that industry in such a manner as its produce may be of greatest value, he intends only his own gain, and he is in this, as in many other cases, led by an invisible hand to promote an end which was no part of his intention."

—Adam Smith (1776)

Cooperation in Different Cultures (A) The Machiguenga of Peru collaborate little with others outside their family and gave little in the ultimatum game. (B) The Lamerala of Indonesia collaborate extensively in fishing and gave a lot.

The first finding of note was how cooperative humans are in the variety of cultures studied. An economist of the rational self-interest view might argue that the sensible offer of the allocator is a small amount such as 10 percent of the good ($1 if the allocator has been given $10). This approach would advance the material wealth of both allocator and responder. In contrast, Henrich and colleagues observed a pattern of results that would puzzle Adam Smith. In the 15 cultures, allocators offered, on average, 39 percent of the good to anonymous strangers. (In other research across Western cultures, 71 percent of the allocators offered the responder between 40 and 50 percent of the money; Fehr & Schmidt, 1999.)

Henrich and colleagues then looked closely at the 15 cultures to determine what cultural factors predict the likelihood of cooperative generosity in the ultimatum game. One factor stood out—how much the individuals in a culture needed to collaborate with others to gather resources to survive. The more the members of a culture depended on one another to gather food and see to other survival needs, the more they offered to a stranger when they were allocators in the ultimatum game. For example, the Machiguenga people of Peru rarely collaborate with members outside of their family to produce food. Their average allocation in the ultimatum game was 26 percent of the resource. The Lamerala of Indonesia, by contrast, fish in highly collaborative groups of individuals from different families. Cooperation is essential to their livelihood and subsistence. Their average gift in the ultimatum game was 58 percent. Interdependence increases people's cooperation and generosity.

Evolution and Cooperation: Tit for Tat

In *The Evolution of Cooperation* (1984), political scientist Robert Axelrod asked the following question: How might cooperation emerge in competitive environments governed by the ruthless pursuit of self-interest? In the context of human evolution, how might non-kin begin to act with an eye toward advancing the welfare of others?

Axelrod assumed that cooperation was part of our evolutionary heritage, given its universality and its emergence in even the most unlikely of social contexts. For example, in the trenches of World War I, British and French soldiers were separated from their enemies, the Germans, by a few hundred yards of no-man's-land (Axelrod, 1984). Brutal assaults by one side were typically met with equally fierce counterattacks by the other. And yet even here cooperation frequently emerged, allowing soldiers to eat meals peacefully, to enjoy long periods of nonconfrontation, and even to fraternize with one another. The two sides would fly special flags, make verbal agreements, and fire deliberately misguided shots, all to signal and maintain peaceful cooperation between episodes of attack in which each side was bent on exterminating the other.

Axelrod conducted a study that helps illuminate the evolutionary origins of cooperation. Although simple in design, this study yields profound lessons. Axelrod ran a tournament in which players—academics, prize-winning mathematicians, computer hackers, and common folk—were invited to submit computer programs that specified what choices to make on a round of the prisoner's dilemma game, given what had happened on previous rounds (Axelrod, 1984). In Axelrod's first tournament, 14 strategies were submitted. Each strategy played 200 rounds of the prisoner's dilemma game with each other strategy. The points were tallied, and the most effective strategy was announced. The winner? It was a so-called tit-for-tat strategy, submitted by mathematical psychologist Anatol Rapaport.

The **tit-for-tat strategy** is disarmingly simple: It cooperates on the first round with every opponent and then reciprocates whatever the opponent did on the previous round. An opponent's cooperation was rewarded with immediate cooperation; defection was punished with immediate defection. In other words, start out cooperatively, and reciprocate your partner's previous move. Axelrod held a second tournament that attracted the submission of 62 strategies. All of the entrants knew the results of the first round—that the tit-for-tat strategy had won. In the second tournament, the tit-for-tat strategy again prevailed. Note that the tit-for-tat strategy did not win every round when pitted against all the different strategies. Instead, it did better overall against the diversity of strategies. What makes the tit-for-tat strategy special, and why might it be relevant to your own life?

Axelrod contends that the tit-for-tat strategy is based on a set of principles that we would all be well advised to follow as we form friendships, deal with the occasional difficult personality at work, negotiate with bosses, persevere in long-term romantic bonds, and raise children. Five factors make it an especially compelling strategy. First, it is *cooperative*, and thus it encourages mutually supportive action toward a shared goal. Second, it is *not envious*: a partner using this strategy can do extremely well without resorting to competitive behavior. Third, it is *not exploitable*—that is, it is not blindly prosocial. If you defect on the tit-for-tat, it will defect on you. Fourth, the tit-for-tat *forgives*—that is, it is willing to cooperate at the first cooperative action of its partner, even after long runs of defection and competition. Finally, the tit-for-tat is *easy to read*—that is, it should not take long for others to know that the tit-for-tat strategy is being played.

As Axelrod put it, "Its niceness prevents it from getting into unnecessary trouble. Its retaliation discourages the other side from persisting whenever defection is tried. Its forgiveness helps restore mutual cooperation. And its clarity makes it intelligible to the other player, thereby eliciting long-term cooperation" (Axelrod, 1984, p. 54). Being nice, stalwart, forgiving, and clear—not a bad set of principles to live by.

Cooperation is part of our evolutionary heritage. The prisoner's dilemma game models the many situations in everyday life when defection is the best solution for each individual but cooperation benefits the two in combination. Situational factors, such as the kind of person you are interacting with, influence levels of cooperation and competition. So, too, do construal processes: people can be primed to cooperate or defect. Studies of different cultures find that cooperation is a human universal and that cultures characterized by economic interdependence show greater cooperation. The tit-for-tat strategy involves initial cooperation and then reciprocation of whatever your opponent has done in the previous round. It is a useful strategy to follow because it encourages cooperation and does not blindly permit an opponent to take advantage.

tit-for-tat strategy A strategy in which the individual's first move is cooperative and thereafter the individual mimics the other person's behavior, whether cooperative or competitive.

Chapter Review

Summary

Altruism

- People help others out of selfish motives, including to reduce their felt distress and to gain social rewards such as praise, attention, or gratitude.

- A form of pure, undiluted altruism is based on *empathic concern*—the feeling of concern for another person after observing and being moved by that person's needs. Experimenters have found clever ways to distinguish between people who help for empathic and nonempathic reasons. Those who help for egoistic distress avoidance reasons show different physiological patterns than those who help for empathic reasons.

- Empathic concern also motivates volunteerism, actions people take to enhance the welfare of others (for example, tending to the sick or dying when there is no expectation of compensation).

- Situational determinants of altruism can be far stronger than our intuitions tell us they should be. Being late reduced the likelihood of a seminary student's helping a victim from 60 percent to 10 percent.

- Whether someone offers help to a victim or not (*bystander intervention*) also depends greatly on the number of people who observe the incident. The presence of others leads to a *diffusion of responsibility*, in which no individual takes responsibility for helping the victim.

- *Pluralistic ignorance* occurs when people are uncertain about what is happening and do nothing, often out of fear of embarrassment in case nothing is really wrong. Their reaction reinforces everyone's erroneous conclusion that the events are innocuous.

- *Victim characteristics* that increase the likelihood of being helped include whether the victim is similar to the target, whether the victim screams and makes his or her distress known, and whether the victim is female.

- People who live in rural settings are more likely to help others than people who live in urban settings.

- People from lower-class backgrounds are more empathetic than people from upper-class backgrounds and are more likely to give resources to strangers and assist people in need.

- Exposure to religious concepts increases levels of altruism.

- Evolutionary approaches to altruism lead initially to a puzzle as to why it would exist at all. From the standpoint of evolution, all our actions should serve to increase the likelihood of survival and reproduction. The *kin selection* hypothesis explains, however, that people will help others to preserve the genes of close kin so as to benefit their own gene pool.

- Another kind of helping behavior, *reciprocal altruism*, also arises out of selfish motives. People help others or grant favors in the belief that those whom they have helped will at some future time grant them favors of similar value.

Cooperation

- Cooperation is part of our evolutionary heritage, and it is evident in almost all societies.

- The prisoner's dilemma game is used to study cooperation. It tempts participants to maximize their own outcomes at the expense of another person by defecting. This strategy backfires if the other person also defects. The optimum outcome is for both to settle for something less than the maximum by cooperating.

- Interacting with more cooperative individuals leads to higher rates of cooperation.

- Knowing a person's reputation as cooperative or competitive influences levels of cooperation in profound ways.

- Being primed with cooperative concepts leads to increased cooperation.

- Cooperation is widespread in certain types of cultures, particularly in those whose members are dependent on one another to gather resources.

- The *tit-for-tat strategy* in the prisoner's dilemma game is a reciprocal strategy that is cooperative, nonenvious, nonexploitable, forgiving, and easy to read. This strategy helps maximize outcomes in potentially competitive situations that occur in real life.

Key Terms

altruism (p. 530)
bystander intervention (p. 538)
diffusion of responsibility (p. 538)
empathic concern (p. 532)

kin selection (p. 549)
personal distress (p. 531)
reciprocal altruism (p. 550)
reputation (p. 554)

social rewards (p. 531)
tit-for-tat strategy (p. 559)
volunteerism (p. 535)

Further Reading

Batson, C. D. (1991). *The altruism question: Toward a social-psychological answer*. Hillsdale, NJ: Erlbaum. An outstanding review of the evidence regarding the different motives for altruism.

Schroeder, D. A., Penner, L. A., Dovidio, J. F., & Piliavin, J. A. (1995). *The psychology of helping and altruism*. New York: McGraw-Hill. An excellent review of 30 years of literature on altruism.

Sober, E., & Wilson, D. S. (1998). *Unto others: The evolution and psychology of unselfish behavior*. Cambridge, MA: Harvard University Press. A philosopher and evolutionary theorist combine talents to consider how altruism could have emerged in evolution.

Social Psychology and Health

MARIE ANTOINETTE WAS A NOTORIOUS QUEEN OF FRANCE during the late eighteenth century. Fond of gambling, fine clothes, behind-the-scenes political maneuvers, and extramarital affairs, she was a favorite target of the revolutionaries when they overthrew the monarchy during the French Revolution. Legend has it that after her capture, during the night that she awaited her execution by guillotine, Marie Antoinette's hair turned white.

People now know that it is physiologically impossible for hair to turn white during the course of a day. But stress—in Marie Antoinette's case caused by her imminent demise, her husband's execution, and the political upheaval she helped bring about—can damage our bodies. Evolution has crafted the stress response to help us handle immediate pressures in the short run, but when chronically active it can lead to myriad health problems. For example, physicians now estimate that about 1 to 2 percent of the cases in which people present with the symptoms of a heart attack actually reflect a syndrome known as apical ballooning syndrome (ABS). This condition arises when stress hormones such as epinephrine flood the left ventricle of the heart, causing it to balloon to dangerous levels. ABS is often triggered by extreme emotional stress—the death of a child, the loss of a spouse, or exposure to warfare and extreme violence. In 1 percent of the cases, ABS can prove fatal.

Stress is only one among many emotional and social factors that can affect our health. Elements of culture, such as social class, influence our health, leading people from lower-class backgrounds to suffer more frequently from almost every kind of health problem. Our social situations, particularly the richness of our social connections, can improve our health. Even certain construal processes—perceptions of control and optimism—can make for healthier lives.

Marie Antoinette

EVOLUTION AND HEALTH: SHORT-TERM AND CHRONIC STRESS

As the day of her execution approached, Marie Antoinette must have experienced incredible levels of stress. She wouldn't have used the term *stress*, or its French equivalent, because this term we so commonly use today was coined only in the past century. But stress must have colored her every waking thought.

Psychological stress results from the sense that our challenges and demands surpass our current capacities, resources, and energies (Lazarus, 1966; Sapolsky, 1994). Not all challenges or demands trigger stress equally, though. As a review of over 200 stress studies reveals, the challenges that threaten our social identity and our connection to others are particularly likely to trigger stress (Dickerson & Kemeny, 2004). In our modern lives, the demands that we face often exceed our capacities. As a result, stress can arise in almost any situation: pressures at work, the loss of a loved one, economic hardship, conflicts with family members, trying times in a marriage. Even positive events in life can be surprisingly stressful: graduations, new jobs, planning a wedding, the early stages of marriage. And young children, while introducing incomparable joys, place new demands on us and create unexpected stress. In any of these circumstances, we may feel that we don't have the energy or skill to handle the demands of life effectively; as a result, we feel stress.

How does stress harm our physical health? The process begins in a system of the body known as the hypothalamic-pituitary-adrenal (HPA) axis and the stress-related hormone *cortisol* (**Figure A1.1**). Stressful events activate the amygdala, a region of the brain that processes information related to threat. The amygdala stimulates the paraventricular nucleus of the hypothalamus, which sends electrochemical signals to the anterior pituitary, which produces adrenocorticotropic hormone (ACTH). ACTH stimulates the adrenal glands (near our kidneys) to release the stress hormone cortisol into our bloodstream.

Cortisol has many effects on the body. Most notably, cortisol increases heart rate and blood pressure, distributing blood to appropriate muscle groups involved in fight-or-flight behavior. Our hands sweat—a process that some think evolved to facilitate grasping. Cortisol suppresses the activity of our immune system, keeping precious resources available for metabolically demanding fight-or-flight behavior. It is even involved in forming flashbulb, stress-related memories in the hippocampus, helping us form enduring memories about the serious sources of danger in our environment.

In the short run, activation of the HPA axis and the accompanying increase in cortisol in our bloodstream help us respond to immediate threats to our survival.

psychological stress The sense that your challenges and demands surpass your current capacities, resources, and energies.

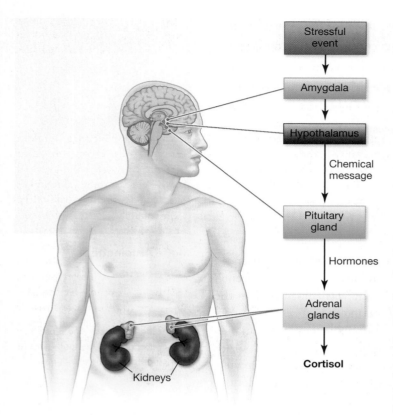

FIGURE A1.1 The Hypothalamic-Pituitary-Adrenal (HPA) Axis

Stressful event

Amygdala

Hypothalamus

Chemical message

Pituitary gland

Hormones

Adrenal glands

Cortisol

Kidneys

rumination The tendency to think about some stressful event over and over again.

During early hominid evolution, this stress response enabled our ancestors to detect an approaching predator or an enraged rival and to respond quickly with appropriate action. Today, this same stress response helps us power through lecture notes to study for an exam, avoid danger, or stay up until the wee hours of the morning taking care of a sick friend or child. Not surprisingly, elevated levels of cortisol have been observed in race car drivers, parachute jumpers, and students taking exams (Coriell & Adler, 2001).

People's troubles begin when they experience chronic stress, which is frequently the result of **rumination**, the tendency to think about some stressful event over and over again (Nolen-Hoeksema, 1987). When we ruminate, we take a specific event, and by thinking of all its deep causes and extensive ramifications, turn that specific event into an enduring, general source of stress that touches on all facets of our lives. Say your boss offers some criticism about how to sharpen up a proposal you have been working on. If you were to ruminate about it, you would take the specific event—the criticism about the project—and elaborate on how that event reflects more general problems you have at work, how you're never living up to expectations, how you'll let your parents down yet again. People who ruminate about a negative event experience prolonged stress compared to people who distract themselves from the event (Lyubomirsky & Nolen-Hoeksema, 1995; Morrow & Nolen-Hoeksema, 1990). Through rumination, our specific stresses become chronic ones: a marital spat begins to feel like the fast road to divorce; a dip in the economy feels like a prolonged depression; a transient health problem feels like a verdict of deteriorating health.

And chronic stress can kill. Psychologists studying stress have found that chronic stress can lead to ulcers, heart disease, cancer, and even cell death in the hippocampus and consequent memory loss, in part because chronically high levels of cortisol damage different cells and organs in the body (Sapolsky, 1994). Feeling chronically stressed makes you more vulnerable to the common cold (Cohen et al., 2008). Chronic stress can even prematurely age parts of your cells. Elissa Epel and her colleagues found that premenopausal women who reported elevated levels of stress showed shortened telomeres, parts of cells that shorten with age (Epel et al., 2004). The telomeres of the most stressed-out women in this study had prematurely aged by ten years.

The message from the literature on stress and cortisol couldn't be clearer. Evolution has equipped humans with an immediate stress response, associated with elevated HPA activation and cortisol release, that enables adaptive responses to pressing problems in our lives. However, short-term stresses can sometimes become chronic stressors, triggering chronically high levels of cortisol that damage our health. Ruminating over stressful or negative events can have precisely that effect.

How to Stop Ruminating

One thing you're probably ruminating about right now is how to stop ruminating and avoid the toxic effects of chronic stress. Susan Nolen-Hoeksema, the leading scholar in the study of rumination, offers several tips for reducing your tendency to ruminate (Nolen-Hoeksema, 2003). Here are a few. First, *break loose* from your pattern of rumination; turn your attention away from those ruminative thoughts. Nolen-Hoeksema has documented how engaging in distracting activities during stressful periods—doing the crossword puzzle, knitting, reading a novel, or working on that Sudoku problem—quiets the ruminative mind and calms you during stressful times.

A second strategy is the *stop* strategy. Here Nolen-Hoeksema recommends that you simply say "Stop" to yourself, even shout it, when you find yourself ruminating. Shift your attention to other matters in your life rather than what you are ruminating about: think of the things you need to do to get ready for grad school, where you might travel in the upcoming years, or friends you need to contact.

Finally, Nolen-Hoeksema recommends that if you are a dyed-in-the-wool ruminator, simply set aside 30 minutes of ruminating time each day, ideally when you're feeling pretty calm. Knowing that you will have time each day to ruminate reduces the likelihood that you'll be overcome

unexpectedly by rumination at random times during the day. Ethan Kross and his colleagues have shown that even for that deliberate period of rumination, it is helpful to engage in **self-distancing**, focusing on your feelings from the perspective of a detached observer (Kross, Ayduk, & Mischel, 2005). Revisiting a situation not from the perspective you initially had, but from the standpoint of a real or imagined observer of the situation, allows you to reflect over stressful thoughts and feelings without becoming overwhelmed by negative affect and arousal (Ayduk & Kross, 2008; Kross & Ayduk, 2008).

CULTURE AND HEALTH: CLASS, STRESS, AND HEALTH OUTCOMES

self-distancing The ability to focus on one's feelings from the perspective of a detached observer.

In a celebrated but perhaps apocryphal exchange, F. Scott Fitzgerald told Ernest Hemingway that "the rich are different from you and me." Hemingway retorted, "Yes, they have more money." Hemingway could have added that the rich also lead healthier and longer lives.

Social scientists think of wealth in terms of class, or what is often called socioeconomic status (SES). We often refer to social class by using categories like "working class" or "upper class." Social scientists measure people's social class in terms of three variables: our family wealth and income, our educational achievement (and that of our parents), and the prestige of our work (and our parents' work) (Oakes & Rossi, 2003; Snibbe & Markus, 2005).

As you have learned in different places in this book, social class is an important cultural dimension of our identity. People of different social class backgrounds tend to prefer different kinds of music (Snibbe & Markus, 2005), they explain economic and political events in different fashion (Chapter 5), and they appear to be prone to different levels of altruism (Chapter 14).

What does social class have to do with your physical health? A great deal, it turns out. Dozens of recent studies have looked at the association between an individual's social class and indicators of physical health. Just about every health problem is more prevalent in lower-SES individuals (see Adler et al., 1994; Coriell & Adler, 2001). Lower-SES newborns are more likely to have a low birth

Low- and High-SES Neighborhoods Lower-SES neighborhoods (A) have fewer green spaces and play structures than higher-SES neighborhoods (B), which allow for more stress-reducing play and relaxation.

weight—a major predictor of later health problems. Lower-SES children are more likely to suffer from asthma, diabetes, and obesity, again all early predictors of other health problems later in life. In adulthood, lower-SES individuals are more likely to suffer from high blood pressure, cardiovascular disease, diabetes, respiratory illness, and poor metabolic functioning related to blood glucose levels. They are also more likely to experience poor health subjectively in terms of symptoms ranging from stomach upset to headaches and bad backs (Adler et al., 1994; Gallo, Bogart, Vranceanu, & Matthews, 2005; Lehman, Taylor, Kiefe, & Seeman, 2005; Singh-Manoux, Adler, & Marmot, 2003).

Class, Neighborhood, and Stress

How would you explain these class-based differences in physical health? Your first inclination might be to take a situationist view and to think about how the physical environments of lower-SES individuals might give rise to health-impairing chronic stress. Situations matter, and so do physical environments. Live close to someone, and you're more likely to become friends with that person (see Chapter 10). Generous acts are more common in rural settings than in urban settings (see Chapter 14). And it is clear that people from lower- and upper-SES backgrounds inhabit very different social and physical environments (see Coriell & Adler, 2001).

People living in poorer neighborhoods are more often exposed to air and water pollution, pesticides, and hazardous wastes. These kinds of toxins harm the nervous system directly, and they can also boost levels of stress. Lower-SES neighborhoods have fewer recreational spaces and parks, so lower-SES individuals have fewer opportunities to exercise, to be outdoors, to relax, to calm down,

While the survival rates are improving every year, the psychological ramifications of breast cancer are complex. Upon being diagnosed, women often feel anxiety, fear, shame, and even hostility—just the kinds of emotions that trigger the HPA axis and cortisol release and perhaps worsen the effects of the disease.

In studying these interviews, Taylor found that women diagnosed with breast cancer did not passively accept their condition. Instead, they actively constructed narratives about this new dimension to their identities. For example, many women found reasons to be grateful in surprising kinds of social comparisons. Women who were diagnosed with breast cancer later in life felt grateful it hadn't happened to them as young women, while they were raising their children and starting their careers; they appreciated having had the chance to live a full life without cancer. Younger women, by contrast, were grateful that they weren't older when they received their diagnosis, for they felt they had the physical robustness to respond to the disease.

One construal process that seems to benefit health is cultivating a sense of control—a sense of mastery, autonomy, and efficacy in influencing important life outcomes (Shapiro, Schwartz, & Astin, 1996). In Taylor's study of breast cancer patients, perceived control proved to be a source of good health. Taylor found that over two-thirds of the women with breast cancer reported a sense of control over the disease. The cancer patients assumed that through diet, exercise, or positive beliefs, they could control the course of their disease. (People suffering from other conditions—HIV/AIDS and coronary problems, for example—similarly express beliefs that they have control over the progression of their disease.) And the more the patient reported a sense of control over her breast cancer, the better she responded to the disease, as assessed by her physician (Taylor, Wood, & Lichtman, 1983; Taylor, Lichtman, & Wood, 1984). More generally, people who report a more pronounced sense of control enjoy better health outcomes (Cohen & Herbert, 1996). Diseases and other health problems threaten our basic beliefs about the control we enjoy over our bodies and lives; this sense of lacking control is stressful in its own right and activates the HPA axis and cortisol. Cultivating beliefs in control can counter these kinds of stresses and promote better health.

These findings raise an intriguing possibility: Might introducing the sense of control into the lives of people whose health is on the decline improve physical health? That question motivated a striking study by Ellen Langer and Judith Rodin (1976) of elderly individuals in a nursing home. As people age into their later years, they often experience a pronounced loss of control in many realms: the loss of eyesight and physical coordination and strength makes simple physical tasks more challenging; the loss of memory can make for more difficult social interactions. These age-related trends are only amplified, many believe, by the conditions of nursing homes. Once in the nursing home, people can lose even more control—over their schedules, their meals, and their social activities.

So Langer and Rodin did something ingenious. They decided to explore the effects of increasing the sense of control in a nursing home in Connecticut. The participants were all healthy, ambulatory 65- to 90-year-olds living in the home. On one floor, individuals were brought together and led in a discussion by a young male staff member about personal responsibility and about the various ways they had control in the home, ranging from planning their free time to voicing complaints to the staff. Each participant then received a small plant and was asked to take care of it. In a second condition, on a neighboring floor, participants were told about all the things in the home available to them, but no mention of their control was made. They, too, each received a plant but were told that the nurses would water and care for the plants.

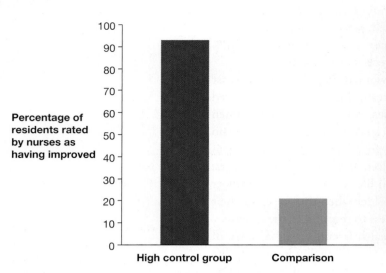

FIGURE A1.4 **Personal Control and Happiness** This older woman appears to be experiencing little control in her nursing home. (Source: Adapted from Langer & Rodin, 1976.)

Before these discussions and again three weeks later, Langer and Rodin gathered several measures of how well the elderly residents were faring (**Figure A1.4**). Sure enough, participants on the floor that emphasized personal control showed greater increases in happiness compared with those on the neighboring floor. They were more likely to attend a free movie. They were ten times as likely to participate in a game proposed by the staff. And as rated by the nurses, nearly four times as many of the participants with the uplifted sense of control were judged to have improved in their overall functioning. Cultivating a sense of control appears to quiet the emotions that activate the HPA axis.

A second construal that has emerged as quite important in health is optimism (see Chapter 5). Highly optimistic people have positive expectations about the future. They are likely to endorse the item "In uncertain times, I usually expect the best" and disagree with the item "If something can go wrong for me, it will." And people who report higher levels of optimism report greater happiness and well-being—and they enjoy better health outcomes. For example, Charles Carver and Michael Scheier have found that individuals who report higher levels of optimism respond with greater robustness and recover more quickly to coronary artery bypass surgery and breast cancer (Carver & Scheier, 1982). Self-reports of pessimism have been found to predict a more rapid aging of the immune system (O'Donovan et al., 2009). In George Valliant's longitudinal study of men who graduated from Harvard in 1945, those individuals who reported higher levels of optimism at age 21 reported higher levels of physical health 35 years later (Peterson, Seligman, & Valliant, 1988).

Taylor and colleagues have argued that beliefs in control and optimism benefit health in several ways. With an increased sense of control, people are likely to respond to stress with less HPA reactivity. Moreover, people with a heightened sense of control and a sense of optimism are likely to engage in better health practices. In one study, optimistic HIV patients showed better health habits (Taylor et al., 1992). These patients are more likely to build good networks of social support, and they are more likely to engage in better health-related behaviors, all of which improve their health.

Summary

Evolution and Health: Short-Term and Chronic Stress

- Evolution has provided us with the hypothalamic-pituitary-adrenal (HPA) axis, which produces the stress hormone *cortisol*. Constant release of cortisol results in chronic stress, which can be alleviated if you avoid rumination, or thinking about some stressful event over and over again.

Culture and Health: Class, Stress, and Health Outcomes

- Lower-SES individuals have much worse health than higher-SES individuals, in part because they are subjected to more stress. But even subjectively lower status, such as being a subordinate executive, results in more stress-related illnesses.

Situational Factors and Health: The Benefits of Social Connection

- People with more meaningful connections to others are healthier. Having a sympathetic person with you when you are undergoing stress significantly reduces the physiological and psychological indicators of stress.

Construal and Health: The Benefits of Perceived Control and Optimism

- Having a sense of control over your fate also reduces stress and yields health benefits.

Key Terms

psychological stress (p. 563) rumination (p. 564) self-distancing (p. 565)

Further Reading

Sapolsky, R. M. (1994). *Why zebras don't get ulcers*. New York: Freeman. Sapolsky details the workings of stress-related physiology, explaining how chronic stress damages different branches of our nervous system. The book also includes several useful tips for managing stress.

Taylor, S. E. (2012). *Health psychology* (8th ed.). New York: McGraw-Hill.

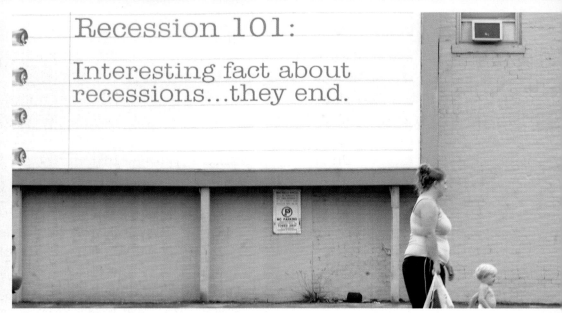

Recession 101:

Interesting fact about
recessions...they end.

Social Psychology and Personal Finance

ON OCTOBER 10, 2007, the Dow Jones industrial average, a widely cited index of the U.S. stock market and the health of the U.S. economy, stood at $14,164. People with heavy investments in the stock market were flush. Exactly one year later, however, the Dow closed at $8,579, wiping out 40 percent of the retirement savings and college funds of a great many families. Six months later, the Dow closed at $6,547, less than half of what it was at its peak. Unemployment at the beginning of this period was 4.6 percent; a year and a half later, it was twice as high. The United States and most of the developed world has been in an economic slump ever since. What happened?

Nothing. That is, there was no great calamity that diminished the productivity of U.S. firms or the country's ability to produce goods and services. No hurricane wiped out our refining capacity. No new war was started. Oil-exporting countries did not boycott the United States. As Franklin Delano Roosevelt famously said with equal truth about an earlier economic depression, "We are stricken by no plague of locusts."

What happened was the accumulation of human error in millions upon millions of economic transactions. People borrowed money against their homes and, since they still owned the house and had more money in their pockets, concluded that they were wealthier than they actually were. Banks approved mortgages to people with very shaky finances and then sold the mortgages on a secondary market to buyers who didn't fully know what they were getting. "Irrational exuberance" (Greenspan, 1996; Shiller, 2000) convinced people that housing and stock prices could only go up, so they had to "get in the game," with borrowed money if necessary.

The Stock Market Collapse
In the fall of 2008, housing and stock markets throughout the world experienced steep declines, sending the United States and much of the world into the worst economic downturn since the Great Depression.

But housing and stock prices don't only go up. And when they went down, just a bit at first, people and institutions that had borrowed heavily couldn't meet their obligations. If they couldn't borrow even more money, they had to sell. The selling reduced the prices of what they owned, further weakening their balance sheets, which produced more selling. And so on. The housing market sank, pulling down large segments of the banking system and the construction industry, and its decline reverberated into every area of the economy.

According to standard economic thinking, this sort of cascade of human error shouldn't—indeed, couldn't—happen. The field of traditional economics is based on two fundamental assumptions: that people are rational and that people are selfish. Economists assume, in other words, that people can accurately assess how much pleasure or pain they would derive from different outcomes, that they can estimate how likely those different outcomes are with as much accuracy as the available information permits, and that they pursue courses of action that are most likely to advance their self-interests. Traditionally, economists have viewed the behavior of financial markets and the actions of individuals as they work, spend, save, and invest through the filter of these two assumptions.

"Money is better than poverty, if only for financial reasons."

—Woody Allen

Psychologists know better. It is certainly true that people are often rational and can be counted on to pursue their self-interests reasonably well most of the time. But as discussed in Chapter 4, human judgment is often distorted by predictable biases. And as discussed in Chapter 14, people are (thankfully) concerned about more than their own self-interest. Knowing when and why people are likely to violate these twin assumptions of economics is essential to a true understanding of human economic behavior. Beginning in the 1980s, a group of psychologists and economists became concerned that standard economic theory didn't recognize or address important shortcomings in individual judgment and decision making, shortcomings that could combine to influence the performance of the economy as a whole. They created a new field, typically referred to as **behavioral economics**,

behavioral economics A discipline that uses insights from psychology to create realistic and accurate models of economic behavior.

that was dedicated to taking insights from psychology about how the mind works and applying them to create more realistic and accurate models of economic behavior. Behavioral economics started out as something of a renegade area within economics and only gradually won over adherents. After the severe recession in the fall of 2008, however, it has reached a much wider audience and won much greater acceptance.

This module reviews some of the most important ideas from the field of behavioral economics and considers some of the ways that people make questionable decisions as they spend, shop, save, and invest. The section ends with some specific advice about how you should start, *right now*, to think about your money and how to handle it.

IRRATIONALITY IN FINANCIAL MARKETS

"People who think money can't buy happiness don't know where to shop."

—Dolly Parton

If people were entirely rational, their buy and sell decisions would not be influenced by factors that have no bearing on the intrinsic value of what they are buying and selling. But such decisions *are* swayed by extraneous factors. For example, people sometimes try to lift themselves out of a bad mood by going shopping, only to end up buying things they regret. But maybe, you might say, these attempts are entirely rational if they succeed in lifting a person's mood. Who is to say a better mood isn't worth the price of spending "too much" and experiencing later regret? Maybe "when the going gets tough, the tough go shopping" is an entirely rational strategy.

But what if people's moods influence their presumably more sober and consequential investment decisions or influence entire markets? It would be harder to defend the rationality of those outcomes. And it turns out that even the most consequential financial transactions *are* influenced by such things as transitory, irrelevant mood states. An analysis of stock market performance in 26 countries over a 15-year period found that the amount of sunshine on a given day is positively correlated with market performance. The market tends to go up more often on sunny days and down more often on gloomy days, a result that the investigators argue is due to investors attributing their good spirits to positive economic circumstances rather than the true source—sunshine (Hirshleifer & Shumway, 2003; Kamstra, Kramer, & Levi, 2003). Another study found that a country's stock exchange tends to decline when that country's soccer team is eliminated from important tournaments, such as the World Cup, and that similar dips occur in countries following losses in other sports (cricket, rugby, basketball) popular in those countries (Edmans, Garcia, & Norli, 2007). It's hard to argue that this effect is rational.

It is also hard to maintain that it was rational for investors to bid up the stock of Computer Literacy Inc. by 33 percent in a single day simply because it changed its name to the edgier, more hip-sounding fatbrain.com. (Cooper, Dimitrov, & Rau, 2001; Zweig, 2007). The irrationality of stock movements (or at least the irrationality of *initial* stock movements) was further demonstrated in a study that examined the relationship between the name of a company newly listed on the stock exchange and its performance (Alter & Oppenheimer, 2006). Stocks in companies with easy-to-pronounce names (for example, Belden Inc., Accenture Ltd.) performed better the day after and one week after they were listed than companies with hard-to-pronounce names (for example, Magyar Tavkozlesi Rt., Inspat International NV). Those who initially got taken in by the sound of a stock's name later paid a price for doing so, as the prices of easy-to-pronounce stocks were not higher six months later. Eventually, the performance of the company—its profitability, not its name—carried the day.

LOSS AVERSION

Suppose that ten years ago, your grandparents bought you 1,000 shares of stock in ABC corporation at $25 a share and 1,000 shares of XYZ corporation at $75 dollars a share. Suppose further that the stock of both companies is now selling for $50 a share. This means (lucky you!) that you own $50,000 of stock in each company.

Now suppose you want to pay off your $25,000 student loan by selling some of your stock. You can sell shares in only one of the companies. Which would you sell, half your shares in ABC or half your shares in XYZ? Amazingly, the evidence suggests that most people would rather sell their stock in the company that had gone up in price (ABC, from $25 to $50) than the stock in the company that had gone down (XYZ, from $75 to $50). People are more inclined to sell their winners, in other words, than their losers.

Although this example might seem fanciful, Terrance Odean (1998) found that people treat their investments precisely this way. He tracked the buy and sell decisions made by over 10,000 individuals who traded stocks with a discount brokerage firm. What he found was that investors were more likely to sell shares of the stocks that had gone up in price than the stocks that had gone down. And they paid a price for their loss aversion. Over the next year, the stocks they sold (their winners) outperformed those they held onto (their losers) by 3.4 percent. If you take that 3.4 percent annual difference and compound it over a lifetime, it can make the difference between being very rich and not nearly so rich.

Why on earth would people make decisions that are so clearly to their disadvantage? The culprit appears to be the psychological phenomenon known as **loss aversion**, or the tendency for a loss of a given magnitude (for example, losing $100) to have more psychological impact than an equivalent gain (winning $100). Note that loss aversion is a particular instance of the broader phenomenon discussed in Chapters 4 and 7 of bad things hurting more than equivalent good things feel good. Finding or winning $100 feels great, but not to the same degree that losing $100 feels bad. Because of loss aversion, people are likely to go to great lengths to avoid taking a loss—or go to great lengths to create the *illusion* that they haven't taken a loss. So if you sell shares of the stock that has gone up in price, you're realizing a gain. That feels good. But if you sell shares of the stock that has gone down in price, you're sustaining a loss. And that feels terrible. People are willing to take a risk to avoid that feeling—the risk being that the losing stock will decline even more in value. (Note, by the way, that there are tax advantages of selling stocks that have declined in value rather than those that have gone up: the amount of the loss, up to a certain amount, can be deducted from your income.)

loss aversion The tendency for a loss of a given magnitude to have more psychological impact than an equivalent gain.

Loss Aversion and Framing

Central to the principle of construal, which is discussed throughout this book, is the idea that the same stimulus can be interpreted in different ways—and that how something is construed profoundly affects people's behavior. When it comes to economic transactions, the same outcome can be construed as a loss or a gain, depending on how it is framed. For instance, many years ago, it was illegal for commercial establishments to charge two different prices for their products—a higher price for a credit card transaction and a lower price for those who paid cash. But because companies pay a fee to the credit card institution (a fee they pass on to the customer in the form of higher prices), a single-price system could be considered unfair to those who pay cash. Cash customers end up subsidizing the credit transactions of others. As a result, Congress agreed to change the laws to permit a two-tiered pricing system. Credit card companies lobbied vigorously to control how the two-tiered system would be labeled. They preferred that it be called a "cash discount" rather than a "credit card surcharge." Because losses have greater psychological impact than gains, the credit card companies wisely reasoned that people would be less inclined to use their credit cards if they had to pay a surcharge to do so. Paying a surcharge is experienced as a direct cost, or loss, whereas declining a cash discount is experienced as a forgone *gain*.

A few years ago, one of your textbook authors conducted a survey for a large life insurance company in which half the respondents were asked whether they could comfortably save 20 percent of their income. Only half of them said they could. Another group was asked whether they could comfortably live on 80 percent of their income. Nearly 80 percent of them said they could. Of course, saving 20 percent means living on 80 percent, so rationally there should be no difference between the two groups. But saving 20 percent is experienced as a loss of current spending resources, whereas living on 80 percent makes that missing 20 percent feel more like a forgone gain.

The asymmetry in people's reactions to outright losses versus forgone gains makes it easier for the government to pay for programs by granting tax breaks rather than by making cash payments. Paying for something (for example, using tax dollars to pay for public housing) is experienced as a cost, or a loss. Granting a tax break (for example, to companies that invest in public housing) is experienced as a forgone gain—tax revenue that would have been collected, but is not. This difference may help explain why populist reformers have made little headway in attacking "corporate welfare." Much of the voting public is easily riled by welfare to the poor because it involves direct payments from the government and is therefore construed as a loss. It is harder to get the public as upset over corporate welfare because it typically comes in the form of tax deductions rather than direct payments.

How outcomes are framed has a particularly strong effect on whether people are likely to make risky or conservative financial decisions. Consider the following example, adapted from Tversky and Kahneman (1986):

> You are first given $300 and then you must choose between:
> a sure gain of $100 or
> a 50 percent chance to gain $200 and a 50 percent chance to gain
>   nothing.

"Wealth is the slave of a wise man. The master of a fool."

—Seneca

Nearly three-quarters of those who are presented with this problem say they would take the sure $100. They don't want to gamble; they are risk averse. But now consider the following, only slightly different, problem:

You are first given $500 and then you must choose between:
a sure loss of $100 or
a 50 percent chance to lose nothing and a 50 percent chance to lose $200.

In this case, nearly two-thirds say they would take the gamble. They are risk seeking. This result is really quite interesting because if you look closely at both pairs of options, you'll notice that they are objectively identical. In each problem, you must choose between having a final outcome of $400 for sure or a 50 percent chance of $500 and a 50 percent chance of $300. But one version forces you to think of the choice as between two possible gains and the other as between two possible losses. When choosing between possible gains, most people prefer the sure thing over a risky chance of a bigger prize. This **risk aversion** when it comes to gains is due to what economists call "diminishing marginal utility"—that is, the more dollars you already own, the less utility each additional dollar you receive yields. So, in this case, a gain of $100 is experienced as more than half as valuable as a gain of $200, so why gamble to get $200? Because diminishing marginal utility works for losses as well, people tend to be **risk seeking** when it comes to choosing between a sure loss of $100 and a risky chance to lose nothing or lose $200. A loss of $100 is more than half as painful as a loss of $200, so why not gamble on the possibility of avoiding a loss altogether?

Loss Aversion and the Sunk Cost Fallacy

Imagine that you paid $800 six months in advance for airfare and lodging for a beach vacation with some of your friends over spring break. Over those six months, however, you've had a falling out with two of your "friends" and you find it unpleasant to be around them. As the trip draws near, you're also not feeling well and you are at risk of falling catastrophically behind in your course work. Would you still go on the vacation, or would you stay home, get well, and take care of your course work?

Now imagine that everything is the same except that you won the airfare and lodging in a raffle. Would you still go on the trip?

Most people say that they would be much more likely to take the trip if they had paid for it than if they had won it in a raffle. This is the **sunk cost fallacy**, a reluctance to "waste" money that leads people to look backward rather than forward when making decisions. In this case, whether or not the vacation was free or was paid for makes no difference in whether it will be rewarding to go. If you paid for the vacation, you're not getting the money back whether you go or not. The key question, in both cases, is whether your overall welfare, or utility, will be advanced more by staying home or by going. Rationally, historical costs should not factor into a decision. Only the future costs and benefits of different options should be weighed when deciding between them.

As this example illustrates, however, people are not always entirely rational. Most of us pay a great deal of attention to historical costs. Consider a study in which people interested in a season-ticket subscription to the Ohio University Theater were randomly assigned to one of three groups. One group paid the regular ticket price ($15), another group was given a $2 discount on each ticket, and a

risk aversion The reluctance to pursue an uncertain option with an average payoff that equals or exceeds the payoff attainable by another, certain option.

risk seeking The opposite of risk aversion; the tendency to forgo a certain outcome in favor of a risky option with an equal or more negative average payoff.

sunk cost fallacy A reluctance to "waste" money that leads people to continue with an endeavor, whether it serves their future interests or not, because they have already invested money, effort, or time in it.

The Intensity of Possible Losses

Consider another study of loss aversion and framing, also by Tversky and Kahneman (1981). One group of participants was asked to imagine that the United States is preparing for the outbreak of a rare disease expected to kill 600 people. Two alternative programs to combat the disease have been proposed:

> If program A is adopted, 200 people will be saved.
>
> If program B is adopted, there is a one-third probability that 600 people will be saved and a two-thirds probability that no one will be saved.

Among these participants, 72 percent preferred program A, the "safe" option. Saving 200 "for sure" is more appealing than trying to save all 600 lives at the risk of saving none.

Another group of participants was given the same introduction as before, but with the following options:

> If program C is adopted, 400 people will die.
>
> If program D is adopted, there is a one-third probability that nobody will die and a two-thirds probability that 600 people will die.

Of these participants, 78 percent preferred program D, the risky option. A one-third probability that no one will die is preferable to the certain death of 400 people. Note, however, that program A in the first version is identical to program C in the second version (200 people saved is equivalent to 400 people who die). Similarly, program B is identical to program D (a one-third probability that 600 people will be saved is equivalent to a one-third probability that nobody will die).

Chances are you found yourself thinking that you would make the same choice as the majority in each case. The first one, in fact, probably seemed like a no-brainer. If you can save 200 lives, better do it. End of story. In fact, when people in a brain scanner (fMRI machine) are choosing this option, their pattern of brain activation shows just how easy the choice is. When considering the sure gain, there is very little activation along the intraparietal sulcus, a region associated with imagining hypothetical events and their outcomes (top left of **Figure A2.1**; Gonzalez, Dana, Koshino, & Just, 2005). But when these participants consider the risky gain—trying to save all 600 lives at the risk of saving no one—the activity in the intraparietal sulcus is intense (top right of Figure A2.1). Most of us make the easy choice, the one less fraught with uncertainty and agitation.

But look what happens when participants think about losses. As the bottom of Figure A2.1 indicates, there is considerable activation along the intraparietal sulcus when they think about the smaller, certain loss or the larger, uncertain loss. Here the decision is more difficult and more stressful. They don't want to accept 400 deaths, but they also don't want to risk having 600 people die. For most people, the decision is resolved, and made easier, by seizing on the fact that a chance that no one will die feels better than the certainty that most of them will die.

These brain activation patterns show the neural foundation of both loss aversion (greater activity when considering losses rather than gains) and framing (outcomes described as gains yield a very different pattern of activation than identical outcomes described as losses).

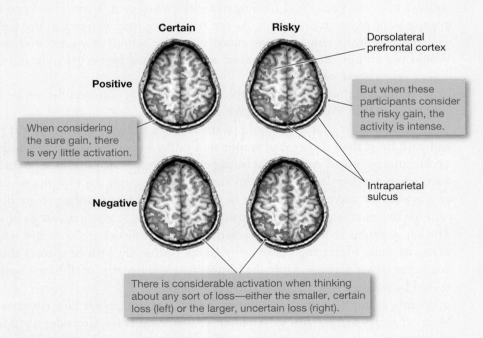

Certain **Risky**

Dorsolateral prefrontal cortex

Positive

When considering the sure gain, there is very little activation.

But when these participants consider the risky gain, the activity is intense.

Negative

Intraparietal sulcus

There is considerable activation when thinking about any sort of loss—either the smaller, certain loss (left) or the larger, uncertain loss (right).

FIGURE A2.1 Activity along the Intraparietal Sulcus (Source: From Gonzalez, Dana, Koshino, & Just, 2005.)

third group received a $7 discount on each ticket. The investigators kept track of how often people in each of these three groups actually attended the theater after paying for all of their tickets up front. What they found was that those who paid the most (regular ticket price) attended more often than those who paid a bit less ($2 discount), who in turn attended more often than those who paid even less ($7 discount) (Arkes & Blumer, 1985). The more people paid for their tickets, the greater their sunk costs, and the more importance they attached to seeing the plays. A similar effect occurs in the area of health and medicine. People benefit more from an inert pill—a placebo—the more they paid for it (Waber, Shiv, Carmon & Ariely, 2008).

To really drive home how irrational and yet how compelling the sunk cost fallacy is, the same investigators presented people with the following hypothetical scenario:

> On your way home you buy a TV dinner on sale for $3 at the local grocery store. A few hours later you decide it is time for dinner, so you get ready to put the TV dinner in the oven. Then you get an idea. You call up your friend to ask if he would like to come over for a quick TV dinner and then watch a good movie on TV. Your friend says sure. You go out to buy a second TV dinner. However, all the on-sale TV dinners are gone. You therefore have to spend $5 (the regular price) for the TV dinner identical to the one you just bought for $3. You go home and put both dinners in the oven. When the two dinners are fully cooked, you get a phone call. Your friend is ill and cannot come. You are not hungry enough to eat both dinners. You cannot freeze one. You must eat one and discard the other. Which one do you eat?

Not surprisingly, most participants expressed no preference. After all, everything is the same regardless of which one you eat—you'll have paid $8 and eaten one TV dinner. But a very substantial minority said they would eat the $5 dinner. Almost no one said they would eat the $3 dinner. Because we honor sunk costs, throwing out the $5 dinner seems more wasteful than throwing out (the same) $3 dinner—even when, rationally, it is not.

MENTAL ACCOUNTING

Imagine that you decided to take a trip during spring break, and you go to the Bahamas, where there is casino gambling. You've allotted yourself $100 to gamble, and you sit down to play blackjack. How careful would you be with your bets?

Now suppose that luck is with you, and soon you're ahead $100. You take your original $100 stake and put it in your pocket, and you are now going to limit yourself to playing with just the $100 you've won. How careful would you now be with your bets?

Many people report that they would be more conservative initially when they were betting with their own money, but that they would bet more boldly with the "house money." This scenario highlights another principle in behavioral economics known as **mental accounting**, or the tendency to treat money differently depending on how it was acquired and to what mental category it is attached. Note that the $100 a person earns at the casino is truly "their" money and should be treated every bit as seriously as the rest of their money. But when they think of it as "house money," it becomes much easier to treat frivolously. Easy come, easy

mental accounting The tendency to treat money differently depending on how it is acquired and the mental category to which it is attached.

go. (By the way, the casino never treats the money it receives from you as "patron's money"; it's theirs the second you lose it.)

The influence of mental accounting can also be seen in a thought experiment adapted from one of the founders of behavioral economics, economist Richard Thaler (1980): Imagine that you've bought a $200 ticket to see a play, a sporting event, or a rock concert. As you approach the entrance, you realize that you've lost your ticket. You can, however, fork over another $200 and get another ticket. Would you do so? Many people report that they would not, on the grounds that $400 is too much to see a play, a sporting event, or a concert.

But now imagine a slightly different scenario. You have reserved a ticket and will pay the $200 when you arrive. As you approach the entrance, however, you notice that you've lost $200 somewhere in the parking lot. You still have enough money to buy your ticket to the event. Would you do so? In this case, most people say, "Of course. I want to see the event, it's worth $200 to me, and I have the money."

But note that these two scenarios don't differ in any meaningful way. In both cases, the decision you face is the same: you're $200 poorer than you were a moment ago, and you have to decide whether it's worth it to pay $200 to attend—and you have the money to do so. Rationally, then, people should make the same choice in the two circumstances. But that's not what most people do. In one version, the lost $200 is mentally "charged" to the cost of the event, making it seem too steep at $400. In the other case, the lost $200 is mentally charged to some other "accident" or "general expenses" account, keeping the psychological cost of the ticket the same as it was originally—$200.

To make the best use of your money, economists will tell you that you should integrate all of your assets and liabilities into one overall account. But people nevertheless set up different mental accounts all the time, with rather peculiar—and important—implications for how they spend and invest the money they receive. For example, an economist at the Bank of Israel examined the economic behavior of a group of Israelis who were receiving regular payments from the German government as restitution for war crimes during World War II (Landsberger, 1966). Some of them received relatively large payments; others received relatively modest payments (depending on their family's financial situation back in Nazi Germany). What he found was a striking example of mental accounting. Those who received the largest sums treated the money very seriously, spending relatively little and saving a lot. On average, they spent 23 cents of every dollar they received. Those who received smaller sums treated the money less seriously, spending a lot and saving little. In fact, these individuals spent $2 for every dollar they received in restitution money! Because the sums weren't large, these individuals "put" the money into some sort of "slush fund" or "everyday expense" account and spent it as quickly as spending opportunities arose. Those who received the larger payments "put" the money into a more serious "asset" or "savings" account and therefore were reluctant to use it for more frivolous purposes.

This mistake comes in many guises. A friend of one of the authors was constantly getting parking tickets. She justified this expense by saying that she didn't eat out at lunchtime, so she had a little nest egg to spend to avoid the trouble of rushing out to the parking meter in the middle of work. The parking tickets were "charged" to an entirely mental account funded by her thrifty lunchtime habits.

Consider the implications of this sort of mental accounting for national economic policy. On several occasions in the last few decades, the federal government has tried to stimulate the economy by giving people tax rebates. In 2001, for

"The only way not to think about money is to have a great deal of it."

—Edith Wharton

example, the government gave out $38 billion to taxpayers in the form of rebates of $300 to $600; in 2008, the government gave out rebates of $600 to $1,200. The rationale behind the rebate programs is that people will spend more if they have more money to spend. Although the rationale has to be true at some level, it seems that it is not as true as government officials hope. Neither the 2001 nor the 2008 rebate program was as successful as policy makers expected, and the culprit seems to have been mental accounting. By describing the money given out to taxpayers as "rebates," recipients were encouraged to think of it as their own money being returned to them. They thus treated it very seriously and put quite a bit of it in the bank. Given what we know about mental accounting, the government would have been better off labeling the payments "tax bonuses."

Such a simple change in wording has been shown to influence spending rather dramatically. In one study conducted at Harvard University (**Figure A2.2**), participants who showed up for an experiment were given, unexpectedly, a $50 check. They were told that it was from the investigator's research budget, which was

---

FIGURE A2.2 Scientific Method: Mental Accounting

Hypothesis: People think of their money as belonging to different "mental accounts" and spend it differently if it is given to them as a "bonus" versus a "rebate."

Research Method:

1. Participants who showed up for an experiment were given, unexpectedly, a $50 check.

2. They were told the money was either a "rebate" or a "bonus."

3. Participants were then told they could purchase items from a "Harvard lab store" on their way out.

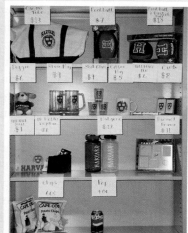

Results: Those who received their money as a rebate spent substantially less than those who received their money as a bonus.

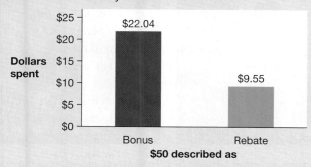

CONCLUSION: Mental accounting matters. People treat bonus money less seriously than rebate money.

Source: Adapted from Epley, Mak, & Idson (2006).

financed by tuition dollars. The investigators described the check to some participants as a "rebate." Others were told it was a "bonus." When the participants were contacted a week later and asked what they had done with the money, those who received a "rebate" reported spending less than half as much of it ($9.55) as those who received a "bonus" ($22.04). The same effect was observed in a follow-up experiment in which participants could purchase items from a "Harvard lab store" on their way out. Those who received their money as a rebate spent substantially less of it than those who received their money as a bonus (Epley, Mak, & Idson, 2006).

Thus, the terminology people use to describe their money leads them to assign it to more serious or less serious mental accounts, with pronounced effects on whether they spend it. As one of the authors of these studies put it, "Getting a rebate is more like being reimbursed for travel expenses than like getting a year-end bonus. Reimbursements send people on trips to the bank. Bonuses send people on trips to the Bahamas" (Epley, 2008).

DECISION PARALYSIS

Suppose you go to the grocery store to buy a pint of gourmet ice cream. Would you rather shop at a store that offers 45 flavors from five different vendors or a store with 18 flavors from two different vendors? It's a no-brainer, right? It's better to have more options so you can maximize your chances of getting *exactly* what you want. To economists, certainly, it is always better to have more options.

But psychologically, it's another story. Making decisions is hard, and people aren't equipped to deal with an abundance of choices all the time. With so many options, we can find ourselves suffering from decision paralysis, unable to decide which option we should select. Consider a study conducted in an upscale grocery store in Menlo Park, California. Catering to the local elite, the store offers its customers over 300 types of jams, 250 different mustards, and 75 varieties of olive oil. The store permitted two social psychologists, Sheena Iyengar and Mark Lepper, the opportunity to set up a tasting booth where they set out a selection of jams. They rotated the selection every hour, so that half the time 6 jams were on display and half the time 24 were on display. Shoppers who stopped by

The Effect of a Large or Small Choice Set To examine the effect of the number of choices available on whether customers would end up making a purchase, Iyengar and Lepper (2000) displayed samples of 6 (A) or 24 (B) different jams. The bar-code labels attached to each jam allowed them to assess whether customers were more likely to buy if they had examined a set of 6 jams or a set of 24 jams.

the booth were given a coupon for $1 off any jam purchased in the store. These coupons had a bar code that allowed the investigators to keep track of whether anyone who ended up purchasing a jar of jam had visited the booth when it had 6 or 24 items on display. Iyengar and Lepper were interested in whether shoppers would be stymied by the 24 jams on display, unable to decide what to buy and hence less likely to make a purchase. They found that although many more people visited the booth when it displayed the large assortment of jams, ten times as many customers actually bought a jar when they examined the smaller assortment (Iyengar & Lepper, 2000). Having a large assortment looks good and draws a lot of customers. But it makes deciding hard—so hard, in fact, that many people never decide at all.

But failing to make a decision, of course, is still a decision—often a costly one. To see how costly, consider the decision faced by new employees who must choose whether and how to participate in their company's retirement plan. In today's world, most of these decisions involve the question of which 401(k) plan is best. In these plans, part of the employee's salary is invested in a stock, bond, or money market fund, often with the employer matching, dollar for dollar, what the employee contributes up to a certain amount (say, 5 percent of the employee's salary). For example, if you make $50,000 you might have $2,500 taken out of your paychecks over the year and invested in one of your company's 401(k) funds; your employer would then kick in an additional $2,500. Because of the employer match, it doesn't make economic sense not to participate. Failing to participate leaves "money on the table."

But nowadays, employees have a bewildering array of funds in which to invest. Picking a fund, or the right mix of funds, can be daunting. Many people become overwhelmed, telling themselves, "I'll decide later." But many never do, depriving themselves of the "free money" that comes with the employer's match and severely hurting their long-term financial profile. The scope of the problem can be seen in **Figure A2.3**, which depicts the percentage of employees in different firms who enroll in their company's 401(k) plans as a function of how many plans the companies offer (Sethi-Iyengar, Huberman, & Jiang, 2004). As you can see, the more plans that are offered, the harder the choice becomes—so hard, in fact, that many people avoid making it, at considerable cost to their financial future. Sometimes having more options is not such a good thing.

A final example, one relevant to life on a college campus, should drive the point home. Amos Tversky and Eldar Shafir (1992) offered students $5 to complete a lengthy questionnaire. Some were given five days to complete it, others were given three weeks, and a third group wasn't given a deadline. Of those who were

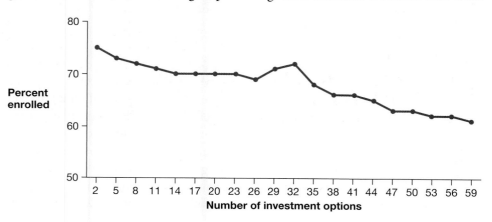

FIGURE A2.3 Overwhelmed by Choice The percentage of employees choosing to enroll in their company's 401(k) retirement savings plans as a function of the number of different investment funds from which the employee could choose. (Source: Adapted from Sethi-Iyengar, Huberman, & Jiang, 2004.)

given only five days to complete the questionnaire, 60 percent turned it in on time versus 42 percent of those who were given three weeks. And only 25 percent of those who weren't given a deadline ever turned it in at all. Does this situation ring a bell? If so, you might consider asking your professors to give you tight deadlines for all assignments. It seems that the more time we have to complete a task, the less pressure we feel to get started, so we often fail to get started at all.

GETTING STARTED ON YOUR OWN FINANCIAL PLANNING

All of the biases discussed in this module can lead you to make less than ideal decisions when you shop, save, and invest. So what can you do about it? What should you keep in mind as you plan your own financial future? What can you do now to make it more likely that you will be financially secure later in life? Five simple ideas—call them the Five Pillars of Financial Wisdom—will improve anyone's financial prospects, regardless of their current economic situation.

Start Early

The key to having sufficient savings later in life is to start saving as soon as possible. The earlier you invest, the more the miracle of compound interest works in your favor. Belsky and Gilovich (1999) illustrate this idea with the following example:

> Meet Jill and John, 21-year-old twins who just graduated from college. Jill, immediately upon entering the workforce, began contributing $50 a month to a stock mutual fund and continued to do so for the next eight years, until she got married and found more pressing uses for her money. John, who married his college sweetheart immediately upon graduating and soon after started a family, didn't start investing until he was 29. Still, he too contributed $50 a month to the same stock fund, but he continued doing so for 37 years until he retired at age 65. All told, John invested $22,200, while Jill contributed just $4,800. At age 65, which of the two siblings had the most money, assuming they earned an average of 10 percent a year? (p. 121)

The amazing result is that Jill, who invested just $4,800, ends up with more money ($256,650) than her brother John ($217,830), even though he invested over four times as much. If you get a late start on saving, it's hard to catch up. Let the math (compound interest) work for you, not against you.

Diversify

You have lived through two of the biggest boom-and-bust events in U.S. economic history—the stock market dive in 2001 and the collapse of the real estate market in 2008. Both episodes point to the difficulty of knowing when a particular class of investments is likely to do well or poorly, making you richer or poorer. But different assets—stocks, bonds, real estate, currency, even precious metals like gold—tend not to rise or fall in sync, so owning something in each class is a good way to protect your savings. A diversified portfolio of investments is less likely to suffer a wrenching decline even during historic busts like those of 2001 and 2008.

Invest in Mutual Funds

Of course, you probably don't have the financial resources to be able to buy a diverse group of stocks or an assortment of bonds, let alone property. But you don't have to. You can start by buying small pieces of each of these assets by purchasing shares in mutual funds. Mutual funds pool your money with that of other investors to buy stocks in a broad range of companies. Because the range of companies can be broad, a mutual fund provides quite a bit of diversification on its own. You can also purchase mutual funds that invest in bonds or in combinations of different assets to further diversify your investments.

Different funds charge investors different fees for investing your money, and you should look for those with very low fees. Predicting market performance—which most mutual fund managers must do—is very difficult, and fund managers who do well one year often fail to do so the next. Therefore, paying the high fees that are often charged by "hot" funds with celebrity fund managers are typically not worth the extra expense. "Index" funds don't try to outfox the market; instead, they merely invest in a broad portfolio of stocks that mirror the market as a whole. Because they are not managed so actively, they typically have the lowest fees and hence represent particularly good investments.

Set Up a Payroll Deduction Plan

Once you get a job and start receiving a regular paycheck, you should enroll in a payroll deduction plan that takes some of your wages and invests them, without your seeing the money first, into a savings account, or a stock, bond, or money market mutual fund. Setting aside the money at the outset is much better than trying to do the saving and investing yourself. If you get your paycheck and then try to put some of it away for savings, the amount you save will feel like a loss of income. If it's automatically invested before you see your paycheck, the investment feels instead like a forgone gain—which, as discussed earlier, is easier to accept than an outright loss. If your employer matches your payroll deductions with an additional payment by the company, you should take the maximum allowable deduction. To do otherwise is to leave money on the table.

Pay Off Credit Card Debt

Many people have money in a savings account but don't use it to pay off the balance on their credit cards. It might sound reasonable ("I need some money stashed away for emergencies"), but it's not. Savings accounts earn very low interest (typically less than 2 percent as we write this), but an unpaid credit card balance accrues hefty interest (usually over 16 percent). The difference between the two rates is money going out the door—from you to the credit card companies. If you don't pay off your credit cards, you're fighting the power of compound interest when you want it working for you. By all means you should be saving money, but not at the expense of absorbing the punishing interest charges on an unpaid credit card balance. If dipping into your savings still makes you nervous, note that those same credit card companies that want you to keep a balance on your card will be perfectly happy to lend you money should an emergency arise. And once you pay off your credit card, *then* you can start to put away money for emergencies.

Summary

- *Behavioral economics* is the effort by psychologists and economists to create more realistic economic models that take into account people's occasional irrationality when making choices.

Irrationality in Financial Markets

- Examples of irrationality can be found in the tendency of the stock market to go up on sunny days and down on cloudy days and to go up in a country whose national soccer team wins (and down when it loses).

Loss Aversion

- People tend to be *risk averse* for possible gains and *risk seeking* for possible losses. Framing choices as losses versus gains therefore yields irrational—or at any rate, inconsistent—patterns of choice.
- People are susceptible to the *sunk cost fallacy*. They are inclined to consume something (for example, go to a play or a sporting event), even when it no longer has positive value to them, in order to be "economical" and not "waste" the money already paid for the item.

Mental Accounting

- People keep separate *mental accounts* when they would be better off having a single mental account for all of their assets.

Decision Paralysis

- Too many choices can result in decision paralysis. The more things you have to choose from, the less likely you might be to choose anything.

Getting Started on Your Own Financial Planning

- Some simple rules about money will have a big impact on your wealth: save early and often, diversify, invest in mutual funds rather than specific stocks or bonds, set up a payroll deduction plan, and for heaven's sake, avoid paying the huge interest on credit card balances.

Key Terms

behavioral economics (p. 575)
loss aversion (p. 577)

mental accounting (p. 581)
risk aversion (p. 579)

risk seeking (p. 579)
sunk cost fallacy (p. 579)

Further Reading

Belsky, G., & Gilovich, T. (2010). *Why smart people make big money mistakes*. New York: Simon & Schuster. An accessible guide to the field of behavioral economics and how findings in that hybrid of psychology and economics can help the average person make better financial decisions.

Zweig, J. (2007). *Your money and your brain*. New York: Simon & Schuster. An entertaining review of what goes on in the brain when people make financial decisions and why so many financial decisions turn out badly.

Social Psychology and Education

OVERHEARD IN PALO ALTO: One European-American high school senior to another, upon hearing of her friend's super-high SAT scores. "Good grief, Jessica, those scores are positively Asian."

On average, Asian-American students' achievements in the academic realm are undeniably impressive, and Asian students regularly outperform American students in math and science. Why do you suppose they do? What could be done to help European-American and African-American students perform at Asian levels? Or do you think that such a thing is highly unlikely or impossible?

Social psychologists have studied some of the reasons for students' better or poorer performance in school. More important, they have investigated ways in which their findings might improve educational outcomes, especially for certain minority students, who often perform at less than their capacity.

As we will see, social psychology has provided excellent tools for improving critical thinking—and these can be sharpened by educational interventions that are remarkably brief but effective.

PYGMALION IN THE CLASSROOM

How much influence does a teacher have on the academic progress of students? The idea that one person can transform another—even create an extraordinary person from ordinary raw material—has been a theme of literature going back to Greek mythology: a sculptor named Pygmalion made a statue so beautiful that he fell in love with it, and with the help of the goddess Venus he brought it to life. A more recent version of the myth is the musical *My Fair Lady*, about an eccentric English phonetics professor who coaches a flower girl in manners and accent, helping her pass for a lady in British high society.

In 1968, Robert Rosenthal and Lenore Jacobson (1968) published a study—they called it "Pygmalion in the Classroom"—that created an uproar in the fields of both psychology and education. All students in a particular school were given an IQ test. Allegedly on the basis of the test, Rosenthal and Jacobson told the teachers at the beginning of the school year that some of their students were "late bloomers"—that is, they were expected to show substantial IQ growth over the course of the school year. About 20 percent of the children in each classroom were designated—ostensibly on the basis of the test, but in fact by random assignment—as being such late bloomers. The investigators reported that the designated late bloomers made substantial IQ gains over the course of the year. The gains for young children were shockingly high—15 points for first graders and 10 points for second graders. These increases seemed to indicate that teachers' expectations for children operated as a powerful self-fulfilling prophecy: if the teacher believed that the child was going to gain in intelligence, the teacher behaved in such a way toward the child as to ensure that such gains would occur. Unnervingly, the children in the control group who showed achievement gains that the teacher did not expect of them were rated by the teacher as less interesting, less affectionate, and not as well adjusted. Education critics argued that the results showed that teacher bias, presumably in favor of white middle-class children, was a significant reason that these children performed better in school and scored higher on IQ tests. Conversely, the scores of African-American, Hispanic, and children of lower socioeconomic status (SES) were being pulled down because of teachers' negative expectations for them.

The furor over the Rosenthal and Jacobson experiment persists to this day. Claims range from outright accusations of fraud to allegations that the results were an underestimate of what goes on in the classroom all the time. Lee Jussim and Kent Harber (2005) reviewed the almost 400 (!) studies conducted in the first 35 years after the initial report and found several important patterns. First, the extremely large effects found by Rosenthal and Jacobson proved to be exceptional; subsequent investigators almost never found the huge effects that they did. Second, it is clear—when expectations are manipulated—that sometimes teacher expectations affect children's IQ and academic performance. (If expectations are not manipulated, a correlation between the teacher's expectation and children's performance could be due to accuracy on the teacher's part. Children who are believed to be—and are—more talented do better in school.) Third, teacher expectation effects are rarely very strong: about 3 IQ points is as large as is generally obtained, and often the effects of teacher expectations are literally zero. Fourth, teacher expectation effects occur only if expectations are

How to Tutor: The Five Cs

Social psychologist Mark Lepper made an intriguing discovery while studying college-student tutors of elementary school students who were having trouble in math. Some tutors had big—and fast—impacts on their pupils. Others had no effect. He then went to work to determine the difference between the effective and the ineffective tutors. Which of the following behaviors do you think would be helpful, and which unhelpful?

1. When a student starts to make even a minor mistake, stop the student immediately to avoid reinforcing the incorrect behavior.
2. If the student makes a mistake, carefully state the rule that the student needs to know to successfully solve the problem.
3. Keep the problems simple so as to avoid damaging self-esteem.
4. Praise the student often for doing work well.
5. Don't get emotionally involved with the student's difficulties, since this

could create a dependent stance on the part of the student.

Actually, all of these approaches are unhelpful and are avoided by effective tutors. They violate one or another of the strategies that characterize the successful tutor. Lepper and his colleagues offer Five Cs for effective tutoring (Lepper & Woolverton, 2001; Lepper, Woolverton, Mumme, & Gurtner, 1993):

Foster a sense of *control* in the student, making the student feel that he or she has command of the material.

Challenge the student—but at a level of difficulty that is within the student's capability.

Instill *confidence* in the student by maximizing success (expressing confidence in the student, assuring the student that the problem he or she just solved was a difficult one) and by minimizing failure (providing excuses for mistakes and emphasizing the part of the problem the student got right).

Foster *curiosity* through Socratic methods (asking leading questions)

and by linking the problem to other problems the student has seen that appear on the surface to be different.

Contextualize by placing the problem in a real-world context or in a context from a movie or TV show.

Expert tutors have a number of strategies that set them apart. They don't bother to correct minor errors like forgetting to write down a plus sign. If the student is about to make a mistake, they gently suggest a problem-solving path that would prevent it from occurring. Or sometimes they let the student make the mistake when they think it can provide a valuable learning experience. They never dumb down the material for the sake of self-esteem, but instead change the way they present it. Most of what good tutors do is ask questions. They ask leading questions. They ask students to explain their reasoning. They are actually less likely to give *positive* feedback than are less effective tutors, because, Lepper theorizes, doing so makes the tutoring session feel too evaluative. And finally, expert tutors are always nurturing and empathic.

---

manipulated early in the school year—within the first two weeks. Fifth, teacher expectation effects are greater for first- and second-grade children than for older children. Sixth, and most important, teacher expectation effects can be genuinely large for low-achieving, lower-SES children and for African-American children (Jussim, Eccles, & Madon, 1996). So a modified version of the original claims appears to be correct: a teacher's belief that lower-achieving, lower-SES, and African-American students can do well intellectually can enhance those students' performance.

INTELLIGENCE: THING OR PROCESS?

Self-fulfilling prophecies can result not only from teachers' expectations but also from students' beliefs about their own intellectual abilities. Carol Dweck and her colleagues (Dweck, 2007; Dweck & Leggett, 1988) have shown that different people have very different views about the nature of intelligence. Some people

incrementalist theory of intelligence The belief that intelligence is something you can improve by dint of working.

entity theory of intelligence The belief that intelligence is something you are born with and cannot change.

believe that intelligence is a malleable quality that can be improved with effort. Dweck and her colleagues call this an **incrementalist theory of intelligence**. Other people think that intelligence is a fixed, predetermined "thing" that people have to one degree or another and that there is not much they can do to change it. Dweck and colleagues call this an **entity theory of intelligence.**

People who are incremental theorists believe that they can increase their ability, and they attribute failure to lack of effort or to the difficulty of the task (Henderson & Dweck, 1990). As a result, they work more toward goals that will increase their ability—even at the risk of exposing their ignorance—and spend less effort trying to document their ability. In contrast, people who are entity theorists are less confident that what they do will make them any smarter. They blame their failures on a lack of intellectual ability, and they are inclined to feel that they can do little to improve because they just don't have what it takes. Entity theorists also tend to choose tasks that are likely to provide positive views of their intellectual ability—but such tasks provide no opportunity to learn something new. It should be clear which attitude is more likely to result in an increase in intellectual skills, not to mention self-esteem.

Henderson and Dweck (1990) found that students entering junior high school who were incrementalists ended up getting better grades than students who were entity theorists. Moreover, incrementalists got better grades regardless of prior academic achievement: whether the students had a history of good or poor grades in elementary school, they got better grades in junior high if they believed that their ability was under their control. In another study, Henderson and Dweck found that students who were about equal in their math performance at the beginning of junior high progressively increased their math grades over the course of two years in high school if they were incrementalists but tended not to improve their grades if they were entity theorists (Blackwell, Trzesniewski, & Dweck, 2007).

But who is right—the entity theorist or the incrementalist? Neither. Or rather, both. If you are an entity theorist, on the one hand, you are not likely to increase as much in intellectual skills. So you're right: you don't believe that your ability is under your control, so in fact it doesn't increase as much, and your genes exert a greater influence on your ability than they would if you believed otherwise. On the other hand, if you're an incrementalist, you're also right: you believe that your ability is under your control and you act accordingly, thereby building on your genetic strengths and increasing your ability (Nisbett, 2009).

CULTURE AND ACHIEVEMENT

Why do Asians—especially Chinese, Japanese, and Koreans and their Asian-American counterparts—tend to show above-average performance on academic tasks? Are they intrinsically smarter than people of European culture? Does something about their genes lead to intellectual superiority?

In fact, there is no good evidence that people of Asian heritage have a genetic advantage over Americans of Western origin. Cross-cultural comparisons of Asians with Westerners find no evidence that Asians have higher IQs, though admittedly it can be difficult to compare IQs across different cultures and languages (Flynn, 1991; Nisbett, 2009). A comparison of the IQs of children about to begin first grade in Minneapolis, in Sendai (in Japan), and in Taipei (in Taiwan) found that the American children had slightly higher IQs than either group of Asian children (Stevenson et al., 1990). Considering the socialization practices of Asians and Americans, this finding should not be surprising: Asians focus on social and emotional growth during the early years, and Americans, especially middle-class and upper-middle-class Americans, are more likely to focus on intellectual skills (Stevenson et al., 1990). By fifth grade, the IQ differences were gone, but the Asian children were light-years ahead of the Americans in math—partly a result of better teaching of math and longer school years in the Asian countries (Stevenson & Stigler, 1992), but also a result of the Asian children working harder at math (Stevenson & Lee, 1996). Asian (and Asian-American) students study many more hours a week on average than European-Americans do.

The best evidence available on the IQ differences between Asian-Americans and European-Americans comes from a massive study of the high school seniors of the class of 1966 (Flynn, 1991). Almost all of these students were Americans, though some were first-generation Americans. The IQs of the Asian-Americans were trivially lower than those of the European-Americans—not surprising given that many of them came from homes where English was not the native language. However, Asian-Americans' SAT scores were substantially higher. SAT scores, of course, are partly a reflection of the kinds of skills measured by IQ tests and partly a reflection of motivational factors that result in a capacity for hard work. Even more striking, when the study participants were adults, fully 55 percent of

BOX A3.2   FOCUS ON CULTURE

Confucius and Theories about Ability

Asian-Americans whose forebears came from the "Confucian cultures" of China, Japan, and Korea achieve at levels higher than would be predicted given their ability scores. Such outcomes could be expected based on ancient theories about talent. Confucius—the founding father of modern East Asian cultures—was quite clear that although some of our ability is, as he said, a gift from heaven, most of it is due to hard work. For 2,000 years, it was possible for a young person to go from being a poor peasant to being the highest magistrate in China by dint of study and hard work. In no other country until modern times has there been that degree of social mobility. As you might expect, East Asians and Americans who spring from that region are devout incrementalists: they believe, much more than European-Americans, that intellectual achievement is mostly a matter of hard work (Chen & Stevenson, 1995; Choi, Nisbett, & Norenzayan, 1999; Heine et al., 2001; Holloway, 1988; Stevenson et al., 1990). When Japanese and Canadians were told that they had either succeeded or failed on a task that presumably measured creativity, the Canadians worked longer on a similar task if they had succeeded on the first one, and the Japanese worked longer if they had failed (Heine et al., 2001).

Confucius

the Chinese-Americans, the largest group of the Asian-Americans, ended up in professional, technical, or managerial positions. Only a third of European-Americans ended up in those jobs. The Asian-Americans capitalized on their ability to a far greater extent than did the European-Americans.

BLOCKING STEREOTYPE THREAT IN THE CLASSROOM

Other minority groups, such as African-Americans and Hispanics, have lower average IQ scores and lower academic achievement than either Asian-Americans or European-Americans. There are numerous social reasons for these differences. Most of these factors are in flux, however, and in recent years the IQ and achievement gaps have begun to lessen substantially (Nisbett, 2009).

In an investigation of one of these factors, Claude Steele and Joshua Aronson demonstrated that women and minorities often perform more poorly on ability tests because they are afraid of confirming stereotypes about the abilities of their group (see Chapter 11). With Catherine Good and Michael Inzlicht, Aronson decided to see what would happen if poor minority students could be convinced that their abilities were under their control. They performed an intervention with poor Hispanic students in Texas (Good, Aronson, & Inzlicht, 2003). All students in the study were assigned college student mentors. Control group mentors gave the students cautionary information about drugs and encouraged their students to avoid taking them. Experimental group mentors told their charges that intelligence was changeable and under their control to a substantial extent and taught them how the brain can make new connections throughout life. Students were shown a web page that reinforced the mentor's message. For students in the experimental group, this website showed animated pictures of the brain, including pictures of neurons and dendrites, along with explanations of how the brain forms new connections when novel problems are being solved. The mentors also helped the students design their own web pages, using their own words and pictures, which reinforced the message of the malleability of intelligence.

The experimental intervention had a very large effect. On a statewide academic achievement test, the boys exposed to the intervention scored much higher in math than those not exposed to the intervention. For the girls, who tend to worry that their gender makes them less talented in math, the difference was even greater. In tests of reading skills, both boys and girls exposed to the intervention did substantially better than students in the control group.

Dweck and her colleagues (Blackwell et al., 2007) performed a similar intervention with poor African-American and Latino seventh-grade students in New York City. Like the Texas students, the New York students in the experimental group were given convincing demonstrations of the changes in knowledge and intelligence that are produced by work and study. Junior high is a difficult time for many students, but it seems to be particularly difficult for disadvantaged minority children. The math performance of control students in the study grew worse and worse as junior high school went on. But the decline was arrested for students who received the intervention. They had held entity beliefs about intelligence and initially thought they were doomed to poor performance because they were incorrigibly unintelligent. Simply being made to believe that their intelligence was under their control had a significant impact on their academic performance.

Daphna Oyserman and her coworkers carried out a quite different intervention with poor African-American junior high students in Detroit (Oyserman, Bybee, & Terry, 2006). They asked the students to think about what kind of future they wanted to have, what difficulties they would likely have along the way, how they could deal with those difficulties, and which of their friends would be most helpful in dealing with the difficulties. Oyserman and colleagues supplemented these sessions by having students work in small groups on how to deal with everyday problems, with social difficulties, with academic problems, and with the process of getting to high school graduation. The intervention had a modest effect on grade point average and on standardized tests and a very large effect on the likelihood of being held back a grade in school.

A study by Geoffrey Cohen and his colleagues showed that simply having minority students write about their most important values at the beginning of middle school substantially improved their grades over the subsequent years (Cohen, Garcia, Apfel, & Master, 2006). The students were enrolled in a mostly middle-class integrated suburban school. As is frequently the case in such schools, the African-American students in the past had had significantly lower grades than the white students. The African-American students were well aware of this, and the social psychologists who conducted the study assumed that these students were subject to the worries prompted by stereotype threat. The social psychologists reasoned that if the students were encouraged to think about their most important values, this self-affirmation in the school context would produce a sense of efficacy and belongingness. In fact, black students who were exposed to the affirmation intervention performed better over the term than black students in the control group (**Figure A3.1**). In the course in which the intervention took

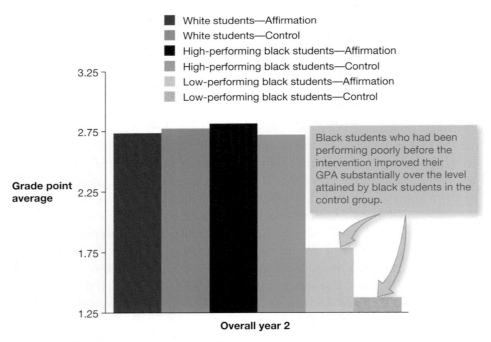

FIGURE A3.1 Blocking Stereotype Threat Mean GPA scores in core courses the year after some students experienced an affirmation intervention (by being asked to write out their most important values). Black students were split into low- and high-performing groups, reflecting their relative standing within their class. (Source: Adapted from Cohen, Garcia, Purdie-Vaughns, Apfel, & Brzustoski, 2009.)

place, the students in the affirmation condition reduced the achievement gap with white students by 40 percent, and their likelihood of getting a D or worse was reduced by half. Cohen and colleagues followed the students over the next two years and found that the effects of the intervention were fully sustained (Cohen, Garcia, Purdie-Vaughns, Apfel, & Brzustoski, 2009). The likelihood of needing remediation was reduced from 18 percent to 5 percent. Interestingly, the intervention had no effect on black students who had performed well before entering middle school; presumably they were sufficiently confident that the affirmation manipulation was unnecessary. Nor did the affirmation manipulation have any effect on white students, whether previously high performing or not.

SOCIAL FEARS AND ACADEMIC ACHIEVEMENT

Cohen, together with Gregory Walton, studied the effects of other types of concerns on the performance of minority students, this time in a college context (Walton & Cohen, 2007). Most beginning students worry about social acceptance and fitting in on campus, but for minority students these issues can be particularly worrisome. If they fail to make friends, because there are typically not that many minority students on campus and because they may feel ill at ease with students from other backgrounds, they may begin to wonder if they belong on campus. Because of these concerns, minority students' motivation may flag, and their GPAs may suffer as they go through school.

Walton and Cohen reasoned that lagging performance could be nipped in the bud if minority students knew that worries about social acceptance are common for all students, regardless of ethnicity, and that their experience was likely to improve in the future (Walton & Cohen, 2007). The researchers performed a modest intervention with black students at a prestigious private university. They invited black and white freshmen to participate in a psychology study at the end of their freshman year. The experimenters intended to convince an intervention group that worries about social acceptance were common for students of all ethnicities but tended to vanish as time went on and they made more friends. The experimenters expected that this information would help black students realize that the best way to understand their social difficulties was not in terms of their race ("I guess my kind of people don't really belong at this kind of place") but as part of the student experience that is common to everyone ("I guess everybody has these kinds of problems"). The researchers believed that recognition of their common problem—and its likely solution—would help keep the students from worrying about belonging and help them focus on academic achievement.

To drive the point home, Walton and Cohen had students in the intervention group write an essay about the likelihood of improvement in their social situation in the future and deliver a speech in front of a video camera, which they were told would be shown to new students at the school "so that they know what college will be like." This standard dissonance manipulation for the students—getting them to say publicly something that was actually somewhat different from their own views—was intended to enhance the persuasive communications they had received.

Walton and Cohen measured behavior related to academic achievement over the next week, as well as students' GPAs the subsequent semester. The intervention

had a large positive effect on blacks but not on whites. In the period after the intervention, blacks reported studying more, making more contacts with professors, and attending more review sessions and study group meetings. The subsequent term, grades of the black students in the intervention group reflected these behaviors: their grades were much higher than those of black students in the control group.

College is also a social challenge for students who are the first in their working-class families to go beyond high school. The attitudes and values they encounter are typically different from those they have been exposed to in their families and neighborhoods. Working-class people are more interdependent than middle- and upper-middle-class people. For students of working-class origin, going to college is not so much an individual achievement as it is an accomplishment having deep social and interpersonal meaning. Nicole Stephens and her colleagues (Stephens, Townsend, Markus, & Phillips, 2012) created two different welcome letters for new university students. One, which was modeled on the actual university welcome letter, emphasized independent values such as exploring personal interests, expressing ideas and opinions, and participating in independent research. The other emphasized learning by being part of a community, working with and learning from others, and participating in collaborative research. Students were then asked to give a 5-minute speech about their college goals. The investigators examined stress during the speech by measures of cortisol (a hormone that increases with stress) and emotional content of the speech. The cortisol level of first-generation students was greater after reading the independent welcome letter than after reading the interdependent letter, whereas the type of letter had no effect on continuing-generation students. The emotional content of the speech was more negative for first-generation students who read the independent letter than for those who read the interdependent letter, whereas this manipulation also had no effect on the content of continuing-generation students' speeches. The investigators concluded that there is a mismatch between the values of working-class students and the new college environment—a mismatch that may impair academic performance.

TEACHING WITH TELENOVELAS

Which reality television show depicting young people traveling around the countryside features such contests as how to repulse the advances of someone of the opposite sex? And in which states does the show air? We're guessing you couldn't come up with answers. It's *Haath Se Haath Milaa* ("Hand in Hand Together"), and it airs in the states of Rajasthan, Haryana, Delhi, Uttar Pradesh, and Uttaranchal (India). It's designed to alert young people to the risks of HIV/AIDS, which exists in epidemic proportions in India. The young people, by the way, travel in separate his-and-hers buses. The program is part of a worldwide network of TV shows collectively called **entertainment-education**.

Albert Bandura is a learning theorist—a scientist who studies how animals and humans learn connections between events in order to learn which events signal impending rewards and which signal impending punishments. He was one of the first such scientists to approach the question of how people learn appropriate and effective social behavior (Bandura, 1973). A fundamental principle of his theory is that people learn what to approach and what to avoid simply by watching

entertainment-education Media presentations that are meant to both entertain and persuade people to act in their own (or in society's) best interests.

relevant others. They observe other people's behavior and its consequences and adopt the behaviors that seem to be successful and avoid those that are punished. The people who are considered relevant to the individual are *role models* for that individual.

A Mexican television producer named Miguel Sabido read about Bandura's principles of social learning and decided to create television programs that would educate people about effective and rewarding social behaviors and persuade them to avoid dangerous and unproductive behavior. He produced the original entertainment-education telenovelas (similar to soap operas) in the 1970s and 1980s.

Sabido's telenovelas are yearlong stories that center on a specific value. Each one presents three types of characters: positive role models, negative role models, and "doubters," those who fall in between (Singhal, Rogers, & Brown, 1993). There are typically four positive role models complemented by four negative role models. There is always a character who approves of the value being promoted (and one who disapproves), one who promotes the value (and one who does not), one who exercises the value (and one who does not), and one who validates the value (and one who does not). There are also three doubters. One of the doubters accepts the value about a third of the way through the series, one about two-thirds of the way through, and one never accepts the value. (The third doubter usually dies a painful death.) In general, those who accept the value are immediately rewarded, and those who don't are punished. Additionally, throughout the series, epilogues are inserted in which a famous individual speaks to the audience in order to reinforce the value.

The television programs clearly have an effect on behavior, although much of the early evidence has to be categorized as anecdotal, coming from Bandura's own account of the success of the programs (Bandura, 2004). One early telenovela by Sabido urged viewers to enroll in a literacy program. The day after the tele-novela appeared, about 25,000 people descended on the distribution center in downtown Mexico City to obtain their reading materials. The result was a monumental traffic jam in the city. The name of the series was *Ven Conmigo* ("Come with Me"), and in the year it aired, enrollment in literacy classes went up tenfold—from about 90,000 to about 900,000. Another drama, *Acompaname* ("Accompany Me"), emphasized family planning. Those who viewed the program were more inclined to think that having fewer children was likely to have social, economic, and psychological benefits. There was a 32 percent increase in new contraceptive users, and national sales of contraceptives went up markedly.

Sabido's telenovelas have been widely imitated. An Indian drama inspired by Sabido's work promoted female rights and family plan-

Teaching with Telenovelas
Actors running through a scene on the set of the Mexican telenovela *Heridas de Amor* ("Wounds of Love").

ning. Amazingly, enrollment of girls in elementary schools rose from 10 per-cent to 38 percent during the year the show was broadcast. After a family planning telenovela aired in Kenya (Westoff & Rodriguez, 1995), contra-ception practices changed for people across the spectrum of social classes.

A program designed to combat the spread of HIV in Tanzania (Vaughn, Rogers, Singhal, & Swalehe, 2000) spanned four years. For the first two years the radio soap opera was not broadcast in a particular region in Tanzania, in order to provide a comparison group. The soap opera was found to reduce the number of sexual partners and increase condom use in the parts of Tanzania where the program was shown. The mediating factors that seemed to be crucial in producing behavior change were increased self-efficacy, increased communication about HIV, and increased risk awareness. In interviews, viewers of the program made it clear that they identified with the characters in the telenovela and tried to emulate them, consistent with social learning theory expectations.

STATISTICS, SOCIAL SCIENCE METHODOLOGY, AND CRITICAL THINKING

Consider the following problems.

1. David is a high school senior choosing between two colleges. He has friends at both. His friends at college A like it a lot on social and academic grounds. His friends at college B are not so satisfied, being generally unenthusiastic about the college. He visits both of the colleges for a day and meets some students at college A who are not very interesting and a professor who gives him a curt brushoff. He meets several students at college B who are lively and intelligent, and a couple of professors take a personal interest in him. Which college do you think he should go to? Why?
2. Medical research has established that drinking a moderate amount of alcohol is associated with reduced likelihood of getting cancer or heart disease. Assume you are a teetotaler on economic and moral grounds. Should you start modest tippling?

If you answered for question 1 that David should go to college B because he has to choose for himself (not let his friends choose for him), you are in good company with most undergraduates. However, you should also have considered the possibility that although David's samples of the two colleges were based on his own personal experience, the samples were not very large, and the experiences he could expect to have at the two colleges might be very different from his one-day sample. His friends, while they are not David, to be sure, at least have the advantage of having much larger samples of the two schools. Their opinions ought to give David, and you, pause. Moreover, more energy may have been put into ensuring that David got a biased sample of events at college B than at college A. For example, if a friend at college B was particularly eager to get David to go there, he or she might have arranged things so that David would be favorably impressed.

If you answered for question 2 that it might be best to keep your wallet in your pocket and your foot off the bar rail, then you recognized that correlation does not establish causation. Indeed, after decades of hearing from researchers that alcohol in moderation is a disease preventive, some scientists are now saying that the association between moderate drinking and health may be a self-selection effect. People who don't drink at all may avoid it because their health is already poor or because their income discourages them from drinking (and income is strongly correlated with health). And people who drink a lot may be damaging their health.

Why is social psychology relevant to these statistical and methodological analyses of everyday life events? Because principles like these are taught in social psychology courses and are central to social psychological research. Taking statistics courses and science courses that emphasize research principles is an excellent start toward being a good critic of research by recognizing flawed data in many scientific fields. And once you have this statistical and methodological knowledge under your belt, you are better able to apply statistical and methodological principles in everyday life situations.

Darrin Lehman and Richard Nisbett studied the effects of four years in college for students majoring in the humanities, the natural sciences, the social sciences, and psychology. Students majoring in psychology and the social sciences showed a 65 percent improvement in their ability to reason using appropriate statistical and methodological principles like the ones just discussed. Students in the humanities and natural sciences improved by only about 25 percent. (Lest you think few advantages in reasoning come from the study of the humanities and the natural sciences, however, students in those fields improved by 65 percent in various kinds of logical reasoning, and students in psychology and the social sciences improved not at all.)

Two years of graduate-level training in psychology have a huge impact on people's ability to apply statistical and methodological principles to everyday life—but only if the area of psychology the student specializes in deals with ordinary human behavior (Lehman, Lempert, & Nisbett, 1988). This includes the fields of social psychology, developmental psychology, personality psychology, and developmental psychology. It does not include the fields of biopsychology, cognitive psychology, or cognitive neuroscience, even though students in those fields are trained in statistics and methodology. Students of chemistry and law gain absolutely nothing along those lines.

Is it necessary to major in the behavioral sciences to be able to use statistical and methodological principles for understanding everyday life events? No. Research by social psychologists shows that statistical and methodological principles, as well as economic concepts such as the cost-benefit principle, can be taught in very brief sessions (Fong, Krantz, & Nisbett, 1986; Larrick, Morgan, & Nisbett, 1990; Larrick, Nisbett, & Morgan, 1993; Nisbett, Fong, Lehman, & Cheng, 1987). In fact, Richard Larrick and his colleagues taught participants about the sunk cost fallacy (discussed in the Social Psychology and Personal Finance module) in a session lasting only a few minutes (Larrick et al., 1990). Several weeks later, they phoned the participants in the guise of pollsters conducting an "opinion survey." The survey presented various personal and institutional dilemmas that involved undertaking something undesirable that had already been paid for. The trained participants were much more likely to recognize that such behavior was actually uneconomical. When the underlying principles are presented in abstract form, people can be shown how to apply them to everyday life events. People can readily generalize from such sessions to a wide range of situations and scientific claims.

Module Review

Summary

Intelligence: Thing or Process?

- *Entity* theorists, who believe that intelligence is an unchangeable thing (entity) that they have no control over, are less likely to learn new things by taking on challenges and are likely to attribute small failures to lack of ability. People who believe that intelligence can be changed are *incrementalists*; they take on challenges and attribute failure to task difficulty or failure to work hard.

Culture and Achievement

- East Asians constitute one large group who tend to be incrementalists and who thereby gain the benefit of hard work and improved ability.

Blocking Stereotype Threat in the Classroom

- When minority group members are persuaded that their ability is under their control, they perform at higher levels. The same is true when they are asked to think about their goals in life and how to achieve them.

Social Fears and Academic Achievement

- Social fears can hold back minority group members from immersing themselves in the academic enterprise.

Teaching with Telenovelas

- *Entertainment-education*, based on Albert Bandura's social learning theory, can have a big impact on the likelihood that people will avoid risky behavior and pursue beneficial goals.

Statistics, Social Science Methodology, and Critical Thinking

- Statistics and social science methodology, including social psychology, increase people's critical thinking skills, making them more likely to spot the errors in reported scientific studies and more likely to avoid errors of judgment in their own lives.

Key Terms

entertainment-education (p. 597)

entity theory of intelligence (p. 592)

incrementalist theory of intelligence (p. 592)

Further Reading

Dweck, C. S. (2007). *Mindset: The new psychology of success.* New York: Ballantine Books.

Stephens, N. M., Fryberg, S. A., & Markus, H. R. (in press). It's your choice: How the middle-class model of independence disadvantages working-class Americans. In S. T. Fiske & H. R. Markus (Eds.), *Facing social class: Social psychology of social class.* New York: Russell Sage Foundation.

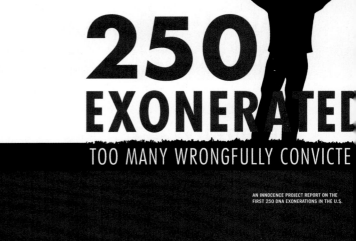

250
EXONERATED

TOO MANY WRONGFULLY CONVICTE

INNOCENCE PROJECT

100 FIFTH AVENUE, 3RD FLOOR
NEW YORK, NEW YORK 10011
WWW.INNOCENCEPROJECT.ORG

BENJAMIN N. CARDOZO SCHOOL OF LAW,
YESHIVA UNIVERSITY

AN INNOCENCE PROJECT REPORT ON THE
FIRST 250 DNA EXONERATIONS IN THE U.S.

BENJAMIN N. CARDOZO SCHOOL OF LAW, YESHIVA UNIVERSITY

Social Psychology and the Law

ON A BRIGHT WINTER DAY in 1989, 29-year-old Eileen Franklin suddenly recalled a horror. She remembered that 20 years before, she had seen her best friend, 8-year-old Susan Nason, murdered. The murderer, silhouetted by the sun, lifted a heavy rock and crushed Susan Nason's skull. Eileen recalled covering her ears so as not to hear the bones of Susan's head shattering. But as her memory grew even sharper, she realized that the murderer had been her own father, George Franklin. In subsequent days, more details of the incident flooded her mind. She finally went to the police and told them about her recovered memory. Her father was ultimately sentenced to life imprisonment based solely on his daughter's testimony, even though some of Eileen's remarkably detailed memories were consistent with botched newspaper accounts rather than the actual facts of the case (Loftus & Ketcham, 1994). Franklin was convicted despite the testimony of psychologist Elizabeth Loftus that "recovered" memories can be utterly mistaken—that people can "remember" things that never happened. And in fact, Eileen's memory was inaccurate: after serving six years in prison for the murder, George Franklin was proved innocent and released. Loftus's testimony, which was at odds with the views of memory held not only by the general public but also by many cognitive psychologists at the time, highlights the important role that psychology can play in understanding—and improving—the procedures that take place in a court of law.

The processes involved in a court case can be separated into three distinct phases: (1) pretrial events including, in the case of criminal trials, eyewitness identification, attempts to elicit confessions, and efforts to distinguish lies from sincere efforts to tell the truth; (2) issues related to the trial itself, including jury selection, jury deliberation, and jury size; and (3) issues of punishment and fairness. Social psychologists have made important contributions to each of these aspects of jurisprudence through their research, often by identifying flaws in existing practices and suggesting improvements. The criminal justice system has instituted quite a few changes in police practice and judicial procedures in response to these findings—a testimony to how the discoveries of social psychology can be used to improve a social institution.

BEFORE A CASE COMES TO TRIAL

You have probably seen many legal dramas on television that unfold in a fairly predictable way: a crime occurs, the police investigate, witnesses identify one or more suspects, those suspects are interrogated, and the criminal does or does not confess. In real life, however, the process is not always so simple or straightforward.

Eyewitness Testimony

Almost nothing that comes before the jury in a criminal trial is more convincing than a witness who, pointing to the defendant, says, "I am certain that that is the man." (Or "the woman," but since the great majority of defendants are men, suspects and defendants are referred to here as men.) Every year, 75,000 eyewitnesses testify against suspects in criminal cases. But those identifications are wrong about a third of the time (Liptak, 2011). In fact, eyewitness errors have been found to be involved in more than half of the cases of wrongful conviction (Kovera & Borgida, in press). In some cases where people have been exonerated by DNA evidence establishing that they could not have been the person who committed the crime, more than one person had wrongly identified the convicted person as the perpetrator.

Social psychologists have studied many factors that can influence the accuracy of eyewitness testimony. Before you read on, however, take the following test. Indicate which of the statements about the accuracy of eyewitness identification seem to you to be true and which false. Pencil in T or F next to each statement to keep yourself honest before you turn to the answers on page 605. You don't want to fall prey to the knew-it-all-along effect!

1. Accurate eyewitnesses are generally more confident than inaccurate ones.
2. Witnesses are generally as accurate about identifying perpetrators of a race different from their own as they are in identifying perpetrators of their own race.

3. When the circumstances of a crime are highly stressful and arousing, the memory of an eyewitness is likely to be more accurate than when the events are less arousing.
4. Witnesses with correct memory for many details about the crime context (for example, how many doors were in the room) generally are more accurate in their testimony about perpetrators than witnesses with less correct memory for details.
5. Asking witnesses to help construct a face composite of the perpetrator generally improves the accuracy of identification of the perpetrator.
6. Asking witnesses to describe a perpetrator before they attempt to identify him from photos or a lineup generally increases accuracy of recognition.
7. Witnesses who rapidly single out an individual from photos or a lineup are generally less accurate than those who take a longer time to consider who they believe to be the perpetrator.
8. Juries are generally capable of distinguishing correct testimony from incorrect testimony.

"Memory can change the shape of a room; it can change the color of a car. And memories can be distorted. They're just an interpretation, they're not a record."

—Leonard Shelby, the protagonist of Christopher Nolan's film *Memento*

The Persistence of Memory One of the greatest triumphs in the field of psychology is the discovery that memory is not a passive registry of the information a person has encountered. Instead, irrefutable evidence shows that memory is an active, constructive process in which inferences about "what must have been" guide memories of "what was." Much of that evidence was compiled by Elizabeth Loftus. In a series of ingenious studies beginning in the late 1970s and early 1980s, she established that memories are inferences, not stored photographs or infallible representations, and that they can be affected by all kinds of information that becomes available after an event has occurred.

In one striking demonstration, participants were shown a series of slides of an automobile accident (Loftus, Miller, & Burns, 1978; **Figure A4.1**). What was depicted on one of the slides varied slightly. A red Datsun was shown stopped at either a stop sign or a yield sign. Participants were asked questions about the accident they had "witnessed." One crucial question was different for two groups

FIGURE A4.1 Effect of Misleading Questions Participants saw either the picture on the left or the one on the right. Many of those asked about the "stop sign" later reported that they had seen the stop sign picture even if they had actually seen the yield sign; many of those asked about the "yield sign" reported that they had seen the yield sign picture even if they had seen the stop sign.

of participants. Participants were asked either "Did another car pass the red Datsun while it was stopped at the stop sign?" or "Did another car pass the red Datsun while it was stopped at the yield sign?" Later, the participants were shown the two pictures and asked which one they had actually seen before. Of participants who had been asked about the sign they had actually seen (stop sign or yield sign), 75 percent identified the correct picture. Of those who had been asked about the sign they hadn't actually seen, only 41 percent identified the correct picture. In other research, Loftus and her colleagues (Loftus, 2001) found that people could be led to think that a robber had a mustache when he didn't and that a red light was green. Of course, most of the time when investigators give misleading information to witnesses, they are not deliberately trying to mislead them. Instead, investigators often operate with patchy or mistaken information and may convey such misinformation to witnesses. In the courtroom, however, attorneys sometimes exercise poetic license in their phraseology in order to lead witnesses in a certain direction.

Loftus's research is relevant to the claims of psychotherapists that their patients have "recovered" memories that they had forgotten or repressed for decades. People have been convicted of heinous crimes based on reports of adults who are "helped to remember" by their therapists episodes of abuse or even murder. People are also sometimes convicted of child abuse based solely on the testimony of children who have been questioned by police. Undoubtedly, some of these recovered memories are valid. But consider a demonstration reported by Loftus and Pickrell (1995), who successfully "implanted" memories in 24 University of Washington students. Loftus and Pickrell persuaded the students' relatives to tell stories about several events that occurred around the time the student in question was 5 years old. They were also asked to generate a plausible story about that child (the student) having been lost—although the event had not occurred. Six of the participants eventually "recalled" the event, sometimes providing substantial detail over a series of interviews. Thus 25 percent of randomly selected university students were rather easily persuaded of the existence of a non-event—and could even provide details about it. Upon being told that one of the episodes never occurred, most of those students could not even correctly identify which one it was.

In similar studies with children, Stephen Ceci and Maggie Bruck (1995) asked preschoolers to remember as much as they could, in sessions once a week for ten weeks, about the time they went "to the hospital with a mousetrap on your finger." When they were interviewed later by another adult, 58 percent were able to give detailed stories about the (non)event. One boy was able to remember that "we went to the hospital, and my mommy, daddy, and Colin drove me there, to the hospital in our van, because it was far away. And the doctor put a bandage on this finger." Researchers including Loftus, Ceci, and their colleagues have thus established that memories, like perceptions and judgments, should be considered inferences rather than direct readouts of reality.

Factors Affecting Eyewitness Accuracy Given the generalization that memory is highly imperfect and highly susceptible to information provided after an event (or non-event) occurs, it is not surprising that eyewitness testimony is far from completely reliable. What factors influence whether such testimony is accurate and whether it is believed? Recall the statements about eyewitness testimony you read at the beginning of this chapter. If you guessed that each statement was false, you were 100 percent correct. Otherwise, your intuitions fell short to one degree or another.

Improving Eyewitness Identification Procedures   Fortunately, a massive amount of research by social psychologists on the accuracy of eyewitness testimony has had an equally massive effect on the law. Canada convened a panel of researchers, lawyers, and police to hammer out a set of procedures to reduce eyewitness errors. A decade later, a similar task force in the United States produced *Eyewitness Evidence: A Guide for Law Enforcement*, which established a set of best practices that are used by most U.S. law enforcement agencies.

It is greatly to the credit of psychologists that they have produced so much useful knowledge about the reliability of eyewitness testimony and the possible biases of jurors, and greatly to the credit of policy makers that this research has been allowed to transform police and judicial practice.

Getting the Truth from Suspects

Guilty persons sometimes confess their crimes, in which case the trial proceedings are relatively simple. Juries and judges simply attempt to arrive at a punishment that fits the admitted crime. But sometimes guilty people do not admit the crime. In days past, torture was frequently used to elicit confessions from the guilty. The assumption was that if people were truly innocent, they would never confess. But in fact people sometimes will confess—without torture—to crimes they did not commit.

False Confessions   In 1989, five teenage boys were arrested for a horrific assault and rape of a woman who had been jogging in Central Park in New York. The woman was beaten nearly to death and was initially not expected to survive, though in a recovery regarded as miraculous she suffered only minor permanent damage. All five of the boys confessed to the crime, and they were given long prison sentences. Thirteen years after the crime, Matias Reyes, who was not one of the five boys, admitted to having been the sole perpetrator of the crime. DNA evidence, which had not been presented at the boys' trial, corroborated Reyes's admission.

Why would the boys have confessed to a crime they had not committed? First, they had in fact been up to no good in the park. They had been assaulting people, and during the interrogation they were probably in a state of extreme stress because they knew they were in fact guilty of something. In addition, they were subjected to pretty much standard operating procedure for the police. First, the suspect is placed in a bare, soundproof room—a situation that has the effect of making the suspect feel alone and helpless. The most widely used manual for police interrogators (Inbau, Reid, Buckley, & Jayne, 2001) advises a ninefold process for questioning suspects in that situation. (1) Insist that the suspect committed the crime; (2) give the suspect helpful excuses for why he might have committed the crime; (3) cut the suspect off when he tries to maintain his innocence; (4) defeat the suspect's objections to the charges; (5) don't let the increasingly silent suspect succeed in ignoring the interrogator; (6) express sympathy for why the suspect might have committed the crime in an effort to get him to admit the crime; (7) offer the suspect an explanation for the crime that would make him

Certain, but Wrong

In 1984 I was a 22-year-old college student. One night someone broke into my apartment, put a knife to my throat and raped me.

During my ordeal I studied every single detail on the rapist's face. I looked at his hairline; I looked for scars, for tattoos, for anything that would help me identify him. When and if I survived the attack, I was going to make sure that he was put in prison and he was going to rot.

Looking at a series of photos at the Police Department, I identified my attacker. I knew this was the man. I was completely confident. I was sure.

I picked the same man in a lineup. Again, I was sure. I knew it. I had picked the right guy, and he was going to go to jail. If there was the possibility of a death sentence, I wanted him to die. I wanted to flip the switch.

Based on my testimony, Ronald Junior Cotton was sentenced to prison for life. It was the happiest day of my life because I could begin to put it all behind me.

In 1995, 11 years after I had first identified Ronald Cotton, I was asked to provide a blood sample so that DNA tests could be run on evidence from the rape.

Poole   Cotton

Bobby Poole and Ronald Cotton Note the close resemblance between Poole, the perpetrator, and Cotton, the falsely accused man.

I will never forget the day I learned about the DNA results. The detective and the prosecuting attorney told me, "Ronald Cotton didn't rape you. It was a man named Bobby Poole."

The man I had identified so emphatically was absolutely innocent.

Ronald Cotton was released from prison after serving 11 years. He and

I are the same age, so I knew what he had missed during those 11 years. My life had gone on. I had gotten married. I had graduated from college. I worked. I was a parent. Ronald Cotton hadn't gotten to do any of that.

(Excerpted from "I Was Certain, But I Was Wrong," by Jennifer Thompson. *New York Times*, June 18, 2000.)

---

feel justified in committing it; (8) if possible, get the suspect to spell out details of the crime; (9) convert those details into a written confession. If those tactics don't suffice, police may offer sympathy and promise leniency in light of the supposed extenuating circumstances. These procedures often succeed in getting suspects to confess.

The problem, as in the case of the Central Park jogger, is that these police tactics can be altogether too effective, sometimes eliciting false confessions. In fact, in cases where defendants are convicted and later proved innocent by DNA tests, as many as one-fifth had confessed to the crime (Garrett, 2008). The young and inexperienced may be particularly susceptible. The five teenagers in the Central Park jogger case were interrogated for up to 30 hours before they gave their confessions, which were videotaped. The defendants later testified that they had been

Yusef Salaam and Matias Reyes (A) Yusef Salaam, one of five individuals sentenced to prison for their alleged role in the Central Park jogger case. (B) Matias Reyes admitted to being the sole perpetrator of the assault, thereby exonerating the five individuals who were wrongly convicted years earlier.

threatened and that promises of various kinds had been made if they would confess. (These charges were denied by the police.) In their naiveté, the boys reported believing that they would be allowed to go home if they just admitted to what they had done.

Juries and Confessions Saul Kassin and Holly Sukel (1997) suspected that confessions made under dubious circumstances might still be taken at face value by jurors. To examine this hypothesis, they presented mock jurors with an account of a murder trial. In one condition, the suspect never admitted to the crime. In this condition, the jurors voted guilty 19 percent of the time. In a condition where it was reported that the suspect had confessed, the conviction rate rose to 62 percent. In a third condition, the suspect had confessed, but in a situation in which he was afraid and in pain while he was handcuffed behind his back. Participants generally recognized that the confession had been coerced, but 50 percent of them voted for conviction anyway. Although they recognized that coercion had probably occurred, they nevertheless chose to believe the defendant's confession. These participants insisted that the confession had not influenced their judgments. This finding is consistent with research showing that people can be quite poor at recognizing just what factors have influenced their judgments (Nisbett & Wilson, 1977).

Can jurors recognize whether a confession is real or fake when they are allowed to watch a videotape of the interrogation? Not necessarily. Kassin, Meissner, & Norwick (2005) videotaped prison inmates confessing either to a crime they had actually committed or to one they had not committed. College students and police investigators watched the videotapes and indicated whether the inmate had or had not actually commit-

"Budget cuts—I'm good cop and bad cop."

ted the crime. Neither the students nor the police were particularly accurate, but the police were for the most part quite confident in their judgments.

In response to research by Kassin and colleagues as well as others, some state and local governments now require that the entire interrogation of suspects be videotaped. But as Kassin's research shows, doing so provides no guarantee that confessions are genuine or that jurors can recognize which confessions are genuine and which are not.

IN THE COURTROOM

The Sixth Amendment to the U.S. Constitution stipulates that "In all criminal prosecutions, the accused shall enjoy the right to a speedy and public trial, by an impartial jury of the State and district wherein the crime shall have been committed." How does the government in the relevant state and district assemble an impartial jury? And how large should the jury be? We typically think of juries of 12, but would a smaller number suffice? Finally, what decision rule should the jury follow in rendering a verdict? A unanimous decision is typically required, but some jurisdictions allow less stringent agreement. How do these differences affect the nature of the jury's deliberation and the kind of verdicts that are announced? Social psychologists have conducted research on all of these questions in an effort to find out which procedures best serve the cause of justice.

Jury Selection

The first step in creating a jury takes place out of the public eye. Local governments—typically county or municipal courts—use a variety of public records such as phone books and voter registration rolls to compile a list of potential jurors. When a trial is to be held, the court randomly selects individuals from this list. These individuals then appear in court and are interviewed by the judge, the prosecution, and the defense in a jury-selection procedure known as **voir dire** (from old French, meaning "to speak the truth"). All three parties ask questions designed to find out whether a potential juror is reasonably impartial, although the prosecution and defense are usually interested in ensuring that a juror is not biased *against* their side. To do so, the prosecuting and defense attorneys consult their intuitions about human nature and how certain types of people are likely to react to different types of arguments and evidence. Many attorneys believe, for example, that engineers are stoic (and therefore unlikely to be moved by emotional appeals), that bearded men are unconventional (and therefore unlikely to be moved by threats to the status quo), or that someone of German descent is likely to be strict and conservative. Many attorneys also proceed under the assumption that particular types of jurors have special concerns that make them likely to be prejudiced for or against defendants in certain cases—that mothers are especially sympathetic to claims about crimes involving children, that the rich are especially sympathetic to alleged crimes against property, that blacks are especially sympathetic to charges of police misconduct, and so on.

Based on potential jurors' responses to questions during voir dire, the defense and prosecution can ask the judge to excuse someone "for cause"—that is, because the person in question would not be impartial. Each side is also allowed a number of *peremptory challenges*, or the right to exclude a potential juror without offering

voir dire The portion of a trial in U.S. courts in which potential jurors are questioned about potential biases and a jury is selected.

any justification. Although a great deal of time and energy goes into the jury-selection process, psychological research shows that neither lawyers' intuitions about certain kinds of people nor jurors' responses to questions during voir dire are reliable guides to the decisions jurors are likely to reach (Kerr, Kramer, Carroll, & Alfini, 1991; Olczak, Kaplan, & Penrod, 1991; Zeisel & Diamond, 1978).

Scientific Jury Selection Recognizing the limits of their intuitions and the informativeness of potential jurors' responses during voir dire, attorneys have turned increasingly to the practice of **scientific jury selection**, a statistical approach to selecting (or excluding) jurors likely to be predisposed to certain claims or appeals. Jury-selection specialists hired by defense and prosecuting attorneys conduct surveys and compile statistics on what sorts of demographic variables (income, gender, ethnicity, and so forth) are related to, say, an inclination to trust the government, to admire corporate executives, to care about the environment, or to distrust the police. Note that in scientific jury selection, the potential jurors themselves are not questioned. Rather, general associations between certain attitudes and demographic categories are established in the community at large. Research has established that the practice can be quite successful (Moran, Cutler, & DeLisa, 1994; Seltzer, 2006), enabling lawyers to know with reasonable accuracy, for example, whether a potential juror has relatively pro-business or anti-business attitudes (Hans, 2000).

Death-Qualified Juries As you are surely aware, the death penalty is a highly controversial component of the U.S. penal system. All but 14 states have the death penalty, although opponents question its effectiveness as a deterrent to crime, the consistency with which it is applied, and the very morality of its use. States with the death penalty do not have lower homicide rates than those without. And the homicide rate does not tend to go down when a state adopts the death penalty, nor does it go up when a state abolishes it (Costanzo, 1997; Haney & Logan, 1994). The overwhelming majority of those who are sentenced to death are poor and cannot afford the kind of defense that wealthy defendants use to maximize their chances of acquittal or, barring that, at least receiving a lesser sentence. In recent years, DNA evidence has exonerated a great many individuals who were convicted of capital crimes they did not commit.

In many jurisdictions, the jury decides not only the guilt or innocence of the individual charged with a capital crime but also whether to administer the death penalty. If you were on a jury in a capital case that found the accused guilty, would you be willing to sentence the defendant to death? If the answer is no, should you be excluded from the sentencing phase of the trial? Indeed, should individuals with profound reservations about the death penalty be allowed to serve on the jury in capital cases at all?

The courts have maintained that it is not a good idea to have such people serve as jurors in capital cases, and they have allowed the practice of *death qualification* whereby the judge may exclude potential jurors who say they would never vote for the death sentence. But does the systematic exclusion of people with such strong reservations about the death penalty alter the verdicts rendered by death-qualified juries? Psychological research indicates that it does indeed. People who are willing to recommend

scientific jury selection A statistical approach to jury selection whereby members of different demographic groups in the community are asked their attitudes toward various issues related to a trial, and defense and prosecuting attorneys try to influence the selection of jurors accordingly.

"Ninety percent of all executions are carried out in just four countries: China, Iran, Saudi Arabia, and the United States."

—Jimmy Carter,
Our Endangered Values

"Good news. Your execution was overturned on appeal."

the death penalty—and hence death-qualified juries as a whole—tend to be more concerned about crime and more trusting of police than people who are unwilling to recommend capital punishment. They also tend to be more skeptical of civil liberty procedures that protect the rights of the accused and to have relatively negative views of defense lawyers as a whole (Fitzgerald & Ellsworth, 1984; Haney, Hurtado, & Vega, 1994). In experiments in which participants are assembled into mock juries and asked to render a hypothetical verdict after looking at a videotape of a real trial, death-qualified juries are more likely to convict than juries in which individuals with reservations about the death penalty are not excluded (Cowan, Thompson, & Ellsworth, 1984). In another notable study, merely hearing the questions typically asked in the death-qualification part of the voir dire procedure tended to bias the jurors toward conviction, presumably because such questions contain an implication of guilt (Haney, 1984). Given these differences between death-qualified and unqualified juries, many have questioned whether death-qualified juries really are impartial (Bersoff, 1987). Nevertheless, the U.S. Supreme Court has upheld the permissibility of death-qualified juries, first in *Witherspoon v. Illinois* (1968) and then again in *Lockhart v. McCree* (1986).

Jury Deliberation

In cinematic depictions of courtroom drama, it's not uncommon for a steadfast and enlightened minority to overcome the impassioned but flawed view of the majority. Although scenes like these make good drama, they rarely happen in real life. In a landmark study of jury decision making, Kalven and Zeisel (1966) interviewed members of 225 juries. In 215 of these cases, there was a majority that leaned in one direction or the other at the time of the initial straw vote, and the jury ended up handing down a verdict consistent with that initial majority 209 times. Similar results have been obtained in studies using mock juries in which groups of paid participants are given information presented in a real trial and are asked to render a hypothetical verdict. In such studies, the initial majority almost always wins the day (Kerr, 1981; Stasser & Davis, 1981). Given what is known about conformity pressures and social influence, it is no surprise that the initial majority so often gets its way. Indeed, studies of the nature of jury deliberation have found that the majority succeeds in doing so through the very processes of informational and normative social influence discussed in Chapter 9 (Kaplan & Schersching, 1981; Stasser & Davis, 1981). Note, however, that even though a minority rarely succeeds in producing the verdict that they initially think is correct, they are able to get the majority to move in their direction a bit when it comes to sentencing (Pennington & Hastie, 1990).

Jury Size Most juries have 12 members, but that number is not specified in the U.S. Constitution, and some states allow smaller juries in noncapital cases. If you were convicted by a six-person jury, would you think you had received a fair trial? When Johnny Williams was in this very situation—found guilty of robbery by a six-person jury in Florida—he understandably thought that the outcome might have been different with a larger jury, so he appealed. The Supreme Court, in *Williams v. Florida* (1970), upheld the conviction and affirmed the permissibility of six-person juries, arguing that "there is no discernible difference between the

Jury Deliberation in Film In the film *12 Angry Men*, Henry Fonda plays the only juror who does not vote to convict the accused on the initial ballot. Slowly, employing one deft persuasion move after another, he wins over the other 11 members of the jury and engineers an acquittal.

"Justice delayed is justice denied."

—British Prime Minister
William Gladstone

results reached" by juries of different sizes. Later, in *Ballew v. Georgia* (1978), the Court reaffirmed its earlier opinion but ruled that juries of fewer than six people are unconstitutional.

In ruling that there is "no discernible difference" in the verdicts likely to be rendered by six- and 12-person juries, the Supreme Court based its claim in part on the conformity research discussed in Chapter 9. One concern that many legal scholars have is to guard against the "tyranny of the majority"— that is, a nearly unanimous majority intimidating a slim minority into swallowing their convictions and caving in to the others. The Court maintained that Asch's (1956) research established that the amount of conformity pressure felt by the minority is proportional to the size of the majority. By this logic, minorities in a 5-to-1 and a 10-to-2 split are equally likely to give in to the majority. But as you'll recall from Chapter 9, that is not what Asch found. Having an ally makes an enormous difference in allowing the minority to stick to their convictions, so the lone holdout in a 5-to-1 split has a much harder time standing firm than either of the two individuals has in a 10-to-2 split. And on purely numerical grounds, someone who dissents from the majority is more likely to have an ally—a bracing partner in dissent—in a group of 12 than in a group of six. The Supreme Court simply misread the relevant evidence. Indeed, research conducted after the two Supreme Court verdicts has found that six-person juries are more likely to arrive at a unanimous decision and to do so with less deliberation (Saks & Marti, 1997).

Jury Decision Rule Recall that the Sixth Amendment guarantees us all "a speedy and public trial." Having juries with fewer than 12 members is one way to try to accelerate the flow of cases through the courts. Another way to speed up the pace of trials is to allow less than unanimous verdicts. The Supreme Court has twice upheld the permissibility of less than unanimous verdicts in state but not federal criminal trials. In *Apodaca, Cooper, and Madden v. Oregon* (1972), the court upheld the convictions of three defendants found guilty using a 10-of-12 majority rule. In *Johnson v. Louisiana* (1972), the court upheld a conviction obtained under a 9-of-12 decision rule. The Court maintained that a "conscientious juror" is concerned with justice, not with simply arriving at a verdict, so having a less than unanimous decision rule should not truncate either the length or vigor of a jury's deliberation. Robust discussion, the Court argued, would continue well after a sufficiently large majority opinion has developed.

At the heart of the Court's ruling, then, was an empirical claim, one that social psychologists quickly set out to test. In one especially ambitious study, Hastie, Penrod, and Pennington (1983) recruited over 800 people and assembled them into 69 mock juries that watched a filmed reenactment of a real-world criminal trial and rendered verdicts using different decision rules (unanimous, 10-of-12, or 8-of-12). The results were clear-cut: although the verdicts rendered by juries operating under different decision rules were not significantly different, the juries that did not have to achieve unanimity spent significantly less time discussing the facts of the case and questions of law. The 8-of-12 juries, for example, typically deliberated for less than 5 minutes after reaching a majority of eight or more.

After the criterion was met, in other words, they all but ignored the holdouts, ended discussion, and announced their verdicts. Similar results were obtained from an analysis of videotaped civil trials with nonunanimous decision rules in Arizona: minority opinions were given little attention once a sufficient majority view was reached (Diamond, Rose, & Murphy, 2006). Note that these differences in how minority views are treated in juries with unanimous versus nonunanimous decision rules are important even if the two types of juries end up making the same decisions (as they often will if the case is relatively straightforward). The mock jurors in Hastie and colleagues' (1983) study later rated the quality of their deliberations, and those required to reach unanimity thought more highly of the thoroughness and seriousness of their discussions. Support for the legal system is enhanced when all participants come away convinced that justice has been served—a sentiment that is much more likely when a unanimous opinion must be reached.

Damage Awards Deciding the guilt or innocence of a defendant can sometimes be wrenchingly difficult, but at least there are only a few possible outcomes to consider—guilty versus not guilty, homicide versus manslaughter, and so on. In contrast, jurors in civil trials must often make decisions in which the response options are nearly boundless. For example, jurors must often decide how much a successful plaintiff should be paid in compensatory and punitive damages. How do jurors cope with such complexity, and how effective are they at awarding damages? Psychological research into these questions provides both encouraging and discouraging news (Kahneman, Schkade, & Sunstein, 1998; Sunstein, Kahneman, Schkade, & Ritov, 2002).

Compensatory damage can be straightforward: it represents the amount the plaintiff should receive to compensate for any loss or harm sustained. The compensatory damages that jurors can award are often tightly constrained by economic analyses of the harm done. Punitive damages are more subjective: they are designed to deter the defendant and others from acting in a similarly negligent manner or with similar intent in the future, and jurors often have much more discretion in what to award. What amount should a clothing manufacturer pay a child for burns she sustained because her pajamas were not sufficiently flame retardant? How much should a gas company pay if, in playing fast and loose with environmental laws, it contaminated local residents' drinking water?

Research indicates that jurors go about making such decisions by first consulting their sense of outrage at the defendant's behavior. As **Figure A4.2** shows, this sense of outrage tends to be affected by how recklessly the defendant behaved and how much malice seemed to be involved in the defendant's actions. Jurors then translate their sense of outrage into punitive intent, which is also influenced by the amount of harm experienced by the plaintiff and by the plaintiff's identity (harm to children or koalas is likely to inspire more punitive intent than similar harm to CEOs or hyenas). The difficulty lies in the next step: translating one's sense of punitive intent into an actual dollar figure. How much more should someone pay if you feel strongly that he should be punished than if you merely believe he should be punished?

The good news is that people tend to agree about how outraged they are about a defendant's actions and about their desire to punish. People tend to agree that injuries to children merit more punishment than injuries to healthy retirees, that willful negligence calls for harsher treatment than simple carelessness,

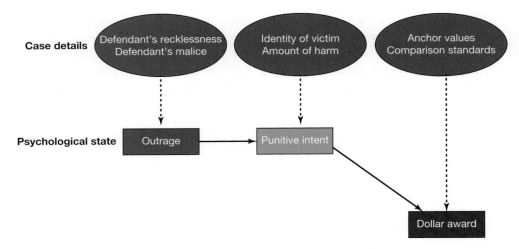

FIGURE A4.2 A Model of the Psychology of Punitive Damage Awards When making punitive damage awards, jurors first assess how outraged they are by the facts of the case and then, considering who the victim is and the amount of harm suffered, develop a sense of their intent to punish. The translation of punitive intent can be difficult and is often influenced by such extraneous considerations as an available anchor value or comparison standards that spring to mind. (Adapted from Kahneman, Schkade, & Sunstein, 1998.)

and that awards that might deter the killing of dolphins or whales should be stiffer than those that might inhibit the killing of carp or mollusks.

The bad news is that the last step, translating punitive intent into an actual dollar award, can be influenced by all sorts of extraneous variables and therefore can be arbitrary. For example, various standards of comparison that are naturally evoked by a given case might introduce a troublesome degree of arbitrariness to the awards handed out. Suppose you hear about a company that allowed a toxic chemical to pollute the water supply used by a small nursing home, leading to the early deaths of several residents. You would no doubt be outraged, but your outrage would likely be affected by comparing this incident to other cases of lethal pollution you've heard about—cases involving larger communities and a wider range of victims, including very young children. Such comparisons might lead you to think that this case, though outrageous, is not as problematic as some, and therefore the punitive damages should not be so high. In fact, research has shown that people can end up recommending higher damages for harm done to appealing species such as dolphins than for harm done to human beings (Kahneman et al., 1998; Sunstein et al., 2002). Converting our moral sentiments into dollars is a difficult translation, one that is prone to predictable biases.

In other cases, an accessible anchor value or a spontaneously invoked comparison might influence the compensation awarded. In a famous case that inspired calls for reform in civil trials, a jury awarded 79-year-old Stella Liebeck $2.7 million because she suffered third-degree burns after spilling a cup of McDonald's coffee on her lap. The jury accepted Liebeck's attorneys' argument that McDonald's coffee was too hot (and inadequately labeled as hot), and they appeared to be influenced by her counsel's suggestion that McDonald's should be penalized an amount equal to one to two days of its average revenue from the sale of coffee ($1.35 million per day). But what would the award have been if another reasonable figure had been cited instead, such as one to two days of McDonald's *net profit* on coffee sales or the average person's earnings during the period of Liebeck's recuperation? A different anchor value would almost certainly have yielded a different result. (The judge reduced the jury's award to $480,000; Liebeck appealed that ruling and reached a settlement with McDonald's for an undisclosed amount believed to be less than $600,000.)

PUNISHMENT: WHY WE PUNISH AND WHAT MAKES IT FAIR

Social psychologists have studied the nature of punishment—what societies do with those who break the rules—and the forms it has taken across time and cultures. Hunter-gatherer societies had no courts or juries or judges or written laws, but individuals who transgressed tribal law—through stealing, cheating, or sexual infidelity, for example—were often subject to violent acts of revenge (Boehm, 1999). The Middle Ages and Renaissance in Europe were times of spectacularly brutal punishment—beheadings, hangings, drawing and quartering, and whipping were regular practices, often in town squares for all community members to see. Even minor transgressions were subject to extreme punishment. In parts of Europe, if a baker sold bread that weighed less than advertised, he would receive the equivalent of today's water boarding. In fifteenth-century Scotland, individuals falsely posing as town fools were subject to having their ears nailed to a post or their fingers amputated.

Today, punishment largely has been subsumed by the criminal justice system, which determines the guilt or innocence of an individual alleged to have committed a crime as well as the punishment that person must undergo if convicted. Within the criminal justice system are people such as police officers, lawyers, judges, and jurors, who make judgments about guilt or innocence and about appropriate punishments. Punishment is an act of the human mind, and social psychologists have uncovered important underpinnings of why we punish and what makes punishment seem to be fair.

Motives and Kinds of Punishment: Just Desserts versus Deterrence

Punishment is referred to as retributive justice, requiring people to make amends for harm and social transgressions. Within the domain of retributive justice, social psychologists differentiate between two motives that govern preferences for different kinds of punishment (Carlsmith, Darley, & Robinson, 2002; Weiner, Graham, & Reyna, 1997). One motive for punishment is called the *just desserts* motive. In common parlance, this is eye-for-an-eye justice; the goal is to avenge a prior evil deed rather than prevent future ones. Such punishments are calibrated to the moral offensiveness of the crime. Empirical studies of U.S. college students find that their recommended punishments closely track their feelings of moral outrage; people prefer punishments that match the perceived severity of the harm caused by the alleged crime (Carlsmith & Darley, 2008).

Just Desserts Punishments (A) In earlier times, people who were guilty of various crimes were subjected to public ridicule by being kept in stocks in public venues. (B) Several hundred years ago in Europe, women who gossiped too much might be forced to wear a "shame mask" like this one. These punishments were guided by just desserts—the requirement that the punishment match the crime.

A second motive that can guide punitive judgments is *deterrence*. Deterrence has the goal of reducing the likelihood of future crimes committed by the criminal or by others. People guided by the motive of deterrence assume that punishments change the cost-benefit analyses of committing crimes; they make more salient the costs of committing a crime (such as prison time or fines), which should outweigh any potential benefits of committing a crime and thus deter people from criminal acts. Punishments guided by the deterrence motive can take many forms. The criminal can be rehabilitated through special programs or engagement in the community. The prisoner can be incarcerated, an obvious way to prevent the individual from committing future crimes. More specific punishments practiced today and in the past reflect the deterrence motive. Lawyers who violate the law or their code of ethics are disbarred from practicing again. Priests are defrocked for immoral acts. Sexual offenders have been castrated. In many countries in the past and present, thieves' hands have been cut off. The underlying logic is that these more specific punishments prevent the perpetrator from committing similar crimes in the future.

An Attributional Account of Punishment

The just desserts and deterrence motives are useful for thinking about why we punish. For example, these motives may be at play in interesting cultural variations in punishment. In Japan and Norway, for example, prisons are much more open, and prisoners are integrated more readily into the nearby community. This approach to punishment appears to be guided by a deterrence-based practice of rehabilitation. The United States, by contrast, has much more severe sentencing

Incarceration across Cultures (A) In the United States, prison sentences tend to be longer than in other industrialized countries, and the prisons themselves more aggressively segregate prisoners from the rest of the population. (B) In many other countries, such as Norway and Japan, prisoners are more readily integrated into local communities.

practices, which might be in part the product of the greater influence of the just desserts motive (although it could readily be argued that severe sentences serve to deter criminals as well). What construal processes might account for such cultural variations, and, more generally, for preferences for just desserts versus deterrence-oriented punishments?

Bernard Weiner and his colleagues have offered one answer to this question. Their theory draws on the idea that emotion-based intuitions drive different punitive judgments (Weiner et al., 1997). According to Weiner's account, two attributions lead individuals to feel anger about a criminal act: (1) the belief that the perpetrator is responsible for the crime and intended it to happen, and (2) the belief that the crime reflects a stable part of the perpetrator's character. Numerous studies find that once angered, people prefer just desserts forms of punishment—they want the perpetrator of the transgression to suffer in proportion to the harm caused (Lerner, Goldberg, & Tetlock, 1998).

A different set of attributions leads individuals to feel sympathy rather than anger for the perpetrator of the criminal act. Specifically, people tend to feel sympathy when they believe (1) that situational factors including the perpetrator's past history (for example, as a victim of abuse) in part led to the crime, and (2) that the crime does not reflect a stable part of the perpetrator's character. These two attributions reduce the inclination to see the perpetrator suffer in proportion to the harm caused (Rudolph, Roesch, Greitemeyer, & Weiner, 2004). Feeling sympathy also increases forgiveness and makes people prefer punishments that protect the criminal and society, such as forms of rehabilitation (Weiner et al., 1997).

Weiner and colleagues have tested this framework in studies of teachers' attitudes toward punishing students for breaking rules, and U.S. citizens' attitudes toward punishing the famous football player O. J. Simpson when he was on trial for murdering his wife. The findings are in keeping with their framework: attributions give rise to feelings of anger or sympathy, and these emotions lead to different punitive judgments. Similar principles may be at play in the legal strategies typically taken by the prosecution (focusing on the responsibility and poor character of the defendant) and the defense (focusing on the role of circumstance). Or consider recent debates about the relevance of defendants' life history in the courtroom (Toobin, 2011). Many perpetrators of violent acts have suffered profound physical abuse as children, and increasingly this evidence is being considered in trials, particularly in death penalty cases. This kind of information, if allowed at trial, is likely to generate more sympathy for the defendant and more lenient punitive judgments.

Bias in the Criminal Justice System

The United States incarcerates a higher percentage of its citizens than any industrialized country except Russia. More than 2 million individuals are in prison, nearly 1 percent of the adult population (Bureau of Justice Statistics, 2011). Social scientists have long grappled with a disturbing fact: black and Latino men are represented in higher numbers in U.S. prisons than they are represented in the general population. Might this overrepresentation be due at least in part to bias in the system, to people's stereotypes and prejudices about blacks and Latinos? One fact might suggest that it is. Young blacks and Latinos are more likely to serve time for drug-related charges—the most common crime that sends people to prison—even though the most rigorous recent surveys indicate that they are no more likely to use drugs than are whites of comparable age and class background (Youth Risk Behavior Survey, 2007).

Social psychologists Jennifer Eberhardt, Phoebe Ellsworth, and Jack Glaser have argued in different ways that stereotype-based decision making may in part account for potential biases in the criminal justice system (Eberhardt, Davies, Purdie-Vaughns, & Johnson, 2006; Ellsworth, 2009; Glaser, 2012). Their reasoning is that cultural stereotypes of blacks and Latinos hold that they are more dangerous, prone to violence, and likely to use drugs. These stereotypes then guide the many decisions people in the criminal justice system make, thus giving rise to race-related biases in who is convicted and punished for different crimes (Plant & Peruche, 2005). Stereotypes, for example, are likely to influence which people police officers pull over and whether they search for drugs or actually write up a ticket for an offense. For similar reasons, stereotypes may shape how jurors assign responsibility for crimes, the degree to which they feel anger or sympathy, and their likelihood of conviction and sentencing length.

Evidence in support of a stereotype-based account of bias in the criminal justice system is mounting (for a summary, see Glaser, in press). For example, the Supreme Court has granted police officers a great deal of latitude in which people they can pull over and search without probable cause. Recent Bureau of Justice statistics find that blacks and Latinos are three times more likely to be searched when pulled over, even though these searches are no more likely to yield incriminating evidence (Durose, Smith, & Langan, 2007; Plant & Peruche, 2005). Once on trial, blacks and Latinos may not receive equivalent treatment: mock jurors are more likely to convict a black than a white defendant in a hypothetical trial for the same crime (Sommers & Ellsworth, 2001). Outside the laboratory, a summary of sentences given to 77,000 offenders found that blacks were given longer sentences than whites for similar crimes (Mustard, 2001). Taken together, these findings suggest that racial stereotypes may in part explain racial biases in police behavior and conviction rates and sentencing within the criminal justice system.

PERCEPTIONS OF FAIRNESS OF THE CRIMINAL JUSTICE SYSTEM

Theoretically, laws and punishments should instill a sense of order in society. In practice, our criminal justice system and the influence of its laws and punishments depend critically on another kind of justice studied by social psychologists—**procedural justice**, which refers to assessments of whether the processes resulting in distribution of rewards and punishments are perceived to be fair. Procedural justice depends on how rewards and punishments are given out. Our concern about procedural justice is salient, for example, when we mull over whether employers use the same criteria to give out bonuses, when there are conflicts about which criteria to use for admitting students to colleges and universities, or when we are concerned about whether the likelihood of arrest and the length of prison sentences depends on the race or social class of the individual.

Three factors shape our sense of procedural justice, according to social psychologist Tom Tyler (1994). First, there is a concern for the *neutrality* of the authority figure. When figure-skating judges give substantially higher ratings to skaters from their own country, their neutrality is clearly in question, and the sense of procedural justice is jeopardized. With respect to punishment, a citizen's sense of procedural justice will depend critically on whether the legal system is seen as evenhanded. Second, there must be *trust* in the system. We must have confidence that authority figures—police officers, lawyers, judges—will be fair, that they will treat others according to consistent principles and standards. Finally, the individual must feel that he or she is treated with *respect*. Do authority figures meting out justice—police officers giving out traffic tickets or judges delivering sentences, for example—treat those they are punishing politely? Respect on the part of authority figures, Tyler reasons, gives people a sense that the legal system is fair.

Tyler and colleagues contend that these three facets of procedural justice have as much influence on our sense that outcomes—punishments and rewards in particular—are fair as does the actual content, good or bad, of the outcome itself (Tyler, 1994). In survey research, they have contacted people who have had recent experiences with authority figures. In one study, participants had recently received sentences for crimes they had committed (Tyler, 1987; Tyler & Caine, 1981). Participants indicated what punishment they had received—for example, how long they had been sentenced to prison. Participants also indicated the extent to which they believed that the authority figure had been neutral and trustworthy and had treated them with respect. The dependent measure of interest was the participant's feelings about the authority figure's fairness.

Two findings stand out. First, the magnitude of the punishment people received in their recent experience with the criminal justice system was not correlated with their sense of procedural justice. This is an important finding because it suggests that people separate how the punishment is delivered from the punishment itself. Second, and perhaps more striking, people's ratings of neutrality, trust, and respect were stronger determinants of their belief in the fairness of the criminal justice system than the actual punishment they received.

Our sense of justice thus revolves around more than personal gains or losses. We care profoundly about the neutrality of authority figures, the trustworthiness of the system, and the respect we receive from others. On the one hand, you might take heart from these results: a society can build a prevailing sense of

procedural justice People's assessments of whether the processes leading to legal outcomes are fair.

justice in groups and communities by ensuring that the distribution of reward and punishment is neutral, trustworthy, and respectful—and it can do so without changing the allocation of material resources. On the other hand, a more sinister implication of Tyler's findings is that authority figures might hand out all sorts of outcomes, from job layoffs to unwarranted prison sentences, without encountering protest, as long as they deliver them in a neutral, trustworthy, and respectful fashion.

Module Review

Summary

Before a Case Comes to Trial

- Eyewitnesses, even though trying their best to tell the truth, can be mistaken in their identification of perpetrators. Laypeople's guesses about what kinds of factors influence witness accuracy can be wide of the mark. Police investigators and jurors have less than perfect ability to assess witness accuracy. Fortunately, police and courts have instituted procedures that lessen the likelihood of conviction due to mistaken identification.

- Some confessions are false, even when coercion is not great. In response to this evidence, some jurisdictions require videotaping of all interrogations. Jurors are poor judges of whether confessions are false or not.

In the Courtroom

- Jury selection begins with a process called *voir dire*, in which the judge and the prosecuting and defense attorneys try to determine whether potential jurors are impartial. Using *scientific jury selection*, attorneys accept or reject juror candidates on the basis of demographic and statistical data. There is controversy over whether only jurors who would sentence a criminal to death should serve in capital cases. Studies have shown that *death-qualified juries* are more likely to convict than those in which some jurors have reservations about the death penalty.

- In cases where a minority of jurors dissent from their fellow jurors' verdict, the initial majority verdict usually is ultimately handed down. Juries smaller than 12 people are allowed in some jurisdictions, but social psychological studies on conformity suggest that larger juries are more likely to consider the opinions of a minority of jurors. When verdicts do not need to be unanimous among jurors, juries spend less time deliberating after the necessary majority is reached.

- *Compensatory damage awards* are intended to make up for any loss the plaintiff has suffered; *punitive damage awards* are intended to deter the defendant and others from acting similarly in the future. Compensatory damages are often straightforward, but punitive damages can be highly subjective and based on arbitrary comparisons and anchors.

Punishment: Why We Punish and What Makes It Fair

- Two motives that guide punishment are the *just desserts* motive, intended to avenge a crime, and *deterrence*, intended to prevent the crime from happening again.

- Differing attributions and emotions may lead to variations in preferred forms of punishment. Believing that a criminal has acted willfully and is responsible for his actions leads to feelings of anger and a preference for *just desserts* forms of punishment. Believing that situational factors led, in large part, to the criminal act leads to feelings of sympathy and a preference for more *deterrence-oriented* punishment.

- Social psychological studies have produced evidence for racial bias in the U.S. criminal justice system. Stereotypes about blacks and Latinos being more likely to commit crimes may lead to a greater likelihood that people in those groups will be investigated, convicted, and punished.

Perceptions of Fairness of the Criminal Justice System

- *Procedural justice* refers to people's assessments of whether the processes that result in the distribution of rewards and punishments are fair. If people feel that the system is neutral and trustworthy and that they have been treated with respect, they are more likely to believe that outcomes are fair, regardless of the magnitude of the punishment or reward.

Key Terms

procedural justice (p. 619)

scientific jury selection (p. 610)

voir dire (p. 609)

Further Reading and Films

Hastie, R., Penrod, S. D., & Pennington, N. (1983). *Inside the jury*. Cambridge, MA: Harvard University Press. An overview of jury selection, deliberation, and effectiveness based on a path-breaking program of research.

Lumet, S. (Director). (1957). *12 Angry Men* [Motion picture]. United States: Orion-Nova Productions. A classic film in which a sole dissenting juror (Henry Fonda) uses insightful persuasion techniques to change the minds of his fellow jurors and prevent an innocent man from being convicted.

Nolan, C. (Director). (2000). *Memento* [Motion picture]. United States: Newmarket Capital Group. A psychologically sophisticated film about a man with anterograde amnesia (the inability to create new memories) who seeks to avenge the death of his wife.

Schacter, D. L. (2001). *The seven sins of memory: How the mind forgets and remembers*. Boston: Houghton Mifflin. A well-written overview of what is known about memory and memory problems, including why people have false memories.

Credits

middle) From The Expression of the Emotions in Man and Animals by Charles Darwin; p. 201 (bottom) Pictorial Press Ltd/Alamy; p. 202 Photographs courtesy Professor Dacher Keltner.; p. 203 Adapted from Ekman, Sorenson, & Friesen (1969); p. 204 (left) © Radius Images/ Corbis; (right) Courtesy Dacher Keltner; p. 206 Haidt & Keltner, 1999; p. 208 Joe Giron/Corbis; p. 209 Alamy; p. 210 © Pierre Lahalle/ TempSport/Corbis; p. 211 (left) ImageState/Alamy; (right) AP/ Corbis.

CHAPTER 7

Photos: p. 232 © Tom Radenz/Demotix/Demotix/Corbis; p. 234 (top left) Bettmann/Corbis; (top right) AP/Wide World Photos; (bottom right) Alamy; p. 237 David M. Dennis/Photolibrary; p. 238 Natalie Fobes/Corbis; p. 240 Timothy A. Clary/AFP/Getty Images; p. 242 © Owen Franken/Corbis; p. 244 Alamy; p. 245 Rob Rogers, © 1994 The Pittsburgh Post-Gazette/Distributed by United Feature Syndicate, Inc.; p. 246 (top) Kevin R. Morris/Corbis; (bottom) 1982 Karen Zebuion, Courtesy New School Public Relations Department; p. 247 Photo courtesy of Terp Weekly EditionPhoto courtesy of Terp Weekly Edition; p. 253 DILBERT, © 1999 Scott Adams/ Distributed by United Feature Syndicate; p. 261 © David Young-Wolff; p. 266 Romilly Lockyer/Getty Images; p. 267 Bill Woodman/ The New Yorker Collection, from cartoonbank.com; p. 268 © Damian Dovarganes/AP/Corbis.

Drawn art: Fig. 7.8: Lee, S. W. S., & Schwarz, N. Figure from "Dirty hands and dirty mouths: Embodiment of the moral-purity metaphor is specific to the motor modality involved in moral transgression." *Psychological Science*, 21, 1423–1425. Copyright © 2010 Blackwell Publishers, Ltd. Reprinted with permission.

CHAPTER 8

Photos: p. 272 The Photo Works; p. 274 (left) Lee Snider/Photo Images/Corbis; (right) Viviane Moos/Corbis; p. 276 (top) AP/Wide World Photos; (bottom) The New Yorker Collection, 1928 Carl Rose, from cartoonbank.com; p. 277 Gary Crabbe/AgeFotostock; p. 278 (left) © Pavel Wolberg/epa/Corbis; (right) © Kayte M. Deioma/ PhotoEdit Inc.; p. 286 Robin Nelson/Photo Edit; p. 287 Hulton-Deutsch Collection/Corbis; p. 288 AP/Wide World Photos/Daily Sentinel; p. 290 © Howard Davies/Corbis; p. 291 (left) Swim Ink 2, LLC/Corbis; (right) Courtesy U.S. Army; p. 292 Corbis; p. 296 (left) Benjamin J. Myers/Corbis; (right) Gordon M. Grant/Alamy; (bottom) Courtesy of the National Youth Anti-Drug Media Campaign and Ogilvy & Mather; p. 299 The New Yorker Collection, 2003 Mick Stevens, from Cartoonbank.com.

CHAPTER 9

Photos: p. 308 Jeff Morgan social issues/Alamy; p. 310 (left) © Trinity Mirror/Mirrorpix/Alamy; (right) © Scott Legato /Retna Ltd./Corbis; p. 312 (left) Al Fenn/Contributor/ Time & Life Pictures/Getty Images; (right) Alamy; p. 312 (bottom) The New Yorker Collection, 2000 Mick Stevens, from cartoonbank.com; p. 314 Barbara Kinney/ William J. Clinton Presidential Library and Museum; p. 316 Courtesy of Swathmore College; p. 317 Adapted from Asch (1956); p. 319 Nick Doan/WireImage for Relevent PR/Getty Images; p. 322 Stephen Chernin/Getty Images; p. 323 (left) Alamy; (right) Mauricio Piffer/ AP Photo; p. 326 (left) Bettmann/Corbis;(right) Bettmann/Corbis; p. 328 Alexandra Milgram; p. 329 (left) From the film Obedience, © 1965 by Stanley Milgram and distributed by Penn State Media Sales; p. 330 From the film Obedience, © 1965 Stanley Milgram and distributed by Penn State Media Sales; p. 331 © Paul J Fearn/Alamy;

p. 335 Courtesy of Jerry Burger; p. 336 (left) From Obedience to Authority: An Experimental View by Stanley Milgram, Harper & Row, Publishers (right) © 1974 by Stanley Milgram; p. 339 Reed Kaestner/Corbis; p. 341 Alamy; p. 344 Stephen Lovekin/Getty Images for UNICEF; p. 345 Bettmann/Corbis; p. 348 Chuck Savage/Corbis; p. 349 Alamy; p. 350 Pars International.

CHAPTER 10

Photos: p. 354 Jeremy Horner/Panos Pictures; p. 356 Alamy; p. 358 (left) David Katzenstein/ Corbis; (center) Eleonora Ghioldi/Corbis; (right) Ralph Reinhold/Photolibrary; p. 359 Harlow 1959; p. 360 Gallo Images/Corbis; p. 362 The New Yorker Collection, 1991 Mischa Richter, from cartoonbank.com; p. 364 (top left) The New Yorker Collection, 1976 Ed Koren, from cartoonbank.com; (bottom row) Courtesy the Estate of Mary Ainsworth; p. 371 (left) Natalie Fobes/ Corbis; (right) Craig Lovell/Corbis; p. 372 AP Photo/Rick Bowmer; p. 374 Glowimages/Getty Images; p. 376 Rob & Sas/Corbis; p. 378 The New Yorker Collection, 1999 Barbara Smaller, from cartoonbank. com; p. 379 The New Yorker Collection 2005 Marisa Acocella Marchetto from cartoonbank.com; p. 380 Trevor Hoey/New Yorker Magazine; p. 382 (left) Photo: Erich Lessing/Art Resource; (left middle) Nimatallah/Art Resource, NY; (right middle) Sunset Boulevard/ Corbis; (right) Frank Trapper/Corbis; p. 384 (left) Archivo Icono-grafico, S.A./Corbis; (right) Evan Agostini/Getty Images; (bottom images) Professor Judith Hall Langlois, University of Texas at Austin; p. 385 Copyright 1994 Macmillan Publishers, Ltd. Photos courtesy of Professor David Perrett, University of St. Andrews, Scotland; p. 387 The New Yorker Collection, 1997 Frank Cotham, from cartoonbank. com; p. 391 Menstrual cycles alters face preference, I. S. Penton-Voak, D. I. Perrett, D. L. Castles, T. Kobayashi, D. M. Burt, L. K. Murray & R. Minamisawa, Nature 399, 741–742 (24 June 1999), Fig. 1; p. 392 (left) Wally Herbert/AgeFotostock; (center) R. Matina/AgeFotostock; (right) Tao Images/AgeFotostock; p. 399 Thinkstock/AgeFotostock; p. 401 (left and right) Redchopsticks Collect/AgeFotostock.

Drawn art: Fig. 10.11: Sternberg, R.J. From "A Triangular Theory of Love." *Psychological Review*, 93 (2), pp. 119–135. Copyright © 1986 American Psychological Association. Reprinted with permission.

CHAPTER 11

Photos: p. 406 Courtesy of We Are Part Of You.org; p. 408 Stapleton Collection/Corbis; p. 410 (top) Yellow Dog Productions/Getty Images; (bottom) © Janine Wiedel Photolibrary/Alamy; p. 417 (all) Archives of the History of American Psychology, University of Akron; The Carolyn and Muzafer Sherif Papers; p. 419 Scott Olson/Getty Images; p. 423 Alamy; p. 423 (left) Scott J. Ferrell/Congressional Quarterly/Getty Images; p. 424 © Dustin Bradford /Icon SMI/ Corbis; p. 427 Steve Grayson/WireImage.com; p. 430 The New Yorker Collection, 2000 David Sipress, from cartoonbank.com; p. 431 Photo by Jesse Grant/WireImage.com/ABC; p. 434 Curtis Means/NBC NewsWire/AP Photo; p. 436 Scott Olson/Getty Images; p. 440 Payne, Lambert, & Jacoby 2002; p. 441 © Mike Stewart/Sygma/Corbis; p. 445 Corbis; p. 448 Alamy.

CHAPTER 12

Photos: p. 452 Derek Love-Art Director/Copywriter; Kristopher Blake-Copywriter; Agency-Adhouse NYC; p. 454 (left) Alamy; (right) Alamy; p. 456 Andreas Rentz/Bongarts/Getty Images; p. 457 Hazel Markus; p. 459 Rubes cartoon by permission of Leigh Rubin and Creators Syndicate, Inc; p. 465 Charles Gupton/Corbis; p. 469 AP/Wide World Photos; p. 471 The New Yorker Collection 1994 Mike Twohy, from cartoonbank.com; p. 477 (all) George Tames/The New York Times/Redux; p. 481 (left and right) Alamy; p. 484 The New Yorker Collection, 1995 Leo Cullum, from cartoonbank.com. All Rights Reserved; p. 485 (left) Roger Ressmeyer/Corbis; (right) John Storey/San Francisco Chronicle; p. 486 Reuters/Corbis; p. 487 Peter Turnley/Corbis; p. 488 Archivo Iconografico, S.A./Corbis; p. 489 Doug Steley/Alamy; p. 492 Corbis.

Drawn art: Fig. 12.2: Zajonc, et al., figure from "Social enhancement and impairment of performance in the cockroach," *Journal of Personality and Social Psychology* 13.2, 83–92. Copyright © 1969, American Psychological Association. Reprinted with permission.

CHAPTER 13
Photos: p. 496 Tim Boyle/Getty Images; p. 498 (left) Bettmann/Corbis; (right) Scott Peterson/Getty Images; p. 500 Alamy; p. 503 (left) Sunset Boulevard/Sygma/Corbis; (right) AFP/Getty Images; p. 504 (left) IGN Entertainment, Inc.; (right) Reuters/Corbis; p. 511 Focus on Sport/Getty Images; p. 514 (left) Robert van der Hilst/Corbis; (right) Dr. Napoleon A. Chagnon; p. 516 © DK Limited/Corbis; p. 518 (left) Leonard de Selva/Corbis; (right) Bettmann/Corbis; p. 519 © Michael Gibson/Paramount Picture/Bureau L.A. Collection/Corbis; p. 520 Alamy.

Drawn art: Fig. 13.3: Wilkinson, F., & Pickett, K. Figure 10.2 from *Spirit Level: Why Greater Equality Makes Societies Stronger*, 2009, p. 135. Reprinted by permission of Bloomsbury Publishing House via The Copyright Clearance Center.

CHAPTER 14
Photos: p. 529 © Alistair Laming/Alamy; p. 530 (top left) Nick Brooks/Newsday/AP Photo; (top right) Jim Young/Reuters/Corbis; (bottom) Carlo Allegri/Getty Images; p. 531 (left) Alan Levenson/Time Life Pictures/Getty Images; (right) Courtesy Debra DiPaolo; p. 533 Blaine Harrington III/Corbis; p. 537 The New York Times Photo Archives/Redux; p. 541 Gideon Mendel/Corbis; p. 542 The New Yorker Collection, 2004 Michael Crawford, from cartoonbank.com; p. 544 (left) Ed Kashi/Corbis; (right) Vario images GmbH & Co. KG/Alamy; p. 551 Michael and Patricia Fogden/Corbis; p. 552 Illustrated London News/Bridgeman Art Library; p. 553 Melanie Stetson Freeman/The Christian Science Monitor/Getty Images; p. 555 David James/© 2000 Warner Bros. & Bel Air Pictures, LLC/Newsmakers; p. 557 (left) Loren McIntyre/Photolibrary; (right) Michael Patrick O'Neill/Alamy.

APPLICATION MODULE 1
Photos: p. 562 Courtesy of The Foundation for a Better Life; p. 563 The London Art Archive/Alamy; p. 566 (left) Spencer Grant/Photo Edit; (right) Craig Lovell/Eagle Visions Photography/Alamy; p. 569 Paula Lerner/Aurora Photos; p. 572 Dennis MacDonald/Alamy.

APPLICATION MODULE 2
Photos: p. 574 Pat Auckerman/AP; p. 575 Spencer Platt/Getty Images; p. 583 Courtesy Nicholas Epley; p. 584 Courtesy Sheena Iyengar. Iyengar, S. S., & Lepper, M. R. (2000). When choice is demotivating: Can one desire too much of a good thing? Journal of Personality and Social Psychology, 79, 995–1006.

APPLICATION MODULE 3
Photos: p. 589 © Carl & Ann Purcell/Corbis; p. 593 Vanni/Art Resource, NY; p. 598 Gregory Bull/AP.

APPLICATION MODULE 4
Photos: p. 602 Courtesy of Innocence Project, Inc./BENJAMIN N. CARDOZO SCHOOL OF LAW, YESHIVA UNIVERSITY; p. 604 Loftus, Miller, & Burns, 1978: Semantic integration of verbal information into a visual memory; p. 607 AP Photo/HO/Burlington Police Department; p. 608 (left) Clarence Davis/NY Daily News Archive via Getty Images; (right) William LaForce Jr./NY Daily News Archive via Getty Images; (bottom) David Sipress/The New Yorker Collection/www.cartoonbank.com; p. 610 Robert Mankoff/The New Yorker Collection/www.cartoonbank.com; p. 612 Alamy; p. 616 (left) © Corbis; p. 616 (right) © Cynthia Hart Designer/Corbis; p. 617 (left) © Andrew Lichtenstein/Sygma/Corbis; (right) © Alex Masi/Corbis.

Box A4.1: Thompson-Cannino, J. 317 word excerpt from "I was certain but I was wrong." Originally published in *The New York Times*, June 18, 2000. Reprinted in *Picking Cotton: Our Memoir of Injustice*, 2009. St. Martin's Press.

References

Aarts, H., & Dijksterhuis, A. (2003). The silence of the library: Environment, situational norm, and social behavior. *Journal of Personality and Social Psychology, 84,* 18–28.

Aarts, H., Gollwitzer, P. M., & Hassin, R. R. (2004). Goal contagion: Perceiving is for pursuing. *Journal of the Personality and Social Psychology, 87,* 23–37.

Abell, G. O. (1981). Astrology. In G. O. Abell & B. Singer (Eds.), *Science and the paranormal: Probing the existence of the supernatural.* New York: Charles Scribner's Sons.

Abrams, D., Viki, G. T., Masser, B., & Bohner, G. (2003). Perceptions of stranger and acquaintance rape: The role of benevolent and hostile sexism in victim blame and rape proclivity. *Journal of Personality and Social Psychology, 84,* 111–125.

Abu-Lughod, L. (1986). *Veiled sentiments.* Berkeley, CA: University of California Press.

Acevedo, B. P., & Aron, A. (2009). Does a long-term relationship kill romantic love? *Review of General Psychology, 13,* 59–65.

Adler, N. E., Boyce, T., Chesney, M. A., Cohen, S., Folkman, S., Kahn, R. L., et al. (1994). Socioeconomic status and health: The challenge of the gradient. *American Psychologist, 49,* 15–24.

Agnew, C. R., Van Lange, P. A. M., Rusbult, C. E., & Langston, C. A. (1998). Cognitive interdependence: Commitment and the mental representation of close relationships. *Journal of Personality and Social Psychology, 74,* 939–954.

Ainsworth, M. D. S. (1993). Attachment as related to mother-infant interaction. *Advances in Infancy Research, 8,* 1–50.

Ainsworth, M. D. S., Blehar, M., Waters, E., & Wall, S. (1978). *Patterns of attachment.* Hillsdale, NJ: Erlbaum.

Ajzen, I. (1977). Intuitive theories of events and the effects of base-rate information on prediction. *Journal of Personality and Social Psychology, 35,* 303–314.

Ajzen, I. (1987). Attitudes, traits, and actions: Dispositional prediction of behavior in personality and social psychology. In L. Berkowitz (Ed.), *Advances in experimental social psychology* (Vol. 20, pp. 1–63). San Diego, CA: Academic Press.

Akerlof, G. A., Yellen, J. L., & Katz, M. L. (1996). An analysis of out-of-wedlock childbearing in the United States. *Quarterly Journal of Economics, 111,* 277–317.

Aldag, R. J., & Fuller, S. R. (1993). Beyond fiasco: A reappraisal of the groupthink phenomenon and a new model of group decision processes. *Psychological Bulletin, 113,* 533–552.

Alicke, M. D., & Govorun, O. (2005). The better-than-average effect. In M. D. Alicke, D. A. Dunning, & J. I. Krueger (Eds.), *The self in social judgment* (pp. 85–106). New York: Psychology Press.

Allan, G. A. (1979). *A sociology of friendship and kinship.* London: Allen & Unwin.

Allee, W. C., & Masure, R. H. (1936). A comparison of maze behavior in paired and isolated shell-parakeets (*Melopsittacus undulatus Shaw*) in a two-alley problem box. *Journal of Comparative Psychology, 3,* 159–182.

Allen, M., Emmers-Sommer, T. M., Gebhardt, L., & Giery, M. (1995). Pornography and rape myth acceptance. *Journal of Communication, 45,* 5–26.

Allen, V. L. (1965). Situational factors in conformity. In L. Berkowitz (Ed.), *Advances in experimental social psychology* (Vol. 2, pp. 133–175). New York: Academic Press.

Allen, V. L., & Wilder, D. A. (1979). Group categorization and attribution of belief similarity. *Small Group Behavior, 10,* 73–80.

Allport, F. H. (1920). The influence of the group upon association and thought. *Journal of Experimental Psychology, 3,* 159–182.

Alluisi, E. A., & Adams, O. S. (1962). Predicting letter preferences: Aesthetics and filtering in man. *Perceptual and Motor Skills, 14,* 123–131.

Alter, A. L., & Oppenheimer, D. M. (2006). Predicting stock price fluctuations using processing fluency. *Proceedings of the National Academy of Sciences, 103,* 9369–9372.

Alter, A. L., Oppenheimer, D. M., Epley, N., & Eyre, R. N. (2007). Overcoming intuition: Metacognitive difficulty activates analytic reasoning. *Journal of Experimental Psychology: General, 136,* 569–576.

Alterovitz, S. S., & Mendelsohn, G. A. (2009). Partner preferences across the life span: Online dating by older adults. *Psychology and Aging, 24*(2), 513–517.

Al-Zahrani, S. S. A., & Kaplowitz, S. A. (1993). Attributional biases in individualistic and collectivistic cultures: A comparison of Americans with Saudis. *Social Psychology Quarterly, 56,* 223–233.

Amato, P. R., & Keith, B. (1991). Parental divorce and well-being of children. *Psychological Bulletin, 110,* 26–46.

Ambady, N., Hallahan, M., & Rosenthal, R. (1995). On judging and being judged in zero-acquaintance situations. *Journal of Personality and Social Psychology, 69,* 518–529.

Ambady, N., & Rosenthal, R. (1993). Haifa minute: Predicting teacher evaluations from thin slices of nonverbal behavior and physical attractiveness. *Journal of Personality and Social Psychology, 64,* 431–441.

Amodio, D. M. (2008). The social neuroscience of intergroup relations. *European Review of Social Psychology, 19,* 1–54.

Amodio, D. M., & Devine, P. G. (2006). Stereotyping and evaluation in implicit race bias: Evidence for independent constructs and unique effects on behavior. *Journal of Personality and Social Psychology, 91,* 652–661.

Amodio, D. M., Harmon-Jones, E., Devine, P. G., Curtin, J. J., Hartley, S. L., & Covert, A. E. (2004). Neural signals for the detection of unintentional race bias. *Psychological Science, 15,* 88–93.

Amodio, D. M., & Lieberman, M. D. (2009). Pictures in our heads: Contributions of fMRI to the study of prejudice and stereotyping. In T. Nelson (Ed.), *Handbook of prejudice, stereotyping, and discrimination* (pp. 347–366). New York: Erlbaum Press.

Andersen, S. M., & Chen, S. (2002). The relational self: An interpersonal social-cognitive theory. *Psychological Review, 109,* 619–645.

Andersen, S. M., Glassman, N. S., Chen, S., & Cole, S. W. (1995). Transference in social perception: The role of chronic accessibility in significant-other representations. *Journal of Personality and Social Psychology, 69,* 41–57.

Andersen, S. M., & Ross, L. (1984). Self-knowledge and social influence I: The impact of cognitive/affective and behavioral data. *Journal of Personality and Social Psychology, 46,* 280–293.

Anderson, C., John, O. P., Keltner, D., & Kring, A. (2001). Social status in naturalistic face-to-face groups: Effects of personality and physical attractiveness in men and women. *Journal of Personality and Social Psychology, 81,* 1108–1129.

Anderson, C., Keltner, D., & John, O. P. (2003). Emotional convergence between people over time. *Journal of Personality and Social Psychology, 84,* 1054–1068.

Anderson, C., & Kilduff, G. J. (2009). Why do dominant personalities attain influence in face-to-face groups? The competence-signaling effects of trait dominance. *Journal of Personality and Social Psychology, 96,* 491–503.

Anderson, C. A. (1987). Temperature and aggression: Effects on quarterly, yearly, and city rates of violent and nonviolent crime. *Journal of Personality and Social Psychology, 52,* 1161–1173.

Anderson, C. A. (1989). Temperature and aggression: Ubiquitous effects of heat on occurrences of human violence. *Psychological Bulletin, 106,* 74–96.

Anderson, C. A. (1991). How people think about causes: Examination of the typical phenomenal organization of attributions for success and failure. *Social Cognition, 9,* 295–329.

Anderson, C. A., Berkowitz, L., Donnerstein, E., Huesmann, L. R., Johnson, J., Linz, D., et al. (2003). The influence of media violence on youth. *Psychological Science in the Public Interest, 4,* 81–110.

Anderson, C., & Brown, C. E. (2010). The functions and dysfunctions of hierarchies. *Review of Organizational Behavior, 30,* 55–89.

Anderson, C. A., & Bushman, B. J. (2001). Effects of violent video games on aggressive behavior, aggressive cognition, aggressive affect, physiological arousal, and prosocial behavior: A meta-analytic review of the scientific literature. *Psychological Science, 12,* 353–359.

Anderson, C. A., & Deuser, W. E. (1993). The primacy of control in causal thinking and attributional style: An attributional functionalism perspective. In G. Weary, F. Gleicher, & K. L. Marsh (Eds.), *Control motivation and social cognition* (pp. 94–121). New York: Springer-Verlag.

Anderson, C. A., & Dill, K. E. (2000). Video games and aggressive thoughts, feelings, and behavior in the laboratory and in life. *Journal of Personality and Social Psychology, 78,* 772–790.

Anderson, C. A., Krull, D. S., & Weiner, B. (1996). Explanations: Processes and consequences. In E. T. Higgins & A. W. Kruglanski (Eds.), *Social psychology: Handbook of basic principles* (pp. 271–296). New York: Guilford Press.

Anderson, J. L., Crawford, C. B., Nadeau, J., & Lindberg, T. (1992). Was the duchess of Windsor right? A cross-cultural review of the socioecology of ideals of female body shape. *Ethology and Sociobiology, 13,* 197–227.

Anderson, R., & Nida, S. A. (1978). Effect of physical attractiveness on opposite- and same-sex evaluations. *Journal of Personality, 46,* 401–413.

Anderson, R. C., & Pichert, J. W. (1978). Recall of previously unrecallable information following a shift in perspective. *Journal of Verbal Learning and Verbal Behavior, 17,* 1–12.

Ansolabehere, S., & Iyengar, S. (1995). *Going negative: How political ads shrink and polarize the electorate.* New York: Free Press.

Antill, J. K. (1983). Sex role complementarity versus similarity in married couples. *Journal of Personality and Social Psychology, 45,* 145–155.

Arden, R., Gottfredson, L. S., Miller, G., & Pierce, A. (2008). Intelligence and semen quality are positively correlated [Electronic version]. *Intelligence.* Retrieved from 10.1016/j.intell.2008.11.001

Arendt, H. (1963). *Eichmann in Jerusalem: A report on the banality of evil.* New York: Viking Press.

Argyle, M. (1999). Causes and correlates of happiness. In D. Kahneman, E. Diener, & N. Schwarz (Eds.), *Well-being: The foundations of hedonic psychology* (pp. 353–373). New York: Russell Sage.

Arkes, H., & Blumer, C. (1985). The psychology of sunk cost. *Organizational Behavior and Human Decision Processes, 35,* 124–140.

Arkin, R. M., & Baumgardner, A. H. (1985). Basic issues in attribution theory and research. In J. H. Harvey & G. Weary (Eds.), *Self-handicapping* (pp. 169–202). New York: Academic Press.

Arkin, R. M., & Maruyama, G. M. (1979). Attribution, affect, and college exam performance. *Journal of Educational Psychology, 71,* 85–93.

Arndt, J., Schimel, J., & Goldenberg, J. L. (2003). Death can be good for your health: Fitness intentions as a proximal and distal defense against mortality salience. *Journal of Applied Social Psychology, 33,* 1726–1746.

Aron, A., & Aron, E. N. (1997). Self-expansion motivation and including the other in self. In S. Duck (Ed.), *Handbook of personal relationships: Theory, research, and interventions* (2nd ed., pp. 251–270). Chichester, England: Wiley.

Aron, A., Aron, E. N., & Allen, J. (1989). *The motivation for unrequited love: A self-expansion perspective.* Paper presented at the International Conference on Personal Relationships, Iowa City, IA.

Aron, A., Aron, E. N., Tudor, M., & Nelson, G. (1991). Close relationships as including other in self. *Journal of Personality and Social Psychology, 60,* 241–253.

Aron, A., & Fraley, B. (1999). Relationship closeness as including other in the self: Cognitive underpinnings and measures. *Social Cognition, 17,* 140–160.

Aron, A., Norman, C. C., Aron, E. N., McKenna, C., & Heyman, R. E. (2000). Couples' shared participation in novel and arousing activities and experienced relationship quality. *Journal of Personality and Social Psychology, 78,* 273–284.

Aronson, E. (1969). The theory of cognitive dissonance: A current perspective. In L. Berkowitz (Ed.), *Advances in experimental social psychology* (Vol. 4, pp. 1–34). New York: Academic Press.

Aronson, E., & Carlsmith, J. M. (1963). Effect of severity of threat in the devaluation of forbidden behavior. *Journal of Abnormal and Social Psychology, 66,* 584–588.

Aronson, E., Ellsworth, P. C., Carlsmith, J. M., & Gonzalez, M. H. (1990). *Methods of research in social psychology* (2nd ed.). New York: McGraw-Hill.

Aronson, E., Fried, C., & Stone, J. (1991). Overcoming denial and increasing the intention to use condoms through the induction of hypocrisy. *American Journal of Public Health, 81*, 1636–1638.

Aronson, E., & Mills, J. (1959). The effect of severity of initiation on liking for a group. *Journal of Abnormal and Social Psychology, 59*, 177–181.

Aronson, E., Stephan, C., Sikes, J., Blaney, N., & Snapp, M. (1978). *The jigsaw classroom.* Beverly Hills, CA: Sage.

Aronson, E., & Thibodeau, R. (1992). The jigsaw classroom: A cooperative strategy for reducing prejudice. In J. Lynch, C. Modgil, & S. Modgil (Eds.), *Cultural diversity in the schools* (pp. 110–118). London: Falmer Press.

Aronson, J., Fried, C. B., & Good, C. (2002). Reducing stereotype threat and boosting academic achievement of African-American students: The role of conceptions of intelligence. *Journal of Experimental Social Psychology, 38*, 113–125.

Aronson, J. M., Lustina, M. J., Good, C., Keough, K., Steele, C. M., & Brown, J. (1999). When white men can't do math: Necessary and sufficient factors in stereotype threat. *Journal of Experimental Social Psychology, 35*, 29–46.

Asch, S. E. (1940). Studies in the principles of judgments and attitudes: II. Determination of judgments by group and by ego standards. *Journal of Social Psychology, 12*, 584–588.

Asch, S. E. (1946). Forming impressions on personality. *Journal of Abnormal and Social Psychology, 41*, 258–290.

Asch, S. (1951). Effects of group pressure upon the modification and distortion of judgments. In G. Guetzkow (Ed.), *Groups, leadership, and men* (pp. 177–190). Pittsburgh, PA: Carnegie Press.

Asch, S. (1952). *Social psychology.* Englewood Cliffs, NJ: Prentice-Hall.

Asch, S. (1956). Studies of independence and conformity: A minority of one against a unanimous majority. *Psychological Monographs, 70* (Whole No. 416).

Asch, S. E., & Zukier, H. (1984). Thinking about persons. *Journal of Personality and Social Psychology, 46*, 1230–1240.

Asendorpf, J. B., Penke, L., & Back, M. D. (2011). From dating to mating and relating: Predictors of initial and long-term outcomes of speed-dating in a community sample. *European Journal of Personality, 25*(1), 16–30.

Ashburn-Nardo, L., Voils, C. I., & Monteith, M. J. (2001). Implicit associations as the seeds of intergroup bias: How easily do they take root? *Journal of Personality and Social Psychology, 81*, 789–799.

Aspinwall, L. G., & Taylor, S. E. (1993). Effects of social comparison direction, threat and self-esteem on affect, evaluation, and expected success. *Journal of Personality and Social Psychology, 64*, 708–722.

Axelrod, R. (1984). *The evolution of cooperation.* New York: Basic Books.

Ayduk, O., Downey, G., Testa, A., Yen, Y., & Shoda, Y. (1999). Does rejection elicit hostility in rejection sensitive women? *Social Cognition, 17*, 245–271.

Ayduk, O., & Kross, E. (2008). Enhancing the pace of recovery: Self-distanced analysis of negative experiences reduces blood pressure reactivity. *Psychological Science, 19*, 229–231.

Bachorowski, J. A., & Owren, M. J. (2001). Not all laughs are alike: Voiced but not unvoiced laughter readily elicits positive affect. *Psychological Science, 12*, 252–257.

Bain, L. L., Wilson, T., & Chaikind, E. (1989). Participant perceptions of exercise programs for overweight women. *Research Quarterly for Exercise and Sport, 60*, 134–143.

Baldwin, M. W., Keelan, J. P. R., Fehr, B., Enns, V., & Koh-Rangarajoo, E. (1996). Social-cognitive conceptualizations of attachment working models: Availability and accessibility effects. *Journal of Personality and Social Psychology, 71*, 94–109.

Bamshad, M. J., & Olson, S. E. (2003, December). Does race exist? *Scientific American*, 78–85.

Banaji, M., Hardin, C. C., & Rothman, A. J. (1993). Implicit stereotyping in person judgement. *Journal of Personality and Social Psychology, 65*, 272–281.

Banaji, M. R., & Steele, C. M. (1989). Alcohol and self-evaluation: Is a social cognitive approach beneficial? *Social Cognition, 7*, 139–153.

Bandura, A. (1973). *Social learning theory.* Englewood Cliffs, NJ: Prentice Hall.

Bandura, A. (2004). Social cognitive theory for personal and social change by enabling media. In M. J. Singhal, E. M. Cody, E. M. Rogers, & M. Sabido (Eds.), *Entertainment education and social change: History, research and practice* (pp. 75–96). Mahwah, NJ: Erlbaum.

Banks, T., & Dabbs, J. M., Jr. (1996). Salivary testosterone and cortisol in delinquents and violent urban culture. *Journal of Social Psychology, 136*, 49–56.

Bargh, J. A. (1996). Automaticity in social psychology. In E. T. Higgins & A. W. Kruglanski (Eds.), *Social psychology: Handbook of basic principles* (Vol. 1, pp. 1–40). New York: Guilford Press.

Bargh, J. A., Chaiken, S., Raymond, P., & Hymes, C. (1996). The automatic evaluation effect: Unconditional automatic activation with a pronunciation task. *Journal of Experimental Social Psychology, 31*, 104–128.

Bargh, J. A., Chen, M., & Burrows, L. (1996). Automaticity of social behavior: Direct effects of trait construct and stereotype activation on action. *Journal of Personality and Social Psychology, 71*, 230–244.

Bargh, J. A., Gollwitzer, P. M., Lee-Chai, A., Barndollar, K., & Trotschel, R. (2001). The automated will: Nonconscious activation and pursuit of behavioral goals. *Journal of Personality and Social Psychology, 81*, 1014–1027.

Bargh, J. A., & Pietromonaco, P. (1982). Automatic information processing and social perception: The influence of trait information presented outside of conscious awareness on impression formation. *Journal of Personality and Social Psychology, 43*, 437–449.

Bargh, J. A., Raymond, P., Pryor, J. B., & Strack, F. (1995). Attractiveness of the underling: An automatic power-sex association and its consequences for sexual harassment and aggression. *Journal of Personality and Social Psychology, 68*(5), 768–781.

Bar-Hillel, M. (1980). The base-rate fallacy in probability judgments. *Acta Psychologica, 44*, 211–233.

Bar-Hillel, M., & Fischhoff, B. (1981). When do base-rates affect predictions? *Journal of Personality and Social Psychology, 41*, 671–680.

Barker, R. G., & Wright, H. F. (1954). *Midwest and its children: The psychological ecology of an American town.* New York: Row, Peterson and Company.

Baron, R. S. (1986). Distraction-conflict theory: Progress and problems. In L. Berkowitz (Ed.), *Advances in experimental social psychology* (Vol. 19, pp. 1–40). New York: Academic Press.

Baron, R. S., Moore, D., & Sanders, G. S. (1978). Distraction as a source of drive in social facilitation research. *Journal of Personality and Social Psychology, 36*, 816–824.

Baron, R. S., Vandello, J. A., & Brunsman, B. (1996). The forgotten variable in conformity research: Impact of task importance on social influence. *Journal of Personality and Social Psychology, 71*, 915–927.

Barrett, L. F. (2006). Are emotions natural kinds? *Perspectives on Psychological Science, 1*, 28–58.

Barrett, L. F., Mesquita, B., Ochsner, K. N., & Gross, J. J. (2007). The experience of emotion. *Annual Review of Psychology, 58*, 373–403.

Barsalou, L. W. (2008). Grounded cognition. *Annual Review of Psychology, 59*, 617–645.

Bar-Tal, D. (1990). Causes and consequences of delegitimization: Models of conflict and ethnocentrism. *Journal of Social Issues, 46*, 65–81.

Bar-Tal, D., & Saxe, L. (1976). Perceptions of similarly and dissimilarly attractive couples and individuals. *Journal of Personality and Social Psychology, 33*, 772–781.

Bartholomew, K., & Horowitz, L. M. (1991). Attachment styles among young adults: A test for a four-category model. *Journal of Personality and Social Psychology, 61*, 226–244.

Bartholow, B. D., & Anderson, C. A. (2002). Effects of violent videogames on aggressive behavior: Potential sex differences. *Journal of Experimental Social Psychology, 38*, 283–290.

Bartholow, B. D., Anderson, C. A., Carnagey, N. L., & Benjamin, A. J. (2005). Interactive effects of life experience and situational cues on aggression: The weapons priming effect in hunters and non-hunters. *Journal of Experimental Social Psychology, 41*, 48–60.

Bartlett, F. A. (1932). *Remembering: A study in experimental psychology.* Cambridge, England: Cambridge University Press.

Bartsch, R. A., Judd, C. M., Louw, D. A., Park, B., & Ryan, C. S. (1997). Cross-national outgroup homogeneity: United States and South African stereotypes. *South African Journal of Psychology, 27*(3), 166–170.

Bassili, J. N. (1996). Meta-judgmental versus operative indexes of psychological attributes: The case of measures of attitude strength. *Journal of Personality and Social Psychology, 71*, 637–653.

Batson, C. D., Engel, C. L., & Fridell, S. R. (1999). Value judgments: Testing the somatic-marker hypothesis using false physiological feedback. *Personality and Social Psychology Bulletin, 25*, 1021–1032.

Batson, C. D., O'Quin, K., Fultz, J., Vanderplas, M., & Isen, A. (1983). Self-reported distress and empathy and egoistic versus altruistic motivation for helping. *Journal of Personality and Social Psychology, 45*, 706–718.

Batson, C. D., & Shaw, L. L. (1991). Evidence for altruism: Toward a pluralism of prosocial motives. *Psychological Inquiry, 2*, 107–122.

Baumeister, R. F. (1982). A self-presentational view of social interaction. *Psychological Bulletin, 91*, 3–26.

Baumeister, R. F. (1987). How the self became a problem: A psychological review of historical research. *Journal of Personality and Social Psychology, 52*, 163–176.

Baumeister, R. F., Bratslavsky, E., Finkenauer, C., & Vohs, K. D. (2001). Bad is stronger than good. *Review of General Psychology, 5*, 323–370.

Baumeister, R. F., Bratslavsky, E., Muraven, M., & Tice, D. M. (1998). Ego depletion: Is the active self a limited resource? *Journal of Personality and Social Psychology, 74*, 1252–1265.

Baumeister, R. F., Campbell, J. D., Krueger, J. I., & Vohs, K. D. (2003). Does high self-esteem cause better performance, interpersonal success, happiness, or healthier lifestyles? *Psychological Science in the Public Interest, 4*, 1–44.

Baumeister, R. F., & Leary, M. R. (1995). The need to belong: Desire for interpersonal attachments as a fundamental human motivation. *Psychological Bulletin, 117*, 497–529.

Baumeister, R. F., Smart, L., & Boden, J. M. (1996). Relation of threatened egotism to violence and aggression: The dark side to high self-esteem. *Psychological Review, 103*, 5–33.

Baumeister, R. F., Stillwell, A. M., & Heatherton, T. F. (1994). Guilt: An interpersonal approach. *Psychological Bulletin, 115*, 243–267.

Baumeister, R. F., Vohs, K. D., & Tice, D. M. (2007). The strength model of self-control. *Current Directions in Psychological Science, 16*, 396–403.

Baxter, L. A. (1984). Forms and functions of intimate play in personal relationships. *Human Communication Research, 18*, 336–363.

Beaman, A. L., Klentz, B., Diener, E., & Svanum, S. (1979). Self-awareness and transgression in children: Two field studies. *Journal of Personality and Social Psychology, 37*, 1835–1946.

Beck, S. P., Ward-Hull, C. I., & McLear, P. M. (1976). Variables related to women's somatic preferences of the male and female body. *Journal of Personality and Social Psychology, 34*, 1200–1210.

Becker, E. (1973). *The denial of death.* New York: Simon & Schuster.

Becker, M. H., & Josephs, J. G. (1988). Aids and behavioral change to reduce risk: A review. *American Journal of Public Health, 78*, 394–410.

Beckman, L. (1970). Effects of students' performance on teachers' and observers' attributions of causality. *Journal of Educational Psychology, 61*, 76–82.

Bedard, K., & Dhuey, E. (2006). The persistence of early childhood maturity: International evidence of long-run age effects. *Quarterly Journal of Economics, 121*, 1437–1472.

Beer, J., Heerey, E. A., Keltner, D., Scabini, D., & Knight, R. (2003). The regulatory function of self-conscious emotion: Insights from patients with orbitofrontal damage. *Journal of Personality and Social Psychology, 85*, 594–604.

Bell, B. E., & Loftus, E. F. (1989). Trivial persuasion in the courtroom: The power of (a few) minor details. *Journal of Personality and Social Psychology, 56*, 669–679.

Bell, S. T., Kuriloff, P. J., & Lottes, I. (1994). Understanding attributions of blame in stranger-rape and date-rape situations: An examination of gender, race, identification, and students' social perceptions of rape victims. *Journal of Applied Social Psychology, 24*, 1719–1734.

Belsky, G., & Gilovich, T. (1999). *Why smart people make big money mistakes, and how to correct them.* New York: Simon & Schuster.

Bem, D. J. (1967). Self-perception: An alternative interpretation of cognitive dissonance phenomena. *Psychological Review, 74*, 183–200.

Bem, D. J. (1972). Self-perception theory. In L. Berkowitz (Ed.), *Advances in experimental social psychology* (Vol. 6, pp. 1–62). New York: Academic Press.

Bem, S. L. (1993). *The lenses of gender: Transforming the debate on sexual inequality.* New Haven, CT: Yale University Press.

Benet-Martinez, V., Leu, J., Lee, F., & Morris, M. W. (2002). Negotiating biculturalism: Cultural frame switching in biculturals with oppositional versus compatible cultural identities. *Journal of Cross-Cultural Psychology, 33*, 492–516.

Ben-Zeev, T., Fein, S., & Inzlicht, M. (2005). Arousal and stereotype threat. *Journal of Experimental Social Psychology, 41*, 174–181.

Berg, J. H., & McQuinn, R. D. (1986). Attraction and exchange in continuing and noncontinuing dating relationships. *Journal of Personality and Social Psychology, 50*, 942–952.

Berglas, S., & Jones, E. E. (1978). Drug choice as a self-handicapping strategy in response to non-contingent success. *Journal of Personality and Social Psychology, 36*, 405–417.

Berk, M. S., & Andersen, S. M. (2000). The impact of past relationships on interpersonal behavior: Behavioral confirmation in the social-cognitive process of transference. *Journal of Personality and Social Psychology, 79*, 546–562.

Berkman, L. F. (1995). The role of social relations in health promotion. *Psychosomatic Medicine*, 57, 245–254.

Berkman, L. F., & Syme, S. L. (1979). Social networks, host resistance, and mortality: A nine-year follow-up study of Alameda County residents. *American Journal of Epidemiology*, 100, 186–204.

Berkowitz, L. (1965). Some aspects of observed aggression. *Journal of Personality and Social Psychology*, 2, 359–369.

Berkowitz, L. (1989). The frustration-aggression hypothesis: An examination and reformulation. *Psychological Bulletin*, 106, 59–73.

Berkowitz, L. (1993). *Aggression*. New York: McGraw-Hill.

Berkowitz, L., & LePage, A. (1967). Weapons as aggression-eliciting stimuli. *Journal of Personality and Social Psychology*, 7, 202–207.

Berkowitz, L., & Troccoli, B. T. (1990). Feelings, direction of attention, and expressed evaluation of others. *Cognition and Emotion*, 4, 305–325.

Berman, M., Jonides, J., & Kaplan, S. (2008). The cognitive benefits of interacting with nature. *Psychological Science*, 19, 1207–1212.

Bernieri, F. J., Zuckerman, M., Koestner, R., & Rosenthal, R. (1994). Measuring person perception accuracy: Another look at self-other agreement. *Personality and Social Psychology Bulletin*, 20, 367–378.

Bernstein, I. H., Lin, T., & McClellan, P. (1982). Cross- vs. within-racial judgments of attractiveness. *Perception and Psychophysics*, 32, 495–503.

Berry, D. S. (1991). Accuracy in social perception: Contributions of facial and vocal information. *Journal of Personality and Social Psychology*, 61, 298–307.

Berry, D. S., & Brownlow, S. (1989). Were the physiognomists right? Personality correlates of facial babyishness. *Personality and Social Psychology Bulletin*, 15, 266–279.

Berry, D. S., & McArthur, L. Z. (1986). Perceiving character in faces: The impact of age-related craniofacial changes in social perception. *Psychological Bulletin*, 100, 3–18.

Berry, D. S., & Zebrowitz-McArthur, L. (1986). Perceiving character in faces: The impact of age-related craniofacial changes in social perception. *Psychological Bulletin*, 100, 3–18.

Berscheid, E., Dion, K., Walster, E., & Walster, G. W. (1971). Physical attractiveness and dating choice: A test of the matching hypothesis. *Journal of Experimental Social Psychology*, 7, 173–189.

Berscheid, E., & Reis, H. T. (1998). Attraction and close relationships. In D. T. Gilbert, S. T. Fiske, & G. Lindzey (Eds.), *The handbook of social psychology* (4th ed., Vol. 2, pp. 193–281). New York: McGraw-Hill.

Bersoff, D. N. (1987). Social science data and the Supreme Court: Lockhart as a case in point. *American Psychologist*, 42, 52–58.

Bessenoff, G. R., & Sherman, J. W. (2000). Automatic and controlled components of prejudice toward fat people: Evaluation versus stereotype activation. *Social Cognition*, 18, 329–353.

Bettencourt, B. A., Brewer, M. B., Croak, M. R., & Miller, N. (1992). Cooperation and the reduction of intergroup bias: The role of reward structure and social orientation. *Journal of Experimental Psychology*, 28, 301–319.

Biernat, M., Manis, M., & Kobrynowicz, D. (1997). Simultaneous assimilation and contrast effects in judgments of self and others. *Journal of Personality and Social Psychology*, 73, 254–269.

Bird, K. (2002). Advertise or die: Advertising and market share dynamics revisited. *Applied Economic Letters*, 9, 763–767.

Blackwell, L., Trzesniewski, K., & Dweck, C. S. (2007). Implicit theories of intelligence predict achievement across an adolescent transition: A longitudinal study and an intervention. *Child Development*, 78, 246–263.

Blair, I. V., Judd, C. M., & Chapleau, K. M. (2004). The influence of Afrocentric facial features in criminal sentencing. *Psychological Science*, 15, 674–679.

Blair, I. V., Judd, C. M., & Fallman, J. L. (2004). The automaticity of race and Afrocentric facial features in social judgments. *Journal of Personality and Social Psychology*, 87, 763–778.

Blair, I. V., Judd, C., Sadler, M. S., & Jenkins, C. (2002). The role of Afrocentric features in person perception: Judging by features and categories. *Journal of Personality and Social Psychology*, 83, 5–25.

Blair, J., Mitchell, D., & Blair, K. (2005). *The psychopath: Emotion and the brain*. Malden, MA: Blackwell Publishing.

Blair, R. J. R., Jones, R. L., Clark, R., and Smith, M. (1997). The psychopathic individual: A lack of responsiveness to distress cues? *Psychophysiology*, 34(2), 192–198.

Blanton, H., Buunk, B. P., Gibbons, F. X., & Kuyper, H. (1999). When better-than-others compare upward: Choice of comparison and comparative evaluation as independent predictors of academic performance. *Journal of Personality & Social Psychology*, 76, 420–430.

Blanton, H., & Jaccard, J. (2008). Unconscious racism: A concept in pursuit of a measure. *Annual Review of Sociology*, 34, 277–297.

Blanton, H., Jaccard, J., Klick, J., Mellers, B., Mitchell, G., & Tetlock, P. E. (2009). Strong claims and weak evidence: Reassessing the predictive validity of the IAT. *Journal of Applied Psychology*, 94, 567–582.

Blanton, H., Pelham, B. W., De Hart, T., & Kuyper, H. (1999). When better-than-others compare upward: Choice of comparison and comparative evaluation as independent predictors of academic performance. *Journal of Personality and Social Psychology*, 76, 420–430.

Blascovich, J., Mendes, W. B., Hunter, S. B., & Salomon, K. (1999). Social "facilitation" as challenge and threat. *Journal of Personality and Social Psychology*, 77, 68–77.

Blass, T. (1999). The Milgram paradigm after 35 years: Some things we now know about obedience to authority. *Journal of Applied Social Psychology*, 29, 955–978.

Blass, T. (2000). *Obedience to authority: Current perspectives on the Milgram paradigm*. Mahwah, NJ: Erlbaum.

Blass, T. (2004). *The man who shocked the world: The life and legacy of Stanley Milgram*. New York: Basic Books.

Bless, H., Clore, G. L., Schwarz, N., Golisano, V., Rabe, C., & Wölk, M. (1996). Mood and the use of scripts: Does a happy mood really lead to mindlessness? *Journal of Personality and Social Psychology*, 71(4), 665–679.

Block, J., & Robins, R. W. (1993). A longitudinal study of consistency and change in self-esteem from early adolescence to early adulthood. *Child Development*, 64, 909–923.

Bloom, B. L., White, S. W., & Asher, S. J. (1979). Marital disruption as a stressful life event. In G. Levinger & O. C. Moles (Eds.), *Divorce and separation: Context, causes, and consequences* (pp. 184–200). New York: Basic Books.

Bochner, S. (1994). Cross-cultural differences in the self-concept. *Journal of Cross-Cultural Psychology*, 25, 273–283.

Bodenhausen, G. V. (1988). Stereotypic biases in social decision making and memory: Testing process models of stereotype use. *Journal of Personality and Social Psychology*, 55, 726–737.

Bodenhausen, G. V. (1990). Stereotypes as judgmental heuristics: Evidence of circadian variations in discrimination. *Psychological Science*, 1, 319–322.

Bodenhausen, G. V., Macrae, C. N., & Sherman, J. W. (1999). On the dialectics of discrimination: Dual processes in social stereotyping.

In S. Chaiken & Y. Trope (Eds.), *Dual process theories in social psychology* (pp. 271–290). New York: Guilford Press.

Bodenhausen, G., Sheppard, L., & Kramer, G. (1994). Negative affect and social judgment: The different impact of anger and sadness. *European Journal of Social Psychology, 24,* 45–62.

Boehm, C. (1999). *Hierarchy in the forest: The evolution of egalitarian behavior.* Cambridge, MA: Harvard University Press.

Boice, R., Quanty, C. B., & Williams, R. C. (1974). Competition and possible dominance in turtles, toads, and frogs. *Journal of Comparative and Physiological Psychology, 86,* 1116–1131.

Bond, M. H., & Cheung, T. (1983). College students' spontaneous self-concept. *Journal of Cross-Cultural Psychology, 14,* 154–171.

Bond, R., & Smith, P. B. (1996). Culture and conformity: A meta-analysis of studies using Asch's line judgment task. *Psychological Bulletin, 119,* 111–137.

Borg, J. S., Hyunes, C., Van Horn, J., Grafton, S., & Sinnott-Armstrong, W. (2006). Consequences, action, and intention as factors in moral judgments: An fMRI investigation. *Journal of Cognitive Neuroscience, 18,* 803–817.

Borg, J. S., Lieberman, D., & Kiehl, K. A. (2008). Infection, incest, and iniquity: Investigating the neural correlates of disgust and morality. *Journal of Cognitive Neuroscience, 20,* 1529–1546.

Borgida, E., Conner, C., & Manteufel, L. (1992). Understanding living kidney donations: A behavioral decision-making perspective. In S. Spacapan & S. Oskamp (Eds.), *Helping and being helped.* Newbury Park, CA: Sage.

Bornstein, R. F. (1989). Exposure and affect: Overview and meta-analysis of research, 1968–1987. *Psychological Bulletin, 106,* 265–289.

Boster, F. J., & Mongeau, P. (1984). Fear-arousing persuasive messages. In R. N. Bostrom (Ed.), *Communication yearbook* (Vol. 8, pp. 330–375). Beverly Hills, CA: Sage.

Boucher, J. D., & Brandt, M. E. (1981). Judgment of emotion: American and Malay antecedents. *Journal of Cross-Cultural Psychology, 12,* 272–283.

Bowlby, J. (1982). *Attachment and loss* (2nd ed., Vol. 1). New York: Basic Books.

Boyd, R., & Richerson, P. J. (1985). Frequency-dependent bias and the evolution of cooperation. In R. Boyd & P. J. Richardson (Eds.), *Culture and the evolutionary process* (pp. 204–240). Chicago: University of Chicago Press.

Boyden, T., Carroll, J. S., & Maier, R. A. (1984). Similarity and attraction in homosexual males: The effects of age and masculinity-femininity. *Sex Roles, 10,* 939–948.

Bradbury, T. N., & Fincham, F. D. (1990). Attributions in marriage: Review and critique. *Psychological Bulletin, 107,* 3–33.

Bradbury, T. N., & Karney, B. R. (1993). Longitudinal study of marital interaction and dysfunction. *Clinical Psychology Review, 13,* 15–27.

Bradfield, A., & Wells, G. L. (2005). Not the same old hindsight bias: Outcome information distorts a broad range of retrospective judgments. *Memory and Cognition, 33,* 120–130.

Bransford, J. D., & Johnson, M. K. (1973). Considerations of some problems of comprehension. In W. G. Chase (Ed.), *Visual information processing* (pp. 383–438). New York: Academic Press.

Brauer, M., Chambres, P., Niedenthal, P. M., & Chatard-Pannetier, A. (2004). The relationship between expertise and evaluative extremity: The moderating role of experts' task characteristics. *Journal of Personality and Social Psychology, 86,* 5–18.

Breckler, S. J. (1984). Empirical validation of affect, behavior, and cognition as distinct components of attitude. *Journal of Personality and Social Psychology, 47,* 1191–1205.

Brehm, J. W. (1956). Post-decision changes in desirability of alternatives. *Journal of Abnormal and Social Psychology, 52,* 384–389.

Brendl, C. M., Higgins, E. T., & Lemm, K. M. (1995). Sensitivity to varying gains and losses: The role of self-discrepancies and event framing. *Journal of Personality and Social Psychology, 69,* 1028–1051.

Brendl, C. M., Markman, A. B., & Messner, C. (2001). How do indirect measures of evaluation work? Evaluating the inference of prejudice in the implicit association test. *Journal of Personality and Social Psychology, 81,* 760–773.

Brennan, K. A., Clark, C. L., & Shaver, P. R. (1998). Self-report measurement of adult attachment: An integrative overview. In J. A. Simpson & W. S. Rholes (Eds.), *Attachment theory and close relationships* (pp. 46–76). New York: Guilford Press.

Brennan, K. A., & Shaver, P. R. (1993). Attachment styles and parental divorce. *Journal of Divorce and Remarriage, 21,* 161–175.

Brewer, M. B. (1979). In-group bias in the minimal intergroup situation: A cognitive-motivational analysis. *Psychological Bulletin, 86,* 307–324.

Brewer, M. B. (1988). A dual process model of impression formation. In T. K. Srull & R. S. Wyer (Eds.), *Advances in social cognition.* Hillsdale, NJ: Erlbaum.

Brewer, M. B., & Brown, R. J. (1998). Intergroup relations. In D. T. Gilbert, S. T. Fiske, & G. Lindzey (Eds.), *The handbook of social psychology* (4th ed., Vol. 2, pp. 554–594). New York: McGraw-Hill.

Brewer, M. B., & Gardner, W. (1996). Who is the "we"? Levels of collective identity and self-representations. *Journal of Personality and Social Psychology, 71,* 83–93.

Brewer, M. B., & Kramer, R. M. (1985). The psychology of intergroup attitudes and behavior. *Annual Review of Psychology, 36,* 219–243.

Brewer, M. B., & Miller, N. (1988). Contact and cooperation: When do they work? In P. Katz & D. Taylor (Eds.), *Eliminating racism: Profiles in controversy* (pp. 315–326). New York: Plenum Press.

Brewer, M. B., & Nakamura, G. V. (1984). The nature and functions of schemas. In R. S. Wyer & T. K. Srull (Eds.), *The handbook of social cognition* (Vol. 1). Hillsdale, NJ: Erlbaum.

Briggs, J. L. (1960). *Never in anger: Portrait of an Eskimo family.* Cambridge, MA: Harvard University Press.

Brigham, J. C. (1993). College students' racial attitudes. *Journal of Applied Social Psychology, 23,* 1933–1967.

Brigham, J., Bennett, L., Meissner, C., & Mitchell, T. (2007). The influence of race on eyewitness memory. In R. C. L. Lindsay, D. F. Ross, D. J. Read, & M. P. Toglia (Eds.), *The handbook of eyewitness psychology.* Mahwah, NJ: Erlbaum.

Brislin, R. W., & Lewis, S. A. (1968). Dating and physical attractiveness: Replication. *Psychological Reports, 22,* 976.

Brockner, J. (1979). The effects of self-esteem, success-failure, and self-consciousness on task performance. *Journal of Personality and Social Psychology, 37,* 1732–1741.

Brockner, J., Guzzi, B., Kane, J., Levine, E., & Shaplen, K. (1984). Organizational fundraising: Further evidence on the effects of legitimizing small donations. *Journal of Consumer Research, 11,* 611–614.

Brown, D. E. (1991). *Human universals.* New York: McGraw-Hill.

Brown, J. D. (1998). *The self.* New York: McGraw-Hill.

Brown, J. D., & Dutton, K. A. (1995). The thrill of victory, the complexity of defeat: Self-esteem and people's emotional reactions to success and failure. *Journal of Personality and Social Psychology, 68,* 712–722.

Brown, P., & Levinson, S. C. (1987). *Politeness: Some universals in language usage.* Cambridge, England: Cambridge University Press.

Brown, R. (1986). *Social psychology* (2nd ed.). New York: Free Press.

Brown, S. L., Nesse, R. M., Vinokur, A. D., & Smith, D. M. (2003). Providing social support may be more beneficial than receiving it: Results from a prospective study of mortality. *Psychological Science, 14*(4), 320–327.

Browning, C. R. (1992). *Ordinary men: Reserve police battalion 101 and the final solution in Poland.* New York: Aaron Asher.

Brownstein, A., Read, S. J., & Simon, D. (2004). Bias at the race-track: Effects of individual expertise and task importance on predecision reevaluation of alternatives. *Personality and Social Psychology Bulletin, 57,* 904–915.

Brownstein, A. L. (2003). Biased predecision processing. *Psychological Bulletin, 129,* 545–568.

Brumberg, J. J. (1997). *The body project: An intimate history of American girls.* New York: Random House.

Buehler, R., Griffin, D., & Ross, M. (1994). Exploring the "planning fallacy": Why people underestimate their task completion times. *Journal of Personality and Social Psychology, 67,* 366–381.

Bureau of Justice Statistics. (2011). Prisoner Statistics. *Correctional Population in the United States, 2011.* Retrieved from http://www.ojp.usdoj.gov/bjs/

Burger, J. M. (1981). Motivational biases in the attribution of responsibility for an accident: A meta-analysis of the defensive-attribution hypothesis. *Psychological Bulletin, 90,* 496–512.

Burger, J. M. (1986). Increasing compliance by improving the deal: The that's-not-all technique. *Journal of Personality and Social Psychology, 51,* 277–283.

Burger, J. M. (1999). The foot-in-the-door compliance procedure: A multiple process analysis and review. *Personality and Social Psychology Review, 3,* 303–325.

Burger, J. M. (2009). Replicating Milgram: Would people still obey today? *American Psychologist, 64,* 1–11.

Burger, J. M., Girgis, Z. M., & Manning, C. C. (2011). In their own words: Explaining obedience to authority through an examination of participants' comments. *Social Psychological and Personality Science, 2,* 460–466.

Burger, J. M., & Guadagno, R. E. (2003). Self-concept clarity and the foot-in-the-door procedure. *Basic and Applied Social Psychology, 25,* 79–86.

Burger, J. M., Reed, M., DeCesare, K., Rauner, S., & Rozolis, J. (1999). The effects of initial request size on compliance: More about the that's-not-all technique. *Basic and Applied Social Psychology, 21,* 243–249.

Burgess, E. W., & Wallin, P. (1953). *Engagement and marriage.* Philadelphia: Lippincott.

Burkhart, K. (1973). *Women in prison.* Garden City, NY: Doubleday.

Burnstein, E. (2005). Kin altruism: The morality of biological systems. In D. M. Buss (Ed.), *The handbook of evolutionary psychology* (pp. 528–551). New York: Wiley.

Burnstein, E., Crandall, C., & Kitayama, S. (1994). Some neo-Darwinian decision rules for altruism: Weighing cues for inclusive fitness as a function of the biological importance of the decision. *Journal of Personality and Social Psychology, 67,* 773–789.

Burnstein, E., & Vinokur, A. (1973). Testing two classes of theories about group-induced shifts in individual choice. *Journal of Experimental Social Psychology, 9,* 123–137.

Burnstein, E., Vinokur, A., & Trope, Y. (1973). Interpersonal comparison versus persuasive argumentation: A more direct test of alternative explanations for group-induced shifts in individual choice. *Journal of Experimental Social Psychology, 9,* 236–245.

Buss, D. M. (1984). Toward a psychology of person-environment (PE) correlation: The role of spouse selection. *Journal of Personality and Social Psychology, 47,* 361–377.

Buss, D. M. (1989). Sex differences in human mate preference: Evolutionary hypothesis tested in 37 cultures. *Behavioral and Brain Sciences, 12,* 1–49.

Buss, D. M. (1994). *The evolution of desire: Strategies of human mating.* New York: Basic Books.

Byrne, D. (1961). Interpersonal attraction and attitude similarity. *Journal of Abnormal and Social Psychology, 62,* 713–715.

Byrne, D., Clore, G. L., & Smeaton, G. (1986). The attraction hypothesis: Do similar attitudes predict anything? *Journal of Personality and Social Psychology, 51,* 1167–1170.

Byrne, D., Griffitt, W., & Stefaniak, D. (1967). Attraction and similarity of personality characteristics. *Journal of Personality and Social Psychology, 5,* 82–90.

Byrne, D., & Nelson, D. (1965). Attraction as a linear function of proportion of positive reinforcements. *Journal of Abnormal and Social Psychology, 1,* 659–663.

Cacioppo, J. T., & Berntson, G. G. (1994). Relationship between attitudes and evaluative space: A critical review with emphasis on the separability of positive and negative substrates. *Psychological Bulletin, 115,* 401–423.

Cacioppo, J. T., & Gardner, W. L. (1999). Emotion. *Annual Review of Psychology, 50,* 191–214.

Cacioppo, J. T., Petty, R. E., Feinstein, J., & Jarvis, B. (1996). Individual differences in cognitive motivation: The life and times of people varying in need for cognition. *Psychological Bulletin, 119,* 197–253.

Cacioppo, J. T., Petty, R. E., & Morris, K. J. (1983). Effects of need for cognition on message evaluation, recall, and persuasion. *Journal of Personality and Social Psychology, 45,* 805–818.

Cacioppo, J. T., Petty, R. E., & Sidera, J. (1982). The effects of salient self-schema on the evaluation of proattitudinal editorials: Top-down versus bottom-up message processing. *Journal of Experimental Social Psychology, 18,* 324–338.

Cacioppo, J. T., Priester, J. R., & Berntson, G. G. (1993). Rudimentary determinants of attitude. II. Arm flexion and extension have differential effects on attitudes. *Journal of Personality and Social Psychology, 65,* 5–17.

Cadinu, M., Maass, A., Rosabianca, A., & Kiesner, J. (2005). Why do women underperform under stereotype threat? Evidence for the role of negative thinking. *Psychological Science, 16,* 572–578.

Campbell, D. T. (1975). On the conflicts between biological and social evolution and between psychology and moral tradition. *American Psychologist, 30,* 1103–1126.

Campbell, J. D., & Fairey, P. J. (1989). Informational and normative routes to conformity: The effect of faction size as a function of norm extremity and attention to the stimulus. *Journal of Personality and Social Psychology, 57,* 457–468.

Carli, L. L. (1999). Cognitive reconstruction, hindsight, and reactions to victims and perpetrators. *Personality and Social Psychology Bulletin, 25,* 966–979.

Carlsmith, J. M., & Gross, A. E. (1969). Some effects of guilt on compliance. *Journal of Personality and Social Psychology, 11,* 232–239.

Carlsmith, K. M., & Darley, J. M. (2008). Psychological aspects of retributive justice. *Advances in Experimental Social Psychology, 40,* 193–236.

Carlsmith, K. M., Darley, J. M., & Robinson, P. H. (2002). Why do we punish? Deterrence and just deserts as motives for punishment. *Journal of Personality and Social Psychology, 83*, 284–299.

Carlson, J. A., & Davis, C. M. (1971). Cultural values and the risky shift: A cross-cultural test in Uganda and the United States. *Journal of Personality and Social Psychology, 20*, 236–245.

Carlson, M., Charlin, V., & Miller, N. (1988). Positive mood and helping behavior: A test of six hypotheses. *Journal of Personality and Social Psychology, 55*, 211–229.

Carlston, D. E., & Skowronski, J. J. (1994). Savings in the relearning of trait information as evidence for spontaneous inference generation. *Journal of Personality and Social Psychology, 66*, 840–880.

Carnevale, P. J., & Isen, A. M. (1986). The influence of positive affect and visual access on the discovery of integrative solutions in bilateral negotiation. *Organizational Behavior and Human Decision Processes, 37*, 1–13.

Carney, D., Cuddy, A. J. C., & Yap, A. J. (2010). Power posing: Brief nonverbal displays affect neuroendocrine levels and risk tolerance. *Psychological Science, 21*, 1363–1368.

Carter, C. S. (1998). Neuroendocrine perspectives on social attachment and love. *Psychoneuroendocrinology, 23*(8), 779–818.

Carter, J., & Irons, M. (1991). Are economists different, and if so, why? *Journal of Economic Perspectives, 5*, 171–177.

Carter, T., Ferguson, M. J., & Hassin, R. R. (2011). A single exposure to the American flag shifts support toward Republicanism up to 8 months later. *Psychological Science, 22*(8), 341–359.

Cartwright, D., & Zander, A. (1968). *Group dynamics: Research and theory.* New York: Harper & Row.

Carver, C. S. (1974). Facilitation of physical aggression through objective self-awareness. *Journal of Experimental Social Psychology, 10*, 365–370.

Carver, C. S., DeGregorio, E., & Gillis, R. (1980). Ego-defensive attribution among two categories of observers. *Personality and Social Psychology Bulletin, 6*, 4–50.

Carver, C. S., & Scheier, M. F. (1981). The self-attention-induced feedback loop and social facilitation. *Journal of Experimental Social Psychology, 17*, 545–568.

Carver, C. S., & Scheier, M. F. (1982). Control theory: A useful conceptual framework for personality-social, clinical, and health psychology. *Psychological Bulletin, 92*, 111–135.

Cash, T. F., & Duncan, N. C. (1984). Physical attractiveness stereotyping among black American college students. *Journal of Social Psychology, 122*, 71–77.

Cash, T. F., & Kilcullen, R. N. (1985). The eye of the beholder: Susceptibility to sexism and beautyism in the evaluation of managerial applicants. *Journal of Applied Social Psychology, 15*, 591–605.

Cash, T. F., & Trimer, C. A. (1984). Sexism and beautyism in women's evaluations of peer performance. *Sex Roles, 10*, 87–98.

Caspi, A., & Herbener, E. S. (1990). Continuity and change: Assortative marriage and the consistency of personality in adulthood. *Journal of Personality and Social Psychology, 58*, 250–258.

Caspi, A., McClay, J., Moffitt, T. E., Mill, J., Martin, J., Craig, I. W., et al. (2002). Role of genotype in the cycle of violence in maltreated children. *Science, 297*, 851–854.

Cate, R. M., Lloyd, S. A., Henton, J. M., & Larson, J. H. (1982). Fairness and reward level as predictors of relationship satisfaction. *Social Psychology Quarterly, 45*, 177–181.

Ceci, S. J., & Bruck, M. (1995). *Jeopardy in the courtroom: A scientific analysis of children's testimony.* Washington, DC: American Psychological Association.

Center for Media and Public Affairs. (July–August 2000). The media at the millennium: The networks' top topics, trends, and joke targets of the 1990s. *Media Monitor, 14*, 1–6.

Centers for Disease Control & Prevention. (2010). Vital signs: Current cigarette smoking among adults aged ≥ 18 years—United States, 2009. *Morbidity and Mortality Weekly Report, 59*(35), 1135–1140.

Central Intelligence Agency. (2011). The World Factbook. Retrieved from https://www.cia.gov/library/publications/the-world-factbook/rankorder/2172rank.html

Cesario, J., Plaks, J. E., & Higgins, E. T. (2006). Automatic social behavior as motivated preparation to interact. *Journal of Personality and Social Psychology, 90*, 893–910.

Cha, J.-H., & Nam, K. D. (1985). A test of Kelley's cube theory of attribution: A cross-cultural replication of McArthur's study. *Korean Social Science Journal, 12*, 151–180.

Chagnon, N. A. (1997). *Yanomamö.* New York: Harcourt, Brace, Jovanovich.

Chaiken, S. (1980). Heuristic versus systematic information processing in the use of source versus message cues in persuasion. *Journal of Personality and Social Psychology, 39*, 752–766.

Chaiken, S., & Baldwin, M. W. (1981). Affective-cognitive consistency and the effect of salient behavioral information on the self-perception of attitudes. *Journal of Personality and Social Psychology, 41*, 1–12.

Chaiken, S., & Eagly, A. H. (1976). Communication modality as a determinant of persuasion: The role of communicator salience. *Journal of Personality and Social Psychology, 45*, 241–256.

Chaiken, S., Liberman, A., & Eagly, A. H. (1989). Heuristic and systematic processing within and beyond the persuasion context. In J. S. Uleman & J. A. Bargh (Eds.), *Unintended thought* (pp. 212–252). New York: Guilford Press.

Chaiken S., & Maheswaran, D. (1994). Heuristic processing can bias systematic processing: effects of source credibility, argument ambiguity, and task importance on attitude judgment. *Journal of Personality and Social Psychology, 66*, 460–473.

Chapman, L. J., & Chapman, J. (1967). Genesis of popular but erroneous diagnostic observations. *Journal of Abnormal Psychology, 72*, 193–204.

Chartrand, T. L., & Bargh, J. A. (1999). The chameleon effect: The perception-behavior link and social interaction. *Journal of Personality and Social Psychology, 76*, 893–910.

Chen, C., Boucher, H., & Tapias, M. P. (2006). The relational self revealed: Integrative conceptualization and implications for interpersonal life. *Psychological Bulletin, 132*(2), 151–179.

Chen, C., & Stevenson, H. W. (1995). Motivation and mathematics achievement: A comparative study of Asian-American, Caucasian-American and East Asian high school students. *Child Development, 66*, 1215–1234.

Chen, M., & Bargh, J. A. (1999). Consequences of automatic evaluation: Immediate behavioral predispositions to approach or avoid the stimulus. *Personality and Social Psychology Bulletin, 25*, 215–224.

Chen, S., & Chaiken, S. (1999). The heuristic-systematic model in its broader context. In S. Chaiken & Y. Trope (Eds.), *Dual-process theories in social and cognitive psychology* (pp. 73–96). New York: Guilford Press.

Chen, S., Lee-Chai, A. Y., & Bargh, J. A. (2001). Relationship orientation as moderator of the effects of social power. *Journal of Personality and Social Psychology, 80*, 183–187.

Chen, S. C. (1937). Social modification of the activity of ants in nest-building. *Physiological Zoology, 10*, 420–436.

Cheng, P. W., & Novick, L. R. (1990). A probabilistic contrast model of causal induction. *Journal of Personality and Social Psychology, 58,* 545–567.

Cheryan, S., & Bodenhausen, G. V. (2000). When positive stereotypes threaten intellectual performance: The psychological hazards of "model minority" status. *Psychological Review, 11,* 399–402.

Cheung, F. M., Leung, K., Zhang, J. X., Sun, H. F., Gan, Y. Q., Song, W. Z., & Dong, X. (2001). Indigenous Chinese personality constructs: Is the five-factor model complete? *Journal of Cross-Cultural Psychology, 32,* 407–433.

Choi, I., & Nisbett, R. E. (1998). Situational salience and cultural differences in the correspondence bias and in the actor-observer bias. *Personality and Social Psychology Bulletin, 24,* 949–960.

Choi, I., Nisbett, R. E., & Norenzayan, A. (1999). Causal attribution across cultures: Variation and universality. *Psychological Bulletin, 125,* 47–63.

Choi, J. N., & Kim, M. U. (1999). The organizational application of groupthink and its limitations in organizations. *Journal of Applied Psychology, 84,* 297–306.

Christakis, N. A., & Fowler, J. H. (2009). *Connected.* New York: Little, Brown.

Chua, H., Leu, J., & Nisbett, R. E. (2005). Culture and the diverging views of social events. *Personality and Social Psychology Bulletin, 31,* 925–934.

Cialdini, R. B. (1984). *Influence: How and why people agree to things.* New York: Quill.

Cialdini, R. B., Borden, R. J., Thorne, A., Walker, M. R., Freeman, S., & Sloan, L. R. (1976). Basking in reflected glory: Three (football) field studies. *Journal of Personality and Social Psychology, 34,* 366–375.

Cialdini, R. B., Darby, B. L., & Vincent, J. E. (1973). Transgression and altruism: A case for hedonism. *Journal of Experimental Social Psychology, 9,* 502–516.

Cialdini, R. R., Demaine, L. J., Sagarin, B. J., Barrett, D. W., Rhoads, K., & Winters, K. (2006). Activating and aligning social norms for persuasive impact. *Social Influence, 1,* 3–15.

Cialdini, R. B., & Fultz, J. (1990). Interpreting the negative mood-helping literature via "mega" analysis: A contrarian view. *Psychological Bulletin, 107,* 210–214.

Cialdini, R. B., Kallgren, C. A., & Reno, R. R. (1991). A focus theory of normative conduct: A theoretical refinement and reevaluation of the role of norms in human behavior. In M. P. Zanna (Ed.), *Advances in experimental social psychology* (Vol. 24, pp. 201–234). San Diego, CA: Academic Press.

Cialdini, R. B., & Kenrick, D. T. (1976). Altruism as hedonism: A social development perspective on the relationship of negative mood state and helping. *Journal of Personality and Social Psychology, 34,* 907–914.

Cialdini, R. B., Schaller, M., Houlihan, D., Arps, K., Fultz, J., & Beaman, A. L. (1987). Empathy-based helping: Is it selflessly or selfishly motivated? *Journal of Personality and Social Psychology, 52,* 749–758.

Cialdini, R. B., & Schroeder, D. A. (1976). Increasing compliance by legitimizing paltry contributions: When even a penny helps. *Journal of Personality and Social Psychology, 34,* 599–604.

Cialdini, R. B., & Trost, M. R. (1998). Social influence: Social norms, conformity, and compliance. In D. T. Gilbert, S. T. Fiske, & G. Lindzey (Eds.), *The handbook of social psychology* (4th ed., Vol. 2, pp. 151–192). New York: McGraw-Hill.

Cialdini, R. B., Vincent, J. E., Lewis, S. K., Catalan, J., Wheeler, D., & Darby, B. L. (1975). Reciprocal concessions procedure for inducing compliance: The door-in-the-face technique. *Journal of Personality and Social Psychology, 31,* 206–215.

Clancy, S. M., & Dollinger, S. J. (1993). Photographic depictions of the self: Gender and age differences in social connectedness. *Sex Roles, 15,* 145–158.

Clark, H. H. (1996). *Using language.* Cambridge, England: Cambridge University Press.

Clark, M., & Isen, A. M. (1982). Toward understanding the relationship between feeling states and social behavior. In A. H. Hastorf & A. M. Isen (Eds.), *Cognitive social psychology* (pp. 73–108). New York: Elsevier.

Clark, M. S. (1992). Research on communal and exchange relationships viewed from a functionalist perspective. In D. A. Owens & M. Wagner (Eds.), *Progress in modern psychology: The legacy of American functionalism* (pp. 241–258). Westport, CT: Praeger.

Clark, M. S., & Mills, J. (1979). Interpersonal attraction in exchange and communal relationships. *Journal of Personality and Social Psychology, 37,* 12–24.

Clark, M. S., & Mills, J. (1993). The difference between communal and exchange relationships: What is and is not. *Personality and Social Psychology Bulletin, 19,* 684–691.

Clark, R., Crockett, W., & Archer, R. (1971). Risk-as-value hypothesis: The relationship between perception of self, others, and the risky shift. *Journal of Personality and Social Psychology, 20,* 425–429.

Clark, R. D. I., & Word, L. E. (1972). Why don't bystanders help? Because of ambiguity? *Journal of Personality and Social Psychology, 24,* 392–400.

Clore, G. L. (1992). Cognitive phenomenology: Feelings and the construction of judgment. In L. L. Martin & A. Tesser (Eds.), *The construction of social judgments* (pp. 133–163). Hillsdale, NJ: Erlbaum.

Clore, G. L., & Byrne, D. (1974). A reinforcement-effect model of attraction. In T. L. Huston (Ed.), *Foundations of interpersonal attraction* (pp. 143–170). New York: Academic Press.

Clore, G. L., Gasper, K., & Garvin, E. (2001). Affect as information. In J. P. Forgas (Ed.), *Handbook of affect and social cognition* (pp. 121–144). Mahwah, NJ: Erlbaum.

Clore, G. L., & Gormly, J. B. (1974). Knowing, feeling, and liking: A psychophysical study of attraction. *Journal of Research in Personality, 8,* 218–230.

Clore, G. L., & Parrott, W. G. (1991). Moods and their vicissitudes: The informational properties of affective thoughts and feelings. In J. Forgas (Ed.), *Emotion and social judgments* (pp. 107–123). Elmsford, NY: Pergamon Press.

Coan, J. A., Schaefer, H. S., & Davidson, R. J. (2006). Lending a hand: Social regulation of the neural response to threat. *Psychological Science, 17,* 1032–1039.

Cohen, C. E. (1981). Person categories and social perception: Testing some boundaries of the processing effects of prior knowledge. *Journal of Personality and Social Psychology, 40,* 441–452.

Cohen, D., & Gunz, A. (2002). *As seen by the other . . . : The self from the "outside in" and the "inside out" in the memories and emotional perceptions of Easterners and Westerners.* Unpublished manuscript, University of Waterloo.

Cohen, D., & Nisbett, R. E. (1997). Field experiments examining the culture of honor: The role of institutions in perpetuating norms about violence. *Personality and Social Psychology Bulletin, 23,* 1188–1199.

Cohen, D., Nisbett, R. E., Bowdle, B., & Schwarz, N. (1996). Insult, aggression, and the Southern culture of honor: An "experimental ethnography." *Journal of Personality and Social Psychology, 70,* 945–960.

Cohen, G., Aronson, J., & Steele, C. M. (2000). When beliefs yield to evidence: Reducing biased evaluation by affirming the self. *Personality and Social Psychology Bulletin, 26,* 1151–1164.

Cohen, G. L., Garcia, J., Apfel, N., & Master, A. (2006). Reducing the racial achievement gap: A social-psychological intervention. *Science, 313,* 1307–1310.

Cohen, G. L., Garcia, J., Purdie-Vaughns, V., Apfel, N., & Brzustoski, P. (2009). Recursive processes in self-affirmation: Intervening to close the minority achievement gap. *Science, 324,* 400–403.

Cohen, S., Alper, C. M., Doyle, W. J., Adler, N., Treanor, J. J., & Turner, R. B. (2008). Objective and subjective socioeconomic status and susceptibility to the common cold. *Health Psychology, 27*(2), 268–274.

Cohen, S., & Herbert, T. B. (1996). Health psychology: Psychological factors and physical disease from the perspective of human psychoneuroimmunology. *Annual Review of Psychology, 47,* 113–142.

Coie, J. D., Cillessen, A. H. N., Dodge, K. A., Hubbard, J. A., Schwartz, D., Lemerise, E. D., et al. (1999). It takes two to fight: A test of relational factors and a method for assessing aggressive dyads. *Developmental Psychology, 35,* 1179–1188.

Collins, N. L., & Miller, L. C. (1994). Self-disclosure and liking: A meta-analytic review. *Psychological Bulletin, 116,* 457–475.

Collins, N. L., & Read, S. J. (1994). Cognitive representations of attachment: The structure and function of working models. In K. Bartholomew & D. Perlman (Eds.), *Attachment processes in adulthood: Advances in personal relationships* (Vol. 5, pp. 53–90). London: Kingsley.

Collins, R. L., Taylor, S. E., Wood, J. V., & Thompson, S. C. (1988). The vividness effect: Elusive or illusory? *Journal of Experimental Social Psychology, 24,* 1–18.

Columbus, C. (1492/1990). *Journal of the first voyage.* Warminster, England: Aris and Phillips Ltd.

Colvin, C. R., & Block, J. (1994). Do positive illusions foster mental health? An examination of the Taylor and Brown formulation. *Psychological Bulletin, 116,* 3–20.

Colvin, C. R., Block, J., & Funder, D. C. (1995). Overly positive self-evaluations and personality: Negative implications for mental health. *Journal of Personality and Social Psychology, 68,* 1152–1162.

Colvin, C. R., & Griffo, R. (2008). On the psychological costs of self-enhancement. In E. C. Chang (Ed.), *Self-criticism and self-enhancement: Theory, research, and clinical implications* (pp. 123–140). Washington, DC: American Psychological Association.

Condon, P., & DeSteno, D. (2011). Compassion for one reduces punishment for another. *Journal of Experimental Social Psychology, 47,* 698–701.

Condry, J., & Condry, S. (1976). Sex differences: A study of the eye of the beholder. *Child Development, 47,* 812–819.

Connolly, K. (1968). The social facilitation of preening behavior of *Drosophila melanogaster. Animal Behavior, 16,* 385–391.

Conway, L. G., & Schaller, M. (2002). On the verifiability of evolutionary psychological theories. *Personality and Social Psychology, 6,* 152–166.

Cooley, C. H. (1902). *Human nature and the social order.* New York: Charles Scribner's Sons.

Coontz, S. (2005). *Marriage, a history: From obedience to intimacy, or how love conquered marriage.* New York: Viking Press.

Cooper, J. (1971). Personal responsibility and dissonance: The role and foreseen consequences. *Journal of Personality and Social Psychology, 18,* 354–363.

Cooper, J., & Worchel, S. (1970). Role of undesired consequences in arousing cognitive dissonance. *Journal of Personality and Social Psychology, 16,* 199–206.

Cooper, J., Zanna, M. P., & Taves, T. A. (1978). Arousal as a necessary condition for attitude change following induced compliance. *Journal of Personality and Social Psychology, 36,* 1101–1106.

Cooper, M. J., Dimitrov, O., & Rau, P. R. (2001). A Rose.com by any other name. *Journal of Finance, 56,* 2371–2388.

Cooper, M. L., Shaver, P., & Collins, N. L. (1998). Attachment styles, emotion regulation, and adjustment in adolescence. *Journal of Personality and Social Psychology, 74,* 1380–1397.

Coriell, M., & Adler, N. E. (2001). Social ordering and health. In B. S. McEwen (volume Ed.) and H. M. Goodman (section Ed.), *Handbook of physiology. Section 7: The endocrine system* (pp. 533–546). New York: American Physiological Society and Oxford University Press.

Correll, J., & Park, B. (2005). A model of the ingroup as a social resource. *Personality and Social Psychology Review, 9,* 341–359.

Correll, J., Park, B., Judd, C. M., & Wittenbrink, B. (2002). The police officer's dilemma: Using ethnicity to disambiguate potentially threatening individuals. *Journal of Personality and Social Psychology, 83,* 1314–1329.

Correll, J., Park, B., Judd, C. M., Wittenbrink, B., Sadler, M. S., & Keesee, T. (2007). Across the thin blue line: Police officers and racial bias in the decision to shoot. *Journal of Personality and Social Psychology, 92*(6), 1006–1023.

Correll, J., Spencer, S. J., & Zanna, M. (2004). An affirmed self and an open mind: Self-affirmation and sensitivity to argument strength. *Journal of Experimental Social Psychology, 40,* 350–356.

Correll, J., Urland, G. R., & Ito, T. A. (2006). Event-related potentials and the decision to shoot: The role of threat perception and cognitive control. *Journal of Experimental Social Psychology, 42,* 120–128.

Cortes, B. P., Demoulin, S., Rodriguez, R. T., Rodriguez, A. P., & Leyens, J. P. (2005). Infrahumanization or familiarity? Attribution of uniquely human emotions to the self, the ingroup, and the outgroup. *Personality and Social Psychology Bulletin, 32*(2), 243–253.

Costanzo, M. (1997). *Just revenge: Costs and consequences of the death penalty.* New York: St. Martin's Press.

Cota, A. A., & Dion, K. L. (1986). Salience of gender and sex composition of ad hoc groups: An experimental test of the distinctiveness theory. *Journal of Personality and Social Psychology, 50,* 770–776.

Côté, S., & Miners, C. T. H. (2006). Emotional intelligence, cognitive intelligence, and job performance. *Administrative Science Quarterly, 51,* 1–28.

Cotterell, N., Eisenberger, R., & Speicher, H. (1992). Inhibiting effects of reciprocation wariness on interpersonal relationships. *Journal of Personality and Social Psychology, 62,* 658–668.

Cottrell, N. B., Wack, D. L., Sekerak, G. J., & Rittle, R. H. (1968). Social facilitation of dominant responses by the presence of an audience and the mere presence of others. *Journal of Personality and Social Psychology, 9,* 245–250.

Cousins, S. D. (1989). Culture and self-perception in Japan and the United States. *Journal of Personality and Social Psychology, 56,* 124–131.

Cowan, C. L., Thompson, W. C., & Ellsworth, P. C. (1984). The effects of death qualification on jurors' predisposition to convict and on the quality of deliberation. *Law and Human Behavior, 8,* 53–80.

Crandall, C. S. (1988). Social contagion of binge eating. *Journal of Personality and Social Psychology, 55,* 588–598.

Crandall, C. S., & Eshleman, A. (2003). A justification-suppression model of the expression and experience of prejudice. *Psychological Bulletin, 129,* 414–446.

Crandall, V. C., Katkovsky, W., & Crandall, V. J. (1965). Children's beliefs in their own control of reinforcements in intellectual-academic achievement situations. *Child Development, 36,* 91–109.

Crano, W. D. (1970). Effects of sex, response order, and expertise in conformity: A dispositional approach. *Sociometry, 33,* 239–252.

Crocker, J. (1982). Biased questions in judgment of covariation studies. *Personality and Social Psychology Bulletin, 8,* 214–220.

Crocker, J., Hannah, D. B., & Weber, R. (1983). Person memory and causal attributions. *Journal of Personality and Social Psychology, 44,* 55–66.

Crocker, J., & Luhtanen, R. (1990). Collective self-esteem and ingroup bias. *Journal of Personality and Social Psychology, 58,* 60–67.

Crocker, J., Luhtanen, R. K., Cooper, M. L., & Bouvrette, A. (2003). Contingencies of self-worth in college students: Theory and measurement. *Journal of Personality and Social Psychology, 85,* 894–908.

Crocker, J., Major, B., & Steele, C. (1998). Social stigma. In D. T. Gilbert, S. T. Fiske, & G. Lindzey (Eds.), *The handbook of social psychology* (4th ed., Vol. 2, pp. 504–553). New York: McGraw-Hill.

Crocker, J., & Park, L. E. (2003). Seeking self-esteem: Construction, maintenance, and protection of self-worth. In M. R. Leary & J. P. Tangney (Eds.), *Handbook of self and identity* (pp. 291–313). New York: Guilford Press.

Crocker, J., & Park, L. E. (2004). The costly pursuit of self-esteem. *Psychological Bulletin, 130,* 392–414.

Crocker, J., Sommers, S. R., & Luhtanen, R. K. (2002). Hopes dashed and dreams fulfilled: Contingencies of self-worth and graduate school admissions. *Personality and Social Psychology Bulletin, 28,* 1275–1286.

Crocker, J., Voelkl, K., Testa, M., & Major, B. (1991). Social stigma: The affective consequences of attributional ambiguity. *Journal of Personality and Social Psychology, 60,* 218–228.

Crocker, J., & Wolfe, C. T. (2001). Contingencies of self-worth. *Psychological Review, 108,* 593–623.

Cross, H. A., Halcomb, C. G., & Matter, W. W. (1967). Imprinting or exposure learning in rats given early auditory stimulation. *Psychonomic Science, 7,* 233–234.

Cross, J. F., & Cross, J. (1971). Age, sex, race, and the perception of facial beauty. *Developmental Psychology, 5,* 433–459.

Cross, S. E., & Madson, L. (1997). Models of the self: Self-construals and gender. *Psychological Bulletin, 122,* 5–37.

Cross, S., & Markus, H. (1991). Possible selves across the life span. *Human Development, 34,* 230–255.

Croyle, R. T., & Cooper, J. (1983). Dissonance arousal: Physiological evidence. *Journal of Personality and Social Psychology, 45,* 782–791.

Cullen, D. (2009). *Columbine.* New York: Twelve Publishing.

Cunningham, M. R., Roberts, A. R., Barbee, A. P., Druen, P. B., & Wu, C. (1995). "Their ideas of beauty are, on the whole, the same as ours": Consistency and variability in the cross-cultural perception of female physical attractiveness. *Journal of Personality and Social Psychology, 68,* 261–279.

Cunningham, W. A., Johnson, M. K., Raye, C. L., Gatenby, J. C., Gore, J. C., & Banaji, M. R. (2004). Separable neural components in the processing of black and white faces. *Psychological Science, 15,* 806–813.

Curran, J. P., & Lippold, S. (1975). The effects of physical attractiveness and attitude similarity on attraction in dating dyads. *Journal of Personality, 43,* 528–539.

Curry, R. L. (1988). Influence of kinship on helping behavior in Galápagos mockingbirds. *Behavioral Ecology and Sociobiology, 38,* 181–192.

Cutrona, C. E. (1982). Transition to college: Loneliness and the process of social adjustment. In L. A. Peplau & D. Perlman (Eds.), *Loneliness: A sourcebook of current theory, research, and therapy* (pp. 291–309). New York: Wiley.

Czopp, A. M., & Monteith, M. J. (2006). Thinking well of African Americans: Measuring complimentary stereotypes and negative prejudice. *Basic and Applied Social Psychology, 28,* 233–250.

Dabbs, J. M., Jr. (2000). *Heroes, rogues and lovers.* New York: McGraw-Hill.

Daly, M., & Wilson, M. (1988). *Homicide.* New York: De Gruyter.

Daly, M., & Wilson, M. I. (1996). Violence against stepchildren. *Current Directions in Psychological Science, 5,* 77–81.

Daly, M., Wilson, M., & Vasdev, S. (2001). Income inequality and homicide rates in Canada and the United States. *Canadian Journal of Criminology,* 219–236.

Damasio, A. R. (1994). *Descartes' error: Emotion, reason, and the human brain.* New York: Free Press.

Danner, D., Snowdon, D., & Friesen, W. (2001). Positive emotions in early life and longevity: Findings from the nun study. *Journal of Personality and Social Psychology, 80,* 804–813.

Darley, J. M., & Batson, C. D. (1973). From Jerusalem to Jericho: A study of situational and dispositional variables in helping behavior. *Journal of Personality and Social Psychology, 27,* 100–119.

Darley, J. M., & Berscheid, E. (1967). Increased liking as a result of the anticipation of personal contact. *Human Relations, 20,* 29–40.

Darley, J. M., & Latané, B. (1968). Bystander intervention in emergencies: Diffusion of responsibility. *Journal of Personality and Social Psychology, 8,* 377–383.

Darley, J. M., Teger, A. I., & Lewis, L. D. (1973). Do groups always inhibit individuals' responses to potential emergencies? *Journal of Personality and Social Psychology, 26,* 395–399.

Darlington, R. B., & Macker, C. E. (1966). Displacement of guilt-produced altruistic behavior. *Journal of Personality and Social Psychology, 4,* 442–443.

Darwin, C. (1871). *The descent of man, and selection in relation to sex.* London: John Murray.

Darwin, C. (1872/1998). *The expression of emotions in man and animals* (3rd ed.). New York: Oxford University Press.

Dasgupta, N., DeSteno, D., Williams, L. A., & Hunsinger, M. (2009). Fanning the flames: The influence of specific incidental emotions on implicit prejudice. *Emotion, 9,* 585–591.

Dashiell, J. F. (1930). An experimental analysis of some group effects. *Journal of Abnormal and Social Psychology, 25,* 190–199.

Davidson, A. R., Yantis, S., Norwood, M., & Montano, D. E. (1985). Amount of information about the attitude object and attitude-behavior consistency. *Journal of Personality and Social Psychology, 49,* 1184–1198.

Davidson, R. J., Kabat-Zinn, J., Schumacher, J., Rosenkranz, M., Muller, D., Santorelli, S. F., et al. (2003). Alterations in brain and immune function produced by mindfulness meditation. *Psychosomatic Medicine, 65,* 564–570.

Davidson, R. J., Pizzagalli, D., Nitzschke, J. B., & Kalin, N. H. (2003). Parsing the subcomponents of emotion and disorders: Perspectives from affective neuroscience. In R. J. Davidson, K. Scherer, & H. H. Goldsmith (Eds.), *Handbook of affective science* (pp. 8–24). New York: Oxford University Press.

Davis, M. H., & Franzoi, S. L. (1991). Stability and change in adolescent self-consciousness and empathy. *Journal of Research in Personality, 25,* 70–87.

Davis, M. H., & Stephan, W. G. (1980). Attributions for exam performance. *Journal of Applied Social Psychology, 10,* 235–248.

Dawes, R. M. (1980). Social dilemmas. *Annual Review of Psychology, 31,* 169–193.

Dawes, R. M. (1988). *Rational choice in an uncertain world.* San Diego, CA: Harcourt, Brace, Jovanovich.

Dawson, E., Gilovich, T., & Regan, D. T. (2002). Motivated reasoning and performance on the Wason selection task. *Personality and Social Psychology Bulletin, 28,* 1379–1387.

Dearing, J. W., & Rogers, E. M. (1996). *Agenda-setting.* Thousand Oaks, CA: Sage.

Deaux, K., & Emswiller, T. (1974). Explanations of successful performance on sex-linked tasks: What is skill for the male is luck for the female. *Journal of Personality and Social Psychology, 29,* 80–85.

Deaux, K., Reid, A., Mizrahi, K., & Ethier, K. A. (1995). Parameters of social identity. *Journal of Personality and Social Psychology, 68,* 280–291.

Debner, J. A., & Jacoby, L. L. (1994). Unconscious perception: Attention, awareness, and control. *Journal of Experimental Psychology: Learning, Memory and Cognition, 20,* 304–317.

Decety, J., & Michalska, K. (2010). Neurodevelopmental changes in the circuits underlying empathy and sympathy from childhood to adulthood. *Developmental Science, 13,* 886–899.

Dechesne, M., Greenberg, J., Arndt, J., & Schimel, J. (2000). Terror management and sports fan affiliation: The effects of mortality salience on fan identification and optimism. *European Journal of Social Psychology, 30,* 813–835.

Dechesne, M., Pyszczynski, T., Arndt, J., Ransom, S., Sheldon, K. M., van Knippenberg, A., et al. (2003). Literal and symbolic immortality: The effect of evidence of literal immortality on self-esteem striving in response to mortality salience. *Journal of Personality and Social Psychology, 84,* 722–737.

Deci, E. L., & Ryan, R. M. (1985). *Intrinsic motivation and self-determination in human behavior.* New York: Plenum Press.

Dempster, F. N. (1992). The rise and fall of the inhibitory mechanism: Toward a unified theory of cognitive development and aging. *Developmental Review, 12,* 45–75.

Denes-Raj, V., & Epstein, S. (1994). Conflict between intuitive and rational processing: When people behave against their better judgment. *Journal of Personality and Social Psychology, 66,* 819–829.

DePaulo, B. M., & Friedman, H. S. (1998). Nonverbal communication. In D. T. Gilbert, S. T. Fiske, & G. Lindzey (Eds.), *Handbook of social psychology* (4th ed., Vol. 2, pp. 3–40). New York: McGraw-Hill.

DePaulo, B. M., Lanier, K., & Davis, T. (1983). Detecting the deceit of the motivated liar. *Journal of Personality and Social Psychology, 43,* 1096–1103.

Deppe, R. K., & Harackiewicz, J. M. (1996). Self-handicapping and intrinsic motivation: Buffering intrinsic motivation from the threat of failure. *Journal of Personality and Social Psychology, 70,* 868–876.

Dermer, M., & Theil, D. (1975). When beauty may fail. *Journal of Personality and Social Psychology, 31,* 1168–1177.

DeSteno, D., Dasgupta, N., Bartlett, M. Y., & Cajdric, A. (2004). Prejudice from thin air: The effect of emotion on automatic intergroup attitudes. *Psychological Science, IS,* 319–324.

DeSteno, D., Petty, R., Wegener, D., & Rucker, D. (2000). Beyond valence in the perception of likelihood: The role of emotion specificity. *Journal of Personality and Social Psychology, 78,* 397–416.

DeSteno, D. A., & Salovey, P. (1996). Jealousy and the characteristics of one's rival: A self-evaluation maintenance perspective. *Personality and Social Psychology, 22,* 920–932.

Destin, M., & Oyserman, D. (2009). From assets to school outcomes: How finances shape children's perceived possibilities and planned effort. *Psychological Science, 20,* 414–418.

Deutsch, M., & Gerard, H. B. (1955). A study of normative and informational social influence upon individual judgment. *Journal of Abnormal and Social Psychology, 51,* 629–636.

Devine, P. G. (1989a). Automatic and controlled processes in prejudice: The roles of stereotypes and personal beliefs. In A. R. Pratkanis, S. J. Breckler, & A. G. Greenwald (Eds.), *Attitude structure and function.* Hillsdale, NJ: Erlbaum.

Devine, P. G. (1989b). Stereotypes and prejudice: Their automatic and controlled components. *Journal of Personality and Social Psychology, 56,* 5–18.

Devine, P. G., & Baker, S. M. (1991). Measurement of racial stereotype subtyping. *Personality and Social Psychology Bulletin, 17,* 44–50.

Devine, P. G., & Elliot, A. J. (1995). Are racial stereotypes really fading? The Princeton trilogy revisited. *Personality and Social Psychology Bulletin, 21,* 1139–1150.

Devine, P. G., & Monteith, M. J. (1999). Automaticity and control in stereotyping. In S. Chaiken & Y. Trope (Eds.), *Dual process theories in social psychology* (pp. 339–360). New York: Guilford Press.

Devine, P. G., Monteith, M. J., Zuwerink, J. R., & Elliot, A. J. (1991). Prejudice with and without compunction. *Journal of Personality and Social Psychology, 60,* 817–830.

Devine, P. G., Plant, E. A., Amodio, D. M., Harmon-Jones, E., & Vance, S. L. (2002). Exploring the relationship between implicit and explicit prejudice: The role of motivations to respond without prejudice. *Journal of Personality and Social Psychology, 82,* 835–848.

Devine, P. G., Plant, E. A., & Blair, I. V. (2001). Classic and contemporary analyses of racial prejudice. In R. Brown & S. Gaertner (Eds.), *Blackwell handbook of social psychology: Intergroup processes* (pp. 198–217). Oxford, UK: Blackwell.

de Waal, F. B. M. (1986). The integration of dominance and social bonding in primates. *Quarterly Review of Biology, 61,* 459–479.

de Waal, F. B. M. (1996). *Good natured: The origins of right and wrong in humans and other animals.* Cambridge, MA: Harvard University Press.

de Wall, C. N., MacDonald, G., Webster, G. D., Masten, C., Baumeister, R. F., Powell, C., et al. (2010). Acetaminophen reduces social pain: Behavioral and neural evidence. *Psychological Science, 21,* 931–937.

Dhawan, N., Roseman, I. J., Naidu, R. K., Thapa, K., & Rettek, S. I. (1995). Self-concepts across two cultures: India and the United States. *Journal of Cross-Cultural Psychology, 26,* 606–621.

Diamond, L. M. (2003). What does sexual orientation orient? A biobehavioral model distinguishing romantic love and sexual desire. *Psychological Review, 110,* 173–192.

Diamond, S. S., Rose, M. R., & Murphy, B. (2006). Revisiting the unanimity requirement: The behavior of the non-unanimous civil jury. *Northwestern Law Review, 100,* 201–230.

Dickerson, S. S., & Kemeny, M. E. (2004). Acute stressors and cortisol responses: A theoretical integration and synthesis of laboratory research. *Psychological Bulletin, 130,* 355–391.

Diener, E. (1980). Deindividuation: The absence of self-awareness and self-regulation in group members. In P. Paulus (Ed.), *The psychology of group influence* (pp. 209–242). Hillsdale, NJ: Erlbaum.

Diener, E. (2000). Subjective well-being: The science of happiness, and some policy implications. *American Psychologist, 55,* 34–43.

Diener, E., Fraser, S. C., Beaman, A. L., & Kelem, R. T. (1976). Effects of deindividuation variables on stealing among Halloween trick-or-treaters. *Journal of Personality and Social Psychology, 33,* 178–183.

Diener, E., & Wallbom, M. (1976). Effects of self-awareness on antinormative behavior. *Journal of Research in Personality, 10,* 107–111.

Diener, E., Wolsic, B., & Fujita, F. (1995). Physical attractiveness and subjective well-being. *Journal of Personality and Social Psychology, 69,* 207–213.

Dienstbier, R. A., & Munter, P. O. (1971). Cheating as a function of the labeling of natural arousal. *Journal of Personality and Social Psychology, 17,* 208–213.

Dijksterhuis, A., & Aarts, H. (2003). On wildebeests and humans: The preferential detection of negative stimuli. *Psychological Science, 14,* 14–18.

Dijksterhuis, A., Aarts, H., Bargh, J. A., & van Knippenberg, A. (2000). On the relation between associative strength and automatic behavior. *Journal of Experimental Social Psychology, 36,* 531–544.

Dijksterhuis, A., Aarts, H., & Smith, P. K. (2005). The power of the subliminal: On subliminal persuasion and other potential applications. In R. R. Hassin, J. S. Uleman, & J. A. Bargh (Eds.), *The new unconscious.* New York: Oxford University Press.

Dijksterhuis, A., & van Knippenberg, A. (1998). The relation between perception and behavior, or how to win a game of Trivial Pursuit. *Journal of Personality and Social Psychology, 74,* 865–877.

Dimberg, U., & Öhman, A. (1996). Behold the wrath: Psychophysiological responses to facial stimuli. *Motivation and Emotion, 20,* 149–182.

Dion, K. K., Berscheid, E., & Walster, E. (1972). What is a beautiful good? *Journal of Personality and Social Psychology, 24,* 285–290.

Dion, K. K., & Dion, K. L. (1993). Individualistic and collectivistic perspectives on gender and the cultural context of love and intimacy. *Journal of Social Issues, 49,* 53–69.

Ditto, P. H., Jemmott, J. B., & Darley, J. M. (1988). Appraising the threat of illness: A mental representational approach. *Health Psychology, 7,* 183–200.

Ditto, P. H., & Lopez, D. F. (1992). Motivated skepticism: Use of differential decision criteria for preferred and nonpreferred conclusions. *Journal of Personality and Social Psychology, 63,* 568–584.

Dodge, K. A., & Schwartz, D. (1997). Social information mechanisms in aggressive behavior. In D. M. Stoff & J. Breiling (Eds.), *Handbook of antisocial behavior* (pp. 171–180). New York: Wiley.

Dollard, J., Doob, L. W., Miller, N. E., Mowrer, H. H., & Sears, R. R. (1939). *Frustration and aggression.* New Haven: Yale University Press.

Donnellan, M. B., Trzesniewski, K. H., Robins, R. W., Moffitt, T. E., & Caspi, A. (2005). Low self-esteem is related to aggression, antisocial behavior, and delinquency. *Psychological Science, 16,* 328–335.

Donnerstein, E. (1980). Aggressive erotica and violence against women. *Journal of Personality and Social Psychology, 39,* 269–277.

Donnerstein, E., & Berkowitz, L. (1981). Victim reactions in aggressive erotic films as a factor in violence against women. *Journal of Personality and Social Psychology, 41,* 710–724.

Doob, A. N., & MacDonald, G. E. (1979). Television and fear of victimization: Is the relationship *causal? Journal of Personality and Social Psychology, 37,* 170–179.

Dovidio, J. F. (1984). Helping behavior and altruism: An empirical and conceptual overview. In L. Berkowitz (Ed.), *Advances in experimental social psychology* (pp. 361–427). New York: Academic Press.

Dovidio, J. F., & Gaertner, S. L. (1981). The effects of race, status, ability on helping behavior. *Social Psychology Quarterly, 44,* 192–203.

Dovidio, J. F., & Gaertner, S. L. (2004). Aversive racism. In M. P. Zanna (Ed.), *Advances in experimental social psychology* (Vol. 36, pp. 1–52). San Diego, CA: Elsevier.

Dovidio, J. F., Kawakami, K., & Gaertner, S. L. (2002). Implicit and explicit prejudice and interracial interaction. *Journal of Personality and Social Psychology, 82,* 62–68.

Dovidio, J. F., Smith, J. K., Donella, A. G., & Gaertner, S. L. (1997). Racial attitudes and the death penalty. *Journal of Applied Social Psychology, 27,* 1468–1487.

Dovidio, J. F., ten Vergert, M., Stewart, T. L., Gaertner, S. L., Johnson, J. D., Esses, V. M., et al. (2004). Perspective and prejudice: Antecedents and mediating mechanisms. *Personality and Social Psychology Bulletin, 30,* 1537–1549.

Downey, G., & Feldman, S. (1996). Implications of rejection sensitivity for intimate relationships. *Journal of Personality and Social Psychology, 70,* 1327–1343.

Downey, G., Feldman, S., & Ayduk, O. (2000). Rejection sensitivity and male violence in romantic relationships. *Personal Relationships, 7,* 45–61.

Downey, G., Freitas, A. L., Michaelis, B., & Khouri, H. (1998). The self-fulfilling prophecy in close relationships: Rejection sensitivity and rejection by romantic partners. *Journal of Personality and Social Psychology, 75,* 545–560.

Downing, C. J., Sternberg, R. J., & Ross, B. H. (1985). Multicausal inference: Evaluation of evidence in causally complex situations. *Journal of Experimental Psychology: General, 114,* 239–263.

Downing, J. W., Judd, C. M., & Brauer, M. (1992). Effects of repeated expression of attitudes on attitude extremity. *Journal of Personality and Social Psychology, 63,* 17–29.

Draine, S. C., & Greenwald, A. G. (1998). Replicable unconscious semantic priming. *Journal of Experimental Psychology: General, 127,* 286–303.

Duck, J. M., & Mullin, B. (1995). The perceived impact of the mass media: Reconsidering the third-person effect. *European Journal of Social Psychology, 25,* 77–93.

Duflo, E., & Saez, E. (2003). The role of information and social interactions in retirement plan decisions: Evidence from a randomized experiment. *Quarterly Journal of Economics, 118*(3), 815–842.

Duncan, B. L. (1976). Differential social perception and attribution on intergroup violence: Testing the lower limits of stereotyping of blacks. *Journal of Personality and Social Psychology, 34,* 590–598.

Dunn, E. W., Aknin, L., & Norton, M. I. (2008). Spending money on others promotes happiness. *Science, 319,* 1687–1688.

Dunn, J., & Munn, P. (1985). Becoming a family member: Family conflict and the development of social understanding in the second year. *Child Development, 56,* 480–492.

Dunning, D., Meyerowitz, J. A., & Holzberg, A. (1989). Ambiguity and self-evaluation: The role of idiosyncratic trait definitions in self-serving assessments of ability. *Journal of Personality and Social Psychology, 57,* 1082–1090.

Dunning, D., & Perretta, S. (2002). Automaticity and eyewitness accuracy: A 10-12-second rule for distinguishing accurate from inaccurate positive identifications. *Journal of Applied Psychology, 87,* 951–962.

Dunning, D., & Sherman, D. A. (1997). Stereotypes and tacit inference. *Journal of Personality and Social Psychology, 73,* 459–471.

Dunning, D., & Stern, L. B. (1994). Distinguishing accurate from inaccurate eyewitness identifications via inquiries about decision-making processes. *Journal of Personality and Social Psychology, 67,* 818–835.

Durose, M. R., Smith, E. L., & Langan, P. A. (2007). *Bureau of Justice Statistics Special Report: Contacts between police and the public, 2005.* Washington, DC: U.S. Department of Justice.

Dutton, D. G. (2002). The neurobiology of abandonment homicide. *Aggression and Violent Behavior, 7,* 407–421.

Dutton, D. G., & Aron, A. P. (1974). Some evidence for heightened sexual attraction under conditions of high anxiety. *Journal of Personality and Social Psychology, 30,* 510–517.

Duval, T. S., & Lalwani, N. (1999). Objective self-awareness and causal attributions for self-standard discrepancies: Changing self or changing standards of correctness. *Personality and Social Psychology Bulletin, 25,* 1220–1229.

Duval, T. S., & Wicklund, R. A. (1972). *A theory of objective self-awareness.* New York: Academic Press.

Dweck, C. S. (1975). The role of expectations and attributions in the alleviation of learned helplessness. *Journal of Personality and Social Psychology, 31,* 674–685.

Dweck, C. S. (1986). Motivational processes affecting learning. *American Psychologist, 41,* 1040–1048.

Dweck, C. S. (1999). *Self-theories: Their role in motivation, personality and development.* Philadelphia: Taylor and Francis/Psychology Press.

Dweck, C. S. (2007). *Mindset: The new psychology of success.* New York: Ballantine Books.

Dweck, C. S., Chiu, C., & Hong, Y. (1995). Implicit theories and their role in judgments and reactions: A world from two perspectives. *Psychological Inquiry, 6,* 267–285.

Dweck, C. S., Davidson, W., Nelson, S., & Enna, B. (1978). Sex differences in learned helplessness: (II) The contingencies of evaluative feedback in the classroom and (III) An experimental analysis. *Developmental Psychology, 14,* 268–276.

Dweck, C. S., Hong, Y. Y., & Chiu, C. Y. (1993). Implicit theories and individual differences in the likelihood and meaning of dispositional inference. *Personality and Social Psychology Bulletin, 19,* 644–656.

Dweck, C. S., & Leggett, E. L. (1988). A social-cognitive approach to motivation and personality. *Psychological Review, 95,* 256–273.

Dweck, C. S., & Reppucci, N. D. (1973). Learned helplessness and reinforcement responsibility in children. *Journal of Personality and Social Psychology, 25,* 109–116.

Eagly, A. H. (1987). *Sex differences in social behavior: A social-role interpretation.* Hillsdale, NJ: Erlbaum.

Eagly, A. H., Ashmore, R. D., Makhijani, M. G., & Longo, L. C. (1991). What is beautiful is good, but . . . : A meta-analytic review of research on the physical attractiveness stereotype. *Psychological Bulletin, 110,* 109–128.

Eagly, A. H., & Carli, L. L. (1981). Sex of researchers and sex-typed communications as determinants of sex differences in influenceability: A meta-analysis of social influence studies. *Psychological Bulletin, 110,* 109–128.

Eagly, A. H., & Chaiken, S. (1993). *The psychology of attitudes.* Fort Worth, TX: Harcourt Brace.

Eagly, A. H., & Chaiken, S. (1998). Attitude structure and function. In D. T. Gilbert, S. T. Fiske, & G. Lindzey (Eds.), *Handbook of social psychology* (4th ed., Vol. 1, pp. 269–322). New York: McGraw-Hill.

Eagly, A. H., & Chrvala, C. (2006). Sex differences in conformity: Status and gender role interpretations. *Psychology of Women Quarterly, 10,* 203–220.

Eagly, A. H., & Wood, W. (1999). The origins of sex differences in human behavior: Evolved dispositions vs. social roles. *American Psychologist, 54,* 408–423.

Eastwick, P. W., & Finkel, E. J. (2008). Sex differences in mate preferences revisited: Do people know what they initially desire in a romantic partner? *Journal of Personality and Social Psychology, 94*(2), 245–264.

Eastwick, P. W., Finkel, E. J., Mochon, D., & Ariely, D. (2007). Selective versus unselective romantic desire: Not all reciprocity is created equal. *Psychological Science, 18,* 317–319.

Eberhardt, J. L., Davies, P. G., Purdie-Vaughns, V. J., & Johnson, S. L. (2006). Looking deathworthy: Perceived stereotypicality of black defendants predicts capital sentencing outcomes. *Psychological Science, 17,* 383–386.

Eckland, B. (1968). Theories of mate selection. *Social Biology, 15,* 71–84.

Edmans, A., Garcia, D., & Norli, O. (2007). Sports sentiment and stock returns. *Journal of Finance, 62,* 1967–1998.

Efran, M. G. (1974). The effect of physical appearance on judgments of guilt, interpersonal attractiveness, and severity of recommended punishment in a simulated jury task. *Journal of Research in Personality, 8,* 45–54.

Eibach, R. P., Libby, L. K., & Gilovich, T. (2003). When change in the self is mistaken for change in the world. *Journal of Personality and Social Psychology, 84,* 917–931.

Eibach, R. P., & Mock, S. E. (2011). Idealizing parenthood to rationalize parental investments. *Psychological Science, 22,* 203–208.

Eibl-Eibesfeldt, I. (1989). *Human ethology.* New York: Aldine de Gruyter Press.

Eisenberg, N., Fabes, R. A., Miller, P. A., Fultz, J., Shell, R., Mathy, R. M., et al. (1989). Relation of sympathy and distress to prosocial behavior: A multimethod study. *Journal of Personality and Social Psychology, 57,* 55–66.

Eisenberg, N., & Lennon, R. (1983). Sex differences in empathy and related capacities. *Psychological Bulletin, 94,* 100–131.

Eisenberger, N. I., Lieberman, M. D., & Williams, K. D. (2003). Does rejection hurt? An fMRI study of social exclusion. *Science, 302,* 290–292.

Ekman, P. (1984). Expression and the nature of emotion. In K. Scherer & P. Ekman (Eds.), *Approaches to emotion.* Hillsdale, NJ: Erlbaum.

Ekman, P. (1992). An argument for basic emotions. *Cognition and Emotion, 6,* 169–200.

Ekman, P. (1993). Facial expression and emotion. *American Psychologist, 48,* 384–392.

Ekman, P., & Davidson, R. J. (1993). Voluntary smiling changes regional brain activity. *Psychological Science, 4,* 342–345.

Ekman, P., Davidson, R. J., & Friesen, W. V. (1990). The Duchenne smile: Emotional expression and brain physiology II. *Journal of Personality and Social Psychology, 58,* 342–353.

Ekman, P., & Friesen, W. V. (1969). The repertoire of nonverbal behavior: Categories, origins, usage, and coding. *Semiotica, 1,* 49–98.

Ekman, P., & Friesen, W. V. (1971). Constants across cultures in the face and emotion. *Journal of Personality and Social Psychology, 17,* 124–129.

Ekman, P., Friesen, W. V., & Ellsworth, P. C. (1982a). *Emotion in the human face.* Cambridge, England: Cambridge University Press.

Ekman, P., Friesen, W. V., & Ellsworth, P. C. (1982b). What are the similarities and differences in facial behavior across cultures? In P. Ekman (Ed.), *Emotion in the human face.* Cambridge, England: Cambridge University Press.

Ekman, P., & O'Sullivan, M. (1991). Who can catch a liar? *American Psychologist, 46,* 913–920.

Ekman, P., O'Sullivan, M., Friesen, W. V., & Scherer, K. R. (1991). Face, voice and body in detecting deception. *Journal of Nonverbal Behavior, 15*, 125–135.

Ekman, P., Sorenson, E. R., & Friesen, W. V. (1969). Pan cultural elements in facial displays of emotions. *Science, 164*, 86–88.

Elfenbein, H. A., & Ambady, N. (2002). On the universality and cultural specificity of emotion recognition: A meta-analysis. *Psychological Bulletin, 128*, 203–235.

Elfenbein, H. A., & Ambady, N. (2003). Universal and cultural differences in recognizing emotions. *Current Directions in Psychological Science, 12*, 159–164.

Elkin, R. A., & Leippe, M. R. (1986). Physiological arousal, dissonance, and attitude change: Evidence for a dissonance-arousal link and a "don't remind me" effect. *Journal of Personality and Social Psychology, 51*, 55–65.

Elliot, A. J., & Devine, P. G. (1994). On the motivational nature of cognitive dissonance: Dissonance as psychological discomfort. *Journal of Personality and Social Psychology, 67*, 382–394.

Ellis, B. (1992). The evolution of sexual attraction: Evaluative mechanisms in women. In J. H. Barkow, L. Cosmides, & J. Tooby (Eds.), *The adapted mind* (pp. 267–288). New York: Oxford University Press.

Ellsworth, P. C. (1994). Sense, culture and sensibility. In S. Kitayama & H. R. Markus (Eds.), *Emotion and culture*. Washington, DC: American Psychological Association.

Ellsworth, P. C. (2009). Race salience in juror decision-making: Misconceptions, clarifications, and unanswered questions. *Behavioral Science & Law, 27*(4), 599–609.

Ellyson, S. L., & Dovidio, J. F. (Eds.). (1985). *Power, dominance, and nonverbal behavior*. New York: Springer-Verlag.

eMarketer Inc. (2011). Retrieved from www.emarketer.com

Emler, N. (1994). Gossip, reputation, and social adaptation. In R. F. Goodman & A. Ben-Ze'ev (Eds.), *Good gossip* (pp. 117–138). Wichita: University Press of Kansas.

Emmons, R. A., McCullough, M. E., & Tsang, J. (2003). Counting blessings versus burdens: An experimental investigation of gratitude and subjective well-being in daily life. *Journal of Personality and Social Psychology, 84*, 377–389.

English, T., & Chen, S. (2007). Culture and self-concept stability: Consistency across and within contexts among Asian- and European-Americans. *Journal of Personality and Social Psychology, 93*, 478–490.

Epel, E. S., Blackburn, E. H., Lin, J., Dhabhar, F. S., Adler, N. E., Morrow, J. D., et al. (2004). Accelerated telomere shortening in response to life stress. *Proceedings of the National Academy of Sciences of the USA. 101*, 17312–17315.

Epley, N. (2008, January 31). Rebate psychology. *New York Times*, p. A27.

Epley, N., & Gilovich, T. (2001). Putting adjustment back in the anchoring and adjustment heuristic: Divergent processing of self-generated and experimenter-provided anchors. *Psychological Science, 12*, 391–396.

Epley, N., & Gilovich, T. (2004). Are adjustments insufficient? *Personality and Social Psychology Bulletin, 30*, 447–460.

Epley, N., Mak, D., & Idson, L. (2006). Bonus or rebate? The impact of income framing on spending and saving. *Journal of Behavioral Decision Making, 19*, 213–227.

Epley, N., Savitsky, K., & Gilovich, T. (2002). Empathy neglect: Reconciling the spotlight effect and the correspondence bias. *Journal of Personality and Social Psychology, 83*, 300–312.

Epstein, S. (1991). Cognitive-experiential self-theory: An integrative theory of personality. In R. Curtis (Ed.), *The self with others:*

Convergences in psychoanalytic, social, and personality psychology (pp. 111–137). New York: Guilford Press.

Erber, R., & Tesser, A. (1994). Self-evaluation maintenance: A social psychological approach to interpersonal relationships. In R. Erber & R. Gilmour (Eds.), *Theoretical frameworks for personal relationships* (pp. 211–233). Hillsdale, NJ: Erlbaum.

Esser, J. K. (1998). Alive and well after 25 years: A review of groupthink research. *Organizational Behavior and Human Decision Processes, 73*, 116–141.

Esser, J. K., & Lindoerfer, J. S. (1989). Groupthink and the space shuttle *Challenger* accident: Toward a quantitative case analysis. *Journal of Behavioral Decision Making, 2*, 167–177.

Essock-Vitale, S. M., & McGuire, M. T. (1985). Women's lives viewed from an evolutionary perspective II. Patterns of helping. *Ethology and Sociobiology, 6*, 155–173.

Ettinger, R. F., Marino, C. J., Endler, N. S., Geller, S. H., & Natziuk, T. (1971). Effects of agreement and correctness on relative competence and conformity. *Journal of Personality and Social Psychology, 19*, 204–212.

Evans, J. St. B.T. (2007). *Hypothetical thinking: Dual processes in reasoning and judgment*. New York: Psychology Press.

Evans, R. (1980). *The making of social psychology*. New York: Gardner Press.

Fallon, A. (1990). Culture in the mirror: Sociocultural determinants of body image. In T. F. Cash & T. Pruzinsky (Eds.), *Body images: Development, deviance, and change* (pp. 80–109). New York: Guilford Press.

Fallon, A. E., & Rozin, P. (1985). Sex differences in perceptions of desirable body shape. *Journal of Abnormal Psychology, 94*, 102–105.

Farber, P. D., Khavari, K. A., & Douglass, F. M., IV. (1980). A factor analytic study of reasons for drinking: Empirical validation of positive and negative reinforcement dimensions. *Journal of Consulting and Clinical Psychology, 48*, 780–781.

Farley, F. (1986, May). The big *T* in personality. *Psychology Today*, pp. 44–52.

Fazio, R. H. (1995). Attitudes as object-evaluation associations: Determinants, consequences, and correlates of attitude accessibility. In R. E. Petty & J. A. Krosnick (Eds.), *Attitude strength: Antecedents and consequences* (pp. 247–282). Mahwah, NJ: Erlbaum.

Fazio, R. H., & Hilden, L. E. (2001). Emotional reactions to a seemingly prejudiced response: The role of automatically activated racial attitudes and motivation to control prejudiced reactions. *Personality and Social Psychology Bulletin, 27*, 538–549.

Fazio, R. H., Jackson, J. R., Dunton, B. C., & Williams, C. J. (1995). Variability in automatic activation as an unobtrusive measure of racial attitudes: A bona fide pipeline? *Journal of Personality and Social Psychology, 69*, 1013–1027.

Fazio, R. H., & Olson, M. A. (2003). Implicit measures in social cognition research: Their meaning and use. *Annual Review of Psychology, 54*, 297–327.

Fazio, R. H., Sanbonmatsu, D. M., Powell, M. C., & Kardes, F. R. (1986). On the automatic activation of attitudes. *Journal of Personality and Social Psychology, 50*, 229–238.

Fazio, R. H., & Williams, C. J. (1986). Attitude accessibility as a moderator of the attitude-perception and attitude-behavior relations: An investigation of the 1984 presidential election. *Journal of Personality and Social Psychology, 51*, 505–514.

Fazio, R. H., & Zanna, M. P. (1978). Attitudinal qualities relating to the strength of the attitude-behavior relationship. *Journal of Experimental Social Psychology, 14*, 398–408.

Fazio, R. H., Zanna, M., & Cooper, J. (1977). Dissonance and self-perception theory: An integrative view of each theory's proper domain of application. *Journal of Experimental Social Psychology, 13*, 464–479.

Fehr, B. (1994). Prototype-based assessment of laypeoples' views of love. *Personal Relationships, 1*, 309–331.

Fehr, B., & Russell, J. A. (1991). The concept of love viewed from a prototype perspective. *Journal of Personality & Social Psychology, 60*, 425–438.

Fehr, E., & Schmidt, K. M. (1999). A theory of fairness, competition, and cooperation. *Quarterly Journal of Economics, 114*, 817–868.

Feigenson, N., Park, J., & Salovey, P. (2001). The role of emotions in comparative negligence judgments. *Journal of Applied Social Psychology, 31*, 576–603.

Fein, S., & Spencer, S. (1997). Prejudice as a self-esteem maintenance: Affirming the self through derogating others. *Journal of Personality and Social Psychology, 73*, 31–44.

Feinberg, M., Willer, R., & Keltner, D. (2012). Flustered and faithful: Embarrassment as a signal of prosocial behavior. *Journal of Personality and Social Psychology, 102*, 81–97.

Feingold, A. (1984). Correlates of physical attractiveness among college students. *Journal of Social Psychology, 122*, 139–140.

Feingold, A. (1990). Gender differences in effects of physical attractiveness on romantic attraction: A comparison across five research paradigms. *Journal of Personality and Social Psychology, 59*, 981–993.

Feingold, A. (1992a). Gender differences in mate selection preferences: A test of the parental investment model. *Psychological Bulletin, 112*, 125–139.

Feingold, A. (1992b). Good-looking people are not what we think. *Psychological Bulletin, 111*, 304–341.

Felson, R. B. (1993). The somewhat social self: How others affect self-appraisals. In J. M. Suls (Ed.), *The self in social perspective* (pp. 1–26). Hillsdale, NJ: Erlbaum.

Fenigstein, A., Scheier, M. F., & Buss, A. H. (1975). Public and private self-consciousness: Assessment and theory. *Journal of Consulting and Clinical Psychology, 43*, 522–527.

Ferguson, M. J. (2008). On becoming ready to pursue a goal you don't know you have: Effects of nonconscious goals on evaluative readiness. *Journal of Personality and Social Psychology, 95*, 1268–1294.

Ferguson, M. J., & Bargh, J. A. (2008). Evaluative readiness: The motivational nature of automatic evaluation. In A. J. Elliott (Ed.), *Handbook of approach and avoidance motivation* (pp. 289–306). New York: Psychology Press.

Ferguson, M. J., Bargh, J. A., & Nayak, D. (2005). After-affects: How automatic evaluations influence the interpretation of subsequent, unrelated stimuli. *Journal of Experimental Social Psychology, 41*, 182–191.

Ferguson, M. J., & Hassin, R. R. (2007). On the automatic association between America and aggression in news-watchers. *Personality and Social Psychology Bulletin, 33*, 1632–1647.

Ferguson, M. J. & Zayas, V. (2009). Nonconscious evaluation. *Current Directions in Psychological Science, 18*, 362–366.

Festinger, L. (1954). A theory of social comparison processes. *Human Relations, 7*, 117–140.

Festinger, L. (1957). *A theory of cognitive dissonance*. Stanford, CA: Stanford University Press.

Festinger, L. (1964). *Conflict, decision, and dissonance*. Stanford, CA: Stanford University Press.

Festinger, L., & Carlsmith, J. M. (1959). Cognitive consequences of forced compliance. *Journal of Abnormal and Social Psychology, 47*, 382–389.

Festinger, L., Pepitone, A., & Newcomb, T. (1952). Some consequences of deindividuation in a group. *Journal of Abnormal and Social Psychology, 47*, 382–389.

Festinger, L., Schachter, S., & Back, K. (1950). *Social pressures in informal groups*. Stanford, CA: Stanford University Press.

Fiedler, K. (2000). Illusory correlations: A simple associative algorithm provides a convergent account of seemingly divergent paradigms. *Review of General Psychology, 4*, 25–58.

Fiedler, K. (2007). Construal level theory as an integrative framework for behavioral decision-making research and consumer psychology. *Journal of Consumer Psychology, 17*(2), 101–106.

Fiedler, K., & Freytag, P. (2004). Pseudocontingencies. *Journal of Personality and Social Psychology, 87*, 453–467.

Fiedler, K., Walther, E., & Nickel, S. (1999). Covariation-based attribution: On the ability to assess multiple covariations of an effect. *Personality and Social Psychology Bulletin, 25*, 607–622.

Finkel, E. J., & Eastwick, P. W. (2008). Speed-dating. *Current Directions in Psychological Science, 17*, 193–197.

Fishbach, A., Friedman, R. S., & Kruglanski, A. W. (2003). Leading us not unto temptation: Momentary allurements elicit overriding goal activation. *Journal of Personality and Social Psychology, 84*, 296–309.

Fishbach, A., & Shah, J. Y. (2006). Self control in action: Implicit dispositions toward goals and away from temptations. *Journal of Personality and Social Psychology, 90*, 820–832.

Fischhoff, B., Gonzalez, R., Lerner, J. S., & Small, D. A. (2005). Evolving judgments of terror risks: Foresight, hindsight, and emotion. *Journal of Applied Social Psychology, 23*, 124–139.

Fishbein, M., & Ajzen, I. (1975). *Belief, attitude, intention, and behavior: An introduction to theory and research*. Reading, MA: Addison-Wesley.

Fisher, H. E., Aron, A., & Brown, L. L. (2006). Romantic love: A mammalian brain system for mate choice. *Philosophical Transactions of the Royal British Society, 361*, 2173–2186.

Fiske, A. P. (1991). *Structures of social life: The four elementary forms of human relations*. New York: Free Press.

Fiske, A. P. (1992). The four elementary forms of sociality: Framework for a unified theory of social relations. *Psychological Review, 99*, 689–723.

Fiske, A. P., Kitayama, S., Markus, H. R., & Nisbett, R. E. (1998). The cultural matrix of social psychology. In D. T. Gilbert, S. T. Fiske, & G. Lindzey (Eds.), *Handbook of social psychology* (4th ed., pp. 915–981). New York: McGraw-Hill.

Fiske, S. T. (1993). Controlling other people: The impact of power on stereotyping. *American Psychologist, 48*(6), 621–628.

Fiske, S. T., & Taylor, S. E. (1991). *Social cognition*. New York: McGraw-Hill.

Fitzgerald, R., & Ellsworth, P. C. (1984). Due process vs. crime control: Death qualification and jury attitudes. *Law and Human Behavior, 8*, 31–52.

Fivush, R. (1989). Exploring sex differences in the emotional content of mother-child conversations about the past. *Sex Roles, 20*, 675–691.

Fivush, R. (1991). Gender and emotion in mother-child conversations about the past. *Journal of Narrative and Life History, 1*, 325–341.

Fivush, R. (1992). Gender differences in parent-child conversations about past emotions. *Sex Roles, 27*, 683–698.

Fleming, J. H., & Darley, J. M. (1989). Perceiving choice and constraint: The effects of contextual and behavioral cues on attitude attribution. *Journal of Personality and Social Psychology, 56*, 27–40.

Flynn, J. R. (1991). *Asian Americans: Achievement beyond IQ*. Hillsdale, NJ: Erlbaum.

Fong, C. (2001). Social preferences, self-interest, and the demand for redistribution. *Journal of Public Economics, 82*, 225–246.

Fong, G. T., Krantz, D. H., & Nisbett, R. E. (1986). The effects of statistical training on thinking about everyday problems. *Cognitive Psychology, 18*, 253–292.

Ford, C. S., & Beach, F. A. (1951). *Patterns of sexual behavior*. New York: Harper & Row.

Ford, T. E., & Kruglanski, A. (1995). Effects of epistemic motivations on the use of momentarily accessible constructs in social judgment. *Personality and Social Psychology Bulletin, 21*, 950–962.

Forgas, J. P. (1992). Mood and the perception of unusual people: Affective asymmetry in memory and social judgments. *European Journal of Social Psychology, 22*, 531–547.

Forgas, J. P. (1995). Mood and judgment: The affect infusion model (AIM). *Psychological Bulletin, 117*(1), 39–66.

Forgas, J. P. (1998a). Asking nicely? Mood effects on responding to more or less polite requests. *Personality and Social Psychology Bulletin, 24*, 173–185.

Forgas, J. P. (1998b). On being happy and mistaken: Mood effects on the fundamental attribution error. *Journal of Personality and Social Psychology, 75*(2), 318–331.

Forgas, J. P. (Ed.). (2000). *Feeling and thinking: The role of affect in social cognition*. New York: Cambridge University Press.

Forgas, J. P. (2003). Affective influences on attitudes and judgments. In R. J. Davidson, K. R. Scherer, & H. H. Goldsmith (Eds.), *Handbook of affective sciences* (pp. 596–618). New York: Oxford University Press.

Forgas, J. P., & Bower, G. H. (1987). Mood effects on person perception judgments. *Journal of Personality and Social Psychology, 53*, 53–60.

Forgas, J. P., & Moylan, S. (1987). After the movies: The effect of mood on social judgments. *Personality and Social Psychology Bulletin, 13*, 465–477.

Forster, J., & Strack, F. (1996). Influence of overt head movements on memory for valenced words: A case of conceptual-motor compatibility. *Journal of Personality and Social Psychology, 71*, 421–430.

Forsterling, F. (1985). Attributional retraining: A review. *Psychological Bulletin, 98*, 495–512.

Forsterling, F. (1989). Models of covariation and attribution: How do they relate to the analogy of analysis of variance? *Journal of Personality and Social Psychology, 57*, 615–625.

Fortune, J. L., & Newby-Clark, I. R. (2008). My friend is embarrassing me: Exploring the guilty by association effect. *Journal of Personality and Social Psychology, 95*, 1440–1449.

Foushee, M. C. (1984). Dyads and triads at 35,000 feet. *American Psychologist, 39*, 885–893.

Fowler, J., Baker, L. A., & Dawes, C. T. (2008). Genetic variation in political participation. *American Political Science Review, 102*, 233–248.

Fowler, J. H., & Christakis, N. A. (2010). Cooperative behavior cascades in social networks. *Proceedings of the National Academy of Sciences of the USA, 107*, 5334–5338.

Fox, J. A., & Pierce, G. L. (1987). *Supplementary homicide reports 1976–1986* [Machine-readable data file]. Ann Arbor, Michigan.

Fraley, R. C., & Spieker, S. J. (2003). Are infant attachment patterns continuously or categorically distributed? A taxometric analysis of strange situation behavior. *Developmental Psychology, 34*, 387–404.

Francis, D., & Meaney, M. J. (1999). Maternal care and the development of stress responses. *Development, 9*, 128–134.

Frank, M. G., Ekman, P., & Friesen, W. V. (1993). Behavioral markers and recognizability of the smile of enjoyment. *Journal of Personality and Social Psychology, 64*, 83–93.

Frank, M. G., & Gilovich, T. (1988). The dark side of self and social perception: Black uniforms and aggression in professional sports. *Journal of Personality and Social Psychology, 54*, 74–85.

Frank, M. G., & Gilovich, T. (1989). The effect of memory perspective on retrospective causal attributions. *Journal of Personality and Social Personality, 57*, 399–403.

Frank, R. H. (1988). *Passions within reason*. New York: Norton.

Frank, R. H., Gilovich, T., & Regan, D. T. (1993). Does studying economics inhibit cooperation? *Journal of Economic Perspectives, 7*, 159–171.

Frederick, S. (2005). Cognitive reflection and decision making. *Journal of Economic Perspectives, 19*, 24–42.

Fredrickson, B. L. (1998). What good are positive emotions? *Review of General Psychology, 2*, 300–319.

Fredrickson, B. L. (2001). The role of positive emotions in positive psychology: The broaden-and-build theory of positive emotions. *American Psychologist, 56*, 218–226.

Fredrickson, B. L., Cohn, M. A., Coffey, K. A., Pek, J., & Finkel, S. M. (2008). Open hearts build lives: Positive emotions, induced through loving-kindness meditation, build consequential personal resources. *Journal of Personality and Social Psychology, 95*, 1045–1062.

Fredrickson, B. L., & Kahneman, D. (1993). Duration neglect in retrospective evaluations of affective episodes. *Journal of Personality and Social Psychology, 65*, 45–55.

Fredrickson, B. L., & Roberts, T. (1997). Objectification theory: Toward understanding women's lived experiences and mental health risks. *Psychology of Women Quarterly, 21*, 173–206.

Freedman, J. L. (1965). Long-term behavioral effects of cognitive dissonance. *Journal of Experimental Social Psychology, 1*, 145–155.

Freedman, J. L., & Fraser, S. C. (1966). Compliance without pressure: The foot-in-the-door-technique. *Journal of Personality and Social Psychology, 4*, 195–203.

French, H. W. (2001, August 7). Hypothesis: A scientific gap. Conclusion: Japanese custom. *New York Times*, p. Al.

French, J., & Raven, B. (1959). The bases of social power. In D. Cartwright (Ed.), *Studies of social power* (pp. 150–167). Ann Arbor, MI: Institute for Social Research.

Frenkel, O. J., & Doob, A. N. (1976). Post-decision dissonance at the polling booth. *Canadian Journal of Behavioral Science, 8*, 347–350.

Friedman, R. S., & Forster, J. (2000). The effects of approach and avoidance motor actions on the elements of creative thought. *Journal of Personality and Social Psychology, 79*, 477–492.

Friese, M., Hofmann, W., & Schmitt, M. (2008). When and why do implicit measures predict behaviour? Empirical evidence for the moderating role of opportunity, motivation, and process reliance. *European Review of Social Psychology, 19*, 285–338.

Frieze, I. H., Olson, J. E., & Russell, J. (1991). Attractiveness and income for men and women in management. *Journal of Applied Social Psychology, 21*, 1039–1057.

Frijda, N. H., & Mesquita, B. (1994). The social roles and functions of emotions. In S. Kitayama & H. Markus (Eds.), *Emotion and culture: Empirical studies of mutual influence* (pp. 51–87). Washington, DC: American Psychological Association.

Frodi, A. (1975). The effect of exposure to weapons on aggressive behavior from a cross-cultural perspective. *International Journal of Psychology, 10*, 283–292.

Froming, W. J., Walker, G. R., & Lopyan, K. J. (1982). Public and private self-awareness: When personal attitudes conflict with societal expectations. *Journal of Experimental Social Psychology, 18*, 476–487.

Fujita, K., Henderson, M. D., Eng, J., Trope, Y., & Liberman, N. (2006). Spatial distance and mental construal of social events. *Psychological Science, 17*, 278–282.

Fultz, J., Batson, C. D., Fortenbach, V. A., McCarthy, P. M., & Varney, L. (1986). Social evaluation and the empathy-altruism hypothesis. *Journal of Personality and Social Psychology, 50*, 761–769.

Gable, S. L., Gonzaga, G., & Strachman, A. (2006). Will you be there for me when things go right? Social support for positive events. *Journal of Personality and Social Psychology, 91*, 904–917.

Gable, S. L., Reis, H. T., Impett, E. A., & Asher, E. R. (2004). What do you do when things go right? The intrapersonal and interpersonal benefits of sharing positive events. *Journal of Personality and Social Psychology, 87*, 228–245.

Gaertner, S. L., & Dovidio, J. F. (1977). The subtlety of white racism, arousal, and helping behavior. *Journal of Personality and Social Psychology, 35*, 691–707.

Gaertner, S. L., & Dovidio, J. F. (1986). The aversive form of racism. In J. F. Dovidio & S. L. Gaertner (Eds.), *Prejudice, discrimination, and racism* (pp. 61–89). Orlando, FL: Academic Press.

Gaertner, S. L., & Dovidio, J. F. (2000). Reducing intergroup bias: The common ingroup identity model. Philadelphia, PA: Psychology Press.

Gaertner, S. L., & Dovidio, J. F. (2009). A common intergroup identity: A categorization-based approach for reducing intergroup bias. In T.D. Nelson (Ed.), *Handbook of prejudice, stereotyping, and discrimination* (pp. 489–505). New York: Psychology Press.

Gaertner, S. L., Mann, J., Dovidio, J. F., Murrell, A., & Pomare, M. (1990). How does cooperation reduce intergroup bias? *Journal of Personality and Social Psychology, 59*, 692–704.

Gaertner, S. L., Murrell, A., & Dovidio, J. F. (1989). Reducing intergroup bias: The benefits of recategorization. *Journal of Personality and Social Psychology, 57*, 239–249.

Gailliot, M. T., Baumeister, R. F., DeWall, C. N., Maner, J. K., Plant, E. A., Tice, D. M., et al. (2007). Self-control relies on glucose as a limited energy source: Willpower is more than a metaphor. *Journal of Personality and Social Psychology, 92*, 325–336.

Galinsky, A. D., Stone, J., & Cooper, J. (2000). The reinstatement of dissonance and psychological discomfort following failed affirmations. *European Journal of Social Psychology, 30*, 123–147.

Gallo, L. C., Bogart, L. M., Vranceanu, A., & Matthews, K. A. (2005). Socioeconomic status, resources, psychological experiences, and emotional responses: A test of the reserve capacity model. *Journal of Personality and Social Psychology, 88*(2), 386–399.

Galton, F. (1878). Composite portraits. *Journal of the Anthropological Institute of Great Britain and Ireland, 8*, 132–142.

Gangestad, S. W., Simpson, J. A., Cousins, A. J., Garver-Apgar, C. E., & Christensen, P. N. (2004). Women's preferences for male behavioral displays change across the menstrual cycle. *Psychological Science, 15*, 203–207.

Gangestad, S. W., & Snyder, M. (2000). Self-monitoring: Appraisal and reappraisal. *Psychological Bulletin, 126*, 530–555.

Gangestad, S. W., & Thornhill, R. (1998). Menstrual cycle variation in women's preference for the scent of symmetrical men. *Proceedings of the Royal Society of London B, 265*, 727–733.

Garcia-Marques, L., & Hamilton, D. L. (1996). Resolving the apparent discrepancy between the incongruency effect and the expectancy-based illusory correlation effect: The TRAP mode. *Journal of Personality and Social Psychology, 71*, 845–860.

Gardner, W. L., Gabriel, S., & Lee, A. Y. (1999). "I" value freedom, but "we" value relationships: Self-construal priming mirrors cultural differences in judgment. *Psychological Science, 10*, 321–326.

Garner, D. M., Garfinkel, P. E., Schwartz, D., & Thompson, M. (1980). Cultural expectations of thinness in women. *Psychological Reports, 47*, 483–491.

Garofalo, J. (1981). Crime and the mass media: A selective review of research. *Journal of Research in Crime and Delinquency, 18*, 319–350.

Garrett, B. (2008). Judging innocence. *Columbia Law Review, 108*, 55–142.

Gates, G. S. (1924). The effects of an audience upon performance. *Journal of Abnormal and Social Psychology, 18*, 334–342.

Gawronski, B. (2003). Implicational schemata and the correspondence bias: On the diagnostic value of situationally constrained behavior. *Journal of Personality and Social Psychology, 84*, 1154–1171.

Gawronski, B., Cunningham, W. A., LeBel, E. P., & Deutsch, R. (2010). Attentional influences on affective priming: Does categorization influence spontaneous evaluations of multiply categorizable objects? *Cognition and Emotion, 24*, 1008–1025.

Gawronski, B., & Payne, B. K. (Eds.). (2010). *Handbook of implicit social cognition: Measurement, theory, and applications.* New York: Guilford Press.

Gawronski, B., Walther, E., & Blank, H. (2005). Cognitive consistency and the formation of interpersonal attitudes: Cognitive balance affects the encoding of social information. *Journal of Experimental Social Psychology, 41*, 618–626.

Geen, R. G. (1989). Alternative conceptions of social facilitation. In P. B. Paulus (Ed.), *Psychology of group influence* (2nd ed., pp. 15–51). Hillsdale, NJ: Erlbaum.

Geen, R. G. (1998). Aggression and antisocial behavior. In D. T. Gilbert, S. T. Fiske, & G. Lindzey (Eds.), *The handbook of social psychology* (4th ed., Vol. 2, pp. 317–356). New York: McGraw-Hill.

Geeraert, N. Y., Yzerbyt, V. Y., Corneille, O., & Wigboldus, D. (2004). The return of dispositionalism: On the linguistic consequences of dispositional suppression. *Journal of Experimental Social Psychology, 40*, 264–272.

Gelfand, M. J., Raver, J. L., Nishii, L., Leslie, L. M., Lun, J., Lim, B. C., . . . , & S. Yamaguchi. (2011). Differences between tight and loose cultures: A 33-nation study. *Science, 332*, 1100–1104.

Gentile, D. A. (2009). Pathological video game use among youth 8 to 18: A national study. *Psychological Science, 20*, 594–602.

Gerard, H. B., Wilhelmy, R. A., & Conolley, E. S. (1968). Conformity and group size. *Journal of Personality and Social Psychology, 8*, 79–82.

Gerber, A. S., & Rogers, T. (2009). Descriptive social norms and motivation to vote: Everyone's voting and so should you. *Journal of Politics, 71*, 178–191.

Gerbner, G., Gross, L., Morgan, M., & Signorielli, N. (1980). The "mainstreaming" of America: Violence profile no. 11. *Journal of Communication, 30*, 10–29.

Gerbner, G., Gross, L., Morgan, M., & Signorielli, N. (1986). Living with television: The dynamics of the cultivation process. In J. Bryant & D. Zillman (Eds.), *Perspectives on media effects* (pp. 17–40). Hillsdale, NJ: Erlbaum.

Gibbons, F. X. (1978). Sexual standards and reactions to pornography: Enhancing behavioral consistency through self-focused attention. *Journal of Personality and Social Psychology, 36*, 976–987.

Gigerenzer, G. (1991). How to make cognitive illusions disappear: Beyond "heuristics and biases." In W. Stroche & M. Hewstone (Eds.), *European review of social psychology* (Vol. 2, pp. 83–115). Chichester, England: Wiley.

Gilbert, D. T. (1989). Thinking lightly about others: Automatic components of the social inference process. In J. S. Uleman & J. A. Bargh (Eds.), *Unintended thought*. New York: Guilford Press.

Gilbert, D. T. (2002). Inferential correction. In T. Gilovich, D. W. Griffin, & D. Kahneman (Eds.), *Heuristics and biases: The psychology of intuitive judgment*. New York: Cambridge University Press.

Gilbert, D. T., Brown, R. P., Pinel, E. E., & Wilson, T. D. (2000). The illusion of external agency. *Journal of Personality and Social Psychology, 79,* 690–700.

Gilbert, D. T., & Jones, E. E. (1986). Perceiver-induced constraint: Interpretations of self-generated reality. *Journal of Personality and Social Psychology, 50,* 269–280.

Gilbert, D. T., & Malone, P. S. (1995). The correspondence bias. *Psychological Bulletin, 117,* 21–38.

Gilbert, D. T., Pinel, E. C., Wilson, T. D., Blumberg, S. J., & Wheatley, T. (1998). Immune neglect: A source of durability bias in affective forecasting. *Journal of Personality and Social Psychology, 75,* 617–638.

Gilbert, S. J. (1981). Another look at the Milgram obedience studies: The role of the gradated series of shocks. *Personality and Social Psychology Bulletin, 4,* 690–695.

Gilmour, T. M., & Reid, D. W. (1979). Locus of control and causal attribution for positive and negative outcomes on university examinations. *Journal of Research in Personality, 13,* 154–160.

Gilovich, T. (1981). Seeing the past in the present: The effect of associations to familiar events on judgments and decisions. *Journal of Personality and Social Psychology, 40,* 797–808.

Gilovich, T. (1983). Biased evaluation and persistence in gambling. *Journal of Personality and Social Psychology, 44,* 1110–1126.

Gilovich, T. (1991). *How we know what isn't so: The fallibility of human reason in everyday life.* New York: Free Press.

Gilovich, T., Griffin, D. W., & Kahneman, D. (Eds.). (2002). *Heuristics and biases: The psychology of intuitive judgment.* New York: Cambridge University Press.

Gilovich, T., Kruger, J., & Medvec, V. H. (2002). The spotlight effect revisited: Overestimating the manifest variability in our actions and appearance. *Journal of Experimental Social Psychology, 38,* 93–99.

Gilovich, T., Medvec, V. H., & Savitsky, K. (2000). The spotlight effect in social judgment: An egocentric bias in estimates of the salience of one's own actions and appearance. *Journal of Personality and Social Psychology, 79,* 211–222.

Gilovich, T., & Savitsky, K. (2002). Like goes with like: The role of representativeness in erroneous and pseudo-scientific beliefs. In T. Gilovich, D. W. Griffin, & D. Kahneman (Eds.), *Heuristics and biases: The psychology of intuitive judgment* (pp. 617–624). New York: Cambridge University Press.

Ginosar, Z., & Trope, Y. (1980). The effects of base rates and individuating information on judgments about another person. *Journal of Experimental Social Psychology, 16,* 228–242.

Givens, D. B. (1983). *Love signals: How to attract a mate.* New York: Crown.

Gladwell, M. (2011). Foreword to L. Ross & R. E. Nisbett, *The person and the situation: Perspectives of social psychology* (2nd. ed.). London: Pinter & Martin.

Glanz, J., & Schwartz, J. (2003, September 26). Dogged engineer's effort to assess shuttle damage. *New York Times,* p. A1.

Glaser, J. (in press). Suspect race: Psychological bases and policy implications of racial profiling. Oxford University Press.

Glasman, L. R., & Albarracin, D. (2006). Forming attitudes that predict future behavior: A meta-analysis of the attitude-behavior relation. *Psychological Bulletin, 132,* 778–822.

Glenn, N. D. (1991). The recent trend in marital success in the United States. *Journal of Marriage and the Family, 53,* 261–270.

Glick, P., & Fiske, S. T. (2001a). Ambivalent sexism. In M. P. Zanna (Ed.), *Advances in experimental social psychology* (Vol. 33, pp. 115–188). Thousand Oaks, CA: Academic Press.

Glick, P., & Fiske, S. T. (2001b). An ambivalent alliance: Hostile and benevolent sexism as complementary justifications of gender inequality. *American Psychologist, 56,* 109–118.

Glied, S., & Neidell, M. (2008). The economic value of teeth. National Bureau of Economic Research Working Paper 13879.

Goethals, G. R., Cooper, J., & Naficy, A. (1979). Role of foreseen, foreseeable, and unforeseeable behavioral consequences in the arousal of cognitive dissonance. *Journal of Personality and Social Psychology, 37,* 1179–1185.

Goetz, J., Keltner, D., & Simon-Thomas, E. (2010). Compassion: An evolutionary analysis and empirical review. *Psychological Bulletin, 136*(3), 351–374.

Goffman, E. (1959). *The presentation of self in everyday life.* Garden City, NY: Doubleday.

Goffman, E. (1961). *Encounters: Two studies in the sociology of interaction.* New York: Penguin.

Goffman, E. (1966). *Behavior in public places.* New York: Free Press.

Goffman, E. (1967). *Interaction ritual: Essays on face-to-face behavior.* New York: Doubleday.

Goldman, W., & Lewis, P. (1977). Beautiful is good: Evidence that the physically attractive are more socially skillful. *Journal of Experimental Social Psychology, 13,* 125–130.

Goldstein, N. J., Cialdini, R. B., & Griskevicius, V. (2008). A room with a viewpoint: Using social norms to motivate environmental conservation in hotels. *Journal of Consumer Research, 35,* 472–482.

Goleman, D. (1985). *Vital lies, simple truths: The psychology of self-deception.* New York: Simon & Schuster.

Gologor, E. (1977). Group polarization in a non-risk-taking culture. *Journal of Cross-Cultural Psychology, 8,* 331–346.

Gonzaga, G. C., Keltner, D., Londahl, E. A., & Smith, M. (2001). Love and the commitment problem in romantic relations and friendship. *Journal of Personality and Social Psychology, 81,* 247–262.

Gonzaga, G. C., Keltner, D., & Ward, D. (2008). Power in mixed-sex interactions. *Cognition and Emotion, 22,* 1555–1568.

Gonzaga, G. C., Turner, R. A., Keltner, D., Campos, B., & Altemus, M. (2006). Romantic love and sexual desire in close bonds. *Emotion, 6,* 163–179.

Gonzalez, C., Dana, J., Koshino, H., & Just, M. (2005). The framing effect and risky decisions: Examining cognitive functions with fMRI. *Journal of Economic Psychology, 26,* 1–20.

Gonzalez, R., & Griffin, D. (1997). On the statistics of interdependence: Treating dyadic data with respect. In S. Duck (Ed.), *Handbook of personal relationships: Theory, research, and interventions* (2nd ed., pp. 271–302). Chichester, England: Wiley.

Good, C., Aronson, J., & Inzlicht, M. (2003). Improving adolescents' standardized test performance: An intervention to reduce the effects of stereotype threat. *Applied Developmental Psychology, 24,* 645–662.

Goodwin, S. A., Gubin, A., Fiske, S. T., & Yzerbyt, V. Y. (2000). Power can bias impression processes: Stereotyping subordinates by default and by design. *Group Processes and Intergroup Relations, 3,* 227–256.

Gosling, S. D., Ko, S. J., Mannarelli, T., & Morris, M. E. (2002). A room with a cue: Judgments of personality based on offices and bedrooms. *Journal of Personality and Social Psychology, 82,* 379–398.

Gottman, J. M. (1993). *Why marriages succeed or fail.* New York: Simon & Schuster.

Gottman, J. M., & Levenson, R. W. (1992). Marital processes predictive of later dissolution: Behavior, physiology, and health. *Journal of Personality and Social Psychology, 63,* 221–233.

Gottman, J. M., & Levenson, R. W. (1999). Rebound from marital conflict and divorce prediction. *Family Processes, 38,* 287–292.

Gottman, J. M., & Levenson, R. W. (2000). The timing of divorce: Predicting when a couple will divorce over a 14-year period. *Journal of Marriage and the Family, 62,* 737–745.

Gouldner, A. W. (1960). The norm of reciprocity: A preliminary statement. *American Sociological Review, 25,* 161–178.

Gourevitch, P. (1998). *We wish to inform you that tomorrow we will be killed with our families.* New York: Picador Press.

Grabe, S., Ward, L. M., & Hyde, J. S. (2008). The role of the media in body image concern among women: A meta-analysis of experimental and correlational studies. *Psychological Bulletin, 134,* 460–476.

Green, D. P., Wong, J., & Strolovitch, D. (1996). *The effects of demographic change on hate crime.* New Haven: Institution for Social and Policy Studies, Yale University.

Greenberg, J., Eloul, L., Markus, H. R., & Tsai, J. (2012). *"Neither East nor West": Conformity and self-enhancement in the Muslim Middle East.* Stanford, CA: Stanford University.

Greenberg, J., Pyszczynski, T., & Solomon, S. (1982). The self-serving attributional bias: Beyond self-presentation. *Journal of Experimental Social Psychology, 18,* 56–67.

Greenberg, J., Pyszczynski, T., Solomon, S., Rosenblatt, A., Veeder, M., Kirkland, S., et al. (1990). Evidence for terror management theory II: The effects of mortality salience on reactions to those who threaten or bolster the cultural worldview. *Journal of Personality and Social Psychology, 58,* 308–318.

Greenberg, J., Simon, L., Porteus, J., Pyszczynski, T., & Solomon, S. (1995). Evidence of a terror management function of cultural icons: The effects of mortality salience on the inappropriate use of cherished cultural symbols. *Personality and Social Psychology Bulletin, 21,* 1221–1228.

Greene, D., Sternberg, B., & Lepper, M. R. (1976). Overjustification in a token economy. *Journal of Personality and Social Psychology, 34,* 1219–1234.

Greene, J. D., & Haidt, J. (2002). How (and where) does moral judgment work? *Trends in Cognitive Sciences, 6,* 517–523.

Greene, J. D., Sommerville, R. B., Nystrom, L. E., Darley, J. M., & Cohen, J. D. (2001). An fMRI investigation of emotional engagement in moral judgment. *Science, 293,* 2105–2108.

Greenspan, A. (1996). The challenge of central banking in a democratic society. Speech given to the American Enterprise Institute, December 5.

Greenwald, A. G. (1980). The totalitarian ego: Fabrication and revision of personal history. *American Psychologist, 35,* 603–618.

Greenwald, A. G., & Banaji, M. R. (1995). Implicit social cognition: Attitudes, self-esteem, and stereotypes. *Psychological Review, 102,* 4–27.

Greenwald, A. G., Klinger, M. R., & Liu, T. J. (1989). Unconscious processing of dichotically masked words. *Memory and Cognition, 17,* 35–47.

Greenwald, A. G., McGhee, D. E., & Schwartz, D. L. K. (1998). Measuring individual differences in implicit cognition: The Implicit Association Test. *Journal of Personality and Social Psychology, 74,* 1464–1480.

Gresham, L. G., & Shimp, T. A. (1985). Attitude toward advertisement and brand attitude: A classical conditioning perspective. *Journal of Advertising, 14,* 10–17.

Greve, F. (2009, May 23). America's poor are its most generous. *The Seattle Times.* Retrieved from http://seattletimes.nwsource.com

Grice, H. P. (1975). *Logic and conversation.* New York: Academic Press.

Gries, P. H., & Peng, K. (2002). Culture clash? Apologies East and West. *Journal of Contemporary China, 11,* 173–178.

Griffin, D., & Tversky, A. (1992). The weighing of evidence and the determinants of confidence. *Cognitive Psychology, 24,* 411–435.

Griffitt, W., & Veitch, R. (1971). Hot and crowded: Influences of population density and temperature on interpersonal affective behavior. *Journal of Personality and Social Psychology, 17,* 92–98.

Griffitt, W., & Veitch, R. (1974). Preacquaintance attitude similarity and attraction revisited: Ten days in a fall-out shelter. *Sociometry, 37,* 163–173.

Groff, B. D., Baron, R. S., & Moore, D. L. (1983). Distraction, attentional conflict, and drivelike behavior. *Journal of Experimental Social Psychology, 19,* 359–380.

Gross, J. J. (1998). Antecedent-and-response-focused emotion regulation: Divergent consequences for experience, expression, and physiology. *Journal of Personality and Social Psychology, 74,* 224–237.

Grush, J. E. (1980). Impact of candidate expenditures, regionality, and prior outcomes on the 1976 presidential primaries. *Journal of Personality and Social Psychology, 38,* 337–347.

Guerin, B. (1993). *Social facilitation.* New York: Cambridge University Press.

Guilbault, R. L., Bryant, F. B., Brockway, J. H., & Posavac, E. J. (2004). A meta-analysis of research on hindsight bias. *Basic and Applied Social Psychology, 26,* 103–117.

Guinote, A. (2007). Power and goal pursuit. *Personality and Social Psychology Bulletin, 33*(8), 1076–1087.

Guinote, A., Judd, C. M., & Brauer, M. (2002). Effects of power on perceived and objective group variability: Evidence that more powerful groups are more powerful. *Journal of Personality and Social Psychology, 82,* 708–721.

Gunnell, J., & Ceci, S. J. (2010). When emotionality trumps reason: A study of individual processing style and juror bias. *Behavioral Science and the Law, 28,* 850–877.

Gustavsson, L., Johnsson, J. I., & Uller, T. (2008). Mixed support for sexual selection theories of mate preferences in the Swedish population. *Evolutionary Psychology, 6*(4), 575–585.

Haberstroh, S., Oyserman, D., Schwarz, N., Kiihnen, U., & Ji, L.-J. (2002). Is the interdependent self more sensitive to question context than the independent self? Self-construal and the observation of conversational norms. *Journal of Experimental Social Psychology, 38,* 323–329.

Haddock, G., Zanna, M. P., & Esses, V. M. (1993). Assessing the structure of prejudicial attitudes: The case of attitudes toward homosexuals. *Journal of Personality and Social Psychology, 65,* 1105–1118.

Haidt, J. (2001). The emotional dog and its rational tail: A social intuitionist approach to moral judgment. *Psychological Review, 108,* 814–834.

Haidt, J. (2003). The moral emotions. In R. J. Davidson, K. R. Scherer, & H. H. Goldsmith (Eds.), *Handbook of affective sciences* (pp. 852–870). New York: Oxford University Press.

Haidt, J., & Keltner, D. (1999). Culture and facial expression: Open-ended methods find more faces and a gradient of universality. *Cognition and Emotion, 13,* 225–266.

Haidt, J., Koller, S. H., & Dias, M. G. (1993). Affect, culture, and morality, or Is it wrong to eat your dog? *Journal of Personality and Social Psychology, 65,* 613–628.

Halberstadt, J. B., & Rhodes, G. (2000). The attractivenes of non-face averages: Implications for an evolutionary explanation of the attractiveness of average faces. *Psychological Science, 11,* 285–289.

Halberstadt, J. B., & Rhodes, G. (2003). It's not just average faces that are attractive: Computer-manipulated averageness makes birds, fish, and automobiles attractive. *Psychonomic Bulletin and Review, 10,* 149–156.

Halberstam, D. (1969). *The best and the brightest.* New York: Random House.

Hall, J. A. (1984). *Nonverbal gender differences: Accuracy of communication and expressive style.* Baltimore, MD: Johns Hopkins University Press.

Hamermesh, D., & Biddle, J. (1994). Beauty and the labor market. *American Economic Review, 84,* 1174–1194.

Hamill, R., Wilson, T. D., & Nisbett, R. E. (1980). Insensitivity to sample bias: Generalizing from atypical cases. *Journal of Personality and Social Psychology, 39,* 578–589.

Hamilton, D. L., & Gifford, R. K. (1976). Illusory correlation in interpersonal perception: A cognitive basis of stereotypic judgments. *Journal of Experimental Social Psychology, 12,* 392–407.

Hamilton, D. L., & Sherman, S. J. (1989). Illusory correlations: Implications for stereotype theory and research. In D. Bar-Tal, C. F. Graumann, A. W. Kruglanski, & W. Stroebe (Eds.), *Stereotypes and prejudice: Changing conceptions* (pp. 59–82). New York: Springer-Verlag.

Hamilton, D. L., Stroessner, S., & Mackie, D. M. (1993). The influence of affect on stereotyping: The case of illusory correlations. In D. M. Mackie & D. L. Hamilton (Eds.), *Affect, cognition, and stereotyping: Interactive processes in group perception* (pp. 39–61). San Diego, CA: Academic Press.

Hamilton, D. L., & Trolier, T. K. (1986). Stereotypes and stereotyping: An overview of the cognitive approach. In J. F. Dovidio & S. L. Gaertner (Eds.), *Prejudice, discrimination and racism* (pp. 127–163). Orlando, FL: Academic Press.

Hamilton, D. L., & Zanna, M. P. (1974). Context effects in impression formation: Changes in connotative meaning. *Journal of Personality and Social Psychology, 29,* 649–654.

Hamilton, W. D. (1964). The genetical evolution of social behavior. *Journal of Theoretical Biology, 7,* 1–52.

Hampden-Turner, C., & Trompenaars, A. (1993). *The seven cultures of capitalism: Value systems for creating wealth in the United States, Japan, Germany, France, Britain, Sweden, and the Netherlands.* New York: Doubleday.

Han, S., & Shavitt, S. (1994). Persuasion and culture: Advertising appeals in individualistic and collectivistic societies. *Journal of Experimental Social Psychology, 30,* 326–350.

Haney, C. (1984). On the selection of capital juries: The biasing effects of the death-qualification process. *Law and Human Behavior, 8,* 121–132.

Haney, C., Banks, C., & Zimbardo, P. G. (1973). Interpersonal dynamics in a simulated prison. *International Journal of Criminology and Penology, 1,* 69–97.

Haney, C., Hurtado, A., & Vega, L. (1994). "Modern" death qualification: New data on its biasing effects. *Law and Human Behavior, 18,* 619–633.

Haney, C., & Logan, D. D. (1994). Broken promise: The Supreme Court's response to social science research on capital punishment. *Journal of Social Issues, 50,* 75–101.

Hanna, J. (1989, September 25). Sexual abandon: The condom is unpopular on the campus. *Maclean's,* p. 48.

Hans, V. P. (2000). *Business on trial: The civil jury and corporate responsibility.* New Haven, CT: Yale University Press.

Hansen, C. H., & Hansen, R. D. (1988). Finding the face in a crowd: An anger superiority effect. *Journal of Personality and Social Psychology, 54,* 917–924.

Harackiewicz, J. M., Manderlink, G., & Sansone, C. (1984). Rewarding pinball wizardry: Effects of evaluation and cue value on intrinsic interest. *Journal of Personality and Social Psychology, 47,* 287–300.

Harari, H., Mohr, D., & Hosey, K. (1980). Faculty helpfulness to students: A comparison of compliance techniques. *Personality and Social Psychology Bulletin, 6,* 373–377.

Harber, K. (1998). Feedback to minorities: Evidence of a positive bias. *Journal of Personality and Social Psychology, 74,* 622–628.

Hardy, C. L., & van Vugt, M. (2006). Nice guys finish first: The competitive altruism hypothesis. *Personality and Social Psychology Bulletin, 32,* 1402–1413.

Hare, R. D. (1991). *The Hare Psychopathy Checklist—Revised.* Toronto, Ontario: Multi-Health Systems.

Hare, R. D. (1993). *Without conscience: The disturbing world of the psychopaths among us.* New York: Simon & Schuster/Pocket.

Harlow, H. F. (1959). Love in infant monkeys. *Scientific American, 200,* 68–86.

Harmon, A. (Dec 26, 2011). Navigating love and autism. *New York Times.*

Harmon-Jones, E. (2000). Cognitive dissonance and experienced negative affect: Evidence that dissonance increases experienced negative affect even in the absence of aversive consequences. *Personality and Social Psychology Bulletin, 26,* 1490–1501.

Harmon-Jones, E., Brehm, J. W., Greenberg, J., Simon, L., & Nelson, D. E. (1996). Evidence that the production of aversive consequences is not necessary to create cognitive dissonance. *Journal of Personality and Social Psychology, 70,* 5–16.

Harris, C. R. (2001). Cardiovascular responses of embarassment and effects of emotional suppression in a social setting. *Journal of Personality and Social Psychology, 81,* 886–897.

Harris, M. B. (1974). Mediators between frustration and aggression in a field experiment. *Journal of Experimental Social Psychology, 10,* 561–571.

Harris, R. J., Benson, S. M., & Hall, C. L. (1975). The effects of confession on altruism. *Journal of Social Psychology, 96,* 187–192.

Harrison, A. A., & Saeed, L. (1977). Let's make a deal: An analysis of revelations and stipulations in lonely hearts advertisements. *Journal of Personality and Social Psychology, 35,* 257–264.

Hart, D., Lucca-Irizarry, N., & Damon, W. (1986). The development of self-understanding in Puerto Rico and the United States. *Journal of Early Adolescence, 6,* 293–304.

Hass, R. G., & Linder, D. E. (1972). Counterargument availability and the effects of message structure on persuasion. *Journal of Personality and Social Psychology, 23,* 219–233.

Hassin, R. R., Ferguson, M. J., Shidlovsky, D., & Gross, T. (2007). Waved by invisible flags: The effects of subliminal exposure to flags on political thought and behavior. *Proceedings of the National Academy of Sciences of the USA, 104,* 19757–19761.

Hastie, R. (1981). Schematic principles in human memory. In E. T. Higgins, C. P. Herman, & M. P. Zanna (Eds.), *Social cognition: The Ontario Symposium* (Vol. 1, pp. 39–88). Hillsdale, NJ: Erlbaum.

Hastie, R., Penrod, S. D., & Pennington, N. (1983). *Inside the jury.* Cambridge, MA: Harvard University Press.

Hatfield, E., Cacioppo, J. T., & Rapson, R. L. (1994). *Emotional contagion.* New York: Cambridge University Press.

Haugtvedt, C. P., & Petty, R. E. (1992). Personality and persuasion: Need for cognition moderates the persistence and resistance of attitude changes. *Journal of Personality and Social Psychology, 63,* 308–319.

Hauser, C. (2004, May 6). Many Iraqis are skeptical of Bush TV appeal. *New York Times,* p. 13.

Havas, D.A., Glenberg, A. M., Gutowski, K. A., Lucarelli, M. J., & Davidson, R. J. (2010). Cosmetic use of botulinum toxin-A affects processing of emotional language. *Psychological Science, 21,* 895–900.

Hazan, C., & Shaver, P. (1987). Romantic love conceptualized as an attachment process. *Journal of Personality and Social Psychology, 52,* 511–524.

Hazan, C., & Shaver, P. (1994). Attachment as an organizational framework for research on close relationships. *Psychological Inquiry, 5,* 1–22.

Heatherton, T. F., Macrae, C. N., & Kelley, W. M. (2004). What the social brain sciences can tell us about the self. *Current Directions in Psychological Science, 13,* 190–193.

Heatherton, T. F., & Polivy, J. (1991). Development and validation of a scale for measuring state self-esteem. *Journal of Personality and Social Psychology, 60,* 895–910.

Heatherton, T. F., Wyland, C. L., McCrae, C. N., Demos, K. E., Denny, B. T., & Keley, W. M. (2006). Medial prefrontal activity differentiates self from close others. *Social Cognitive Affective Neuroscience, 1,* 18–25.

Hebl, M. R., Foster, J. B., Mannix, L. M., & Dovidio, J. F. (2002). Formal and interpersonal discrimination: A field study of bias toward homosexual applicants. *Personality and Social Psychology Bulletin, 28,* 815–825.

Hebl, M., & Heatherton, T. F. (1997). The stigma of obesity in women: The difference is black and white. *Personality and Social Psychology Bulletin, 24,* 417–426.

Hedden, T., Ji, L., Jing, Q., Jiao, S., Yao, C., Nisbett, R. E., et al. (2000). *Culture and age differences in recognition memory for social dimensions.* Paper presented at the Cognitive Aging Conference, Atlanta, GA.

Hedden, T., Ketay, S., Aron, A., Markus, H. R., & Gabrieli, J. D. E. (2008). Cultural influences on neural substrates of attentional control. *Psychological Science, 19,* 12–17.

Heider, F. (1946). Attitudes and cognitive organization. *Journal of Psychology, 21,* 107–112.

Heider, F. (1958). *The psychology of interpersonal relations.* New York: Wiley.

Heine, S. J. (2005). Constructing good selves in Japan and North America. In *Culture and social behavior: The Tenth Ontario Symposium* (pp. 115–143). Hillsdale, NJ: Erlbaum.

Heine, S. J., Kitayama, S., Lehman, D. R., Takata, T., Ide, E., Leung, C., & Matsumoto, H. (2001). Divergent consequences of success and failure in Japan and North America: An investigation of self-improving motivations and malleable selves. *Journal of Personality and Social Psychology, 81,* 599–615.

Heine, S. J., & Lehman, D. R. (1997). Culture, dissonance, and self-affirmation. *Personality and Social Psychology Bulletin, 23,* 389–400.

Heine, S. J., & Lehman, D. R. (2003). Move the body, change the self: Acculturative effects on the self-concept. In M. Schaller & C. S. Crandall (Eds.), *Psychological foundations of culture* (pp. 305–331). Mahwah, NJ: Erlbaum.

Heine, S. J., Lehman, D. R., Markus, H. R., & Kitayama, S. (1999). Is there a universal need for positive self-regard? *Psychological Review, 106,* 766–794.

Helgeson, V. S., & Mickelson, K. D. (1995). Motives for social comparison. *Personality and Social Psychology Bulletin, 21,* 1200–1209.

Henderson, V. L., & Dweck, C. S. (1990). Achievement and motivation in adolescence: A new model and data. In S. Feldman & G. Elliott (Eds.), *At the threshold: The developing adolescent.* Cambridge, MA: Harvard University Press.

Henley, N. M., & LaFrance, M. (1984). Gender as culture: Difference and dominance in nonverbal behavior. In A. Wolfgang (Ed.), *Nonverbal behavior: Perspectives, applications, intercultural insights.* Lewiston, NY: C. J. Hogrefe.

Henningsen, D. D., Henningsen, M. L. M., Eden, J., & Cruz, M. G. (2006). Examining the symptoms of groupthink and retrospective sensemaking. *Small Group Research, 37,* 36–64.

Henrich, J., & Boyd, R. (1998). The evolution of conformist transmission and the emergence of between-group differences. *Evolution and Human Behavior, 19,* 215–242.

Henrich, J., Boyd, R., Bowles, S., Camerer, C., Gintis, H., McElreath, R., et al. (2001). In search of *Homo economicus:* Experiments in 15 small-scale societies. *American Economic Review, 91*(2), 73–79.

Henrich, J., Heine, S. J., & Norenzayan, A. (2010). The weirdest people in the world? *Behavioral and Brain Sciences, 33,* 61–83.

Hepworth, J. T., & West, S. G. (1988). Lynchings and the economy: A time-series reanalysis of Hovland and Sears (1940). *Journal of Personality and Social Psychology, 55,* 239–247.

Herek, G. M. (1998). *Stigma and sexual orientation: Understanding prejudice against lesbians, gay men, and bisexuals.* Thousand Oaks, CA: Sage.

Herr, P. M. (1986). Consequences of priming: Judgment and behavior. *Journal of Personality and Social Psychology, 51,* 1106–1115.

Hertenstein, M. J. (2002). Touch: Its communicative functions in infancy. *Human Development, 45,* 70–94..

Hertenstein, M. J., Keltner, D., App, B., Bulleit, B. A., & Jaskolka, A. R. (2006). Touch communicates distinct emotions. *Emotion, 6,* 528–533.

Hess, U., Banse, R., & Kappas, A. (1995). The intensity of facial expression is determined by underlying affective states and social situations. *Journal of Personality and Social Psychology, 69,* 280–288.

Hewstone, M., & Jaspers, J. (1983). A re-examination of the roles of consensus, consistency, & distinctiveness: Kelley's cube revisited. *British Journal of Social Psychology, 22,* 41–50.

Hewstone, M., & Jaspers, J. (1987). Covariation and causal attribution: A logical model of the intuitive analysis of variance. *Journal of Personality and Social Psychology, 53,* 663–672.

Higgins, E. T. (1987). Self discrepancy: A theory relating self and affect. *Psychological Review, 94,* 319–340.

Higgins, E. T. (1996). Ideals, oughts, and regulatory focus: Affect and motivation from distinct pains and pleasures. In P. M. Gollwitzer & J. A. Bargh (Eds.), *The psychology of action: Linking cognition and motivation to behavior* (pp. 91–114). New York: Guilford Press.

Higgins, E. T. (1999). Promotion and prevention as motivational duality: Implications for evaluative processes. In S. Chaiken & Y. Trope (Eds.), *Dual-process theories in social psychology.* New York: Guilford Press.

Higgins, E. T., & Brendl, M. (1995). Accessibility and applicability: Some "activation rules" influencing judgment. *Journal of Experimental Social Psychology, 31,* 218–243.

Higgins, E. T., King, G. A., & Mavin, G. H. (1982). Individual construct accessibility and subjective impressions and recall. *Journal of Personality and Social Psychology, 43,* 35–47.

Higgins, E. T., & Rholes, W. S. (1976). Impression formation and role fulfillment: A "holistic reference" approach. *Journal of Experimental Social Psychology, 12,* 422–435.

Higgins, E. T., Rholes, W. S., & Jones, C. R. (1977). Category accessibility and impression formation. *Journal of Experimental Social Psychology, 13,* 141–154.

Higgins, E. T., Shah, J., & Friedman, R. (1997). Emotional responses to goal attainment: Strength of regulatory focus as a moderator. *Journal of Personality and Social Psychology, 72,* 515–525.

Hill, A. L., Rand, D. G., Nowak, M. A., & Christakis, N. C. (2010). Infectious disease modeling of social contagion in networks. *PLoS Computational Biology, 6,* e1000968.

Hilton, D. J., & Slugoski, B. R. (1986). Knowledge-based causal attribution: The abnormal conditions focus model. *Psychological Review, 93,* 75–88.

Hilton, D. J., Smith, R. H., & Kim, S. H. (1995). Process of causal explanation and dispositional attribution. *Journal of Personality and Social Psychology, 68,* 377–387.

Hinkley, K., & Andersen, S. M. (1996). The working self-concept in transference: Significant-other activation and self change. *Journal of Personality and Social Psychology, 71,* 1279–1295.

Hinsz, V. B., Tindale, R. S., & Vollrath, D. A. (1997). The emerging conceptualization of groups as information processors. *Psychological Bulletin, 121,* 43–64.

Hirshleifer, D., & Shumway, T. (2003). Good day sunshine: Stock returns and the weather. *Journal of Finance, 58*(3), 1009–1032.

Hirt, E. R. (1990). Do I see only what I expect? Evidence for an expectancy-guided retrieval model. *Journal of Personality and Social Psychology, 58,* 937–951.

Hirt, E. R., MacDonald, H. E., & Erikson, G. A. (1995). How do I remember thee? The role of encoding set and delay in reconstructive memory processes. *Journal of Experimental Social Psychology, 31,* 379–409.

Hirt, E. R., McCrea, S. M., & Kimble, C. E. (2000). Public self-focus and sex differences in behavioral self-handicapping: Does increasing self-threat still make it just a man's game? *Personality and Social Psychology Bulletin, 26,* 1131–1141.

Hirt, E. R., Zillman, D., Erickson, G. A., & Kennedy, C. (1992). Costs and benefits of allegiance: Changes in fans' self-ascribed competencies after team victory versus defeat. *Journal of Personality and Social Psychology, 63,* 724–738.

Ho, C., & Jackson, J. W. (2001). Attitudes toward Asian Americans: Theory and measurement. *Journal of Applied Social Psychology, 31,* 1553–1581.

Hobart, C. (1991). Conflict in remarriages. *Journal of Divorce and Remarriage, 15,* 69–86.

Hodson, G., Dovidio, J. F., & Gaertner, S. L. (2002). Processes in racial discrimination: Differential weighting of conflicting information. *Personality and Social Psychology Bulletin, 28,* 460–471.

Hoeksema-van Orden, C. Y. D., Gaillard, A. W. K., & Buunk, B. P. (1998). Social loafing under fatigue. *Journal of Personality and Social Psychology, 75,* 1179–1190.

Hofstede, G. (1980). *Culture's consequences: International differences in work-related values.* Beverly Hills, CA: Sage.

Hogg, M. A., & Williams, K. D. (2000). From *I* to *we*: Social identity and the collective self. *Group Dynamics: Theory, Research, and Practice. Special Issue: One hundred years of group research, 4,* 81–97.

Holland, R. W., Hendricks, M., & Aarts, H. (2005). Smells like clean spirit: Nonconscious effects of scent on cognition and behavior. *Psychological Science, 16,* 689–693.

Holloway, S. (1988). Concepts of ability and effort in Japan and the United States. *Review of Educational Research, 58,* 327–345.

Holtgraves, T., & Lasky, B. (1999). Linguistic power and persuasion. *Journal of Language and Social Psychology, 18,* 196–205.

Holyoak, K. J., & Thagard, P. (1995). *Mental leaps: Analogy in creative thought.* Cambridge, MA: MIT Press.

Homans, G. C. (1965). Group factors in worker productivity. In H. Proshansky & L. Seidenberg (Eds.), *Basic studies in social psychology.* New York: Holt.

Hong, Y., Chiu, C., & Kung, T. (1997). Bringing culture out in front: Effects of cultural meaning system activation on social cognition. In K. Leung, U. Kim, S. Yamaguchi, & Y. Kashima (Eds.), *Progress in Asian social psychology* (Vol. 1, pp. 135–146). Singapore: Wiley.

Hoorens, V., & Ruiter, S. (1996). The optimal impact phenomenon: Beyond the third person effect. *European Journal of Social Psychology, 26,* 599–610.

Horberg, E. J., Oveis, C., Keltner, D., & Cohen, A. B. (2009). Disgust and the moralization of purity. *Journal of Personality and Social Psychology, 97,* 963–976.

Hosey, G. R., Wood, M., Thompson, R. J., & Druck, P. L. (1985). Social facilitation in a non-social animal, the centipede *Lithobius forficatus. Behavioral Processes, 10,* 123–130.

Hoshino-Browne, E., Zanna, A. S., Spencer, S. J., & Zanna, M. P. (2004). Investigating attitudes cross-culturally: A case of cognitive dissonance among East Asians and North Americans. In G. Haddock & G. R. Maio (Eds.), *Contemporary perspectives on the psychology of attitudes* (pp. 375–397). East Sussex, England: Psychology Press.

Hosman, L. A. (1989). The evaluative consequences of hedges, hesitations, and intensifiers: Powerful and powerless speech styles. *Human Communication Research, 15,* 383–406.

Hovland, C. I., Janis, I. L., & Kelley, H. H. (1953). *Communication and persuasion: Psychological studies of opinion change.* New Haven, CT: Yale University Press.

Hovland, C. J., Lumsdaine, A. A., & Sheffield, F. D. (1949). *Experiments on mass communication.* Princeton, NJ: Princeton University Press.

Hovland, C. J., & Sears, R. R. (1940). Minor studies in aggression: VI. Correlation of lynchings with economic indices. *Journal of Abnormal and Social Psychology, 9,* 301–310.

Hovland, C. J., & Weiss, W. (1951). The influence of source credibility on communication effectiveness. *Public Opinion Quarterly, 15,* 635–660.

Howard, J. W., & Rothbart, M. (1980). Social categorization and memory for ingroup and outgroup behavior. *Journal of Personality and Social Psychology, 38,* 301–310.

Hrdy, S. B. (1999). *Mother nature: A history of mothers, infants, and natural selection.* New York: Pantheon.

Hsiang, S. M., Meng, K. C., & Cane, M. A. (2011). Civil conflicts are associated with the global climate. *Nature, 476,* 438–441.

Hsu, F. L. K. (1953). *Americans and Chinese: Two ways of life.* New York: Schuman.

Hubschman, J. H., & Stack, M. A. (1992). Parasite-induced changes in *Chironomus decorus* (Diptera: Chironomidae). *Journal of Parasitology, 78,* 872–875.

Huesmann, L. R. (1986). Psychological processes promoting the relations between exposure to media violence and aggressive behavior by the viewer. *Journal of Social Issues, 42,* 125–139.

Huesmann, L. R., Moise-Titus, J., Podolski, C.-L., & Eron, L. D. (2003). Longitudinal relations between children's exposure to TV violence and their aggressive and violent behavior in young adulthood: 1977–1992. *Developmental Psychology, 39*, 201–221.

Hughes, M. E., & Waite, L. J. (2009). Marital biography and health at midlife. *Journal of Health and Social Behavior, 50*(3), 344–358.

Huguet, P., Galvaing, M. P., Monteil, J. M., & Dumas, F. (1999). Social presence effects in the Stroop task: Further evidence for an attentional view of social facilitation. *Journal of Personality and Social Psychology, 77*, 1011–1025.

Hummert, M. L., Crockett, W. H., & Kemper, S. (1990). Processing mechanisms underlying use of the balance schema. *Journal of Personality and Social Psychology, 58*, 5–21.

Hunter, J. E., & Hunter, R. F. (1984). Validity and utility of alternative predictors of job performance. *Psychological Bulletin, 96*, 72–98.

Huntley, J. (1990). *The elements of astrology.* Shaftesbury, Dorset, England: Element Books Unlimited.

Ijerman, H., & Semin, G. R. (2009). The thermometer of social relations: Mapping social proximity on temperature. *Psychological Science, 20*, 1214–1210.

Iliffe, A. H. (1960). A study of preferences in feminine beauty. *British Journal of Psychology, 51*, 267–273.

Inbar, Y., Pizarro, D. A., & Bloom, P. (in press). Disgusting smells cause decreased liking of gay men. *Emotion.*

Inbau, F. E., Reid, J. E., Buckley, J. P., & Jayne, B. C. (2001). *Criminal interrogation and confessions* (4th ed.). Gaithersburg, MD: Aspen.

Independent Sector. (2002). *Giving and volunteering in the United States.* Washington, DC: Independent Sector.

Innes, J. M., & Zeitz, H. (1988). The public's view of the impact of the mass media: A test of the "third person" effect. *European Journal of Social Psychology, 18*, 457–463.

Insel, T. R., Young, L., & Zuoxin, W. (1997). Molecular aspects of monogamy. In C. S. Carter & I. I. Lederhendler (Eds.), *Annals of the New York Academy of Sciences* (Vol. 807, pp. 302–316). New York: New York Academy of Sciences.

Insko, C. A. (1984). Balance theory, the Jordan paradigm, and the Wiest tetrahedron. In L. Berkowitz (Ed.), *Advances in experimental social psychology* (Vol. 18, pp. 89–140). San Diego, CA: Academic Press.

Insko, C. A., Smith, R. H., Alicke, M. D., Wade, J., & Taylor, S. (1985). Conformity and group size: The concern with being right and the concern with being liked. *Personality and Social Psychology Bulletin, 11*, 41–50.

Inzlicht, M., & Ben-Zeev, T. (2000). A threatening intellectual environment: Why females are susceptible to experiencing problem-solving deficits in the presence of males. *Psychological Science, 11*, 365–371.

Ip, G. W. M., & Bond, M. H. (1995). Culture, values, and the spontaneous self-concept. *Asian Journal of Psychology, 1*, 29–35.

Isen, A. M. (1987). Positive affect, cognitive processes, and social behavior. In L. Berkowitz (Ed.), *Advances in experimental social psychology* (pp. 203–253). New York: Academic Press.

Isen, A. M. (1993). Positive affect and decision making. In M. Lewis & J. M. Haviland-Jones (Eds.), *Handbook of emotions* (pp. 261–278). New York: Guilford Press.

Isen, A. M. (1999). Positive affect. In T. Dalgleish & M. J. Power (Eds.), *Handbook of cognition and emotion* (pp. 521–539). Chichester, England: Wiley.

Isen, A. M., Clark, M., & Schwartz, M. F. (1976). Duration of the effect of good mood on helping: Footprints on the sands of time. *Journal of Personality and Social Psychology, 34*, 385–393.

Isen, A. M., & Levin, P. F. (1972). Effect of feeling good on helping: Cookies and kindness. *Journal of Personality and Social Psychology, 21*, 384–388.

Ito, T. A., Larsen, J. T., Smith, N. K., & Cacioppo, J. T. (1998). Negative information weighs more heavily on the brain: The negativity bias in evaluative categorizations. *Journal of Personality and Social Psychology, 75*, 887–900.

Iyengar, S. (2004). Engineering consent: The renaissance of mass communications research in politics. In J. T. Jost, M. R. Banaji, & D. Prentice (Eds.), *Perspectives in social psychology: The yin and the yang of scientific progress: Perspectives on the social psychology of thought systems.* Washington, DC: APA Press.

Iyengar, S., & Kinder, D. (1987). *News that matters: Television and American opinion.* Chicago: University of Chicago Press.

Iyengar, S. S., & Lepper, M. R. (2000). When choice is demotivating: Can one desire too much of a good thing? *Journal of Personality and Social Psychology, 79*, 995–1006.

Izard, C. E. (1971). *The face of emotion.* New York: Appleton-Century-Crofts.

Izard, C. E. (1994). Innate and universal facial expressions: Evidence from developmental and cross-cultural research. *Psychological Bulletin, 115*, 288–299.

Jackson, L. A., Hunter, J. E., & Hodge, C. N. (1995). Physical attractiveness and intellectual competence: A meta-analytic review. *Social Psychology Quarterly, 58*, 108–122.

Jacobson, G. C. (1978). The effects of campaign spending in house elections. *American Political Science Review, 72*, 469–1191.

Jacoby, L. L., & Dallas, M. (1981). On the relationship between autobiographical memory and perceptual learning. *Journal of Experimental Psychology, 3*, 306–340.

Jacoby, L. L., Woloshyn, V., & Kelley, C. (1989). Becoming famous without being recognized: Unconscious influences of memory produced by dividing attention. *Journal of Experimental Psychology: General, 118*, 115–125.

James, W. (1884). What is an emotion? *Mind, 9*, 188–205.

James, W. (1890). *Principles of psychology.* New York: Holt.

Janes, L. M., & Olson, J. M. (2000). Jeer pressure: The behavioral effects of observing ridicule of others. *Personality and Social Psychology Bulletin, 26*, 474–485.

Janis, I. L. (1972). *Victims of groupthink.* Boston: Houghton Mifflin.

Janis, I. L. (1982). *Groupthink: Psychological studies of policy decisions and fiascos* (2nd ed.). Boston: Houghton Mifflin.

Janis, I. L., Kaye, D., & Kirschner, P. (1965). Facilitating effects of eating while reading on responsiveness to persuasive communications. *Journal of Personality and Social Psychology, 1*, 181–186.

Janis, I. L., & Mann, L. (1977). *Decision making.* New York: Free Press.

Jeffery, R. W. (1996). Does weight cycling present a health risk? *American Journal of Clinical Nutrition, 63*, 452S–455S.

Jellison, J. M., & Riskind, J. (1970). A social comparison of abilities interpretation of risk-taking behavior. *Journal of Personality and Social Psychology, 15*, 375–390.

Jemmott, J. B. III, Jemmott, L. S., Braverman, P. K., & Fong, G. T. (2005). HIV/STD risk reduction interventions for African American and Latino adolescent girls at an inner-city adolescent medicine clinic: A randomized controlled trial. *Archives of Pediatrics and Adolescent Medicine, 159*, 440–449.

Jemmott, J. B. III, Jemmott, L. S., & Fong, G. T. (1998). Abstinence and safer sex: A randomized controlled trial of HIV sexual risk-reduction interventions for young African American adolescents. *Journal of the American Medical Association, 279*, 1529–1536.

Ji, L., Schwarz, N., & Nisbett, R. E. (2000). Culture, autobiographical memory, and social comparison: Measurement issues in cross-cultural studies. *Personality and Social Psychology Bulletin, 26,* 585–593.

Ji, L. J., Nisbett, R. E., & Su, Y. (2001). Culture, change, and prediction. *Psychological Science, 12,* 450–456.

Ji, L. J., Zhang, Z., & Guo, T. (2008). To buy or to sell: Cultural differences in stock market decisions based on stock price trends. *Journal of Behavioral Decision Making, 21,* 399–413.

Job, R. F. S. (1988). Effective and ineffective use of fear in health promotion campaigns. *American Journal of Public Health, 78,* 163–167.

John, O. P., & Robins, R. W. (1994). Accuracy and bias in self-perception: Individual differences in self-enhancement and the role of narcissism. *Journal of Personality & Social Psychology, 66(1),* 206–219.

Johnson, J. T. (1986). The knowledge of what might have been: Affective and attributional consequences of near outcomes. *Personality and Social Psychology Bulletin, 12,* 51–62.

Johnson, K. J., & Fredrickson, B. L. (2005). We all look the same to me: Positive emotions eliminate the own-race-bias in face recognition. *Psychological Science, 16,* 875–881.

Jones, C., & Aronson, E. (1973). Attribution of fault to a rape victim as a function of the respectability of the victim. *Journal of Personality and Social Psychology, 26,* 415–419.

Jones, E. E. (1964). *Ingratiation.* New York: Appleton-Century-Crofts.

Jones, E. E., & Berglas, S. (1978). Control of attributions about the self through self-handicapping strategies: The appeal of alcohol and the role of underachievement. *Personality and Social Psychology Bulletin, 4,* 200–206.

Jones, E. E., & Davis, K. E. (1965). From acts to dispositions: The attribution process in person perception. In L. Berkowitz (Ed.), *Advances in experimental social psychology* (Vol. 2, pp. 219–266). New York: Academic Press.

Jones, E. E., Davis, K. E., & Gergen, K. J. (1961). Role-playing variations and their informational value for person perception. *Journal of Abnormal and Social Psychology, 63,* 302–310.

Jones, E. E., Farina, A., Hastorf, A. H., Markus, H., Miller, D. T., & Scott, R. A. (1984). *Social stigma: The psychology of marked relationships.* New York: Freeman.

Jones, E. E., & Harris, V. A. (1967). The attribution of attitudes. *Journal of Experimental Social Psychology, 3,* 1–24.

Jones, E. E., & Nisbett, R. E. (1972). The actor and the observer: Divergent perceptions of the causes of behavior. In E. E. Jones, D. E. Kanouse, H. H. Kelley, R. E. Nisbett, S. Valins, & B. Weiner (Eds.), *Attribution: Perceiving the causes of behavior.* Morristown, NJ: General Learning Press.

Jost, J. T. (1997). An experimental replication of the depressed entitlement effect among women. *Psychology of Women Quarterly, 21,* 387–393.

Jost, J. T., & Banaji, M. R. (1994). The role of stereotyping in system justification and the production of false consciousness. *British Journal of Social Psychology, 33,* 1–27.

Jost, J. T., Banaji, M. R., & Nosek, B. A. (2004). A decade of system justification theory: Accumulated evidence of conscious and unconscious bolstering of the status quo. *Political Psychology, 25,* 881–919.

Jost, J. T., Glaser, J., Kruglanski, A. W., & Sulloway, F. (2003). Political conservatism as motivated social cognition. *Psychological Bulletin, 129,* 339–375.

Jost, J. T., & Kay, A. C. (2005). Exposure to benevolent sexism and complementary gender stereotypes: Consequences for specific and diffuse forms of system justification. *Journal of Personality and Social Psychology, 88,* 498–509.

Jost, J. T., Pelham, B. W., Sheldon, O., & Sullivan, B. N. (2003). Social inequality and the reduction of ideological dissonance on behalf of the system: Evidence of enhanced system justification among the disadvantaged. *European Journal of Social Psychology, 33,* 13–36.

Jostmann, N. B., Lakens, D., & Schubert, T. W. (2009). Weight as an embodiment of importance. *Psychological Science, 20(9),* 1169–1174.

Jourard, S. M. (1966). An exploratory study of body accessibility. *British Journal of Social and Clinical Psychology, 5,* 221–231.

Judd, C. M., Blair, I. V., & Chapleau, K. M. (2004). Automatic stereotypes vs. automatic prejudice: Sorting out the possibilities in the Payne (2001) weapon paradigm. *Journal of Experimental Social Psychology, 40,* 75–81.

Judd, C. M., Drake, R. A., Downing, J. W., & Krosnick, J. A. (1991). Some dynamic properties of attitude structures: Context induced responses facilitation and polarization. *Journal of Personality and Social Psychology, 60,* 193–202.

Judd, C. M., Kenny, D. A., & Krosnick, J. A. (1983). Judging the positions of political candidates: Models of assimilation and contrast. *Journal of Personality and Social Psychology, 46,* 1193–1207.

Judd, C. M., & Lusk, C. M. (1984). Knowledge structures and evaluative judgments: Effects of structural variables on judgment extremity. *Journal of Personality and Social Psychology, 46,* 1193–1207.

Judd, C. M., & Park, B. (1993). The assessment of accuracy of social stereotypes. *Psychological Review, 100,* 109–128.

Judge, T. A., Bono, J. E., Hies, R., & Gerhardt, M. W. (2002). Personality and leadership: A qualitative and quantitative review. *Journal of Applied Psychology, 87,* 765–780.

Jussim, L. (1986). Self-fulfilling prophecies: A theoretical and integrative review. *Psychological Review, 93,* 429–445.

Jussim, L., Eccles, J., & Madon, S. J. (1996). Social perception, social stereotypes, and teacher expectations: Accuracy and the quest for the powerful self-fulfilling prophecy. *Advances in Experimental Social Psychology, 29,* 281–388.

Jussim, L., & Harber, K. (2005). Teacher expectations and self-fulfilling prophecies: Knowns and unknowns, resolved and unresolved controversies. *Personality and Social Psychology Review, 9,* 131–155.

Kahneman, D. (1999). Objective happiness. In D. Kahneman, E. Diener, & N. Schwarz (Eds.), *Hedonic psychology.* New York: Cambridge University Press.

Kahneman, D., & Frederick, S. (2002). Representativeness revisited: Attribute substitution in intuitive judgment. In T. Gilovich, D. W. Griffin, & D. Kahneman (Eds.), *Heuristics and biases: The psychology of intuitive judgment* (pp. 49–81). New York: Cambridge University Press.

Kahneman, D., & Lovallo, D. (1993). Timid choices and bold forecasts: A cognitive perspective on risk taking. *Management Science, 39,* 17–31.

Kahneman, D., & Miller, D. T. (1986). Norm theory: Comparing reality to its alternatives. *Psychological Review, 93,* 136–153.

Kahneman, D., Schkade, D., & Sunstein, C. R. (1998). Shared outrage and erratic awards: The psychology of punitive damages. *Journal of Risk and Uncertainty, 16,* 49–86.

Kahneman, D., Slovic, P., & Tversky, A. (1982). *Judgment under uncertainty: Heuristics and biases.* New York: Cambridge University Press.

Kahneman, D., & Tversky, A. (1972). Subjective probability: A judgment of representativeness. *Cognitive Psychology, 3,* 430–454.

Kahneman, D., & Tversky, A. (1973a). Availability: A heuristic for judging frequency and probability. *Cognitive Psychology, 4,* 207–232.

Kahneman, D., & Tversky, A. (1973b). On the psychology of prediction. *Psychological Review, 80,* 237–251.

Kahneman, D., & Tversky, A. (1982a). The simulation heuristic. In D. Kahneman, P. Slovic, & A. Tversky (Eds.), *Judgment under certainty: Heuristics and biases* (pp. 201–208). New York: Cambridge University Press.

Kahneman, D., & Tversky, A. (1982b). Variants of uncertainty. *Cognition, 11,* 143–157.

Kahneman, D., & Tversky, A. (1995). On the reality of cognitive illusions. *Psychological Review, 103,* 582–591.

Kaid, L. L. (1981). Political advertising. In D. D. Nimmo & K. R. Sanders (Eds.), *Handbook of political communication.* Beverly Hills, CA: Sage.

Kalven, H., & Zeisel, H. (1966). *The American jury.* Boston: Little, Brown.

Kamarck, T. W., Manuch, S., & Jennings, J. R. (1990). Social support reduces cardiovascular reactivity to psychological challenge: A laboratory model. *Psychosomatic Medicine, 52,* 42–58.

Kamstra, M. J., Kramer, L. A., & Levi, M. D. (2003). Winter blues: Seasonal affective disorder (SAD) and stock market returns. *American Economic Review, 93,* 324–343.

Kaplan, M. F., & Schersching, C. (1981). Juror deliberation: An information integration analysis. In B. Sales (Ed.), *The trial process* (pp. 235–262). New York: Plenum.

Karau, S. J., & Williams, K. D. (1995). Social loafing: Research findings, implications, and future directions. *Current Directions in Psychological Science, 4,* 134–140.

Karney, B. R., & Bradbury, T. N. (1995). The longitudinal course of marital quality and stability: A review of theory, method, and research. *Psychological Bulletin, 118,* 3–34.

Karney, B. R., & Bradbury, T. N. (1997). Neuroticism, marital interaction, and the trajectory of marital satisfaction. *Journal of Personality and Social Psychology, 72,* 1075–1092.

Karney, B. R., & Bradbury, T. N. (2000). Attributions in marriage: State or trait? A growth curve analysis. *Journal of Personality and Social Psychology, 78,* 295–309.

Karney, B. R., Bradbury, T. N, Fincham, F. D., & Sullivan, K. T. (1994). The role of negative affectivity in the association between attributions and marital satisfaction. *Journal of Personality and Social Psychology, 66,* 413–424.

Karpinski, A., & Hilton, J. L. (2001). Attitudes and the Implicit Association Test. *Journal of Personality and Social Psychology, 81,* 774–788.

Kashima, Y., Siegal, M., Tanaka, K., & Kashima, E. S. (1992). Do people believe behaviours are consistent with attitudes? Towards a cultural psychology of attribution processes. *British Journal of Social Psychology, 37,* 111–124.

Kashima, Y., Yamaguchi, S., Kim, U., Choi, S.-C, Gelfand, M. J., & Yuki, M. (1995). Culture, gender, and self: A perspective from individualism-collectivism research. *Journal of Personality and Social Psychology, 69,* 925–937.

Kasser, T., & Sheldon, K. M. (2000). Of wealth and death: Materialism, mortality salience, and consumption behavior. *Psychological Science, 11,* 348–351.

Kassin, S. M., Meissner, C., & Norwick, R. J. (2005). "I'd know a false confession if I saw one": A comparative study of college students and police investigators. *Law and Human Behavior, 29,* 211–227.

Kassin, S. M., & Sukel, H. (1997). Coerced confessions and the jury: An experimental test of the "harmless error" rule. *Law and Human Behavior, 21,* 27–46.

Katz, I., Glucksberg, S., & Krauss, R. (1960). Need satisfaction and Edwards PPS scores in married couples. *Journal of Consulting Psychology, 24,* 205–208.

Kay, A. C., & Jost, J. T. (2003). Complementary justice: Effects of "poor but happy" and "poor but honest" stereotype exemplars on system justification and implicit activation of the justice motive. *Journal of Personality and Social Psychology, 85,* 823–837.

Kay, A. C., Wheeler, S. C., Bargh, J. A., & Ross, L. (2004). Material priming: The influence of mundane physical objects on situation construal and competitive behavioral choice. *Organizational Behavior and Human Decision Processes, 95,* 83–96.

Kelley, H. H. (1967). Attribution theory in social psychology. In D. Levine (Ed.), *Nebraska Symposium on Motivation* (Vol. 15, pp. 192–238). Lincoln: University of Nebraska Press.

Kelley, H. H. (1973). The processes of causal attribution. *American Psychologist, 28,* 107–128.

Kelley, H. H., & Stahelski, A. J. (1970). The social interaction basis of cooperators' and competitors' beliefs about others. *Journal of Personality and Social Psychology, 16,* 66–91.

Kelley, H. H., & Thibaut, J. W. (1978). *Interpersonal relations: A theory of interdependence.* New York: Wiley.

Kelly, J. R., & Karau, S. J. (1999). Group decision making: The effects of initial preference and time pressure. *Personality and Social Psychology Bulletin, 25,* 1342–1354.

Kelman, H. C. (1958). Compliance, identification, and internalization: Three processes of attitude change. *Journal of Conflict Resolution, 2,* 51–60.

Keltner, D. (1995). The signs of appeasement: Evidence for the distinct displays of embarrassment, amusement, and shame. *Journal of Personality and Social Psychology, 68,* 441–454.

Keltner, D. (2009). *Born to be good: The science of a meaningful life.* New York: Norton.

Keltner, D., & Anderson, C. (2000). Saving face for Darwin: Functions and uses of embarrassment. *Current Directions in Psychological Science, 9,* 187–191.

Keltner, D., & Bonanno, G. A. (1997). A study of laughter and dissociation: The distinct correlates of laughter and smiling during bereavement. *Journal of Personality and Social Psychology, 73,* 687–702.

Keltner, D., & Buswell, B. N. (1997). Embarrassment: Its distinct form and appeasement functions. *Psychological Bulletin, 122,* 250–270.

Keltner, D., Capps, L. M., Kring, A. M., Young, R. C., & Heerey, E. A. (2001). Just teasing: A conceptual analysis and empirical review. *Psychological Bulletin, 127,* 229–248.

Keltner, D., Ellsworth, P. C., & Edwards, K. (1993). Beyond simple pessimism: Effects of sadness and anger on social perception. *Journal of Personality and Social Psychology, 64,* 740–752.

Keltner, D., Gruenfeld, D. H., & Anderson, C. A. (2003). Power, approach, and inhibition. *Psychological Review, 110,* 265–284.

Keltner, D., & Haidt, J. (1999). Social functions of emotions at four levels of analysis. *Cognition and Emotion, 13,* 505–521.

Keltner, D., & Haidt, J. (2003). Approaching awe: A moral, spiritual, and aesthetic emotion. *Cognition and Emotion, 17,* 297–314.

Keltner, D., Locke, K. D., & Audrain, P. C. (1993). The influence of attributions on the relevance of negative feelings to personal satisfaction. *Personality and Social Psychology Bulletin, 19,* 21–29.

Keltner, D., Moffitt, T., & Stouthamer-Loeber, M. (1995). Facial expressions of emotion and psychopathology in adolescent boys. *Journal of Abnormal Psychology, 104,* 644–652.

Keltner, D., Van Kleef, G. A., Chen, S., & Kraus, M. W. (2008). A reciprocal influence model of social power: Emerging principles and lines of inquiry. *Advances in Experimental Social Psychology, 40,* 151–192.

Keltner, D., Young, R. C., Heerey, E. A., Oemig, C., & Monarch, N. D. (1998). Teasing in hierarchial and intimate relations. *Journal of Personality and Social Psychology, 75,* 1231–1247.

Kemper, T. D. (1991). Predicting emotions from social relations. *Social Psychology Quarterly, 54,* 330–342.

Kenny, D. A., & DePaulo, B. M. (1993). Do people know how others view them? An empirical and theoretical account. *Psychological Bulletin, 114,* 145–161.

Kenrick, D. T., & Keefe, R. C. (1992). Age preferences in mates reflect sex differences in reproductive strategies. *Behavioral and Brain Sciences, 15,* 75–133.

Kenrick, D. T., & MacFarlane, S. W. (1984). Ambient temperature and horn-honking: A field study of the heat/aggression relationship. *Environment and Behavior, 18,* 179–191.

Kerr, N. L. (1981). Social transition schemes: Charting the group's road to agreement. *Journal of Personality and Social Psychology, 41,* 684–702.

Kerr, N. L., Kramer, G. P., Carroll, J. S., & Alfini, J. J. (1991). On the effectiveness of voir dire in criminal cases with prejudicial pretrial publicity: An empirical study. *American University Law Review, 40,* 665–701.

Kerr, N. L., MacCoun, R. J., & Kramer, G. P. (1996). Bias in judgment: Comparing individuals and groups. *Psychological Review, 103,* 687–719.

Ketelaar, T. (2005). Emotions and economic decision-making: The role of moral sentiments in experimental economics. In D. De Cremer, K. Murnighan, &. M. Zeelenberg, (Eds.), *Social psychology and experimental economics.* Mahwah, NJ: Erlbaum.

Kiecolt-Glaser, J. K., & Glaser, R. (1995). Psychoneuroimmunology and health consequences: Data and shared mechanisms. *Psychosomatic Medicine, 57,* 269–274.

Kiecolt-Glaser, J. K., Malarkey, W. B., Cacioppo, J. T., & Glaser, R. (1994). Stressful personal relationships: Immune and endocrine function. In R. Glaser & Kiecolt-Glaser (Eds.), *Handbook of human stress and immunity* (pp. 321–339). San Diego, CA: Academic Press.

Kiesler, S. B. (1971). *The psychology of commitment: Experiments linking behavior to belief.* New York: Academic Press.

Kiesler, S. B., & Mathog, R. (1968). The distraction hypothesis in attitude change. *Psychological Reports, 23,* 1123–1133.

Kim, H., & Baron, R. S. (1988). Exercise and illusory correlation: Does arousal heighten stereotypic processes? *Journal of Experimental Social Psychology, 24,* 366–380.

Kim, H., & Markus, H. R. (1999). Deviance or uniqueness, harmony or conformity? A cultural analysis. *Journal of Personality and Social Psychology, 77,* 785–800.

Kimmel, M. S. (2004). *The gendered society* (2nd ed.). New York: Oxford University Press.

Kinder, D. R., & Sears, D. O. (1981). Prejudice and politics: Symbolic racism versus racial threats to the good life. *Journal of Personality and Social Psychology, 40,* 414–431.

King, E. B., Knight, J. L., & Hebl, M. R. (2010). The influence of economic conditions on aspects of stigmatization. *Journal of Social Issues, 66,* 446–460.

King, L. A., & Miner, K. N. (2000). Writing about the perceived benefits of traumatic events: Implications for physical health. *Personality and Social Psychology Bulletin, 26,* 220–230.

Kirkpatrick, L. A., & Hazan, C. (1994). Attachment styles and close relationships: A four-year prospective study. *Personal Relationships, 1,* 123–142.

Kitayama, S., Duffy, S., Kawamura, T., & Larsen, J. T. (2002). Perceiving an object in its context in different cultures: A cultural look at the New Look. *Psychological Science, 14,* 201–206.

Kitayama, S., Karasawa, M., & Mesquita, B. (2004). Collective and personal processes in regulating emotions: Emotion and self in Japan and the United States. In P. Philipot & R. S. Feldman (Eds.), *The regulation of emotion* (pp. 251–273). Hillsdale, NJ: Erlbaum.

Kitayama, S., Markus, H. R., & Kurokawa, M. (2000). Culture, emotion, and well-being: Good feelings in Japan and the United States. *Cognition and Emotion, 14,* 93–124.

Kitayama, S., Markus, H. R., Matsumoto, H., & Norasakkunkit, V. (1997). Individual and collective processes in the construction of the self: Self-enhancement in the United States and self-depreciation in Japan. *Journal of Personality and Social Psychology, 72,* 1245–1267.

Kitayama, S., & Masuda, T. (1997). Shaiaiteki ninshiki no bunkateki baikai model: taiousei bias no bunkashinrigakuteki kentou. [Cultural psychology of social inference: The correspondence bias in Japan.] In K. Kashiwagi, S. Kitayama, & H. Azuma (Eds.), *Bunkashinrigaju: riron tojisho.* [*Cultural psychology: Theory and evidence*]. Tokyo: University of Tokyo Press.

Kitayama, S., Mesquita, B., & Karasawa, M. (2005). *Culture and emotional experience: Socially engaging and disengaging emotions in Japan and the United States.* Unpublished manuscript.

Kitayama, S., Snibbe, A. C., Markus, H. R., & Suzuki, T. (2004). Is there any "free" choice? Self and dissonance in two cultures. *Psychological Science, 15,* 527–533.

Klauer, K. C., & Meiser, T. (2000). A source-monitoring analysis of illusory correlations. *Personality and Social Psychology Bulletin, 26,* 1074–1093.

Klayman, J., & Ha, Y. (1987). Confirmation, disconfirmation, and information in hypothesis testing. *Psychological Review, 94,* 211–228.

Klein, S. B., & Kihlstrom, J. F. (1986). Elaboration, organization, and the self-reference effect in memory. *Journal of Experimental Psychology: General, 115,* 26–38.

Klein, S. B., & Loftus, J. (1988). The nature of self-referent encoding: The contributions of elaborative and organizational processes. *Journal of Personality and Social Psychology, 55,* 5–11.

Kleinhesselink, R. R., & Edwards, R. E. (1975). Seeking and avoiding belief-discrepant information as a function of its perceived refutability. *Journal of Personality and Social Psychology, 31,* 787–790.

Klinger, M. R., Burton, P. C., & Pitts, G. S. (2000). Mechanisms of unconscious priming I: Response competition, not spreading activation. *Journal of Experimental Psychology: Learning, Memory, and Cognition, 26,* 441–455.

Klohnen, E. C., & Bera, S. J. (1998). Behavioral and experiential patterns of avoidantly and securely attached women across adulthood: A 30-year longitudinal perspective. *Journal of Personality and Social Psychology, 74,* 211–223.

Kniffin, K. M., & Wilson, D. S. (2004). The effect of nonphysical traits on the perception of physical attractiveness: Three naturalistic studies. *Evolution and Human Behavior, 25,* 88–101.

Knox, R. E., & Inkster, J. A. (1968). Postdecision dissonance at posttime. *Journal of Personality and Social Psychology, 8,* 319–323.

Knutson, B. (1996). Facial expressions of emotion influence interpersonal trait inferences. *Journal of Nonverbal Behavior, 20,* 165–182.

Knutson, B., Wimmer, G. E., Rick, S., Hollon, N. G., Prelec, D., & Loewenstein, G. (2008). Neural antecedents of the endowment effect. *Neuron, 58,* 814–822.

Kohn, M. L. (1969). *Class and conformity: A study in values.* Homewood, IL: Dorsey Press.

Kolbert, E. (2009, November 9). The things people say. *The New Yorker,* p. 112.

Konner, M. (2003). *The tangled wing: Biological constraints on the human spirit.* New York: Holt.

Konrath, S., O'Brien, E., & Hsing, C. (2011). Changes in dispositional empathy in American college students over time: A meta-analysis. *Personality and Social Psychology Review, 15,* 180–198.

Korpela, U., & Kinnunen, K. (2009). How is leisure time interacting with nature related to the need for recovery from work demands? Testing multiple mediators. *Leisure Sciences, 33,* 1–14.

Kosfeld, M., Heinrichs, M., Zak, P. J., Fishbacher, U., & Fehr, E. (2005). Oxytocin increases trust in humans. *Nature, 435,* 673–676.

Koslowsky, M., & Schwarzwald, J. (2001). The power interaction model: Theory, methodology, and empirical applications. In A. Y. Lee-Chai & J. A. Bargh (Eds.), *The use and abuse of power: Multiple perspectives on the causes of corruption* (pp. 195–214). Philadelphia: Psychology Press.

Kovera, M. B., & Borgida, E. (in press). Social psychology and law. In S. T. Fiske, D. T. Gilbert & G. Lindzey (Eds.), *Handbook of social psychology* (5th ed.). New York: Oxford University Press.

Kraus, M. W., Côté, S., & Keltner, D. (2010). Social class, contextualism, and empathic accuracy, *Psychological Science, 21,* 1716–1723.

Kraus, M. W., Huang, C., & Keltner, D. (2010). Tactile communication, cooperation, and performance: An ethological study of the NBA, *Emotion, 10,* 745–749.

Kraus, M. W., Piff, P. K., & Keltner, D. (2009). Social class, sense of control, and social explanation, *Journal of Personality and Social Psychology, 97,* 992–1004.

Kraus, M. W., Piff, P. K., & Keltner, D. (2011). Social class as culture: The convergence of resources and rank in the social realm. *Current Directions in Psychological Science, 100,* 246–250.

Kristof, N. D., & WuDunn, S. (2009). *Half the sky.* New York: Knopf.

Krosnick, J. A. (1988). The role of attitude importance in social evaluation: A study of policy preferences, presidential candidate evaluations, and voting behavior. *Journal of Personality and Social Psychology, 55,* 196–210.

Krosnick, J. A., Betz, A. L., Jussim, L. J., & Lynn, A. R. (1992). Subliminal conditioning of attitudes. *Personality and Social Psychology Bulletin, 18,* 152–162.

Krosnick, J. A., & Petty, R. E. (1995). Attitude strength: An overview. In R. E. Petty & J. A. Krosnick (Eds.), *Attitude strength: Antecedents and consequences* (pp. 1–24). Mahwah, NJ: Erlbaum.

Kross, E., & Ayduk, O. (2008). Facilitating adaptive emotional analysis: Distinguishing distanced-analysis of depressive experiences from immersed-analysis and distraction. *Personality and Social Psychology Bulletin, 34,* 924–938.

Kross, E., Ayduk, O., & Mischel, W. (2005). When asking "why" does not hurt: Distinguishing rumination from reflective processing of negative emotions. *Psychological Science, 16,* 709–715.

Kruger, J., Wirtz, D., & Miller, D. (2005). Counterfactual thinking and the first instinct fallacy. *Journal of Personality and Social Psychology, 88,* 725–735.

Kruglanski, A. W., & Mayseless, O. (1990). Classic and current social comparison research: Expanding the perspective. *Psychological Bulletin, 108*(2), 195–208.

Kruglanski, A. W., & Webster, D. M. (1991). Group members' reactions to opinion deviates and conformists at varying degrees of proximity to decision deadline and of environmental noise. *Journal of Personality and Social Psychology, 61,* 212–225.

Kruglanski, A. W., & Webster, D. M. (1996). Motivated closing of the mind: "Seizing" and "freezing." *Psychological Review, 103,* 263–283.

Krull, D. S. (1993). Does the grist change the mill? The effect of the perceiver's inferential goal on the process of social inference. *Personality and Social Psychology Bulletin, 19,* 340–348.

Krull, D. S., & Dill, J. C. (1996). On thinking first and responding fast: Flexibility in social inference processes. *Personality and Social Psychology Bulletin, 22,* 949–959.

Krull, D. S., & Erickson, D. J. (1995). Inferential hopscotch: How people draw social inferences from behavior. *Current Directions in Psychological Science, 4,* 35–38.

Krull, D. S., Loy, M., Lin, J., Wang, C.-F., Chen, S., & Zhao, X. (1996). *The fundamental attribution error: Correspondence bias in independent and interdependent cultures.* Paper presented at the 13th Congress of the International Association for Cross-Cultural Psychology, Montreal, Quebec, Canada.

Kuhlmeier, V., Wynn, K., & Bloom, P. (2003). Attribution of dispositional states by 12-month-olds. *Psychological Science, 5,* 402–408.

Kuhn, M. H., & McPartland, T. S. (1954). An empirical investigation of self-attitudes. *American Sociological Review, 19,* 68–76.

Kühnen, U., & Oyserman, D. (2002). *Thinking about the self influences thinking in general: Cognitive consequences of salient self-concept.* Ann Arbor: University of Michigan Press.

Kulik, J. A. (1983). Confirmatory attribution and the perpetuation of social beliefs. *Journal of Personality and Social Psychology, 44,* 1171–1181.

Kunda, Z. (1990). The case for motivated reasoning. *Psychological Bulletin, 108,* 480–496.

Kunda, Z., Davies, P. G., Adams, B., & Spencer, S. J. (2002). The dynamic time course of stereotype activation: Activation, dissipation, and resurrection. *Journal of Personality and Social Psychology, 82,* 283–299.

Kunda, Z., & Oleson, K. C. (1995). Maintaining stereotypes in the face of disconfirmation: Constructing grounds for subtyping deviants. *Journal of Personality and Social Psychology, 68,* 565–579.

Kunda, Z., & Sherman-Williams, B. (1993). Stereotypes and the construal of individuating information. *Personality and Social Psychology Bulletin, 19,* 90–99.

Kunda, Z., & Thagard, P. (1996). Forming impressions from stereotypes, traits, and behaviors: A parallel-constraint-satisfaction theory. *Psychological Review, 103,* 646–657.

Kunstman, J., & Maner, J. K. (2011). Sexual overperception: Power, mating goals, and biases in social judgment. *Journal of Personality and Social Psychology, 100,* 282–294.

Kunz, P. R., & Woolcott, M. (1976). Season's greetings: From my status to yours. *Social Research, 5,* 269–278.

Kuo, F. E., & Sullivan, W. C. (2001). Environment and crime in the inner city. Does vegetation reduce crime? *Environment and Behavior, 33,* 343–367.

Kurdek, L. A. (1993). Predicting marital dissolution: A 5-year prospective longitudinal study of newlywed couples. *Journal of Personality and Social Psychology, 64,* 221–242.

Kurzban, R. (2001). The social psychophysics of cooperation: Non-verbal communication in a public goods game. *Journal of Nonverbal Behavior, 25,* 241–259.

LaBrie, J. W., Hummer, J. F., Neighbors, C., & Pedersen, E. R. (2008). Live interactive group-specific normative feedback reduces misperceptions and drinking in college students: A randomized cluster trial. *Psychology of Addictive Behaviors, 22,* 141–148.

LaFrance, M., Henley, N. M., Hall, J. A., & Halberstadt, A. G. (1997). Nonverbal behavior: Are women's superior skills caused by their oppression? In M. R. Walsh (Ed.), *Women, men, and gender: Ongoing debates.* New Haven: Yale University Press.

Lakin, J. L., & Chartrand, T. L. (2003). Using nonconscious behavioral mimicry to create affiliation and rapport. *Psychological Science, 14,* 334–339.

Lakoff, G. (2004). *Don't think of an elephant: Know your values and frame the debate.* White River Junction, VT: Chelsea Green Publishing.

Lakoff, G., & Johnson, M. (1980). *Metaphors we live by.* Chicago: University of Chicago Press.

Lambert, A. J., Burroughs, T., & Nguyen, T. (1999). Perceptions of risk and the buffering hypothesis: The role of just world beliefs and right-wing authoritarianism. *Personality and Social Psychology Bulletin, 25,* 643–656.

Lambert, A. J., Payne, B. K., Jacoby, L. L., Shaffer, L. M., Chasteen, A. L., & Khan, S. R. (2003). Stereotypes as dominant responses: On the "social facilitation" of prejudice in anticipated public contexts. *Journal of Personality and Social Psychology, 84,* 277–295.

Lammers, J., Stapel, D. A., & Galinsky, A. D. (2011). Power increases hypocrisy: Moralizing in reasoning, immorality in behavior. *Psychological Science, 21,* 737–744.

Landau, M. J., Solomon, S., Greenberg, J., Cohen, F., & Pyszczynski, T. (2004). Deliver us from evil: The effects of mortality salience and reminders of 9/11 on support for President George W. Bush. *Personality and Social Psychology Bulletin, 30,* 1136–1150.

Landes, E. M., & Rosenfield, A. M. (1994). Durability of advertising revisited. *Journal of Industrial Economics, 43,* 263–277.

Landsberger, M. (1966). Windfall income and consumption: Comment. *American Economic Review, 56,* 534–540.

Landy, D., & Sigall, H. (1974). Beauty is talent: Task evaluation as a function of the performer's physical attractiveness. *Journal of Personality and Social Psychology, 29,* 299–304.

Lane, K. A., Banaji, M. R., Nosek, B. A., & Greenwald, A. G. (2007). Understanding and using the Implicit Association Test: IV: Procedures and validity. In B. Wittenbrink & N. Schwarz (Eds.), *Implicit measures of attitudes: Procedures and controversies* (pp. 59–102). New York: Guilford Press.

Langer, E. J., & Rodin, J. (1976). The effects of choice and enhanced personal responsibility for the aged: A field experiment in an institutional setting. *Journal of Personality and Social Psychology, 34,* 191–198.

Langlois, J. H., Kalakanis, L., Rubenstein, A. J., Larson, A., Hallam, M., & Smoot, M. (2000). Maxims or myths of beauty? A meta-analytic review and theoretical review. *Psychological Bulletin, 126,* 390–423.

Langlois, J. H., Ritter, J. M., Roggman, L. A., & Vaughn, L. S. (1991). Facial diversity and infant preferences for attractive faces. *Developmental Psychology, 27,* 79–84.

Langlois, J. H., & Roggman, L. A. (1990). Attractive faces are only average. *Psychological Science, 1,* 115–121.

Langlois, J. H., Roggman, L. A., Casey, R. J., Ritter, J. M., Rieser-Danner, L. A., & Jenkins, V. Y. (1987). Infant preferences for attractive faces: Rudiments of a stereotype. *Developmental Psychology, 23,* 363–369.

LaPiere, R. T. (1934). Attitudes versus actions. *Social Forces, 13,* 230–237.

Larrick, R. P., Morgan, J. N., & Nisbett, R. E. (1990). Teaching the use of cost-benefit reasoning in everyday life. *Psychological Science, 1,* 362–370.

Larrick, R. P., Nisbett, R. E., & Morgan, J. N. (1993). Who uses the cost-benefit rules of choice? Implications for the normative status of microeconomic theory. *Organizational Behavior and Human Decision Processes, 56,* 331–347.

Larrick, R. P., Timmerman, T. A., Carton, A. M., & Abrevaya, J. (2011). Temper, temperature, and temptation: Heat-related retaliation in baseball. *Psychological Science, 22,* 423–428.

Lassiter, G. D., Geers, A. L., Munhall, P. J., Ploutz-Snyder, R. J., & Breitenbecher, D. L. (2002). Illusory causation: Why it occurs. *Psychological Science, 13,* 299–305.

Latané, B., & Darley, J. M. (1968). Group inhibition of bystander intervention in emergencies. *Journal of Personality and Social Psychology, 10,* 215–221.

Latané, B., & Nida, S. (1981). Ten years of research on group size and helping. *Psychological Bulletin, 89,* 308–324.

Latané, B., Williams, K., & Harkins, S. (1979). Many hands make the work light: The causes and consequences of social loafing. *Journal of Personality and Social Psychology, 37,* 822–832.

Lau, G., Kay, A. C., & Spencer, S. J. (2008). Loving those who justify inequality: The effects of system threat on attraction to women who embody benevolent sexist ideals. *Psychological Science, 19*(1), 20–21.

Lau, R. R., & Russell, D. (1980). Attributions in the sports pages: A field test of some current hypotheses about attribution research. *Journal of Personality and Social Psychology, 39,* 29–38.

Laughlin, P. R. (1988). Collective induction: Group performance, social combination processes, and mutual majority and minority influence. *Journal of Personality and Social Psychology, 54,* 254–267.

Laughlin, P. R., & Ellis, A. L. (1986). Demonstrability and social combination processes on mathematical intellective tasks. *Journal of Experimental Social Psychology, 22,* 177–189.

Laughlin, P. R., Hatch, E. C., Silver, J. S., & Boh, L. (2006). Groups perform better than the best individuals on letters-to-numbers problems: Effects of group size. *Journal of Personality and Social Psychology, 90,* 644–651.

Lawler, K. A., Younger, J. W., Piferi, R. L., Billington, E., Jobe, R., Edmondson, K., et al. (2003). A change of heart: Cardiovascular correlates of forgiveness in response to interpersonal conflict. *Journal of Behavioral Medicine, 26,* 373–393.

Lazarus, R. S. (1966). *Psychological stress and the coping process.* New York: McGraw-Hill.

Lazarus, R. S. (1991). *Emotion and adaptation.* New York: Oxford University Press.

Lea, M., Spears, R., & de Groot, D. (2001). Knowing me, knowing you: Anonymity effects on social identity processes within groups. *Personality and Social Psychology Bulletin, 27,* 526–537.

Leary, M. R. (2007). Motivational and emotional aspects of the self. *Annual Review of Psychology, 58,* 317–344.

Leary, M. R., & Jones, J. L. (1993). The social psychology of tanning and sunscreen use: Self-presentational motives as a predictor of health risk. *Journal of Applied Social Psychology, 23,* 1390–1406.

Leary, M. R., & Kowalski, R. M. (1990). Impression management: A literature review and two-component model. *Psychological Bulletin, 107,* 34–47.

Leary, M. R., Kowalski, R. M., Smith, L., & Phillips, S. (2003). Teasing, rejection, and violence: Case studies of the school shootings. *Aggressive Behavior, 29*, 202–214.

Leary, M. R., Tambor, E. S., Terdal, S. K., & Downs, D. L. (1995). Self-esteem as an interpersonal monitor: The sociometer hypothesis. *Journal of Personality and Social Psychology, 68*, 518–530.

Leary, M. R., Tchividjian, L. R., & Kraxberger, B. E. (1994). Self-presentation can be hazardous to your health: Impression management and health risk. *Health Psychology, 13*, 451–470.

LeBon, G. (1895). *The crowd*. London: Unwin.

LeDoux, J. E. (1989). Cognitive-emotional interactions in the brain. *Cognition and Emotion, 3*, 267–289.

LeDoux, J. E. (1993). Emotional networks in the brain. In M. Lewis & J. M. Haviland (Eds.), *Handbook of emotions* (pp. 109–118). New York: Guilford Press.

LeDoux, J. E. (1996). *The emotional brain*. New York: Simon & Schuster.

Lee, F., Hallahan, M., & Herzog, T. (1996). Explaining real-life events: How culture and domain shape attributions. *Personality and Social Psychology Bulletin, 22*, 732–741.

Lee, S. W. S., & Schwarz, N. (2010). Dirty hands and dirty mouths: Embodiment of the moral-purity metaphor is specific to the motor modality involved in moral transgression. *Psychological Science, 21*, 1423–1425.

Lee, S. W. S., & Schwarz, N. (2011). Clean slate effects: The psychological consequences of physical cleansing. *Current Directions in Psychological Science, 20*, 307–311.

Lee, Y., Jussim, L., & McCauley, C. R. (1995). *Stereotype accuracy: Toward appreciating group differences*. Washington, DC: American Psychological Association.

Lehman, B. J., Taylor, S. E., Kiefe, C. I., & Seeman, T. E. (2005). Relation of childhood socioeconomic status and family environment to adult metabolic functioning in the CARDIA study. *Psychosomatic Medicine, 67*, 846–854.

Lehman, D. R., Lempert, R. O., & Nisbett, R. E. (1988). The effects of graduate training on reasoning: Formal discipline and thinking about everyday life events. *American Psychologist, 43*, 431–443.

Leighton, J., Bird, G., Orsini, C., & Heyes, C. (2010). Social attitudes modulate automatic imitation. *Journal of Experimental Social Psychology, 46*, 905–910.

Leippe, M. R., & Elkin, R. A. (1987). When motives clash: Issue involvement and response involvement as determinants of persuasion. *Journal of Personality and Social Psychology, 52*, 269–278.

Lemyre, L., & Smith, P. M. (1985). Intergroup discrimination and self-esteem in the minimal group paradigm. *Journal of Personality and Social Psychology, 49*, 660–670.

Lepore, L., & Brown, R. (1997). Category and stereotype activation: Is prejudice inevitable? *Journal of Personality and Social Psychology, 72*, 275–287.

Lepore, S. J., Allen, K. M., & Evans, G. W. (1993). Social support lowers cardiovascular reactivity to an acute stressor. *Psychosomatic Medicine, 55*, 518–524.

Lepper, M. R. (1973). Dissonance, self-perception, and honesty in children. *Journal of Personality and Social Psychology, 23*, 65–74.

Lepper, M. R., & Greene, D. (1978). *The hidden costs of reward*. Hillsdale, NJ: Erlbaum.

Lepper, M. R., Greene, D., & Nisbett, R. E. (1973). Undermining children's intrinsic interest with extrinsic reward: A test of the overjustification hypothesis. *Journal of Personality and Social Psychology, 28*, 129–137.

Lepper, M. R., Ross, L., Vallone, R., & Keavney, M. (unpublished data). Biased perceptions of victory and media hostility in network coverage of presidential debates.

Lepper, M. R., Sagotsky, G., Dafoe, J., & Greene, D. (1982). Consequences of superfluous social constraints: Effect on young children's social inferences and subsequent intrinsic interest. *Journal of Personality and Social Psychology, 42*, 51–65.

Lepper, M. R., & Woolverton, M. (2001). The wisdom of practice: Lessons learned from the study of highly effective tutors. In J. Aronson (Ed.), *Improving academic achievement: Contributions of social psychology*. Orlando, FL: Academic Press.

Lepper, M. R., Woolverton, M., Mumme, D. L., & Gurtner, J.-L. (1993). Motivational techniques of expert human tutors: Lessons for the design of computer-based tutors. In S. P. Lajoie & S. J. Derry (Eds.), *Computers as cognitive tools*. Hillsdale, NJ: Erlbaum.

Lerner, J. S., Goldberg, J. H., & Tetlock, P. E. (1998). Sober second thoughts: The effects of accountability, anger, and authoritarianism on attributions of responsibility. *Personality and Social Psychology Bulletin, 24*, 563–574.

Lerner, J. S., & Gonzalez, R. M. (2005). Forecasting one's future based on fleeting subjective experiences. *Personality and Social Psychology Bulletin, 31*(4), 454–466.

Lerner, J. S., Gonzalez, R. M., Small, D. A., & Fischhoff, B. (2003). Effects of fear and anger on perceived risks of terrorism: A national field experiment. *Psychological Science, 14*(2), 144–150.

Lerner, J. S., & Keltner, D. (2001). Fear, anger, and risk. *Journal of Personality and Social Psychology, 81*, 146–159.

Lerner, J. S., Small, D. A., & Loewenstein, G. (2004). Heart strings and purse strings: Carryover effects of emotions on economic decisions. *Psychological Science, 15*, 337–341.

Lerner, M. J. (1980). *The belief in a just world: A fundamental delusion*. New York: Plenum Press.

Lerner, M. J., & Miller, D. T. (1978). Just world research and the attribution process: Looking back and ahead. *Psychological Bulletin, 85*, 1030–1051.

Lerner, M. J., & Simmons, C. H. (1966). Observer's reactions to the "innocent victim": Compassion or rejection? *Journal of Personality and Social Psychology, 4*, 203–210.

Leslie, A. (2000). "Theory of mind" as a mechanism of selective attention. In M. S. Gazzaniga (Ed.), *The new cognitive neurosciences* (pp. 1235–1247). Cambridge, MA: MIT Press.

Levenson, R. W. (2003). Autonomic specificity and emotion. In R. J. Davidson, K. R. Scherer, & H. H. Goldsmith (Eds.), *Handbook of affective sciences* (pp. 212–224). New York: Oxford University Press.

Levenson, R. W., & Gottman, J. M. (1983). Marital interaction: Physiological linkage and affective exchange. *Journal of Personality and Social Psychology, 45*, 587–597.

Leventhal, H. (Ed.). (1970). *Findings and theory in the study of fear communications*. New York: Academic Press.

Leventhal, H., Singer, R. P., & Jones, S. H. (1965). The effects of fear and specificity of recommendation upon attitudes and behavior. *Journal of Personality and Social Psychology, 2*, 20–29.

Leventhal, H., Watts, J. C., & Pagano, F. (1967). Effects of fear and instructions on how to cope with danger. *Journal of Personality and Social Psychology, 6*, 313–321.

Levin, I. P., & Gaeth, G. J. (1988). Framing of attribute information before and after consuming the product. *Journal of Consumer Research, 15*, 374–378.

Levine, J. M. (1989). Reaction to opinion deviance in small groups. In P. B. Paulus (Ed.), *Psychology of group influence* (2nd ed., pp. 187–231). Hillsdale, NJ: Erlbaum.

Levine, J. M., Higgins, E. T., & Choi, H. S. (2000). Development of strategic norms in groups. *Organizational Behavior and Human Decision Processes, 82,* 88–101.

Levine, J. M., & Moreland, R. L. (1990). Progress in small group research. *Annual Review of Psychology, 41,* 585–634.

Levine, J. M., & Moreland, R. L. (1998). Small groups. In D. T. Gilbert, S. T. Fiske, & G. Lindzey (Eds.), *The handbook of social psychology* (4th ed., Vol. 2, pp. 415–469). New York: McGraw-Hill.

LeVine, R. A., & Campbell, D. T. (1972). *Ethnocentrism.* New York: Wiley.

Levinger, G. (1964). Note on need complementarity in marriage. *Psychological Bulletin, 61,* 153–157.

Levinger, G., & Schneider, D. J. (1969). Test of the "risk as a value" hypothesis. *Journal of Personality and Social Psychology, 11,* 165–169.

Levinger, G., Senn, D. J., & Jorgensen, B. W. (1970). Progress toward permanence in courtship: A test of the Kerckhoff-Davis hypothesis. *Sociometry, 33,* 427–433.

Levitt, S. D. (1994). Using repeat challengers to estimate the effect of campaign spending on election outcomes in the U.S. House. *Journal of Political Economy, 102,* 777–798.

Lewin, K. (1935). The conflict between Aristotelian and Galilean modes of thought in contemporary psychology. *Journal of General Psychology, 5,* 141–177.

Lewin, K. (1952). Group decision and social change. In G. E. Swanson, T. M. Newcomb, & E. L. Hartley (Eds.), *Readings in social psychology.* New York: Holt.

Lewis, M., & Sullivan, M. W. (2005). The development of self-conscious emotions. In A. J. Elliot & C. S. Dweck (Eds.), *Handbook of competence and motivation.* New York: Guilford Press.

Lewis, M. A., & Neighbors, C. (2004). Gender-specific misperceptions of college student drinking norms. *Psychology of Addictive Behaviors, 18,* 334–339.

Leyens, J. P., Camino, L., Parke, R. D., & Berkowitz, L. (1975). Effects of movie violence on aggression in a field setting as a function of group dominance and cohesion. *Journal of Personality and Social Psychology, 32,* 346–360.

Leyens, J. P., Cisneros, T., & Hossay, J. F. (1976). Decentration as a means of reducing aggression after exposure to violent stimuli. *European Journal of Social Psychology, 6,* 459–473.

Leyens, J. P., & Picus, S. (1973). Identification with the winner of a fight and name mediation: Their differential effects upon subsequent aggressive behavior. *British Journal of Social and Clinical Psychology, 12,* 374–377.

Leyens, J. P., Rodriguez, A. P, Rodriguez, R. T., Gaunt, R., Paladino, M. P., Vaes, J., & Demoulin, S. (2001). Psychological essentialism and the differential attribution of uniquely human emotions to ingroups and outgroups. *European Journal of Social Psychology, 31,* 395–411.

Li, Y., Johnson, E. J., & Zaval, L. (2011). Local warming: Daily temperature change influences belief in global warming. *Psychological Science, 22,* 454–459.

Li, J., Wang, L., & Fischer, K. W. (2004). The organization of Chinese shame concepts. *Cognition and Emotion, 18*(6), 767–797.

Libby, L. K., & Eibach, R. P. (2011). Visual perspective in mental imagery: A representational tool that functions in judgment, emotion, and self-insight. In J. M. Olson & M. P. Zanna (Eds.), *Advances in experimental social psychology* (Vol. 44, pp. 185–245). Burlington, VT: Academic Press.

Libby, L. K., Shaeffer, E. M., Eibach, R. P., & Slemmer, J. A. (2007). Picture yourself at the polls: Visual perspective in mental imagery affects self-perception and behavior. *Psychological Science, 18,* 199–203.

Libby, L. K., Valenti, G., Pfent, A., & Eibach, R. P. (2011). Seeing failure in your life: Third-person imagery causes self-esteem to shape reactions to recalled and imagined failure. Manuscript under review.

Liberman, N., Sagristano, M., & Trope, Y. (2002). The effect of temporal distance on level of construal. *Journal of Experimental Social Psychology, 38,* 523–535.

Liberman, V., Samuels, S. M., & Ross, L. (2002). The name of the game: Predictive power of reputations vs. situational labels in determining Prisoner's Dilemma game moves. *Personality and Social Psychology Bulletin, 30,* 1175–1185.

Lieberman, M. D. (2007). Social cognitive neuroscience: A review of core processes. *Annual Review of Psychology, 58,* 259–289.

Lieberman, M. D., Hariri, A., Jarcho, J. M., Eisenberger, N. I., & Bookheimer, S. Y. (2005). An fMRI investigation of race-related amygdala activity in African-American and Caucasian-American individuals. *Nature Neuroscience, 8,* 720–722.

Linder, D. E., Cooper, J., & Jones, E. E. (1967). Decision freedom as a determinant of the role of incentive magnitude in attitude change. *Journal of Personality and Social Psychology, 6,* 245–254.

Linville, P. W. (1982). The complexity-extremity effect and age-based stereotyping. *Journal of Personality and Social Psychology, 42,* 193–211.

Linville, P. W. (1985). Self-complexity and affective extremity: Don't put all of your eggs in one cognitive basket. *Social Cognition, 3,* 94–120.

Linville, P. W. (1987). Self-complexity as a cognitive buffer against stress-related illness and depression. *Journal of Personality and Social Psychology, 52,* 663–676.

Linville, P. W., & Carlston, D. E. (1994). Social cognition of the self. In P. G. Devine, D. L. Hamilton, & T. M. Ostrom (Eds.), *Social Cognition: Impact on Social Psychology* (pp. 143–193). San Diego: Academic Press.

Linville, P. W., Fischer, G. W., & Fischhoff, B. (1993). AIDS risk perceptions and decision biases. In J. B. Pryor and G. D. Reeder (Eds.), *The social psychology of HIV infection* (pp. 5–38). Hillsdale, NJ: Erlbaum.

Linville, P. W., Fischer, G. W., & Salovey, P. (1989). Perceived distributions of the characteristics of in-group and out-group members: Empirical evidence and a computer simulation. *Journal of Personality and Social Psychology, 57,* 165–188.

Lipkus, I. M., Dalbert, C., & Siegler, I. C. (1996). The importance of distinguishing the belief in a just world for self versus for others: Implications for psychological well-being. *Personality and Social Psychology Bulletin, 22,* 666–677.

Lippmann, W. (1922). *Public opinion.* New York: Harcourt Brace.

Liptak, A. (2011, August 23). 34 years later, Supreme Court will revisit eyewitness IDs. *New York Times.* Retrieved from http://www.nytimes.com/2011/08/23/us/23bar.html?scp= 1&sq=eyewitness%20identification&st=cse

Livingston, R. W., & Brewer, M. B. (2002). What are we really priming? Cue-based versus category-based processing of facial stimuli. *Journal of Personality and Social Psychology, 82,* 5–18.

Livshits, G., & Kobyliansky, E. (1991). Fluctuating asymmetry as a possible measure of developmental homeostasis in humans: A review. *Human Biology, 63*, 441–466.

Locke, K. D., & Horowitz, L. M. (1990). Satisfaction in interpersonal interactions as a function of similarity in level of dysphoria. *Journal of Personality and Social Psychology, 58*, 823–831.

Lockwood, P. (2002). Could it happen to you? Predicting the impact of downward social comparisons on the self. *Journal of Personality and Social Psychology, 82*, 343–358.

Loewenstein, G., & Lerner, J. S. (2003). The role of affect in decision making. In R. J. Davidson, K. R. Scherer, & H. H. Goldsmith (Eds.), *Handbook of affective sciences* (pp. 619–642). New York: Oxford University Press.

Loftus, E. F. (1993). The reality of repressed memories. *American Psychologist, 48*, 518–537.

Loftus, E. F. (2001). Imagining the past. *The Psychologist, 14*, 584–587.

Loftus, E. F. (2003). The dangers of memory. In R. J. Sternberg (Ed.), *Psychologists defying the crowd: Stories of those who battled the establishment and won* (pp. 105–117). Washington, DC: American Psychological Association.

Loftus, E. F., & Ketcham, K. (1994). *The myth of repressed memory.* New York: St. Martin's Press.

Loftus, E. F., Miller, D. G. & Burns, H. J. (1978). Semantic integration of verbal information into a visual memory. *Human Learning and Memory, 4*, 19–31.

Loftus, E. F., & Pickrell, J. E. (1995). The formation of false memories. *Psychiatric Annals, 25*, 720–725.

Longley, J., & Pruitt, D. G. (1980). Groupthink: A critique of Janis' theory. In L. Wheeler (Ed.), *Review of personality and social psychology.* Beverly Hills, CA: Sage.

Lord, C. G., Desforges, D. M., Ramsey, S. L., Trezza, G. R., & Lepper, M. R. (1991). Typicality effects in attitude-behavior consistency: Effects of category discrimination and category knowledge. *Journal of Experimental Social Psychology, 27*, 550–575.

Lord, C. G., Lepper, M. R., & Mackie, D. (1984). Attitude prototypes as determinants of attitude-behavior consistency. *Journal of Personality and Social Psychology, 46*, 1254–1266.

Lord, C., Ross, L., & Lepper, M. (1979). Biased assimilation and attitude polarization: The effects of prior theories on subsequently considered evidence. *Journal of Personality and Social Psychology, 37*, 2098–2109.

Lord, C. G., Scott, K. O., Pugh, M. A., & Desforges, D. M. (1997). Leakage beliefs and the correspondence bias. *Personality and Social Psychology Bulletin, 23*, 824–836.

Lorenz, K. (1971/1950). Part and parcel in animal and human societies. In *Studies in animal and human behaviour* (Vol. 2, pp. 115–195). Cambridge, MA: Harvard University Press.

Losch, M. E., & Cacioppo, J. T. (1990). Cognitive dissonance may enhance sympathetic tonus, but attitudes are changed to reduce negative affect rather than arousal. *Journal of Experimental Social Psychology, 26*, 289–304.

Lott, A. J., & Lott, B. E. (1961). Group cohesiveness, communication level, and conformity. *Journal of Abnormal and Social Psychology, 62*, 408–412.

Lott, A. J., & Lott, B. E. (1974). The role of reward in formation of positive interpersonal attitudes. In T. L. Huston (Ed.), *Foundations of interpersonal attraction* (pp. 171–189). New York: Academic Press.

Lowery, B. S., Unzueta, M. M., Knowles, E. D., & Goff, P. A. (2006). Concern for the ingroup and opposition to affirmative action. *Journal of Personality and Social Psychology, 90*, 961–974.

Luo, S., & Zhang, G. (2009). What leads to romantic attraction: Similarity, reciprocity, security, or beauty? Evidence from a speed-dating study. *Journal of Personality, 77*(4), 933–964.

Lutz, C. A. (1988). *Unnatural emotions: Everyday sentiments on a Micronesian atoll and their challenge to Western theory.* Chicago: University of Chicago Press.

Lydon, J., Zanna, M. P., & Ross, M. (1988). Bolstering attitudes by autobiographical recall: Attitude persistence and selective memory. *Personality and Social Psychology Bulletin, 14*, 78–86.

Lynam, D. R., Milich, R., Zimmerman, R., Novak, S. P., Logan, T. K., Martin, C. E., et al. (1999). Project DARE: No effects at 10-year follow-up. *Journal of Consulting and Clinical Psychology, 67*, 590–593.

Lynch, J. J. (1979). *The broken heart: The medical consequences of loneliness.* New York: Basic Books.

Lyubomirsky, S. (2007). *The how of happiness.* New York: Penguin Press.

Lyubomirsky, S., King, L., & Diener, E. (2005). The benefits of frequent positive affect: Does happiness lead to success? *Psychological Bulletin, 131*, 803–855.

Lyubomirsky, S., & Nolen-Hoeksema, S. (1995). Effects of self-focused rumination on negative thinking and interpersonal problem solving. *Journal of Personality and Social Psychology, 69*, 176–190.

Lyubomirsky, S., Sheldon, K. M., & Schkade, D. (2005). Pursuing happiness: The architecture of sustainable change. *Review of General Psychology, 9*, 111–131.

Ma, D. S., & Correll, J. (2011). Target prototypicality moderates racial bias in the decision to shoot. *Journal of Experimental Social Psychology, 47*, 391–396.

Ma, V., & Schoeneman, T. J. (1997). Individualism versus collectivism: A comparison of Kenyan and American self-concepts. *Basic and Applied Social Psychology, 19*, 261–273.

Maass, A., & Clark, R. D. III (1983). Internalization versus compliance: Different processes underlying minority influence and conformity. *European Journal of Social Psychology, 13*, 197–215.

Maass, A., Salvi, D., Arcuri, L., & Semin, G. (1989). Language use in intergroup contexts: The linguistic intergroup bias. *Journal of Personality and Social Psychology, 57*, 981–993.

Maccoby, E. E. (1990). Gender and relationships: A developmental account. *American Psychologist, 45*, 513–520.

Maccoby, E. E., & Jacklin, C. N. (1974). *The psychology of sex differences.* Stanford, CA: Stanford University Press.

MacCoun, R. (1993). Blaming others to a fault. *Chance, 6*, 31–33.

MacDonald, G., & Leary, M. R. (2005). Why does social exclusion hurt? The relationship between social and physical pain. *Psychological Bulletin, 131*(2), 202–223.

Machiavelli, N. (1532/2003). *The prince* (G. Bull, Trans.). New York: Penguin Classics.

Macintyre, S., Maciver, S., & Solomon, A. (1993). Area, class, and health: Should we be focusing on places or people? *Journal of Social Policy, 22*, 213–234.

Mackie, D. M. (1987). Systematic and nonsystematic processing of majority and minority persuasive communications. *Journal of Personality and Social Psychology, 53*, 41–52.

Mackie, D. M., Silver, L. A., & Smith, E. R. (2004). Intergroup emotions: Emotion as an intergroup phenomenon. In L. Z. Tiedens & C. W. Leach (Eds.), *The social life of emotions* (pp. 227–246). New York: Cambridge University Press.

Mackie, D. M., & Worth, L. T. (1989). Cognitive deficits and the mediation of positive affect in persuasion. *Journal of Personality and Social Psychology, 57*, 27–40.

Macrae, C. N., Alnwick, K. A., Milne, A. B., & Schloerscheidt, A. M. (2002). Person perception across the menstrual cycle: Hormonal influences on social-cognitive functioning. *Psychological Science, 13,* 532–536.

Macrae, C. N., & Bodenhausen, G. V. (2000). Social cognition: Thinking categorically about others. *Annual Review of Psychology, 51,* 93–120.

Macrae, C. N., Hewstone, M., & Griffiths, R. J. (1993). Processing load and memory for stereotype-based information. *European Journal of Social Psychology, 23,* 77–87.

Macrae, C. N., Milne, A. B., & Bodenhausen, G. V. (1994). Stereotypes as energy-saving devices: A peek inside the cognitive toolbox. *Journal of Personality and Social Psychology, 66,* 37–47.

Macrae, C. N., Stangor, C., & Milne, A. B. (1994). Activating social stereotypes: A functional analysis. *Journal of Experimental Social Psychology, 30,* 370–389.

Magee, J. C., Galinsky, A. D., Inesi, M. E., & Gruenfeld, D. H. (2006). Power and perspectives not taken. *Psychological Science, 17*(12), 1068–1074.

Major, B. (1994). From social inequality to personal entitlement: The role of social comparisons, legitimacy appraisals, and group membership. *Advances in Experimental Social Psychology, 26,* 293–355.

Malle, B. F. (1999). How people explain behavior: A new theoretical framework. *Personality and Social Psychology Review, 3,* 23–48.

Malle, B. F. (2001). Folk explanations of intentional actions. In B. F. Malle, L. J. Moses, & D. A. Baldwin (Eds.), *Intentions and intentionality: Foundations of social cognition.* Cambridge, MA: MIT Press.

Malle, B. F., Moses, L. J., & Baldwin, D. A. (2001). *Intentions and intentionality: Foundations of social cognition.* Cambridge, MA: MIT Press.

Mann, L. (1981). The baiting crowd in episodes of threatened suicide. *Journal of Personality and Social Psychology, 41,* 703–709.

Manning, J. T., & Hartley, M. A. (1991). Symmetry and ornamentation are correlated in the peacock's train. *Animal Behavior, 42,* 1020–1021.

Maret, S. M. (1983). Attractiveness ratings of photographs of blacks by Cruzans and Americans. *Journal of Psychology, 115,* 113–116.

Maret, S. M., & Harling, G. A. (1985). Cross cultural perceptions of physical attractiveness: Ratings of photos of whites by Cruzans and Americans. *Perceptual and Motor Skills, 60,* 163–166.

Margolin, L., & White, L. (1987). The continuing role of physical attractiveness in marriage. *Journal of Marriage and the Family, 49,* 21–27.

Markow, T. A., & Ricker, J. P. (1992). Male size, developmental stability, and mating success in natural populations on three *Drosophila* species. *Heredity, 69,* 122–127.

Markus, H. (1977). Self-schemata and processing information about the self. *Journal of Personality and Social Psychology, 35,* 63–78.

Markus, H. (1978). The effect of mere presence on social facilitation. An unobtrusive test. *Journal of Experimental Social Psychology, 14,* 389–397.

Markus, H. R., & Kitayama, S. (1991). Culture and the self: Implications for cognition, emotion, and motivation. *Psychological Review, 98,* 224–253.

Markus, H., & Nurius, P. S. (1986). Possible selves. *American Psychologist, 41,* 954–969.

Markus, H., & Wurf, E. (1987). The dynamic self-concept: A social psychological perspective. *Annual Review in Psychology, 38,* 299–337.

Marmot, M. G., Shipley, S., & Rose, G. (1984). Inequalities in death—Specific explanations of a general pattern. *Lancet, 1,* 1003–1006.

Marsh, H. L. (1991). A comparative analysis of crime coverage in newspapers in the United States and other countries from 1960–1989: A review of the literature. *Journal of Criminal Justice, 19,* 67–79.

Marsh, H. W., & Parker, J. W. (1984). Determinants of student self-concept: Is it better to be a relatively large fish in a small pond even if you don't learn to swim as well? *Journal of Personality and Social Psychology, 47,* 213–231.

Martin, G. G., & Clark, R. D. I. (1982). Distress crying in infants: Species and peer specificity. *Developmental Psychology, 18,* 3–9.

Martin, T., & Bumpass, L. (1989). Recent trends in marital disruption. *Demography, 26,* 37–52.

Maruyama, G., & Miller, N. (1980). Physical attractiveness, race, and essay evaluation. *Personality and Social Psychology Bulletin, 6,* 384–390.

Marwell, G., & Ames, R. (1981). Economists free ride, does anyone else? Experiments on the provision of public goods, IV. *Journal of Public Economics, 15,* 295–310.

Masuda, T., Ellsworth, P. C., Mesquita, B., Leu, J., & van de Veerdonk, E. (2004). *A face in the crowd or a crowd in the face: Japanese and American perceptions of others' emotions.* Unpublished manuscript, Hokkaido University.

Mathur, V. A., Harada, T., Lipke, T., & Chiao, J. Y. (2010). Neural basis of extraordinary empathy and altruistic motivation. *Neuroimage, 51,* 1468–1475.

Matsumoto, D., Keltner, D., Shiota, M. N., O'Sullivan, M., & Frank, M. (2008). Facial expressions of emotion. In M. Lewis, J. M. Haviland-Jones, & L. F. Barrett (Eds.), *Handbook of emotions* (pp. 211–234). New York: Guilford Press.

Matsumoto, D., & Willingham, B. (2006). The thrill of victory and the agony of defeat: Spontaneous expressions of medal winners of the 2004 Athens Olympic games. *Journal of Personality and Social Psychology, 91,* 568–581.

Matza, D. (1964). *Delinquency and drift.* New York: Wiley.

Mauro, R., Sato, K., & Tucker, J. (1992). The role of appraisal in human emotions: A cross-cultural study. *Journal of Personality and Social Psychology, 62,* 301–317.

Mayer, J. D., Barsade, S. G., & Roberts, R. D. (2008). Human abilities: Emotional intelligence. *Annual Review of Psychology, 59,* 507–536.

McAdams, D. P. (2008). Personal narratives and the life story. In O. P. John, R. Robins, & L. Pervin (Eds.), *Handbook of personality: Theories and research* (3rd ed., pp. 242–262). New York: Guilford Press.

McArthur, L. Z. (1972). The how and what of why: Some determinants and consequences of causal attribution. *Journal of Personality and Social Psychology, 13,* 733–742.

McArthur, L. Z., & Baron, R. M. (1983). Toward an ecological theory of social perception. *Psychological Review, 90,* 215–238.

McArthur, L. Z., & Post, D. L. (1977). Figural emphasis and person perception. *Journal of Experimental Social Psychology, 13,* 520–533.

McCauley, C. (1989). The nature of social influence in groupthink: Compliance and internalization. *Journal of Personality and Social Psychology, 57,* 250–260.

McCauley, C. (1998). Group dynamics in Janis's theory of groupthink: Backward and forward. *Organizational Behavior and Human Decision Processes, 73,* 142–162.

McConahay, J. B. (1986). Modern racism, ambivalence, and the modern racism scale. In J. F. Dovidio & S. L. Gaertner (Eds.), *Prejudice, discrimination, and racism* (pp. 91–126). Orlando, FL: Academic Press.

McConahay, J. B., Hardee, B. B., & Batts, V. (1981). Has racism declined in America? It depends upon who is asking and what is asked. *Journal of Conflict Resolution, 25,* 563–579.

McConnell, A. R., & Leibold, J. M. (2001). Relations among the implicit association test, discriminatory behavior, and explicit measures of racial attitudes. *Journal of Experimental Social Psychology, 37,* 435–442.

McCoy, S. K., & Major, B. (2003). Group identification moderates emotional responses to perceived prejudice. *Personality and Social Psychology Bulletin, 29,* 1005–1017.

McCrae, R. R., Costa, P. T., & Yik, M. S. M. (1996). Universal aspects of Chinese personality structure. In M. H. Bond (Ed.), *The handbook of Chinese psychology* (pp. 189–207). Hong Kong: Oxford University Press.

McCullough, M. C., Kilpatrick, S. D., Emmons, R. A., & Larson, D. B. (2001). Is gratitude a moral affect? *Psychological Bulletin, 127,* 249–266.

McCullough, M. E. (2008). *Beyond revenge: The evolution of the forgiveness instinct.* New York: Basic Books.

McCullough, M. E., Fincham, F. D., & Tsang, J. (2003). Forgiveness, forbearance, and time: The temporal unfolding of transgression-related interpersonal motivations. *Journal of Personality and Social Psychology, 84,* 540–557.

McFayden-Ketchum, M., Bates, S. A., Dodge, K. A., & Pettit, G. S. (1996). Patterns of change in early childhood aggressive-disruptive behavior: Gender differences in predictions from early coercive and affectionate mother-child interactions. *Child Development, 67,* 2417–2433.

McGill, A. L. (1989). Context effects in judgments of causation. *Journal of Personality and Social Psychology, 57,* 189–200.

McGlone, M. S., & Tofighbakhsh, J. (2000). Birds of a feather flock conjointly(?): Rhyme as reason in aphorisms. *Psychological Science, 11,* 424–428.

McGrath, J. (1984). *Groups: Interaction and performance.* Englewood Cliffs, NJ: Prentice-Hall.

McGuire, W. J. (1985). Attitudes and attitude change. In G. Lindzey & E. Aronson (Eds.), *Handbook of social psychology* (3rd ed., Vol. 2, pp. 233–346). New York: Random House.

McGuire, W. J. (1986). The myth of massive media impact: Savagings and salvagings. *Public Communication and Behavior, 1,* 173–257.

McGuire, W. J., & Padawer-Singer, A. (1978). Trait salience in the spontaneous self-concept. *Journal of Personality and Social Psychology, 33,* 743–754.

McGuire, W. J., & Papageorgis, D. (1961). The relative efficacy of various types of prior belief-defense in producing immunity against persuasion. *Journal of Abnormal and Social Psychology, 62,* 327–337.

McKenna, K. Y. A., & Bargh, J. A. (1998). Coming out in the age of the Internet: Identity demarginalization through virtual group participation. *Journal of Personality and Social Psychology, 75,* 681–694.

McMahon, D. M. (2006). *Happiness: A history.* New York: Grove Press.

McNeil, B. J., Pauker, S. G., Sox, H. C., & Tversky, A. (1982). On the elicitation of preferences for alternative therapies. *New England Journal of Medicine, 306,* 1259–1262.

McNulty, J. K., & Karney, B. R. (2001). Attributions in marriage: Integrating specific and global evaluations of a relationship. *Personality and Social Psychology Bulletin, 27,* 943–955.

McPherson, K. (1983). Opinion-related information seeking: Personal and situational variables. *Personality and Social Psychology Bulletin, 9,* 116–124.

McQueen, A., & Klein, W. (2006). Experimental manipulations of self-affirmation: A systematic review. *Self and Identity, 5,* 289–354.

Mead, G. H. (1934). *Mind, self, and society.* Chicago: University of Chicago Press.

Medcoff, J. W. (1990). PEAT: An integrative model of attribution processes. In M. P. Zanna (Ed.), *Advances in experimental social psychology* (Vol. 23, pp. 111–209). New York: Academic Press.

Medvec, V. H., Madey, S. F., & Gilovich, T. (1995). When less is more: Counterfactual thinking and satisfaction among Olympic medalists. *Journal of Personality and Social Psychology, 69,* 603–610.

Mehrabian, A., & Williams, M. (1969). Nonverbal concomitants of perceived and intended persuasiveness. *Journal of Personality and Social Psychology, 13,* 37–58.

Merton, R. (1957). *Social theory and social structure.* Glencoe, IL: Free Press.

Mesquita, B. (2001). Emotions in collectivist and individualist contexts. *Journal of Personality and Social Psychology, 80,* 68–74.

Mesquita, B. (2003). Emotions as dynamic cultural phenomena. In R. J. Davidson, K. R. Scherer, & H. H. Goldsmith (Eds.), *Handbook of affective sciences* (pp. 871–890). New York: Oxford University Press.

Mesquita, B., & Ellsworth, P. C. (2001). The role of culture in appraisal. In K. R. Scherer & A. Schorr (Eds.), *Appraisal processes in emotion: Theory, methods, research.* New York: Oxford University Press.

Mesquita, B., & Frijda, N. H. (1992). Cultural variations in emotions: A review. *Psychological Bulletin, 112,* 179–204.

Mesquita, B., & Karasawa, M. (2002). Different emotional lives. *Cognition and Emotion, 16,* 127–141.

Mesquita, B., & Leu, J. (2007). The cultural psychology of emotion. In S. Kitayama & D. Cohen (Eds.), *The handbook of cultural psychology* (pp. 734–759). New York: Guilford Press.

Meyer, J. P., & Pepper, S. (1977). Need compatibility and marital adjustment in young married couples. *Journal of Personality and Social Psychology, 35,* 331–342.

Michaels, J. W., Blommel, J. M., Brocato, R. M., Linkous, R. A., & Rowe, J. S. (1982). Social facilitation and inhibition in a natural setting. *Replications in Social Psychology, 2,* 21–24.

Mikulincer, M., & Shaver, P. R. (2003). The attachment behavioral system in adulthood: Activation, psychodynamics, and interpersonal processes. In M. P. Zanna (Ed.), *Advances in experimental social psychology* (Vol. 35, pp. 53–152). New York: Academic Press.

Mikulincer, M., Shaver, P. R., Gillath, O., & Nitzberg, R. E. (2005). Attachment, caregiving, and altruism: Boosting attachment security increases compassion and helping. *Journal of Personality and Social Psychology, 89,* 817–839.

Milgram, S. (1961). Nationality and conformity. *Scientific American, 205,* 45–51.

Milgram, S. (1963). Behavioral study of obedience. *Journal of Abnormal and Social Psychology, 67,* 371–378.

Milgram, S. (1965). Some conditions of obedience and disobedience to authority. *Human Relations, 18,* 57–75.

Milgram, S. (1970). The experience of living in cities. *Science, 167,* 1461–1468.

Milgram, S. (1974). *Obedience to authority: An experimental view.* New York: Harper & Row.

Millar, M., & Tesser, A. (1986). Effects of affective and cognitive focus on the attitude-behavior relation. *Journal of Personality and Social Psychology, 51,* 270–276.

Miller, A. G. (1986). *The obedience experiments: A case study of controversy in social science.* New York: Praeger.

Miller, A. G., Ashton, W., & Mishal, M. (1990). Beliefs concerning the features of constrained behavior: A basis for the fundamental attribution error. *Journal of Personality and Social Psychology, 59*, 635–650.

Miller, A. G., Jones, E. E., & Hinkle, S. (1981). A robust attribution error in the personality domain. *Journal of Experimental Social Psychology, 17*, 587–600.

Miller, D. T., & McFarland, C. (1986). Counterfactual thinking and victim compensation: A test of norm theory. *Personality and Social Psychology Bulletin, 12*, 513–519.

Miller, D. T., & McFarland, C. (1991). When social comparison goes awry: The case of pluralistic ignorance. In J. M. Suls & T. A. Wills (Eds.), *Social comparison: Contemporary theory and research* (pp. 287–313). Hillsdale, NJ: Erlbaum.

Miller, D. T., & Taylor, B. R. (1995). Counterfactual thought, regret, and superstition: How to avoid kicking yourself. In N. J. Roese & J. M. Olson (Eds.), *What might have been: The social psychology of counterfactual thinking*. Mahwah, NJ: Erlbaum.

Miller, N., & Brewer, M. B. (1986). Categorization effects on ingroup and outgroup perception. In J. F. Dovidio & S. L. Gaertner (Eds.), *Prejudice, discrimination, and racism* (pp. 209–230). Orlando, FL: Academic Press.

Miller, N. E. (1941). The frustration-aggression hypothesis. *Psychological Review, 48*, 337–342.

Miller, N. E., & Bugelski, R. (1948). Minor studies of aggression: II. The influence of frustrations imposed by the in-group on attitudes expressed toward out-groups. *Journal of Psychology, 25*, 437–442.

Miller, R. S. (1992). The nature and severity of self-reported embarrassing circumstances. *Personality and Social Psychology Bulletin, 18*, 190–198.

Miller, R. S. (1996). *Embarrassment: Poise and peril in everyday life.* New York: Guilford Press.

Miller, R. S., & Leary, M. R. (1992). Social sources and interactive functions of embarrassment. In M. Clark (Ed.), *Emotion and social behavior*. Newbury Park, CA: Sage.

Miller, R. S., & Tangney, J. P. (1994). Differentiating embarrassment from shame. *Journal of Social and Clinical Psychology, 13*, 273–287.

Miller, S. L., & Maner, J. K. (2010). Scent of a woman: Men's testosterone responses to olfactory ovulation cues. *Psychological Science, 21*(2), 276–283.

Miller, S. L., & Maner, J. K. (2011). Ovulation as a male mating prime: Subtle signs of women's fertility influence men's mating cognition and behavior. *Journal of Personality and Social Psychology, 100*(2), 295–308.

Mineka, S., Rafaeli, E., & Yovel, I. (2003). Cognitive biases in emotional disorders: Information processing and social-cognitive perspectives. In R. J. Davidson, K. R. Scherer, & H. H. Goldsmith (Eds.), *Handbook of affective sciences* (pp. 976–1009). New York: Oxford University Press.

Mischel, W., & Shoda, Y. (1995). A cognitive-affective system theory of personality: Reconceptualizing situations, dispositions, dynamics, and invariance in personality structures. *Psychological Review, 102*, 246–268.

Mita, T. H., Dermer, M., & Knight, J. (1977). Reversed facial images and the mere-exposure hypothesis. *Journal of Personality and Social Psychology, 35*, 597–601.

Mithen, S. (1996). *The prehistory of the mind: The cognitive origins of art and science.* London: Thames and Hudson.

Moller, A. P. (1992a). Female swallow preference for symmetrical male sexual ornaments. *Nature, 357*, 238–240.

Moller, A. P. (1992b). Parasites differentially increase the degree of fluctuating asymmetry in secondary sexual characteristics. *Journal of Evolutionary Biology, 5*, 691–699.

Moore, J. S., Graziano, W. G., & Millar, M. G. (1987). Physical attractiveness, sex role orientation, and the evaluation of adults and children. *Personality and Social Psychology Bulletin, 13*, 95–102.

Moran, G., Cutler, B. L., & De Lisa, A. (1994). Attitudes toward tort reform, scientific jury selection, and juror bias: Verdict inclination in criminal and civil trials. *Law and Psychology Review, 18*, 309–328.

Moreland, R. L., & Beach, S. R. (1992). Exposure effects in the classroom: The development of affinity among students. *Journal of Experimental Social Psychology, 28*, 255–276.

Moreland, R. L., & Levine, J. M. (1989). Newcomers and oldtimers in small groups. In P. Paulus (Ed.), *Psychology of group influence* (2nd ed., pp. 143–186). Hillsdale, NJ: Erlbaum.

Morelli, G. A., & Rothbaum, F. (2007). Situating the child in context: Attachment relationships and self-regulation in different cultures. In *Handbook of Cultural Psychology* (pp. 500–527). New York: Guilford Press.

Morgan, C. A., III, Hazlett, G., Doran, A., Garrett, S., Hoyt, G., et al. (2004). Accuracy of eyewitness memory for persons encountered during exposure to highly intense stress. *International Journal of Law and Psychiatry, 27*, 265–279.

Morris, M. W., & Peng, K. (1994). Culture and cause: American and Chinese attributions for social and physical events. *Journal of Personality and Social Psychology, 67*, 949–971.

Morrow, J., & Nolen-Hoeksema, S. (1990). Effects of responses to depression on the remediation of depressive affect. *Journal of Personality and Social Psychology, 58*, 519–527.

Moscovici, S. (1985). Social influence and conformity. In G. Lindzey & E. Aronson (Eds.), *The handbook of social psychology* (3rd ed., Vol. 2, pp. 347–412). New York: Random House.

Moscovici, S., Lage, E., & Naffrechoux, M. (1969). Influences of a consistent minority on the responses of a majority in a color perception task. *Sociometry, 32*, 365–380.

Moscovici, S., & Zavalloni, M. (1969). The group as a polarizer of attitudes. *Journal of Personality and Social Psychology, 12*, 125–135.

Moskowitz, D. S. (1994). Cross-situational generality and the interpersonal circumplex. *Journal of Personality and Social Psychology, 66*, 921–933.

Moskowitz, J. T., Epel, E. S., & Acree, M. (2008). Positive affect uniquely predicts lower risk of mortality in people with diabetes. *Health Psychology, 27*, 73–82.

Mullen, B., & Riordan, C. A. (1988). Self-serving attributions for performance in naturalistic settings: A meta-analytic review. *Journal of Applied Social Psychology, 18*, 3–22.

Munro, D. (1985). Introduction. In D. Munro (Ed.), *Individualism and holism: Studies in Confucian and Taoist values* (pp. 1–34). Ann Arbor: Center for Chinese Studies, University of Michigan.

Muraven, M. R., & Baumeister, R. F. (2000). Self-regulation and depletion of limited resources: Does self-control resemble a muscle? *Psychological Bulletin, 126*, 247–259.

Muraven, M., & Slessareva, E. (2003). Mechanisms of self-control failure: Motivation and limited resources. *Personality and Social Psychology Bulletin, 29*, 894–906.

Murphy, S. T., & Zajonc, R. B. (1993). Affect, cognition, and awareness: Affective priming with optimal and suboptimal stimulus exposures. *Journal of Personality and Social Psychology, 64*, 723–739.

Murray, S. L., & Holmes, J. G. (1993). Seeing virtues in faults: Negativity and the transformation of interpersonal narratives in close relationships. *Journal of Personality and Social Psychology, 65,* 707–723.

Murray, S. L., & Holmes, J. G. (1997). A leap of faith? Positive illusions in romantic relationships. *Personality and Social Psychology Bulletin, 23,* 586–604.

Murray, S. L., & Holmes, J. G. (1999). The (mental) ties that bind: Cognitive structures that predict relationship resilience. *Journal of Personality and Social Psychology, 77,* 1228–1244.

Murray, S. L., Holmes, J. G., Dolderman, D., & Griffin, D. W. (2000). What the motivated mind sees: Comparing friends' perspectives to married partners' views of each other. *Journal of Experimental Social Psychology, 36,* 600–620.

Murray, S. L., Holmes, J. G., & Griffin, D. W. (1996). The benefits of positive illusions: Idealization and the construction of satisfaction in close relationships. *Journal of Personality and Social Psychology, 70,* 79–98.

Murray, S. L., Holmes, J. G., MacDonald, G., & Ellsworth, P. C. (1998). Through the looking glass darkly? When self-doubts turn into relationship insecurities. *Journal of Personality and Social Psychology, 75,* 1459–1480.

Mussweiler, T. (2003). Comparison processes in social judgment: Mechanisms and consequences. *Psychological Review, 110,* 472–489.

Mussweiler, T., & Rüter, K. (2003). What friends are for! The use of routine standards in social comparison. *Journal of Personality and Social Psychology, 85,* 467–481.

Mustard, D. B. (2001). Racial, ethnic, and gender disparities in sentencing: Evidence from the U.S. federal courts. *Journal of Law and Economics, 19,* 285–314.

Mwaniki, M. K. (1973). *The relationship between self-concept and academic achievement in Kenyan pupils.* Unpublished doctoral dissertation, Stanford University, California.

Myers, D. G. (1999). Close relationships and quality of life. In K. Kahneman, E. Diener, & N. Schwarz (Eds.), *Well-being: The foundations of hedonic psychology* (pp. 374–391). New York: Russell Sage Foundation.

Myers, D. G. (2000a). *The American paradox.* New Haven: Yale University Press.

Myers, D. G. (2000b). The funds, friends, and faith of happy people. *American Psychologist, 55,* 56–67.

Myers, D. G., & Bishop, G. D. (1971). Enhancement of dominant attitudes in group discussion. *Journal of Personality and Social Psychology, 20,* 386–391.

Na, J., & Kitayama, S. (2011). Spontaneous trait inference is culture-specific: Behavioral and neural evidence. *Psychological Science, 22,* 1025–1032.

Nahemow, L., & Lawton, M. P. (1975). Similarity and propinquity in friendship formation. *Journal of Personality and Social Psychology, 32,* 205–213.

Neff, L. A., & Karney, B. R. (2002). Judgments of a relationship partner: Specific accuracy but global enhancement. *Journal of Personality, 70,* 1079–1112.

Neighbors, C., Larimer, M. E., & Lewis, M. A. (2004). Targeting misperceptions of descriptive drinking norms: Efficacy of a computer-delivered personalized normative feedback intervention. *Journal of Consulting and Clinical Psychology, 72,* 434–447.

Neimeyer, R. A., & Mitchell, K. A. (1988). Similarity and attraction: A longitudinal study. *Journal of Social and Personal Relationships, 5,* 131–148.

Nel, E., Helmreich, R., & Aronson, E. (1969). Opinion change in the advocate as a function of the persuasibility of his audience: A clarification on the meaning of dissonance. *Journal of Personality and Social Psychology, 12,* 117–124.

Nelson, L. D., & Morrison, E. L. (2005). Judgments of food and finances influence preferences for potential partners. *Psychological Science, 16,* 167–173.

Nemeroff, C., & Rozin, P. (1989). "You are what you eat": Applying the demand-free "impressions" technique to an unacknowledged belief. *Ethos, 17,* 50–69.

Nemeth, C. (1986). Differential contributions of majority and minority influence. *Psychological Review, 93,* 23–32.

Nesse, R. (1990). Evolutionary explanations of emotions. *Human Nature, 1,* 261–289.

Neuberg, S. L. (1988). Behavioral implications of information presented outside of conscious awareness: The effect of subliminal presentation of trait information on behavior in the Prisoner's Dilemma game. *Social Cognition, 6,* 207–230.

Neuberg, S. L., & Fiske, S. T. (1987). Motivational influences on impression formation: Outcome dependency, accuracy-driven attention, and individuating processes. *Journal of Personality and Social Psychology, 53,* 431–444.

Newcomb, T. M. (1956). The prediction of interpersonal attraction. *American Psychologist, 1,* 575–586.

Newcomb, T. M. (1958). Attitude development as a function of reference groups. In E. E. Maccoby, T. M. Newcomb, & E. L. Hartley (Eds.), *Readings in social psychology* (3rd ed.). New York: Holt, Rinehart and Winston.

Newcomb, T. M. (1961). *The acquaintance process.* New York: Holt, Rinehart and Winston.

Newman, L. S. (1991). Why are traits inferred spontaneously? A developmental approach. *Social Cognition, 9,* 221–253.

Newman, L. S. (1993). How individualists interpret behavior: Idiocentrism and spontaneous trait inference. *Social Cognition, 11,* 243–269.

Niedenthal, P. M. (2008). Emotion concepts. In M. Lewis, J. M. Haviland-Jones, & L. F. Barrett (Eds.), *Handbook of emotions* (pp. 587–600). New York: Guilford Press.

Niedenthal, P. M., Barsalou, L. W., Winkielman, P., Krauth-Gruber, S., & Ric, F. (2005). Embodiment in attitudes, social perception, and emotion. *Personality and Social Psychology Review, 9,* 184–211.

Niedenthal, P. M., Mermillod, M., Maringer, M., & Hess, U (2010). The Simulation of Smiles (SIMS) model: Embodied simulation and the meaning of facial expression. *Behavioral and Brain Sciences, 33,* 417–433.

Niemi, R. G., & Jennings, M. K. (1991). Issues and inheritance in the formation of party identification. *American Journal of Political Science, 35,* 970–988.

Nier, J. A., Gaertner, S. L., Dovidio, J. F., Banker, B. S. & Ward, C. M. (2001). Changing interracial evaluations and behavior: The benefits of a common ingroup identity. *Group Processes and Intergroup Relations, 4,* 299–316.

Nisbett, R. E. (1993). Violence and U.S. regional culture. *American Psychologist, 48,* 441–449.

Nisbett, R. E. (2003). *The geography of thought: Why we think the way we do.* New York: Free Press.

Nisbett, R. E. (2009). *Intelligence and how to get it: Why schools and cultures count.* New York: Norton.

Nisbett, R. E., Caputo, C., Legant, P., & Maracek, J. (1973). Behavior as seen by the actor and as seen by the observer. *Journal of Personality and Social Psychology, 27,* 154–164.

Nisbett, R. E., & Cohen, D. (1996). *Culture of honor: The psychology of violence in the South.* Boulder, CO: Westview Press.

Nisbett, R. E., Fong, G. T., Lehman, D. R., & Cheng, P. W. (1987). Teaching reasoning. *Science, 238,* 625–631.

Nisbett, R. E., & Ross, L. (1980). *Human inference: Strategies and shortcomings of social judgment.* Englewood Cliffs, NJ: Prentice-Hall.

Nisbett, R. E., & Wilson, T. D. (1977). Telling more than we can know: Verbal reports on mental processes. *Psychological Review, 84,* 231–259.

Nitschke, J. B., Nelson, E. E., Rosch, B. D., Fox, A. S., Oakes, T. R., & Davidson, R. J. (2004). Orbitofrontal cortex tracks positive mood in mothers viewing pictures of their newborn infants. *Neuro-Image, 21,* 583–592.

Nolen-Hoeksema, S. (1987). Sex differences in unipolar depression: Evidence and theory. *Psychological Bulletin, 101,* 259–282.

Nolen-Hoeksema, S. (2003). *Women who think too much.* New York: Holt.

Norenzayan, A., Choi, I., & Nisbett, R. E. (1999). Eastern and Western perceptions of causality for social behavior: Lay theories about personalities and social situations. In D. Prentice & D. Miller (Eds.), *Cultural divides: Understanding and overcoming group conflict* (pp. 239–272). New York: Russell Sage Foundation.

Norenzayan, A., & Heine, S. J. (2004). *Psychological universals: What are they and how can we know?* Vancouver: University of British Columbia.

Norenzayan, A., & Shariff, A. F. (2008). The origin and evolution of religious prosociality. *Science, 322,* 58–62.

North, A. C., Hargreaves, D. J., and McKendrick, J. (1999). The influence of in-store music on wine selections. *Journal of Applied Psychology, 84,* 271–276.

Norton, M. I., Monin, B., Cooper, J., & Hogg, M. (2003). Vicarious dissonance: Attitude change from the inconsistency of others. *Journal of Personality and Social Psychology, 85,* 47–62.

Norton, M. I., Sommers, S. R., Apfelbaum, E. P., Pura, N., & Ariely, A. (2006). Color blindness and interracial interaction: Playing the political correctness game. *Psychological Science, 17,* 949–953.

Norton, M. I., Vandello, J. A., & Darley, J. M. (2004). Casuistry and social category bias. *Journal of Personality and Social Psychology, 87,* 817–831.

Nosek, B. A., Banaji, M. R., & Greenwald, A. G. (2002). Harvesting implicit group attitudes and beliefs from demonstration web site. *Group Dynamics: Theory, Research, and Practice, 6,* 101–115.

Nowak, M. A., Page, K. M., & Sigmund, K. (2000). Fairness versus reason in the ultimatum game. *Science, 289,* 1773–1775.

Nowak, M. A., & Sigmund, K. (1998). Evolution of indirect reciprocity by image scoring. *Nature, 393,* 573–576.

Oakes, J. M., & Rossi, R. H. (2003). The measurement of SES in health research: Current practice and steps toward a new approach. *Social Science and Medicine, 56,* 769–784.

Oakes, P. J., & Turner, J. C. (1980). Social categorization and intergroup behavior: Does minimal intergroup discrimination make social identity more positive? *European Journal of Social Psychology, 10,* 295–301.

Oatley, K. (1993). Social construction in emotion. In M. Lewis & J. Haviland (Eds.), *Handbook of emotions* (pp. 342–352). New York: Guilford Press.

Oatley, K. (2003). Creative expression and communication of emotions in the visual and narrative arts. In R. J. Davidson, K. R. Scherer, & H. H. Goldsmith (Eds.). *Handbook of affective sciences* (pp. 481–502). New York: Oxford University Press.

Oatley, K. (2004). *Emotions: A brief history.* Malden, MA: Blackwell.

Oatley, K., & Jenkins, J. M. (1992). Human emotions: Function and dysfunction. *Annual Review of Psychology, 43,* 55–85.

Oatley, K., Keltner, D., & Jenkins, J. (2006). *Understanding emotions* (2nd ed.). Malden, MA: Blackwell.

Ochsner, K. N., & Lieberman, M. D. (2001). The emergence of social cognitive neuroscience. *American Psychologist, 56,* 717–734.

Odean, T. (1998). Are investors reluctant to realize their losses? *Journal of Finance, 53,* 1775–1798.

O'Donovan, A., Lin, J., Dhabhar, F. S., Wolkowitz, O., Tillie, J. M., Blackburn, E., et al. (2009). Pessimism correlates with leukocyte telomere shortness and elevated interleukin-6 in post-menopausal women. *Brain Behavior Immunology, 23*(4), 446–449.

Ogbu, J. U. (1991). Low performance as an adaptation: The case of blacks in Stockton, California. In M. A. Gibson & J. U. Ogbu (Eds.), *Minority status and schooling* (pp. 249–285). New York: Garland.

Ogbu, J. U., & Davis, A. (2003). *Black American students in an affluent suburb: A study of academic disengagement.* Mahwah, NJ: Erlbaum.

Öhman, A. (1986). Face the beast and fear the face: Animal and social fears as prototypes for evolutionary analysis of emotions. *Psychophysiology, 23,* 123–145.

O'Keefe, D. J., & Figgé, M. (1997). A guilt-based explanation of the door-in-the-face influence strategy. *Human Communication Research, 24,* 64–81.

O'Keefe, D. J., & Hale, S. L. (1998). The door-in-the-face influence strategy: A random-effects meta-analytic review. In M. E. Roloff (Ed.), *Communication yearbook* (Vol. 21, pp. 1–33). Thousand Oaks, CA: Sage.

O'Keefe, D. J., & Hale, S. L. (2001). An odds-ratio-based meta-analysis of research on the door-in-the-face influence strategy. *Communication Reports, 14,* 31–38.

Olczak, P. V., Kaplan, M. F., & Penrod, S. (1991). Attorneys' lay psychology and its effectiveness in selecting jurors: Three empirical studies. *Journal of Social Behavior and Personality, 6,* 431–452.

Oliner, S., & Oliner, P. (1988). *The altruistic personality.* New York: Free Press.

Olweus, D. (1979). Stability of aggressive reaction patterns in males: A review. *Psychological Bulletin, 86,* 852–875.

Olweus, D. (1980). Familial and temperamental determinants of aggressive behavior in adolescent boys: A causal analysis. *Developmental Psychology, 16,* 644–660.

Omoto, A. M., Malsch, A. M., & Barraza, J. A. (2009). Compassionate acts: Motivations for and correlates of volunteerism among older adults. In B. Fehr, S. Sprecher, & L. G. Underwood (Eds.), *The science of compassionate love: Theory, research, and applications* (pp. 257–282). Malden, MA: Wiley-Blackwell.

Omoto, A. M., & Snyder, M. (1995). Sustained helping without obligation: Motivation, longevity of service, and perceived attitude change among AIDS volunteers. *Journal of Personality and Social Psychology, 68,* 671–686.

Oppenheimer, D. M. (2008). The secret life of fluency. *Trends in Cognitive Sciences, 12,* 237–241.

Orians, G. H., & Heerwagen, J. H. (1992). Evolved responses to landscapes. In J. H. Barlow, L. Cosmides, & J. Tooby (Eds.), *The adapted mind* (pp. 555–580). New York: Oxford University Press.

Ostrom, T. M., & Sedikides, C. (1992). Out-group homogeneity effects in natural and minimal groups. *Psychological Bulletin, 112,* 536–552.

Oveis, C., Horberg, E. J., & Keltner, D. (2010). Compassion, pride, and social intuitions of self-other similarity. *Journal of Personality and Social Psychology, 98,* 618–630.

Oxman, T. E., & Hull, J. G. (1997). Social support, depression, and activities of daily living in older heart surgery patients. *Journal of Gerontology: Psychological Sciences, 52,* 1–14.

Oyserman, D., Bybee, D., & Terry, K. (2006). Possible selves and academic outcomes: How and when possible selves impel action. *Journal of Personality and Social Psychology, 91,* 188–204.

Pallak, M. S., Mueller, M., Dollar, K., & Pallak, J. (1972). Effects of commitment on responsiveness to an extreme consonant communication. *Journal of Personality and Social Psychology, 23,* 429–436.

Park, B., & Judd, C. M. (1990). Measures and models of perceived group variability. *Journal of Personality and Social Psychology, 59,* 173–191.

Park, B., & Rothbart, M. (1982). Perception of out-group homogeneity and levels of social categorization: Memory for the subordinate attributes of in-group and out-group members. *Journal of Personality and Social Psychology, 42,* 1051–1068.

Parrott, W. G. (2001). Implications of dysfunctional emotions for understanding how emotions function. *Review of General Psychology, 5,* 180–186.

Parrott, W. G., & Smith, S. F. (1991). Embarrassment: Actual vs. typical cases, classical vs. prototypical representations. *Cognition and Emotion, 5,* 467–488.

Payne, B. K. (2001). Prejudice and perception: The role of automatic and controlled processes in misperceiving a weapon. *Journal of Personality and Social Psychology, 81,* 181–192.

Payne, B. K. (2006). Weapons bias: Split-second decisions and unintended stereotyping. *Current Directions in Psychological Science, 15,* 287–291.

Payne, B. K., Lambert, A. J., & Jacoby, L. L. (2002). Best laid plans: Effect of goals on accessibility bias and cognitive control in race-based misperceptions of weapons. *Journal of Experimental Social Psychology, 38,* 384–396.

Pearson, C. M., & Porath, C. L. (1999). *Workplace incivility: The target's-eye view.* Paper presented at the Annual Meeting of the Academy of Management, Chicago.

Peng, K., & Knowles, E. (2003). Culture, ethnicity and the attribution of physical causality. *Personality and Social Psychology Bulletin, 29,* 1272–1284.

Pennebaker, J. W. (1989). Confession, inhibition, and disease. In L. Berkowitz (Ed.), *Advances in experimental social psychology* (Vol. 22, pp. 211–244). New York: Academic Press.

Pennebaker, J. W. (1993). Putting stress into words: Health, linguistic and therapeutic implications. *Behavioral Research and Therapy, 31,* 539–548.

Pennebaker, J. W., Hughes, C. F., & O'Heeron, R. C. (1987). The psychophysiology of confession: Linking inhibitory and psychosomatic processes. *Journal of Personality and Social Psychology, 52,* 781–793.

Pennebaker, J. W., Mayne, T. J., & Francis, M. (1997). Linguistic predictors of adaptive bereavement. *Journal of Personality and Social Psychology, 72,* 863–871.

Pennebaker, J. W., & Roberts, T. A. (1992). Toward a his and hers theory of emotion: Gender differences in visceral perception. *Journal of Social and Clinical Psychology, 11,* 199–212.

Penner, L. A., Dovidio, J. F., Piliavin, J. A., & Schroeder, D. A. (2005). Prosocial behavior: Multi-level perspectives. *Annual Review of Psychology, 56,* 365–392.

Pennington, N., & Hastie, R. (1990). Practical implications of psychological research on juror and jury decision making. *Personality and Social Psychology Bulletin, 16,* 90–105.

Penton-Voak, I. S., Perrett, D. I., Castles, D. L., Kobayashi, T., Burt, D. M., Murray, L. K., et al. (1999). Menstrual cycle alters face preference. *Nature, 399,* 741–742.

Penton-Voak, I. S., Pound, N., Little, A. C., & Perrett, D. I. (2006). Personality judgments from natural and composite facial images: More evidence for a "kernel of truth" in social perception. *Social Cognition, 24,* 607–640.

Perkins, H. W., & Craig, D. W. (2006). A successful social norms campaign to reduce alcohol misuse among college student-athletes. *Journal of Studies on Alcohol, 67,* 880–889.

Perkins, H. W., Haines, M. P., & Rice, R. (2005). Misperceiving the college drinking norm and related problems: A nationwide study of exposure to prevention information, perceived norms and student alcohol misuse. *Journal of Studies on Alcohol, 66,* 470–478.

Perloff, R. M. (1993). Third-person effect research 1983–1992: A review and synthesis. *International Journal of Public Opinion Research, 5,* 167–184.

Perner, J., Frith, U., Leslie, A. M., & Leekam, S. R. (1989). Exploration of the autistic child's theory of mind: Knowledge, belief and communication. *Child Development, 60,* 689–700.

Perper, T. (1985). *Sex signals: The biology of love.* Philadelphia: ISI Press.

Perrett, D. I., Lee, K., Penton-Voak, I., Burt, D. M., Rowland, D., Yoshikawa, S., et al. (1998). Sexual dimorphism and facial attractiveness. *Nature, 394,* 884–886.

Perrett, D. I., May, K. A., & Yoshikawa, S. (1994). Facial shape and judgments of female attractiveness. *Nature, 368,* 239–242.

Perrin, S., & Spencer, C. (1981). Independence of conformity in the Asch experiment as a reflection of cultural or situational factors. *British Journal of Social Psychology, 20,* 205–209.

Pessin, J. (1933). The comparative effects of social and mechanical stimulation on memorizing. *American Journal of Psychology, 45,* 263–270.

Pessin, J., & Husband, R. W. (1933). Effect of social stimulation on human maze learning. *Journal of Abnormal and Social Psychology, 28,* 148–154.

Peterson, C. (2000). The future of optimism. *American Psychologist, 55,* 44–55.

Peterson, C., & Barrett, L. C. (1987). Explanatory style and academic performance among university freshmen. *Journal of Personality and Social Psychology, 53,* 603–607.

Peterson, C., Maier, S., & Seligman, M. E. P. (1993). *Learned helplessness.* New York: Oxford University Press.

Peterson, C., Seligman, M. E. P., & Vaillant, G. E. (1988). Pessimistic explanatory style is a risk factor for physical illness: A thirty-five-year longitudinal study. *Journal of Personality and Social Psychology, 55,* 23–27.

Pettigrew, T. (1979). The ultimate attribution error: Extending Allport's cognitive analysis to prejudice. *Personality and Social Psychology Bulletin, 5,* 461–476.

Pettigrew, T. F., & Tropp, L. R. (2000). Does intergroup contact reduce prejudice? Recent meta-analytic findings. In S. Oskamp (Ed.), *Reducing prejudice and discrimination: The Claremont Symposium on Applied Social Psychology* (pp. 93–114). Mahwah, NJ: Erlbaum.

Pettigrew, T. F., & Tropp, L. R. (2006). A meta-analytic test of intergroup contact theory. *Journal of Personality and Social Psychology, 90,* 751–783.

Pettigrew, T. F., & Tropp, L. R. (2008). How does intergroup contact reduce prejudice? Meta-analytic tests of three mediators. *European Journal of Social Psychology, 38,* 922–934.

Petty, R. E. (1997). The evolution of theory and research in social psychology: From single to multiple effect and process models. In C. McGarty & S. A. Haslam (Eds.), *The message of social* psychology: Perspectives on mind in society (pp. 268–290). Oxford, England: Blackwell.

Petty, R. E., & Brinol, P. (2008). Persuasion: From single to multiple to metacognitive processes. *Perspectives on Psychological Science, 3,* 137–147.

Petty, R. E., & Cacioppo, J. T. (1979). Issue involvement can increase or decrease persuasion by enhancing message-relevant cognitive responses. *Journal of Personality and Social Psychology, 37,* 1915–1926.

Petty, R. E., & Cacioppo, J. T. (1984). The effects of involvement on responses to argument quantity and quality: Central and peripheral routes to persuasion. *Journal of Personality and Social Psychology, 46,* 69–81.

Petty, R. E., & Cacioppo, J. T. (1986). The elaboration likelihood model of persuasion. In L. Berkowitz (Ed.), *Advances in experimental social psychology* (Vol. 19, pp. 123–205). New York: Academic Press.

Petty, R. E., Cacioppo, J. T., & Goldman, R. (1981). Personal involvement as a determinant of argument-based persuasion. *Journal of Personality and Social Psychology, 41,* 847–855.

Petty, R. E., Cacioppo, J. T., & Schumann, D. W. (1983). Central and peripheral routes to advertising effectiveness: The moderating role of involvement. *Journal of Consumer Research, 10,* 135–146.

Petty, R. E., Haugtvedt, C. P., & Smith, S. M. (1995). Elaboration as a determinant of attitude strength. In R. E. Petty & J. A. Krosnick (Eds.), *Attitude strength: Antecedents and consequences* (pp. 93–130). Mahwah, NJ: Erlbaum.

Petty, R. E., & Wegener, D. (1998). Attitude change: Multiple roles for persuasion variables. In D. T. Gilbert, S. T. Fiske, & G. Lindzey (Eds.), *Handbook of social psychology* (4th ed., pp. 323–390). New York: McGraw-Hill.

Pew Research Center. (2007, January 9). How young people view their lives, futures, and politics: A portrait of "generation next."

Pfeifer, J. H., Masten, C. L., Borofsky, L. A., Dapretto, M., Fuligni, A. J., & Lieberman, M. D. (2009). Neural correlates of direct and reflected self-appraisals in adolescents and adults: When social perspective taking informs self-perception. *Child Development, 80,* 1016–1038.

Phelps, E. A., O'Connor, K. J., Cunningham, W. A., Funayama, E. S., Gatenby, J. C., Gore, J. C., et al. (2000). Performance on indirect measure of race evaluation predicts amygdala activation. *Journal of Cognitive Neuroscience, 12,* 729–738.

Phillips, D. P. (1986). Natural experiments on the effects of mass media violence on fatal aggression: Strengths and weakness of a new approach. In L. Berkowitz (Ed.), *Advances in experimental social psychology* (Vol. 19, pp. 207–250). Orlando, FL: Academic Press.

Piedmont, R. L., & Chase, J. H. (1997). Cross-cultural generality of the five-factor model of personality: Development and validation of the NEO-PI-R for Koreans. *Journal of Cross-Cultural Psychology, 28,* 131–155.

Pietromonaco, P. R., & Feldman-Barrett, L. (2000). Internal working models: What do we know about knowing the self in relation to others? *Review of General Psychology, 4,* 155–175.

Piff, P. K., Kraus, M. W., Côté, S., Cheng, B., & Keltner, D. (2010). Having less, giving more: The influence of social class on prosocial behavior, *Journal of Personality and Social Psychology, 99,* 771–784.

Piliavin, J. A., & Piliavin, I. M. (1972). The effects of blood on reactions to a victim. *Journal of Personality and Social Psychology, 23,* 253–261.

Piliavin, J. A., Piliavin, I. M., & Broll, L. (1976). Time of arousal at an emergency and likelihood of helping. *Personality and Social Psychology Bulletin, 2,* 273–276.

Piliavin, J. A., & Unger, R. K. (1985). The helpful but helpless female: Myth or reality? In V. O'Leary, R. K. Unger, & B. S. Wallston (Eds.), *Women, gender, and social psychology* (pp. 149–186). Hillsdale, NJ: Erlbaum.

Pinel, E. (1999). Stigma consciousness: The psychological legacy of social stereotypes. *Journal of Personality and Social Psychology, 76,* 114–128.

Pinker, S. (1994). *The language instinct.* New York: HarperCollins.

Pinker, S. (2002). *The blank slate: The modern denial of human nature.* New York: Viking.

Pinker, S. (2007). A history of violence [Electronic version]. *The New Republic Online.* Retrieved March 16, 2009.

Pinker, S. (2011). *The better angels of our nature: Why violence has declined.* New York: Viking.

Plaks, J. E., & Higgins, E. T. (2000). Pragmatic use of stereotyping in teamwork: Social loafing and compensation as a function of inferred partner–situation fit. *Journal of Personality and Social Psychology, 79,* 962–974.

Plant, E. A., & Devine, P. G. (1998). Internal and external motivation to respond without prejudice. *Journal of Personality and Social Psychology, 75,* 811–832.

Plant, E. A., Kling, K. C., & Smith, G. L. (2004). The influence of gender and social role on the interpretation of facial expressions. *Sex Roles, 51,* 187–196.

Plant, E. A., & Peruche, B. M. (2005). The consequences of race for police officers' responses to criminal suspects. *Psychological Science, 16,* 180–183.

Plant, E. A., Peruche, B. M., & Butz, D. A. (2005). Eliminating automatic racial bias: Making race non-diagnostic for responses to criminal suspects. *Journal of Experimental Social Psychology, 41,* 141–156.

Platania, J., & Moran, G. P. (2001). Social facilitation as a function of the mere presence of others. *Journal of Social Psychology, 141,* 190–197.

Platt, J. J., & James, W. T. (1966). Social facilitation of eating behavior in young opossums: I. Group vs. solitary feeding. *Psychonomic Science, 6,* 421–422.

Platt, J. J., Yaksh, T., & Darby, C. L. (1967). Social facilitation of eating behavior in armadillos. *Psychological Reports, 20,* 1136.

Plous, S. (1985). Perceptual illusions and military realities. *Journal of Conflict Resolution, 29,* 363–389.

Podratz, K. E., Halverson, S. K., & Dipboye, R. L. (2004). Physical attractiveness biases in ratings of employment suitability: Tracking down the "beauty is beastly." Manuscript submitted for publication.

Polak, M. (1993). Parasitic infection increases fluctuating asymmetry of male *Drosophila nigrospiracula*: Implications for sexual selection. *Genetica, 89,* 255–265.

Pollock, C. L., Smith, S. D., Knowles, E. S., & Bruce, H. J. (1998). Mindfulness limits compliance with the that's-not-all technique. *Personality and Social Psychology Bulletin, 24,* 1153–1157.

Porter, R. H., Cernoch, J. M., & Balogh, R. D. (1984). Recognition of neonates by facial-visual characteristics. *Pediatrics, 74,* 501–504.

Porter, R. H., Cernoch, J. M., & McLauglin, F. J. (1983). Maternal recognition of neonates through olfactory cues. *Physiology and Behavior, 30,* 151–154.

Postmes, T., & Spears, R. (1998). Deindividuation and antinormative behavior: A meta-analysis. *Psychological Bulletin, 123,* 238–259.

Postmes, T., Spears, R., & Cihangir, S. (2001). Quality of decision making and group norms. *Journal of Personality and Social Psychology, 80,* 918–930.

Pound, N., Penton-Voak, I. S., & Brown, W. M. (2007). Facial symmetry is positively associated with self-reported extraversion. *Personality and Individual Differences, 43,* 1572–1582.

Pratkanis, A. R., & Aronson, E. (2000). *Age of propaganda.* New York: Freeman.

Pratkanis, A. R., Breckler, S. J., & Greenwald, A. G. (Eds.). (1989). *Attitude structure and function.* Hillsdale, NJ: Erlbaum.

Pratkanis, A. R., Greenwald, A. G., Leippe, M. R., & Baumgardner, M. H. (1988). In search of reliable persuasion effects: III. The sleeper effect is dead. Long live the sleeper effect. *Journal of Personality and Social Psychology, 54,* 203–218.

Pratto, F., & Bargh, J. A. (1991). Stereotyping based upon apparently individuating information: Trait and global components of sex stereotypes under attention overload. *Journal of Experimental Psychology, 27,* 26–47.

Pratto, F., & John, O. P. (1991). Automatic vigilance: The attention-grabbing power of negative social information. *Journal of Personality and Social Psychology, 61,* 380–391.

Prentice, D. A. (1990). Familiarity and differences in self- and other-representations. *Journal of Personality and Social Psychology, 59,* 369–383.

Prentice, D. A., & Miller, D. T. (1993). Pluralistic ignorance and alcohol use on campus: Some consequences of misperceiving the social norm. *Journal of Personality and Social Psychology, 64,* 243–256.

Prentice-Dunn, S., & Rogers, R. W. (1989). Deindividuation and self-regulation of behavior. In P. Paulus (Ed.), *The psychology of group influence* (2nd ed., pp. 87–109). Hillsdale, NJ: Erlbaum.

Preston, C. E., & Harris, S. (1965). Psychology of drivers in traffic accidents. *Journal of Applied Psychology, 49,* 284–288.

Preston, S. D., & de Waal, F. B. M. (2002). Empathy: Its ultimate and proximate bases. *Behavioral and Brain Sciences, 25,* 1–72.

Preuschoft, S. (1992). "Laughter" and "smile" in Barbary macaques (*Macaca sylvanus*). *Ethology, 91,* 220–236.

Price, K. H., Harrison, D. A., & Gavin, J. H. (2006). Withholding inputs in team contexts: Member composition, interaction processes, evaluation structure, and social loafing. *Journal of Applied Social Psychology, 90,* 197–209.

Profet, M. (1992). Pregnancy sickness as adaptation: A deterrent to maternal ingestion of teratogens. In J. H. Barlow, L. Cosmides, & J. Tooby (Eds.), *The adapted mind* (pp. 327–366). New York: Oxford University Press.

Pronin, E., Berger, J., & Molouki, S. (2007). Alone in a crowd of sheep: Asymmetric perceptions of conformity and their roots in an introspection illusion. *Journal of Personality and Social Psychology, 92,* 585–595.

Pronin, E., Gilovich, T., & Ross, L. (2004). Objectivity in the eye of the beholder: Divergent perceptions of bias in self versus others. *Psychological Review, 111,* 781–799.

Pronin, E., Lin, D. Y., & Ross, L. (2002). The bias blind spot: Perceptions of bias in self versus others. *Personality and Social Psychology Bulletin, 28,* 369–381.

Provine, R. R. (1992). Contagious laughter: Laughter is a sufficient stimulus for laughs and smiles. *Bulletin of the Psychonomic Society, 30,* 1–4.

Ptacek, J. T., & Dodge, K. L. (1995). Coping strategies and relationship satisfaction in couples. *Personality and Social Psychology Bulletin, 21,* 76–84.

Puts, D. A. (2005). Mating context and menstrual phase affect women's preferences for male voice pitch. *Evolution and Human Behavior, 26,* 388–397.

Pyszczynski, T., Abdollahi, A., Solomon, S., Greenberg, J., Cohen, F., & Weise, D. (2006). Mortality salience, martyrdom, and military might: The great Satan versus the Axis of Evil. *Personality and Social Psychology Bulletin, 32,* 525–537.

Pyszczynski, T., & Greenberg, J. (1987). Toward an integration of cognitive and motivational perspectives on social inference: A biased hypothesis-testing model. In L. Berkowitz (Ed.), *Advances in experimental social psychology* (Vol. 20, pp. 297–340). New York: Academic Press.

Quattrone, G. A., & Jones, E. E. (1980). The perception of variability within in-groups and out-groups: Implications for the law of small numbers. *Journal of Personality and Social Psychology, 38,* 141–152.

Queller, S., & Smith, E. R. (2002). Subtyping versus bookkeeping in stereotype learning and change: Connectionist simulations and empirical findings. *Journal of Personality and Social Psychology, 82,* 300–313.

Quigley, B., & Tedeschi, J. (1996). Mediating effects of blame attributions on feelings of anger. *Personality and Social Psychology Bulletin, 22,* 1280–1288.

Rajecki, D. W., Bledsoe, S. B., & Rasmussen, J. L. (1991). Successful personal ads: Gender differences and similarities in offers, stipulations, and outcomes. *Basic and Applied Psychology, 12,* 457–469.

Rajecki, D. W., Ickes, W., Corcoran, C., & Lenerz, K. (1977). Social facilitation of human performance: Mere presence effects. *Journal of Social Psychology, 102,* 297–310.

Raskin, R., & Terry, H. (1988). A principal-components analysis of the Narcissistic Personality Inventory and further evidence of its construct validity. *Journal of Personality and Social Psychology, 54,* 890–902.

Raz, N., Gunning, F. M., Head, D., Dupuis, J. H., McQuain, J., Briggs, S. D., et al. (1997). Selective aging of the human cerebral cortex observed in vivo: Differential vulnerability of the prefrontal gray matter. *Cerebral Cortex, 7,* 268–282.

Razran, G. H. S. (1940). Conditioned response changes in rating and appraising sociopolitical slogans. *Psychological Bulletin, 37,* 481.

Read, A. W., et al. (1978). *Funk and Wagnalls new comprehensive international dictionary of the English language.* New York: Publishers Guild Press.

Read, S. J. (1984). Analogical reasoning social judgment: The importance of causal theories. *Journal of Personality and Social Psychology, 46,* 14–25.

Read, S. J. (1987). Similarity and causality in the use of social analogies. *Journal of Experimental Social Psychology, 23,* 189–207.

Read, S. J., & Urada, S. I. (2003). A neural network simulation of the outgroup homogeniety effect. *Personality and Social Psychology Review, 7,* 146–159.

Reber, R., Schwarz, N., & Winkielman, P. (2004). Processing fluency and aesthetic pleasure: Is beauty in the perceiver's processing experience? *Personality and Social Psychology Review, 8,* 364–382.

Reber, R., Winkielman, P., & Schwarz, N. (1998). Effects of perceptual fluency on affective judgments. *Psychological Science, 9,* 45–48.

Reed, J. (1981). Below the Smith and Wesson line: Reflections on Southern violence. In M. Black & J. Reed (Eds.), *Perspectives on the American South: An annual review of society, politics, and culture.* New York: Gordon and Breach Science Publications.

Reed, J. S. (1990). Billy, the fabulous moolah, and me. In J. S. Reed (Ed.), *Whistling Dixie* (pp. 119–122). San Diego, CA: Harcourt Brace Jovanovich.

Reeder, G. D., Monroe, A. E., & Pryor, J. B. (2008). Impressions of Milgram's obedient teachers: Situational cues inform inferences about motives and traits. *Journal of Personality and Social Psychology, 95,* 1–17.

Reeves, R. A., Baker, G. A., Boyd, J. G., & Cialdini, R. B. (1991). The door-in-the-face technique: Reciprocal concessions vs. self-presentational explanations. *Journal of Social Behavior and Personality, 6,* 645–658.

Reeves, R. A., Macolini, R. M., & Martin, R. C. (1987). Legitimizing paltry contributions: On-the-spot vs. mail-in requests. *Journal of Applied Social Psychology, 7,* 731–738.

Reeves-Sanday, P. (1997). The socio-cultural context of rape: A cross-cultural study. In L. L. O'Toole (Ed.), *Gender violence: Interdisciplinary perspectives.* New York: New York University Press.

Regan, D. T. (1971). Effects of a favor and liking on compliance. *Journal of Experimental Social Psychology, 7,* 627–639.

Regan, D. T., & Fazio, R. (1977). On the consistency between attitudes and behavior: Look to the method of attitude formation. *Journal of Experimental Social Psychology, 13,* 28–45.

Regan, D. T., & Kilduff, M. (1988). Optimism about elections: Dissonance reduction at the ballot box. *Political Psychology, 9,* 101–107.

Regan, D. T., Williams, M., & Sparling, S. (1972). Voluntary expiation of guilt: A field experiment. *Journal of Personality and Social Psychology, 24,* 42–45.

Regan, J. W. (1971). Guilt, perceived injustice, and altruistic behavior. *Journal of Personality and Social Psychology, 18,* 124–132.

Reifman, A. S., Larrick, R. P., & Fein, S. (1991). Temper and temperature on the diamond: The heat-aggression relationship in major league baseball. *Personality and Social Psychology Bulletin, 17,* 580–585.

Reis, H. T., Nezlek, J., & Wheeler, L. (1980). Physical attractiveness in social interaction. *Journal of Personality and Social Psychology, 38,* 604–617.

Reis, H. T., Wheeler, L., Speigel, N., Kernis, M. H., Nezlek, J., & Perri, M. (1982). Physical attractiveness in social interaction: 2. Why does appearance affect social experience? *Journal of Personality and Social Psychology, 43,* 979–996.

Remley, A. (1988, October). From obedience to independence. *Psychology Today,* 56–59.

Rhee, E., Uleman, J. S., Lee, H. K., & Roman, R. J. (1995). Spontaneous self-descriptions and ethnic identities in individualistic and collectivist cultures. *Journal of Personality and Social Psychology, 69,* 142–152.

Rhine, R. J., & Severance, L. J. (1970). Ego-involvement, discrepancy, source credibility, and attitude *change. Journal of Personality and Social Psychology, 16,* 175–190.

Rhodes, G. (2006). The evolutionary psychology of facial beauty. *Annual Review of Psychology, 57,* 199–226.

Rhodes, G., Yoshikawa, S., Clark, A., Lee, K., McKay, R., & Aka-matsu, S. (2001). Attractiveness of facial averageness and symmetry in non-Western cultures: In search of biologically based standards of beauty. *Perception, 30,* 611–625.

Richards, Z., & Hewstone, M. (2001). Subtyping and subgrouping: Processes for the prevention and promotion of stereotype change. *Personality and Social Psychology Review, 5,* 52–73.

Riggio, R. E., & Friedman, H. S. (1983). Individual differences and cues to deception. *Journal of Personality and Social Psychology, 45,* 899–915.

Riggio, R. E., & Woll, S. B. (1984). The role of nonverbal cues and physical attractiveness in the selection of dating partners. *Journal of Social and Personal Relationships, 1,* 347–357.

Rilling, J. K., Gutman, D. A., Zeh, T. R., Pagnoni, G., Berns, G. S., & Kilts, C. D. (2002). A neural basis for cooperation. *Neuron, 35,* 395–405.

Risen, J. L., & Critcher, C. R. (2011). Visceral fit: While in a visceral state, associated states of the world seem more likely. *Journal of Personality and Social Psychology, 100,* 777–785.

Risen, J. L., & Gilovich, T. (2007). Another look at why people are reluctant to exchange lottery tickets. *Journal of Personality and Social Psychology, 93,* 12–22.

Risen, J. L., & Gilovich, T. (2008). Why people are reluctant to tempt fate. *Journal of Personality and Social Psychology, 95,* 293–307.

Risen, J. L., Gilovich, T., & Dunning, D. (2007). One-shot illusory correlations and stereotyping. *Personality and Social Psychology Bulletin, 33,* 1492–1502.

Robberson, M. R., & Rogers, R. W. (1988). Beyond fear appeals: Negative and positive persuasive appeals to health and self-esteem. *Journal of Applied Social Psychology, 18,* 277–287.

Roberts, T. A., & Pennebaker, J. W. (1995). Gender differences in perceiving internal state: Toward a his-and-hers model of perceptual cue use. In M. Zanna (Ed.), *Advances in experimental social psychology* (Vol. 27, pp. 143–176). New York: Academic Press.

Robins, R. W., & Beer, J. S. (2001). Positive illusions about the self: Short-term benefits and long-term costs. *Journal of Personality and Social Psychology, 80,* 340–352.

Robinson, J., & McArthur, L. Z. (1982). Impact of salient vocal qualities on causal attribution for a speaker's behavior. *Journal of Personality and Social Psychology, 43,* 236–247.

Robinson, R., Keltner, D., Ward, A., & Ross, L. (1995). Actual versus assumed differences in construal: "Naive realism" in intergroup perception and conflict. *Journal of Personality and Social Psychology, 68,* 404–417.

Rodriguez Mosquera, P. M., Fischer, A. H., & Manstead, A. S. R. (2000). The role of honor-related values in the elicitation, experience, and communication of pride, shame, and anger: Spain and the Netherlands compared. *Personality and Social Psychology Bulletin, 26,* 833–844.

Rodriguez Mosquera, P. M., Fischer, A. H., & Manstead, A. S. R. (2004). Inside the heart of emotion: On culture and relational concerns. In L. Z. Tiedens & C. W. Leach, *The social life of emotions* (pp. 187–202). New York: Cambridge University Press.

Roesch, S. C., & Amirkhan, J. H. (1997). Boundary conditions for self-serving attributions: Another look at the sports pages. *Journal of Applied Social Psychology, 27,* 245–261.

Roese, N. J. (1997). Counterfactual thinking. *Psychological Bulletin, 121,* 133–148.

Roese, N. J., & Olson, J. M. (Eds.). (1995). *What might have been: The social psychology of counterfactual thinking.* Mahwah, NJ: Erlbaum.

Rogers, R. W., & Mewborn, C. R. (1976). Fear appeals and attitude change: Effects of a threat's noxiousness, probability of occurrence and the efficacy of coping responses. *Journal of Personality and Social Psychology, 34,* 54–61.

Rogers, T. B., Kuiper, N. A., & Kirker, W. S. (1977). Self-reference and the encoding of personal information. *Journal of Personality and Social Psychology, 35,* 677–688.

Rohrer, J. H., Baron, S. H., Hoffman, E. L., & Swander, D. V. (1954). The stability of autokinetic judgments. *Journal of Abnormal and Social Psychology, 49,* 595–597.

Rolls, E. T. (2000). The orbitofrontal cortext and reward. *Cerebral Cortex, 10,* 284–294.

Roseman, I. J. (1991). Appraisal determinants of discrete emotions. *Cognition and Emotion, 5,* 161–200.

Rosenberg, L. A. (1961). Group size, prior experience, and conformity. *Journal of Abnormal and Social Psychology, 63*, 436–437.

Rosenberg, M. (1965). *Society and the adolescent self-image*. Princeton, NJ: Princeton University Press.

Rosenblatt, A., & Greenberg, J. (1988). Depression and interpersonal attraction: The role of perceived similarity. *Journal of Personality and Social Psychology, 55*, 112–119.

Rosenblatt, A., Greenberg, J., Solomon, S., Pyszczynski, T., & Lyon, D. (1989). Evidence for terror management theory I: The effects of mortality salience on reactions to those who violate or uphold cultural values. *Journal of Personality and Social Psychology, 57*, 681–690.

Rosenthal, R., & Jacobson, L. (1968). *Pygmalion in the classroom: Teacher expectation and student intellectual development*. New York: Holt, Rinehart, and Winston.

Ross, L. (1977). The intuitive psychologist and his shortcomings. In L. Berkowitz (Ed.), *Advances in experimental social psychology* (Vol. 10, pp. 173–220). New York: Academic Press.

Ross, L. (1988). Situationist perspectives on the obedience experiments. *Contemporary Psychology, 33*, 101–104.

Ross, L., Amabile, T. M., & Steinmetz, J. L. (1977). Social roles, social control, and biases on social-perception processes. *Journal of Personality and Social Psychology, 35*, 485–494.

Ross, L., Bierbrauer, G., & Hoffman, S. (1976). The role of attribution process in conformity and dissent: Revisiting the Asch situation. *American Psychologist, 31*, 148–157.

Ross, L., & Nisbett, R. E. (1991/2011). *The person and the situation: Perspectives of social psychology*. London: Pinter & Martin.

Ross, L., & Stillinger, C. (1991). Barriers to conflict resolution. *Negotiation Journal, 8*, 389–404.

Ross, L., & Ward, A. (1995). Psychological barriers to dispute resolution. In M. P. Zanna (Ed.), Advances in experimental social psychology (Vol. 27, pp. 255–304). San Diego, CA: Academic Press.

Ross, M., & Sicoly, F. (1979). Egocentric biases in availability and attribution. *Journal of Personality and Social Psychology, 32*, 880–892.

Ross, S., & Ross, J. G. (1949). Social facilitation of feeding behavior in dogs: I. Group and solitary feeding. *Journal of Genetic Psychology, 74*, 97–108.

Roszell, P., Kennedy, D., & Grabb, E. (1989). Physical attractiveness and income attainment among Canadians. *Journal of Psychology, 123*, 547–559.

Rothbart, M., Evans, M., & Fulero, S. (1979). Recall for confirming events: Memory processes and the maintenance of social stereotyping. *Journal of Experimental Social Psychology, 15*, 343–355.

Rothberg, J. M., & Jones, F. D. (1987). Suicide in the U.S. Army: Epidemiological and periodic aspects. *Suicide and Life-Threatening Behavior, 17*, 119–132.

Rotton, J., & Frey, J. (1985). Air pollution, weather, and violent crime: Concomitant time-series analysis of archival data. *Journal of Personality and Social Psychology, 49*, 1207–1220.

Rozin, P. (1996). Towards a psychology of food and eating: From motivation to module to model to marker, morality, meaning, and metaphor. *Current Directions in Psychological Science, 5*, 18–24.

Rozin, P., & Kalat, J. (1971). Specific hungers and poison avoidance as adaptive specialization of learning. *Psychological Review, 78*, 459–486.

Rozin, P., Lowery, L., Imada, S., & Haidt, J. (1999). The CAD triad hypothesis: A mapping between three moral emotions (contempt, anger, and disgust) and three moral codes (community, autonomy, divinity). *Journal of Personality and Social Psychology, 66*, 870–881.

Rozin, P., & Royzman, E. B. (2001). Negativity bias, negativity dominance, and contagion. *Personality and Social Psychology Review, 5*, 296–320.

Rozin, P., & Singh, L. (1999). The moralization of cigarette smoking in America. *Journal of Consumer Behavior, 8*, 321–337.

Ruch, W. (1995). Will the real relationship between facial expression and affective experience please stand up? The case of exhilaration. *Cognition and Emotion, 9*, 33–58.

Rudman, L. A., & Ashmore, R. D. (2007). Discrimination and the IAT. *Group Processes and Intergroup Relations, 10*, 359–372.

Rudman, L. A., & Borgida, E. (1995). The afterglow of construct accessibility: The behavioral consequences of priming men to view women as sexual objects. *Journal of Experimental Social Psychology, 31*, 493–517.

Rudolph, U., Roesch, S. C., Greitemeyer, T., & Weiner, B. (2004). A meta-analytic review of help giving and aggression from an attributional perspective: Contributions to a general theory of motivation. *Cognition and Emotion, 18*, 815–848.

Rusbult, C. E. (1980). Commitment and satisfaction in romantic associations: A test of the investment model. *Journal of Experimental Social Psychology, 17*, 172–186.

Rusbult, C. E. (1983). A longitudinal test of the investment model: The development (and deterioration) of satisfaction and commitment in heterosexual involvements. *Journal of Personality and Social Psychology, 45*, 101–117.

Rushton, J. P., & Bons, T. A. (2005). Mate choice and friendship in twins: Evidence for genetic similarity. *Psychological Science, 16*, 555–559.

Rushton, J. P., Russell, R. J. H., & Wells, P. A. (1984). Genetic similarity theory: Beyond kin selection altruism. *Behavioral Genetics, 14*, 179–193.

Russell, J. A. (1991). Culture and categorization of emotion. *Psychological Bulletin, 110*, 426–450.

Russell, J. A. (2003). Core affect and the psychological construction of emotion. *Psychological Review, 110*, 145–172.

Russo, J. E., Medvec, V. H., & Meloy, M. G. (1996). The distortion of information during decisions. *Organizational Behavior and Human Decision Processes, 66*, 102–110.

Russo, J. E., Meloy, M. G., & Medvec, V. H. (1998). Predecisional distortion of product information. *Journal of Marketing Research, 35*, 438–452.

Ryckman, D. B., & Peckham, P. (1987). Gender differences in attributions for success and failure situations across subject areas. *Journal of Educational Research, 81*, 120–125.

Sabini, J. (1995). *Social psychology* (2nd ed.). New York: Norton.

Sacks, O. (1985). *The man who mistook his wife for a hat and other clinical tales*. New York: Summit Books.

Sagar, H. A., & Schofield, J. W. (1980). Racial and behavioral cues in black and white children's perceptions of ambiguously aggressive acts. *Journal of Personality and Social Psychology, 39*, 590–598.

Said, C. P., & Todorov, A. (2011). A statistical model of facial attractiveness. *Psychological Science, 22*(9), 1183–1190.

Sakai, H. (1981). Induced compliance and opinion change. *Japanese Psychological Research, 23*, 1–8.

Saks, M. J., & Marti, M. W. (1997). A meta-analysis of the effects of jury size. *Law and Human Behavior, 21*, 451–468.

Salancik, G., & Meindl, J. R. (1984). Corporate attributions as strategic illusions of management control. *Administrative Science Quarterly, 29*, 238–254.

Salovey, P., & Mayer, J. D. (1990). Emotional intelligence. *Imagination, Cognition, and Personality, 9*(3), 185–211.

Salovey, P., & Rodin, J. (1989). Envy and jealousy in close relationships. *Review of Personality and Social Psychology, 10*, 221–246.

Salovey, P., & Rothman, A. J. (1991). Jealousy and envy: Self and society. In P. Salovey (Ed.), *The psychology of jealousy and envy* (pp. 271–286). New York: Guilford Press.

Sampson, R. J., Raudenbush, S., & Earls, F. (1997). Neighborhoods and violent crime: A multilevel study of collective efficacy. *Science, 277*, 918–924.

Samuels, C. A., & Ewy, R. (1985). Aesthetic perception of faces during infancy. *British Journal of Developmental Psychology, 3*, 221–228.

Sanchez-Burks, J. (2002). Protestant relational ideology and (in) attention to relational cues in work settings. *Journal of Personality and Social Psychology, 83*(4), 919–929.

Sanchez-Burks, J. (2004). Protestant relational ideology: The cognitive underpinnings and organizational implications of an American anomaly. In B. Staw & R. Kramer (Eds.), *Research in organizational behavior* (Vol. 26, pp. 265–305). San Diego, CA: Elsevier, JAI Press.

Sanchez-Burks, J., Bartel, C. A., & Blount, S. (2009). Performance in intercultural interactions at work: Cross-cultural differences in response to behavioral mirroring. *Journal of Applied Psychology, 94*, 216–223.

Sanchez-Burks, J., Nisbett, R. E., & Ybarra, O. (2000). Cultural styles, relationship schemas, and prejudice against outgroups. *Journal of Personality and Social Psychology, 79*, 174–189.

Sanday, P. R. (1981). The socio-cultural context of rape: A cross-cultural study. Journal *of Social Issues, 37*, 5–27.

Sanday, P. R. (1997). The socio-cultural context of rape: A cross-cultural study. In L. L. O'Toole (Ed.), *Gender violence: Interdisciplinary perspectives*. New York: New York University Press.

Sanders, G. S. (1981). Driven by distraction: An integrative review of social facilitation theory and research. *Journal of Experimental Social Psychology, 17*, 227–251.

Sanders, G. S., & Baron, R. S. (1975). The motivating effects of distraction on task performance. *Journal of Personality and Social Psychology, 32*, 956–963.

Sanna, L. J. (1992). Self-efficacy theory: Implications for social facilitation and social loafing. *Journal of Personality and Social Psychology, 62*, 774–786.

Sanna, L. J. (2000). Mental simulation, affect, and personality: A conceptual framework. *Current Directions in Psychological Science, 9*, 168–173.

Sansone, C., & Harackiewicz, J. M. (Eds.). (2000). *Intrinsic and extrinsic motivation: The search for optimal motivation and performance*. San Diego, CA: Academic Press.

Sapolsky, R. M. (1982). The endocrine stress-response and social status in the wild baboon. *Hormones and Behavior, 16*(3), 279–292.

Sapolsky, R. M. (1994). *Why zebras don't get ulcers*. New York: Freeman.

Sastry, J., & Ross, C. E. (1998). Asian ethnicity and the sense of personal control. *Social Psychology Quarterly, 61*, 101–120.

Saucier, D. A., Miller, C. T., & Doucet, N. (2005). Differences in helping whites and blacks: A meta-analysis. *Personality and Social Psychology Review, 9*, 2–16.

Saulnier, K., & Perlman, D. (1981). The actor-observer bias is alive and well in prison: A sequel to Wells. *Personality and Social Psychology Bulletin, 7*, 559–564.

Savani, K., Markus, H. R., & Conner, A. L. (2008). Let your preference be your guide: Preferences and choices are more tightly linked for North Americans than for Indians. *Journal of Personality and Social Psychology, 95*, 861–876.

Savin-Williams, R. C. (1977). Dominance in a human adolescent group. *Animal Behavior, 25*, 400–406.

Savitsky, K., Epley, N., & Gilovich, T. (2001). Is it as bad as we fear? Overestimating the extremity of others' judgments. *Journal of Personality and Social Psychology, 81*, 44–56.

Schachter, S. (1951). Deviation, rejection and communication. *Journal of Abnormal and Social Psychology, 46*, 190–207.

Schachter, S., & Singer, J. E. (1962). Cognitive, social and psychological determinants of emotional state. *Psychological Review, 69*, 379–399.

Schacter, D. L. (2001). *The seven sins of memory: How the mind forgets and remembers*. Boston: Houghton Mifflin.

Schaller, M., Simpson, J. A., & Kenrick, D. T. (2006). *Evolution and social psychology*. New York: Psychology Press.

Schanie, C. F., & Sundel, M. (1978). A community mental health innovation in mass media preventive education: The alternative project. *American Journal of Community Psychology, 6*(6), 573–581.

Schank, R., & Abelson, R. P. (1977). *Scripts, plans, goals, and understanding: An inquiry into human knowledge structures*. Hillsdale, NJ: Erlbaum.

Scheib, J. E., Gangestad, S. W., & Thornhill, R. (1999). Facial attractiveness, symmetry, and cues of good genes. *Proceedings of the Royal Society London B, 266*, 1913–1917.

Scheier, M. F., Fenigstein, A., & Buss, A. H. (1974). Self-awareness and physical aggression. *Journal of Experimental Social Psychology, 10*, 264–273.

Schelling, T. C. (1978). *Micromotives and macrobehavior*. New York: Norton.

Scherer, K. R. (1997). The role of culture in emotion-antecedent appraisal. *Journal of Personality and Social Psychology, 73*, 902–922.

Scherer, K. R., Johnstone, T., & Klasmeyer, G. (2003). Vocal expression of emotion. In R. J. Davidson, K. R. Scherer, & H. H. Goldsmith (Eds.), *Handbook of affective science* (pp. 433–456). New York: Oxford University Press.

Schick, T., & Vaughn, L. (1995). *How to think about weird things: Critical thinking for a new age*. Mountain View, CA: Mayfield.

Schimmack, U., Oishi, S., & Diener, E. (2002). Cultural influences on the relation between pleasant emotions and unpleasant emotions: Asian dialectic philosophies or individualism-collectivism? *Cognition and Emotion, 16*, 705–719.

Schlenker, B. R. (1980). *Impression management: The self-concept, social identity, and interpersonal relations*. Monterey, CA: Brooks/Cole.

Schlenker, B. R., & Leary, M. R. (1982). Social anxiety and self-presentation: A conceptualization and a model. *Psychological Bulletin, 92*, 641–669.

Schmeichel, B. J., & Martens, A. (2005). Self-affirmation and mortality salience: Affirming values reduces worldview defense and death-thought accessibility. *Personality and Social Psychology Bulletin, 31*, 658–667.

Schmitt, B. H., Gilovich, T., Goore, N., & Joseph, L. (1986). Mere presence and social facilitation: One more time. *Journal of Experimental Social Psychology, 22*, 242–248.

Schmitt, D. P. (2003). Universal sex differences in the desire for sexual variety: Tests from 52 nations, 6 continents, and 13 islands. *Journal of Personality and Social Psychology, 85*, 85–104.

Schnall, E., Wassertheil-Smoller, S., Swencionis, C., Zemon, V., Tinker, L., O'Sullivan, J., et. al. (2008). The relationship between religion and cardiovascular outcomes and all-cause mortality in the women's health initiative observational study [Electronic version]. *Psychology and Health*, 1–15. Retrieved from http://dx.doi.org/10.1080/08870440802311322

Schoeneman, T. J., & Rubanowitz, D. E. (1985). Attributions in the advice columns: Actors and observers, causes and reasons. *Personality and Social Psychology Bulletin, 11*, 315–325.

Schooler, J. W., & Engstler-Schooler, T. Y. (1990). Verbal overshadowing of visual memories: Some things are better left unsaid. *Cognitive Psychology, 22*, 36–71.

Schroeder, C. M., & Prentice, D. A. (1998). Exposing pluralistic ignorance to reduce alcohol use among college students. *Journal of Applied Social Psychology, 28*, 2150–2180.

Schroeder, D. A., Penner, L. A., Dovidio, J. F., & Piliavin, J. A. (1995). *The psychology of helping and altruism*. New York: McGraw-Hill.

Schultz, P. W., Nolan, J. M., Cialdini, R. B., Goldstein, N. J., & Griskevicius, V. (2007). The constructive, destructive, and reconstructive power of social norms. *Psychological Science, 18*, 429–434.

Schulz-Hardt, S., Frey, D., Luthgens, C., & Moscovici, S. (2000). Biased information search in group decision making. *Journal of Personality and Social Psychology, 78*, 655–669.

Schwartz, J. (2004, May 6). Simulated prison in '71 showed a fine line between "normal" and "monster." *New York Times*, A14.

Schwartzwald, J., Bizman, A., & Raz, M. (1983). The foot-in-the-door paradigm: Effects of second request size on donation probability and donor generosity. *Personality and Social Psychology Bulletin, 9*, 443–450.

Schwarz, N., & Bless, H. (1992). Constructing reality and its alternatives: An inclusion/exclusion model of assimilation and contrast in social judgment. In L. L. Martin & A. Tesser (Eds.), *The construction of social judgments* (pp. 217–245). Hillsdale, NJ: Erlbaum.

Schwarz, N., Bless, H., Strack, F., Klumpp, G., Rittenauer-Schatka, H., & Simons, A. (1991). Ease of retrieval as information: Another look at the availability heuristic. *Journal of Personality and Social Psychology, 61*, 195–202.

Schwarz, N., & Clore, G. L. (1983). Mood, misattribution, and judgments of well-being: Informative and directive functions of affective states. *Journal of Personality and Social Psychology, 45*, 513–523.

Schwarz, N., Strack, F., & Mai, H. P. (1991). Assimilation-contrast effects in part-whole question sequences: A conversational logic analysis. *Public Opinion Quarterly, 55*, 3–23.

Schwarz, N., & Vaughn, L. A. (2002). The availability heuristic revisited: Ease of recall and content of recall as distinct sources of information. In T. Gilovich, D. W. Griffin, & D. Kahneman (Eds.), *Heuristics and biases: The psychology of intuitive judgment* (pp. 103–119). New York: Cambridge University Press.

Searle, J. R. (1983). *Intentionality: An essay in the philosophy of mind*. Cambridge, England: Cambridge University Press.

Sears, D. O. (1986). College students in the laboratory: Influences of a narrow database on social psychology's view of human nature. *Journal of Personality and Social Psychology, 51*, 515–530.

Sears, D. O. (1988). Symbolic racism. In P. A. Katz & D. A. Taylor (Eds.), *Eliminating racism: Profiles in controversy* (pp. 53–84). New York: Plenum Press.

Sears, D. O., & Henry, P. J. (2005). Over thirty years later: A contemporary look at symbolic racism. In M. P. Zanna (Ed.), *Advances in experimental social psychology* (Vol. 37, pp. 95–150). San Diego, CA: Elsevier.

Sears, D. O., & Kinder, D. R. (1985). Whites' opposition to busing: On conceptualizing and operationalizing group conflict. *Journal of Personality and Social Psychology, 48*, 1141–1147.

Sedikides, C., & Brewer, M. B. (2001). *Individual self, relational self, collective self*. Philadelphia: Psychology Press.

Sedikides, C., & Gregg, A. (2008). Self-enhancement: Food for thought. *Perspectives on Psychological Science, 3*, 102–116.

Segal, N. L. (1984). Cooperation, competition, and altruism within twin sets: A reappraisal. *Ethology and Sociobiology, 5*, 163–177.

Seibt, B., & Forster, J. (2004). Stereotype threat and performance: How self-stereotypes influence processing by inducing regulatory foci. *Journal of Personality and Social Psychology, 87*, 38–56.

Select Committee on Intelligence. United States Senate. (2004). Report on the U.S. intelligence community's prewar intelligence assessments on Iraq. Ordered reported on July 7, 2004. 108th Congress.

Seligman, M. E. P. (1970). On the generality of the laws of learning. *Psychological Review, 77*, 127–190.

Seligman, M. E. P. (1975). *Helplessness: On depression, development, and death*. San Francisco: Freeman.

Seligman, M. E. P. (1988). Boomer blues. *Psychology Today, 22*, 50–53.

Seligman, M. E. P., Maier, S. F., & Geer, J. H. (1968). Alleviation of learned helplessness in the dog. *Journal of Abnormal Psychology, 73*, 256–262.

Seltzer, R. (2006). Scientific jury selection: Does it work? *Journal of Applied Social Psychology, 36*, 2417–2435.

Semin, G. R., & Manstead, A. S. R. (1982). The social implications of embarrassment displays and restitution behavior. *European Journal of Social Psychology, 12*, 367–377.

Sen, A. (1990, January 20). More than 100 million women are missing. *The New York Review of Books*.

Seta, C. E., & Seta, J. J. (1992). Increments and decrements in mean arterial pressure levels as a function of audience composition: An averaging and summation analysis. *Personality and Social Psychology Bulletin, 18*, 173–181.

Sethi-Iyengar, S., Huberman, G., and Jiang, W. (2004). How much choice is too much? Contributions to 401(k) retirement plans. In O. S. Mitchell & S. Utkus (Eds.), *Pension design and structure: New lessons from behavioral finance* (pp. 83–95). New York: Oxford University Press.

Shah, J., & Higgins, E. T. (2001). Regulatory concerns and appraisal efficiency: The general impact of promotion and prevention. *Journal of Personality and Social Psychology, 80*, 693–705.

Shah, J. Y. (2003). Automatic for the people: How representations of significant others implicitly affect goal pursuit. *Journal of Personality and Social Psychology, 84*, 661–681.

Shapin, S. (2006, January 16). Eat and run. *The New Yorker*, 76–82.

Shapiro, D. H., Schwartz, C. E., & Astin, J. A. (1996). Controlling ourselves, controlling our world. *American Psychologist, 51*, 1213–1230.

Shariff, A. F., & Norenzayan, A. (2007). God is watching you: Priming God concepts increases prosocial behavior in an anonymous economic game. *Psychological Science, 18*, 803–809.

Shaver, P. R., & Brennan, K. A. (1992). Attachment style and the "big five" of personality traits: Their connections with each other and with romantic relationship outcomes. *Personality and Social Psychology Bulletin, 18*, 536–545.

Shavitt, S., Sanbonmatsu, D. M., Smittipatana, S., & Posavac, S. S. (1999). Broadening the conditions for illusory correlation formation: Implications for judging minority groups. *Basic and Applied Social Psychology, 21*, 263–279.

Shearn, D., Bergman, E., Hill, K., Abel, A., & Hinds, L. (1992). Blushing as a function of audience size. *Psychophysiology, 29*, 431–436.

Shedler, L., & Manis, M. (1986). Can the availability heuristic explain vividness effects? *Journal of Personality and Social Psychology, 51*, 26–36.

Sheley, J. F., & Askins, C. D. (1981). Crime, crime news, and crime views. *Public Opinion Quarterly, 45,* 492–506.

Shelley, H. P. (1965). Eating behavior: Social facilitation or social inhibition. *Psychonomic Science, 3,* 521–522.

Shelton, J. N, & Richeson, J. A. (2005). Intergroup contact and pluralistic ignorance. *Journal of Personality and Social Psychology, 88,* 91–107.

Shelton, J. N., Richeson, J. A., & Salvatore, J. (2005). Expecting to be the target of prejudice: Implications for interethnic interactions. *Personality and Social Psychology Bulletin, 31,* 1189–1202.

Sheppard, J. A. (1995). Remedying motivation and productivity loss in collective settings. *Current Directions in Psychological Science, 4,* 131–134.

Sheppard, J. A., & Taylor, K. M. (1999). Social loafing and expectancy-value theory. *Personality and Social Psychology Bulletin, 25,* 1147–1158.

Sherif, M. (1936). *The psychology of social norms.* New York: Harper.

Sherif, M., Harvey, O. J., White, B. J., Hood, W., & Sherif, C. (1961). *Intergroup conflict and cooperation: The robbers cave experiment.* Norman: University of Oklahoma Institute of Group Relations.

Sherman, D. K., & Cohen, G. L. (2002). Accepting threatening information: Self-affirmation and the reduction of defensive biases. *Current Directions in Psychological Science, 11,* 119–123.

Sherman, D. K., & Cohen, G. L. (2006). The psychology of self-defense: Self-affirmation theory. In M. P. Zanna (Ed.), *Advances in experimental social psychology* (Vol. 38, pp. 183–242). San Diego, CA: Academic Press.

Sherman, J. W., Gawronski, B., Gonsalkorale, K., Hugenberg, K., Allen, T. J., & Groom, C. J. (2008). The self-regulation of automatic associations and behavioral impulses. *Psychological Review, 115,* 314–335.

Sherman, L., & Strang, H. (2007). *Restorative justice: The evidence.* London: Smith Institute.

Sherman, P. W. (1985). Alarm calls of Belding's ground squirrels to aerial predators: Nepotism or self-preservation? *Behavioral Ecology and Sociobiology, 17,* 313–323.

Sherman, S. J., & Gorkin, L. (1980). Attitude bolstering when behavior is inconsistent with central attitudes. *Journal of Experimental Social Psychology, 16,* 388–403.

Sherman, S. J., Mackie, D. M., & Driscoll, D. M. (1990). Priming and the differential use of dimensions in evaluation. *Personality and Social Psychology Bulletin, 16,* 405–418.

Shermer, M. (1997). *Why people believe weird things: Pseudoscience, superstition, and other contusions of our time.* New York: Freeman.

Shiller, R. J. (2000). *Irrational exuberance.* Princeton, NJ: Princeton University Press.

Shimamura, A.P. (1994). Neuropsychological perspectives on memory and cognitive decline in normal human aging. *Seminars in the Neurosciences, 6,* 387–394.

Shook, N. J., & Fazio, R. H. (2008). An experimental field test of the contact hypothesis. *Psychological Science, 19,* 717–723.

Shrauger, J. S., & Shoeneman, T. J. (1979). Symbolic interactionist view of self-concept: Through the looking glass darkly. *Psychological Bulletin, 86,* 549–573.

Shweder, R. A., & Bourne, E. J. (1984). Does the concept of the person vary cross-culturally? In R. A. Shweder & R. A. LeVine (Eds.), *Culture theory: Essays on mind, self, and emotion* (pp. 158–199). Cambridge, England: Cambridge University Press.

Shweder, R. A., Jensen, L. A., & Goldstein, W. M. (1995). Who sleeps by whom revisited: A method for extracting moral goods implicit in practice. *New Directions in Child Development, 67,* 21–39.

Sidanius, J., & Pratto, F. (1999). *Social dominance: An intergroup theory of social hierarchy and oppression.* New York: Cambridge University Press.

Sieverding, M., Decker, S., & Zimmermann, F. (2010). Information about low participation in cancer screening demotivates other people. *Psychological Science, 21,* 941–943.

Sigall, H., & Ostrove, N. (1975). Beautiful but dangerous: Effects of offender attractiveness and nature of the crime on juridic judgment. *Journal of Personality and Social Psychology, 31,* 410–414.

Silverstein, B., Perdue, L., Peterson, L., & Kelly, E. (1986). The role of the mass media in promoting a thin standard of bodily attractiveness for women. *Sex Roles, 14,* 519–532.

Simon, B., Mlicki, P., Johnston, L., Caetano, A., Warowicki, M., Van Knippenberg, A., et al. (1990). The effects of ingroup and outgroup homogeneity on ingroup favouritism, stereotyping, and overestimation of relative ingroup size. *European Journal of Social Psychology, 20*(6), 519–523.

Simon, D., Krawczyk, D. C., & Holyoak, K. J. (2004). Construction of preferences by constraint satisfaction. *Psychological Science, IS,* 331–336.

Simon, D., Pham, L. B., Le, Q. A., & Holyoak, K. J. (2001). The emergence of coherence over the course of decision making. *Journal of Experimental Psychology: Learning, Memory and Cognition, 27,* 1250–1260.

Simons, D. J., & Chabris, C. F. (1999). Gorillas in our midst: Sustained inattentional blindness for dynamic events. *Perception, 28,* 1059–1074.

Simpson, G. E., & Yinger, J. M. (1985). *Racial and cultural minorities: An analysis of prejudice and discrimination.* New York: Plenum Press.

Simpson, J. A. (1987). The dissolution of romantic relationships: Factors involved in relationship stability and emotional distress. *Journal of Personality and Social Psychology, S3,* 683–692.

Simpson, J. A., & Rholes, W. S. (1998). *Attachment theory and close relationships.* New York: Guilford Press.

Sinaceur, M., & Tiedens, L. Z. (2006). Get mad and get more than even: When and why anger expression is effective in negotiations. *Journal of Experimental Social Psychology, 42*(3), 314–322.

Sinclair, L., & Kunda, Z. (1999). Reactions to a black professional: Motivated inhibition and activation of conflicting stereotypes. *Journal of Personality and Social Psychology, 77,* 885–904.

Singer, J. E., Brush, C. A., & Lublin, S. C. (1965). Some aspects of deindividuation: Identification and conformity. *Journal of Experimental Social Psychology, 1,* 356–378.

Singer, T., Seymour, B., O'Doherty, J., Kaube, H., Dolan, R. J., & Frith, C. D. (2004). Empathy for pain involves the affective but not sensory components of pain. *Science, 303,* 1157–1162.

Singh, D. (1993). Adaptive significance of female physical attractiveness: Role of waist-to-hip ratio. *Journal of Personality and Social Psychology, 65,* 293–307.

Singhal, A., Rogers, E. M., & Brown, W. J. (1993). Harnessing the potential of entertainment-education telenovelas. *Gazette, 51,* 1–18.

Singh-Manoux, A., Adler, N. E., & Marmot, M. G. (2003). Subjective social status: Its determinants and its association with measures of ill health in the Whitehall II study. *Social Science & Medicine, 56*(6), 1321–1333.

Sistrunk, F., & McDavid, J. W. (1971). Sex variable in conforming behavior. *Journal of Personality and Social Psychology, 17,* 200–207.

Skov, R. B., & Sherman, S. J. (1986). Information-gathering processes: Diagnosticity, hypothesis-confirmatory strategies, and perceived hypothesis confirmation. *Journal of Experimental Social Psychology, 22*, 93–121.

Slater, A., von der Shulenburg, C., Brown, E., Badenoch, M., Butterworth, G., Parsons, S., et al. (1998). Newborn infants prefer attractive faces. *Infant Behavior and Development, 21*, 345–354.

Slavin, R. E. (1995). *Cooperative learning: Theory, research, and practice* (2nd ed.). Boston: Allyn & Bacon.

Sloman, S. A. (2002). Two systems of reasoning. In T. Gilovich, D. W. Griffin, & D. Kahneman (Eds.), *Heuristics and biases: The psychology of intuitive judgement* (pp. 379–396). New York: Cambridge University Press.

Slovic, P., Fischoff, B., & Lichtenstein, S. (1982). Facts versus fears: Understanding perceived risk. In D. Kahneman, P. Slovic, & A. Tversky (Eds.), *Judgment under uncertainty: Heuristics and biases* (pp. 463–489). New York: Cambridge University Press.

Small Arms Survey. (2011). *The Small Arms Survey 2011: States of security.* Retrieved from http://en.wikipedia.org/wiki/List_of_countries_by_gun_ownership

Smith, A. (1776/1998). *The wealth of nations.* Washington, DC: Regnery Publishing.

Smith, A. E., Jussim, L., & Eccles, J. S. (1999). Do self-fulfilling prophecies accumulate, dissipate, or remain stable over time? *Journal of Personality and Social Psychology, 77*, 548–565.

Smith, C., & Ellsworth, P. (1985). Patterns of cognitive appraisal in emotion. *Journal of Personality and Social Psychology, 48*, 813–838.

Smith, E. R., & Miller, F. D. (1979). Salience and the cognitive mediation of attribution. *Journal of Personality and Social Psychology, 37*, 2240–2252.

Smith, E. R., & Zarate, M. A. (1990). Exemplar and prototype use in social categorization. *Social Cognition, 8*, 243–262.

Smith, P. K., Jostmann, N. B., Galinsky, A. D., & van Dijk, W. W (2008). Lacking power impairs executive functions. *Psychological Science, 19*(5), 441–447.

Smith, P. K., & Trope, Y. (2006). You focus on the forest when you're in charge of the trees: Power priming and abstract information processing. *Journal of Personality and Social Psychology, 90*, 578–596.

Smith, S. S., & Richardson, D. (1983). Amelioration of deception and harm in psychological research: The important role of debriefing. *Journal of Personality and Social Psychology, 44*, 1075–1082.

Smith, T. W. (2009). Loving and caring in the United States: Trends and correlates of empathy, altruism, and related constructs. In B. Fehr, S. Sprecher, & L. G. Underwood (Eds.), *The science of compassionate love: Theory, research, and applications* (pp. 81–120). Malden, MA: Wiley-Blackwell.

Smoski, M. J., & Bachorowski, J.-A. (2003). Antiphonal laughter between friends and strangers. *Cognition and Emotion, 17*, 327–340.

Smyth, J. M. (1998). Written emotional expression: Effect sizes, outcome types, and moderating variables. *Journal of Consulting and Clinical Psychology, 66*, 174–184.

Snibbe, A. C., & Markus, H. R., (2005). You can't always get what you want: Educational attainment, agency, and choice. *Journal of Personality and Social Psychology, 88*, 703–720.

Snyder, M. (1974). Self-monitoring of expressive behavior. *Journal of Personality and Social Psychology, 30*, 526–537.

Snyder, M. (1979). Self-monitoring processes. In L. Berkowitz (Ed.), *Advances in experimental social psychology* (Vol. 12, pp. 85–128). New York: Academic Press.

Snyder, M., & Swann, W. B. (1978). Hypothesis-testing in social interaction. *Journal of Personality and Social Psychology, 36*, 1202–1212.

Snyder, M., Tanke, E. D., & Berscheid, E. (1977). Social perception and interpersonal behavior: On the self-fulfilling nature of social stereotypes. *Journal of Personality and Social Psychology, 35*, 656–666.

Sommer, K. L., & Baumeister, R. F. (2002). Self-evaluation, persistence, and performance following implicit rejection: The role of trait self-esteem. *Personality and Social Psychology Bulletin, 28*, 926–938.

Sommers, S. R. (2006). On racial diversity and group decision making: Identifying multiple effects of racial composition on jury deliberations. *Journal of Personality and Social Psychology, 90*, 597–612.

Sommers, S. R., & Ellsworth, P. C. (2001). White juror bias: An investigation of prejudice against black defendants in the American courtroom. *Psychology and Public Policy & Law, 7*(1), 201–229.

Song, H., & Schwarz, N. (2008). If it's hard to read, it's hard to do. *Psychological Science, 19*, 986–988.

Spears, R. (2011). Group identities: The social identity perspective. In S. J. Schwartz, K. Luyckx, & V. L. Vignoles (Eds.), *Handbook of identity theory and research* (Vols. 1 and 2; pp. 201–224). New York: Springer.

Speer, N. K., Reynolds, J. R., Swallow, K. M., & Zacks, J. M. (2009). Reading stories activates neural representations of visual and motor experiences. *Psychological Science, 20*, 989–999.

Spellman, B. A., & Holyoak, K. J. (1992). If Saddam is Hitler then who is George Bush? Analogical mapping between systems of social roles. *Journal of Personality and Social Psychology, 62*, 913–933.

Spencer, S. J., Steele, C. M., & Quinn, D. M. (1999). Stereotype threat and women's math performance. *Journal of Experimental Social Psychology, 35*, 4–28.

Sperber, D. (1996). *Explaining culture: A naturalistic approach.* Oxford, England: Blackwell.

Spiegel, D., Bloom, J. R., Kraemer, H. C., & Gottheil, E. (1989). Effect of psychosocial treatment on survival of patients with metastatic breast cancer. *Lancet, 2*, 888–891.

Spivey, C. B., & Prentice-Dunn, S. (1990). Assessing the directionality of deindividuated behavior: Effects of deindividuation, modeling, and private self-consciousness on aggressive and pro-social responses. *Basic and Applied Psychology, 11*, 387–403.

Sprecher, S., & Regan, P. C. (1998). Passionate and companionate love in courting and young married couples. *Sociological Inquiry, 68*, 163–185.

Sritharan, R., & Gawronski, B. (2010). Changing implicit and explicit prejudice: Insights from the associative-propositional evaluation model. *Social Psychology, 41*(3), 113–123.

Srull, T. K., & Wyer, R. S. (1979). The role of category accessibility in the interpretation of information about persons: Some determinants and implications. *Journal of Personality and Social Psychology, 37*, 1660–1672.

Srull, T. K., & Wyer, R. S. (1980). Category accessibility and social perception: Some implications for the study of person memory and interpersonal judgments. *Journal of Personality and Social Psychology, 38*, 841–856.

Staats, A. W., & Staats, C. K. (1958). Attitudes established by classical conditioning. *Journal of Abnormal and Social Psychology, 57*, 37–40.

Stangor, C., & Duan, C. (1991). Effects of multiple task demands upon memory for information about social groups. *Journal of Experimental Social Psychology, 27*, 357–378.

Stangor, C., & Lange, J. E. (1994). Mental representation of social groups: Advances in understanding stereotypes and stereotyping. In M. P. Zanna (Ed.), *Advances in experimental social psychology* (Vol. 26). San Diego, CA: Academic Press.

Stangor, C., & McMillan, D. (1992). Memory for expectancy-congruent and expectancy-incongruent information: A review of the social and social developmental literatures. *Psychological Bulletin, 111,* 42–61.

Stanovich, K. E., & West, R. F. (2002). Individual differences in reasoning: Implications for the rationality debate. In T. Gilovich, D. W. Griffin, & D. Kahneman (Eds.), *Heuristics and biases: The psychology of intuitive judgment* (pp. 421–440). New York: Cambridge University Press.

Stapel, D. A., Koomen, W., & van der Plight, J. (1997). Categories of category accessibility: The impact of trait versus exemplar priming on person judgments. *Journal of Experimental Social Psychology, 33* 44–76.

Stasser, G. (1999). The uncertain role of unshared information in collective choice. In L. L. Thomson, J. M. Levine, & D. M. Messic (Eds.), *Shared cognition in organizations: The management of knowledge* (pp. 46–69). Mahwah, NJ: Erlbaum.

Stasser, G., & Davis, J. H. (1981). Group decision making and social influence: A social interaction sequence model. *Psychological Review, 88,* 523–551.

Stasser, G., & Titus, W. (1985). Pooling of unshared information in group decision making: Biased information sampling during discussion. *Journal of Personality and Social Psychology, 48,* 1467–1478.

Staub, E. (1989). *The roots of evil: The origins of genocide and other group violence.* Cambridge, England: Cambridge University Press.

Steblay, N. M. (1987). Helping behavior in rural and urban environments: A meta-analysis. *Psychological Bulletin, 102,* 346–356.

Steele, C. M. (1988). The psychology of self-affirmation: Sustaining the integrity of the self. In L. Berkowitz (Ed.), *Advances in experimental social psychology* (Vol. 21). Orlando, FL: Academic Press.

Steele, C. M. (1997). A threat in the air: How stereotypes shape intellectual identity and performance. *American Psychologist, 52,* 613–629.

Steele, C. M., & Aronson, J. (1995). Stereotype threat and the intellectual test performance of African Americans. *Journal of Personality and Social Psychology, 69,* 797–811.

Steele, C. M., Spencer, S. J., & Aronson, J. (2002). Contending with group image: The psychology of stereotype and social identity threat. In M. P. Zanna (Ed.), *Advances in experimental social psychology* (Vol. 34, pp. 379–440). San Diego, CA: Academic Press.

Steele, C. M., Spencer, S. J., & Lynch, M. (1993). Self-image resilience and dissonance: The role of affirmational resources. *Journal of Personality and Social Psychology, 64,* 885–896.

Stel, M., van Baaren, R. B., Blascovich, J., van Dijk, E., McCall, C., Pollmann, M. M. H., . . . , & Vonk, R. (2010). Effects of a priori liking on the elicitation of mimicry. *Experimental Psychology, 57*(6), 412–418.

Stephan, W. G. (1986). The effect of school desegregation: An evaluation 30 years after *Brown.* In M. J. Saks & L. Saxe (Eds.), *Advances in applied social psychology* (Vol. 3, pp. 181–206). Hillsdale, NJ: Erlbaum.

Stephan, W. G., & Stephan, C. W. (1996). *Intergroup relations.* Madison, WI: Brown & Benchmark.

Stephens, N. M., Fryberg, S. A., & Markus, H. R. (2011). When choice does not equal freedom: A sociocultural analysis of agency in working-class American contexts. *Social and Personality Psychology Science, 2,* 33–41.

Stephens, N. M., Markus, H. R., & Townsend, S. S. M. (2007). Choice as an act of meaning: The case of social class. *Journal of Personality and Social Psychology, 93,* 814–830.

Stephens, N. M., Townsend, S. S. M., Markus, H. R., & Phillips, L. T. (2012). A cultural mismatch: Independent cultural norms contribute to increased stress among first-generation college students in American universities. Evanston, IL: Northwestern University.

Sternberg, R. J. (1986). A triangular theory of love. *Psychological Review, 93,* 119–135.

Sternberg, R. J. (1988). Triangulating love. In R. J. Sternberg & M. L. Barnes (Eds.), *The psychology of love.* New Haven, CT: Yale University Press.

Stevenson, H. W., & Lee, S. (1996). The academic achievement of Chinese students. In M. H. Bond (Ed.), *The handbook of Chinese psychology* (pp. 124–142). New York: Oxford University Press.

Stevenson, H. W., Lee, S. Y., Chen, C., Stigler, J. W., Hsu, C. C., & Kitamura, S. (1990). Contexts of achievement: A study of American, Chinese and Japanese children. *Monographs of the Society for Research in Child Development, 55,* 1–2, Serial No. 221.

Stevenson, H. W., & Stigler, J. W. (1992). *The learning gap: Why our schools are failing and what we can learn from Japanese and Chinese education.* New York: Summit Books.

Stewart, J. E. (1980). Defendant's attractiveness as a factor in the outcome of criminal trials: An observational study. *Journal of Applied Social Psychology, 10,* 348–361.

Stone, J., Lynch, C. I., Sjomeling, M., & Darley, J. M. (1999). Stereotype threat effects on black and white athletic performance. *Journal of Personality and Social Psychology, 77,* 1213–1227.

Stone, J., Perry, Z., & Darley, J. (1997). "White men can't jump": Evidence for perceptual confirmation of racial stereotypes following a basketball game. *Basic and Applied Social Psychology, 19,* 291–306.

Stoner, J. A. F. (1961). *A comparison of individual and group decisions involving risk.* Unpublished Master's thesis, MIT, Cambridge, Massachusetts.

Storms, M. D. (1973). Videotape and the attribution process: Reversing actors' and observers' points of view. *Journal of Personality and Social Psychology, 27,* 165–175.

Strack, F., & Deutsch, R. (2004). Reflective and impulsive determinants of social behavior. *Personality and Social Psychology Review, 8,* 220–247.

Strack, F., Martin, L. L., & Schwarz, N. (1988). Priming and communication: The social determinants of information use in judgments of life satisfaction. *European Journal of Social Psychology, 18,* 429–442.

Strack, F., Martin, L. L., & Stepper, S. (1988). Inhibiting and facilitating conditions of the human smile: A nonobtrusive test of the facial feedback hypothesis. *Journal of Personality and Social Psychology, 53,* 768–777.

Strahan, E. J., Spencer, S. J., & Zanna, M. P. (2002). Subliminal priming and persuasion: Striking while the iron is hot. *Journal of Experimental Social Psychology, 38,* 556–568.

Strauman, T. J., & Higgins, E. T. (1987). Automatic activation of self-discrepancies and emotional syndromes: When cognitive structures influence affect. *Journal of Personality and Social Psychology, 53,* 1004–1014.

Strobel, M. G. (1972). Social facilitation of operant behavior in satiated rats. *Journal of Comparative Physiological Psychology, 80,* 502–508.

Stroebe, K., Spears, R., & Lodewijkx, H. (2007) Contrasting and integrating social identity and interdependence approaches to intergroup discrimination in the minimal group paradigm.

In M. Hewstone, H. A. W. Schut, J. B. F. De Wit, K. Van Den Bos, & M. S. Stroebe (Eds.), *The scope of social psychology: Theory and applications* (pp. 173–190). New York: Psychology Press.

Strohmetz, D., Rind, B., Fisher, R. & Lynn, M. (2002). Sweetening the till: The use of candy to increase restaurant tipping. *Journal of Applied Social Psychology, 32,* 300–309.

Studd, M. V. (1996). Sexual harassment. In D. M. Buss & N. M. Malamuth (Eds.), *Sex, power, and conflict: Evolutionary and feminist perspectives.* New York: Oxford University Press.

Suedfeld, P., & Tetlock, P. E. (1977). Integrative complexity of communications in international crises. *Journal of Conflict Resolution, 21,* 169–184.

Suh, E., Diener, E., Oishi, S., & Triandis, H. C. (1998). The shifting basis of life satisfaction judgments across cultures: Emotions versus norms. *Journal of Personality and Social Psychology, 74,* 482–493.

Sulloway, F. J. (1996). *Born to rebel: Birth order, family dynamics, and creative lives.* New York: Pantheon Books.

Sulloway, F. J. (2001). Birth order, sibling competition, and human behavior. In H. R. Halcomb III (Ed.), *Conceptual challenges in evolutionary psychology: Innovative research strategic Studies in cognitive systems* (Vol. 27, pp. 39–83). Dordrecht, the Netherlands: Kluwer Academic Publishers.

Suls, J., Martin, R., & Wheeler, L. (2002). Social comparison: Why, with whom and with what effect? *Current Directions in Psychological Science, 11*(5), 159–163.

Suls, J. M., & Wheeler, L. (2000). *Handbook of social comparison: Theory and research.* New York: Kluwer Academic/Plenum.

Summers, G., & Feldman, N. S. (1984). Blaming the victim versus blaming the perpetrator: An attributional analysis of spouse abuse. *Journal of Applied Social and Clinical Psychology, 2,* 339–347.

Sunstein, C. (2007). *Republic.com 2.0.* Princeton, NJ: Princeton University Press.

Sunstein, C. R., Kahneman, D., Schkade, D., & Ritov, I. (2002). Predictably incoherent judgments. *Stanford Law Review, 54,* 1153–1215.

Surowieki, J. (2004). *The wisdom of crowds.* New York: Random House.

Svenson, O. (1981). Are we all less risky and more skillful than our fellow drivers? *Acta Psychologica, 47,* 143–148.

Swann, W. B., Jr. (1990). To be adored or to be known: The interplay of self-enhancement and self-verification. In R. M. Sorrentino & E. T. Higgins (Eds.). *Handbook of motivation and cognition* (Vol. 2, pp. 408–448). New York: Guilford Press.

Swann, W. B., Jr., De La Ronde, C., & Hixon, J. G. (1994). Authenticity and positivity strivings in marriage and courtship. *Journal of Personality and Social Psychology, 66,* 857–869.

Swann, W. B., Griffin, J. J., Predmore, S. C., & Gaines, B. (1987). The cognitive-affective cross: When self-consistency confronts self-enhancement. *Journal of Personality and Social Psychology, 52,* 881–889.

Swann, W. B., Jr., & Read, S. J. (1981). Self-verification processes: How we sustain our self-conceptions. *Journal of Experimental Social Psychology, 17,* 351–372.

Swann, W. B., Jr., Wenzlaff, R. M., Krull, D. S., & Pelham, B. W. (1992). The allure of negative feedback: Self-verification strivings among depressed persons. *Journal of Abnormal Psychology, 101,* 293–306.

Sweeney, P. D., & Gruber, K. L. (1984). Selective exposure: Voter information preferences and the Watergate affair. *Journal of Personality and Social Psychology, 46,* 1208–1221.

Swim, J. K., Aikin, K. J., Hall, W. S., & Hunter, B. A. (1995). Sexism and racism: Old-fashioned and modern prejudices. *Journal of Personality and Social Psychology, 68,* 199–214.

Swim, J. K., & Campbell, B. (2001). Sexism: Attitudes, beliefs, and behaviors. In R. Brown & S. Gaertner (Eds.), *Blackwell handbook of social psychology: Intergroup processes* (pp. 198–217). Oxford, UK: Blackwell.

Swim, J. K., & Sanna, L. (1996). He's skilled, she's lucky: A meta-analysis of observers' attributions for women's and men's successes and failures. *Personality and Social Psychology Bulletin, 22,* 507–519.

Tajfel, H., & Billig, M. G. (1974). Familiarity and categorization in intergroup behavior. *Journal of Experimental Social Psychology, 10,* 159–170.

Tajfel, H., Billig, M. G., Bundy, R. P., & Flament, C. (1971). Social categorization and intergroup behavior. *European Journal of Social Psychology, 1,* 149–177.

Tajfel, H., & Turner, J. (1979). An integrative theory of intergroup conflict. In W. G. Austin & S. Worchel (Eds.), *The social psychology of intergroup relations.* Monterey, CA: Brooks/Cole.

Tajfel, H., & Turner, J. C. (1986). The social identity theory of intergroup behavior. In S. Worchel & W. G. Austin (Eds.), *Psychology of intergroup relations* (pp. 7–24). Chicago: Nelson-Hall.

Tajfel, H., & Wilkes, A. (1963). Classifications and quantitative judgment. *British Journal of Social Psychology, 54,* 101–114.

Tan, D. T. Y., & Singh, R. (1995). Attitudes and attraction: A developmental study of the similarity-attraction dissimilarity-repulsion hypotheses. *Personality and Social Psychology Bulletin, 21,* 975–986.

Tangney, J. P., Miller, R. S., Flicker, L., & Barlow, D. H. (1996). Are shame, guilt, and embarrassment distinct emotions? *Journal of Personality and Social Psychology, 70,* 1256–1264.

Taubman-Ben-Ari, O., Florian, V., & Mikulincer, M. (1999). The impact of mortality salience on reckless driving—A test of terror management mechanisms. *Journal of Personality and Social Psychology, 76,* 35–45.

Taylor, A. F., & Kuo, F. E. (2009). Children with attention deficits concentrate better after a walk in the park. *Journal of Attention Disorders, 12,* 402–409.

Taylor, D. M., & Jaggi, V. (1974). Ethnocentrism and causal attribution in a South Indian context. *Journal of Cross-Cultural Psychology, 5,* 162–171.

Taylor, S. E. (1983). Adjustment to threatening events: A theory of cognitive adaptation. *American Psychologist, 38,* 1161–1173.

Taylor, S. E. (1989). *Positive illusions: Creative self-deception and the healthy mind.* New York: Basic Books.

Taylor, S. E. (1991). Asymmetrical effects of positive and negative events: The mobilization-minimization hypothesis. *Psychological Bulletin, 110,* 67–85.

Taylor, S. E. (2002). *The tending instinct.* New York: Holt.

Taylor, S. E., & Brown, J. D. (1988). Illusion and well-being: A social psychological perspective on mental health. *Psychological Bulletin, 103,* 193–210.

Taylor, S. E., & Brown, J. D. (1994). Positive illusions and well-being revisited: Separating fact from fiction. *Psychological Bulletin, 116,* 21–27.

Taylor, S. E., Burklund, L. J., Eisenberger, N. I., Lehman, B. J., Hilmert, C. J., & Lieberman, M. D. (2008). Neural bases of moderation of cortisol stress responses by psychosocial resources. *Journal of Personality and Social Psychology, 95,* 197–211.

Taylor, S. E., & Crocker, J. (1981). Schematic bases of social information processing. In E. T. Higgins, C. P. Herman, & M. P. Zanna

(Eds.), *Social cognition: The Ontario Symposium* (Vol. 1, pp. 89–134). Hillsdale, NJ: Erlbaum.

Taylor, S. E., & Fiske, S. T. (1975). Point of view and perceptions of causality. *Journal of Personality and Social Psychology, 32,* 439–445.

Taylor, S. E., Kemeny, M., Aspinwall, L. G., Schneider, S. G., Rodriguez, R., & Herbert, M. (1992). Optimism, coping, psychological distress, and high-risk sexual behavior among men at risk for AIDS. *Journal of Personality and Social Psychology, 63,* 460–473.

Taylor, S. E., Klein, L. C., Lewis, B. P., Gruenewal, T. L., Gurung, R. A. R., & Updegraff, J. A. (2000). Biobehavioral responses to stress in females: Tend-and-befriend, not fight-or-flight. *Psychological Review, 107,* 411–429.

Taylor, S. E., Lerner, J. S., Sherman, D. K., Sage, R. M., & McDowell, N. K. (2003). Are self-enhancing cognitions associated with healthy or unhealthy biological profiles? *Journal of Personality and Social Psychology, 85,* 605–615.

Taylor, S. E., Lichtman, R. R., & Wood, J. V. (1984). Attributions, beliefs about control, and adjustment to breast cancer. *Journal of Personality and Social Psychology, 46,* 489–502.

Taylor, S. E., & Lobel, M. (1989). Social comparison activity under threat: Downward evaluation and upward contacts. *Psychological Review, 96,* 569–575.

Taylor, S. E., & Thompson, S. C. (1982). Stalking the elusive "vividness" effect. *Psychological Review, 89,* 155–181.

Taylor, S. E., Wood, J. V., & Lichtman, R. R. (1983). It could be worse: Selective evaluation as a response to victimization. *Journal of Social Issues, 39,* 19–40.

Teger, A. I., & Pruitt, D. G. (1967). Components of group risk taking. *Journal of Experimental Social Psychology, 3,* 189–205.

Tesser, A. (1988). Toward a self-evaluation maintenance model of social behavior. In L. Berkowitz (Ed.), *Advances in experimental social psychology* (Vol. 21, pp. 181–227). San Diego, CA: Academic Press.

Tesser, A. (1993). The importance of heritability in psychological research: The case of attitudes. *Psychological Review, 100,* 129–142.

Tesser, A., Campbell, J. D., & Mickler, S. (1983). The role of social pressure, attention to the stimulus, and self-doubt in conformity. *European Journal of Social Psychology, 13,* 217–233.

Tesser, A., & Conlee, M. C. (1975). Some effects of time and thought on attitude polarization. *Journal of Personality and Social Psychology, 31,* 262–270.

Tesser, A., Martin, L., & Mendolia, M. (1995). The impact of thought on attitude extremity and attitude-behavior consistency. In R. E. Petty & J. Krosnick (Eds.), *Attitude strength: Antecedents and consequences.* Mahwah, NJ: Erlbaum.

Tesser, A., & Smith, J. (1980). Some effects of friendship and task relevance on helping: You don't always help the one you like. *Journal of Experimental Social Psychology, 16,* 582–590.

Tetlock, P. E. (1981). Pre- to post-election shifts in presidential rhetoric: Impression management or cognitive adjustment. *Journal of Personality and Social Psychology, 41,* 207–212.

Tetlock, P. E. (1984). Cognitive style and political belief systems in the British House of Commons. *Journal of Personality and Social Psychology, 46,* 365–375.

Tetlock, P. E., Peterson, R. S., McGuire, C., Chang, S., & Feld, P. (1992). Assessing political group dynamics: A test of the group-think model. *Journal of Personality and Social Psychology, 20,* 142–146.

Thakerar, J. N., & Iwawaki, S. (1979). Cross-cultural comparisons in interpersonal attraction of females toward males. *Journal of Social Psychology, 108,* 121–122.

Thaler, R. H. (1980). Toward a positive theory of consumer choice. *Journal of Economic Behavior and Organization, 1,* 39–60.

Thomas, S. L., Skitka, L. J., Christen, S., & Jurgena, M. (2002). Social facilitation and impression formation. *Basic and Applied Social Psychology, 24,* 67–70.

Thompson, J. (2000, June 18). "I was certain, but I was wrong." New York Times, June 18, 2000. Retrieved from http://www.nytimes.com/2000/06/18/opinion/i-was-certain-but-i-was-wrong.html

Thompson, L. (2005). *The heart and mind of the negotiator* (3rd ed.). Upper Saddle River, NJ: Pearson Education.

Thompson, L., & Hrebec, D. (1996). Lose-lose arguments in interdependent decision making. *Psychological Bulletin, 120,* 396–409.

Thornhill, R., & Gangestad, S. W. (1993). Human facial beauty: Averageness, symmetry, and parasite resistance. *Human Nature, 4,* 237–269.

Thornhill, R., & Gangestad, S. W. (1999). The scent of symmetry: A human sex pheromone that signals fitness? *Evolution and Human Behavior, 20,* 175–201.

Thornhill, R., & Gangestad, S. W. (2005). Facial sexual dimorphism, developmental stability, and susceptibilty to disease in men and women. *Evolution and Human Behavior, 27,* 131–144.

Thornhill, R., Gangestad, S. W., Miller, R., Scheyd, G., McCollough, J., & Franklin, M. (2003). MHC, symmetry and body scent attractiveness in men and women (*Homo sapiens*). *Behavioral Ecology, 14,* 668–768.

Tice, D. M. (1993). Self-concept change and self-presentation: The looking glass self is also a magnifying glass. *Journal of Personality and Social Psychology, 63,* 435–451.

Tice, D. M., Baumeister, R. F., Shmueli, D., & Muraven, M. (2007). Restoring the self: Positive affect helps improve self-regulation following ego depletion. *Journal of Experimental Social Psychology, 43,* 379–384.

Tice, D. M., & Wallace, H. M. (2005). The reflected self: Creating yourself as (you think) others see you. In M. R. Leary & J. P. Tangney (Eds.), *Handbook of self and identity* (pp. 91–105). New York: Guilford Press.

Tiedens, L. Z. (2001). Anger and advancement versus sadness and subjugation: The effect of negative emotion expressions on social status conferral. *Journal of Personality and Social Psychology, 80*(1), 86–94.

Tiedens, L. Z., & Leach, C. W. (2004). *The social life of emotions.* New York: Cambridge University Press.

Tiedens, L. Z., & Linton, S. (2001). Judgment under emotional certainty and uncertainty: The effects of specific emotions on information processing. *Journal of Personality and Social Psychology, 81,* 973–988.

Todorov, A., & Bargh, J. A. (2002). Automatic sources of aggression. *Aggression and Violent Behavior, 7,* 53–68.

Todorov, A., Mandisodza, A. N., Goren, A., & Hall, C. C. (2005). Inferences of competence from faces predict election outcomes. *Science, 308,* 1623–1626.

Todorov, A., Said, C. P., Engell, A. D., & Oosterhof, N. N. (2008). Understanding evaluation of faces on social dimensions. *Trends in Cognitive Sciences, 12,* 455–460.

Todorov, A., & Uleman, J. S. (2003). The efficiency of binding spontaneous trait inferences to actors' faces. *Journal of Experimental Social Psychology, 39,* 549–562.

Tom, S. M., Fox, C. R., Trepel, C., & Poldrack, R. A. (2007). The neural basis of loss aversion in decision-making under risk. *Science, 315,* 515–518.

Tomkins, S. S. (1962). *Affect, imagery, consciousness: I. The positive affects*. New York: Springer.

Tomkins, S. S. (1963). *Affect, imagery, consciousness: II. The negative affects*. New York: Springer.

Toobin, J. (2011, May 9). The mitigator: A new way of looking at the death penalty. *The New Yorker*.

Tooby, J., & Cosmides, L. (1992). The psychological foundations of culture. In J. H. Barkow, L. Cosmides, & J. Tooby (Eds.), *The adapted mind: Evolutionary psychology and the generation of culture*. New York: Oxford University Press.

Tormala, Z. L., Brinol, P., & Petty, R. E. (2007). Multiple roles for source credibility under high elaboration: It's all in the timing. *Social Cognition, 25*, 536–552.

Tormala, Z. L., Clarkson, J. J., & Petty, R. E. (2006). Resisting persuasion by the skin of one's teeth: The hidden success of resisted persuasive messages. *Journal of Personality and Social Psychology, 91*, 423–435.

Tormala, Z. L., & Petty, R. E. (2002). What doesn't kill me makes me stronger: The effects of resisting persuasion on attitude certainty. *Journal of Personality and Social Psychology, 83*, 1298–1313.

Tormala, Z. L., & Petty, R. E. (2004a). Resistance to persuasion and attitude certainty: The moderating role of elaboration. *Personality and Social Psychology Bulletin, 30*, 1446–1457.

Tormala, Z. L., & Petty, R. E. (2004b). Source credibility and attitude certainty: A metacognitive analysis of resistance to persuasion. *Journal of Consumer Psychology, 14*, 427–442.

Torrance, E. P. (1955). Some consequences of power differences in decision making in permanent and temporary 3-man groups. In A. P. Hare, E. F. Bogatta, & R. F. Bales (Eds.), *Small groups: Studies in social interaction*. New York: Knopf.

Tourangeau, R., Rasinski, K., & Bradburn, N. (1991). Measuring happiness in surveys: A test of the subtraction hypothesis. *Public Opinion Quarterly, 55*, 255–266.

Tracy, J. L., & Matsumoto, D. (2008). The spontaneous display of pride and shame: Evidence for biologically innate nonverbal displays. *Proceedings of the National Academy of Sciences of the USA, 105*, 11655–11660.

Tracy, J. L., & Robins, R. W. (2004). Show your pride: Evidence for a discrete emotion expression. *Psychological Science, 15*, 94–97.

Tracy, J. L., & Robins, R. W. (2007). Emerging insights into the nature and function of pride. *Current Directions in Psychological Science, 16*, 147–150.

Trafimow, D., Triandis, H. C., & Goto, S. G. (1991). Some tests of the distinction between the private self and the collective self. *Journal of Personality and Social Psychology, 60*, 649–655.

Travis, L. E. (1925). The effect of a small audience upon eye-hand coordination. *Journal of Abnormal and Social Psychology, 20*, 142–146.

Triandis, H. C. (1987). Individualism and social psychological theory. In C. Kagitcibasi (Ed.), *Growth and progress in cross-cultural psychology* (pp. 78–83). New York: Swets North America.

Triandis, H. C. (1989). The self and social behavior in differing cultural contexts. *Psychological Review, 96*, 269–289.

Triandis, H. C. (1994). *Culture and social behavior*. New York: McGraw-Hill.

Triandis, H. C. (1995). *Individualism and collectivism*. Boulder, CO: Westview Press.

Triandis, H. C., McCusker, C., & Hui, C. H. (1990). Multimethod probes of individualism and collectivism. *Journal of Personality and Social Psychology, 56*, 1006–1020.

Triplett, N. (1898). The dynamogenic factors in pacemaking and competition. *American Journal of Psychology, 9*, 507–533.

Trivers, R. L. (1971). The evolution of reciprocal altruism. *Quarterly Review of Biology, 46*, 35–57.

Trivers, R. L. (1985). *Social evolution*. Menlo Park, CA: Benjamin Cummings.

Trope, Y. (1986). Identification and inferential processes in dispositional attribution. *Psychological Review, 93*, 239–257.

Trope, Y., & Liberman, N. (2003). Temporal construal. *Psychological Review, 110*, 403–421.

Trope, Y., & Liberman, N. (2010). Construal-level theory of psychological distance. *Psychological Review, 117*, 440–463.

Trzesniewski, K. H., Donnellan, M. B., Caspi, A., Moffitt, T. E., Robins, R. W., & Poultin, R. (2006). Adolescent low self-esteem is a risk factor for adult poor health, criminal behavior, and limited economic prospects. *Developmental Psychology, 42*, 38–390.

Tsai, J. L. (2007). Ideal affect: Cultural causes and behavioral consequences. *Perspectives on Psychological Science, 2*, 242–259.

Tsai, J. L., Knutson, B., & Fung, H. H. (2006). Cultural variation in affect valuation. *Journal of Personality and Social Psychology, 90*, 288–307.

Tsai, J. L., & Levenson, R. W. (1997). Cultural influences on emotional responding: Chinese American and European American dating couples during interpersonal conflict. *Journal of Cross-Cultural Psychology, 28*, 600–625.

Turnbull, C. (1965). *Wayward servants*. New York: Natural History Press.

Turner, C., & Leyens, J. (1992). The weapons effect revisited: The effects of firearms on aggressive behavior. In P. Suedfeld & P. E. Tetlock (Eds.), *Psychology and social policy* (pp. 201–221). New York: Hemisphere.

Turner, M. E., & Pratkanis, A. R. (1998). Twenty-five years of groupthink theory and research: Lessons from the evaluation of a theory. *Organizational Behavior and Human Decision Processes, 73*, 105–115.

Tversky, A., & Kahneman, D. (1974). Judgment under uncertainty: Heuristics and biases. *Science, 185*, 1124–1131.

Tversky, A., & Kahneman, D. (1981). The framing of decisions and the psychology of choice. *Science, 211*, 453–458.

Tversky, A., & Kahneman, D. (1982). Evidential impact of base rates. In D. Kahneman, P. Slovic, & A. Tversky (Eds.), *Judgment under uncertainty: Heuristics and biases* (pp. 153–160). New York: Cambridge University Press.

Tversky, A., & Kahneman, D. (1986). Rational choice and the framing of decisions. *Journal of Business, 59*, 5251–5278.

Tversky, A., & Shafir, E. (1992). Choice under conflict: The dynamics of deferred decision. *Psychological Science, 3*(6), 358–361.

Twenge, J. M. (2002). Birth cohort, social change, and personality: The interplay of dysphoria and individualism in the 20th century. In D. Cervone & W. Mischel (Eds.), *Advances in personality science*. New York: Guilford Press.

Twenge, J. M., Baumeister, R. F., Tice, D. M., & Stucke, T. S. (2001). If you can't join them, beat them: Effects of social exclusion on aggressive behavior. *Journal of Personality and Social Psychology, 81*, 1058–1069.

Twenge, J. M., & Campbell, W. K. (2001). Age and birth cohort differences in self-esteem: A cross-temporal analysis. *Personality and Social Psychology Review, 5*, 321–344.

Tyler, T. R. (1984). Assessing the risk of crime victimization: The integration of personal victimization experience and socially transmitted information. *Journal of Social Issues, 40*, 27–38.

Tyler, T. R. (1987). Conditions leading to value-expressive effects in judgments of procedural justice: A test of four models. *Journal of Personality and Social Psychology, 52*, 333–344.

Tyler, T. R. (1994). Psychological models of the justice motive: Antecedents of distributive and procedural justice. *Journal of Personality and Social Psychology, 67,* 850–863.

Tyler, T. R., & Caine, A. (1981). The influence of outcomes and procedures on satisfaction with formal leaders. *Journal of Personality and Social Psychology, 41,* 642–655.

Uchino, B. N., Cacioppo, J. T., & Kiecolt-Glaser, J. K. (1996). The relationship between social support and physiological process: A review with emphasis on underlying mechanisms and implications for health. *Psychological Bulletin, 119,* 88–531.

Uematsu, T. (1970). Social facilitation of feeding behavior in freshwater fish. I. *Rhodeus, Acheilognathus* and *Rhinogobius. Annual of Animal Psychology, 20,* 87–95.

Uleman, J. S. (1987). Consciousness and control: The case of spontaneous trait inferences. *Personality and Social Psychology Bulletin, 13,* 337–354.

Umberson, D., & Hughes, M. (1987). The impact of physical attractiveness on achievement and psychological well-being. *Social Psychology Quarterly, 50,* 227–236.

UN Women. (2011). Virtual Knowledge Centre to End Violence against Women and Girls. Retrieved from www.endvawnow.org

Updegraff, J. A., & Taylor, S. E. (2000). From vulnerability to growth: Positive and negative effects of stressful life events. In J. H. Harvey & E. D. Miller (Eds.), *Loss and trauma: General and close relationship perspectives* (pp. 3–28). New York: Brunner-Routledge.

Uranowitz, S. W. (1975). Helping and self-attributions: A field experiment. *Journal of Personality and Social Psychology, 31,* 852–854.

Vaes, J., Paladino, M. P., Castelli, L., Leyens, J. Ph., Giovanazzi, A. (2003). On the behavioral consequences of infra-humanization: The implicit role of uniquely human emotions in intergroup relations. *Journal of Personality and Social Psychology, 85,* 1016–1034

Valdesolo, P., & DeSteno, D. (2011). Synchrony and the social tuning of compassion. *Emotion, 11,* 262–266.

Valenti, A. C., & Downing, L. L. (1975). Differential effects of jury size on verdicts following deliberations as a function of the apparent guilt of a defendant. *Journal of Personality and Social Psychology, 32,* 655–663.

Vallacher, R. R., & Wegner, D. M. (1985). *A theory of action identification.* Hillsdale, NJ: Erlbaum.

Vallacher, R. R., & Wegner, D. M. (1987). What do people think they're doing? Action identification and human behavior. *Psychological Review, 94,* 3–15.

Vallone, R. P., Ross, L., & Lepper, M. R. (1985). The hostile media phenomenon: Biased perception and perceptions of media bias in coverage of the Beirut massacre. *Journal of Personality and Social Psychology, 49,* 577–585.

Van Baaren, R. B., Holland, R. W., Kawakami, K., & van Knippenberg, A. (2004). Mimicry and pro-social behavior. *Psychological Science, 15,* 71–74.

Van Baaren, R. B., Holland, R. W., Steenaert, B., & van Knippenberg, A. (2003). Mimicry for money: Behavioral consequences of imitation. *Journal of Experimental Social Psychology, 39,* 393–398.

Van Boven, L., Kamada, A., & Gilovich, T. (1999). The perceiver as perceived: Everyday intuitions about the correspondence bias. *Journal of Personality and Social Psychology, 77,* 1188–1199.

van Dijk, C., de Jong, P. J., & Peters, M. L. (2009). The remedial value of blushing in the context of transgressions and mishaps. *Emotion, 9,* 287–291.

Van Dort, B. E., & Moos, R. H. (1976). Distance and the utilization of a student health center. *Journal of the American College Health Association, 24,* 159–162.

Van Kleef, G. A., De Dreu, C. K. W., Pietroni, D., & Manstead, A. S. R. (2006). Power and emotion in negotiation: Power moderates the interpersonal effects of anger and happiness on concession making. *European Journal of Social Psychology*: Special issue on social power, 36, 557–581.

Vandello, J., & Cohen, D. (1999). Patterns of individualism and collectivism across the United States. *Journal of Personality and Social Psychology, 77,* 279–292.

Vanneman, R. D., & Pettigrew, T. F. (1972). Race and relative deprivation in the urban United States. *Race, 13,* 461–486.

Vasquez, K., Keltner, D., Ebenbach, D. H., & Banaszynski, T. L. (2001). Cultural variation and similarity in moral rhetorics: Voices from the Philippines and United States. *Journal of Cross-Cultural Psychology, 32,* 93–120.

Vasquez, N. A., & Buehler, R. (2007). Seeing future success: Does imagery perspective influence achievement motivation? *Personality and Social Psychology Bulletin, 33,* 1392–1405.

Vaughn, P. W., Rogers, E. M., Singhal, A., & Swalehe, R. M. (2000). Entertainment-education and HIV/AIDS prevention: A field experiment in Tanzania. *Journal of Health Communication, 5,* 81–100.

Vescio, T. K., Gervais, S. J., Heidenreich, S., & Snyder, M. (2006). The effects of prejudice level and social influence strategy on powerful people's responding to racial outgroup members. *European Journal of Social Psychology, 36,* 435–450.

Vescio, T. K., Gervais, S. J., Snyder, M., & Hoover, A. (2005). Power and the creation of patronizing environments: The stereotype-based behaviors of the powerful and their effects on female performance in masculine domains. *Journal of Personality and Social Psychology, 88*(4), 658–672.

Vescio, T. K., Snyder, M., & Butz, D. (2003). Power in stereotypically masculine domains: A social influence strategy × stereotype match model. *Journal of Personality and Social Psychology, 85*(6), 1062–1078.

Vohs, K. D., & Heatherton, T. F. (2001). Self-esteem and threats to self: Implications for self construals and interpersonal perceptions. *Journal of Personality and Social Psychology, 81,* 1103–1118.

von Hippel, W., Sekaquaptewa, D., & Vargas, P. (1995). On the role of encoding processes in stereotype maintenance. In M. P. Zanna (Ed.), *Advances in experimental social psychology* (Vol. 27, pp. 177–254). San Diego, CA: Academic Press.

Vonk, R. (1999). Effects of outcome dependency on the correspondence bias. *Personality and Social Psychology Bulletin, 25,* 382–389.

Vonk, R. (2002). Self-serving interpretations of flattery: Why ingratiation works. *Journal of Personality and Social Psychology, 82,* 515–526.

Waber, R., Shiv, B., Carmon, Z., & Ariely, D. (2008). Commercial features of placebo and therapeutic efficacy. *Journal of the American Medical Association, 299*(9), 1016–1017.

Wagner, R. C. (1975). Complementary needs, role expectations, interpersonal attraction, and the stability of work relationships. *Journal of Personality and Social Psychology, 32,* 116–124.

Wallach, M. A., Kogan, N., & Bem, D. J. (1962). Group influences on individual risk taking. *Journal of Abnormal and Social Psychology, 65,* 75–86.

Wallerstein, J. S., Lewis, J., & Blakeslee, S. (2000). *The unexpected legacy of divorce: The 25-year landmark study.* New York: Hyperion.

Walster, E. (1966). Assignment of responsibility for an accident. *Journal of Personality and Social Psychology, 3,* 73–79.

Walster, E., Aronson, E., & Abrahams, D. (1966). On increasing the persuasiveness of a low prestige communicator. *Journal of Experimental Social Psychology, 2*, 325–342.

Walster, E., Aronson, V., Abrahams, D., & Rottman, L. (1966). Importance of physical attractiveness in dating behavior. *Journal of Personality and Social Psychology, 4*, 508–516.

Walton, G. M., & Cohen, G. L. (2007). A question of belonging: Race, social fit, and achievement. *Journal of Personality and Social Psychology, 92*, 82–96.

Waterman, C. K. (1969). The facilitating and interfering effects of cognitive dissonance on simple and complex paired associates learning tasks. *Journal of Experimental Social Psychology, 5*, 31–42.

Watson, D. (1982). The actor and the observer: How are their perceptions of causality divergent? *Psychological Bulletin, 92*, 682–700.

Watson, R. I. (1973). Investigation into deindividuation using a cross-cultural survey technique. *Journal of Personality and Social Psychology, 25*, 342–345.

Waugh, C. E., & Fredrickson, B. L. (2006). Nice to know you: Positive emotions, self-other overlap, and complex understanding in the formation of a new relationship. *Journal of Positive Psychology, 1*, 93–106.

Weber, M. (1947). *The theory of social and economic organization* (A. M. Henderson & T. Parsons, Trans.). New York: Oxford University Press.

Weber, R., & Crocker, J. (1983). Cognitive processes in the revision of stereotypic beliefs. *Journal of Personality and Social Psychology, 45*, 961–977.

Wedekind, C., & Milinski, M. (2000). Cooperation through image scoring in humans. *Science, 288*, 850–852.

Wegener, D. T., & Petty, R. E. (1994). Mood management across affective states: The hedonic contingency hypothesis. *Journal of Personality and Social Psychology, 66*, 1034–1048.

Wegener, D. T., Petty, R. E., & Smith, S. M. (1995). Positive mood can increase or decrease message scrutiny: The hedonic contingency view of mood and message processing. *Journal of Personality and Social Psychology, 69*, 5–15.

Wegner, D. M. (1994). Ironic processes of mental control. *Psychological Review, 101*, 34–52.

Wegner, D. M., Ansfield, M., & Pilloff, D. (1998). The putt and the pendulum: Ironic effects of the mental control of action. *Psychological Science, 9*, 196–199.

Weiner, B. (1986). *An attributional theory of achievement and motivation.* New York: Springer-Verlag.

Weiner, B., Graham, S., & Reyna, C. (1997). An attributional examination of retributive versus utilitarian philosophies of punishment. *Social Justice Research, 10*, 431–452.

Wellman, H. M. (1990). *The child's theory of mind.* Cambridge, MA: MIT Press.

Wells, G. L., Charman, S. D., & Olson, E. A. (2005). Building face composites can harm lineup identification performance. *Journal of Experimental Psychology, 11*, 147–156.

Wells, G. L., & Gavanski, I. (1989). Mental simulation of causality. *Journal of Personality and Social Psychology, 56*, 161–169.

Wells, G. L., & Leippe, M. R. (1981). How do triers of fact enter the accuracy of eyewitness identification? *Journal of Applied Psychology, 66*, 682–687.

Wells, G. L., Lindsay, R. C. L., & Ferguson, T. (1979). Accuracy, confidence and juror perceptions in eyewitness identification. *Journal of Applied Psychology, 64*, 440–448.

Wells, G. L., Memon, A., & Penrod, S. D. (2006). Eyewitness evidence: Improving its probative value. *Psychological Science in the Public Interest, 7*, 45–75.

Wells, G. L., & Petty, R. E. (1980). The effects of overt head movements on persuasion: Compatibility and incompatibility of responses. *Basic and Applied Social Psychology, 1*, 219–230.

West, S. G., & Brown, T. J. (1975). Physical attractiveness, the severity of the emergency, and helping: A field experiment and interpersonal simulation. *Journal of Experimental Social Psychology, 11*, 531–538.

West, T. V., Pearson, A. R., Dovidio, J. F., Shelton, J. N., & Trail, T. E. (2009). Superordinate identity and intergroup roommate friendship development. *Journal of Experimental Social Psychology, 45*, 1266–1272.

Westoff, C. F., & Rodriguez, G. (1995). The mass media and family planning in Kenya. *International Family Planning Perspectives, 21*(1), 26–31, 35.

Wetzel, C. G. (1982). Self-serving biases in attribution: A Bayesian analysis. *Journal of Personality and Social Psychology, 43*, 197–209.

Weyant, J. M. (1984). Applying social psychology to induce charitable donations. *Journal of Applied Social Psychology, 14*, 441–447.

Whatley, M. A., Webster, J. M., Smith, R. H., & Rhodes, A. (1999). The effect of a favor on public and private compliance: How internalized is the norm of reciprocity? *Basic and Applied Social Psychology, 21*, 251–259.

Wheatley, T., & Haidt, J. (2005). Hypnotic disgust makes moral judgments more severe. *Psychological Science, 16*, 780–785.

Wheeler, L., & Kim, Y. (1997). What is beautiful is culturally good: The physical attractiveness stereotype has different content in collectivistic cultures. *Personality and Social Psychology Bulletin, 23*, 795–800.

Wheeler, L., & Nezlek, J. (1977). Sex differences in social participation. *Journal of Personality and Social Psychology, 35*, 742–754.

White, G. L., & Kight, T. D. (1984). Misattribution of arousal and attraction: Effects of salience of explanations of arousal. *Journal of Experimental Social Psychology, 20*, 55–64.

White, H. (1997). Longitudinal perspective on alcohol and aggression during adolescence. In M. Galanter (Ed.), *Recent developments in alcoholism: Alcohol and violence: Epidemiology, neurobiology, psychology, and family issues* (Vol. 13, pp. 81–103). New York: Plenum Press.

White, L. K., & Booth, A. (1991). Divorce over the life course: The role of marital happiness. *Review of Personality and Social Psychology, 12*, 265–289.

White, P. A. (2002). Causal attribution from covariation information: The evidential evaluation model. *European Journal of Social Psychology, 32*, 667–684.

Whitely, B. E. (1990). The relationship of heterosexuals' attributions for the causes of homosexuality to attitudes towards lesbians and gay men. *Personality and Social Psychology Bulletin, 16*, 369–377.

Whittlesea, B. W., & Leboe, J. P. (2000). The heuristic basis of remembering and classification: Fluency, generation, and resemblance. *Journal of Experimental Psychology: General, 129*, 84–106.

Wicker, A. W. (1969). Attitudes versus actions: The relationship of verbal and overt behavioral responses to attitude objects. *Journal of Social Issues, 25*, 41–78.

Wieselquist, J., Rusbult, C. E., Agnew, C. R., & Foster, C. A. (1999). Commitment, pro-relationship behavior, and trust in close relationships. *Journal of Personality and Social Psychology, 77*, 942–966.

Wigboldus, D. H. J., Sherman, J. W., Franzese, H. L., & van Knippenberg, A. (2004). Capacity and comprehension: Spontaneous stereotyping under cognitive load. *Social Cognition, 22*, 292–309.

Wiggins, J. S., Wiggins, N., & Conger, J. C. (1968). Correlates of heterosexual somatic preference. *Journal of Personality and Social Psychology, 10*, 82–90.

Wilder, D. A. (1984). Predictions of belief homogeneity and similarity following social categorization. *British Journal of Social Psychology, 23*, 323–333.

Wilder, D. A. (1986). Social categorization: Implications for creation and reduction of intergroup bias. In L. Berkowitz (Ed.), *Advances in experimental social psychology* (Vol. 19, pp. 291–355). San Diego, CA: Academic Press.

Wiley, M. G., Crittenden, K. S., & Birg, L. D. (1979). Why a rejection? Causal attribution of a career achievement event. *Social Psychology Quarterly, 42*, 214–222.

Wilkinson, F., & Pickett, K. (2009). *Spirit level: Why greater equality makes societies stronger.* New York: Bloomsbury Press.

Wilkinson, G. (1990, February). Food sharing in vampire bats. *Scientific American*, 76–82.

Wilier, R. (2004). The effects of government-issued terror warnings on presidential approval ratings. *Current Research in Social Psychology, 10*, 1–12.

Willer, R. (2009). Groups reward individual sacrifice: The status solution to the collective action problem. *American Sociological Review, 74*, 23–43.

Williams, D. R., & Collins, C. (1995). U.S. socioeconomic and racial differences in health: Patterns and explanations. *Annual Review of Sociology, 21*, 349–386.

Williams, E. F., & Gilovich, T. (in press). The better-than-my-average effect: The relative impact of peak and typical performances in judging the self and others. *Journal of Experimental Social Psychology.*

Williams, E. F., Gilovich, T., & Dunning, D. (in press). Being all that you can be: How potential performances influence assessments of self and others. *Personality and Social Psychology Bulletin.*

Williams, J. R., Insel, T. R., Harbaugh, C. R., & Carter, C. S. (1994). Oxytocin administered centrally facilitates formation of a partner preference in female prairie voles (*Microtus ochrogaster*). *Journal of Neuroendocrinology, 6*, 247–250.

Williams, K. D. (2007). Ostracism. *Annual Review of Psychology, 58*, 425–452.

Williams, K. D., Harkins, S., & Latané, B. (1981). Identifiability as a deterrent to social loafing: Two cheering experiments. *Journal of Personality and Social Psychology, 40*, 303–311.

Willis, F. N., & Hamm, H. K. (1980). The use of interpersonal touch in securing compliance. *Journal of Nonverbal Behavior, 5*(1), 49–55.

Willis, J., & Todorov, A. (2006). First impressions: Making up your mind after a 100-ms exposure to a face. *Psychological Science, 17*, 592–598.

Wilson, M. I., Daly, M., & Weghorst, S. J. (1980). Household composition and the risk of child abuse and neglect. *Journal of Biological Science, 12*, 333–340.

Wilson, T., & Brekke, N. (1994). Mental contamination and mental correction: Unwanted influences on judgments and evaluations. *Psychological Bulletin, 116*, 117–142.

Wilson, T., Centerbar, D., & Brekke, N. (2002). Mental contamination and the debiasing problem. In T. Gilovich, D. W. Griffin, & D. Kahneman (Eds.), *Heuristics and biases: The psychology of intuitive judgment* (pp. 185–200). New York: Cambridge University Press.

Wilson, T. D., & Dunn, D. S. (1986). Effects of introspection on attitude-behavior consistency: Analyzing reasons versus focusing on feelings. *Journal of Experimental Social Psychology, 22*, 249–263.

Wilson, T. D., Dunn, D. S., Bybee, J. A., Hyman, D. B., & Rotondo, J. A. (1984). Effects of analyzing reasons on attitude-behavior consistency. *Journal of Personality and Social Psychology, 47*, 5–16.

Wilson, T. D., & Gilbert, D. T. (2008). Explaining why. A model of affective adaptation. *Perspectives in Psychological Science, 3*, 372–388.

Wilson, T. D., Lisle, D., Schooler, J. W., Hodges, S. D., Klaaren, K. J., & LaFleur, S. J. (1993). Introspecting about reasons can reduce post-choice satisfaction. *Personality and Social Psychology Bulletin, 19*, 331–339.

Wilson, T. D., & Schooler, J. W. (1991). Thinking too much: Introspection can reduce the quality of preferences and decisions. *Journal of Personality and Social Psychology, 60*, 181–192.

Wilson, T. D., Wheatley, T., Kurtz, J., Dunn, & Gilbert, D. T. (2004). When to fire: Anticipatory versus postevent reconstrual of uncontrollable events. *Personality and Social Psychology Bulletin, 30*, 1–12.

Wilson, T. D., Wheatley, T., Meyers, J. M., Gilbert, D. T., & Axson, D. (2000). Focalism: A source of durability bias in affective forecasting. *Journal of Personality and Social Psychology, 78*, 821–836.

Winch, R. F. (1955). The theory of complementary needs in mate selection: A test of one kind of complementariness. *American Sociological Review, 20*, 52–56.

Winch, R. F., Ktanes, T., & Ktanes, V. (1954). The theory of complementary needs in mate selection: An analytic and descriptive study. *American Sociological Review, 19*, 241–249.

Winch, R. F., Ktanes, T., & Ktanes, V. (1955). Empirical elaboration of the theory of complementary needs in mate selection. *Journal of Abnormal and Social Psychology, 51*, 508–513.

Windhauser, J., Seiter, J., & Winfree, T. (1991). Crime news in the Louisiana press. *Journalism Quarterly, 45*, 72–78.

Wink, P. (1991). Two faces of narcissism. *Journal of Personality and Social Psychology, 61*, 590–597.

Winkielman, P., & Cacioppo, J. T. (2001). Mind at ease puts a smile on the face: Psychophysiological evidence that processing facilitation increases positive affect. *Journal of Personality and Social Psychology, 81*, 989–1000.

Winter, D. G. (1973). *The power motive.* New York: Free Press.

Winter, D. G. (1988). The power motive in women and men. *Journal of Personality and Social Psychology, 54*, 510–519.

Winter, D. G., & Barenbaum, N. B. (1985). Responsibility and the power motive in women and men. *Journal of Personality, 53*, 335–355.

Winter, L., & Uleman, J. S. (1984). When are social judgments made? Evidence for the spontaneousness of trait inferences. *Journal of Personality and Social Psychology, 47*, 237–252.

Wiseman, C. V., Gray, J. J., Mosimann, J. E., & Ahrens, A. H. (1992). Cultural expectations of thinness in women: An update. *International Journal of Eating Disorders, 11*, 85–89.

Wisman, A., and Goldenberg, J. (2005). From the grave to the cradle: Evidence that mortality salience engenders a desire for offspring. *Journal of Personality and Social Psychology, 89*, 46–61.

Wittenbrink, B. (2004). Ordinary forms of prejudice. *Psychological Inquiry, 15*, 306–310.

Wittenbrink, B., Judd, C. M., & Park, B. (1997). Evidence for racial prejudice at the implicit level and its relationship with questionnaire measures. *Journal of Personality and Social Psychology, 72*, 262–274.

Wittenbrink, B., & Schwarz, N. (Eds.). (2007). *Implicit measures of attitudes.* New York: Guilford Press.

Wolf, S. (1985). Manifest and latent influence on majorities and minorities. *Journal of Personality and Social Psychology, 48*, 899–908.

Wolfe, T. (1979). *The right stuff.* New York: Farrar, Straus & Giroux.

Wolfe, T. (1987). *The bonfire of the vanities*. New York: Farrar, Straus & Giroux.

Woll, S. (1986). So many to choose from: Decision strategies in videodating. *Journal of Social and Personal Relationships*, 3, 43–52.

Wood, J. V. (1989). Theory and research concerning social comparisons of personal attributes. *Psychological Bulletin*, 106, 231–248.

Wood, J. V. (1996). What is social comparison and how should we study it? *Personality and Social Psychology Bulletin*, 22, 520–537.

Wood, W. (1982). Retrieval of attitude-relevant information from memory: Effects of susceptibility to persuasion and on intrinsic motivation. *Journal of Personality and Social Psychology*, 42, 798–810.

Wood, W., & Eagly, A. H. (2002). A cross-cultural analysis of the behavior of women and men: Implications for the origin of sex differences. *Psychological Bulletin*, 126, 699–727.

Wood, W., & Kallgren, C. A. (1988). Communicator attributes and persuasion: Recipients access to attitude-relevant information in memory. *Personality and Social Psychology Bulletin*, 14, 172–182.

Wood, W., Lundgren, S., Ouellette, J. A., Busceme, S., & Blackstone, T. (1994). Minority influence: A meta-analytic review of social influence processes. *Psychological Bulletin*, 115, 323–345.

Wooley, S. C., & Wooley, O. W. (1980). Eating disorders: Obesity and anorexia. In A. M. Brodsky & R. T. Hare-Mustin (Eds.), *Women and psychotherapy: An assessment of research and practice* (pp. 135–158). New York: Guilford Press.

Woolger, R. J. (1988). *Other lives, other selves: A Jungian psychotherapist discovers past lives*. New York: Bantam.

Worchel, S. (1974). The effects of three types of arbitrary thwarting on the instigation to aggression. *Journal of Personality*, 42, 301–318.

Word, C. O., Zanna, M. P., & Cooper, J. (1974). The nonverbal mediation of self-fulfilling prophecies in interracial interaction. *Journal of Experimental Social Psychology*, 10, 109–120.

Wright, D. B., & Stroud, J. N. (2002). Age differences in lineup identification accuracy: People are better with their own age. *Law and Human Behavior*, 26, 641–654.

Wright, R. (2000). *Nonzero: The logic of human destiny*. New York: Pantheon Books.

Wright, S., Aron, A., McLaughlin-Volpe, T., & Ropp, S. (1997). The extended contact effect: Knowledge of cross-group friendships and prejudice. *Journal of Personality and Social Psychology*, 73, 73–90.

Wu, C., & Shaffer, D. R. (1987). Susceptibility to persuasive appeals as a function of source credibility and prior experience with the attitude object. *Journal of Personality and Social Psychology*, 52, 677–688.

Wyer, R. S., & Srull, T. K. (1981). Category accessibility: Some theoretical and empirical issues concerning the processing of social stimulus information. In E. T. Higgins, C. P. Herman, & M. P. Zanna (Eds.), *Social cognition: The Ontario Symposium* (pp. 161–197). Hillsdale, NJ: Erlbaum.

Wyer, R. S., Srull, T. K., Gordon, S. E., & Hartwick, J. (1982). Effects of processing objectives on the recall of prose material. *Journal of Personality and Social Psychology*, 43, 674–688.

Yamagishi, T., Mifune, N., Liu, J. H., & Pauling, J. (2008). Exchanges of group-based favors: Ingroup bias in the prisoner's dilemma game with minimal groups in Japan and New Zealand. *Asian Journal of Social Psychology*, 11(3), 196–207.

Yang, M. H., & Bond, M. H. (1990). Exploring implicit personality theories with indigenous or imported constructs: The Chinese case. *Journal of Personality and Social Psychology*, 58, 1087–1095.

Youth Risk Behavior Survey. (2007). *Health risk behaviors by race/ethnicity*. Atlanta, GA: Centers for Disease Control.

Yuchida, Y., & Kitayama, S. (2009). *Happiness and unhappiness in East and West*. Kyoto, Japan: Kyoto University.

Yudko, E., Blanchard, D., Henne, J., & Blanchard, R. (1997). Emerging themes in preclinical research on alcohol and aggression. In M. Galanter (Ed.), *Recent developments in alcoholism: Alcohol and violence: Epidemiology, neurobiology, psychology, and family issues* (Vol. 13, pp. 123–138). New York: Plenum Press.

Zadny, J., & Gerard, H. B. (1974). Attributed intentions and informational selectivity. *Journal of Experimental Social Psychology*, 10, 34–52.

Zajonc, R. B. (1965). Social facilitation. *Science*, 149, 269–274.

Zajonc, R. B. (1968). The attitudinal effects of mere exposure. *Journal of Personality and Social Psychology*, 9 (monographs), 1–27.

Zajonc, R. B. (1980). Feeling and thinking: Preferences need no inferences. *American Psychologist*, 35, 151–175.

Zajonc, R. B. (2001). Mere exposure: A gateway to the subliminal. *Current Directions in Psychological Science*, 10, 224–228.

Zajonc, R. B. (2002). The zoomorphism of human collective violence. In L. S. Newman & R. Erber (Eds.), *Understanding genocide: The social psychology of the Holocaust* (pp. 222–240). New York: Oxford University Press.

Zajonc, R. B., Adelmann, P. K., Murphy, S. T., & Niedenthal, P. M. (1987). Convergence in the physical appearance of spouses. *Motivation and Emotion*, 11, 335–346.

Zajonc, R. B., Heingartner, A., & Herman, E. M. (1969). Social enhancement and impairment of performance in the cockroach. *Journal of Personality and Social Psychology*, 13, 83–92.

Zanna, M. P., & Cooper, J. (1974). Dissonance and the pill: An attribution approach to studying the arousal properties of dissonance. *Journal of Personality and Social Psychology*, 29, 703–709.

Zanna, M. P., Kiesler, C. A., & Pilkonis, P. A. (1970). Positive and negative attitudinal affect established by classical conditioning. *Journal of Personality and Social Psychology*, 14, 321–328.

Zanna, M. P., & Rempel, J. K. (1988). Attitudes: A new look at an old concept. In D. Bar-Tal & A. W. Kruglanski (Eds.), *The social psychology of knowledge* (pp. 315–334). Cambridge, England: Cambridge University Press.

Zarate, M. A., Uleman, J. S., & Voils, C. I. (2001). Effects of culture and processing goals on the activation and binding of trait concepts. *Social Cognition*, 19, 295–323.

Zebrowitz, L. (1997). *Reading faces: Window to the soul?* Boulder, CO: Westview Press.

Zebrowitz, L. A., Andreoletti, C., Collins, M. A., Lee, S. Y., & Blumenthal, J. (1998). Bright, bad, babyfaced boys: Appearance stereotypes do not always yield self-fulfilling prophecy effects. *Journal of Personality and Social Psychology*, 75, 1300–1320.

Zebrowitz, L. A., & McDonald, S. M. (1991). The impact of litigants' babyfacedness and attractiveness on adjudications in small claims courts. *Law and Human Behavior*, 15, 603–624.

Zebrowitz, L. A., & Montepare, J. M. (2005). Appearance DOES matter. *Science*, 308, 1565–1566.

Zebrowitz, L. A., Olson, K., & Hoffman, K. (1993). Stability of babyfaceness and attractiveness across the life span. *Journal of Personality and Social Psychology*, 64, 453–466.

Zebrowitz, L. A., Tenenbaum, D. R., & Goldstein, L. H. (1991). The impact of job applicants' facial maturity, gender, and academic achievement on hiring recommendations. *Journal of Applied Social Psychology*, 21, 525–548.

Zebrowitz, L. A., Voinescu, L., & Collins, M. A. (1996). "Wide-eyed" and "crooked-faced": Determinants of perceived and real honesty across the life span. *Personality and Social Psychology Bulletin, 22,* 1258–1269.

Zeisel, H., & Diamond, S. (1978). The effect of peremptory challenges on jury and verdict: An experiment in a federal district court. *Stanford Law Review, 30,* 491–531.

Zhong, C. B., & Leonardelli, G. J. (2008). Cold and lonely: Does social exclusion literally feel cold? *Psychological Science, 19,* 838–842.

Zhong, C. B., & Liljenquist, K. (2006). Washing away your sins: Threatened morality and physical cleansing. *Science, 313,* 1451–1452.

Zhu, Y., Zhang, L., Fan, J., & Han, S. (2007). Neural basis of cultural influences on self-representation. *Neuroimage, 34,* 1310–1316.

Zimbardo, P. G. (1970). *The human choice: Individuation, reason and order versus deindividuation, impulse and chaos.* Paper presented at the Nebraska Symposium on Motivation (1969), Lincoln, Nebraska.

Zimbardo, P. G., & Leippe, M. R. (1991). *The psychology of attitude change and social influence.* New York: McGraw-Hill.

Zimet, G., Dalhem, W., Zimet, S. & Farley, G. (1988). The Multidimensional Scale of Perceived Social Support. *Journal of Personality Assessment, 52*(1), 30–41.

Zuber, J. A., Crott, H. W., & Werner, J. (1992). Choice shift and group polarization: An analysis of the status of arguments and social decision schemes. *Journal of Personality and Social Psychology, 62,* 50–61.

Zusne, L., & Jones, W. H. (1982). *Anomalistic psychology.* Hillsdale, NJ: Erlbaum.

Zuwerink, J. R., & Devine, P. G. (1996). Attitude importance and resistance to persuasion: It's not just the thought that counts. *Journal of Personality and Social Psychology, 70,* 931–944.

Zweig, J. (2007). *Your money and your brain.* New York: Simon & Schuster.

Glossary

A

actor-observer difference A difference in attribution based on who is making the causal assessment: the actor (who is relatively disposed to make situational attributions) or the observer (who is relatively disposed to make dispositional attributions).

actual self The self that people believe they are.

affective forecasting Predicting future emotions—for example, whether an event will result in happiness or anger or sadness, and for how long.

agenda control Efforts of the media to select certain events and topics to emphasize, thereby shaping which issues and events people think are important.

altruism Unselfish behavior that benefits others without regard to consequences for the self.

anxious-preoccupied style An attachment style characterized by dependency or "clinginess." People with an anxious-preoccupied style tend not to have a positive view of themselves, but they value and seek out intimacy.

applied science Science concerned with solving some real-world problem of importance.

appraisal processes The ways people evaluate events and objects in their environment based on their relation to current goals.

approach/inhibition theory A theory that maintains that high-power individuals are inclined to go after their goals and make quick judgments, whereas low-power individuals are more likely to constrain their behavior and attend to others carefully.

attachment theory A theory about how our early attachments with our parents shape our relationships for the rest of our lives.

attitude An evaluation of an object in a positive or negative fashion that includes the three elements of affect, cognition, and behavior.

attitude inoculation Small attacks on people's beliefs that engage their attitudes, prior commitments, and knowledge structures, enabling them to counteract a subsequent larger attack and be resistant to persuasion.

attribution theory An umbrella term used to describe the set of theoretical accounts of how people assign causes to the events around them and the effects that people's causal assessments have.

augmentation principle The idea that people should assign greater weight to a particular cause of behavior if other causes are present that normally would produce the opposite outcome.

authority Power that derives from institutionalized roles or arrangements.

availability heuristic The process whereby judgments of frequency or probability are based on how readily pertinent instances come to mind.

B

balance theory A theory holding that people try to maintain balance among their beliefs, cognitions, and sentiments.

base-rate information Information about the relative frequency of events or of members of different categories in the population.

basic science Science concerned with trying to understand some phenomenon in its own right, with a view toward using that understanding to build valid theories about the nature of some aspect of the world.

basking in reflected glory The tendency for people to take pride in the accomplishments of those with whom they are in some way associated, as when fans identify with a winning team.

behavioral economics A discipline that uses insights from psychology to create realistic and accurate models of economic behavior.

better-than-average effect The finding that most people think they are above average on various trait and ability dimensions.

bottom-up processes "Data-driven" mental processing, in which an individual forms conclusions based on the stimuli encountered through experience.

broaden-and-build hypothesis The hypothesis that positive emotions broaden thought and action repertoires, helping people build social resources.

bystander intervention Giving assistance to someone in need on the part of those who have witnessed an emergency. Bystander intervention is generally reduced as the number of observers increases, because each person feels that someone else will probably help.

C

causal attribution Linking an event to a cause, such as inferring that a personality trait was responsible for a behavior.

central (systematic) route A persuasive route wherein people think carefully and deliberately about the content of a message, attending to its logic, cogency, and arguments as well as to related evidence and principles.

channel factors Certain situational circumstances that appear unimportant on the surface but that can have great consequences for behavior, either facilitating or blocking it or guiding behavior in a particular direction.

cognitive dissonance theory A theory that maintains that inconsistencies among a person's thoughts, sentiments, and actions create an aversive emotional state (dissonance) that leads to efforts to restore consistency.

collective self Beliefs about our identities as members of social groups to which we belong.

communal relationships Relationships in which the individuals feel a special responsibility for one another and give and receive according to the principle of need; such relationships are often long term.

complementarity The tendency for people to seek out others with characteristics that are different from and that complement their own.

compliance Responding favorably to an explicit request by another person.

confirmation bias The tendency to test a proposition by searching for evidence that would support it.

conformity Changing one's behavior or beliefs in response to explicit or implicit pressure (whether real or imagined) from others.

consensus What most people would do in a given situation—that is, whether most people would behave the same way or few or no other people would behave that way.

consistency What an individual does in a given situation on different occasions—that is, whether next time under the same circumstances, the person would behave the same or differently.

construal People's interpretation and inference about the stimuli or situations they confront.

construal level theory A theory that outlines the relationship between psychological distance and the concreteness versus abstraction of thought. Psychologically distant actions and events are thought about in abstract terms; actions and events that are close at hand are thought about in concrete terms.

contingencies of self-worth An account of self-esteem that maintains that self-esteem is contingent on successes and failures in domains on which a person has based his or her self-worth.

control condition A condition comparable to the experimental condition in every way except that it lacks the one ingredient hypothesized to produce the expected effect on the dependent variable.

core-relational themes Distinct themes, such as danger or offense or fairness, that define the core of each emotion.

correlational research Research that does not involve random assignment to different situations, or conditions, and that psychologists conduct just to see whether there is a relationship between the variables.

counterfactual thoughts Thoughts of what might have, could have, or should have happened "if only" something had been done differently.

covariation principle The idea that behavior should be attributed to potential causes that co-occur with the behavior.

culture of honor A culture that is defined by its members' strong concerns about their own and others' reputations, leading to sensitivity to slights and insults and a willingness to use violence to avenge any perceived wrong or insult.

D

debriefing In preliminary versions of an experiment, asking participants straightforwardly if they understood the instructions, found the setup to be reasonable, and so forth. In later versions, debriefings are used to educate participants about the questions being studied.

deception research Research in which the participants are misled about the purpose of the research or the meaning of something that is done to them.

dehumanization The tendency to attribute nonhuman characteristics to groups other than one's own—for example, by referring to them as rats, dogs, pigs, or vermin.

deindividuation The reduced sense of individual identity accompanied by diminished self-regulation that comes over people when they are in a large group.

dependent variable In experimental research, the variable that is measured (as opposed to manipulated); it is hypothesized to be affected by manipulation of the independent variable.

descriptive norms People's perceptions of how most people behave in a given context.

diffusion of responsibility A reduction of a sense of urgency to help someone involved in an emergency or dangerous situation under the assumption that others who are also observing the situation will help.

discounting principle The idea that people should assign reduced weight to a particular cause of behavior if other plausible causes might have produced it.

discrimination Unfair treatment of members of a particular group based on their membership in that group.

dismissive-avoidant style An attachment style characterized by independence and self-reliance. People with a dismissive-avoidant style seek less intimacy with others and deny the importance of close relationships.

display rules Culturally specific rules that govern how and when and to whom people express emotion.

dispositions Internal factors such as beliefs, values, personality traits, or abilities that guide a person's behavior.

distinctiveness What an individual does in different situations—that is, whether the behavior is unique to a particular situation or occurs in all situations.

distraction-conflict theory A theory based on the idea that being aware of another person's presence creates a conflict between attending to that person and attending to the task at hand, and that this attentional conflict is arousing and produces social facilitation effects.

dominance Behavior enacted with the goal of acquiring or demonstrating power.

dominant response In an individual's hierarchy of responses, the response he or she is most likely to make.

door-in-the-face technique (reciprocal concessions technique) Asking someone for a very large favor that he or she will certainly refuse and then following that request with one for a smaller favor (which tends to be seen as a concession that the target will feel compelled to honor).

duration neglect The relative unimportance of the length of an emotional experience, be it pleasurable or unpleasant, in judgements of the overall experience.

E

effort justification People's tendency to reduce dissonance by justifying the time, effort, or money they have devoted to something that has turned out to be unpleasant or disappointing.

ego depletion A state, produced by acts of self-control, in which people lack the energy or resources to engage in further acts of self-control.

ego-defensive function An attitudinal function that enables people to maintain cherished beliefs about themselves and their world by protecting them from contradictory information.

elaboration likelihood model (ELM) A model of persuasion that maintains that there are two different routes of persuasion: the central route and the peripheral route.

emotion accents Culturally specific ways that individuals from different cultures express particular emotions, such as the tongue bite as an expression of embarrassment in India.

emotional amplification A ratcheting up of an emotional reaction to an event that is proportional to how easy it is to imagine the event not happening.

emotions Brief, specific psychological and physiological responses that help humans meet goals, many of which are social.

empathic concern Identifying with another person—feeling and understanding what that person is experiencing—accompanied by the intention to help the person in need.

encoding Filing information away in memory based on what information is attended to and the initial interpretation of the information.

entertainment-education Media presentations that are meant to both entertain and persuade people to act in their own (or in society's) best interests.

entity theory of intelligence The belief that intelligence is something you are born with and cannot change.

equity theory A theory that maintains that people are motivated to pursue fairness, or equity, in their relationships; rewards and costs are shared roughly equally among individuals.

ethnocentrism Glorifying one's own group while vilifying other groups.

evaluation apprehension People's concern about how they might appear in the eyes of others—that is, about being evaluated.

exchange relationships Relationships in which individuals feel little responsibility toward one another; giving and receiving are governed by concerns about equity and reciprocity.

experimental research In social psychology, research that randomly assigns people to different conditions, or situations, and that enables researchers to make strong inferences about how these different conditions affect people's behavior.

explanatory style A person's habitual way of explaining events, typically assessed along three dimensions: internal/external, stable/unstable, and global/specific.

external validity An experimental setup that closely resembles real-life situations so that results can safely be generalized to such situations.

F

face The public image of ourselves that we want others to believe.

fearful-avoidant style An attachment style characterized by ambivalence and discomfort toward close relationships. People with a fearful-avoidant style desire closeness with others but feel unworthy of others' affection and so do not seek out intimacy.

feelings-as-information perspective A theory that since many judgments are too complex for people to thoroughly review all the relevant evidence, they rely on their emotions to provide them with rapid, reliable information about events and conditions within their social environment.

field experiment An experiment set up in the real world, usually with participants who are not aware that they are in a study of any kind.

fluency The feeling of ease associated with processing information.

focal emotions Emotions that are especially common within a particular culture.

focalism A tendency to focus too much on a central aspect of an event while neglecting to consider the impact of ancillary aspects of the event or the impact of other events.

foot-in-the-door technique A compliance technique in which a person makes an initial small request with which nearly everyone complies, followed by a larger request involving the real behavior of interest.

framing effect The influence on judgment resulting from the way information is presented, such as the order of presentation or how it is worded.

frustration The internal state that accompanies the thwarting of an attempt to achieve some goal.

frustration-aggression theory A theory that elaborates the idea that frustration leads to aggression.

functional distance The tendency of an architectural layout to encourage or inhibit certain activities, including contact between people.

fundamental attribution error The failure to recognize the importance of situational influences on behavior, and the corresponding tendency to overemphasize the importance of dispositions or traits on behavior.

G

Gestalt psychology Based on the German word *gestalt*, meaning "form" or "figure," this approach stresses the fact that people perceive objects not by means of some automatic registering device but by active, usually unconscious interpretation of what the object represents as a whole.

group polarization The tendency for group decisions to be more extreme than those made by individuals. Whatever way the individuals are leaning, group discussion tends to make them lean further in that direction.

groupthink A kind of faulty thinking by highly cohesive groups in which the critical scrutiny that should be devoted to the issues at hand is subverted by social pressures to reach consensus.

H

halo effect The common belief—accurate or not—that attractive individuals possess a host of positive qualities beyond their physical appearance.

heuristics Intuitive mental operations that allow us to make a variety of judgments quickly and efficiently.

heuristic-systematic model A model of persuasion that maintains that there are two different routes of persuasion: the systematic route and the heuristic route.

hindsight bias People's tendency to be overconfident about whether they could have predicted a given outcome.

hostile aggression Behavior intended to harm another, either physically or psychologically, and motivated by feelings of anger and hostility.

hypercognize To represent a particular emotion with numerous words and concepts.

hypothesis A prediction about what will happen under particular circumstances.

I

ideal self The self that embodies people's wishes and aspirations as held by themselves and by other people for them.

identifiable victim effect The tendency to be more moved by the plight of a single, vivid individual than by a more abstract number of individuals.

ideomotor action The phenomenon whereby merely thinking about a behavior makes its actual performance more likely.

illusory correlation The belief that two variables are correlated when in fact they are not.

immune neglect The tendency for people to underestimate their capacity to be resilient in responding to difficult life events, which leads them to overestimate the extent to which life's difficulties will reduce their personal well-being.

Implicit Association Test (IAT) A technique for revealing nonconscious prejudices toward particular groups.

implicit attitude measures Indirect measures of attitudes that do not involve self-report.

inclusive fitness The evolutionary tendency to look out for ourselves, our offspring, and our close relatives together with their offspring, so that our genes will survive and be passed on in future generations.

incrementalist theory of intelligence The belief that intelligence is something you can improve by dint of working.

independent (individualistic) cultures Cultures in which people tend to think of themselves as distinct social entities, tied to each other by voluntary bonds of affection and organizational memberships but essentially separate from other people and having attributes that exist in the absence of any connection to others.

independent variable In experimental research, the variable that is manipulated; it is hypothesized to be the cause of a particular outcome.

individual self Beliefs about our unique personal traits, abilities, preferences, tastes, talents, and so forth.

individuation An enhanced sense of individual identity produced by focusing attention on the self, which generally leads people to act carefully and deliberately and in accordance with their sense of propriety and values.

induced (forced) compliance Subtly compelling individuals to behave in a manner that is inconsistent with their beliefs, attitudes, or values, in order to elicit dissonance—and therefore a change in their original attitudes or values.

informational social influence The influence of other people that results from taking their comments or actions as a source of information about what is correct, proper, or effective.

informed consent Participants' willingness to participate in a procedure or research study after learning all relevant aspects about the procedure or study.

infrahumanization The tendency to be reluctant to attribute more complex emotions, such as pride or compassion, to outgroup members.

institutional review board (IRB) A university committee that examines research proposals and makes judgments about the ethical appropriateness of the research.

instrumental aggression Behavior intended to harm another in the service of motives other than pure hostility (for example, to attract attention, to acquire wealth, or to advance political and ideological causes).

interdependent (collectivistic) cultures Cultures in which people tend to define themselves as part of a collective, inextricably tied to others in their group and placing less importance on individual freedom or personal control over their lives.

internal validity In experimental research, confidence that only the manipulated variable could have produced the results.

internalization Private acceptance of a proposition, orientation, or ideology.

intersex attraction The interest in and attraction toward a member of the opposite sex.

intervention An effort to change people's behavior.

intrasex competition Direct competition between two or more males or two or more females for access to members of the opposite sex.

investment model of interpersonal relationships A model of interpersonal relationships that maintains that three things make partners more committed to each other: rewards, few alternative partners, and investments in the relationship.

J

just world hypothesis The belief that people get what they deserve in life and deserve what they get.

K

kin selection The tendency for natural selection to favor behaviors that increase the chances of survival of genetic relatives.

knowledge function An attitudinal function whereby attitudes help organize people's understanding of the world, guiding how they attend to, store, and retrieve information.

L

learned helplessness Passive and depressed responses that individuals show when their goals are blocked and they feel that they have no control over their outcomes.

Likert scale A numerical scale used to assess people's attitudes; it includes a set of possible answers with labeled anchors on each extreme.

longitudinal study A study conducted over a long period of time with the same population, which is periodically assessed regarding a particular behavior.

loss aversion The tendency for a loss of a given magnitude to have more psychological impact than an equivalent gain.

M

measurement validity The correlation between some measure and some outcome that the measure is supposed to predict.

mental accounting The tendency to treat money differently depending on how it is acquired and the mental category to which it is attached.

mere exposure effect The finding that repeated exposure to a stimulus (for example, an object or person) leads to greater liking of the stimulus.

message characteristics Aspects of the message itself, including the quality of the evidence and the explicitness of its conclusions.

minimal group paradigm An experimental paradigm in which researchers create groups based on arbitrary and seemingly meaningless criteria and then examine how the members of these "minimal groups" are inclined to behave toward one another.

modern racism Prejudice directed at other racial groups that exists alongside rejection of explicitly racist beliefs.

N

natural experiments Naturally occurring events or phenomena having somewhat different conditions that can be compared with almost as much rigor as in experiments where the investigator manipulates the conditions.

natural selection An evolutionary process that molds animals and plants so that traits that enhance the probability of survival and reproduction are passed on to subsequent generations.

naturalistic fallacy The claim that the way things *are* is the way they *should be.*

negative state relief hypothesis The idea that people engage in certain actions, such as agreeing to a request, to relieve their negative feelings and feel better about themselves.

norm of reciprocity A norm dictating that people should provide benefits to those who benefit them.

normative social influence The influence of other people that comes from the individual's desire to avoid their disapproval, harsh judgments, and other social sanctions (for example, barbs, ostracism).

O

obedience In an unequal power relationship, submitting to the demands of the more powerful person.

ought self The self that is concerned with the duties, obligations, and external demands people feel they are compelled to honor.

outgroup homogeneity effect The tendency for people to assume that within-group similarity is much stronger for outgroups than for ingroups.

P

paired distinctiveness The pairing of two distinctive events that stand out even more because they co-occur.

parental investment The evolutionary principle that costs and benefits are associated with reproduction and the nurturing of offspring. Because these costs and benefits are different for males and females, one sex will normally value and invest more in each child than will the other sex.

peripheral (heuristic) route A persuasive route wherein people attend to relatively simple, superficial cues related to the message, such as the length of the message or the expertise or attractiveness of the communicator.

personal distress A motive for helping those in distress that may arise from a need to reduce our *own* distress.

planning fallacy The tendency for people to be unrealistically optimistic about how quickly they can complete a project.

pluralistic ignorance Misperception of a group norm that results from observing people who are acting at variance with their private beliefs out of a concern for the social consequences—actions that reinforce the erroneous group norm.

possible selves Hypothetical selves that a person aspires to be in the future.

power The ability to control our own outcomes and those of others; the freedom to act.

prejudice A negative attitude or affective response toward a certain group and its individual members.

prescriptive (injunctive) norms People's perceptions of what behaviors are generally approved of or frowned on by others.

prevention focus Regulating behavior with respect to ought standards, entailing a focus on avoiding negative outcomes and avoidance-related behaviors.

primacy effect The disproportionate influence on judgment by information presented first in a body of evidence.

primary appraisal stage An initial, automatic positive or negative evaluation of ongoing events based on whether they are congruent or incongruent with an individual's goals.

prime To momentarily activate a concept and hence make it accessible. (Also used as a noun—a stimulus presented to activate a concept.)

priming A procedure used to increase the accessibility of a concept or schema (for example, a stereotype).

principle of serviceable habits Charles Darwin's thesis that emotional expressions are remnants of full-blown behaviors that helped our primate and mammalian predecessors meet important goals in the past.

prisoner's dilemma A situation involving payoffs to two people, who must decide whether to "cooperate" or "defect." In the end, trust and cooperation lead to higher joint payoffs than mistrust and defection.

procedural justice People's assessments of whether the processes leading to legal outcomes are fair.

processing style perspective A theory that different emotions lead people to reason in different ways—for example, that anger facilitates reliance on preexisting heuristics and stereotypes, whereas sadness facilitates more careful attention to situational details.

promotion focus Regulating behavior with respect to ideal self standards, entailing a focus on attaining positive outcomes and approach-related behaviors.

propinquity Physical proximity.

psychological stress The sense that your challenges and demands surpass your current capacities, resources, and energies.

R

random assignment Assigning participants in experimental research to different groups randomly, such that they are as likely to be assigned to one condition as to another.

rape-prone cultures Cultures in which rape tends to be used as an act of war against enemy women, as a ritual act, and as a threat against women so that they will remain subservient to men.

reactance theory The idea that people reassert their prerogatives in response to the unpleasant state of arousal they experience when they believe their freedoms are threatened.

reactive devaluation The tendency to attach less value to an offer in a negotiation once the opposing group makes it.

realistic group conflict theory A theory that group conflict, prejudice, and discrimination are likely to arise over competition between groups for limited resources.

receiver characteristics Characteristics of the person who receives the message, including age, mood, personality, and motivation to attend to the message.

recency effect The disproportionate influence on judgment by information presented last in a body of evidence.

reciprocal altruism The tendency to help others with the expectation that they are likely to help us in return at some future time.

reference groups Groups whose opinions matter to a person and that affect the person's opinions and beliefs.

reflected self-appraisals Beliefs about what others think of our social selves.

relational self Beliefs about our identities in specific relationships.

reliability The degree to which the particular way that researchers measure a given variable is likely to yield consistent results.

representativeness heuristic The process whereby judgments of likelihood are based on assessments of similarity between individuals and group prototypes or between cause and effect.

reproductive fitness The capacity to get one's genes passed on to subsequent generations.

reputation The beliefs, evaluations, and impressions people hold about an individual within a social network.

response latency The time it takes an individual to respond to a stimulus, such as an attitude question.

retrieval The extraction of information from memory.

reverse causation When variable 1 is assumed to cause variable 2, yet the opposite direction of causation may be the case.

risk aversion The reluctance to pursue an uncertain option with an average payoff that equals or exceeds the payoff attainable by another, certain option.

risk seeking The opposite of risk aversion; the tendency to forgo a certain outcome in favor of a risky option with an equal or more negative average payoff.

risky shift The tendency for groups to make riskier decisions than individuals would.

rumination The tendency to think about some stressful event over and over again.

S

schema A knowledge structure consisting of any organized body of stored information.

scientific jury selection A statistical approach to jury selection whereby members of different demographic groups in the community are asked their attitudes toward various issues related to a trial, and defense and prosecuting attorneys try to influence the selection of jurors accordingly.

secondary appraisal stage A subsequent evaluation in which people determine why they feel the way they do about an event, consider possible ways of responding to the event, and weigh future consequences of different courses of action.

secure attachment style An attachment style characterized by feelings of security in relationships. Individuals with this style are comfortable with intimacy and want to be close to others during times of threat and uncertainty.

self-affirmation Bolstering our identity and self-esteem by taking note of important elements of our identity, such as our important values.

self-awareness theory A theory that maintains that when people focus their attention inward on themselves, they become concerned with self-evaluation and how their current behavior conforms to their internal standards and values.

self-censorship The tendency to withhold information or opinions in group discussions.

self-complexity The tendency to define the self in terms of multiple domains that are relatively distinct from one another in content.

self-discrepancy theory A theory that behavior is motivated by standards reflecting ideal and ought selves. Falling short of these standards produces specific emotions—dejection-related emotions for actual-ideal discrepancies, and agitation-related emotions for actual-ought discrepancies.

self-distancing The ability to focus on one's feelings from the perspective of a detached observer.

self-esteem The positive or negative overall evaluation that each person has of himself or herself.

self-evaluation maintenance (SEM) model A model that maintains that people are motivated to view themselves in a favorable light and that they do so through two processes: reflection and social comparison.

self-fulfilling prophecy The tendency for people to act in ways that bring about the very thing they expect to happen.

self-handicapping People's tendency to engage in self-defeating behavior in order to have a ready excuse should they perform poorly or fail.

self-monitoring The tendency for people to monitor their behavior in such a way that it fits situational demands (the current situation).

self-perception theory A theory that people come to know their own attitudes by looking at their behavior and the context in which it occurred and *inferring* what their attitudes must be.

self-presentation Presenting the person that we would like others to believe we are.

self-reference effect The tendency for information that is related to the self to be more thoroughly processed and integrated with existing self-knowledge, thereby making it more memorable.

self-regulation Processes that people use to initiate, alter, and control their behavior in the pursuit of goals, including the ability to resist short-term awards that thwart the attainment of long-term goals.

self-schemas Cognitive structures, derived from past experience, that represent a person's beliefs and feelings about the self in particular domains.

self-selection A problem that arises when the participant, rather than the investigator, selects his or her level on each variable, bringing with this value unknown other properties that make causal interpretation of a relationship difficult.

self-serving attributional bias The tendency to attribute failure and other bad events to external circumstances, but to attribute success and other good events to oneself.

self-verification theory A theory that holds that people strive for stable, subjectively accurate beliefs about the self because such beliefs give them a sense of coherence.

sleeper effect An effect that occurs when messages from unreliable sources initially exert little influence but later cause individuals' attitudes to shift.

social class The amount of wealth, education, and occupational prestige a person and his or her family enjoy.

social comparison theory The hypothesis that people compare themselves to other people in order to obtain an accurate assessment of their own opinions, abilities, and internal states.

social exchange theory A theory based on the idea that all relationships have costs and rewards, and that how people feel about a relationship depends on their assessments of its costs and rewards and the costs and rewards available to them in other relationships.

social facilitation Initially a term for enhanced performance in the presence of others; now a broader term for the effect—positive or negative—of the presence of others on performance.

social identity theory A theory that a person's self-concept and self-esteem derive not only from personal identity and accomplishments but also from the status and accomplishments of the various groups to which the person belongs.

social influence The many ways that people affect one another, including changes in attitudes, beliefs, feelings, and behavior that result from the comments, actions, or even the mere presence of others.

social loafing The tendency to exert less effort when working on a group task in which individual contributions cannot be monitored.

social psychology The scientific study of the feelings, thoughts, and behaviors of individuals in social situations.

social rewards Benefits like praise, positive attention, tangible rewards, honors, and gratitude that may be gained from helping others.

sociometer hypothesis A hypothesis that maintains that self-esteem is an internal, subjective index or marker of the extent to which a person is included or looked on favorably by others.

source characteristics Characteristics of the person who delivers the message, including the person's attractiveness, credibility, and expertise.

spotlight effect People's conviction that other people are attending to them—to their appearance and behavior—more than they actually are.

statistical significance A measure of the probability that a given result could have occurred by chance.

status The outcome of an evaluation of attributes that produces differences in respect and prominence, which in part determines an individual's power within a group.

stereotype threat People's fear of confirming the stereotypes that others have regarding a group of which they are a member.

stereotypes Beliefs that certain attributes are characteristic of members of particular groups.

strange situation An experimental situation designed to assess an infant's attachment to the caregiver. An infant's reactions are observed after her caregiver has left her alone in an unfamiliar room with a stranger and then when the caregiver returns to the room (the reunion).

subliminal Below the threshold of conscious awareness.

subtyping Explaining away exceptions to a given stereotype by creating a subcategory of the stereotyped group that can be expected to differ from the group as a whole.

sunk cost fallacy A reluctance to "waste" money that leads people to continue with an endeavor, whether it serves their future interests or not, because they have already invested money, effort, or time in it.

superordinate goals Goals that transcend the interests of any one group and that can be achieved more readily by two or more groups working together.

system justification theory The theory that people are motivated to see the existing political and social status quo as desirable, fair, and legitimate.

T

terror management theory (TMT) The theory that people deal with the potentially paralyzing anxiety that comes with the knowledge of the inevitability of death by striving for symbolic immortality through the preservation of a valued worldview and the conviction that they have lived up to its values and prescriptions.

that's-not-all technique Adding something to an original offer, thus creating some pressure to reciprocate.

theory A body of related propositions intended to describe some aspect of the world.

theory of mind The understanding that other people have beliefs and desires.

third variable When variable 1 does not cause variable 2 and variable 2 does not cause variable 1, but rather some other variable exerts a causal influence on both.

third-person effect The assumption by most people that "other people" are more prone to being influenced by persuasive messages (such as those in media campaigns) than they themselves are.

thought polarization hypothesis The hypothesis that more extended thought about a particular issue tends to produce more extreme, entrenched attitudes.

tit-for-tat strategy A strategy in which the individual's first move is cooperative and thereafter the individual mimics the other person's behavior, whether cooperative or competitive.

top-down processes "Theory-driven" mental processing, in which an individual filters and interprets new information in light of preexisting knowledge and expectations.

triangular theory of love A theory that states that love has three major components—passion, intimacy, and commitment—which can be combined in different ways.

U

utilitarian function An attitudinal function that serves to alert people to rewarding objects and situations they should approach and costly or punishing objects or situations they should avoid.

V

value-expressive function An attitudinal function whereby attitudes help people express their most cherished values—usually in groups in which these values can be supported and reinforced.

voir dire The portion of a trial in U.S. courts in which potential jurors are questioned about potential biases and a jury is selected.

volunteerism Nonmonetary assistance an individual regularly provides to another person or group with no expectation of compensation.

W

working self-concept Subset of self-knowledge that is brought to mind in a particular context.

Name Index

Note: Material in figures or tables is indicated by italic page numbers.

Berkman, L. F., 568
Berkowitz, L., 502, 509, 510, 512–513, 517, 527
Berman, M., 507
Bernieri, F. J., 75
Berns, G. S., 553
Bernstein, I. H., 381
Berntson, G. G., 21, 235, 263
Berry, D. S., 110, 111, 363
Berscheid, E., 280, 370, 375, 378, 379, 380, 397
Bersoff, D. N., 611
Bessenoff, G. R., 415
Bettencourt, B. A., 419
Betz, A. L., 285
Beyonce, 244
Biddle, J., 379
Bierbrauer, G., 325
Biernat, M., 117
Billig, M. G., 421
Billington, E., 229, 524
Bird, G., 313
Bird, K., 295
Birg, L. D., 168
Bishop, G. D., 472
Bizman, A., 342
Blackburn, E., 572
Blackburn, E. H., 564
Blackstone, T., 327
Blackwell, L., 59, 158, 592, 594
Blair, I. V., 20, 408, 441, 442
Blair, J., 520
Blair, K., 520
Blair, R. J. R., 217, 220
Blake, W., 401
Blakeslee, S., 397
Blanchard, D., 499
Blanchard, R., 499
Blaney, N., 420
Blank, H., 244
Blanton, H., 76, 414
Blascovich, J., 313, 461
Blass, T., 330, 333, 353
Bledsoe, S. B., 388
Blehar, M., 364
Bless, H., 129, 138, 262, 293
Block, J., 83, 92
Blommel, J. M., 461
Bloom, B. L., 359
Bloom, J. R., 569
Bloom, P., 24, 221
Blount, S., 212, 314–315
Blumberg, S. J., 224–225
Blumenthal, J., 111
Blumer, C., 581
Bochner, S., 30
Boden, J. M., 88
Bodenhausen, G., 221–222
Bodenhausen, G. V., 428, 429, 434, 438, 446
Boehm, C., 615
Bogart, L. M., 566
Boh, L., 465
Bohner, G., 175
Boice, R., 456
Bonanno, G. A., 200
Bond, M. H., 30, 189
Bond, R., 323, 324
Bono, 286
Bono, J. E., 478
Bons, T. A., 375
Bookheimer, S. Y., 439
Booth, A., 395
Borden, R. J., 423–424
Borg, J. S., 27
Borgida, E., 481, 550, 603
Bornstein, R. F., 371
Borofsky, L. A., 68–70
Boster, F. J., 290

Bouazizi, M., 453
Boucher, H., 67
Boucher, J. D., 198
Bourne, E. J., 185
Bouvrette, A., 84
Bowdle, B., 53–54, 57, 60–61, 514
Bower, G. H., 343
Bowlby, J., 357, 363–364, 404, 405
Bowles, S., 557–558
Boyce, T., 477, 565, 566, 567
Boyd, J. G., 340
Boyd, R., 312, 557–558
Boyden, T., 377
Bradburn, N., 117
Bradbury, T. N., 356, 397, 398, 399
Bradfield, A., 43
Brandt, M. E., 198
Bransford, J. D., 124, 126
Bratslavsky, E., 97, 116, 119, 237
Brauer, M., 302, 479, 481
Braverman, P. K., 297
Breckler, S. J., 235, 275
Brehm, J. W., 245, 259, 350
Breitenbecher, D. L., 177
Brekke, N., 228
Brendl, C. M., 96, 414
Brendl, M., 132
Brennan, K. A., 365, 366
Brewer, M. B., 20, 67, 125, 419, 421, 422, 442, 522
Briggs, J. L., 205
Briggs, S. D., 27
Brigham, J., 605
Brigham, J. C., 412, 439
Brillat-Savarin, J. A., 382
Brinol, P., 284
Brislin, R. W., 378
Brocato, R. M., 461
Brockner, J., 81, 342
Brockway, J. H., 43
Broll, L., 541
Brown, C. E., 476, 477, 478
Brown, D. E., 219
Brown, E., 381
Brown, J., 445
Brown, J. D., 71, 83, 92, 100
Brown, L. L., 402
Brown, P., 103
Brown, R., 131, 427–428, 439
Brown, R. J., 422
Brown, R. P., 224
Brown, S. L., 536
Brown, T., 239
Brown, T. J., 379
Brown, W. J., 598
Brown, W. M., 111
Browning, C. R., 333
Brownlow, S., 111
Brownstein, A., 246
Brownstein, A. L., 246
Bruce, H. J., 341
Bruck, M., 605
Brumberg, J. J., 382
Brunsman, B., 316, 325
Brush, C. A., 486
Bryant, F. B., 43
Brzustoski, P., 595, 596
Buckley, J. P., 606
Buddha, 227
Buehler, R., 144–145, 182
Buffett, W., 545
Bugelski, R., 426
Bulleit, B. A., 209, 210
Bumpass, L., 396
Bundy, R. P., 421
Bundy, T., 142
Burger, J. M., 175, 329, 334–335, 341, 342
Burgess, E. W., 375

Burkhart, K., 358
Burklund, L. J., 569
Burns, H. J., 604
Burnstein, E., 288, 472, 550
Burr, A., 42
Burroughs, T., 175
Burrows, L., 20, 128
Burt, D. M., 390, 391
Burton, P. C., 131
Buscema, S., 327
Bush, G. W., 268, 269, 298, 467, 529
Bushman, B. J., 503–504, 505
Buss, A. H., 492
Buss, D. M., 375, 388, 389, 390
Buswell, B. N., 204, 220
Butler, S., 550
Butterworth, G., 381
Butz, D., 479–480
Butz, D. A., 441
Buunk, B. P., 76, 464
Bybee, D., 95, 228, 595
Bybee, J. A., 240
Byrne, D., 362, 375

C
Cacioppo, J. T., 21, 210, 235, 237, 258, 263, 281, 283, 284, 286, 287, 288, 292, 359, 373, 374, 397
Cadinu, M., 446
Caen, H., 371
Caetano, A., 431
Caine, A., 619
Cajdric, A., 426
Caldwell, A., 474
Camerer, C., 557–558
Camino, L., 502
Campbell, B., 408
Campbell, D. T., 416, 531
Campbell, J. D., 87, 316, 320
Campbell, W. K., 86
Campos, B., 213, 214
Cane, M. A., 501
Capps, L. M., 483
Caputo, C., 182
Carli, L. L., 126, 127, 324
Carlsmith, J. M., 56, 63, 248–250, 251, 252, 254, 344
Carlsmith, K. M., 615
Carlson, J. A., 474
Carlson, M., 343
Carlston, D. E., 72, 178
Carmon, Z., 581
Carnagey, N. L., 513
Carnegie, D., 362
Carnevale, P. J., 222
Carney, D., 481
Carroll, J. S., 377, 610
Carter, C. S., 213
Carter, J., 279, 298, 557, 610
Carter, T., 129
Carton, A. M., 500
Cartwright, D., 455
Carver, C. S., 95, 168, 492, 572
Casey, R. J., 381
Cash, T. F., 379
Caspi, A., 82, 88, 375, 499
Castelli, L., 216
Castles, D. L., 391
Castro, F., 466
Catalan, J., 340
Cate, R. M., 395
Ceci, S. J., 379, 605
Centerbar, D., 228
Cernoch, J. M., 549
Cesario, J., 128, 314
Cha, J.-H., 186
Chabris, C. F., 125
Chagnon, N., 513

Chaiken, S., 235, 261, 275, 279, 281, 282, 283, 284, 286, 287, 288, 299, 307
Chaikind, E., 102
Chambres, P., 479
Chang, S., 467
Chapleau, K. M., 441, 442
Chapman, J., 148–149
Chapman, L. J., 148–149
Charlin, V., 343
Charman, S. D., 605
Chartrand, T. L., 210, 313, 314
Chase, J. H., 189
Chasteen, A. L., 459
Chatard-Pannetier, A., 479
Chen, C., 67, 593
Chen, M., 20, 128, 235, 263
Chen, S., 72, 132, 186, 284, 359–360, 479, 484, 554
Chen, S. C., 456
Cheng, B., 546
Cheng, P. W., 149, 160, 600
Cheryan, S., 446
Chesney, M. A., 477, 565, 566, 567
Cheung, F. M., 189
Cheung, T., 30
Chiao, J. Y., 541
Chiu, C., 59, 187, 189
Chiu, C. Y., 189
Choi, H. S., 316
Choi, I., 186, 189, 593
Choi, J. N., 467
Choi, S.-C., 36
Christakis, N. A., 555
Christakis, N. C., 346
Christen, S., 459, 461
Christensen, P. N., 391
Chrvala, C., 324
Chua, H., 77
Churchill, W., 26, 157
Cialdini, R. B., 318, 322, 340, 342, 345, 346, 347, 349, 353, 423–424, 531
Ciano, G., 424
Cicero, 339
Cihangir, S., 475
Cillessen, A. H. N., 519
Cisneros, T., 503
Clancy, S. M., 75
Clark, A., 381
Clark, C. L., 365
Clark, H. H., 103
Clark, M., 343, 344
Clark, M. S., 361, 404
Clark, R., 217, 220, 472
Clark, R. D. I., 531, 540, 541
Clark, R. D. III, 327
Clarkson, J. J., 304
Cliff, J., 350
Clinton, H. R., 125
Clinton, W., 314, 479
Clooney, G., 456
Clore, G. L., 216, 217, 218, 293, 362, 375, 377
Coan, J. A., 210
Coffey, K. A., 227
Cohen, A. B., 221
Cohen, C. E., 125, 127
Cohen, D., 35, 41–42, 46, 48–49, 53–54, 56, 57, 60–61, 77, 514–515, 527
Cohen, F., 268
Cohen, G., 254
Cohen, G. L., 228, 254, 595, 596
Cohen, J. D., 27, 220
Cohen, S., 477, 564, 565, 566, 567, 571
Cohn, M. A., 227
Coie, J. D., 519

Gross, T., 129
Gruber, K. L., 299
Gruenewal, T. L., 570
Gruenfeld, D. H., 479, *480*
Grush, J. E., 295
Guadagno, R. E., 342
Gubin, A., 479
Guerin, B., 461, 464
Guilbault, R. L., 43
Guinote, A., 479, 481
Gunnell, J., 379
Gunning, F. M., 27
Gunz, A., 77
Guo, T., 146
Gurtner, J.-L., 591
Gurung, R. A. R., 570
Gustavsson, L., 388
Gutman, D. A., 553
Gutowski, K. A., 265
Guzzi, B., 342

H
Ha, Y., 121
Haberstroh, S., 117
Habyarimana, J., 497
Hacker, A., 287
Hackman, R., 495
Haddock, G., 411
Haidt, J., 197, 198, 203, 205, *206*, 216, 219, 220, 221
Haines, M. P., 347
Halberstadt, A. G., 479
Halberstadt, J. B., 374
Halberstam, D., 233
Halcomb, C. G., 372, *373*
Hale, S. L., 340
Hall, C. C., 112
Hall, C. L., 344
Hall, J. A., 75, 479
Hall, W. S., 411
Hallahan, M., 75, 185
Hallam, M., 380, 381
Halverson, S. K., 379
Hamermesh, D., 379
Hamill, R., 288
Hamilton, A., 42, 475
Hamilton, D. L., 117, 280, 432–434
Hamilton, W. D., 549
Hamm, H. K., 210
Hampden-Turner, C., 32, 34
Han, S., 73, 291
Haney, C., 6–7, 610, 611
Hanna, J., 102
Hannah, D. B., 436
Hannity, S., 298
Hans, V. P., 610
Hansen, C. H., 116
Hansen, R. D., 116
Harackiewicz, J. M., 101, 261
Harada, T., 541
Harari, H., 341
Harbaugh, C. R., 213
Harber, K., 412, 590
Hardee, B. B., 412
Hardin, C. C., 132, 415
Hardy, C. L., 531
Hare, R. D., 88, 520
Hargreaves, D. J., 128
Hariri, A., 439
Harkins, S., 464
Harling, G. A., 381
Harlow, H. F., 358, *359*
Harmon, A., 209
Harmon-Jones, E., 19, 258, 259, 277, 413
Harris, C. R., 204
Harris, E., 504, 505
Harris, M. B., 509

Harris, R. J., 344
Harris, S., 89
Harris, V. A., 171, *172*, 186
Harrison, A. A., 388
Harrison, D. A., 464
Harry (Prince Henry of Wales), 69
Hart, D., 187
Hartley, M. A., 385
Hartley, S. L., 413
Hartwick, J., 126
Harvey, O. J., 416
Hass, R. G., 288
Hassin, R. R., 129
Hastie, R., 125, 151, 611, 612, 613, 621
Hastorf, A. H., 444
Hatch, E. C., 465
Hatfield, E., 210
Haugtvedt, C. P., 286, 292, 302
Hauser, C., 6
Havas, D. A., 265
Hazan, C., 363, 365, 366
Hazlett, G., 605
Head, D., 27
Heath, S. B., 45
Heatherton, T. F., 26, 73, 83, 87, 220, 381
Hebl, M., 381
Hebl, M. R., 416, 447
Hedden, T., 184, 185
Heerey, E. A., 220, 400, 477–478, 483
Heerwagen, J. H., 276
Heidenreich, S., 480
Heider, F., 160, 190, 244, 245
Heine, S. J., 28, 30, 39, 86, 87, 92, 255, 593
Heingartner, A., 458, *460*
Heinrichs, M., 213
Helgeson, V. S., 76
Helmreich, R., 254
Hemingway, E., 565
Henderson, M. D., 121
Henderson, V. L., 59, 592
Hendricks, M., 130
Henley, N. M., 479
Henne, J., 499
Henningsen, D. D., 467
Henningsen, M. L. M., 467
Henrich, J., 28, 39, 312, 557–558
Henry, P. J., 411
Henton, J. M., 395
Hepworth, J. T., 427
Herbener, E. S., 375
Herbert, M., 572
Herbert, T. B., 571
Herek, G. M., 444, 451
Herman, E. M., 458, *460*
Herr, P. M., 129
Hertenstein, M. J., 198, 209, *210*
Herzog, T., 185
Hess, U., 200, 212
Hewstone, M., 160, 162, 428, 435
Heyes, C., 313
Heyman, R. E., 400
Hies, R., 478
Higgins, E. T., 95, 96, 105, 117, 127, 128, 129, 131, 132, 220, 314, 316, 464
Hilden, L. E., 415
Hill, A. L., 346
Hill, K., 212
Hilmert, C. J., 569
Hilton, D. J., 160, 162
Hilton, J. L., 414
Hinckley, J., Jr., 501–502, *503*
Hinds, L., 212
Hinkle, S., 171
Hinkley, K., 360

Hinsz, V. B., 465
Hirshleifer, D., 576
Hirt, E. R., 83, 101, 127, 134, 424
Hitler, A., 8, 11, 133, 274, 292, 478, 511
Hixon, J. G., 94
Ho, C., 412
Hobart, C., 518
Hobbes, T., 26
Hodge, C. N., 379
Hodges, S. D., 240
Hodson, G., 411
Hoeksema-van Orden, C. Y. D., 464
Hoffman, E. L., 315
Hoffman, K., 378
Hoffman, S., 325
Hofmann, W., 415
Hofstede, G., 29, 32, *33*, 34
Hogg, M., 258
Hogg, M. A., 67
Hogue, J., 99–100, 101
Holder, E., 435
Holland, R. W., 130, 314
Hollon, N. G., 27
Hollopeter, C., 529
Holloway, S., 593
Holmes, J. G., 378, 397, 401, 402
Holmes, O. W., 321
Holtgraves, T., 482
Holyoak, K. J., 132, 246–247
Holzberg, A., 89
Homans, G. C., 464
Hong, Y., 59, 187, 189
Hong, Y. Y., 189
Hood, W., 416
Hoorens, V., 294
Hoover, A., 479, 480
Hoover, H., 523
Hopkins, A., *520*
Horberg, E. J., 199, 221
Horowitz, L. M., 365, 375
Hosey, G. R., 456
Hosey, K., 341
Hoshino-Browne, E., 256
Hosman, L. A., 482
Hossay, J. F., 503
Houlihan, D., 345
Hovland, C. I., 286
Hovland, C. J., 287, 288, 427
Howard, J. W., 126
Hoyt, G., 605
Hrdy, S. B., 363
Hrebec, D., 522
Hsiang, S. M., 501
Hsing, C., 535
Hsu, C. C., 593
Hsu, F. L. K., 29, 30
Huang, C., 210
Hubbard, J. A., 519
Huberman, G., 585
Hubschman, J. H., 385
Huesmann, L. R., 502, 503
Hugenberg, K., 438
Hughes, C. F., 228
Hughes, M., 379
Hughes, M. E., 359
Huguet, P., 464
Hui, C. H., 30
Hull, J. G., 359
Hume, D., 217
Hummer, J. F., 349
Hummert, M. L., 244
Hunsinger, M., 221
Hunter, B. A., 411
Hunter, J. E., 181, 379
Hunter, R. F., 181
Hunter, S. B., 461
Huntley, J., *147*

Hurley, E., 383
Hurtado, A., 611
Husband, R. W., 457
Hussein, King of Jordan, *314*
Hussein, S., 322, 478
Hyde, J. S., 298
Hyman, D. B., 240
Hymes, C., 235
Hyunes, C., 27

I
Ickes, W., 463
Ide, E., 87, 593
Idson, L., *583*, 584
Ijerman, H., 264
Iliffe, A. H., 381
Imada, S., 198, 221
Impett, E. A., 400
Inbar, Y., 221
Inbau, F. E., 606
Inesi, M. E., 479, *480*
Inkster, J. A., 245–246
Innes, J. M., 294
Insel, T. R., 213
Insko, C. A., 244, 320
Inzlicht, M., 445, 446, 459, 594
Ip, G. W. M., 30
Irons, M., 557
Isen, A., 532
Isen, A. M., 216, 222, 343, 344
Ito, T. A., 237, 441
Iwawaki, S., 381
Iyengar, S., 204, 295, 297
Iyengar, S. S., 584–585
Izard, C. E., 201, 202, 203

J
Jaccard, J., 414
Jacklin, C. N., 74
Jackson, J. R., 235, 439, 440
Jackson, J. W., 412
Jackson, L. A., 379
Jacobson, G. C., 295
Jacobson, L., 134, 590
Jacoby, L. L., 131, 140, 440, 459
Jaggi, V., 436
James, J., 416
James, W., 20, 67, 197, 313, 357
James, W. T., 456
Janes, L. M., 320
Janis, I. L., 276, 286, 466–468, 495
Jarcho, J. M., 439
Jarvis, B., 292
Jaskolka, A. R., 209, *210*
Jaspers, J., 160, 162
Jayne, B. C., 606
Jefferson, T., 18, 135
Jeffery, R. W., 50
Jellison, J. M., 474
Jemmott, J. B., 300
Jemmott, J. B., III, 297
Jemmott, L. S., 297
Jenkins, C., 442
Jenkins, J., 212
Jenkins, J. M., 197
Jenkins, V. Y., 381
Jennings, J. R., 568
Jennings, M. K., 277
Jensen, L. A., 367
Ji, L., 184
Ji, L. J., 117, 146
Jiang, W., 585
Jiao, S., 184
Jing, Q., 184
Job, R. F. S., 291
Jobe, R., 229, 524
John, O. P., 92, 116, 212, 476, 478
Johnson, E. J., 265
Johnson, J., 502

Subject Index

Note: Material in figures or tables is indicated by italic page numbers.

attitude inoculation, 302–3, *304*
attitudes
    accessibility of, 236, 270
    advertising and associations, 276
    affect (affective component), 235, 239
    association with behaviors, 235
    attitude inoculation, 302–3, *304*
    automatic behavior that bypasses attitudes, 243
    balance theory, 45, 244–45, 271
    Bennington College study, 278–79, 293
    centrality of, 236, 270
    changes in attitude certainty, 303–5
    cognition (cognitive component), 235, 239
    conflict with other determinant of behavior, 239
    consistency between attitudes and behavior,
        234–35
    definition, 235
    ego-defensive function of, 276–77, 306
    general attitudes and specific targets, 242–43
    genetic basis, 301
    implicit attitude measures, 236, 270
    inconsistent attitudes, 239, 240, *240*
    induced compliance and attitude change, 243–44,
        248–50, 253, 262–63, 270
    introspecting about reasons for, 240–41
    knowledge function of, 279–80, 306
    measurement of, 235–38, 270
    motor cortex activation by attitudes, 235
    predicting attitudes from behavior, 242–57
    predicting behavior from attitudes, 238–43, 270
    reference groups and, 277, 278, 306
    response latency, 236
    secondhand information, effect of, 240–41
    strength of negative and positive stimuli, 237
    system justification theory, 266, 271
    thought polarization hypothesis, 302, 307
    toward gays, 159, 221, 242–43, 447
    utilitarian function of, 275–76, 306
    value-expressive function of, 277–79, 306
    see also cognitive dissonance theory; persuasion;
        self-perception theory; terror management
        theory; violence, attitudes toward
Attitudes toward Blacks Scale, 411, 412, 439, 440
attraction, 368–92
    to average faces, 384–85, *386*
    biology and, 382–86
    cognitive fluency, 373, 374
    evolutionary basis, 382–83, 385, 386–88,
        390–91
    intersex attraction, 386, 404
    mere exposure effect, 370–73, 392, 404
    overview, 368, 392, 404
    physical attractiveness, 378–86, 392, 404
    proximity, 368–74, 392, 404
    reproductive fitness, 382–83, 386, 392, 404
    sex differences in mate preferences, 386–91,
        404–5
    similarity, 370, 375–78, 392, 404
    universality of attractiveness, 381
    see also relationships; romantic relationships
attribution, causal. *see* causal attribution
attributional ambiguity, 444, 447, 451
attribution theory, 155, 168
augmentation principle, 163, *164*, 192
authority, definition, 478
autism and theory of mind, 25
autokinetic illusion, 315, *316*, 352
automatic mimicry
    cultural differences, 314–15
    emotional mimicry, 210, 212–13, 230
    experiments, 312–13
    ideomotor action, 313, *314*
    overview, 312
    as preparation for interaction, 313–14
    reasons for mimicry, 313–14
automatic processing
    attitudes toward outgroups, 19–20, 437–47, 451
    automatic behavior that bypasses attitudes, 243
    automatic characterizations, 178–80

automatic self-control strategies, 98–99, 104
    construal, 21, 38
    controlled processing and, 19–21
    efficiency of, 21
    functions of, 21
    implicit attitudes and beliefs, 20
    skill acquisition, 20
    stereotypes and prejudice, 437–41, 443, 451
    types of unconscious processing, 20–21
    see also controlled processing
automatic self-control strategies, 98–99, 104
availability heuristic, 136–41, 147–49, 150–51
    see also heuristics
avoidant attachment in children, 364

B

balance theory, 45,
    244–45, 271
Ballew v. Georgia, 612
base-rate information, 142–44
basic science, 58–59, 62
basking in reflected glory, 90, 423–24
Bay of Pigs, 466, 468, 469
beauty, 374
    see also physical attractiveness
behavior
    consistency between attitudes and behavior,
        234–35
    effect of situations, 7, 8–9
    explaining with social psychology, 6–7
    predicting attitudes from behavior, 242–57
    predicting behavior from attitudes, 238–43, 270
    prevailing norms of behavior, effect of, 239
    universal behaviors, reactions, and institutions, 23
behavioral economics
    corporate welfare, 578
    cultural differences, 146
    decision paralysis, 584–86, 588
    definition, 575
    framing effects, 578–79, 580, 588
    irrationality in financial markets, 575, 576–77, 588
    loss aversion, 577–81
    mental accounting, 581–84, 588
    outright losses *vs.* forgone gains, 578
    overview, 575–76, 588
    personal financial planning basics, 586–87, 588
    risk aversion, 579, 588
    risk seeking, 579, 588
    stock market and real estate collapse in 2008,
        574–75, 586
    sunk cost fallacy, 579, 581, 588, 600
    see also economic perspective on prejudice and
        discrimination; economics
Bennington College, 278–79, 293
better-than-average effect, 89
"Big Five" personality dimensions, 189
birth order and personality, 69
Black Power, 211
blame in romantic relationships, 398–99, 405
Blond Bather (Renoir), 382
bogus stranger paradigm, 375–76
bonobos, 478, 551
Bosnia, 332, 408, 516
Boston Red Sox, *169*
botox, 265
bottom-up processes, 124, 133, 182
brain
    activation in smiling, 200
    age effects, 27
    amygdala, 52, 217, 237, 402, 414, 439, 563
    anterior cingulate and pain, 506
    the brain in love, 402
    the cooperative brain, 553
    effects of emotion, 198
    frontal lobes, access to emotions, 217
    fronto-parietal activity and perceptual judgments,
        185
    functional magnetic resonance imaging (fMRI),
        27, 69–70, 185, 220, 402, 506, 580

hippocampus, 563, 564
hypothalamus, 210, 213, 563
intraparietal sulcus, 580
meditation effects, 227
the moral brain, 220
motor cortex activation by attitudes, 235
orbitofrontal cortex, 198–99, 209, 550, 555
paraventricular nucleus, 563
periaqueductal grey and sympathy, 198–99
prefrontal cortex, 69, 73, 439, 541
regions related to stress, 210
thalamus, 237
ventral striatum and rewards, 402
see also neuroscience
breast cancer, 76, 569, 570–71, 572
broaden-and-build hypothesis, 222, 230
Brown v. Board of Education of Topeka, 7, 215, 447
bulimia, 319, 382, 383
bullies and bullying, *286*, 507, 509, *541*
bystander intervention, 538–40, 542–43, 560

C

California self-esteem task force, 81–82, 87
causal attribution, 152–93
    actor–observer differences, 154, 181–83, 192
    of athletes and coaches, 165, *166*, 168–69, 185
    attitudes toward punishment, 616–18, 620–21
    attribution theory, 155, 168
    augmentation principle, 163, *164*, 192
    cognition and, 177–80
    consensus and covariation information, 161–62
    consistency and covariation information, 161–62
    controllability and, 158, 159
    counterfactual thoughts and, 164–65, *166*,
        168, 192
    covariation and, 160–62
    covariation principle, 160–62, 170, 171, 192
    cultural differences, 183–90, 192–93
    culture and attention to context, 184–85
    definition, 155
    discounting principle and, 162–63, *164*, 178,
        179, 192
    dispositional inference and attribution, 175,
        178–79, 186–87
    dispositions, flexibility of, 188–89
    explanatory style, 156–59, 192
    first- and third-person perspectives in memory
        and imagining, 182
    gender and attribution style, 158–59
    global/specific dimension, 156–57, 158, 159, 192
    heat and aggression, 501
    imagining alternative actors and outcomes,
        162–67
    in independent and interdependent cultures, 185,
        192–93
    influence of exceptions *vs.* routines, 166–67
    and intentions of actors, 190–91, 193
    internal/external dimension, 156–57,
        159–60, 192
    perceptual salience and, 177, *178*, 183
    persuasiveness and importance of, 156
    priming cultures, 187–88, 193
    processes of, 159–68
    self-serving attributional bias, 168–71, 183, 192
    social attribution, definition, 154
    social class and, 188, 193
    stable/unstable dimension, 156–57, 159, 192
    and theory of mind, 191
    tutoring experiment, 169–70
    see also fundamental attribution error
causality, cultural differences, 190
Celts, 490, 515
Central Artery/Tunnel Project (the "Big Dig") in
    Boston, *145*
central (systematic) route to persuasion, 281,
    282–83, 294, 306
    see also persuasion
Challenger space shuttle, 466
channel factors, 13

children's readers, 31, 36
chimpanzees, 22, 24, 203, 478, 551
cigarette advertising, *40*, 59, 273–74
civil rights and race relations
    Black Power, 211
    Brown v. Board of Education of Topeka, 7, 215, 447
    Civil Rights Act, 3
    history, 3–5
    Rosa Parks and segregated buses, *326*
    see also discrimination; prejudice; stereotypes
class differences. *see* social class
climate change. *see* global warming
coaching, 456, 459–61
cognitive consistency theories, 235, 244, 245, 250, 270
    see also balance theory; cognitive dissonance theory; rationalization
cognitive dissonance theory
    cultural differences, 255–56
    decisions and dissonance, 245–47
    definition, 245
    dissonance reduction, 245–47, 256, 259
    effort justification, 247–48, 270
    "forbidden toy" paradigm, 251–52
    forseeability and dissonance, 254
    free choice and dissonance, 253, 255–56, 256, 270
    group initiation and liking for the group, 247–48
    induced compliance and attitude change, 243–44, 248–50, 253, 270
    induced compliance and extinguishing undesired behavior, 251–52
    insufficient justification and dissonance, 253, 270
    negative consequences and dissonance, 253–54, 270
    post-decision paradigm, 246, 255, 256
    reconciling with self-perception theory, 259–62
    self-affirmation and dissonance, 254–55, 270
    testing for arousal, 258–59
    why inconsistency produces dissonance, 252–54
    see also attitudes; self-perception theory
cognitive perspective on prejudice and discrimination, 428–43
    automatic and controlled processing, 437–41, 443, 451
    construal processes and biased assessments, 429–35, 450
    definition, 408–9
    evaluation of, 441–43
    expectations and biased information processing, 434–35
    explaining away exceptions to stereotypes, 435–37
    illusory correlations, 147–49, 432–34, 438, 450
    ingroup similarity and outgroup difference assumptions, 430–31
    outgroup homogeneity effect, 431–32, 434, 438, 443, 450
    overview, 428, 443, 450–51
    stereotypes and conservation of mental reserves, 428–29, 443
    stereotype subtyping, 435–36, 437
    see also discrimination; prejudice
cognitive psychology, 8
Cognitive Reflection Task, 140–41
collective self, 67
collectivistic cultures. *see* interdependent cultures
Columbia space shuttle, 466
Columbine High School shootings, 504, 505, 506
commitment in romantic relationships, 393–94, 395–96, 405
communal relationships, 361–62, 367, 404
communication
    emotional communication through touch, 209–10, 230
    flirtation and nonverbal display, 211
    intergroup conflict and, 524
    off-record communication, 103, 105
    on-record communication, 103, 105

companionate love, 394, 403
comparison and self-enhancement, 90–92, 94
compassion and prosocial behavior, 221
compensatory awards in civil trials, 613, 620
competition
    economic theory and, 556–57
    intrasex competition, 385, 386–87, 404
    quiz-show competition, 175, *176*
    shifts between competition and cooperation, 551, 552, 553
    situational determinants, 554–55
complementarity, 376–77
compliance, 338–51
    definition, 311, 352
    descriptive norms, 349
    door-in-the-face (reciprocal concessions) technique, 340–41, 351
    emotion-based approaches, 342–46, 350, 351, 352–53
    "even a penny" technique, 342
    friendly touch and increased compliance, 210
    negative mood and, 344–46, 351
    negative state relief hypothesis, 345–46, 351, 353
    norm-based approaches, 346–50, 351, 353
    norm of reciprocity, 338–40, 341, 351, 352
    overview, 311, 338, 351, 352–53
    positive mood and, 342–44, 351, 352–53
    prescriptive (injunctive) norms, 349, 351
    reason-based approaches, 338–42, 351, 352
    that's-not-all technique, 341, 351
    see also conformity; induced compliance; social influence
Computer Center Corporation (CCC), 153
concern and prosocial behavior, 221
confirmation bias, 121–24, 150
conformity, 311–27
    anonymity, effect of, 325, 352
    automatic mimicry, 316–20
    definition, 311, 352
    evolution and, 312
    expertise and status, effect of, 321–22, 352
    factors affecting conformity pressure, 320–25, 352
    and free speech, 321
    gender differences, 324, 352
    group size effect, 320–21, 327, 352
    interdependent *vs.* independent cultures, 322–23, 327, 352
    jury deliberations, 611, 612
    minority opinion influence on the majority, 326–27, 352, 611
    overview, 311–12
    Sherif's conformity experiment, 315–16, 317, 318, 324, 328
    task difficulty or ambiguity, effect of, 316, 318, 324–25, 352
    unanimity, effect of, 321, 327, 352
    see also Asch's conformity experiment; compliance; social influence
Con Man (Moss), 99
consensus and covariation information, 161–62
consistency and covariation information, 161–62
consistency theories, 235, 244, 245, 250, 270
    see also balance theory; cognitive dissonance theory; rationalization
construal, 14–19, 38
    aggression and, 508–16
    altruism and construal processes, 541–43, 551
    automatic processing, 21, 38
    better-than-average effect, 89
    breast cancer and, 76, 570–71, 572
    in conflict and peacemaking, 521–25
    construal level theory, 120
    cooperation and, 555–56, 559
    definition, 14
    expectations and biased information processing, 434–35
    gestalt principles, 14, *15*
    illusory correlations, 147–49, 432–34, 438, 450

independent self-construal, 73–74, 75
ingroup similarity and outgroup difference assumptions, 430–31
interdependent self-construal, 73–74, 75
and judgments about social world, 15–16
in Milgram experiment, 14
outgroup homogeneity effect, 431–32, 434, 438, 443, 450
prisoner's dilemma game, 15–16, 555–56
and schemas, 17–18, 38, 127
self-construal and gender, 74–75
self-construal and the brain, 73
self-serving construals, 89–90, 94, 104
socioeconomic status, 567
stereotypes, concrete *vs.* abstract construal, 436–37
stereotypes and, 18–19
stereotypes and biased assessments, 429–35, 450
and visual perception, 14–15
consummate love, 394
contempt in romantic relationships, 398, 399, 400, 403, 405
contingencies of self-worth, 83–84, 88, 104
control condition, definition, 52
controlled processing
    attitudes toward outgroups, 19, 437–47, 451
    automatic processing and, 19–21
    explicit attitudes and beliefs, 20
    stereotypes and prejudice, 437–41, 443, 451
    see also automatic processing
cooperation, 551–59, 560
    construal processes and, 555–56, 559
    contagious nature of, 555
    culture and, 556–58, 560
    evolution and, 551, 558–59, 560
    reputation and, 554–55
    shifts between competition and cooperation, 551, 552, 553
    situational determinants of, 554–55, 559
    tit-for-tat strategy, 559, 560
    ultimatum game, 557–58
    between World War I enemies, 552, 558
    see also prisoner's dilemma game
copycat violence, 501–2, *503*, 526
core-relational themes, 198
corporate welfare, 578
correlational research
    causation and correlation, 49–51, 54–55
    definition, 49
    illusory correlations, 147–49
    longitudinal studies, 52
    reverse causation, 49
    scatterplots and correlation, 49–50
    self-selection, 49, 62
    strength of relationships, 49–50
    value of correlational findings, 51–52
cortisol
    benefits of social connection, 569
    in culture of honor, 514
    effects on the body, 563, 564
    in high self-enhancers, 92
    hypothalamic-pituitary-adrenal (HPA) axis, 563–64, 567, 568–69, 571, 573
    increase in low-power postures, 481
    meditation and, 570
    oxytocin and, 570
    reduction by touch, 209
    social rejection and, 505
    stress measurement and, 52
cost-benefit analysis, 250
counterfactual thoughts, 164–65, *166*, 168, 192
courtroom events and procedures
    compensatory awards, 613, 620
    damage awards in civil trials, 613–14, 620
    death-qualified juries, 610–11, 620
    jury decision rule, 612–13, 620
    jury deliberation, 611–15
    jury selection, 609–11, 620
    jury size, 611–12

social benefits of, 204–5
subordinate status and, 215, 216, 230
tongue bite, 205, 206, 208
emblems, 211
embodied cognition and emotion, 262–65, 271
embodied metaphors, 264
emergent properties of groups, 486, 487
emotion accents, 205, 208, 230
emotional amplification, 165, 192
emotional intelligence, 214, 216, 230
emotions, 194–231
appraisal processes and, 198, 199, 230
broaden-and-build hypothesis, 222, 230
components of, 197–99
core-relational themes and, 198
creativity and positive emotions, 222, 225
cross-cultural research on emotional expression, 201–3
cultural specificity, 199–200, 205–8
culture and ideal or valued emotions, 207–8, 230
definition and characteristics, 196–99
de-intensifying of emotional expression, 207–8
display rules, 207–8
emotion accents, 205, 208, 230
emotional amplification, 165, 192
emotional intelligence, 214, 216, 230
emotional mimicry, 210, 212–13, 230
emotion-based approaches to compliance, 342–46, 350, 351, 352–53
expression by blind and sighted individuals, 201, 205
expression in other animals, 22–24, 203–5
flirtation and nonverbal display, 211
focal emotions, 206–7, 208, 230
in friendship and intimate relationships, 209–14
as grammar of social relationships, 206, 209, 214
and group boundaries, 215–16
in group dynamics, overview, 214
harm-related emotions, 221
hypercognized emotions, 207
influence on reasoning, 221–22
as information for judgments, 217–18, 222, 230
intensifying of emotional expression, 207
in judgments of complex matters, 218
Kirsten and Jack's relationship, 209, 210, 213, 214
as magical transformations, 196
masking of emotional expression, 207–8
and moral judgment, 219–21, 222, 230
neutralizing of emotional expression, 208
other-condemning emotions, 221
other-praising emotions, 220
primary appraisal stage, 198, 199, 230
processing style perspective, 221–22, 230
reason vs. emotions in decision making, 216–17
and role negotiation within groups, 215
secondary appraisal stage, 198, 199, 230
self-conscious emotions, 206–7
self-critical emotions, 220
sympathy breakthroughs, 195–96, 198
touch and closeness, 209–10, 216, 230
universality, evolutionary approach, 199, 200–201
universality of facial expressions, 22, 24, 201–5, 208
empathic concern, 532–33, 534–37, 540, 543, 546, 560
empathy
among newborns, 531, 533
decrease in young adults today, 535
deficits in psychopaths, 520
empathic concern, 532–33, 534–37, 540, 543, 546, 560
greater empathy in women, 520
and Milgram's experiments, 332, 335
physiological indicators, 534–35
power and empathy failures, 479, 480
volunteerism and, 535–36
"empty" love, 394
encoding, 126–27
Enron, 350, 482

entertainment-education, 597–99, 601
entity theory of intelligence, 592, 594, 601
equity theory, 363, 367–68
ethical concerns
experimental research, 51, 55, 60–61, 334, 488
informed consent, 60, 62
institutional review boards (IRBs), 60–61, 62
power and, 483–84
ethnocentrism, 416
evaluation apprehension, 461–63, 464, 494
"even a penny" technique, 342
evolution, 22–27, 38
aggression and, 517–20, 526
altruism and, 548–51, 560
attraction, 382–83, 385, 386–88, 390–91
conformity and, 312
cooperation, 551, 558–59, 560
Darwin on, 22, 45, 200–201
emotions, universality, 199, 200–201
friendship and, 357
gender roles, 25, 75
group living, 24, 455
human emotional expression and, 22–24, 199, 200–205
human universals, 22–24
income inequality and aggression, 508
kin selection and, 549–50, 551, 560
landscape preferences, 276, 277
language, 24
naturalistic fallacy and, 26
natural selection, 22, 45, 548
neuroscience and, 26–27
parental investment, 25, 27, 38, 386–87, 404
physical attractiveness, 382–83, 385
reciprocal altruism and, 550–51, 560
relationships, 357
sex differences in mate preferences, 386–91, 404–5
social neuroscience and, 26–27
social rejection and, 505
stress response, 562, 563–64
theory of mind, 24–25
threat defense system and, 505
universals and, 22–24
use in understanding situations, 36–37
exchange relationships, 361–62, 367, 404
experimental research
control condition, 52–53
definition, 49
dependent variables, 52, 62
ethical concerns, 51, 55, 60–61, 334, 488
field experiments, 56, 62, 218, 420
independent variables, 52, 62
longitudinal studies, 52, 357, 366, 396, 405
natural experiments, 55, 187, 358
overview, 52–55, 62
random assignment, 52, 57
see also methods of social psychology; scientific method
explanatory style
attribution and, 156–59, 192
controllability and attribution, 158
correlation with later physical health, 157–58
definition, 156
explanatory style index, 157
gender and attribution style, 158–59
global/specific dimension, 156–57, 158, 159, 192
internal/external dimension, 156–57, 159, 192
stable/unstable dimension, 156–57, 159, 192
Expression of Emotions in Man and Animals, The (Darwin), 200
extended families, 355–56
external validity in experiments, 55–56, 58, 62
eyewitness testimony
eyewitness errors, 602, 603–4, 605–6, 607
improving eyewitness identification procedures, 606
overview, 603–4, 620
persistence of memory, 604–5
recovered memories, 602, 605

F
face, definition, 100
facial expressions
blind and sighted individuals, 201, 205
cultural differences, 201–3, 206–7
Darwin on, 201, 203, 205
Mechanism of Human Facial Expression, The (Duchenne de Boulogne), 200
universality of, 22, 24, 201–5, 208
see also emotions
Fairness and Accuracy in Reporting (FAIR), 298
false confessions, 603–6, 620
fear, influence on judgments, 218
fear and persuasiveness, 290–91
fearful-avoidant attachment style, 365
feelings-as-information perspective, 217–18, 230
field experiments, 56, 62, 218, 420
firsthand information, 112–13, 347–48, 541, 542–43, 551
Five Cs for effective tutoring, 591
flirtation and nonverbal display, 211
fluency, 140–41, 373, 374
focal emotions, 206–7, 208, 230
focalism, 225
food preferences, utilitarian function of, 275
footbridge dilemma, 220
foot-in-the-door technique, 341–42, 351, 352
"forbidden toy" paradigm, 251–52
forced compliance. see induced compliance
Fore (Papua New Guinea), 202–3
"Four Horsemen of the Apocalypse," 397–98
framing effects
construal level theory and, 120
definition, 117
loss aversion and, 578–79, 580, 588
order effects, 20–21, 116–17, 150
positive and negative framing, 118–20
primacy effects, 117, 121, 150
recency effects, 117, 121, 150
in social cognition, 117–20, 121, 149, 150
spin framing, 106, 118, 150
temporal framing, 120–21, 150
fraternity hazing, 247
free speech and conformity, 321
friendship
emotions in, 209–14
evolution, 357
How to Win Friends and Influence People (Carnegie), 362
limitation number of close friends, 358
proximity and, 368–70
similarity and, 370
Westgate West apartment friendship research, 368–70
fronto-parietal activity and perceptual judgments, 185
frustration, definition, 509
frustration-aggression theory, 426–27, 428, 450, 509–10, 526
Fuegians of Tierra del Fuego, Chile, 199
functional distance, 369
functional magnetic resonance imaging (fMRI), 27, 69–70, 185, 220, 402, 506, 580
fundamental attribution error
automatic characterizations, 178–80
Castro essay experiment, 171–72
cognition and attribution, 177–80
consequences of, 180–81
cultural differences, 185–87
definition, 13, 171, 192
derogation of victims, 177
dispositions and, 12–13, 175, 177, 178–79, 180–81
essay and attitude experiments, 171–72, 177–78, 186
just world hypothesis, 175, 177, 192
Milgram study of obedience, 171
motivational influences, 175
perceiver-induced constraint paradigm, 172–73

fundamental attribution error (*continued*)
    perception of advantage and disadvantage, 153–54, 173–74, 175, 176
    perceptual salience, 177, *178*, 183
    quiz-show competition, 175, *176*
    salience of people *vs.* situations, 177, 180, 185–86, 192
    situational factors, 12–13, 171, 177–79, 180–81
    see also causal attribution

G

gay marriage, *278*
gender
    aggression and, 519–20
    attribution style and, 158–59
    effect on conformity, 324, 352
    gender socialization, 36, 75, 324, 520
    impact of physical attractiveness, 380–81, 387–88, *389*
    sex differences in mate preferences, 386–91, 404–5
    the social self and gender, 74–75
gender roles
    cultural differences, 34–35, 75
    evolution, 25, 75
    gender socialization, 36, 75, 325, 520
    lifetime monogamy, 35
    parental investment and, 25, 27, 38, 386–87, 404
    polyandry, 25, 35
    polygyny, 25, 35
    serial monogamy, 35
    the social self and gender, 74–75
    universal aspects, 25, 34
genocide
    after social upheavals, 335
    Bosnia, 332, 408, 516
    Darfur (Sudan), 310, 332, 408, 497–98, 499, 516, 519
    Rwanda, 332, 408, 497–99, 516, 519, 521, 524
    Somalia, 408
    step-by-step guide to genocide, 337
    see also Holocaust
Genovese, Kitty, murder, 536–37, 538
gestalt psychology, 14–15
global warming
    greenhouse gases, 272
    heat and aggression, 500–501
    persuasion and, 272, 280–81, 288, 289, 290, 293
    rationalization and, 234
    room temperature effect on global warming belief, 265
    steps to control carbon emissions, 280
Golden Gate Bridge, 374
Golden Rule across cultures and religions, 547
Good Samaritan study with seminarians, 11–12, 54, 537–38
green spaces and aggression, 506, 507
group living, evolution, 24, 455
group polarization
    definition, 472
    in homogeneous groups, 475, 494
    in modern life, 475, 494
    persuasive arguments account, 472, 473, 476, 494
    and risk, 471–72, 473–74, 494
    risky shift, 472, 474
    social comparison interpretation account, 472–73, 476, 494
groups, 452–95
    being a member of a stigmatized group, 443–47, 451
    definition, 455
    emergent properties of, 486, 487
    evolution of group living, 24, 455
    group decision making, 465–76, 494
    group justification, 266
    measuring attitudes about groups, 412–15
    nature and purpose of group living, 455
    reference groups, 277, 278, 306
    risky shift, 469–71, 472, 474, 494

spotlight effect, 492–93, 495
    see also group polarization; groupthink; intergroup conflict; mob psychology; power; social facilitation
groupthink
    Bay of Pigs decision making, 466, 468, 469
    in Bush administration, 467
    cultural differences, 469
    definition, 466
    devil's advocate role, 468, 469, 476
    incestuous amplification in military, 467
    Janis's groupthink hypothesis, 466–68
    overview, 466, 475–76, 494
    prevention, 468–69
    self-censorship, 467, 494
    strong leaders and, 467, 468, 476
    symptoms and sources, 467
    see also groups; social facilitation
guilt
    agitation and, 96
    and compliance, 344–45, 353
    and moral judgment, 219, 220
    shame- or guilt-prone cultures, 206
    survivor guilt, 167

H

Haath Se Haath Milaa ("Hand in Hand Together"), 597
Halloween, 489–90, 491
halo effect, 379–80, 404
happiness
    affective forecasting, 224–25
    creativity and positive emotions, 222, 225
    cultivating happiness, 226–29
    determinants of pleasure, 223
    effects of getting tenure, 224–25
    effects of romantic breakups, 224
    environmental factors, 226–27
    genetic factors, 226
    marriage and, 49, 55, 225
    meaning of, 223
    meditation and, 227
    money and, 226
    Olympic medal winners, 165, *166*
    personal narratives, 225, 227–28, 229
    predicting happiness, 224–25
    relationships and, 226
    sources of, 225–26
Harlow's monkey "mother surrogates" research, 309, *310*
hasham, 215
health
    construal and, 563, 567, 570–72, 573
    correlation with explanatory style, 157–58
    heuristics in health and medicine, 146–47
    human health risks without relationships, 359
    optimism, benefits of, 572
    perceived control, benefits of, 571–72, 573
    smoking and risk, 273, 299
    social connection, benefits of, 568–70, 573
    socioeconomic status and, 477, 563, 565–67, 573
    see also stress
heat and aggression, 500–501, 506, 509
heuristic route to persuasion, *281*, 282–83, 294, 306
heuristics
    availability heuristic, 136–41, 147–49, 150–51
    base-rate information and, 142–44
    biased assessments of risk, 139
    biased estimates of joint project contributions, 139–40
    definitions, 136
    ease of retrieval *vs.* amount of information retrieved, 137–38
    fluency and, 140–41
    in health and medicine, 146–47
    heuristic route to persuasion, *281*, 282–83, 294, 306
    illusory correlations, 147–49

inside *vs.* outside perspective, 144–45, 149
    intuition and, 135–36, 149
    mistaken judgment and, 136
    planning fallacy, 144–45
    predictions by Americans and East Asians, 146
    pseudoscience, 147
    representativeness heuristic, 136, 141–47, 148–49, 151
    resemblance between cause and effect, 145–47
    see also social cognition
heuristic-systematic model of persuasion, 281, 282, 294
    see also elaboration likelihood model (ELM) of persuasion; persuasion
hindsight bias, 43
hippocampus, 563, 564
HIV/AIDS, 280, 289–90, 572, 597, 599
hockey players, 176
Holocaust
    concentration camps, 195, 333, 337, *498*
    deportations in freight trains, 134
    ineffective resistance of German soldiers, 333–34
    Jewish genocide, 134, 310, 333, 337–38
    rescues of Jews by civilians, *345*, 350, 536
    role of social influence, 310, 332–33, 350
    step-by-step guide to genocide, 337
    trauma of survivors, 227–28
    see also genocide; World War II
homicide *vs.* suicide rates, 139
homosexuality
    attitudes toward gays, 159, 221, 242–43, 447
    cultural differences, 35
    gay marriage, 278
    prejudice and gay people, 242–43, 406
    "typical" gay man stereotype, 242
Hong Kong, causal attribution, 185, 187
honor, culture of. *see* culture of honor
hostile aggression, 498, 526
How to Win Friends and Influence People (Carnegie), 362
human universals. *see* universals
Hutus, 332, 497–98, 521, 530, 551, 553
hypercognize, definition, 207
hypothalamic-pituitary-adrenal (HPA) axis, 563–64, 567, 568, 569, 573
hypothalamus, 210, 213, 563, *564*
hypotheses, 43, 44–45, 53

I

ideal self, 95–96, 104
identifiable victim effect, 289–90, 306
identity cues and self-verification, 93–94
ideological distortions, 113–14
ideomotor action, 313–14
illusory correlations, 147–49, 432–34, 438, 450
illustrators, 211
Implicit Association Test (IAT), 236, 413–14, 415, 439–40, 443, 450
implicit attitude measures, 236, 270
incest, 24, 219
inclusive fitness, 518, 549
incrementalist theory of intelligence, 592, 593, 601
independent cultures
    causal attribution, 185, 193
    class differences, 36
    conformity and, 352
    definition, 29
    emotional expression, 207, 208
    independent self-construal, 73–74
    independent *vs.* interdependent cultures, 29
    sleeping arrangements of children, 367
independent variables, 52, 62
India–Pakistan arms race, 553
individualistic cultures. *see* independent cultures
individual self, definition, 67
individuation, 486, 490, 491–93, 495
    see also deindividuation; self-awareness theory; spotlight effect

induced compliance
    and attitude change, 243–44, 248–50, 253,
        262–63, 270
    definition, 248
    effect of reward or coercion amount, 249–50,
        260–61
    extinguishing undesired behavior, 251–52
    see also compliance
infantile facial features, personality ratings, 110, 111
infatuation, 394
information
    availability for social cognition, 109–16
    confirmation bias and, 121–24, 150
    different reactions to positive and negative
        information, 115–16, 119, 139, 150
    encoding in memory, 126–27
    how information is presented, 116–21
    how we seek information, 121–24
    mistakes as source of information, 108
    order effects, 20–21, 116–17, 150
    pluralistic ignorance, 112–13, 150, 347–48, 541,
        542–43, 551
    retrieval from memory, 126–27, 137–39
    see also schemas
informational social influence
    anonymity, effect of, 325
    Asch's conformity experiment, 318
    cultural differences, 322
    definition, 315, 352
    effects of uncertainty and ambiguity, 316, 318,
        324–25
    expertise, effect of, 321–22
    expertise and status and, 322
    group size effect, 320–21
    group unanimity and, 321
    internalization and, 325
    in jury deliberations, 611
    Sherif's conformity experiment, 315–16, 324
    task difficulty and, 324–25
    see also normative social influence; social
        influence
Information Sciences, Inc. (ISI), 153–54
informed consent, 60, 62
infrahumanization, 216, 230
ingroup favoritism
    minimal group paradigm, 422
    in modern racism, 411
    preserving cultural identity or way of life, 410
    Robbers Cave experiment, 418
    social identity theory and, 422, 423, 450
injunctive norms, 349
institutional review boards (IRBs), 60–61, 62
instrumental aggression, 498, 509, 526
intelligence, and work at school, 59
intelligence, nature of, 591–92, 601
interahamwe, 497, 498, 530
interdependent cultures
    causal attribution, 185, 188, 189, 192–93
    conformity, 322–23, 327, 352
    definition, 30
    emotion expression, 207, 208
    focal emotions in, 206–7
    independent vs. interdependent cultures, 29
    interdependent self-construal, 73–74
    media message content, 291, 306
    persuasion and message targeting, 291
    self-concept, 29–30, 30
    self-esteem levels, 86
    sleeping arrangements of children, 367
    social influence and, 322–23, 327, 352
    social priming, 256
    "Who Am I" test, 28, 30–32
    in the workplace, 32, 33, 34
intergroup conflict
    automatic and controlled processing of
        stereotypes and prejudice, 437–41
    basking in reflected glory, 90, 423–24
    being a member of a stigmatized group,
        443–47, 451

benevolent racism and sexism, 412
    characterizing intergroup bias, 409–15
    communication and, 524
    complex vs. simplistic reasoning and rhetoric,
        523–24, 526
    contact hypothesis, 418, 447–49, 451
    dehumanization and, 521, 525, 526
    frustration-aggression theory, 426–27, 428, 450
    illusory correlations, 147–49, 432–34, 438, 450
    ingroup favoritism, 422, 423, 450
    ingroup similarity and outgroup difference
        assumptions, 430–31
    measuring attitudes about groups, 412–15
    minimal group paradigm, 421–22, 423,
        430–31, 450
    misperception and, 521–23, 524
    modern racism, 410–12
    outgroup homogeneity effect, 431–32
    overview, 407–8, 450–51
    peacemaking and, 521–25, 526
    realistic group conflict theory, 416, 450
    reconciliation and, 524–25
    reducing stereotypes, prejudice, and
        discrimination, 418–19, 420, 447–49,
        450, 451
    reduction through superordinate goals, 417,
        418–19, 420, 450
    self-esteem and boosting ingroup status, 423
    self-esteem and derogating outgroups, 424–25,
        426, 428
    social identity theory, 422–26, 450
    see also cognitive perspective on prejudice and
        discrimination; discrimination; economic
        perspective on prejudice and discrimination;
        groups; motivational perspective on prejudice
        and discrimination; prejudice; stereotypes
intergroup emotion theory, 215–16
internalization, definition, 325
Internal Motivation to Respond Without Prejudice
    Scale, 412
internal validity in experiments, 57, 58, 62
intersex attraction, 386, 404
intervention, definition, 59
intimacy in romantic relationships, 393–94, 405
intraparietal sulcus, 580
intrasex competition, 385, 386–87, 404
intuition, 135–36, 149
    see also heuristics
Inuit of Alaska, 205, 513, 514
investment model of interpersonal relationships,
    395–96, 405

J

Janis's groupthink hypothesis, 466–68
Japan and Japanese
    cognitive dissonance, 255–56, 271
    context and causal attribution, 184–85
    earthquake relief efforts in 2011, 114
    gender and the social self, 74
    groupthink, 469
    Harajuku-inspired fashion, 94
    language and the social self, 74, 85
    and positive illusions, 92
    relational and collective self-definition, 67
    self-esteem and everyday experiences, 86–87
    smile workshop for businessmen, 74
"jigsaw" classrooms, 420
Johnson v. Louisiana, 612
Judas Priest rock band, 285
juries
    Apodaca, Cooper, and Madden v. Oregon, 612
    Ballew v. Georgia, 612
    compensatory awards, 613, 620
    confessions and, 608–9, 620
    damage awards in civil trials, 613–14, 620
    death-qualified juries, 610–11, 620
    Johnson v. Louisiana, 612
    jury decision rule, 612–13, 620
    jury deliberation, 611–15

    jury selection, 609–11, 620
    jury size, 611–12
    Lockhart v. McCree, 611
    punitive awards, 613–15, 620
    scientific jury selection, 610, 620
    voir dire, 609–10, 611, 620
    Williams v. Florida, 611–12
    Witherspoon v. Illinois, 611
just world hypothesis, 175, 177, 192

K

Kenya, self-characterization in, 30–32
kin selection, 549–50, 551, 560
Kirsten and Jack's relationship, 209, 210, 213, 214
knowledge function of attitudes, 279–80, 360
knowledge structures. see schemas
Korea and Koreans
    and consensus information, 186
    and fundamental attribution error, 186
    halo effect, 379
    interdependent culture, 30
    magazine advertisements, 291
    on malleability of personality, 189
    media message content, 291
Korean War, 274
Korsakoff's syndrome, 78

L

landscape preferences, utilitarian function of, 276,
    277
language and evolution, 24
law and social psychology, 602–21
    see also courtroom events and procedures;
        criminal justice system; pretrial events
leadership, 476–78
    see also groups; power
learned helplessness, 510
Lecter, Hannibal, 520
legal system. see criminal justice system
Lie to Me, 289
Likert scale, 235–36, 270
Lockhart v. McCree, 611
longitudinal studies, 52, 357, 366, 396, 405
loss aversion
    definition, 577
    framing effects, 578–79, 580, 588
    overview, 577, 588
    reactions to outright losses vs. forgone gains, 578
    risk aversion, 579, 588
    risk seeking, 579, 588
    sunk cost fallacy and, 579, 581, 588
love
    brain and, 402
    companionate love, 394, 403
    consummate love, 394
    "empty" love, 394
    fatuous love, 394
    nonverbal signs of romantic love, 213
    oxytocin and, 214, 402
    triangular theory of love, 393–94, 405
    see also romantic relationships
lying, 289

M

marketing
    cigarette advertising, 40, 59, 273–74
    culture and, 291
    how information is presented, 116
    message characteristics, 288
    spin framing in, 118
marriage
    arranged marriages, 392, 402–3, 405
    cultural difference, 392, 401–3, 405
    divorce frequency, 396
    "Four Horsemen of the Apocalypse," 397–98
    gay marriage, 278
    happiness and, 49, 55, 225
    marital dissatisfaction, 396–99, 405
    predictors of divorce, 397

off-record communication, 103, 105
Olympic medalists and counterfactual thinking, 165, *166*
on-record communication, 103, 105
orbicularis oculi muscle, 200
orbitofrontal cortex, 198–99, 209, 550, 555
order effects, 20–21, 116–17, 150
Organization Man, The (Whyte), 368
ought self, 95–96, 104
outgroup homogeneity effect, 431–32, 434, 438, 443, 450
Outliers (Gladwell), 153, 176
overjustification effect, 260
overlearned skills, 20
oxytocin
  activation of brain regions, 198, 213, 402
  and cortisol, 570
  and trust, 213–14, 216, 230, 402, 570

P

paired distinctiveness, 432–33, *434*, 438, 450
Pakistan–India arms race, 553
paraventricular nucleus (hypothalamus), 563
parental investment, 25, 27, 38, 386–87, 404
participant, definition, 14
participant observation, 45–46, 62
passion in romantic relationships, 393–94, 405
Pay It Forward (movie), 555
perceptual psychologists, 108
peripheral route to persuasion, *281*, 282–83, 294, 306
personal distress motive in altruism, 531, 532–33, 536
personal financial planning, 586–87, 588
  see also behavioral economics
personality, "Big Five" personality dimensions, 189
personality psychology, 8, 188–89
persuasion, 272–307
  advertising and associations, 276
  attentional biases and resistance, 299–301
  attitude inoculation, 302–3, *304*
  audience age and, 293
  central (systematic) route, *281*, 282–83, 294, 306
  changes in attitude certainty, 303–5
  fear and, 290–91
  global warming, 272, 280–81, 288, 289, 293
  heuristic-systematic model, 281, 282, 294
  identifiable victim effect, 289–90, 306
  knowledge and resistance, 302
  lying as persuasion, 289
  media and, 294–98, 306
  message characteristics, 288–91, 306
  message quality and, 288
  message targeting to particular cultures, 291
  message vividness and, 288–90, 306
  mood and, 292–93, 306, 342–46, 351, 352–53
  need for cognition and, 292, 306
  peripheral (heuristic) route, *281*, 282–83, 294, 306
  previous commitments and resistance, 301–2
  resistance to, 274, 299–305, 307
  sleeper effect, 287–88, 306
  source attractiveness and, 286–87
  source credibility and, 287, *288*, 306
  subliminal cues, 284, 285
  third-person effect, 294, 306
  two-process approach, 281–86
  see also attitudes; elaboration likelihood model (ELM) of persuasion
Petrified Forest National Park, 349
PGA Tournament Golf, 505
physical attractiveness, 378–86, 392, 404
  and attraction, overview, 378, 392, 404
  of average faces, 384–85, 386
  bilateral symmetry, 385–86, 390
  biology and, 382–86
  body weight, 380–81, 382
  evolutionary theory, 382–83, 385
  gender and, 380–81, 387–88, *389*

halo effect, 379–80, 404
  impact of, 378–79, 380–81
  reproductive fitness, 382–83, 386, 392, 404
  universality of, 381
planning fallacy, 144–45
pleasure, determinants of, 223
pluralistic ignorance, 112–13, 150, 347–48, *541*, 542–43, 551, 560
poker face, 208
political conservatism, 276–77
polyandry, 25, 35
polygyny, 25, 35
possible selves, 95, 96, 99, 104
power
  accountability and, 482
  approach-inhibition theory, 479–84, 495
  definition, 478
  disinhibition of high-power people, 480–81, 482–84
  effect on social perception, 479–80
  influence on behavior, 478–84
  inhibition of low-power people, 481–82
  intimidation and, 477
  leadership and, 476–78
  Machiavelli on, 477
  overview, 478, 494–95
  postures and poses of power, *477, 481*
  reduced empathy with power, 479, *480*
  teasing and, 482–83
  see also groups
Pravda, 287
prefrontal cortex, 69, 73, 439, 541
prejudice
  attributional ambiguity and, 444, 447, 451
  automatic and controlled processing, 437–41, 443, 451
  being a member of a stigmatized group, 443–47, 451
  benevolent racism and sexism, 412
  definition, 409
  economic perspective on, 415–21, 450
  Implicit Association Test (IAT), 236, 413–14, 415, 439–40, 443, 450
  measuring attitudes about groups, 412–15
  modern racism, 410–12
  motivational perspective on, 421–28, 450
  priming and implicit prejudice, 414–15, 450
  self-esteem and boosting ingroup status, 423
  self-esteem and derogating outgroups, 424–25, 426
  self-esteem and racial prejudice, 425, *426*
  self-fulfilling prophecies, 134, 380, 446–47, 451
  social facilitation, 459
  see also cognitive perspective on prejudice and discrimination; discrimination; stereotypes
prescriptive (injunctive) norms, 349, 351, 353
pretrial events
  eyewitness testimony, 602, 603–6, 607, 620
  false confessions, 603–6, 620
  juries and confessions, 608–9, 620
  police interrogation procedures, 606–7
  see also courtroom events and procedures; criminal justice system
prevention focus, 96, 99, 104
Pride and Prejudice (Austen), 387
primacy effects, 117, 121, 150
primary appraisal stage, 198, 199, 230
prime, definition, 129
priming
  aggression, *512*, 513
  cognitive dissonance and social priming, 256
  culture and cognitive dissonance, 256
  cultures, 187–88, 193
  definition, 129
  implicit prejudice, 414–15, 450
  power, 480
  in prisoner's dilemma game, 556, 560
  schemas, 128, 129, 131–33, 134
  similarity or feature matching, 132–33

  stereotypes, 128, 132–33
  subliminal, 131–32, 285
  weapons and aggression, 512–13
primogeniture, 35
principle of serviceable habits, 200–201
Principles of Psychology, The (James), 67
prisoner's dilemma game
  "community game," 16
  competitive players, 16, 554–55, 560
  computer programs and, 558–59
  construal, 15–16, 555+556
  cooperative players, 16, 554–55
  cooperative strategy, 15–16
  defecting strategy, 15–16, 552–53
  economics majors as players, 557
  overview, 15, 552–53, 554, 559, 560
  payoff matrix, *16*, 552, 554
  priming, 556, 560
  reputation of players, 554–55, 560
  tit-for-tat strategy, 559, 560
  "Wall Street game," 16
  see also cooperation
prisons
  Abu Ghraib prisoner abuse, 6–7, 8, 332, 334, 336
  cultural differences, 616–17
  kinship-like ties formed by prisoners, 358
  social influence and prisoner abuse, 309
  Zimbardo prison study, 6–7
procedural justice, 619–20, 621
processing style perspective, 221–22, 230
projective tests, 148
promotion focus, 96, 99, 104
propinquity, 368
proximity, 368–74, 392, 404
  anticipation of interactions, 370
  diversity and, 370
  friendship, 368–70
  functional distance, 369
  mere exposure effect, 370–73, 392, 404
  proximity version of Milgram experiment, 330
  studies of attraction and, 368–70
  touch-proximity version of Milgram experiment, 330
  Westgate West apartment houses, 368–70
pseudoscience, 147
psycholinguists, 108
psychological stress, 563
psychopaths and psychopathologies, 88, 148, 520
public self and self-presentation, 99–103, 105
punishment
  attributional account of, 616–18, 620–21
  death penalty, 123, 442, 610–11, 620
  deterrence motive, 613–14, 616–17, 620, 621
  just desserts motive, 615, 616–17, 620
  overview, 615, 620–21
  sympathy, effect on judgment, 221, 617
punitive awards in civil trials, 613–15, 620
"Pygmalion in the Classroom," 590–91

R

racism
  Attitudes toward Blacks Scale, 411, 412, 439, 440
  Internal Motivation to Respond Without Prejudice Scale, 412
  Modern Racism Scale, 412, 414, 438
  racial bias in criminal justice system, 618, 621
  see also civil rights and race relations; discrimination; prejudice; stereotypes
random assignment, 52, 57
rape-prone cultures, 516–17, 526
rationalization
  after making decisions, 245–46
  dissonance reduction, 245–46
  induced compliance, 250, 253
  before making decisions, 246–47
  sweet lemons rationalization, 247
  see also balance theory; cognitive dissonance theory

rational system and reason, 135–36, 149
reactance theory, 350
reactive devaluation, 522
realistic group conflict theory, 416, 450
receiver characteristics, 292–93, 306
recency effects, 117, 121, 150
reciprocal altruism, 550–51, 560
reciprocity
    among animals, 339
    door-in-the-face (reciprocal concessions)
        technique, 340–41, 351
    exchange relationships, 361
    norm of reciprocity, 338–40, 341, 351, 352
    promotion by touch, 210
    reciprocal altruism, 550–51
recovered memories, 602, 605
reference groups, 277, 278, 306
reflected self-appraisals, 68–70, 104
reflection and self-enhancement, 90–92, 94
regulators, 211
related disciplines compared with social
        psychology, 8
relational self, 67, 360, 361, 367, 404
relationships, 354–405
    biology and the need to belong, 357–58,
        404, 455
    communal relationships, 361–62, 367, 404
    effect of past on current interactions,
        360–61, 366
    equity theory, 363, 367–68
    evolutionary basis, 357, 360, 363, 404
    exchange relationships, 361–62, 367, 404
    extended families, 355–56
    human health risks without relationships, 359
    importance of, 357–59
    longitudinal studies, 357, 366, 396, 405
    relational self, 67, 360, 361, 367, 404
    research methods and challenges, 356–57
    reward framework for relationships, 362–63
    and sense of self, 359–61
    social exchange theory, 363, 404
    universal features, 357–58, 403
    see also attachment; attraction; romantic
        relationships
reliability, 57, 58, 62
representativeness heuristic, 141–47, 148–49, 151
    base-rate information and, 142–44
    definition, 136
    in health and medicine, 146–47
    inside vs. outside perspective, 144–45, 149
    planning fallacy, 144–45
    predictions by Americans and East Asians, 146
    pseudoscience, 147
    resemblance between cause and effect, 145–47
    use of, overview, 141–42
    see also heuristics
reproductive fitness, 382–83, 386, 392, 404
reputation, 554–55, 560
research methods. see methods of social psychology
response cries, 100
response latency, 236
restorative justice, 525
retributive justice. see punishment
retrieval, definition, 126
reverse causation, definition, 49
rewards
    in induced compliance, 249–50, 260–61
    orbitofrontal cortex and, 209
    overjustification effect, 260–61
    performance-contingent rewards, 261
    reward framework for relationships, 362–63
    social rewards motive in altruism, 531, 532, 533,
        536, 551, 560
    task-contingent rewards, 261
    ventral striatum and, 402
rhesus monkey "mother surrogates" research, 309,
        310
risk aversion, 470, 471, 473, 579, 588
risk seeking, 471, 579, 588

risky shift, 469–71, 472, 474, 494
role distance, 464
romantic relationships, 392–403, 405
    blame, 398–99, 405
    commitment, 393–94, 395–96, 405
    companionate love, 394, 403
    consummate love, 394
    contempt in, 398, 399, 400, 403, 405
    creating stronger romantic bonds, 400–401
    criticism in, 398, 400, 403, 405
    cultural differences in marriage, 392,
        401–3, 405
    defensiveness in, 398, 400, 403, 405
    effects of romantic breakups on happiness, 224
    "empty" love, 394
    fatuous love, 394
    "Four Horsemen of the Apocalypse," 397–98
    illusions and idealization in, 402
    infatuation, 394
    intimacy, 393–94, 405
    investment model of interpersonal relationships,
        395–96, 405
    marital dissatisfaction, 396–99, 405
    nonverbal signs of romantic love, 213
    oxytocin and, 214, 402
    passion, 393–94, 405
    playfulness in, 400, 401
    predictors of divorce, 397
    stonewalling, 398, 400, 401, 403, 405
    triangular theory of love, 393–94, 405
    universal features, 403
    see also attraction; relationships
Rorschach inkblots, 148
rumination, 564, 565, 573
Rwanda
    altruism, 530
    cooperation, 551, 553
    genocide, 332, 408, 497–99, 516, 519, 521, 524
    ideological distortion, 114, 521
    legitimizing ideology, 336
    rapes, 516, 519
    reconciliation, 521, 524
Ryan White Care Act, 289–90

S

Saudi Arabian students and fundamental
        attribution error, 186
scatterplots and correlation, 49–50
schemas, 124–35, 150
    activation, consciousness of, 131
    activation, recent, 129–30
    activation, subliminal, 131–32
    activation and behavior, 20, 128–29
    activation by expectations, 134
    chronic accessibility, 130–31
    in construal, 17–18, 38, 127
    definition, 17, 38, 125
    Donald studies, 127, 129, 132–33
    and encoding of information, 126–27
    influence on attention, 125
    influence on behavior, 128–29
    influence on memory, 78–80, 125–27
    influence on social judgment, 17–18
    innate vs. learned knowledge, 130
    misleading similarities, 133–34
    priming, 128, 129, 131–33, 134
    and retrieval of information, 126–27
    self-schemas, 78–81, 104
    similarity or feature matching, 132–34
    and stereotypes, 18, 38, 125–26, 128–29
    top-down processes, 124, 127, 133, 150
    use in persuasion, 18
    see also social cognition
scientific jury selection, 610, 620
scientific method
    Albert Einstein on, 43
    attitude inoculation, 304
    comparison and self-esteem, 91
    correlations and, 51

counterfactual thinking by Olympic medalists,
        166
distinctiveness and illusory correlation, 433
empathy and altruism, 534
health benefits of social connection, 569
honor experiments, 53
induced compliance and attitude change, 249
mental accounting, 583
normative social influence, 317
power of situation and helping, 12
priming of anger-related aggression, 512
selective attention, 126
social facilitation on simple and complex
        tasks, 460
universality of facial expressions, 203
see also experimental research; methods of social
        psychology
secondary appraisal stage, 198, 199, 230
secondhand information, 113–16, 150, 240–41
    see also eyewitness testimony
secure attachment style, 364, 365, 366, 367, 404
selective attention, 125, 126, 299–300, 303
selective evaluation, 300, 303
self-adaptors, 211
self-affirmation, 254–55, 270
self-awareness theory, 491–93, 495
    see also individuation; spotlight effect
self-censorship, 467, 494
self-complexity, 80–81, 84, 104
self-concept
    gender and self-concept, 74–75
    independent vs. interdependent societies, 28–30
    "Who Am I" test, 28, 30–32
    working self-concept, 71, 72, 83
    see also self-esteem; self-knowledge
self-control, 95, 97–99, 104
self-discrepancy theory, 95–96, 104
self-distancing, 565
self-enhancement
    adaptive value of positive illusions, 92–93
    better-than-average effect, 89
    comparison and reflection processes, 90–92, 94
    definition, 89, 94, 104
    self-evaluation maintenance model (SEM), 90
    self-serving construals, 89–90, 94, 104
self-esteem, 81–88, 104
    aggression or violence, 88
    better-than-average effect, 89
    and boosting ingroup status, 423
    California self-esteem task force, 81–82, 87
    comparison and reflection processes, 83,
        90–92, 94
    contingencies of self-worth, 83–84, 88, 104
    costs of self-esteem goals, 84
    cultural differences, 85–87, 88, 104
    definition, 82
    and derogating outgroups, 424–25, 426, 428
    forces driving self-evaluation, 89–94
    gender differences, 83
    good or bad outcomes of high self-esteem,
        87–88
    mortality salience, 267–68
    narcissism and, 87–88, 92, 104
    and racial prejudice, 425, 426
    self-esteem movement, 83, 87
    self-esteem scale, 82
    self-evaluation maintenance model (SEM), 90
    self-improvement efforts vs. self-esteem,
        84, 86, 87, 88
    self-serving construals, 89–90, 94, 104
    self-verification, 93–94, 104
    situationism and, 86–87
    social acceptance and self-esteem, 85
    sociometer hypothesis, 85, 88
    state self-esteem, 83, 85, 88, 104
    terror management theory and, 267
    trait self-esteem, 82–83, 88, 104
    see also self-concept; self-enhancement; social self
self-evaluation maintenance model (SEM), 90

social self (*continued*)
   protecting others' face, 103
   reflected self-appraisals, 68–70, 104
   relational self, 67, 360, 361, 367, 404
   self-complexity, 80–81, 84, 104
   self-construal and gender, 74–75
   self-control, 95, 97–99, 104
   self-discrepancy theory, 95–96, 104
   self-handicapping, 101–2, 105
   self-monitoring, 101, 105
   self-presentation, 99–103
   self-reference effect, 79–80
   self-regulation, 95, 97–99, 104
   sibling dynamics, 69
   siblings and, 69
   situationism and, 70–72, 86–87
   social comparison theory, 75–77, 90, 104, 472–74, 476, 494
   working self-concept, 71, 72, 83
   see also self-esteem; self-knowledge
socioeconomic status (SES)
   in arranged marriages, 402
   and causal attribution, 188, 193
   construal and, 567
   definition, 397
   and divorce, 397
   health, 477, 563, 565–67, 573
   and health, 477
   ladder measure, 567
   see also social class
sociology, 8
sociometer hypothesis, 85, 88
Somalia, 408
source characteristics and persuasion, 286–88, 306
speed dating, 378, 393
speed-dating, *101*
spin framing, *106*, 118, 150
spotlight effect, 492–93, 495
   see also self-awareness theory
statistical significance, 58
status
   anger and, 215, 230
   conformity and, 321–22, 352
   definition, 478
   embarrassment and subordinate status, 215, 216, 230
   role negotiation within groups, 215
   social influence and, 321–22
   see also socioeconomic status (SES)
stepfamilies and violence, 517–19, 526
stereotypes
   activation of, 20, 128–29
   attributional ambiguity and, 444, 447, 451
   automatic and controlled processing, 437–41, 443, 451
   being a member of a stigmatized group, 443–47, 451
   and bias in criminal justice system, 618, 621
   as cognitive categories, 428, 450
   cognitive perspective on, 428–43, 450–51
   concrete *vs.* abstract construal, 436–37
   conservation of mental reserves, 428–29, 443
   and construal, 18–19, 38
   construal processes and biased assessments, 429–35, 450
   definition, 18, 409
   disconfirmation, 435, 436, 443
   expectations and biased information processing, 434–35
   explaining away exceptions, 435–37
   facial features and criminal sentences, 442
   illusory correlations, 147–49, 432–34, 438, 450
   ingroup similarity and outgroup difference assumptions, 430–31
   outgroup homogeneity effect, 431–32, 434, 438, 443, 450
   physical attractiveness and social skills, 380
   priming, 128, 132–33
   processing style perspective and, 221–22, 230
   schemas and, 18, 38, 125–26, 128–29

self-fulfilling prophecies, 134, 380, 446–47, 451
   social facilitation and, 459
   stereotype threat, 444–46, 447, 451, 594–96, 601
   subtyping, 435–36, 437
   system justification theory, 266, 271
   "typical" gay man, 242
   see also discrimination; prejudice
stereotype threat, 444–46, 447, 451, 594–96, 601
stock market collapse in 2008, 574–75
stonewalling in romantic relationships, 398, 400, *401*, 403, 405
stress
   biological responses to, 92
   brain regions related to, 210
   cardiovascular arousal and, 227, 505, 568
   chronic stress, 564–65, 566, 567, 573
   cortisol and, 52, 92, 209, 481
   evolution and, 562, 563–64
   and health, 563–65
   HPA (hypothalamic-pituitary-adrenal) axis, 563–64, 567–68, 569, 573
   hypothalamic-pituitary-adrenal (HPA) axis, 563–64, 567–68, 569, 573
   Marie Antoinette, 562, 563
   marital conflict and, 396–97
   neighborhoods and, 566–67
   participants in Milgram study, 334, 335, 336
   psychological stress, 563
   rumination, 564, 565, 573
   self-enhancement and, 92
   self-esteem and, 84, 92
   short-term stress, 563, 564
   social class and, 566–67
   soothing effect of touch, 209–10
   tips for reducing stress, 570
   see also health
subjectivist view of beauty, 374
subliminal stimuli, 131–32, 284, 285
subtyping, 435–36, 437
suicide, copycat, 502, 526
suicide baiting, 488, 491
sunk cost fallacy, 579, 581, 588, 600
superordinate goals, 417, 418–19, 420, 450
surveys, 46–49, 55, 62
Sydney Opera House, 144, *145*
symbolic interactionism, 68
sympathy, 195–96, 198–99, 217, 221
systematic route. *see* central (systematic) route to persuasion
system justification theory, 266, 271

T

Taoism, 146
Tao symbol, 146
tattoos, 309, *310*
Taxi Driver (movie), 501–2, *503*
teasing and power, 482–83
telenovelas, 597–99, 601
telomeres, 564
temporal framing, 120–21, 150
terrorist attacks on 9/11, 19, 216, 218, 228, 268, 416
terror management theory
   certainty of death, 266–67, 268, 271
   definition, 267
   mortality salience, 267–68, *269*, 276
   symbolic immortality, 267, 269, 271, 276
   see also attitudes
testosterone, 53, 54, 391, 481, 499, 514
thalamus, 237
that's-not-all technique, 341, 351
Thematic Apperception Test, 482
theory, definition, 45
theory of mind, 24–25, 27, 38, 190–91
The Prince (Machiavelli), 477
Thinks (Lodge), 362
thinness and physical attractiveness, 382–83
third-person effect, 294, 306
third variable, definition, 49
thought polarization hypothesis, 302, 307
threat defense system and, 505

tit-for-tat strategy, 559, 560
top-down processes, 124, 127, 133, 150
   see also schemas
TransAmerica building, *371*
Trends in International Mathematics and Science Study, 176
trials. *see* courtroom events and procedures
triangular theory of love, 393–94, 405
trolley dilemma, 220
trust game, the, 213
tutoring effectiveness: the Five Cs, 591
Tutsis, 332, 497–98, 521, 530, 532, 551, *553*
12 Angry Men (movie), 612
"Twinkie defense," 484
two-system theory of moral judgment, 221, 222

U

ultimatum game, 557–58
unconscious processing. *see* automatic processing
UNICEF, *290*, *344*
universals
   attractiveness, 381
   evolution and, 22–24, 199, 200–201
   facial expressions, 22, *24*, 201–5, 208
   gender roles, universal aspects, 25, 34
   physical attractiveness, 381
   romantic relationships, 403
   universal behaviors, reactions, and institutions, *23*
U.S. surveillance plane collision with Chinese fighter, 190
utilitarian function of attitudes, 275–76, 306

V

value-expressive function of attitudes, 277–79, 306
vampire bats, 550–51
Ven Conmigo ("Come with Me"), 598
ventral striatum, 402
Venus before a Mirror (Rubens), *382*
video games
   aggression and video game violence, 295, 503–5
   Columbine High School shootings and, 504, 505
   Doom, 504
   Mortal Kombat, 504–5
   obsession and addiction, 504
   PGA Tournament Golf, 505
Vietnam War, 133–34, 233–34, 466
violence, attitudes toward
   dueling tradition, *42*
   insult-related homicides, 46, 53, 514–15
   job applicant with felony conviction, 41–42, 56
   South *vs.* Northern regions, 41–42, 48–49, 53–54, 56, 514–15
   survey questions, 48, 50
   violence on TV and fear of victimization, 114
   see also aggression; attitudes
voir dire, 609–10, 611, 620
volunteerism, 535–36, 560

W

Way I Am, The (Eminem), 65–66
Westgate West apartment friendship research, 368–70
"Who Am I" test, *28*, 30–32
Witherspoon v. Illinois, 611
Wizard of Oz, The, 137
working self-concept, 71, 72, 83
World War II
   argument for intervention, 133–34
   Jewish genocide, 134, 333, 337
   Pearl Harbor attack, 466
   propaganda, 59, 286, *291*
   see also Holocaust

Y

Yanomami, 513, *514*
yin and yang, 146, 377

Z

Zajonc's model of social facilitation, 457–64, *465*, 494
Zelig (Woody Allen), 70
zygomatic major muscle, 200, 374